HARPER COLLINS
GERMAN
DICTIONARY

HARPER COLLINS
GERMAN
DICTIONARY
GERMAN · ENGLISH ENGLISH · GERMAN

HarperResource
An Imprint of HarperCollinsPublishers

ISBN 0-06-273750-3

The HarperCollins website address is
www.harpercollins.com

The HarperCollins UK website address is
www.**fire**and**water**.com

Harper*Resource*   A Division of HarperCollins*Publishers*
10 East 53rd Street, New York, N.Y. 10022

first published 1990
second edition 2000

First Harper*Resource* printing: 2000

Typeset by Wordcraft, Glasgow
Printed in the United States of America

20 19 18 17 16 15 14 13 12

Harper*Resource* and colophons are trademarks of
HarperCollins*Publishers*

INHALT

CONTENTS

EINLEITUNG

Wir freuen uns, dass Sie sich zum Kauf dieses Collins Wörterbuchs entschlossen haben und hoffen, dass es Ihnen in der Schule, zu Hause, im
Urlaub oder im Büro nützlich ist und Freude macht.

Diese Einleitung enthält Tipps, wie Sie das Beste aus ihrem Wörterbuch herausholen können – nicht nur aus der umfangreichen Wortliste, sondern
auch aus den Informationen, die in jedem Artikel stehen. Das wird Ihnen
dabei helfen, modernes Englisch zu lesen und zu verstehen und sich auf
Englisch auszudrücken und zu verständigen.

Vorn in diesem Wörterbuch steht eine Liste der im Text verwendeten
Abkürzungen und eine Erläuterung der Symbole der Lautschrift. Hinten finden Sie deutsche Verbtabellen und englische unregelmäßige Verben.

ZUM GEBRAUCH IHRES COLLINS WÖRTERBUCHS

Das Wörterbuch enthält eine Fülle von Informationen, die mithilfe von
unterschiedlichen Schriften und Schriftgrößen, Symbolen, Abkürzungen
und Klammern vermittelt werden. Die dabei verwendeten Regeln und
Symbole werden in den folgenden Abschnitten erklärt.

Stichwörter

Die Wörter, die Sie im Wörterbuch nachschlagen – „Stichwörter" – sind
alphabetisch geordnet. Sie sind **fett** gedruckt, damit man sie schnell
erkennt. Die beiden Stichwörter oben auf jeder Seite geben das erste und
letzte Wort an, das auf der betreffenden Seite behandelt wird.

Informationen zur Verwendung oder zur Form bestimmter Stichwörter stehen in Klammern hinter der Lautschrift. Sie erscheinen meist in abgekürzter Form und sind kursiv gedruckt (z. B. (*fam*), (*COMM*)).

Wo es angebracht ist, werden mit dem Stichwort verwandte Wörter im selben Artikel behandelt (z. B. **accept, acceptance**). Sie sind wie das
Stichwörter fett, aber etwas kleiner gedruckt.
Häufig verwendete Ausdrücke, in denen das Stichwort vorkommt (z. B. **to
be cold**), sind in einer anderen Schrift halbfett gedruckt.

Lautschrift

Die Lautschrift für jedes Stichwort (zur Angabe seiner Aussprache), steht in
eckigen Klammern direkt hinter dem Stichwort (z. B. **Quark** [kvark], **knead**
[niːd]). Die Symbole der Lautschrift sind auf Seite xv erklärt.

Übersetzungen

Die Übersetzungen des Stichworts sind normal gedruckt. Wenn es mehr als
eine Bedeutung oder Verwendung des Stichworts gibt, sind diese durch ein
Semikolon voneinander getrennt. Vor den Übersetzungen stehen oft andere, kursiv gedruckte Wörter in Klammern. Sie geben an, in welchem

Zusammenhang das Stichwort erscheinen könnte (z. B. **rough** (*voice*) oder (*weather*)), oder sie sind Synonyme (z. B. **rough** (*violent*)).

Schlüsselwörter

Besonders behandelt werden bestimmte deutsche und englische Wörter, die man als „Schlüsselwörter" der jeweiligen Sprache betrachten kann. Diese Wörter kommen beispielsweise sehr häufig vor oder werden unterschiedlich verwendet (z. B. **sein, auch; get, that**). Mithilfe von Rauten und Ziffern können Sie die verschiedenen Wortarten und Verwendungen unterscheiden. Weitere nützliche Hinweise finden Sie kursiv und in Klammern in der jeweiligen Sprache des Benutzers.

Grammatische Informationen

Wortarten stehen in abgekürzter Form kursiv gedruckt hinter der Aussprache des Stichworts (z. B. *vt, adv, conj*).

Die unregelmäßigen Formen englischer Substantive und Verben stehen in Klammern vor der Wortart (z. B. **man** (*pl* **men**) *n*, **give** (*pt* **gave**, *pp* **given**) *vt*).

Die deutsche Rechtschreibreform

Dieses Wörterbuch folgt durchweg der reformierten deutschen Rechtschreibung. Alle Stichwörter auf der deutsch-englischen Seite, die von der Rechtschreibreform betroffen sind, sind mit ▲ gekennzeichnet. Alte Schreibungen, die sich wesentlich von der neuen Schreibung unterscheiden und an einem anderen alphabetischen Ort erscheinen, sind jedoch weiterhin aufgeführt und werden zur neuen Schreibung verwiesen. Diese alten Schreibungen sind mit △ gekennzeichnet.

INTRODUCTION

We are delighted you have decided to buy the Collins German dictionary and hope you will enjoy and benefit from using it at school, at home, on holiday or at work.

This introduction gives you a few tips on how to get the most out of your dictionary – not simply from its comprehensive wordlist but also from the information provided in each entry. This will help you to read and understand modern German, as well as communicate and express yourself in the language.

The Collins German Dictionary begins by listing the abbreviations used in the text and illustrating the sounds shown by the phonetic symbols. You will find German verb tables and English irregular verbs at the back.

USING YOUR COLLINS DICTIONARY

A wealth of information is presented in the dictionary, using various typefaces, sizes of type, symbols, abbreviations and brackets. The conventions and symbols used are explained in the following sections.

Headwords

The words you look up in a dictionary – "headwords" – are listed alphabetically. They are printed in **bold type** for rapid identification. The two headwords appearing at the top of each page indicate the first and last word dealt with on the page in question.

Information about the usage or form of certain headwords is given in brackets after the phonetic spelling. This usually appears, in abbreviated form and in italics (e.g. (*umg*), (*comm*)).

Where appropriate, words related to headwords are grouped in the same entry (**Glück, glücken**) in a slightly smaller bold type than the headword.

Common expressions in which the headword appears are shown in a different bold type (e.g. **Glück haben**).

Phonetic spellings

The phonetic spelling of each headword (indicating its pronunciation) is given in square brackets immediately after the headword (e.g. **Quark** [kvark]). A list of these symbols is given on page xv.

Meanings

Headword translations are given in ordinary type and, where more than one meaning or usage exists, these are separated by a semi-colon. You will often find other words in italics in brackets before the translations. These offer suggested contexts in which the headword might appear (e.g. **eng**

(*Kleidung*) or (*Freundschaft*)) or provide synonyms (e.g. **eng** (*fig: Horizont*)).

"Key" words

Special status is given to certain German and English words which are considered as "key" words in each language. They may, for example, occur very frequently or have several types of usage (e.g. **sein, auch; get, that**). A combination of lozenges and numbers helps you to distinguish different parts of speech and different meanings. Further helpful information is provided in brackets and in italics in the relevant language for the user.

Grammatical information

Parts of speech are given in abbreviated form in italics after the phonetic spellings of headwords (e.g. *vt, adv, konj*).

Genders of German nouns are indicated as follows: *m* for a masculine and *f* for a feminine and *nt* for a neuter noun. The genitive and plural forms of regular nouns are shown on the table on page xiv. Nouns which do not follow these rules have the genitive and plural in brackets immediately preceding the gender (e.g. **Spaß (-es, ̈e)** *m*).

Adjectives are normally shown in their basic form (e.g. **groß** *adj*), but where they are only used attributively (i.e. before a noun), feminine and neuter endings follow in brackets (**hohe(r, s)** *adj attrib*).

The German spelling reform

The German spelling reform has been fully implemented in this dictionary. All headwords on the German-English side which are affected by the spelling changes are marked ▲. Old spellings which are significantly different from the new ones and have a different alphabetical position are still listed and are cross-referenced to the new spellings. The old spellings are marked △.

ABKÜRZUNGEN

ABBREVIATIONS

Abkürzung	**abk, abbr**	abbreviation
Adjektiv	**adj**	adjective
Akkusativ	**acc**	accusative
Adverb	**adv**	adverb
Landwirtschaft	**AGR**	agriculture
Akkusativ	**akk**	accusative
Anatomie	**ANAT**	anatomy
Architektur	**ARCHIT**	architecture
Astrologie	**ASTROL**	astrology
Astronomie	**ASTRON**	astronomy
attributiv	**attrib**	attributive
Kraftfahrzeuge	**AUT**	automobiles
Hilfsverb	**aux**	auxiliary
Luftfahrt	**AVIAT**	aviation
besonders	**bes**	especially
Biologie	**BIOL**	biology
Botanik	**BOT**	botany
britisch	**BRIT**	British
Chemie	**CHEM**	chemistry
Film	**CINE**	cinema
Konjunktion	**conj**	conjunction
Handel	**COMM**	commerce
Komparativ	**compar**	comparative
Computer	**COMPUT**	computing
Kochen und Backen	**COOK**	cooking
zusammengesetztes Wort	**cpd**	compound
Dativ	**dat**	dative
bestimmter Artikel	**def art**	definite article
dekliniert	**dekl**	decline
Diminutiv	**dimin**	diminutive
kirchlich	**ECCL**	ecclesiastical
Eisenbahn	**EISENB**	railways
Elektrizität	**ELEK, ELEC**	electricity
besonders	**esp**	especially
und so weiter	**etc**	et cetera
etwas	**etw**	something
Euphemismus, Hüllwort	**euph**	euphemism
Interjektion, Ausruf	**excl**	exclamation
Femininum	**f**	feminine
übertragen	**fig**	figurative
Finanzwesen	**FIN**	finance
nicht getrennt gebraucht	**fus**	(phrasal verb) inseparable
Genitiv	**gen**	genitive
Geografie	**GEOG**	geography
Geologie	**GEOL**	geology
gewöhnlich	**gew**	usually
Grammatik	**GRAM**	grammar
Geschichte	**HIST**	history
unpersönlich	**impers**	impersonal

ABKÜRZUNGEN

ABBREVIATIONS

unbestimmter Artikel	**indef art**	indefinite article
umgangssprachlich (! vulgär)	**inf(!)**	informal (! particularly offensive)
Infinitiv, Grundform	**infin**	infinitive
nicht getrennt gebraucht	**insep**	inseparable
unveränderlich	**inv**	invariable
unregelmäßig	**irreg**	irregular
jemand	**jd**	somebody
jemandem	**jdm**	(to) somebody
jemanden	**jdn**	somebody
jemandes	**jds**	somebody's
Rechtswesen	**JUR**	law
Kochen und Backen	**KOCH**	cooking
Komparativ	**kompar**	comparative
Konjunktion	**konj**	conjunction
Sprachwissenschaft	**LING**	linguistics
Literatur	**LITER**	of literature
Maskulinum	**m**	masculine
Mathematik	**MATH**	mathematics
Medizin	**MED**	medicine
Meteorologie	**MET**	meteorology
Militär	**MIL**	military
Bergbau	**MIN**	mining
Musik	**MUS**	music
Substantiv, Hauptwort	**n**	noun
nautisch, Seefahrt	**NAUT**	nautical, naval
Nominativ	**nom**	nominative
Neutrum	**nt**	neuter
Zahlwort	**num**	numeral
Objekt	**obj**	object
oder	**od**	or
sich	**o.s.**	oneself
Parlament	**PARL**	parliament
abschätzig	**pej**	pejorative
Fotografie	**PHOT**	photography
Physik	**PHYS**	physics
Plural	**pl**	plural
Politik	**POL**	politics
Präposition	**präp, prep**	preposition
Typografie	**PRINT**	printing
Pronomen, Fürwort	**pron**	pronoun
Psychologie	**PSYCH**	psychology
1. Vergangenheit, Imperfekt	**pt**	past tense
Partizip Perfekt	**pp**	past participle
Radio	**RAD**	radio
Eisenbahn	**RAIL**	railways
Religion	**REL**	religion
jemand(-en, -em)	**sb**	someone, somebody

ABKÜRZUNGEN

ABBREVIATIONS

Schulwesen	**SCH**	school
Naturwissenschaft	**SCI**	science
Singular, Einzahl	**sg**	singular
etwas	**sth**	something
Konjunktiv	**sub**	subjunctive
Subjekt	**subj**	(grammatical) subject
Superlativ	**superl**	superlative
Technik	**TECH**	technology
Nachrichtentechnik	**TEL**	telecommunications
Theater	**THEAT**	theatre
Fernsehen	**TV**	television
Typografie	**TYP**	printing
umgangssprachlich (! vulgär)	**umg(!)**	colloquial (! particularly offensive)
Hochschulwesen	**UNIV**	university
unpersönlich	**unpers**	impersonal
unregelmäßig	**unreg**	irregular
(nord)amerikanisch	**US**	(North) America
gewöhnlich	**usu**	usually
Verb	**vb**	verb
intransitives Verb	**vi**	intransitive verb
reflexives Verb	**vr**	reflexive verb
transitives Verb	**vt**	transitive verb
Zoologie	**ZOOL**	Zoology
zusammengesetztes Wort	**zW**	compound
zwischen zwei Sprechern	—	change of speaker
ungefähre Entsprechung	≈	cultural equivalent
eingetragenes Warenzeichen	®	registered trademark

REGULAR GERMAN NOUN ENDINGS

noun		gen	pl
-ant	m	-anten	-anten
-anz	f	-anz	-anzen
-ar	m	-ar(e)s	-are
-chen	nt	-chens	-chen
-e	f	-	-n
-ei	f	-ei	-eien
-elle	f	-elle	-ellen
-ent	m	-enten	-enten
-enz	f	-enz	-enzen
-ette	f	-ette	-etten
-eur	m	-eurs	-eure
-euse	f	-euse	-eusen
-heit	f	-heit	-heiten
-ie	f	-ie	-ien
-ik	f	-ik	-iken
-in	f	-in	-innen
-ine	f	-ine	-inen
-ion	f	-ion	-ionen
-ist	m	-isten	-isten
-ium	nt	-iums	-ien
-ius	m	-ius	-iusse
-ive	f	-ive	-iven
-keit	f	-keit	-keiten
-lein	nt	-leins	-lein
-ling	m	-lings	-linge
-ment	nt	-ments	-mente
-mus	m	-mus	-men
-schaft	f	-schaft	-schaften
-tät	f	-tät	-täten
-tor	m	-tors	-toren
-ung	f	-ung	-ungen
-ur	f	-ur	-uren

PHONETIC SYMBOLS / LAUTSCHRIFT

all vowel sounds are approximate only
alle Vokallaute sind nur ungefähre Entsprechungen

bet	b	Ball			e	Metall
dim	d	dann			e:	geben
face	f	Fass	set	ɛ	hässlich
go	g	Gast			ɛ̃:	Cousin
hit	h	Herr	pity	ɪ	Bischof
you	j	ja			i	vital
cat	k	kalt	green	i:	viel
lick	l	Last	rot	ɔ	Post
must	m	Mast	board	ɔ:	
nut	n	Nuss			o	Moral
bang	ŋ	lang			o:	oben
pepper	p	Pakt			õ	Champignon
red	r	Regen			ø	ökonomisch
sit	s	Rasse			œ	gönnen
shame	ʃ	Schal	full	u	kulant
tell	t	Tal	root	u:	Hut
chat	tʃ	tschüs	come	ʌ	
vine	v	was			ʊ	Pult
wine	w				y	physisch
loch	x	Bach			y:	für
	ç	ich			ʏ	Müll
zero	z	Hase	above	ə	bitte
leisure	ʒ	Genie	girl	ə:	
join	dʒ					
thin	θ		lie	aɪ	weit
this	ð		now	au	
				aʊ	Haut
	a	Hast	day	eɪ	
hat	æ		fair	ɛə	
	a:	Bahn	beer	ɪə	
farm	ɑ:		toy	ɔɪ	
	ã	Ensemble		ɔy	Heu
fiancé	ã:		pure	uə	

Other signs/Andere Zeichen

: *length mark / Längezeichen*

ˈ *stress mark / Betonung*

| *glottal stop / Knacklaut*

ʳ *can be pronounced before a vowel / Bindungs-R*

DEUTSCH – ENGLISCH
GERMAN – ENGLISH

A, a

Aal |a:l| (-(e)s, -e) *m* eel
Aas |a:s| (-es, -e *od* **Äser**) *nt* carrion

ab |ap| *präp +dat* from; **Kinder ab 12 Jahren** children from the age of 12; **ab morgen** from tomorrow; **ab sofort** as of now
♦ *adv* **1** off; **links ab** to the left; **der Knopf ist ab** the button has come off; **ab nach Hause!** off you go home
2 (*zeitlich*): **von da ab** from then on; **von heute ab** from today, as of today
3 (*auf Fahrplänen*): **München ab 12.20** leaving Munich 12.20
4: **ab und zu** *od* **an** now and then *od* again

Abänderung |ˈapˌɛndərʊŋ| *f* alteration
Abbau |ˈapbaʊ| (-(e)s) *m* (+*gen*) dismantling; (*Verminderung*) reduction (in); (*Verfall*) decline (in); (*MIN*) mining; quarrying; (*CHEM*) decomposition; **a~en** *vt* to dismantle; (*MIN*) to mine; to quarry; (*verringern*) to reduce; (*CHEM*) to break down
abbeißen |ˈapbaɪsən| (*unreg*) *vt* to bite off
abbekommen |ˈapbəkɔmən| (*unreg*) *vt* (*Deckel, Schraube, Band*) to loosen; **etwas ~** (*beschädigt werden*) to get damaged; (: *Person*) to get injured
abbestellen |ˈapbəʃtɛlən| *vt* to cancel
abbezahlen |ˈapbatsaːlən| *vt* to pay off
abbiegen |ˈapbiːgən| (*unreg*) *vi* to turn off; (*Straße*) to bend ♦ *vt* to bend; (*verhindern*) to ward off
abbilden |ˈapbɪldən| *vt* to portray; **Abbildung** *f* illustration
abblenden |ˈapblɛndən| *vt, vi* (*AUT*) to dip (*BRIT*), to dim (*US*)
Abblendlicht |ˈapblɛntlɪçt| *nt* dipped (*BRIT*) *od* dimmed (*US*) headlights *pl*
abbrechen |ˈapbrɛçən| (*unreg*) *vt, vi* to break off; (*Gebäude*) to pull down; (*Zelt*) to take down; (*aufhören*) to stop; (*COMPUT*) to abort
abbrennen |ˈapbrɛnən| (*unreg*) *vt* to burn off; (*Feuerwerk*) to let off ♦ *vi* (*aux sein*) to burn down
abbringen |ˈapbrɪŋən| (*unreg*) *vt*: **jdn von etw ~** to dissuade sb from sth; **jdn vom Weg ~** to divert sb
abbröckeln |ˈapbrœkəln| *vt, vi* to crumble

off *od* away
Abbruch |ˈapbrʊx| *m* (*von Verhandlungen etc*) breaking off; (*von Haus*) demolition; **jdm/etw ~ tun** to harm sb/sth; **a~reif** *adj* only fit for demolition
abbrühen |ˈapbryːən| *vt* to scald; **abgebrüht** (*umg*) hard-boiled
abbuchen |ˈapbuːxən| *vt* to debit
abdanken |ˈapdaŋkən| *vi* to resign; (*König*) to abdicate; **Abdankung** *f* resignation; abdication
abdecken |ˈapdɛkən| *vt* (*Loch*) to cover; (*Tisch*) to clear; (*Plane*) to uncover
abdichten |ˈapdɪçtən| *vt* to seal; (*NAUT*) to caulk
abdrehen |ˈapdreːən| *vt* (*Gas*) to turn off; (*Licht*) to switch off; (*Film*) to shoot ♦ *vi* (*Schiff*) to change course
Abdruck |ˈapdrʊk| *m* (*Nachdrucken*) reprinting; (*Gedrucktes*) reprint; (*Gipsabdruck, Wachsabdruck*) impression; (*Fingerabdruck*) print; **a~en** *vt* to print, to publish
abdrücken |ˈapdrʏkən| *vt* (*Waffe*) to fire; (*Person*) to hug, to squeeze
Abend |ˈaːbənt| (-s, -e) *m* evening; **guten ~** good evening; **zu ~ essen** to have dinner *od* supper; **heute ~** this evening; **~brot** *nt* supper; **~essen** *nt* supper; **~garderobe** *f* evening dress; **~kasse** *f* box office; **~kleid** *nt* evening dress; **~kurs** *m* evening classes *pl*; **~land** *nt* (*Europa*) West; **a~lich** *adj* evening; **~mahl** *nt* Holy Communion; **~rot** *nt* sunset; **a~s** *adv* in the evening
Abenteuer |ˈaːbəntɔyər| (-s, -) *nt* adventure; **a~lich** *adj* adventurous; **~urlaub** *m* adventure holiday
Abenteurer (-s, -) *m* adventurer; **~in** *f* adventuress
aber |ˈaːbər| *konj* but; (*jedoch*) however ♦ *adv*: **das ist ~ schön** that's really nice; **nun ist ~ Schluss!** now that's enough!; **vielen Dank ~ ~ bitte!** thanks a lot — you're welcome; **A~glaube** *m* superstition; **~gläubisch** *adj* superstitious
aberkennen |ˈapˌɛrkɛnən| (*unreg*) *vt* (*JUR*): **jdm etw ~** to deprive sb of sth, to take sth (away) from sb
abermals |ˈaːbəmaːls| *adv* once again
abertausend, Abertausend

|ˈaːbərtaʊzənt| *indef pron*: **tausend** *od*
Tausend und ~ thousands upon thousands
Abf. *abk* (= *Abfahrt*) dep.
abfahren |ˈapfaːrən| (*unreg*) *vi* to leave, to
depart ♦ *vt* to take *od* cart away; (*Strecke*) to
drive; (*Reifen*) to wear; (*Fahrkarte*) to use
Abfahrt |ˈapfaːrt| *f* departure; (*SKI*) descent;
(*Piste*) run; **~szeit** *f* departure time
Abfall |ˈapfal| *m* waste; (*von Speisen etc*)
rubbish (*BRIT*), garbage (*US*); (*Neigung*)
slope; (*Verschlechterung*) decline; **~eimer** *m*
rubbish bin (*BRIT*), garbage can (*US*); **a~en**
(*unreg*) *vi* (*auch fig*) to fall *od* drop off; (*sich
neigen*) to fall *od* drop away
abfällig |ˈapfɛlɪç| *adj* disparaging,
deprecatory
abfangen |ˈapfaŋən| (*unreg*) *vt* to intercept;
(*Person*) to catch; (*unter Kontrolle bringen*) to
check
abfärben |ˈapfɛrbən| *vi* to lose its colour;
(*Wäsche*) to run; (*fig*) to rub off
abfassen |ˈapfasən| *vt* to write, to draft
abfertigen |ˈapfɛrtɪgən| *vt* to prepare for
dispatch, to process; (*an der Grenze*) to
clear; (*Kundschaft*) to attend to
Abfertigungsschalter *m* (*Flughafen*)
check-in desk
abfeuern |ˈapfɔʏərn| *vt* to fire
abfinden |ˈapfɪndən| (*unreg*) *vt* to pay off
♦ *vr* to come to terms; **sich mit jdm ~/nicht
~** to put up with/not get on with sb
Abfindung *f* (*von Gläubigern*) payment;
(*Geld*) sum in settlement
abflauen |ˈapflaʊən| *vi* (*Wind, Erregung*) to
die away, to subside; (*Nachfrage, Geschäft*)
to fall *od* drop off
abfliegen |ˈapfliːgən| (*unreg*) *vi* (*Flugzeug*) to
take off; (*Passagier auch*) to fly ♦ *vt* (*Gebiet*)
to fly over
abfließen |ˈapfliːsən| (*unreg*) *vi* to drain
away
Abflug |ˈapfluːk| *m* departure; (*Start*) take-
off; **~halle** *f* departure lounge; **~zeit** *f*
departure time
Abfluss ▲ |ˈapflʊs| *m* draining away;
(*Öffnung*) outlet; **~rohr** ▲ *nt* drain pipe;
(*von sanitären Anlagen auch*) waste pipe
abfragen |ˈapfraːgən| *vt* (*bes SCH*) to test
orally (on)
Abfuhr |ˈapfuːr| (-, **-en**) *f* removal; (*fig*) snub,
rebuff
abführen |ˈapfyːrən| *vt* to lead away; (*Gelder,
Steuern*) to pay ♦ *vi* (*MED*) to have a laxative
effect
Abführmittel |ˈapfyːrmɪtəl| *nt* laxative,
purgative
abfüllen |ˈapfʏlən| *vt* to draw off; (*in
Flaschen*) to bottle
Abgabe |ˈapgaːbə| *f* handing in; (*von Ball*)
pass; (*Steuer*) tax; (*eines Amtes*) giving up;
(*einer Erklärung*) giving

Abgang |ˈapgaŋ| *m* (*von Schule*) leaving;
(*THEAT*) exit; (*Abfahrt*) departure; (*der Post,
von Waren*) dispatch
Abgas |ˈapgaːs| *nt* waste gas; (*AUT*) exhaust
abgeben |ˈapgeːbən| (*unreg*) *vt* (*Gegenstand*)
to hand *od* give in; (*Ball*) to pass; (*Wärme*)
to give off; (*Amt*) to hand over; (*Schuss*) to
fire; (*Erklärung, Urteil*) to give; (*darstellen,
sein*) to make ♦ *vr*: **sich mit jdm/etw ~** to
associate with sb/bother with sth; **jdm etw
~** (*überlassen*) to let sb have sth
abgebrüht |ˈapgəbryːt| (*umg*) *adj* (*skrupellos*)
hard-boiled
abgehen |ˈapgeːən| (*unreg*) *vi* to go away, to
leave; (*THEAT*) to exit; (*Knopf etc*) to come
off; (*Straße*) to branch off ♦ *vt* (*Strecke*) to
go *od* walk along; **etw geht jdm ab** (*fehlt*)
sb lacks sth
abgelegen |ˈapgəleːgən| *adj* remote
abgemacht |ˈapgəmaxt| *adj* fixed; **~!** done!
abgeneigt |ˈapgənaɪkt| *adj* disinclined
abgenutzt |ˈapgənʊtst| *adj* worn
Abgeordnete(r) |ˈapgəɔrdnətə(r)| *f(m)*
member of parliament; elected
representative
abgeschlossen |ˈapgəʃlɔsən| *adj attrib*
(*Wohnung*) self-contained
abgeschmackt |ˈapgəʃmakt| *adj* tasteless
abgesehen |ˈapgəzeːən| *adj*: **es auf jdn/etw
~ haben** to be after sb/sth; **~ von ... apart
from ...**
abgespannt |ˈapgəʃpant| *adj* tired out
abgestanden |ˈapgəʃtandən| *adj* stale; (*Bier
auch*) flat
abgestorben |ˈapgəʃtɔrbən| *adj* numb;
(*BIOL, MED*) dead
abgetragen |ˈapgətraːgən| *adj* shabby, worn
out
abgewinnen |ˈapgəvɪnən| (*unreg*) *vt*: **einer
Sache etw/Geschmack ~** to get sth/
pleasure from sth
abgewöhnen |ˈapgəvøːnən| *vt*: **jdm/sich
etw ~** to cure sb of sth/give sth up
abgrenzen |ˈapgrɛntsən| *vt* (*auch fig*) to
mark off; to fence off
Abgrund |ˈapgrʊnt| *m* (*auch fig*) abyss
abhacken |ˈaphakən| *vt* to chop off
abhaken |ˈaphaːkən| *vt* (*auf Papier*) to tick
off
abhalten |ˈaphaltən| (*unreg*) *vt*
(*Versammlung*) to hold; **jdn von etw ~** (*fern
halten*) to keep sb away from sth; (*hindern*)
to keep sb from sth
abhanden |apˈhandən| *adj*: **~ kommen** to
get lost
Abhandlung |ˈaphandlʊŋ| *f* treatise,
discourse
Abhang |ˈaphaŋ| *m* slope
abhängen |ˈaphɛŋən| *vt* (*Bild*) to take down;
(*Anhänger*) to uncouple; (*Verfolger*) to shake
off ♦ *vi* (*unreg*: *Fleisch*) to hang; **von jdm/**

etw ~ to depend on sb/sth

abhängig ['aphɛŋıç] *adj:* ~ **(von)** dependent (on); **A~keit** *f:* A~keit **(von)** dependence (on)

abhärten ['ɑphɛrtən] *vt, vr* to toughen (o.s.) up; **sich gegen etw** ~ to inure o.s. to sth

abhauen ['aphaʊən] *(unreg) vt* to cut off; *(Baum)* to cut down ♦ *vi (umg)* to clear off *od* out

abheben ['aphe:bən] *(unreg) vt* to lift (up); *(Karten)* to cut; *(Geld)* to withdraw, to take out ♦ *vi (Flugzeug)* to take off; *(Rakete)* to lift off ♦ *vr* to stand out

abheften ['aphɛftən] *vt (Rechnungen etc)* to file away

abhetzen ['aphɛtsən] *vr* to wear *od* tire o.s. out

Abhilfe ['aphılfə] *f* remedy; ~ **schaffen** to put things right

abholen ['apho:lən] *vt (Gegenstand)* to fetch, to collect; *(Person)* to call for; *(am Bahnhof etc)* to pick up, to meet

abholzen ['aphɔltsən] *vt (Wald)* to clear

abhorchen ['aphɔrçən] *vt (MED)* to listen to a patient's chest

abhören ['aphø:rən] *vt (Vokabeln)* to test; *(Telefongespräch)* to tap; *(Tonband etc)* to listen to

Abhörgerät *nt* bug

Abitur [abi'tu:r] *(-s, -e) nt* German school-leaving examination; **~i'ent(in)** *m(f)* candidate for school-leaving certificate

Abk. *abk (= Abkürzung)* abbr.

abkapseln ['apkapsəln] *vr* to shut *od* cut o.s. off

abkaufen ['apkaʊfən] *vt:* **jdm etw** ~ *(auch fig)* to buy sth from sb

abkehren ['apke:rən] *vt (Blick)* to avert, to turn away ♦ *vr* to turn away

abklingen ['apklıŋən] *(unreg) vi* to die away; *(Radio)* to fade out

abknöpfen ['apknœpfən] *vt* to unbutton; **jdm etw** ~ *(umg)* to get sth off sb

abkochen ['apkɔxən] *vt* to boil

abkommen ['apkɔmən] *(unreg) vi* to get away; **von der Straße/von einem Plan** ~ to leave the road/give up a plan; **A~ (-s, -)** *nt* agreement

abkömmlich ['apkœmlıç] *adj* available, free

abkratzen ['apkratsən] *vt* to scrape off ♦ *vi (umg)* to kick the bucket

abkühlen ['apky:lən] *vt* to cool down ♦ *vr (Mensch)* to cool down *od* off; *(Wetter)* to get cool; *(Zuneigung)* to cool

abkürzen ['apkʏrtsən] *vt* to shorten; *(Wort auch)* to abbreviate; **den Weg** ~ to take a short cut

Abkürzung *f (Wort)* abbreviation; *(Weg)* short cut

abladen ['apla:dən] *(unreg) vt* to unload

Ablage ['apla:gə] *f (für Akten)* tray; *(für Kleider)* cloakroom

ablassen ['aplasən] *(unreg) vt (Wasser, Dampf)* to let off; *(vom Preis)* to knock off ♦ *vi:* **von etw** ~ to give sth up, to abandon sth

Ablauf ['aplaʊf] *m (Abfluss)* drain; *(von Ereignissen)* course; *(einer Frist, Zeit)* expiry *(BRIT)*, expiration *(US)*; **a~en** *(unreg) vi (abfließen)* to drain away; *(Ereignisse)* to happen; *(Frist, Zeit, Pass)* to expire ♦ *vt (Sohlen)* to wear (down *od* out)

ablegen ['aple:gən] *vt* to put *od* lay down; *(Kleider)* to take off; *(Gewohnheit)* to get rid of; *(Prüfung)* to take, to sit; *(Zeugnis)* to give

Ableger **(-s, -)** *m* layer; *(fig)* branch, offshoot

ablehnen ['aple:nən] *vt* to reject; *(Einladung)* to decline, to refuse ♦ *vi* to decline, to refuse

ablehnend *adj (Haltung, Antwort)* negative; *(Geste)* disapproving; **ein ~er Bescheid** a rejection

Ablehnung *f* rejection; refusal

ableiten ['aplaɪtən] *vt (Wasser)* to divert; *(deduzieren)* to deduce; *(Wort)* to derive; **Ableitung** *f* diversion; deduction; derivation; *(Wort)* derivative

ablenken ['aplɛŋkən] *vt* to turn away, to deflect; *(zerstreuen)* to distract ♦ *vi* to change the subject; **Ablenkung** *f* distraction

ablesen ['aple:zən] *(unreg) vt* to read out; *(Messgeräte)* to read

ablichten ['aplıçtən] *vt* to photocopy

abliefern ['apli:fərn] *vt* to deliver; **etw bei jdm** ~ to hand sth over to sb

Ablieferung *f* delivery

ablösen ['aplø:zən] *vt (abtrennen)* to take off, to remove; *(in Amt)* to take over from; *(Wache)* to relieve

Ablösung *f* removal; relieving

abmachen ['apmaxən] *vt* to take off; *(vereinbaren)* to agree; **Abmachung** *f* agreement

abmagern ['apma:gərn] *vi* to get thinner

Abmagerungskur *f* diet; **eine ~ machen** to go on a diet

abmarschieren ['apmarʃi:rən] *vi* to march off

abmelden ['apmɛldən] *vt (Zeitungen)* to cancel; *(Auto)* to take off the road ♦ *vr* to give notice of one's departure; *(im Hotel)* to check out; **jdn bei der Polizei** ~ to register sb's departure with the police

abmessen ['apmɛsən] *(unreg) vt* to measure; **Abmessung** *f* measurement

abmontieren ['apmɔnti:rən] *vt* to take off

abmühen ['apmy:ən] *vr* to wear o.s. out

Abnahme ['apna:mə] *f (+gen)* removal;

(COMM) buying; (Verringerung) decrease (in)

abnehmen ['apneːmən] (unreg) vt to take off, to remove; (Führerschein) to take away; (Prüfung) to hold; (Maschen) to decrease ♦ vi to decrease; (schlanker werden) to lose weight; (jdm) etw ~ (Geld) to get sth (out of sb); (kaufen, umg: glauben) to buy sth (from sb); **jdm Arbeit ~** to take work off sb's shoulders

Abnehmer (-s, -) m purchaser, customer

Abneigung ['apnaɪɡʊŋ] f aversion, dislike

abnorm [ap'nɔrm] adj abnormal

abnutzen ['apnʊtsən] vt to wear out; **Abnutzung** f wear (and tear)

Abo ['abo] (umg) nt abk = **Abonnement**

Abonnement [abɔn(ə)'maː] (-s, -s) nt subscription; **Abonnent(in)** [abɔ'nɛnt(ɪn)] m(f) subscriber; **abonnieren** vt to subscribe to

Abordnung ['apˌɔrdnʊŋ] f delegation

abpacken ['appakən] vt to pack

abpassen ['appasən] vt (Person, Gelegenheit) to wait for

Abpfiff ['appfɪf] m final whistle

abplagen ['applaːɡən] vr to wear o.s. out

abprallen ['applalən] vi to bounce off; to ricochet

abraten ['apraːtən] (unreg) vi: **jdm von etw ~** to advise od warn sb against sth

abräumen ['aprɔʏmən] vt to clear up od away

abreagieren ['apreagiːrən] vt: **seinen Zorn (an jdm/etw) ~** to work one's anger off (on sb/sth) ♦ vr to calm down

abrechnen ['aprɛçnən] vt to deduct, to take off ♦ vi to settle up; (fig) to get even

Abrechnung f settlement; (Rechnung) bill

Abrede ['apreːdə] f: **etw in ~ stellen** to deny od dispute sth

Abreise ['apraɪzə] f departure; **a~n** vi to leave, to set off

abreißen ['apraɪsən] (unreg) vt (Haus) to tear down; (Blatt) to tear off

abrichten ['apmçtən] vt to train

abriegeln ['apriːɡəln] vt (Straße, Gebiet) to seal off

Abruf ['apruːf] m: **auf ~ on call; a~en** (unreg) vt (Mensch) to call away; (COMM: Ware) to request delivery of

abrunden ['aprʊndən] vt to round off

abrupt [a'brʊpt] adj abrupt

abrüsten ['aprʏstən] vi to disarm; **Abrüstung** f disarmament

abrutschen ['aprʊtʃən] vi to slip; (AVIAT) to sideslip

Abs. abk (= Absender) sender, from

Absage ['apzaːɡə] f refusal; **a~n** vt to cancel, to call off; (Einladung) to turn down ♦ vi to cry off; (ablehnen) to decline

absahnen ['apzaːnən] vt to skim ♦ vi (fig) to rake in

Absatz ['apzats] m (COMM) sales pl; (Bodensatz) deposit; (neuer Abschnitt) paragraph; (Treppensatz) landing; (Schuhabsatz) heel; **~gebiet** nt (COMM) market

abschaffen ['apʃafən] vt to abolish, to do away with; **Abschaffung** f abolition

abschalten ['apʃaltən] vt, vi (auch umg) to switch off

abschätzen ['apʃɛtsən] vt to estimate; (Lage) to assess; (Person) to size up

abschätzig ['apʃɛtsɪç] adj disparaging, derogatory

Abschaum ['apʃaʊm] (-(e)s) m scum

Abscheu ['apʃɔʏ] (-(e)s) m loathing, repugnance; **~ erregend** repulsive, loathsome; **a~lich** [ap'ʃɔʏlɪç] adj abominable

abschicken ['apʃɪkən] vt to send off

abschieben ['apʃiːbən] (unreg) vt to push away; (Person) to pack off; (: POL) to deport

Abschied ['apʃiːt] (-(e)s, -e) m parting; (von Armee) discharge; **(von jdm) ~ nehmen** to say goodbye (to sb), to take one's leave (of sb); **seinen ~ nehmen** (MIL) to apply for discharge; **~sbrief** m farewell letter; **~sfeier** f farewell party

abschießen ['apʃiːsən] (unreg) vt (Flugzeug) to shoot down; (Geschoss) to fire

abschirmen ['apʃɪrmən] vt to screen

abschlagen ['apʃlaːɡən] (unreg) vt (abhacken, COMM) to knock off; (ablehnen) to refuse; (MIL) to repel

abschlägig ['apʃlɛːɡɪç] adj negative

Abschlagszahlung f interim payment

Abschlepp- ['apʃlɛp] zW: **~dienst** m (AUT) breakdown service (BRIT), towing company (US); **a~en** vt to (take in) tow; **~seil** nt towrope

abschließen ['apʃliːsən] (unreg) vt (Tür) to lock; (beenden) to conclude, to finish; (Vertrag, Handel) to conclude ♦ vr (sich isolieren) to cut o.s. off; **~d** adj concluding

Abschluss ▲ ['apʃlʊs] m (Beendigung) close, conclusion; (COMM: Bilanz) balancing; (von Vertrag, Handel) conclusion; **zum ~** in conclusion; **~feier** ▲ f (SCH) end of term party; **~prüfung** ▲ f final exam

abschneiden ['apʃnaɪdən] (unreg) vt to cut off ♦ vi to do, to come off

Abschnitt ['apʃnɪt] m section; (MIL) sector; (Kontrollabschnitt) counterfoil; (MATH) segment; (Zeitabschnitt) period

abschrauben ['apʃraʊbən] vt to unscrew

abschrecken ['apʃrɛkən] vt to deter, to put off; (mit kaltem Wasser) to plunge in cold water; **~d** adj deterrent; **~des Beispiel** warning

abschreiben ['apʃraɪbən] (unreg) vt to copy; (verloren geben) to write off; (COMM) to deduct

Abschrift ['apʃrɪft] f copy

Abschuss ▲ ['apʃʊs] *m* (*eines Geschützes*) firing; (*Herunterschießen*) shooting down; (*Tötung*) shooting

abschüssig ['apʃʏsɪç] *adj* steep

abschwächen ['apʃvɛçən] *vt* to lessen; (*Behauptung, Kritik*) to tone down ♦ *vr* to lessen

abschweifen ['apʃvaɪfən] *vi* to digress

abschwellen ['apʃvɛlən] (*unreg*) *vi* (*Geschwulst*) to go down; (*Lärm*) to die down

abschwören ['apʃvøːrən] *vi +dat* to renounce

absehbar ['apzeːbaːr] *adj* foreseeable; **in ~er Zeit** in the foreseeable future; **das Ende ist ~** the end is in sight

absehen ['apzeːən] (*unreg*) *vt* (*Ende, Folgen*) to foresee ♦ *vi*: **von etw ~** to refrain from sth; (*nicht berücksichtigen*) to leave sth out of consideration

abseilen ['apzaɪlən] *vr* (*Bergsteiger*) to abseil (down)

abseits ['apzaɪts] *adv* out of the way ♦ *präp +gen* away from; **A~** *nt* (*SPORT*) offside

absenden ['apzɛndən] (*unreg*) *vt* to send off, to dispatch

Absender (**-s, -**) *m* sender

absetzen ['apzɛtsən] *vt* (*niederstellen, aussteigen lassen*) to put down; (*abnehmen*) to take off; (*COMM: verkaufen*) to sell; (*FIN: abziehen*) to deduct; (*entlassen*) to dismiss; (*König*) to depose; (*streichen*) to drop; (*hervorheben*) to pick out ♦ *vr* (*sich entfernen*) to clear off; (*sich ablagern*) to be deposited

Absetzung *f* (*FIN: Abzug*) deduction; (*Entlassung*) dismissal; (*von König*) deposing

absichern ['apzɪçərn] *vt* to make safe; (*schützen*) to safeguard ♦ *vr* to protect o.s.

Absicht ['apzɪçt] *f* intention; **mit ~** on purpose; **a~lich** *adj* intentional, deliberate

absinken ['apzɪŋkən] (*unreg*) *vi* to sink; (*Temperatur, Geschwindigkeit*) to decrease

absitzen ['apzɪtsən] (*unreg*) *vi* to dismount ♦ *vt* (*Strafe*) to serve

absolut [apzoˈluːt] *adj* absolute; **A~ismus** *m* absolutism

absolvieren [apzɔlˈviːrən] *vt* (*SCH*) to complete

absonder- ['apzɔndər] *zW*: **~lich** *adj* odd, strange; **~n** *vt* to separate; (*ausscheiden*) to give off, to secrete ♦ *vr* to cut o.s. off; **A~ung** *f* separation; (*MED*) secretion

abspalten ['apʃpaltən] *vt* to split off

abspannen ['apʃpanən] *vt* (*Pferde*) to unhitch; (*Wagen*) to uncouple

abspeisen ['apʃpaɪzən] *vt* (*fig*) to fob off

abspenstig ['apʃpɛnstɪç] *adj*: (**jdm**) **~ machen** to lure away (from sb)

absperren ['apʃpɛrən] *vt* to block *od* close

off; (*Tür*) to lock; **Absperrung** *f* (*Vorgang*) blocking *od* closing off; (*Sperre*) barricade

abspielen ['apʃpiːlən] *vt* (*Platte, Tonband*) to play; (*SPORT: Ball*) to pass ♦ *vr* to happen

Absprache ['apʃpraːxa] *f* arrangement

absprechen ['apʃprɛçən] (*unreg*) *vt* (*vereinbaren*) to arrange; **jdm etw ~** to deny sb sth

abspringen ['apʃprɪŋən] (*unreg*) *vi* to jump down/off; (*Farbe, Lack*) to flake off; (*AVIAT*) to bale out; (*sich distanzieren*) to back out

Absprung ['apʃprɔŋ] *m* jump

abspülen ['apʃpyːlən] *vt* to rinse; (*Geschirr*) to wash up

abstammen ['apʃtamən] *vi* to be descended; (*Wort*) to be derived; **Abstammung** *f* descent; derivation

Abstand ['apʃtant] *m* distance; (*zeitlich*) interval; **davon ~ nehmen, etw zu tun** to refrain from doing sth; **mit ~ der Beste** by far the best

abstatten ['apʃtatən] *vt* (*Dank*) to give; (*Besuch*) to pay

abstauben ['apʃtaʊbən] *vt, vi* to dust; (*umg: stehlen*) to pinch; (: *schnorren*) to scrounge

Abstecher ['apʃtɛçər] (**-s, -**) *m* detour

abstehen ['apʃteːən] (*unreg*) *vi* (*Ohren, Haare*) to stick out; (*entfernt sein*) to stand away

absteigen ['apʃtaɪgən] (*unreg*) *vi* (*vom Rad etc*) to get off, to dismount; (**in die zweite Liga**) **~** to be relegated (to the second division)

abstellen ['apʃtɛlən] *vt* (*niederstellen*) to put down; (*entfernt stellen*) to pull out; (*hinstellen: Auto*) to park; (*ausschalten*) to turn *od* switch off; (*Missstand, Unsitte*) to stop

Abstellraum *m* storage room

abstempeln ['apʃtɛmpəln] *vt* to stamp

absterben ['apʃtɛrbən] (*unreg*) *vi* to die; (*Körperteil*) to go numb

Abstieg ['apʃtiːk] (**-(e)s, -e**) *m* descent; (*SPORT*) relegation; (*fig*) decline

abstimmen ['apʃtɪmən] *vi* to vote ♦ *vt*: **~ (auf +akk)** (*Instrument*) to tune (to); (*Interessen*) to match (with); (*Termine, Ziele*) to fit in (with) ♦ *vr* to agree

Abstimmung *f* vote

Abstinenz [apstiˈnɛnts] *f* abstinence; teetotalism; **~ler(in)** (**-s, -**) *m(f)* teetotaller

abstoßen ['apʃtoːsən] (*unreg*) *vt* to push off *od* away; (*verkaufen*) to unload; (*anekeln*) to repel, to repulse; **~d** *adj* repulsive

abstrakt [apˈstrakt] *adj* abstract ♦ *adv* abstractly, in the abstract

abstreiten ['apʃtraɪtən] (*unreg*) *vt* to deny

Abstrich ['apʃtrɪç] *m* (*Abzug*) cut; (*MED*) smear; **~e machen** to lower one's sights

---

Spelling reform: ▲ *new spelling* △ *old spelling (to be phased out)*

abstufen ['apʃtuːfən] *vt* (*Hang*) to terrace; (*Farben*) to shade; (*Gehälter*) to grade

Absturz ['apʃturts] *m* fall; (*AVIAT*) crash

abstürzen ['apʃtʏrtsən] *vi* to fall; (*AVIAT*) to crash

absuchen ['apzuːxən] *vt* to scour, to search

absurd [ap'zʊrt] *adj* absurd

Abszess ▲ [aps'tsɛs] (**-es, -e**) *m* abscess

Abt [apt] (**-(e)s, ⁼e**) *m* abbot

Abt. *abk* (= *Abteilung*) dept.

abtasten ['aptastən] *vt* to feel, to probe

abtauen ['aptaʊən] *vt, vi* to thaw

Abtei [ap'taɪ] (**-, -en**) *f* abbey

Abteil [ap'taɪl] (**-(e)s, -e**) *nt* compartment; **'a~en** *vt* to divide up; (*abtrennen*) to divide off; **~ung** *f* (*in Firma, Kaufhaus*) department; (*in Krankenhaus*) section; (*MIL*) unit

abtippen ['aptɪpən] *vt* (*Text*) to type up

abtransportieren ['aptranspɔrtiːrən] *vt* to take away, to remove

abtreiben ['aptraɪbən] (*unreg*) *vt* (*Boot, Flugzeug*) to drive off course; (*Kind*) to abort ♦ *vi* to be driven off course; to abort

Abtreibung *f* abortion

abtrennen ['aptrɛnən] *vt* (*lostrennen*) to detach; (*entfernen*) to take off; (*abteilen*) to separate off

abtreten ['aptreːtən] (*unreg*) *vt* to wear out; (*überlassen*) to hand over, to cede ♦ *vi* to go off; (*zurücktreten*) to step down

Abtritt ['aptrɪt] *m* resignation

abtrocknen ['aptrɔknən] *vt, vi* to dry

abtun ['aptuːn] (*unreg*) *vt* (*fig*) to dismiss

abwägen ['apvɛːgən] (*unreg*) *vt* to weigh up

abwälzen ['apvɛltsən] *vt* (*Schuld, Verantwortung*): **~ (auf** +*akk*) to shift (onto)

abwandeln ['apvandəln] *vt* to adapt

abwandern ['apvandərn] *vi* to move away; (*FIN*) to be transferred

abwarten ['apvartən] *vt* to wait for ♦ *vi* to wait

abwärts ['apvɛrts] *adv* down

Abwasch ['apvaʃ] (**-(e)s**) *m* washing-up; **a~en** (*unreg*) *vt* (*Schmutz*) to wash off; (*Geschirr*) to wash (up)

Abwasser ['apvasər] (**-s, -wässer**) *nt* sewage

abwechseln ['apvɛksəln] *vi, vr* to alternate; (*Personen*) to take turns; **~d** *adj* alternate; **Abwechslung** *f* change; **abwechslungsreich** *adj* varied

abwegig ['apveːgɪç] *adj* wrong

Abwehr ['apveːr] (**-**) *f* defence; (*Schutz*) protection; (*-dienst*) counterintelligence (service); **a~en** *vt* to ward off; (*Ball*) to stop

abweichen ['apvaɪçən] (*unreg*) *vi* to deviate; (*Meinung*) to differ

abweisen ['apvaɪzən] (*unreg*) *vt* to turn away; (*Antrag*) to turn down; **~d** *adj* (*Haltung*) cold

abwenden ['apvɛndən] (*unreg*) *vt* to avert ♦ *vr* to turn away

abwerfen ['apvɛrfən] (*unreg*) *vt* to throw off; (*Profit*) to yield; (*aus Flugzeug*) to drop; (*Spielkarte*) to discard

abwerten ['apveːrtən] *vt* (*FIN*) to devalue

abwertend *adj* (*Worte, Sinn*) pejorative

Abwertung *f* (*von Währung*) devaluation

abwesend ['apveːzənt] *adj* absent

Abwesenheit ['apveːzənhaɪt] *f* absence

abwickeln ['apvɪkəln] *vt* to unwind; (*Geschäft*) to wind up

abwimmeln ['apvɪməln] (*umg*) *vt* (*Menschen*) to get shot of

abwischen ['apvɪʃən] *vt* to wipe off *od* away; (*putzen*) to wipe

Abwurf ['apvʊrf] *m* throwing off; (*von Bomben etc*) dropping; (*von Reiter, SPORT*) throw

abwürgen ['apvʏrgən] (*umg*) *vt* to scotch; (*Motor*) to stall

abzahlen ['aptsaːlən] *vt* to pay off

abzählen ['aptsɛːlən] *vt, vi* to count (up)

Abzahlung *f* repayment; **auf ~ kaufen** to buy on hire purchase

abzapfen ['aptsapfən] *vt* to draw off; **jdm Blut ~** to take blood from sb

abzäunen ['aptsɔʏnən] *vt* to fence off

Abzeichen ['aptsaɪçən] *nt* badge; (*Orden*) decoration

abzeichnen ['aptsaɪçnən] *vt* to draw, to copy; (*Dokument*) to initial ♦ *vr* to stand out; (*fig: bevorstehen*) to loom

abziehen ['aptsiːən] (*unreg*) *vt* to take off; (*Tier*) to skin; (*Bett*) to strip; (*Truppen*) to withdraw; (*subtrahieren*) to take away, to subtract; (*kopieren*) to run off ♦ *vi* to go away; (*Truppen*) to withdraw

abzielen ['aptsiːlən] *vi*: **~ auf** +*akk* to be aimed at

Abzug ['aptsuːk] *m* departure; (*von Truppen*) withdrawal; (*Kopie*) copy; (*Subtraktion*) subtraction; (*Betrag*) deduction; (*Rauchabzug*) flue; (*von Waffen*) trigger

abzüglich ['aptsyːklɪç] *präp* +*gen* less

abzweigen ['aptsvaɪgən] *vi* to branch off ♦ *vt* to set aside

Abzweigung *f* junction

ach [ax] *excl* oh; **~ ja!** (oh) yes; **~ so!** I see; **mit A~ und Krach** by the skin of one's teeth

Achse ['aksə] *f* axis; (*AUT*) axle

Achsel ['aksəl] (**-, -n**) *f* shoulder; **~höhle** *f* armpit

acht [axt] *num* eight; **~ Tage** a week; **A~¹** (**-, -en**) *f* eight; (*beim Eislaufen etc*) figure eight

Acht² (**-, -en**) *f*: **~ geben (auf** +*akk*) to pay attention (to); **sich in ~ nehmen (vor** +*dat*) to be careful (of), to watch out (for); **etw außer ~ lassen** to disregard sth; **a~bar** *adj* worthy

acht- *zW*: **~e(r, s)** *adj* eighth; **A~el** *num*

eighth; **~en** vt to respect ♦ vi: **~en (auf +akk)** to pay attention (to); **~en, dass ...** to be careful that ...

ächten [ˈɛçtən] vt to outlaw, to ban

Achterbahn [ˈaxtər-] f roller coaster

acht- zW: **~fach** adj eightfold; **~geben** △ (unreg) vi siehe **Acht²**; **~hundert** num eight hundred; **~los** adj careless; **~mal** adv eight times; **~sam** adj attentive

Achtung [ˈaxtʊŋ] f attention; (Ehrfurcht) respect ♦ excl look out!; (MIL) attention!; **alle ~!** good for you/him etc!

achtzehn num eighteen

achtzig num eighty

ächzen [ˈɛçtsən] vi to groan

Acker [ˈakər] (-s, ") m field; **a~n** vt, vi to plough; (umg) to slog away

ADAC [aːdeːˈaːtseː] abk (= Allgemeiner Deutscher Automobil-Club) ≈ AA, RAC

Adapter [aˈdaptər] (-s, -) m adapter

addieren [aˈdiːrən] vt to add (up); **Addition** [aditsiˈoːn] f addition

Adel [ˈaːdəl] (-s) m nobility; **a~ig** adj noble; **a~n** vt to raise to the peerage

Ader [ˈaːdər] (-, -n) f vein

Adjektiv [ˈatjɛktiːf] (-s, -e) nt adjective

Adler [ˈaːdlər] (-s, -) m eagle

adlig adj noble

Adopt- zW: **a~ieren** [adɔpˈtiːrən] vt to adopt; **~ion** [adɔptsiˈoːn] f adoption; **~iveltern** pl adoptive parents; **~ivkind** nt adopted child

Adressbuch ▲ nt directory; (privat) address book

Adress- zW: **~e** [aˈdrɛsə] f address; **a~ieren** [adrɛˈsiːrən] vt: **a~ieren (an +akk)** to address (to)

Adria [ˈaːdria] (-) f Adriatic

Advent [atˈvɛnt] (-(e)s, -e) m Advent; **~skalender** m Advent calendar; **~skranz** m Advent wreath

Adverb [atˈvɛrp] nt adverb

Aerobic [aeˈroːbik] nt aerobics sg

Affäre [aˈfɛːrə] f affair

Affe [ˈafə] (-n, -n) m monkey

Affekt [aˈfɛkt] (-(e)s, -e) m: **im ~ handeln** to act in the heat of the moment; **a~iert** [afɛkˈtiːrt] adj affected

Affen- zW: **a~artig** adj like a monkey; **mit a~artiger Geschwindigkeit** like a flash; **~hitze** (umg) f incredible heat

affig [ˈafɪç] adj affected

Afrika [ˈaːfrika] (-s) nt Africa; **~ner(in)** [-ˈkaːnər(ɪn)] (-s, -) m(f) African; **a~nisch** [-ˈkaːnɪʃ] adj African

AG [aːˈgeː] abk (= Aktiengesellschaft) ≈ plc (BRIT), inc (US)

Agent [aˈgɛnt] m agent; **~ur** f agency

Aggregat [agreˈgaːt] (-(e)s, -e) nt aggregate;

(TECH) unit

Aggress- zW: **~ion** [agrɛsiˈoːn] f aggression; **a~iv** [agrɛˈsiːf] adj aggressive; **~ivität** [agrɛsiviˈtɛːt] f aggressiveness

Agrarpolitik [aˈgraːr-] f agricultural policy

Ägypten [ɛˈgʏptən] (-s) nt Egypt; **ägyptisch** adj Egyptian

aha [aˈhaː] excl aha

ähneln [ˈɛːnəln] vi +dat to be like, to resemble ♦ vr to be alike od similar

ahnen [ˈaːnən] vt to suspect; (Tod, Gefahr) to have a presentiment of

ähnlich [ˈɛːnlɪç] adj (+dat) similar (to); **Ä~keit** f similarity

Ahnung [ˈaːnʊŋ] f idea, suspicion; presentiment; **a~slos** adj unsuspecting

Ahorn [ˈaːhɔrn] (-s, -e) m maple

Ähre [ˈɛːrə] f ear

Aids [eːdz] nt AIDS sg

Airbag [ˈɛːbɛk] (-s, -s) m airbag

Akademie [akadeˈmiː] f academy; **Aka'demiker(in)** (-s, -) m(f) university graduate; **akademisch** adj academic

akklimatisieren [aklimatiˈziːrən] vr to become acclimatized

Akkord [aˈkɔrt] (-(e)s, -e) m (MUS) chord; **im ~ arbeiten** to do piecework

Akkordeon [aˈkɔrdeɔn] (-s, -s) nt accordion

Akku [ˈaku] (-s, -s) m rechargeable battery

Akkusativ [ˈakuzatiːf] (-s, -e) m accusative

Akne [ˈaknə] f acne

Akrobat(in) [akroˈbaːt(ɪn)] (-en, -en) m(f) acrobat

Akt [akt] (-(e)s, -e) m act; (KUNST) nude

Akte [ˈaktə] f file

Akten- zW: **~koffer** m attaché case; **a~kundig** adj on the files; **~schrank** m filing cabinet; **~tasche** f briefcase

Aktie [ˈaktsiə] f share

Aktien- zW: **~gesellschaft** f public limited company; **~index** (-(es), -e od -indices) m share index; **~kurs** m share price

Aktion [aktsiˈoːn] f campaign; (Polizeiaktion, Suchaktion) action

Aktionär [aktsioˈnɛːr] (-s, -e) m shareholder

aktiv [akˈtiːf] adj active; (MIL) regular; **~ieren** [-ˈviːrən] vt to activate; **A~ität** f activity

Aktualität [aktualiˈtɛːt] f topicality; (einer Mode) up-to-dateness

aktuell [aktuˈɛl] adj topical; up-to-date

Akupunktur [akupʊŋkˈtuːər] f acupuncture

Akustik [aˈkʊstik] f acoustics pl

akut [aˈkuːt] adj acute

Akzent [akˈtsɛnt] m accent; (Betonung) stress

akzeptabel [aktsɛpˈtaːbl] adj acceptable

akzeptieren [aktsɛpˈtiːrən] vt to accept

Alarm [aˈlarm] (-(e)s, -e) m alarm; **a~bereit** adj standing by; **~bereitschaft** f stand-by; **a~ieren** [-ˈmiːrən] vt to alarm

Albanien |al'ba:niən| (-s) nt Albania
albanisch adj Albanian
albern ['albərn] adj silly
Albtraum ▲ |'alptraʊm| m nightmare
Album ['album] (-s, **Alben**) nt album
Alge ['algə] f algae
Algebra ['algebra] (-) f algebra
Algerier(in) |al'ge:riər(ın)| (-s, -) m(f)
Algerian
algerisch adj Algerian
alias ['a:lias] adv alias
Alibi ['a:libi] (-s, -s) nt alibi
Alimente |ali'mentə| pl alimony sg
Alkohol ['alkohɔl] (-s, -e) m alcohol; **a~frei**
adj non-alcoholic; **~iker(in)**
|alko'ho:likər(ın)| (-s, -) m(f) alcoholic;
a~isch adj alcoholic; **~verbot** nt ban on
alcohol
All |al| (-s) nt universe
all'abendlich adj every evening
'allbekannt adj universally known

SCHLÜSSELWORT

alle(r, s) ['alə(r, s)] adj 1 (*sämtliche*) all; **wir
alle** all of us; **alle Kinder waren da** all the
children were there; **alle Kinder mögen ...**
all children like ...; **alle beide** both of us/
them; **sie kamen alle** they all came; **alles
Gute** all the best; **alles in allem** all in all
2 (*mit Zeit- oder Maßangaben*) every; **alle
vier Jahre** every four years; **alle fünf
Meter** every five metres
♦ *pron* everything; **alles was er sagt**
everything he says, all that he says
♦ *adv* (*zu Ende, aufgebraucht*) finished; **die
Milch ist alle** the milk's all gone, there's no
milk left; **etw alle machen** to finish sth up

Allee |a'le:| f avenue
allein |a'laın| adv alone; (*ohne Hilfe*) on one's
own, by oneself ♦ konj but, only; **nicht ~**
(*nicht nur*) not only; **~ stehend** single;
A~erziehende(r) f(m) single parent;
A~gang m: **im A~gang** on one's own
allemal ['alə'ma:l] adv (*jedes Mal*) always;
(*ohne weiteres*) with no bother; siehe **Mal**
allenfalls ['alən'fals] adv at all events;
(*höchstens*) at most
aller- |'alər| zW: **~beste(r, s)** adj very best;
~dings adv (*zwar*) admittedly; (*gewiss*)
certainly
Allergie |aler'gi:| f allergy; **al'lergisch** adj
allergic
aller- zW: **~hand** (*umg*) adj inv all sorts of;
das ist doch ~hand! that's a bit much!;
~hand! (*lobend*) good show!; **A~heiligen**
nt All Saints' Day; **~höchstens** adv at the
very most; **~lei** adj inv all sorts of;
~letzte(r, s) adj very last; **A~seelen** (-s) nt
All Souls' Day; **~seits** adv on all sides; **prost
~seits!** cheers everyone!

Allerwelts- in zW (*Durchschnitts-*) common;
(*nichts sagend*) commonplace
alles pron everything; **~ in allem** all in all; **~
Gute!** all the best!
Alleskleber (-s, -) m multi-purpose glue
allgemein ['algəmaın] adj general; **im A~en**
in general; **~ gültig** generally accepted;
A~wissen nt general knowledge
Alliierte(r) |ali'i:rtə(r)| m ally
all- zW: **~jährlich** adj annual; **~mächtig** adj
almighty; **~mählich** adj gradual; **A~tag** m
everyday life; **~täglich** adj, adv daily;
(*gewöhnlich*) commonplace; **~tags** adv on
weekdays; **~'wissend** adj omniscient; **~zu**
adv all too; **~zu oft** all too often; **~zu viel**
too much
Allzweck- ['altsvek-] in zW multi-purpose
Alm |alm| (-, **-en**) f alpine pasture
Almosen ['almo:zən] (-s, -) nt alms pl
Alpen ['alpən] pl Alps; **~vorland** nt foothills
pl of the Alps
Alphabet |alfa'be:t| (-(e)s, -e) nt alphabet;
a~isch adj alphabetical
Alptraum |'alptraʊm| siehe **Albtraum**

SCHLÜSSELWORT

als |als| konj 1 (*zeitlich*) when; (*gleichzeitig*)
as; **damals, als ...** (in the days) when ...;
gerade, als ... just as ...
2 (*in der Eigenschaft*) than; **als Antwort** as
an answer; **als Kind** as a child
3 (*bei Vergleichen*) than; **ich kam später als
er** I came later than he (did) od later than
him; **lieber ... als** ... rather ... than ...;
nichts als Ärger nothing but trouble
4: **als ob/wenn** as if

---

also ['alzo:] konj so; (*folglich*) therefore; **~ gut
od schön!** okay then; **~, so was!** well
really!; **na ~!** there you are then!
Alsterwasser |'alstər-| nt shandy (BRIT),
beer and lemonade
Alt |alt| (-s, -e) m (MUS) alto
alt adj old; **alles beim A~en lassen** to leave
everything as it was
Altar |al'ta:r| (-(e)s, **-äre**) m altar
Alt- zW: **~bau** m old building; **a~bekannt**
adj long-known; **~bier** nt top-fermented
German dark beer; **~eisen** nt scrap iron
Alten(wohn)heim nt old people's home
Alter ['altər] (-s, -) nt age; (*hohes*) old age;
im ~ von at the age of; **a~n** vi to grow old,
to age
Alternativ- |alterna'ti:f| in zW alternative; **~e**
f alternative
Alters- zW: **~grenze** f age limit; **~heim** nt
old people's home; **~rente** f old age
pension; **a~schwach** adj (*Mensch*) frail;
~versorgung f old age pension
Altertum ['altərtu:m] nt antiquity
alt- zW: **A~glas** nt glass for recycling;

A~glascontainer *m* bottle bank; **~klug** *adj* precocious; **~modisch** *adj* old-fashioned; **A~papier** *nt* waste paper; **A~stadt** *f* old town

Alufolie |ˈaːlufoːliə| *f* aluminium foil

Aluminium |aluˈmiːniʊm| (**-s**) *nt* aluminium, aluminum (*US*)

Alzheimerkrankheit |ˈaltshaɪ-mərˈkraŋkhaɪt| *f* Alzheimer's (disease)

am |am| = **an dem**; **~ Schlafen** (*umg*) sleeping; **~ 15. März** on March 15th; **~ besten/schönsten** best/most beautiful

Amateur |amaˈtøːr| *m* amateur

Amboss ▲ |ˈambɔs| (**-es, -e**) *m* anvil

ambulant |ambuˈlant| *adj* outpatient; **Ambulanz** *f* outpatients *sg*

Ameise |ˈaːmaɪzə| *f* ant

Ameisenhaufen *m* ant hill

Amerika |aˈmeːrika| (**-s**) *nt* America; **~ner(in)** |-ˈkaːnər(ɪn)| (**-s, -**) *m(f)* American; **a~nisch** |-ˈkaːnɪʃ| *adj* American

Amnestie |amnɛsˈtiː| *f* amnesty

Ampel |ˈampəl| (**-, -n**) *f* traffic lights *pl*

amputieren |ampuˈtiːrən| *vt* to amputate

Amsel |ˈamzəl| (**-, -n**) *f* blackbird

Amt |amt| (**-(e)s, ̈er**) *nt* office; (*Pflicht*) duty; (*TEL*) exchange; **a~ieren** |amˈtiːrən| *vi* to hold office; **a~lich** *adj* official

Amts- *zW:* **~richter** *m* district judge; **~stunden** *pl* office hours; **~zeichen** *nt* dialling tone; **~zeit** *f* period of office

amüsant |amyˈzant| *adj* amusing

amüsieren |amyˈziːrən| *vt* to amuse ♦ *vr* to enjoy o.s.

Amüsierviertel *nt* nightclub district

an |an| *präp +dat* **1** (*räumlich: wo?*) at; (*auf, bei*) on; (*nahe bei*) near; **an diesem Ort** at this place; **an der Wand** on the wall; **zu nahe an etw** too near to sth; **unten am Fluss** down by the river; **Köln liegt am Rhein** Cologne is on the Rhine

2 (*zeitlich: wann?*) on; **an diesem Tag** on this day; **an Ostern** at Easter

3: **arm an Fett** low in fat; **an etw sterben** to die of sth; **an (und für) sich** actually

♦ *präp +akk* **1** (*räumlich: wohin?*) to; **er ging ans Fenster** he went (over) to the window; **etw an die Wand hängen/schreiben** to hang/write sth on the wall

2 (*zeitlich: woran?*): **an etw denken** to think of sth

3 (*gerichtet an*) to; **ein Gruß/eine Frage an dich** greetings/a question to you

♦ *adv* **1** (*ungefähr*) about; **an die hundert** about a hundred

2 (*auf Fahrplänen*): **Frankfurt an 18.30** arriving Frankfurt 18.30

3 (*ab*): **von dort/heute an** from there/today onwards

4 (*angeschaltet, angezogen*) on; **das Licht ist an** the light is on; **ohne etwas an** with nothing on; *siehe auch* **am**

analog |anaˈloːk| *adj* analogous; **A~ie** |-ˈgiː| *f* analogy

Analphabet(in) |anʔalfaˈbeːt(ɪn)| (**-en, -en**) *m(f)* illiterate (person)

Analyse |anaˈlyːzə| *f* analysis

analysieren |analyˈziːrən| *vt* to analyse

Ananas |ˈananas| (**-, - od -se**) *f* pineapple

Anarchie |anarˈçiː| *f* anarchy

Anatomie |anatoˈmiː| *f* anatomy

anbahnen |ˈanbaːnən| *vt, vr* to open up

Anbau |ˈanbaʊ| *m* (*AGR*) cultivation; (*Gebäude*) extension; **a~en** *vt* (*AGR*) to cultivate; (*Gebäudeteil*) to build on

anbehalten |ˈanbəhaltən| (*unreg*) *vt* to keep on

anbei |anˈbaɪ| *adv* enclosed

anbeißen |ˈanbaɪsən| (*unreg*) *vt* to bite into ♦ *vi* to bite; (*fig*) to swallow the bait; **zum A~** (*umg*) good enough to eat

anbelangen |ˈanbəlaŋən| *vt* to concern; **was mich anbelangt** as far as I am concerned

anbeten |ˈanbeːtən| *vt* to worship

Anbetracht |ˈanbətraxt| *m*: **in ~ +gen** in view of

anbieten |ˈanbiːtən| (*unreg*) *vt* to offer ♦ *vr* to volunteer

anbinden |ˈanbɪndən| (*unreg*) *vt* to tie up; **kurz angebunden** (*fig*) curt

Anblick |ˈanblɪk| *m* sight; **a~en** *vt* to look at

anbraten |ˈanbraːtən| *vt* to brown

anbrechen |ˈanbreçən| (*unreg*) *vt* to start; (*Vorräte*) to break into ♦ *vi* to start; (*Tag*) to break; (*Nacht*) to fall

anbrennen |ˈanbrɛnən| (*unreg*) *vi* to catch fire; (*KOCH*) to burn

anbringen |ˈanbrɪŋən| (*unreg*) *vt* to bring; (*Ware*) to sell; (*festmachen*) to fasten

Anbruch |ˈanbrʊx| *m* beginning; **~ des Tages/der Nacht** dawn/nightfall

anbrüllen |ˈanbrʏlən| *vt* to roar at

Andacht |ˈandaxt| (**-, -en**) *f* devotion; (*Gottesdienst*) prayers *pl*; **andächtig** |ˈandɛçtɪç| *adj* devout

andauern |ˈandaʊərn| *vi* to last, to go on; **~d** *adj* continual

Anden |ˈandən| *pl* Andes

Andenken |ˈandɛŋkən| (**-s, -**) *nt* memory; souvenir

andere(r, s) |ˈandərə(r, z)| *adj* other; (*verschieden*) different; **ein ~s Mal** another time; **kein ~r** nobody else; **von etw ~m sprechen** to talk about something else; **~rseits** *adv* on the other hand

andermal *adv*: **ein ~** some other time

ändern ['ɛndərn] *vt* to alter, to change ♦ *vr* to change

andernfalls ['andərnfals] *adv* otherwise

anders ['andərs] *adv*: **~ (als)** differently (from); **wer ~?** who else?; **jd/irgendwo ~** sb/somewhere else; **~ aussehen/klingen** to look/sound different; **~artig** *adj* different; **~herum** *adv* the other way round; **~wo** *adv* somewhere else; **~woher** *adv* from somewhere else

anderthalb ['andərt'halp] *adj* one and a half

Änderung ['ɛndəruŋ] *f* alteration, change

Änderungsschneiderei *f* tailor (*who does alterations*)

anderweitig ['andər'vaitiç] *adj* other ♦ *adv* otherwise; (*anderswo*) elsewhere

andeuten ['andɔytən] *vt* to indicate; (*Wink geben*) to hint at; **Andeutung** *f* indication; hint

Andrang ['andraŋ] *m* crush

andrehen ['andre:ən] *vt* to turn *od* switch on; **jdm etw ~** (*umg*) to unload sth onto sb

androhen ['andro:ən] *vt*: **jdm etw ~** to threaten sb with sth

aneignen ['anaignən] *vt*: **sich** *dat* **etw ~** to acquire sth; (*widerrechtlich*) to appropriate sth

aneinander |an|ai'nandər| *adv* at/on/to *etc* one another *od* each other; **~ geraten** to clash

Anekdote |anɛk'do:tə| *f* anecdote

anekeln ['an|e:kəln] *vt* to disgust

anerkannt ['an|ɛrkant] *adj* recognized, acknowledged

anerkennen ['an|ɛrkɛnən] (*unreg*) *vt* to recognize, to acknowledge; (*würdigen*) to appreciate; **~d** *adj* appreciative

Anerkennung *f* recognition, acknowledgement; appreciation

anfachen ['anfaxən] *vt* to fan into flame; (*fig*) to kindle

anfahren ['anfa:rən] (*unreg*) *vt* to deliver; (*fahren gegen*) to hit; (*Hafen*) to put into; (*fig*) to bawl out ♦ *vi* to drive up; (*losfahren*) to drive off

Anfahrt ['anfa:rt] *f* (*Anfahrtsweg, Anfahrtszeit*) journey

Anfall ['anfal] *m* (*MED*) attack; **a~en** (*unreg*) *vt* to attack; (*fig*) to overcome ♦ *vi* (*Arbeit*) to come up; (*Produkt*) to be obtained

anfällig ['anfɛlıç] *adj* delicate; **~ für etw** prone to sth

Anfang ['anfaŋ] (-(e)s, -fänge) *m* beginning, start; **von ~ an** right from the beginning; **zu ~** at the beginning; **~ Mai** at the beginning of May; **a~en** (*unreg*) *vt*, *vi* to begin, to start; (*machen*) to do

Anfänger(in) ['anfɛŋər(ın)] (-s, -) *m(f)* beginner

anfänglich ['anfɛŋlıç] *adj* initial

anfangs *adv* at first; **A~buchstabe** *m* initial *od* first letter; **A~gehalt** *nt* starting salary

anfassen ['anfasən] *vt* to handle; (*berühren*) to touch ♦ *vi* to lend a hand ♦ *vr* to feel

anfechten ['anfɛçtən] (*unreg*) *vt* to dispute

anfertigen ['anfɛrtıgən] *vt* to make

anfeuern ['anfɔyərn] *vt* (*fig*) to spur on

anflehen ['anfle:ən] *vt* to implore

anfliegen ['anfli:gən] (*unreg*) *vt* to fly to

Anflug ['anflu:k] *m* (*AVIAT*) approach; (*Spur*) trace

anfordern ['anfɔrdərn] *vt* to demand; (*COMM*) to requisition

Anforderung *f* (+*gen*) demand (for)

Anfrage ['anfra:gə] *f* inquiry; **a~n** *vi* to inquire

anfreunden ['anfrɔyndən] *vr* to make friends

anfügen ['anfy:gən] *vt* to add; (*beifügen*) to enclose

anfühlen ['anfy:lən] *vt*, *vr* to feel

anführen ['anfy:rən] *vt* to lead; (*zitieren*) to quote; (*umg*: *betrügen*) to lead up the garden path

Anführer *m* leader

Anführungszeichen *pl* quotation marks, inverted commas

Angabe ['anga:bə] *f* statement; (*TECH*) specification; (*umg*: *Prahlerei*) boasting; (*SPORT*) service

angeben ['ange:bən] (*unreg*) *vt* to give; (*anzeigen*) to inform on; (*bestimmen*) to set ♦ *vi* (*umg*) to boast; (*SPORT*) to serve

Angeber (-s, -) (*umg*) *m* show-off; **Angebe'rei** (*umg*) *f* showing off

angeblich ['ange:plıç] *adj* alleged

angeboren ['angəbo:rən] *adj* inborn, innate

Angebot ['angəbo:t] *nt* offer; **~ (an** +*dat*) (*COMM*) supply (of)

angebracht ['angəbraxt] *adj* appropriate, in order

angegriffen ['angəgrıfən] *adj* exhausted

angeheitert ['angəhaitərt] *adj* tipsy

angehen ['ange:ən] (*unreg*) *vt* to concern; (*angreifen*) to attack; (*bitten*): **jdn ~ (um)** to approach sb (for) ♦ *vi* (*Feuer*) to light; (*umg*: *beginnen*) to begin; **~d** *adj* prospective

angehören ['angəhø:rən] *vi* +*dat* to belong to; (*Partei*) to be a member of

Angehörige(r) *f(m)* relative

Angeklagte(r) ['angəkla:ktə(r)| *f(m)* accused

Angel ['aŋəl] (-, -n) *f* fishing rod; (*Türangel*) hinge

Angelegenheit ['angələgənhait] *f* affair, matter

Angel- *zW*: **~haken** *m* fish hook; **a~n** *vt* to catch ♦ *vi* to fish; **~n** (-s) *nt* angling, fishing; **~rute** *f* fishing rod; **~schein** *m* fishing permit

angemessen ['angəmɛsən] *adj* appropriate,

suitable

angenehm [ˈangəneːm] *adj* pleasant; ~! (*bei Vorstellung*) pleased to meet you

angeregt [angəˈreːkt] *adj* animated, lively

angesehen [ˈangəzeːən] *adj* respected

angesichts [ˈangəzɪçts] *präp +gen* in view of, considering

angespannt [ˈangəʃpant] *adj* (*Aufmerksamkeit*) close; (*Arbeit*) hard

Angestellte(r) [ˈangəʃtɛltə(r)] *f(m)* employee

angestrengt [ˈangəʃtrɛŋt] *adv* as hard as one can

angetan [ˈangətaːn] *adj*: **von jdm/etw ~ sein** to be impressed by sb/sth; **es jdm ~ haben** to appeal to sb

angetrunken [ˈangətrʊŋkən] *adj* tipsy

angewiesen [ˈangəviːzən] *adj*: **auf jdn/etw ~ sein** to be dependent on sb/sth

angewöhnen [ˈangəvøːnən] *vt*: **jdm/sich etw ~** to get sb/become accustomed to sth

Angewohnheit [ˈangəvoːnhaɪt] *f* habit

angleichen [ˈanglaɪçən] (*unreg*) *vt, vr* to adjust

Angler [ˈaŋlər] (**-s, -**) *m* angler

angreifen [ˈangraɪfən] (*unreg*) *vt* to attack; (*beschädigen*) to damage

Angreifer (**-s, -**) *m* attacker

Angriff [ˈangrɪf] *m* attack; **etw in ~ nehmen** to make a start on sth

Angst (**-, ⁻e**) *f* fear; **jdm ist a~** sb is afraid od scared; **~ haben (vor** +*dat*) to be afraid od scared (of); **~ haben um jdn/etw** to be worried about sb/sth; **jdm ~ machen** to scare sb; **~hase** (*umg*) *m* chicken, scaredy-cat

ängst- [ˈɛŋst] *zW*: **~igen** *vt* to frighten ♦ *vr*: **sich ~igen (vor** +*dat* od **um)** to worry (o.s.) (about); **~lich** *adj* nervous; (*besorgt*) worried; **Ä~lichkeit** *f* nervousness

anhaben [ˈanhaːbən] (*unreg*) *vt* to have on; **er kann mir nichts ~** he can't hurt me

anhalt- [ˈanhalt] *zW*: **~en** (*unreg*) *vt* to stop ♦ *vi* to stop; (*andauern*) to persist; (**jdm**) **etw ~en** to hold sth up (against sb); **jdn zur Arbeit/Höflichkeit ~en** to make sb work/be polite; **~end** *adj* persistent; **A~er(in)** (**-s, -**) *m(f)* hitch-hiker; **per A~er fahren** to hitch-hike; **A~spunkt** *m* clue

anhand [anˈhant] *präp +gen* with

Anhang [ˈanhaŋ] *m* appendix; (*Leute*) family; supporters *pl*

anhäng- [ˈanhɛŋ] *zW*: **~en** (*unreg*) *vt* to hang up; (*Wagen*) to couple up; (*Zusatz*) to add (on); **A~er** (**-s, -**) *m* supporter; (*AUT*) trailer; (*am Koffer*) tag; (*Schmuck*) pendant; **A~erschaft** *f* supporters *pl*; **~lich** *adj* devoted; **A~lichkeit** *f* devotion; **A~sel** (**-s, -**) *nt* appendage

Anhäufung [ˈanhɔyfʊŋ] *f* accumulation

anheben [ˈanheːbən] (*unreg*) *vt* to lift up; (*Preise*) to raise

anheizen [ˈanhaɪtsən] *vt* (*Stimmung*) to lift; (*Moral*) to boost

Anhieb [ˈanhiːb] *m*: **auf ~** at the very first go; (*kurz entschlossen*) on the spur of the moment

Anhöhe [ˈanhøːə] *f* hill

anhören [ˈanhøːrən] *vt* to listen to; (*anmerken*) to hear ♦ *vr* to sound

animieren [aniˈmiːrən] *vt* to encourage, to urge on

Anis [aˈniːs] (**-es, -e**) *m* aniseed

Ank. *abk* (= *Ankunft*) arr.

Ankauf [ˈankaʊf] *m* (*von Wertpapieren, Devisen, Waren*) purchase; **a~en** *vt* to purchase, to buy

Anker [ˈaŋkər] (**-s, -**) *m* anchor; **vor ~ gehen** to drop anchor

Anklage [ˈanklaːgə] *f* accusation; (*JUR*) charge; **~bank** *f* dock; **a~n** *vt* to accuse; **jdn (eines Verbrechens) a~n** (*JUR*) to charge sb (with a crime)

Ankläger [ˈanklɛːgər] *m* accuser

Anklang [ˈanklaŋ] *m*: **bei jdm ~ finden** to meet with sb's approval

Ankleidekabine *f* changing cubicle

ankleiden [ˈanklaɪdən] *vt, vr* to dress

anklopfen [ˈanklɔpfən] *vi* to knock

anknüpfen [ˈanknʏpfən] *vt* to fasten od tie on; (*fig*) to start ♦ *vi* (*anschließen*): **~ an** +*akk* to refer to

ankommen [ˈankɔmən] (*unreg*) *vi* to arrive; (*näher kommen*) to approach; (*Anklang finden*): **bei jdm (gut) ~** to go down well with sb; **es kommt darauf an** it depends; (*wichtig sein*) that (is what) matters; **es darauf ~ lassen** to let things take their course; **gegen jdn/etw ~** to cope with sb/sth; **bei jdm schlecht ~** to go down badly with sb

ankreuzen [ˈankrɔytsən] *vt* to mark with a cross; (*hervorheben*) to highlight

ankündigen [ˈankʏndɪgən] *vt* to announce; **Ankündigung** *f* announcement

Ankunft [ˈankʊnft] (**-, -künfte**) *f* arrival; **~szeit** *f* time of arrival

ankurbeln [ˈankʊrbəln] *vt* (*fig*) to boost

Anlage [ˈanlaːgə] *f* disposition; (*Begabung*) talent; (*Park*) gardens *pl*; (*Beilage*) enclosure; (*TECH*) plant; (*FIN*) investment; (*Entwurf*) layout

Anlass ▲ [ˈanlas] (**-es, -lässe**) *m*: **~ (zu)** cause (for); (*Ereignis*) occasion (for); **aus ~** +*gen* on the occasion of ; **~ zu etw geben** to give rise to sth; **etw zum ~ nehmen** to take the opportunity of sth

anlassen (*unreg*) *vt* to leave on; (*Motor*) to

start ♦ vr (umg) to start off

Anlasser (-s, -) m (AUT) starter

anlässlich ▲ ['anlɛslɪç] präp +gen on the occasion of

Anlauf ['anlaʊf] m run-up; **a~en** (unreg) vi to begin; (neuer Film) to show; (SPORT) to run up; (Fenster) to mist up; (Metall) to tarnish ♦ vt to call at; **rot a~en** to blush; **angelaufen kommen** to come running up

anlegen ['anle:gən] vt to put; (anziehen) to put on; (gestalten) to lay out; (Geld) to invest ♦ vi to dock; **etw an etw** akk ~ to put sth against od on sth; **ein Gewehr ~ (auf +akk)** to aim a weapon (at); **es auf etw** akk ~ to be out for sth/to do sth; **sich mit jdm ~** (umg) to quarrel with sb

Anlegestelle f landing place

anlehnen ['anle:nən] vt to lean; (Tür) to leave ajar; **(sich) an etw** akk ~ to lean on/against sth

Anleihe ['anlaɪə] f (FIN) loan

anleiten ['anlaɪtən] vt to instruct; **Anleitung** f instructions pl

anliegen ['anli:gən] (unreg) vi (Kleidung) to cling; **A~** (-s, -) nt matter; (Wunsch) wish; **~d** adj adjacent; (beigefügt) enclosed

Anlieger (-s, -) m resident; **„~ frei"** "residents only"

anmachen ['anmaxən] vt to attach; (Elektrisches) to put on; (Zigarette) to light; (Salat) to dress

anmaßen ['anma:sən] vt: **sich** dat **etw ~** (Recht) to lay claim to sth; **~d** adj arrogant

Anmaßung f presumption

anmelden ['anmɛldən] vt to announce ♦ vr (sich ankündigen) to make an appointment; (polizeilich, für Kurs etc) to register

Anmeldung f announcement; appointment; registration

anmerken ['anmɛrkən] vt to observe; (anstreichen) to mark; **sich** dat **nichts ~ lassen** to not give anything away

Anmerkung f note

anmieten ['anmi:tən] vt to rent; (auch Auto) to hire

Anmut ['anmu:t] (-) f grace; **a~en** vt to give a feeling; **a~ig** adj charming

annähen ['annɛ:ən] vt to sew on

annähern ['annɛ:ərn] vr to get closer; **~d** adj approximate

Annäherung f approach

Annäherungsversuch m advances pl

Annahme ['anna:mə] f acceptance; (Vermutung) assumption

annehm- ['anne:m] zW: **~bar** adj acceptable; **~en** (unreg) vt to accept; (Namen) to take; (Kind) to adopt; (vermuten) to suppose, to assume ♦ vr (+gen) to take care (of); **A~lichkeit** f comfort

Annonce [a'nõ:sə] f advertisement

annoncieren [anõ'si:rən] vt, vi to advertise

annullieren [anʊ'li:rən] vt to annul

anonym [ano'ny:m] adj anonymous

Anorak ['anorak] (-s, -s) m anorak

anordnen ['anʔɔrdnən] vt to arrange; (befehlen) to order

Anordnung f arrangement; order

anorganisch ['anʔɔrga:nɪʃ] adj inorganic

anpacken ['anpakən] vt to grasp; (fig) to tackle; **mit ~** to lend a hand

anpassen ['anpasən] vt: **(jdm) ~** to fit (on sb); (fig) to adapt ♦ vr to adapt

anpassungsfähig adj adaptable

Anpfiff ['anpfɪf] m (SPORT) (starting) whistle; kick-off; (umg) rocket

anprallen ['anpralən] vi: **~ (gegen** od **an +akk)** to collide (with)

anprangern ['anpraŋərn] vt to denounce

anpreisen ['anpraɪzən] (unreg) vt to extol

Anprobe ['anpro:bə] f trying on

anprobieren ['anprobi:rən] vt to try on

anrechnen ['anrɛçnən] vt to charge; (fig) to count; **jdm etw hoch ~** to value sb's sth greatly

Anrecht ['anrɛçt] nt: **~ (auf +akk)** right (to)

Anrede ['anre:də] f form of address; **a~n** vt to address; (belästigen) to accost

anregen ['anre:gən] vt to stimulate; **angeregte Unterhaltung** lively discussion; **~d** adj stimulating

Anregung f stimulation; (Vorschlag) suggestion

anreichern ['anraɪçərn] vt to enrich

Anreise ['anraɪzə] f journey; **a~n** vi to arrive

Anreiz ['anraɪts] m incentive

Anrichte ['anrɪçtə] f sideboard; **a~n** vt to serve up; **Unheil a~n** to make mischief

anrüchig ['anrʏçɪç] adj dubious

anrücken ['anrʏkən] vi to approach; (MIL) to advance

Anruf ['anru:f] m call; **~beantworter** [-bə'antvɔrtər] (-s, -) m answering machine; **a~en** (unreg) vt to call out to; (bitten) to call on; (TEL) to ring up, to phone, to call

ans [ans] = an das

Ansage ['anza:gə] f announcement; **a~n** vt to announce ♦ vr to say one will come; **~r(in)** (-s, -) m(f) announcer

ansammeln ['anzaməln] vt (Reichtümer) to amass ♦ vr (Menschen) to gather, to assemble; (Wasser) to collect;
Ansammlung f collection; (Leute) crowd

ansässig ['anzɛsɪç] adj resident

Ansatz ['anzats] m start; (Haaransatz) hairline; (Halsansatz) base; (Verlängerungsstück) extension; (Veranschlagung) estimate; **~punkt** m starting point

anschaffen ['anʃafən] vt to buy, to purchase; **Anschaffung** f purchase

anschalten ['anʃaltən] vt to switch on

anschau- ['anʃau] zW: **~en** vt to look at; **~lich** adj illustrative; **A~ung** f (Meinung) view; **aus eigener A~ung** from one's own experience

Anschein ['anʃain] m appearance; **allem ~ nach** to all appearances; **den ~ haben** to seem, to appear; **a~end** adj apparent

anschieben ['anʃiːbən] vt to push

Anschlag ['anʃlaːk] m notice; (Attentat) attack; (COMM) estimate; (auf Klavier) touch; (Schreibmaschine) character; **a~en** ['anʃlaːgən] (unreg) vt to put up; (beschädigen) to chip; (Akkord) to strike; (Kosten) to estimate ♦ vi to hit; (wirken) to have an effect; (Glocke) to ring; **an etw** akk **a~en** to hit against sth

anschließen ['anʃliːsən] (unreg) vt to connect up; (Sender) to link up ♦ vi: **an etw** akk ~ to adjoin sth; (zeitlich) to follow sth ♦ vr: **sich jdm/etw** ~ to join sb/sth; (beipflichten) to agree with sb/sth; **sich an etw** akk ~ to adjoin sth; **~d** adj adjacent; (zeitlich) subsequent ♦ adv afterwards

Anschluss ▲ ['anʃlʊs] m (ELEK, EISENB) connection; (von Wasser etc) supply; **im ~ an** +akk following; **~ finden** to make friends; **~flug** ▲ m connecting flight

anschmiegsam ['anʃmiːkzaːm] adj affectionate

anschnallen ['anʃnalən] vt to buckle on ♦ vr to fasten one's seat belt

anschneiden ['anʃnaidən] (unreg) vt to cut into; (Thema) to introduce

anschreiben ['anʃraibən] (unreg) vt to write (up); (COMM) to charge up; (benachrichtigen) to write to

anschreien ['anʃraiən] (unreg) vt to shout at

Anschrift ['anʃrift] f address

Anschuldigung ['anʃʊldigʊŋ] f accusation

anschwellen ['anʃvelən] (unreg) vi to swell (up)

anschwindeln ['anʃvindəln] vt to lie to

ansehen ['anzeːən] (unreg) vt to look at; **jdm etw** ~ to see sth (from sb's face); **jdn/etw als etw** ~ to look on sb/sth as sth; **~ für** to consider; **A~** (-s) nt respect; (Ruf) reputation

ansehnlich ['anzeːnlɪç] adj fine-looking; (beträchtlich) considerable

ansetzen ['anzetsən] vt (festlegen) to fix; (entwickeln) to develop; (Fett) to put on; (Blätter) to grow; (zubereiten) to prepare ♦ vi (anfangen) to start, to begin; (Entwicklung) to set in; (dick werden) to put on weight ♦ vr (Rost etc) to start to develop; **~ an** +akk (anfügen) to fix on to; (anlegen, an Mund etc) to put to

Ansicht ['anzɪçt] f (Anblick) sight; (Meinung) view, opinion; **zur ~** on approval; **meiner ~ nach** in my opinion; **~skarte** f picture

postcard; **~ssache** f matter of opinion

ansonsten [an'zɔnstən] adv otherwise

anspannen ['anʃpanən] vt to harness; (Muskel) to strain; **Anspannung** f strain

anspielen ['anʃpiːlən] vi (SPORT) to start play; **auf etw** akk ~ to refer od allude to sth

Anspielung f: ~ **(auf** +akk) reference (to), allusion (to)

Anspitzer ['anʃpɪtsər] (-s, -) m pencil sharpener

Ansporn ['anʃpɔrn] (-(e)s) m incentive

Ansprache ['anʃpraːxə] f address

ansprechen ['anʃpreçən] (unreg) vt to speak to; (bitten, gefallen) to appeal to ♦ vi: **(auf etw** akk) ~ to react (to sth); **jdn auf etw** akk **(hin)** ~ to ask sb about sth; **~d** adj attractive

anspringen ['anʃprɪŋən] (unreg) vi (AUT) to start ♦ vt to jump at

Anspruch ['anʃprʊx] m (Recht): ~ **(auf** +akk) claim (to); **hohe Ansprüche stellen/haben** to demand/expect a lot; **jdn/etw in ~ nehmen** to occupy sb/take up sth; **a~slos** adj undemanding; **a~svoll** adj demanding

anstacheln ['anʃtaxəln] vt to spur on

Anstalt ['anʃtalt] (-, -en) f institution; **~en machen, etw zu tun** to prepare to do sth

Anstand ['anʃtant] m decency

anständig ['anʃtendɪç] adj decent; (umg) proper; (groß) considerable

anstandslos adv without any ado

anstarren ['anʃtarən] vt to stare at

anstatt [an'ʃtat] präp +gen instead of ♦ konj: ~ **etw zu tun** instead of doing sth

Ansteck- ['anʃtek] zW: **a~en** vt to pin on; (MED) to infect; (Pfeife) to light; (Haus) to set fire to ♦ vr: **ich habe mich bei ihm angesteckt** I caught it from him ♦ vi (fig) to be infectious; **a~end** adj infectious; **~ung** f infection

anstehen ['anʃteːən] (unreg) vi to queue (up) (BRIT), to line up (US)

ansteigen ['anʃtaigən] vi (Straße) to climb; (Gelände, Temperatur, Preise) to rise

anstelle [an'ʃtelə] präp +gen in place of; **~n** [an'-] vt (einschalten) to turn on; (Arbeit geben) to employ; (machen) to do ♦ vr to queue (up) (BRIT), to line up (US) (umg) to act

Anstellung f employment; (Posten) post, position

Anstieg ['anʃtiːk] (-(e)s, -e) m (+gen) climb; (fig: von Preisen etc) increase (in)

anstiften ['anʃtiftən] vt (Unglück) to cause; **jdn zu etw** ~ to put sb up to sth

anstimmen ['anʃtimən] vt (Lied) to strike up with; (Geschrei) to set up

Anstoß ['anʃtoːs] m impetus; (Ärgernis) offence; (SPORT) kick-off; **der erste** ~ the initiative; ~ **nehmen an** +*dat* to take offence at; **a~en** (*unreg*) *vt* to push; (*mit Fuß*) to kick ♦ *vi* to knock, to bump; (*mit der Zunge*) to lisp; (*mit Gläsern*): **a~en (auf** +*akk*) to drink (to), to drink a toast (to)

anstößig [ˈanʃtøːsɪç] *adj* offensive, indecent

anstreichen [ˈanʃtraɪçən] (*unreg*) *vt* to paint

anstrengen [ˈanʃtrɛŋən] *vt* to strain; (*JUR*) to bring ♦ *vr* to make an effort; **~d** *adj* tiring

Anstrengung *f* effort

Anstrich [ˈanʃtrɪç] *m* coat of paint

Ansturm [ˈanʃtʊrm] *m* rush; (*MIL*) attack

Antarktis [antˈʔarktɪs] (-) *f* Antarctic

antasten [ˈantastən] *vt* to touch; (*Recht*) to infringe upon; (*Ehre*) to question

Anteil [ˈantaɪl] (-s, -e) *m* share; (*Mitgefühl*) sympathy; ~ **nehmen (an** +*dat*) to share (in); (*sich interessieren*) to take an interest (in); **~nahme** (-) *f* sympathy

Antenne [anˈtɛnə] *f* aerial

Anti- [ˈanti] *in zW* anti; **~alko'holiker** *m* teetotaller; **a~autori'tär** *adj* antiauthoritarian; **~babypille** *f* contraceptive pill; **~biotikum** [antibiˈoːtikʊm] (-s, -ka) *nt* antibiotic

antik [anˈtiːk] *adj* antique; **A~e** *f* (*Zeitalter*) ancient world

Antiquariat [antikvariˈaːt] (-(e)s, -e) *nt* secondhand bookshop

Antiquitäten [antikviˈtɛːtən] *pl* antiques; **~händler** *m* antique dealer

Antrag [ˈantraːk] (-(e)s, -träge) *m* proposal; (*PARL*) motion; (*Gesuch*) application; **~steller(in)** (-s, -) *m(f)* claimant; (*für Kredit*) applicant

antreffen [ˈantrɛfən] (*unreg*) *vt* to meet

antreiben [ˈantraɪbən] (*unreg*) *vt* to drive on; (*Motor*) to drive

antreten [ˈantreːtən] (*unreg*) *vt* (*Amt*) to take up; (*Erbschaft*) to come into; (*Beweis*) to offer; (*Reise*) to start, to begin ♦ *vi* (*MIL*) to fall in; (*SPORT*) to line up; **gegen jdn** ~ to play/fight (against) sb

Antrieb [ˈantriːp] *m* (*auch fig*) drive; **aus eigenem** ~ of one's own accord

antrinken [ˈantrɪŋkən] (*unreg*) *vt* (*Flasche, Glas*) to start to drink from; **sich** *dat* **Mut/ einen Rausch** ~ to give o.s. Dutch courage/ get drunk; **angetrunken sein** to be tipsy

Antritt [ˈantrɪt] *m* beginning, commencement; (*eines Amts*) taking up

antun [ˈantuːn] (*unreg*) *vt*: **jdm etw** ~ to do sth to sb; **sich** *dat* **Zwang** ~ to force o.s.; **sich** *dat* **etwas** ~ to (try to) take one's own life

Antwort [ˈantvɔrt] (-, -en) *f* answer, reply; **a~en** *vi* to answer, to reply

anvertrauen [ˈanfɛrtrauən] *vt*: **jdm etw** ~ to entrust sb with sth; **sich jdm** ~ to confide in sb

anwachsen [ˈanvaksən] (*unreg*) *vi* to grow; (*Pflanze*) to take root

Anwalt [ˈanvalt] (-(e)s, -wälte) *m* solicitor; lawyer; (*fig*) champion

Anwältin [ˈanvɛltɪn] *f siehe* **Anwalt**

Anwärter [ˈanvɛrtər] *m* candidate

anweisen [ˈanvaɪzən] (*unreg*) *vt* to instruct; (*zuteilen*) to assign

Anweisung *f* instruction; (*COMM*) remittance; (*Postanweisung, Zahlungsanweisung*) money order

anwend- [ˈanvɛnd] *zW*: **~bar** [ˈanvɛnt-] *adj* practicable, applicable; **~en** (*unreg*) *vt* to use, to employ; (*Gesetz, Regel*) to apply; **A~ung** *f* use; application

anwesend [ˈanveːzənt] *adj* present; **die A~en** those present

Anwesenheit *f* presence

anwidern [ˈanviːdərn] *vt* to disgust

Anwohner(in) [ˈanvoːnər(ɪn)] (-s, -) *m(f)* neighbour

Anzahl [ˈantsaːl] *f*: ~ **(an** +*dat*) number (of); **a~en** *vt* to pay on account; **~ung** *f* deposit, payment on account

Anzeichen [ˈantsaɪçən] *nt* sign, indication

Anzeige [ˈantsaɪgə] *f* (*Zeitungsanzeige*) announcement; (*Werbung*) advertisement; (*bei Polizei*) report; ~ **erstatten gegen jdn** to report sb (to the police); **a~n** *vt* (*zu erkennen geben*) to show; (*bekannt geben*) to announce; (*bei Polizei*) to report

anziehen [ˈantsiːən] (*unreg*) *vt* to attract; (*Kleidung*) to put on; (*Mensch*) to dress; (*Seil*) to pull tight; (*Schraube*) to tighten; (*Knie*) to draw up ♦ *vr* to get dressed; **~d** *adj* attractive

Anziehung *f* (*Reiz*) attraction; **~skraft** *f* power of attraction; (*PHYS*) force of gravitation

Anzug [ˈantsuːk] *m* suit; (*Herankommen*): **im** ~ **sein** to be approaching

anzüglich [ˈantsyːklɪç] *adj* personal; (*anstößig*) offensive; **A~keit** *f* offensiveness; (*Bemerkung*) personal remark

anzünden [ˈantsyndən] *vt* to light

anzweifeln [ˈantsvaɪfəln] *vt* to doubt

apathisch [aˈpaːtɪʃ] *adj* apathetic

Apfel [ˈapfəl] (-s, ᵕ) *m* apple; **~saft** *m* apple juice; **~sine** [-ˈziːnə] *f* orange; **~wein** *m* cider

Apostel [aˈpɔstəl] (-s, -) *m* apostle

Apotheke [apoˈteːkə] *f* chemist's (shop), drugstore (*US*); **a~npflichtig** [-pflɪçtɪç] *adj* available only at a chemist's shop (*BRIT*) or pharmacy; **~r(in)** (-s, -) *m(f)* chemist, druggist (*US*)

Apparat [apaˈraːt] (-(e)s, -e) *m* piece of apparatus; camera; telephone; (*RAD, TV*) set; **am** ~! speaking!; **~ur** [-ˈtuːr] *f* apparatus

Appartement [apart(ə)ˈmãː] (-s, -s) *nt* flat

appellieren [apɛˈliːrən] *vi*: ~ **(an** +*akk*) to appeal (to)

Appetit [apeˈtiːt] (-(e)s, -e) *m* appetite;

guten ~! enjoy your meal!; **a~lich** adj appetizing; **~losigkeit** f lack of appetite
Applaus [aˈplaʊs] **(-es, -e)** m applause
Aprikose [apriˈkoːzə] f apricot
April [aˈprɪl] **(-(s), -e)** m April
Aquarell [akvaˈrɛl] **(-s, -e)** nt watercolour
Äquator [ɛˈkvaːtɔr] **(-s)** m equator
Arab- [ˈarab] zW: **~er(in) (-s, -)** m(f) Arab; **~ien** [aˈraːbiən] **(-s)** nt Arabia; **a~isch** [aˈraːbɪʃ] adj Arabian
Arbeit [ˈarbaɪt] **(-, -en)** f work no art; (Stelle) job; (Erzeugnis) piece of work; (wissenschaftliche) dissertation; (Klassenarbeit) test; **das war eine ~** that was a hard job; **a~en** vi to work ♦ vt to work, to make; **~er(in) (-s, -)** m(f) worker; (ungelernt) labourer; **~erschaft** f workers pl, labour force; **~geber (-s, -)** m employer; **~nehmer (-s, -)** m employee
Arbeits- in zW labour; **a~am** adj industrious; **~amt** nt employment exchange; **~erlaubnis** f work permit; **a~fähig** adj fit for work, able-bodied; **~gang** m operation; **~kräfte** pl (Mitarbeiter) workforce; **a~los** adj unemployed, out-of-work; **~lose(r)** f(m) unemployed person; **~losigkeit** f unemployment; **~markt** m job market; **~platz** m job; place of work; **a~scheu** adj workshy; **~tag** m work(ing) day; **a~unfähig** adj unfit for work; **~zeit** f working hours pl; **~zimmer** nt study
Archäologe [arçɛoˈloːgə] **(-n, -n)** m archaeologist
Architekt(in) [arçiˈtekt(ɪn)] **(-en, -en)** m(f) architect; **~ur** [-ˈtuːr] f architecture
Archiv [arˈçiːf] **(-s, -e)** nt archive
arg [ark] adj bad, awful ♦ adv awfully, very
Argentinien [argenˈtiːniən] **(-s)** nt Argentina, the Argentine
argentinisch adj Argentinian
Ärger [ˈɛrgər] **(-s)** m (Wut) anger; (Unannehmlichkeit) trouble; **ä~lich** adj (zornig) angry; (lästig) annoying, aggravating; **ä~n** vt to annoy ♦ vr to get annoyed
arg- zW: **~listig** adj cunning, insidious; **~los** adj guileless, innocent
Argument [arguˈment] nt argument
argwöhnisch adj suspicious
Arie [ˈaːriə] f aria
Aristokrat [aristoˈkraːt] **(-en, -en)** m aristocrat; **~ie** [-ˈtiː] f aristocracy
Arktis [ˈarktɪs] **(-)** f Arctic
Arm [arm] **(-(e)s, -e)** m arm; (Flussarm) branch
arm adj poor
Armatur [armaˈtuːr] f (ELEK) armature; **~enbrett** nt instrument panel; (AUT) dashboard

Armband nt bracelet; **~uhr** f (wrist) watch
Arme(r) f(m) poor man (woman); **die ~n** the poor
Armee [arˈmeː] f army
Ärmel [ˈɛrməl] **(-s, -)** m sleeve; **etw aus dem ~ schütteln** (fig) to produce sth just like that; **~kanal** m English Channel
ärmlich [ˈɛrmlɪç] adj poor
armselig adj wretched, miserable
Armut [ˈarmuːt] **(-)** f poverty
Aroma [aˈroːma] **(-s, Aromen)** nt aroma; **~therapie** f aromatherapy; **a~tisch** [aroˈmaːtɪʃ] adj aromatic
arrangieren [arãˈʒiːrən] vt to arrange ♦ vr to come to an arrangement
Arrest [aˈrɛst] **(-(e)s, -e)** m detention
arrogant [aroˈgant] adj arrogant
Arsch [arʃ] **(-es, ̈e)** (umg!) m arse (BRIT!), ass (US!)
Art [aːrt] **(-, -en)** f (Weise) way; (Sorte) kind, sort; (BIOL) species; **eine ~ (von) Frucht** a kind of fruit; **Häuser aller ~** houses of all kinds; **es ist nicht seine ~, das zu tun** it's not like him to do that; **ich mache das auf meine ~** I do that my (own) way
Arterie [arˈteːriə] f artery; **~nverkalkung** f arteriosclerosis
artig [ˈaːrtɪç] adj good, well-behaved
Artikel [arˈtiːkəl] **(-s, -)** m article
Artillerie [artɪləˈriː] f artillery
Artischocke [artiˈʃɔkə] f artichoke
Artist(in) [arˈtɪst(ɪn)] **(-en, -en)** m(f) (circus/variety) artiste od performer
Arznei [aːrtsˈnaɪ] f medicine; **~mittel** nt medicine, medicament
Arzt [aːrtst] **(-es, ̈e)** m doctor; **~helferin** f (doctor's) receptionist
Ärztin [ˈɛːrtstɪn] f doctor
ärztlich [ˈɛːrtstlɪç] adj medical
As △ [as] **(-ses, -se)** nt siehe Ass
Asche [ˈaʃə] f (-, -n) ash, cinder
Aschen- zW: **~bahn** f cinder track; **~becher** m ashtray
Aschermittwoch m Ash Wednesday
Äser [ˈɛːzər] pl von Aas
Asiat(in) [aziˈaːt(ɪn)] **(-en, -en)** m(f) Asian; **a~isch** [-ˈaːtɪʃ] adj Asian
Asien [ˈaːziən] **(-s)** nt Asia
asozial [ˈazotsiaːl] adj antisocial; (Familien) asocial
Aspekt [asˈpɛkt] **(-(e)s, -e)** m aspect
Asphalt [asˈfalt] **(-(e)s, -e)** m asphalt; **a~ieren** vt to asphalt
Ass ▲ [as] **(-es, -e)** nt ace
aß etc [aːs] vb siehe essen
Assistent(in) [asɪsˈtent(ɪn)] m(f) assistant
Assoziation [asotsiatsiˈoːn] f association
Ast [ast] **(-(e)s, ̈e)** m bough, branch
ästhetisch [ɛsˈteːtɪʃ] adj aesthetic

Asthma ['astma] (-s) nt asthma; **~tiker(in)** (-s, -) m(f) asthmatic

Astro- |astro| zW: **~'loge** (-n, -n) m astrologer; **~lo'gie** f astrology; **~'naut** (-en, -en) m astronaut; **~'nom** (-en, -en) m astronomer; **~no'mie** f astronomy

Asyl |a'zy:l| (-s, -e) nt asylum; (Heim) home; (Obdachlosenasyl) shelter; **~ant(in)** |azy'lant(ın)| (-en, -en) m(f) asylum-seeker

Atelier |atali'e:| (-s, -s) nt studio

Atem ['a:təm] (-s) m breath; **den ~ anhalten** to hold one's breath; **außer ~** out of breath; **a~beraubend** adj breathtaking; **a~los** adj breathless; **~not** f difficulty in breathing; **~pause** f breather; **~zug** m breath

Atheismus |ate'ısmos| m atheism

Atheist m atheist; **a~isch** adj atheistic

Athen |a'te:n| (-s) nt Athens

Äthiopien |ɛti'o:piən| (-s) nt Ethiopia

Athlet |at'le:t| (-en, -en) m athlete

Atlantik |at'lantık| (-s) m Atlantic (Ocean)

Atlas ['atlas] (- od -ses, -se od **Atlanten**) m atlas

atmen ['a:tmən] vt, vi to breathe

Atmosphäre |atmo'sfe:rə| f atmosphere; **atmosphärisch** adj atmospheric

Atmung ['a:tmoŋ] f respiration

Atom |a'to:m| (-s, -e) nt atom; **a~'ar** adj atomic; **~bombe** f atom bomb; **~energie** f atomic od nuclear energy; **~kern** m atomic nucleus; **~kraftwerk** nt nuclear power station; **~krieg** m nuclear od atomic war; **~müll** m atomic waste; **~strom** m (electricity generated by) nuclear power; **~versuch** m atomic test; **~waffen** pl atomic weapons; **a~waffenfrei** adj nuclear-free; **~zeitalter** nt atomic age

Attentat |aten'ta:t| (-(e)s, -e) nt: ~ (auf +akk) (attempted) assassination (of)

Attentäter |aten'tɛ:tər| m (would-be) assassin

Attest |a'tɛst| (-(e)s, -e) nt certificate

Attraktion |atrakstsi'o:n| f (Tourismus, Zirkus) attraction

attraktiv |atrak'ti:f| adj attractive

Attrappe |a'trapə| f dummy

Attribut |atri'bu:t| (-(e)s, -e) nt (GRAM) attribute

ätzen ['ɛtsən] vi to be caustic; **~d** adj (Säure) corrosive; (fig: Spott) cutting

au |au| excl ouch!; **~ ja!** oh yes!

Aubergine |obɛr'ʒi:nə| f aubergine, eggplant

auch |aux| adv 1 (ebenfalls) also, too, as well; **das ist auch schön** that's nice too od as well; **er kommt – ich auch** he's coming – so am I, me too; **auch nicht** not ... either; **ich auch nicht** nor I, me neither; **oder auch** or; **auch das noch!** not that as well!

2 (selbst, sogar) even; **auch wenn das Wetter schlecht ist** even if the weather is bad; **ohne auch nur zu fragen** without even asking

3 (wirklich) really; **du siehst müde aus – bin ich auch** you look tired – (so) I am; **so sieht es auch aus** it looks like it too

4 (auch immer): **wer auch** whoever; **was auch** whatever; **wie dem auch sei** be that as it may; **wie sehr er sich auch bemühte** however much he tried

auf |auf| präp +dat (wo?) on; **auf dem Tisch** on the table; **auf der Reise** on the way; **auf der Post/dem Fest** at the post office/party; **auf der Straße** on the road; **auf dem Land/der ganzen Welt** in the country/the whole world

♦ präp +akk 1 (wohin?) on(to); **auf den Tisch** on(to) the table; **auf die Post gehen** go to the post office; **auf das Land** into the country; **etw auf einen Zettel schreiben** to write sth on a piece of paper

2: **auf Deutsch** in German; **auf Lebenszeit** for my/his lifetime; **bis auf ihn** except for him; **auf einmal** at once; **auf seinen Vorschlag (hin)** at his suggestion

♦ adv 1 (offen) open; **auf sein** (umg: Tür, Geschäft) to be open; **das Fenster ist auf** the window is open

2 (hinauf) up; **auf und ab** up and down; **auf und davon** up and away; **auf!** (los!) come on!

3 (aufgestanden) up; **auf sein** to be up; **ist er schon auf?** is he up yet?

♦ konj: **auf dass** (so) that

aufatmen ['aufʔa:tmən] vi to heave a sigh of relief

aufbahren ['aufba:rən] vt to lay out

Aufbau ['aufbau] m (Bauen) building, construction; (Struktur) structure; (aufgebautes Teil) superstructure; **a~en** vt to erect, to build (up); (Existenz) to make; (gestalten) to construct; **a~en (auf +dat)** (gründen) to found od base (on)

aufbauschen ['aufbau:ʃən] vt to puff out; (fig) to exaggerate

aufbekommen ['aufbəkɔmən] (unreg) vt (öffnen) to get open; (Hausaufgaben) to be given

aufbessern ['aufbɛsərn] vt (Gehalt) to increase

aufbewahren ['aufbəva:rən] vt to keep; (Gepäck) to put in the left-luggage office (BRIT) od baggage check (US)

Aufbewahrung f (safe)keeping; (Gepäckaufbewahrung) left-luggage office (BRIT), baggage check (US)

aufbieten |ˈaʊfbiːtən| (unreg) vt (Kraft) to summon (up); (Armee, Polizei) to mobilize

aufblasen |ˈaʊfblaːzən| (unreg) vt to blow up, to inflate ♦ vr (umg) to become bigheaded

aufbleiben |ˈaʊfblaɪbən| (unreg) vi (Laden) to remain open; (Person) to stay up

aufblenden |ˈaʊfblɛndən| vt (Scheinwerfer) to switch on full beam ♦ vi (Fahrer) to have the lights on full beam ♦ vt (AUT: Scheinwerfer) to be on full beam

aufblicken |ˈaʊfblɪkən| vi to look up; ~ zu look up at; (fig) to look up to

aufblühen |ˈaʊfblyːən| vi to blossom, to flourish

aufbrauchen |ˈaʊfbraʊxən| vt to use up

aufbrausen |ˈaʊfbraʊzən| vi (fig) to flare up; ~d adj hot-tempered

aufbrechen |ˈaʊfbrɛçən| (unreg) vt to break od prise (BRIT) open ♦ vi to burst open; (gehen) to start, to set off

aufbringen |ˈaʊfbrɪŋən| (unreg) vt (öffnen) to open; (in Mode) to bring into fashion; (beschaffen) to procure; (FIN) to raise; (ärgern) to irritate; **Verständnis für etw ~** to be able to understand sth

Aufbruch |ˈaʊfbrʊx| m departure

aufbrühen |ˈaʊfbryːən| vt (Tee) to make

aufbürden |ˈaʊfbyrdən| vt: **jdm etw ~** to burden sb with sth

aufdecken |ˈaʊfdɛkən| vt to uncover

aufdrängen |ˈaʊfdrɛŋən| vt: **jdm etw ~** to force sth on sb ♦ vr (Mensch): **sich jdm ~** to intrude on sb

aufdrehen |ˈaʊfdreːən| vt (Wasserhahn etc) to turn on; (Ventil) to open up

aufdringlich |ˈaʊfdrɪŋlɪç| adj pushy

aufeinander |aʊfaɪˈnandər| adv on top of each other; (schießen) at each other; (vertrauen) each other; ~ **folgen** to follow one another; ~ **folgend** consecutive; ~ **prallen** to hit one another

Aufenthalt |ˈaʊfɛnthalt| m stay; (Verzögerung) delay; (EISENB: Halten) stop; (Ort) haunt

Aufenthaltserlaubnis f residence permit

auferlegen |ˈaʊfɛrleːɡən| vt: **(jdm) ~** to impose (upon sb)

Auferstehung |ˈaʊfɛrʃteːʊŋ| f resurrection

aufessen |ˈaʊfɛsən| (unreg) vt to eat up

auffahr- |ˈaʊfaːr| zW: **~en** (unreg) vi (herankommen) to draw up; (hochfahren) to jump up; (wütend werden) to flare up; (in den Himmel) to ascend ♦ vt (Kanonen, Geschütz) to bring up; **~en auf** +akk (Auto) to run od crash into; **~end** adj hot-tempered; **A~t** f (Hausauffahrt) drive; (Autobahnauffahrt) slip road (BRIT), (freeway) entrance (US); **A~unfall** m pile-up

auffallen |ˈaʊffalən| (unreg) vi to be noticeable; **jdm ~** to strike sb

auffällig |ˈaʊffɛlɪç| adj conspicuous, striking

auffangen |ˈaʊffaŋən| (unreg) vt to catch; (Funkspruch) to intercept; (Preise) to peg

auffassen |ˈaʊffasən| vt to understand, to comprehend; (auslegen) to see, to view

Auffassung f (Meinung) opinion; (Auslegung) view, concept; (auch: **~sgabe**) grasp

auffindbar |ˈaʊffɪntbaːr| adj to be found

auffordern |ˈaʊffɔrdərn| vt (befehlen) to call upon, to order; (bitten) to ask

Aufforderung f (Befehl) order; (Einladung) invitation

auffrischen |ˈaʊffrɪʃən| vt to freshen up; (Kenntnisse) to brush up; (Erinnerungen) to reawaken ♦ vi (Wind) to freshen

aufführen |ˈaʊffyːrən| vt (THEAT) to perform; (in einem Verzeichnis) to list, to specify ♦ vr (sich benehmen) to behave

Aufführung f (THEAT) performance; (Liste) specification

Aufgabe |ˈaʊfɡaːbə| f task; (SCH) exercise; (Hausaufgabe) homework; (Verzicht) giving up; (von Gepäck) registration; (von Post) posting; (von Inserat) insertion

Aufgang |ˈaʊfɡaŋ| m ascent; (Sonnenaufgang) rise; (Treppe) staircase

aufgeben |ˈaʊfɡeːbən| (unreg) vt (verzichten) to give up; (Paket) to send, to post; (Gepäck) to register; (Bestellung) to give; (Inserat) to insert; (Rätsel, Problem) to set ♦ vi to give up

Aufgebot |ˈaʊfɡəboːt| nt supply; (Eheaufgebot) banns pl

aufgedunsen |ˈaʊfɡədʊnzən| adj swollen, puffed up

aufgehen |ˈaʊfɡeːən| (unreg) vi (Sonne, Teig) to rise; (sich öffnen) to open; (klar werden) to become clear; (MATH) to come out exactly; (in +dat) (sich widmen) to be absorbed (in); **in Rauch/Flammen ~** to go up in smoke/ flames

aufgelegt |ˈaʊfɡəleːkt| adj: **gut/schlecht ~ sein** to be in a good/bad mood; **zu etw ~ sein** to be in the mood for sth

aufgeregt |ˈaʊfɡəreːkt| adj excited

aufgeschlossen |ˈaʊfɡəʃlɔsən| adj open, open-minded

aufgeweckt |ˈaʊfɡəvɛkt| adj bright, intelligent

aufgießen |ˈaʊfɡiːsən| (unreg) vt (Wasser) to pour over; (Tee) to infuse

aufgreifen |ˈaʊfɡraɪfən| (unreg) vt (Thema) to take up; (Verdächtige) to pick up, to seize

aufgrund, auf Grund |aʊfˈɡrʊnt| präp +gen on the basis of; (wegen) because of

aufhaben |ˈaʊfhaːbən| (unreg) vt to have on; (Arbeit) to have to do

---

Spelling reform: ▲ *new spelling* △ *old spelling (to be phased out)*

aufhalsen |'aofhalzən| (umg) vt: **jdm etw ~** to saddle od lumber sb with sth

aufhalten |'aofhaltən| (unreg) vt (Person) to detain; (Entwicklung) to check; (Tür, Hand) to hold open; (Augen) to keep open ♦ vr (wohnen) to live; (bleiben) to stay; **sich mit etw ~** to waste time over sth

aufhängen |'aofhɛŋən| (unreg) vt (Wäsche) to hang up; (Menschen) to hang ♦ vr to hang o.s.

Aufhänger (-s, -) m (am Mantel) loop; (fig) peg

aufheben |'aofhe:bən| (unreg) vt (hochheben) to raise, to lift; (Sitzung) to wind up; (Urteil) to annul; (Gesetz) to repeal, to abolish; (aufbewahren) to keep ♦ vr to cancel itself out; **bei jdm gut aufgehoben sein** to be well looked after at sb's; **viel A~(s) machen (von)** to make a fuss (about)

aufheitern |'aofhaɪtərn| vt, vr (Himmel, Miene) to brighten; (Mensch) to cheer up

aufhellen |'aofhɛlən| vt, vr to clear up; (Farbe, Haare) to lighten

aufhetzen |'aofhɛtsən| vt to stir up

aufholen |'aofho:lən| vt to make up ♦ vi to catch up

aufhorchen |'aofhɔrçən| vi to prick up one's ears

aufhören |'aofhø:rən| vi to stop; **~, etw zu tun** to stop doing sth

aufklappen |'aofklapən| vt to open

aufklären |'aofklɛ:rən| vt (Geheimnis etc) to clear up; (Person) to enlighten; (sexuell) to tell the facts of life to; (MIL) to reconnoitre ♦ vr to clear up

Aufklärung f (von Geheimnis) clearing up; (Unterrichtung, Zeitalter) enlightenment; (sexuell) sex education; (MIL, AVIAT) reconnaissance

aufkleben |'aofkle:bən| vt to stick on; **Aufkleber** (-s, -) m sticker

aufknöpfen |'aofknœpfən| vt to unbutton

aufkommen |'aofkɔmən| (unreg) vi (Wind) to come up; (Zweifel, Gefühl) to arise; (Mode) to start; **für jdn/etw ~** to be liable od responsible for sb/sth

aufladen |'aofla:dən| (unreg) vt to load

Auflage |'aofla:gə| f edition; (Zeitung) circulation; (Bedingung) condition

auflassen |'aoflasən| (unreg) vt (offen) to leave open; (aufgesetzt) to leave on

auflauern |'aoflaoərn| vi: **jdm ~** to lie in wait for sb

Auflauf |'aoflaof| m (KOCH) pudding; (Menschenauflauf) crowd

aufleben |'aofle:bən| vi (Mensch, Gespräch) to liven up; (Interesse) to revive

auflegen |'aofle:gən| vt to put on; (Telefon) to hang up; (TYP) to print

auflehnen |'aofle:nən| vt to lean on ♦ vr to rebel

Auflehnung f rebellion

auflesen |'aofle:zən| (unreg) vt to pick up

aufleuchten |'aoflɔyçtən| vi to light up

auflisten |'aoflistən| vt to list

auflockern |'aoflɔkərn| vt to loosen; (fig: Eintönigkeit etc) to liven up

auflösen |'aoflø:zən| vt to dissolve; (Haare etc) to loosen; (Missverständnis) to sort out ♦ vr to dissolve; to come undone; to be resolved; **(in Tränen) aufgelöst sein** to be in tears

Auflösung f dissolving; (fig) solution

aufmachen |'aofmaxən| vt to open; (Kleidung) to undo; (zurechtmachen) to do up ♦ vr to set out

Aufmachung f (Kleidung) outfit, get-up; (Gestaltung) format

aufmerksam |'aofmɛrkza:m| adj attentive; **jdn auf etw** akk **~ machen** to point sth out to sb; **A~keit** f attention, attentiveness

aufmuntern |'aofmontərn| vt (ermutigen) to encourage; (erheitern) to cheer up

Aufnahme |'aofna:mə| f reception; (Beginn) beginning; (in Verein etc) admission; (in Liste etc) inclusion; (Notieren) taking down; (PHOT) shot; (auf Tonband etc) recording; **a~fähig** adj receptive; **~prüfung** f entrance test

aufnehmen |'aofne:mən| (unreg) vt to receive; (hochheben) to pick up; (beginnen) to take up; (in Verein etc) to admit; (in Liste etc) to include; (fassen) to hold; (notieren) to take down; (fotografieren) to photograph; (auf Tonband, Platte) to record; (FIN: leihen) to take out; **es mit jdm ~ können** to be able to compete with sb

aufopfern |'aofɔpfərn| vt, vr to sacrifice; **~d** adj selfless

aufpassen |'aofpasən| vi (aufmerksam sein) to pay attention; **auf jdn/etw ~** to look after od watch sb/sth; **aufgepasst!** look out!

Aufprall |'aofpral| (-s, -e) m impact; **a~en** vi to hit, to strike

Aufpreis |'aofpraɪs| m extra charge

aufpumpen |'aofpompən| vt to pump up

aufräumen |'aofrɔymən| vt, vi (Dinge) to clear away; (Zimmer) to tidy up

aufrecht |'aofrɛçt| adj (auch fig) upright; **~erhalten** (unreg) vt to maintain

aufreg- |'aofrɛ:g| zW: **~en** vt to excite ♦ vr to get excited; **~end** adj exciting; **A~ung** f excitement

aufreibend |'aofraɪbənt| adj strenuous

aufreißen |'aofraɪsən| (unreg) vt (Umschlag) to tear open; (Augen) to open wide; (Tür) to throw open; (Straße) to take up

aufreizen |'aofraɪtsən| vt to incite, to stir up; **~d** adj exciting, stimulating

aufrichten |'aofrɪçtən| vt to put up, to erect; (moralisch) to console ♦ vr to rise;

(*moralisch*): **sich ~ (an** +*dat*) to take heart (from)

aufrichtig |'aʊfrɪçtɪç| *adj* sincere, honest; **A~keit** *f* sincerity

aufrücken |'aʊfrʏkən| *vi* to move up; (*beruflich*) to be promoted

Aufruf |'aʊfruːf| *m* summons; (*zur Hilfe*) call; (*des Namens*) calling out; **a~en** (*unreg*) *vt* (*Namen*) to call out; (*auffordern*): **jdn a~en** (**zu**) to call upon sb (for)

Aufruhr |'aʊfruːr| (**-(e)s, -e**) *m* uprising, revolt

aufrührerisch |'aʊfryːrərɪʃ| *adj* rebellious

aufrunden |'aʊfrʊndən| *vt* (*Summe*) to round up

Aufrüstung |'aʊfrʏstʊŋ| *f* rearmament

aufrütteln |'aʊfrʏtəln| *vt* (*auch fig*) to shake up

aufs |aʊfs| = **auf das**

aufsagen |'aʊfzaːɡən| *vt* (*Gedicht*) to recite

aufsässig |'aʊfzɛsɪç| *adj* rebellious

Aufsatz |'aʊfzats| *m* (*Geschriebenes*) essay; (*auf Schrank etc*) top

aufsaugen |'aʊfzaʊɡən| (*unreg*) *vt* to soak up

aufschauen |'aʊfʃaʊən| *vi* to look up

aufscheuchen |'aʊfʃɔʏçən| *vt* to scare *od* frighten away

aufschieben |'aʊfʃiːbən| (*unreg*) *vt* to push open; (*verzögern*) to put off, to postpone

Aufschlag |'aʊfʃlaːk| *m* (*Ärmelaufschlag*) cuff; (*Jackenaufschlag*) lapel; (*Hosenaufschlag*) turn-up; (*Aufprall*) impact; (*Preisaufschlag*) surcharge; (*Tennis*) service; **a~en** [-ɡən] (*unreg*) *vt* (*öffnen*) to open; (*verwunden*) to cut; (*hochschlagen*) to turn up; (*aufbauen: Zelt, Lager*) to pitch, to erect; (*Wohnsitz*) to take up ♦ *vi* (*aufprallen*) to hit; (*teurer werden*) to go up; (*Tennis*) to serve

aufschließen |'aʊfʃliːsən| (*unreg*) *vt* to open up, to unlock ♦ *vi* (*aufrücken*) to close up

aufschlussreich ▲ *adj* informative, illuminating

aufschnappen |'aʊfʃnapən| *vt* (*umg*) to pick up ♦ *vi* to fly open

aufschneiden |'aʊfʃnaɪdən| (*unreg*) *vt* (*Brot*) to cut up; (*MED*) to lance ♦ *vi* to brag

Aufschneider (**-s, -**) *m* boaster, braggart

Aufschnitt |'aʊfʃnɪt| *m* (slices of) cold meat

aufschrauben |'aʊfʃraʊbən| *vt* (*festschrauben*) to screw on; (*lösen*) to unscrew

aufschrecken |'aʊfʃrɛkən| *vt* to startle ♦ *vi* (*unreg*) to start up

aufschreiben |'aʊfʃraɪbən| (*unreg*) *vt* to write down

aufschreien |'aʊfʃraɪən| (*unreg*) *vi* to cry out

Aufschrift |'aʊfʃrɪft| *f* (*Inschrift*) inscription; (*auf Etikett*) label

Aufschub |'aʊfʃuːp| (**-(e)s, -schübe**) *m* delay, postponement

Aufschwung |'aʊfʃvʊŋ| *m* (*Elan*) boost; (*wirtschaftlich*) upturn, boom; (*SPORT*) circle

aufsehen |'aʊfzeːən| (*unreg*) *vi* to look up; **~ zu** to look up at; (*fig*) to look up to; **A~** (**-s**) *nt* sensation, stir; **A~ erregend** sensational

Aufseher(in) (**-s, -**) *m(f)* guard; (*im Betrieb*) supervisor; (*Museumsaufseher*) attendant; (*Parkaufseher*) keeper

aufsein △ *siehe* **auf**

aufsetzen |'aʊfzɛtsən| *vt* to put on; (*Dokument*) to draw up ♦ *vr* to sit up(right) ♦ *vi* (*Flugzeug*) to touch down

Aufsicht |'aʊfzɪçt| *f* supervision; **die ~ haben** to be in charge

Aufsichtsrat *m* (supervisory) board

aufsitzen |'aʊfzɪtsən| (*unreg*) *vi* (*aufrecht hinsitzen*) to sit up; (*aufs Pferd, Motorrad*) to mount, to get on; (*Schiff*) to run aground; **jdm ~** (*umg*) to be taken in by sb

aufsparen |'aʊfʃpaːrən| *vt* to save (up)

aufsperren |'aʊfʃpɛrən| *vt* to unlock; (*Mund*) to open wide

aufspielen |'aʊfʃpiːlən| *vr* to show off

aufspießen |'aʊfʃpiːsən| *vt* to spear

aufspringen |'aʊfʃprɪŋən| (*unreg*) *vi* (*hochspringen*) to jump up; (*sich öffnen*) to spring open; (*Hände, Lippen*) to become chapped; **auf etw akk ~** to jump onto sth

aufspüren |'aʊfʃpyːrən| *vt* to track down, to trace

aufstacheln |'aʊfʃtaxəln| *vt* to incite

Aufstand |'aʊfʃtant| *m* insurrection, rebellion; **aufständisch** |'aʊfʃtɛndɪʃ| *adj* rebellious, mutinous

aufstehen |'aʊfʃteːən| (*unreg*) *vi* to get up; (*Tür*) to be open

aufsteigen |'aʊfʃtaɪɡən| (*unreg*) *vi* (*hochsteigen*) to climb; (*Rauch*) to rise; **auf etw akk ~** to get onto sth

aufstellen |'aʊfʃtɛlən| *vt* (*aufrecht stellen*) to put up; (*aufreihen*) to line up; (*nominieren*) to nominate; (*formulieren: Programm etc*) to draw up; (*leisten: Rekord*) to set up

Aufstellung *f* (*SPORT*) line-up; (*Liste*) list

Aufstieg |'aʊfʃtiːk| (**-(e)s, -e**) *m* (*auf Berg*) ascent; (*Fortschritt*) rise; (*beruflich, SPORT*) promotion

aufstocken |'aʊfʃtɔkən| *vt* (*Kapital*) to increase

aufstoßen |'aʊfʃtoːsən| (*unreg*) *vt* to push open ♦ *vi* to belch

aufstützen |'aʊfʃtʏtsən| *vt* (*Körperteil*) to prop, to lean; (*Person*) to prop up ♦ *vr*: **sich auf etw akk ~** to lean on sth

aufsuchen |'aʊfzuːxən| *vt* (*besuchen*) to visit; (*konsultieren*) to consult

Auftakt |'aʊftakt| *m* (*MUS*) upbeat; (*fig*)

Spelling reform: ▲ *new spelling* △ *old spelling (to be phased out)*

prelude

auftanken [ˈaʊftaŋkən] vi to get petrol (BRIT) od gas (US) ♦ vt to refuel

auftauchen [ˈaʊftaʊxən] vi to appear; (aus Wasser etc) to emerge; (U-Boot) to surface; (Zweifel) to arise

auftauen [ˈaʊftaʊən] vt to thaw ♦ vi to thaw; (fig) to relax

aufteilen [ˈaʊftaɪlən] vt to divide up; (Raum) to partition; **Aufteilung** f division; partition

Auftrag [ˈaʊftraːk] (-(e)s, -träge) m order; (Anweisung) commission; (Aufgabe) mission; **im ~ von** on behalf of; **a~en** (-gən) (unreg) vt (Essen) to serve; (Farbe) to put on; (Kleidung) to wear out; **jdm etw a~en** to tell sb sth; **dick a~en** (fig) to exaggerate; **~geber** (-s, -) m (COMM) purchaser, customer

auftreiben [ˈaʊftraɪbən] (unreg) vt (umg: beschaffen) to raise

auftreten [ˈaʊftreːtən] (unreg) vt to kick open ♦ vi to appear; (mit Füßen) to tread; (sich verhalten) to behave; **A~** (-s) nt (Vorkommen) appearance; (Benehmen) behaviour

Auftrieb [ˈaʊftriːp] m (PHYS) buoyancy, lift; (fig) impetus

Auftritt [ˈaʊftrɪt] m (des Schauspielers) entrance; (Szene: auch fig) scene

aufwachen [ˈaʊfvaxən] vi to wake up

aufwachsen [ˈaʊfvaksən] (unreg) vi to grow up

Aufwand [ˈaʊfvant] (-(e)s) m expenditure; (Kosten auch) expense; (Luxus) show

aufwändig [ˈaʊfvɛndɪç] adj costly

aufwärmen [ˈaʊfvɛrmən] vt to warm up; (alte Geschichten) to rake up

aufwärts [ˈaʊfvɛrts] adv upwards; **A~entwicklung** f upward trend

Aufwasch [ˈaʊfvaʃ] m washing-up

aufwecken [ˈaʊfvɛkən] vt to wake up, to waken up

aufweisen [ˈaʊfvaɪzən] (unreg) vt to show

aufwenden [ˈaʊfvɛndən] (unreg) vt to expend; (Geld) to spend; (Sorgfalt) to devote

aufwendig adj siehe **aufwändig**

aufwerfen [ˈaʊfvɛrfən] (unreg) vt (Fenster etc) to throw open; (Probleme) to throw up, to raise

aufwerten [ˈaʊfvɛrtən] vt (FIN) to revalue; (fig) to raise in value

aufwickeln [ˈaʊfvɪkəln] vt (aufrollen) to roll up; (umg: Haar) to put in curlers

aufwiegen [ˈaʊfviːgən] (unreg) vt to make up for

Aufwind [ˈaʊfvɪnt] m up-current

aufwirbeln [ˈaʊfvɪrbəln] vt to whirl up; **Staub ~** (fig) to create a stir

aufwischen [ˈaʊfvɪʃən] vt to wipe up

aufzählen [ˈaʊftsɛːlən] vt to list

aufzeichnen [ˈaʊftsaɪçnən] vt to sketch;

(schriftlich) to jot down; (auf Band) to record

Aufzeichnung f (schriftlich) note; (Tonbandaufzeichnung) recording; (Filmaufzeichnung) record

aufzeigen [ˈaʊftsaɪgən] vt to show, to demonstrate

aufziehen [ˈaʊftsiːən] (unreg) vt (hochziehen) to raise, to draw up; (öffnen) to pull open; (Uhr) to wind; (umg: necken) to tease; (großziehen: Kinder) to raise, to bring up; (Tiere) to rear

Aufzug [ˈaʊftsuːk] m (Fahrstuhl) lift, elevator; (Aufmarsch) procession, parade; (Kleidung) get-up; (THEAT) act

aufzwingen [ˈaʊftsvɪŋən] (unreg) vt: **jdm etw ~** to force sth upon sb

Augapfel [ˈaʊkapfəl] m eyeball; (fig) apple of one's eye

Auge [ˈaʊgə] (-s, -n) nt eye; (Fettauge) globule of fat; **unter vier ~n** in private

Augen- zW: **~blick** m moment; **im ~blick** at the moment; **a~blicklich** adj (sofort) instantaneous; (gegenwärtig) present; **~braue** f eyebrow; **~optiker(in)** m(f) optician; **~weide** f sight for sore eyes; **~zeuge** m eye witness

August [aʊˈgʊst] (-(e)s od -, -e) m August

Auktion [aʊktsiˈoːn] f auction

Aula [ˈaʊla] (-, Aulen od -s) f assembly hall

SCHLÜSSELWORT

aus [aʊs] präp +dat **1** (räumlich) out of; (von ... her) from; **er ist aus Berlin** he's from Berlin; **aus dem Fenster** out of the window **2** (gemacht/hergestellt aus) made of; **ein Herz aus Stein** a heart of stone **3** (auf Ursache deutend) from; **aus Mitleid** out of sympathy; **aus Erfahrung** from experience; **aus Spaß** for fun **4**: **aus ihr wird nie etwas** she'll never get anywhere

♦ adv **1** (zu Ende) finished, over; **aus sein** to be over; **aus und vorbei** over and done with

2 (ausgeschaltet, ausgezogen) out; (Aufschrift an Geräten) off; **aus sein** (nicht brennen) to be out; (abgeschaltet sein: Radio, Herd) to be off; **Licht aus!** lights out!

3 (nicht zu Hause): **aus sein** to be out

4 (in Verbindung mit von): **von Rom aus** from Rome; **vom Fenster aus** out of the window; **von sich aus** (selbstständig) of one's own accord; **von ihm aus** as far as he's concerned

---

ausarbeiten [ˈaʊsarbaɪtən] vt to work out

ausarten [ˈaʊsartən] vi to degenerate

ausatmen [ˈaʊsaːtmən] vi to breathe out

ausbaden [ˈaʊsbaːdən] (umg) vt: **etw ~ müssen** to carry the can for sth

Ausbau [ˈaʊsbaʊ] m extension, expansion;

removal; **a~en** vt to extend, to expand; (herausnehmen) to take out, to remove; **a~fähig** adj (fig) worth developing

ausbessern ['ausbɛsərn] vt to mend, to repair

ausbeulen ['ausbɔylən] vt to beat out

Ausbeute ['ausbɔytə] f yield; (Fische) catch; **a~n** vt to exploit; (MIN) to work

ausbild- ['ausbɪld] zW: **~en** vt to educate; (Lehrling, Soldat) to instruct, to train; (Fähigkeiten) to develop; (Geschmack) to cultivate; **A~er (-s, -)** m instructor; **A~ung** f education; training, instruction; development; cultivation

ausbleiben ['ausblaɪbən] (unreg) vi (Personen) to stay away, not to come; (Ereignisse) to fail to happen, not to happen

Ausblick ['ausblɪk] m (auch fig) prospect, outlook, view

ausbrechen ['ausbrɛçən] (unreg) vi to break out ♦ vt to break off; **in Tränen/Gelächter ~** to burst into tears/out laughing

ausbreiten ['ausbraɪtən] vt to spread (out); (Arme) to stretch out ♦ vr to spread; **sich über ein Thema ~** to expand od enlarge on a topic

ausbrennen ['ausbrɛnən] (unreg) vt to scorch; (Wunde) to cauterize ♦ vi to burn out

Ausbruch ['ausbrʊx] m outbreak; (von Vulkan) eruption; (Gefühlsausbruch) outburst; (von Gefangenen) escape

ausbrüten ['ausbry:tən] vt (auch fig) to hatch

Ausdauer ['ausdauər] f perseverance, stamina; **a~nd** adj persevering

ausdehnen ['ausde:nən] vt, vr (räumlich) to expand; (zeitlich, auch Gummi) to stretch; (Nebel, fig: Macht) to extend

ausdenken ['ausdɛŋkən] (unreg) vt: **sich dat etw ~** to think sth up

Ausdruck ['ausdrʊk] m expression, phrase; (Kundgabe, Gesichtsausdruck) expression; (COMPUT) print-out, hard copy; **a~en** vt (COMPUT) to print out

ausdrücken ['ausdrykən] vt (auch vr: formulieren, zeigen) to express; (Zigarette) to put out; (Zitrone) to squeeze

ausdrücklich adj express, explicit

ausdrucks- zW: **~los** adj expressionless, blank; **~voll** adj expressive; **A~weise** f mode of expression

auseinander [ausʔaɪ'nandər] adv (getrennt) apart; **~ schreiben** to write as separate words; **~ bringen** to separate; **~ fallen** to fall apart; **~ gehen** (Menschen) to separate; (Meinungen) to differ; (Gegenstand) to fall apart; **~ halten** to tell apart; **~ nehmen** to take to pieces, to dismantle; **~ setzen** to set forth, to explain ♦ vr (sich verständigen) to

come to terms, to settle; (sich befassen) to concern o.s.; **A~setzung** f argument

ausfahren ['ausfa:rən] (unreg) vt (spazieren fahren: im Auto) to take for a drive; (: im Kinderwagen) to take for a walk; (liefern) to deliver

Ausfahrt f (des Zuges etc) leaving, departure; (Autobahnausfahrt) exit; (Garagenausfahrt etc) exit, way out; (Spazierfahrt) drive, excursion

Ausfall ['ausfal] m loss; (Nichtstattfinden) cancellation; (MIL) sortie; (radioaktiv) fall-out; **a~en** vi (Zähne, Haare) to fall od come out; (nicht stattfinden) to be cancelled; (wegbleiben) to be omitted; (Person) to drop out; (Lohn) to be stopped; (nicht funktionieren) to break down; (Resultat haben) to turn out; **~straße** f arterial road

ausfertigen ['ausfɛrtɪgən] vt (förmlich: Urkunde, Pass) to draw up; (Rechnung) to make out

Ausfertigung ['ausfɛrtɪgʊŋ] f drawing up; making out; (Exemplar) copy

ausfindig ['ausfɪndɪç] adj: **~ machen** to discover

ausfließen ['ausfli:sən] (unreg) vt (herausfließen): **~ (aus)** to flow out (of); (auslaufen: Öl etc): **~ (aus)** to leak (out of)

Ausflucht ['ausflʊxt] (-, -flüchte) f excuse

Ausflug ['ausflu:k] m excursion, outing; **Ausflügler** ['ausfly:klər] (-s, -) m tripper

Ausflugslokal nt tourist café

Ausfluss ▲ ['ausflʊs] m outlet; (MED) discharge

ausfragen ['ausfra:gən] vt to interrogate, to question

ausfressen ['ausfrɛsən] (unreg) vt to eat up; (aushöhlen) to corrode; (umg: anstellen) to be up to

Ausfuhr ['ausfu:r] (-, -en) f export, exportation ♦ in zW export

ausführ- ['ausfy:r] zW: **~en** vt (verwirklichen) to carry out; (Person) to take out; (Hund) to take for a walk; (COMM) to export; (erklären) to give details of; **~lich** adj detailed ♦ adv in detail; **A~lichkeit** f detail; **A~ung** f execution, performance; (Durchführung) completion; (Herstellungsart) version; (Erklärung) explanation

ausfüllen ['ausfʏlən] vt to fill up; (Fragebogen etc) to fill in; (Beruf) to be fulfilling for

Ausgabe ['ausga:bə] f (Geld) expenditure, outlay; (Aushändigung) giving out; (Gepäckausgabe) left-luggage office; (Buch) edition; (Nummer) issue; (COMPUT) output

Ausgang ['ausgaŋ] m way out, exit; (Ende) end; (Ausgangspunkt) starting point; (Ergebnis) result; (Ausgehtag) free time, time off; **kein ~** no exit

Ausgangs- zW: **~punkt** m starting point;
~sperre f curfew

ausgeben ['aʊsgeːbən] (unreg) vt (Geld) to
spend; (austeilen) to issue, to distribute ♦ vr:
sich für etw/jdn ~ to pass o.s. off as sth/sb

ausgebucht ['aʊsgəbuːxt] adj (Vorstellung,
Flug, Maschine) fully booked

ausgedient ['aʊsgədiːnt] adj (Soldat)
discharged; (verbraucht) no longer in use; **~
haben** to have done good service

ausgefallen ['aʊsgəfalən] adj (ungewöhnlich)
exceptional

ausgeglichen ['aʊsgəɡlɪçən] adj
(well-)balanced; **A~heit** f balance; (von
Mensch) even-temperedness

ausgehen ['aʊsgeːən] (unreg) vi to go out;
(zu Ende gehen) to come to an end; (Benzin) to
run out; (Haare, Zähne) to fall od come
out; (Feuer, Ofen, Licht) to go out; (Strom)
to go off; (Resultat haben) to turn out; **mir
ging das Benzin aus** I ran out of petrol
(BRIT) od gas (US); **von etw ~** (wegführen) to
lead away from sth; (herrühren) to come
from sth; (zugrunde legen) to proceed from
sth; **wir können davon ~, dass ...** we can
take as our starting point that ...; **leer ~** to
get nothing

ausgelassen ['aʊsgəlasən] adj boisterous,
high-spirited

ausgelastet ['aʊsgəlastət] adj fully occupied

ausgelernt ['aʊsgəlɛrnt] adj trained,
qualified

ausgemacht ['aʊsgəmaxt] adj settled; (umg:
Dummkopf etc) out-and-out, downright; **es
war eine ~e Sache, dass ...** it was a
foregone conclusion that ...

ausgenommen ['aʊsgənɔmən] präp +gen
except ♦ konj except; **Anwesende sind ~**
present company excepted

ausgeprägt ['aʊsgəprɛːkt] adj distinct

ausgerechnet ['aʊsgərɛçnət] adv just,
precisely; **~ du/heute** you of all people/
today of all days

ausgeschlossen ['aʊsgəʃlɔsən] adj
(unmöglich) impossible, out of the question

ausgeschnitten ['aʊsgəʃnɪtən] adj (Kleid)
low-necked

ausgesprochen ['aʊsgəʃprɔxən] adj
(Faulheit, Lüge etc) out-and-out;
(uɪ... nnbar) marked ♦ adv decidedly

ausgezeichnet ['aʊsgətsaɪçnət] adj excellent

ausgiebig ['aʊsgiːbɪç] adj (Gebrauch)
thorough, good; (Essen) generous, lavish; **~
schlafen** to have a good sleep

ausgießen ['aʊsgiːsən] vt to pour out;
(Behälter) to empty

Ausgleich ['aʊsglaɪç] (-(e)s, -e) m balance;
(Vermittlung) reconciliation; (SPORT)
equalization; **zum ~ einer Sache** gen in
order to offset sth; **a~en** (unreg) vt to
balance (out); to reconcile; (Höhe) to even

up ♦ vi (SPORT) to equalize

ausgraben ['aʊsgraːbən] (unreg) vt to dig
up; (Leichen) to exhume; (fig) to unearth

Ausgrabung f excavation; (Ausgraben auch)
digging up

Ausguss ▲ ['aʊsgʊs] m (Spüle) sink; (Abfluss)
outlet; (Tülle) spout

aushalten ['aʊshaltən] (unreg) vt to bear, to
stand; (Geliebte) to keep ♦ vi to hold out;
das ist nicht zum A~ that is unbearable

aushandeln ['aʊshandəln] vt to negotiate

aushändigen ['aʊshɛndɪgən] vt: **jdm etw ~**
to hand sth over to sb

Aushang ['aʊshaŋ] m notice

aushängen ['aʊshɛŋən] (unreg) vt (Meldung)
to put up; (Fenster) to take off its hinges ♦ vi
to be displayed

ausharren ['aʊsharən] vi to hold out

ausheben ['aʊsheːbən] (unreg) vt (Erde) to
lift out; (Grube) to hollow out; (Tür) to take
off its hinges; (Diebesnest) to clear out; (MIL)
to enlist

aushecken ['aʊshɛkən] (umg) vt to cook up

aushelfen ['aʊshɛlfən] (unreg) vi: **jdm ~** to
help sb out

Aushilfe ['aʊshɪlfə] f help, assistance;
(Person) (temporary) worker

Aushilfs- zW: **~kraft** f temporary worker;
a~weise adv temporarily, as a stopgap

ausholen ['aʊshoːlən] vi to swing one's arm
back; (zur Ohrfeige) to raise one's hand;
(beim Gehen) to take long strides

aushorchen ['aʊshɔrçən] vt to sound out, to
pump

auskennen ['aʊskɛnən] (unreg) vr to know a
lot; (an einem Ort) to know one's way
about; (in Fragen etc) to be knowledgeable

Ausklang ['aʊsklaŋ] m end

auskleiden ['aʊsklaɪdən] vr to undress ♦ vt
(Wand) to line

ausklingen ['aʊsklɪŋən] (unreg) vi (Ton, Lied)
to die away; (Fest) to peter out

ausklopfen ['aʊsklɔpfən] vt (Teppich) to
beat; (Pfeife) to knock out

auskochen ['aʊskɔxən] vt to boil; (MED) to
sterilize; **ausgekocht** (fig) out-and-out

Auskommen (-s) nt: **sein ~ haben** to have
a regular income

auskommen (unreg) vi: **mit jdm ~** to get
on with sb; **mit etw ~** to get by with sth

auskosten ['aʊskɔstən] vt to enjoy to the full

auskundschaften ['aʊskʊntʃaftən] vt to spy
out; (Gebiet) to reconnoitre

Auskunft ['aʊskʊnft] (-, -künfte) f
information; (nähere) details pl, particulars
pl; (Stelle) information office; (TEL) directory
inquiries sg

auslachen ['aʊslaxən] vt to laugh at, to
mock

ausladen ['aʊslaːdən] (unreg) vt to unload;
(umg: Gäste) to cancel an invitation to

Auslage [ˈaʊslaːɡə] f shop window (display);
~n pl (Ausgabe) outlay sg

Ausland [ˈaʊslant] nt foreign countries pl; **im
~** abroad; **ins ~** abroad

Ausländer(in) [ˈaʊslɛndər(ɪn)] (-s, -) m(f)
foreigner

ausländisch adj foreign

Auslands- zW: **~gespräch** nt international
call; **~reise** f trip abroad; **~schutzbrief** m
international travel cover

auslassen [ˈaʊslasən] (unreg) vt to leave out;
(Wort etc auch) to omit; (Fett) to melt;
(Kleidungsstück) to let out ♦ vr: **sich über
etw** akk **~** to speak one's mind about sth;
seine Wut etc **an jdm ~** to vent one's rage
etc on sb

Auslassung f omission

Auslauf [ˈaʊslaʊf] m (für Tiere) run; (Ausfluss)
outflow, outlet; **a~en** (unreg) vi to run out;
(Behälter) to leak; (NAUT) to put out (to sea);
(langsam aufhören) to run down

Ausläufer [ˈaʊslɔʏfər] m (von Gebirge) spur;
(Pflanze) runner; (MET: von Hoch) ridge;
(: von Tief) trough

ausleeren [ˈaʊsleːrən] vt to empty

auslegen [ˈaʊsleːɡən] vt (Waren) to lay out;
(Köder) to put down; (Geld) to lend;
(bedecken) to cover; (Text etc) to interpret

Auslegung f interpretation

ausleiern [ˈaʊslaɪərn] vi (Gummi) to wear
out

Ausleihe [ˈaʊslaɪə] f issuing; (Stelle) issue
desk; **a~n** (unreg) vt (verleihen) to lend; **sich**
dat **etw a~n** to borrow sth

Auslese [ˈaʊsleːzə] f selection; (Elite) elite;
(Wein) choice wine; **a~n** (unreg) vt to select;
(umg: zu Ende lesen) to finish

ausliefern [ˈaʊsliːfərn] vt to deliver (up), to
hand over; (COMM) to deliver; **jdm/etw
ausgeliefert sein** to be at the mercy of sb/
sth

auslöschen [ˈaʊslœʃən] vt to extinguish; (fig)
to wipe out, to obliterate

auslosen [ˈaʊsloːzən] vt to draw lots for

auslösen [ˈaʊsløːzən] vt (Explosion, Schuss) to
set off; (hervorrufen) to cause, to produce;
(Gefangene) to ransom; (Pfand) to redeem

ausmachen [ˈaʊsmaxən] vt (Licht, Radio) to
turn off; (Feuer) to put out; (entdecken) to
make out; (vereinbaren) to agree; (beilegen)
to settle; (Anteil darstellen, betragen) to
represent; (bedeuten) to matter; **macht es
Ihnen etwas aus, wenn …?** would you
mind if …?

ausmalen [ˈaʊsmaːlən] vt to paint; (fig) to
describe; **sich** dat **etw ~** to imagine sth

Ausmaß [ˈaʊsmaːs] nt dimension; (fig auch)
scale

ausmessen [ˈaʊsmɛsən] (unreg) vt to

measure

Ausnahme [ˈaʊsnaːmə] f exception; **~fall** m
exceptional case; **~zustand** m state of
emergency

ausnahms- zW: **~los** adv without
exception; **~weise** adv by way of exception,
for once

ausnehmen [ˈaʊsneːmən] (unreg) vt to take
out, to remove; (Tier) to gut; (Nest) to rob;
(umg: Geld abnehmen) to clean out;
(ausschließen) to make an exception of ♦ vr
to look, to appear; **~d** adj exceptional

ausnützen [ˈaʊsnʏtsən] vt (Zeit, Gelegenheit)
to use, to turn to good account; (Einfluss) to
use; (Mensch, Gutmütigkeit) to exploit

auspacken [ˈaʊspakən] vt to unpack

auspfeifen [ˈaʊspfaɪfən] (unreg) vt to hiss/
boo at

ausplaudern [ˈaʊsplaʊdərn] vt (Geheimnis)
to blab

ausprobieren [ˈaʊsprobiːrən] vt to try (out)

Auspuff [ˈaʊspʊf] (-(e)s, -e) m (TECH)
exhaust; **~rohr** nt exhaust (pipe)

ausradieren [ˈaʊsradiːrən] vt to erase, to rub
out; (fig) to annihilate

ausrangieren [ˈaʊsrãʒiːrən] (umg) vt to
chuck out

ausrauben [ˈaʊsraʊbən] vt to rob

ausräumen [ˈaʊsrɔʏmən] vt (Dinge) to clear
away; (Schrank, Zimmer) to empty;
(Bedenken) to dispel

ausrechnen [ˈaʊsrɛçnən] vt to calculate, to
reckon

Ausrede [ˈaʊsreːdə] f excuse; **a~n** vi to have
one's say ♦ vt: **jdm etw a~n** to talk sb out
of sth

ausreichen [ˈaʊsraɪçən] vi to suffice, to be
enough; **~d** adj sufficient, adequate; (SCH)
adequate

Ausreise [ˈaʊsraɪzə] f departure; **bei der ~**
when leaving the country; **~erlaubnis** f exit
visa; **a~n** vi to leave the country

ausreißen [ˈaʊsraɪsən] (unreg) vt to tear od
pull out ♦ vi (Riss bekommen) to tear; (umg)
to make off, to scram

ausrenken [ˈaʊsrɛŋkən] vt to dislocate

ausrichten [ˈaʊsrɪçtən] vt (Botschaft) to
deliver; (Gruß) to pass on; (Hochzeit etc) to
arrange; (in gerade Linie bringen) to get in a
straight line; (angleichen) to bring into line;
(TYP) to justify; **ich werde es ihm ~** I'll tell
him; **etwas/nichts bei jdm ~** to get
somewhere/nowhere with sb

ausrotten [ˈaʊsrɔtən] vt to stamp out, to
exterminate

Ausruf [ˈaʊsruːf] m (Schrei) cry, exclamation;
(Bekanntmachung) proclamation; **a~en**
(unreg) vt to cry out, to exclaim; to call out;
~ezeichen nt exclamation mark

ausruhen ['ausruːən] *vt*, *vr* to rest

ausrüsten ['ausrystən] *vt* to equip, to fit out

Ausrüstung *f* equipment

ausrutschen ['ausrutʃən] *vi* to slip

Aussage ['auszaːgə] *f* (JUR) statement; **a~n** *vt* to say, to state ♦ *vi* (JUR) to give evidence

ausschalten ['ausʃaltən] *vt* to switch off; (fig) to eliminate

Ausschank ['ausʃaŋk] (-(e)s, -schänke) *m* dispensing, giving out; (COMM) selling; (Theke) bar

Ausschau ['ausʃau] *f*: ~ **halten (nach)** to look out (for), to watch (for); **a~en** *vi*: **a~en (nach)** to look out (for), to be on the lookout (for)

ausscheiden ['ausʃaidən] (unreg) *vt* to take out; (MED) to secrete ♦ *vi*: ~ **(aus)** to leave; (SPORT) to be eliminated (from) *od* knocked out (of)

Ausscheidung *f* separation; secretion; elimination; (aus Amt) retirement

ausschenken ['ausʃeŋkən] *vt* (Alkohol, Kaffee) to pour out; (COMM) to sell

ausschildern ['ausʃildərn] *vt* to signpost

ausschimpfen ['ausʃimpfən] *vt* to scold, to tell off

ausschlafen ['ausʃlaːfən] (unreg) *vi*, *vr* to have a good sleep ♦ *vt* to sleep off; **ich bin nicht ausgeschlafen** I didn't have *od* get enough sleep

Ausschlag ['ausʃlaːk] *m* (MED) rash; (Pendelausschlag) swing; (Nadelausschlag) deflection; **den ~ geben** (fig) to tip the balance; **a~en** [-gən] (unreg) *vt* to knock out; (auskleiden) to deck out; (verweigern) to decline ♦ *vi* (Pferd) to kick out; (BOT) to sprout; **a~gebend** *adj* decisive

ausschließen ['ausʃliːsən] (unreg) *vt* to shut *od* lock out; (fig) to exclude

ausschließlich *adj* exclusive ♦ *adv* exclusively ♦ *präp* +gen exclusive of, excluding

Ausschluss ▲ ['ausʃlus] *m* exclusion

ausschmücken ['ausʃmykən] *vt* to decorate; (fig) to embellish

ausschneiden ['ausʃnaidən] (unreg) *vt* to cut out; (Büsche) to trim

Ausschnitt ['ausʃnit] *m* (Teil) section; (von Kleid) neckline; (Zeitungsausschnitt) cutting; (aus Film etc) excerpt

ausschreiben ['ausʃraibən] (unreg) *vt* (ganz schreiben) to write out (in full); (ausstellen) to write (out); (Stelle, Wettbewerb etc) to announce, to advertise

Ausschreitung ['ausʃraitʊŋ] *f* (usu pl) riot

Ausschuss ▲ ['ausʃus] *m* committee, board; (Abfall) waste, scraps pl; (COMM: auch: ~ware) reject

ausschütten ['ausʃytən] *vt* to pour out; (Eimer) to empty; (Geld) to pay ♦ *vr* to shake (with laughter)

ausschweifend ['ausʃvaifənt] *adj* (Leben) dissipated, debauched; (Fantasie) extravagant

aussehen ['ausze:ən] (unreg) *vi* to look; **es sieht nach Regen aus** it looks like rain; **es sieht schlecht aus** things look bad; **A~ (-s)** *nt* appearance

aussein △ *siehe* aus

außen ['ausən] *adv* outside; (nach ~) outwards; ~ **ist es rot** it's red (on the) outside

Außen- *zW*: ~**dienst** *m*: **im ~dienst sein** to work outside the office; ~**handel** *m* foreign trade; ~**minister** *m* foreign minister; ~**ministerium** *nt* foreign office; ~**politik** *f* foreign policy; **a~politisch** *adj* (Entwicklung, Lage) foreign; ~**seite** *f* outside; ~**seiter (-s, -)** *m* outsider; ~**stände** *pl* outstanding debts; ~**stehende(r)** *f(m)* outsider; ~**welt** *f* outside world

außer ['ausər] *präp* +dat (räumlich) out of; (abgesehen von) except ♦ *konj* (ausgenommen) except; ~ **Gefahr** out of danger; ~ **Zweifel** beyond any doubt; ~ **Betrieb** out of order; ~ **Dienst** retired; ~ **Landes** abroad; ~ **sich** dat **sein** to be beside o.s.; ~ **sich** akk **geraten** to go wild; ~ **wenn** unless; ~ **dass** except; ~**dem** *konj* besides, in addition

äußere(r, s) ['ɔysərə(r, s)] *adj* outer, external

außergewöhnlich *adj* unusual

außerhalb *präp* +gen outside ♦ *adv* outside

äußerlich *adj* external

äußern *vt* to utter, to express; (zeigen) to show ♦ *vr* to give one's opinion; (Krankheit etc) to show itself

außerordentlich *adj* extraordinary

außerplanmäßig *adj* unscheduled

äußerst ['ɔysərst] *adv* extremely, most; ~**e(r, s)** *adj* utmost; (räumlich) farthest; (Termin) last possible; (Preis) highest

Äußerung *f* remark, comment

aussetzen ['auszɛtsən] *vt* (Kind, Tier) to abandon; (Boote) to lower; (Belohnung) to offer; (Urteil, Verfahren) to postpone ♦ *vi* (aufhören) to stop; (Pause machen) to have a break; **jdm/etw ausgesetzt sein** to be exposed to sb/sth; **an jdm/etw etwas ~** to find fault with sb/sth

Aussicht ['auszɪçt] *f* view; (in Zukunft) prospect; **etw in ~ haben** to have sth in view

Aussichts- *zW*: **a~los** *adj* hopeless; ~**punkt** *m* viewpoint; **a~reich** *adj* promising; ~**turm** *m* observation tower

aussöhnen ['auszøːnən] *vt* to reconcile ♦ *vr* to reconcile o.s., to become reconciled

aussondern ['auszɔndərn] *vt* to separate, to select

aussortieren ['auszɔrtiːrən] *vt* to sort out

ausspannen ['ausʃpanən] *vt* to spread *od*

stretch out; (*Pferd*) to unharness; (*umg:*
Mädchen): **(jdm) jdn ~** to steal sb (from sb)
♦ *vi* to relax
aussperren |ˈaʊsʃpɛrən| *vt* to lock out
ausspielen |ˈaʊsʃpiːlən| *vt* (*Karte*) to lead;
(*Geldprämie*) to offer as a prize ♦ *vi* (*KARTEN*)
to lead; **jdn gegen jdn ~** to play sb off
against sb; **ausgespielt haben** to be
finished
Aussprache |ˈaʊsʃpraːxə| *f* pronunciation;
(*Unterredung*) (frank) discussion
aussprechen |ˈaʊsʃprɛçən| (*unreg*) *vt* to
pronounce; (*äußern*) to say, to express ♦ *vr*
(*sich äußern*): **sich ~ (über** +*akk*) to speak
(about); (*sich anvertrauen*) to unburden o.s.
(about *od* on); (*diskutieren*) to discuss ♦ *vi*
(*zu Ende sprechen*) to finish speaking
Ausspruch |ˈaʊsʃprɔx| *m* saying, remark
ausspülen |ˈaʊsʃpyːlən| *vt* to wash out;
(*Mund*) to rinse
Ausstand |ˈaʊsʃtant| *m* strike; **in den ~
treten** to go on strike
ausstatten |ˈaʊsʃtatən| *vt* (*Zimmer etc*) to
furnish; (*Person*) to equip, to kit out
Ausstattung *f* (*Ausstatten*) provision;
(*Kleidung*) outfit; (*Aufmachung*) make-up;
(*Einrichtung*) furnishing
ausstechen |ˈaʊsʃtɛçən| (*unreg*) *vt* (*Augen,
Rasen, Graben*) to dig out; (*Kekse*) to cut
out; (*übertreffen*) to outshine
ausstehen |ˈaʊsʃteːən| (*unreg*) *vt* to stand, to
endure ♦ *vi* (*noch nicht da sein*) to be
outstanding
aussteigen |ˈaʊsʃtaɪgən| (*unreg*) *vi* to get
out, to alight
ausstellen |ˈaʊsʃtɛlən| *vt* to exhibit, to
display; (*umg: ausschalten*) to switch off ;
(*Rechnung etc*) to make out; (*Pass, Zeugnis*)
to issue
Ausstellung *f* exhibition; (*FIN*) drawing up;
(*einer Rechnung*) making out; (*eines Passes
etc*) issuing
aussterben |ˈaʊsʃtɛrbən| (*unreg*) *vi* to die
out
Aussteuer |ˈaʊsʃtɔyər| *f* dowry
Ausstieg |ˈaʊsʃtiːk| (**-(e)s, -e**) *m* exit
ausstopfen |ˈaʊsʃtɔpfən| *vt* to stuff
ausstoßen |ˈaʊsʃtoːsən| (*unreg*) *vt* (*Luft,
Rauch*) to give off, to emit; (*aus Verein etc*)
to expel, to exclude; (*Auge*) to poke out
ausstrahlen |ˈaʊsʃtraːlən| *vt*, *vi* to radiate;
(*RAD*) to broadcast
Ausstrahlung *f* radiation; (*fig*) charisma
ausstrecken |ˈaʊsʃtrɛkən| *vt*, *vr* to stretch
out
ausstreichen |ˈaʊsʃtraɪçən| (*unreg*) *vt* to
cross out; (*glätten*) to smooth (out)
ausströmen |ˈaʊsʃtrøːmən| *vi* (*Gas*) to pour
out, to escape ♦ *vt* to give off; (*fig*) to

radiate
aussuchen |ˈaʊszuːxən| *vt* to select, to pick
out
Austausch |ˈaʊstaʊʃ| *m* exchange; **a~bar**
adj exchangeable; **a~en** *vt* to exchange, to
swap
austeilen |ˈaʊstaɪlən| *vt* to distribute, to give
out
Auster |ˈaʊstər| (**-, -n**) *f* oyster
austoben |ˈaʊstoːbən| *vr* (*Kind*) to run wild;
(*Erwachsene*) to sow one's wild oats
austragen |ˈaʊstraːgən| (*unreg*) *vt* (*Post*) to
deliver; (*Streit etc*) to decide; (*Wettkämpfe*)
to hold
Australien |aʊsˈtraːliən| (**-s**) *nt* Australia;
Australier(in) (**-s, -**) *m(f)* Australian;
australisch *adj* Australian
austreiben |ˈaʊstraɪbən| (*unreg*) *vt* to drive
out, to expel; (*Geister*) to exorcize
austreten |ˈaʊstreːtən| (*unreg*) *vi* (*zur
Toilette*) to be excused ♦ *vt* (*Feuer*) to tread
out, to trample; (*Schuhe*) to wear out;
(*Treppe*) to wear down; **aus etw ~** to leave
sth
austrinken |ˈaʊstrɪŋkən| (*unreg*) *vt* (*Glas*) to
drain; (*Getränk*) to drink up ♦ *vi* to finish
one's drink, to drink up
Austritt |ˈaʊstrɪt| *m* emission; (*aus Verein,
Partei etc*) retirement, withdrawal
austrocknen |ˈaʊstrɔknən| *vt*, *vi* to dry up
ausüben |ˈaʊslyːbən| *vt* (*Beruf*) to practise, to
carry out; (*Funktion*) to perform; (*Einfluss*) to
exert; **einen Reiz auf jdn ~** to hold an
attraction for sb; **eine Wirkung auf jdn ~** to
have an effect on sb
Ausverkauf |ˈaʊsfɛrkaʊf| *m* sale; **a~en** *vt* to
sell out; (*Geschäft*) to sell up; **a~t** *adj*
(*Karten, Artikel*) sold out; (*THEAT: Haus*) full
Auswahl |ˈaʊsvaːl| *f*: **eine ~ (an** +*dat*) a
selection (of), a choice (of)
auswählen |ˈaʊsvɛːlən| *vt* to select, to
choose
Auswander- |ˈaʊsvandər| *zW*: **~er** *m*
emigrant; **a~n** *vi* to emigrate; **~ung** *f*
emigration
auswärtig |ˈaʊsvɛrtɪç| *adj* (*nicht am/vom
Ort*) out-of-town; (*ausländisch*) foreign
auswärts |ˈaʊsvɛrts| *adv* outside; (*nach
außen*) outwards; **~ essen** to eat out
Auswärtsspiel |ˈaʊsvɛrtsʃpiːl| *nt* away
game
auswechseln |ˈaʊsvɛksəln| *vt* to change, to
substitute
Ausweg |ˈaʊsveːk| *m* way out; **a~los** *adj*
hopeless
ausweichen |ˈaʊsvaɪçən| (*unreg*) *vi*: **jdm/
etw ~** to move aside *od* make way for sb/
sth; (*fig*) to sidestep sb/sth; **~d** *adj* evasive
ausweinen |ˈaʊsvaɪnən| *vr* to have a

Spelling reform: ▲ *new spelling* △ *old spelling (to be phased out)*

(good) cry
Ausweis |'aosvaıs| (-es, -e) *m* identity card; passport; (*Mitgliedsausweis*, *Bibliotheksausweis etc*) card; **a~en** |-zən| (*unreg*) *vt* to expel, to banish ♦ *vr* to prove one's identity; **~kontrolle** *f* identity check; **~papiere** *pl* identity papers; **~ung** *f* expulsion
ausweiten |'aosvaıtən| *vt* to stretch
auswendig |'aosvendıç| *adv* by heart
auswerten |'aosvertən| *vt* to evaluate; **Auswertung** *f* evaluation, analysis; (*Nutzung*) utilization
auswirken |'aosvırkən| *vr* to have an effect; **Auswirkung** *f* effect
auswischen |'aosvıʃən| *vt* to wipe out; **jdm eins ~** (*umg*) to put one over on sb
Auswuchs |'aosvu:ks| *m* (out)growth; (*fig*) product
auszahlen |'aostsa:lən| *vt* (*Lohn*, *Summe*) to pay out; (*Arbeiter*) to pay off; (*Miterbe*) to buy out ♦ *vr* (*sich lohnen*) to pay
auszählen |'aostse:lən| *vt* (*Stimmen*) to count
auszeichnen |'aostsaıçnən| *vt* to honour; (*MIL*) to decorate; (*COMM*) to price ♦ *vr* to distinguish o.s.
Auszeichnung *f* distinction; (*COMM*) pricing; (*Ehrung*) awarding of decoration; (*Ehre*) honour; (*Orden*) decoration; **mit ~** with distinction
ausziehen |'aostsi:ən| (*unreg*) *vt* (*Kleidung*) to take off; (*Haare*, *Zähne*, *Tisch etc*) to pull out; (*nachmalen*) to trace ♦ *vr* to undress ♦ *vi* (*aufbrechen*) to leave; (*aus Wohnung*) to move out
Auszubildende(r) |'aostsobıldəndə(r)| *f(m)* trainee
Auszug |'aostsu:k| *m* (*aus Wohnung*) removal; (*aus Buch etc*) extract; (*Kontoauszug*) statement; (*Ausmarsch*) departure
Auto |'aoto| (-s, -s) *nt* (motor)car; **~ fahren** to drive; **~atlas** *m* road atlas; **~bahn** *f* motorway; **~bahndreieck** *nt* motorway junction; **~bahngebühr** *f* toll; **~bahnkreuz** *nt* motorway intersection; **~bus** *m* bus; **~fähre** *f* car ferry; **~fahrer(in)** *m(f)* motorist, driver; **~fahrt** *f* drive
autogen |-'ge:n| *adj* autogenous
Auto- *zW:* **~'gramm** *nt* autograph; **~'mat** (-en, -en) *m* machine; **~'matik** |aoto'ma:tık| *f* (*AUT*) automatic; **a~'matisch** *adj* automatic; **a~nom** |-'no:m| *adj* autonomous
Autor(in) |'aotor(ın)| (-s, -en) *m(f)* author
Auto- *zW:* **~radio** *nt* car radio; **~reifen** *m* car tyre; **~reisezug** *m* motorail train; **~rennen** *nt* motor racing
autoritär |aotori'te:r| *adj* authoritarian
Autorität *f* authority
Auto- *zW:* **~telefon** *nt* car phone; **~unfall** *m*

car *od* motor accident; **~vermietung** *f* car hire (*BRIT*) *od* rental (*US*); **~waschanlage** *f* car wash
Axt |akst| (-, ⁼e) *f* axe

B, b

Baby |'be:bi| (-s, -s) *nt* baby; **~nahrung** *f* baby food; **~sitter** (-s, -) *m* baby-sitter
Bach |bax| (-(e)s, ⁼e) *m* stream, brook
Backe |'bakə| *f* cheek
backen |'bakən| (*unreg*) *vt*, *vi* to bake
Backenzahn *m* molar
Bäcker(in) |'bɛkər(ın)| (-s, -) *m* baker; **~ei** *f* bakery; (*~eiladen*) baker's (shop)
Back- *zW:* **~form** *f* baking tin; **~obst** *nt* dried fruit; (*~ofen*) *m* oven; **~pflaume** *f* prune; **~pulver** *nt* baking powder; **~stein** *m* brick
Bad |ba:t| (-(e)s, ⁼er) *nt* bath; (*Schwimmen*) bathe; (*Ort*) spa
Bade- |'ba:də| *zW:* **~anstalt** *f* (swimming) baths *pl*; **~anzug** *m* bathing suit; **~hose** *f* bathing *od* swimming trunks *pl*; **~kappe** *f* bathing cap; **~mantel** *m* bath(ing) robe; **~meister** *m* baths attendant; **b~n** *vi* to bathe, to have a bath ♦ *vt* to bath; **~ort** *m* spa; **~tuch** *nt* bath towel; **~wanne** *f* bath (tub); **~zimmer** *nt* bathroom
Bagatelle |baga'tɛlə| *f* trifle
Bagger |'bagər| (-s, -) *m* excavator; (*NAUT*) dredger; **b~n** *vt* to excavate; to dredge
Bahn |ba:n| (-, -en) *f* railway, railroad (*US*); (*Weg*) road, way; (*Spur*) lane; (*Rennbahn*) track; (*ASTRON*) orbit; (*Stoffbahn*) length; **b~brechend** *adj* pioneering; **~Card** ® |'ba:nka:rd| (-, -s) *f* = railcard; **~damm** *m* railway embankment; **b~en** *vt*: **sich/jdm einen Weg b~en** to clear a way/a way for sb; **~fahrt** *f* railway journey; **~fracht** *f* rail freight; **~hof** (-, -s) *m* station; **auf dem ~hof** at the station; **~hofshalle** *f* station concourse; **~linie** *f* (railway) line; **~steig** *m* platform; **~übergang** *m* level crossing, grade crossing (*US*)
Bahre |'ba:rə| *f* stretcher
Bakterien |bak'te:riən| *pl* bacteria *pl*
Balance |ba'lã:sə| *f* balance, equilibrium
balan'cieren *vt*, *vi* to balance
bald |balt| *adv* (*zeitlich*) soon; (*beinahe*) almost; **~ig** |'baldıç| *adj* early, speedy
Baldrian |'baldria:n| (-s, -e) *m* valerian
Balkan |'balkan| (-s) *m*: **der ~** the Balkans *pl*
Balken |'balkən| (-s, -) *m* beam; (*Tragbalken*) girder; (*Stützbalken*) prop
Balkon |bal'kõ:| (-s, -s *od* -e) *m* balcony; (*THEAT*) (dress) circle
Ball |bal| (-(e)s, ⁼e) *m* ball; (*Tanz*) dance, ball
Ballast |'balast| (-(e)s, -e) *m* ballast; (*fig*)

27 **Ballen → Bauch**

weight, burden

Ballen |'balən| (-s, -) *m* bale; (ANAT) ball; **b~** *vt* (formen) to make into a ball; (Faust) to clench ♦ *vr* (Wolken etc) to build up; (Menschen) to gather

Ballett |ba'lɛt| (-(e)s, -e) *nt* ballet

Ballkleid *nt* evening dress

Ballon |ba'lõː| (-s, -s od -e) *m* balloon

Ballspiel *nt* ball game

Ballungsgebiet |'balʊŋsɡəbiːt| *nt* conurbation

Baltikum |'baltikʊm| (-s) *nt*: **das ~** the Baltic States

Banane |ba'naːnə| *f* banana

Band¹ |bant| (-(e)s, ¨e) *m* (Buchband) volume

Band² (-(e)s, ¨er) *nt* (Stoffband) ribbon, tape; (Fließband) production line; (Tonband) tape; (ANAT) ligament; **etw auf ~ aufnehmen** to tape sth; **am laufenden ~** (umg) non-stop

Band³ (-(e)s, -e) *nt* (Freundschaftsband etc) bond

Band⁴ |bɛnt| (-, -s) *f* band, group

band *etc vb siehe* **binden**

Bandage |ban'daːʒə| *f* bandage

banda'gieren *vt* to bandage

Bande |'bandə| *f* band; (Straßenbande) gang

bändigen |'bɛndɪɡən| *vt* (Tier) to tame; (Trieb, Leidenschaft) to control, to restrain

Bandit |ban'diːt| (-en, -en) *m* bandit

Band- zW: **~nudel** *f* (KOCH: gew pl) ribbon noodles *pl*; **~scheibe** *f* (ANAT) disc; **~wurm** *m* tapeworm

bange |'baŋə| *adj* scared; (besorgt) anxious; **jdm wird es ~** sb is becoming scared; **jdm B~ machen** to scare sb; **~n** *vi*: **um jdn/etw ~n** to be anxious or worried about sb/sth

Bank¹ |baŋk| (-, ¨e) *f* (Sitzbank) bench; (Sandbank etc) (sand)bank, (sand)bar

Bank² (-, -en) *f* (Geldbank) bank; **~anweisung** *f* banker's order; **~einzug** *m* direct debit

Bankett |baŋ'kɛt| (-(e)s, -e) *nt* (Essen) banquet; (Straßenrand) verge (BRIT), shoulder (US)

Bankier |baŋki'eː| (-s, -s) *m* banker

Bank- zW: **~konto** *m* bank account; **~leitzahl** *f* bank sort code number; **~note** *f* banknote; **~raub** *m* bank robbery

Bankrott |baŋ'krɔt| (-(e)s, -e) *m* bankruptcy; **~ machen** to go bankrupt; **b~** *adj* bankrupt

Bankverbindung *f* banking arrangements *pl*; **geben Sie bitte Ihre ~** please give your account details

Bann |ban| (-(e)s, -e) *m* (HIST) ban; (Kirchenbann) excommunication; (fig: Zauber) spell; **b~en** *vt* (Geister) to exorcize; (Gefahr) to avert; (bezaubern) to enchant; (HIST) to banish

Banner (-s, -) *nt* banner, flag

Bar (-, -s) *f* bar

bar |baːr| *adj* (+gen) (unbedeckt) bare; (frei von) lacking (in); (offenkundig) utter, sheer; **~e(s) Geld** cash; **etw (in) ~ bezahlen** to pay sth (in) cash; **etw für ~e Münze nehmen** (fig) to take sth at its face value

Bär |bɛːr| (-en, -en) *m* bear

Baracke |ba'rakə| *f* hut

barbarisch |bar'baːrɪʃ| *adj* barbaric, barbarous

Bar- zW: **b~fuß** *adj* barefoot; **~geld** *nt* cash, ready money; **b~geldlos** *adj* non-cash

Barkauf *m* cash purchase

Barkeeper |'baːrkiːpər| (-s, -) *m* barman, bartender

barmherzig |barm'hɛrtsɪç| *adj* merciful, compassionate

Baron |ba'roːn| (-s, -e) *m* baron; **~in** *f* baroness

Barren |'barən| (-s, -) *m* parallel bars *pl*; (Goldbarren) ingot

Barriere |bari'ɛːrə| *f* barrier

Barrikade |bari'kaːdə| *f* barricade

Barsch |barʃ| (-(e)s, -e) *m* perch

barsch |barʃ| *adj* brusque, gruff

Bar- zW: **~schaft** *f* ready money; **~scheck** *m* open od uncrossed cheque (BRIT), open check (US)

Bart |baːrt| (-(e)s, ¨e) *m* beard; (Schlüsselbart) bit; **bärtig** |'bɛːrtɪç| *adj* bearded

Barzahlung *f* cash payment

Base |'baːzə| *f* (CHEM) base; (Kusine) cousin

Basel |'baːzəl| *nt* Basle

Basen *pl von* **Base, Basis**

basieren |ba'ziːrən| *vt* to base ♦ *vi* to be based

Basis |'baːzɪs| (-, Basen) *f* basis

Bass ▲ |bas| (-es, ¨e) *m* bass

Bassin |ba'sɛ̃ː| (-s, -s) *nt* pool

Bassstimme ▲ *f* bass voice

Bast |bast| (-(e)s, -e) *m* raffia

basteln |'bastəln| *vt* to make ♦ *vi* to do handicrafts

bat *etc* |baːt| *vb siehe* **bitten**

Bataillon |batal'joːn| (-s, -e) *nt* battalion

Batik |'baːtɪk| *f* (Verfahren) batik

Batterie |batə'riː| *f* battery

Bau |bau| (-(e)s) *m* (Bauen) building, construction; (Aufbau) structure; (Körperbau) frame; (~stelle) building site; (pl Baue: Tierbau) hole, burrow; (: MIN) working(s); (pl Bauten: Gebäude) building; **sich im ~ befinden** to be under construction; **~arbeiten** *pl* building od construction work *sg*; **~arbeiter** *m* building worker

Bauch |baux| (-(e)s, Bäuche) *m* belly; (ANAT auch) stomach, abdomen; **~fell** *nt* peritoneum; **b~ig** *adj* bulbous; **~nabel** *m* navel; **~redner** *m* ventriloquist;

Spelling reform: ▲ new spelling △ old spelling (to be phased out)

~schmerzen pl stomachache; **~weh** nt stomachache

Baudenkmal nt historical monument

bauen ['bauən] vt, vi to build; (TECH) to construct; **auf jdn/etw ~** to depend od count upon sb/sth

Bauer¹ ['bauər] (-n od -s, -n) m farmer; (Schach) pawn

Bauer² ['bauər] (-s, -) nt od m (bird)cage

Bäuerin ['bɔʏrɪn] f farmer; (Frau des Bauers) farmer's wife

bäuerlich adj rustic

Bauern- zW: **~haus** nt farmhouse; **~hof** m farm(yard)

Bau- zW: **b~fällig** adj dilapidated; **~gelände** f building site; **~genehmigung** f building permit; **~gerüst** nt scaffolding; **~herr** m purchaser; **~kasten** m box of bricks; **~land** nt building land; **b~lich** adj structural

Baum [baum] (-(e)s, Bäume) m tree

baumeln ['bauməln] vi to dangle

bäumen ['bɔʏmən] vr to rear (up)

Baum- zW: **~schule** f nursery; **~stamm** m tree trunk; **~stumpf** m tree stump; **~wolle** f cotton

Bau- zW: **~plan** m architect's plan; **~platz** m building site

bauspar- zW: **~en** vi to save with a building society; **B~kasse** f building society; **B~vertrag** m building society savings agreement

Bau- zW: **~stein** m building stone, freestone; **~stelle** f building site; **~teil** nt prefabricated part (of building); **~ten** pl von Bau; **~unternehmer** m building contractor; **~weise** f (method of) construction; **~werk** nt building; **~zaun** m hoarding

Bayern ['baiərn] nt Bavaria

bayrisch ['bairɪʃ] adj Bavarian

Bazillus [ba'tsɪlʊs] (-, Bazillen) m bacillus

beabsichtigen [bə'apzɪçtɪgən] vt to intend

beacht- [bə'axt] zW: **~en** vt to take note of; (Vorschrift) to obey; (Vorfahrt) to observe; **~lich** adj considerable; **B~ung** f notice, attention, observation

Beamte(r) [bə'amtə(r)] (-n, -n) m official; (Staatsbeamte) civil servant; (Bankbeamte etc) employee

Beamtin f siehe Beamte(r)

beängstigend [bə'ɛŋstɪgənt] adj alarming

beanspruchen [bə'anʃprʊxən] vt to claim; (Zeit, Platz) to take up, to occupy; **jdn ~** to take up sb's time

beanstanden [bə'anʃtandən] vt to complain about, to object to

beantragen [bə'antra:gən] vt to apply for, to ask for

beantworten [bə'antvɔrtən] vt to answer; **Beantwortung** f (+gen) reply (to)

bearbeiten [bə'arbaitən] vt to work; (Material) to process; (Thema) to deal with;

(Land) to cultivate; (CHEM) to treat; (Buch) to revise; (umg: beeinflussen wollen) to work on

Bearbeitung f processing; cultivation; treatment; revision

Bearbeitungsgebühr f handling charge

Beatmung [bə'a:tmʊŋ] f respiration

beaufsichtigen [bə'aufzɪçtɪgən] vt to supervise; **Beaufsichtigung** f supervision

beauftragen [bə'auftra:gən] vt to instruct; **jdn mit etw ~** to entrust sb with sth

Beauftragte(r) f(m) (dekl wie adj) representative

bebauen [bə'bauən] vt to build on; (AGR) to cultivate

beben ['be:bən] vi to tremble, to shake; **B~** (-s, -) nt earthquake

Becher ['bɛçər] (-s, -) m mug; (ohne Henkel) tumbler

Becken ['bɛkən] (-s, -) nt basin; (MUS) cymbal; (ANAT) pelvis

bedacht [bə'daxt] adj thoughtful, careful; **auf etw** akk **sein** to be concerned about sth

bedächtig [bə'dɛçtɪç] adj (umsichtig) thoughtful, reflective; (langsam) slow, deliberate

bedanken [bə'daŋkən] vr: **sich (bei jdm) ~** to say thank you (to sb)

Bedarf [bə'darf] (-(e)s) m need, requirement; (COMM) demand; **je nach ~** according to demand; **bei ~** if necessary; **~ an etw** dat **haben** to be in need of sth

Bedarfs- zW: **~fall** m case of need; **~haltestelle** f request stop

bedauerlich [bə'dauərlɪç] adj regrettable

bedauern [bə'dauərn] vt to be sorry for; (bemitleiden) to pity; **B~** (-s) nt regret; **~swert** adj (Zustände) regrettable; (Mensch) pitiable, unfortunate

bedecken [bə'dɛkən] vt to cover

bedeckt adj covered; (Himmel) overcast

bedenken [bə'dɛŋkən] (unreg) vt to think over, to consider

Bedenken (-s, -) nt (Überlegen) consideration; (Zweifel) doubt; (Skrupel) scruple

bedenklich adj doubtful; (bedrohlich) dangerous, risky

Bedenkzeit f time to think

bedeuten [bə'dɔʏtən] vt to mean; to signify; (wichtig sein) to be of importance; **~d** adj important; (beträchtlich) considerable

bedeutsam adj (wichtig) significant

Bedeutung f meaning; significance; (Wichtigkeit) importance; **b~slos** adj insignificant, unimportant; **b~svoll** adj momentous, significant

bedienen [bə'di:nən] vt to serve; (Maschine) to work, to operate ♦ vr (beim Essen) to help o.s.; **sich jds/einer Sache ~** to make use of sb/sth

Bedienung f service; (*Kellnerin*) waitress; (*Verkäuferin*) shop assistant; (*Zuschlag*) service (charge)

Bedienungsanleitung f operating instructions pl

bedingen [bəˈdɪŋən] vt (*verursachen*) to cause

bedingt adj (*Richtigkeit, Tauglichkeit*) limited; (*Zusage, Annahme*) conditional

Bedingung f condition; (*Voraussetzung*) stipulation; **b~slos** adj unconditional

bedrängen [bəˈdrɛŋən] vt to pester, to harass

bedrohen [bəˈdroːən] vt to threaten; **Bedrohung** f threat, menace

bedrücken [bəˈdrʏkən] vt to oppress, to trouble

bedürf- [bəˈdʏrf] zW: **~en** (*unreg*) vi +gen to need, to require; **B~nis (-ses, -se)** nt need; **~tig** adj in need, poor, needy

beeilen [bəˈʔaɪlən] vr to hurry

beeindrucken [bəˈʔaɪndrʊkən] vt to impress, to make an impression on

beeinflussen [bəˈʔaɪnflʊsən] vt to influence

beeinträchtigen [bəˈʔaɪntrɛçtɪɡən] vt to affect adversely; (*Freiheit*) to infringe upon

beend(ig)en [bəˈʔɛnd(ɪɡ)ən] vt to end, to finish, to terminate

beengen [bəˈʔɛŋən] vt to cramp; (*fig*) to hamper, to oppress

beerben [bəˈʔɛrbən] vt: **jdn ~** to inherit from sb

beerdigen [bəˈʔeːrdɪɡən] vt to bury; **Beerdigung** f funeral, burial

Beere [ˈbeːrə] f berry; (*Traubenbeere*) grape

Beet [beːt] (-(e)s, -e) nt bed

befähigen [bəˈfɛːɪɡən] vt to enable

befähigt adj (*begabt*) talented; **~ (für)** (*fähig*) capable (of)

Befähigung f capability; (*Begabung*) talent, aptitude

befahrbar [bəˈfaːrbaːr] adj passable; (*NAUT*) navigable

befahren [bəˈfaːrən] (*unreg*) vt to use, to drive over; (*NAUT*) to navigate ♦ adj used

befallen [bəˈfalən] (*unreg*) vt to come over

befangen [bəˈfaŋən] adj (*schüchtern*) shy, self-conscious; (*voreingenommen*) biased

befassen [bəˈfasən] vr to concern o.s.

Befehl [bəˈfeːl] (-(e)s, -e) m command, order; **b~en** (*unreg*) vt to order ♦ vi to give orders; **jdm etw b~en** to order sb to do sth; **~sverweigerung** f insubordination

befestigen [bəˈfɛstɪɡən] vt to fasten; (*stärken*) to strengthen; (*MIL*) to fortify; **~ an** +dat to fasten to

Befestigung f fastening; strengthening; (*MIL*) fortification

befeuchten [bəˈfɔʏçtən] vt to damp(en), to moisten

befinden [bəˈfɪndən] (*unreg*) vr to be; (*sich fühlen*) to feel ♦ vt: **jdn/etw für** od **als etw ~** to deem sb/sth to be sth ♦ vi: **~ (über +akk)** to decide (on), to adjudicate (on); **B~ (-s)** nt health, condition; (*Meinung*) view, opinion

befolgen [bəˈfɔlɡən] vt to comply with, to follow

befördern [bəˈfœrdərn] vt (*senden*) to transport, to send; (*beruflich*) to promote; **Beförderung** f transport; promotion

befragen [bəˈfraːɡən] vt to question

befreien [bəˈfraɪən] vt to set free; (*erlassen*) to exempt; **Befreiung** f liberation, release; (*Erlassen*) exemption

befreunden [bəˈfrɔʏndən] vr to make friends; (*mit Idee etc*) to acquaint o.s.

befreundet adj friendly

befriedigen [bəˈfriːdɪɡən] vt to satisfy; **~d** adj satisfactory

Befriedigung f satisfaction, gratification

befristet [bəˈfrɪstət] adj limited

befruchten [bəˈfrʊxtən] vt to fertilize; (*fig*) to stimulate

Befruchtung f: **künstliche ~** artificial insemination

Befugnis [bəˈfuːknɪs] (-, -se) f authorization, powers pl

befugt adj authorized, entitled

Befund [bəˈfʊnt] (-(e)s, -e) m findings pl; (*MED*) diagnosis

befürchten [bəˈfʏrçtən] vt to fear; **Befürchtung** f fear, apprehension

befürworten [bəˈfyːrvɔrtən] vt to support, to speak in favour of; **Befürworter (-s, -)** m supporter, advocate

begabt [bəˈɡaːpt] adj gifted

Begabung [bəˈɡaːbʊŋ] f talent, gift

begann etc [bəˈɡan] vb siehe **beginnen**

begeben [bəˈɡeːbən] (*unreg*) vr (*gehen*) to betake o.s.; (*geschehen*) to occur; **sich ~ nach** od **zu** to proceed to(wards); **B~heit** f occurrence

begegnen [bəˈɡeːɡnən] vi: **jdm ~** to meet sb; (*behandeln*) to treat sb; **einer Sache** dat **~** to meet with sth

Begegnung f meeting

begehen [bəˈɡeːən] (*unreg*) vt (*Straftat*) to commit; (*abschreiten*) to cover; (*Straße etc*) to use, to negotiate; (*Feier*) to celebrate

begehren [bəˈɡeːrən] vt to desire

begehrt adj in demand; (*Junggeselle*) eligible

begeistern [bəˈɡaɪstərn] vt to fill with enthusiasm, to inspire ♦ vr: **sich für etw ~** to get enthusiastic about sth

begeistert adj enthusiastic

Begierde [bəˈɡiːrdə] f desire, passion

begierig |bə'giːrɪç| adj eager, keen

begießen |bə'giːsən| (unreg) vt to water; (mit Alkohol) to drink to

Beginn |bə'gɪn| (-(e)s) m beginning; **zu** ~ at the beginning; **b~en** (unreg) vt, vi to start, to begin

beglaubigen |bə'glaʊbɪgən| vt to countersign; **Beglaubigung** f counter-signature

begleichen |bə'glaɪçən| (unreg) vt to settle, to pay

Begleit- |bə'glaɪt| zW: **b~en** vt to accompany; (MIL) to escort; ~**er** (-s, -) m companion; (Freund) escort; (MUS) accompanist; ~**schreiben** nt covering letter; ~**umstände** pl concomitant circumstances; ~**ung** f company; (MIL) escort; (MUS) accompaniment

beglücken |bə'glʏkən| vt to make happy, to delight

beglückwünschen |bə'glʏkvʏnʃən| vt: ~ (zu) to congratulate (on)

begnadigen |bə'gnaːdɪgən| vt to pardon; **Begnadigung** f pardon, amnesty

begnügen |bə'gnyːgən| vr to be satisfied, to content o.s.

begonnen etc |bə'gɔnən| vb siehe **beginnen**

begraben |bə'graːbən| (unreg) vt to bury; **Begräbnis** |bə'grɛːpnɪs| (-ses, -se) nt burial, funeral

begreifen |bə'graɪfən| (unreg) vt to understand, to comprehend

begreiflich |bə'graɪflɪç| adj understandable

begrenzen |bə'grɛntsən| vt (beschränken) to limit

Begrenztheit |bə'grɛntsthaɪt| f limitation, restriction; (fig) narrowness

Begriff |bə'grɪf| (-(e)s, -e) m concept, idea; **im ~ sein, etw zu tun** to be about to do sth; **schwer von ~** (umg) slow, dense

begriffsstutzig adj slow, dense

begründ- |bə'grʏnd| zW: **~en** vt (Gründe geben) to justify; **~et** adj well-founded, justified; **B~ung** f justification, reason

begrüßen |bə'gryːsən| vt to greet, to welcome; **Begrüßung** f greeting, welcome

begünstigen |bə'gʏnstɪgən| vt (Person) to favour; (Sache) to further, to promote

begutachten |bə'guːtʔaxtən| vt to assess

begütert |bə'gyːtərt| adj wealthy, well-to-do

behaart |bə'haːrt| adj hairy

behagen |bə'haːgən| vi: **das behagt ihm nicht** he does not like it

behaglich |bə'haːklɪç| adj comfortable, cosy; **B~keit** f comfort, cosiness

behalten |bə'haltən| (unreg) vt to keep, to retain; (im Gedächtnis) to remember

Behälter |bə'hɛltər| (-s, -) m container, receptacle

behandeln |bə'handəln| vt to treat; (Thema) to deal with; (Maschine) to handle

Behandlung f treatment; (von Maschine) handling

beharren |bə'harən| vi: **auf etw** dat ~ to stick od keep to sth

beharrlich |bə'harlɪç| adj (ausdauernd) steadfast, unwavering; (hartnäckig) tenacious, dogged; **B~keit** f steadfastness; tenacity

behaupten |bə'haʊptən| vt to claim, to assert, to maintain; (sein Recht) to defend ♦ vr to assert o.s.

Behauptung f claim, assertion

beheben |bə'heːbən| (unreg) vt to remove

behelfen |bə'hɛlfən| (unreg) vr: **sich mit etw** ~ to make do with sth

behelfsmäßig adj improvised, makeshift; (vorübergehend) temporary

behelligen |bə'hɛlɪgən| vt to trouble, to bother

beherbergen |bə'hɛrbɛrgən| vt to put up, to house

beherrsch- |bə'hɛrʃ| zW: **~en** vt (Volk) to rule, to govern; (Situation) to control; (Sprache, Gefühle) to master ♦ vr to control o.s.; **~t** adj controlled; **B~ung** f rule; control; mastery

beherzigen |bə'hɛrtsɪgən| vt to take to heart

beherzt adj courageous, brave

behilflich |bə'hɪlflɪç| adj helpful; **jdm** ~ **sein (bei)** to help sb (with)

behindern |bə'hɪndərn| vt to hinder, to impede

Behinderte(r) f(m) disabled person

Behinderung f hindrance; (Körperbehinderung) handicap

Behörde |bə'høːrdə| f (auch pl) authorities pl

behördlich |bə'høːrtlɪç| adj official

behüten |bə'hyːtən| vt to guard; **jdn vor etw** dat ~ to preserve sb from sth

behutsam |bə'huːtzaːm| adj cautious, careful; **B~keit** f caution, carefulness

bei |baɪ| präp +dat **1** (nahe bei) near; (zum Aufenthalt) at, with; (unter, zwischen) among; **bei München** near Munich; **bei uns** at our place; **bei Firma** at the hairdresser's; **bei seinen Eltern wohnen** to live with one's parents; **bei einer Firma arbeiten** to work for a firm; **etw bei sich haben** to have sth on one; **jdn bei sich haben** to have sb with one; **bei Goethe** in Goethe; **beim Militär** in the army

2 (zeitlich) at, on; (während) during; (Zustand, Umstand) in; **bei Nacht** at night; **bei Nebel** in fog; **bei Regen** if it rains; **bei solcher Hitze** in such heat; **bei meiner Ankuft** on my arrival; **bei der Arbeit** when I'm etc working; **beim Fahren** while driving

beibehalten |'baɪbəhaltən| (unreg) vt to keep, to retain

beibringen |'baɪbrɪŋən| (unreg) vt (Beweis, Zeugen) to bring forward; (Gründe) to adduce; **jdm etw ~** (lehren) to teach sb sth; (zu verstehen geben) to make sb understand sth; (zufügen) to inflict sth on sb

Beichte ['baɪçtə] f confession; **b~n** vt to confess ♦ vi to go to confession

beide(s) ['baɪdə(s)| pron, adj both; **meine ~n Brüder** my two brothers, both my brothers; **die ersten ~n** the first two; **wir ~** we both; **einer von ~n** one of the two; **alles ~s** both (of them)

beider- ['baɪdər| zW: **~lei** adj inv of both; **~seitig** adj mutual, reciprocal; **~seits** adv mutually ♦ präp +gen on both sides of

beieinander |baɪ'a'nandər| adv together

Beifahrer ['baɪfaːrər] m passenger

Beifall |'baɪfal| (-(e)s) m applause; (Zustimmung) approval

beifügen ['baɪfyːgən] vt to enclose

beige ['beːʒ] adj beige, fawn

beigeben |'baɪgeːbən| (unreg) vt (zufügen) to add; (mitgeben) to give ♦ vi (nachgeben) to give in

Beihilfe ['baɪhɪlfə] f aid, assistance; (Studienbeihilfe) grant; (JUR) aiding and abetting

beikommen ['baɪkɔmən] (unreg) vi +dat to get at; (einem Problem) to deal with

Beil [baɪl] (-(e)s, -e) nt axe, hatchet

Beilage |'baɪlaːgə| f (Buchbeilage etc) supplement; (KOCH) vegetables and potatoes pl

beiläufig |'baɪlɔyfɪç| adj casual, incidental ♦ adv casually, by the way

beilegen ['baɪleːgən] vt (hinzufügen) to enclose, to add; (beimessen) to attribute, to ascribe; (Streit) to settle

Beileid ['baɪlaɪt] nt condolence, sympathy; **herzliches ~** deepest sympathy

beiliegend ['baɪliːgənt] adj (COMM) enclosed

beim [baɪm] = bei dem

beimessen ['baɪmesən] (unreg) vt (+dat) to attribute (to), to ascribe (to)

Bein [baɪn] (-(e)s, -e) nt leg

beinah(e) |'baɪnaː(ə)| adv almost, nearly

Beinbruch m fracture of the leg

beinhalten [bə'ɪnhaltən] vt to contain

Beipackzettel ['baɪpaktsetəl] m instruction leaflet

beipflichten ['baɪpflɪçtən] vi: **jdm/etw ~** to agree with sb/sth

beisammen [baɪ'zamən] adv together; **B~sein** (-s) nt get-together

Beischlaf ['baɪʃlaːf] m sexual intercourse

Beisein |'baɪzaɪn| (-s) nt presence

beiseite [baɪ'zaɪtə] adv to one side, aside; (stehen) on one side, aside; **etw ~ legen** (sparen) to put sth by

beisetzen ['baɪzetsən] vt to bury; **Beisetzung** f funeral

Beisitzer ['baɪzɪtsər] (-s, -) m (bei Prüfung) assessor

Beispiel |'baɪʃpiːl| (-(e)s, -e) nt example; **sich +dat an jdm ein ~ nehmen** to take sb as an example; **zum ~** for example; **b~haft** adj exemplary; **b~los** adj unprecedented; **b~sweise** adv for instance od example

beißen ['baɪsən] (unreg) vt, vi to bite; (stechen: Rauch, Säure) to burn ♦ vr (Farben) to clash; **~d** adj biting, caustic; (fig auch) sarcastic

Beistand ['baɪʃtant] (-(e)s, ̈e) m support, help; (JUR) adviser

beistehen ['baɪʃteːən] (unreg) vi: **jdm ~** to stand by sb

beisteuern ['baɪʃtɔyərn] vt to contribute

Beitrag ['baɪtraːk] (-(e)s, ̈e) m contribution; (Zahlung) fee, subscription; (Versicherungsbeitrag) premium; **b~en** [baɪtraːgən] (unreg) vt, vi: **b~en (zu)** to contribute (to); (mithelfen) to help (with)

beitreten ['baɪtreːtən] (unreg) vi +dat to join

Beitritt ['baɪtrɪt] m joining, membership

Beiwagen ['baɪvaːgən] m (Motorradbeiwagen) sidecar

beizeiten [baɪ'tsaɪtən] adv in time

bejahen [bə'jaːən] vt (Frage) to say yes to, to answer in the affirmative; (gutheißen) to agree with

bekämpfen [bə'kempfən] vt (Gegner) to fight; (Seuche) to combat ♦ vr to fight; **Bekämpfung** f fight, struggle

bekannt [bə'kant] adj (well-)known; (nicht fremd) familiar; **~ geben** to announce publicly; **~ machen** to announce; **mit jdm ~ sein** to know sb; **jdn mit jdm ~ machen** to introduce sb to sb; **das ist mir ~** I know that; **es/sie kommt mir ~ vor** it/she seems familiar; **B~e(r)** f(m) acquaintance; friend; **B~enkreis** m circle of friends; **~lich** adv as is well known, as you know; **B~machung** f publication; announcement; **B~schaft** f acquaintance

bekehren [bə'keːrən] vt to convert ♦ vr to be od become converted

bekennen [bə'kenən] (unreg) vt to confess; (Glauben) to profess; **Farbe ~** (umg) to show where one stands

Bekenntnis [bə'kentnɪs] (-ses, -se) nt admission, confession; (Religion) confession, denomination

beklagen [bə'klaːgən] vt to deplore, to lament ♦ vr to complain

bekleiden [bə'klaɪdən] vt to clothe; (Amt) to occupy, to fill

Bekleidung f clothing

beklemmen [bə'klemən] vt to oppress

beklommen |bə'klɔmən| *adj* anxious, uneasy

bekommen |bə'kɔmən| *(unreg) vt* to get, to receive; *(Kind)* to have; *(Zug)* to catch, to get ♦ *vi*: **jdm ~** to agree with sb

bekömmlich |bə'kœmlıç| *adj* easily digestible

bekräftigen |bə'krɛftıgən| *vt* to confirm, to corroborate

bekreuzigen |bə'krɔytsıgən| *vr* to cross o.s.

bekunden |bə'kundən| *vt (sagen)* to state; *(zeigen)* to show

belächeln |bə'lɛçəln| *vt* to laugh at

beladen |bə'la:dən| *(unreg) vt* to load

Belag |bə'la:k| *(-(e)s, ²e) m* covering, coating; *(Brotbelag)* spread; *(Zahnbelag)* tartar; *(auf Zunge)* fur; *(Bremsbelag)* lining

belagern |bə'la:gərn| *vt* to besiege; **Belagerung** *f* siege

Belang |bə'laŋ| *(-(e)s) m* importance; **~e** *pl* *(Interessen)* interests, concerns; **b~los** *adj* trivial, unimportant

belassen |bə'lasən| *(unreg) vt (in Zustand, Glauben)* to leave; *(in Stellung)* to retain

belasten |bə'lastən| *vt* to burden; *(fig: bedrücken)* to trouble, to worry; *(COMM: Konto)* to debit; *(JUR)* to incriminate ♦ *vr* to weigh o.s. down; *(JUR)* to incriminate o.s.; **~d** *adj (JUR)* incriminating

belästigen |bə'lɛstıgən| *vt* to annoy, to pester; **Belästigung** *f* annoyance, pestering

Belastung |bə'lastuŋ| *f* load; *(fig: Sorge etc)* weight; *(COMM)* charge, debit(ing); *(JUR)* incriminatory evidence

belaufen |bə'laufən| *(unreg) vr*: **sich ~ auf** +*akk* to amount to

beleben |bə'le:bən| *vt (anregen)* to liven up; *(Konjunktur, jds Hoffnungen)* to stimulate ♦ *vr (Augen)* to light up; *(Stadt)* to come to life

belebt |bə'le:pt| *adj (Straße)* busy

Beleg |bə'le:k| *(-(e)s, -e) m (COMM)* receipt; *(Beweis)* documentary evidence, proof; *(Beispiel)* example; **b~en** *vt* to cover; *(Kuchen, Brot)* to spread; *(Platz)* to reserve, to book; *(Kurs, Vorlesung)* to register for; *(beweisen)* to verify, to prove; *(MIL: mit Bomben)* to bomb; **~schaft** *f* personnel, staff; **b~t** *adj*: **b~tes Brot** open sandwich

belehren |bə'le:rən| *vt* to instruct, to teach; **Belehrung** *f* instruction

beleibt |bə'laıpt| *adj* stout, corpulent

beleidigen |bə'laıdıgən| *vt* to insult, to offend; **Beleidigung** *f* insult; *(JUR)* slander, libel

beleuchten |bə'lɔyçtən| *vt* to light, to illuminate; *(fig)* to throw light on

Beleuchtung *f* lighting, illumination

Belgien |'bɛlgiən| *nt* Belgium; **Belgier(in)** *m(f)* Belgian; **belgisch** *adj* Belgian

belichten |bə'lıçtən| *vt* to expose

Belichtung *f* exposure; **~smesser** *m* exposure meter

Belieben |bə'li:bən| *nt*: **(ganz) nach ~** (just) as you wish

beliebig |bə'li:bıç| *adj* any you like ♦ *adv* as you like; **ein ~es Thema** any subject you like *od* want; **~ viel/viele** as much/many as you like

beliebt |bə'li:pt| *adj* popular; **sich bei jdm ~ machen** to make o.s. popular with sb; **B~heit** *f* popularity

beliefern |bə'li:fərn| *vt* to supply

bellen |'bɛlən| *vi* to bark

belohnen |bə'lo:nən| *vt* to reward; **Belohnung** *f* reward

Belüftung |bə'lʏftuŋ| *f* ventilation

belügen |bə'ly:gən| *(unreg) vt* to lie to, to deceive

belustigen |bə'lustıgən| *vt* to amuse; **Belustigung** *f* amusement

bemalen |bə'ma:lən| *vt* to paint

bemängeln |bə'mɛŋəln| *vt* to criticize

bemerk- |bə'mɛrk| *zW*: **~bar** *adj* perceptible, noticeable; **sich ~bar machen** *(Person)* to make *od* get o.s. noticed; *(Unruhe)* to become noticeable; **~en** *vt (wahrnehmen)* to notice, to observe; *(sagen)* to say, to mention; **~enswert** *adj* remarkable, noteworthy; **B~ung** *f* remark; *(schriftlich auch)* note

bemitleiden |bə'mıtlaıdən| *vt* to pity

bemühen |bə'my:ən| *vr* to take trouble *od* pains; **Bemühung** *f* trouble, pains *pl*, effort

benachbart |bə'naxba:rt| *adj* neighbouring

benachrichtigen |bə'na:xrıçtıgən| *vt* to inform; **Benachrichtigung** *f* notification, information

benachteiligen |bə'na:xtaılıgən| *vt* to put at a disadvantage; to victimize

benehmen |bə'ne:mən| *(unreg) vr* to behave; **B~** *(-s) nt* behaviour

beneiden |bə'naıdən| *vt* to envy; **~swert** *adj* enviable

benennen |bə'nɛnən| *(unreg) vt* to name

Bengel |'bɛŋəl| *(-s, -) m (little)* rascal *od* rogue

benommen |bə'nɔmən| *adj* dazed

benoten |bə'no:tən| *vt* to mark

benötigen |bə'nø:tıgən| *vt* to need

benutzen |bə'nutsən| *vt* to use

Benutzer **(-s, -)** *m* user

Benutzung *f* utilization, use

Benzin |bɛnt'si:n| *(-s, -e) nt (AUT)* petrol *(BRIT)*, gas(oline) *(US)*; **~kanister** *m* petrol *(BRIT) od* gas *(US)* can; **~tank** *m* petrol tank *(BRIT)*, gas tank *(US)*; **~uhr** *f* petrol *(BRIT) od* gas *(US)* gauge

beobachten |bə'o:baxtən| *vt* to observe; **Beobachter** **(-s, -)** *m* observer; *(eines Unfalls)* witness; *(PRESSE, TV)* correspondent; **Beobachtung** *f* observation

bepacken |bə'pakən| *vt* to load, to pack

bequem |bəˈkveːm| *adj* comfortable; (*Ausrede*) convenient; (*Person*) lazy, indolent; **~en** *vr*: **sich ~en(, etw zu tun)** to condescend (to do sth); **B~lichkeit** |-lɪçkaɪt| *f* convenience, comfort; (*Faulheit*) laziness, indolence

beraten |bəˈraːtən| (*unreg*) *vt* to advise; (*besprechen*) to discuss, to debate ♦ *vr* to consult; **gut/schlecht ~ sein** to be well/ill advised; **sich ~ lassen** to get advice

Berater **(-s, -)** *m* adviser

Beratung *f* advice; (*Besprechung*) consultation; **~sstelle** *f* advice centre

berauben |bəˈraʊbən| *vt* to rob

berechenbar |bəˈrɛçənbaːr| *adj* calculable

berechnen |bəˈrɛçnən| *vt* to calculate; (*COMM: anrechnen*) to charge; **~d** *adj* (*Mensch*) calculating, scheming

Berechnung *f* calculation; (*COMM*) charge

berechtigen |bəˈrɛçtɪgən| *vt* to entitle; to authorize; (*fig*) to justify

berechtigt |bəˈrɛçtɪçt| *adj* justifiable, justified

Berechtigung *f* authorization; (*fig*) justification

bereden |bəˈreːdən| *vt* (*besprechen*) to discuss; (*überreden*) to persuade ♦ *vr* to discuss

Bereich |bəˈraɪç| **(-(e)s, -e)** *m* (*Bezirk*) area; (*PHYS*) range; (*Ressort, Gebiet*) sphere

bereichern |bəˈraɪçərn| *vt* to enrich ♦ *vr* to get rich

bereinigen |bəˈraɪnɪgən| *vt* to settle

bereisen |bəˈraɪzən| *vt* (*Land*) to travel through

bereit |bəˈraɪt| *adj* ready, prepared; **zu etw ~ sein** to be ready for sth; **sich ~ erklären** to declare o.s. willing; **~en** *vt* to prepare, to make ready; (*Kummer, Freude*) to cause; **~halten** (*unreg*) *vt* to keep in readiness; **~legen** *vt* to lay out; **~machen** *vt*, *vr* to prepare, to get ready; **~s** *adv* already; **B~schaft** *f* readiness; (*Polizei*) alert; **B~schaftsdienst** *m* emergency service; **~stehen** (*unreg*) *vi* (*Person*) to be prepared; (*Ding*) to be ready; **~stellen** *vt* (*Kisten, Pakete etc*) to put ready; (*Geld etc*) to make available; (*Truppen, Maschinen*) to put at the ready; **~willig** *adj* willing, ready; **B~willigkeit** *f* willingness, readiness

bereuen |bəˈrɔʏən| *vt* to regret

Berg |bɛrk| **(-(e)s, -e)** *m* mountain; hill; **b~ab** *adv* downhill; **~arbeiter** *m* miner; **b~auf** *adv* uphill; **~bahn** *f* mountain railway; **~bau** *m* mining

bergen |ˈbɛrgən| (*unreg*) *vt* (*retten*) to rescue; (*Ladung*) to salvage; (*enthalten*) to contain

Berg- *zW*: **~führer** *m* mountain guide; **~gipfel** *m* peak, summit; **b~ig** |ˈbɛrgɪç| *adj* mountainous, hilly; **~kette** *f* mountain range; **~mann** (*pl* **-leute**) *m* miner; **~rettungsdienst** *m* mountain rescue team; **~rutsch** *m* landslide; **~steigen** *nt* mountaineering; **~steiger(in)** **(-s, -)** *m(f)* mountaineer, climber; **~tour** *f* mountain climb

Bergung |ˈbɛrgʊŋ| *f* (*von Menschen*) rescue; (*von Material*) recovery; (*NAUT*) salvage

Berg- *zW*: **~wacht** *f* mountain rescue service; **~wanderung** *f* hike in the mountains; **~werk** *nt* mine

Bericht |bəˈrɪçt| **(-(e)s, -e)** *m* report, account; **b~en** *vt*, *vi* to report; **~erstatter** **(-s, -)** *m* reporter; (*newspaper*) correspondent

berichtigen |bəˈrɪçtɪgən| *vt* to correct; **Berichtigung** *f* correction

Bernstein |ˈbɛrnʃtaɪn| *m* amber

bersten |ˈbɛrstən| (*unreg*) *vi* to burst, to split

berüchtigt |bəˈrʏçtɪçt| *adj* notorious, infamous

berücksichtigen |bəˈrʏkzɪçtɪgən| *vt* to consider, to bear in mind; **Berücksichtigung** *f* consideration

Beruf |bəˈruːf| **(-(e)s, -e)** *m* occupation, profession; (*Gewerbe*) trade; **b~en** (*unreg*) *vt*: **b~en zu** to appoint to ♦ *vr*: **sich auf jdn/etw b~en** to refer *od* appeal to sb/sth ♦ *adj* competent, qualified; **b~lich** *adj* professional

Berufs- *zW*: **~ausbildung** *f* job training; **~berater** *m* careers adviser; **~beratung** *f* vocational guidance; **~geheimnis** *nt* professional secret; **~leben** *nt* professional life; **~schule** *f* vocational *od* trade school; **~sportler** |-ʃpɔrtlər| *m* professional (sportsman); **b~tätig** *adj* employed; **b~unfähig** *adj* unfit for work; **~verkehr** *m* rush-hour traffic

Berufung *f* vocation, calling; (*Ernennung*) appointment; (*JUR*) appeal; **~ einlegen** to appeal

beruhen |bəˈruːən| *vi*: **auf etw** *dat* **~** to be based on sth; **etw auf sich ~ lassen** to leave sth at that

beruhigen |bəˈruːɪgən| *vt* to calm, to pacify, to soothe ♦ *vr* (*Mensch*) to calm (o.s.) down; (*Situation*) to calm down

Beruhigung *f* soothing; (*der Nerven*) calming; **zu jds ~** (in order) to reassure sb; **~smittel** *nt* sedative

berühmt |bəˈryːmt| *adj* famous; **B~heit** *f* (*Ruf*) fame; (*Mensch*) celebrity

berühren |bəˈryːrən| *vt* to touch; (*gefühlsmäßig bewegen*) to affect; (*flüchtig erwähnen*) to mention, to touch on ♦ *vr* to meet, to touch

Berührung *f* contact

besagen |bəˈzaːgən| *vt* to mean

besänftigen |bəˈzɛnftɪgən| *vt* to soothe,

to calm

Besatz [bə'zats] (**-es, ⸚e**) *m* trimming, edging

Besatzung [bə'zatsuŋ] *f* garrison; (NAUT, AVIAT) crew

Besatzungsmacht *f* occupying power

beschädigen [bə'ʃɛːdɪɡən] *vt* to damage; **Beschädigung** *f* damage; (*Stelle*) damaged spot

beschaffen [bə'ʃafən] *vt* to get, to acquire ♦ *adj*: **das ist so ~, dass** that is such that; **B~heit** *f* (*von Mensch*) constitution, nature

Beschaffung *f* acquisition

beschäftigen [bə'ʃɛftɪɡən] *vt* to occupy; (*beruflich*) to employ ♦ *vr* to occupy od concern o.s.

beschäftigt *adj* busy, occupied

Beschäftigung *f* (*Beruf*) employment; (*Tätigkeit*) occupation; (*Befassen*) concern

beschämen [bə'ʃɛːmən] *vt* to put to shame; **~d** *adj* shameful; (*Hilfsbereitschaft*) shaming

beschämt *adj* ashamed

Bescheid [bə'ʃait] (**-(e)s, -e**) *m* information; (*Weisung*) directions *pl*; **~ wissen (über** +*akk*) to be well-informed (about); **ich weiß ~** I know; **jdm ~ geben** od **sagen** to let sb know

bescheiden [bə'ʃaidən] (*unreg*) *vr* to content o.s. ♦ *adj* modest; **B~heit** *f* modesty

bescheinen [bə'ʃainən] (*unreg*) *vt* to shine on

bescheinigen [bə'ʃainɪɡən] *vt* to certify; (*bestätigen*) to acknowledge

Bescheinigung *f* certificate; (*Quittung*) receipt

beschenken [bə'ʃɛŋkən] *vt*: **jdn mit etw ~** to give sb sth as a present

bescheren [bə'ʃeːrən] *vt*: **jdm etw ~** to give sb sth as a Christmas present; **jdn ~** to give Christmas presents to sb

Bescherung *f* giving of Christmas presents; (*umg*) mess

beschildern [bə'ʃildərn] *vt* to put signs/a sign on

beschimpfen [bə'ʃimpfən] *vt* to abuse; **Beschimpfung** *f* abuse; insult

Beschlag [bə'ʃlaːk] (**-(e)s, ⸚e**) *m* (*Metallband*) fitting; (*auf Fenster*) condensation; (*auf Metall*) tarnish; finish; (*Hufeisen*) horseshoe; **jdn/etw in ~ nehmen** od **mit ~ belegen** to monopolize sb/sth; **b~en** [bə'ʃlaːɡən] (*unreg*) *vt* to cover; (*Pferd*) to shoe ♦ *vi, vr* (*Fenster etc*) to mist over; **b~en sein (in** od **auf** +*dat*) to be well versed (in); **b~nahmen** *vt* to seize, to confiscate; to requisition; **~nahmung** *f* confiscation, sequestration

beschleunigen [bə'ʃlɔynɪɡən] *vt* to accelerate, to speed up ♦ *vi* (AUT) to accelerate; **Beschleunigung** *f* acceleration

beschließen [bə'ʃliːsən] (*unreg*) *vt* to decide on; (*beenden*) to end, to close

Beschluss ▲ [bə'ʃlʊs] (**-es, ⸚e**) *m* decision, conclusion; (*Ende*) conclusion, end

beschmutzen [bə'ʃmʊtsən] *vt* to dirty, to soil

beschönigen [bə'ʃøːnɪɡən] *vt* to gloss over

beschränken [bə'ʃrɛŋkən] *vt, vr*: (**sich**) ~ (**auf** +*akk*) to limit od restrict (o.s.) (to)

beschränk- *zW*: **~t** *adj* confined, restricted; (*Mensch*) limited, narrow-minded; **B~ung** *f* limitation

beschreiben [bə'ʃraibən] (*unreg*) *vt* to describe; (*Papier*) to write on

Beschreibung *f* description

beschriften [bə'ʃriftən] *vt* to mark, to label; **Beschriftung** *f* lettering

beschuldigen [bə'ʃʊldɪɡən] *vt* to accuse; **Beschuldigung** *f* accusation

Beschuss ▲ [bə'ʃʊs] *m*: **jdn/etw unter ~ nehmen** (MIL) to open fire on sb/sth

beschützen [bə'ʃytsən] *vt*: ~ (**vor** +*dat*) to protect (from); **Beschützer** (**-s, -**) *m* protector

Beschwerde [bə'ʃveːrdə] *f* complaint; (*Mühe*) hardship; **~n** *pl* (*Leiden*) trouble

beschweren [bə'ʃveːrən] *vt* to weight down; (*fig*) to burden ♦ *vr* to complain

beschwerlich *adj* tiring, exhausting

beschwichtigen [bə'ʃvɪçtɪɡən] *vt* to soothe, to pacify

beschwindeln [bə'ʃvindəln] *vt* (*betrügen*) to cheat; (*belügen*) to fib to

beschwingt [bə'ʃviŋt] *adj* in high spirits

beschwipst [bə'ʃvipst] (*umg*) *adj* tipsy

beschwören [bə'ʃvøːrən] (*unreg*) *vt* (*Aussage*) to swear to; (*anflehen*) to implore; (*Geister*) to conjure up

beseitigen [bə'zaitɪɡən] *vt* to remove; **Beseitigung** *f* removal

Besen ['beːzən] (**-s, -**) *m* broom; **~stiel** *m* broomstick

besessen [bə'zɛsən] *adj* possessed

besetz- [bə'zɛts] *zW*: **~en** *vt* (*Haus, Land*) to occupy; (*Platz*) to take, to fill; (*Posten*) to fill; (*Rolle*) to cast; (*mit Edelsteinen*) to set; **~t** *adj* full; (TEL) engaged, busy; (*Platz*) taken; (WC) engaged; **B~tzeichen** *nt* engaged tone; **B~ung** *f* occupation; filling; (*von Rolle*) casting; (*die Schauspieler*) cast

besichtigen [bə'zɪçtɪɡən] *vt* to visit, to have a look at; **Besichtigung** *f* visit

Besied(e)lung [bə'ziːd(ə)lʊŋ] *f* population

besiegen [bə'ziːɡən] *vt* to defeat, to overcome

besinn- [bə'zin] *zW*: **~en** (*unreg*) *vr* (*nachdenken*) to think, to reflect; (*erinnern*) to remember; **sich anders ~en** to change one's mind; **B~ung** *f* consciousness; **zur B~ung kommen** to recover consciousness; (*fig*) to come to one's senses; **~ungslos** *adj* unconscious

Besitz [bə'zits] (**-es**) *m* possession; (*Eigentum*) property; **b~en** (*unreg*) *vt* to possess, to own; (*Eigenschaft*) to have;

~er(in) (**-s, -**) m(f) owner, proprietor;
~ergreifung f occupation, seizure
besoffen [bəˈzɔfən] (umg) adj drunk, stoned
besohlen [bəˈzoːlən] vt to sole
Besoldung [bəˈzɔldʊŋ] f salary, pay
besondere(r, s) [bəˈzɔndərə(r, s)] adj
special; (eigen) particular; (gesondert)
separate; (eigentümlich) peculiar
Besonderheit [bəˈzɔndərhait] f peculiarity
besonders [bəˈzɔndərs] adv especially,
particularly; (getrennt) separately
besonnen [bəˈzɔnən] adj sensible, level-
headed
besorg- [bəˈzɔrg] zW: **~en** vt (beschaffen) to
acquire; (kaufen auch) to purchase;
(erledigen: Geschäfte) to deal with; (sich
kümmern um) to take care of; **B~nis** (**-, -se**)
f anxiety, concern; **~t** [bəˈzɔrçt] adj anxious,
worried; **B~ung** f acquisition; (Kauf)
purchase
bespielen [bəˈʃpiːlən] vt to record
bespitzeln [bəˈʃpɪtsəln] vt to spy on
besprechen [bəˈʃprɛçən] (unreg) vt to
discuss; (Tonband etc) to record, to speak
onto; (Buch) to review ♦ vr to discuss, to
consult; **Besprechung** f meeting,
discussion; (von Buch) review
besser [ˈbɛsər] adj better; **es geht ihm ~** he
is feeling better; **~n** vt to make better, to
improve ♦ vr to improve; (Menschen) to
reform; **B~ung** f improvement; **gute
B~ung!** get well soon!; **B~wisser** (**-s, -**) m
know-all
Bestand [bəˈʃtant] (**-(e)s, ̈e**) m (Fortbestehen) duration, stability; (Kassen-
bestand) amount, balance; (Vorrat) stock;
~ haben, von ~ sein to last long, to
endure
beständig [bəˈʃtɛndɪç] adj (ausdauernd: auch
fig) constant; (Wetter) settled; (Stoffe)
resistant; (Klagen etc) continual
Bestandsaufnahme [bəˈʃtantsaufnaːmə] f
stocktaking
Bestandteil m part, component; (Zutat)
ingredient
bestärken [bəˈʃtɛrkən] vt: **jdn in etw** dat **~**
to strengthen od confirm sb in sth
bestätigen [bəˈʃtɛːtɪgən] vt to confirm;
(anerkennen, COMM) to acknowledge;
Bestätigung f confirmation; acknowledgement
bestatten [bəˈʃtatən] vt to bury
Bestattung f funeral
Bestattungsinstitut nt funeral director's
bestaunen [bəˈʃtaunən] vt to marvel at, to
gaze at in wonder
beste(r, s) [ˈbɛstə(r, s)] adj best; **so ist es
am ~n** it's best that way; **am ~n gehst du
gleich** you'd better go at once; **jdn zum**

B~n haben to pull sb's leg; **einen Witz** etc
zum B~n geben to tell a joke etc; **aufs B~
od ~** in the best possible way; **zu jds B~n**
for the benefit of sb
bestechen [bəˈʃtɛçən] (unreg) vt to bribe;
bestechlich adj corruptible; **Bestechung** f
bribery, corruption
Besteck [bəˈʃtɛk] (**-(e)s, -e**) nt knife, fork and
spoon, cutlery; (MED) set of instruments
bestehen [bəˈʃteːən] (unreg) vi to be; to
exist; (andauern) to last ♦ vt (Kampf, Probe,
Prüfung) to pass; **~ auf** +dat to insist on; **~
aus** to consist of
bestehlen [bəˈʃteːlən] (unreg) vt: **jdn (um
etw) ~** to rob sb (of sth)
besteigen [bəˈʃtaigən] (unreg) vt to climb, to
ascend; (Pferd) to mount; (Thron) to ascend
Bestell- [bəˈʃtɛl] zW: **~buch** nt order book;
b~en vt to order; (kommen lassen) to
arrange to see; (nominieren) to name;
(Acker) to cultivate; (Grüße, Auftrag) to pass
on; **~formular** nt order form; **~nummer** f
order code; **~ung** f (COMM) order; (~en)
ordering
bestenfalls [ˈbɛstənˈfals] adv at best
bestens [ˈbɛstəns] adv very well
besteuern [bəˈʃtɔyərn] vt (jdn, Waren) to tax
Bestie [ˈbɛstiə] f (auch fig) beast
bestimm- [bəˈʃtɪm] zW: **~en** vt (Regeln) to
lay down; (Tag, Ort) to fix; (beherrschen) to
characterize; (vorsehen) to mean; (ernennen)
to appoint; (definieren) to define;
(veranlassen) to induce; **~t** adj (entschlossen)
firm; (gewiss) certain, definite; (Artikel)
definite ♦ adv (gewiss) definitely, for sure;
suchen Sie etwas B~tes? are you looking
for something in particular?; **B~theit** f
firmness; certainty; **B~ung** f (Verordnung)
regulation; (Festsetzen) determining;
(Verwendungszweck) purpose; (Schicksal)
fate; (Definition) definition; **B~ungsland** nt
(country of) destination; **B~ungsort** m
(place of) destination
Bestleistung f best performance
bestmöglich adj best possible
bestrafen [bəˈʃtraːfən] vt to punish;
Bestrafung f punishment
bestrahlen [bəˈʃtraːlən] vt to shine on; (MED)
to treat with X-rays
Bestrahlung f (MED) X-ray treatment,
radiotherapy
Bestreben [bəˈʃtreːbən] (**-s**) nt endeavour,
effort
bestreiten [bəˈʃtraitən] (unreg) vt (abstreiten)
to dispute; (finanzieren) to pay for, to
finance
bestreuen [bəˈʃtrɔyən] vt to sprinkle, to
dust; (Straße) to grit
bestürmen [bəˈʃtyrmən] vt (mit Fragen,

Bitten etc) to overwhelm, to swamp
bestürzend [bə'ʃtʏrtsənd] *adj* (*Nachrichten*) disturbing
bestürzt [bə'ʃtʏrtst] *adj* dismayed
Bestürzung *f* consternation
Besuch [bə'zu:x] (**-(e)s, -e**) *m* visit; (*Person*) visitor; **einen ~ machen bei jdm** to pay sb a visit *od* call; **~ haben** to have visitors; **bei jdm auf** *od* **zu ~ sein** to be visiting sb; **b~en** *vt* to visit; (*SCH etc*) to attend; **gut b~t** well-attended; **~er(in)** (**-s, -**) *m(f)* visitor, guest; **~szeit** *f* visiting hours *pl*
betätigen [bə'tɛːtɪɡən] *vt* (*bedienen*) to work, to operate ♦ *vr* to involve o.s.; **sich als etw ~** to work as sth
Betätigung *f* activity; (*beruflich*) occupation; (*TECH*) operation
betäuben [bə'tɔybən] *vt* to stun; (*fig: Gewissen*) to still; (*MED*) to anaesthetize
Betäubung *f* (*Narkose*): **örtliche ~** local anaesthesia
Betäubungsmittel *nt* anaesthetic
Bete ['beːtə] *f*: **Rote ~** beetroot (*BRIT*), beet (*US*)
beteilig- [bə'taɪlɪɡ] *zW*: **~en** *vr*: **sich ~en (an** +*dat*) to take part (in), to participate (in), to share (in); (*an Geschäft: finanziell*) to have a share (in) ♦ *vt*: **jdn ~en (an** +*dat*) to give sb a share *od* interest (in); **B~te(r)** *f(m)* (*Mitwirkender*) partner; (*finanziell*) shareholder; **B~ung** *f* participation; (*Anteil*) share, interest; (*Besucherzahl*) attendance
beten ['beːtən] *vt, vi* to pray
beteuern [bə'tɔyərn] *vt* to assert; (*Unschuld*) to protest
Beton [be'tɔ̃ː] (**-s, -s**) *m* concrete
betonen [bə'toːnən] *vt* to stress
betonieren [beto'niːrən] *vt* to concrete
Betonung *f* stress, emphasis
betr. *abk* (= *betrifft*) re
Betracht [bə'traxt] *m*: **in ~ kommen** to be considered *od* relevant; **etw in ~ ziehen** to take sth into consideration; **außer ~ bleiben** not to be considered; **b~en** *vt* to look at; (*fig*) to look at, to consider; **~er(in)** (**-s, -**) *m(f)* observer
beträchtlich [bə'trɛçtlɪç] *adj* considerable
Betrachtung *f* (*Ansehen*) examination; (*Erwägung*) consideration
Betrag [bə'traːk] (**-(e)s, ⁼e**) *m* amount; **b~en** (*unreg*) *vt* to amount to ♦ *vr* to behave; **~en** (**-s**) *nt* behaviour
Betreff *m*: **~ Ihr Schreiben vom ...** re your letter of ...
betreffen [bə'trɛfən] (*unreg*) *vt* to concern, to affect; **was mich betrifft** as for me; **~d** *adj* relevant, in question
betreffs [bə'trɛfs] *präp* +*gen* concerning, regarding; (*COMM*) re
betreiben [bə'traɪbən] (*unreg*) *vt* (*ausüben*) to practise; (*Politik*) to follow; (*Studien*) to

pursue; (*vorantreiben*) to push ahead; (*TECH: antreiben*) to drive
betreten [bə'treːtən] (*unreg*) *vt* to enter; (*Bühne etc*) to step onto ♦ *adj* embarrassed; **B~ verboten** keep off/out
Betreuer(in) [bə'trɔyər(ɪn)] (**-s, -**) *m(f)* (*einer Person*) minder; (*eines Gebäudes, Arbeitsgebiets*) caretaker; (*SPORT*) coach
Betreuung *f* care
Betrieb [bə'triːp] (**-(e)s, -e**) *m* (*Firma*) firm, concern; (*Anlage*) plant; (*Tätigkeit*) operation; (*Treiben*) traffic; **außer ~ sein** to be out of order; **in ~ sein** to be in operation
Betriebs- *zW*: **~ausflug** *m* works outing; **b~bereit** *adj* operational; **b~fähig** *adj* in working order; **~ferien** *pl* company holidays (*BRIT*), company vacation *sg* (*US*); **~klima** *nt* (working) atmosphere; **~kosten** *pl* running costs; **~rat** *m* workers' council; **b~sicher** *adj* safe (to operate); **~störung** *f* breakdown; **~system** *nt* (*COMPUT*) operating system; **~unfall** *m* industrial accident; **~wirtschaft** *f* economics
betrinken [bə'trɪŋkən] (*unreg*) *vr* to get drunk
betroffen [bə'trɔfən] *adj* (*bestürzt*) full of consternation; **von etw ~ werden** *od* **sein** to be affected by sth
betrüben [bə'tryːbən] *vt* to grieve
betrübt [bə'tryːpt] *adj* sorrowful, grieved
Betrug [bə'truːk] (**-(e)s**) *m* deception; (*JUR*) fraud
betrügen [bə'tryːɡən] (*unreg*) *vt* to cheat; (*JUR*) to defraud; (*Ehepartner*) to be unfaithful to ♦ *vr* to deceive o.s.
Betrüger (**-s, -**) *m* cheat, deceiver; **b~isch** *adj* deceitful; (*JUR*) fraudulent
betrunken [bə'trʊŋkən] *adj* drunk
Bett [bɛt] (**-(e)s, -en**) *nt* bed; **ins** *od* **zu ~ gehen** to go to bed; **~bezug** *m* duvet cover; **~decke** *f* blanket; (*Daunenbett*) quilt; (*Überwurf*) bedspread
Bettel- ['bɛtəl] *zW*: **b~arm** *adj* very poor, destitute; **~ei** [bɛtə'laɪ] *f* begging; **b~n** *vi* to beg
bettlägerig ['bɛtlɛːɡərɪç] *adj* bedridden
Bettlaken *nt* sheet
Bettler(in) ['bɛtlər(ɪn)] (**-s, -**) *m(f)* beggar
Bett- *zW*: **~tuch** ▲ *nt* sheet; **~vorleger** *m* bedside rug; **~wäsche** *f* bed linen; **~zeug** *nt* bed linen *pl*
beugen ['bɔyɡən] *vt* to bend; (*GRAM*) to inflect ♦ *vr* (*sich fügen*) to bow
Beule ['bɔylə] *f* bump, swelling
beunruhigen [bə'ʊnruːɪɡən] *vt* to disturb, to alarm ♦ *vr* to become worried
Beunruhigung *f* worry, alarm
beurlauben [bə'uːrlaʊbən] *vt* to give leave *od* a holiday to (*BRIT*), to grant vacation time to (*US*)
beurteilen [bə'ʊrtaɪlən] *vt* to judge; (*Buch*

etc) to review
Beurteilung *f* judgement; review; (*Note*) mark
Beute ['bɔytə] (-) *f* booty, loot
Beutel (-s, -) *m* bag; (*Geldbeutel*) purse; (*Tabakbeutel*) pouch
Bevölkerung [bə'fœlkəruŋ] *f* population
bevollmächtigen [bə'fɔlmɛçtɪgən] *vt* to authorize
Bevollmächtigte(r) *f(m)* authorized agent
bevor [bə'foːr] *konj* before; ~**munden** *vt insep* to treat like a child; ~**stehen** (*unreg*) *vi*: (*jdm*) ~**stehen** to be in store (for sb); ~**stehend** *adj* imminent, approaching; ~**zugen** *vt insep* to prefer
bewachen [bə'vaxən] *vt* to watch, to guard
Bewachung *f* (*Bewachen*) guarding; (*Leute*) guard, watch
bewaffnen [bə'vafnən] *vt* to arm
Bewaffnung *f* (*Vorgang*) arming; (*Ausrüstung*) armament, arms *pl*
bewahren [bə'vaːrən] *vt* to keep; **jdn vor jdm/etw** ~ to save sb from sb/sth
bewähren [bə'vɛːrən] *vr* to prove o.s.; (*Maschine*) to prove its worth
bewahrheiten [bə'vaːrhaɪtən] *vr* to come true
bewährt *adj* reliable
Bewährung *f* (*JUR*) probation
bewältigen [bə'vɛltɪgən] *vt* to overcome; (*Arbeit*) to finish; (*Portion*) to manage
bewandert [bə'vandərt] *adj* expert, knowledgeable
bewässern [bə'vɛsərn] *vt* to irrigate
Bewässerung *f* irrigation
bewegen [bə'veːgən] *vt, vr* to move; **jdn zu etw** ~ to induce sb to do sth; ~**d** *adj* touching, moving
Beweg- [bə'veːg] *zW*: ~**grund** *m* motive; **b~lich** *adj* movable, mobile; (*flink*) quick; **b~t** *adj* (*Leben*) eventful; (*Meer*) rough; (*ergriffen*) touched
Bewegung *f* movement, motion; (*innere*) emotion; (*körperlich*) exercise; ~**sfreiheit** *f* freedom of movement; (*fig*) freedom of action; **b~slos** *adj* motionless
Beweis [bə'vaɪs] (-es, -e) *m* proof; (*Zeichen*) sign; **b~en** [-zən] (*unreg*) *vt* to prove; (*zeigen*) to show; ~**mittel** *nt* evidence
Bewerb- [bə'vɛrb] *zW*: **b~en** (*unreg*) *vr* to apply (for); ~**er(in)** (-s, -) *m(f)* applicant; ~**ung** *f* application
bewerkstelligen [bə'vɛrkʃtɛlɪgən] *vt* to manage, to accomplish
bewerten [bə'vɛːrtən] *vt* to assess
bewilligen [bə'vɪlɪgən] *vt* to grant, to allow
Bewilligung *f* granting
bewirken [bə'vɪrkən] *vt* to cause, to bring about

bewirten [bə'vɪrtən] *vt* to feed, to entertain (to a meal)
bewirtschaften [bə'vɪrtʃaftən] *vt* to manage
Bewirtung *f* hospitality
bewog *etc* [bə'voːk] *vb siehe* **bewegen**
bewohn- [bə'voːn] *zW*: ~**bar** *adj* habitable; ~**en** *vt* to inhabit, to live in; **B~er(in)** (-s, -) *m(f)* inhabitant; (*von Haus*) resident
bewölkt [bə'vœlkt] *adj* cloudy, overcast
Bewölkung *f* clouds *pl*
Bewunder- [bə'vundər] *zW*: ~**er** (-s, -) *m* admirer; **b~n** *vt* to admire; **b~nswert** *adj* admirable, wonderful; ~**ung** *f* admiration
bewusst ▲ [bə'vust] *adj* conscious; (*absichtlich*) deliberate; **sich gen einer Sache** *dat* ~ **sein** to be aware of sth; ~**los** ▲ *adj* unconscious; **B~losigkeit** ▲ *f* unconsciousness; **B~sein** ▲ *nt* consciousness; **bei B~sein** conscious
bezahlen [bə'tsaːlən] *vt* to pay for
Bezahlung *f* payment
bezaubern [bə'tsaubərn] *vt* to enchant, to charm
bezeichnen [bə'tsaɪçnən] *vt* (*kennzeichnen*) to mark; (*nennen*) to call; (*beschreiben*) to describe; (*zeigen*) to show, to indicate; ~**d** *adj*: ~**d** (**für**) characteristic (of), typical (of)
Bezeichnung *f* (*Zeichen*) mark, sign; (*Beschreibung*) description
bezeugen [bə'tsɔygən] *vt* to testify to
Bezichtigung [bə'tsɪçtɪguŋ] *f* accusation
beziehen [bə'tsiːən] (*unreg*) *vt* (*mit Überzug*) to cover; (*Bett*) to make; (*Haus, Position*) to move into; (*Standpunkt*) to take up; (*erhalten*) to receive; (*Zeitung*) to subscribe to, to take ♦ *vr* (*Himmel*) to cloud over; **etw auf jdn/etw** ~ to relate sth to sb/sth; **sich** ~ **auf** +*akk* to refer to
Beziehung *f* (*Verbindung*) connection; (*Zusammenhang*) relation; (*Verhältnis*) relationship; (*Hinsicht*) respect; ~**en haben** (*vorteilhaft*) to have connections *od* contacts; **b~sweise** *adv* or; (*genauer gesagt auch*) that is, or rather
Bezirk [bə'tsɪrk] (-(e)s, -e) *m* district
Bezug [bə'tsuːk] (-(e)s, -̈e) *m* (*Hülle*) covering; (*COMM*) ordering; (*Gehalt*) income, salary; (*Beziehung*): ~ (**zu**) relation(ship) (to); **in** ~ **auf** +*akk* with reference to; ~ **nehmen auf** +*akk* to refer to
bezüglich [bə'tsyːklɪç] *präp* +*gen* concerning, referring to ♦ *adj* (*GRAM*) relative; **auf etw** *akk* ~ relating to sth
bezwecken [bə'tsvɛkən] *vt* to aim at
bezweifeln [bə'tsvaɪfəln] *vt* to doubt, to query
BH *m abk von* **Büstenhalter**
Bhf. *abk* (= *Bahnhof*) station
Bibel ['biːbəl] (-, -n) *f* Bible

Biber ['bi:bər] (-s, -) m beaver
Biblio- [bi:blio] zW: **~grafie** ▲ |-'gra'fi:| f bibliography; **~thek** [-'te:k| (-, -en) f library; **~thekar(in)** [-te'ka:r(ɪn)] (-s, -e) m(f) librarian
biblisch ['bi:blɪʃ] adj biblical
bieder ['bi:dər] adj upright, worthy; (Kleid etc) plain
bieg- ['bi:g] zW: **~en** (unreg) vt, vr to bend ♦ vi to turn; **~sam** ['bi:k-| adj flexible; **B~ung** f bend, curve
Biene ['bi:nə] f bee
Bienenhonig m honey
Bienenwachs nt beeswax
Bier |bi:r| (-(e)s, -e) nt beer; **~deckel** m beer mat; **~garten** m beer garden; **~krug** m beer mug; **~zelt** nt beer tent
Biest [bi:st] (-s, -er) (umg: pej) nt (Tier) beast, creature; (Mensch) beast
bieten ['bi:tən] (unreg) vt to offer; (bei Versteigerung) to bid ♦ vr (Gelegenheit): **sich jdm ~** to present itself to sb; **sich** dat **etw ~ lassen** to put up with sth
Bikini [bi'ki:ni] (-s, -s) m bikini
Bilanz [bi'lants] f balance; (fig) outcome; **~ ziehen (aus)** to take stock (of)
Bild [bɪlt] (-(e)s, -er) nt (auch fig) picture; photo; (Spiegelbild) reflection; **~bericht** m photographic report
bilden ['bɪldən] vt to form; (erziehen) to educate; (ausmachen) to constitute ♦ vr to arise; (erziehen) to educate o.s.
Bilderbuch nt picture book
Bilderrahmen m picture frame
Bild- zW: **~fläche** f screen; (fig) scene; **~hauer** (-s, -) m sculptor; **b~hübsch** adj lovely, pretty as a picture; **b~lich** adj figurative; pictorial; **~schirm** m television screen; (COMPUT) monitor; **b~schön** adj lovely
Bildung |-dʊŋ| f formation; (Wissen, Benehmen) education
Billard ['bɪljart] (-s, -e) nt billiards sg; **~kugel** f billiard ball
billig ['bɪlɪç] adj cheap; (gerecht) fair, reasonable; **~en** ['bɪlɪgən] vt to approve of
Binde ['bɪndə] f bandage; (Armbinde) band; (MED) sanitary towel; **~gewebe** nt connective tissue; **~glied** nt connecting link; **~hautentzündung** f conjunctivitis; **b~n** (unreg) vt to bind, to tie; **~strich** m hyphen
Bindfaden ['bɪnt-] m string
Bindung f bond, tie; (Skibindung) binding
binnen ['bɪnən] präp (+dat od gen) within; **B~hafen** m river port; **B~handel** m internal trade
Bio- [bio-] in zW bio-; **~chemie** f biochemistry; **~grafie** ▲ [-gra'fi:] f biography; **~laden** m wholefood shop; **~loge** [-'lo:gə] (-n, -n) m biologist; **~logie** [-lo'gi:] f biology; **b~logisch** [-'lo:gɪʃ] adj biological;

~top m od nt biotope
Birke ['bɪrkə] f birch
Birne ['bɪrnə] f pear; (ELEK) (light) bulb

SCHLÜSSELWORT

bis |bɪs| präp +akk, adv **1** (zeitlich) till, until; (bis spätestens) by; **Sie haben bis Dienstag Zeit** you have until od till Tuesday; **bis Dienstag muss es fertig sein** it must be ready by Tuesday; **bis auf weiteres** until further notice; **bis in die Nacht** into the night; **bis bald/gleich** see you later/soon **2** (räumlich) (up) to; **ich fahre bis Köln** I'm going to od I'm going as far as Cologne; **bis an unser Grundstück** (right od up) to our plot; **bis hierher** this far
3 (bei Zahlen) up to; **bis zu** up to
4: bis auf etw akk; (außer) except sth; (einschließlich) including sth
♦ konj **1** (mit Zahlen) to; **10 bis 20** 10 to 20 **2** (zeitlich) till, until; **bis es dunkel wird** till od until it gets dark; **von … bis …** from … to …

Bischof ['bɪʃɔf] (-s, ⁼e) m bishop; **bischöflich** ['bɪʃøːflɪç] adj episcopal
bisher [bɪs'he:r] adv till now, hitherto; **~ig** adj till now
Biskuit [bɪs'kvi:t] (-(e)s, -s od -e) m od nt (fatless) sponge
Biss ▲ |bɪs| (-es, -e) m bite
biss etc ▲ vb siehe **beißen**
bisschen ▲ ['bɪsçən] adj, adv bit
Bissen ['bɪsən] (-s, -) m bite, morsel
bissig ['bɪsɪç] adj (Hund) snappy; (Bemerkung) cutting, biting
bist [bɪst] vb siehe **sein**
bisweilen [bɪs'vaɪlən] adv at times, occasionally
Bitte ['bɪtə] f request; **b~** excl please; (wie b~?) (I beg your) pardon? ♦ interj (als Antwort auf Dank) you're welcome; **darf ich? – aber b~!** may I? – please do; **b~ schön!** it was a pleasure; **b~n** (unreg) vt, vi: **b~n (um)** to ask (for); **b~nd** adj pleading, imploring
bitter ['bɪtər] adj bitter; **~böse** adj very angry; **B~keit** f bitterness; **~lich** adj bitter
Blähungen ['blɛːʊŋən] pl (MED) wind sg
blamabel [bla'ma:bəl] adj disgraceful
Blamage [bla'ma:ʒə] f disgrace
blamieren [bla'mi:rən] vr to make a fool of o.s., to disgrace o.s. ♦ vt to let down, to disgrace
blank |blaŋk| adj bright; (unbedeckt) bare; (sauber) clean, polished; (umg: ohne Geld) broke; (offensichtlich) blatant
blanko ['blaŋko] adv blank; **B~scheck** m blank cheque
Blase ['bla:zə] f bubble; (MED) blister; (ANAT) bladder; **~balg** (-(e)s, -bälge) m bellows pl;

b~n (*unreg*) *vt, vi* to blow; **~nentzündung** *f* cystitis

Blas- |'blɑːs| *zW:* **~instrument** *nt* wind instrument; **~kapelle** *f* brass band

blass ▲ |blas| *adj* pale

Blässe |'blɛsə| (-) *f* paleness, pallor

Blatt |blat| (-(e)s, =er) *nt* leaf; (*von Papier*) sheet; (*Zeitung*) newspaper; (*KARTEN*) hand

blättern |'blɛtərn| *vi:* **in etw** *dat* **~** to leaf through sth

Blätterteig *m* flaky *od* puff pastry

blau |blau| *adj* blue; (*umg*) drunk, stoned; (*KOCH*) boiled; (*Auge*) black; **~er Fleck** bruise; **Fahrt ins B~e** mystery tour; **~äugig** *adj* blue-eyed

Blech |blɛç| (-(e)s, -e) *nt* tin, sheet metal; (*Backblech*) baking tray; **~büchse** *f* tin, can; **~dose** *f* tin, can; **b~en** (*umg*) *vt, vi* to fork out; **~schaden** *m* (*AUT*) damage to bodywork

Blei |blai| (-(e)s, -e) *nt* lead

Bleibe |'blaibə| *f* roof over one's head; **b~n** (*unreg*) *vi* to stay, to remain; **b~n lassen** to leave (alone); **b~nd** *adj* (*Erinnerung*) lasting; (*Schaden*) permanent

bleich |blaiç| *adj* faded, pale; **~en** *vt* to bleach

Blei- *zW:* **b~ern** *adj* leaden; **b~frei** *adj* (*Benzin*) lead-free; **~stift** *m* pencil

Blende |'blɛndə| *f* (*PHOT*) aperture; **b~n** *vt* to blind, to dazzle; (*fig*) to hoodwink; **b~nd** (*umg*) *adj* grand; **b~nd aussehen** to look smashing

Blick |blik| (-(e)s, -e) *m* (*kurz*) glance, glimpse; (*Anschauen*) look; (*Aussicht*) view; **b~en** *vi* to look; **sich b~en lassen** to put in an appearance; **~fang** *m* eye-catcher

blieb *etc* |bliːp| *vb siehe* **bleiben**

blind |blint| *adj* blind; (*Glas etc*) dull; **~er Passagier** stowaway; **B~darm** *m* appendix; **B~darmentzündung** *f* appendicitis; **B~enschrift** |'blindən-| *f* Braille; **B~heit** *f* blindness; **~lings** *adv* blindly

blink- |'bliŋk| *zW:* **~en** *vi* to twinkle, to sparkle; (*Licht*) to flash, to signal; (*AUT*) to indicate ♦ *vt* to flash, to signal; **B~er** (-s, -) *m* (*AUT*) indicator; **B~licht** *nt* (*AUT*) indicator; (*an Bahnübergängen usw*) flashing light

blinzeln |'blintsəln| *vi* to blink, to wink

Blitz |blits| (-es, -e) *m* (*flash of*) lightning; **~ableiter** *m* lightning conductor; **b~en** *vi* (*aufleuchten*) to flash, to sparkle; **es b~t** (*MET*) there's a flash of lightning; **~licht** *nt* flashlight; **b~schnell** *adj* lightning ♦ *adv* (as) quick as a flash

Block |blɔk| (-(e)s, =e) *m* block; (*von Papier*) pad; **~ade** |blɔ'kaːdə| *f* blockade; **~flöte** *f* recorder; **b~frei** *adj* (*POL*) unaligned; **~haus**

nt log cabin; **b~ieren** |blɔ'kiːrən| *vt* to block ♦ *vi* (*Räder*) to jam; **~schrift** *f* block letters *pl*

blöd |bløːt| *adj* silly, stupid; **~eln** |'bløːdəln| (*umg*) *vi* to act the goat (*fam*), to fool around; **B~sinn** *m* nonsense; **~sinnig** *adj* silly, idiotic

blond |blɔnt| *adj* blond, fair-haired

bloß |bloːs| *adj* **1** (*unbedeckt*) bare; (*nackt*) naked; **mit der bloßen Hand** with one's bare hand; **mit bloßem Auge** with the naked eye

2 (*alleinig, nur*) mere; **der bloße Gedanke** the very thought; **bloßer Neid** sheer envy ♦ *adv* only, merely; **lass das bloß!** just don't do that!; **wie ist das bloß passiert?** how on earth did that happen?

└────────────────────────────────────

Blöße |'bløːsə| *f* bareness; nakedness; (*fig*) weakness

bloßstellen *vt* to show up

blühen |'blyːən| *vi* to bloom (*lit*), to be in bloom; (*fig*) to flourish; **~d** *adj* (*Pflanze*) blooming; (*Aussehen*) blooming, radiant; (*Handel*) thriving, booming

Blume |'bluːmə| *f* flower; (*von Wein*) bouquet

Blumen- *zW:* **~kohl** *m* cauliflower; **~topf** *m* flowerpot; **~zwiebel** *f* bulb

Bluse |'bluːzə| *f* blouse

Blut |bluːt| (-(e)s) *nt* blood; **b~arm** *adj* anaemic; (*fig*) penniless; **b~befleckt** *adj* bloodstained; **~bild** *nt* blood count; **~druck** *m* blood pressure

Blüte |'blyːtə| *f* blossom; (*fig*) prime

Blut- *zW:* **b~en** *vi* to bleed; **~er** *m* (*MED*) haemophiliac; **~erguss ▲** *m* haemorrhage; (*auf Haut*) bruise

Blütezeit *f* flowering period; (*fig*) prime

Blut- *zW:* **~gruppe** *f* blood group; **b~ig** *adj* bloody; **b~jung** *adj* very young; **~probe** *f* blood test; **~spender** *m* blood donor; **~transfusion** *f* (*MED*) blood transfusion; **~ung** *f* bleeding, haemorrhage; **~vergiftung** *f* blood poisoning; **~wurst** *f* black pudding

Bö |bøː| (-, -en) *f* squall

Bock |bɔk| (-(e)s, =e) *m* buck, ram; (*Gestell*) trestle, support; (*SPORT*) buck; **~wurst** *f* type of pork sausage

Boden |'boːdən| (-s, =) *m* ground; (*Fußboden*) floor; (*Meeresboden, Fassboden*) bottom; (*Speicher*) attic; **b~los** *adj* bottomless; (*umg*) incredible; **~nebel** *m* ground mist; **~personal** *nt* (*AVIAT*) ground staff; **~schätze** *pl* mineral resources; **~see** *m:* **der ~see** Lake Constance; **~turnen** *nt* floor exercises *pl*

Böe |'bøːə| *f* squall

Bogen |ˈboːɡən| (**-s**, **-**) m (Biegung) curve; (ARCHIT) arch; (Waffe, MUS) bow; (Papier) sheet

Bohne |ˈboːnə| f bean

bohnern vt to wax, to polish

Bohnerwachs nt floor polish

Bohr- |ˈboːr| zW: **b~en** vt to bore; **~er** (**-s**, **-**) m drill; **~insel** f oil rig; **~maschine** f drill; **~turm** m derrick

Boiler |ˈbɔylər| (**-s**, **-**) m (hot-water) tank

Boje |ˈboːjə| f buoy

Bolzen |ˈbɔltsən| (**-s**, **-**) m bolt

bombardieren |bɔmbarˈdiːrən| vt to bombard; (aus der Luft) to bomb

Bombe |ˈbɔmbə| f bomb

Bombenangriff m bombing raid

Bombenerfolg (umg) m smash hit

Bon |bɔŋ| (**-s**, **-s**) m voucher, chit

Bonbon |bõˈbõ| (**-s**, **-s**) m od nt sweet

Boot |boːt| (**-(e)s**, **-e**) nt boat

Bord |bɔrt| (**-(e)s**, **-e**) m (AVIAT, NAUT) board ♦ nt (Brett) shelf; **an ~** on board

Bordell |bɔrˈdɛl| (**-s**, **-e**) nt brothel

Bordstein m kerb(stone)

borgen |ˈbɔrɡən| vt to borrow; **jdm etw ~** to lend sb sth

borniert |bɔrˈniːrt| adj narrow-minded

Börse |ˈbœːrzə| f stock exchange; (Geldbörse) purse; **~nmakler** m stockbroker

Borte |ˈbɔrtə| f edging; (Band) trimming

bös |bøːs| adj = **böse**

bösartig |ˈbøːz-| adj malicious

Böschung |ˈbœʃʊŋ| f slope; (Uferböschung etc) embankment

böse |ˈbøːzə| adj bad, evil; (zornig) angry

boshaft |ˈboːshaft| adj malicious, spiteful

Bosheit f malice, spite

Bosnien |ˈbɔsniən| (**-s**) nt Bosnia; **~ und Herzegowina** |-hɛrtsəˈɡoːvina| nt Bosnia (and) Herzegovina

böswillig |ˈbøːsvɪlɪç| adj malicious

bot etc |boːt| vb siehe **bieten**

Botanik |boˈtaːnɪk| f botany; **botanisch** adj botanical

Bot- |ˈboːt| zW: **~e** (**-n**, **-n**) m messenger; **~schaft** f message, news; (POL) embassy; **~schafter** (**-s**, **-**) m ambassador

Bottich |ˈbɔtɪç| (**-(e)s**, **-e**) m vat, tub

Bouillon |bʊˈljõ| (**-**, **-s**) f consommé

Bowle |ˈboːlə| f punch

Box- |ˈbɔks| zW: **b~en** vi to box; **~er** (**-s**, **-**) m boxer; **~kampf** m boxing match

boykottieren |bɔykɔˈtiːrən| vt to boycott

brach etc |braːx| vb siehe **brechen**

brachte etc |ˈbraxtə| vb siehe **bringen**

Branche |ˈbrãːʃə| f line of business

Branchenverzeichnis nt Yellow Pages ® pl

Brand |brant| (**-(e)s**, **-e**) m fire; (MED) gangrene; **b~en** |ˈbrandən| vi to surge; (Meer) to break; **b~marken** vt to brand; (fig) to stigmatize; **~salbe** f ointment for burns; **~stifter** |-ʃtɪftər| m arsonist, fire raiser; **~stiftung** f arson; **~ung** f surf

Branntwein |ˈbrantvain| m brandy

Brasilien |braˈziːliən| nt Brazil

Brat- |ˈbraːt| zW: **~apfel** m baked apple; **b~en** (unreg) vt to roast; to fry; **~en** (**-s**, **-**) m roast, joint; **~hähnchen** nt roast chicken; **~huhn** nt roast chicken; **~kartoffeln** pl fried od roast potatoes; **~pfanne** f frying pan

Bratsche |ˈbraːtʃə| f viola

Bratspieß m spit

Bratwurst f grilled/fried sausage

Brauch |braox| (**-(e)s**, **Bräuche**) m custom; **b~bar** adj usable, serviceable; (Person) capable; **b~en** vt (bedürfen) to need; (müssen) to have to; (umg: verwenden) to use

Braue |ˈbraoə| f brow

brauen |ˈbraoən| vt to brew

Brauerei f brewery

braun |braon| adj brown; (von Sonne auch) tanned; **~ gebrannt** tanned

Bräune |ˈbrɔynə| (**-**) f brownness; (Sonnenbräune) tan; **b~n** vt to make brown; (Sonne) to tan

Brause |ˈbraozə| f shower bath; (von Gießkanne) rose; (Getränk) lemonade; **b~n** vi to roar; (auch vr: duschen) to take a shower

Braut |braot| (**-**, **Bräute**) f bride; (Verlobte) fiancée

Bräutigam |ˈbrɔytiɡam| (**-s**, **-e**) m bridegroom; fiancé

Brautpaar nt bride and (bride)groom, bridal pair

brav |braːf| adj (artig) good; (ehrenhaft) worthy, honest

bravo |ˈbraːvo| excl well done

BRD |beːʔɛrˈdeː| (**-**) f abk = **Bundesrepublik Deutschland**

Brech- |ˈbrɛç| zW: **~eisen** nt crowbar; **b~en** (unreg) vt, vi to break; (Licht) to refract; (fig: Mensch) to crush; (speien) to vomit; **~reiz** m nausea, retching

Brei |brai| (**-(e)s**, **-e**) m (Masse) pulp; (KOCH) gruel; (Haferbrei) porridge

breit |brait| adj wide, broad; **sich ~ machen** to spread o.s. out; **B~e** f width; (bes bei Maßangaben) breadth; (GEOG) latitude; **~en** vt: **etw über etw** akk **~en** to spread sth over sth; **B~engrad** m degree of latitude; **~treten** (unreg) (umg) vt to go on about

Brems- |ˈbrɛms| zW: **~belag** m brake lining; **~e** |-zə| f brake; (ZOOL) horsefly; **b~en** |-zən| vi to brake ♦ vt (Auto) to brake; (fig) to slow down; **~flüssigkeit** f brake fluid; **~licht** nt brake light; **~pedal** nt brake pedal; **~spur** f skid mark (as pl); **~weg** m braking distance

Brenn- |ˈbrɛn| zW: **b~bar** adj inflammable;

b~en (unreg) vi to burn, to be on fire; (Licht, Kerze etc) to burn ♦ vt (Holz etc) to burn; (Ziegel, Ton) to fire; (Kaffee) to roast; **darauf b~en, etw zu tun** to be dying to do sth; **~nessel** ▲ f stinging nettle; **~punkt** m (PHYS) focal point; (Mittelpunkt) focus; **~stoff** m fuel

brenzlig ['brɛntslɪç] adj (fig) precarious

Bretagne [brə'tanjə] f: **die ~** Brittany

Brett [brɛt] (-(e)s, -er) nt board, plank; (Bord) shelf; (Spielbrett) board; **~er** pl (SKI) skis; (THEAT) boards; **schwarzes ~** notice board; **~erzaun** m wooden fence; **~spiel** nt board game

Brezel ['bre:tsəl] (-, -n) f pretzel

brichst etc [brɪçst] vb siehe **brechen**

Brief [bri:f] (-(e)s, -e) m letter; **~freund** m penfriend; **~kasten** m letterbox; **b~lich** adj, adv by letter; **~marke** f (postage) stamp; **~papier** nt notepaper; **~tasche** f wallet; **~träger** m postman; **~umschlag** m envelope; **~waage** f letter scales; **~wechsel** m correspondence

briet etc [bri:t] vb siehe **braten**

Brikett [bri'kɛt] (-s, -s) nt briquette

brillant [brɪl'jant] adj (fig) brilliant; **B~** (-en, -en) m brilliant, diamond

Brille ['brɪlə] f spectacles pl; (Schutzbrille) goggles pl; (Toilettenbrille) (toilet) seat; **~ngestell** nt (spectacle) frames

bringen ['brɪŋən] (unreg) vt to bring; (mitnehmen, begleiten) to take; (einbringen: Profit) to bring in; (veröffentlichen) to publish; (THEAT, CINE) to show; (RAD, TV) to broadcast; (in einen Zustand versetzen) to get; (umg: tun können) to manage; **jdn dazu ~, etw zu tun** to make sb do sth; **jdn nach Hause ~** to take sb home; **jdn um etw ~** to make sb lose sth; **jdn auf eine Idee ~** to give sb an idea

Brise ['bri:zə] f breeze

Brit- ['bri:t] zW: **~e m** Briton; **~in** f Briton; **b~isch** adj British

bröckelig ['brœkəlɪç] adj crumbly

Brocken ['brɔkən] (-s, -) m piece, bit; (Felsbrocken) lump of rock

brodeln ['bro:dəln] vi to bubble

Brokkoli ['brɔkoli] pl (BOT) broccoli

Brombeere ['brɔmbe:rə] f blackberry, bramble (BRIT)

Bronchien ['brɔnçiən] pl bronchia(l tubes) pl

Bronchitis [brɔn'çi:tɪs] (-) f bronchitis

Bronze ['brõ:sə] f bronze

Brosche ['brɔʃə] f brooch

Broschüre [brɔ'ʃy:rə] f pamphlet

Brot [bro:t] (-(e)s, -e) nt bread; (Laib) loaf

Brötchen ['brø:tçən] nt roll

Bruch [brʊx] (-(e)s, -̈e) m breakage; (zerbrochene Stelle) break; (fig) split, breach;

(MED: Eingeweidebruch) rupture, hernia; (Beinbruch etc) fracture; (MATH) fraction

brüchig ['brʏçɪç] adj brittle, fragile; (Haus) dilapidated

Bruch- zW: **~landung** f crash landing; **~strich** m (MATH) line; **~stück** nt fragment; **~teil** m fraction; **~zahl** f (MATH) fraction

Brücke ['brʏkə] f bridge; (Teppich) rug

Bruder ['bru:dər] (-s, -̈) m brother; **brüderlich** adj brotherly

Brühe ['bry:ə] f broth, stock; (pej) muck

brüllen ['brʏlən] vi to bellow, to roar

brummen ['brʊmən] vi (Bär, Mensch etc) to growl; (Insekt) to buzz; (Motoren) to roar; (murren) to grumble

brünett [brʏ'nɛt] adj brunette, dark-haired

Brunnen ['brʊnən] (-s, -) m fountain; (tief) well; (natürlich) spring

Brust [brʊst] (-, -̈e) f breast; (Männerbrust) chest

brüsten ['brʏstən] vr to boast

Brust- zW: **~kasten** m chest; **~schwimmen** nt breast-stroke

Brüstung ['brʏstʊŋ] f parapet

Brut [bru:t] (-, -en) f brood; (Brüten) hatching

brutal [bru'ta:l] adj brutal; **B~ität** f brutality

brüten ['bry:tən] vi (auch fig) to brood

Brutkasten m incubator

brutto ['brʊto] adv gross; **B~einkommen** nt gross salary; **B~gehalt** nt gross salary; **B~gewicht** nt gross weight; **B~lohn** m gross wages pl; **B~sozialprodukt** nt gross national product

BSE f abk (= Bovine Spongiforme Enzephalopathie) BSE

Bube ['bu:bə] (-n, -n) m (Schurke) rogue; (KARTEN) jack

Buch [bu:x] (-(e)s, -̈er) nt book; (COMM) account book; **~binder** m bookbinder; **~drucker** m printer

Buche f beech tree

buchen vt to book; (Betrag) to enter

Bücher- ['by:çər] zW: **~brett** nt bookshelf; **~ei** [-'raɪ] f library; **~regal** nt bookshelves pl, bookcase; **~schrank** m bookcase

Buch- zW: **~führung** f book-keeping, accounting; **~halter(in)** (-s, -) m(f) book-keeper; **~handel** m book trade; **~händler(in)** m(f) bookseller; **~handlung** f bookshop

Büchse ['bʏksə] f tin, can; (Holzbüchse) box; (Gewehr) rifle; **~nfleisch** nt tinned meat; **~nmilch** f (KOCH) evaporated milk, tinned milk; **~nöffner** m tin od can opener

Buch- zW: **~stabe** (-ns, -n) m letter (of the alphabet); **b~stabieren** [bu:xʃta'bi:rən] vt to spell; **b~stäblich** ['bu:xʃtε:plɪç] adj literal

Bucht [bʊxt] (-, -en) f bay

Buchung |'bu:xʊŋ| f booking; (COMM) entry
Buckel ['bʊkəl] (-s, -) m hump
bücken ['bʏkən] vr to bend
Bude ['bu:də] f booth, stall; (umg) digs pl (BRIT)
Büfett [bv'fɛt] (-s, -s) nt (Anrichte) sideboard; (Geschirrschrank) dresser; **kaltes ~** cold buffet
Büffel ['bʏfəl] (-s, -) m buffalo
Bug [bu:k] (-(e)s, -e) m (NAUT) bow; (AVIAT) nose
Bügel ['by:gəl] (-s, -) m (Kleiderbügel) hanger; (Steigbügel) stirrup; (Brillenbügel) arm; **~brett** nt ironing board; **~eisen** nt iron; **~falte** f crease; **b~frei** adj crease-resistant, noniron; **b~n** vt, vi to iron
Bühne ['by:nə] f stage; **~nbild** nt set, scenery
Buhruf ['bu:ru:f] m boo
buk etc [bu:k] vb siehe **backen**
Bulgarien [bul'ga:riən] nt Bulgaria
Bull- ['bʊl] zW: **~auge** nt (NAUT) porthole; **~dogge** f bulldog; **~dozer** ['bʊldo:zər] (-s, -) m bulldozer; **~e** (-n, -n) m bull
Bumerang ['bu:məraŋ] (-s, -e) m boomerang
Bummel ['bʊməl] (-s, -) m stroll; (Schaufensterbummel) window-shopping; **~ant** [-'lant] m slowcoach; **~ei** [-'laɪ] f wandering; dawdling; skiving; **b~n** vi to wander, to stroll; (trödeln) to dawdle; (faulenzen) to skive, to loaf around; **~streik** ['bʊməlʃtraɪk] m go-slow
Bund¹ [bʊnt] (-(e)s, ²e) m (Freundschaftsbund etc) bond; (Organisation) union; (POL) confederacy; (Hosenbund, Rockbund) waistband
Bund² (-(e)s, -e) nt bunch; (Strohbund) bundle
Bündel ['bʏndəl] (-s, -) nt bundle, bale; **b~n** vt to bundle
Bundes- ['bʊndəs] in zW Federal; **~bürger** m German citizen; **~hauptstadt** f Federal capital; **~kanzler** m Federal Chancellor; **~land** nt Land; **~liga** f football league; **~präsident** m Federal President; **~rat** m upper house of German Parliament; **~regierung** f Federal government; **~republik** f Federal Republic (of Germany); **~staat** m Federal state; **~straße** f Federal road; **~tag** m German Parliament; **~wehr** f German Armed Forces pl; **b~weit** adj nationwide
Bündnis ['bʏntnɪs] (-ses, -se) nt alliance
Bunker ['bʊŋkər] (-s, -) m bunker
bunt [bʊnt] adj coloured; (gemischt) mixed; **jdm wird es zu ~** it's getting too much for sb; **B~stift** m coloured pencil, crayon
Burg [bʊrk] (-, -en) f castle, fort
Bürge ['bʏrgə] (-n, -n) m guarantor; **b~n** vi: **b~n für** to vouch for
Bürger(in) ['bʏrgər(ɪn)] (-s, -) m(f) citizen;

member of the middle class; **~krieg** m civil war; **b~lich** adj (Rechte) civil; (Klasse) middle-class; (pej) bourgeois; **~meister** m mayor; **~recht** nt civil rights pl; **~schaft** f (Vertretung) City Parliament; **~steig** m pavement
Bürgschaft f surety; **~ leisten** to give security
Büro [by'ro:] (-s, -s) nt office; **~angestellte(r)** f(m) office worker; **~klammer** f paper clip; **~kra'tie** f bureaucracy; **b~'kratisch** adj bureaucratic; **~schluss** ▲ m office closing time
Bursche ['bʊrʃə] (-n, -n) m lad, fellow; (Diener) servant
Bürste ['bʏrstə] f brush; **b~n** vt to brush
Bus [bʊs] (-ses, -se) m bus; **~bahnhof** m bus/coach (BRIT) station
Busch [bʊʃ] (-(e)s, ²e) m bush, shrub
Büschel ['bʏʃəl] (-s, -) nt tuft
buschig adj bushy
Busen ['bu:zən] (-s, -) m bosom; (Meerbusen) inlet, bay
Bushaltestelle f bus stop
Buße ['bu:sə] f atonement, penance; (Geld) fine
büßen ['by:sən] vi to do penance, to atone ♦ vt to do penance for, to atone for
Bußgeld ['bu:sgɛlt] nt fine; **~bescheid** m notice of payment due (for traffic offence etc)
Büste ['bʏstə] f bust; **~nhalter** m bra
Butter ['bʊtər] (-) f butter; **~blume** f buttercup; **~brot** nt (piece of) bread and butter; (umg) sandwich; **~brotpapier** nt greaseproof paper; **~dose** f butter dish; **~milch** f buttermilk; **b~weich** ['bʊtərvaɪç] adj soft as butter; (fig, umg) soft
b. w. abk (= bitte wenden) p.t.o.
bzgl. abk (= bezüglich) re
bzw. abk = beziehungsweise

C, c

ca. [ka] abk (= circa) approx.
Café [ka'fe:] (-s, -s) nt café
Cafeteria [kafete'ri:a] (-, -s) f cafeteria
Camcorder m camcorder
Camp- ['kɛmp] zW: **c~en** vi to camp; **~er** (-s, -) m camper; **~ing** (-s) nt camping; **~ingführer** m camping guide (book); **~ingkocher** m camping stove; **~ingplatz** m camp(ing) site
CD-Spieler m CD (player)
Cello ['tʃɛlo] (-s, -s od Celli) nt cello
Celsius ['tsɛlziʊs] (-) nt centigrade
Champagner [ʃam'panjər] (-s, -) m champagne
Champignon ['ʃampɪnjõ] (-s, -s) m button mushroom
Chance ['ʃã:s(ə)] f chance, opportunity

Chaos |'ka:ɔs| (-, -) nt chaos; **chaotisch**
[ka'o:tɪʃ] adj chaotic

Charakter |ka'raktər, pl karak'te:rə| (-s, -e) m
character; **c~fest** adj of firm character,
strong; **c~i'sieren** vt to characterize;
c~istisch [karakte'rɪstɪʃ] adj: **c~istisch (für)**
characteristic (of), typical (of); **c~los** adj
unprincipled; **~losigkeit** f lack of principle;
~schwäche f weakness of character;
~stärke f strength of character; **~zug** m
characteristic, trait

charmant |ʃar'mant| adj charming

Charme |ʃarm| (-s) m charm

Charterflug |'tʃartərflu:k| m charter flight

Chauffeur |ʃɔ'fø:r| m chauffeur

Chauvinist |ʃovi'nɪst| m chauvinist, jingoist

Chef |ʃɛf| (-s, -s) m head; (umg) boss; **~arzt**
m senior consultant; **~in** (umg) f boss

Chemie |çe'mi:| (-) f chemistry; **~faser** f
man-made fibre

Chemikalie |çemi'ka:liə| f chemical

Chemiker ['çe:mikər| (-s, -) m (industrial)
chemist

chemisch |'çe:mɪʃ| adj chemical; **~e**
Reinigung dry cleaning

Chicorée |ʃiko're:| (-s) m od f chicory

Chiffre |'ʃifrə| f (Geheimzeichen) cipher; (in
Zeitung) box number

Chile |'tʃi:le| nt Chile

Chin- |çi:n| zW: **~a** nt China; **~akohl** m
Chinese leaves; **~ese** [-'ne:zə] m Chinese;
~esin f Chinese; **c~esisch** adj Chinese

Chip |tʃip| (-s, -s) m (Kartoffelchips crisp
(BRIT), chip (US); (COMPUT) chip; **~karte** f
smart card

Chirurg |çi'rʊrg| (-en, -en) m surgeon; **~ie**
[-'gi:] f surgery; **c~isch** adj surgical

Chlor |klo:r| (-s) nt chlorine; **~o'form** (-s) nt
chloroform

cholerisch |ko'le:rɪʃ| adj choleric

Chor |ko:r| (-(e)s, ²e) m choir; (Musikstück,
THEAT) chorus; **~al** |ko'ra:l| (-s, -äle) m chorale

Choreograf ▲ |koreo'gra:f| (-en, -en) m
choreographer

Christ |krɪst| (-en, -en) m Christian; **~baum**
m Christmas tree; **~entum** nt Christianity;
~in f Christian; **~kind** nt ≈ Father
Christmas; (Jesus) baby Jesus; **c~lich** adj
Christian; **~us** (-) m Christ

Chrom |kro:m| (-s) nt (CHEM) chromium;
chrome

Chron- |'kro:n| zW: **~ik** f chronicle; **c~isch**
adj chronic; **c~ologisch** [-o'lo:gɪʃ] adj
chronological

circa ['tsɪrka] adv about, approximately

Clown |klaʊn| (-s, -s) m clown

Cocktail ['kɔkte:l| (-s, -s) m cocktail

Cola |'ko:la| (-, -s) f Coke ®

Computer |kɔm'pju:tər| (-s, -) m computer;

~spiel nt computer game

Cord |kɔrt| (-s) m cord, corduroy

Couch |kaʊtʃ| (-, -es od -en) f couch

Coupon |ku'põ:| (-s, -s) m = **Kupon**

Cousin |ku'zɛ:| (-s, -s) m cousin; **~e**
|ku'zi:nə| f cousin

Creme |kre:m| (-, -s) f cream; (Schuhcreme)
polish; (Zahncreme) paste; (KOCH) mousse;
c~farben adj cream(-coloured)

cremig |'kre:mɪç| adj creamy

Curry ['kari| (-s) m od nt curry powder;
~pulver nt curry powder; **~wurst** f curried
sausage

D, d

da [da:] adv 1 (örtlich) there; (hier) here; **da**
draußen out there; **da sein** to be there; **da**
bin ich here I am; **da, wo** where; **ist noch**
Milch da? is there any milk left?
2 (zeitlich) then; (folglich) so
3: **da haben wir Glück gehabt** we were
lucky there; **da kann man nichts machen**
nothing can be done about it
♦ konj (weil) as, since

dabehalten (unreg) vt to keep

dabei |da'baɪ| adv (räumlich) close to it;
(noch dazu) besides; (zusammen mit) with
them; (zeitlich) during this; (obwohl doch)
but, however; **was ist schon ~?** what of it?;
es ist doch nichts ~, wenn ... it doesn't
matter if ...; **bleiben wir ~** let's leave it at
that; **es bleibt ~** that's settled; **das**
Dumme/Schwierige ~ the stupid/difficult
part of it; **er war gerade ~, zu gehen** he
was just leaving; **~ sein** (anwesend) to be
present; (beteiligt) to be involved; **~stehen**
(unreg) vi to stand around

Dach |dax| (-(e)s, ²er) nt roof; **~boden** m
attic, loft; **~decker** (-s, -) m slater, tiler;
~fenster nt skylight; **~gepäckträger** m
roof rack; **~luke** f skylight; **~pappe** f
roofing felt; **~rinne** f gutter

Dachs |daks| (-es, -e) m badger

dachte etc |'daxtə| vb siehe **denken**

Dackel |'dakəl| (-s, -) m dachshund

dadurch |da'dʊrç| adv (räumlich) through it;
(durch diesen Umstand) thereby, in that way;
(deshalb) because of that, for that reason
♦ konj: **~, dass** because

dafür |da'fy:r| adv for it; (anstatt) instead; **er**
kann nichts ~ he can't help it; **er ist**
bekannt ~ he is well-known for that; **was**
bekomme ich ~? what will I get for it?

dagegen |da'ge:gən| adv against it; (im

Vergleich damit) in comparison with it; *(bei Tausch)* for it/them ♦ *konj* however; **ich habe nichts ~** I don't mind; **ich war ~** I was against it; **~ kann man nichts tun** one can't do anything about it; **~halten** *(unreg) vt (vergleichen)* to compare with it; *(entgegnen)* to object to it; **~sprechen** *(unreg) vi:* **es spricht nichts ~** there's no reason why not

daheim [daˈhaɪm] *adv* at home; **D~ (-s)** *nt* home

daher [daˈheːr] *adv (räumlich)* from there; *(Ursache)* from that ♦ *konj (deshalb)* that's why

dahin [daˈhɪn] *adv (räumlich)* there; *(zeitlich)* then; *(vergangen)* gone; **~ gehend** on this matter; **~'gegen** *konj* on the other hand; **~gestellt** *adv:* **~gestellt bleiben** to remain to be seen; **~gestellt sein lassen** to leave open *od* undecided

dahinten [daˈhɪntən] *adv* over there

dahinter [daˈhɪntɐ] *adv* behind it; **~ kommen** to get to the bottom of it

dalli [ˈdali] *(umg) adv* chop chop

damalig [ˈdaːmaːlɪç] *adj* of that time, then

damals [ˈdaːmaːls] *adv* at that time, then

Dame [ˈdaːmə] *f* lady; *(SCHACH, KARTEN)* queen; *(Spiel)* draughts *sg;* **~nbinde** *f* sanitary towel *od* napkin *(US);* **d~nhaft** *adj* ladylike; **~ntoilette** *f* ladies' toilet *od* restroom *(US);* **~nwahl** *f* ladies' excuse-me

damit [daˈmɪt] *adv* with it; *(begründend)* by that ♦ *konj* in order that, in order to; **was meint er ~?** what does he mean by that?; **genug ~!** that's enough!

dämlich [ˈdɛːmlɪç] *(umg) adj* silly, stupid

Damm [dam] **(-(e)s, ²e)** *m* dyke; *(Staudamm)* dam; *(Hafendamm)* mole; *(Bahndamm, Straßendamm)* embankment

dämmen [ˈdɛmən] *vt (Wasser)* to dam up; *(Schmerzen)* to keep back

dämmer- *zW:* **~ig** *adj* dim, faint; **~n** *vi (Tag)* to dawn; *(Abend)* to fall; **D~ung** *f* twilight; *(Morgendämmerung)* dawn; *(Abenddämmerung)* dusk

Dampf [dampf] **(-(e)s, ²e)** *m* steam; *(Dunst)* vapour; **d~en** *vi* to steam

dämpfen [ˈdɛmpfən] *vt (KOCH)* to steam; *(bügeln)* to iron with a damp cloth; *(fig)* to dampen, to subdue

Dampf- *zW:* **~schiff** *nt* steamship; **~walze** *f* steamroller

danach [daˈnaːx] *adv* after that; *(zeitlich)* after that, afterwards; *(gemäß)* accordingly; according to which; according to that; **er sieht ~ aus** he looks it

Däne [ˈdɛːnə] **(-n, -n)** *m* Dane

daneben [daˈneːbən] *adv* beside it; *(im Vergleich)* in comparison; **~benehmen** *(unreg) vr* to misbehave; **~gehen** *(unreg) vi* to miss; *(Plan)* to fail

Dänemark [ˈdɛːnəmark] *nt* Denmark; **Dänin**

f Dane; **dänisch** *adj* Danish

Dank [daŋk] **(-(e)s)** *m* thanks *pl;* **vielen** *od* **schönen ~** many thanks; **jdm ~ sagen** to thank sb; **d~** *präp (+dat od gen)* thanks to; **d~bar** *adj* grateful; *(Aufgabe)* rewarding; **~barkeit** *f* gratitude; **d~e** *excl* thank you, thanks; **d~en** *vi +dat* to thank; **d~enswert** *adj (Arbeit)* worthwhile; rewarding; *(Bemühung)* kind; **d~sagen** *vi* to express one's thanks

dann [dan] *adv* then; **~ und wann** now and then

daran [daˈran] *adv* on it; *(stoßen)* against it; **es liegt ~, dass ...** the cause of it is that ...; **gut/schlecht ~ sein** to be well-/badly off; **das Beste/Dümmste ~** the best/stupidest thing about it; **ich war nahe ~ zu ...** I was on the point of *od* of ...; **er ist ~ gestorben** he died from it *od* of it; **~gehen** *(unreg) vi* to start; **~setzen** *vt* to stake

darauf [daˈraʊf] *adv (räumlich)* on it; *(zielgerichtet)* towards it; *(danach)* afterwards; **es kommt ganz ~ an, ob ...** it depends whether ...; **die Tage ~** the days following *od* thereafter; **am Tag ~** the next day; **~ folgend** *(Tag, Jahr)* next, following; **~ legen** to lay *od* put on top

daraus [daˈraʊs] *adv* from it; **was ist ~ geworden?** what became of it?; **~ geht hervor, dass ...** this means that ...

Darbietung [ˈdaːrbiːtʊŋ] *f* performance

darf *etc* [darf] *vb siehe* **dürfen**

darin [daˈrɪn] *adv* in (there), in it

darlegen [ˈdaːrleːgən] *vt* to explain, to expound, to set forth; **Darlegung** *f* explanation

Darleh(e)n **(-s, -)** *nt* loan

Darm [darm] **(-(e)s, ²e)** *m* intestine; *(Wurstdarm)* skin; **~grippe** *f (MED)* gastric influenza *od* flu

darstell- [ˈdaːrʃtɛl] *zW:* **~en** *vt (abbilden, bedeuten)* to represent; *(THEAT)* to act; *(beschreiben)* to describe ♦ *vr* to appear to be; **D~er(in)** **(-s, -)** *m(f)* actor (actress); **D~ung** *f* portrayal, depiction

darüber [daˈryːbɐ] *adv (räumlich)* over it, above it; *(fahren)* over it; *(mehr)* more; *(währenddessen)* meanwhile; *(sprechen, streiten)* about it; **~ geht nichts** there's nothing like it

darum [daˈrʊm] *adv (räumlich)* round it ♦ *konj* that's why; **er bittet ~** he is pleading for it; **es geht ~, dass ...** the thing is that ...; **er würde viel ~ geben, wenn ...** he would give a lot to ...; **ich tue es ~, weil ...** I am doing it because ...

darunter [daˈrʊntɐ] *adv (räumlich)* under it; *(dazwischen)* among them; *(weniger)* less; **ein Stockwerk ~** one floor below (it); **was verstehen Sie ~?** what do you understand by that?

das [das] *def art* the ♦ *pron* that

Dasein ['daːzaɪn] (**-s**) *nt* (*Leben*) life;
(*Anwesenheit*) presence; (*Bestehen*) existence
dasein ▲ *siehe* **da**
dass ▲ [das] *konj* that
dasselbe |das'zɛlbə| *art, pron* the same
dastehen ['daːʃteːən] (*unreg*) *vi* to stand
there
Datei [da'taɪ] *f* file
Daten- ['daːtən] *zW:* **~bank** *f* database;
~schutz *m* data protection;
~verarbeitung *f* data processing
datieren [da'tiːrən] *vt* to date
Dativ ['daːtiːf] (**-s, -e**) *m* dative (case)
Dattel ['datəl] (**-, -n**) *f* date
Datum ['daːtʊm] (**-s, Daten**) *nt* date; **Daten**
pl (*Angaben*) data *pl*
Dauer ['daʊər] (**-, -n**) *f* duration; (*gewisse
Zeitspanne*) length; (*Bestand, Fortbestehen*)
permanence; **es war nur von kurzer ~** it
didn't last long; **auf die ~** in the long run;
(*auf längere Zeit*) indefinitely; **~auftrag** *m*
standing order; **d~haft** *adj* lasting, durable;
~karte *f* season ticket; **~lauf** *m* jog(ging);
d~n *vi* to last; **es hat sehr lang gedauert,
bis er ...** it took him a long time to ...;
d~nd *adj* constant; **~parkplatz** *m* long-stay
car park; **~welle** *f* perm, permanent wave;
~wurst *f* German salami; **~zustand** *m*
permanent condition
Daumen ['daʊmən] (**-s, -**) *m* thumb
Daune ['daʊnə] *f* down; **~ndecke** *f* down
duvet, down quilt
davon [da'fɔn] *adv* of it; (*räumlich*) away;
(*weg von*) from it; (*Grund*) because of it;
das kommt ~! that's what you get!; **~
abgesehen** apart from that; **~ sprechen/
wissen** to talk/know of *od* about it; **was
habe ich ~?** what's the point?; **~kommen**
(*unreg*) *vi* to escape; **~laufen** (*unreg*) *vi* to
run away
davor [da'foːr] *adv* (*räumlich*) in front of it;
(*zeitlich*) before (that); **~ warnen** to warn
about it
dazu [da'tsuː] *adv* (*legen, stellen*) by it; (*essen,
singen*) with it; **und ~ noch** and in addition;
ein Beispiel/seine Gedanken ~ one
example for/his thoughts on this; **wie
komme ich denn ~?** why should I?; **~ fähig
sein** to be capable of it; **sich ~ äußern** to
say something on it; **~gehören** *vi* to belong
to it; **~kommen** (*unreg*) *vi* (*Ereignisse*) to
happen too; (*an einen Ort*) to come along
dazwischen [da'tsvɪʃən] *adv* in between;
(*räumlich auch*) between (them); (*zusammen
mit*) among them; **~kommen** (*unreg*) *vi*
(*hineingeraten*) to get caught in it; **es ist
etwas ~gekommen** something cropped up;
~reden *vi* (*unterbrechen*) to interrupt; (*sich
einmischen*) to interfere; **~treten** (*unreg*) *vi*

to intervene
Debatte [de'batə] *f* debate
Deck |dɛk| (**-(e)s, -s** *od* **-e**) *nt* deck; **an ~
gehen** to go on deck
Decke *f* cover; (*Bettdecke*) blanket;
(*Tischdecke*) tablecloth; (*Zimmerdecke*)
ceiling; **unter einer ~ stecken** to be hand in
glove; **~l** (**-s, -**) *m* lid; **d~n** *vt* to cover ♦ *vr* to
coincide
Deckung *f* (*Schützen*) covering; (*Schutz*)
cover; (*SPORT*) defence; (*Übereinstimmen*)
agreement
Defekt |de'fɛkt| (**-(e)s, -e**) *m* fault, defect; **d~**
adj faulty
defensiv |defen'siːf| *adj* defensive
definieren [defi'niːrən] *vt* to define;
Definition |definitsi'oːn| *f* definition
Defizit ['deːfitsɪt] (**-s, -e**) *nt* deficit
deftig ['dɛftɪç] *adj* (*Essen*) large; (*Witz*)
coarse
Degen ['deːgən] (**-s, -**) *m* sword
degenerieren [degene'riːrən] *vi* to
degenerate
dehnbar ['deːnbaːr] *adj* elastic; (*fig: Begriff*)
loose
dehnen *vt, vr* to stretch
Deich |daɪç| (**-(e)s, -e**) *m* dyke, dike
deichseln (*umg*) *vt* (*fig*) to wangle
dein(e) |daɪn(ə)| *adj* your; **~e(r, s)** *pron*
yours; **~er** (*gen von* **du**) *pron* of you;
~erseits *adv* on your part; **~esgleichen**
pron people like you; **~etwegen** *adv* (*für
dich*) for your sake; (*wegen dir*) on your
account; **~etwillen** *adv:* **um ~etwillen =
deinetwegen; ~ige** *pron:* **der/die/das ~ige**
od **D~ige** yours
Deklination |deklinatsi'oːn| *f* declension
deklinieren |dɛkli'niːrən| *vt* to decline
Dekolleté, Dekolletee |dekɔl'teː| (**-s, -s**)
nt low neckline
Deko- |deko| *zW:* **~rateur** |-ra'tøːr| *m*
window dresser; **~ration** |-ratsi'oːn| *f*
decoration; (*in Laden*) window dressing;
d~rativ |-ra'tiːf| *adj* decorative; **d~rieren**
|-'riːrən| *vt* to decorate; (*Schaufenster*) to dress
Delegation |delegatsi'oːn| *f* delegation
delegieren |dele'giːrən| *vt:* **~ an** +*akk*
(*Aufgaben*) to delegate to
Delfin ▲ |dɛl'fiːn| (**-s, -e**) *m* dolphin
delikat |deli'kaːt| *adj* (*zart, heikel*) delicate;
(*köstlich*) delicious
Delikatesse |delika'tɛsə| *f* delicacy; **~n** *pl*
(*Feinkost*) delicatessen food; **~ngeschäft** *nt*
delicatessen
Delikt |de'lɪkt| (**-(e)s, -e**) *nt* (*JUR*) offence
Delle |'dɛlə| (*umg*) *f* dent
Delphin △ |dɛl'fiːn| (**-s, -e**) *m siehe* **Delfin**
dem |de(:)m| *art dat von* **der**
Demagoge |dema'goːgə| (**-n, -n**) *m*

demagogue

dementieren |demɛn'tiːrən| vt to deny

dem- zW: **~gemäß** adv accordingly; **~nach** adv accordingly; **~nächst** adv shortly

Demokrat |demo'kraːt| (**-en, -en**) m democrat; **~ie** |-'tiː| f democracy; **d~isch** adj democratic; **d~isieren** |-i'ziːrən| vt to democratize

demolieren |demo'liːrən| vt to demolish

Demon- |demɔn| zW: **~strant(in)** |-'strant(ɪn)| m(f) demonstrator; **~stration** |stratsi'oːn| f demonstration; **d~strativ** |-stra'tiːf| adj demonstrative; (Protest) pointed; **d~strieren** |-'striːrən| vt, vi to demonstrate

Demoskopie |demosko'piː| f public opinion research

Demut ['deːmuːt] (**-**) f humility

demütig ['deːmyːtɪç] adj humble; **~en** ['deːmyːtɪgən] vt to humiliate; **D~ung** f humiliation

demzufolge ['deːmtsu'fɔlgə] adv accordingly

den |de(ː)n| art akk von **der**

denen ['deːnən] pron dat pl von **der, die, das**

Denk- |'dɛŋk| zW: **d~bar** adj conceivable; **~en (-s)** nt thinking; **d~en** (unreg) vt, vi to think; **d~faul** adj lazy; **~fehler** m logical error; **~mal (-s, ⁼er)** nt monument; **~malschutz** m protection of historical monuments; **unter ~malschutz stehen** to be classified as a historical monument; **d~würdig** adj memorable; **~zettel** m: **jdm einen ~zettel verpassen** to teach sb a lesson

denn |dɛn| konj for ♦ adv then; (nach Komparativ) than; **warum ~?** why?

dennoch |'dɛnɔx| konj nevertheless

Denunziant |denʊntsi'ant| m informer

Deodorant |deodo'rant| (**-s, -s** od **-e**) nt deodorant

Deponie |depo'niː| f dump

deponieren |depo'niːrən| vt (COMM) to deposit

Depot |de'poː| (**-s, -s**) nt warehouse; (Busdepot, EISENB) depot; (Bankdepot) strongroom, safe (US)

Depression |depresi'oːn| f depression; **depres'siv** adj depressive

deprimieren |depri'miːrən| vt to depress

SCHLÜSSELWORT

der |de(ː)r| (f **die**, nt **das**, gen **des, der, des**, dat **dem, der, dem**, akk **den, die, das**, pl **die**) def art the; (demonstrativ) **der Rhein** the Rhine; **der Klaus** (umg) Klaus; **die Frau** (im Allgemeinen) women; **der Tod/das Leben** death/life; **der Fuß des Berges** the foot of the hill; **gib es der Frau** give it to the woman; **er hat sich die Hand verletzt** he has hurt his hand

♦ relativ pron (bei Menschen) who, that; (bei Tieren, Sachen) which, that; **der Mann, den ich gesehen habe** the man who od whom od that I saw

♦ demonstrativ pron he/she/it; (jener, dieser) that; (pl) those; **der/die war es** it was him/her; **der mit der Brille** the one with glasses; **ich will den (da)** I want that one

---

derart ['deːr'aːrt] adv so; (solcher Art) such; **~ig** adj such, this sort of

derb |dɛrp| adj sturdy; (Kost) solid; (grob) coarse

der- zW: **'~gleichen** pron such; **'~jenige** pron he; she; it; the one (who); that (which); **'~maßen** adv to such an extent, so; **~'selbe** art, pron the same; **'~'weil(en)** adv in the meantime; **'~'zeitig** adj present, current; (damalig)

des |dɛs| art gen von **der**

desertieren |dezɛr'tiːrən| vi to desert

desgleichen ['dɛs'glaiçən] adv likewise, also

deshalb ['dɛs'halp] adv therefore, that's why

Desinfektion |dɛzɪnfɛktsi'oːn| f disinfection; **~smittel** nt disinfectant

desinfizieren |dɛzɪnfi'tsiːrən| vt to disinfect

dessen ['dɛsən] pron gen von **der, das**; **~ ungeachtet** nevertheless, regardless

Dessert |dɛ'seːr| (**-s, -s**) nt dessert

destillieren |dɛstɪ'liːrən| vt to distil

desto ['dɛsto] adv all the, so much the; **~ besser** all the better

deswegen ['dɛs've:gən] konj therefore, hence

Detail |de'tai| (**-s, -s**) nt detail

Detektiv |detɛk'tiːf| (**-s, -e**) m detective

deut- ['dɔʏt] zW: **~en** vt to interpret, to explain ♦ vi: **~en (auf +akk)** to point (to od at); **~lich** adj clear; (Unterschied) distinct; **D~lichkeit** f clarity; distinctness

Deutsch |dɔʏtʃ| nt German

deutsch adj German; **auf D~** in German; **D~e Demokratische Republik** (HIST) German Democratic Republic, East Germany; **~es Beefsteak** ≈ hamburger; **D~e** f German; **D~er** m German; **ich bin D~er** I am German; **D~land** nt Germany

Devise |de'viːzə| f motto, device; **~n** pl (FIN) foreign currency, foreign exchange

Dezember |de'tsɛmbər| (**-s, -**) m December

dezent |de'tsɛnt| adj discreet

dezimal |detsi'maːl| adj decimal; **D~system** nt decimal system

d. h. abk (= das heißt) i.e.

Dia ['diːa] (**-s, -s**) nt (PHOT) slide, transparency

Diabetes |dia'beːtɛs| (**-, -**) m (MED) diabetes

Diagnose |dia'gnoːzə| f diagnosis

diagonal |diago'naːl| adj diagonal

Dialekt |dia'lɛkt| (**-(e)s, -e**) m dialect; **d~isch** adj dialectal; (Logik) dialectical

Dialog |dia'loːk| (**-(e)s, -e**) m dialogue

Diamant |dia'mant| *m* diamond
Diaprojektor |'di:aprojɛktɔr| *m* slide
projector
Diät |di'ɛ:t| (-, -en) *f* diet
dich |dıç| (*akk von* du) *pron* you; yourself
dicht |dıçt| *adj* dense; (*Nebel*) thick; (*Gewebe*)
close; (*undurchlässig*) (water)tight; (*fig*)
concise ♦ *adv*: ~ **an/bei** close to; ~
bevölkert densely *od* heavily populated;
D~e *f* density; thickness; closeness;
(water)tightness; (*fig*) conciseness
dichten *vt* (*dicht machen*) to make
watertight, to seal; (*NAUT*) to caulk; (*LITER*)
to compose, to write ♦ *vi* to compose, to
write
Dichter(in) (-s, -) *m(f)* poet; (*Autor*) writer;
d~isch *adj* poetical
dichthalten (*unreg*) (*umg*) *vi* to keep one's
mouth shut
Dichtung *f* (*TECH*) washer; (*AUT*) gasket;
(*Gedichte*) poetry; (*Prosa*) (piece of) writing
dick |dık| *adj* thick; (*fett*) fat; **durch ~ und
dünn** through thick and thin; **D~darm** *m*
(*ANAT*) colon; **D~e** *f* thickness; fatness;
~flüssig *adj* viscous; **D~icht** (-s, -e) *nt*
thicket; **D~kopf** *m* mule; **D~milch** *f* soured
milk
die |di:| *def art siehe* **der**
Dieb(in) |di:p, 'di:bın| (-(e)s, -e) *m(f)* thief;
d~isch *adj* thieving; (*umg*) immense;
~stahl (-(e)s, -e) *m* theft;
~stahlversicherung *f* insurance against
theft
Diele |'di:lə| *f* (*Brett*) board; (*Flur*) hall, lobby
dienen |'di:nən| *vi*: **(jdm) ~** to serve (sb)
Diener (-s, -) *m* servant; **~in** *f* (maid)servant;
~schaft *f* servants *pl*
Dienst |di:nst| (-(e)s, -e) *m* service; **außer ~**
retired; **~ haben** to be on duty; **d~ habend**
(*Arzt*) on duty
Dienstag |'di:nsta:k| *m* Tuesday; **d~s** *adv* on
Tuesdays
Dienst- *zW*: **~bote** *m* servant; **~geheimnis**
nt official secret; **~gespräch** *nt* business
call; **~leistung** *f* service; **d~lich** *adj* official;
~mädchen *nt* (house)maid; **~reise** *f*
business trip; **~stelle** *f* office; **~vorschrift** *f*
official regulations *pl*; **~weg** *m* official
channels *pl*; **~zeit** *f* working hours *pl*; (*MIL*)
period of service
dies- |di:s| *pron* (*demonstrativ: sg*) this; (: *pl*)
these; **~bezüglich** *adj* (*Frage*) on this
matter; **~e(r, s)** |'di:zə(r, s)| *pron* this (one)
Diesel |'di:zəl| *m* (*Kraftstoff*) diesel
dieselbe |di:'zɛlbə| *pron, art* the same
Dieselmotor *m* diesel engine
diesig |'di:zıç| *adj* drizzly
dies- *zW*: **~jährig** *adj* this year's; **~mal** *adv*
this time; **~seits** *präp +gen* on this side;

D~seits (-) *nt* this life
Dietrich |'di:trıç| (-s, -e) *m* picklock
diffamieren |dıfa'mi:rən| (*pej*) *vt* to defame
Differenz |dıfə'rɛnts| (-, -en) *f* (*Unterschied*)
difference; **~en** *pl* (*Meinungsverschiedenheit*)
difference (of opinion); **d~ieren** *vt* to make
distinctions in; **d~iert** *adj* (*Mensch etc*)
complex
digital |digi'ta:l| *adj* digital
Dikt- |dıkt| *zW*: **~afon**, **~aphon** |-a'fo:n| *nt*
dictaphone; **~at** |-'ta:t| (-(e)s, -e) *nt*
dictation; **~ator** |-'ta:tɔr| *m* dictator;
d~atorisch |-a'to:rıʃ| *adj* dictatorial; **~atur**
|-a'tu:r| *f* dictatorship; **d~ieren** |-'ti:rən| *vt*
to dictate
Dilemma |di'lɛma| (-s, -s *od* -ta) *nt* dilemma
Dilettant |dile'tant| *m* dilettante, amateur;
d~isch *adj* amateurish, dilettante
Dimension |dimɛnzi'o:n| *f* dimension
DIN *f abk* (= *Deutsche Industrie-Norm*) German
Industrial Standard
Ding |dıŋ| (-(e)s, -e) *nt* thing, object; **d~lich**
adj real, concrete; **~s(bums)** |'dıŋks(bʊms)|
(-) (*umg*) *nt* thingummybob
Diplom |di'plo:m| (-(e)s, -e) *nt* diploma,
certificate; **~at** |-'ma:t| (-en, -en) *m*
diplomat; **~atie** |-a'ti:| *f* diplomacy;
d~atisch |-'ma:tıʃ| *adj* diplomatic;
~ingenieur *m* qualified engineer
dir |di:r| (*dat von* du) *pron* (to) you
direkt |di'rɛkt| *adj* direct; **D~flug** *m* direct
flight; **D~or** *m* director; (*SCH*) principal,
headmaster; **D~übertragung** *f* live broadcast
Dirigent |diri'gɛnt| *m* conductor
dirigieren |diri'gi:rən| *vt* to direct; (*MUS*) to
conduct
Diskette |dıs'kɛtə| *f* diskette, floppy disk
Diskont |dıs'kɔnt| (-s, -e) *m* discount; **~satz**
m rate of discount
Diskothek |dısko'te:k| (-, -en) *f*
disco(theque)
diskret |dıs'kre:t| *adj* discreet; **D~ion** *f*
discretion
diskriminieren |dıskrimi'ni:rən| *vt* to
discriminate against
Diskussion |dıskʊsi'o:n| *f* discussion,
debate; **zur ~ stehen** to be under discussion
diskutieren |dıskʊ'ti:rən| *vt, vi* to discuss; to
debate
Distanz |dıs'tants| *f* distance; **distan'zieren**
vr: **sich von jdm/etw d~ieren** to distance
o.s. from sb/sth
Distel |'dıstəl| (-, -n) *f* thistle
Disziplin |dıstsi'pli:n| *f* discipline
Dividende |divi'dɛndə| *f* dividend
dividieren |divi'di:rən| *vt*: **(durch etw) ~** to
divide (by sth)
DM |de:'ʔɛm| *abk* (= *Deutsche Mark*) German
Mark

Spelling reform: ▲ *new spelling* △ *old spelling (to be phased out)*

D-Mark ['deːmark] f D Mark, German Mark

SCHLÜSSELWORT

doch |dɔx| adv 1 (dennoch) after all; (sowieso) anyway; **er kam doch noch** he came after all; **du weißt es ja doch besser** you know better than I do anyway; **und doch ...** and yet ...
2 (als bejahende Antwort) yes I do/it does etc; **das ist nicht wahr – doch!** that's not true – yes it is!
3 (auffordernd): **komm doch** do come; **lass ihn doch** just leave him; **nicht doch!** oh no!
4: **sie ist doch noch so jung** but she's still so young; **Sie wissen doch, wie das ist** you know how it is(, don't you?); **wenn doch** if only
♦ konj (aber) but; (trotzdem) all the same; **und doch hat er es getan** but still he did it

Docht |dɔxt| (-(e)s, -e) m wick
Dock |dɔk| (-s, -s od -e) nt dock
Dogge ['dɔgə] f bulldog
Dogma ['dɔgma] (-s, -men) nt dogma; **d~tisch** adj dogmatic
Doktor ['dɔktɔr, pl -'toːrən] (-s, -en) m doctor
Dokument |doku'mɛnt| nt document
Dokumentar- |dokumɛn'taːr| zW: **~bericht** m documentary; **~film** m documentary (film); **d~isch** adj documentary
Dolch |dɔlç| (-(e)s, -e) m dagger
dolmetschen ['dɔlmɛtʃən] vt, vi to interpret; **Dolmetscher(in)** (-s, -) m(f) interpreter
Dom |doːm| (-(e)s, -e) m cathedral
dominieren |domi'niːrən| vt to dominate ♦ vi to predominate
Donau ['doːnau] f Danube
Donner ['dɔnər] (-s, -) m thunder; **d~n** vi unpers to thunder
Donnerstag ['dɔnərstaːk] m Thursday
doof |doːf| (umg) adj daft, stupid
Doppel ['dɔpəl] (-s, -) nt duplicate; (SPORT) doubles; **~bett** nt double bed; **d~deutig** adj ambiguous; **~fenster** nt double glazing; **~gänger** (-s, -) m double; **~punkt** m colon; **~stecker** m two-way adaptor; **d~t** adj double; **in d~ter Ausführung** in duplicate; **~verdiener** m person with two incomes; (pl: Paar) two-income family; **~zentner** m 100 kilograms; **~zimmer** nt double room
Dorf |dɔrf| (-(e)s, -er) nt village; **~bewohner** m villager
Dorn |dɔrn| (-(e)s, -en) m (BOT) thorn; **d~ig** adj thorny
Dörrobst ['dœro:pst] nt dried fruit
Dorsch |dɔrʃ| (-(e)s, -e) m cod
dort |dɔrt| adv there; **~ drüben** over there; **~her** adv from there; **~hin** adv (to) there;

~ig adj of that place; in that town
Dose ['doːzə] f box; (Blechdose) tin, can
Dosen pl von Dose, Dosis
Dosenöffner m tin od can opener
Dosis ['doːzɪs] (-, Dosen) f dose
Dotter ['dɔtər] (-s, -) m (egg) yolk
Drache ['draxə] (-n, -n) m (Tier) dragon
Drachen (-s, -) m kite; **~fliegen** (-s) nt hang-gliding
Draht |draːt| (-(e)s, -e) m wire; **auf ~ sein** to be on the ball; **d~ig** adj (Mann) wiry; **~seil** nt cable; **~seilbahn** f cable railway, funicular
Drama ['draːma] (-s, Dramen) nt drama, play; **~tiker** [-'maːtikər] (-s, -) m dramatist; **d~tisch** [-'maːtɪʃ] adj dramatic
dran |dran| (umg) adv: **jetzt bin ich ~!** it's my turn now; siehe **daran**
Drang |draŋ| (-(e)s, -e) m (Trieb): **~ (nach)** impulse (for), urge (for), desire (for); (Druck) pressure (for)
drängeln ['drɛŋəln] vt, vi to push, to jostle
drängen ['drɛŋən] vt (schieben) to push, to press; (antreiben) to urge ♦ vi (eilig sein) to be urgent; (Zeit) to press; **auf etw** akk **~** to press for sth
drastisch ['drastɪʃ] adj drastic
drauf |drauf| (umg) adv = **darauf**; **D~gänger** (-s, -) m daredevil
draußen ['drausən] adv outside, out-of-doors
Dreck |drɛk| (-(e)s) m mud, dirt; **d~ig** adj dirty, filthy
Dreh- ['dreː] zW: **~arbeiten** pl (CINE) shooting sg; **~bank** f lathe; **~buch** nt (CINE) script; **d~en** vt to turn, to rotate; (Zigaretten) to roll; (Film) to shoot ♦ vi to turn, to rotate ♦ vr to turn; (handeln von): **es d~t sich um ...** it's about ...; **~orgel** f barrel organ; **~tür** f revolving door; **~ung** f (Rotation) rotation; (Umdrehung, Wendung) turn; **~zahl** f rate of revolutions; **~zahlmesser** m rev(olution) counter
drei |drai| num three; **~ viertel** three-quarters; **D~eck** nt triangle; **~eckig** adj triangular; **~einhalb** num three and a half; **~erlei** adj inv of three kinds; **~fach** adj triple, treble ♦ adv three times; **~hundert** num three hundred; **D~'königsfest** nt Epiphany; **~mal** adv three times; **~malig** adj three times
dreinreden ['drainreːdən] vi: **jdm ~** (dazwischenreden) to interrupt sb; **~** (sich einmischen) to interfere with sb
Dreirad nt tricycle
dreißig ['draisɪç] num thirty
dreist |draist| adj bold, audacious
drei- zW: **~viertel** △ siehe **drei**; **D~viertelstunde** f three-quarters of an hour; **~zehn** num thirteen
dreschen ['drɛʃən] (unreg) vt (Getreide) to thresh; (umg: verprügeln) to beat up

dressieren [drɛ'si:rən] *vt* to train
drillen ['drɪlən] *vt* (*bohren*) to drill, to bore; (*MIL*) to drill; (*fig*) to train
Drilling *m* triplet
drin [drɪn] (*umg*) *adv* = **darin**
dringen ['drɪŋən] (*unreg*) *vi* (*Wasser, Licht, Kälte*): ~ **(durch/in** +*akk***)** to penetrate (through/into); **auf etw** *akk* ~ to insist on sth
dringend ['drɪŋənt] *adj* urgent
Dringlichkeit *f* urgency
drinnen ['drɪnən] *adv* inside, indoors
dritte(r, s) [drɪtə(r, s)] *adj* third; **D~ Welt** Third World; **D~s Reich** Third Reich; **D~l** (**-s, -**) *nt* third; **~ns** *adv* thirdly
DRK [de:|ɛr'ka:] *nt abk* (= *Deutsches Rotes Kreuz*) German Red Cross
droben ['dro:bən] *adv* above, up there
Droge ['dro:gə] *f* drug
drogen *zW*: **~abhängig** *adj* addicted to drugs; **D~händler** *m* drug pedlar, pusher
Drogerie [dro:gə'ri:] *f* chemist's shop
Drogist [dro'gɪst] *m* pharmacist, chemist
drohen ['dro:ən] *vi*: **(jdm)** ~ to threaten (sb)
dröhnen ['drø:nən] *vi* (*Motor*) to roar; (*Stimme, Musik*) to ring, to resound
Drohung ['dro:ʊŋ] *f* threat
drollig ['drɔlɪç] *adj* droll
Drossel ['drɔsəl] (**-, -n**) *f* thrush
drüben ['dry:bən] *adv* over there, on the other side
drüber ['dry:bər] (*umg*) *adv* = **darüber**
Druck [drʊk] (**-(e)s, -e**) *m* (*PHYS, Zwang*) pressure; (*TYP*: *Vorgang*) printing; (: *Produkt*) print; (*fig*: *Belastung*) burden, weight; **~buchstabe** *m* block letter
drücken ['drʏkən] *vt* (*Knopf, Hand*) to press; (*zu eng sein*) to pinch; (*fig*: *Preise*) to keep down; (: *belasten*) to oppress, to weigh down ♦ *vi* to press; to pinch ♦ *vr*: **sich vor etw** *dat* ~ to get out of (doing) sth; **~d** *adj* oppressive
Drucker (**-s, -**) *m* printer
Drücker (**-s, -**) *m* button; (*Türdrücker*) handle; (*Gewehrdrücker*) trigger
Druck- *zW*: **~e'rei** *f* printing works, press; **~erschwärze** *f* printer's ink; **~fehler** *m* misprint; **~knopf** *m* press stud, snap fastener; **~sache** *f* printed matter; **~schrift** *f* block *od* printed letters *pl*
drum [drʊm] (*umg*) *adv* = **darum**
drunten ['drʊntən] *adv* below, down there
Drüse ['dry:zə] *f* gland
Dschungel ['dʒʊŋəl] (**-s, -**) *m* jungle
du [du:] (*nom*) *pron* you; **D~ sagen** = **duzen**
Dübel ['dy:bəl] (**-s, -**) *m* Rawlplug ®
ducken ['dʊkən] *vt* (*Kopf, Person*) to duck; (*fig*) to take down a peg or two ♦ *vr* to duck
Duckmäuser ['dʊkmɔʏzər] (**-s, -**) *m* yes man
Dudelsack ['du:dəlzak] *m* bagpipes *pl*
Duell [du'ɛl] (**-s, -e**) *nt* duel
Duft [dʊft] (**-(e)s, ¨e**) *m* scent, odour; **d~en** *vi* to smell, to be fragrant; **d~ig** *adj* (*Stoff, Kleid*) delicate, diaphanous
dulden ['dʊldən] *vt* to suffer; (*zulassen*) to tolerate ♦ *vi* to suffer
dumm [dʊm] *adj* stupid; (*ärgerlich*) annoying; **der D~e sein** to be the loser; **~erweise** *adv* stupidly; **D~heit** *f* stupidity; (*Tat*) blunder, stupid mistake; **D~kopf** *m* blockhead
dumpf [dʊmpf] *adj* (*Ton*) hollow, dull; (*Luft*) musty; (*Erinnerung, Schmerz*) vague
Düne ['dy:nə] *f* dune
düngen ['dʏŋən] *vt* to manure
Dünger (**-s, -**) *m* dung, manure; (*künstlich*) fertilizer
dunkel ['dʊŋkəl] *adj* dark; (*Stimme*) deep; (*Ahnung*) vague; (*rätselhaft*) obscure; (*verdächtig*) dubious, shady; **im D~n tappen** (*fig*) to grope in the dark
Dunkel- *zW*: **~heit** *f* darkness; (*fig*) obscurity; **~kammer** *f* (*PHOT*) darkroom; **d~n** *vi unpers* to grow dark; **~ziffer** *f estimated number of unreported cases*
dünn [dʏn] *adj* thin; **~flüssig** *adj* watery, thin
Dunst [dʊnst] (**-es, ¨e**) *m* vapour; (*Wetter*) haze
dünsten ['dʏnstən] *vt* to steam
dunstig ['dʊnstɪç] *adj* vaporous; (*Wetter*) hazy, misty
Duplikat [dupli'ka:t] (**-(e)s, -e**) *nt* duplicate
Dur [du:r] (**-, -**) *nt* (*MUS*) major

SCHLÜSSELWORT

durch [dʊrç] *präp* +*akk* **1** (*hindurch*) through; **durch den Urwald** through the jungle; **durch die ganze Welt reisen** to travel all over the world
2 (*mittels*) through, by (means of); (*aufgrund*) due to, owing to; **Tod durch Herzschlag/den Strang** death from a heart attack/by hanging; **durch die Post** by post; **durch seine Bemühungen** through his efforts
♦ *adv* **1** (*hindurch*) through; **die ganze Nacht durch** all through the night; **den Sommer durch** during the summer; **8 Uhr durch** past 8 o'clock; **durch und durch** completely
2 (*durchgebraten etc*): **(gut) durch** well-done

durch- *zW*: **~arbeiten** *vt, vi* to work through ♦ *vr* to work one's way through; **~'aus** *adv* completely; (*unbedingt*) definitely; **~aus nicht** absolutely not

Durchblick ['dʊrçblɪk] *m* view; (*fig*) comprehension; **d~en** *vi* to look through; (*umg: verstehen*): **(bei etw) d~en** to understand (sth); **etw d~en lassen** (*fig*) to hint at sth

durchbrechen ['dʊrçbrɛçən] (*unreg*) *vt, vi* to break

durch'brechen [dʊrç'brɛçən] (*unreg*) *vt insep* (*Schranken*) to break through; (*Schallmauer*) to break; (*Gewohnheit*) to break free from

durchbrennen ['dʊrçbrɛnən] (*unreg*) *vi* (*Draht, Sicherung*) to burn through; (*umg*) to run away

durchbringen (*unreg*) *vt* (*Kranken*) to pull through; (*umg: Familie*) to support; (*durchsetzen: Antrag, Kandidat*) to get through; (*vergeuden: Geld*) to get through, to squander

Durchbruch ['dʊrçbrʊx] *m* (*Öffnung*) opening; (*MIL*) breach; (*von Gefühlen etc*) eruption; (*der Zähne*) cutting; (*fig*) breakthrough; **zum ~ kommen** to break through

durch- *zW:* **~dacht** [-'daxt] *adj* well thought-out; **~'denken** (*unreg*) *vt* to think out; **~drehen** *vt* (*Fleisch*) to mince ♦ *vi* (*umg*) to crack up

durcheinander [dʊrçʔaɪ'nandər] *adv* in a mess, in confusion; (*umg: verwirrt*) confused; **~ bringen** to mess up; (*verwirren*) to confuse; **~ reden** to talk at the same time; **D~ (-s)** *nt* (*Verwirrung*) confusion; (*Unordnung*) mess

durch- *zW:* **~fahren** (*unreg*) *vi* (*durch Tunnel usw*) to drive through; (*ohne Unterbrechung*) to drive straight through; (*ohne anzuhalten*): **der Zug fährt bis Hamburg ~** the train runs direct to Hamburg; (*ohne Umsteigen*): **können wir ~fahren?** can we go direct?, can we go non-stop?; **D~fahrt** *f* transit; (*Verkehr*) thoroughfare; **D~fall** *m* (*MED*) diarrhoea; **~fallen** (*unreg*) *vi* to fall through; (*in Prüfung*) to fail; **~finden** (*unreg*) *vr* to find one's way through; **~fragen** *vr* to find one's way by asking

durchführ- ['dʊrçfyːr] *zW:* **~bar** *adj* feasible, practicable; **~en** *vt* to carry out; **D~ung** *f* execution, performance

Durchgang ['dʊrçgaŋ] *m* passage(way); (*bei Produktion, Versuch*) run; (*SPORT*) round; (*bei Wahl*) ballot; **„~ verboten"** "no thoroughfare"

Durchgangsverkehr *m* through traffic

durchgefroren ['dʊrçgəfroːrən] *adj* (*Mensch*) frozen stiff

durchgehen ['dʊrçgeːən] (*unreg*) *vt* (*behandeln*) to go over ♦ *vi* to go through; (*ausreißen: Pferd*) to break loose; (*Mensch*) to run away; **mein Temperament ging mit mir durch** my temper got the better of me;

jdm etw ~ lassen to let sb get away with sth; **~d** *adj* (*Zug*) through; (*Öffnungszeiten*) continuous

durch- *zW:* **~greifen** (*unreg*) *vi* to take strong action; **~halten** (*unreg*) *vi* to last out ♦ *vt* to keep up; **~kommen** (*unreg*) *vi* to get through; (*überleben*) to pull through; **~'kreuzen** *vt insep* to thwart, to frustrate; **~lassen** (*unreg*) *vt* (*Person*) to let through; (*Wasser*) to let in; **~lesen** (*unreg*) *vt* to read through; **~'leuchten** *vt insep* to X-ray; **~machen** *vt* to go through; **die Nacht ~machen** to make a night of it

Durchmesser (**-s, -**) *m* diameter

durch- *zW:* **~'nässen** *vt insep* to soak (through); **~nehmen** (*unreg*) *vt* to go over; **~nummerieren** ▲ *vt* to number consecutively; **~'queren** [dʊrç'kveːrən] *vt insep* to cross; **D~reise** *f* transit; **auf der D~reise** passing through; (*Güter*) in transit; **~ringen** (*unreg*) *vr* to reach a decision after a long struggle

durchs [dʊrçs] = **durch das**

Durchsage ['dʊrçzaːgə] *f* intercom *od* radio announcement

durchschauen ['dʊrçʃaʊən] *vi* to look *od* see through; (*Person, Lüge*) to see through

durchscheinen ['dʊrçʃaɪnən] (*unreg*) *vi* to shine through; **~d** *adj* translucent

Durchschlag ['dʊrçʃlaːk] *m* (*Doppel*) carbon copy; (*Sieb*) strainer; **d~en** [-gən] (*unreg*) *vt* (*entzweischlagen*) to split (in two); (*sieben*) to sieve ♦ *vi* (*zum Vorschein kommen*) to emerge, to come out ♦ *vr* to get by

durchschlagend *adj* resounding

durchschneiden ['dʊrçʃnaɪdən] (*unreg*) *vt* to cut through

Durchschnitt ['dʊrçʃnɪt] *m* (*Mittelwert*) average; **über/unter dem ~** above/below average; **im ~** on average; **d~lich** *adj* average ♦ *adv* on average

Durchschnittswert *m* average

durch- *zW:* **D~schrift** *f* copy; **~sehen** (*unreg*) *vt* to look through; **~setzen** *vt* to enforce ♦ *vr* (*Erfolg haben*) to succeed; (*sich behaupten*) to get one's way; **seinen Kopf ~setzen** to get one's way; **~'setzen** *vt insep* to mix

Durchsicht ['dʊrçzɪçt] *f* looking through, checking; **d~ig** *adj* transparent

durch- *zW:* **'~sprechen** (*unreg*) *vt* to talk over; **'~stehen** (*unreg*) *vt* to live through; **~stellen** *vt* (*an Telefon*) to put through; **~stöbern** (*auch untr*) *vt* (*Kisten*) to rummage through, to rifle through; (*Haus, Wohnung*) to ransack; **'~streichen** (*unreg*) *vt* to cross out; **'~suchen** *vt insep* to search; **D~'suchung** *f* search; **~'wachsen** *adj* (*Speck*) streaky; (*fig: mittelmäßig*) so-so; **D~wahl** *f* (*TEL*) direct dialling; **~weg** *adv* throughout, completely;

~ziehen (unreg) vt (Faden) to draw through ♦ vi to pass through; **D~zug** m (Luft) draught; (von Truppen, Vögeln) passage

---

SCHLÜSSELWORT

---

dürfen ['dʏrfən] (unreg) vi **1** (Erlaubnis haben) to be allowed to; **ich darf das** I'm allowed to (do that); **darf ich?** may I?; **darf ich ins Kino?** can od may I go to the cinema?; **es darf geraucht werden** you may smoke

2 (in Verneinungen): **er darf das nicht** he's not allowed to (do that); **das darf nicht geschehen** that must not happen; **da darf sie sich nicht wundern** that shouldn't surprise her

3 (in Höflichkeitsformeln): **darf ich Sie bitten, das zu tun?** may od could I ask you to do that?; **was darf es sein?** what can I do for you?

4 (können): **das dürfen Sie mir glauben** you can believe me

5 (Möglichkeit): **das dürfte genug sein** that should be enough; **es dürfte Ihnen bekannt sein, dass** ... as you will probably know ...

---

dürftig ['dʏrftɪç] adj (ärmlich) needy, poor; (unzulänglich) inadequate

dürr [dʏr] adj dried-up; (Land) arid; (mager) skinny, gaunt; **D~e** f aridity; (Zeit) drought; (Magerkeit) skinniness

Durst [dʊrst] (-(e)s) m thirst; **~ haben** to be thirsty; **d~ig** adj thirsty

Dusche ['dʊʃə] f shower; **d~en** vi, vr to have a shower

Düse ['dy:zə] f nozzle; (Flugzeugdüse) jet

Düsen- zW: **~antrieb** m jet propulsion; **~flugzeug** nt jet (plane); **~jäger** m jet fighter

Dussel ['dʊsəl] (-s, -) (umg) m twit

düster ['dy:stər] adj dark; (Gedanken, Zukunft) gloomy

Dutzend ['dʊtsənt] (-s, -e) nt dozen; **~(e)** od **dutzend(e) Mal** a dozen times

duzen ['du:tsən] vt: **(jdn) ~** to use the familiar form of address "du" (to od with sb)

Dynamik [dy'na:mɪk] f (PHYS) dynamics sg; (fig: Schwung) momentum; (von Mensch) dynamism; **dynamisch** adj (auch fig) dynamic

Dynamit [dyna'mi:t] (-s) nt dynamite

Dynamo [dy'na:mo] (-s, -s) m dynamo

DZ nt abk = **Doppelzimmer**

D-Zug ['de:tsu:k] m through train

E, e

Ebbe ['ɛbə] f low tide

eben ['e:bən] adj level, flat; (glatt) smooth ♦ adv just; (bestätigend) exactly; **~ deswegen** just because of that; **~bürtig** adj: **jdm ~bürtig sein** to be sb's equal; **E~e** f (fig) level; **~falls** adv likewise; **~so** adv just as

Eber ['e:bər] (-s, -) m boar

ebnen ['e:bnən] vt to level

Echo ['ɛço] (-s, -s) nt echo

echt |ɛçt| adj genuine; (typisch) typical; **E~heit** f genuineness

Eck- ['ɛk] zW: **~ball** m corner (kick); **~e** f corner; (MATH) angle; **e~ig** adj angular; **~zahn** m eye tooth

ECU [e'ky:] (-, -s) m (FIN) ECU

edel ['e:dəl] adj noble; **E~metall** nt rare metal; **E~stahl** m high-grade steel; **E~stein** m precious stone

EDV [e:de:'fau] (-) f abk (= elektronische Datenverarbeitung) electronic data processing

Efeu ['e:fɔy] (-s) m ivy

Effekt [ɛ'fɛkt] (-s, -e) m effect

Effekten [ɛ'fɛktən] pl stocks

effektiv [ɛfɛk'ti:f] adj effective, actual

EG ['e:'ge:] f abk (= Europäische Gemeinschaft) EC

egal [e'ga:l] adj all the same

Ego- |e:go| zW: **~ismus** |-'ɪsmʊs| m selfishness, egoism; **~ist** [-'ɪst] m egoist; **e~istisch** adj selfish, egoistic

Ehe ['e:ə] f marriage

ehe konj before

Ehe- zW: **~beratung** f marriage guidance (counselling); **~bruch** m adultery; **~frau** f married woman; wife; **~leute** pl married people; **e~lich** adj matrimonial; (Kind) legitimate

ehemalig adj former

ehemals adv formerly

Ehe- zW: **~mann** m married man; husband; **~paar** nt married couple

eher ['e:ər] adv (früher) sooner; (lieber) rather, sooner; (mehr) more

Ehe- zW: **~ring** m wedding ring; **~schließung** f marriage ceremony

eheste(r, s) ['e:əstə(r, s)] adj (früheste) first, earliest; **am ~n** (liebsten) soonest; (meist) most; (wahrscheinlichst) most probably

Ehr- |'e:r| zW: **e~bar** adj honourable, respectable; **~e** f honour; **e~en** vt to honour

Ehren- |'e:rən| zW: **e~amtlich** adj honorary; **~gast** m guest of honour; **e~haft** adj honourable; **~platz** m place of honour od

---

(US) honor; ~runde f lap of honour; ~sache f point of honour; e~voll adj honourable; ~wort nt word of honour

Ehr- zW: ~furcht f awe, deep respect; e~fürchtig adj reverent; ~gefühl nt sense of honour; ~geiz m ambition; e~geizig adj ambitious; e~lich adj honest; ~lichkeit f honesty; e~los adj dishonourable; ~ung f honour(ing); e~würdig adj venerable

Ei [aɪ] (-(e)s, -er) nt egg

Eich- zW: ~e ['aɪçə] f oak (tree); ~el (-, -n) f acorn; ~hörnchen nt squirrel

Eichmaß nt standard

Eid ['aɪt] (-(e)s, -e) m oath

Eidechse ['aɪdɛksə] f lizard

eidesstattlich adj: ~e Erklärung affidavit

Eidgenosse m Swiss

Eier- zW: ~becher m eggcup; ~kuchen m omelette; pancake; ~likör m advocaat; ~schale f eggshell; ~stock m ovary; ~uhr f egg timer

Eifer ['aɪfər] (-s) m zeal, enthusiasm; ~sucht f jealousy; e~süchtig adj: e~süchtig (auf +akk) jealous (of)

eifrig ['aɪfrɪç] adj zealous, enthusiastic

Eigelb ['aɪgɛlp] (-(e)s, -) nt egg yolk

eigen ['aɪgən] adj own; (~artig) peculiar; mit der/dem ihm ~en ... with that ... peculiar to him; sich dat etw zu E~ machen to make sth one's own; E~art f peculiarity; characteristic; ~artig adj peculiar; E~bedarf m: zum E~bedarf for (one's) personal use/domestic requirements; der Vermieter machte E~bedarf geltend the landlord showed he needed the house/flat for himself; ~händig adj with one's own hand; E~heim nt owner-occupied house; E~heit f peculiarity; ~mächtig adj high-handed; E~name m proper name; ~s adv expressly, on purpose; E~schaft f quality, property, attribute; E~sinn m obstinacy; ~sinnig adj obstinate; ~tlich adj actual, real ♦ adv actually, really; E~tor nt own goal; E~tum nt property; E~tümer(in) (-s, -) m(f) owner, proprietor; ~tümlich adj peculiar; E~tümlichkeit f peculiarity; E~tumswohnung f freehold flat

eignen ['aɪgnən] vr to be suited; Eignung f suitability

Eil- zW: ~bote m courier; ~brief m express letter; ~e f haste; es hat keine ~e there's no hurry; e~en vi (Mensch) to hurry; (dringend sein) to be urgent; e~ends adv hastily; ~gut nt express goods pl, fast freight (US); e~ig adj hasty, hurried; (dringlich) urgent; es e~ig haben to be in a hurry; ~zug m semi-fast train, limited stop train

Eimer ['aɪmər] (-s, -) m bucket, pail

ein [aɪn] adv: nicht ~ noch aus wissen not to know what to do

ein(e) ['aɪn(ə)] num one ♦ indef art a, an

einander [aɪ'nandər] pron one another, each other

einarbeiten ['aɪnˌarbaɪtən] vt to train ♦ vr: sich in etw akk ~ to familiarize o.s. with sth

einatmen ['aɪnˌaːtmən] vt, vi to inhale, to breathe in

Einbahnstraße ['aɪnbaːnˌʃtraːsə] f one-way street

Einband ['aɪnbant] m binding, cover

einbauen ['aɪnbaʊən] vt to build in; (Motor) to install, to fit

Einbaumöbel pl built-in furniture sg

einbegriffen ['aɪnbəgrɪfən] adj included

einberufen ['aɪnbəruːfən] (unreg) vt to convene; (MIL) to call up

Einbettzimmer nt single room

einbeziehen ['aɪnbətsiːən] (unreg) vt to include

einbiegen ['aɪnbiːgən] (unreg) vi to turn

einbilden ['aɪnbɪldən] vt: sich dat etw ~ to imagine sth

Einbildung f imagination; (Dünkel) conceit; ~skraft f imagination

Einblick ['aɪnblɪk] m insight

einbrechen ['aɪnbrɛçən] (unreg) vi (in Haus) to break in; (Nacht) to fall; (Winter) to set in; (durchbrechen) to break; ~ in +akk (MIL) to invade

Einbrecher (-s, -) m burglar

einbringen ['aɪnbrɪŋən] (unreg) vt to bring in; (Geld, Vorteil) to yield; (mitbringen) to contribute

Einbruch ['aɪnbrʊx] m (Hauseinbruch) break-in, burglary; (Eindringen) invasion; (des Winters) onset; (Durchbrechen) breach; (MET) approach; (MIL) penetration; (bei/vor) ~ der Nacht at/before nightfall; e~sicher adj burglar-proof

einbürgern ['aɪnbʏrgərn] vt to naturalize ♦ vr to become adopted

einbüßen ['aɪnbyːsən] vt to lose, to forfeit

einchecken ['aɪntʃɛkən] vt, vi to check in

eincremen ['aɪnkreːmən] vt to put cream on

eindecken ['aɪndɛkən] vr: sich (mit etw) ~ to lay in stocks (of sth); to stock up (with sth)

eindeutig ['aɪndɔʏtɪç] adj unequivocal

eindringen ['aɪndrɪŋən] (unreg) vi: ~ (in +akk) to force one's way in(to); (in Haus) to break in(to); (in Land) to invade; (Gas, Wasser) to penetrate; (auf jdn) ~ (mit Bitten) to pester (sb)

eindringlich ['aɪndrɪŋlɪç] adj forcible, urgent

Eindringling m intruder

Eindruck ['aɪndrʊk] m impression

eindrücken ['aɪndrʏkən] vt to press in

eindrucksvoll adj impressive

eine(r, s) pron one; (jemand) someone

eineiig ['aɪnaɪɪç] adj (Zwillinge) identical

eineinhalb ['aɪnaɪn'halp] num one and a half

einengen |'aɪn|ɛŋən| vt to confine, to restrict

einer- |'aɪnər| zW: **'E~'lei (-s)** nt sameness; **'~'lei** adj (gleichartig) the same kind of; **es ist mir ~lei** it is all the same to me; **~seits** adv on the one hand

einfach |'aɪnfax| adj simple; (nicht mehrfach) single ♦ adv simply; **E~heit** f simplicity

einfädeln |'aɪnfɛːdəln| vt (Nadel, Faden) to thread; (fig) to contrive

einfahren |'aɪnfaːrən| (unreg) vt to bring in; (Barriere) to knock down; (Auto) to run in ♦ vi to drive in; (Zug) to pull in; (MIN) to go down

Einfahrt f (Vorgang) driving in; pulling in; (MIN) descent; (Ort) entrance

Einfall |'aɪnfal| m (Idee) idea, notion; (Lichteinfall) incidence; (MIL) raid; **e~en** (unreg) vi (Licht) to fall; (MIL) to raid; (einstürzen) to fall in, to collapse; (einstimmen): **(in etw akk) e~en** to join in (with sth); **etw fällt jdm ein** sth occurs to sb; **das fällt mir gar nicht ein** I wouldn't dream of it; **sich** dat **etwas e~en lassen** to have a good idea

einfältig |'aɪnfɛltɪç| adj simple(-minded)

Einfamilienhaus |aɪnfaˈmiːliənhaʊs| nt detached house

einfarbig |'aɪnfarbɪç| adj all one colour; (Stoff etc) self-coloured

einfetten |'aɪnfɛtən| vt to grease

einfließen |'aɪnfliːsən| (unreg) vi to flow in

einflößen |'aɪnfløːsən| vt: **jdm etw ~** to give sb sth; (fig) to instil sth in sb

Einfluss ▲ |'aɪnflʊs| m influence; **~bereich** ▲ m sphere of influence

einförmig |'aɪnfœrmɪç| adj uniform; **E~keit** f uniformity

einfrieren |'aɪnfriːrən| (unreg) vi to freeze (up) ♦ vt to freeze

einfügen |'aɪnfyːgən| vt to fit in; (zusätzlich) to add

Einfuhr |'aɪnfuːr| (-) f import; **~beschränkung** f import restrictions pl; **~bestimmungen** pl import regulations

einführen |'aɪnfyːrən| vt to bring in; (Mensch, Sitten) to introduce; (Ware) to import

Einführung f introduction

Eingabe |'aɪngaːbə| f petition; (COMPUT) input

Eingang |'aɪngaŋ| m entrance; (COMM: Ankunft) arrival; (Erhalt) receipt

eingeben |'aɪngeːbən| (unreg) vt (Arznei) to give; (Daten etc) to enter

eingebildet |'aɪngəbɪldət| adj imaginary; (eitel) conceited

Eingeborene(r) |'aɪngəboːrənə(r)| f(m) native

Eingebung f inspiration

eingefleischt |'aɪngəflaɪʃt| adj (Gewohnheit, Vorurteile) deep-rooted

eingehen |'aɪngeːən| (unreg) vi (Aufnahme finden) to come in; (Sendung, Geld) to be received; (Tier, Pflanze) to die; (Firma) to fold; (schrumpfen) to shrink ♦ vt to enter into; (Wette) to make; **auf etw** akk **~** to go into sth; **auf jdn ~** to respond to sb; **jdm ~** (verständlich sein) to be comprehensible to sb; **~d** adj exhaustive, thorough

Eingemachte(s) |'aɪngəma:xtə(s)| nt preserves pl

eingenommen |'aɪngənɔmən| adj: **~ (von)** fond (of), partial (to); **~ (gegen)** prejudiced (against)

eingeschrieben |'aɪngəʃriːbən| adj registered

eingespielt |'aɪngəʃpiːlt| adj: **aufeinander ~ sein** to be in tune with each other

Eingeständnis |'aɪngəʃtɛntnɪs| (-ses, -se) nt admission, confession

eingestehen |'aɪngəʃteːən| (unreg) vt to confess

eingestellt |'aɪngəʃtɛlt| adj: **auf etw ~ sein** to be prepared for sth

eingetragen |'aɪngətraːgən| adj (COMM) registered

Eingeweide |'aɪngəvaɪdə| (-s, -) nt innards pl, intestines pl

Eingeweihte(r) |'aɪngəvaɪtə(r)| f(m) initiate

eingewöhnen |'aɪngəvøːnən| vr: **sich ~ in** +akk to settle (down) in

eingleisig |'aɪnglaɪzɪç| adj single-track

eingreifen |'aɪngraɪfən| (unreg) vi to intervene, to interfere; (Zahnrad) to mesh

Eingriff |'aɪngrɪf| m intervention, interference; (Operation) operation

einhaken |'aɪnhaːkən| vt to hook in ♦ vr: **sich bei jdm ~** to link arms with sb ♦ vi (sich einmischen) to intervene

Einhalt |'aɪnhalt| m: **~ gebieten** +dat to put a stop to; **e~en** (unreg) vt (Regel) to keep ♦ vi to stop

einhändigen |'aɪnhɛndɪgən| vt to hand in

einhängen |'aɪnhɛŋən| vt to hang; (Telefon) to hang up ♦ vi (TEL) to hang up; **sich bei jdm ~** to link arms with sb

einheimisch |'aɪnhaɪmɪʃ| adj native; **E~e(r)** f(m) local

Einheit |'aɪnhaɪt| f unity; (Maß, MIL) unit; **e~lich** adj uniform; **~spreis** m standard price

einholen |'aɪnhoːlən| vt (Tau) to haul in; (Fahne, Segel) to lower; (Vorsprung aufholen) to catch up with; (Verspätung) to make up; (Rat, Erlaubnis) to ask ♦ vi (einkaufen) to shop

einhüllen |'aɪnhʏlən| vt to wrap up

einhundert |'aɪn'hʊndərt| num one

Spelling reform: ▲ *new spelling* △ *old spelling (to be phased out)*

hundred, a hundred

einig ['aɪnɪç] adj (vereint) united; **~ gehen** to agree; **sich** dat **~ sein** to be in agreement; **~ werden** to agree

einige(r, s) ['aɪnɪgə(r, s)] adj, pron some ♦ pl some; (mehrere) several; **~ Mal** a few times

einigen vt to unite ♦ vr: **sich ~ (auf** +akk) to agree (on)

einigermaßen adv somewhat; (leidlich) reasonably

einig- zW: **E~keit** f unity; (Übereinstimmung) agreement; **E~ung** f agreement; (Vereinigung) unification

einkalkulieren ['aɪnkalkuliːrən] vt to take into account, to allow for

Einkauf ['aɪnkaʊf] m purchase; **e~en** vt to buy ♦ vi to shop; **e~en gehen** to go shopping

Einkaufs- zW: **~bummel** m shopping spree; **~korb** m shopping basket; **~wagen** m shopping trolley; **~zentrum** nt shopping centre

einklammern ['aɪnklamərn] vt to put in brackets, to bracket

Einklang ['aɪnklaŋ] m harmony

einklemmen ['aɪnklɛmən] vt to jam

einkochen ['aɪnkɔxən] vt to boil down; (Obst) to preserve, to bottle

Einkommen ['aɪnkɔmən] (-s, -) nt income; **~(s)steuer** f income tax

Einkünfte ['aɪnkʏnftə] pl income sg, revenue sg

einladen ['aɪnlaːdən] (unreg) vt (Person) to invite; (Gegenstände) to load; **jdn ins Kino ~** to take sb to the cinema

Einladung f invitation

Einlage ['aɪnlaːgə] f (Programmeinlage) interlude; (Spareinlage) deposit; (Schuheinlage) insole; (Fußstütze) support; (Zahneinlage) temporary filling; (KOCH) noodles pl, vegetables pl etc in soup

einlagern ['aɪnlaːgərn] vt to store

Einlass ▲ ['aɪnlas] (-es, ⁼e) m (Zutritt) admission

einlassen ['aɪnlasən] (unreg) vt to let in; (einsetzen) to set in ♦ vr: **sich mit jdm/auf etw** akk **~** to get involved with sb/sth

Einlauf ['aɪnlaʊf] m arrival; (von Pferden) finish; (MED) enema; **e~en** (unreg) vi to arrive, to come in; (in Hafen) to enter; (SPORT) to finish; (Wasser) to run in; (Stoff) to shrink ♦ vt (Schuhe) to break in ♦ vr (SPORT) to warm up; (Motor, Maschine) to run in; **jdm das Haus e~en** to invade sb's house

einleben ['aɪnleːbən] vr to settle down

einlegen ['aɪnleːgən] vt (einfügen: Blatt, Sohle) to insert; (KOCH) to pickle; (Pause) to have; (Protest) to make; (Veto) to use; (Berufung) to lodge; (AUT: Gang) to engage

einleiten ['aɪnlaɪtən] vt to introduce, to start;

(Geburt) to induce; **Einleitung** f introduction; induction

einleuchten ['aɪnlɔʏçtən] vi: (jdm) **~** to be clear od evident (to sb); **~d** adj clear

einliefern ['aɪnliːfərn] vt: **~ (in** +akk) to take (into)

Einlieferungsschein m certificate of posting

Einliegerwohnung ['aɪnliːgərvoːnʊŋ] f self-contained flat; (für Eltern, Großeltern) granny flat

einlösen ['aɪnløːzən] vt (Scheck) to cash; (Schuldschein, Pfand) to redeem; (Versprechen) to keep

einmachen ['aɪnmaxən] vt to preserve

einmal ['aɪnmaːl] adv once; (erstens) first; (zukünftig) sometime; **nehmen wir ~ an** just let's suppose; **noch ~** once more; **nicht ~** not even; **auf ~** all at once; **es war ~** once upon a time there was/were; **E~'eins** nt multiplication tables pl; **~ig** adj unique; (nur ~ erforderlich) single; (prima) fantastic

Einmarsch ['aɪnmarʃ] m entry; (MIL) invasion; **e~ieren** vi to march in

einmischen ['aɪnmɪʃən] vr: **sich ~ (in** +akk) to interfere (with)

einmütig ['aɪnmyːtɪç] adj unanimous

Einnahme ['aɪnnaːmə] f (von Medizin) taking; (MIL) capture, taking; **~n** pl (Geld) takings, revenue sg; **~quelle** f source of income

einnehmen ['aɪnneːmən] (unreg) vt to take; (Stellung, Raum) to take up; **~ für/gegen** to persuade in favour of/against; **~d** adj charming

einordnen ['aɪnɔrdnən] vt to arrange, to fit in ♦ vr to adapt; (AUT) to get into lane

einpacken ['aɪnpakən] vt to pack (up)

einparken ['aɪnparkən] vt to park

einpendeln ['aɪnpɛndəln] vr to even out

einpflanzen ['aɪnpflantsən] vt to plant; (MED) to implant

einplanen ['aɪnplaːnən] vt to plan for

einprägen ['aɪnprɛːgən] vt to impress, to imprint; (beibringen): (jdm) **~** to impress (on sb); **sich** dat **etw ~** to memorize sth

einrahmen ['aɪnraːmən] vt to frame

einräumen ['aɪnrɔʏmən] vt (ordnend) to put away; (überlassen: Platz) to give up; (zugestehen) to admit, to concede

einreden ['aɪnreːdən] vt: **jdm/sich etw ~** to talk sb/o.s. into believing sth

einreiben ['aɪnraɪbən] (unreg) vt to rub in

einreichen ['aɪnraɪçən] vt to hand in; (Antrag) to submit

Einreise ['aɪnraɪzə] f entry; **~bestimmungen** pl entry regulations; **~erlaubnis** f entry permit; **~genehmigung** f entry permit; **e~n** vi: (in ein Land) **e~n** to enter (a country)

einrichten ['aɪnrɪçtən] vt (Haus) to furnish;

(*schaffen*) to establish, to set up; (*arrangieren*) to arrange; (*möglich machen*) to manage ♦ *vr* (*in Haus*) to furnish one's house; **sich ~ (auf** +*akk*) (*sich vorbereiten*) to prepare o.s. (for); (*sich anpassen*) to adapt (to)

Einrichtung *f* (*Wohnungseinrichtung*) furnishings *pl*; (*öffentliche Anstalt*) organization; (*Dienste*) service

einrosten ['aınrɔstən] *vi* to get rusty

einrücken ['aınrʏkən] *vi* (*MIL: in Land*) to move in

Eins [aıns] (-, **-en**) *f* one; **e~** *num* one; **es ist mir alles e~** it's all one to me

einsam ['aınzaːm] *adj* lonely, solitary; **E~keit** *f* loneliness, solitude

einsammeln ['aınzaməln] *vt* to collect

Einsatz ['aınzats] *m* (*Teil*) inset; (*an Kleid*) insertion; (*Verwendung*) use, employment; (*Spieleinsatz*) stake; (*Risiko*) risk; (*MIL*) operation; (*MUS*) entry; **im ~** in action; **e~bereit** *adj* ready for action

einschalten ['aınʃaltən] *vt* (*einfügen*) to insert; (*Pause*) to make; (*ELEK*) to switch on; (*Anwalt*) to bring in ♦ *vr* (*dazwischentreten*) to intervene

einschärfen ['aınʃɛrfən] *vt*: **jdm etw ~ to** impress sth (up)on sb

einschätzen ['aınʃɛtsən] *vt* to estimate, to assess ♦ *vr* to rate o.s.

einschenken ['aınʃɛŋkən] *vt* to pour out

einschicken ['aınʃıkən] *vt* to send in

einschl. *abk* (= *einschließlich*) incl.

einschlafen ['aınʃlaːfən] (*unreg*) *vi* to fall asleep, to go to sleep

einschläfernd ['aınʃlɛːfərnt] *adj* (*MED*) soporific; (*langweilig*) boring; (*Stimme*) lulling

Einschlag ['aınʃlaːk] *m* impact; (*fig: Beimischung*) touch, hint; **e~en** [-gən] (*unreg*) *vt* to knock in; (*Fenster*) to smash, to break; (*Zähne, Schädel*) to smash in; (*AUT: Räder*) to turn; (*kürzer machen*) to take up; (*Ware*) to pack, to wrap up; (*Weg, Richtung*) to take ♦ *vi* to hit; (*sich einigen*) to agree; (*Anklang finden*) to work, to succeed; **in etw akk/auf jdn e~en** to hit sth/sb

einschlägig ['aınʃlɛːgıç] *adj* relevant

einschließen ['aınʃliːsən] (*unreg*) *vt* (*Kind*) to lock in; (*Häftling*) to lock up; (*Gegenstand*) to lock away; (*Bergleute*) to cut off; (*umgeben*) to surround; (*MIL*) to encircle; (*fig*) to include, to comprise ♦ *vr* to lock o.s. in

einschließlich *adv* inclusive ♦ *präp* +*gen* inclusive of, including

einschmeicheln ['aınʃmaıçəln] *vr*: **sich ~ (bei)** to ingratiate o.s. (with)

einschnappen ['aınʃnapən] *vi* (*Tür*) to click

to; (*fig*) to be touchy; **eingeschnappt sein** to be in a huff

einschneidend ['aınʃnaıdənt] *adj* drastic

Einschnitt ['aınʃnıt] *m* cutting; (*MED*) incision; (*Ereignis*) decisive point

einschränken ['aınʃrɛŋkən] *vt* to limit, to restrict; (*Kosten*) to cut down, to reduce ♦ *vr* to cut down (on expenditure); **Einschränkung** *f* restriction, limitation; reduction; (*von Behauptung*) qualification

Einschreib- ['aınʃraıb] *zW*: **~(e)brief** *m* recorded delivery letter; **e~en** (*unreg*) *vt* to write in; (*Post*) to send recorded delivery ♦ *vr* to register; (*UNIV*) to enrol; **~en** *nt* recorded delivery letter

einschreiten ['aınʃraıtən] (*unreg*) *vi* to step in, to intervene; **~ gegen** to take action against

einschüchtern ['aınʃʏçtərn] *vt* to intimidate

einschulen ['aınʃuːlən] *vt*: **eingeschult werden** (*Kind*) to start school

einsehen ['aınzeːən] (*unreg*) *vt* (*hineinsehen in*) to realize; (*Akten*) to have a look at; (*verstehen*) to see; **E~ (-s)** *nt* understanding; **ein E~ haben** to show understanding

einseitig ['aınzaıtıç] *adj* one-sided

Einsend- ['aınzɛnd] *zW*: **e~en** (*unreg*) *vt* to send in; **~er (-s, -)** *m* sender, contributor; **~ung** *f* sending in

einsetzen ['aınzɛtsən] *vt* to put (in); (*in Amt*) to appoint, to install; (*Geld*) to stake; (*verwenden*) to use; (*MIL*) to employ ♦ *vi* (*beginnen*) to set in; (*MUS*) to enter, to come in ♦ *vr* to work hard; **sich für jdn/etw ~** to support sb/sth

Einsicht ['aınzıçt] *f* insight; (*in Akten*) look, inspection; **zu der ~ kommen, dass ...** to come to the conclusion that ...; **e~ig** *adj* (*Mensch*) judicious; **e~slos** *adj* unreasonable; **e~svoll** *adj* understanding

einsilbig ['aınzılbıç] *adj* (*auch fig*) monosyllabic; (*Mensch*) uncommunicative

einspannen ['aınʃpanən] *vt* (*Papier*) to insert; (*Pferde*) to harness; (*umg: Person*) to rope in

Einsparung ['aınʃpaːrʊŋ] *f* economy, saving

einsperren ['aınʃpɛrən] *vt* to lock up

einspielen ['aınʃpiːlən] *vr* (*SPORT*) to warm up ♦ *vt* (*Film: Geld*) to bring in; (*Instrument*) to play in; **sich aufeinander ~** to become attuned to each other; **gut eingespielt** running smoothly

einsprachig ['aınʃpraːxıç] *adj* monolingual

einspringen ['aınʃprıŋən] (*unreg*) *vi* (*aushelfen*) to help out, to step into the breach

Einspruch ['aınʃprʊx] *m* protest, objection; **~srecht** *nt* veto

einspurig ['aınʃpuːrıç] *adj* (*EISENB*) single-

track; (AUT) single-lane
einst |aɪnst| adv once; (zukünftig) one day, some day
einstecken |ˈaɪnʃtɛkən| vt to stick in, to insert; (Brief) to post; (ELEK: Stecker) to plug in; (Geld) to pocket; (mitnehmen) to take; (überlegen sein) to put in the shade; (hinnehmen) to swallow
einstehen |ˈaɪnʃteːən| (unreg) vi: **für jdn/ etw ~** to guarantee sb/sth; (verantworten): **für etw ~** to answer for sth
einsteigen |ˈaɪnʃtaɪɡən| (unreg) vi to get in od on; (in Schiff) to go on board; (sich beteiligen) to come in; (hineinklettern) to climb in
einstellen |ˈaɪnʃtɛlən| vt (aufhören) to stop; (Geräte) to adjust; (Kamera etc) to focus; (Sender, Radio) to tune in; (unterstellen) to put; (in Firma) to employ, to take on ♦ vi (Firma) to take on staff/workers ♦ vr (anfangen) to set in; (kommen) to arrive; **sich auf jdn ~** to adapt to sb; **sich auf etw akk ~** to prepare o.s. for sth
Einstellung f (Aufhören) suspension, cessation; adjustment; focusing; (von Arbeiter etc) appointment; (Haltung) attitude
Einstieg |ˈaɪnʃtiːk| (-(e)s, -e) m entry; (fig) approach
einstig |ˈaɪnstɪç| adj former
einstimmig |ˈaɪnʃtɪmɪç| adj unanimous; (MUS) for one voice
einstmals adv once, formerly
einstöckig |ˈaɪnʃtœkɪç| adj two-storeyed
Einsturz |ˈaɪnʃtʊrts| m collapse
einstürzen |ˈaɪnʃtʏrtsən| vi to fall in, to collapse
einst- zW: **~weilen** adv meanwhile; (vorläufig) temporarily, for the time being; **~weilig** adj temporary
eintägig |ˈaɪntɛːɡɪç| adj one-day
eintauschen |ˈaɪntaʊʃən| vt: **~ (gegen od für)** to exchange (for)
eintausend |aɪnˈtaʊzənt| num one thousand
einteilen |ˈaɪntaɪlən| vt (in Teile) to divide (up); (Menschen) to assign
einteilig adj one-piece
eintönig |ˈaɪntøːnɪç| adj monotonous
Eintopf |ˈaɪntɔpf| m stew
Eintracht |ˈaɪntraxt| (-) f concord, harmony;
einträchtig |ˈaɪntrɛçtɪç| adj harmonious
Eintrag |ˈaɪntraːk| (-(e)s, ⁼e) m entry; **amtlicher ~** entry in the register; **e~en** |-ɡən| (unreg) vt (in Buch) to enter; (Profit) to yield ♦ vr to put one's name down
einträglich |ˈaɪntrɛːklɪç| adj profitable
eintreffen |ˈaɪntrɛfən| (unreg) vi to happen; (ankommen) to arrive
eintreten |ˈaɪntreːtən| (unreg) vi to occur; (sich einsetzen) to intercede ♦ vt (Tür) to kick open; **~ in +akk** to enter; (in Klub, Partei) to join

Eintritt |ˈaɪntrɪt| m (Betreten) entrance; (Anfang) commencement; (in Klub etc) joining
Eintritts- zW: **~geld** nt admission charge; **~karte** f (admission) ticket; **~preis** m admission charge
einüben |ˈaɪnyːbən| vt to practise
Einvernehmen |ˈaɪnfɛrneːmən| (-s, -) nt agreement, harmony
einverstanden |ˈaɪnfɛrʃtandən| excl agreed, okay ♦ adj: **~ sein** to agree, to be agreed
Einverständnis |ˈaɪnfɛrʃtɛntnɪs| nt understanding; (gleiche Meinung) agreement
Einwand |ˈaɪnvant| (-(e)s, ⁼e) m objection
Einwand- zW: **~erer** m immigrant; **e~ern** vi to immigrate; **~erung** f immigration
einwandfrei adj perfect ♦ adv absolutely
Einweg- |ˈaɪnveːɡ-| zW: **~flasche** f no-deposit bottle; **~spritze** f disposable syringe
einweichen |ˈaɪnvaɪçən| vt to soak
einweihen |ˈaɪnvaɪən| vt (Kirche) to consecrate; (Brücke) to open; (Gebäude) to inaugurate; **~ (in +akk) (Person)** to initiate (in); **Einweihung** f consecration; opening; inauguration; initiation
einweisen |ˈaɪnvaɪzən| (unreg) vt (in Amt) to install; (in Arbeit) to introduce; (in Anstalt) to send
einwenden |ˈaɪnvɛndən| (unreg) vt: **etwas ~ gegen** to object to, to oppose
einwerfen |ˈaɪnvɛrfən| (unreg) vt to throw in; (Brief) to post; (Geld) to put in, to insert; (Fenster) to smash; (äußern) to interpose
einwickeln |ˈaɪnvɪkəln| vt to wrap up; (fig: umg) to outsmart
einwilligen |ˈaɪnvɪlɪɡən| vi: **~ (in +akk)** to consent (to), to agree (to); **Einwilligung** f consent
einwirken |ˈaɪnvɪrkən| vi: **auf jdn/etw ~** to influence sb/sth
Einwohner |ˈaɪnvoːnər| (-s, -) m inhabitant; **~'meldeamt** nt registration office; **~schaft** f population, inhabitants pl
Einwurf |ˈaɪnvʊrf| m (Öffnung) slot; (von Münze) insertion; (von Brief) posting; (Einwand) objection; (SPORT) throw-in
Einzahl |ˈaɪntsaːl| f singular; **e~en** vt to pay in; **~ung** f paying in; **~ungsschein** m paying-in slip, deposit slip (US)
einzäunen |ˈaɪntsɔʏnən| vt to fence in
Einzel |ˈaɪntsəl| (-s, -) nt (TENNIS) singles; **~fahrschein** m one-way ticket; **~fall** m single instance, individual case; **~handel** m retail trade; **~handelspreis** m retail price; **~heit** f particular, detail; **~kind** nt only child; **e~n** adj single; (vereinzelt) the odd ♦ adv singly; **e~n angeben** to specify; **der/ die ~ne** the individual; **das ~ne** the particular; **ins ~ne gehen** to go into detail(s); **~teil** nt component (part); **~zimmer** nt single room; **~zimmerzuschlag**

m single room supplement

einziehen ['aɪntsiːən] (*unreg*) *vt* to draw in, to take in; (*Kopf*) to duck; (*Fühler, Antenne, Fahrgestell*) to retract; (*Steuern, Erkundigungen*) to collect; (*MIL*) to draft, to call up; (*aus dem Verkehr ziehen*) to withdraw; (*konfiszieren*) to confiscate ♦ *vi* to move in; (*Friede, Ruhe*) to come; (*Flüssigkeit*) to penetrate

einzig ['aɪntsɪç] *adj* only; (*ohnegleichen*) unique; **das E~e** the only thing; **der/die E~e** the only one; **~artig** *adj* unique

Einzug ['aɪntsuːk] *m* entry, moving in

Eis [aɪs] (*-es, -*) *nt* ice; (*Speiseeis*) ice cream; **~bahn** *f* ice *od* skating rink; **~bär** *m* polar bear; **~becher** *m* sundae; **~bein** *nt* pig's trotters *pl*; **~berg** *m* iceberg; **~café** *nt* ice-cream parlour (*BRIT*) *od* parlor (*US*); **~decke** *f* sheet of ice; **~diele** *f* ice-cream parlour

Eisen ['aɪzən] (*-s, -*) *nt* iron

Eisenbahn *f* railway, railroad (*US*); **~er** (*-s, -*) *m* railwayman, railway employee, railroader (*US*); **~schaffner** *m* railway guard; **~wagen** *m* railway carriage

Eisenerz *nt* iron ore

eisern ['aɪzərn] *adj* iron; (*Gesundheit*) robust; (*Energie*) unrelenting; (*Reserve*) emergency

Eis- *zW*: **e~frei** *adj* clear of ice; **~hockey** *nt* ice hockey; **e~ig** ['aɪzɪç] *adj* icy; **e~kalt** *adj* icy cold; **~kunstlauf** *m* figure skating; **~laufen** *vi* ice skating; **~pickel** *m* ice axe; **~schrank** *m* fridge, icebox (*US*); **~würfel** *m* ice cube; **~zapfen** *m* icicle; **~zeit** *f* ice age

eitel ['aɪtəl] *adj* vain; **E~keit** *f* vanity

Eiter ['aɪtər] (*-s*) *m* pus; **e~ig** *adj* suppurating; **e~n** *vi* to suppurate

Eiweiß (*-es, -e*) *nt* white of an egg; (*CHEM*) protein

Ekel¹ ['eːkəl] (*-s*) *nt* (*umg: Mensch*) nauseating person

Ekel² ['eːkəl] (*-s*) *m* nausea, disgust; **~erregend** nauseating, disgusting; **e~haft** *adj* nauseating, disgusting; **e~ig** *adj* nauseating, disgusting; **e~n** *vt* to disgust ♦ *vr*: **sich e~n vor** (*+dat*) to loathe, to be disgusted (at); **es e~t jdn** *od* **jdm** sb is disgusted; **eklig** *adj* nauseating, disgusting

Ekstase [ɛkˈstaːzə] *f* ecstasy

Ekzem [ɛkˈtseːm] (*-s, -e*) *nt* (*MED*) eczema

Elan [eˈlãː] (*-s*) *m* elan

elastisch [eˈlastɪʃ] *adj* elastic

Elastizität [elastitsiˈtɛːt] *f* elasticity

Elch [ɛlç] (*-(e)s, -e*) *m* elk

Elefant [eleˈfant] *m* elephant

elegant [eleˈgant] *adj* elegant

Eleganz [eleˈgants] *f* elegance

Elek- [eˈlɛk] *zW*: **~triker** [-trikər] (*-s, -*) *m* electrician; **e~trisch** [-trɪʃ] *adj* electric; **e~trisieren** [-triˈziːrən] *vt* (*auch fig*) to

electrify; (*Mensch*) to give an electric shock to ♦ *vr* to get an electric shock; **~trizität** [-tritsiˈtɛːt] *f* electricity; **~trizitätswerk** *nt* power station; (*Gesellschaft*) electric power company

Elektro- [eˈlɛktro] *zW*: **~de** [-ˈtroːdə] *f* electrode; **~gerät** *nt* electrical appliance; **~herd** *m* electric cooker; **~n** (*-s, -en*) *nt* electron; **~nenrechner** [elɛkˈtroːnən-] *m* computer; **~nik** *f* electronics *sg*; **e~nisch** *adj* electronic; **~rasierer** *m* electric razor; **~technik** *f* electrical engineering

Element [eleˈment] (*-s, -e*) *nt* element; (*ELEK*) cell, battery; **e~ar** [-ˈtaːr] *adj* elementary; (*naturhaft*) elemental

Elend ['eːlɛnt] (*-(e)s*) *nt* misery; **e~** *adj* miserable; **~sviertel** *nt* slum

elf [ɛlf] *num* eleven; **E~** (*-, -en*) *f* (*SPORT*) eleven

Elfe *f* elf

Elfenbein *nt* ivory

Elfmeter *m* (*SPORT*) penalty (kick)

Elite [eˈliːtə] *f* elite

Ell- *zW*: **~bogen** *m* elbow; **~e** *f* ell; (*Maß*) yard; **~enbogen** *m* elbow; **~(en)bogenfreiheit** *f* (*fig*) elbow room

Elsass ▲ ['ɛlzas] (*- od -es*) *nt*: **das ~** Alsace

Elster ['ɛlstər] (*-, -n*) *f* magpie

Eltern ['ɛltərn] *pl* parents; **~beirat** *m* (*SCH*) ≈ PTA (*BRIT*), parents' council; **~haus** *nt* home; **e~los** *adj* parentless

E-mail ['iːmeːl] (*-, -s*) *f* E-mail

Emaille [eˈmaljə] (*-s, -s*) *f* enamel

emaillieren [emaˈjiːrən] *vt* to enamel

Emanzipation [emantsipatsiˈoːn] *f* emancipation

emanzi'pieren *vt* to emancipate

Embryo ['ɛmbryo] (*-s, -s od* **Embryonen**) *m* embryo

Emi- *zW*: **~'grant(in)** *m(f)* emigrant; **~gration** *f* emigration; **e~grieren** *vi* to emigrate

Emissionen [emisiˈoːnən] *fpl* emissions

Empfang [ɛmˈpfaŋ] (*-(e)s, -̈e*) *m* reception; (*Erhalten*) receipt; **in ~ nehmen** to receive; **e~en** (*unreg*) *vt* to receive ♦ *vi* (*schwanger werden*) to conceive

Empfäng- [ɛmˈpfɛŋ] *zW*: **~er** (*-s, -*) *m* receiver; (*COMM*) addressee, consignee; **~erabschnitt** *m* receipt slip; **e~lich** *adj* receptive, susceptible; **~nis** (*-, -se*) *f* conception; **~nisverhütung** *f* contraception

Empfangs- *zW*: **~bestätigung** *f* acknowledgement; **~dame** *f* receptionist; **~schein** *m* receipt; **~zimmer** *nt* reception room

empfehlen [ɛmˈpfeːlən] (*unreg*) *vt* to recommend ♦ *vr* to take one's leave; **~swert**

adj recommendable

Empfehlung f recommendation

empfiehlst *etc* [ɛm'pfi:lst] *vb siehe* **empfehlen**

empfind- [ɛm'pfɪnt] *zW:* **~en** [-dən] (*unreg*) *vt* to feel; **~lich** *adj* sensitive; (*Stelle*) sore; (*reizbar*) touchy; **~sam** *adj* sentimental; **E~ung** [-duŋ] f feeling, sentiment

empfohlen *etc* [ɛm'pfoːlən] *vb siehe* **empfehlen**

empor [ɛm'poːr] *adv* up, upwards

empören [ɛm'pøːrən] *vt* to make indignant; to shock ♦ *vr* to become indignant; **~d** *adj* outrageous

Emporkömmling [ɛm'poːrkœmlɪŋ] m upstart, parvenu

Empörung f indignation

emsig ['ɛmzɪç] *adj* diligent, busy

End- ['ɛnt] *in zW* final; **~e** (-s, -n) nt end; **am ~e** at the end; (*schließlich*) in the end; **am ~e sein** to be at the end of one's tether; **~e Dezember** at the end of December; **zu ~e sein** to be finished; **e~en** *vi* to end; **e~gültig** ['ɛnt-] *adj* final, definite

Endivie [ɛn'diːviə] f endive

End- *zW:* **e~lich** *adj* final; (*MATH*) finite ♦ *adv* finally; **e~lich!** at last!; **komm e~lich!** come on!; **e~los** *adj* endless, infinite; **~spiel** nt final(s); **~spurt** m (*SPORT*) final spurt; **~station** f terminus; **~ung** f ending

Energie [enɛr'giː] f energy; **~bedarf** m energy requirement; **e~los** *adj* lacking in energy, weak; **~verbrauch** m energy consumption; **~versorgung** f supply of energy; **~wirtschaft** f energy industry

energisch [e'nergɪʃ] *adj* energetic

eng [ɛŋ] *adj* narrow; (*Kleidung*) tight; (*fig: Horizont*) narrow, limited; (*Freundschaft, Verhältnis*) close; **~ an etw** *dat* close to sth

Engagement [ãgaʒə'mãː] (-s, -s) nt engagement; (*Verpflichtung*) commitment

engagieren [ãga'ʒiːrən] *vt* to engage ♦ *vr* to commit o.s.

Enge ['ɛŋə] f (*auch fig*) narrowness; (*Landenge*) defile; (*Meerenge*) straits *pl*; **jdn in die ~ treiben** to drive sb into a corner

Engel ['ɛŋəl] (-s, -) m angel; **e~haft** *adj* angelic

England ['ɛŋlant] nt England; **Engländer(in)** m(f) Englishman(-woman); **englisch** *adj* English

Engpass ▲ m defile, pass; (*fig, Verkehr*) bottleneck

en gros [ã'groː] *adv* wholesale

engstirnig ['ɛŋʃtɪrnɪç] *adj* narrow-minded

Enkel ['ɛŋkəl] (-s, -) m grandson; **~in** f granddaughter; **~kind** nt grandchild

enorm [e'nɔrm] *adj* enormous

Ensemble [ã'sãbəl] (-s, -s) nt company, ensemble

entbehr- [ɛnt'beːr] *zW:* **~en** *vt* to do

without, to dispense with; **~lich** *adj* superfluous; **E~ung** f deprivation

entbinden [ɛnt'bɪndən] (*unreg*) *vt* (+*gen*) to release (from); (*MED*) to deliver ♦ *vi* (*MED*) to give birth; **Entbindung** f release; (*MED*) confinement; **Entbindungsheim** nt maternity hospital

entdeck- [ɛnt'dɛk] *zW:* **~en** *vt* to discover; **E~er** (-s, -) m discoverer; **E~ung** f discovery

Ente ['ɛntə] f duck; (*fig*) canard, false report

enteignen [ɛnt'aɪɡnən] *vt* to expropriate; (*Besitzer*) to dispossess

enterben [ɛnt'ɛrbən] *vt* to disinherit

entfallen [ɛnt'falən] (*unreg*) *vi* to drop, to fall; (*wegfallen*) to be dropped; **jdm ~** (*vergessen*) to slip sb's memory; **auf jdn ~** to be allotted to sb

entfalten [ɛnt'faltən] *vt* to unfold; (*Talente*) to develop ♦ *vr* to open; (*Mensch*) to develop one's potential; **Entfaltung** f unfolding; (*von Talenten*) development

entfern- [ɛnt'fɛrn] *zW:* **~en** *vt* to remove; (*hinauswerfen*) to expel ♦ *vr* to go away, to withdraw; **~t** *adj* distant; **weit davon ~t sein, etw zu tun** to be far from doing sth; **E~ung** f distance; (*Wegschaffen*) removal

entfremden [ɛnt'frɛmdən] *vt* to estrange, to alienate; **Entfremdung** f alienation, estrangement

entfrosten [ɛnt'frɔstən] *vt* to defrost

Entfroster (-s, -) m (*AUT*) defroster

entführ- [ɛnt'fyːr] *zW:* **~en** *vt* to carry off, to abduct; to kidnap; **E~er** m kidnapper; **E~ung** f abduction; kidnapping

entgegen [ɛnt'geːɡən] *präp* +*dat* contrary to, against ♦ *adv* towards; **~bringen** (*unreg*) *vt* to bring; **jdm etw ~bringen** (*fig*) to show sb sth; **~gehen** (*unreg*) *vi* +*dat* to go to meet, to go towards; **~gesetzt** *adj* opposite; (*widersprechend*) opposed; **~halten** (*unreg*) *vt* (*fig*) to object; **E~kommen** nt obligingness; **~kommen** (*unreg*) *vi* +*dat* to approach; to meet; (*fig*) to accommodate; **~kommend** *adj* obliging; **~nehmen** (*unreg*) *vt* to receive, to accept; **~sehen** (*unreg*) *vi* +*dat* to await; **~setzen** *vt* to oppose; **~treten** (*unreg*) *vi* +*dat* to step up to; (*fig*) to oppose, to counter; **~wirken** *vi* +*dat* to counteract

entgegnen [ɛnt'geːɡnən] *vt* to reply, to retort

entgehen [ɛnt'geːən] (*unreg*) *vi* (*fig*): **jdm ~** to escape sb's notice; **sich** *dat* **etw ~ lassen** to miss sth

Entgelt [ɛnt'gɛlt] (-(e)s, -e) nt compensation, remuneration

entgleisen [ɛnt'glaɪzən] *vi* (*EISENB*) to be derailed; (*fig: Person*) to misbehave; **~ lassen** to derail

entgräten [ɛnt'grɛːtən] *vt* to fillet, to bone

Enthaarungscreme [ɛnt'haːrʊŋs-] f hair-

removing cream
enthalten [ɛnt'haltən] (unreg) vt to contain
♦ vr: **sich (von etw)** ~ to abstain (from sth),
to refrain (from sth)
enthaltsam [ɛnt'haltza:m] adj abstinent,
abstemious
enthemmen [ɛnt'hɛmən] vt: **jdn** ~ to free
sb from his inhibitions
enthüllen [ɛnt'hʏlən] vt to reveal, to unveil
Enthusiasmus [ɛntuzi'asmʊs] m enthusiasm
entkommen [ɛnt'kɔmən] (unreg) vi: ~ **(aus**
od +dat) to get away (from), to escape
(from)
entkräften [ɛnt'krɛftən] vt to weaken, to
exhaust; (Argument) to refute
entladen [ɛnt'la:dən] (unreg) vt to unload;
(ELEK) to discharge ♦ vr (ELEK: Gewehr) to
discharge; (Ärger etc) to vent itself
entlang [ɛnt'laŋ] adv along; ~ **dem Fluss,**
den Fluss ~ along the river; **~gehen**
(unreg) vi to walk along
entlarven [ɛnt'larfən] vt to unmask, to
expose
entlassen [ɛnt'lasən] (unreg) vt to discharge;
(Arbeiter) to dismiss; **Entlassung** f discharge; dismissal
entlasten [ɛnt'lastən] vt to relieve; (Achse) to
relieve the load on; (Angeklagten) to
exonerate; (Konto) to clear
Entlastung f relief; (COMM) crediting
Entlastungszug m relief train
entlegen [ɛnt'le:gən] adj remote
entlocken [ɛnt'lɔkən] vt: **jdm etw** ~ to
elicit (sth from sb)
entmutigen [ɛnt'mu:tɪgən] vt to discourage
entnehmen [ɛnt'ne:mən] (unreg) vt (+dat)
to take out (of), to take (from); (folgern) to
infer (from)
entreißen [ɛnt'raɪsən] (unreg) vt: **jdm etw** ~
to snatch sth (away) from sb
entrichten [ɛnt'rɪçtən] vt to pay
entrosten [ɛnt'rɔstən] vt to remove rust
from
entrümpeln [ɛnt'rʏmpəln] vt to clear
out
entrüst- [ɛnt'rʏst] zW: **~en** vt to incense, to
outrage ♦ vr to be filled with indignation;
~et adj indignant, outraged; **E~ung** f
indignation
entschädigen [ɛnt'ʃɛ:dɪgən] vt to compensate; **Entschädigung** f compensation
entschärfen [ɛnt'ʃɛrfən] vt to defuse; (Kritik)
to tone down
Entscheid [ɛnt'ʃaɪt] (-(e)s, -e) m decision;
e~en [-dən] (unreg) vt, vi, vr to decide; **e~end**
adj decisive; (Stimme) casting; **~ung** f decision
entschieden [ɛnt'ʃi:dən] adj decided;
(entschlossen) resolute; **E~heit** f firmness,
determination

entschließen [ɛnt'ʃli:sən] (unreg) vr to
decide
entschlossen [ɛnt'ʃlɔsən] adj determined,
resolute; **E~heit** f determination
Entschluss ▲ [ɛnt'ʃlʊs] m decision;
e~freudig ▲ adj decisive; **~kraft** ▲ f
determination, decisiveness
entschuldigen [ɛnt'ʃʊldɪgən] vt to excuse
♦ vr to apologize
Entschuldigung f apology; (Grund) excuse;
jdn um ~ bitten to apologize to sb; **~!**
excuse me; (Verzeihung) sorry
entsetz- [ɛnt'zɛts] zW: **~en** vt to horrify;
(MIL) to relieve ♦ vr to be horrified od
appalled; **E~en** (-s) nt horror, dismay; **~lich**
adj dreadful, appalling; **~t** adj horrified
Entsorgung [ɛnt'zɔrgʊŋ] f (von Kraftwerken,
Chemikalien) (waste) disposal
entspannen [ɛnt'ʃpanən] vt, vr (Körper) to
relax; (POL: Lage) to ease
Entspannung f relaxation, rest; (POL)
détente; **~spolitik** f policy of détente
entsprechen [ɛnt'ʃprɛçən] (unreg) vi +dat to
correspond to; (Anforderungen, Wünschen) to
meet, to comply with; **~d** adj appropriate
♦ adv accordingly
entspringen [ɛnt'ʃprɪŋən] (unreg) vi (+dat)
to spring (from)
entstehen [ɛnt'ʃte:ən] (unreg) vi: ~ **(aus** od
durch) to arise (from), to result (from)
Entstehung f genesis, origin
entstellen [ɛnt'ʃtɛlən] vt to disfigure;
(Wahrheit) to distort
entstören [ɛnt'ʃtø:rən] vt (RAD) to eliminate
interference from
enttäuschen [ɛnt'tɔʏʃən] vt to disappoint;
Enttäuschung f disappointment
entwaffnen [ɛnt'vafnən] vt (lit, fig) to
disarm
entwässern [ɛnt'vɛsərn] vt to drain;
Entwässerung f drainage
entweder [ɛnt've:dər] konj either
entwenden [ɛnt'vɛndən] (unreg) vt to
purloin, to steal
entwerfen [ɛnt'vɛrfən] (unreg) vt
(Zeichnung) to sketch; (Modell) to design;
(Vortrag, Gesetz etc) to draft
entwerten [ɛnt've:rtən] vt to devalue;
(stempeln) to cancel
Entwerter (-s, -) m ticket punching machine
entwickeln [ɛnt'vɪkəln] vt, vr (auch PHOT) to
develop; (Mut, Energie) to show (o.s.), to
display (o.s.)
Entwicklung [ɛnt'vɪklʊŋ] f development;
(PHOT) developing
Entwicklungs- zW: **~hilfe** f aid for
developing countries; **~land** nt developing
country
entwöhnen [ɛnt'vø:nən] vt to wean;

(*Süchtige*): (**einer Sache** *dat od* **von etw**) ~ to cure (of sth)

Entwöhnung *f* weaning; cure, curing

entwürdigend [ɛnt'vyrdɪgənt] *adj* degrading

Entwurf [ɛnt'vʊrf] *m* outline, design; (*Vertragsentwurf, Konzept*) draft

entziehen [ɛnt'tsiːən] (*unreg*) *vt* (+*dat*) to withdraw (from), to take away (from); (*Flüssigkeit*) to draw (from), to extract (from) ♦ *vr* (+*dat*) to escape (from); (*jds Kenntnis*) to be outside od beyond; (*der Pflicht*) to shirk (from)

Entziehung *f* withdrawal; **~sanstalt** *f* drug addiction/alcoholism treatment centre; **~skur** *f* treatment for drug addiction/ alcoholism

entziffern [ɛnt'tsɪfərn] *vt* to decipher; to decode

entzücken [ɛnt'tsʏkən] *vt* to delight; **E~** (**-s**) *nt* delight; **~d** *adj* delightful, charming

entzünden [ɛnt'tsʏndən] *vt* to light, to set light to; (*fig, MED*) to inflame; (*Streit*) to spark off ♦ *vr* (*auch fig*) to catch fire; (*Streit*) to start; (*MED*) to become inflamed

Entzündung *f* (*MED*) inflammation

entzwei [ɛnt'tsvaɪ] *adv* broken; in two; **~brechen** (*unreg*) *vt, vi* to break in two; **~en** *vr* to set at odds ♦ *vr* to fall out; **~gehen** (*unreg*) *vi* to break (in two)

Enzian ['ɛntsiaːn] (**-s, -e**) *m* gentian

Epidemie [epide'miː] *f* epidemic

Epilepsie [epile'psiː] *f* epilepsy

Episode [epi'zoːdə] *f* episode

Epoche [e'pɔxə] *f* epoch; ~ **machend** epoch-making

Epos ['eːpɔs] (**-s, Epen**) *nt* epic (poem)

er [eːr] (*nom*) *pron* he; it

erarbeiten [ɛr'arbaɪtən] *vt* to work for, to acquire; (*Theorie*) to work out

erbarmen [ɛr'barmən] *vr* (+*gen*) to have pity od mercy (on); **E~** (**-s**) *nt* pity

erbärmlich [ɛr'bɛrmlɪç] *adj* wretched, pitiful; **E~keit** *f* wretchedness

erbarmungslos [ɛr'barmʊŋsloːs] *adj* pitiless, merciless

erbau- [ɛr'baʊ] *zW*: **~en** *vt* to build, to erect; (*fig*) to edify; **E~er** (**-s, -**) *m* builder; **~lich** *adj* edifying

Erbe¹ ['ɛrbə] (**-n, -n**) *m* heir

Erbe² ['ɛrbə] *nt* inheritance; (*fig*) heritage

erben *vt* to inherit

erbeuten [ɛr'bɔʏtən] *vt* to carry off; (*MIL*) to capture

Erb- [ɛrb] *zW*: **~faktor** *m* gene; **~folge** *f* (line of) succession; **~in** *f* heiress

erbittern [ɛr'bɪtərn] *vt* to embitter; (*erzürnen*) to incense

erbittert [ɛr'bɪtərt] *adj* (*Kampf*) fierce, bitter

erblassen [ɛr'blasən] *vi* to (turn) pale

erblich ['ɛrplɪç] *adj* hereditary

erblinden [ɛr'blɪndən] *vi* to go blind

erbrechen [ɛr'brɛçən] (*unreg*) *vt, vr* to vomit

Erbschaft *f* inheritance, legacy

Erbse ['ɛrpsə] *f* pea

Erbstück *nt* heirloom

Erd- ['eːrd] *zW*: **~achse** *f* earth's axis; **~atmosphäre** *f* earth's atmosphere; **~beben** *nt* earthquake; **~beere** *f* strawberry; **~boden** *m* ground; **~e** *f* earth; **zu ebener ~e** at ground level; **e~en** *vt* (*ELEK*) to earth

erdenklich [ɛr'dɛŋklɪç] *adj* conceivable

Erd- *zW*: **~gas** *nt* natural gas; **~geschoss** ▲ *nt* ground floor; **~kunde** *f* geography; **~nuss** ▲ *f* peanut; **~öl** *nt* (mineral) oil

erdrosseln [ɛr'drɔsəln] *vt* to strangle, to throttle

erdrücken [ɛr'drʏkən] *vt* to crush

Erd- *zW*: **~rutsch** *m* landslide; **~teil** *m* continent

erdulden [ɛr'dʊldən] *vt* to endure, to suffer

ereignen [ɛr'aɪgnən] *vr* to happen

Ereignis [ɛr'aɪgnɪs] (**-ses, -se**) *nt* event; **e~los** *adj* uneventful; **e~reich** *adj* eventful

ererbt [ɛr'ɛrpt] *adj* (*Haus*) inherited; (*Krankheit*) hereditary

erfahren [ɛr'faːrən] (*unreg*) *vt* to learn, to find out; (*erleben*) to experience ♦ *adj* experienced

Erfahrung *f* experience; **e~sgemäß** *adv* according to experience

erfassen [ɛr'fasən] *vt* to seize; (*fig: einbeziehen*) to include, to register; (*verstehen*) to grasp

erfind- [ɛr'fɪnd] *zW*: **~en** (*unreg*) *vt* to invent; **E~er** (**-s, -**) *m* inventor; **~erisch** *adj* inventive; **E~ung** *f* invention

Erfolg [ɛr'fɔlk] (**-(e)s, -e**) *m* success; (*Folge*) result; ~ **versprechend** promising; **e~en** |-gən| *vi* to follow; (*sich ergeben*) to result; (*stattfinden*) to take place; (*Zahlung*) to be effected; **e~los** *adj* unsuccessful; **~losigkeit** *f* lack of success; **e~reich** *adj* successful

erforderlich *adj* requisite, necessary

erfordern [ɛr'fɔrdərn] *vt* to require, to demand

erforschen [ɛr'fɔrʃən] *vt* (*Land*) to explore; (*Problem*) to investigate; (*Gewissen*) to search; **Erforschung** *f* exploration; investigation; searching

erfreuen [ɛr'frɔʏən] *vr*: **sich ~ an** +*dat* to enjoy ♦ *vt* to delight; **sich einer Sache** *gen* ~ to enjoy sth

erfreulich [ɛr'frɔʏlɪç] *adj* pleasing, gratifying; **~erweise** *adv* happily, luckily

erfrieren [ɛr'friːrən] (*unreg*) *vi* to freeze (to death); (*Glieder*) to get frostbitten; (*Pflanzen*) to be killed by frost

erfrischen [ɛr'frɪʃən] *vt* to refresh; **Erfrischung** *f* refreshment

Erfrischungs- *zW*: **~getränk** *nt* (liquid)

refreshment; **~raum** m snack bar, cafeteria

erfüllen |ɛr'fʏlən| vt (Raum etc) to fill; (fig: Bitte etc) to fulfil ♦ vr to come true

ergänzen |ɛr'gɛntsən| vt to supplement, to complete ♦ vr to complement one another; **Ergänzung** f completion; (Zusatz) supplement

ergeben |ɛr'ge:bən| (unreg) vt to yield, to produce ♦ vr to surrender; (folgen) to result ♦ adj devoted, humble

Ergebnis |ɛr'ge:pnɪs| (**-ses, -se**) nt result; **e~los** adj without result, fruitless

ergehen |ɛr'ge:ən| (unreg) vi to be issued, to go out ♦ vi unpers: **es ergeht ihm gut/schlecht** he's faring od getting on well/badly ♦ vr: **sich in etw** dat **~** to indulge in sth; **etw über sich ~ lassen** to put up with sth

ergiebig |ɛr'gi:bɪç| adj productive

Ergonomie |ɛrgɔnoˈmiː| f ergonomics sg

Ergonomik |ɛrgɔˈnoːmɪk| f = **Ergonomie**

ergreifen |ɛr'graɪfən| (unreg) vt (auch fig) to seize; (Beruf) to take up; (Maßnahmen) to resort to; (rühren) to move; **~d** adj moving, touching

ergriffen |ɛr'grɪfən| adj deeply moved

Erguss ▲ |ɛr'gʊs| m discharge; (fig) outpouring, effusion

erhaben |ɛr'ha:bən| adj raised, embossed; (fig) exalted, lofty; **über etw** akk **~ sein** to be above sth

erhalten |ɛr'haltən| (unreg) vt to receive; (bewahren) to preserve, to maintain; **gut ~** in good condition

erhältlich |ɛr'hɛltlɪç| adj obtainable, available

Erhaltung f maintenance, preservation

erhärten |ɛr'hɛrtən| vt to harden; (These) to substantiate, to corroborate

erheben |ɛr'he:bən| (unreg) vt to raise; (Protest, Forderungen) to make; (Fakten) to ascertain, to establish ♦ vr to rise (up)

erheblich |ɛr'he:plɪç| adj considerable

erheitern |ɛr'haɪtərn| vt to amuse, to cheer (up)

Erheiterung f exhilaration; **zur allgemeinen ~** to everybody's amusement

erhitzen |ɛr'hɪtsən| vt to heat ♦ vr to heat up; (fig) to become heated

erhoffen |ɛr'hɔfən| vt to hope for

erhöhen |ɛr'hø:ən| vt to raise; (verstärken) to increase

erhol- |ɛr'ho:l| zW: **~en** vr to recover; (entspannen) to have a rest; **~sam** adj restful; **E~ung** f recovery; relaxation, rest; **~ungsbedürftig** adj in need of a rest, rundown; **E~ungsgebiet** nt ≈ holiday area; **E~ungsheim** nt convalescent home

erhören |ɛr'hø:rən| vt (Gebet etc) to hear; (Bitte etc) to yield to

erinnern |ɛr'|ɪnərn| vt: **~ (an** +akk) to remind (of) ♦ vr: **sich (an** akk **etw) ~** to remember (sth)

Erinnerung f memory; (Andenken) reminder

erkältet |ɛr'kɛltət| adj with a cold; **~ sein** to have a cold

Erkältung f cold

erkennbar adj recognizable

erkennen |ɛr'kɛnən| (unreg) vt to recognize; (sehen, verstehen) to see

erkennt- zW: **~lich** adj: **sich ~lich zeigen** to show one's appreciation; **E~lichkeit** f gratitude; (Geschenk) token of one's gratitude; **E~nis** (**-, -se**) f knowledge; (das Erkennen) recognition; (Einsicht) insight; **zur E~nis kommen** to realize

Erkennung f recognition

Erkennungszeichen nt identification

Erker |'ɛrkər| (**-s, -**) m bay

erklär- |ɛr'klɛ:r| zW: **~bar** adj explicable; **~en** vt to explain; **~lich** adj explicable; (verständlich) understandable; **E~ung** f explanation; (Aussage) declaration

erkranken |ɛr'kraŋkən| vi to fall ill; **Erkrankung** f illness

erkund- |ɛr'kʊnd| zW: **~en** vt to find out, to ascertain; (bes MIL) to reconnoitre, to scout; **~igen** vr: **sich ~igen (nach)** to inquire (about); **E~igung** f inquiry; **E~ung** f reconnaissance, scouting

erlahmen |ɛr'la:mən| vi to tire; (nachlassen) to flag, to wane

erlangen |ɛr'laŋən| vt to attain, to achieve

Erlass ▲ |ɛr'las| (**-es, ⸚e**) m decree; (Aufhebung) remission

erlassen (unreg) vt (Verfügung) to issue; (Gesetz) to enact; (Strafe) to remit; **jdm etw ~** to release sb from sth

erlauben |ɛr'lauben| vt: **(jdm etw) ~** to allow od permit (sb (to do) sth) ♦ vr to permit o.s., to venture

Erlaubnis |ɛr'laupnɪs| (**-, -se**) f permission; (Schriftstück) permit

erläutern |ɛr'lɔytərn| vt to explain; **Erläuterung** f explanation

erleben |ɛr'le:bən| vt to experience; (Zeit) to live through; (miterleben) to witness; (noch miterleben) to live to see

Erlebnis |ɛr'le:pnɪs| (**-ses, -se**) nt experience

erledigen |ɛr'le:dɪgən| vt to take care of, to deal with; (Antrag etc) to process; (umg: erschöpfen) to wear out; (: ruinieren) to finish; (: umbringen) to do in

erleichtern |ɛr'laɪçtərn| vt to make easier; (fig: Last) to lighten; (lindern, beruhigen) to relieve; **Erleichterung** f facilitation; lightening; relief

erleiden |ɛr'laɪdən| (unreg) vt to suffer, to endure

Spelling reform: ▲ *new spelling* △ *old spelling (to be phased out)*

erlernen |ɛrˈlɛrnən| vt to learn, to acquire

erlesen |ɛrˈleːzən| adj select, choice

erleuchten |ɛrˈlɔʏçtən| vt to illuminate; (fig) to inspire

Erleuchtung f (Einfall) inspiration

Erlös |ɛrˈløːs| (-es, -e) m proceeds pl

erlösen |ɛrˈløːzən| vt to redeem, to save; **Erlösung** f release; (REL) redemption

ermächtigen |ɛrˈmɛçtɪɡən| vt to authorize, to empower; **Ermächtigung** f authorization; authority

ermahnen |ɛrˈmaːnən| vt to exhort, to admonish; **Ermahnung** f admonition, exhortation

ermäßigen |ɛrˈmɛsɪɡən| vt to reduce; **Ermäßigung** f reduction

ermessen |ɛrˈmɛsən| (unreg) vt to estimate, to gauge; **E~** (-s) nt estimation; discretion; **in jds E~ liegen** to lie within sb's discretion

ermitteln |ɛrˈmɪtəln| vt to determine; (Täter) to trace ♦ vi: **gegen jdn ~** to investigate sb

Ermittlung |ɛrˈmɪtlʊŋ| f determination; (Polizeiermittlung) investigation

ermöglichen |ɛrˈmøːklɪçən| vt (+dat) to make possible (for)

ermorden |ɛrˈmɔrdən| vt to murder

ermüden |ɛrˈmyːdən| vt, vi to tire; (TECH) to fatigue; **~d** adj tiring; (fig) wearisome

Ermüdung f fatigue

ermutigen |ɛrˈmuːtɪɡən| vt to encourage

ernähr- |ɛrˈnɛːr| zW: **~en** vt to feed, to nourish; (Familie) to support ♦ vr to support o.s., to earn a living; **sich ~en von** to live on; **E~er** (-s, -) m breadwinner; **E~ung** f nourishment; nutrition; (Unterhalt) maintenance

ernennen |ɛrˈnɛnən| (unreg) vt to appoint; **Ernennung** f appointment

erneu- |ɛrˈnɔʏ| zW: **~ern** vt to renew; to restore; to renovate; **E~erung** f renewal; restoration; renovation; **~t** adj renewed, fresh ♦ adv once more

ernst |ɛrnst| adj serious; **~ gemeint** meant in earnest, serious; **E~** (-es) m seriousness; **das ist mein E~** I'm quite serious; **im E~** in earnest; **E~ machen mit etw** to put sth into practice; **E~fall** m emergency; **~haft** adj serious; **E~haftigkeit** f seriousness; **~lich** adj serious

Ernte |ˈɛrntə| f harvest; **e~n** vt to harvest; (Lob etc) to earn

ernüchtern |ɛrˈnʏçtərn| vt to sober up; (fig) to bring down to earth

Erober- |ɛrˈʔoːbər| zW: **~er** (-s, -) m conqueror; **e~n** vt to conquer; **~ung** f conquest

eröffnen |ɛrˈʔœfnən| vt to open ♦ vr to present itself; **jdm etw ~** to disclose sth to sb

Eröffnung f opening

erörtern |ɛrˈʔœrtərn| vt to discuss

Erotik |eˈroːtɪk| f eroticism; **erotisch** adj erotic

erpress- |ɛrˈprɛs| zW: **~en** vt (Geld etc) to extort; (Mensch) to blackmail; **E~er** (-s, -) m blackmailer; **E~ung** f extortion; blackmail

erprobt |ɛrˈproːpt| adj (Gerät, Medikamente) proven, tested

erraten |ɛrˈraːtən| (unreg) vt to guess

erreg- |ɛrˈreːɡ| zW: **~en** vt to excite; (ärgern) to infuriate; (hervorrufen) to arouse, to provoke ♦ vr to get excited od worked up; **E~er** (-s, -) m causative agent; **E~ung** f excitement

erreichbar adj accessible, within reach

erreichen |ɛrˈraɪçən| vt to reach; (Zweck) to achieve; (Zug) to catch

errichten |ɛrˈrɪçtən| vt to erect, to put up; (gründen) to establish, to set up

erringen |ɛrˈrɪŋən| (unreg) vt to gain, to win

erröten |ɛrˈrøːtən| vi to blush, to flush

Errungenschaft |ɛrˈrʊŋənʃaft| f achievement; (umg: Anschaffung) acquisition

Ersatz |ɛrˈzats| (-es) m substitute; replacement; (Schadenersatz) compensation; (MIL) reinforcements pl; **~dienst** m (MIL) alternative service; **~reifen** m (AUT) spare tyre; **~teil** nt spare (part)

erschaffen |ɛrˈʃafən| (unreg) vt to create

erscheinen |ɛrˈʃaɪnən| (unreg) vi to appear; **Erscheinung** f appearance; (Geist) apparition; (Gegebenheit) phenomenon; (Gestalt) figure

erschießen |ɛrˈʃiːsən| (unreg) vt to shoot (dead)

erschlagen |ɛrˈʃlaːɡən| (unreg) vt to strike dead

erschöpf- |ɛrˈʃœpf| zW: **~en** vt to exhaust; **~end** adj exhaustive, thorough; **E~ung** f exhaustion

erschrecken |ɛrˈʃrɛkən| vt to startle, to frighten ♦ vi to be frightened od startled; **~d** adj alarming, frightening

erschrocken |ɛrˈʃrɔkən| adj frightened, startled

erschüttern |ɛrˈʃʏtərn| vt to shake; (fig) to move deeply; **Erschütterung** f shaking; shock

erschweren |ɛrˈʃveːrən| vt to complicate

erschwinglich adj within one's means

ersetzen |ɛrˈzɛtsən| vt to replace; **jdm Unkosten** etc **~** to pay sb's expenses etc

ersichtlich |ɛrˈzɪçtlɪç| adj evident, obvious

ersparen |ɛrˈʃpaːrən| vt (Ärger etc) to spare; (Geld) to save

Ersparnis (-, -se) f saving

┌─────────────────────────────┐
│ SCHLÜSSELWORT   │
└─────────────────────────────┘

erst |eːrst| adv 1 first; **mach erst mal die Arbeit fertig** finish your work first; **wenn du das erst mal hinter dir hast** once you've got that behind you

2 (*nicht früher als, nur*) only; (*nicht bis*) not till; **erst gestern** only yesterday; **erst morgen** not until tomorrow; **erst als** only when, not until; **wir fahren erst später** we're not going until later; **er ist (gerade) erst angekommen** he's only just arrived **3**: **wäre er doch erst zurück!** if only he were back!

erstatten |ɛrˈʃtatən| *vt* (*Kosten*) to (re)pay; **Anzeige** *etc* **gegen jdn ~** to report sb; **Bericht ~** to make a report

Erstattung *f* (*von Kosten*) refund

Erstaufführung |ˈeːrstauffyːrʊŋ| *f* first performance

erstaunen |ɛrˈʃtaunən| *vt* to astonish ♦ *vi* to be astonished; **E~ (-s)** *nt* astonishment

erstaunlich *adj* astonishing

erst- |ˈeːrst| *zW*: **E~ausgabe** *f* first edition; **~beste(r, s)** *adj* first that comes along; **~e(r, s)** *adj* first

erstechen |ɛrˈʃteçən| (*unreg*) *vt* to stab (to death)

erstehen |ɛrˈʃteːən| (*unreg*) *vt* to buy ♦ *vi* to (a)rise

erstens |ˈeːrstəns| *adv* firstly, in the first place

ersticken |ɛrˈʃtɪkən| *vt* (*auch fig*) to stifle; (*Mensch*) to suffocate; (*Flammen*) to smother ♦ *vi* (*Mensch*) to suffocate; (*Feuer*) to be smothered; **in Arbeit ~** to be snowed under with work

erst- *zW*: **~klassig** *adj* first-class; **~malig** *adj* first; **~mals** *adv* for the first time

erstrebenswert |ɛrˈʃtreːbənsveːrt| *adj* desirable, worthwhile

erstrecken |ɛrˈʃtrɛkən| *vr* to extend, to stretch

ersuchen |ɛrˈzuːxən| *vt* to request

ertappen |ɛrˈtapən| *vt* to catch, to detect

erteilen |ɛrˈtailən| *vt* to give

Ertrag |ɛrˈtraːk| **(-(e)s, ²e)** *m* yield; (*Gewinn*) proceeds *pl*

ertragen |ɛrˈtraːgən| (*unreg*) *vt* to bear, to stand

erträglich |ɛrˈtrɛːklɪç| *adj* tolerable, bearable

ertrinken |ɛrˈtrɪŋkən| (*unreg*) *vi* to drown; **E~ (-s)** *nt* drowning

erübrigen |ɛrˈlyːbrɪgən| *vt* to spare ♦ *vr* to be unnecessary

erwachen |ɛrˈvaxən| *vi* to awake

erwachsen |ɛrˈvaksən| *adj* grown-up; **E~e(r)** *f(m)* adult; **E~enbildung** *f* adult education

erwägen |ɛrˈvɛːgən| (*unreg*) *vt* to consider; **Erwägung** *f* consideration

erwähn- |ɛrˈvɛːn| *zW*: **~en** *vt* to mention; **~enswert** *adj* worth mentioning; **E~ung** *f* mention

erwärmen |ɛrˈvɛrmən| *vt* to warm, to heat ♦ *vr* to get warm, to warm up; **sich ~ für** to

warm to

Erwarten *nt*: **über meinen/unseren** *usw* **~** beyond my/our *etc* expectations; **wider ~** contrary to expectations

erwarten |ɛrˈvartən| *vt* to expect; (*warten auf*) to wait for; **etw kaum ~ können** to be hardly able to wait for sth

Erwartung *f* expectation

erwartungsgemäß *adv* as expected

erwartungsvoll *adj* expectant

erwecken |ɛrˈvɛkən| *vt* to rouse, to awake; **den Anschein ~** to give the impression

Erweis |ɛrˈvais| **(-es, -e)** *m* proof; **e~en** (*unreg*) *vt* to prove ♦ *vr*: **sich e~en (als)** to prove (to be); **jdm einen Gefallen/Dienst e~en** to do sb a favour/service

Erwerb |ɛrˈvɛrp| **(-(e)s, -e)** *m* acquisition; (*Beruf*) trade; **e~en** |-bən| (*unreg*) *vt* to acquire

erwerbs- *zW*: **~los** *adj* unemployed; **E~quelle** *f* source of income; **~tätig** *adj* (gainfully) employed

erwidern |ɛrˈviːdərn| *vt* to reply; (*vergelten*) to return

erwischen |ɛrˈvɪʃən| (*umg*) *vt* to catch, to get

erwünscht |ɛrˈvynʃt| *adj* desired

erwürgen |ɛrˈvyrgən| *vt* to strangle

Erz |eːrts| **(-es, -e)** *nt* ore

erzähl- |ɛrˈtsɛːl| *zW*: **~en** *vt* to tell ♦ *vi*: **sie kann gut ~en** she's a good story-teller; **E~er (-s, -)** *m* narrator; **E~ung** *f* story, tale

Erzbischof *m* archbishop

erzeug- |ɛrˈtsɔyg| *zW*: **~en** *vt* to produce; (*Strom*) to generate; **E~nis (-ses, -se)** *nt* product, produce; **E~ung** *f* production, generation

erziehen |ɛrˈtsiːən| (*unreg*) *vt* to bring up; (*bilden*) to educate, to train; **Erzieher(in) (-s, -)** *m(f)* (*Berufsbezeichnung*) teacher; (*in Kindergarten*) nursery school teacher;

Erziehung *f* bringing up; (*Bildung*) education; **Erziehungsbeihilfe** *f* educational grant; **Erziehungsberechtigte(r)** *f(m)* parent; guardian

erzielen |ɛrˈtsiːlən| *vt* to achieve, to obtain; (*Tor*) to score

erzwingen |ɛrˈtsvɪŋən| (*unreg*) *vt* to force, to obtain by force

es |ɛs| (*nom, akk*) *pron* it

Esel |ˈeːzəl| **(-s, -)** *m* donkey, ass

Eskalation |ɛskalatsiˈoːn| *f* escalation

Ess- ▲ *zW*: **e~bar** ▲ *adj* eatable, edible; **~besteck** ▲ *nt* knife, fork and spoon; **~ecke** ▲ *f* dining area

essen |ˈɛsən| (*unreg*) *vt*, *vi* to eat; **E~ (-s, -)** *nt* meal; food

Essig |ˈɛsɪç| **(-s, -e)** *m* vinegar

Spelling reform: ▲ *new spelling* △ *old spelling (to be phased out)*

Ess- ▲ zW: **~kastanie** ▲ f sweet chestnut;
~löffel ▲ m tablespoon; **~tisch** ▲ m
dining table; **~waren** ▲ pl foodstuffs,
provisions; **~zimmer** ▲ nt dining room

etablieren [eta'bli:rən] vr to become
established; to set up in business

Etage [e'ta:ʒə] f floor, storey; **~nbetten** pl
bunk beds; **~nwohnung** f flat

Etappe [e'tapə] f stage

Etat [e'ta:] (-s, -s) m budget

etc. abk (= et cetera) etc

Ethik ['e:tɪk] f ethics sg; **ethisch** adj ethical

Etikett [eti'ket] (-(e)s, -e) nt label; tag; **~e** f
etiquette, manners pl

etliche ['etlɪçə] pron pl some, quite a few; **~s**
pron a thing or two

Etui [et'vi:] (-s, -s) nt case

etwa ['etva] adv (ungefähr) about; (vielleicht)
perhaps; (beispielsweise) for instance; **nicht ~**
by no means; **~ig** ['etvaɪç] adj possible

etwas pron something; anything; (ein wenig)
a little ♦ adv a little

euch [ɔʏç] pron (akk von **ihr**) you; yourselves
(dat von **ihr**) (to) you

euer ['ɔʏɐr] pron (gen von **ihr**) of you ♦ adj
your

Eule ['ɔʏlə] f owl

eure ['ɔʏrə] adj f siehe **euer**

eure(r, s) ['ɔʏrə(r, s)] pron yours; **~rseits**
adv on your part; **~s** adj nt siehe **euer**;
~sgleichen pron people like you; **~twegen**
adv (für euch) for your sakes; (wegen euch)
on your account; **~twillen** adv: **um
~twillen** = euretwegen

eurige ['ɔʏrɪgə] pron: **der/die/das ~** od **E~**
yours

Euro ['ɔʏro:] (-, -s) nt euro

Euro- zW: **~pa** [ɔʏ'ro:pa] nt Europe;
~päer(in) [ɔʏro'pɛ:ar(ɪn)] m(f) European;
e~päisch adj European; **~pameister**
[ɔʏ'ro:pa-] m European champion;
~paparlament nt European Parliament;
~scheck m (FIN) eurocheque

Euter ['ɔʏtɐr] (-s, -) nt udder

evakuieren [evaku'i:rən] vt to evacuate

evangelisch [evaŋ'ge:lɪʃ] adj Protestant

Evangelium [evaŋ'ge:liʊm] nt gospel

eventuell [eventu'el] adj possible ♦ adv
possibly, perhaps

evtl. abk = **eventuell**

EWG [e:ve:'ge:] (-) f abk (= Europäische
Wirtschaftsgemeinschaft) EEC, Common
Market

ewig ['e:vɪç] adj eternal; **E~keit** f eternity

EWU [e:ve:'lu:] f abk (= Europäische
Währungsunion) EMU

exakt [ɛ'ksakt] adj exact

Examen [ɛ'ksa:mən] (-s, - od **Examina**) nt
examination

Exemplar [ɛksɛm'pla:r] (-s, -e) nt specimen;
(Buchexemplar) copy; **e~isch** adj exemplary

Exil [ɛ'ksi:l] (-s, -e) nt exile

Existenz [ɛksɪs'tɛnts] f existence; (Unterhalt)
livelihood, living; (pej: Mensch) character;
~minimum (-s) nt subsistence level

existieren [ɛksɪs'ti:rən] vi to exist

exklusiv [ɛksklu'zi:f] adj exclusive; **~e** adv
exclusive of, not including ♦ präp +gen
exclusive of, not including

exotisch [ɛ'kso:tɪʃ] adj exotic

Expedition [ɛkspeditsi'o:n] f expedition

Experiment [ɛksperi'mɛnt] nt experiment;
e~ell [-'tɛl] adj experimental; **e~ieren**
[-'ti:rən] vi to experiment

Experte [ɛks'pɛrtə] (-n, -n) m expert,
specialist

Expertin f expert, specialist

explo- [ɛksplo] zW: **~dieren** [-'di:rən] vi to
explode; **E~sion** [-zi'o:n] f explosion; **~siv**
[-'zi:f] adj explosive

Export [ɛks'pɔrt] (-(e)s, -e) m export; **~eur**
[-'tø:r] m exporter; **~handel** m export trade;
e~ieren [-'ti:rən] vt to export; **~land** nt
exporting country

Express- ▲ [ɛks'prɛs] zW: **~gut** ▲ nt
express goods pl, express freight; **~zug** ▲
m express (train)

extra ['ɛkstra] adj inv (umg: gesondert)
separate; (besondere) extra ♦ adv (gesondert)
separately; (speziell) specially; (absichtlich)
on purpose; (vor Adjektiven, zusätzlich) extra;
E~ (-s, -s) nt extra; **E~ausgabe** f special
edition; **E~blatt** nt special edition

Extrakt [ɛks'trakt] (-(e)s, -e) m extract

extravagant [ɛkstrava'gant] adj extravagant

extrem [ɛks'tre:m] adj extreme; **~istisch**
[-'mɪstɪʃ] adj (POL) extremist; **E~itäten**
[-mi'te:tən] pl extremities

exzentrisch [ɛks'tsɛntrɪʃ] adj eccentric

EZ nt abk = **Einzelzimmer**

EZB f abk (= Europäische Zentralbank) ECB

F, f

Fa. abk (= Firma) firm; (in Briefen) Messrs

Fabel ['fa:bəl] (-, -n) f fable; **f~haft** adj
fabulous, marvellous

Fabrik [fa'bri:k] f factory; **~ant** [-'kant] m
(Hersteller) manufacturer; (Besitzer)
industrialist; **~arbeiter** m factory worker;
~at [-'ka:t] (-(e)s, -e) nt manufacture,
product; **~gelände** nt factory site

Fach [fax] (-(e)s, ̈er) nt compartment;
(Sachgebiet) subject; **ein Mann vom ~** an
expert; **~arbeiter** m skilled worker; **~arzt** m
(medical) specialist; **~ausdruck** m technical
term

Fächer ['fɛçər] (-s, -) m fan

Fach- zW: **~geschäft** nt specialist shop;
~hochschule f = technical college; **~kraft** f
skilled worker, trained employee; **f~kundig**

adj expert, specialist; **f~lich** *adj* professional; expert; **~mann** (*pl* **-leute**) *m* specialist; **f~männisch** *adj* professional; **~schule** *f* technical college; **f~simpeln** *vi* to talk shop; **~werk** *nt* timber frame

Fackel ['fakəl] (-, -n) *f* torch

fad(e) [faːt, 'faːdə] *adj* insipid; (*langweilig*) dull

Faden ['faːdən] (-s, :) *m* thread; **f~scheinig** *adj* (*auch fig*) threadbare

fähig ['fɛːɪç] *adj*: ~ (**zu** *od* +*gen*) capable (of); able (to); **F~keit** *f* ability

fahnden ['faːndən] *vi*: ~ **nach** to search for; **Fahndung** *f* search

Fahndungsliste *f* list of wanted criminals, wanted list

Fahne ['faːnə] *f* flag, standard; **eine ~ haben** (*umg*) to smell of drink; **~nflucht** *f* desertion

Fahr- *zW*: **~ausweis** *m* ticket; **~bahn** *f* carriageway (*BRIT*), roadway

Fähre ['fɛːrə] *f* ferry

fahren ['faːrən] (*unreg*) *vt* to drive; (*RAD*) to ride; (*befördern*) to drive, to take; (*Rennen*) to drive in ♦ *vi* (*sich bewegen*) to go; (*Schiff*) to sail; (*abfahren*) to leave; **mit dem Auto/ Zug ~** to go *od* travel by car/train; **mit der Hand ~ über** +*akk* to pass one's hand over

Fahr- *zW*: **~er(in)** (-s, -) *m(f)* driver; **~erflucht** *f* hit-and-run; **~gast** *m* passenger; **~geld** *nt* fare; **~karte** *f* ticket; **~kartenausgabe** *f* ticket office; **~kartenautomat** *m* ticket machine; **~kartenschalter** *m* ticket office; **f~lässig** *adj* negligent; **f~lässige Tötung** *f* manslaughter; **~lehrer** *m* driving instructor; **~plan** *m* timetable; **f~planmäßig** *adj* scheduled; **~preis** *m* fare; **~prüfung** *f* driving test; **~rad** *nt* bicycle; **~radweg** *m* cycle lane; **~schein** *m* ticket; **~scheinentwerter** *m* (automatic) ticket stamping machine

Fährschiff ['fɛːrʃɪf] *nt* ferry(boat)

Fahr- *zW*: **~schule** *f* driving school; **~spur** *f* lane; **~stuhl** *m* lift (*BRIT*), elevator (*US*)

Fahrt [faːrt] (-, -en) *f* journey; (*kurz*) trip; (*AUT*) drive; (*Geschwindigkeit*) speed; **gute ~!** I have a good journey!

Fährte ['fɛːrtə] *f* track, trail

Fahrt- *zW*: **~kosten** *pl* travelling expenses; **~richtung** *f* course, direction

Fahrzeit *f* time for the journey

Fahrzeug *nt* vehicle; **~brief** *m* logbook; **~papiere** *pl* vehicle documents

fair [fɛːr] *adj* fair

Fakt [fakt] (-(e)s, -en) *m* fact

Faktor ['faktɔr] *m* factor

Fakultät [fakʊl'tɛːt] *f* faculty

Falke ['falkə] (-n, -n) *m* falcon

Fall [fal] (-(e)s, :e) *m* (*Sturz*) fall; (*Sachverhalt*: *JUR*, *GRAM*) case; **auf jeden ~, auf alle Fälle**

in any case; (*bestimmt*) definitely; **auf keinen ~!** no way!

Falle *f* trap

fallen (*unreg*) *vi* to fall; **etw ~ lassen** to drop sth; (*Bemerkung*) to make sth; (*Plan*) to abandon sth, to drop sth

fällen ['fɛlən] *vt* (*Baum*) to fell; (*Urteil*) to pass

fällig ['fɛlɪç] *adj* due

falls [fals] *adv* in case, if

Fallschirm *m* parachute; **~springer** *m* parachutist

falsch [falʃ] *adj* false; (*unrichtig*) wrong

fälschen ['fɛlʃən] *vt* to forge

fälsch- *zW*: **~lich** *adj* false; **~licherweise** *adv* mistakenly; **F~ung** *f* forgery

Falte ['faltə] *f* (*Knick*) fold, crease; (*Hautfalte*) wrinkle; (*Rockfalte*) pleat; **f~n** *vt* to fold; (*Stirn*) to wrinkle

faltig ['faltɪç] *adj* (*Hände, Haut*) wrinkled; (*zerknittert*: *Rock*) creased

familiär [famɪliˈɛːr] *adj* familiar

Familie [faˈmiːliə] *f* family

Familien- *zW*: **~betrieb** *m* family business; **~kreis** *m* family circle; **~mitglied** *nt* member of the family; **~name** *m* surname; **~stand** *m* marital status

Fanatiker [faˈnaːtikər] (-s, -) *m* fanatic; **fanatisch** *adj* fanatical

fand *etc* [fant] *vb siehe* **finden**

Fang [faŋ] (-(e)s, :e) *m* catch; (*Jagen*) hunting; (*Kralle*) talon, claw; **f~en** (*unreg*) *vt* to catch ♦ *vr* to get caught; (*Flugzeug*) to level out; (*Mensch: nicht fallen*) to steady o.s.; (*fig*) to compose o.s.; (*in Leistung*) to get back on form

Fantasie ▲ [fanta'ziː] *f* imagination; **f~los** ▲ *adj* unimaginative; **f~ren** ▲ *vi* to fantasize; **f~voll** ▲ *adj* imaginative

fantastisch ▲ [fan'tastɪʃ] *adj* fantastic

Farb- ['farb] *zW*: **~abzug** *m* colour print; **~aufnahme** *f* colour photograph; **~band** *nt* typewriter ribbon; **~e** *f* colour; (*zum Malen etc*) paint; (*Stoffarbe*) dye; **f~echt** *adj* colourfast

färben ['fɛrbən] *vt* to colour; (*Stoff, Haar*) to dye

farben- ['farbən] *zW*: **~blind** *adj* colour-blind; **~freudig** *adj* colourful; **~froh** *adj* colourful, gay

Farb- *zW*: **~fernsehen** *nt* colour television; **~film** *m* colour film; **~foto** *nt* colour photograph; **f~ig** *adj* coloured; **~ige(r)** *f(m)* coloured (person); **~kasten** *m* paintbox; **f~lich** *adj* colour; **f~los** *adj* colourless; **~stift** *m* coloured pencil; **~stoff** *m* dye; **~ton** *m* hue, tone

Färbung ['fɛrbʊŋ] *f* colouring; (*Tendenz*) bias

Farn [farn] (-(e)s, -e) *m* fern; bracken

Fasan [fa'za:n] (-(e)s, -e(n)) *m* pheasant
Fasching ['faʃɪŋ] (-s, -e *od* -s) *m* carnival
Faschismus [fa'ʃɪsmʊs] *m* fascism
Faschist *m* fascist
Faser ['fa:zər] (-, -n) *f* fibre; **f~n** *vi* to fray
Fass ▲ [fas] (-es, ͡er) *nt* vat, barrel; (*für Öl*) drum; **Bier vom ~** draught beer
Fassade [fa'sa:də] *f* façade
fassen ['fasən] *vt* (*ergreifen*) to grasp, to take; (*inhaltlich*) to hold; (*Entschluss etc*) to take; (*verstehen*) to understand; (*Ring etc*) to set; (*formulieren*) to formulate, to phrase ♦ *vr* to calm down; **nicht zu ~** unbelievable
Fassung ['fasʊŋ] *f* (*Umrahmung*) mounting; (*Lampenfassung*) socket; (*Wortlaut*) version; (*Beherrschung*) composure; **jdn aus der ~ bringen** to upset sb; **f~slos** *adj* speechless
fast [fast] *adv* almost, nearly
fasten ['fastən] *vi* to fast; **F~zeit** *f* Lent
Fastnacht *f* Shrove Tuesday; carnival
faszinieren [fastsi'ni:rən] *vt* to fascinate
fatal [fa'ta:l] *adj* fatal; (*peinlich*) embarrassing
faul [faʊl] *adj* rotten; (*Person*) lazy; (*Ausreden*) lame; **daran ist etwas ~** there's something fishy about it; **~en** *vi* to rot; **~enzen** *vi* to idle; **F~enzer** (-s, -) *m* idler, loafer; **F~heit** *f* laziness; **~ig** *adj* putrid
Faust ['faʊst] (-, Fäuste) *f* fist; **auf eigene ~** off one's own bat; **~handschuh** *m* mitten
Favorit [favo'ri:t] (-en, -en) *m* favourite
Fax [faks] (-, -(e)) *nt* fax
faxen ['faksən] *vt* to fax; **jdm etw ~** to fax sth to sb
FCKW *m abk* (= *Fluorchlorkohlenwasserstoff*) CFC
Februar ['fe:brua:r] (-(s), -e) *m* February
fechten ['fɛçtən] (*unreg*) *vi* to fence
Feder ['fe:dər] (-, -n) *f* feather; (*Schreibfeder*) pen nib; (*TECH*) spring; **~ball** *m* shuttlecock; **~bett** *nt* continental quilt; **~halter** *m* penholder, pen; **f~leicht** *adj* light as a feather; **f~n** *vi* (*nachgeben*) to be springy; (*sich bewegen*) to bounce ♦ *vt* to spring; **~ung** *f* (*AUT*) suspension
Fee [fe:] *f* fairy
fegen ['fe:gən] *vt* to sweep
fehl [fe:l] *adj*: **~ am Platz** *od* **Ort** out of place; **F~betrag** *m* deficit; **~en** *vi* to be wanting *od* missing; (*abwesend sein*) to be absent; **etw ~t jdm** sb lacks sth; **du ~st mir** I miss you; **was ~t ihm?** what's wrong with him?; **F~er** (-s, -) *m* mistake, error; (*Mangel, Schwäche*) fault; **~erfrei** *adj* faultless; without any mistakes; **~erhaft** *adj* incorrect; faulty; **~erlos** *adj* flawless, perfect; **F~geburt** *f* miscarriage; **~gehen** (*unreg*) *vi* to go astray; **F~griff** *m* blunder; **F~konstruktion** *f* badly designed thing; **~schlagen** (*unreg*) *vi* to fail; **F~start** *m* (*SPORT*) false start; **F~zündung** *f* (*AUT*) misfire, backfire

Feier ['faɪər] (-, -n) *f* celebration; **~abend** *m* time to stop work; **~abend machen** to stop, to knock off; **jetzt ist ~abend!** that's enough!; **f~lich** *adj* solemn; **~lichkeit** *f* solemnity; **~lichkeiten** *pl* (*Veranstaltungen*) festivities; **f~n** *vt*, *vi* to celebrate; **~tag** *m* holiday
feig(e) [faɪk, 'faɪgə] *adj* cowardly
Feige ['faɪgə] *f* fig
Feigheit *f* cowardice
Feigling *m* coward
Feile ['faɪlə] *f* file
feilschen ['faɪlʃən] *vi* to haggle
fein [faɪn] *adj* fine; (*vornehm*) refined; (*Gehör etc*) keen; **~!** great!
Feind [faɪnt] (-(e)s, -e) *m* enemy; **f~lich** *adj* hostile; **~schaft** *f* enmity; **f~selig** *adj* hostile
Fein- *zW*: **f~fühlig** *adj* sensitive; **~gefühl** *nt* delicacy, tact; **~heit** *f* fineness; refinement; keenness; **~kostgeschäft** *nt* delicatessen (shop); **~schmecker** (-s, -) *m* gourmet; **~wäsche** *f* delicate clothing (*when washing*); **~waschmittel** *nt* mild detergent
Feld [fɛlt] (-(e)s, -er) *nt* field; (*SCHACH*) square; (*SPORT*) pitch; **~herr** *m* commander; **~stecher** (-s, -) *m* binoculars *pl*; **~weg** *m* path; **~zug** *m* (*fig*) campaign
Felge ['fɛlgə] *f* (wheel) rim
Fell [fɛl] (-(e)s, -e) *nt* fur; coat; (*von Schaf*) fleece; (*von toten Tieren*) skin
Fels [fɛls] (-en, -en) *m* rock; (*Klippe*) cliff
Felsen ['fɛlzən] (-s, -) *m* = **Fels**; **f~fest** *adj* firm
feminin [femi'ni:n] *adj* feminine
Fenster ['fɛnstər] (-s, -) *nt* window; **~bank** *f* windowsill; **~laden** *m* shutter; **~leder** *nt* chamois (leather); **~scheibe** *f* windowpane
Ferien ['fe:rɪən] *pl* holidays, vacation *sg* (*US*); **~ haben** to be on holiday; **~bungalow** [-bʊŋgalo] (-s, -s) *m* holiday bungalow; **~haus** *nt* holiday home; **~kurs** *m* holiday course; **~lager** *nt* holiday camp; **~reise** *f* holiday; **~wohnung** *f* holiday apartment
Ferkel ['fɛrkəl] (-s, -) *nt* piglet
fern [fɛrn] *adj, adv* far-off, distant; **~ von hier** a long way (away) from here; **der F~e Osten** the Far East; **~ halten** to keep away; **F~bedienung** *f* remote control; **F~e** *f* distance; **~er** *adj* further ♦ *adv* further; (*weiterhin*) in future; **F~gespräch** *nt* trunk call; **F~glas** *nt* binoculars *pl*; **F~licht** *nt* (*AUT*) full beam; **F~rohr** *nt* telescope; **F~ruf** *m* (*förmlich*) telephone number; **F~schreiben** *nt* telex; **F~sehapparat** *m* television set; **F~sehen** (-s) *nt* television; **im F~sehen** on television; **~sehen** (*unreg*) *vi* to watch television; **F~seher** *m* television; **F~sehturm** *m* television tower; **F~sprecher** *m* telephone; **F~steuerung** *f* remote control; **F~straße** *f* = A road (*BRIT*), highway (*US*); **F~verkehr** *m* long-

distance traffic

Ferse |'ferzə| f heel

fertig |'fertıç| adj (bereit) ready; (beendet) finished; (gebrauchsfertig) ready-made; ~ **bringen** (fähig sein) to be capable of ; ~ **machen** (beenden) to finish; (umg: Person) to finish; (: körperlich) to exhaust; (: moralisch) to get down; **sich ~ machen** to get ready ♦ **fertig stellen** to complete; **F~gericht** nt precooked meal; **F~haus** nt kit house, prefab; **F~keit** f skill

Fessel |'fesəl| (-, -n) f fetter; **f~n** vt to bind; (mit ~n) to fetter; (fig) to spellbind; **f~nd** adj fascinating, captivating

Fest |-(e)s, -e| nt party; festival; **frohes ~!** Happy Christmas!

fest |fest| adj firm; (Nahrung) solid; (Gehalt) regular; **~e Kosten** fixed cost ♦ adv (schlafen) soundly; ~ **angestellt** permanently employed; ~ **halten** to seize, to hold fast; **~binden** (unreg) vt to tie, to fasten; **~bleiben** (unreg) vi to stand firm; **F~essen** nt banquet; **~halten** (unreg) vt (Ereignis) to record ♦ vr: **sich ~halten (an** +dat) to hold on (to); **~igen** vt to strengthen; **F~igkeit** f strength; **F~ival** |'festival| (-s, -s) nt festival; **F~land** nt mainland; **~legen** vt to fix ♦ vr to commit o.s.; **~lich** adj festive; **~liegen** (unreg) vi (~stehen: Termin) to be confirmed, be fixed; **~machen** vt to fasten; (Termin etc) to fix; **F~nahme** f arrest; **~nehmen** (unreg) vt to arrest; **F~preis** m (COMM) fixed price; **F~rede** f address; **~setzen** vt to fix, to settle; **F~spiele** pl (Veranstaltung) festival sg; **~stehen** (unreg) vi to be certain; **~stellen** vt to establish; (sagen) to remark; **F~tag** m feast day, holiday; **F~ung** f fortress; **F~wochen** pl festival

Fett |fet| (-(e)s, -e) nt fat, grease

fett adj fat; (Essen etc) greasy; (TYP) bold; **~arm** adj low fat; **~en** vt to grease; **F~fleck** m grease stain; **~ig** adj greasy, fatty

Fetzen |'fetsən| (-s, -) m scrap

feucht |fɔyçt| adj damp; (Luft) humid; **F~igkeit** f dampness; humidity; **F~igkeitscreme** f moisturizing cream

Feuer |'fɔyər| (-s, -) nt fire; (zum Rauchen) a light; (fig: Schwung) spirit; **~alarm** m fire alarm; **f~fest** adj fireproof; **~gefahr** f danger of fire; **f~gefährlich** adj inflammable; **~leiter** f fire escape ladder; **~löscher** (-s, -) m fire extinguisher; **~melder** (-s, -) m fire alarm; **f~n** vt, vi (auch fig) to fire; **~stein** m flint; **~treppe** f fire escape; **~wehr** (-, -en) f fire brigade; **~wehrauto** nt fire engine; **~wehrmann** m fireman; **~werk** nt fireworks pl; **~zeug** nt (cigarette) lighter

Fichte |'fıçtə| f spruce, pine

Fieber |'fi:bər| (-s, -) nt fever, temperature; **f~haft** adj feverish; **~thermometer** nt thermometer; **fiebrig** adj (Erkältung) feverish

fiel etc |fi:l| vb siehe **fallen**

fies |fi:s| (umg) adj nasty

Figur |fi'gu:r| (-, -en) f figure; (Schachfigur) chessman, chess piece

Filet |fi'le:| (-s, -s) nt (KOCH) fillet

Filiale |fili'a:lə| f (COMM) branch

Film |film| (-(e)s, -e) m film; **~aufnahme** f shooting; **f~en** vt, vi to film; **~kamera** f cine camera

Filter |'fıltər| (-s, -) m filter; **f~n** vt to filter; **~papier** nt filter paper; **~zigarette** f tipped cigarette

Filz |fılts| (-es, -e) m felt; **f~en** vt (umg) to frisk ♦ vi (Wolle) to mat; **~stift** m felt-tip pen

Finale |fi'na:lə| (-s, -(s)) nt finale; (SPORT) final(s)

Finanz |fi'nants| f finance; **~amt** nt Inland Revenue office; **~beamte(r)** m revenue officer; **f~iell** |-'tsi̯el| adj financial; **f~ieren** |-'tsi:rən| vt to finance; **f~kräftig** adj financially strong; **~minister** m Chancellor of the Exchequer (BRIT), Minister of Finance

Find- |find| zW: **f~en** (unreg) vt to find; (meinen) to think ♦ vr to be (found); (sich fassen) to compose o.s.; **ich f~e nichts dabei, wenn ...** I don't see what's wrong if ...; **das wird sich f~en** things will work out; **~er** (-s, -) m finder; **~erlohn** m reward (for sb who finds sth); **f~ig** adj resourceful

fing etc |fıŋ| vb siehe **fangen**

Finger |'fıŋər| (-s, -) m finger; **~abdruck** m fingerprint; **~nagel** m fingernail; **~spitze** f fingertip

fingiert adj made-up, fictitious

Fink |fıŋk| (-en, -en) m finch

Finn- |fın| zW: **~e** (-n, -n) m Finn; **~in** f Finn; **f~isch** adj Finnish; **~land** nt Finland

finster |'fınstər| adj dark, gloomy; (verdächtig) dubious; (verdrossen) grim; (Gedanke) dark; **F~nis** (-) f darkness, gloom

Firma |'fırma| (-, -men) f firm

Firmen- |'fırmən| zW: **~inhaber** m owner of firm; **~schild** nt (shop) sign; **~wagen** m company car; **~zeichen** nt trademark

Fisch |fıʃ| (-(e)s, -e) m fish; **~e** pl (ASTROL) Pisces sg; **f~en** vt, vi to fish; **~er** (-s, -) m fisherman; **~erei** f fishing, fishery; **~fang** m fishing; **~geschäft** nt fishmonger's (shop); **~gräte** f fishbone; **~stäbchen** |-ʃtɛːpçən| nt fish finger (BRIT), fish stick (US)

fit |fıt| adj fit; **F~ness** ▲ (-, -) f (physical) fitness

fix |fıks| adj fixed; (Person) alert, smart; ~ **und fertig** finished; (erschöpft) done in; **F~er(in)** m(f) (umg) junkie; **F~erstube** f (umg) junkie's centre; **~ieren** |fɪˈksiːrən| *vt* to fix; (*anstarren*) to stare at

flach |flax| *adj* flat; (*Gefäß*) shallow

Fläche |ˈflɛçə| *f* area; (*Oberfläche*) surface

Flachland *nt* lowland

flackern |ˈflakərn| *vi* to flare, to flicker

Flagge |ˈflagə| *f* flag; **f~n** *vi* to fly a flag

flämisch |ˈflɛːmɪʃ| *adj* (*LING*) Flemish

Flamme |ˈflamə| *f* flame

Flandern |ˈflandərn| *nt* Flanders

Flanke |ˈflankə| *f* flank; (*SPORT: Seite*) wing

Flasche |ˈflaʃə| *f* bottle; (*umg: Versager*) wash-out

Flaschen- *zW:* **~bier** *nt* bottled beer; **~öffner** *m* bottle opener; **~zug** *m* pulley

flatterhaft *adj* flighty, fickle

flattern |ˈflatərn| *vi* to flutter

flau |flaʊ| *adj* weak, listless; (*Nachfrage*) slack; **jdm ist ~** sb feels queasy

Flaum |flaʊm| (-(e)s) *m* (*Feder*) down; (*Haare*) fluff

flauschig |ˈflaʊʃɪç| *adj* fluffy

Flaute |ˈflaʊtə| *f* calm; (*COMM*) recession

Flechte |ˈflɛçtə| *f* plait; (*MED*) dry scab; (*BOT*) lichen; **f~n** (*unreg*) *vt* to plait; (*Kranz*) to twine

Fleck |flɛk| (-(e)s, -e) *m* spot; (*Schmutzfleck*) stain; (*Stofffleck*) patch; (*Makel*) blemish; **nicht vom ~ kommen** (*auch fig*) not to get any further; **vom ~ weg** straight away

Flecken (-s, -) *m* = **Fleck**; **f~los** *adj* spotless; **~mittel** *nt* stain remover; **~wasser** *nt* stain remover

fleckig *adj* spotted; stained

Fledermaus |ˈfleːdərmaʊs| *f* bat

Flegel |ˈfleːgəl| (-s, -) *m* (*Mensch*) lout; **f~haft** *adj* loutish, unmannerly; **~jahre** *pl* adolescence *sg*

flehen |ˈfleːən| *vi* to implore; **~tlich** *adj* imploring

Fleisch |ˈflaɪʃ| (-(e)s) *nt* flesh; (*Essen*) meat; **~brühe** *f* beef tea, meat stock; **~er** (-s, -) *m* butcher; **~erei** *f* butcher's (shop); **f~ig** *adj* fleshy; **f~los** *adj* meatless, vegetarian

Fleiß |ˈflaɪs| (-es) *m* diligence, industry; **f~ig** *adj* diligent, industrious

fletschen |ˈflɛtʃən| *vt* (*Zähne*) to show

flexibel |flɛˈksiːbəl| *adj* flexible

Flicken |ˈflɪkən| (-s, -) *m* patch; **f~** *vt* to mend

Flieder |ˈfliːdər| (-s, -) *m* lilac

Fliege |ˈfliːgə| *f* fly; (*Kleidung*) bow tie; **f~n** (*unreg*) *vt, vi* to fly; **auf jdn/etw f~n** (*umg*) to be mad about sb/sth; **~npilz** *m* toadstool; **~r** (-s, -) *m* flier, airman

fliehen |ˈfliːən| (*unreg*) *vi* to flee

Fliese |ˈfliːzə| *f* tile

Fließ- |ˈfliːs| *zW:* **~band** *nt* production *od* assembly line; **f~en** (*unreg*) *vi* to flow; **f~end** *adj* flowing; (*Rede, Deutsch*) fluent; (*Übergänge*) smooth

flimmern |ˈflɪmərn| *vi* to glimmer

flink |flɪŋk| *adj* nimble, lively

Flinte |ˈflɪntə| *f* rifle; shotgun

Flitterwochen *pl* honeymoon *sg*

flitzen |ˈflɪtsən| *vi* to flit

Flocke |ˈflɔkə| *f* flake

flog *etc* |floːk| *vb siehe* **fliegen**

Floh |floː| (-(e)s, ꞏe) *m* flea; **~markt** *m* flea market

florieren |floˈriːrən| *vi* to flourish

Floskel |ˈflɔskəl| (-, -n) *f* set phrase

Floß |floːs| (-es, ꞏe) *nt* raft, float

floss *etc* ▲ *vb siehe* **fließen**

Flosse |ˈflɔsə| *f* fin

Flöte |ˈfløːtə| *f* flute; (*Blockflöte*) recorder

flott |flɔt| *adj* lively; (*elegant*) smart; (*NAUT*) afloat; **F~e** *f* fleet, navy

Fluch |fluːx| (-(e)s, ꞏe) *m* curse; **f~en** *vi* to curse, to swear

Flucht |fluxt| (-, -en) *f* flight; (*Fensterflucht*) row; (*Zimmerflucht*) suite; **f~artig** *adj* hasty

flücht- |ˈflʏçt| *zW:* **~en** *vi, vr* to flee, to escape; **~ig** *adj* fugitive; (*vergänglich*) transitory; (*oberflächlich*) superficial; (*eilig*) fleeting; **F~igkeitsfehler** *m* careless slip; **F~ling** *m* fugitive, refugee

Flug |fluːk| (-(e)s, ꞏe) *m* flight; **~blatt** *nt* pamphlet

Flügel |ˈflyːgəl| (-s, -) *m* wing; (*MUS*) grand piano

Fluggast *m* airline passenger

Flug- *zW:* **~gesellschaft** *f* airline (company); **~hafen** *m* airport; **~lärm** *m* aircraft noise; **~linie** *f* airline; **~plan** *m* flight schedule; **~platz** *m* airport; (*klein*) airfield; **~reise** *f* flight; **~schein** *m* (*Ticket*) plane ticket; (*Pilotenschein*) pilot's licence; **~steig** [-staɪk] (-(e)s, -e) *m* gate; **~verbindung** *f* air connection; **~verkehr** *m* air traffic; **~zeug** *nt* (*aero*)plane, airplane (*US*); **~zeugentführung** *f* hijacking of a plane; **~zeughalle** *f* hangar; **~zeugträger** *m* aircraft carrier

Flunder |ˈflʊndər| (-, -n) *f* flounder

flunkern |ˈflʊŋkərn| *vi* to fib, to tell stories

Fluor |ˈfluːɔr| (-s) *nt* fluorine

Flur |fluːr| (-(e)s, -e) *m* hall; (*Treppenflur*) staircase

Fluss ▲ |flʊs| (-es, ꞏe) *m* river; (*Fließen*) flow

flüssig |ˈflʏsɪç| *adj* liquid; **~ machen** (*Geld*) to make available; **F~keit** *f* liquid; (*Zustand*) liquidity

flüstern |ˈflʏstərn| *vt, vi* to whisper

Flut |fluːt| (-, -en) *f* (*auch fig*) flood; (*Gezeiten*) high tide; **f~en** *vi* to flood; **~licht** *nt* floodlight

Fohlen |ˈfoːlən| (-s, -) *nt* foal

Föhn |føːn| (-(e)s, -e) *m* (*warmer Fallwind*) föhn; (*Haartrockner*) hair-dryer

föhnen ▲ *vt* to (blow-)dry

Folge |ˈfɔlgə| *f* series, sequence; (*Fortsetzung*)

instalment; (*Auswirkung*) result; **in rascher ~** in quick succession; **etw zur ~ haben** to result in sth; **~n haben** to have consequences; **einer Sache** *dat* **~ leisten** to comply with sth; **f~n** *vi* +*dat* to follow; (*gehorchen*) to obey; **jdm f~n können** (*fig*) to follow *od* understand sb; **f~nd** *adj* following; **f~ndermaßen** *adv* as follows, in the following way; **f~rn** *vt*: **f~rn (aus)** to conclude (from); **~rung** *f* conclusion

folglich ['fɔlklɪç] *adv* consequently

folgsam ['fɔlkza:m] *adj* obedient

Folie ['fo:liə] *f* foil

Folklore ['fɔlklo:ər] *f* folklore

Folter ['fɔltər] (-, -n) *f* torture; (*Gerät*) rack; **f~n** *vt* to torture

Fön ® [fø:n] (-(e)s, -e) *m* hair-dryer

Fondue [fõdy:] (-s, -s *od* -, -s) *nt od f* (*KOCH*) fondue

fönen △ *vt siehe* **Föhnen**

Fontäne [fɔn'tɛ:nə] *f* fountain

Förder- ['fœrdər] *zW*: **~band** *nt* conveyor belt; **~korb** *m* pit cage; **f~lich** *adj* beneficial

fordern ['fɔrdərn] *vt* to demand

fördern ['fœrdərn] *vt* to promote; (*unterstützen*) to help; (*Kohle*) to extract

Forderung ['fɔrdərʊŋ] *f* demand

Förderung ['fœrdərʊŋ] *f* promotion; help; extraction

Forelle [fo'rɛlə] *f* trout

Form [fɔrm] (-, -en) *f* shape; (*Gestaltung*) form; (*Gussform*) mould; (*Backform*) baking tin; **in ~ sein** to be in good form *od* shape; **in ~ von** in the shape of

Formalität *f* formality

Format [fɔr'ma:t] (-(e)s, -e) *nt* format; (*fig*) distinction

formbar *adj* malleable

Formblatt *nt* form

Formel (-, -n) *f* formula

formell [fɔr'mɛl] *adj* formal

formen *vt* to form, to shape

Formfehler *m* faux pas, gaffe; (*JUR*) irregularity

formieren [fɔr'mi:rən] *vt* to form ♦ *vr* to form up

förmlich ['fœrmlɪç] *adj* formal; (*umg*) real; **F~keit** *f* formality

formlos *adj* shapeless; (*Benehmen etc*) informal

Formular [fɔrmu'la:r] (-s, -e) *nt* form

formulieren [fɔrmu'li:rən] *vt* to formulate

forsch [fɔrʃ] *adj* energetic, vigorous

forsch- *zW*: **~en** *vi*: **~en (nach)** to search (for); (*wissenschaftlich*) to (do) research (into); **~end** *adj* searching; **F~er** (-s, -) *m* research scientist; (*Naturforscher*) explorer; **F~ung** *f* research

Forst [fɔrst] (-(e)s, -e) *m* forest

Förster ['fœrstər] (-s, -) *m* forester; (*für Wild*) gamekeeper

fort [fɔrt] *adv* away; (*verschwunden*) gone; (*vorwärts*) on; **und so ~** and so on; **in einem ~** on and on; **~bestehen** (*unreg*) *vi* to survive; **~bewegen** *vt*, *vr* to move away; **~bilden** *vr* to continue one's education; **~bleiben** (*unreg*) *vi* to stay away; **F~dauer** *f* continuance; **~fahren** (*unreg*) *vi* to depart; (*-setzen*) to go on, to continue; **~führen** *vt* to continue, to carry on; **~gehen** (*unreg*) *vi* to go away; **~geschritten** *adj* advanced; **~pflanzen** *vr* to reproduce; **F~pflanzung** *f* reproduction

fort- *zW*: **~schaffen** *vt* to remove; **~schreiten** (*unreg*) *vi* to advance

Fortschritt ['fɔrtʃrɪt] *m* advance; **~e machen** to make progress; **f~lich** *adj* progressive

fort- *zW*: **~setzen** *vt* to continue; **F~setzung** *f* continuation; (*folgender Teil*) instalment; **F~setzung folgt** to be continued; **~während** *adj* incessant, continual

Foto ['fo:to] (-s, -s) *nt* photo(graph); **~apparat** *m* camera; **~'graf** *m* photographer; **~gra'fie** *f* photography; (*Bild*) photograph; **f~gra'fieren** *vt* to photograph ♦ *vi* to take photographs; **~kopie** *f* photocopy

Fr. *abk* (= *Frau*) Mrs, Ms

Fracht [fraxt] (-, -en) *f* freight; (*NAUT*) cargo; (*Preis*) carriage; **~ zahlt Empfänger** (*COMM*) carriage forward; **~er** (-s, -) *m* freighter, cargo boat; **~gut** *nt* freight

Frack [frak] (-(e)s, ᵉe) *m* tails *pl*

Frage ['fra:gə] (-, -n) *f* question; **jdm eine ~ stellen** to ask sb a question, to put a question to sb; *siehe* **infrage**; **~bogen** *m* questionnaire; **f~n** *vt*, *vi* to ask; **~zeichen** *nt* question mark

fraglich *adj* questionable, doubtful

fraglos *adv* unquestionably

Fragment [fra'gmɛnt] *nt* fragment

fragwürdig ['fra:kvʏrdɪç] *adj* questionable, dubious

Fraktion [fraktsi'o:n] *f* parliamentary party

frankieren [fraŋ'ki:rən] *vt* to stamp, to frank

franko ['fraŋko] *adv* post-paid; carriage paid

Frankreich ['fraŋkraɪç] (-s) *nt* France

Franzose [fran'tso:zə] *m* Frenchman; **Französin** [fran'tsø:zɪn] *f* Frenchwoman; **französisch** *adj* French

fraß *etc* [fra:s] *vb siehe* **fressen**

Fratze ['fratsə] *f* grimace

Frau [fraʊ] (-, -en) *f* woman; (*Ehefrau*) wife; (*Anrede*) Mrs, Ms; **~ Doktor** Doctor

Frauen- *zW*: **~arzt** *m* gynaecologist; **~bewegung** *f* feminist movement; **~haus** *nt* women's refuge; **~zimmer** *nt* female, broad (US)

Fräulein |'frɔylaɪn| nt young lady; (Anrede) Miss, Ms

fraulich |'fraʊlɪç| adj womanly

frech |frɛç| adj cheeky, impudent; **F~heit** f cheek, impudence

frei |fraɪ| adj free; (Stelle, Sitzplatz) free, vacant; (Mitarbeiter) freelance; (unbekleidet) bare; **von etw ~ sein** to be free of sth; **im F~en** in the open air; **~ sprechen** to talk without notes; **~ Haus** (COMM) carriage paid; **~er Wettbewerb** (COMM) fair/open competition; **F~bad** nt open-air swimming pool; **~bekommen** (unreg) vt: **einen Tag ~bekommen** to get a day off; **~beruflich** adj self-employed; **~gebig** adj generous; **~halten** (unreg) vt to keep free; **~händig** adv (fahren) with no hands; **F~heit** f freedom; **~heitlich** adj liberal; **F~heitsstrafe** f prison sentence; **F~karte** f free ticket; **~lassen** (unreg) vt to (set) free; **~legen** vt to expose; **~lich** adv certainly, admittedly; **ja ~lich** yes of course; **F~lichtbühne** f open-air theatre; **F~lichtmuseum** nt open-air museum; **~machen** vt (Post) to frank ♦ vr to arrange to be free; (entkleiden) to undress; **Tage ~machen** to take days off; **~ nehmen** ▲ (unreg) vt: **sich dat einen Tag ~ nehmen** to take a day off; **~sprechen** (unreg) vt: **~sprechen (von)** to acquit (of); **F~spruch** m acquittal; **~stehen** (unreg) vi (leer stehen: Wohnung, Haus) to lie/stand empty; **es steht dir ~, das zu tun** you're free to do that; **~stellen** vt: **jdm etw ~stellen** to leave sth (up) to sb; **F~stoß** m free kick

Freitag m Friday; **~s** adv on Fridays

frei- zW: **~willig** adj voluntary; **F~zeit** f spare od free time; **F~zeitpark** m amusement park; **F~zeitzentrum** nt leisure centre; **~zügig** adj liberal, broad-minded; (mit Geld) generous

fremd |frɛmt| adj (unvertraut) strange; (ausländisch) foreign; (nicht eigen) someone else's; **etw ist jdm ~** sth is foreign to sb; **~artig** adj strange; **F~enführer** |'frɛmdən-| m (tourist) guide; **F~enverkehr** m tourism; **F~enverkehrsamt** nt tourist board; **F~enzimmer** nt guest room; **F~körper** m foreign body; **~ländisch** adj foreign; **F~sprache** f foreign language; **F~wort** nt foreign word

Frequenz |fre'kvɛnts| f (RAD) frequency

fressen |'frɛsən| (unreg) vt, vi to eat

Freude |'frɔydə| f joy, delight

freudig adj joyful, happy

freuen |'frɔyən| vt unpers to make happy od pleased ♦ vr to be glad od happy; **freut mich!** pleased to meet you; **sich auf etw** akk **~** to look forward to sth; **sich über etw** akk **~** to be pleased about sth

Freund |'frɔynt| (-(e)s, -e) m friend; boyfriend; **~in** |-dɪn| f friend; girlfriend; **f~lich** adj kind, friendly; **f~licherweise** adv kindly; **~lichkeit** f friendliness, kindness; **~schaft** f friendship; **f~schaftlich** adj friendly

Frieden |'fri:dən| (-s, -) m peace; **im ~** in peacetime

Friedens- zW: **~schluss** ▲ m peace agreement; **~vertrag** m peace treaty; **~zeit** f peacetime

fried- |'fri:t| zW: **~fertig** adj peaceable; **F~hof** m cemetery; **~lich** adj peaceful

frieren |'fri:rən| (unreg) vt, vi to freeze; **ich friere, es friert mich** I'm freezing, I'm cold

Frikadelle |frika'dɛlə| f rissole

Frikassee |frika'se:| (-s, -s) nt (KOCH) fricassee

frisch |frɪʃ| adj fresh; (lebhaft) lively; **~ gestrichen!** wet paint!; **sich ~ machen** to freshen (o.s.) up; **F~e** f freshness; liveliness; **F~haltefolie** f cling film

Friseur |fri'zøːr| m hairdresser

Friseuse |fri'zøːzə| f hairdresser

frisieren |fri'zi:rən| vt to do (one's hair); (fig: Abrechnung) to fiddle, to doctor ♦ vr to do one's hair

Frisiersalon m hairdressing salon

frisst etc ▲ |frɪst| vb siehe **fressen**

Frist |frɪst| (-, -en) f period; (Termin) deadline; **f~gerecht** adj within the stipulated time od period; **f~los** adj (Entlassung) instant

Frisur |fri'zu:r| f hairdo, hairstyle

frivol |fri'vo:l| adj frivolous

froh |fro:| adj happy, cheerful; **ich bin ~, dass ...** I'm glad that ...

fröhlich |'frøːlɪç| adj merry, happy; **F~keit** f merriness, gaiety

fromm |frɔm| adj pious, good; (Wunsch) idle; **Frömmigkeit** |'frœmɪçkaɪt| f piety

Fronleichnam |fro:n'laɪçna:m| (-(e)s) m Corpus Christi

Front |frɔnt| (-, -en) f front; **f~al** |frɔn'ta:l| adj frontal

fror etc |fro:r| vb siehe **frieren**

Frosch |frɔʃ| (-(e)s, ⁼e) m frog; (Feuerwerk) squib; **~mann** m frogman; **~schenkel** m frog's leg

Frost |frɔst| (-(e)s, ⁼e) m frost; **~beule** f chilblain

frösteln |'frœstəln| vi to shiver

frostig adj frosty

Frostschutzmittel nt antifreeze

Frottier(hand)tuch |frɔ'ti:r(hant)tu:x| nt towel

Frucht |frʊxt| (-, ⁼e) f (auch fig) fruit; (Getreide) corn; **f~bar** adj fruitful, fertile; **~barkeit** f fertility; **f~ig** adj (Geschmack) fruity; **f~los** adj fruitless; **~saft** m fruit juice

früh |fry:| adj, adv early; **heute ~** this morning; **F~aufsteher** (-s, -) m early riser; **F~e** f early morning; **~er** adj earlier;

(ehemalig) former ♦ *adv* formerly; **~er war das anders** that used to be different; **~estens** *adv* at the earliest; **F~jahr** *nt* spring; **F~ling** *m* spring; **~reif** *adj* precocious; **F~stück** *nt* breakfast; **~stücken** *vi* to (have) breakfast; **F~stücksbüfett** *nt* breakfast buffet; **~zeitig** *adj* early; *(pej)* untimely

frustrieren |frus'tri:rən| *vt* to frustrate

Fuchs |fuks| (-es, ⁼e) *m* fox; **f~en** *(umg)* *vt* to rile, to annoy; **f~teufelswild** *adj* hopping mad

Fuge |'fu:gə| *f* joint; *(MUS)* fugue

fügen |'fy:gən| *vt* to place, to join ♦ *vr*: **sich ~ (in** +*akk*) to be obedient (to); *(anpassen)* to adapt oneself (to) ♦ *vr unpers* to happen

fühl- *zW*: **~bar** *adj* perceptible, noticeable; **~en** *vt, vi, vr* to feel; **F~er** (-s, -) *m* feeler

fuhr *etc* |fu:r| *vb siehe* **fahren**

führen |'fy:rən| *vt* to lead; *(Geschäft)* to run; *(Name)* to bear; *(Buch)* to keep ♦ *vi* to lead ♦ *vr* to behave

Führer |'fy:rər| (-s, -) *m* leader; *(Fremdenführer)* guide; **~schein** *m* driving licence

Führung |'fy:rʊŋ| *f* leadership; *(eines Unternehmens)* management; *(MIL)* command; *(Benehmen)* conduct; *(Museumsführung)* conducted tour; **~szeugnis** *nt* certificate of good conduct

Fülle |'fʏlə| *f* wealth, abundance; **f~n** *vt* to fill; *(KOCH)* to stuff ♦ *vr* to fill (up)

Füll- *zW*: **~er** (-s, -) *m* fountain pen; **~federhalter** *m* fountain pen; **~ung** *f* filling; *(Holzfüllung)* panel

fummeln |'fʊməln| *(umg)* *vi* to fumble

Fund |fʊnt| (-(e)s, -e) *m* find

Fundament |fʊnda'mɛnt| *nt* foundation; **fundamen'tal** *adj* fundamental

Fund- *zW*: **~büro** *nt* lost property office, lost and found *(US)*; **~grube** *f (fig)* treasure trove

fundiert |fʊn'di:rt| *adj* sound

fünf |fʏnf| *num* five; **~hundert** *num* five hundred; **~te(r, s)** *adj* fifth; **F~tel** (-s, -) *nt* fifth; **~zehn** *num* fifteen; **~zig** *num* fifty

Funk |fʊŋk| (-s) *m* radio, wireless; **~e** (-ns, -n) *m (auch fig)* spark; **f~eln** *vi* to sparkle; **~en** (-s, -) *m (auch fig)* spark; **f~en** *vi (durch Funk)* to signal, to radio; *(umg: richtig funktionieren)* to work ♦ *vt (Funken sprühen)* to shower with sparks; **~er** (-s, -) *m* radio operator; **~gerät** *nt* radio set; **~rufempfänger** *m* pager, paging device; **~streife** *f* police radio patrol; **~telefon** *nt* cellphone

Funktion |fʊŋktsi'o:n| *f* function; **f~ieren** [-'ni:rən] *vi* to work, to function

für |fy:r| *präp* +*akk* for; **was ~** what kind *od*

sort of; **das F~ und Wider** the pros and cons *pl*; **Schritt ~ Schritt** step by step

Furche |'fʊrçə| *f* furrow

Furcht |fʊrçt| (-) *f* fear; **f~bar** *adj* terrible, frightful

fürchten |'fʏrçtən| *vt* to be afraid of, to fear ♦ *vr*: **sich ~ (vor** +*dat*) to be afraid (of)

fürchterlich *adj* awful

furchtlos *adj* fearless

füreinander |fy:r|aɪ'nandər| *adv* for each other

Furnier |fʊr'ni:r| (-s, -e) *nt* veneer

fürs |fy:rs| = **für das**

Fürsorge |'fy:rzɔrgə| *f* care; *(Sozialfürsorge)* welfare; **~r(in)** (-s, -) *m(f)* welfare worker; **~unterstützung** *f* social security, welfare benefit *(US)*; **fürsorglich** *adj* attentive, caring

Fürsprache *f* recommendation; *(um Gnade)* intercession

Fürsprecher *m* advocate

Fürst |fʏrst| (-en, -en) *m* prince; **~entum** *nt* principality; **~in** *f* princess; **f~lich** *adj* princely

Fuß |fu:s| (-es, ⁼e) *m* foot; *(von Glas, Säule etc)* base; *(von Möbel)* leg; **zu ~** on foot; **~ball** *m* football; **~ballplatz** *m* football pitch; **~ballspiel** *nt* football match; **~ballspieler** *m* footballer; **~boden** *m* floor; **~bremse** *f (AUT)* footbrake; **~ende** *nt* foot; **~gänger(in)** *m(f)* pedestrian; **~gängerzone** *f* pedestrian precinct; **~nagel** *m* toenail; **~note** *f* footnote; **~spur** *f* footprint; **~tritt** *m* kick; *(Spur)* footstep; **~weg** *m* footpath

Futter |'fʊtər| (-s, -) *nt* fodder, feed; *(Stoff)* lining; **~al** [-'ra:l] (-s, -e) *nt* case

füttern |'fʏtərn| *vt* to feed; *(Kleidung)* to line

Futur |fu'tu:r| (-s, -e) *nt* future

G, g

g *abk* = **Gramm**

gab *etc* |ga:p| *vb siehe* **geben**

Gabe |'ga:bə| *f* gift

Gabel |'ga:bəl| (-, -n) *f* fork; **~ung** *f* fork

gackern |'gakərn| *vi* to cackle

gaffen |'gafən| *vi* to gape

Gage |'ga:ʒə| *f* fee; salary

gähnen |'gɛ:nən| *vi* to yawn

Galerie |galə'ri:| *f* gallery

Galgen |'galgən| (-s, -) *m* gallows *sg*; **~frist** *f* respite; **~humor** *m* macabre humour

Galle |'galə| *f* gall; *(Organ)* gall bladder; **~nstein** *m* gallstone

gammeln |'gaməln| *(umg)* *vi* to bum around; **Gammler(in)** (-s, -) *(pej)* *m(f)* layabout, loafer *(inf)*

Gämse → gebildet

Gämse ▲ |'gɛmzə] f chamois
Gang |gaŋ] (-(e)s, ⁻e) m walk; (Botengang)
errand; (-art) gait; (Abschnitt eines
Vorgangs) operation; (Essensgang, Ablauf)
course; (Flur etc) corridor; (Durchgang)
passage; (TECH) gear; in ~ bringen to start
up; (fig) to get off the ground; in ~ sein to
be in operation; (fig) to be under way
gang adj: ~ und gäbe usual, normal
gängig |'gɛŋɪç] adj common, current; (Ware)
in demand, selling well
Gangschaltung f gears pl
Ganove |ga'noːvə] (-n, -n) (umg) m crook
Gans |gans] (-, ⁻e) f goose
Gänse- |'gɛnzə] zW: ~blümchen nt daisy;
~füßchen (umg) pl (Anführungszeichen)
inverted commas; ~haut f goose pimples pl;
~marsch m: im ~marsch in single file;
~rich (-s, -e) m gander
ganz |gants] adj whole; (vollständig) complete
♦ adv quite; (völlig) completely; ~ Europa all
Europe; sein ~es Geld all his money; ~ und
gar nicht not at all; es sieht ~ so aus it
really looks like it; aufs G~e gehen to go for
the lot
gänzlich |'gɛntslɪç] adj complete, entire
♦ adv completely, entirely
Ganztagsschule f all-day school
gar |gaːr] adj cooked, done ♦ adv quite; ~
nicht/nichts/keiner not/nothing/nobody at
all; ~ nicht schlecht not bad at all
Garage |ga'raːʒə] f garage
Garantie |garan'tiː] f guarantee; g~ren vt to
guarantee; er kommt g~rt he's guaranteed
to come
Garbe |'garbə] f sheaf
Garde |'gardə] f guard
Garderobe |gardə'roːbə] f wardrobe;
(Abgabe) cloakroom; ~nfrau f cloakroom
attendant
Gardine |gar'diːnə] f curtain
garen |'gaːrən] vt, vi to cook
gären |'gɛːrən] (unreg) vi to ferment
Garn |garn] (-(e)s, -e) nt thread; yarn (auch
fig)
Garnele |gar'neːlə] f shrimp, prawn
garnieren |gar'niːrən] vt to decorate;
(Speisen, fig) to garnish
Garnison |garni'zoːn] (-, -en) f garrison
Garnitur |garni'tuːr] f (Satz) set;
(Unterwäsche) set of (matching) underwear;
erste ~ top rank; zweite ~ (fig) second
rate
garstig |'garstɪç] adj nasty, horrid
Garten |'gartən] (-s, ⁻) m garden; ~arbeit f
gardening; ~gerät nt gardening tool;
~lokal nt beer garden; ~tür f garden gate
Gärtner(in) |'gɛrtnər(ɪn)] (-s, -) m(f)
gardener; ~ei |-'raɪ] f nursery;
(Gemüsegärtnerei) market garden (BRIT),
truck farm (US)

Gärung |'gɛːrʊŋ] f fermentation
Gas |gaːs] (-es, -e) nt gas; ~ geben (AUT) to
accelerate, to step on the gas; ~hahn m gas
tap; ~herd m gas cooker; ~kocher m gas
cooker; ~leitung f gas pipe; ~pedal nt
accelerator, gas pedal
Gasse |'gasə] f lane, alley
Gast |gast] (-es, ⁻e) m guest; (in Lokal)
patron; bei jdm zu ~ sein to be sb's guest;
~arbeiter(in) m(f) foreign worker
Gäste- |'gɛstə] zW: ~buch nt visitors' book,
guest book; ~zimmer nt guest od spare
room
Gast- zW: g~freundlich adj hospitable;
~geber (-s, -) m host; ~geberin f hostess;
~haus nt hotel, inn; ~hof m hotel, inn;
g~ieren |-'tiːrən] vi (THEAT) to (appear as a)
guest; g~lich adj hospitable; ~rolle f guest
role; ~spiel nt (THEAT) guest performance;
~stätte f restaurant; pub; ~wirt m
innkeeper; ~wirtschaft f hotel, inn
Gaswerk nt gasworks sg
Gaszähler m gas meter
Gatte |'gatə] (-n, -n) m husband, spouse
Gattin f wife, spouse
Gattung |'gatʊŋ] f genus; kind
Gaudi |'gaʊdi] (umg: SÜDD, ÖSTERR) nt od f
fun
Gaul |gaʊl] (-(e)s, Gäule) m horse; nag
Gaumen |'gaʊmən] (-s, -) m palate
Gauner |'gaʊnər] (-s, -) m rogue; ~ei |-'raɪ] f
swindle
geb. abk ~ geboren
Gebäck |gə'bɛk] (-(e)s, -e) nt pastry
gebacken |gə'bakən] adj baked; (gebraten)
fried
Gebälk |gə'bɛlk] (-(e)s) nt timberwork
Gebärde |gə'bɛːrdə] f gesture; g~n vr to
behave
gebären |gə'bɛːrən] (unreg) vt to give birth
to, to bear
Gebärmutter f uterus, womb
Gebäude |gə'bɔʏdə] (-s, -) nt building;
~komplex m (building) complex
geben |'geːbən] (unreg) vt, vi to give; (Karten)
to deal ♦ vb unpers: es gibt there is/are;
there will be ♦ vr (sich verhalten) to behave,
to act; (aufhören) to abate; jdm etw ~ to
give sb sth od sth to sb; was gibt's? what's
up?; was gibt es im Kino? what's on at the
cinema?; sich geschlagen ~ to admit
defeat; das wird sich schon ~ that'll soon
sort itself out
Gebet |gə'beːt] (-(e)s, -e) nt prayer
gebeten |gə'beːtən] vb siehe bitten
Gebiet |gə'biːt] (-(e)s, -e) nt area;
(Hoheitsgebiet) territory; (fig) field; g~en
(unreg) vt to command, to demand;
g~erisch adj imperious
Gebilde |gə'bɪldə] (-s, -) nt object
gebildet adj cultured, educated

Gebirge |gə'bɪrgə| (**-s, -**) nt mountain chain

Gebiss ▲ |gə'bɪs| (**-es, -e**) nt teeth pl; (künstlich) dentures pl

gebissen vb siehe **beißen**

geblieben |gə'bliːbən| vb siehe **bleiben**

geblümt |gə'blyːmt| adj (Kleid, Stoff, Tapete) floral

geboren |gə'boːrən| adj born; (Frau) née

geborgen |gə'bɔrgən| adj secure, safe

Gebot |gə'boːt| (**-(e)s, -e**) nt command; (REL) commandment; (bei Auktion) bid

geboten |gə'boːtən| vb siehe **bieten**

Gebr. abk (= Gebrüder) Bros.

gebracht |gə'braxt| vb siehe **bringen**

gebraten |gə'braːtən| adj fried

Gebrauch |gə'braux| (**-(e)s, Gebräuche**) m use; (Sitte) custom; **g~en** vt to use

gebräuchlich |gə'brɔʏçlɪç| adj usual, customary

Gebrauchs- zW: **~anweisung** f directions pl for use; **g~fertig** adj ready for use; **~gegenstand** m commodity

gebraucht |gə'brauxt| adj used; **G~wagen** m secondhand od used car

gebrechlich |gə'brɛçlɪç| adj frail

Gebrüder |gə'bryːdər| pl brothers

Gebrüll |gə'brʏl| (**-(e)s**) nt roaring

Gebühr |gə'byːr| (**-, -en**) f charge, fee; **nach ~** fittingly; **über ~** unduly; **g~en** vi: **jdm g~en** to be sb's due od due to sb ♦ vr to be fitting; **g~end** adj fitting, appropriate ♦ adv fittingly, appropriately

Gebühren- zW: **~einheit** f (TEL) unit; **~erlass** ▲ m remission of fees; **~ermäßigung** f reduction of fees; **g~frei** adj free of charge; **~ordnung** f scale of charges, tariff; **g~pflichtig** adj subject to a charge

gebunden |gə'bʊndən| vb siehe **binden**

Geburt |gə'buːrt| (**-, -en**) f birth

Geburtenkontrolle f birth control

Geburtenregelung f birth control

gebürtig |gə'bʏrtɪç| adj born in, native of; **~e Schweizerin** native of Switzerland

Geburts- zW: **~anzeige** f birth notice; **~datum** nt date of birth; **~jahr** nt year of birth; **~ort** m birthplace; **~tag** m birthday; **~urkunde** f birth certificate

Gebüsch |gə'bʏʃ| (**-(e)s, -e**) nt bushes pl

gedacht |gə'daxt| vb siehe **denken**

Gedächtnis |gə'dɛçtnɪs| (**-ses, -se**) nt memory; **~feier** f commemoration

Gedanke |gə'daŋkə| (**-ns, -n**) m thought; **sich über etw** akk **~n machen** to think about sth

Gedanken- zW: **~austausch** m exchange of ideas; **g~los** adj thoughtless; **~strich** m dash; **~übertragung** f thought transference, telepathy

Gedeck |gə'dɛk| (**-(e)s, -e**) nt cover(ing); (Speisenfolge) menu; **ein ~ auflegen** to lay a place

gedeihen |gə'daɪən| (unreg) vi to thrive, to prosper

Gedenken nt: **zum ~ an jdn** in memory of sb

gedenken |gə'dɛŋkən| (unreg) vi +gen (beabsichtigen) to intend; (sich erinnern) to remember

Gedenk- zW: **~feier** f commemoration; **~minute** f minute's silence; **~stätte** f memorial; **~tag** m remembrance day

Gedicht |gə'dɪçt| (**-(e)s, -e**) nt poem

gediegen |gə'diːgən| adj (good) quality; (Mensch) reliable, honest

Gedränge |gə'drɛŋə| (**-s**) nt crush, crowd

gedrängt adj compressed; **~ voll** packed

gedrückt |gə'drʏkt| adj (deprimiert) low, depressed

gedrungen |gə'drʊŋən| adj thickset, stocky

Geduld |gə'dʊlt| f patience; **g~en** |gə'dʊldən| vr to be patient; **g~ig** adj patient, forbearing; **~sprobe** f trial of (one's) patience

gedurft |gə'dʊrft| vb siehe **dürfen**

geehrt |gə'|eːrt| adj: **Sehr ~e Frau X!** Dear Mrs X

geeignet |gə'|aɪɡnət| adj suitable

Gefahr |gə'faːr| (**-, -en**) f danger; **~ laufen, etw zu tun** to run the risk of doing sth; **auf eigene ~** at one's own risk

gefährden |gə'fɛːrdən| vt to endanger

Gefahren- zW: **~quelle** f source of danger; **~zulage** f danger money

gefährlich |gə'fɛːrlɪç| adj dangerous

Gefährte |gə'fɛːrtə| (**-n, -n**) m companion; (Lebenspartner) partner

Gefährtin |gə'fɛːrtɪn| f (female) companion; (Lebenspartner) (female) partner

Gefälle |gə'fɛlə| (**-s, -**) nt gradient, incline

Gefallen¹ |gə'falən| (**-s, -**) m favour

Gefallen² |gə'falən| (**-s**) nt pleasure; **an etw** dat **~ finden** to derive pleasure from sth

gefallen pp von **fallen** ♦ vi: **jdm ~** to please sb; **er/es gefällt mir** I like him/it; **das gefällt mir an ihm** that's one thing I like about him; **sich** dat **etw ~ lassen** to put up with sth

gefällig |gə'fɛlɪç| adj (hilfsbereit) obliging; (erfreulich) pleasant; **G~keit** f favour; helpfulness; **etw aus G~keit tun** to do sth out of the goodness of one's heart

gefangen |gə'faŋən| adj captured; (fig) captivated; **~ halten** to keep prisoner; **~ nehmen** to take prisoner; **G~e(r)** f(m) prisoner, captive; **G~nahme** f capture; **G~schaft** f captivity

Gefängnis |gə'fɛŋnɪs| (**-ses, -se**) nt prison; **~strafe** f prison sentence; **~wärter** m

Spelling reform: ▲ *new spelling* △ *old spelling (to be phased out)*

prison warder; **~zelle** f prison cell
Gefäß |gə'fɛːs| (-es, -e) nt vessel; (auch ANAT)
container
gefasst ▲ |gə'fast| adj composed, calm; **auf
etw** akk **~ sein** to be prepared od ready for
sth
Gefecht |gə'fɛçt| (-(e)s, -e) nt fight; (MIL)
engagement
Gefieder |gə'fiːdər| (-s, -) nt plumage,
feathers pl
gefleckt |gə'flɛkt| adj spotted, mottled
geflogen |gə'floːgən| vb siehe **fliegen**
geflossen |gə'flɔsən| vb siehe **fließen**
Geflügel |gə'flyːgəl| (-s) nt poultry
Gefolgschaft |gə'fɔlkʃaft| f following
gefragt |gə'fraːkt| adj in demand
gefräßig |gə'frɛːsɪç| adj voracious
Gefreite(r) |gə'fraitə(r)| m lance corporal;
(NAUT) able seaman; (AVIAT) aircraftman
Gefrierbeutel m freezer bag
gefrieren |gə'friːrən| (unreg) vi to freeze
Gefrier- zW: **~fach** nt icebox; **~fleisch** nt
frozen meat; **g~getrocknet** |-gətrɔknət|
adj freeze-dried; **~punkt** m freezing point;
~schutzmittel nt antifreeze; **~truhe** f
deep-freeze
gefroren |gə'froːrən| vb siehe **frieren**
Gefühl |gə'fyːl| (-(e)s, -e) nt feeling; **etw im
~ haben** to have a feel for sth; **g~los** adj
unfeeling
gefühls- zW: **~betont** adj emotional;
G~duselei |-duːzə'lai| f over-sentimentality;
~mäßig adj instinctive
gefüllt |gə'fʏlt| adj (KOCH) stuffed
gefunden |gə'fundən| vb siehe **finden**
gegangen |gə'gaŋən| vb siehe **gehen**
gegeben |gə'geːbən| vb siehe **geben** ♦ adj
given; **zu ~er Zeit** in good time
gegebenenfalls |gə'geːbənənfals| adv if
need be

SCHLÜSSELWORT

gegen |'geːgən| präp +akk **1** against; **nichts
gegen jdn haben** to have nothing against
sb; **X gegen Y** (SPORT, JUR) X versus Y; **ein
Mittel gegen Schnupfen** something for
colds
2 (in Richtung auf) towards; **gegen Osten**
to(wards) the east; **gegen Abend** towards
evening; **gegen einen Baum fahren** to
drive into a tree
3 (ungefähr) round about; **gegen 3 Uhr**
around 3 o'clock
4 (gegenüber) towards; (ungefähr) around;
gerecht gegen alle fair to all
5 (im Austausch für) for; **gegen bar** for
cash; **gegen Quittung** against a receipt
6 (verglichen mit) compared with

Gegenangriff m counter-attack
Gegenbeweis m counter-evidence

Gegend |'geːgənt| (-, -en) f area, district
Gegen- zW: **g~ei'nander** adv against one
another; **~fahrbahn** f oncoming
carriageway; **~frage** f counter-question;
~gewicht nt counterbalance; **~gift** nt
antidote; **~leistung** f service in return;
~maßnahme f countermeasure; **~mittel** nt
antidote, cure; **~satz** m contrast; **~sätze
überbrücken** to overcome differences;
g~sätzlich adj contrary, opposite;
(widersprüchlich) contradictory; **g~seitig** adj
mutual, reciprocal; **G~ (-s, -)** nt opposite;
help each other; **~spieler** m opponent;
~sprechanlage f (two-way) intercom;
~stand m object; **~stimme** f vote against;
~stoß m counterblow; **~stück** nt
counterpart; **~teil** nt opposite; **im ~teil** on
the contrary; **g~teilig** adj opposite, contrary
gegenüber |geːgən'yːbər| präp +dat
opposite; (zu) to(wards); (angesichts) in the
face of ♦ adv opposite; **G~ (-s, -)** nt person
opposite; **~liegen** (unreg) vr to face each
other; **~stehen** (unreg) vr to be opposed (to
each other); **~stellen** vt to confront; (fig) to
contrast; **G~stellung** f confrontation; (fig)
contrast; **~treten** (unreg) vi +dat to face
Gegen- zW: **~verkehr** m oncoming traffic;
~vorschlag m counterproposal; **~wart** f
present; **g~wärtig** adj present ♦ adv at
present; **das ist mir nicht mehr g~wärtig**
that has slipped my mind; **~wert** m
equivalent; **~wind** m headwind;
g~zeichnen vt, vi to countersign
gegessen |gə'gɛsən| vb siehe **essen**
Gegner |'geːgnər| (-s, -) m opponent;
g~isch adj opposing
gegr. abk (= gegründet) est.
gegrillt |gə'grɪlt| adj grilled
Gehackte(s) |gə'haktə(s)| nt mince(d meat)
Gehalt¹ |gə'halt| (-(e)s, -e) m content
Gehalt² |gə'halt| (-(e)s, ̈er) nt salary
Gehalts- zW: **~empfänger** m salary earner;
~erhöhung f salary increase; **~zulage** f
salary increment
gehaltvoll |gə'haltfɔl| adj (nahrhaft)
nutritious
gehässig |gə'hɛsɪç| adj spiteful, nasty
Gehäuse |gə'hɔyzə| (-s, -) nt case; casing;
(von Apfel etc) core
Gehege |gə'heːgə| (-s, -) nt reserve; (im Zoo)
enclosure
geheim |gə'haim| adj secret; **~ halten** to
keep secret; **G~dienst** m secret service,
intelligence service; **G~nis** (-ses, -se) nt
secret; mystery; **~nisvoll** adj mysterious;
G~polizei f secret police
gehemmt |gə'hɛmt| adj inhibited, self-
conscious
gehen |'geːən| (unreg) vt, vi to go; (zu Fuß ~)
to walk ♦ vb unpers: **wie geht es (dir)?** how
are you od things?; **~ nach** (Fenster) to face;

mir/ihm geht es gut I'm/he's (doing) fine; **geht das?** is that possible?; **gehts noch?** can you manage?; **es geht** not too bad, O.K.; **das geht nicht** that's not on; **es geht um etw** sth is concerned, it's about sth; **sich ~ lassen** (*unbeherrscht sein*) to lose control (of o.s.); **jdn ~ lassen** to let/leave sb alone; **lass mich ~!** leave me alone!

geheuer [gə'hɔyər] *adj*: **nicht ~** eerie; (*fragwürdig*) dubious

Gehilfe [gə'hılfə] (**-n, -n**) *m* assistant; **Gehilfin** *f* assistant

Gehirn [gə'hırn] (**-(e)s, -e**) *nt* brain; **~erschütterung** *f* concussion; **~hautentzündung** *f* meningitis

gehoben [gə'ho:bən] *pp von* **heben** ♦ *adj* (*Position*) elevated; high

geholfen [gə'hɔlfən] *vb siehe* **helfen**

Gehör [gə'hø:r] (**-(e)s**) *nt* hearing; **musikalisches ~** ear; **~ finden** to gain a hearing; **jdm ~ schenken** to give sb a hearing

gehorchen [gə'hɔrçən] *vi +dat* to obey

gehören [gə'hø:rən] *vi* to belong ♦ *vr unpers* to be right *od* proper

gehörig *adj* proper; **~ zu** *od +dat* belonging to; part of

gehörlos *adj* deaf

gehorsam [gə'ho:rza:m] *adj* obedient; **G~** (**-s**) *m* obedience

Geh- ['ge:-] *zW*: **~steig** *m* pavement, sidewalk (*US*); **~weg** *m* pavement, sidewalk (*US*)

Geier ['gaɪər] (**-s, -**) *m* vulture

Geige ['gaɪgə] *f* violin; **~r** (**-s, -**) *m* violinist

geil [gaɪl] *adj* randy (*BRIT*), horny (*US*)

Geisel ['gaɪzəl] (**-, -n**) *f* hostage

Geist [gaɪst] (**-(e)s, -er**) *m* spirit; (*Gespenst*) ghost; (*Verstand*) mind

geisterhaft *adj* ghostly

Geistes- *zW*: **g~abwesend** *adj* absent-minded; **~blitz** *m* brainwave; **~gegenwart** *f* presence of mind; **g~krank** *adj* mentally ill; **~kranke(r)** *f(m)* mentally ill person; **~krankheit** *f* mental illness; **~wissenschaften** *pl* the arts; **~zustand** *m* state of mind

geist- *zW*: **~ig** *adj* intellectual; mental; (*Getränke*) alcoholic; **~ig behindert** mentally handicapped; **~lich** *adj* spiritual, religious; clerical; **G~liche(r)** *m* clergyman; **G~lichkeit** *f* clergy; **~los** *adj* uninspired, dull; **~reich** *adj* clever; witty; **~voll** *adj* intellectual; (*weise*) wise

Geiz [gaɪts] (**-es**) *m* miserliness, meanness; **g~en** *vi* to be miserly; **~hals** *m* miser; **g~ig** *adj* miserly, mean; **~kragen** *m* miser

gekannt [gə'kant] *vb siehe* **kennen**

gekonnt [gə'kɔnt] *adj* skilful ♦ *vb siehe*
können

gekünstelt [gə'kynstəlt] *adj* artificial, affected

Gel [ge:l] (**-s, -e**) *nt* gel

Gelächter [gə'lɛçtər] (**-s, -**) *nt* laughter

geladen [gə'la:dən] *adj* loaded; (*ELEK*) live; (*fig*) furious

gelähmt [gə'lɛ:mt] *adj* paralysed

Gelände [gə'lɛndə] (**-s, -**) *nt* land, terrain; (*von Fabrik, Sportgelände*) grounds *pl*; (*Baugelände*) site; **~lauf** *m* cross-country race

Geländer [gə'lɛndər] (**-s, -**) *nt* railing; (*Treppengeländer*) banister(s)

gelangen [gə'laŋən] *vi*: **~ (an** +*akk od* **zu)** to reach; (*erwerben*) to attain; **in jds Besitz ~** to come into sb's possession

gelangweilt [gə'laŋvaɪlt] *adj* bored

gelassen [gə'lasən] *adj* calm, composed; **G~heit** *f* calmness, composure

Gelatine [ʒelatiːnə] *f* gelatine

geläufig [gə'lɔyfıç] *adj* (*üblich*) common; **das ist mir nicht ~** I'm not familiar with it

gelaunt [gə'laʊnt] *adj*: **schlecht/gut ~** in a bad/good mood; **wie ist er ~?** what sort of mood is he in?

gelb [gɛlp] *adj* yellow; (*Ampellicht*) amber; **~lich** *adj* yellowish; **G~sucht** *f* jaundice

Geld [gɛlt] (**-(e)s, -er**) *nt* money; **etw zu ~ machen** to sell sth off; **~anlage** *f* investment; **~automat** *m* cash dispenser; **~beutel** *m* purse; **~börse** *f* purse; **~geber** (**-s, -**) *m* financial backer; **g~gierig** *adj* avaricious; **~schein** *m* banknote; **~schrank** *m* safe, strongbox; **~strafe** *f* fine; **~stück** *nt* coin; **~wechsel** *m* exchange (of money)

Gelee [ʒe'le:] (**-s, -s**) *nt od m* jelly

gelegen [gə'le:gən] *adj* situated; (*passend*) convenient, opportune ♦ *vb siehe* **liegen**; **etw kommt jdm ~** sth is convenient for sb

Gelegenheit [gə'le:gənhaɪt] *f* opportunity; (*Anlaß*) occasion; **bei jeder ~** at every opportunity; **~sarbeit** *f* casual work; **~skauf** *m* bargain

gelegentlich [gə'le:gəntlıç] *adj* occasional ♦ *adv* occasionally; (*bei Gelegenheit*) some time (or other) ♦ *präp +gen* on the occasion of

gelehrt [gə'le:rt] *adj* learned; **G~e(r)** *f(m)* scholar; **G~heit** *f* scholarliness

Geleise [gə'laɪzə] (**-s, -**) *nt* = **Gleis**

Geleit [gə'laɪt] (**-(e)s, -e**) *nt* escort; **g~en** *vt* to escort

Gelenk [gə'lɛŋk] (**-(e)s, -e**) *nt* joint; **g~ig** *adj* supple

gelernt [gə'lɛrnt] *adj* skilled

Geliebte(r) [gə'li:ptə(r)] *f(m)* sweetheart, beloved

geliehen [gə'li:ən] *vb siehe* **leihen**

gelind(e) |gə'lɪnd(ə)| adj mild, light; (fig: Wut) fierce; **gelinde gesagt** to put it mildly

gelingen |gə'lɪŋən| (unreg) vi to succeed; **es ist mir gelungen, etw zu tun** I succeeded in doing sth

geloben |gə'lo:bən| vt, vi to vow, to swear

gelten |'gɛltən| (unreg) vt (wert sein) to be worth ♦ vi (gültig sein) to be valid; (erlaubt sein) to be allowed ♦ vb unpers: **es gilt, etw zu tun** it is necessary to do sth; **jdm viel/ wenig ~** to mean a lot/not to mean much to sb; **was gilt die Wette?** what do you bet?; **etw ~ lassen** to accept sth; **als od für etw ~** to be considered to apply to sth; **jdm od für jdn ~** (betreffen) to apply to od for sb; **~d** adj prevailing; **etw ~d machen** to assert sth; **sich ~d machen** to make itself/o.s. felt

Geltung |'gɛltʊŋ| f: **~ haben** to have validity; **sich/etw** dat **~ verschaffen** to establish one's position/the position of sth; **etw zur ~ bringen** to show sth to its best advantage; **zur ~ kommen** to be seen/heard etc to its best advantage

Geltungsbedürfnis nt desire for admiration

Gelübde |gə'lʏpdə| (-s, -) nt vow

gelungen |gə'lʊŋən| adj successful

gemächlich |gə'mɛːçlɪç| adj leisurely

Gemahl |gə'ma:l| (-(e)s, -e) m husband; **~in** f wife

Gemälde |gə'mɛːldə| (-s, -) nt picture, painting

gemäß |gə'mɛːs| präp +dat in accordance with ♦ adj (+dat) appropriate (to)

gemäßigt adj moderate; (Klima) temperate

gemein |gə'maɪn| adj common; (niederträchtig) mean; **etw ~ haben (mit)** to have sth in common with

Gemeinde |gə'maɪndə| f district, community; (Pfarrgemeinde) parish; (Kirchengemeinde) congregation; **~steuer** f local rates pl; **~verwaltung** f local administration; **~wahl** f local election

Gemein- zW: **g~gefährlich** adj dangerous to the public; **~heit** f commonness; mean thing to do/to say; **g~nützig** adj charitable; **g~nütziger Verein** non-profit-making organization; **g~sam** adj joint, common (auch MATH) ♦ adv together, jointly; **g~same Sache mit jdm machen** to be in cahoots with sb; **etw g~sam haben** to have sth in common; **~samkeit** f community, having in common; **~schaft** f community; **in ~schaft mit** jointly od together with; **g~schaftlich** adj = gemeinsam; **~schaftsarbeit** f teamwork; team effort; **~sinn** m public spirit

Gemenge |gə'mɛŋə| (-s, -) nt mixture; (Handgemenge) scuffle

gemessen |gə'mɛsən| adj measured

Gemetzel |gə'mɛtsəl| (-s, -) nt slaughter, carnage, butchery

Gemisch |gə'mɪʃ| (-es, -e) nt mixture; **g~t** adj mixed

gemocht |gə'mɔxt| vb siehe **mögen**

Gemse △ |'gɛmzə| f = **Gämse**

Gemurmel |gə'mʊrməl| (-s) nt murmur(ing)

Gemüse |gə'my:zə| (-s, -) nt vegetables pl; **~garten** m vegetable garden; **~händler** m greengrocer

gemusst ▲ |gə'mʊst| vb siehe **müssen**

gemustert |gə'mʊstərt| adj patterned

Gemüt |gə'my:t| (-(e)s, -er) nt disposition, nature; person; **sich** dat **etw zu ~e führen** (umg) to indulge in sth; **die ~er erregen** to arouse strong feelings; **g~lich** adj comfortable, cosy; (Person) good-natured; **~lichkeit** f comfortableness, cosiness; amiability

Gemüts- zW: **~mensch** m sentimental person; **~ruhe** f composure; **~zustand** m state of mind

Gen |ge:n| (-s, -e) nt gene

genannt |gə'nant| vb siehe **nennen**

genau |gə'nau| adj exact, precise ♦ adv exactly, precisely; **etw ~ nehmen** to take sth seriously; **~ genommen** strictly speaking; **G~igkeit** f exactness, accuracy; **~so** adv just the same; **~so gut** just as good

genehm |gə'ne:m| adj agreeable, acceptable; **~igen** vt to approve, to authorize; **sich** dat **etw ~igen** to indulge in sth; **G~igung** f approval, authorization; (Schriftstück) permit

General |gene'ra:l| (-s, -e od =e) m general; **~direktor** m director general; **~konsulat** nt consulate general; **~probe** f dress rehearsal; **~streik** m general strike; **g~überholen** vt to overhaul thoroughly; **~versammlung** f general meeting

Generation |generatsi'o:n| f generation

Generator |gene'ra:tɔr| m generator, dynamo

generell |genə'rɛl| adj general

genesen |ge'ne:zən| (unreg) vi to convalesce, to recover; **Genesung** f recovery, convalescence

genetisch |ge'ne:tɪʃ| adj genetic

Genf |'gɛnf| nt Geneva; **der ~er See** Lake Geneva

genial |geni'a:l| adj brilliant

Genick |gə'nɪk| (-(e)s, -e) nt (back of the) neck

Genie |ʒe'ni:| (-s, -s) nt genius

genieren |ʒe'ni:rən| vt to bother ♦ vr to feel awkward od self-conscious

genieß- zW: **~bar** adj edible; drinkable; **~en** |gə'ni:sən| (unreg) vt to enjoy; to eat; to drink; **G~er** (-s, -) m epicure; pleasure lover; **~erisch** adj appreciative ♦ adv with relish

genmanipuliert |'ge:nmanipuli:rt| adj genetically modified

genommen |gə'nɔmən| vb siehe **nehmen**

Genosse |gə'nɔsə| (-n, -n) m (bes POL)

comrade, companion; **~nschaft** *f*
cooperative (association)

Genossin *f (bes POL)* comrade, companion

Gentechnik ['gɛntɛçnɪk] *f* genetic
engineering

genug [gə'nuːk] *adv* enough

Genüge [gə'nyːgə] *f*: **jdm/etw ~ tun** *od*
leisten to satisfy sb/sth; **g~n** *vi (+dat)* to be
enough (for); **g~nd** *adj* sufficient

genügsam [gə'nyːkzaːm] *adj* modest, easily
satisfied; **G~keit** *f* moderation

Genugtuung [gə'nuːktuːʊŋ] *f* satisfaction

Genuss ▲ [gə'nʊs] **(-es, ÷e)** *m* pleasure;
(Zusichnehmen) consumption; **in den ~ von**
etw kommen to receive the benefit of sth

genüsslich ▲ [gə'nʏslɪç] *adv* with relish

Genussmittel ▲ *pl* (semi-)luxury items

geöffnet [gə'œfnət] *adj* open

Geograf ▲ [geo'graːf] **(-en, -en)** *m*
geographer; **Geografie ▲** *f* geography;
g~isch ▲ *adj* geographical

Geologe [geo'loːgə] **(-n, -n)** *m* geologist;
Geologie *f* geology

Geometrie [geome'triː] *f* geometry

Gepäck [gə'pɛk] **(-(e)s)** *nt* luggage,
baggage; **~abfertigung** *f* luggage office;
~annahme *f* luggage office;
~aufbewahrung *f* left-luggage office
(BRIT), baggage check *(US)*; **~aufgabe** *f*
luggage office; **~ausgabe** *f* luggage office
(AVIAT) luggage reclaim; **~netz** *nt* luggage
rack; **~träger** *m* porter; *(Fahrrad)* carrier;
~versicherung *f* luggage insurance; **~wagen**
m luggage van *(BRIT)*, baggage car *(US)*

gepflegt [gə'pfleːkt] *adj* well-groomed; *(Park*
etc) well looked after

Gerade [gə'raːdə] *f* straight line

SCHLÜSSELWORT

gerade [gə'raːdə] *adj* straight; *(aufrecht)*
upright; **eine gerade Zahl** an even number
♦ *adv* 1 *(genau)* just, exactly; *(speziell)*
especially; **gerade deshalb** that's just *od*
exactly why; **das ist es ja gerade!** that's
just it!; **gerade du** you especially; **warum**
gerade ich? why me (of all people)?; **jetzt**
gerade nicht! not now!; **gerade neben**
right next to

2 *(eben, soeben)* just; **er wollte gerade**
aufstehen he was just about to get up;
gerade erst only just; **gerade noch** (only)
just

gerade- *zW*: **~'aus** *adv* straight ahead;
~he'raus *adv* straight out, bluntly;
~stehen *(unreg)* *vi*: **für jdn/etw g~stehen**
to be answerable for sb('s actions)/sth;
~wegs *adv* direct, straight; **~zu** *adv*
(beinahe) virtually, almost

gerannt [gə'rant] *vb siehe* **rennen**

Gerät [gə'rɛːt] **(-(e)s, -e)** *nt* device;
(Werkzeug) tool; *(SPORT)* apparatus;
(Zubehör) equipment *no pl*

geraten [gə'raːtən] *(unreg)* *vi (gedeihen)* to
thrive; *(gelingen)*: **(jdm) ~** to turn out well
(for sb); **gut/schlecht ~** to turn out well/
badly; **an jdn ~** to come across sb; **in etw**
akk **~** to get into sth; **nach jdm ~** to take
after sb

Geratewohl [gəraːtə'voːl] *nt*: **aufs ~** on the
off chance; *(bei Wahl)* at random

geräuchert [gə'rɔʏçərt] *adj* smoked

geräumig [gə'rɔʏmɪç] *adj* roomy

Geräusch [gə'rɔʏʃ] **(-(e)s, -e)** *nt* sound,
noise; **g~los** *adj* silent

gerben ['gɛrbən] *vt* to tan

gerecht [gə'rɛçt] *adj* just, fair; **jdm/etw ~**
werden to do justice to sb/sth; **G~igkeit** *f*
justice, fairness

Gerede [gə'reːdə] **(-s)** *nt* talk, gossip

geregelt [gə'reːgəlt] *adj (Arbeit)* steady,
regular; *(Mahlzeiten)* regular, set

gereizt [gə'raɪtst] *adj* irritable; **G~heit** *f*
irritation

Gericht [gə'rɪçt] **(-(e)s, -e)** *nt* court; *(Essen)*
dish; **mit jdm ins ~ gehen** *(fig)* to judge sb
harshly; **das Jüngste ~** the Last Judgement;
g~lich *adj* judicial, legal ♦ *adv* judicially,
legally

Gerichts- *zW*: **~barkeit** *f* jurisdiction; **~hof**
m court (of law); **~kosten** *pl* (legal) costs;
~medizin *f* forensic medicine; **~saal** *m*
courtroom; **~verfahren** *nt* legal
proceedings *pl*; **~verhandlung** *f* trial;
~vollzieher *m* bailiff

gerieben [gə'riːbən] *adj* grated; *(umg:*
schlau) smart, wily ♦ *vb siehe* **reiben**

gering [gə'rɪŋ] *adj* slight, small; *(niedrig)* low;
(Zeit) short; **~fügig** *adj* slight, trivial;
~schätzig *adj* disparaging

geringste(r, s) *adj* slightest, least; **~nfalls**
adv at the very least

gerinnen [gə'rɪnən] *(unreg)* *vi* to congeal;
(Blut) to clot; *(Milch)* to curdle

Gerippe [gə'rɪpə] **(-s, -)** *nt* skeleton

gerissen [gə'rɪsən] *adj* wily, smart

geritten [gə'rɪtən] *vb siehe* **reiten**

gern(e) ['gɛrn(ə)] *adv* willingly, gladly; **~**
haben, ~ mögen to like; **etwas ~ tun** to
like doing something; **ich möchte ~ ...** I'd
like ...; **ja, ~** yes, please; yes, I'd like to; **~**
geschehen it's a pleasure

gerochen [gə'rɔxən] *vb siehe* **riechen**

Geröll [gə'rœl] **(-(e)s, -e)** *nt* scree

Gerste ['gɛrstə] *f* barley; **~nkorn** *nt (im Auge)*
stye

Geruch [gə'rʊx] **(-(e)s, ÷e)** *m* smell, odour;
g~los *adj* odourless

Spelling reform: ▲ *new spelling* △ *old spelling (to be phased out)*

Gerücht |gə'rʏçt| (-(e)s, -e) nt rumour

geruhsam |gə'ru:za:m| adj (Leben) peaceful; (Nacht, Zeit) peaceful, restful; (langsam: Arbeitsweise, Spaziergang) leisurely

Gerümpel |gə'rʏmpəl| (-s) nt junk

Gerüst |gə'rʏst| (-(e)s, -e) nt (Baugerüst) scaffold(ing); frame

gesalzen |gə'zaltsən| pp von **salzen** ♦ adj (umg: Preis, Rechnung) steep

gesamt |gə'zamt| adj whole, entire; (Kosten) total; (Werke) complete; **im G~en** all in all; **~deutsch** adj all-German; **G~eindruck** m general impression; **G~heit** f totality, whole; **G~schule** f ≈ comprehensive school

gesandt |gə'zant| vb siehe **senden**

Gesandte(r) |gə'zantə(r)| m envoy

Gesandtschaft |gə'zantʃaft| f legation

Gesang |gə'zaŋ| (-(e)s, ²e) m song; (Singen) singing; **~buch** nt (REL) hymn book

Gesäß |gə'zɛːs| (-es, -e) nt seat, bottom

Geschäft |gə'ʃɛft| (-(e)s, -e) nt business; (Laden) shop; (Geschäftsabschluß) deal; **g~ig** adj active, busy; (pej) officious; **g~lich** adj commercial ♦ adv on business

Geschäfts- zW: **~bedingungen** pl terms of business; **~bericht** m financial report; **~frau** f businesswoman; **~führer** m manager; (Klub) secretary; **~geheimnis** nt trade secret; **~jahr** nt financial year; **~lage** f business conditions pl; **~mann** m businessman; **g~mäßig** adj businesslike; **~partner** m business partner; **~reise** f business trip; **~schluss** ▲ m closing time; **~stelle** f office, place of business; **g~tüchtig** adj business-minded; **~viertel** nt business quarter; **~wagen** m company car; **~zeit** f business hours pl

geschehen |gə'ʃeːən| (unreg) vi to happen; **es war um ihn ~** that was the end of him

gescheit |gə'ʃaɪt| adj clever

Geschenk |gə'ʃɛŋk| (-(e)s, -e) nt present, gift

Geschichte |gə'ʃɪçtə| f story; (Sache) affair; (Historie) history

geschichtlich adj historical

Geschick |gə'ʃɪk| (-(e)s, -e) nt aptitude; (Schicksal) fate; **~lichkeit** f skill, dexterity; **g~t** adj skilful

geschieden |gə'ʃiːdən| adj divorced

geschienen |gə'ʃiːnən| vb siehe **scheinen**

Geschirr |gə'ʃɪr| (-(e)s, -e) nt crockery; pots and pans pl; (Pferdegeschirr) harness; **~spülmaschine** f dishwasher; **~spülmittel** nt washing-up liquid; **~tuch** nt dish cloth

Geschlecht |gə'ʃlɛçt| (-(e)s, -er) nt sex; (GRAM) gender; (Gattung) race; family; **g~lich** adj sexual

Geschlechts- zW: **~krankheit** f venereal disease; **~teil** nt genitals pl; **~verkehr** m sexual intercourse

geschlossen |gə'ʃlɔsən| adj shut ♦ vb siehe

schließen

Geschmack |gə'ʃmak| (-(e)s, ²e) m taste; **nach jds ~** to sb's taste; **~ finden an etw** dat to (come to) like sth; **g~los** adj tasteless; (fig) in bad taste; **~ssinn** m sense of taste; **g~voll** adj tasteful

geschmeidig |gə'ʃmaɪdɪç| adj supple; (formbar) malleable

Geschnetzelte(s) |gə'ʃnɛtsalta(s)| nt (KOCH) strips of meat stewed to produce a thick sauce

geschnitten |gə'ʃnɪtən| vb siehe **schneiden**

Geschöpf |gə'ʃœpf| (-(e)s, -e) nt creature

Geschoss |gə'ʃɔs| (-es, -e), **Geschoß** |gə'ʃoːs| (ÖSTERR) (-sses, -sse) nt (MIL) projectile, missile; (Stockwerk) floor

geschossen |gə'ʃɔsən| vb siehe **schießen**

geschraubt |gə'ʃraʊpt| adj stilted, artificial

Geschrei |gə'ʃraɪ| (-s) nt cries pl, shouting; (fig: Aufheben) noise, fuss

geschrieben |gə'ʃriːbən| vb siehe **schreiben**

Geschütz |gə'ʃʏts| (-es, -e) nt gun, cannon; **ein schweres ~ auffahren** (fig) to bring out the big guns

geschützt adj protected

Geschw. abk = **Geschwister**

Geschwätz |gə'ʃvɛts| (-es) nt chatter, gossip; **g~ig** adj talkative

geschweige |gə'ʃvaɪgə| adv: **~ (denn)** let alone, not to mention

geschwind |gə'ʃvɪnt| adj quick, swift; **G~igkeit** |-dɪçkaɪt| f speed, velocity; **G~igkeitsbeschränkung** f speed limit; **G~igkeitsüberschreitung** f exceeding the speed limit

Geschwister |gə'ʃvɪstər| pl brothers and sisters

geschwommen |gə'ʃvɔmən| vb siehe **schwimmen**

Geschworene(r) |ge'ʃvoːrənə(r)| f(m) juror; **~n** pl jury

Geschwulst |gə'ʃvʊlst| (-, ²e) f swelling; growth, tumour

geschwungen |gə'ʃvʊŋən| pp von **schwingen** ♦ adj curved, arched

Geschwür |gə'ʃvyːr| (-(e)s, -e) nt ulcer

Gesell- [gə'zɛl| zW: **~e (-n, -n)** m fellow; (Handwerkgeselle) journeyman; **g~ig** adj sociable; **~igkeit** f sociability; **~schaft** f society; (Begleitung, COMM) company; (Abendgesellschaft etc) party; **g~schaftlich** adj social; **~schaftsordnung** f social structure; **~schaftsschicht** f social stratum

gesessen |gə'zɛsən| vb siehe **sitzen**

Gesetz |gə'zɛts| (-es, -e) nt law; **~buch** nt statute book; **~entwurf** m (draft) bill; **~gebung** f legislation; **g~lich** adj legal, lawful; **g~licher Feiertag** statutory holiday; **g~los** adj lawless; **g~mäßig** adj lawful; **g~t** adj (Mensch) sedate; **g~widrig** adj illegal, unlawful

Gesicht [gə'zɪçt] (-(e)s, -er) nt face; **das zweite ~** second sight; **das ist mir nie zu ~ gekommen** I've never laid eyes on that

Gesichts- zW: **~ausdruck** m (facial) expression; **~creme** f face cream; **~farbe** f complexion; **~punkt** m point of view; **~wasser** nt face lotion; **~züge** pl features

Gesindel [gə'zɪndəl] (-s) nt rabble

gesinnt [gə'zɪnt] adj disposed, minded

Gesinnung [gə'zɪnʊŋ] f disposition; (Ansicht) views pl

gesittet [gə'zɪtət] adj well-mannered

Gespann [gə'ʃpan] (-(e)s, -e) nt team; (umg) couple

gespannt adj tense, strained; (begierig) eager; **ich bin ~, ob** I wonder if od whether; **auf etw/jdn ~ sein** to look forward to sth/ meeting sb

Gespenst [gə'ʃpɛnst] (-(e)s, -er) nt ghost, spectre

gesperrt [gə'ʃpɛrt] adj closed off

Gespött [gə'ʃpœt] (-(e)s) nt mockery; **zum ~ werden** to become a laughing stock

Gespräch [gə'ʃprɛːç] f (-(e)s, -e) nt conversation; discussion(s); (Anruf) call; **g~ig** adj talkative

gesprochen [gə'ʃprɔxən] vb siehe **sprechen**

gesprungen [gə'ʃprʊŋən] vb siehe **springen**

Gespür [gə'ʃpyːr] (-s) nt feeling

Gestalt [gə'ʃtalt] (-, -en) f form, shape; (Person) figure; **in ~ von** in the form of; **~ annehmen** to take shape; **g~en** vt (formen) to shape, to form; (organisieren) to arrange, to organize ♦ vr: **sich g~en (zu)** to turn out (to be); **~ung** f formation; organization

gestanden [gə'ʃtandən] vb siehe **stehen**

Geständnis [gə'ʃtɛntnɪs] (-ses, -se) nt confession

Gestank [gə'ʃtaŋk] (-(e)s) m stench

gestatten [gə'ʃtatən] vt to permit, to allow; **~ Sie?** may I?; **sich** dat **~, etw zu tun** to take the liberty of doing sth

Geste ['gɛstə] f gesture

gestehen [gə'ʃteːən] (unreg) vt to confess

Gestein [gə'ʃtaɪn] (-(e)s, -e) nt rock

Gestell [gə'ʃtɛl] (-(e)s, -e) nt frame; (Regal) rack, stand

gestern ['gɛstərn] adv yesterday; **~ Abend/ Morgen** yesterday evening/morning

Gestirn [gə'ʃtɪrn] (-(e)s, -e) nt star; (Sternbild) constellation

gestohlen [gə'ʃtoːlən] vb siehe **stehlen**

gestorben [gə'ʃtɔrbən] vb siehe **sterben**

gestört [gə'ʃtøːrt] adj disturbed

gestreift [gə'ʃtraɪft] adj striped

gestrichen [gə'ʃtrɪçən] adj cancelled

gestrig ['gɛstrɪç] adj yesterday's

Gestrüpp [gə'ʃtrʏp] (-(e)s, -e) nt undergrowth

Gestüt [gə'ʃtyːt] (-(e)s, -e) nt stud farm

Gesuch [gə'zuːx] (-(e)s, -e) nt petition; (Antrag) application; **g~t** adj (COMM) in demand; wanted; (fig) contrived

gesund [gə'zʊnt] adj healthy; **wieder ~ werden** to get better; **G~heit** f health(iness); **G~heit!** bless you!; **~heitlich** adj health attrib, physical ♦ adv: **wie geht es Ihnen ~heitlich?** how's your health?; **~heitsschädlich** adj unhealthy; **G~heitswesen** nt health service; **G~heitszustand** m state of health

gesungen [gə'zʊŋən] vb siehe **singen**

getan [gə'taːn] vb siehe **tun**

Getöse [gə'tøːzə] (-s) nt din, racket

Getränk [gə'trɛŋk] (-(e)s, -e) nt drink; **~ekarte** f wine list

getrauen [gə'traʊən] vr to dare, to venture

Getreide [gə'traɪdə] (-s, -) nt cereals pl, grain; **~speicher** m granary

getrennt [gə'trɛnt] adj separate

Getriebe [gə'triːbə] (-s, -) nt (Leute) bustle; (AUT) gearbox

getrieben [gə'triːbən] vb siehe **treiben**

getroffen [gə'trɔfən] vb siehe **treffen**

getrost [gə'troːst] adv without any bother

getrunken [gə'trʊŋkən] vb siehe **trinken**

Getue [gə'tuːə] (-s) nt fuss

geübt [gə'yːpt] adj experienced

Gewächs [gə'vɛks] (-es, -e) nt growth; (Pflanze) plant

gewachsen [gə'vaksən] adj: **jdm/etw ~ sein** to be sb's equal/equal to sth

Gewächshaus nt greenhouse

gewagt [gə'vaːkt] adj daring, risky

gewählt [gə'vɛːlt] adj (Sprache) refined, elegant

Gewähr [gə'vɛːr] (-) f guarantee; **keine ~ übernehmen für** to accept no responsibility for; **g~en** vt to grant; (geben) to provide; **g~leisten** vt to guarantee

Gewahrsam [gə'vaːrzaːm] (-s, -e) m safekeeping; (Polizeigewahrsam) custody

Gewalt [gə'valt] (-, -en) f power; (große Kraft) force; (~taten) violence; **mit aller ~** with all one's might; **~anwendung** f use of force; **g~ig** adj tremendous; (Irrtum) huge; **~marsch** m forced march; **g~sam** adj forcible; **g~tätig** adj violent

Gewand [gə'vant] (-(e)s, ⁻er) nt gown, robe

gewandt [gə'vant] adj deft, skilful; (erfahren) experienced; **G~heit** f dexterity, skill

gewann etc [gə'van] vb siehe **gewinnen**

Gewässer [gə'vɛsər] (-s, -) nt waters pl

Gewebe [gə'veːbə] (-s, -) nt (Stoff) fabric; (BIOL) tissue

Gewehr [gə'veːr] (-(e)s, -e) nt gun; rifle; **~lauf** m rifle barrel

Geweih [gə'vaɪ] (-(e)s, -e) nt antlers pl

Gewerb- [gəˈvɛrb] zW: **~e** (-s, -) nt trade, occupation; **Handel und ~e** trade and industry; **~eschule** f technical school; **~ezweig** m line of trade

Gewerkschaft [gəˈvɛrkʃaft] f trade union; **~ler** (-s, -) m trade unionist; **~sbund** m trade unions federation

gewesen [gəˈveːzən] pp von **sein**

Gewicht [gəˈvɪçt] (-(e)s, -e) nt weight; (fig) importance

gewieft [gəˈviːft] adj shrewd, cunning

gewillt [gəˈvɪlt] adj willing, prepared

Gewimmel [gəˈvɪməl] (-s) nt swarm

Gewinde [gəˈvɪndə] (-s, -) nt (Kranz) wreath; (von Schraube) thread

Gewinn [gəˈvɪn] (-(e)s, -e) m profit; (bei Spiel) winnings pl; **~ bringend** profitable; **etw mit ~ verkaufen** to sell sth at a profit; **~- und Verlustrechnung** (COMM) profit and loss account; **~beteiligung** f profit-sharing; **g~en** (unreg) vt to win; (erwerben) to gain; (Kohle, Öl) to extract ♦ vi to win; (profitieren) to gain; **an etw** dat **g~en** to gain (in) sth; **g~end** adj (Lächeln, Aussehen) winning, charming; **~er(in)** (-s, -) m(f) winner; **~spanne** f profit margin; **~ung** f winning; gaining; (von Kohle etc) extraction

Gewirr [gəˈvɪr] (-(e)s, -e) nt tangle; (von Straßen) maze

gewiss ▲ [gəˈvɪs] adj certain ♦ adv certainly

Gewissen [gəˈvɪsən] (-s, -) nt conscience; **g~haft** adj conscientious; **g~los** adj unscrupulous

Gewissens- zW: **~bisse** pl pangs of conscience, qualms; **~frage** f matter of conscience; **~konflikt** m moral conflict

gewissermaßen [gəvɪsərˈmaːsən] adv more or less, in a way

Gewissheit ▲ [gəˈvɪshait] f certainty

Gewitter [gəˈvɪtər] (-s, -) nt thunderstorm; **g~n** vi unpers: **es g~t** there's a thunderstorm

gewitzt [gəˈvɪtst] adj shrewd, cunning

gewogen [gəˈvoːgən] adj (+dat) well-disposed (towards)

gewöhnen [gəˈvøːnən] vt: **jdn an etw** akk **~** to accustom sb to sth; (erziehen zu) to teach sb sth ♦ vr: **sich an etw** akk **~** to get used to/accustomed to sth

Gewohnheit [gəˈvoːnhait] f habit; (Brauch) custom; **aus ~** from habit; **zur ~ werden** to become a habit

Gewohnheits- zW: **~mensch** m creature of habit; **~recht** nt common law

gewöhnlich [gəˈvøːnlɪç] adj usual; ordinary; (pej) common; **wie ~** as usual

gewohnt [gəˈvoːnt] adj usual; **etw ~ sein** to be used to sth

Gewöhnung f: **~ (an** +akk) getting accustomed (to)

Gewölbe [gəˈvœlbə] (-s, -) nt vault

gewollt [gəˈvɔlt] adj affected, artificial

gewonnen [gəˈvɔnən] vb siehe **gewinnen**

geworden [gəˈvɔrdən] vb siehe **werden**

geworfen [gəˈvɔrfən] vb siehe **werfen**

Gewühl [gəˈvyːl] (-(e)s) nt throng

Gewürz [gəˈvʏrts] (-es, -e) nt spice, seasoning; **g~t** adj spiced

gewusst ▲ [gəˈvʊst] vb siehe **wissen**

Gezeiten [gəˈtsaitən] pl tides

gezielt [gəˈtsiːlt] adj with a particular aim in mind, purposeful; (Kritik) pointed

gezogen [gəˈtsoːgən] vb siehe **ziehen**

Gezwitscher [gəˈtsvɪtʃər] (-s) nt twitter(ing), chirping

gezwungen [gəˈtsvʊŋən] adj forced; **~ermaßen** adv of necessity

ggf. abk von **gegebenenfalls**

gibst etc [ɡiːpst] vb siehe **geben**

Gicht [ɡɪçt] (-) f gout

Giebel [ˈɡiːbəl] (-s, -) m gable; **~dach** nt gable(d) roof; **~fenster** nt gable window

Gier [ɡiːr] (-) f greed; **g~ig** adj greedy

gießen [ˈɡiːsən] (unreg) vt to pour; (Blumen) to water; (Metall) to cast; (Wachs) to mould

Gießkanne f watering can

Gift [ɡɪft] (-(e)s, -e) nt poison; **g~ig** adj poisonous; (fig: boshaft) venomous; **~müll** m toxic waste; **~stoff** m toxic substance; **~zahn** m fang

ging etc [ɡɪŋ] vb siehe **gehen**

Gipfel [ˈɡɪpfəl] (-s, -) m summit, peak; (fig: Höhepunkt) height; **g~n** vi to culminate; **~treffen** nt summit (meeting)

Gips [ɡɪps] (-es, -e) m plaster; (MED) plaster (of Paris); **~abdruck** m plaster cast; **g~en** vt to plaster; **~verband** m plaster (cast)

Giraffe [ɡiˈrafə] f giraffe

Girlande [ɡɪrˈlandə] f garland

Giro [ˈʒiːro] (-s, -s) nt giro; **~konto** nt current account

Gitarre [ɡiˈtarə] f guitar

Gitter [ˈɡɪtər] (-s, -) nt grating, bars pl; (für Pflanzen) trellis; (Zaun) railing(s); **~bett** nt cot; **~fenster** nt barred window; **~zaun** m railing(s)

Glanz [ɡlants] (-es) m shine, lustre; (fig) splendour

glänzen [ˈɡlɛntsən] vi to shine (also fig) to gleam ♦ vt to polish; **~d** adj shining; (fig) brilliant

Glanz- zW: **~leistung** f brilliant achievement; **g~los** adj dull; **~zeit** f heyday

Glas [ɡlaːs] (-es, ⁼er) nt glass; **~er** (-s, -) m glazier; **~faser** f fibreglass; **g~ieren** [ɡlaˈziːrən] vt to glaze; **g~ig** adj glassy; **~scheibe** f pane; **~ur** [ɡlaˈzuːr] f glaze; (KOCH) icing

glatt [ɡlat] adj smooth; (rutschig) slippery; (Absage) flat; (Lüge) downright; **Glätte** f smoothness; slipperiness

Glatteis nt (black) ice; **jdn aufs ~ führen** (fig) to take sb for a ride

glätten vt to smooth out

Glatze ['glatsə] f bald head; **eine ~ bekommen** to go bald

Glaube ['glaubə] (**-ns, -n**) m: **~ (an** +akk) faith (in); belief (in); **g~n** vt, vi to believe; to think; **jdm g~n** to believe sb; **an etw** akk **g~n** to believe in sth; **daran g~n müssen** (umg) to be for it

glaubhaft ['glaubhaft] adj credible

gläubig ['glɔybɪç] adj (REL) devout; (vertrauensvoll) trustful; **G~e(r)** f(m) believer; **die G~en** the faithful; **G~er** (**-s, -**) m creditor

glaubwürdig ['glaubvvrdɪç] adj credible; (Mensch) trustworthy; **G~keit** f credibility; trustworthiness

gleich [glaɪç] adj equal; (identisch) (the) same, identical ♦ adv equally; (sofort) straight away; (bald) in a minute; **es ist mir ~** it's all the same to me; **~ bleibend** constant; **~ gesinnt** like-minded; **2 mal 2 ~ 4** 2 times 2 is od equals 4; **~ groß** the same size; **~ nach/an** right after/at; **~altrig** adj of the same age; **~artig** adj similar; **~bedeutend** adj synonymous; **G~berechtigung** f equal rights pl; **~en** (unreg) vi: **jdm/etw ~en** to be like sb/sth ♦ vr to be alike; **~falls** adv likewise; **danke ~falls!** the same to you; **G~förmigkeit** f uniformity; **G~gewicht** nt equilibrium, balance; **~gültig** adj indifferent; (unbedeutend) unimportant; **G~gültigkeit** f indifference; **G~heit** f equality; **~kommen** (unreg) vi +dat to be equal to; **~mäßig** adj even, equal; **~sam** adv as it were; **G~schritt** m: **im G~schritt gehen** to walk in step; **~stellen** vt (rechtlich etc) to treat as (an) equal; **G~strom** m (ELEK) direct current; **~tun** (unreg) vi: **es jdm ~tun** to match sb; **G~ung** f equation; **~viel** adv no matter; **~wertig** adj (Geld) of the same value; (Gegner) evenly matched; **~zeitig** adj simultaneous

Gleis [glaɪs] (**-es, -e**) nt track, rails pl; (Bahnsteig) platform

gleiten ['glaɪtən] (unreg) vi to glide; (rutschen) to slide

Gleitzeit f flex(i)time

Gletscher ['glɛtʃər] (**-s, -**) m glacier; **~spalte** f crevasse

Glied [gliːt] (**-(e)s, -er**) nt member; (Arm, Bein) limb; (von Kette) link; (MIL) rank(s); **g~ern** [-dərn] vt to organize, to structure; **~erung** f structure, organization

glimmen ['glɪmən] (unreg) vi to glow, to gleam

glimpflich ['glɪmpflɪç] adj mild, lenient; **~ davonkommen** to get off lightly

glitschig ['glɪtʃɪç] adj (Fisch, Weg) slippery

glitzern ['glɪtsərn] vi to glitter; to twinkle

global [glo'baːl] adj global

Globus ['gloːbʊs] (**- od -ses, Globen** od **-se**) m globe

Glocke ['glɔkə] f bell; **etw an die große ~ hängen** (fig) to shout sth from the rooftops

Glocken- zW: **~blume** f bellflower; **~geläut** nt peal of bells; **~spiel** nt chime(s); (MUS) glockenspiel; **~turm** m bell tower

Glosse ['glɔsə] f comment

glotzen ['glɔtsən] (umg) vi to stare

Glück [glʏk] (**-(e)s**) nt luck, fortune; (Freude) happiness; **~ haben** to be lucky; **viel ~!** good luck!; **zum ~** fortunately; **g~en** vi to succeed; **es g~te ihm, es zu bekommen** he succeeded in getting it

gluckern ['glʊkərn] vi to glug

glück- zW: **~lich** adj fortunate; (froh) happy; **~licherweise** adv fortunately; **~'selig** adj blissful

Glücks- zW: **~fall** m stroke of luck; **~kind** nt lucky person; **~sache** f matter of luck; **~spiel** nt game of chance

Glückwunsch m congratulations pl, best wishes pl

Glüh- [ˈglyː] zW: **~birne** f light bulb; **g~en** vi to glow; **~wein** m mulled wine; **~würmchen** nt glow-worm

Glut [gluːt] (**-, -en**) f (Röte) glow; (Feuersglut) fire; (Hitze) heat; (fig) ardour

GmbH [geːʔɛmbeːˈhaː] f abk (= Gesellschaft mit beschränkter Haftung) ≈ limited company, Ltd

Gnade ['gnaːdə] f (Gunst) favour; (Erbarmen) mercy; (Milde) clemency

Gnaden- zW: **~frist** f reprieve, respite; **g~los** adj merciless; **~stoß** m coup de grâce

gnädig ['gnɛːdɪç] adj gracious; (voll Erbarmen) merciful

Gold [gɔlt] (**-(e)s**) nt gold; **g~en** adj golden; **~fisch** m goldfish; **~grube** f goldmine; **g~ig** ['gɔldɪç] (umg) adj (fig: allerliebst) sweet, adorable; **~regen** m laburnum; **~schmied** m goldsmith

Golf[1] [gɔlf] (**-(e)s, -e**) m gulf

Golf[2] [gɔlf] (**-s**) nt golf; **~platz** m golf course; **~schläger** m golf club

Golfstrom m Gulf Stream

Gondel ['gɔndəl] (**-, -n**) f gondola; (Seilbahn) cable car

gönnen ['gœnən] vt: **jdm etw ~** not to begrudge sb sth; **sich** dat **etw ~** to allow o.s. sth

Gönner (**-s, -**) m patron; **g~haft** adj patronizing

Gosse ['gɔsə] f gutter

Gott [gɔt] (**-(e)s, ⁼er**) m god; **mein ~!** for heaven's sake!; **um ~es willen!** for heaven's sake!; **grüß ~!** hello; **~ sei Dank!** thank

Godl; **~heit** f deity

Göttin [ˈɡœtɪn] f goddess

göttlich adj divine

gottlos adj godless

Götze [ˈɡœtsə] (-n, -n) m idol

Grab [ɡraːp] (-(e)s, ⁼er) nt grave; **g~en** [ˈɡraːbən] (unreg) vt to dig; **~en** (-s, ⁼) m ditch; (MIL) trench; **~stein** m gravestone

Grad [ɡraːt] (-(e)s, -e) m degree

Graf [ɡraːf] (-en, -en) m count, earl

Gram [ɡraːm] (-(e)s) m grief, sorrow

grämen [ˈɡrɛːmən] vr to grieve

Gramm [ɡram] (-s, -e) nt gram(me)

Grammatik [ɡraˈmatɪk] f grammar

Granat [ɡraˈnaːt] (-(e)s, -e) m (Stein) garnet

Granate f (MIL) shell; (Handgranate) grenade

Granit [ɡraˈniːt] (-s, -e) m granite

Grafiker(in) ▲ [ˈɡraːfɪkər(ɪn)] (-s, -) m(f) graphic designer

grafisch ▲ [ˈɡraːfɪʃ] adj graphic

Gras [ɡraːs] (-es, ⁼er) nt grass; **g~en** [ˈɡraːzən] vi to graze; **~halm** m blade of grass

grassieren [ɡraˈsiːrən] vi to be rampant, to rage

grässlich ▲ [ˈɡrɛslɪç] adj horrible

Grat [ɡraːt] (-(e)s, -e) m ridge

Gräte [ˈɡrɛːtə] f fishbone

gratis [ˈɡraːtɪs] adj, adv free (of charge); **G~probe** f free sample

Gratulation [ɡratulatsiˈoːn] f congratulation(s)

gratulieren [ɡratuˈliːrən] vi: **jdm ~ (zu etw)** to congratulate sb (on sth); **(ich) gratuliere!** congratulations!

grau [ɡrau] adj grey

Gräuel ▲ [ˈɡrɔʏəl] (-s, -) m horror, revulsion; **etw ist jdm ein ~** sb loathes sth

Grauen (-s) nt horror; **g~** vi unpers: **es graut jdm vor etw** sb dreads sth, sb is afraid of sth ♦ vr: **sich g~ vor** to dread, to have a horror of; **g~haft** adj horrible

grauhaarig adj grey-haired

gräulich [ˈɡrɔʏlɪç] ▲ adj horrible

grausam [ˈɡrauzaːm] adj cruel; **G~keit** f cruelty

Grausen [ˈɡrauzən] (-s) nt horror; **g~** vb = **grauen**

gravieren [ɡraˈviːrən] vt to engrave; **~d** adj grave

graziös [ɡratsiˈøːs] adj graceful

greifbar adj tangible, concrete; **in ~er Nähe** within reach

greifen [ˈɡraɪfən] (unreg) vt to seize; to grip; **nach etw ~** to reach for sth; **um sich ~** (fig) to spread; **zu etw ~** (fig) to turn to sth

Greis [ɡraɪs] (-es, -e) m old man; **g~enhaft** adj senile; **~in** f old woman

grell [ɡrɛl] adj harsh

Grenz- [ˈɡrɛnts] zW: **~beamte(r)** m frontier official; **~e** f boundary; (Staatsgrenze) frontier; (Schranke) limit; **g~en** vi: **g~en (an +akk)** to border (on); **g~enlos** adj boundless; **~fall** m borderline case; **~kontrolle** f border control; **~übergang** m frontier crossing

Greuel △ [ˈɡrɔʏəl] (-s, -) m = **Gräuel**; **greulich** △ adj = **gräulich**

Griech- [ˈɡriːç] zW: **~e** (-n, -n) m Greek; **~enland** nt Greece; **~in** f Greek; **g~isch** adj Greek

griesgrämig [ˈɡriːsɡrɛːmɪç] adj grumpy

Grieß [ɡriːs] (-es, -e) m (KOCH) semolina

Griff [ɡrɪf] (-(e)s, -e) m grip; (Vorrichtung) handle; **g~bereit** adj handy

Grill [ɡrɪl] m grill; **~e** f cricket; **g~en** vt to grill; **~fest** nt barbecue party

Grimasse [ɡriˈmasə] f grimace

grimmig [ˈɡrɪmɪç] adj furious; (heftig) fierce, severe

grinsen [ˈɡrɪnzən] vi to grin

Grippe [ˈɡrɪpə] f influenza, flu

grob [ɡroːp] adj coarse, gross; (Fehler, Verstoß) gross; **G~heit** f coarseness; coarse expression

grölen [ˈɡrøːlən] (pej) vt to bawl, to bellow

Groll [ɡrɔl] (-(e)s) m resentment; **g~en** vi (Donner) to rumble; **g~en (mit od +dat)** to bear ill will (towards)

groß [ɡroːs] adj big, large; (hoch) tall; (fig) great ♦ adv greatly; **im G~en und Ganzen** on the whole; **bei jdm ~ geschrieben werden** to be high on sb's list of priorities; **~artig** adj great, splendid; **G~aufnahme** f (CINE) close-up; **G~britannien** nt Great Britain

Größe [ˈɡrøːsə] f size; (Höhe) height; (fig) greatness

Groß- zW: **~einkauf** m bulk purchase; **~eltern** pl grandparents; **g~enteils** adv mostly; **~format** nt large size; **~handel** m wholesale trade; **~händler** m wholesaler; **~macht** f great power; **~mutter** f grandmother; **~rechner** m mainframe (computer); **g~schreiben** (unreg) vt (Wort) to write in block capitals; siehe **groß**; **g~spurig** adj pompous; **~stadt** f city, large town

größte(r, s) [ˈɡrøːstə(r, s)] adj superl von **groß**; **~nteils** adv for the most part

Groß- zW: **g~tun** (unreg) vi to boast; **~vater** m grandfather; **g~ziehen** (unreg) vt to raise; **g~zügig** adj generous; (Planung) on a large scale

grotesk [ɡroˈtɛsk] adj grotesque

Grotte [ˈɡrɔtə] f grotto

Grübchen [ˈɡryːpçən] nt dimple

Grube [ˈɡruːbə] f pit; mine

grübeln [ˈɡryːbəln] vi to brood

Gruft [ɡruft] (-, ⁼e) f tomb, vault

grün [ɡryːn] adj green; **der ~e Punkt** green spot symbol on recyclable packaging

Grünanlage f park

Grund |grʊnt| (-(e)s, ˀe) m ground; (von See, Gefäß) bottom; (fig) reason; **im ~e genommen** basically; siehe **aufgrund**; **~ausbildung** f basic training; **~besitz** m land(ed property), real estate; **~buch** nt land register

gründen |grʏndən| vt to found ♦ vr: **sich ~ (auf** +dat) to be based (on); **~ auf** +akk to base on

Gründer (-s, -) m founder

Grund- zW: **~gebühr** f basic charge; **~gesetz** nt constitution; **~lage** f foundation; **g~legend** adj fundamental

gründlich adj thorough

Grund- zW: **g~los** adj groundless; **~regel** f basic rule; **~riss ▲** m plan; (fig) outline; **~satz** m principle; **g~sätzlich** adj fundamental; (Frage) of principle ♦ adv fundamentally; (prinzipiell) on principle; **~schule** f elementary school; **~stein** m foundation stone; **~stück** nt estate; plot

Grundwasser nt ground water

Grünstreifen m central reservation

grunzen |grʊntsən| vi to grunt

Gruppe |ˈgrʊpə| f group; **~nermäßigung** f group reduction; **g~nweise** adv in groups

gruppieren |grʊˈpiːrən| vt, vr to group

gruselig adj creepy

gruseln |ˈgruːzəln| vi unpers: **es gruselt jdm vor einer ~** sth gives sb the creeps ♦ vr to have the creeps

Gruß |gruːs| (-es, ˀe) m greeting; (MIL) salute; **viele Grüße** best wishes; **mit freundlichen Grüßen** yours sincerely; **Grüße an** +akk regards to

grüßen |ˈgryːsən| vt to greet; (MIL) to salute; **jdn von jdm ~** to give sb sb's regards; **jdn ~ lassen** to send sb one's regards

gucken |ˈgʊkən| vi to look

gültig |ˈgʏltɪç| adj valid; **G~keit** f validity

Gummi |ˈgʊmi| (-s, -s) nt od m rubber; (~harze) gum; **~band** nt rubber od elastic band; (Hosenband) elastic; **~bärchen** nt ≈ jelly baby (BRIT); **~baum** m rubber plant; **g~eren** |gʊˈmiːrən| vt to gum; **~stiefel** m rubber boot

günstig |ˈgʏnstɪç| adj convenient; (Gelegenheit) favourable; **das habe ich ~ bekommen** it was a bargain

Gurgel |ˈgʊrgəl| (-, -n) f throat; **g~n** vi to gurgle; (im Mund) to gargle

Gurke |ˈgʊrkə| f cucumber; **saure ~** pickled cucumber, gherkin

Gurt |gʊrt| (-(e)s, -e) m belt

Gürtel |ˈgʏrtəl| (-s, -) m belt; (GEOG) zone; **~reifen** m radial tyre

GUS f abk (= Gemeinschaft unabhängiger Staaten) CIS

Guss ▲ |gʊs| (-es, ˀe) m casting; (Regen~) down-

pour; (KOCH) glazing; **~eisen** nt cast iron

SCHLÜSSELWORT
---

gut adj good; **alles Gute** all the best; **also gut** all right then
♦ adv well; **gut gehen** to work, to come off; **es geht jdm gut** sb's doing fine; **gut gemeint** well meant; **gut schmecken** to taste good; **jdm gut tun** to do sb good; **gut, aber ...** OK, but ...; **(na) gut, ich komme** all right, I'll come; **gut drei Stunden** a good three hours; **das kann gut sein** that may well be; **lass es gut sein** that'll do

---

Gut |guːt| (-(e)s, ˀer) nt (Besitz) possession; **Güter** pl (Waren) goods; **~achten** (-s, -) nt (expert) opinion; **~achter** (-s, -) m expert; **g~artig** adj good-natured; (MED) benign; **g~bürgerlich** adj (Küche) (good) plain; **~dünken** nt: **nach ~dünken** at one's discretion

Güte |ˈgyːtə| f goodness, kindness; (Qualität) quality

Güter- zW: **~abfertigung** f (EISENB) goods office; **~bahnhof** m goods station; **~wagen** m goods waggon (BRIT), freight car (US); **~zug** m goods train (BRIT), freight train (US)

Gütezeichen nt quality mark; ≈ kite mark

gut- zW: **~gehen** △ (unreg) vi unpers siehe **gut**; **~gemeint** △ adj siehe **gut**; **~gläubig** adj trusting; **G~haben** (-s) nt credit; **~heißen** (unreg) vt to approve (of)

gütig |ˈgyːtɪç| adj kind

Gut- zW: **g~mütig** adj good-natured; **~schein** m voucher; **g~schreiben** (unreg) vt to credit; **~schrift** f (Betrag) credit; **g~tun** △ (unreg) vi siehe **gut**; **g~willig** adj willing

Gymnasium |gʏmˈnaːziʊm| nt grammar school (BRIT), high school (US)

Gymnastik |gʏmˈnastɪk| f exercises pl, keep fit

H, h

Haag |haːk| m: **Den ~** the Hague

Haar |haːr| (-(e)s, -e) nt hair; **um ein ~** nearly; **an den ~en herbeigezogen** (umg: Vergleich) very far-fetched; **~bürste** f hairbrush; **h~en** vi, vr to lose hair; **~esbreite** f: **um ~esbreite** by a hair's-breadth; **~festiger** (-s, -) m (hair) setting lotion; **h~genau** adv precisely; **h~ig** adj hairy; (fig) nasty; **~klammer** f hairgrip; **~nadel** f hairpin; **h~scharf** adv (beobachten) very sharply; (daneben) by a

hair's breadth; **~schnitt** *m* haircut;
~spange *f* hair slide; **h~sträubend** *adj*
hair-raising; **~teil** *nt* hairpiece;
~waschmittel *nt* shampoo
Habe ['ha:bə] (-) *f* property
haben ['ha:bən] (*unreg*) *vt, vb aux* to have;
Hunger/Angst ~ to be hungry/afraid;
woher hast du das? where did you get
that from?; **was hast du denn?** what's the
matter (with you)?; **du hast zu schweigen**
you're to be quiet; **ich hätte gern** I would
like; **H~ (-s, -)** *nt* credit
Habgier *f* avarice; **h~ig** *adj* avaricious
Habicht ['ha:bɪçt] (-s, -e) *m* hawk
Habseligkeiten ['ha:pze:lɪçkaɪtən] *pl*
belongings
Hachse ['haksə] *f* (*KOCH*) knuckle
Hacke ['hakə] *f* hoe; (*Ferse*) heel; **h~n** *vt* to
hack, to chop; (*Erde*) to hoe
Hackfleisch *nt* mince, minced meat
Hafen ['ha:fən] (-s, ⸚) *m* harbour, port;
~arbeiter *m* docker; **~rundfahrt** *f* boat trip
round the harbour; **~stadt** *f* port
Hafer ['ha:fər] (-s) *m* oats *pl*; **~flocken** *pl*
rolled oats; **~schleim** *m* gruel
Haft [haft] (-) *f* custody; **h~bar** *adj* liable,
responsible; **~befehl** *m* warrant (for arrest);
h~en *vi* to stick, to cling; **h~en für** to be
liable *od* responsible for; **h~en bleiben (an**
+*dat*) to stick (to)
Häftling *m* prisoner
Haft- *zW:* **~pflicht** *f* liability; **~pflicht-
versicherung** *f* (*AUT*) third party insurance;
~schalen *pl* contact lenses; **~ung** *f* liability;
~ungsbeschränkung *f* limitation of
liability
Hagebutte ['ha:gəbʊtə] *f* rose hip
Hagel ['ha:gəl] (-s) *m* hail; **h~n** *vi unpers* to
hail
hager ['ha:gər] *adj* gaunt
Hahn [ha:n] (-(e)s, ⸚e) *m* cock; (*Wasserhahn*)
tap, faucet (*US*)
Hähnchen ['hɛ:nçən] *nt* cockerel; (*KOCH*)
chicken
Hai(fisch) ['haɪ(fɪʃ)] (-(e)s, -e) *m* shark
häkeln ['hɛ:kəln] *vt* to crochet
Haken ['ha:kən] (-s, -) *m* hook; (*fig*) catch;
~kreuz *nt* swastika; **~nase** *f* hooked nose
halb [halp] *adj* half; **~ eins** half past twelve; **~
offen** half-open; **ein ~es Dutzend** half a
dozen; **H~dunkel** *nt* semi-darkness
halber ['halbər] *präp* +*gen* (*wegen*) on
account of; (*für*) for the sake of
Halb- *zW:* **~heit** *f* half-measure; **h~ieren** *vt*
to halve; **~insel** *f* peninsula; **~jahr** *nt* six
months; (*auch: COMM*) half-year; **h~jährlich**
adj half-yearly; **~kreis** *m* semicircle; **~leiter**
m semiconductor; **~mond** *m* half-moon;
(*fig*) crescent; **~pension** *f* half-board; **~rechte(r)** *mf*
(*SPORT*) inside right; **~schuh** *m* shoe;

h~tags *adv:* **h~tags arbeiten** to work part-
time, to work mornings/afternoons;
h~wegs *adv* halfway; **h~wegs besser**
more or less better; **~zeit** *f* (*SPORT*) half;
(*Pause*) half-time
Halde ['haldə] *f* (*Kohlen*) heap
half [half] *vb siehe* **helfen**
Hälfte ['hɛlftə] *f* half
Halfter ['halftər] (-s, -) *m od nt* (*für Tiere*)
halter
Halle ['halə] *f* hall; (*AVIAT*) hangar; **h~n** *vi* to
echo, to resound; **~nbad** *nt* indoor
swimming pool
hallo [ha'lo:] *excl* hello
Halluzination [halutsinatsi'o:n] *f*
hallucination
Halm ['halm] (-(e)s, -e) *m* blade; stalk
Halogenlampe [halo'ge:nlampə] *f* halogen
lamp
Hals [hals] (-es, ⸚e) *m* neck; (*Kehle*) throat; **~
über Kopf** in a rush; **~band** *nt* (*von Hund*)
collar; **~kette** *f* necklace; **~-Nasen-Ohren-
Arzt** *m* ear, nose and throat specialist;
~schmerzen *pl* sore throat *sg*; **~tuch** *nt* scarf
Halt [halt] (-(e)s, -e) *m* stop; (*fester ~*) hold;
(*innerer ~*) stability; **~ od halt!** stop!, halt!;
h~ machen to stop; **h~bar** *adj* durable;
(*Lebensmittel*) non-perishable; (*MIL, fig*)
tenable; **~barkeit** *f* durability; (*non-*)
perishability
halten ['haltən] (*unreg*) *vt* to keep;
(*festhalten*) to hold ♦ *vi* to hold; (*frisch
bleiben*) to keep; (*stoppen*) to stop ♦ *vr* (*frisch
bleiben*) to keep; (*sich behaupten*) to hold
out; **~ für** to regard as; **~ von** to think of;
an sich ~ to restrain o.s.; **sich rechts/links
~** to keep to the right/left
Halte- *zW:* **~stelle** *f* stop; **~verbot** *nt:* **hier
ist ~verbot** there's no waiting here
Halt- *zW:* **h~los** *adj* unstable; **h~ma-
chen** △ *vi siehe* **Halt**; **~ung** *f* posture; (*fig*)
attitude; (*Selbstbeherrschung*) composure
Halunke [ha'lʊŋkə] (-n, -n) *m* rascal
hämisch ['hɛ:mɪʃ] *adj* malicious
Hammel ['haməl] (-s, ⸚ *od* -) *m* wether;
~fleisch *nt* mutton
Hammer ['hamər] (-s, ⸚) *m* hammer
hämmern ['hɛmərn] *vt, vi* to hammer
Hämorr(ho)iden [hemɔrɔˈiːdən,
hemɔˈriːdn] *pl* haemorrhoids
Hamster ['hamstər] (-s, -) *m* hamster; **~ei**
[-ˈraɪ] *f* hoarding; **h~n** *vi* to hoard
Hand [hant] (-, ⸚e) *f* hand; **~arbeit** *f* manual
work; (*Nadelarbeit*) needlework; **~ball** *m*
(*SPORT*) handball; **~bremse** *f* handbrake;
~buch *nt* handbook, manual
Händedruck ['hɛndədrʊk] *m* handshake
Handel ['handəl] (-s) *m* trade; (*Geschäft*)
transaction
Handeln ['handəln] (-s) *nt* action
handeln *vi* to trade; (*agieren*) to act ♦ *vr*

unpers: **sich ~ um** to be a question of, to be about; **~ von** to be about

Handels- *zW*: **~bilanz** *f* balance of trade; **~kammer** *f* chamber of commerce; **~reisende(r)** *m* commercial traveller; **~schule** *f* business school; **h~üblich** *adj* customary; (*Preis*) going *attrib*; **~vertreter** *m* sales representative

Hand- *zW*: **~feger (-s, -)** *m* hand brush; **h~fest** *adj* hefty; **h~gearbeitet** *adj* handmade; **~gelenk** *nt* wrist; **~gemenge** *nt* scuffle; **~gepäck** *nt* hand luggage; **h~geschrieben** *adj* handwritten; **h~greiflich** (*-s, -*) *nt* palpable; **h~greiflich werden** to become violent; **~griff** *m* flick of the wrist; **h~haben** *vt insep* to handle

Händler ['hɛndlər] (*-s, -*) *m* trader, dealer

handlich ['hantlɪç] *adj* handy

Handlung ['handluŋ] *f* act(ion); (*in Buch*) plot; (*Geschäft*) shop

Hand- *zW*: **~schelle** *f* handcuff; **~schrift** *f* handwriting; (*Text*) manuscript; **~schuh** *m* glove; **~stand** *m* (*SPORT*) handstand; **~tasche** *f* handbag; **~tuch** *nt* towel; **~umdrehen** *nt*: **im ~umdrehen** in the twinkling of an eye; **~werk** *nt* trade, craft; **~werker (-s, -)** *m* craftsman, artisan; **~werkzeug** *nt* tools *pl*

Handy ['hɛndi] (*-s, -s*) *nt* mobile (telephone)

Hanf [hanf] (*-(e)s*) *m* hemp

Hang [haŋ] (*-(e)s, ≈e*) *m* inclination; (*Abhang*) slope

Hänge- ['hɛŋə] *in zW* hanging; **~brücke** *f* suspension bridge; **~matte** *f* hammock

hängen ['hɛŋən] (*unreg*) *vi* to hang ♦ *vt*: **etw (an etw** *akk*) **~** to hang sth (on sth); **~ an** +*dat* (*fig*) to be attached to; **sich ~ an** +*akk* to hang on to, to cling to; **~ bleiben** to be caught; (*fig*) to remain, to stick; **~ bleiben an** +*dat* to catch *od* get caught on; **~ lassen** (*vergessen*) to leave; **den Kopf ~ lassen** to get downhearted

Hannover [ha'noːfər] (*-s*) *nt* Hanover

hänseln ['hɛnzəln] *vt* to tease

Hansestadt ['hanzəʃtat] *f* Hanse town

hantieren [han'tiːrən] *vi* to work, to be busy; **mit etw ~** to handle sth

hapern ['haːpərn] *vi unpers*: **es hapert an etw** *dat* there is a lack of sth

Happen ['hapən] (*-s, -*) *m* mouthful

Harfe ['harfə] *f* harp

Harke ['harkə] *f* rake; **h~n** *vt, vi* to rake

harmlos ['harmloːs] *adj* harmless; **H~igkeit** *f* harmlessness

Harmonie [harmo'niː] *f* harmony; **h~ren** *vi* to harmonize

harmonisch [har'moːnɪʃ] *adj* harmonious

Harn ['harn] (*-(e)s, -e*) *m* urine; **~blase** *f* bladder

Harpune [har'puːnə] *f* harpoon

harren ['harən] *vi*: **~ (auf** +*akk*) to wait (for)

hart [hart] *adj* hard; (*fig*) harsh; **~ gekocht** hard-boiled

Härte ['hɛrtə] *f* hardness; (*fig*) harshness

hart- *zW*: **~herzig** *adj* hard-hearted; **~näckig** *adj* stubborn; **H~näckigkeit** *f* stubbornness

Harz [haːrts] (*-es, -e*) *nt* resin

Haschee [ha'ʃeː] (*-s, -s*) *nt* hash

Haschisch ['haʃɪʃ] (*-*) *nt* hashish

Hase ['haːzə] (*-n, -n*) *m* hare

Haselnuss ▲ ['haːzəlnʊs] *f* hazelnut

Hasenscharte *f* harelip

Hass ▲ [has] (*-es*) *m* hate, hatred

hassen ['hasən] *vt* to hate

hässlich ▲ ['hɛslɪç] *adj* ugly; (*gemein*) nasty; **H~keit** *f* ugliness; nastiness

Hast [hast] *f* haste

hast *vb siehe* **haben**

hasten *vi* to rush

hastig *adj* hasty

hat [hat] *vb siehe* **haben**

hatte *etc* ['hatə] *vb siehe* **haben**

Haube ['haʊbə] *f* hood; (*Mütze*) cap; (*AUT*) bonnet, hood (*US*)

Hauch [haʊx] (*-(e)s, -e*) *m* breath; (*Lufthauch*) breeze; (*fig*) trace; **h~dünn** *adj* extremely thin

Haue ['haʊə] *f* hoe, pick; (*umg*) hiding; **h~n** (*unreg*) *vt* to hew, to cut; (*umg*) to thrash

Haufen ['haʊfən] (*-s, -*) *m* heap; (*Leute*) crowd; **ein ~ (x)** (*umg*) loads *od* a lot (of x); **auf einem ~** in one heap

häufen ['hɔʏfən] *vt* to pile up ♦ *vr* to accumulate

haufenweise *adv* in heaps; in droves; **etw ~ haben** to have piles of sth

häufig ['hɔʏfɪç] *adj* frequent ♦ *adv* frequently; **H~keit** *f* frequency

Haupt [haʊpt] (*-(e)s, Häupter*) *nt* head; (*Oberhaupt*) chief ♦ *in zW* main; **~bahnhof** *m* central station; **h~beruflich** *adv* as one's main occupation; **~darsteller(in)** *m(f)* leading actor (actress); **~fach** *nt* (*SCH, UNIV*) main subject, major (*US*); **~gericht** *nt* (*KOCH*) main course

Häuptling ['hɔʏptlɪŋ] *m* chief(tain)

Haupt- *zW*: **~mann** (*pl* **-leute**) *m* (*MIL*) captain; **~person** *f* central figure; **~quartier** *nt* headquarters *pl*; **~rolle** *f* leading part; **~sache** *f* main thing; **h~sächlich** *adj* chief ♦ *adv* chiefly; **~saison** *f* high season, peak season; **~schule** *f* ≈ secondary school; **~stadt** *f* capital; **~straße** *f* main street; **~verkehrszeit** *f* rush-hour, peak traffic hours *pl*

Haus [haʊs] (*-es, Häuser*) *nt* house; **~ halten** (*sparen*) to economize; **nach ~e** home; **zu**

Spelling reform: ▲ *new spelling* △ *old spelling (to be phased out)*

~e at home; ~**apotheke** f medicine cabinet; ~**arbeit** f housework; (SCH) homework; ~**arzt** m family doctor; ~**aufgabe** f (SCH) homework; ~**besitzer(in)** m(f) house owner; ~**besuch** m (von Arzt) house call; ~**durchsuchung** f police raid; **h~eigen** adj belonging to a/the hotel/firm

Häuser- ['hɔyzər] zW: ~**block** m block (of houses); ~**makler** m estate agent (BRIT), real estate agent (US)

Haus- zW: ~**flur** m hallway; ~**frau** f housewife; **h~gemacht** adj home-made; ~**halt** m household; (POL) budget

haushalten △ (unreg) vi siehe **Haus**; ~**hälterin** f housekeeper; ~**haltsgeld** nt housekeeping (money); ~**haltsgerät** nt domestic appliance; ~**herr** m host; (Vermieter) landlord; **h~hoch** adv: **h~hoch verlieren** to lose by a mile

hausieren [hau'zi:rən] vi to peddle

Hausierer (-s, -) m pedlar (BRIT), peddler (US)

häuslich ['hɔyslıç] adj domestic

Haus- zW: ~**meister** m caretaker, janitor; ~**nummer** f street number; ~**ordnung** f house rules pl; ~**putz** m house cleaning; ~**schlüssel** m front door key; ~**schuh** m slipper; ~**tier** nt pet; ~**tür** f front door; ~**wirt** m landlord; ~**wirtschaft** f domestic science; ~**zelt** nt frame tent

Haut [haut] (-, **Häute**) f skin; (Tierhaut) hide; ~**creme** f skin cream; **h~eng** adj skin-tight; ~**farbe** f complexion; ~**krebs** m skin cancer

Haxe ['haksə] f = **Hachse**

Hbf. abk = **Hauptbahnhof**

Hebamme ['he:plamə] f midwife

Hebel ['he:bal] (-s, -) m lever

heben ['he:bən] (unreg) vt to raise, to lift

Hecht [hɛçt] (-(e)s, -e) m pike

Heck [hɛk] (-(e)s, -e) nt stern; (von Auto) rear

Hecke ['hɛkə] f hedge

Heckenschütze m sniper

Heckscheibe f rear window

Heer [he:r] (-(e)s, -e) nt army

Hefe ['he:fə] f yeast

Heft [hɛft] (-(e)s, -e) nt exercise book; (Zeitschrift) number; (von Messer) haft; **h~en** vt: **h~en (an +akk)** to fasten (to); (nähen) to tack ((on) to); **etw an etw akk h~en** to fasten sth to sth; ~**er** (-s, -) m folder

heftig adj fierce, violent; **H~keit** f fierceness, violence

Heft- zW: ~**klammer** f paper clip; ~**pflaster** nt sticking plaster; ~**zwecke** f drawing pin

hegen ['he:gən] vt (Wild, Bäume) to care for, to tend; (fig, geh: empfinden: Wunsch) to cherish; (: Misstrauen) to feel

Hehl [he:l] m od nt: **kein(en)** ~ **aus etw machen** to make no secret of sth; ~**er** (-s, -) m receiver (of stolen goods), fence

Heide¹ ['haidə] (-n, -n) m heathen, pagan

Heide² ['haidə] f heath, moor; ~**kraut** nt heather

Heidelbeere f bilberry

Heidentum nt paganism

Heidin f heathen, pagan

heikel ['haikəl] adj awkward, thorny

Heil [hail] (-(e)s) nt well-being; (Seelenheil) salvation; **h~** adj in one piece, intact; ~**and** (-(e)s, -e) m saviour; **h~bar** adj curable; **h~en** vt to cure ♦ vi to heal; **h~froh** adj very relieved

heilig ['hailıç] adj holy; ~ **sprechen** to canonize; **H~abend** m Christmas Eve; **H~e(r)** f(m) saint; ~**en** vt to sanctify, to hallow; **H~enschein** m halo; **H~keit** f holiness; **H~tum** nt shrine; (Gegenstand) relic

Heil- zW: **h~los** adj unholy; (fig) hopeless; ~**mittel** nt remedy; ~**praktiker(in)** m(f) non-medical practitioner; **h~sam** adj (fig) salutary; ~**sarmee** f Salvation Army; ~**ung** f cure

Heim [haim] (-(e)s, -e) nt home; **h~** adv home

Heimat ['haima:t] (-, -en) f home (town/ country etc); ~**land** nt homeland; **h~lich** adj native, home attrib; (Gefühle) nostalgic; **h~los** adj homeless; ~**ort** m home town/ area

Heim- zW: ~**computer** m home computer; **h~fahren** (unreg) vi to drive home; ~**fahrt** f journey home; **h~gehen** (unreg) vi to go home; (sterben) to pass away; **h~isch** adj (gebürtig) native; **sich h~isch fühlen** to feel at home; ~**kehr** (-, -en) f homecoming; **h~kehren** vi to return home; **h~lich** adj secret; ~**lichkeit** f secrecy; ~**reise** f journey home; ~**spiel** nt (SPORT) home game; **h~suchen** vt to afflict; (Geist) to haunt; ~**trainer** m exercise bike; **h~tückisch** adj malicious; ~**weg** m way home; ~**weh** nt homesickness; ~**werker** (-s, -) m handyman; **h~zahlen** vt: **jdm etw h~zahlen** to pay sb back for sth

Heirat ['haira:t] (-, -en) f marriage; **h~en** vt to marry ♦ vi to marry, to get married ♦ vr to get married; ~**santrag** m proposal

heiser ['haizər] adj hoarse; **H~keit** f hoarseness

heiß [hais] adj hot; ~**e(s) Eisen** (umg) hot potato; **h~blütig** adj hot-blooded

heißen ['haisən] (unreg) vi to be called; (bedeuten) to mean ♦ vt to command; (nennen) to name ♦ vi unpers: **es heißt** it says; it is said; **das heißt** that is (to say)

Heiß- zW: ~**hunger** m ravenous hunger; **h~laufen** (unreg) vi, vr to overheat

heiter ['haitər] adj cheerful; (Wetter) bright; **H~keit** f cheerfulness; (Belustigung) amusement

Heiz- ['haits] *zW:* **h~bar** *adj* heated; *(Raum)* with heating; **h~en** *vt* to heat; **~körper** *m* radiator; **~öl** *nt* fuel oil; **~sonne** *f* electric fire; **~ung** *f* heating

hektisch ['hɛktɪʃ] *adj* hectic

Held [hɛlt] **(-en, -en)** *m* hero; **h~enhaft** *adj* heroic; **~in** *f* heroine

helfen ['hɛlfən] *(unreg) vi* to help; *(nützen)* to be of use ♦ *vb unpers:* **es hilft nichts, du musst** ... it's no use, you'll have to ...; **jdm (bei etw)** ~ to help sb (with sth); **sich** *dat* **zu** ~ **wissen** to be resourceful

Helfer (-s, -) *m* helper, assistant; **~shelfer** *m* accomplice

hell [hɛl] *adj* clear, bright; *(Farbe, Bier)* light; **~blau** *adj* light blue; **~blond** *adj* ash blond; **H~e (-)** *f* clearness, brightness; **~hörig** *adj (Wand)* paper-thin; **~hörig werden** *(fig)* to prick up one's ears; **H~seher** *m* clairvoyant; **~wach** *adj* wide-awake

Helm ['hɛlm] **(-(e)s, -e)** *m (auf Kopf)* helmet

Hemd [hɛmt] **(-(e)s, -en)** *nt* shirt; *(Unterhemd)* vest; **~bluse** *f* blouse

hemmen ['hɛmən] *vt* to check, to hold up; **gehemmt sein** to be inhibited; **Hemmung** *f* check; *(PSYCH)* inhibition; **hemmungslos** *adj* unrestrained, without restraint

Hengst [hɛŋst] **(-es, -e)** *m* stallion

Henkel ['hɛŋkəl] **(-s, -)** *m* handle

Henker (-s, -) *m* hangman

Henne ['hɛnə] *f* hen

SCHLÜSSELWORT

her [heːr] *adv* **1** *(Richtung):* **komm her zu mir** come here (to me); **von England her** from England; **von weit her** from a long way away; **her damit!** hand it over!; **wo hat er das her?** where did he get that from?; **wo bist du her?** where do you come from?

2 *(Blickpunkt):* **von der Form her** as far as the form is concerned

3 *(zeitlich):* **das ist 5 Jahre her** that was 5 years ago; **ich kenne ihn von früher her** I know him from before

---

herab [hɛ'rap] *adv* down(ward(s)); **~hängen** *(unreg) vi* to hang down; **~lassen** *(unreg) vt* to let down ♦ *vr* to condescend; **~lassend** *adj* condescending; **~setzen** *vt* to lower, to reduce; *(fig)* to belittle, to disparage

heran [hɛ'ran] *adv:* **näher ~!** come up closer!; **~ zu mir!** come up to me!; **~bringen** *(unreg) vt:* **~bringen (an** +*akk)* to bring up (to); **~fahren** *(unreg) vi:* **~fahren (an** +*akk)* to drive up (to); **~kommen** *(unreg) vi:* **(an jdn/etw) ~kommen** to approach (sb/sth), to come near (to sb/sth); **~machen** *vr:* **sich an jdn**

~machen to make up to sb; **~treten** *(unreg) vi:* **mit etw an jdn ~treten** to approach sb with sth; **~wachsen** *(unreg) vi* to grow up; **~ziehen** *(unreg) vt* to pull nearer; *(aufziehen)* to raise; *(ausbilden)* to train; **jdn zu etw ~ziehen** to call upon sb to help in sth

herauf [hɛ'rauf] *adv* up(ward(s)), up here; **~beschwören** *(unreg) vt* to conjure up, to evoke; **~bringen** *(unreg) vt* to bring up; **~setzen** *vt (Preise, Miete)* to raise, put up

heraus [hɛ'raus] *adv* out; **~bekommen** *(unreg) vt* to get out; *(fig)* to find *od* figure out; **~bringen** *(unreg) vt* to bring out; *(Geheimnis)* to elicit; **~finden** *(unreg) vt* to find out; **~fordern** *vt* to challenge; **H~forderung** *f* challenge; provocation; **~geben** *(unreg) vt* to hand over, to surrender; *(zurückgeben)* to give back; *(Buch)* to edit; *(veröffentlichen)* to publish; **H~geber (-s, -)** *m* editor; *(Verleger)* publisher; **~gehen** *(unreg) vi:* **aus sich ~gehen** to come out of one's shell; **~halten** *(unreg) vr:* **sich aus etw ~halten** to keep out of sth; **~hängen**[1] *vt* to hang out; **~hängen**[2] *(unreg) vi* to hang out; **~holen** *vt:* **~holen (aus)** to get out (of); **~kommen** *(unreg) vi* to come out; **dabei kommt nichts ~** nothing will come of it; **~nehmen** *(unreg) vt* to remove (from), take out (of); **sich** *dat* **etw ~nehmen** to take liberties; **~reißen** *(unreg) vt* to tear out; to pull out; **~rücken** *vt (Geld)* to fork out; to hand over; **mit etw ~rücken** *(fig)* to come out with sth; **~stellen** *vr:* **sich ~stellen (als)** to turn out (to be); **~suchen** *vt:* **sich** *dat* **jdn/etw ~suchen** to pick sb/sth out; **~ziehen** *(unreg) vt* to pull out, to extract

herb [hɛrp] *adj* (slightly) bitter, acid; *(Wein)* dry; *(fig: schmerzlich)* bitter

herbei [hɛr'bai] *adv (over)* here; **~führen** *vt* to bring about; **~schaffen** *vt* to procure

herbemühen ['heːrbəmyːən] *vr* to take the trouble to come

Herberge ['hɛrbɛrgə] *f* shelter; hostel, inn

Herbergsmutter *f* warden

Herbergsvater *m* warden

herbitten *(unreg) vt* to ask to come (here)

Herbst [hɛrpst] **(-(e)s, -e)** *m* autumn, fall *(US)*; **h~lich** *adj* autumnal

Herd [heːrt] **(-(e)s, -e)** *m* cooker; *(fig, MED)* focus, centre

Herde ['heːrdə] *f* herd; *(Schafherde)* flock

herein [hɛ'rain] *adv* in (here), here; **~!** come in!; **~bitten** *(unreg) vt* to ask in; **~brechen** *(unreg) vi* to set in; **~bringen** *(unreg) vt* to bring in; **~fallen** *(unreg) vi* to be caught, to be taken in; **~fallen auf** +*akk* to fall for; **~kommen** *(unreg) vi* to come in; **~lassen**

Spelling reform: ▲ *new spelling* △ *old spelling (to be phased out)*

(*unreg*) *vt* to admit; **~legen** *vt*: **jdn ~legen** to take sb in; **~platzen** (*umg*) *vi* to burst in

Her- *zW*: **~fahrt** *f* journey here; **h~fallen** (*unreg*) *vi*: **h~fallen über** +*akk* to fall upon; **~gang** *m* course of events; **h~geben** (*unreg*) *vt* to give, to hand (over); **sich zu etw h~geben** to lend one's name to sth; **h~gehen** (*unreg*) *vi*: **hinter jdm h~gehen** to follow sb; **es geht hoch h~** there are a lot of goings-on; **h~halten** (*unreg*) *vt* to hold out; **h~halten müssen** (*umg*) to have to suffer; **h~hören** *vi* to listen

Hering ['heːrɪŋ] (**-s, -e**) *m* herring

her- |her| *zW*: **~kommen** (*unreg*) *vi* to come; **komm mal ~!** come here!; **~kömmlich** *adj* traditional; **H~kunft** (**-, -künfte**) *f* origin; **H~kunftsland** *nt* country of origin; **H~kunftsort** *m* place of origin; **~laufen** (*unreg*) *vi*: **~laufen hinter** +*dat* to run after

hermetisch |her'meːtɪʃ| *adj* hermetic ♦ *adv* hermetically

her'nach *adv* afterwards

Heroin [hero'iːn] (**-s**) *nt* heroin

Herr [her] (**-(e)n, -en**) *m* master; (*Mann*) gentleman; (*REL*) Lord; (*vor Namen*) Mr.; **mein ~!** sir!; **meine ~en!** gentlemen!

Herren- *zW*: **~haus** *nt* mansion; **~konfektion** *f* menswear; **h~los** *adj* ownerless; **~toilette** *f* men's toilet *od* restroom (*US*)

herrichten ['heːrrɪçtn] *vt* to prepare

Herr- *zW*: **~in** *f* mistress; **h~isch** *adj* domineering; **h~lich** *adj* marvellous, splendid; **~lichkeit** *f* splendour, magnificence; **~schaft** *f* power, rule; (**~ und ~in**) master and mistress; **meine ~schaften!** ladies and gentlemen!

herrschen ['herʃən] *vi* to rule; (*bestehen*) to prevail, to be

Herrscher(in) (**-s, -**) *m(f)* ruler

her- *zW*: **~rühren** *vi* to arise, to originate; **~sagen** *vt* to recite; **~stellen** *vt* to make, to manufacture; **H~steller** (**-s, -**) *m* manufacturer; **H~stellung** *f* manufacture

herüber |hɛ'ryːbər| *adv* over (here), across

herum [hɛ'rom] *adv* about, (a)round; **um etw ~** around sth; **~führen** *vi* to show around; **~gehen** (*unreg*) *vi* to walk about; **um etw ~gehen** to walk *od* go round sth; **~kommen** (*unreg*) *vi* (*um Kurve etc*) to come round, to turn (round); **~kriegen** (*umg*) *vt* to bring *od* talk around; **~lungern** (*umg*) *vi* to hang about *od* around; **~sprechen** (*unreg*) *vr* to get around, to be spread; **~treiben** *vi, vr* to drift about; **~ziehen** *vi, vr* to wander about

herunter |hɛ'rontər| *adv* downward(s), down (there); **~gekommen** *adj* run-down; **~kommen** (*unreg*) *vi* to come down; (*fig*) to come down in the world; **~machen** *vt* to take down; (*schimpfen*) to have a go at

hervor [hɛr'foːr] *adv* out, forth; **~bringen** (*unreg*) *vt* to produce; (*Wort*) to utter; **~gehen** (*unreg*) *vi* to emerge, to result; **~heben** (*unreg*) *vt* to stress; (*als Kontrast*) to set off; **~ragend** *adj* (*fig*) excellent; **~rufen** (*unreg*) *vt* to cause, to give rise to; **~treten** (*unreg*) *vi* to come out (from behind/ between/below); (*Adern*) to be prominent

Herz [herts] (**-ens, -en**) *nt* heart; (*KARTEN*) hearts *pl*; **~anfall** *m* heart attack; **~fehler** *m* heart defect; **h~haft** *adj* hearty

herziehen ['hɛːrtsiːən] (*unreg*) *vi*: **über jdn/ etw ~** (*umg: auch fig*) to pull sb/sth to pieces (*inf*)

Herz- *zW*: **~infarkt** *m* heart attack; **~klopfen** *nt* palpitation; **h~lich** *adj* cordial; **h~lichen Glückwunsch** congratulations *pl*; **h~liche Grüße** best wishes; **h~los** *adj* heartless

Herzog ['hɛrtsoːk] (**-(e)s, ̈e**) *m* duke; **~tum** *nt* duchy

Herz- *zW*: **~schlag** *m* heartbeat; (*MED*) heart attack; **~stillstand** *m* cardiac arrest; **h~zerreißend** *adj* heartrending

Hessen ['hɛsən] (**-s**) *nt* Hesse

hessisch *adj* Hessian

Hetze ['hɛtsə] *f* (*Eile*) rush; **h~n** *vt* to hunt; (*verfolgen*) to chase ♦ *vi* (*eilen*) to rush; **jdn/ etw auf jdn/etw h~n** to set sb/sth on sb/ sth; **h~n gegen** to stir up feeling against; **h~n zu** to agitate for

Heu |hɔy| (**-(e)s**) *nt* hay; **Geld wie ~** stacks of money

Heuch- ['hɔyç] *zW*: **~elei** [-ə'laɪ] *f* hypocrisy; **h~eln** *vt* to pretend, to feign ♦ *vi* to be hypocritical; **~ler(in)** (**-s, -**) *m(f)* hypocrite; **h~lerisch** *adj* hypocritical

heulen ['hɔylən] *vi* to howl; to cry

Heurige(r) ['hɔyrɪgə(r)] *m* new wine

Heu- *zW*: **~schnupfen** *m* hay fever; **'~schrecke** *f* grasshopper; locust

heute ['hɔytə] *adv* today; **~ Abend/früh** this evening/morning

heutig ['hɔytɪç] *adj* today's

heutzutage ['hɔyttsutaːgə] *adv* nowadays

Hexe ['hɛksə] *f* witch; **h~n** *vi* to practise witchcraft; **ich kann doch nicht h~n** I can't work miracles; **~nschuss** ▲ *m* lumbago; **~'rei** *f* witchcraft

Hieb [hiːp] (**-(e)s, -e**) *m* blow; (*Wunde*) cut, gash; (*Stichelei*) cutting remark; **~e bekommen** to get a thrashing

hielt *etc* |hiːlt| *vb siehe* **halten**

hier [hiːr] *adv* here; **~auf** *adv* thereupon; (*danach*) after that; **~behalten** to keep here; **~ bleiben** to stay here; **~ lassen** to leave here; **~bei** *adv* herewith, enclosed; **~durch** *adv* by this means; (*örtlich*) through here; **~her** *adv* this way, here; **~hin** *adv* here; **~mit** *adv* hereby; **~nach** *adv* hereafter; **~von** *adv* about this, hereof; **~zulande, ~ zu Lande** *adv* in this country

hiesig |'hiːzıç| adj of this place, local

hieß etc |hiːs| vb siehe **heißen**

Hilfe |'hılfə| f help; aid; **erste ~** first aid; **~!** help!

Hilf- zW: **h~los** adj helpless; **~losigkeit** f helplessness; **h~reich** adj helpful

Hilfs- zW: **~arbeiter** m labourer; **h~bedürftig** adj needy; **h~bereit** adj ready to help; **~kraft** f assistant, helper

hilfst |hılfst| vb siehe **helfen**

Himbeere |'hımbeːrə| f raspberry

Himmel |'hıməl| (-s, -) m sky; (REL, auch fig) heaven; **~bett** nt four-poster bed; **h~blau** adj sky-blue; **~fahrt** f Ascension; **~srichtung** f direction

himmlisch |'hımlıʃ| adj heavenly

SCHLÜSSELWORT

hin |hın| adv 1 (Richtung): **hin und zurück** there and back; **hin und her** to and fro; **bis zur Mauer hin** up to the wall; **wo ist er hin?** where has he gone?; **Geld hin, Geld her** money or no money

2 (auf ... hin): **auf meine Bitte hin** at my request; **auf seinen Rat hin** on the basis of his advice

3: **mein Glück ist hin** my happiness has gone

hinab |hı'nap| adv down; **~gehen** (unreg) vi to go down; **~sehen** (unreg) vi to look down

hinauf |hı'nauf| adv up; **~arbeiten** vr to work one's way up; **~steigen** (unreg) vi to climb

hinaus |hı'naus| adv out; **~gehen** (unreg) vi to go out; **~gehen über** +akk to exceed; **~laufen** (unreg) vi to run out; **~laufen auf** +akk to come to, to amount to; **~schieben** (unreg) vt to put off, to postpone; **~werfen** (unreg) vt (Gegenstand, Person) to throw out; **~wollen** vi to want to go out; **~wollen auf** +akk to drive at, to get at

Hinblick |'hınblık| m: **in** od **im ~ auf** +akk in view of

hinder- |'hındər| zW: **~lich** adj: **~lich sein** to be a hindrance od nuisance; **~n** vt to hinder, to hamper; **jdn an etw** dat **~n** to prevent sb from doing sth; **H~nis** (-ses, -se) nt obstacle; **H~nisrennen** nt steeplechase

hindeuten |'hındɔytən| vi: **~ auf** +akk to point to

hindurch |hın'dʊrç| adv through; across; (zeitlich) through(out)

hinein |hı'naın| adv in; **~fallen** (unreg) vi to fall in; **~fallen in** +akk to fall into; **~gehen** (unreg) vi to go in; **~gehen in** +akk to go into, to enter; **~geraten** (unreg) vi: **~geraten in** +akk to get into; **~passen** vi to

fit in; **~passen in** +akk to fit into; (fig) to fit in with; **~steigern** vr to get worked up; **~versetzen** vr: **sich ~versetzen in** +akk to put o.s. in the position of; **~ziehen** (unreg) vt to pull in ♦ vi to go in

hin- |'hın| zW: **~fahren** (unreg) vi to go; to drive ♦ vt to take; to drive; **H~fahrt** f journey there; **~fallen** (unreg) vi to fall (down); **~fällig** adj frail; (fig: ungültig) invalid; **H~flug** m outward flight; **H~gabe** f devotion; **~geben** (unreg) vr +dat to give o.s. up to, to devote o.s. to; **~gehen** (unreg) vi to go; (Zeit) to pass; **~halten** (unreg) vt to hold out; (warten lassen) to put off, to stall

hinken |'hıŋkən| vi to limp; (Vergleich) to be unconvincing

hinkommen (unreg) vi (an Ort) to arrive

hin- |'hın| zW: **~legen** vt to put down ♦ vr to lie down; **~nehmen** (unreg) vt (fig) to put up with, to take; **H~reise** f journey out; **~reißen** (unreg) vt to carry away, to enrapture; **sich ~reißen lassen, etw zu tun** to get carried away and do sth; **~richten** vt to execute; **H~richtung** f execution; **~setzen** vt to put down ♦ vr to sit down; **~sichtlich** präp +gen with regard to; **~stellen** vt to put (down) ♦ vr to place o.s.

hinten |'hıntən| adv at the back; behind; **~herum** adv round the back; (fig) secretly

hinter |'hıntər| präp (+dat od akk) behind; (: nach) after; **~ jdm her sein** to be after sb; **H~achse** f rear axle; **H~bliebene(r)** f(m) surviving relative; **~e(r, s)** adj rear, back; **~einander** adv one after the other; **H~gedanke** m ulterior motive; **~gehen** (unreg) vt to deceive; **H~grund** m background; **H~halt** m ambush; **~hältig** adj underhand, sneaky; **~her** adv afterwards, after; **H~hof** m backyard; **H~kopf** m back of one's head; **~'lassen** (unreg) vt to leave; **~'legen** vt to deposit; **H~list** f cunning, trickery; (Handlung) trick, dodge; **~listig** adj cunning, crafty; **H~mann** m person behind; **H~rad** nt back wheel; **H~radantrieb** m (AUT) rear wheel drive; **~rücks** adv from behind; **H~tür** f back door; (fig: Ausweg) loophole; **~'ziehen** (unreg) vt (Steuern) to evade

hinüber |hı'nyːbər| adv across, over; **~gehen** (unreg) vi to go over od across

hinunter |hı'nʊntər| adv down; **~bringen** (unreg) vt to take down; **~schlucken** vt (auch fig) to swallow; **~steigen** (unreg) vi to descend

Hinweg |'hınveːk| m journey out

hinweghelfen |hın'vɛk-| (unreg) vi: **jdm über etw** akk **~** to help sb to get over sth

hinwegsetzen |hın'vɛk-| vr: **sich ~ über**

+*akk* to disregard

hin- |'hɪn| *zW:* **H~weis (-es, -e)** *m* (*Andeutung*) hint; (*Anweisung*) instruction; (*Verweis*) reference; **~weisen** (*unreg*) *vi:* **~weisen auf** +*akk* (*anzeigen*) to point to; (*sagen*) to point out, to refer to; **~werfen** (*unreg*) *vt* to throw down; **~ziehen** (*unreg*) *vr* (*fig*) to drag on

hinzu |hɪn'tsuː| *adv* in addition; **~fügen** *vt* to add; **~kommen** (*unreg*) *vi* (*Mensch*) to arrive, to turn up; (*Umstand*) to ensue

Hirn |hɪrn| **(-(e)s, -e)** *nt* brain(s); **~gespinst (-(e)s, -e)** *nt* fantasy

Hirsch |hɪrʃ| **(-(e)s, -e)** *m* stag

Hirt |'hɪrt| **(-en, -en)** *m* herdsman; (*Schafhirt, fig*) shepherd

hissen |'hɪsən| *vt* to hoist

Historiker |hɪs'toːrikar| **(-s, -)** *m* historian

historisch |hɪs'toːrɪʃ| *adj* historical

Hitze |'hɪtsə| **(-)** *f* heat; **h~beständig** *adj* heat-resistant; **h~frei** *adj:* **h~frei haben** *to have time off school because of excessively hot weather;* **~welle** *f* heat wave

hitzig |'hɪtsɪç| *adj* hot-tempered; (*Debatte*) heated

Hitzkopf *m* hothead

Hitzschlag *m* heatstroke

hl. *abk von* **heilig**

H-Milch |'haːmɪlç| *f* long-life milk

Hobby |'hɔbi| **(-s, -s)** *nt* hobby

Hobel |'hoːbal| **(-s, -)** *m* plane; **~bank** *f* carpenter's bench; **h~n** *vt, vi* to plane; **~späne** *pl* wood shavings

Hoch (-s, -s) *nt* (*Ruf*) cheer; (*MET*) anticyclone

hoch |hoːx| *adj high* (*attrib* **hohe(r, s)**) ♦ *adv:* **~ achten** to respect; **~ begabt** extremely gifted; **~ dotiert** highly paid; **H~achtung** *f* respect, esteem; **~achtungsvoll** *adv* yours faithfully; **H~amt** *nt* high mass; **~arbeiten** *vr* to work one's way up; **H~betrieb** *m* intense activity; (*COMM*) peak time; **H~burg** *f* stronghold; **H~deutsch** *nt* High German; **H~druck** *m* high pressure; **H~ebene** *f* plateau; **H~form** *f* top form; **H~gebirge** *nt* high mountains *pl*; **H~glanz** *m* (*PHOT*) high gloss print; **etw auf H~glanz bringen** to make sth sparkle like new; **~halten** (*unreg*) *vt* to hold up; (*fig*) to uphold, to cherish; **H~haus** *nt* multi-storey building; **~heben** (*unreg*) *vt* to lift (up); **H~konjunktur** *f* boom; **H~land** *nt* highlands *pl*; **~leben** *vi:* **jdn ~leben lassen** to give sb three cheers; **H~mut** *m* pride; **~mütig** *adj* proud, haughty; **~näsig** *adj* stuck-up, snooty; **H~ofen** *m* blast furnace; **~prozentig** *adj* (*Alkohol*) strong; **H~rechnung** *f* projection; **H~saison** *f* high season; **H~schule** *f* college; university; **H~sommer** *m* middle of summer; **H~spannung** *f* high tension; **H~sprung** *m*

high jump

höchst |høːçst| *adv* highly, extremely

Hochstapler |'hoːxstaːplar| **(-s, -)** *m* swindler

höchste(r, s) *adj* highest; (*äußerste*) extreme

Höchst- *zW:* **h~ens** *adv* at the most; **~geschwindigkeit** *f* maximum speed; **h~persönlich** *adv* in person; **~preis** *m* maximum price; **h~wahrscheinlich** *adv* most probably

Hoch- *zW:* **~verrat** *m* high treason; **~wasser** *nt* high water; (*Überschwemmung*) floods *pl*

Hochzeit |'hɔxtsaɪt| **(-, -en)** *f* wedding; **~sreise** *f* honeymoon

hocken |'hɔkən| *vi, vr* to squat, to crouch

Hocker (-s, -) *m* stool

Höcker |'hœkar| **(-s, -)** *m* hump

Hoden |'hoːdən| **(-s, -)** *m* testicle

Hof |hoːf| **(-(e)s, ⸗e)** *m* (*Hinterhof*) yard; (*Bauernhof*) farm; (*Königshof*) court

hoff- |'hɔf| *zW:* **~en** *vi:* **~en (auf** +*akk***)** to hope (for); **~entlich** *adv* I hope, hopefully; **H~nung** *f* hope

Hoffnungs- *zW:* **h~los** *adj* hopeless; **~losigkeit** *f* hopelessness; **h~voll** *adj* hopeful

höflich |'høːflɪç| *adj* polite, courteous; **H~keit** *f* courtesy, politeness

hohe(r, s) |'hoːə(r, s)| *adj attrib siehe* **hoch**

Höhe |'høːə| *f* height; (*Anhöhe*) hill

Hoheit |'hoːhaɪt| *f* (*POL*) sovereignty; (*Titel*) Highness

Hoheits- *zW:* **~gebiet** *nt* sovereign territory; **~gewässer** *nt* territorial waters *pl*

Höhen- |'høːən| *zW:* **~luft** *f* mountain air; **~messer (-s, -)** *m* altimeter; **~sonne** *f* sun lamp; **~unterschied** *m* difference in altitude

Höhepunkt *m* climax

höher *adj, adv* higher

hohl |hoːl| *adj* hollow

Höhle |'høːlə| *f* cave, hole; (*Mundhöhle*) cavity; (*fig, ZOOL*) den

Hohlmaß *nt* measure of volume

Hohn |hoːn| **(-(e)s)** *m* scorn

höhnisch *adj* scornful, taunting

holen |'hoːlən| *vt* to get, to fetch; (*Atem*) to take; **jdn/etw ~ lassen** to send for sb/sth

Holland |'hɔlant| *nt* Holland; **Holländer** |'hɔlɛndar| *m* Dutchman; **holländisch** *adj* Dutch

Hölle |'hœlə| *f* hell

höllisch |'hœlɪʃ| *adj* hellish, infernal

holperig |'hɔlpərɪç| *adj* rough, bumpy

Holunder |ho'lʊndar| **(-s, -)** *m* elder

Holz |hɔlts| **(-es, ⸗er)** *nt* wood

hölzern |'hœltsərn| *adj* (*auch fig*) wooden

Holz- *zW:* **~fäller (-s, -)** *m* lumberjack, woodcutter; **h~ig** *adj* woody; **~kohle** *f*

charcoal; ~**schuh** m clog; ~**weg** m (fig) wrong track; ~**wolle** f fine wood shavings pl
Homöopathie [homøopa'tiː] f homeopathy
homosexuell [homozɛksuˈɛl] adj homosexual
Honig ['hoːnɪç] (-s, -e) m honey; ~**melone** f (BOT, KOCH) honeydew melon; ~**wabe** f honeycomb
Honorar [hono'raːr] (-s, -e) nt fee
Hopfen ['hɔpfən] (-s, -) m hops pl
hopsen ['hɔpsən] vi to hop
Hörapparat m hearing aid
hörbar adj audible
horchen ['hɔrçən] vi to listen; (pej) to eavesdrop
Horde ['hɔrdə] f horde
hör- ['høːr] zW: ~**en** vt, vi to hear; **Musik/ Radio** ~en to listen to music/the radio; **H~er** (-s, -) m hearer; (RAD) listener; (UNIV) student; (Telefonhörer) receiver; **H~funk** (-s) m radio; ~**geschädigt** [-gəʃɛːdɪçt] adj hearing-impaired
Horizont [hori'tsɔnt] (-(e)s, -e) m horizon; **h~al** [-'taːl] adj horizontal
Hormon [hɔr'moːn] (-s, -e) nt hormone
Hörmuschel f (TEL) earpiece
Horn [hɔrn] (-(e)s, ⁼er) nt horn; ~**haut** f horny skin
Hornisse [hɔr'nɪsə] f hornet
Horoskop [horo'skoːp] (-s, -e) nt horoscope
Hörspiel nt radio play
Hort [hɔrt] (-(e)s, -e) m (SCH) day centre for schoolchildren whose parents are at work
horten ['hɔrtən] vt to hoard
Hose ['hoːzə] f trousers pl, pants pl (US)
Hosen- zW: ~**anzug** m trouser suit; ~**rock** m culottes pl; ~**tasche** f (trouser) pocket; ~**träger** m braces pl (BRIT), suspenders pl (US)
Hostie ['hɔstiə] f (REL) host
Hotel [ho'tɛl] (-s, -s) nt hotel; ~**ier** [hoteli'eː] (-s, -s) m hotelkeeper, hotelier; ~**verzeichnis** nt hotel register
Hubraum ['huːp-] m (AUT) cubic capacity
hübsch [hʏpʃ] adj pretty, nice
Hubschrauber ['huːpʃrauber] (-s, -) m helicopter
Huf ['huːf] (-(e)s, -e) m hoof; ~**eisen** nt horseshoe
Hüft- ['hʏft] zW: ~**e** f hip; ~**gürtel** m girdle; ~**halter** (-s, -) m girdle
Hügel ['hyːgəl] (-s, -) m hill; **h~ig** adj hilly
Huhn [huːn] (-(e)s, ⁼er) nt hen; (KOCH) chicken
Hühner- ['hyːnər] zW: ~**auge** nt corn; ~**brühe** f chicken broth
Hülle ['hʏlə] f cover(ing); wrapping; **in ~ und Fülle** galore; **h~n** vt: **h~n (in** +akk) to cover (with); to wrap (in)

Hülse ['hʏlzə] f husk, shell; ~**nfrucht** f pulse
human [hu'maːn] adj humane; ~**i'tär** adj humanitarian; **H~i'tät** f humanity
Hummel ['hʊməl] (-, -n) f bumblebee
Hummer ['hʊmər] (-s, -) m lobster
Humor [hu'moːr] (-s, -e) m humour; ~ **haben** to have a sense of humour; ~**ist** [-'rɪst] m humorist; **h~voll** adj humorous
humpeln ['hʊmpəln] vi to hobble
Humpen ['hʊmpən] (-s, -) m tankard
Hund [hʊnt] (-(e)s, -e) m dog
Hunde- [hʊndə] zW: ~**hütte** f (dog) kennel; **h~müde** (umg) adj dog-tired
hundert ['hʊndərt] num hundred; **H~'jahrfeier** f centenary; ~**prozentig** adj, adv one hundred per cent
Hundesteuer f dog licence fee
Hündin ['hʏndɪn] f bitch
Hunger ['hʊŋər] (-s) m hunger; ~ **haben** to be hungry; **h~n** vi to starve; ~**snot** f famine
hungrig ['hʊŋrɪç] adj hungry
Hupe ['huːpə] f horn; **h~n** vi to hoot, to sound one's horn
hüpfen ['hʏpfən] vi to hop; to jump
Hürde ['hʏrdə] f hurdle; (für Schafe) pen; ~**nlauf** m hurdling
Hure ['huːrə] f whore
hurtig ['hʊrtɪç] adj brisk, quick ♦ adv briskly, quickly
huschen ['hʊʃən] vi to flit; to scurry
Husten ['huːstən] (-s) m cough; **h~** vi to cough; ~**anfall** m coughing fit; ~**bonbon** m od nt cough drop; ~**saft** m cough mixture
Hut¹ [huːt] (-(e)s, ⁼e) m hat
Hut² [huːt] (-) f care; **auf der ~ sein** to be on one's guard
hüten ['hyːtən] vt to guard ♦ vr to watch out; **sich ~, zu** to take care not to; **sich ~ (vor)** to beware (of), to be on one's guard (against)
Hütte ['hʏtə] f hut; cottage; (Eisenhütte) forge
Hütten- zW: ~**käse** m (KOCH) cottage cheese; ~**schuh** m slipper sock
Hydrant [hy'drant] m hydrant
hydraulisch [hy'drauliʃ] adj hydraulic
Hygiene [hygi'eːnə] (-) f hygiene
hygienisch [hygi'eːnɪʃ] adj hygienic
Hymne ['hʏmnə] f hymn; anthem
Hypno- [hʏp'noː] zW: ~**se** f hypnosis; **h~tisch** adj hypnotic; ~**tiseur** [-ti'zøːr] m hypnotist; **h~ti'sieren** vt to hypnotize
Hypothek [hypo'teːk] (-, -en) f mortgage
Hypothese [hypo'teːzə] f hypothesis
Hysterie [hyste'riː] f hysteria
hysterisch [hʏs'teːrɪʃ] adj hysterical

Spelling reform: ▲ *new spelling* △ *old spelling (to be phased out)*

I, i

ICE [iːtseːˈʔeː] *m abk* = **Intercity-Expresszug**
Ich (**-(s)**, **-(s)**) *nt* self; (*PSYCH*) ego
ich [ɪç] *pron* I; **~ bins!** it's me!
Ideal [ideˈaːl] (**-s**, **-e**) *nt* ideal; **i~** *adj* ideal;
i~istisch [-ˈlɪstɪʃ] *adj* idealistic
Idee [iˈdeː, *pl* iˈdeːən] *f* idea
identifizieren [identifiˈtsiːrən] *vt* to
identify
identisch [iˈdɛntɪʃ] *adj* identical
Identität [identiˈtɛːt] *f* identity
Ideo- [ideo] *zW*: **~loge** [-ˈloːgə] (**-n**, **-n**) *m*
ideologist; **~logie** [-loˈgiː] *f* ideology;
i~logisch [-ˈloːgɪʃ] *adj* ideological
Idiot [idiˈoːt] (**-en**, **-en**) *m* idiot; **i~isch** *adj*
idiotic
idyllisch [iˈdʏlɪʃ] *adj* idyllic
Igel [ˈiːgəl] (**-s**, **-**) *m* hedgehog
ignorieren [ɪɡnoˈriːrən] *vt* to ignore
ihm [iːm] (*dat von* **er**, **es**) *pron* (to) him; (to)
it
ihn [iːn] (*akk von* **er**, **es**) *pron* him; it; **~en**
(*dat von* **sie** *pl*) *pron* (to) them; **I~en** (*dat
von* **Sie** *pl*) *pron* (to) you

ihr [iːr] *pron* 1 (*nom pl*) you; **ihr seid es** it's
you
  2 (*dat von* **sie**) to her; **gib es ihr** give it to
her; **er steht neben ihr** he is standing
beside her
♦ *possessiv pron* 1 (*sg*) her; (: *bei Tieren,
Dingen*) its; **ihr Mann** her husband
  2 (*pl*) their; **die Bäume und ihre Blätter**
the trees and their leaves

ihr(e) [iːr] *adj* (*sg*) her, its; (*pl*) their; **Ihr(e)**
adj your
ihre(r, s) *pron* (*sg*) hers, its; (*pl*) theirs; **I~(r,
s)** *pron* yours; **~r** (*gen von* **sie** *sg/pl*) *pron* of
her/them; **I~r** (*gen von* **Sie**) *pron* of you;
~rseits *adv* for her/their part; **~sgleichen**
pron people like her/them; (*von Dingen*)
others like it; **~twegen** *adv* (*für sie*) for her/
its/their sake; (*wegen ihr*) on her/its/their
account; **~twillen** *adv*: **um ~twillen** =
ihretwegen
ihrige [ˈiːrɪɡə] *pron*: **der/die/das ~** *od* **Ihrige**
hers; its; theirs
illegal [ˈɪleɡaːl] *adj* illegal
Illusion [ɪluziˈoːn] *f* illusion
illusorisch [ɪluˈzoːrɪʃ] *adj* illusory
illustrieren [ɪlusˈtriːrən] *vt* to illustrate
Illustrierte *f* magazine
im [ɪm] = **in dem**
Imbiss ▲ [ˈɪmbɪs] (**-es**, **-e**) *m* snack; **~-
Stube** ▲ *f* snack bar
imitieren [imiˈtiːrən] *vt* to imitate
Imker [ˈɪmkər] (**-s**, **-**) *m* beekeeper

immatrikulieren [ɪmatrikuˈliːrən] *vi*, *vr* to
register
immer [ˈɪmər] *adv* always; **~ wieder** again
and again; **~ noch** still; **~ noch nicht** still
not; **für ~** forever; **~ wenn ich ...** every time
I ...; **~ schöner/trauriger** more and more
beautiful/sadder and sadder; **was/wer
(auch) ~** whatever/whoever; **~hin** *adv* all
the same; **~zu** *adv* all the time
Immobilien [ɪmoˈbiːliən] *pl* real estate *sg*;
~makler *m* estate agent (*BRIT*), realtor (*US*)
immun [ɪˈmuːn] *adj* immune; **I~ität** [-iˈtɛːt] *f*
immunity; **I~system** *nt* immune system
Imperfekt [ˈɪmpɛrfɛkt] (**-s**, **-e**) *nt* imperfect
(tense)
Impf- [ˈɪmpf] *zW*: **i~en** *vt* to vaccinate;
~stoff *m* vaccine, serum; **~ung** *f*
vaccination
imponieren [ɪmpoˈniːrən] *vi* +*dat* to impress
Import [ɪmˈpɔrt] (**-(e)s**, **-e**) *m* import; **~eur**
m importer; **i~ieren** *vt* to import
imposant [ɪmpoˈzant] *adj* imposing
impotent [ˈɪmpotɛnt] *adj* impotent
imprägnieren [ɪmprɛˈɡniːrən] *vt* to
(water)proof
improvisieren [ɪmproviˈziːrən] *vt*, *vi* to
improvise
Impuls [ɪmˈpʊls] (**-es**, **-e**) *m* impulse; **i~iv**
[-ˈziːf] *adj* impulsive
imstande, **im Stande** [ɪmˈʃtandə] *adj*: **~
sein** to be in a position; (*fähig*) to be able

in [ɪn] *präp* +*akk* 1 (*räumlich: wohin?*) in, into;
in die Stadt into town; **in die Schule
gehen** to go to school
  2 (*zeitlich*): **bis ins 20. Jahrhundert** into
od up to the 20th century
♦ *präp* +*dat* 1 (*räumlich: wo*) in; **in der Stadt**
in town; **in der Schule sein** to be at school
  2 (*zeitlich: wann*): **in diesem Jahr** this year;
(*in jenem Jahr*) in that year; **heute in zwei
Wochen** two weeks today

Inanspruchnahme [ɪnˈʔanʃpruxnaːmə] *f*
(+*gen*) demands *pl* (on)
Inbegriff [ˈɪnbəɡrɪf] *m* embodiment,
personification; **i~en** *adj* included
indem [ɪnˈdeːm] *konj* while; **~ man etw
macht** (*dadurch*) by doing sth
Inder(in) [ˈɪndər(ɪn)] *m(f)* Indian
indes(sen) [ɪnˈdes(ən)] *adv* however;
(*inzwischen*) meanwhile ♦ *konj* while
Indianer(in) [ɪndiˈaːnər(ɪn)] (**-s**, **-**) *m(f)*
American Indian, native American;
indianisch *adj* Red Indian
Indien [ˈɪndiən] *nt* India
indirekt [ˈɪndirɛkt] *adj* indirect
indisch [ˈɪndɪʃ] *adj* Indian
indiskret [ˈɪndɪskreːt] *adj* indiscreet
indiskutabel [ˈɪndɪskutaːbəl] *adj* out of the

question
individuell |ɪndividu'ɛl| *adj* individual
Individuum |ɪndi'vi:duʊm| (**-s, -en**) *nt* individual
Indiz |ɪn'di:ts| (**-es, -ien**) *nt* (*JUR*) clue; ~ (**für**) sign (of)
industrialisieren |ɪndʊstriali'zi:rən| *vt* to industrialize
Industrie |ɪndʊs'tri:| *f* industry ♦ *in zW* industrial; **~gebiet** *nt* industrial area; **~- und Handelskammer** *f* chamber of commerce; **~zweig** *m* branch of industry
ineinander |ɪn|aɪ'nandər| *adv* in(to) one another *od* each other
Infarkt |ɪn'farkt| (**-(e)s, -e**) *m* coronary (thrombosis)
Infektion |ɪnfɛktsi'o:n| *f* infection; **~skrankheit** *f* infectious disease
Infinitiv |'ɪnfiniti:f| (**-s, -e**) *m* infinitive
infizieren |ɪnfi'tsi:rən| *vt* to infect ♦ *vr*: **sich (bei jdm)** ~ to be infected (by sb)
Inflation |ɪnflatsi'o:n| *f* inflation
inflationär |ɪnflatsio'nɛ:r| *adj* inflationary
infolge |ɪn'fɔlgə| *präp +gen* as a result of, owing to; **~dessen** |-'dɛsən| *adv* consequently
Informatik |ɪnfɔr'ma:tɪk| *f* information studies *pl*
Information |ɪnfɔrmatsi'o:n| *f* information *no pl*
informieren |ɪnfɔr'mi:rən| *vt* to inform ♦ *vr*: **sich ~ (über +akk)** to find out (about)
infrage, in Frage *adv*: **~ stellen** to question sth; **nicht ~ kommen** to be out of the question
Ingenieur |ɪnʒeni'ø:r| *m* engineer; **~schule** *f* school of engineering
Ingwer |'ɪŋvər| (**-s**) *m* ginger
Inh. *abk* (= *Inhaber*) prop.; (= *Inhalt*) contents
Inhaber(in) |'ɪnha:bər(ɪn)| (**-s, -**) *m(f)* owner; (*Hausinhaber*) occupier; (*Lizenzinhaber*) licensee, holder; (*FIN*) bearer
inhaftieren |ɪnhaf'ti:rən| *vt* to take into custody
inhalieren |ɪnha'li:rən| *vt, vi* to inhale
Inhalt |'ɪnhalt| (**-(e)s, -e**) *m* contents *pl*; (*eines Buchs etc*) content; (*MATH*) area; volume; **i~lich** *adj* as regards content
Inhalts- *zW*: **~angabe** *f* summary; **~verzeichnis** *nt* table of contents
inhuman |'ɪnhuma:n| *adj* inhuman
Initiative |initsia'ti:və| *f* initiative
inklusive |ɪnklu'zi:və| *präp +gen* inclusive of ♦ *adv* inclusive
In-Kraft-Treten |ɪn'kraftre:tən| (**-s**) *nt* coming into force
Inland |'ɪnlant| (**-(e)s**) *nt* (*GEOG*) inland; (*POL, COMM*) home (country); **~flug** *m* domestic flight

inmitten |ɪn'mɪtən| *präp +gen* in the middle of; ~ **von** amongst
innehaben |'ɪnəha:bən| (*unreg*) *vt* to hold
innen |'ɪnən| *adv* inside; **I~architekt** *m* interior designer; **I~einrichtung** *f* (interior) furnishings *pl*; **I~hof** *m* inner courtyard; **I~minister** *m* minister of the interior, Home Secretary (*BRIT*); **I~politik** *f* domestic policy; **~politisch** *adj* (*Entwicklung, Lage*) internal, domestic; **I~stadt** *f* town/city centre
inner- |'ɪnər| *zW*: **~e(r, s)** *adj* inner; (*im Körper, inländisch*) internal; **I~e(s)** *nt* inside; (*Mitte*) centre; (*fig*) heart; **I~eien** |-'raɪən| *pl* innards; **~halb** *adv* within; (*räumlich*) inside ♦ *präp +gen* within; inside; **~lich** *adj* internal; (*geistig*) inward; **~ste(r, s)** *adj* innermost; **I~ste(s)** *nt* heart
innig |'ɪnɪç| *adj* (*Freundschaft*) close
inoffiziell |'ɪn|ofitsiɛl| *adj* unofficial
ins |ɪns| = **in das**
Insasse |'ɪnzasə| (**-n, -n**) *m* (*Anstalt*) inmate; (*AUT*) passenger
Insassenversicherung *f* passenger insurance
insbesondere |ɪnsbə'zɔndərə| *adv* (e)specially
Inschrift |'ɪnʃrɪft| *f* inscription
Insekt |ɪn'zɛkt| (**-(e)s, -en**) *nt* insect
Insektenschutzmittel *nt* insect repellent
Insel |'ɪnzəl| (**-, -n**) *f* island
Inser- *zW*: **~at** |ɪnzeˈraːt| (**-(e)s, -e**) *nt* advertisement; **~ent** |ɪnzeˈrɛnt| *m* advertiser; **i~ieren** |ɪnzeˈriːrən| *vt, vi* to advertise
insgeheim |ɪnsɡəˈhaɪm| *adv* secretly
insgesamt |ɪnsɡəˈzamt| *adv* altogether, all in all
insofern |ɪnzoˈfɛrn| *adv* in this respect ♦ *konj* if; (*deshalb*) (and) so; ~ **als** in so far as
insoweit |ɪnzoˈvaɪt| = **insofern**
Installateur |ɪnstalaˈtøːr| *m* electrician; plumber
Instandhaltung |ɪnˈʃtanthaltʊŋ| *f* maintenance
inständig |ɪnˈʃtɛndɪç| *adj* urgent
Instandsetzung |ɪnˈʃtant-| *f* overhaul; (*eines Gebäudes*) restoration
Instanz |ɪnˈʃtants| *f* authority; (*JUR*) court
Instinkt |ɪnˈʃtɪŋkt| (**-(e)s, -e**) *m* instinct; **i~iv** |-ˈtiːf| *adj* instinctive
Institut |ɪnstiˈtuːt| (**-(e)s, -e**) *nt* institute
Instrument |ɪnstruˈmɛnt| *nt* instrument
Intell- |ɪntɛl| *zW*: **i~ektuell** |-ɛktuˈɛl| *adj* intellectual; **i~igent** |-iˈɡɛnt| *adj* intelligent; **~igenz** |-iˈɡɛnts| *f* intelligence; (*Leute*) intelligentsia *pl*
Intendant |ɪntɛnˈdant| *m* director
intensiv |ɪntɛnˈziːf| *adj* intensive; **I~station** *f* intensive care unit
Intercity- |ɪntərˈsɪti| *zW*: **~-Expresszug** ▲ *m* high-speed train; **~-Zug** *m* intercity

---

Spelling reform: ▲ *new spelling* △ *old spelling (to be phased out)*

(train); **~-Zuschlag** m intercity supplement

Interess- zW: **i~ant** [ɪntɛrɛˈsant] adj interesting; **i~anterweise** adv interestingly enough; **~e** [ɪntɛˈrɛsə] (-s, -n) nt interest; **~e haben an** +dat to be interested in; **~ent** [ɪntɛrɛˈsɛnt] m interested party; **i~ieren** [ɪntɛrɛˈsiːrən] vt to interest ♦ vr: **sich i~ieren für** to be interested in

intern [ɪnˈtɛrn] adj (Angelegenheiten, Regelung) internal; (Besprechung) private

Internat [ɪntɛrˈnaːt] (-(e)s, -e) nt boarding school

inter- [ɪntɛr] zW: **~national** [-natsioˈnaːl] adj international; **I~net** [ˈɪntənɛt] (-s) nt: **das I~net** the Internet; **I~net-Café** nt Internet café; **~pretieren** [-preˈtiːrən] vt to interpret; **I~vall** [-ˈval] (-s, -e) nt interval; **I~view** [-ˈvjuː] (-s, -s) nt interview; **~viewen** [-ˈvjuːən] vt to interview

intim [ɪnˈtiːm] adj intimate; **I~ität** f intimacy

intolerant [ˈɪntolɛrant] adj intolerant

Intrige [ɪnˈtriːgə] f intrigue, plot

Invasion [ɪnvaziˈoːn] f invasion

Inventar [ɪnvɛnˈtaːr] (-s, -e) nt inventory

Inventur [ɪnvɛnˈtuːr] f stocktaking; **~ machen** to stocktake

investieren [ɪnvɛsˈtiːrən] vt to invest

inwie- [ɪnviː] zW: **~fern** adv how far, to what extent; **~weit** adv how far, to what extent

inzwischen [ɪnˈtsvɪʃən] adv meanwhile

Irak [iˈraːk] (-s) m: **der ~** Iraq; **i~isch** adj Iraqi

Iran [iˈraːn] (-s) m: **der ~** Iran; **i~isch** adj Iranian

irdisch [ˈɪrdɪʃ] adj earthly

Ire [ˈiːrə] (-n, -n) m Irishman

irgend [ˈɪrgɛnt] adv at all; **wann/was/wer ~** whenever/whatever/whoever; **~etwas ▲** pron something/anything; **~jemand ▲** pron somebody/anybody; **~ein(e, s)** adj some, any; **~einmal** adv sometime or other; (fragend) ever; **~wann** adv sometime; **~wie** adv somehow; **~wo** adv somewhere; anywhere; **~wohin** adv somewhere; anywhere

Irin [ˈiːrɪn] f Irishwoman

Irland [ˈɪrlant] (-s) nt Ireland

Ironie [iroˈniː] f irony; **ironisch** [iˈroːnɪʃ] adj ironic(al)

irre [ˈɪrə] adj crazy, mad; **I~(r)** f(m) lunatic; **~führen** vt to mislead; **~machen** vt to confuse; **~n** vi to be mistaken; (umherirren) to wander, to stray ♦ vr to be mistaken; **I~nanstalt** f lunatic asylum

Irr- zW: **~garten** m maze; **i~ig** [ˈɪrɪç] adj incorrect, wrong; **i~itieren** [ɪriˈtiːrən] vt (verwirren) to confuse; (ärgern) to irritate; (stören) to annoy; **i~sinnig** adj mad, crazy; (umg) terrific; **~tum** (-s, -tümer) m mistake, error; **i~tümlich** adj mistaken

Island [ˈiːslant] (-s) nt Iceland

Isolation [izolatsiˈoːn] f isolation; (ELEK) insulation

Isolier- [izoˈliːr] zW: **~band** nt insulating

tape; **i~en** vt to isolate; (ELEK) to insulate; **~station** f (MED) isolation ward; **~ung** f isolation; (ELEK) insulation

Israel [ˈɪsraeːl] (-s) nt Israel; **~i** [-ˈeːli] (-s, -s) m Israeli; **i~isch** adj Israeli

isst ▲ [ɪst] vb siehe **essen**

ist [ɪst] vb siehe **sein**

Italien [iˈtaːliən] (-s) nt Italy; **~er(in)** (-s) m(f) Italian; **i~isch** adj Italian

i. V. abk = **in Vertretung**

J, j

ja [jaː] adv **1** yes; **haben Sie das gesehen? – ja** did you see it? – yes(, I did); **ich glaube ja** (yes,) I think so
2 (fragend) really?; **ich habe gekündigt – ja?** I've quit – have you?; **du kommst, ja?** you're coming, aren't you?
3: **sei ja vorsichtig** do be careful; **Sie wissen ja, dass ...** as you know, ...; **tu das ja nicht!** don't do that!; **ich habe es ja gewusst** I just knew it; **ja, also ...** well you see ...

Jacht [jaxt] (-, -en) f yacht

Jacke [ˈjakə] f jacket; (Wolljacke) cardigan

Jackett [ʒaˈkɛt] (-s, -s od -e) nt jacket

Jagd [jaːkt] (-, -en) f hunt; (Jagen) hunting; **~beute** f kill; **~flugzeug** nt fighter; **~hund** m hunting dog

jagen [ˈjaːgən] vi to hunt; (eilen) to race ♦ vt to hunt; (wegjagen) to drive (off); (verfolgen) to chase

Jäger [ˈjɛːgər] (-s, -) m hunter; **~schnitzel** nt (KOCH) pork in a spicy sauce with mushrooms

jäh [jɛː] adj sudden, abrupt; (steil) steep, precipitous

Jahr [jaːr] (-(e)s, -e) nt year; **j~elang** adv for years

Jahres- zW: **~abonnement** nt annual subscription; **~abschluss ▲** m end of the year; (COMM) annual statement of account; **~beitrag** m annual subscription; **~karte** f yearly season ticket; **~tag** m anniversary; **~wechsel** m turn of the year; **~zahl** f date; year; **~zeit** f season

Jahr- zW: **~gang** m age group; (von Wein) vintage; **~'hundert** (-s, -e) nt century; **jährlich** [ˈjɛːrlɪç] adj, adv yearly; **~markt** m fair; **~tausend** nt millennium; **~'zehnt** nt decade

Jähzorn [ˈjɛːtsɔrn] m sudden anger; hot temper; **j~ig** adj hot-tempered

Jalousie [ʒaluˈziː] f venetian blind

Jammer [ˈjamər] (-s) m misery; **es ist ein ~, dass ...** it is a crying shame that ...

jämmerlich [ˈjɛmərlɪç] adj wretched, pathetic

jammern vi to wail ♦ vt unpers: **es jammert jdn** it makes sb feel sorry
Januar ['janua:r] (-**s**, -**e**) m January
Japan ['ja:pan] (-**s**) nt Japan; ~**er(in)** [-'pa:nər(ın)] (-**s**) m(f) Japanese; **j~isch** adj Japanese
jäten ['jɛ:tən] vt: **Unkraut ~** to weed
jauchzen ['jauxtsən] vi to rejoice
jaulen ['jaulən] vi to howl
jawohl [ja'vo:l] adv yes (of course)
Jawort ['ja:vɔrt] nt consent
Jazz [dʒɛz] (-) m Jazz

SCHLÜSSELWORT
---

je [je:] adv **1** (jemals) ever; **hast du so was je gesehen?** did you ever see anything like it? **2** (jeweils) every, each; **sie zahlten je 3 Mark** they paid 3 marks each ♦ konj **1**: **je nach** depending on; **je nachdem** it depends; **je nachdem, ob …** depending on whether … **2**: **je eher, desto** od **umso besser** the sooner the better

Jeans [dʒi:nz] pl jeans
jede(r, s) ['je:də(r, s)] adj every, each ♦ pron everybody; (~ Einzelne) each; ~ **Mal** every time, each time; **ohne ~ x** without any x
jedenfalls adv in any case
jedermann pron everyone
jederzeit adv at any time
jedoch [je'dɔx] adv however
jeher ['je:he:r] adv: **von/seit ~** always
jemals ['je:ma:ls] adv ever
jemand ['je:mant] pron somebody; anybody
jene(r, s) ['je:nə(r, s)] adj that ♦ pron that one
jenseits ['je:nzaɪts] adv on the other side ♦ präp +gen on the other side of, beyond
Jenseits nt: **das ~** the hereafter, the beyond
jetzig ['jɛtsıç] adj present
jetzt [jɛtst] adv now
jeweilig adj respective
jeweils adv: ~ **zwei zusammen** two at a time; **zu ~ 5 DM** at 5 marks each; ~ **das Erste** the first each time
Jh. abk = **Jahrhundert**
Job [dʒɔp] (-**s**, -**s**) m (umg) job; **j~ben** ['dʒɔbən] vi (umg) to work
Jockei ['dʒɔke] (-**s**, -**s**) m jockey
Jod [jo:t] (-**(e)s**) nt iodine
jodeln ['jo:dəln] vi to yodel
joggen ['dʒɔgən] vi to jog
Jog(h)urt ['jo:gurt] (-**s**, -**s**) m od nt yogurt
Johannisbeere [jo'hanısbe:rə] f redcurrant; **schwarze ~** blackcurrant
johlen ['jo:lən] vi to yell
jonglieren [ʒõ'gli:rən] vi to juggle
Journal- [ʒʊrnal] zW: ~**ismus** [-'lısmʊs] m

journalism; ~**ist(in)** [-'lıst(ın)] m(f) journalist; **journa'listisch** adj journalistic
Jubel ['ju:bəl] (-**s**) m rejoicing; **j~n** vi to rejoice
Jubiläum [jubi'lɛ:ʊm] (-**s**, **Jubiläen**) nt anniversary; jubilee
jucken ['jʊkən] vi to itch ♦ vt: **es juckt mich am Arm** my arm is itching
Juckreiz ['jʊkraıts] m itch
Jude ['ju:də] (-**n**, -**n**) m Jew
Juden- zW: ~**tum** (-) nt Judaism; Jewry; ~**verfolgung** f persecution of the Jews
Jüdin ['jy:dın] f Jewess
jüdisch ['jy:dıʃ] adj Jewish
Jugend ['ju:gənt] (-) f youth; **j~frei** adj (CINE) U (BRIT), G (US), suitable for children; ~**herberge** f youth hostel; ~**herbergsausweis** m youth hostelling card; **j~lich** adj youthful; ~**liche(r)** f(m) teenager, young person
Jugoslaw- [jugo'sla:v] zW: ~**ien** (-**s**) nt Yugoslavia; **j~isch** adj Yugoslavian
Juli ['ju:li] (-**(s)**, -**s**) m July
jun. abk (= junior) jr.
jung [jʊŋ] adj young; **J~e** (-**n**, -**n**) m boy, lad ♦ nt young animal; **J~en** pl (von Tier) young pl
Jünger ['jyŋər] (-**s**, -) m disciple
jünger adj younger
Jung- zW: ~**frau** f virgin; (ASTROL) Virgo; ~**geselle** m bachelor; ~**gesellin** f unmarried woman
jüngst [jyŋst] adv lately, recently; ~**e(r, s)** adj youngest; (neueste) latest
Juni ['ju:ni] (-**(s)**, -**s**) m June
Junior ['ju:niɔr] (-**s**, -**en**) m junior
Jurist [ju'rıst] m jurist, lawyer; **j~isch** adj legal
Justiz [jʊs'ti:ts] (-) f justice; ~**beamte(r)** m judicial officer; ~**irrtum** m miscarriage of justice; ~**minister** m ≈ Lord (High) Chancellor (BRIT), Attorney General (US)
Juwel [ju've:l] (-**s**, -**en**) nt od m jewel
Juwelier [juve'li:r] (-**s**, -**e**) m jeweller; ~**geschäft** nt jeweller's (shop)
Jux [jʊks] (-**es**, -**e**) m joke, lark

K, k

Kabarett [kaba'rɛt] (-**s**, -**e** od -**s**) nt cabaret; ~**ist** [-'tıst] m cabaret artiste
Kabel ['ka:bəl] (-**s**, -) nt (ELEK) wire; (stark) cable; ~**fernsehen** nt cable television
Kabeljau ['ka:bəljau] (-**s**, -**e** od -**s**) m cod
Kabine [ka'bi:nə] f cabin; (Zelle) cubicle
Kabinenbahn f cable railway
Kabinett [kabi'nɛt] (-**s**, -**e**) nt (POL) cabinet
Kachel ['kaxəl] (-, -**n**) f tile; **k~n** vt to tile;

~ofen m tiled stove
Käfer ['kɛːfər] (-s, -) m beetle
Kaffee ['kafe] (-s, -s) m coffee; **~haus** nt café; **~kanne** f coffeepot; **~löffel** m coffee spoon
Käfig ['kɛːfɪç] (-s, -e) m cage
kahl [kaːl] adj bald; **~ geschoren** shaven, shorn; **~köpfig** adj bald-headed
Kahn [kaːn] (-(e)s, ⁼e) m boat, barge
Kai [kaɪ] (-s, -e od -s) m quay
Kaiser ['kaɪzər] (-s, -) m emperor; **~in** f empress; **k~lich** adj imperial; **~reich** nt empire; **~schnitt** m (MED) Caesarian (section)
Kakao [ka'kaːo] (-s, -s) m cocoa
Kaktee [kak'teː(ə)] (-, -n) f cactus
Kaktus ['kaktus] (-, -teen) m cactus
Kalb [kalp] (-(e)s, ⁼er) nt calf; **k~en** ['kalbən] vi to calve; **~fleisch** nt veal; **~sleder** nt calf(skin)
Kalender [ka'lɛndər] (-s, -) m calendar; (Taschenkalender) diary
Kaliber [ka'liːbər] (-s, -) nt (auch fig) calibre
Kalk [kalk] (-(e)s, -e) m lime; (BIOL) calcium; **~stein** m limestone
kalkulieren [kalku'liːrən] vt to calculate
Kalorie [kalo'riː] f calorie
kalt [kalt] adj cold; **mir ist (es) ~** I am cold; **~ bleiben**; (fig) to remain unmoved; **~ stellen** to chill; **~blütig** adj cold-blooded; (ruhig) cool
Kälte ['kɛltə] (-) f cold; coldness; **~grad** m degree of frost od below zero; **~welle** f cold spell
kalt- zW: **~herzig** adj cold-hearted; **~schnäuzig** adj cold, unfeeling; **~stellen** vt (fig) to leave out in the cold
kam etc [kaːm] vb siehe **kommen**
Kamel [ka'meːl] (-(e)s, -e) nt camel
Kamera ['kaməra] (-, -s) f camera
Kamerad [kamə'raːt] (-en, -en) m comrade, friend; **~schaft** f comradeship; **k~schaftlich** adj comradely
Kameramann (-(e)s, -männer) m cameraman
Kamille [ka'mɪlə] f camomile; **~ntee** m camomile tea
Kamin [ka'miːn] (-s, -e) m (außen) chimney; (innen) fireside, fireplace; **~kehrer** (-s, -) m chimney sweep
Kamm [kam] (-(e)s, ⁼e) m comb; (Bergkamm) ridge; (Hahnenkamm) crest
kämmen ['kɛmən] vt to comb ♦ vr to comb one's hair
Kammer ['kamər] (-, -n) f chamber; small bedroom; **~diener** m valet
Kampagne [kam'panjə] f campaign
Kampf [kampf] (-(e)s, ⁼e) m fight, battle; (Wettbewerb) contest; (fig: Anstrengung) struggle; **k~bereit** adj ready for action
kämpfen ['kɛmpfən] vi to fight

Kämpfer (-s, -) m fighter, combatant
Kampf- zW: **~handlung** f action; **k~los** adj without a fight; **~richter** m (SPORT) referee; (TENNIS) umpire; **~stoff** m: **chemischer/biologischer ~stoff** chemical/biological weapon
Kanada ['kanada] (-s) nt Canada; **Ka'nadier(in)** [ka'naːdiər(ın)] (-s, -) m(f) Canadian; **ka'nadisch** adj Canadian
Kanal [ka'naːl] (-s, Kanäle) m (Fluss) canal; (Rinne, Ärmelkanal) channel; (für Abfluss) drain; **~inseln** pl Channel Islands; **~isation** [-izatsi'oːn] f sewage system; **~tunnel** m: **der ~tunnel** the Channel Tunnel
Kanarienvogel [ka'naːrianfoːgəl] m canary
kanarisch [ka'naːrɪʃ] adj: **K~e Inseln** Canary Islands, Canaries
Kandi- [kandi] zW: **~dat** [-'daːt] (-en, -en) m candidate; **~datur** [-da'tuːr] f candidature, candidacy; **k~dieren** [-'diːrən] vi to stand, to run
Kandis(zucker) ['kandıs(tsʊkər)] (-) m candy
Känguru ▲ ['kɛŋguru] (-s, -s) nt kangaroo
Kaninchen [ka'niːnçən] nt rabbit
Kanister [ka'nıstər] (-s, -) m can, canister
Kännchen ['kɛnçən] nt pot
Kanne ['kanə] f (Krug) jug; (Kaffeekanne) pot; (Milchkanne) churn; (Gießkanne) can
kannst etc [kanst] vb siehe **können**
Kanone [ka'noːnə] f gun; (HIST) cannon; (fig: Mensch) ace
Kante ['kantə] f edge
Kantine [kan'tiːnə] f canteen
Kanton [kan'toːn] (-s, -e) m canton
Kanu ['kaːnu] (-s, -s) nt canoe
Kanzel ['kantsəl] (-, -n) f pulpit
Kanzler ['kantslər] (-s, -) m chancellor
Kap [kap] (-s, -s) nt cape (GEOG)
Kapazität [kapatsi'tɛːt] f capacity; (Fachmann) authority
Kapelle [ka'pɛlə] f (Gebäude) chapel; (MUS) band
kapieren [ka'piːrən] (umg) vt, vi to get, to understand
Kapital [kapi'taːl] (-s, -e od -ien) nt capital; **~anlage** f investment; **~ismus** [-'lɪsmʊs] m capitalism; **~ist** [-'lɪst] m capitalist; **k~istisch** adj capitalist
Kapitän [kapi'tɛːn] (-s, -e) m captain
Kapitel [ka'pɪtəl] (-s, -) nt chapter
Kapitulation [kapitulatsi'oːn] f capitulation
kapitulieren [kapitu'liːrən] vi to capitulate
Kappe ['kapə] f cap; (Kapuze) hood
kappen vt to cut
Kapsel ['kapsəl] (-, -n) f capsule
kaputt [ka'pʊt] (umg) adj kaput, broken; (Person) exhausted, finished; **am Auto ist etwas ~** there's something wrong with the car; **~gehen** (unreg) vi to break; (Schuhe) to fall apart; (Firma) to go bust; (Stoff) to wear out; (sterben) to cop it (umg); **~machen** vt

to break; (*Mensch*) to exhaust, to wear out
Kapuze [ka'pu:tsə] *f* hood
Karamell ▲ [kara'mɛl] (**-s**) *m* caramel;
~bonbon ▲ *m* od *nt* toffee
Karate [ka'ra:tə] (**-s**) *nt* karate
Karawane [kara'va:nə] *f* caravan
Kardinal [kardi'na:l] (**-s, Kardinäle**) *m*
cardinal; **~zahl** *f* cardinal number
Karfreitag [ka:r'fraita:k] *m* Good Friday
karg [kark] *adj* (*Landschaft, Boden*) barren;
(*Lohn*) meagre
kärglich ['kɛrkliç] *adj* poor, scanty
Karibik [ka'ri:bɪk] (**-**) *f:* **die ~** the Caribbean
karibisch [ka'ri:bɪʃ] *adj:* **K~e Inseln**
Caribbean Islands
kariert [ka'ri:rt] *adj* (*Stoff*) checked; (*Papier*)
squared
Karies ['ka:riɛs] (**-**) *f* caries
Karikatur [karika'tu:r] *f* caricature; **~ist**
[-'rɪst] *m* cartoonist
Karneval ['karnəval] (**-s, -e** od **-s**) *m* carnival
Karo ['ka:ro] (**-s, -s**) *nt* square; (*KARTEN*)
diamonds
Karosserie [karɔsə'ri:] *f* (*AUT*) body(work)
Karotte [ka'rɔtə] *f* carrot
Karpfen ['karpfən] (**-s, -**) *m* carp
Karre ['karə] *f* cart, barrow
Karren (**-s, -**) *m* cart, barrow
Karriere [kari'ɛ:rə] *f* career; **~ machen** to get
on, to get to the top; **~macher** (**-s, -**) *m*
careerist
Karte ['kartə] *f* card; (*Landkarte*) map;
(*Speisekarte*) menu; (*Eintrittskarte, Fahrkarte*)
ticket; **alles auf eine ~ setzen** to put all
one's eggs in one basket
Kartei [kar'tai] *f* card index; **~karte** *f* index card
Kartell [kar'tɛl] (**-s, -e**) *nt* cartel
Karten- *zW:* **~spiel** *nt* card game; pack
of cards; **~telefon** *nt* cardphone;
~vorverkauf *m* advance booking office
Kartoffel [kar'tɔfəl] (**-, -n**) *f* potato; **~brei** *m*
mashed potatoes *pl*; **~mus** *nt* mashed
potatoes *pl*; **~püree** *nt* mashed potatoes *pl*;
~salat *m* potato salad
Karton [kar'tõ:] (**-s, -s**) *m* cardboard;
(*Schachtel*) cardboard box; **k~iert**
[kartɔ'ni:rt] *adj* hardback
Karussell [karu'sɛl] (**-s, -s**) *nt* roundabout
(*BRIT*), merry-go-round
Karwoche ['ka:rvɔxə] *f* Holy Week
Käse ['kɛ:zə] (**-s, -**) *m* cheese; **~glocke** *f*
cheese (plate) cover; **~kuchen** *m*
cheesecake
Kaserne [ka'zɛrnə] *f* barracks *pl*; **~nhof** *m*
parade ground
Kasino [ka'zi:no] (**-s, -s**) *nt* club; (*MIL*)
officers' mess; (*Spielkasino*) casino
Kaskoversicherung ['kasko-] *f* (*Teilkasko*) ≈
third party, fire and theft insurance;

(*Vollkasko*), fully comprehensive insurance
Kasse ['kasə] *f* (*Geldkasten*) cashbox; (*in
Geschäft*) till, cash register; cash desk,
checkout; (*Kinokasse, Theaterkasse etc*) box
office; ticket office; (*Krankenkasse*) health
insurance; (*Sparkasse*) savings bank; **~
machen** to count the money; **getrennte ~
führen** to pay separately; **an der ~** (*in
Geschäft*) at the desk; **gut bei ~ sein** to be
in the money
Kassen- *zW:* **~arzt** *m* panel doctor (*BRIT*);
~bestand *m* cash balance; **~patient** *m*
panel patient (*BRIT*); **~prüfung** *f* audit;
~sturz *m:* **~sturz machen** to check one's
money; **~zettel** *m* receipt
Kassette [ka'sɛtə] *f* small box; (*Tonband,
PHOT*) cassette; (*Bücherkassette*) case
Kassettenrekorder (**-s, -**) *m* cassette
recorder
kassieren [ka'si:rən] *vt* to take ♦ *vi:* **darf ich
~?** would you like to pay now?
Kassierer [ka'si:rər] (**-s, -**) *m* cashier; (*von
Klub*) treasurer
Kastanie [kas'ta:niə] *f* chestnut; (*Baum*)
chestnut tree
Kasten ['kastən] (**-s, ⸚**) *m* (*auch SPORT*) box;
case; (*Truhe*) chest
kastrieren [kas'tri:rən] *vt* to castrate
Katalog [kata'lo:k] (**-(e)s, -e**) *m* catalogue
Katalysator [kataly'za:tɔr] *m* catalyst; (*AUT*)
catalytic converter
katastrophal [katastro'fa:l] *adj* catastrophic
Katastrophe [kata'stro:fə] *f* catastrophe,
disaster
Kat-Auto ['kat|auto] *nt* car fitted with a
catalytic converter
Kategorie [katego'ri:] *f* category
kategorisch [kate'go:rɪʃ] *adj* categorical
Kater ['ka:tər] (**-s, -**) *m* tomcat; (*umg*)
hangover
kath. *abk* (= *katholisch*) Cath.
Kathedrale [kate'dra:lə] *f* cathedral
Katholik [kato'li:k] (**-en, -en**) *m* Catholic
katholisch [ka'to:lɪʃ] *adj* Catholic
Kätzchen ['kɛtsçən] *nt* kitten
Katze ['katsə] *f* cat; **für die Katz** (*umg*) in
vain, for nothing
Katzen- *zW:* **~auge** *nt* cat's eye; (*Fahrrad*)
rear light; **~sprung** (*umg*) *m* stone's throw;
short journey
Kauderwelsch ['kaudərvɛlʃ] (**-(s)**) *nt* jargon;
(*umg*) double Dutch
kauen ['kauən] *vt, vi* to chew
kauern ['kauərn] *vi* to crouch down; (*furchtsam*) to cower
Kauf [kauf] (**-(e)s, Käufe**) *m* purchase, buy;
(*Kaufen*) buying; **ein guter ~** a bargain; **etw
in ~ nehmen** to put up with sth; **k~en** *vt* to
buy

Käufer(in) ['kɔʏfər(ɪn)] (-s, -) m(f) buyer
Kauf- zW: **~frau** f businesswoman; **~haus** nt department store; **~kraft** f purchasing power
käuflich ['kɔʏflɪç] adj purchasable, for sale; (pej) venal ♦ adv: **~ erwerben** to purchase
Kauf- zW: **k~lustig** adj interested in buying; **~mann** (pl **-leute**) m businessman; shopkeeper; **k~männisch** adj commercial; **k~männischer Angestellter** office worker; **~preis** m purchase price; **~vertrag** m bill of sale
Kaugummi ['kaʊgʊmi] m chewing gum
Kaulquappe ['kaʊlkvapə] f tadpole
kaum [kaʊm] adv hardly, scarcely
Kaution [kaʊtsˈoːn] f deposit; (JUR) bail
Kauz [kaʊts] (-es, **Käuze**) m owl; (fig) queer fellow
Kavalier [kava'liːr] (-s, -e) m gentleman, cavalier; **~sdelikt** nt peccadillo
Kaviar ['ka:viar] m caviar
keck [kɛk] adj daring, bold
Kegel ['ke:gəl] (-s, -) m skittle; (MATH) cone; **~bahn** f skittle alley; bowling alley; **k~n** vi to play skittles
Kehle ['ke:lə] f throat
Kehlkopf m larynx
Kehre ['ke:rə] f turn(ing), bend; **k~n** vt, vi (wenden) to turn; (mit Besen) to sweep; **sich an etw** dat **nicht k~n** not to heed sth
Kehricht ['ke:rɪçt] (-s) m sweepings pl
Kehrseite f reverse, other side; wrong side; bad side
kehrtmachen vi to turn about, to about-turn
keifen ['kaɪfən] vi to scold, to nag
Keil [kaɪl] (-(e)s, -e) m wedge; (MIL) arrowhead; **~riemen** m (AUT) fan belt
Keim [kaɪm] (-(e)s, -e) m bud; (MED, fig) germ; **k~en** vi to germinate; **k~frei** adj sterile; **~zelle** f (fig) nucleus
kein [kaɪn] adj no, not ... any; **~e(r, s)** pron no one, nobody; none; **~erlei** adj attrib no ... whatsoever
keinesfalls adv on no account
keineswegs adv by no means
keinmal adv not once
Keks [ke:ks] (-es, -e) m od nt biscuit
Kelch [kɛlç] (-(e)s, -e) m cup, goblet, chalice
Kelle ['kɛlə] f (Suppenkelle) ladle; (Maurerkelle) trowel
Keller ['kɛlər] (-s, -) m cellar
Kellner(in) ['kɛlnər(ɪn)] (-s, -) m(f) waiter(-tress)
keltern ['kɛltərn] vt to press
kennen ['kɛnən] (unreg) vt to know; **~ lernen** to get to know; **sich ~ lernen** to get to know each other; (zum ersten Mal) to meet
Kenner (-s, -) m connoisseur
kenntlich adj distinguishable, discernible; **etw ~ machen** to mark sth

Kenntnis (-, -se) f knowledge no pl; **etw zur ~ nehmen** to note sth; **von etw ~ nehmen** to take notice of sth; **jdn in ~ setzen** to inform sb
Kenn- zW: **~zeichen** nt mark, characteristic; **k~zeichnen** vt insep to characterize; **~ziffer** f reference number
kentern ['kɛntərn] vi to capsize
Keramik [ke'ra:mɪk] (-, -en) f ceramics pl, pottery
Kerbe ['kɛrbə] f notch, groove
Kerker ['kɛrkər] (-s, -) m prison
Kerl [kɛrl] (-s, -e) m chap, bloke (BRIT), guy
Kern [kɛrn] (-(e)s, -e) m (Obstkern) pip, stone; (Nusskern) kernel; (Atomkern) nucleus; (fig) heart, core; **~energie** f nuclear energy; **~forschung** f nuclear research; **~frage** f central issue; **k~gesund** adj thoroughly healthy, fit as a fiddle; **k~ig** adj (kraftvoll) robust; (Ausspruch) pithy; **~kraftwerk** nt nuclear power station; **k~los** adj seedless, without pips; **~physik** f nuclear physics sg; **~spaltung** f nuclear fission; **~waffen** pl nuclear weapons
Kerze ['kɛrtsə] f candle; (Zündkerze) plug; **k~ngerade** adj straight as a die; **~nständer** m candle holder
kess ▲ [kɛs] adj saucy
Kessel ['kɛsəl] (-s, -) m kettle; (von Lokomotive etc) boiler; (GEOG) depression; (MIL) encirclement
Kette ['kɛtə] f chain; **k~n** vt to chain; **~nrauchen** (-s) nt chain smoking; **~nreaktion** f chain reaction
Ketzer ['kɛtsər] (-s, -) m heretic
keuchen ['kɔʏçən] vi to pant, to gasp
Keuchhusten m whooping cough
Keule ['kɔʏlə] f club; (KOCH) leg
keusch [kɔʏʃ] adj chaste; **K~heit** f chastity
kfm. abk = **kaufmännisch**
Kfz [ka:ʔɛf'tset] nt abk = **Kraftfahrzeug**
KG [ka:'ge:] (-, -s) f abk (= Kommandit-gesellschaft) ≈ limited partnership
kg abk = **Kilogramm**
kichern ['kɪçərn] vi to giggle
kidnappen ['kɪtnɛpən] vt to kidnap
Kiefer¹ ['ki:fər] (-s, -) m jaw
Kiefer² ['ki:fər] (-, -n) f pine; **~nzapfen** m pine cone
Kiel [ki:l] (-(e)s, -e) m (Federkiel) quill; (NAUT) keel
Kieme ['ki:mə] f gill
Kies [ki:s] (-es, -e) m gravel
Kilo ['ki:lo] nt kilo; **~gramm** [kilo'gram] nt kilogram; **~meter** [kilo'me:tər] m kilometre; **~meterzähler** m ≈ milometer
Kind [kɪnt] (-(e)s, -er) nt child; **von ~ auf** from childhood
Kinder- ['kɪndər] zW: **~betreuung** f crèche; **~ei** [-'raɪ] f childishness; **~garten** m nursery school, playgroup; **~gärtnerin** f nursery

school teacher; **~geld** nt child benefit (BRIT); **~heim** nt children's home; **~krippe** f crèche; **~lähmung** f poliomyelitis; **k~leicht** adj childishly easy; **k~los** adj childless; **~mädchen** nt nursemaid; **k~reich** adj with a lot of children; **~sendung** f (RAD, TV) children's programme; **~sicherung** f (AUT) childproof safety catch; **~spiel** nt (fig) child's play; **~tagesstätte** f day nursery; **~wagen** m pram, baby carriage (US); **~zimmer** nt (für ~) children's room; (für Säugling) nursery

Kind- zW: **~heit** f childhood; **k~isch** adj childish; **k~lich** adj childlike

Kinn [kɪn] (-(e)s, -e) nt chin; **~haken** m (BOXEN) uppercut

Kino ['kiːnoː] (-s, -s) nt cinema; **~besucher** m cinema-goer; **~programm** nt film programme

Kiosk [kiˈɔsk] (-(e)s, -e) m kiosk

Kippe ['kɪpə] f cigarette end; (umg) fag; **auf der ~ stehen** (fig) to be touch and go

kippen vi to topple over, to overturn ♦ vt to tilt

Kirch- ['kɪrç] zW: **~e** f church; **~enlied** nt hymn; **~ensteuer** f church tax; **~gänger** (-s, -) m churchgoer; **~hof** m churchyard; **k~lich** adj ecclesiastical

Kirmes ['kɪrməs] (-, -sen) f fair

Kirsche ['kɪrʃə] f cherry

Kissen ['kɪsən] (-s, -) nt cushion; (Kopfkissen) pillow; **~bezug** m pillowslip

Kiste ['kɪstə] f box; chest

Kitsch [kɪtʃ] (-(e)s) m kitsch; **k~ig** adj kitschy

Kitt [kɪt] (-(e)s, -e) m putty

Kittel (-s, -) m overall, smock

kitten vt to putty; (fig: Ehe etc) to cement

kitzelig ['kɪtsəlɪç] adj (auch fig) ticklish

kitzeln vi to tickle

Kiwi ['kiːvi] (-, -s) f (BOT, KOCH) kiwi fruit

KKW [kaːkaːˈveː] nt abk = **Kernkraftwerk**

Klage ['klaːɡə] f complaint; (JUR) action; **k~n** vi (wehklagen) to lament, to wail; (sich beschweren) to complain; (JUR) to take legal action

Kläger(in) ['klɛːɡər(ɪn)] (-s, -) m(f) plaintiff

kläglich ['klɛːklɪç] adj wretched

klamm [klam] adj (Finger) numb; (feucht) damp

Klammer ['klamər] (-, -n) f clamp; (in Text) bracket; (Büroklammer) clip; (Wäscheklammer) peg; (Zahnklammer) brace; **k~n** vr: **sich k~n an** +akk to cling to

Klang [klaŋ] (-(e)s, ̈e) m sound; **k~voll** adj sonorous

Klappe ['klapə] f valve; (Ofenklappe) damper; (umg: Mund) trap; **k~n** vi (Geräusch) to click; (Sitz etc) to tip ♦ vt to tip ♦ vb unpers to work

Klapper ['klapər] (-, -n) f rattle; **k~ig** adj run-

down, worn-out; **k~n** vi to clatter, to rattle; **~schlange** f rattlesnake; **~storch** m stork

Klapp- zW: **~messer** nt jackknife; **~rad** nt collapsible bicycle; **~stuhl** m folding chair; **~tisch** m folding table

Klaps [klaps] (-es, -e) m slap

klar [klaːr] adj clear; (NAUT) ready for sea; (MIL) ready for action; **sich** akk **(über etw** dat**) ~ werden** to get (sth) clear in one's mind; **sich** +akk **im K~en sein über** dat to be clear about; **ins K~e kommen** to get clear; **(na) ~!** of course!; **~ sehen** to see clearly

Kläranlage f purification plant

klären ['klɛːrən] vt (Flüssigkeit) to purify; (Probleme) to clarify ♦ vr to clear (itself) up

Klarheit f clarity

Klarinette [klariˈnɛtə] f clarinet

klar- zW: **~legen** vt to clear up, to explain; **~machen** vt (Schiff) to get ready for sea; **jdm etw ~machen** to make sth clear to sb

klarsehen △ (unreg) vi siehe **klar**; **K~sichtfolie** f transparent film; **~stellen** vt to clarify

Klärung ['klɛːrʊŋ] f (von Flüssigkeit) purification; (von Probleme) clarification

klarwerden △ (unreg) vi siehe **klar**

Klasse ['klasə] f class; (SCH) class, form

klasse (umg) adj smashing

Klassen- zW: **~arbeit** f test; **~gesellschaft** f class society; **~lehrer** m form master; **k~los** adj classless; **~sprecher(in)** m(f) form prefect; **~zimmer** nt classroom

klassifizieren [klasifiˈtsiːrən] vt to classify

Klassik ['klasɪk] f (Zeit) classical period; (Stil) classicism; **~er** (-s, -) m classic

klassisch adj (auch fig) classical

Klatsch [klatʃ] (-(e)s, -e) m smack, crack; (Gerede) gossip; **~base** f gossip, scandalmonger; **~e** (umg) f crib; **k~en** vi (Geräusch) to clash; (reden) to gossip; (applaudieren) to applaud, to clap ♦ vt: **jdm Beifall k~en** to applaud sb; **~mohn** m (corn) poppy; **k~nass** ▲ adj soaking wet

Klaue ['klaʊə] f claw; (umg: Schrift) scrawl; **k~n** (umg) vt to pinch

Klausel ['klaʊzəl] (-, -n) f clause

Klausur [klaʊˈzuːr] f seclusion; **~arbeit** f examination paper

Klavier [klaˈviːr] (-s, -e) nt piano

Kleb- ['kleːb] zW: **k~en** ['kleːbən] vt, vi: **k~en (an** +akk**)** to stick (to); **k~rig** adj sticky; **~stoff** m glue; **~streifen** m adhesive tape

kleckern ['klɛkərn] vi to make a mess ♦ vt to spill

Klecks [klɛks] (-es, -e) m blot, stain

Klee [kleː] (-s) m clover; **~blatt** nt cloverleaf; (fig) trio

Kleid [klaɪt] (-(e)s, -er) nt garment;

Spelling reform: ▲ *new spelling* △ *old spelling (to be phased out)*

(*Frauenkleid*) dress; **~er** pl (*Kleidung*) clothes; **k~en** ['klaɪdən] vt to clothe, to dress; to suit ♦ vr to dress

Kleider- ['klaɪdər] zW: **~bügel** m coat hanger; **~bürste** f clothes brush; **~schrank** m wardrobe

Kleid- zW: **k~sam** adj flattering; **~ung** f clothing; **~ungsstück** nt garment

klein [klaɪn] adj little, small; **~ hacken** to chop, to mince; **~ schneiden** to chop up; **K~e(r, s)** mf little one; **K~format** nt small size; **im K~format** small-scale; **K~geld** nt small change; **K~igkeit** f trifle; **K~kind** nt infant; **K~kram** m details pl; **~laut** adj dejected, quiet; **~lich** adj petty, paltry; **K~od** ['klaɪnoːt] (**-s, -odien**) nt gem, jewel; treasure; **K~stadt** f small town; **~städtisch** adj provincial; **~stmöglich** adj smallest possible

Kleister ['klaɪstər] (**-s, -**) m paste

Klemme ['klɛmə] f clip; (*MED*) clamp; (*fig*) jam; **k~n** vt (*festhalten*) to jam; (*quetschen*) to pinch, to nip ♦ vr to catch o.s.; (*sich hineinzwängen*) to squeeze o.s. ♦ vi (*Tür*) to stick, to jam; **sich hinter jdn/etw k~n** to get on to sb/down to sth

Klempner ['klɛmpnər] (**-s, -**) m plumber

Klerus ['kleːrʊs] (**-**) m clergy

Klette ['klɛtə] f burr

Kletter- ['klɛtər] zW: **~er** (**-s, -**) m climber; **k~n** vi to climb; **~pflanze** f creeper

Klient(in) [kli'ɛnt(ɪn)] m(f) client

Klima ['kliːma] (**-s, -s** od **-te**) nt climate; **~anlage** f air conditioning; **~wechsel** m change of air

klimpern ['klɪmpərn] (*umg*) vi (*mit Münzen, Schlüsseln*) to jingle; (*auf Klavier*) to plonk (away)

Klinge ['klɪŋə] f blade; sword

Klingel ['klɪŋəl] (**-, -n**) f bell; **~beutel** m collection bag; **k~n** vi to ring

klingen ['klɪŋən] (*unreg*) vi to sound; (*Gläser*) to clink

Klinik ['kliːnɪk] f hospital, clinic

Klinke ['klɪŋkə] f handle

Klippe ['klɪpə] f cliff; (*im Meer*) reef; (*fig*) hurdle

klipp und klar ['klɪpʊntklaːr] adj clear and concise

klirren ['klɪrən] vi to clank, to jangle; (*Gläser*) to clink; **~de Kälte** biting cold

Klischee [kli'ʃeː] (**-s, -s**) nt (*Druckplatte*) plate, block; (*fig*) cliché; **~vorstellung** f stereotyped idea

Klo [kloː] (**-s, -s**) (*umg*) nt loo (*BRIT*), john (*US*)

Kloake [klo'aːkə] f sewer

klobig ['kloːbɪç] adj clumsy

Klopapier (*umg*) nt loo paper (*BRIT*)

klopfen ['klɔpfən] vi to knock; (*Herz*) to thump ♦ vt to beat; **es klopft** somebody's knocking; **jdm auf die Schulter ~** to tap sb

on the shoulder

Klopfer (**-s, -**) m (*Teppichklopfer*) beater; (*Türklopfer*) knocker

Klops [klɔps] (**-es, -e**) m meatball

Klosett [klo'zɛt] (**-s, -e** od **-s**) nt lavatory, toilet; **~papier** nt toilet paper

Kloß [kloːs] (**-es, ̈-e**) m (*im Hals*) lump; (*KOCH*) dumpling

Kloster ['kloːstər] (**-s, ̈-**) nt (*Männerkloster*) monastery; (*Frauenkloster*) convent; **klösterlich** ['kløːstərlɪç] adj monastic; convent cpd

Klotz [klɔts] (**-es, ̈-e**) m log; (*Hackklotz*) block; **ein ~ am Bein** (*fig*) a drag, a millstone round (sb's) neck

Klub [klʊp] (**-s, -s**) m club; **~sessel** m easy chair

Kluft [klʊft] (**-, ̈-e**) f cleft, gap; (*GEOG*) gorge, chasm

klug [kluːk] adj clever, intelligent; **K~heit** f cleverness, intelligence

Klumpen ['klʊmpən] (**-s, -**) m (*Erdklumpen*) clod; (*Blutklumpen*) clot; (*Goldklumpen*) nugget; (*KOCH*) lump

km abk = **Kilometer**

knabbern ['knabərn] vt, vi to nibble

Knabe [knaːbə] (**-n, -n**) m boy

Knäckebrot ['knɛkəbroːt] nt crispbread

knacken ['knakən] vt, vi (*auch fig*) to crack

Knacks [knaks] (**-es, -e**) m crack; (*fig*) defect

Knall [knal] (**-(e)s, -e**) m bang; (*Peitschenknall*) crack; **~ und Fall** (*umg*) unexpectedly; **~bonbon** nt cracker; **k~en** vi to bang; to crack; **k~rot** adj bright red

knapp [knap] adj tight; (*Geld*) scarce; (*Sprache*) concise; **eine ~e Stunde** just under an hour; **~ unter/neben** just under/by; **jdn (mit etw) ~ halten** to keep sb short (of sth); **K~heit** f tightness; scarcity; conciseness

knarren ['knarən] vi to creak

Knast [knast] (**-(e)s**) (*umg*) m (*Haftstrafe*) porridge, time (*inf*); (*Gefängnis*) slammer (*inf*), clink (*inf*)

knattern ['knatərn] vi to rattle; (*Maschinengewehr*) to chatter

Knäuel ['knɔʏəl] (**-s, -**) m od nt (*Wollknäuel*) ball; (*Menschenknäuel*) knot

Knauf [knaʊf] (**-(e)s, Knäufe**) m knob; (*Schwertknauf*) pommel

Knebel ['kneːbəl] (**-s, -**) m gag

kneifen ['knaɪfən] (*unreg*) vt to pinch ♦ vi to pinch; (*sich drücken*) to back out; **vor etw ~** to dodge sth

Kneipe ['knaɪpə] (*umg*) f pub

kneten ['kneːtən] vt to knead; (*Wachs*) to mould

Knick [knɪk] (**-(e)s, -e**) m (*Sprung*) crack; (*Kurve*) bend; (*Falte*) fold; **k~en** vt, vi (*springen*) to crack; (*brechen*) to break; (*Papier*) to fold; **geknickt sein** to be downcast

Knicks |knıks| (-es, -e) *m* curtsey
Knie |kni:| (-s, -) *nt* knee; **~beuge** *f* knee bend; **~bundhose** *m* knee breeches; **~gelenk** *nt* knee joint; **~kehle** *f* back of the knee; **k~n** *vi* to kneel; **~scheibe** *f* kneecap; **~strumpf** *m* knee-length sock
Kniff |knıf| (-(e)s, -e) *m* (*fig*) trick, knack; **k~elig** *adj* tricky
knipsen |'knıpsən| *vt* (*Fahrkarte*) to punch; (*PHOT*) to take a snap of, to snap ♦ *vi* to take a snap *od* snaps
Knirps |knırps| (-es, -e) *m* little chap (®: *Schirm*) telescopic umbrella
knirschen |'knırʃən| *vi* to crunch; **mit den Zähnen ~** to grind one's teeth
knistern |'knıstərn| *vi* to crackle
Knitter- |'knıtər| *zW*: **~falte** *f* crease; **k~frei** *adj* non-crease; **k~n** *vi* to crease
Knoblauch |'kno:plaʊx| (-(e)s) *m* garlic; **~zehe** *f* (*KOCH*) clove of garlic
Knöchel |'knœçəl| (-s, -) *m* knuckle; (*Fußknöchel*) ankle
Knochen |'knɔxən| (-s, -) *m* bone; **~bruch** *m* fracture; **~gerüst** *nt* skeleton; **~mark** *nt* bone marrow
knöchern |'knœçərn| *adj* bone
knochig |'knɔxıç| *adj* bony
Knödel |'knø:dəl| (-s, -) *m* dumpling
Knolle |'knɔlə| *f* tuber
Knopf |knɔpf| (-(e)s, ⸚e) *m* button; (*Kragenknopf*) stud
knöpfen |'knœpfən| *vt* to button
Knopfloch *nt* buttonhole
Knorpel |'knɔrpəl| (-s, -) *m* cartilage, gristle; **k~ig** *adj* gristly
Knospe |'knɔspə| *f* bud
Knoten |'kno:tən| (-s, -) *m* knot; (*BOT*) node; (*MED*) lump; **k~** *vt* to knot; **~punkt** *m* junction
Knüller |'knʏlər| (-s, -) (*umg*) *m* hit; (*Reportage*) scoop
knüpfen |'knʏpfən| *vt* to tie; (*Teppich*) to knot; (*Freundschaft*) to form
Knüppel |'knʏpəl| (-s, -) *m* cudgel; (*Polizeiknüppel*) baton, truncheon; (*AVIAT*) (joy)stick
knurren |'knʊrən| *vi* (*Hund*) to snarl, to growl; (*Magen*) to rumble; (*Mensch*) to mutter
knusperig |'knʊspərıç| *adj* crisp; (*Keks*) crunchy
k. o. |ka:'o:| *adj* knocked out; (*fig*) done in
Koalition |koalitsi'o:n| *f* coalition
Kobold |'ko:bɔlt| (-(e)s, -e) *m* goblin, imp
Koch |kɔx| (-(e)s, ⸚e) *m* cook; **~buch** *nt* cook(ery) book; **k~en** *vt, vi* to cook; (*Wasser*) to boil; **~er** (-s, -) *m* stove, cooker; **~gelegenheit** *f* cooking facilities *pl*
Köchin |'kœçın| *f* cook

Koch- *zW*: **~löffel** *m* kitchen spoon; **~nische** *f* kitchenette; **~platte** *f* hotplate; **~salz** *nt* cooking salt; **~topf** *m* saucepan, pot
Köder |'kø:dər| (-s, -) *m* bait, lure
ködern *vt* (*Tier*) to trap with bait; (*Person*) to entice, to tempt
Koexistenz |koeksıs'tents| *f* coexistence
Koffein |kɔfe'i:n| (-s) *nt* caffeine; **k~frei** *adj* decaffeinated
Koffer |'kɔfər| (-s, -) *m* suitcase; (*Schrankkoffer*) trunk; **~kuli** *m* (luggage) trolley; **~radio** *nt* portable radio; **~raum** *m* (*AUT*) boot (*BRIT*), trunk (*US*)
Kognak |'kɔnjak| (-s, -s) *m* brandy, cognac
Kohl |ko:l| (-(e)s, -e) *m* cabbage
Kohle |'ko:lə| *f* coal; (*Holzkohle*) charcoal; (*CHEM*) carbon; **~hydrat** (-(e)s, -e) *nt* carbohydrate
Kohlen- *zW*: **~dioxid** (-(e)s, -e) *nt* carbon dioxide; **~händler** *m* coal merchant, coalman; **~säure** *f* carbon dioxide; **~stoff** *m* carbon
Kohlepapier *nt* carbon paper
Koje |'ko:jə| *f* cabin; (*Bett*) bunk
Kokain |koka'i:n| (-s) *nt* cocaine
kokett |ko'ket| *adj* coquettish, flirtatious
Kokosnuss ▲ |'ko:kɔsnʊs| *f* coconut
Koks |ko:ks| (-es, -e) *m* coke
Kolben |'kɔlbən| (-s, -) *m* (*Gewehrkolben*) rifle butt; (*Keule*) club; (*CHEM*) flask; (*TECH*) piston; (*Maiskolben*) cob
Kolik |'ko:lık| *f* colic, the gripes *pl*
Kollaps |kɔ'laps| (-es, -e) *m* collapse
Kolleg |kɔ'le:k| (-s, -s *od* -ien) *nt* lecture course; **~e** |kɔ'le:gə| (-n, -n) *m* colleague; **~in** *f* colleague; **~ium** *nt* working party; (*SCH*) staff
Kollekte |kɔ'lektə| *f* (*REL*) collection
kollektiv |kɔlek'ti:f| *adj* collective
Köln |kœln| (-s) *nt* Cologne
Kolonie |kolo'ni:| *f* colony
kolonisieren |koloni'zi:rən| *vt* to colonize
Kolonne |ko'lɔnə| *f* column; (*von Fahrzeugen*) convoy
Koloss ▲ |ko'lɔs| (-es, -e) *m* colossus; **kolo'ssal** *adj* colossal
Kölsch |kœlʃ| (-, -) *nt* (*Bier*) ≈ (strong) lager
Kombi- |'kɔmbi| *zW*: **~nation** |-natsi'o:n| *f* combination; (*Vermutung*) conjecture; (*Hemdhose*) combinations *pl*; **k~nieren** |-'ni:rən| *vt* to combine ♦ *vi* to deduce, to work out; (*vermuten*) to guess; **~wagen** *m* station wagon; **~zange** *f* (pair of) pliers *pl*
Komet |ko'me:t| (-en, -en) *m* comet
Komfort |kɔm'fo:r| (-s) *m* luxury
Komik |'ko:mık| *f* humour, comedy; **~er** (-s, -) *m* comedian
komisch |'ko:mıʃ| *adj* funny
Komitee |komi'te:| (-s, -s) *nt* committee

Komma |'kɔma| (-s, -s od -ta) nt comma; **2 ~ 3** 2 point 3

Kommand- |kɔ'mand| zW: **~ant** [-'dant] m commander, commanding officer; **k~ieren** [-'di:rən] vt, vi to command; **~o** (-s, -s) nt command, order; (Truppe) detachment, squad; **auf ~o** to order

kommen |'kɔmən| (unreg) vi to come; (näher ~) to approach; (passieren) to happen; (gelangen, geraten) to get; (Blumen, Zähne, Tränen etc) to appear; (in die Schule, das Zuchthaus etc) to go; **~ lassen** to send for; **das kommt in den Schrank** that goes in the cupboard; **zu sich ~** to come round od to; **zu etw ~** to acquire sth; **um etw ~** to lose sth; **nichts auf jdn/etw ~ lassen** to have nothing said against sb/sth; **jdm frech ~** to get cheeky with sb; **auf jeden vierten kommt ein Platz** there's one place for every fourth person; **wer kommt zuerst?** who's first?; **unter ein Auto ~** to be run over by a car; **wie hoch kommt das?** what does that cost?; **komm gut nach Hause!** safe journey (home); **~den Sonntag** next Sunday; **K~** (-s) nt coming

Kommentar |kɔmɛn'ta:r| m commentary; **kein ~** no comment; **k~los** adj without comment

Kommentator |kɔmɛn'ta:tɔr| m (TV) commentator

kommentieren |kɔmɛn'ti:rən| vt to comment on

kommerziell |kɔmɛrtsi'ɛl| adj commercial

Kommilitone |kɔmili'to:nə| (-n, -n) m fellow student

Kommissar |kɔmı'sa:r| m police inspector

Kommission |kɔmısi'o:n| f (COMM) commission; (Ausschuss) committee

Kommode |kɔ'mo:də| f (chest of) drawers

kommunal |kɔmu'na:l| adj local; (von Stadt auch) municipal

Kommune |kɔ'mu:nə| f commune

Kommunikation |kɔmunıkatsi'o:n| f communication

Kommunion |kɔmuni'o:n| f communion

Kommuniqué, Kommunikee |kɔmyni'ke:| (-s, -s) nt communiqué

Kommunismus |kɔmu'nısmʊs| m communism

Kommunist(in) |kɔmu'nıst(ın)| m(f) communist; **k~isch** adj communist

kommunizieren |kɔmuni'tsi:rən| vi to communicate

Komödie |ko'mø:diə| f comedy

Kompagnon |kɔmpan'jöː| (-s, -s) m (COMM) partner

kompakt |kɔm'pakt| adj compact

Kompanie |kɔmpa'ni:| f company

Kompass ▲ |'kɔmpas| (-es, -e) m compass

kompatibel |kɔmpa'ti:bəl| adj compatible

kompetent |kɔmpe'tɛnt| adj competent

Kompetenz f competence, authority

komplett |kɔm'plɛt| adj complete

Komplex |kɔm'plɛks| (-es, -e) m (Gebäudekomplex) complex

Komplikation |kɔmplikatsi'o:n| f complication

Kompliment |kɔmpli'mɛnt| nt compliment

Komplize |kɔm'pli:tsə| (-n, -n) m accomplice

kompliziert |kɔmpli'tsi:rt| adj complicated

komponieren |kɔmpo'ni:rən| vt to compose

Komponist |kɔmpo'nıst(ın)| m composer

Komposition |kɔmpozitsi'o:n| f composition

Kompost |kɔm'pɔst| (-(e)s, -e) m compost

Kompott |kɔm'pɔt| (-(e)s, -e) nt stewed fruit

Kompromiss ▲ |kɔmpro'mıs| (-es, -e) m compromise; **k~bereit** ▲ adj willing to compromise

Kondens- |kɔn'dɛns| zW: **~ation** |kɔndɛnzatsi'o:n| f condensation; **k~ieren** |kɔndɛn'zi:rən| vt to condense; **~milch** f condensed milk

Kondition |kɔnditsi'o:n| f (COMM, FIN) condition; (Durchhaltevermögen) stamina; (körperliche Verfassung) physical condition, state of health

Konditionstraining |kɔnditsi'o:nstrɛnıŋ| nt fitness training

Konditor |kɔn'di:tɔr| m pastry cook; **~ei** [-'rai] f café; cake shop

Kondom |kɔn'do:m| (-s, -e) nt condom

Konferenz |kɔnfe'rɛnts| f conference, meeting

Konfession |kɔnfesi'o:n| f (religious) denomination; **k~ell** [-'nɛl] adj denominational; **k~slos** adj non-denominational

Konfirmand |kɔnfır'mant| m candidate for confirmation

Konfirmation |kɔnfırmatsi'o:n| f (REL) confirmation

konfirmieren |kɔnfır'mi:rən| vt to confirm

konfiszieren |kɔnfıs'tsi:rən| vt to confiscate

Konfitüre |kɔnfi'ty:rə| f jam

Konflikt |kɔn'flıkt| (-(e)s, -e) m conflict

konfrontieren |kɔnfrɔn'ti:rən| vt to confront

konfus |kɔn'fu:s| adj confused

Kongress ▲ |kɔn'grɛs| (-es, -e) m congress; **~zentrum** ▲ nt conference centre

Kongruenz |kɔngru'ɛnts| f agreement, congruence

König |'kø:nıç| (-(e)s, -e) m king; **~in** |'kø:nıgın| f queen; **k~lich** adj royal; **~reich** nt kingdom

Konjugation |kɔnjugatsi'o:n| f conjugation

konjugieren |kɔnju'gi:rən| vt to conjugate

Konjunktion |kɔnjʊŋktsi'o:n| f conjunction

Konjunktiv |'kɔnjʊŋkti:f| (-s, -e) m subjunctive

Konjunktur |kɔnjʊŋkˈtuːr| f economic situation; (*Hochkonjunktur*) boom

konkret |kɔnˈkreːt| adj concrete

Konkurrent(in) |kɔnkʊˈrɛnt(ɪn)| m(f) competitor

Konkurrenz |kɔnkʊˈrɛnts| f competition; **k~fähig** adj competitive; **~kampf** m competition; rivalry, competitive situation

konkurrieren |kɔnkʊˈriːrən| vi to compete

Konkurs |kɔnˈkʊrs| (-es, -e) m bankruptcy

Können (-s) nt ability

SCHLÜSSELWORT

---

können |ˈkœnən| (pt konnte, pp gekonnt od (als Hilfsverb) können) vt, vi **1** to be able to; **ich kann es machen** I can do it, I am able to do it; **ich kann es nicht machen** I can't do it, I'm not able to do it; **ich kann nicht ... I can't ..., I cannot ...; ich kann nicht mehr** I can't go on

2 (wissen, beherrschen) to know; **können Sie Deutsch?** can you speak German?; **er kann gut Englisch** he speaks English well; **sie kann keine Mathematik** she can't do mathematics

3 (dürfen) to be allowed to; **kann ich gehen?** can I go?; **könnte ich ...?** could I ...?; **kann ich mit?** (umg) can I come with you?

4 (möglich sein): **Sie könnten Recht haben** you may be right; **das kann sein** that's possible; **kann sein** maybe

---

Könner m expert

konnte etc |ˈkɔntə| vb siehe **können**

konsequent |kɔnzeˈkvɛnt| adj consistent

Konsequenz |kɔnzeˈkvɛnts| f consistency; (Folgerung) conclusion

Konserv- |kɔnˈzɛrv| zW: **k~ativ** |-aˈtiːf| adj conservative; **~ative(r)** |-aˈtiːvə| f(m) (POL) conservative; **~e** f tinned food; **~enbüchse** f tin, can; **k~ieren** |-ˈviːrən| vt to preserve; **~ierung** f preservation; **~ierungsstoff** m preservatives

Konsonant |kɔnzoˈnant| m consonant

konstant |kɔnˈstant| adj constant

konstru- zW: **~ieren** |kɔnstruˈiːrən| vt to construct; **K~kteur** |kɔnstrukˈtøːr| m designer; **K~ktion** |kɔnstruktsiˈoːn| f construction; **~ktiv** |kɔnstrukˈtiːf| adj constructive

Konsul |ˈkɔnzʊl| (-s, -n) m consul; **~at** |-ˈlaːt| nt consulate

konsultieren |kɔnzʊlˈtiːrən| vt to consult

Konsum |kɔnˈzuːm| (-s) m consumption; **~artikel** m consumer article; **~ent** |-ˈmɛnt| m consumer; **k~ieren** |-ˈmiːrən| vt to consume

Kontakt |kɔnˈtakt| (-(e)s, -e) m contact; **k~arm** adj unsociable; **k~freudig** adj sociable; **~linsen** pl contact lenses

kontern |ˈkɔntərn| vt, vi to counter

Kontinent |ˈkɔntiˈnɛnt| m continent

Kontingent |kɔntɪŋˈgɛnt| (-(e)s, -e) nt quota; (*Truppenkontingent*) contingent

kontinuierlich |kɔntinuˈiːrlɪç| adj continuous

Konto |ˈkɔnto| (-s, Konten) nt account; **~auszug** m statement (of account); **~inhaber(in)** m(f) account holder; **~stand** m balance

Kontra |ˈkɔntra| (-s, -s) nt (KARTEN) double; **jdm ~ geben** (fig) to contradict sb; **~bass ▲** m double bass; **~hent** m (COMM) contracting party; **~punkt** m counterpoint

Kontrast |kɔnˈtrast| (-(e)s, -e) m contrast

Kontroll- |kɔnˈtrɔl| zW: **~e** f control, supervision; (*Passkontrolle*) passport control; **~eur** |-ˈløːr| m inspector; **k~ieren** |-ˈliːrən| vt to control, to supervise; (nachprüfen) to check

Konvention |kɔnvɛntsiˈoːn| f convention; **k~ell** |-ˈnɛl| adj conventional

Konversation |kɔnvɛrzatsiˈoːn| f conversation; **~slexikon** nt encyclop(a)edia

Konvoi |ˈkɔnvɔy| (-s, -s) m convoy

Konzentration |kɔntsɛntratsiˈoːn| f concentration; **~slager** nt concentration camp

konzentrieren |kɔntsɛnˈtriːrən| vt, vr to concentrate

konzentriert adj concentrated ♦ adv (zuhören, arbeiten) intently

Konzern |kɔnˈtsɛrn| (-s, -e) m combine

Konzert |kɔnˈtsɛrt| (-(e)s, -e) nt concert; (Stück) concerto; **~saal** m concert hall

Konzession |kɔntsesiˈoːn| f licence; (Zugeständnis) concession

Konzil |kɔnˈtsiːl| (-s, -e od -ien) nt council

kooperativ |koʔoperaˈtiːf| adj cooperative

koordinieren |koʔɔrdiˈniːrən| vt to coordinate

Kopf |kɔpf| (-(e)s, ⁼e) m head; **~haut** f scalp; **~hörer** m headphones pl; **~kissen** nt pillow; **k~los** adj panic-stricken; **k~rechnen** vi to do mental arithmetic; **~salat** m lettuce; **~schmerzen** pl headache sg; **~sprung** m header, dive; **~stand** m headstand; **~stütze** f (im Auto etc) headrest, head restraint; **~tuch** nt headscarf; **~weh** nt headache; **~zerbrechen** nt: jdm **~zerbrechen machen** to be a headache for sb

Kopie |koˈpiː| f copy; **k~ren** vt to copy

Kopiergerät nt photocopier

Koppel¹ |ˈkɔpəl| (-, -n) f (Weide) enclosure

Koppel² |ˈkɔpəl| (-s, -) m (Gürtel) belt

koppeln vt to couple

Koppelung f coupling

Koralle |koˈralə| f coral

Korb |kɔrp| (-(e)s, ⁼e) m basket; jdm einen **~ geben** (fig) to turn sb down; **~ball** m basketball; **~stuhl** m wicker chair

Kord |kɔrt| (-(e)s, -e) m cord, corduroy

Kordel ['kɔrdəl| (-, -n) f cord, string

Kork |kɔrk| (-(e)s, -e) m cork; ~en (-s, -) m stopper, cork; ~enzieher (-s, -) m corkscrew

Korn |kɔrn| (-(e)s, ⁼er) nt corn, grain; (Gewehr) sight

Körper ['kœrper| (-s, -) m body; ~bau m build; k~behindert adj disabled; ~geruch m body odour; ~gewicht nt weight; ~größe f height; k~lich adj physical; ~pflege f personal hygiene; ~schaft f corporation; ~schaftssteuer f corporation tax; ~teil m part of the body; ~verletzung f bodily od physical injury

korpulent |kɔrpu'lent| adj corpulent

korrekt |kɔ'rekt| adj correct; K~ur |-'tu:r| f (eines Textes) proofreading; (Text) proof; (SCH) marking, correction

Korrespond- |kɔrespɔnd| zW: ~ent(in) |-'dent(ın)| m(f) correspondent; ~enz |-'dents| f correspondence; k~ieren |-'di:rən| vi to correspond

Korridor |'kɔrido:r| (-s, -e) m corridor

korrigieren |kɔri'gi:rən| vt to correct

Korruption |kɔruptsi'o:n| f corruption

Kose- |'ko:zə| zW: ~form f pet form; ~name m pet name; ~wort nt term of endearment

Kosmetik |kɔs'me:tık| f cosmetics pl; ~erin f beautician

kosmetisch adj cosmetic; (Chirurgie) plastic

kosmisch ['kɔsmıʃ| adj cosmic

Kosmo- |kɔsmo| zW: ~naut |-'naot| (-en, -en) m cosmonaut; k~politisch adj cosmopolitan; ~s (-) m cosmos

Kost |kɔst| (-) f (Nahrung) food; (Verpflegung) board; k~bar adj precious; (teuer) costly, expensive; ~barkeit f preciousness; costliness, expensiveness; (Wertstück) valuable

Kosten pl cost(s); (Ausgaben) expenses; auf ~ von at the expense of; k~ vt to cost; (versuchen) to taste ♦ vi to taste; was kostet ...? what does ... cost?, how much is ...?; ~anschlag m estimate; k~los adj free (of charge)

köstlich ['kœstlıç| adj precious; (Einfall) delightful; (Essen) delicious; sich ~ amüsieren to have a marvellous time

Kostprobe f taste; (fig) sample

kostspielig adj expensive

Kostüm |kɔs'ty:m| (-s, -e) nt costume; (Damenkostüm) suit; ~fest nt fancy-dress party; k~ieren |kɔsty'mi:rən| vt, vr to dress up; ~verleih m costume agency

Kot |ko:t| (-(e)s) m excrement

Kotelett |kotə'let| (-(e)s, -e od -s) nt cutlet, chop; ~en pl (Bart) sideboards

Köter |'kø:tər| (-s, -) m cur

Kotflügel m (AUT) wing

kotzen |'kɔtsən| (umg!) vi to puke (umg), to throw up (umg)

Krabbe |'krabə| f shrimp; k~ln vi to crawl

Krach |krax| (-(e)s, -s od -e) m crash; (andauernd) noise; (umg: Streit) quarrel, argument; k~en vi to crash; (beim Brechen) to crack ♦ vr (umg) to argue, to quarrel

krächzen ['kreçtsən| vi to croak

Kraft |kraft| (-, ⁼e) f strength; power; force; (Arbeitskraft) worker; in ~ treten to come into force; k~ präp +gen by virtue of; ~fahrer m (motor) driver; ~fahrzeug nt motor vehicle; ~fahrzeugbrief m logbook; ~fahrzeugsteuer f road tax; ~fahrzeugversicherung f car insurance

kräftig |'kreftıç| adj strong; ~en vt to strengthen

Kraft- zW: k~los adj weak; powerless; (JUR) invalid; ~probe f trial of strength; ~stoff m fuel; k~voll adj vigorous; ~werk nt power station

Kragen |'kra:gən| (-s, -) m collar; ~weite f collar size

Krähe |'kre:ə| f crow; k~n vi to crow

Kralle |'kralə| f claw; (Vogelkralle) talon; k~n vt to clutch; (krampfhaft) to claw

Kram |kra:m| (-(e)s) m stuff, rubbish; k~en vi to rummage; ~laden (pej) m small shop

Krampf |krampf| (-(e)s, ⁼e) m cramp; (zuckend) spasm; ~ader f varicose vein; k~haft adj convulsive; (fig: Versuche) desperate

Kran |kra:n| (-(e)s, ⁼e) m crane; (Wasserkran) tap, faucet (US)

krank |krank| adj ill, sick; K~e(r) f(m) sick person, invalid; patient; ~en vi: an etw dat ~en (fig) to suffer from sth

kränken |'krenkən| vt to hurt

Kranken- zW: ~geld nt sick pay; ~gymnastik f physiotherapy; ~haus nt hospital; ~kasse f health insurance; ~pfleger m nursing orderly; ~schein m health insurance card; ~schwester f nurse; ~versicherung f health insurance; ~wagen m ambulance

Krank- zW: k~haft adj diseased; (Angst etc) morbid; ~heit f illness; disease; ~heitserreger m disease-causing agent

kränklich |'krenklıç| adj sickly

Kränkung f insult, offence

Kranz |krants| (-es, ⁼e) m wreath, garland

krass ▲ |kras| adj crass

Krater |'kra:tər| (-s, -) m crater

Kratz- |'krats| zW: ~bürste f (fig) crosspatch; k~en vt, vi to scratch; ~er (-s, -) m scratch; (Werkzeug) scraper

Kraul |kraol| (-s) nt crawl; ~ schwimmen to do the crawl; k~en vi (schwimmen) to do the crawl ♦ vt (streicheln) to fondle

kraus |kraos| adj crinkly; (Haar) frizzy; (Stirn) wrinkled

Kraut |kraot| (-(e)s, Kräuter) nt plant; (Gewürz) herb; (Gemüse) cabbage

Krawall |kra'val| (-s, -e) m row, uproar
Krawatte |kra'vatə| f tie
kreativ |krea'ti:f| adj creative
Krebs |kre:ps| (-es, -e) m crab; (MED, ASTROL) cancer; **k~krank** adj suffering from cancer
Kredit |kre'di:t| (-(e)s, -e) m credit;
  ~institut nt bank; **~karte** f credit card
Kreide |'kraɪdə| f chalk; **k~bleich** adj as white as a sheet
Kreis |kraɪs| (-es, -e) m circle; (Stadtkreis etc) district; **im ~ gehen** (auch fig) to go round in circles
kreischen |'kraɪʃən| vi to shriek, to screech
Kreis- zW: **~el** |'kraɪzəl| (-s, -) m top; (~verkehr) roundabout (BRIT), traffic circle (US); **k~en** |'kraɪzən| vi to spin; **~lauf** m (MED) circulation; (fig: der Natur etc) cycle; **~säge** f circular saw; **~stadt** f county town; **~verkehr** m roundabout traffic
Krematorium |krema'to:riʊm| nt crematorium
Kreml |'kre:ml| (-s) m Kremlin
krepieren |kre'pi:rən| (umg) vi (sterben) to die, to kick the bucket
Krepp |krep| (-s, -s od -e) m crepe;
  ~papier ▲ nt crepe paper
Kresse |'kresə| f cress
Kreta |'kre:ta| (-s) nt Crete
Kreuz |krɔʏts| (-es, -e) nt cross; (ANAT) small of the back; (KARTEN) clubs; **k~en** vt, vr to cross ♦ vi (NAUT) to cruise; **~er** (-s, -) m (Schiff) cruiser; **~fahrt** f cruise; **~feuer** nt (fig): **ins ~feuer geraten** to be under fire from all sides; **~gang** m cloisters pl; **k~igen** vt to crucify; **~igung** f crucifixion; **~ung** f (Verkehrskreuzung) crossing, junction; (Züchten) cross; **~verhör** nt cross-examination; **~weg** m crossroads sg; (REL) Way of the Cross; **~worträtsel** nt crossword puzzle; **~zug** m crusade
Kriech- |'kri:ç| zW: **k~en** (unreg) vi to crawl, to creep; (pej) to grovel, to crawl; **~er** (-s, -) m crawler; **~spur** f crawler lane; **~tier** nt reptile
Krieg |kri:k| (-(e)s, -e) m war
kriegen |'kri:gən| (umg) vt to get
Kriegs- zW: **~erklärung** f declaration of war; **~fuß** m: **mit jdm/etw auf ~fuß stehen** to be at loggerheads with sb/to have difficulties with sth; **~gefangene(r)** m prisoner of war; **~gefangenschaft** f captivity; **~gericht** nt court-martial; **~schiff** nt warship; **~verbrecher** m war criminal; **~versehrte(r)** m person disabled in the war; **~zustand** m state of war
Krim |krɪm| (-) f Crimea
Krimi |'kri:mi| (-s, -s) (umg) m thriller
Kriminal- |krimi'na:l| zW: **~beamte(r)** m detective; **~i'tät** f criminality; **~'polizei** f ≈

Criminal Investigation Department (BRIT), Federal Bureau of Investigation (US); **~ro'man** m detective story
kriminell |krimi'nɛl| adj criminal; **K~e(r)** m criminal
Krippe |'krɪpə| f crib; (Kinderkrippe) crèche
Krise |'kri:zə| f crisis; **k~ln** vi: **es k~lt** there's a crisis
Kristall |krɪs'tal| (-s, -e) m crystal ♦ nt (Glas) crystal
Kriterium |kri'te:riʊm| nt criterion
Kritik |kri'ti:k| f criticism; (Zeitungskritik) review, write-up; **~er** |'kri:tikər| (-s, -) m critic; **k~los** adj uncritical
kritisch |'kri:tɪʃ| adj critical
kritisieren |kriti'zi:rən| vt, vi to criticize
kritzeln |'krɪtsəln| vt, vi to scribble, to scrawl
Kroatien |kro'a:tsiən| nt Croatia
Krokodil |kroko'di:l| (-s, -e) nt crocodile
Krokus |'kro:kʊs| (-, - od -se) m crocus
Krone |'kro:nə| f crown; (Baumkrone) top
krönen |'krø:nən| vt to crown
Kron- zW: **~korken** m bottle top; **~leuchter** m chandelier; **~prinz** m crown prince
Krönung |'krø:nʊŋ| f coronation
Kropf |krɔpf| (-(e)s, ⁼e) m (MED) goitre; (von Vogel) crop
Kröte |'krø:tə| f toad
Krücke |'krykə| f crutch
Krug |kru:k| (-(e)s, ⁼e) m jug; (Bierkrug) mug
Krümel |'kry:məl| (-s, -) m crumb; **k~n** vt, vi to crumble
krumm |krʊm| adj (auch fig) crooked; (kurvig) curved; **jdm etw ~ nehmen** to take sth amiss; **k~beinig** adj bandy-legged; **~lachen** (umg) vr to laugh o.s. silly
Krümmung |'krymʊŋ| f bend, curve
Krüppel |'krypəl| (-s, -) m cripple
Kruste |'krʊstə| f crust
Kruzifix |krutsi'fɪks| (-es, -e) nt crucifix
Kübel |'ky:bəl| (-s, -) m tub; (Eimer) pail
Kubikmeter |ku'bi:kme:tər| m cubic metre
Küche |'kyçə| f kitchen; (Kochen) cooking, cuisine
Kuchen |'ku:xən| (-s, -) m cake; **~form** f baking tin; **~gabel** f pastry fork
Küchen- zW: **~herd** m cooker, stove; **~schabe** f cockroach; **~schrank** m kitchen cabinet
Kuckuck |'kʊkʊk| (-s, -e) m cuckoo; **~suhr** f cuckoo clock
Kugel |'ku:gəl| (-, -n) f ball; (MATH) sphere; (MIL) bullet; (Erdkugel) globe; (SPORT) shot; **k~förmig** adj spherical; **~lager** nt ball bearing; **k~rund** adj (Gegenstand) round; (umg: Person) tubby; **~schreiber** m ballpoint (pen), Biro ®; **k~sicher** adj bulletproof; **~stoßen** (-s) nt shot put
Kuh |ku:| (-, ⁼e) f cow

kühl |kyːl| adj (auch fig) cool; **K~anlage** f refrigeration plant; **K~e** (-) f coolness; **~en** vt to cool; **K~er** (-s, -) m (AUT) radiator; **K~erhaube** f (AUT) bonnet (BRIT), hood (US); **K~raum** m cold storage chamber; **K~schrank** m refrigerator; **K~truhe** f freezer; **K~ung** f cooling; **K~wasser** nt radiator water

kühn |kyːn| adj bold, daring; **K~heit** f boldness

Kuhstall m byre, cattle shed

Küken |ˈkyːkən| (-s, -) nt chicken

kulant |kuˈlant| adj obliging

Kuli |ˈkuːli| (-s, -s) m coolie; (umg: Kugelschreiber) Biro ®

Kulisse |kuˈlɪsə| f scenery

kullern |ˈkʊlərn| vi to roll

Kult |kʊlt| (-(e)s, -e) m worship, cult; **mit etw einen ~ treiben** to make a cult out of sth

kultivieren |kʊltiˈviːrən| vt to cultivate

kultiviert adj cultivated, refined

Kultur |kʊlˈtuːr| f culture; civilization; (des Bodens) cultivation; **~banause** (umg) m philistine, low-brow; **~beutel** m toilet bag; **k~ell** |-uˈrɛl| adj cultural; **~ministerium** nt ministry of education and the arts

Kümmel |ˈkʏməl| (-s, -) m caraway seed; (Branntwein) kümmel

Kummer |ˈkʊmər| (-s) m grief, sorrow

kümmerlich |ˈkʏmərlɪç| adj miserable, wretched

kümmern |ˈkʏmərn| vt to concern ♦ vr: **sich um jdn ~** to look after sb; **das kümmert mich nicht** that doesn't worry me; **sich um etw ~** to see to sth

Kumpel |ˈkʊmpəl| (-s, -) (umg) m mate

kündbar |ˈkʏntbaːr| adj redeemable, recallable; (Vertrag) terminable

Kunde¹ |ˈkʊndə| (-n, -n) m customer

Kunde² |ˈkʊndə| f (Botschaft) news

Kunden- zW: **~dienst** m after-sales service; **~konto** nt charge account; **~nummer** f customer number

Kund- zW: **k~geben** (unreg) vt to announce; **~gebung** f announcement; (Versammlung) rally

Künd- |ˈkʏnd| zW: **k~igen** vi to give in one's notice ♦ vt to cancel; **jdm k~igen** to give sb his notice; **die Stellung/Wohnung k~igen** to give notice that one is leaving one's job/house; **jdm die Stellung/Wohnung k~igen** to give sb notice to leave his/her job/house; **~igung** f notice; **~igungsfrist** f period of notice; **~igungsschutz** m protection against wrongful dismissal

Kundin f customer

Kundschaft f customers pl, clientele

künftig |ˈkʏnftɪç| adj future ♦ adv in future

Kunst |kʊnst| (-, ⁼e) f art; (Können) skill; **das ist doch keine ~** it's easy; **~dünger** m

artificial manure; **~faser** f synthetic fibre; **~fertigkeit** f skilfulness; **~gegenstand** m art object; **~gerecht** adj skilful; **~geschichte** f history of art; **~gewerbe** nt arts and crafts pl; **~griff** m trick, knack; **~händler** m art dealer

Künstler(in) |ˈkʏnstlər(ɪn)| (-s, -) m(f) artist; **k~isch** adj artistic; **~name** m pseudonym

künstlich |ˈkʏnstlɪç| adj artificial

Kunst- zW: **~sammler** (-s, -) m art collector; **~seide** f artificial silk; **~stoff** m synthetic material; **~stück** nt trick; **~turnen** nt gymnastics sg; **k~voll** adj artistic; **~werk** nt work of art

kunterbunt |ˈkʊntərbʊnt| adj higgledy-piggledy

Kupee |kuˈpeː| (-s, -s) nt = Coupé

Kupfer |ˈkʊpfər| (-s) nt copper; **k~n** adj copper

Kupon |kuˈpõː, kuˈpɔŋ| (-s, -s) m coupon; (Stoffkupon) length of cloth

Kuppe |ˈkʊpə| f (Bergkuppe) top; (Fingerkuppe) tip

Kuppel (-, -n) f dome; **k~n** vi (JUR) to procure; (AUT) to declutch ♦ vt to join

Kupplung f coupling; (AUT) clutch

Kur |kuːr| (-, -en) f cure, treatment

Kür |kyːr| (-, -en) f (SPORT) free exercises pl

Kurbel |ˈkʊrbəl| (-, -n) f crank, winder; (AUT) starting handle; **~welle** f crankshaft

Kürbis |ˈkʏrbɪs| (-ses, -se) m pumpkin; (exotisch) gourd

Kurgast m visitor (to a health resort)

kurieren |kuˈriːrən| vt to cure

kurios |kuriˈoːs| adj curious, odd; **K~i'tät** f curiosity

Kurort m health resort

Kurs |kʊrs| (-es, -e) m course; (FIN) rate; **~buch** nt timetable; **k~ieren** |kʊrˈziːrən| vi to circulate; **k~iv** |kʊrˈziːf| adv in italics; **~us** |ˈkʊrzʊs| (-, Kurse) m course; **~wagen** m (EISENB) through carriage

Kurtaxe |-taksə| (-, -n) f visitors' tax (at health resort or spa)

Kurve |ˈkʊrvə| f curve; (Straßenkurve) curve, bend; **kurvig** adj (Straße) bendy

kurz |kʊrts| adj short; **~ gesagt** in short; **~ halten** to keep short; **zu ~ kommen** to come off badly; **den Kürzeren ziehen** to get the worst of it; **K~arbeit** f short-time work; **~ärm(e)lig** adj short-sleeved

Kürze |ˈkʏrtsə| f shortness, brevity; **k~n** vt to cut short; (in der Länge) to shorten; (Gehalt) to reduce

kurz- zW: **~erhand** adv on the spot; **~fristig** adj short-term; **K~geschichte** f short story; **~halten** △ (unreg) vt siehe kurz; **~lebig** adj short-lived

kürzlich |ˈkʏrtslɪç| adv lately, recently

Kurz- zW: **~schluss** ▲ m (ELEK) short circuit; **k~sichtig** adj short-sighted

Kürzung f (eines Textes) abridgement; (eines Theaterstück, des Gehalts) cut
Kurzwelle f short wave
kuscheln ['kʊʃəln] vr to snuggle up
Kusine [ku'zi:nə] f cousin
Kuss ▲ [kʊs] (-es, ²e) m kiss
küssen ['kʏsən] vt, vr to kiss
Küste ['kʏstə] f coast, shore
Küstenwache f coastguard
Küster ['kʏstər] (-s, -) m sexton, verger
Kutsche ['kʊtʃə] f coach, carriage; ~r (-s, -) m coachman
Kutte ['kʊtə] f habit
Kuvert [ku'vert] (-s, -es od -s) nt envelope; cover
KZ nt abk von **Konzentrationslager**

L, l

l abk = **Liter**
labil [la'bi:l] adj (MED: Konstitution) delicate
Labor [la'bo:r] (-s, -e od -s) nt lab; ~ant(in) m(f) lab(oratory) assistant
Labyrinth [laby'rɪnt] (-s, -e) nt labyrinth
Lache ['laxə] f (Flüssigkeit) puddle; (von Blut, Benzin etc) pool
lächeln ['lɛçəln] vi to smile; **L~** (-s) nt smile
lachen ['laxən] vi to laugh
lächerlich ['lɛçərlɪç] adj ridiculous
Lachgas nt laughing gas
lachhaft adj laughable
Lachs [laks] (-es, -e) m salmon
Lack [lak] (-(e)s, -e) m lacquer, varnish; (von Auto) paint; **l~ieren** [la'ki:rən] vt to varnish; (Auto) to spray; ~ierer [la'ki:rər] (-s, -) m varnisher
Laden ['la:dən] (-s, ²) m shop; (Fensterladen) shutter
laden ['la:dən] (unreg) vt (Lasten) to load; (JUR) to summon; (einladen) to invite
Laden- zW: ~dieb m shoplifter; ~diebstahl m shoplifting; ~schluss ▲ m closing time; ~tisch m counter
Laderaum m freight space; (AVIAT, NAUT) hold
Ladung ['la:dʊŋ] f (Last) cargo, load; (Beladen) loading; (JUR) summons; (Einladung) invitation; (Sprengladung) charge
Lage ['la:gə] f position, situation; (Schicht) layer; **in der ~ sein** to be in a position
Lageplan m ground plan
Lager ['la:gər] (-s, -) nt camp; (COMM) warehouse; (Schlaflager) bed; (von Tier) lair; (TECH) bearing; ~bestand m stocks pl; ~feuer nt campfire; ~haus nt warehouse, store
lagern ['la:gərn] vi (Dinge) to be stored;

(Menschen) to camp ♦ vt to store; (betten) to lay down; (Maschine) to bed
Lagune [la'gu:nə] f lagoon
lahm [la:m] adj lame; ~ legen to paralyse; ~en vi to be lame
lähmen ['lɛ:mən] vt to paralyse
Lähmung f paralysis
Laib [laɪp] (-s, -e) m loaf
Laie ['laɪə] (-n, -n) m layman; **l~nhaft** adj amateurish
Laken ['la:kən] (-s, -) nt sheet
Lakritze [la'krɪtsə] f liquorice
lallen ['lalən] vt, vi to slur; (Baby) to babble
Lamelle [la'mɛlə] f lamella; (ELEK) lamina; (TECH) plate
Lametta [la'mɛta] (-s) nt tinsel
Lamm [lam] (-(e)s, ²er) nt lamb
Lampe ['lampə] f lamp
Lampen- zW: ~fieber nt stage fright; ~schirm m lampshade
Lampion [lampi'õ:] (-s, -s) m Chinese lantern
Land [lant] (-(e)s, ²er) nt land; (Nation, nicht Stadt) country; (Bundesland) state; **auf dem ~(e)** in the country; siehe **hierzulande**; ~besitz m landed property; ~ebahn f runway; **l~en** ['landən] vt, vi to land
Landes- ['landəs] zW: ~farben pl national colours; ~innere(s) nt inland region; ~sprache f national language; ~üblich adj customary; ~verrat m high treason; ~währung f national currency; **l~weit** adj nationwide
Land- zW: ~haus nt country house; ~karte f map; ~kreis m administrative region; **l~läufig** adj customary
ländlich ['lɛntlɪç] adj rural
Land- zW: ~schaft f countryside; (KUNST) landscape; ~schaftsschutzgebiet nt nature reserve; ~sitz m country seat; ~straße f country road; ~streicher (-s, -) m tramp; ~strich m region
Landung ['landʊŋ] f landing; ~sbrücke f jetty, pier
Land- zW: ~weg m: **etw auf dem ~weg befördern** to transport sth by land; ~wirt m farmer; ~wirtschaft f agriculture; ~zunge f spit
lang [laŋ] adj long; (Mensch) tall; ~atmig adj long-winded; ~e adv for a long time; (dauern, brauchen) a long time
Länge ['lɛŋə] f length; (GEOG) longitude
langen ['laŋən] vi (ausreichen) to do, to suffice; (fassen): ~ (nach) to reach (for) ♦ vt: **jdm etw ~** to hand od pass sb sth; **es langt mir** I've had enough
Längengrad m longitude
Längenmaß nt linear measure
lang- zW: **L~eweile** f boredom; ~fristig adj long-term; ~jährig adj (Freundschaft,

Gewohnheit) long-standing; **L~lauf** *m* (*SKI*) cross-country skiing

länglich *adj* longish

längs [lɛŋs] *präp* (+*gen od dat*) along ♦ *adv* lengthwise

lang- *zW*: **~sam** *adj* slow; **L~samkeit** *f* slowness; **L~schläfer(in)** *m(f)* late riser

längst [lɛŋst] *adv*: **das ist ~ fertig** that was finished a long time ago, that has been finished for a long time; **~e(r, s)** *adj* longest

lang- *zW*: **~weilen** *vt* to bore ♦ *vr* to be bored; **~weilig** *adj* boring, tedious; **L~welle** *f* long wave; **~wierig** *adj* lengthy, long-drawn-out

Lanze ['lantsə] *f* lance

Lappalie [la'paːliə] *f* trifle

Lappen ['lapən] (**-s, -**) *m* cloth, rag; (*ANAT*) lobe

läppisch ['lɛpɪʃ] *adj* foolish

Lapsus ['lapsʊs] (**-, -**) *m* slip

Laptop ['lɛptɔp] (**-s, -s**) *m* laptop (computer)

Lärche ['lɛrçə] *f* larch

Lärm [lɛrm] (**-(e)s**) *m* noise; **l~en** *vi* to be noisy, to make a noise

Larve ['larfə] *f* (*BIOL*) larva

lasch [laʃ] *adj* slack

Laser ['leːzər] (**-s, -**) *m* laser

SCHLÜSSELWORT

lassen ['lasən] (*pt* **ließ**, *pp* **gelassen** *od* (*als Hilfsverb*) **lassen**) *vt* 1 (*unterlassen*) to stop; (*momentan*) to leave; **lass das** (**sein**)! don't (do it)!; (*hör auf!*) stop it!; **lass mich!** leave me alone; **lassen wir das!** let's leave it; **er kann das Trinken nicht lassen** he can't stop drinking

2 (*zurücklassen*) to leave; **etw lassen, wie es ist** to leave sth (just) as it is

3 (*überlassen*): **jdn ins Haus lassen** to let sb into the house

♦ *vi*: **lass mal, ich mache das schon** leave it, I'll do it

♦ *Hilfsverb* 1 (*veranlassen*): **etw machen lassen** to have *od* get sth done; **sich** *dat* **etw schicken lassen** to have sth sent (to one)

2 (*zulassen*): **jdn etw wissen lassen** to let sb know sth; **das Licht brennen lassen** to leave the light on; **jdn warten lassen** to keep sb waiting; **das lässt sich machen** that can be done

3: **lass uns gehen** let's go

lässig ['lɛsɪç] *adj* casual; **L~keit** *f* casualness

Last [last] (**-, -en**) *f* load, burden; (*NAUT, AVIAT*) cargo; (*meist pl*: *Gebühr*) charge; **jdm zur ~ fallen** to be a burden to sb; **~auto** *nt* lorry, truck; **l~en** *vi*: **l~en auf** +*dat* to weigh on; **~enaufzug** *m* goods lift *od* elevator (*US*)

Laster ['lastər] (**-s, -**) *nt* vice

lästern ['lɛstərn] *vt, vi* (*Gott*) to blaspheme; (*schlecht sprechen*) to mock

Lästerung *f* jibe; (*Gotteslästerung*) blasphemy

lästig ['lɛstɪç] *adj* troublesome, tiresome

Last- *zW*: **~kahn** *m* barge; **~kraftwagen** *m* heavy goods vehicle; **~schrift** *f* debit; **~wagen** *m* lorry, truck; **~zug** *m* articulated lorry

Latein [la'taɪn] (**-s**) *nt* Latin; **~amerika** *nt* Latin America

latent [la'tɛnt] *adj* latent

Laterne [la'tɛrnə] *f* lantern; (*Straßenlaterne*) lamp, light; **~npfahl** *m* lamppost

latschen ['laːtʃən] (*umg*) *vi* (*gehen*) to wander, to go; (*lässig*) to slouch

Latte ['latə] *f* lath; (*SPORT*) goalpost; (*quer*) crossbar

Latzhose ['latshoːzə] *f* dungarees *pl*

lau [lau] *adj* (*Nacht*) balmy; (*Wasser*) lukewarm

Laub [laup] (**-(e)s**) *nt* foliage; **~baum** *m* deciduous tree; **~frosch** *m* tree frog; **~säge** *f* fretsaw

Lauch [laʊx] (**-(e)s, -e**) *m* leek

Lauer ['laʊər] *f*: **auf der ~ sein** *od* **liegen** to lie in wait; **l~n** *vi* to lie in wait; (*Gefahr*) to lurk

Lauf [lauf] (**-(e)s, Läufe**) *m* run; (*Wettlauf*) race; (*Entwicklung, ASTRON*) course; (*Gewehrlauf*) barrel; **einer Sache** *dat* **ihren ~ lassen** to let sth take its course; **~bahn** *f* career

laufen ['laufən] (*unreg*) *vt, vi* to run; (*umg*: *gehen*) to walk; **~d** *adj* running; (*Monat, Ausgaben*) current; **auf dem ~den sein/halten** to be/keep up to date; **am ~den Band** (*fig*) continuously

Läufer ['lɔyfər] (**-s, -**) *m* (*Teppich, SPORT*) runner; (*Fußball*) half-back; (*Schach*) bishop

Lauf- *zW*: **~masche** *f* run, ladder (*BRIT*); **~pass** ▲ *m*: **jdm den ~pass geben** (*umg*) to send sb packing (*inf*); **~stall** *m* playpen; **~steg** *m* catwalk; **~werk** *nt* (*COMPUT*) disk drive

Lauge ['laugə] *f* soapy water; (*CHEM*) alkaline solution

Laune ['launə] *f* mood, humour; (*Einfall*) caprice; (*schlechte*) temper; **l~nhaft** *adj* capricious, changeable

launisch *adj* moody; bad-tempered

Laus [laus] (**-, Läuse**) *f* louse

lauschen ['laʊʃən] *vi* to eavesdrop, to listen in

lauschig ['laʊʃɪç] *adj* snug

lausig ['laʊzɪç] (*umg*: *pej*) *adj* measly; (*Kälte*) perishing

laut [laut] *adj* loud ♦ *adv* loudly; (*lesen*) aloud ♦ *präp* (+*gen od dat*) according to; **L~** (**-(e)s, -e**) *m* sound

Laute ['lautə] f lute
lauten ['lautən] vi to say; (Urteil) to be
läuten ['lɔytən] vt, vi to ring, to sound
lauter ['lautər] adj (Wasser) clear, pure;
(Wahrheit, Charakter) honest ♦ adj inv
(Freude, Dummheit etc) sheer ♦ adv nothing
but, only
laut- zW: **~hals** adv at the top of one's voice;
~los adj noiseless, silent; **L~schrift** f
phonetics pl; **L~sprecher** m loudspeaker;
~stark adj vociferous; **L~stärke** f (RAD)
volume
lauwarm ['lauvarm] adj (auch fig) lukewarm
Lavendel [la'vɛndəl] (-s, -) m lavender
Lawine [la'vi:nə] f avalanche; **~ngefahr** f
danger of avalanches
lax [laks] adj lax
Lazarett [latsa'rɛt] (-(e)s, -e) nt (MIL)
hospital, infirmary
leasen ['li:zən] vt to lease
Leben (-s, -) nt life
leben ['le:bən] vt, vi to live; **~d** adj living;
~dig [le'bɛndɪç] adj living, alive; (lebhaft)
lively; **L~digkeit** f liveliness
Lebens- zW: **~art** f way of life; **~erwartung**
f life expectancy; **l~fähig** adj able to live;
~freude f zest for life; **~gefahr** f: **~gefahr!**
danger!; **in ~gefahr** dangerously ill;
l~gefährlich adj dangerous; (Verletzung)
critical; **~haltungskosten** pl cost of living
sg; **~jahr** nt year of life; **l~länglich** adj
(Strafe) for life; **~lauf** m curriculum vitae;
~mittel pl food sg; **~mittelgeschäft** nt
grocer's (shop); **~mittelvergiftung** f (MED)
food poisoning; **l~müde** adj tired of life;
~retter m lifesaver; **~standard** m standard
of living; **~unterhalt** m livelihood;
~versicherung f life insurance; **~wandel**
m way of life; **~weise** f lifestyle, way of life;
l~wichtig adj vital, essential; **~zeichen** nt
sign of life
Leber ['le:bər] (-, -n) f liver; **~fleck** m mole;
~tran m cod-liver oil; **~wurst** f liver
sausage
Lebewesen nt creature
leb- ['le:p] zW: **~haft** adj lively, vivacious;
L~kuchen m gingerbread; **~los** adj lifeless
Leck [lɛk] (-(e)s, -e) nt leak; **l~** adj leaky,
leaking; **l~en** vi (Loch haben) to leak;
(schlecken) to lick ♦ vt to lick
lecker ['lɛkər] adj delicious, tasty; **L~bissen**
m dainty morsel
Leder ['le:dər] (-s, -) nt leather; **~hose** f
lederhosen; **l~n** adj leather; **~waren** pl
leather goods
ledig ['le:dɪç] adj single; **einer Sache** gen **~**
sein to be free of sth; **~lich** adv merely,
solely
leer [le:r] adj empty; vacant; **~ machen** to

empty; **~ stehend** empty; **L~e** (-) f
emptiness; **~en** vt, vr to empty; **L~gewicht**
nt weight when empty; **L~gut** nt empties
pl; **L~lauf** m neutral; **L~ung** f emptying;
(Post) collection
legal [le'ga:l] adj legal, lawful; **~i'sieren** vt to
legalize
legen ['le:gən] vt to lay, to put, to place; (Ei)
to lay ♦ vr to lie down; (fig) to subside
Legende [le'gɛndə] f legend
leger [le'ʒɛːr] adj casual
Legierung [le'gi:rʊŋ] f alloy
Legislative [legɪsla'ti:və] f legislature
legitim [legi'ti:m] adj legitimate
legitimieren [legiti'mi:rən] vt to legitimate
♦ vr to prove one's identity
Lehm [le:m] (-(e)s, -e) m loam; **l~ig** adj loamy
Lehne ['le:nə] f arm; back; **l~n** vt, vr to lean
Lehnstuhl m armchair
Lehr- zW: **~amt** nt teaching profession;
~buch nt textbook
Lehre ['le:rə] f teaching, doctrine; (beruflich)
apprenticeship; (moralisch) lesson; (TECH)
gauge; **l~n** vt to teach
Lehrer(in) (-s, -) m(f) teacher; **~zimmer** nt
staff room
Lehr- zW: **~gang** m course; **~jahre** pl
apprenticeship sg; **~kraft** f (förmlich)
teacher; **~ling** m apprentice; **~plan** m
syllabus; **l~reich** adj instructive; **~stelle** f
apprenticeship; **~zeit** f apprenticeship
Leib [laɪp] (-(e)s, -er) m body; **halt ihn mir**
vom ~! keep him away from me!; **l~haftig**
adj personified; (Teufel) incarnate; **l~lich**
adj bodily; (Vater etc) own; **~schmerzen** pl
stomach pains; **~wache** f bodyguard
Leiche ['laɪçə] f corpse; **~nhalle** f mortuary;
~nwagen m hearse
Leichnam ['laɪçna:m] (-(e)s, -e) m corpse
leicht [laɪçt] adj light; (einfach) easy; **jdm ~**
fallen to be easy for sb; **es sich** dat **~**
machen to make things easy for o.s.;
L~athletik f athletics sg; **~fertig** adj
frivolous; **~gläubig** adj gullible, credulous;
~hin adv lightly; **L~igkeit** f easiness; **mit**
L~igkeit with ease; **L~sinn** m carelessness;
~sinnig adj careless
Leid [laɪt] (-(e)s) nt grief, sorrow; **es tut mir/**
ihm ~ I am/he is sorry; **er/das tut mir ~** I
am sorry for him/it; **l~** adj: **etw l~ haben**
od **sein** to be tired of sth; **l~en** ['laɪdən]
(unreg) vt to suffer; (erlauben) to permit ♦ vi
to suffer; **jdn/etw nicht l~en können** not
to be able to stand sb/sth; **~en** ['laɪdən] (-s,
-) nt suffering; (Krankheit) complaint;
~enschaft f passion; **l~enschaftlich** adj
passionate
leider ['laɪdər] adv unfortunately; **ja, ~** yes,
I'm afraid so; **~ nicht** I'm afraid not

Spelling reform: ▲ new spelling △ old spelling (to be phased out)

leidig ['laɪdɪç] adj worrying, troublesome
leidlich [laɪtlɪç] adj tolerable ♦ adv tolerably
Leid- zW: ~tragende(r) f(m) bereaved;
(Benachteiligter) one who suffers; ~wesen
nt: zu jds ~wesen to sb's disappointment
Leier ['laɪər] (-, -n) f lyre; (fig) old story;
~kasten m barrel organ
Leihbibliothek f lending library
Leihbücherei f lending library
leihen ['laɪən] (unreg) vt to lend; sich dat
etw ~ to borrow sth
Leih- zW: ~gebühr f hire charge; ~haus nt
pawnshop; ~wagen m hired car
Leim [laɪm] (-(e)s, -e) m glue; l~en vt to glue
Leine ['laɪnə] f line, cord; (Hundeleine) leash, lead
Leinen ['laɪnən] nt linen; l~ adj linen
Leinwand f (KUNST) canvas; (CINE) screen
leise ['laɪzə] adj quiet; (sanft) soft, gentle
Leiste ['laɪstə] f ledge; (Zierleiste) strip; (ANAT)
groin
leisten ['laɪstən] vt (Arbeit) to do;
(Gesellschaft) to keep; (Ersatz) to supply;
(vollbringen) to achieve; sich dat etw ~
können to be able to afford sth
Leistung f performance; (gute) achievement;
~sdruck m pressure; l~sfähig adj efficient
Leitartikel m leading article
Leitbild nt model
leiten ['laɪtən] vt to lead; (Firma) to manage;
(in eine Richtung) to direct; (ELEK) to conduct
Leiter¹ ['laɪtər] (-s, -) m leader, head; (ELEK)
conductor
Leiter² ['laɪtər] (-, -n) f ladder
Leitfaden m guide
Leitplanke f crash barrier
Leitung f (Führung) direction; (CINE, THEAT
etc) production; (von Firma) management;
directors pl; (Wasserleitung) pipe; (Kabel)
cable; eine lange ~ haben to be slow on
the uptake
Leitungs- zW: ~draht m wire; ~rohr nt
pipe; ~wasser nt tap water
Lektion [lɛktsi'oːn] f lesson
Lektüre [lɛk'tyːrə] f (Lesen) reading;
(Lesestoff) reading matter
Lende ['lɛndə] f loin; ~nstück nt fillet
lenk- ['lɛŋk] zW: ~bar adj (Fahrzeug)
steerable; (Kind) manageable; ~en vt to
steer; (Kind) to guide; (Blick, Aufmerksamkeit): ~en (auf +akk) to direct
(at); L~rad nt steering wheel;
L~radschloss ▲ nt steering (wheel)
lock; L~stange f handlebars pl;
L~ung f steering
Lepra ['leːpra] (-) f leprosy
Lerche ['lɛrçə] f lark
lernbegierig adj eager to learn
lernen ['lɛrnən] vt to learn
lesbar ['leːsbaːr] adj legible
Lesbierin ['lɛsbiərɪn] f lesbian
lesbisch ['lɛsbɪʃ] adj lesbian

Lese ['leːzə] f (Wein) harvest
Lesebrille f reading glasses
Lesebuch nt reading book, reader
lesen (unreg) vt, vi to read; (ernten) to gather,
to pick
Leser(in) (-s, -) m(f) reader; ~brief m
reader's letter; l~lich adj legible
Lesezeichen nt bookmark
Lesung ['leːzʊŋ] f (PARL) reading
letzte(r, s) ['lɛtstə(r, s)] adj last; (neueste)
latest; zum ~n Mal for the last time; ~ns
adv lately; ~re(r, s) adj latter
Leuchte ['lɔyçtə] f lamp, light; l~n vi to
shine, to gleam; ~r (-s, -) m candlestick
Leucht- zW: ~farbe f fluorescent colour;
~rakete f flare; ~reklame f neon sign;
~röhre f strip light; ~turm m lighthouse
leugnen ['lɔygnən] vt to deny
Leukämie [lɔykɛ'miː] f leukaemia
Leukoplast [lɔyko'plast] ® (-(e)s, -e) nt
Elastoplast ®
Leumund ['lɔymʊnt] (-(e)s, -e) m reputation
Leumundszeugnis nt character reference
Leute ['lɔytə] pl people pl
Leutnant ['lɔytnant] (-s, -s od -e) m
lieutenant
leutselig ['lɔytzɛːlɪç] adj amiable
Lexikon ['lɛksikɔn] (-s, Lexiken od Lexika)
nt encyclop(a)edia
Libelle [li'bɛlə] f dragonfly; (TECH) spirit level
liberal [libe'raːl] adj liberal; L~e(r) f(m)
liberal
Licht [lɪçt] (-(e)s, -er) nt light; ~bild nt
photograph; (Dia) slide; ~blick m cheering
prospect; l~empfindlich adj sensitive to
light; l~en vt to clear; (Anker) to weigh ♦ vr
to clear up; (Haar) to thin; l~erloh adv:
l~erloh brennen to be ablaze; ~hupe f
flashing of headlights; ~jahr nt light year;
~maschine f dynamo; ~schalter m light
switch; ~schutzfaktor m protection factor
Lichtung f clearing, glade
Lid [liːt] (-(e)s, -er) nt eyelid; ~schatten m
eyeshadow
lieb [liːp] adj dear; das ist ~ von dir that's
kind of you; ~ gewinnen to get fond of; ~
haben to be fond of; ~äugeln ['liːbɔygəln]
vi insep: mit etw ~äugeln to have one's eye
on sth; mit dem Gedanken ~äugeln, etw
zu tun to toy with the idea of doing sth
Liebe ['liːbə] f love; l~bedürftig adj:
l~bedürftig sein to need love; l~n vt to
love; to like
liebens- zW: ~wert adj lovable; ~würdig
adj kind; ~würdigerweise adv kindly;
L~würdigkeit f kindness
lieber ['liːbər] adv rather, preferably; ich
gehe ~ nicht I'd rather not go; siehe auch
gern, lieb
Liebes- zW: ~brief m love letter; ~kummer
m: ~kummer haben to be lovesick; ~paar

nt courting couple, lovers *pl*
liebevoll *adj* loving
lieb- |li:p| *zW:* **~gewinnen** △ *(unreg)* *vt*
siehe **lieb**; **~haben** △ *(unreg)* *vt* siehe **lieb**;
L~haber (-s, -) *m* lover; **L~habe'rei** *f*
hobby; **~kosen** |'li:pkoːzən| *vt insep* to
caress; **~lich** *adj* lovely, charming; **L~ling** *m*
darling; **L~lings** *in zW* favourite; **~los** *adj*
unloving; **L~schaft** *f* love affair
Lied [liːt] **(-(e)s, -er)** *nt* song; *(REL)* hymn;
~erbuch |'liːdər-| *nt* songbook; hymn book
liederlich |'liːdərlɪç| *adj* slovenly;
(Lebenswandel) loose, immoral; **L~keit** *f*
slovenliness; immorality
lief *etc* |liːf| *vb* siehe **laufen**
Lieferant |liːfə'rant| *m* supplier
Lieferbedingungen *pl* terms of delivery
liefern ['liːfərn] *vt* to deliver; *(versorgen mit)*
to supply; *(Beweis)* to produce
Liefer- *zW:* **~schein** *m* delivery note;
~termin *m* delivery date; **~ung** *f* delivery;
supply; **~wagen** *m* van; **~zeit** *f* delivery
period
Liege ['liːgə] *f* bed
liegen ['liːgən] *(unreg)* *vi* to lie; *(sich
befinden)* to be; **mir liegt nichts/viel daran**
it doesn't matter to me/it matters a lot to
me; **es liegt bei Ihnen, ob ...** it's up to you
whether ...; **Sprachen ~ mir nicht**
languages are not my line; **woran liegt es?**
what's the cause?; **~ bleiben** *(im Bett)* to
stay in bed; *(nicht aufstehen)* to stay lying
down; *(vergessen werden)* to be left
(behind); **~ lassen** *(vergessen)* to leave
behind
Liege- *zW:* **~sitz** *m* *(AUT)* reclining seat;
~stuhl *m* deck chair; **~wagen** *m* *(EISENB)*
couchette
Lift |lɪft| **(-(e)s, -e** *od* **-s)** *m* lift
Likör |li'køːr| **(-s, -e)** *m* liqueur
lila ['liːla] *adj inv* purple, lilac; **L~ (-s, -s)** *nt*
(Farbe) purple, lilac
Lilie ['liːliə] *f* lily
Limonade |limo'naːdə| *f* lemonade
Limone |li'moːnə| *f* lime
Linde ['lɪndə] *f* lime tree, linden
lindern ['lɪndərn] *vt* to alleviate, to soothe;
Linderung *f* alleviation
Lineal |line'aːl| **(-s, -e)** *nt* ruler
Linie ['liːniə] *f* line
Linien- *zW:* **~blatt** *nt* ruled sheet; **~flug** *m*
scheduled flight; **~richter** *m* linesman
linieren |li'niːrən| *vt* to line
Linke ['lɪŋkə] *f* left side; left hand; *(POL)* left
linkisch *adj* awkward, gauche
links [lɪŋks] *adv* left; to on the left; **~ von
mir** to *od* to my left; **L~händer(in) (-s, -)**
m(f) left-handed person; **L~kurve** *f* left-
hand bend; **L~verkehr** *m* driving on the left

Linoleum |li'noːleʊm| **(-s)** *nt* lino(leum)
Linse ['lɪnzə] *f* lentil; *(optisch)* lens *sg*
Lippe ['lɪpə] *f* lip; **~nstift** *m* lipstick
lispeln ['lɪspəln] *vi* to lisp
Lissabon ['lɪsabɔn] **(-s)** *nt* Lisbon
List [lɪst] **(-, -en)** *f* cunning; trick, ruse
Liste ['lɪstə] *f* list
listig ['lɪstɪç] *adj* cunning, sly
Liter ['liːtər] **(-s, -)** *nt od m* litre
literarisch |lite'raːrɪʃ| *adj* literary
Literatur |lɪtera'tuːr| *f* literature
Litfaßsäule ['lɪtfasˌzɔʏlə] *f* advertising pillar
Liturgie |litur'giː| *f* liturgy
liturgisch |li'turgɪʃ| *adj* liturgical
Litze ['lɪtsə] *f* braid; *(ELEK)* flex
Lizenz [li'tsɛnts] *f* licence
Lkw [ɛlkaːveː] **(-(s), -(s))** *m abk* = **Last-
kraftwagen**
Lob |loːp| **(-(e)s)** *nt* praise
Lobby ['lɔbi] *f* lobby
loben ['loːbən] *vt* to praise; **~swert** *adj*
praiseworthy
löblich ['løːplɪç] *adj* praiseworthy, laudable
Loch |lɔx| **(-(e)s, ̈er)** *nt* hole; **l~en** *vt* to
punch holes in; **~er (-s, -)** *m* punch
löcherig ['lœçərɪç] *adj* full of holes
Lochkarte *f* punch card
Lochstreifen *m* punch tape
Locke ['lɔkə] *f* lock, curl; **l~n** *vt* to entice;
(Haare) to curl; **~nwickler (-s, -)** *m* curler
locker ['lɔkər] *adj* loose; **~lassen** *(unreg)* *vi*:
nicht ~lassen not to let up; **~n** *vt* to loosen
lockig ['lɔkɪç] *adj* curly
lodern ['loːdərn] *vi* to blaze
Löffel ['lœfəl] **(-s, -)** *m* spoon
löffeln *vt* to spoon
Loge ['loːʒə] *f* *(THEAT)* box; *(Freimaurer)*
(masonic) lodge; *(Pförtnerloge)* office
Logik ['loːgɪk] *f* logic
logisch ['loːgɪʃ] *adj* logical
Logopäde |logo'pɛːdə| **(-n, -n)** *m* speech
therapist
Lohn |loːn| **(-(e)s, ̈e)** *m* reward; *(Arbeitslohn)*
pay, wages *pl*; **~büro** *nt* wages office;
~empfänger *m* wage earner
lohnen ['loːnən] *vr unpers* to be worth it ♦ *vt*:
(jdm etw) ~ to reward (sb for sth); **~d** *adj*
worthwhile
Lohn- *zW:* **~erhöhung** *f* pay rise; **~steuer** *f*
income tax; **~steuerkarte** *f* (income) tax
card; **~streifen** *m* pay slip; **~tüte** *f* pay
packet
Lokal |loˈkaːl| **(-(e)s, -e)** *nt* pub(lic house)
lokal *adj* local; **~i'sieren** *vt* to localize
Lokomotive |lokomo'tiːvə| *f* locomotive
Lokomotivführer *m* engine driver
Lorbeer ['lɔrbeːr] **(-s, -en)** *m* *(auch fig)*
laurel; **~blatt** *nt* *(KOCH)* bay leaf
Los |loːs| **(-es, -e)** *nt* *(Schicksal)* lot, fate;

Spelling reform: ▲ *new spelling* △ *old spelling (to be phased out)*

(*Lotterielos*) lottery ticket

los |loːs| *adj* (*locker*) loose; **~!** go on!; **etw ~ sein** to be rid of sth; **was ist ~?** what's the matter?; **dort ist nichts/viel ~** there's nothing/a lot going on there; **~binden** (*unreg*) *vt* to untie

Löschblatt |'lœʃblat| *nt* sheet of blotting paper

löschen |'lœʃən| *vt* (*Feuer, Licht*) to put out, to extinguish; (*Durst*) to quench; (*COMM*) to cancel; (*COMPUT*) to delete; (*Tonband*) to erase; (*Fracht*) to unload ♦ *vi* (*Feuerwehr*) to put out a fire; (*Tinte*) to blot

Lösch- *zW*: **~fahrzeug** *nt* fire engine; fire boat; **~gerät** *nt* fire extinguisher; **~papier** *nt* blotting paper

lose |'loːzə| *adj* loose

Lösegeld *nt* ransom

losen |'loːzən| *vi* to draw lots

lösen |'løːzən| *vt* to loosen; (*Rätsel etc*) to solve; (*Verlobung*) to call off; (*CHEM*) to dissolve; (*Partnerschaft*) to break up; (*Fahrkarte*) to buy ♦ *vr* (*aufgehen*) to come loose; (*Zucker etc*) to dissolve; (*Problem, Schwierigkeit*) to (re)solve itself

los- *zW*: **~fahren** (*unreg*) *vi* to leave; **~gehen** (*unreg*) *vi* to set out; (*anfangen*) to start; (*Bombe*) to go off; **auf jdn ~gehen** to go for sb; **~haben** *vt* (*umg*): **etw ~** (*umg*) to be clever; **~kaufen** *vt* (*Gefangene, Geißeln*) to pay ransom for; **~kommen** (*unreg*) *vi*: **von etw ~kommen** to get away from sth; **~lassen** (*unreg*) *vt* (*Seil*) to let go of ; (*Schimpfe*) to let loose; **~laufen** (*unreg*) *vi* to run off

löslich |'løːslɪç| *adj* soluble; **L~keit** *f* solubility

los- *zW*: **~lösen** *vt*: **(sich) ~lösen** to free (o.s.); **~machen** *vt* to loosen; (*Boot*) to unmoor ♦ *vr* to get away; **~schrauben** *vt* to unscrew

Losung |'loːzʊŋ| *f* watchword, slogan

Lösung |'løːzʊŋ| *f* (*Lockermachen*) loosening; (*eines Rätsels, CHEM*) solution; **~smittel** *nt* solvent

los- *zW*: **~werden** (*unreg*) *vt* to get rid of ; **~ziehen** (*unreg*) (*umg*) *vi* (*sich aufmachen*) to set off

Lot |loːt| (-(**e**)**s, -e**) *nt* plumbline; **im ~** vertical; (*fig*) on an even keel

löten |'løːtən| *vt* to solder

Lothringen |'loːtrɪŋən| (**-s**) *nt* Lorraine

Lotse |'loːtsə| (**-n, -n**) *m* pilot; (*AVIAT*) air traffic controller; **l~n** *vt* to pilot; (*umg*) to lure

Lotterie |lɔtə'riː| *f* lottery

Lotto |'lɔto| (**-s, -s**) *nt* national lottery; **~zahlen** *pl* winning lottery numbers

Löwe |'løːvə| (**-n, -n**) *m* lion; (*ASTROL*) Leo; **~nanteil** *m* lion's share; **~nzahn** *m* dandelion

loyal |loa'jaːl| *adj* loyal; **L~ität** *f* loyalty

Luchs |lʊks| (**-es, -e**) *m* lynx

Lücke |'lʏkə| *f* gap

Lücken- *zW*: **~büßer** (**-s, -**) *m* stopgap; **l~haft** *adj* full of gaps; (*Versorgung, Vorräte etc*) inadequate; **l~los** *adj* complete

Luft |lʊft| (**-, ~e**) *f* (*Atem*) breath; **in der ~ liegen** to be in the air; **jdn wie ~ behandeln** to ignore sb; **~angriff** *m* air raid; **~ballon** *m* balloon; **~blase** *f* air bubble; **l~dicht** *adj* airtight; **~druck** *m* atmospheric pressure

lüften |'lʏftən| *vt* to air; (*Hut*) to lift, to raise ♦ *vi* to let some air in

Luft- *zW*: **~fahrt** *f* aviation; **~fracht** *f* air freight; **l~gekühlt** *adj* air-cooled; **~gewehr** *nt* air rifle, airgun; **l~ig** *adj* (*Ort*) breezy; (*Raum*) airy; (*Kleider*) summery; **~kissenfahrzeug** *nt* hovercraft; **~kurort** *m* health resort; **l~leer** *adj*: **l~leerer Raum** vacuum; **~linie** *f*: **in der ~linie** as the crow flies; **~loch** *nt* air hole; (*AVIAT*) air pocket; **~matratze** *f* Lilo ® (*BRIT*) air mattress; **~pirat** *m* hijacker; **~post** *f* airmail; **~pumpe** *f* air pump; **~röhre** *f* (*ANAT*) windpipe; **~schlange** *f* streamer; **~schutzkeller** *m* air-raid shelter; **~verkehr** *m* air traffic; **~verschmutzung** *f* air pollution; **~waffe** *f* air force; **~zug** *m* draught

Lüge |'lyːgə| *f* lie; **jdm/etw ~n strafen** to give the lie to sb/sth; **l~n** (*unreg*) *vi* to lie

Lügner(in) (**-s, -**) *m(f)* liar

Luke |'luːkə| *f* dormer window; hatch

Lump |lʊmp| (**-en, -en**) *m* scamp, rascal

lumpen |'lʊmpən| *vi*: **sich nicht ~ lassen** not to be mean

Lumpen |'lʊmpən| (**-s, -**) *m* rag

lumpig |'lʊmpɪç| *adj* shabby

Lupe |'luːpə| *f* magnifying glass; **unter die ~ nehmen** (*fig*) to scrutinize

Lust |lʊst| (**-, ~e**) *f* joy, delight; (*Neigung*) desire; **~ haben zu** *od* **auf etw** *akk*/**etw zu tun** to feel like sth/doing sth

lüstern |'lʏstərn| *adj* lustful, lecherous

lustig |'lʊstɪç| *adj* (*komisch*) amusing, funny; (*fröhlich*) cheerful

Lust- *zW*: **l~los** *adj* unenthusiastic; **~mord** *m* sex(ual) murder; **~spiel** *nt* comedy

lutschen |'lʊtʃən| *vt, vi* to suck; **am Daumen ~** to suck one's thumb

Lutscher (**-s, -**) *m* lollipop

luxuriös |lʊksuri'øːs| *adj* luxurious

Luxus |'lʊksʊs| (**-**) *m* luxury; **~artikel** *pl* luxury goods; **~hotel** *nt* luxury hotel

Luzern |lu'tsɛrn| (**-s**) *nt* Lucerne

Lymphe |'lʏmfə| *f* lymph

lynchen |'lʏnçən| *vt* to lynch

Lyrik |'lyːrɪk| *f* lyric poetry; **~er** (**-s, -**) *m* lyric poet

lyrisch |'lyːrɪʃ| *adj* lyrical

M, m

m *abk* = **Meter**
Machart *f* make
machbar *adj* feasible

SCHLÜSSELWORT

machen ['maxən] *vt* **1** to do; (*herstellen, zubereiten*) to make; **was machst du da?** what are you doing (there)?; **das ist nicht zu machen** that can't be done; **das Radio leiser machen** to turn the radio down; **aus Holz gemacht** made of wood
2 (*verursachen, bewirken*) to make; **jdm Angst machen** to make sb afraid; **das macht die Kälte** it's the cold that does that
3 (*ausmachen*) to matter; **das macht nichts** that doesn't matter; **die Kälte macht mir nichts** I don't mind the cold
4 (*kosten, ergeben*) to be; **3 und 5 macht 8** 3 and 5 is *od* are 8; **was** *od* **wie viel macht das?** how much does that make?
5: was macht die Arbeit? how's the work going?; **was macht dein Bruder?** how is your brother doing?; **das Auto machen lassen** to have the car done; **machs gut!** take care!; (*viel Glück*) good luck!
♦ *vi:* **mach schnell!** hurry up!; **Schluss machen** to finish (off); **mach schon!** come on!; **das macht müde** it makes you tired; **in etw** *dat* **machen** to be *od* deal in sth
♦ *vr* to come along (nicely); **sich an etw** *akk* **machen** to set about sth; **sich verständlich machen** to make o.s. understood; **sich** *dat* **viel aus jdm/etw machen** to like sb/sth

Macht [maxt] (-, ⸚e) *f* power; **~haber** (-s, -) *m* ruler
mächtig ['mɛçtɪç] *adj* powerful, mighty; (*umg: ungeheuer*) enormous
Macht- *zW:* **m~los** *adj* powerless; **~probe** *f* trial of strength; **~wort** *nt:* **ein ~wort sprechen** to exercise one's authority
Mädchen ['mɛːtçən] *nt* girl; **m~haft** *adj* girlish; **~name** *m* maiden name
Made ['maːdə] *f* maggot
madig ['maːdɪç] *adj* maggoty; **jdm etw ~ machen** to spoil sth for sb
mag *etc* [maːk] *vb siehe* **mögen**
Magazin [maga'tsiːn] (-s, -e) *nt* magazine
Magen ['maːgən] (-s, - *od* ⸚) *m* stomach; **~geschwür** *nt* (*MED*) stomach ulcer; **~schmerzen** *pl* stomachache *sg*
mager ['maːgər] *adj* lean; (*dünn*) thin; **M~keit** *f* leanness; thinness
Magie [ma'giː] *f* magic
magisch ['maːgɪʃ] *adj* magical

Magnet [ma'gneːt] (-s *od* -en, -en) *m* magnet; **m~isch** *adj* magnetic; **~nadel** *f* magnetic needle
mähen ['mɛːən] *vt, vi* to mow
Mahl [maːl] (-(e)s, -e) *nt* meal; **m~en** (*unreg*) *vt* to grind; **~zeit** *f* meal ♦ *excl* enjoy your meal
Mahnbrief *m* reminder
Mähne ['mɛːnə] *f* mane
mahn- ['maːn] *zW:* **~en** *vt* to remind; (*warnend*) to warn; (*wegen Schuld*) to demand payment from; **M~mal** *nt* memorial; **M~ung** *f* reminder; admonition, warning
Mai [maɪ] (-(e)s, -e) *m* May; **~glöckchen** *nt* lily of the valley
Mailand ['maɪlant] *nt* Milan
mailändisch *adj* Milanese
Mais [maɪs] (-es, -e) *m* maize, corn (*US*); **~kolben** *m* corncob; **~mehl** *nt* (*KOCH*) corn meal
Majestät [majɛs'tɛːt] *f* majesty; **m~isch** *adj* majestic
Majonäse [majɔ'nɛːzə] *f* mayonnaise
Major [ma'joːr] (-s, -e) *m* (*MIL*) major; (*AVIAT*) squadron leader
Majoran [majo'raːn] (-s, -e) *m* marjoram
makaber [ma'kaːbər] *adj* macabre
Makel ['maːkəl] (-s, -) *m* blemish; (*moralisch*) stain; **m~los** *adj* immaculate, spotless
mäkeln ['mɛːkəln] *vi* to find fault
Makler(in) ['maːklər(ɪn)] (-s, -) *m(f)* broker
Makrele [ma'kreːlə] *f* mackerel
Mal [maːl] (-(e)s, -e) *nt* mark, sign; (*Zeitpunkt*) time; **ein für alle ~** once and for all; **m~** *adv* times; (*umg*) *siehe* **einmal**
♦ *suffix:* **-mal** -times
malen *vt, vi* to paint
Maler (-s, -) *m* painter; **Male'rei** *f* painting; **m~isch** *adj* picturesque
Malkasten *m* paintbox
Mallorca [ma'jɔrka, ma'lɔrka] (-s) *nt* Majorca
malnehmen (*unreg*) *vt, vi* to multiply
Malz [malts] (-es) *nt* malt; **~bier** *nt* (*KOCH*) malt beer; **~bonbon** *nt* cough drop; **~kaffee** *m* malt coffee
Mama ['mama:] (-, -s) (*umg*) *f* mum(my) (*BRIT*), mom(my) (*US*)
Mami ['mami] (-, -s) = **Mama**
Mammut ['mamʊt] (-s, -e *od* -s) *nt* mammoth
man [man] *pron* one, you; **~ sagt, ...** they *od* people say ...; **wie schreibt ~ das?** how do you write it?, how is it written?
Manager(in) ['mɛnɪdʒər(ɪn)] (-s, -) *m(f)* manager
manch [manç] (*unver*) *pron* many a
manche(r, s) ['mançə(r, s)] *adj* many a; (*pl: einige*) a number of ♦ *pron* some

---

Spelling reform: ▲ *new spelling* △ *old spelling (to be phased out)*

mancherlei |manςər'laɪ| adj inv various
♦ pron inv a variety of things

manchmal adv sometimes

Mandant(in) |man'dant(ɪn)| m(f) (JUR)
client

Mandarine |manda'ri:nə| f mandarin,
tangerine

Mandat |man'da:t| (-(e)s, -e) nt mandate

Mandel |'mandəl| (-, -n) f almond; (ANAT)
tonsil; ~entzündung f (MED) tonsillitis

Manege |ma'ne:ʒə| f ring, arena

Mangel |'maŋəl| (-s, ⁀) m lack; (Knappheit)
shortage; (Fehler) defect, fault; ~ an +dat
shortage of; ~erscheinung f deficiency
symptom; m~haft adj poor; (fehlerhaft)
defective, faulty; m~n vi unpers: es m~t
jdm an etw dat sb lacks sth ♦ vt (Wäsche) to
mangle

mangels präp +gen for lack of

Manie |ma'ni:| f mania

Manier |ma'ni:r| (-) f manner; style; (pej)
mannerism; ~en pl (Umgangsformen)
manners; m~lich adj well-mannered

Manifest |mani'fɛst| (-es, -e) nt manifesto

Maniküre |mani'ky:rə| f manicure

manipulieren |manipu'li:rən| vt to
manipulate

Manko |'maŋko| (-s, -s) nt deficiency;
(COMM) deficit

Mann |man| (-(e)s, ⁀er) m man; (Ehemann)
husband; (NAUT) hand; seinen ~ stehen to
hold one's own

Männchen |'mɛnςən| nt little man; (Tier)
male

Mannequin |manə'kɛ̃:| (-s, -s) nt fashion
model

männlich |'mɛnlɪς| adj (BIOL) male; (fig,
GRAM) masculine

Mannschaft f (SPORT, fig) team; (AVIAT,
NAUT) crew; (MIL) other ranks pl

Manöver |ma'nø:vər| (-s, -) nt manoeuvre

manövrieren |manø'vri:rən| vt, vi to
manoeuvre

Mansarde |man'zardə| f attic

Manschette |man'ʃɛtə| f cuff; (TECH) collar;
sleeve; ~nknopf m cufflink

Mantel |'mantəl| (-s, ⁀) m coat; (TECH)
casing, jacket

Manuskript |manu'skrɪpt| (-(e)s, -e) nt
manuscript

Mappe |'mapə| f briefcase; (Aktenmappe)
folder

Märchen |'mɛːrςən| nt fairy tale; m~haft adj
fabulous; ~prinz m Prince Charming

Margarine |marga'ri:nə| f margarine

Margerite |margə'ri:tə| f (BOT) marguerite

Marienkäfer |ma'ri:ənkɛːfər| m ladybird

Marine |ma'ri:nə| f navy; m~blau adj navy
blue

marinieren |mari'ni:rən| vt to marinate

Marionette |mario'nɛtə| f puppet

Mark¹ |mark| (-, -) f (Münze) mark

Mark² |mark| (-(e)s) nt (Knochenmark)
marrow; jdm durch ~ und Bein gehen to
go right through sb

markant |mar'kant| adj striking

Marke |'markə| f mark; (Warensorte) brand;
(Fabrikat) make; (Rabattmarke, Briefmarke)
stamp; (Essenmarke) ticket; (aus Metall etc)
token, disc

Markenartikel m proprietary article

markieren |mar'ki:rən| vt to mark; (umg) to
act ♦ vi (umg) to act it

Markierung f marking

Markise |mar'ki:zə| f awning

Markstück nt one-mark piece

Markt |markt| (-(e)s, ⁀e) m market;
~forschung f market research; ~lücke f
(COMM) opening, gap in the market; ~platz
m market place; m~üblich adj (Preise,
Mieten) standard, usual; ~wert m (COMM)
market value; ~wirtschaft f market
economy

Marmelade |marmə'la:də| f jam

Marmor |'marmor| (-s, -e) m marble;
m~ieren |-'ri:rən| vt to marble

Marokko |ma'rɔko| (-s) nt Morocco

Marone |ma'ro:nə| (-, -n od Maroni) f
chestnut

Marotte |ma'rɔtə| f fad, quirk

Marsch¹ |marʃ| (-, -en) f marsh

Marsch² |marʃ| (-(e)s, ⁀e) m march ♦ excl
march!; ~befehl m marching orders pl;
m~bereit adj ready to move; m~ieren
|mar'ʃi:rən| vi to march

Märtyrer(in) |'mɛrtyrər(ɪn)| (-s, -) m(f)
martyr

März |mɛrts| (-(es), -e) m March

Marzipan |martsi'pa:n| (-s, -e) nt marzipan

Masche |'maʃə| f mesh; (Strickmasche) stitch;
das ist die neueste ~ that's the latest thing;
~ndraht m wire mesh; m~nfest adj run-
resistant

Maschine |ma'ʃi:nə| f machine; (Motor)
engine; (Schreibmaschine) typewriter; ~
schreiben to type; m~ll |maʃi'nɛl| adj
machine(-); mechanical

Maschinen- zW: ~bauer m mechanical
engineer; ~gewehr nt machine gun;
~pistole f submachine gun; ~schaden m
mechanical fault; ~schlosser m fitter;
~schrift f typescript

Maschinist |maʃi'nɪst| m engineer

Maser |'ma:zər| (-, -n) f (von Holz) grain; ~n
pl (MED) measles sg

Maske |'maskə| f mask; ~nball m fancy-dress
ball

maskieren |mas'ki:rən| vt to mask;
(verkleiden) to dress up ♦ vr to disguise o.s.;
to dress up

Maskottchen |mas'kɔtςən| nt (lucky)
mascot

Maß¹ [maːs] (**-es, -e**) *nt* measure; (*Mäßigung*) moderation; (*Grad*) degree, extent; **~ halten** to exercise moderation

Maß² [maːs] (**-, -(e)**) *f* litre of beer

Massage [ma'saːʒə] *f* massage

Maßanzug *m* made-to-measure suit

Maßarbeit *f* (*fig*) neat piece of work

Masse ['masə] *f* mass

Maßeinheit *f* unit of measurement

Massen- *zW:* **~artikel** *m* mass-produced article; **~grab** *nt* mass grave; **m~haft** *adj* loads of; **~medien** *pl* mass media *pl*; **~veranstaltung** *f* mass meeting; **m~weise** *adv* on a large scale

Masseur [ma'søːr] *m* masseur; **~in** *f* masseuse

maßgebend *adj* authoritative

maßhalten △ (*unreg*) *vi siehe* **Maß¹**

massieren [ma'siːrən] *vt* to massage; (*MIL*) to mass

massig ['masɪç] *adj* massive; (*umg*) massive amount of

mäßig ['mɛːsɪç] *adj* moderate; **~en** ['mɛːsɪgən] *vt* to restrain, to moderate; **M~keit** *f* moderation

Massiv (**-s, -e**) *nt* massif

massiv [ma'siːf] *adj* solid; (*fig*) heavy, rough

Maß- *zW:* **~krug** *m* tankard; **m~los** *adj* extreme; **~nahme** *f* measure, step; **~stab** *m* rule, measure; (*fig*) standard; (*GEOG*) scale; **m~voll** *adj* moderate

Mast [mast] (**-(e)s, -e(n)**) *m* mast; (*ELEK*) pylon

mästen ['mɛstən] *vt* to fatten

Material [materi'aːl] (**-s, -ien**) *nt* material(s); **~fehler** *m* material defect; **~ismus** [-'lɪsmʊs] *m* materialism; **m~istisch** [-'lɪstɪʃ] *adj* materialistic

Materie [ma'teːriə] *f* matter, substance

materiell [materi'ɛl] *adj* material

Mathematik [matema'tiːk] *f* mathematics *sg;* **~er(in)** [mate'maːtikər(ɪn)] (**-s, -**) *m(f)* mathematician

mathematisch [mate'maːtɪʃ] *adj* mathematical

Matjeshering ['matjəsheːrɪŋ] *m* (*KOCH*) young herring

Matratze [ma'tratsə] *f* mattress

Matrixdrucker ['maːtrɪks-] *m* dot-matrix printer

Matrose [ma'troːzə] (**-n, -n**) *m* sailor

Matsch [matʃ] (**-(e)s**) *m* mud; (*Schneematsch*) slush; **m~ig** *adj* muddy; slushy

matt [mat] *adj* weak; (*glanzlos*) dull; (*PHOT*) matt; (*SCHACH*) mate

Matte ['matə] *f* mat

Mattscheibe *f* (*TV*) screen

Mauer ['mauər] (**-, -n**) *f* wall; **m~n** *vi* to build; to lay bricks ♦ *vt* to build

Maul [maʊl] (**-(e)s, Mäuler**) *nt* mouth; **m~en** (*umg*) *vi* to grumble; **~esel** *m* mule; **~korb** *m* muzzle; **~sperre** *f* lockjaw; **~tasche** *f* (*KOCH*) pasta envelopes stuffed and used in soup; **~tier** *nt* mule; **~wurf** *m* mole

Maurer ['maʊrər] (**-s, -**) *m* bricklayer

Maus [maʊs] (**-, Mäuse**) *f* (*auch* COMPUT) mouse

Mause- ['maʊzə] *zW:* **~falle** *f* mousetrap; **m~n** *vi* to catch mice ♦ *vt* (*umg*) to pinch; **m~tot** *adj* stone dead

Maut- [-'maʊt] *zW:* **~gebühr** *f* toll (charge); **~straße** *f* toll road

maximal [maksi'maːl] *adj* maximum ♦ *adv* at most

Mayonnaise [majɔ'nɛːzə] *f* mayonnaise

Mechan- [me'çaːn] *zW:* **~ik** *f* mechanics *sg;* (*Getriebe*) mechanics *pl;* **~iker** (**-s, -**) *m* mechanic, engineer; **m~isch** *adj* mechanical; **~ismus** *m* mechanism

meckern ['mɛkərn] *vi* to bleat; (*umg*) to moan

Medaille [me'daljə] *f* medal

Medaillon [medal'jõː] (**-s, -s**) *nt* (*Schmuck*) locket

Medikament [medika'mɛnt] *nt* medicine

Meditation [meditatsi'oːn] *f* meditation

meditieren [medi'tiːrən] *vi* to meditate

Medizin [medi'tsiːn] (**-, -en**) *f* medicine; **m~isch** *adj* medical

Meer [meːr] (**-(e)s, -e**) *nt* sea; **~enge** *f* straits *pl;* **~esfrüchte** *pl* seafood *sg;* **~esspiegel** *m* sea level; **~rettich** *m* horseradish; **~schweinchen** *nt* guinea pig

Mehl [meːl] (**-(e)s, -e**) *nt* flour; **m~ig** *adj* floury; **~schwitze** *f* (*KOCH*) roux; **~speise** *f* (*KOCH*) flummery

mehr [meːr] *adj, adv* more; **~deutig** *adj* ambiguous; **~ere** *adj* several; **~eres** *pron* several things; **~fach** *adj* multiple; (*wiederholt*) repeated; **M~fahrtenkarte** *f* multi-journey ticket; **M~heit** *f* majority; **~malig** *adj* repeated; **~mals** *adv* repeatedly; **~stimmig** *adj* for several voices; **~stimmig singen** to harmonize; **M~wertsteuer** *f* value added tax; **M~zahl** *f* majority; (*GRAM*) plural

Mehrzweck- *in zW* multipurpose

meiden ['maɪdən] (*unreg*) *vt* to avoid

Meile ['maɪlə] *f* mile; **~nstein** *m* milestone; **m~nweit** *adj* for miles

mein(e) [maɪn] *adj* my; **~e(r, s)** *pron* mine

Meineid ['maɪnʔaɪt] *m* perjury

meinen ['maɪnən] *vi* to think ♦ *vt* to think; (*sagen*) to say; (*sagen wollen*) to mean; **das will ich ~** I should think so

mein- *zW:* **~erseits** *adv* for my part; **~etwegen** *adv* (*für mich*) for my sake;

(*wegen mir*) on my account; (*von mir aus*) as far as I'm concerned; I don't care *od* mind; **~etwillen** *adv:* **um ~etwillen** for my sake, on my account

Meinung ['mainʊŋ] *f* opinion; **ganz meine ~** I quite agree; **jdm die ~ sagen** to give sb a piece of one's mind

Meinungs- *zW:* **~austausch** *m* exchange of views; **~umfrage** *f* opinion poll; **~verschiedenheit** *f* difference of opinion

Meise ['maizə] *f* tit(mouse)

Meißel ['maisəl] (**-s, -**) *m* chisel

meist [maist] *adj* most ♦ *adv* mostly; **am ~en** the most; **~ens** *adv* generally, usually

Meister ['maistər] (**-s, -**) *m* master; (*SPORT*) champion; **m~haft** *adj* masterly; **m~n** *vt* (*Schwierigkeiten etc*) to overcome, conquer; **~schaft** *f* mastery; (*SPORT*) championship; **~stück** *nt* masterpiece; **~werk** *nt* masterpiece

Melancholie [melaŋko'liː] *f* melancholy; **melancholisch** [melaŋ'koːlɪʃ] *adj* melancholy

Melde- ['mɛldə] *zW:* **~frist** *f* registration period; **m~n** *vt* to report ♦ *vr* to report; (*SCH*) to put one's hand up; (*freiwillig*) to volunteer; (*auf etw, am Telefon*) to answer; **sich m~n bei** to report to; to register with; **sich zu Wort m~n** to ask to speak; **~pflicht** *f* obligation to register with the police; **~schluss ▲** *m* closing date; **~stelle** *f* registration office

Meldung ['mɛldʊŋ] *f* announcement; (*Bericht*) report

meliert [me'liːrt] *adj* (*Haar*) greying; (*Wolle*) flecked

melken ['mɛlkən] (*unreg*) *vt* to milk

Melodie [melo'diː] *f* melody, tune

melodisch [me'loːdɪʃ] *adj* melodious, tuneful

Melone [me'loːnə] *f* melon; (*Hut*) bowler (hat)

Membran [mɛm'braːn] (**-, -en**) *f* (*TECH*) diaphragm

Memoiren [memo'aːrən] *pl* memoirs

Menge ['mɛŋə] *f* quantity; (*Menschenmenge*) crowd; (*große Anzahl*) lot (of); **m~n** *vt* to mix ♦ *vr:* **sich m~n in** *+akk* to meddle with; **~nlehre** *f* (*MATH*) set theory; **~nrabatt** *m* bulk discount

Mensch [mɛnʃ] (**-en, -en**) *m* human being, man; person ♦ *excl* hey!; **kein ~** nobody

Menschen- *zW:* **~affe** *m* (*ZOOL*) ape; **m~freundlich** *adj* philanthropical; **~kenner** *m* judge of human nature; **m~leer** *adj* deserted; **m~möglich** *adj* humanly possible; **~rechte** *pl* human rights; **m~unwürdig** *adj* beneath human dignity; **~verstand** *m:* **gesunder ~verstand** common sense

Mensch- *zW:* **~heit** *f* humanity, mankind; **m~lich** *adj* human; (*human*) humane; **~lichkeit** *f* humanity

Menstruation [mɛnstruatsi'oːn] *f* menstruation

Mentalität [mɛntali'tɛːt] *f* mentality

Menü [me'nyː] (**-s, -s**) *nt* (*auch COMPUT*) menu

Merk- ['mɛrk] *zW:* **~blatt** *nt* instruction sheet *od* leaflet; **m~en** *vt* to notice; **sich** *dat* **etw m~en** to remember sth; **m~lich** *adj* noticeable; **~mal** *nt* sign, characteristic; **m~würdig** *adj* odd

messbar ▲ ['mɛsbaːr] *adj* measurable

Messbecher ▲ *m* measuring jug

Messe ['mɛsə] *f* fair; (*ECCL*) mass; **~gelände** *nt* exhibition centre; **~halle** *f* pavilion at a fair

messen (*unreg*) *vt* to measure ♦ *vr* to compete

Messer (**-s, -**) *nt* knife; **~spitze** *f* knife point; (*in Rezept*) pinch

Messestand *m* stall at a fair

Messgerät ▲ *nt* measuring device, gauge

Messing ['mɛsɪŋ] (**-s**) *nt* brass

Metall [me'tal] (**-s, -e**) *nt* metal; **m~isch** *adj* metallic

Meter ['meːtər] (**-s, -**) *nt od m* metre; **~maß** *nt* tape measure

Methode [me'toːdə] *f* method; **methodisch** *adj* methodical

Metropole [metro'poːlə] *f* metropolis

Metzger ['mɛtsgər] (**-s, -**) *m* butcher; **~ei** [-'rai] *f* butcher's (shop)

Meute ['mɔytə] *f* pack; **~'rei** *f* mutiny; **m~rn** *vi* to mutiny

miauen [mi'auən] *vi* to miaow

mich [mɪç] (*akk von* **ich**) *pron* me; myself

Miene ['miːnə] *f* look, expression

mies [miːs] (*umg*) *adj* lousy

Miet- ['miːt] *zW:* **~auto** *nt* hired car; **~e** *f* rent; **zur ~e wohnen** to live in rented accommodation; **m~en** *vt* to rent; (*Auto*) to hire; **~er(in)** (**-s, -**) *m(f)* tenant; **~shaus** *nt* tenement, block of (rented) flats; **~vertrag** *m* lease

Migräne [mi'grɛːnə] *f* migraine

Mikro- ['mikro] *zW:* **~fon, ~phon** [-'foːn] (**-s, -e**) *nt* microphone; **~skop** [-'skoːp] (**-s, -e**) *nt* microscope; **m~skopisch** *adj* microscopic; **~wellenherd** *m* microwave (oven)

Milch [mɪlç] (**-**) *f* milk; **~glas** *nt* frosted glass; **m~ig** *adj* milky; **~kaffee** *m* white coffee; **~mann** (*pl* **-männer**) *m* milkman; **~mixgetränk** *nt* (*KOCH*) milkshake; **~pulver** *nt* powdered milk; **~straße** *f* Milky Way; **~zahn** *m* milk tooth

mild [mɪlt] *adj* mild; (*Richter*) lenient; (*freundlich*) kind, charitable; **M~e** *f* mildness; leniency; **~ern** *vt* to mitigate, to soften; (*Schmerz*) to alleviate; **~ernde Umstände** extenuating circumstances

Milieu [mili'øː] (**-s, -s**) *nt* background,

environment; **m~geschädigt** adj maladjusted

Mili- |mili| zW: **m~tant** |-'tant| adj militant; **~tär** |-'tɛːr| (-s) nt military, army; **~'tärgericht** nt military court; **m~'tärisch** adj military

Milli- |'mili| zW: **~ardär** |-arˈdɛːr| m multimillionaire; **~arde** |-'ardə| f milliard; billion (bes US); **~meter** m millimetre; **~meterpapier** nt graph paper

Million |miliˈoːn| (-, -en) f million; **~är** |-oˈnɛːr| m millionaire

Milz |milts| (-, -en) f spleen

Mimik |'miːmik| f mime

Mimose |miˈmoːzə| f mimosa; (fig) sensitive person

minder |'mindər| adj inferior ♦ adv less; **M~heit** f minority; **~jährig** adj minor; **M~jährige(r)** f(m) minor; **~n** vt, vr to decrease, to diminish; **M~ung** f decrease; **~wertig** adj inferior; **M~wertigkeits- komplex** m inferiority complex

Mindest- |'mindəst| zW: **~alter** nt minimum age; **~betrag** m minimum amount; **m~e(r, s)** adj least; **zum ~en** od **m~en** at least; **m~ens** adv at least; **~haltbarkeitsdatum** nt best-before date; **~lohn** m minimum wage; **~maß** nt minimum

Mine |'miːnə| f mine; (Bleistiftmine) lead; (Kugelschreibermine) refill

Mineral |mineˈraːl| (-s, -e od -ien) nt mineral; **m~isch** adj mineral; **~wasser** nt mineral water

Miniatur |miniaˈtuːr| f miniature

Mini- zW: **~golf** |'miniɡɔlf| nt miniature golf, crazy golf; **m~mal** |miniˈmaːl| adj minimal; **~mum** |'miniːmɔm| nt minimum; **~rock** nt miniskirt

Minister |miˈnistər| (-s, -) m minister; **m~iell** adj ministerial; **~ium** nt ministry; **~präsident** m prime minister

Minus |'miːnɔs| (-, -) nt deficit

minus adv minus; **M~zeichen** nt minus sign

Minute |miˈnuːtə| f minute

Minze |'mintsə| f mint

mir |miːr| (dat von **ich**) pron (to) me; **~ nichts, dir nichts** just like that

Misch- |'miʃ| zW: **~brot** nt bread made from more than one kind of flour; **~ehe** f mixed marriage; **m~en** vt to mix; **~ling** m half- caste; **~ung** f mixture

miserabel |mizəˈraːbəl| (umg) adj (Essen, Film) dreadful

Miss- ▲ |'mis| zW: **~behagen** ▲ nt discomfort, uneasiness; **~bildung** ▲ f deformity; **m~'billigen** ▲ vt insep to disapprove of; **~brauch** ▲ m abuse; (falscher Gebrauch) misuse; **m~'brauchen** ▲ vt insep to abuse; **jdn zu** od **für etw m~brauchen** to use sb for od to do sth;

~erfolg ▲ m failure; **~fallen** ▲ (-s) nt displeasure; **m~'fallen** ▲ (unreg) vi insep: **jdm m~fallen** to displease sb; **~ge- schick** ▲ nt misfortune; **m~glücken** |mɪsˈɡlʏkən| ▲ vi insep to fail; **jdm m-glückt etw** sb does not succeed with sth; **~griff** ▲ m mistake; **~gunst** ▲ f envy; **m~günstig** ▲ adj envious; **m~'handeln** ▲ vt insep to ill-treat; **~'handlung** ▲ f ill-treatment

Mission |misiˈoːn| f mission; **~ar(in)** m(f) missionary

Miss- ▲ zW: **~klang** ▲ m discord; **~kredit** ▲ m discredit; **m~lingen** ▲ |mɪsˈlɪŋən| (unreg) vi insep to fail; **~mut** ▲ m sullenness; **m~mutig** ▲ adj sullen; **m~'raten** ▲ (unreg) vi insep to turn out badly ♦ adj ill-bred; **~stand** ▲ m bad state of affairs; abuse; **m~'trauen** ▲ vi insep to mistrust; **~trauen** ▲ (-s) nt distrust, suspicion; **~trauensantrag** ▲ m (POL) motion of no confidence; **m~trauisch** ▲ adj distrustful, suspicious; **~verhältnis** ▲ nt disproportion; **~verständnis** ▲ nt misunderstanding; **m~verstehen** ▲ (unreg) vt insep to misunderstand; **~wirtschaft** ▲ f mismanagement

Mist |mist| (-(e)s) m dung; dirt; (umg) rubbish

Mistel (-, -n) f mistletoe

Misthaufen m dungheap

mit |mit| präp +dat with; (mittels) by ♦ adv along, too; **~ der Bahn** by train; **~ 10 Jahren** at the age of 10; **wollen Sie ~?** do you want to come along?

Mitarbeit |'mitʔarbait| f cooperation; **m~en** vi to cooperate, to collaborate; **~er(in)** m(f) collaborator; co-worker ♦ pl (Personal) staff

Mit- zW: **~bestimmung** f participation in decision-making; **m~bringen** (unreg) vt to bring along

miteinander |mitʔaiˈnandər| adv together, with one another

miterleben vt to see, to witness

Mitesser |'mitʔɛsər| (-s, -) m blackhead

mitfahr- zW: **~en** vi to accompany; (auf Reise auch) to travel with; **M~gelegenheit** f lift; **M~zentrale** f agency for arranging lifts

mitfühlend adj sympathetic, compassionate

Mit- zW: **m~geben** (unreg) vt to give; **~gefühl** nt sympathy; **m~gehen** (unreg) vi to go/come along; **m~genommen** adj done in, in a bad way; **~gift** f dowry

Mitglied |'mitɡliːt| nt member; **~sbeitrag** m membership fee; **~schaft** f membership

Mit- zW: **m~halten** (unreg) vi to keep up; **m~helfen** (unreg) vi to help; **~hilfe** f help, assistance; **m~hören** vt to listen in to; **m~kommen** (unreg) vi to come along; (verstehen) to keep up, to follow; **~läufer** m

Spelling reform: ▲ new spelling △ old spelling (to be phased out)

hanger-on; (*POL*) fellow traveller
Mitleid nt sympathy; (*Erbarmen*) compassion;
m~ig adj sympathetic; **m~slos** adj pitiless,
merciless
Mit- zW: **m~machen** vt to join in, to take
part in; **~mensch** m fellow man;
m~nehmen (*unreg*) vt to take along/away;
(*anstrengen*) to wear out, to exhaust; **zum**
~nehmen to take away; **m~reden** vi: **bei**
etw m~reden to have a say in sth;
m~reißen (*unreg*) vt to carry away/along;
(*fig*) to thrill, captivate
mitsamt |mɪt'zamt| präp +dat together with
Mitschuld f complicity; **m~ig** adj: **m~ig (an**
+dat) implicated (in); (*an Unfall*) partly
responsible (for)
Mit- zW: **~schüler(in)** m(f) schoolmate;
m~spielen vi to join in, to take part;
~spieler(in) m(f) partner
Mittag |'mɪta:k| (-(e)s, -e) m midday,
lunchtime; (zu) ~ **essen** to have lunch;
heute/morgen ~ today/tomorrow at
lunchtime od noon; **~essen** nt lunch, dinner
mittags adv at lunchtime od noon;
M~pause f lunch break; **M~schlaf** m early
afternoon nap, siesta
Mittäter(in) |'mɪttɛːtər(ɪn)| m(f) accomplice
Mitte |'mɪtə| f middle; (*POL*) centre; **aus**
unserer ~ from our midst
mitteilen |'mɪttaɪlən| vt: **jdm etw ~** to
inform sb of sth, to communicate sth to sb
Mitteilung f communication
Mittel |'mɪtəl| (-s -) nt means; method;
(*MATH*) average; (*MED*) medicine; **ein ~ zum**
Zweck a means to an end; **~alter** nt Middle
Ages pl; **m~alterlich** adj mediaeval; **~ding**
nt cross; **~europa** nt Central Europe;
~gebirge nt low mountain range;
m~mäßig adj mediocre, middling;
~mäßigkeit f mediocrity; **~meer** nt
Mediterranean; **~ohrentzündung** f
inflammation of the middle ear; **~punkt** m
centre; **~stand** m middle class; **~streifen** m
central reservation; **~stürmer** m centre-
forward; **~weg** m middle course; **~welle** f
(*RAD*) medium wave
mitten |'mɪtən| adv in the middle; **~ auf der**
Straße/in der Nacht in the middle of the
street/night
Mitternacht |'mɪtərnaxt| f midnight
mittlere(r, s) |'mɪtlərə(r, s)| adj middle;
(*durchschnittlich*) medium, average; **~ Reife**
≈ O-levels
mittlerweile |'mɪtlər'vaɪlə| adv meanwhile
Mittwoch |'mɪtvɔx| (-(e)s, -e) m
Wednesday; **m~s** adv on Wednesdays
mitunter |mɪt'ʊntər| adv occasionally,
sometimes
Mit- zW: **m~verantwortlich** adj jointly
responsible; **m~wirken** vi: **m~wirken (bei)**
to contribute (to); (*THEAT*) to take part (in);

~wirkung f contribution; participation
Mobbing |'mɔbɪŋ| (-s) nt workplace
bullying
Möbel |'møːbəl| pl furniture sg; **~wagen** m
furniture od removal van
mobil |moˈbiːl| adj mobile; (*MIL*) mobilized;
M~iar |mobiliˈaːr| (-s, -e) nt furnishings pl;
M~machung f mobilization; **M~telefon** nt
mobile phone
möblieren |møːˈbliːrən| vt to furnish;
möbliert wohnen to live in furnished
accommodation
möchte etc |'mœçtə| vb siehe **mögen**
Mode |'moːdə| f fashion
Modell |moˈdɛl| (-s, -e) nt model; **m~ieren**
|-ˈliːrən| vt to model
Modenschau f fashion show
moderig |'moːdərɪç| adj (*Keller*) musty; (*Luft*)
stale
modern |moˈdɛrn| adj modern; (*modisch*)
fashionable; **~isieren** vt to modernize
Mode- zW: **~schau** f fashion show;
~schmuck m fashion jewellery;
~schöpfer(in) m(f) fashion designer;
~wort nt fashionable word, buzz word
modisch |'moːdɪʃ| adj fashionable
Mofa |'moːfa| (-s, -s) nt small moped
mogeln |'moːgəln| (*umg*) vi to cheat

SCHLÜSSELWORT

mögen |'møːgən| (pt **mochte**, pp **gemocht**
od (als Hilfsverb) **mögen**) vt, vi to like;
magst du/mögen Sie ihn? do you like
him?; **ich möchte ...** I would like ..., I'd
like ...; **er möchte in die Stadt** he'd like to
go into town; **ich möchte nicht, dass du**
... I wouldn't like you to ...; **ich mag nicht**
mehr I've had enough
♦ Hilfsverb to like to; (*wollen*) to want;
möchtest du etwas essen? would you
like something to eat?; **sie mag nicht**
bleiben she doesn't want to stay; **das mag**
wohl sein that may well be; **was mag das**
heißen? what might that mean?; **Sie**
möchten zu Hause anrufen could you
please call home?

---

möglich |'møːklɪç| adj possible; **~erweise**
adv possibly; **M~keit** f possibility; **nach**
M~keit if possible; **~st** adv as ... as possible
Mohn |moːn| (-(e)s, -e) m (~**blume**) poppy;
(~**samen**) poppy seed
Möhre |'møːrə| f carrot
Mohrrübe |'moːrryːbə| f carrot
mokieren |moˈkiːrən| vr: **sich ~ über** +akk
to make fun of
Mole |'moːlə| f (harbour) mole
Molekül |moleˈkyːl| (-s, -e) nt molecule
Molkerei |mɔlkəˈraɪ| f dairy
Moll |mɔl| (-, -) nt (*MUS*) minor (key)
mollig adj cosy; (*dicklich*) plump

Moment |mo'mɛnt| (-(e)s, -e) *m* moment ♦ *nt* factor; **im ~** at the moment; **~ (mal)!** just a moment; **m~an** |-'taːn| *adj* momentary ♦ *adv* at the moment

Monarch |mo'narç| (-en, -en) *m* monarch; **~ie** |monar'çiː| *f* monarchy

Monat |'moːnat| (-(e)s, -e) *m* month; **m~elang** *adv* for months; **m~lich** *adj* monthly

Monats- *zW:* **~gehalt** *nt:* **das dreizehnte ~gehalt** Christmas bonus (*of one month's salary*); **~karte** *f* monthly ticket

Mönch |mœnç| (-(e)s, -e) *m* monk

Mond |moːnt| (-(e)s, -e) *m* moon; **~finsternis** *f* eclipse of the moon; **m~hell** *adj* moonlit; **~landung** *f* moon landing; **~schein** *m* moonlight

Mono- |mono| *in zW* mono; **~log** |-'loːk| (-s, -e) *m* monologue; **~pol** |-'poːl| (-s, -e) *nt* monopoly; **m~polisieren** |-poli'ziːrən| *vt* to monopolize; **m~ton** |-'toːn| *adj* monotonous; **~tonie** |-toˈniː| *f* monotony

Montag |'moːntaːk| (-(e)s, -e) *m* Monday

Montage |mɔn'taːʒə| *f* (*PHOT etc*) montage; (*TECH*) assembly; (*Einbauen*) fitting

Monteur |mɔn'tøːr| *m* fitter

montieren |mɔn'tiːrən| *vt* to assemble

Monument |monu'mɛnt| *nt* monument; **m~al** |-'taːl| *adj* monumental

Moor |moːr| (-(e)s, -e) *nt* moor

Moos |moːs| (-es, -e) *nt* moss

Moped |'moːpɛt| (-s, -s) *nt* moped

Moral |moˈraːl| (-, -en) *f* morality; (*einer Geschichte*) moral; **m~isch** *adj* moral

Morast |mo'rast| (-(e)s, -e) *m* morass, mire; **m~ig** *adj* boggy

Mord |mɔrt| (-(e)s, -e) *m* murder; **~anschlag** *m* murder attempt

Mörder(in) |'mœrdar| (-s, -) *m(f)* murderer (murderess)

mörderisch *adj* (*fig: schrecklich*) terrible, dreadful ♦ *adv* (*umg: entsetzlich*) terribly, dreadfully

Mord- *zW:* **~kommission** *f* murder squad; **~sglück** (*umg*) *nt* amazing luck; **m~smäßig** (*umg*) *adj* terrific, enormous; **~verdacht** *m* suspicion of murder; **~waffe** *f* murder weapon

morgen |'mɔrgən| *adv* tomorrow; **~ früh** tomorrow morning; **M~** (-s, -) *m* morning; **M~mantel** *m* dressing gown; **M~rock** *m* dressing gown; **M~röte** *f* dawn; **~s** *adv* in the morning

morgig |'mɔrgıç| *adj* tomorrow's; **der ~e Tag** tomorrow

Morphium |'mɔrfiʊm| *nt* morphine

morsch |mɔrʃ| *adj* rotten

Morsealphabet |'mɔrzəʔalfabeːt| *nt* Morse code

morsen *vi* to send a message by Morse code

Mörtel |'mœrtəl| (-s, -) *m* mortar

Mosaik |moza'iːk| (-s, -en *od* -e) *nt* mosaic

Moschee |mɔ'ʃeː| (-, -n) *f* mosque

Moskito |mɔs'kiːto| (-s, -s) *m* mosquito

Most |mɔst| (-(e)s, -e) *m* (unfermented) fruit juice; (*Apfelwein*) cider

Motel |mo'tɛl| (-s, -s) *nt* motel

Motiv |mo'tiːf| (-s, -e) *nt* motive; (*MUS*) theme; **~ation** |-vatsi'oːn| *f* motivation; **m~ieren** |moti'viːrən| *vt* to motivate

Motor |'moːtɔr, *pl* mo'toːrən| (-s, -en) *m* engine; (*bes ELEK*) motor; **~boot** *nt* motorboat; **~haube** *f* (*von Auto*) bonnet (*BRIT*), hood (*US*); **m~isieren** *vt* to motorize; **~öl** *nt* engine oil; **~rad** *nt* motorcycle; **~roller** *m* (motor) scooter; **~schaden** *m* engine trouble *od* failure

Motte |'mɔtə| *f* moth; **~nkugel** *f* mothball(s)

Motto |'mɔto| (-s, -s) *nt* motto

Möwe |'møːvə| *f* seagull

Mücke |'mʏkə| *f* midge, gnat; **~nstich** *m* midge *od* gnat bite

müde |'myːdə| *adj* tired

Müdigkeit |'myːdıçkaıt| *f* tiredness

Muffel (-s, -) (*umg*) *m* killjoy, sourpuss

muffig *adj* (*Luft*) musty

Mühe |'myːə| *f* trouble, pains *pl*; **mit Müh und Not** with great difficulty; **sich** *dat* **~ geben** to go to a lot of trouble; **m~los** *adj* without trouble, easy; **m~voll** *adj* laborious, arduous

Mühle |'myːlə| *f* mill; (*Kaffeemühle*) grinder

Müh- *zW:* **~sal** (-, -e) *f* tribulation; **m~sam** *adj* arduous, troublesome; **m~selig** *adj* arduous, laborious

Mulde |'mʊldə| *f* hollow, depression

Mull |mʊl| (-(e)s, -e) *m* thin muslin

Müll |mʏl| (-(e)s) *m* refuse; **~abfuhr** *f* rubbish disposal; (*Leute*) dustmen *pl*; **~ablageplatz** *m* rubbish dump

Mullbinde *f* gauze bandage

Müll- *zW:* **~eimer** *m* dustbin, garbage can (*US*); **~haufen** *m* rubbish heap; **~schlucker** (-s, -) *m* garbage disposal unit; **~tonne** *f* dustbin; **~verbrennungsanlage** *f* incinerator

mulmig |'mʊlmıç| *adj* rotten; (*umg*) dodgy; **jdm ist ~** sb feels funny

multiplizieren |mʊltipliˈtsiːrən| *vt* to multiply

Mumie |'muːmiə| *f* mummy

Mumm |mʊm| (-s) (*umg*) *m* gumption, nerve

Mumps |mʊmps| (-) *m od f* (*MED*) mumps

München |'mʏnçən| (-s) *nt* Munich

Mund |mʊnt| (-(e)s, ⁇er) *m* mouth; **~art** *f* dialect

münden |'mʏndən| *vi:* **~ in** +*akk* to flow into

Mund- zW: **m~faul** adj taciturn; **~geruch** m bad breath; **~harmonika** f mouth organ

mündig ['mʏndɪç] adj of age; **M~keit** f majority

mündlich ['mʏntlɪç] adj oral

Mundstück nt mouthpiece; (Zigaretten- mundstück) tip

Mündung ['mʏndʊŋ] f (von Fluss) mouth; (Gewehr) muzzle

Mund- zW: **~wasser** nt mouthwash; **~werk** nt: **ein großes ~werk haben** to have a big mouth; **~winkel** m corner of the mouth

Munition [munitsi'o:n] f ammunition; **~slager** nt ammunition dump

munkeln ['mʊŋkəln] vi to whisper, to mutter

Münster ['mʏnstər] (-s, -) nt minster

munter ['mʊntər] adj lively

Münze ['mʏntsə] f coin; **m~n** vt to coin, to mint

Münzfernsprecher ['mʏntsfɛrnʃprɛçər] m callbox (BRIT), pay phone

mürb(e) ['mʏrb(ə)] adj (Gestein) crumbly; (Holz) rotten; (Gebäck) crisp; **jdn mürbe machen** to wear sb down; **M~eteig** ['mʏrbətaɪç] m shortcrust pastry

murmeln ['mʊrməln] vt, vi to murmur, to mutter

murren ['mʊrən] vi to grumble, to grouse

mürrisch ['mʏrɪʃ] adj sullen

Mus [mu:s] (-es, -e) nt purée

Muschel ['mʊʃəl] (-, -n) f mussel; (~schale) shell; (Telefonmuschel) receiver

Muse ['mu:zə] f muse

Museum [mu'ze:ʊm] (-s, Museen) nt museum

Musik [mu'zi:k] f music; (Kapelle) band; **m~alisch** [-ka:lɪʃ] adj musical; **~ant(in)** [-'kant(ɪn)] (-en, -en) m(f) musician; **~box** f jukebox; **~er** (-s, -) m musician; **~hochschule** f college of music; **~instrument** nt musical instrument

musisch ['mu:zɪʃ] adj (Mensch) artistic

musizieren [muzi'tsi:rən] vi to make music

Muskat [mʊs'ka:t] (-(e)s, -e) m nutmeg

Muskel ['mʊskəl] (-s, -n) m muscle; **~kater** m: **~kater haben** to be stiff

Muskulatur [mʊskula'tu:r] f muscular system

muskulös [mʊsku'lø:s] adj muscular

Müsli ['my:sli] (-s, -) nt (KOCH) muesli

Muss ▲ [mʊs] (-) nt necessity, must

Muße ['mu:sə] (-) f leisure

---

müssen ['mʏsən] (pt musste, pp gemusst od (als Hilfsverb) müssen) vi 1 (Zwang) must (nur im Präsens) to have to; **ich muss es tun** I must do it, I have to do it; **ich musste es tun** I had to do it; **er muss es nicht tun** he doesn't have to do it; **muss ich?** must I?, do I have to?; **wann müsst**

ihr zur Schule? when do you have to go to school?; **er hat gehen müssen** he (has) had to go; **muss das sein?** is that really necessary?; **ich muss mal** (umg) I need the toilet

2 (sollen): **das musst du nicht tun!** you oughtn't to od shouldn't do that; **Sie hätten ihn fragen müssen** you should have asked him

3: **es muss geregnet haben** it must have rained; **es muss nicht wahr sein** it needn't be true

---

müßig ['my:sɪç] adj idle

Muster ['mʊstər] (-s, -) nt model; (Dessin) pattern; (Probe) sample; **m~gültig** adj exemplary; **m~n** vt (Tapete) to pattern; (fig, MIL) to examine; (Truppen) to inspect; **~ung** f (von Stoff) pattern; (MIL) inspection

Mut [mu:t] m courage; **nur ~!** cheer up!; **jdm ~ machen** to encourage sb; **m~ig** adj courageous; **m~los** adj discouraged, despondent

mutmaßlich ['mu:tma:slɪç] adj presumed ♦ adv probably

Mutprobe f test od trial of courage

Mutter¹ ['mʊtər] (-, ⁻) f mother

Mutter² ['mʊtər] (-, -n) f (Schraubenmutter) nut

mütterlich ['mʏtərlɪç] adj motherly; **~erseits** adv on the mother's side

Mutter- zW: **~liebe** f motherly love; **~mal** nt birthmark; **~milch** f mother's milk; **~schaft** f motherhood, maternity; **~schutz** m maternity regulations; **'m~'seelenal'lein** adj all alone; **~sprache** f native language; **~tag** m Mother's Day

Mutti ['mʊti] (-, -s) f mum(my) (BRIT), mom(my) (US)

mutwillig ['mu:tvɪlɪç] adj malicious, deliberate

Mütze ['mʏtsə] f cap

MwSt abk (= Mehrwertsteuer) VAT

mysteriös [mʏsteri'ø:s] adj mysterious

Mythos ['my:tɔs] (-, Mythen) m myth

N, n

na [na] excl well; **~ gut** okay then

Nabel ['na:bəl] (-s, -) m navel; **~schnur** f umbilical cord

---

nach [na:x] präp +dat 1 (örtlich) to; **nach Berlin** to Berlin; **nach links/rechts** (to the) left/right; **nach oben/hinten** up/back

2 (zeitlich) after; **einer nach dem anderen** one after the other; **nach Ihnen!** after you!; **zehn (Minuten) nach drei** ten (minutes) past three

3 (*gemäß*) according to; **nach dem Gesetz** according to the law; **dem Namen nach** judging by his/her name; **nach allem, was ich weiß** as far as I know
♦ *adv*: **ihm nach!** after him!; **nach und nach** gradually, little by little; **nach wie vor** still

nachahmen |'na:x|a:mən| *vt* to imitate
Nachbar(in) |'naxba:r(ın)| **(-s, -n)** *m(f)* neighbour; **~haus** *nt*: **im ~haus** next door; **n~lich** *adj* neighbourly; **~schaft** *f* neighbourhood; **~staat** *m* neighbouring state
nach- *zW*: **~bestellen** *vt*: **50 Stück ~bestellen** to order another 50; **N~bestellung** *f* (*COMM*) repeat order; **N~bildung** *f* imitation, copy; **~blicken** *vi* to gaze after; **~datieren** *vt* to postdate
nachdem |na:x'de:m| *konj* after; (*weil*) since; **je ~ (ob)** it depends (whether)
nachdenken (*unreg*) *vi*: **~ über** +*akk* to think about; **N~ (-s)** *nt* reflection, meditation
nachdenklich *adj* thoughtful, pensive
Nachdruck |'na:xdrʊk| *m* emphasis; (*TYP*) reprint, reproduction
nachdrücklich |'na:xdrʏklıç| *adj* emphatic
nacheinander |na:x|aı'nandər| *adv* one after the other
nachempfinden |'na:x|ɛmpfındən| (*unreg*) *vt*: **jdm etw ~** to feel sth with sb
Nacherzählung |'na:x|ɛrtse:loŋ| *f* reproduction (of a story)
Nachfahr |'na:xfa:r| **(-s, -en)** *m* descendant
Nachfolge |'na:xfɔlgə| *f* succession; **n~n** *vi* +*dat* to follow; **~r(in) (-s, -)** *m(f)* successor
nachforschen *vt*, *vi* to investigate
Nachforschung *f* investigation
Nachfrage |'na:xfra:gə| *f* inquiry; (*COMM*) demand; **n~n** *vi* to inquire
nach- *zW*: **~füllen** *vt* to refill; **~geben** (*unreg*) *vi* to give way, to yield; **N~gebühr** *f* (*POST*) excess postage
nachgehen |'na:xge:ən| (*unreg*) *vi* (+*dat*) to follow; (*erforschen*) to inquire (into); (*Uhr*) to be slow
Nachgeschmack |'na:xgəʃmak| *m* aftertaste
nachgiebig |'na:xgi:bıç| *adj* soft, accommodating; **N~keit** *f* softness
nachhaltig |'na:xhaltıç| *adj* lasting; (*Widerstand*) persistent
nachhause *adv* (*österreichisch, schweizerisch*) home
nachhelfen |'na:xhɛlfən| (*unreg*) *vi* +*dat* to assist, to help
nachher |na:x'he:r| *adv* afterwards
Nachhilfeunterricht |'na:xhılfə|ʊntərrıçt|

m extra tuition
nachholen |'na:xho:lən| *vt* to catch up with; (*Versäumtes*) to make up for
Nachkomme |'na:xkɔmə| **(-, -n)** *m* descendant
nachkommen (*unreg*) *vi* to follow; (*einer Verpflichtung*) to fulfil; **N~schaft** *f* descendants *pl*
Nachkriegszeit |'na:xkri:kstsaıt| *f* postwar period
Nach- *zW*: **~lass ▲ (-es, -lässe)** *m* (*COMM*) discount, rebate; (*Erbe*) estate; **n~lassen** (*unreg*) *vt* (*Strafe*) to remit; (*Summe*) to take off; (*Schulden*) to cancel ♦ *vi* to decrease, to ease off; (*Sturm*) to die down, to ease off; (*schlechter werden*) to deteriorate; **er hat n~gelassen** he has got worse; **n~lässig** *adj* negligent, careless
nachlaufen |'na:xlaʊfən| (*unreg*) *vi* +*dat* to run after, to chase
nachlösen |'na:xlø:zən| *vi* (*Zuschlag*) to pay on the train, pay at the other end; (*zur Weiterfahrt*) to pay the supplement
nachmachen |'na:xmaxən| *vt* to imitate, to copy; (*fälschen*) to counterfeit
Nachmittag |'na:xmıta:k| *m* afternoon; **am ~** in the afternoon; **n~s** *adv* in the afternoon
Nach- *zW*: **~nahme** *f* cash on delivery; **per ~nahme** C.O.D.; **~name** *m* surname; **~porto** *nt* excess postage
nachprüfen |'na:xpry:fən| *vt* to check, to verify
nachrechnen |'na:xrɛçnən| *vt* to check
nachreichen |'na:xraıçən| *vt* (*Unterlagen*) to hand in later
Nachricht |'na:xrıçt| **(-, -en)** *f* (piece of) news; (*Mitteilung*) message; **~en** *pl* (*Neuigkeiten*) news
Nachrichten- *zW*: **~agentur** *f* news agency; **~dienst** *m* (*MIL*) intelligence service; **~sprecher(in)** *m(f)* newsreader; **~technik** *f* telecommunications *sg*
Nachruf |'na:xru:f| *m* obituary
nachsagen |'na:xza:gən| *vt* to repeat; **jdm etw ~** to say sth of sb
Nachsaison |'na:xzɛzõ:| *f* off-season
nachschicken |'na:xʃıkən| *vt* to forward
nachschlagen |'na:xʃla:gən| (*unreg*) *vt* to look up
Nachschlagewerk *nt* reference book
Nachschlüssel *m* duplicate key
Nachschub |'na:xʃu:p| *m* supplies *pl*; (*Truppen*) reinforcements *pl*
nachsehen |'na:xze:ən| (*unreg*) *vt* (*prüfen*) to check ♦ *vi* (*erforschen*) to look and see; **jdm etw ~** to forgive sb sth; **das N~ haben** to come off worst
Nachsendeantrag *m* application to have one's mail forwarded

Spelling reform: ▲ *new spelling* △ *old spelling (to be phased out)*

nachsenden ['naːxzɛndən] (unreg) vt to
send on, to forward
nachsichtig adj indulgent, lenient
nachsitzen ['naːxzɪtsən] (unreg) vi: ~
(müssen) (SCH) to be kept in
Nachspeise ['naːxʃpaɪzə] f dessert, sweet,
pudding
Nachspiel ['naːxʃpiːl] nt epilogue; (fig)
sequel
nachsprechen ['naːxʃpreçən] (unreg) vt:
(jdm) ~ to repeat (after sb)
nächst [neːçst] präp +dat (räumlich) next to;
(außer) apart from; ~**beste(r, s)** adj first
that comes along; (zweitbeste) next best;
N~e(r) f(m) neighbour; ~**e(r, s)** adj next;
(-gelegen) nearest
nachstellen ['naːxʃtɛlən] vt (TECH: neu
einstellen) to adjust
nächst- zW: **N~enliebe** f love for one's
fellow men; ~**ens** adv shortly, soon;
~**liegend** adj nearest; (fig) obvious;
~**möglich** adj next possible
Nacht [naxt] (-, =e) f night; ~**dienst** m night
shift
Nachteil ['naːxtaɪl] m disadvantage; **n~ig** adj
disadvantageous
Nachthemd nt (Herrennachthemd)
nightshirt; (Damennachthemd) nightdress
Nachtigall ['naxtɪgal] (-, -en) f nightingale
Nachtisch ['naːxtɪʃ] m = Nachspeise
Nachtklub m night club
Nachtleben nt nightlife
nächtlich ['nɛçtlɪç] adj nightly
Nachtlokal nt night club
Nach- zW: ~**trag** (-(e)s, -träge) m
supplement; **n~tragen** (unreg) vt to carry;
(zufügen) to add; jdm etw n~tragen to
hold sth against sb; **n~träglich** adj later,
subsequent; additional ♦ adv later,
subsequently; additionally; **n~trauern** vi:
jdm/etw n~trauern to mourn the loss of
sb/sth
Nacht- zW: **n~s** adv at od by night;
~**schicht** f nightshift; ~**schwester** f night
nurse; ~**tarif** m off-peak tariff; ~**tisch** m
bedside table; ~**wächter** m night
watchman
Nach- zW: ~**untersuchung** f checkup;
n~wachsen (unreg) vi to grow again;
~**wahl** f (POL) ≈ by-election
Nachweis ['naːxvaɪs] (-es, -e) m proof;
n~bar adj provable, demonstrable; **n~en**
(unreg) vt to prove; jdm etw n~en to point
sth out to sb; **n~lich** adj evident,
demonstrable
nach- zW: ~**wirken** vi to have aftereffects;
N~wirkung f aftereffect; **N~wort** nt
epilogue; **N~wuchs** m offspring; (beruflich
etc) new recruits pl; ~**zahlen** vt, vi to pay
extra; **N~zahlung** f additional payment;
(zurückdatiert) back pay; ~**ziehen** (unreg) vt

(hinter sich herziehen: Bein) to drag;
N~zügler (-s, -) m straggler
Nacken ['nakən] (-s, -) m nape of the neck
nackt [nakt] adj naked; (Tatsachen) plain,
bare; **N~badestrand** m nudist beach;
N~heit f nakedness
Nadel ['naːdəl] (-, -n) f needle; (Stecknadel)
pin; ~**öhr** nt eye of a needle; ~**wald** m
coniferous forest
Nagel ['naːgəl] (-s, =) m nail; ~**bürste** f
nailbrush; ~**feile** f nailfile; ~**lack** m nail
varnish od polish (BRIT); **n~n** vt, vi to nail;
n~neu adj brand-new; ~**schere** f nail
scissors pl
nagen ['naːgən] vt, vi to gnaw
Nagetier ['naːgətiːr] nt rodent
nah(e) ['naː(ə)] adj (räumlich) near(by);
(Verwandte) near; (Freunde) close; (zeitlich)
near, close ♦ adv near(by); near, close;
(verwandt) closely ♦ präp +dat near (to),
close to; **der Nahe Osten** the Near East; ~
gehen +dat to grieve; ~ **kommen** +dat to
get close (to); jdm etw ~ **legen** to suggest
sth to sb; ~ **liegen** to be obvious; ~**liegend**
obvious; ~ **stehen** +dat to be close (to);
einer Sache ~ **stehen** to sympathize with
sth; ~ **stehend** close; jdm (zu) ~ **treten** to
offend sb
Nahaufnahme f close-up
Nähe ['nɛːə] (-) f nearness, proximity;
(Umgebung) vicinity; **in der** ~ close by; at
hand; **aus der** ~ from close to
nah(e)bei adv nearby
nahen vi, vr to approach, to draw near
nähen ['nɛːən] vt, vi to sew
näher adj, adv nearer; (Erklärung,
Erkundigung) more detailed; (sich) ~
kommen to get closer; **N~e(s)** nt details pl,
particulars pl
Naherholungsgebiet nt recreational area
(close to a town)
nähern vr to approach
nahezu adv nearly
Nähgarn nt thread
Nahkampf m hand-to-hand fighting
Nähkasten m sewing basket, workbox
nahm etc [naːm] vb siehe nehmen
Nähmaschine f sewing machine
Nähnadel f needle
nähren ['nɛːrən] vt to feed ♦ vr (Person) to
feed o.s.; (Tier) to feed
nahrhaft ['naːrhaft] adj nourishing, nutritious
Nahrung ['naːrʊŋ] f food; (fig auch) sustenance
Nahrungs- zW: ~**mittel** nt foodstuffs pl;
~**mittelindustrie** f food industry; ~**suche** f
search for food
Nährwert m nutritional value
Naht [naːt] (-, =e) f seam; (MED) suture;
(TECH) join; **n~los** adj seamless; **n~los**
ineinander übergehen to follow without a
gap

Nah- zW: **~verkehr** m local traffic;
~verkehrszug m local train; **~ziel** nt
immediate objective

Name ['na:mə] (**-ns, -n**) m name; **im ~n von**
on behalf of; **n~ns** adv by the name of;
~nstag m name day, saint's day; **n~ntlich**
adj by name ♦ adv particularly, especially

namhaft ['na:mhaft] adj (berühmt) famed,
renowned; (beträchtlich) considerable; **~
machen** to name

nämlich ['nɛ:mlıç] adv that is to say, namely;
(denn) since

nannte etc ['nantə] vb siehe **nennen**

Napf |napf| (**-(e)s, ⁼e**) m bowl, dish

Narbe |'narbə| f scar; **narbig** adj scarred

Narkose [nar'ko:zə] f anaesthetic

Narr [nar] (**-en, -en**) m fool; **n~en** vt to fool;
Närrin ['nɛrın] f fool; **närrisch** adj foolish,
crazy

Narzisse [nar'tsısə] f narcissus; daffodil

naschen ['naʃən] vt, vi to nibble; (heimlich
kosten) to pinch a bit

naschhaft adj sweet-toothed

Nase ['na:zə] f nose

Nasen- zW: **~bluten** (**-s**) nt nosebleed;
~loch nt nostril; **~tropfen** pl nose drops

naseweis adj pert, cheeky; (neugierig) nosey

Nashorn ['na:shɔrn] nt rhinoceros

nass ▲ |nas| adj wet

Nässe ['nɛsə] (**-**) f wetness; **n~n** vt to wet

nasskalt ▲ adj wet and cold

Nassrasur ▲ f wet shave

Nation [natsi'o:n] f nation

national [natsio'na:l] adj national;
N~feiertag m national holiday; **N~hymne**
f national anthem; **~isieren** [-i'zi:rən] vt to
nationalize; **N~ismus** |-'lısmʊs|
nationalism; **~istisch** [-'lıstıʃ] adj
nationalist; **N~i'tät** f nationality;
N~mannschaft f national team;
N~sozialismus m national socialism

Natron ['na:trɔn] (**-s**) nt soda

Natter ['natər] (**-, -n**) f adder

Natur |na'tu:r| f nature; (körperlich)
constitution; **~ell** (**-s, -e**) nt disposition;
~erscheinung f natural phenomenon od
event; **n~farben** adj natural coloured;
n~gemäß adj natural; **N~i'tät** f law of
nature; **n~getreu** adj true to life;
~katastrophe f natural disaster

natürlich [na'ty:rlıç] adj natural ♦ adv
naturally; **ja, ~!** yes, of course!; **N~keit** f
naturalness

Natur- zW: **~park** m ≈ national park;
~produkt nt natural product; **n~rein** adj
natural, pure; **~schutz** m nature
conservation; **unter ~schutz stehen** to be
legally protected; **~schutzgebiet** nt nature
reserve; **~wissenschaft** f natural science;

~wissenschaftler(in) m(f) scientist

nautisch ['nautıʃ] adj nautical

Nazi ['na:tsi] (**-s, -s**) m Nazi

NB abk (= nota bene) nb

n. Chr. abk (= nach Christus) A.D.

Nebel ['ne:bəl] (**-s, -**) m fog, mist; **n~ig** adj
foggy, misty; **~scheinwerfer** m fog lamp

neben ['ne:bən] präp (+akk od dat) next to;
(+dat: außer) apart from, besides; **~an**
[ne:bən'an] adv next door; **N~anschluss** ▲
m (TEL) extension; **N~ausgang** m side exit;
~bei [ne:bən'baı] adv at the same time;
(außerdem) additionally; (beiläufig)
incidentally; **N~beruf** m second job;
N~beschäftigung f second job;
N~buhler(in) (**-s, -**) m(f) rival; **~einander**
[ne:bən|aı'nandər] adv side by side;
~einander legen to put next to each other;
N~eingang m side entrance; **N~fach** nt
subsidiary subject; **N~fluss** ▲ m tributary;
N~gebäude nt annexe; **N~geräusch** nt
(RAD) atmospherics pl, interference; **~her**
[ne:bən'he:r] adv (zusätzlich) besides;
(gleichzeitig) at the same time; (daneben)
alongside; **N~kosten** pl extra charges,
extras; **N~produkt** nt by-product;
N~sache f trifle, side issue; **~sächlich** adj
minor, peripheral; **N~saison** f low season;
N~straße f side street; **N~verdienst** m
secondary income; **N~wirkung** f side
effect; **N~zimmer** nt adjoining room

neblig ['ne:blıç] adj foggy, misty

Necessaire [nesɛ'sɛ:r] (**-s, -s**) nt (Näh-
necessaire) needlework box; (Nagel-
necessaire) manicure case

necken ['nɛkən] vt to tease

Neckerei [nɛkə'raı] f teasing

Neffe ['nɛfə] (**-n, -n**) m nephew

negativ ['ne:gati:f] adj negative; **N~** (**-s, -e**)
nt (PHOT) negative

Neger ['ne:gər] (**-s, -**) m negro; **~in** f negress

nehmen ['ne:mən] (unreg) vt to take; **jdn zu
sich ~** to take sb in; **sich ernst ~** to take o.s.
seriously; **nimm dir doch bitte** please help
yourself

Neid [naıt] (**-(e)s**) m envy; **~er** (**-s, -**) m
envier; **n~isch** ['naıdıʃ] adj envious, jealous

neigen ['naıgən] vt to incline, to lean; (Kopf)
to bow ♦ vi: **zu etw ~** to tend to sth

Neigung f (des Geländes) slope; (Tendenz)
tendency, inclination; (Vorliebe) liking;
(Zuneigung) affection

nein [naın] adv no

Nektarine [nɛkta'ri:nə] f (Frucht) nectarine

Nelke ['nɛlkə] f carnation, pink; (Gewürz)
clove

Nenn- ['nɛn] zW: **n~en** (unreg) vt to name;
(mit Namen) to call; **wie n~t man ...?** what
do you call ...?; **n~enswert** adj worth

mentioning; **~er** (**-s, -**) m denominator;
~wert m nominal value; (COMM) par

Neon |'ne:ɔn| (**-s**) nt neon; **~licht** nt neon
light; **~röhre** f neon tube

Nerv |nɛrf| (**-s, -en**) m nerve; **jdm auf die
~en gehen** to get on sb's nerves;
n~enaufreibend adj nerve-racking;
~enbündel nt bundle of nerves;
~enheilanstalt f mental home;
n~enkrank adj mentally ill; **~ensäge**
(umg) f pain (in the neck) (umg);
~ensystem nt nervous system;
~enzusammenbruch m nervous
breakdown; **n~lich** adj (Belastung) affecting
the nerves; **n~ös** |nɛrˈvøːs| adj nervous;
~osi'tät f nervousness; **n~tötend** adj
nerve-racking; (Arbeit) soul-destroying

Nerz |nɛrts| (**-es, -e**) m mink

Nessel |'nɛsəl| (**-, -n**) f nettle

Nessessär ▲ |nɛsɛˈsɛːr| (**-s, -s**) nt =
Necessaire

Nest |nɛst| (**-(e)s, -er**) nt nest; (umg: Ort)
dump

nett |nɛt| adj nice; (freundlich) nice, kind;
~erweise adv kindly

netto |'nɛtoː| adv net

Netz |nɛts| (**-es, -e**) nt net; (Gepäcknetz)
rack; (Einkaufsnetz) string bag; (Spinnennetz)
web; (System) network; **jdm ins ~ gehen**
(fig) to fall into sb's trap; **~anschluss** ▲ m
mains connection; **~haut** f retina

neu |nɔy| adj new; (Sprache, Geschichte)
modern; **seit ~estem** (since) recently; **die
~esten Nachrichten** the latest news; **~
schreiben** to rewrite, to write again;
N~anschaffung f new purchase od
acquisition; **~artig** adj new kind of; **N~bau**
m new building; **N~e(r)** f(m) the new man/
woman; **~erdings** adv (kürzlich) (since)
recently; (von ~em) again; **N~erscheinung**
f (Buch) new publication; (Schallplatte) new
release; **N~erung** f innovation, new
departure; **N~gier** f curiosity; **~gierig** adj
curious; **N~heit** f newness; novelty;
N~igkeit f news sg; **N~jahr** nt New Year;
~lich adv recently, the other day; **N~ling** m
novice; **N~mond** m new moon

neun |nɔyn| num nine; **~zehn** num nineteen;
~zig num ninety

neureich adj nouveau riche; **N~e(r)** f(m)
nouveau riche

neurotisch adj neurotic

Neuseeland |nɔyˈzeːlant| nt New Zealand;
Neuseeländer(in) |nɔyˈzeːlɛndər(ɪn)| m(f)
New Zealander

neutral |nɔyˈtraːl| adj neutral; **~i'sieren** vt
to neutralize

Neutrum |'nɔytrʊm| (**-s, -a** od **-en**) nt
neuter

Neu- zW: **~wert** m purchase price;
n~wertig adj (as) new, not used; **~zeit** f

modern age; **n~zeitlich** adj modern, recent

SCHLÜSSELWORT

nicht |nɪçt| adv 1 (Verneinung) not; **er ist es
nicht** it's not him, it isn't him; **er raucht
nicht** (gerade) he isn't smoking;
(gewöhnlich) he doesn't smoke; **ich kann
das nicht – ich auch nicht** I can't do it –
neither od nor can I; **es regnet nicht mehr**
it's not raining any more; **nicht rostend**
stainless
2 (Bitte, Verbot): **nicht!** don't!, no!; **nicht
berühren!** do not touch!; **nicht doch!**
don't!
3 (rhetorisch): **du bist müde, nicht
(wahr)?** you're tired, aren't you?; **das ist
schön, nicht (wahr)?** it's nice, isn't it?
4: **was du nicht sagst!** the things you
say!

Nichtangriffspakt |nɪçtˈʔangrɪfspakt| m
non-aggression pact

Nichte |'nɪçtə| f niece

nichtig |'nɪçtɪç| adj (ungültig) null, void;
(wertlos) futile; **N~keit** f nullity, invalidity;
(Sinnlosigkeit) futility

Nichtraucher(in) m(f) non-smoker

nichts |nɪçts| pron nothing; **für ~ und
wieder ~** for nothing at all; **~ sagend**
meaningless; **N~ (-)** nt nothingness; (pej:
Person) nonentity

Nichtschwimmer m non-swimmer

nichts- zW: **~destoweniger** adv
nevertheless; **N~nutz** (**-es, -e**) m good-for-
nothing; **~nutzig** adj worthless, useless;
N~tun (**-s**) nt idleness

Nichtzutreffende(s) nt: **~s** od **nicht
Zutreffendes (bitte) streichen!** (please)
delete where appropriate

Nickel |'nɪkəl| (**-s**) nt nickel

nicken |'nɪkən| vi to nod

Nickerchen |'nɪkərçən| nt nap

nie |niː| adv never; **~ wieder** od **mehr** never
again; **~ und nimmer** never ever

nieder |'niːdər| adj low; (gering) inferior
♦ adv down; **N~gang** m decline;
~gedrückt adj (deprimiert) dejected,
depressed; **~gehen** (unreg) vi to descend;
(AVIAT) to come down; (Regen) to fall;
(Boxer) to go down; **~geschlagen** adj
depressed, dejected; **N~lage** f defeat;
N~lande pl Netherlands; **N~länder(in)**
m(f) Dutchman(-woman); **~ländisch** adj
Dutch; **~lassen** (unreg) vr (sich setzen) to sit
down; (an Ort) to settle (down); (Arzt,
Rechtsanwalt) to set up a practice;
N~lassung f settlement; (COMM) branch;
~legen vt to lay down; (Arbeit) to stop;
(Amt) to resign; **N~sachsen** nt Lower
Saxony; **N~schlag** m (MET) precipitation;
rainfall; **~schlagen** (unreg) vt (Gegner) to

125 niedlich → Notlage

beat down; (*Gegenstand*) to knock down; (*Augen*) to lower; (*Aufstand*) to put down ♦ *vr* (*CHEM*) to precipitate; **~trächtig** *adj* base, mean; **N~trächtigkeit** *f* meanness, baseness; outrage; **N~ung** *f* (*GEOG*) depression; (*Mündungsgebiet*) flats *pl*
niedlich [ˈniːtlɪç] *adj* sweet, cute
niedrig [ˈniːdrɪç] *adj* low; (*Stand*) lowly, humble; (*Gesinnung*) mean
niemals [ˈniːmaːls] *adv* never
niemand [ˈniːmant] *pron* nobody, no one
Niemandsland [ˈniːmantslant] *nt* no-man's-land
Niere [ˈniːrə] *f* kidney
nieseln [ˈniːzəln] *vi* to drizzle
niesen [ˈniːzən] *vi* to sneeze
Niete [ˈniːtə] *f* (*TECH*) rivet; (*Los*) blank; (*Reinfall*) flop; (*Mensch*) failure; **n~n** *vt* to rivet
Nikotin [nikoˈtiːn] (*-s*) *nt* nicotine
Nilpferd [ˈniːl-] *nt* hippopotamus
Nimmersatt [ˈnɪmərzat] (*-(e)s, -e*) *m* glutton
nimmst [ˈnɪmst] *etc* *vb siehe* **nehmen**
nippen [ˈnɪpən] *vt, vi* to sip
nirgend- [ˈnɪrgənt] *zW:* **~s** *adv* nowhere; **~wo** *adv* nowhere; **~wohin** *adv* nowhere
Nische [ˈniːʃə] *f* niche
nisten [ˈnɪstən] *vi* to nest
Niveau [niˈvoː] (*-s, -s*) *nt* level
Nixe [ˈnɪksə] *f* water nymph
nobel [ˈnoːbəl] *adj* (*großzügig*) generous; (*elegant*) posh (*inf*)

SCHLÜSSELWORT

noch [nɔx] *adv* 1 (*weiterhin*) still; **noch nicht** not yet; **noch nie** never (yet); **noch immer** *od* **immer noch** still; **bleiben Sie doch noch** stay a bit longer
2 (*in Zukunft*) still, yet; **das kann noch passieren** that might still happen; **er wird noch kommen** he'll come (yet)
3 (*nicht später als*): **noch vor einer Woche** only a week ago; **noch am selben Tag** the very same day; **noch im 19. Jahrhundert** as late as the 19th century; **noch heute** today
4 (*zusätzlich*): **wer war noch da?** who else was there?; **noch einmal** once more, again; **noch dreimal** three more times; **noch einer** another one
5 (*bei Vergleichen*): **noch größer** even bigger; **das ist noch besser** that's better still; **und wenn es noch so schwer ist** however hard it is
6: **Geld noch und noch** heaps (and heaps) of money; **sie hat noch und noch versucht**, ... she tried again and again to ...
♦ *konj:* **weder A noch B** neither A nor B

noch- *zW:* **~mal** [ˈnɔxmaːl] *adv* again, once more; **~malig** [ˈnɔxmaːlɪç] *adj* repeated; **~mals** *adv* again, once more
Nominativ [ˈnoːminatiːf] (*-s, -e*) *m* nominative
nominell [nomiˈnɛl] *adj* nominal
Nonne [ˈnɔnə] *f* nun
Nord(en) [ˈnɔrd(ən)] (*-s*) *m* north
Nord'irland *nt* Northern Ireland
nordisch *adj* northern
nördlich [ˈnœrtlɪç] *adj* northerly, northern ♦ *präp +gen* (to the) north of; **~ von** (to the) north of
Nord- *zW:* **~pol** *m* North Pole; **~rhein-Westfalen** *nt* North Rhine-Westphalia; **~see** *f* North Sea; **n~wärts** *adv* northwards
nörgeln [ˈnœrgəln] *vi* to grumble; **Nörgler** (*-s, -*) *m* grumbler
Norm [nɔrm] (*-, -en*) *f* norm; (*Größenvorschrift*) standard; **n~al** [nɔrˈmaːl] *adj* normal; **N~albenzin** *nt* ≈ 2-star petrol (*BRIT*), regular petrol (*US*); **n~alerweise** *adv* normally; **n~ali'sieren** *vt* to normalize ♦ *vr* to return to normal
normen *vt* to standardize
Norwegen [ˈnɔrveːgən] *nt* Norway; **norwegisch** *adj* Norwegian
Nostalgie [nɔstalˈgiː] *f* nostalgia
Not [noːt] (*-, -̈e*) *f* need; (*Mangel*) want; (*Mühe*) trouble; (*Zwang*) necessity; **~leidend** needy; **zur ~** if necessary; (*gerade noch*) just about
Notar [noˈtaːr] (*-s, -e*) *m* notary; **n~i'ell** *adj* notarial
Not- *zW:* **~arzt** *m* emergency doctor; **~ausgang** *m* emergency exit; **~behelf** (*-s, -e*) *m* makeshift; **~bremse** *f* emergency brake; **~dienst** *m* (*Bereitschaftsdienst*) emergency service; **n~dürftig** *adj* scanty; (*behelfsmäßig*) makeshift
Note [ˈnoːtə] *f* note; (*SCH*) mark (*BRIT*), grade (*US*)
Noten- *zW:* **~blatt** *nt* sheet of music; **~schlüssel** *m* clef; **~ständer** *m* music stand
Not- *zW:* **~fall** *m* (case of) emergency; **n~falls** *adv* if need be; **n~gedrungen** *adj* necessary, unavoidable; **etw n~gedrungen machen** to be forced to do sth
notieren [noˈtiːrən] *vt* to note; (*COMM*) to quote
Notierung *f* (*COMM*) quotation
nötig [ˈnøːtɪç] *adj* necessary; **etw ~ haben** to need sth; **~en** [-gən] *vt* to compel, to force; **~enfalls** *adv* if necessary
Notiz [noˈtiːts] (*-, -en*) *f* note; (*Zeitungsnotiz*) item; **~ nehmen** to take notice; **~block** *m* notepad; **~buch** *nt* notebook
Not- *zW:* **~lage** *f* crisis, emergency;

Spelling reform: ▲ *new spelling* △ *old spelling (to be phased out)*

n-landen vi to make a forced cd emergency landing; **n-leidend** △ adj siehe **Not**; **~lösung** f temporary solution; **~lüge** f white lie

notorisch |no'to:rɪʃ| adj notorious

Not- zW: **~ruf** m emergency call; **~rufsäule** f emergency telephone; **~stand** m state of emergency; **~unterkunft** f emergency accommodation; **~verband** m emergency dressing; **~wehr** (-) f self-defence; **n~wendig** adj necessary; **~wendigkeit** f necessity

Novelle |no'vɛlə| f short novel; (JUR) amendment

November |no'vɛmbər| (-s, -) m November

Nu |nu:| m: **im ~** in an instant

Nuance |ny'ã:sə| f nuance

nüchtern |'nʏçtərn| adj sober; (Magen) empty; (Urteil) prudent; **N~heit** f sobriety

Nudel |'nu:dəl| (-, -n) f noodle; **~n** pl (Teigwaren) pasta sg; (in Suppe) noodles

Null |nʊl| (-, -en) f nought, zero; (pej: Mensch) washout; **n~** num zero; (Fehler) no; **n~ Uhr** midnight; **n~ und nichtig** null and void; **~punkt** m zero; **auf dem ~punkt** at zero

numerisch |nu'me:rɪʃ| adj numerical

Nummer |'nɔmər| (-, -n) f number; (Größe) size; **n~ieren** ▲ vt to number; **~nschild** nt (AUT) number od license (US) plate

nun |nu:n| adv now ♦ excl well; **das ist ~ mal so** that's the way it is

nur |nu:r| adv just, only; **wo bleibt er ~?** (just) where is he?

Nürnberg |'nʏrnbɛrk| (-s) nt Nuremberg

Nuss ▲ |nʊs| (-, Nüsse) f nut; **~baum** ▲ m walnut tree; **~knacker** ▲ (-s, -) m nutcracker

nutz |nʊts| adj: **zu nichts ~ sein** to be no use for anything; **~bringend** adj (Verwendung) profitable

nütze |'nʏtsə| adj = **nutz**

Nutzen (-s) m usefulness; (Gewinn) profit; **von ~** useful; **n~** vi to be of use ♦ vt: **etw zu etw n~** to use sth for sth; **was nutzt es?** what's the use?, what use is it?

nützen vi, vt = **nutzen**

nützlich |'nʏtslɪç| adj useful; **N~keit** f usefulness

Nutz- zW: **n~los** adj useless; **~losigkeit** f uselessness; **~nießer** (-s, -) m beneficiary

Nylon |'nailɔn| (-(s)) nt nylon

O, o

Oase |o'a:zə| f oasis

ob |ɔp| konj if, whether; **~ das wohl wahr ist?** can that be true?; **und ~!** you bet!

obdachlos adj homeless

Obdachlose(r) f(m) homeless person;

~nasyl nt shelter for the homeless

Obduktion |ɔpdʊktsi'o:n| f post-mortem

obduzieren |ɔpdu'tsi:rən| vt to do a post-mortem on

O-Beine |'o:bainə| pl bow od bandy legs

oben |'o:bən| adv above; (in Haus) upstairs; **~ erwähnt ~ genannt** above-mentioned; **nach ~** up; **von ~** down; **~ ohne** topless; **jdn von ~ bis unten ansehen** to look sb up and down; **~an** adv at the top; **~auf** adv up above, on the top ♦ adj (munter) in form; **~drein** adv into the bargain

Ober |'o:bər| (-s, -) m waiter; **die ~en** pl (umg) the bosses; (ECCL) the superiors; **~arm** m upper arm; **~arzt** m senior physician; **~aufsicht** f supervision; **~bayern** nt Upper Bavaria; **~befehl** m supreme command; **~befehlshaber** m commander-in-chief; **~bekleidung** f outer clothing; **~'bürgermeister** m lord mayor; **~deck** nt upper od top deck; **o~e(r, s)** adj upper; **~fläche** f surface; **o~flächlich** adj superficial; **~geschoss** ▲ nt upper storey; **o~halb** adv above ♦ präp +gen above; **~haupt** nt head, chief; **~haus** nt (POL) upper house, House of Lords (BRIT); **~hemd** nt shirt; **~herrschaft** f supremacy, sovereignty; **~in** f matron; (ECCL) Mother Superior; **~kellner** m head waiter; **~kiefer** m upper jaw; **~körper** m upper part of body; **~leitung** f direction; (ELEK) overhead cable; **~licht** nt skylight; **~lippe** f upper lip; **~schenkel** m thigh; **~schicht** f upper classes pl; **~schule** f grammar school (BRIT), high school (US); **~schwester** f (MED) matron

Oberst |'o:bərst| (-en od -s, -en od -e) m colonel; **o~e(r, s)** adj very top, topmost

Ober- zW: **~stufe** f upper school; **~teil** nt upper part; **~weite** f bust/chest measurement

obgleich |ɔp'glaiç| konj although

Obhut |'ɔphu:t| (-) f care, protection; **in jds ~ sein** to be in sb's care

obig |'o:biç| adj above

Objekt |ɔp'jɛkt| (-(e)s, -e) nt object; **~iv** |-'ti:f| (-s, -e) nt lens; **o~iv** adj objective; **~ivität** f objectivity

Oblate |o'bla:tə| f (Gebäck) wafer; (ECCL) host

obligatorisch |ɔbliga'to:rɪʃ| adj compulsory, obligatory

Obrigkeit |'o:brɪçkait| f (Behörden) authorities pl, administration; (Regierung) government

obschon |ɔp'ʃo:n| konj although

Observatorium |ɔpzɛrva'to:riɔm| nt observatory

obskur |ɔps'ku:r| adj obscure; (verdächtig) dubious

Obst |o:pst| (-(e)s) nt fruit; **~baum** m fruit

tree; **~garten** *m* orchard; **~händler** *m* fruiterer, fruit merchant; **~kuchen** *m* fruit tart

obszön [ɔpsˈtsøːn] *adj* obscene; **O~i'tät** *f* obscenity

obwohl [ɔpˈvoːl] *konj* although

Ochse [ˈɔksə] **(-n, -n)** *m* ox; **o~n** (*umg*) *vt, vi* to cram, to swot (*BRIT*)

Ochsenschwanzsuppe *f* oxtail soup

Ochsenzunge *f* oxtongue

öd(e) [ˈøːd(ə)] *adj* (*Land*) waste, barren; (*fig*) dull; **Öde** *f* desert, waste(land); (*fig*) tedium

oder [ˈoːdər] *konj* or; **das stimmt, ~?** that's right, isn't it?

Ofen [ˈoːfən] **(-s, ̈)** *m* oven; (*Heizofen*) fire, heater; (*Kohlenofen*) stove; (*Hochofen*) furnace; (*Herd*) cooker, stove; **~rohr** *nt* stovepipe

offen [ˈɔfən] *adj* open; (*aufrichtig*) frank; (*Stelle*) vacant; **~ gesagt** to be honest; **~ bleiben** (*Fenster*) to stay open; (*Frage, Entscheidung*) to remain open; **~ halten** to keep open; **~ lassen** to leave open; **~ stehen** to be open; (*Rechnung*) to be unpaid; **es steht Ihnen ~, es zu tun** you are at liberty to do it; **~bar** *adj* obvious; **~baren** [ɔfənˈbaːrən] *vt* to reveal, to manifest; **O~'barung** *f* (*REL*) revelation; **O~heit** *f* candour, frankness; **~herzig** *adj* candid, frank; (*Kleid*) revealing; **~kundig** *adj* well-known; (*klar*) evident; **~sichtlich** *adj* evident, obvious

offensiv [ɔfɛnˈziːf] *adj* offensive; **O~e** [-ˈziːvə] *f* offensive

öffentlich [ˈœfəntlɪç] *adj* public; **Ö~keit** *f* (*Leute*) public; (*einer Versammlung etc*) public nature; **in aller ~keit** in public; **an die ~ dringen** to reach the public ear

offiziell [ɔfitsiˈɛl] *adj* official

Offizier [ɔfiˈtsiːr] **(-s, -e)** *m* officer; **~skasino** *nt* officers' mess

öffnen [ˈœfnən] *vt, vr* to open; **jdm die Tür ~** to open the door for sb

Öffner [ˈœfnər] **(-s, -)** *m* opener

Öffnung [ˈœfnʊŋ] *f* opening; **~szeiten** *pl* opening times

oft [ɔft] *adv* often

öfter [ˈœftər] *adv* more often *od* frequently; **~s** *adv* often, frequently

oh [oː] *excl* oh; **~ je!** oh dear

OHG *abk* (= *Offene Handelsgesellschaft*) ≈ general partnership

ohne [ˈoːnə] *präp* +*akk* without ♦ *konj* without; **das ist nicht ~** (*umg*) it's not bad; **~ weiteres** without a second thought; (*sofort*) immediately; **~ zu fragen** without asking; **~ dass er es wusste** without him knowing it; **~dies** [oːnəˈdiːs] *adv* anyway; **~gleichen** [oːnəˈglaɪçən] *adj* unsurpassed,

without equal; **~hin** [oːnəˈhɪn] *adv* anyway, in any case

Ohnmacht [ˈoːnmaxt] *f* faint; (*fig*) impotence; **in ~ fallen** to faint

ohnmächtig [ˈoːnmɛçtɪç] *adj* in a faint, unconscious; (*fig*) weak, impotent; **sie ist ~** she has fainted

Ohr [oːr] **(-(e)s, -en)** *nt* ear

Öhr [øːr] **(-(e)s, -e)** *nt* eye

Ohren- *zW*: **~arzt** *m* ear specialist; **o~betäubend** *adj* deafening; **~schmalz** *nt* earwax; **~schmerzen** *pl* earache *sg*

Ohr- *zW*: **~feige** *f* slap on the face; box on the ears; **o~feigen** *vt*: **jdn o~feigen** to slap sb's face; to box sb's ears; **~läppchen** *nt* ear lobe; **~ring** *m* earring; **~wurm** *m* earwig; (*MUS*) catchy tune

Öko- [øko] *zW*: **~laden** *m* wholefood shop; **ö~logisch** [-ˈloːgɪʃ] *adj* ecological; **ö~nomisch** [-ˈnoːmɪʃ] *adj* economical

Oktober [ɔkˈtoːbər] **(-s, -)** *m* October; **~fest** *nt* Munich beer festival

ökumenisch [økuˈmeːnɪʃ] *adj* ecumenical

Öl [øːl] **(-(e)s, -e)** *nt* oil; **~baum** *m* olive tree; **ö~en** *vt* to oil; (*TECH*) to lubricate; **~farbe** *f* oil paint; **~feld** *nt* oilfield; **~film** *m* film of oil; **~heizung** *f* oil-fired central heating; **ö~ig** *adj* oily; **~industrie** *f* oil industry

oliv [oˈliːf] *adj* olive-green; **O~e** *f* olive

Öl- *zW*: **~messstab** ▲ *m* dipstick; **~sardine** *f* sardine; **~stand** *m* oil level; **~standanzeiger** *m* (*AUT*) oil gauge; **~tanker** *m* oil tanker; **~ung** *f* lubrication; oiling; (*ECCL*) anointment; **die Letzte ~ung** Extreme Unction; **~wechsel** *m* oil change

Olymp- [oˈlʏmp] *zW*: **~iade** [olʏmpiˈaːdə] *f* Olympic Games *pl*; **~iasieger(in)** [-iaziˈgər(ɪn)] *m(f)* Olympic champion; **~iateilnehmer(in)** *m(f)* Olympic competitor; **o~isch** *adj* Olympic

Ölzeug *nt* oilskins *pl*

Oma [ˈoːma] **(-, -s)** (*umg*) *f* granny

Omelett [ɔm(ə)ˈlɛt] **(-(e)s, -s)** *nt* omelet(te)

ominös [omiˈnøːs] *adj* (*unheilvoll*) ominous

Omnibus [ˈɔmnibʊs] *m* (omni)bus

Onanie [onaˈniː] *f* masturbation; **o~ren** *vi* to masturbate

Onkel [ˈɔŋkəl] **(-s, -)** *m* uncle

Opa [ˈoːpa] **(-s, -s)** (*umg*) *m* grandpa

Oper [ˈoːpər] **(-, -n)** *f* opera; opera house

Operation [operatsiˈoːn] *f* operation; **~ssaal** *m* operating theatre

Operette [opeˈrɛtə] *f* operetta

operieren [opeˈriːrən] *vt* to operate on ♦ *vi* to operate

Opern- *zW*: **~glas** *nt* opera glasses *pl*; **~haus** *nt* opera house

Opfer [ˈɔpfər] **(-s, -)** *nt* sacrifice; (*Mensch*) victim; **o~n** *vt* to sacrifice; **~ung** *f* sacrifice

opponieren |ɔpoˈniːrən| *vi*: **gegen jdn/etw ~** to oppose sb/sth

Opportunist |ɔpɔrtuˈnɪst| *m* opportunist

Opposition |ɔpozitsiˈoːn| *f* opposition; **o~ell** *adj* opposing

Optik |ˈɔptɪk| *f* optics *sg*; **~er** (**-s, -**) *m* optician

optimal |ɔptiˈmaːl| *adj* optimal, optimum

Optimismus |ɔptiˈmɪsmʊs| *m* optimism

Optimist |ɔptiˈmɪst| *m* optimist; **o~isch** *adj* optimistic

optisch |ˈɔptɪʃ| *adj* optical

Orakel |oˈraːkəl| (**-s, -**) *nt* oracle

oral |oˈraːl| *adj* (*MED*) oral

Orange |oˈrãːʒə| *f* orange; **o~** *adj* orange; **~ade** |orãˈʒaːdə| *f* orangeade; **~at** |orãˈʒaːt| (**-s, -e**) *nt* candied peel

Orchester |ɔrˈkɛstər| (**-s, -**) *nt* orchestra

Orchidee |ɔrçiˈdeːə| *f* orchid

Orden |ˈɔrdən| (**-s, -**) *m* (*ECCL*) order; (*MIL*) decoration; **~sschwester** *f* nun

ordentlich |ˈɔrdəntlɪç| *adj* (*anständig*) decent, respectable; (*geordnet*) tidy, neat; (*umg: annehmbar*) not bad; (: *tüchtig*) real, proper ♦ *adv* properly; **~er Professor** (full) professor; **O~keit** *f* respectability; tidiness, neatness

ordinär |ɔrdiˈnɛːr| *adj* common, vulgar

ordnen |ˈɔrdnən| *vt* to order, to put in order

Ordner (**-s, -**) *m* steward; (*COMM*) file

Ordnung *f* order; (*Ordnen*) ordering; (*Geordnetsein*) tidiness; **~ machen** to tidy up; **in ~!** okay!

Ordnungs- *zW*: **o~gemäß** *adj* proper, according to the rules; **o~liebend** *adj* orderly, methodical; **~strafe** *f* fine; **o~widrig** *adj* contrary to the rules, irregular; **~widrigkeit** |-vɪdrɪçkaɪt| *f* infringement (*of law or rule*); **~zahl** *f* ordinal number

Organ |ɔrˈgaːn| (**-s, -e**) *nt* organ; (*Stimme*) voice; **~isation** |-izatsiˈoːn| *f* organization; **~isator** |-iˈzaːtɔr| *m* organizer; **o~isch** *adj* organic; **o~isieren** |-iˈziːrən| *vt* to organize, to arrange; (*umg: beschaffen*) to acquire ♦ *vr* to organize; **~ismus** |-ˈnɪsmʊs| *m* organism; **~ist** |-ˈnɪst| *m* organist; **~spende** *f* organ donation; **~spenderausweis** *m* donor card

Orgasmus |ɔrˈgasmʊs| *m* orgasm

Orgel |ˈɔrgəl| (**-, -n**) *f* organ

Orgie |ˈɔrgiə| *f* orgy

Orient |ˈoːriɛnt| (**-s**) *m* Orient, east; **o~alisch** |-ˈtaːlɪʃ| *adj* oriental

orientier- *zW*: **~en** |-ˈtiːrən| *vt* (*örtlich*) to locate; (*fig*) to inform ♦ *vr* to find one's way *od* bearings; to inform o.s.; **O~ung** |-ˈtiːrʊŋ| *f* orientation; (*fig*) information; **O~ungssinn** *m* sense of direction; **O~ungsstufe** *f* period during which pupils are selected for different schools

original |origiˈnaːl| *adj* original; **O~** (**-s, -e**) *nt* original; **O~fassung** *f* original version;

O~iˈtät *f* originality

originell |origiˈnɛl| *adj* original

Orkan |ɔrˈkaːn| (**-(e)s, -e**) *m* hurricane; **o~artig** *adj* (*Wind*) gale-force; (*Beifall*) thunderous

Ornament |ɔrnaˈmɛnt| *nt* decoration, ornament; **o~al** |-ˈtaːl| *adj* decorative, ornamental

Ort |ɔrt| (**-(e)s, -e** *od* **˜er**) *m* place; **an ~ und Stelle** on the spot; **o~en** *vt* to locate

ortho- |ɔrto| *zW*: **~dox** |-ˈdɔks| *adj* orthodox; **O~grafie** |-graˈfiː| ▲ *f* spelling, orthography; **~grafisch** ▲ *adj* orthographic; **O~päde** |-ˈpɛːdə| (**-n, -n**) *m* orthopaedist; **O~pädie** |-pɛˈdiː| *f* orthopaedics *sg*; **~ˈpädisch** *adj* orthopaedic

örtlich |ˈœrtlɪç| *adj* local; **Ö~keit** *f* locality

ortsansässig *adj* local

Ortschaft *f* village, small town

Orts- *zW*: **o~fremd** *adj* non-local; **~gespräch** *nt* local (phone)call; **~name** *m* place name; **~netz** *nt* (*TEL*) local telephone exchange area; **~tarif** *m* (*TEL*) tariff for local calls; **~zeit** *f* local time

Ortung *f* locating

Öse |ˈøːzə| *f* loop, eye

Ost'asien |ɔsˈtaːziən| *nt* Eastern Asia

Osten |ˈɔstən| (**-s**) *m* east

Oster- |ˈɔːstər| *zW*: **~ei** *nt* Easter egg; **~fest** *nt* Easter; **~glocke** *f* daffodil; **~hase** *m* Easter bunny; **~montag** *m* Easter Monday; **~n** (**-s, -**) *nt* Easter

Österreich |ˈøːstəraɪç| (**-s**) *nt* Austria; **~er(in)** (**-s, -**) *m(f)* Austrian; **ö~isch** *adj* Austrian

Ostküste *f* east coast

östlich |ˈœstlɪç| *adj* eastern, easterly

Ostsee *f*: **die ~** the Baltic (Sea)

Ouvertüre |uvɛrˈtyːrə| *f* overture

oval |oˈvaːl| *adj* oval

Ovation |ovatsiˈoːn| *f* ovation

Oxid, Oxyd |ɔˈksyːt| (**-(e)s, -e**) *nt* oxide; **o~ieren** *vt, vi* to oxidize; **~ierung** *f* oxidization

Ozean |ˈoːtseaːn| (**-s, -e**) *m* ocean; **~dampfer** *m* (ocean-going) liner

Ozon |oˈtsoːn| (**-s**) *nt* ozone; **~loch** *nt* ozone hole; **~schicht** *f* ozone layer

P, p

Paar |paːr| (**-(e)s, -e**) *nt* pair; (*Ehepaar*) couple; **ein p~** a few; **ein p~ Mal** a few times; **p~en** *vt, vr* to couple; (*Tiere*) to mate; **~lauf** *m* pair skating; **~ung** *f* combination; mating; **p~weise** *adv* in pairs; in couples

Pacht |paxt| (**-, -en**) *f* lease; **p~en** *vt* to lease

Pächter |ˈpɛçtər| (**-s, -**) *m* leaseholder, tenant

Pack¹ |pak| (**-(e)s, -e** *od* **˜e**) *m* bundle, pack

Pack² |pak| (**-(e)s**) *nt* (*pej*) mob, rabble

Päckchen |ˈpɛkçən| *nt* small package;

(*Zigaretten*) packet; (*Postpäckchen*) small parcel

Pack- zW: **p~en** vt to pack; (*fassen*) to grasp, to seize; (*umg: schaffen*) to manage; (*fig: fesseln*) to grip; **~en** (-s, -) m bundle; (*fig: Menge*) heaps of ; **~esel** m (*auch fig*) packhorse; **~papier** nt brown paper, wrapping paper; **~ung** f packet; (*Pralinenpackung*) box; (*MED*) compress; **~ungsbeilage** f enclosed instructions pl for use

Pädagog- [pɛdaˈgoːg] zW: **~e** (-n, -n) m teacher; **~ik** f education; **p~isch** adj educational, pedagogical

Paddel [ˈpadəl] (-s, -) nt paddle; **~boot** nt canoe; **p~n** vi to paddle

Page [ˈpaːʒə] (-n, -n) m page

Paket [paˈkeːt] (-(e)s, -e) nt packet; (*Postpaket*) parcel; **~karte** f dispatch note; **~post** f parcel post; **~schalter** m parcels counter

Pakt [pakt] (-(e)s, -e) m pact

Palast [paˈlast] (-es, **Paläste**) m palace

Palästina [palɛˈstiːna] (-s) nt Palestine

Palme [ˈpalmə] f palm (tree)

Pampelmuse [ˈpampəlmuːzə] f grapefruit

panieren [paˈniːrən] vt (*KOCH*) to bread

Paniermehl [paˈniːrmeːl] nt breadcrumbs pl

Panik [ˈpaːnɪk] f panic

panisch [ˈpaːnɪʃ] adj panic-stricken

Panne [ˈpanə] f (*AUT etc*) breakdown; (*Missgeschick*) slip; **~nhilfe** f breakdown service

panschen [ˈpanʃən] vi to splash about ♦ vt to water down

Pantoffel [panˈtɔfəl] (-s, -n) m slipper

Pantomime [pantoˈmiːmə] f mime

Panzer [ˈpantsər] (-s, -) m armour; (*Platte*) armour plate; (*Fahrzeug*) tank; **~glas** nt bulletproof glass; **p~n** vt to armour ♦ vr (fig) to arm o.s.

Papa [paˈpa:] (-s, -s) (*umg*) m dad, daddy

Papagei [papaˈgai] (-s, -en) m parrot

Papier [paˈpiːr] (-s, -e) nt paper; (*Wertpapier*) security; **~fabrik** f paper mill; **~geld** nt paper money; **~korb** m wastepaper basket; **~taschentuch** nt tissue

Papp- [ˈpap] zW: **~deckel** m cardboard; **~e** f cardboard; **~el** (-, -n) f poplar; **p~en** (*umg*) vt, vi to stick; **p~ig** adj sticky

Paprika [ˈpaprika] (-s, -s) m (*Gewürz*) paprika; (*~schote*) pepper

Papst [pa:pst] (-(e)s, ⁼e) m pope

päpstlich [ˈpɛːpstlɪç] adj papal

Parabel [paˈraːbəl] (-, -n) f parable; (*MATH*) parabola

Parabolantenne [paraboˈlantɛnə] f satellite dish

Parade [paˈraːdə] f (*MIL*) parade, review;

(*SPORT*) parry

Paradies [paraˈdiːs] (-es, -e) nt paradise; **p~isch** adj heavenly

Paradox [paraˈdɔks] (-es, -e) nt paradox; **p~** adj paradoxical

Paragraf ▲ [paraˈgraːf] (-en, -en) m paragraph; (*JUR*) section

parallel [paraˈleːl] adj parallel; **P~e** f parallel

Parasit [paraˈziːt] (-en, -en) m (*auch fig*) parasite

parat [paˈraːt] adj ready

Pärchen [ˈpɛːrçən] nt couple

Parfüm [parˈfyːm] (-s, -s od -e) nt perfume; **~erie** [-əˈriː] f perfumery; **p~frei** adj non-perfumed; **p~ieren** vt to scent, to perfume

parieren [paˈriːrən] vt to parry ♦ vi (*umg*) to obey

Paris [paˈriːs] (-) nt Paris; **~er** adj Parisian ♦ m Parisian; **~erin** f Parisian

Park [park] (-s, -s) m park; **~anlage** f park; (*um Gebäude*) grounds pl; **p~en** vt, vi to park; **~ett** (-(e)s, -e) nt parquet (floor); (*THEAT*) stalls pl; **~gebühr** f parking fee; **~haus** nt multi-storey car park; **~lücke** f parking space; **~platz** m parking place; car park, parking lot (*US*); **~scheibe** f parking disc; **~schein** m car park ticket; **~uhr** f parking meter; **~verbot** nt parking ban

Parlament [parlaˈmɛnt] nt parliament; **~arier** [-ˈtaːriər] (-s, -) m parliamentarian; **p~arisch** [-ˈtaːrɪʃ] adj parliamentary

Parlaments- zW: **~beschluss** ▲ m vote of parliament; **~mitglied** nt member of parliament; **~sitzung** f sitting (of parliament)

Parodie [paroˈdiː] f parody; **p~ren** vt to parody

Parole [paˈroːlə] f password; (*Wahlspruch*) motto

Partei [parˈtai] f party; **~ ergreifen für jdn** to take sb's side; **p~isch** adj partial, bias(s)ed; **p~los** adj neutral, impartial; **~mitglied** nt party member; **~programm** nt (party) manifesto; **~tag** m party conference

Parterre [parˈtɛr] (-s, -s) nt ground floor; (*THEAT*) stalls pl

Partie [parˈtiː] f part; (*Spiel*) game; (*Ausflug*) outing; (*Mann, Frau*) catch; (*COMM*) lot; **mit von der ~ sein** to join in

Partizip [partiˈtsiːp] (-s, -ien) nt participle

Partner(in) [ˈpartnər(ɪn)] (-s, -) m(f) partner; **~schaft** f partnership; (*von Städten*) twinning; **p~schaftlich** adj as partners; **~stadt** f twin town

Party [ˈpaːrti] (-, -s od **Parties**) f party

Pass ▲ [pas] (-es, ⁼e) m pass; (*Ausweis*) passport

passabel [paˈsaːbəl] adj passable, reasonable

Passage [paˈsaːʒə] f passage

Passagier |pasa'ʒi:r| (-s, -e) *m* passenger;
~**flugzeug** *nt* airliner
Passamt ▲ *nt* passport office
Passant |pa'sant| *m* passer-by
Passbild ▲ *nt* passport photograph
passen |'pasən| *vi* to fit; (*Farbe*) to go; (*auf
Frage, KARTEN, SPORT*) to pass; **das passt mir
nicht** that doesn't suit me; ~ **zu** (*Farbe,
Kleider*) to go with; **er passt nicht zu dir**
he's not right for you; ~**d** *adj* suitable;
(*zusammenpassend*) matching; (*angebracht*)
fitting; (*Zeit*) convenient
passier- |pa'si:r| *zW:* ~**bar** *adj* passable; ~**en**
vt to pass; (*durch Sieb*) to strain ♦ *vi* to
happen; **P~schein** *m* pass, permit
Passion |pasi'o:n| *f* passion; **p~iert** |-'ni:rt|
adj enthusiastic, passionate; ~**sspiel** *nt*
Passion Play
passiv |'pasi:f| *adj* passive; **P~** (-s, -e) *nt*
passive; **P~a** *pl* (*COMM*) liabilities; **P~i'tät** *f*
passiveness; **P~rauchen** *nt* passive smoking
Pass- ▲ *zW:* ~**kontrolle** ▲ *f* passport
control; ~**stelle** ▲ *f* passport office;
~**straße** ▲ *f* (mountain) pass
Paste |'pastə| *f* paste
Pastete |pas'te:tə| *f* pie
pasteurisieren |pastøri'zi:rən| *vt* to
pasteurize
Pastor |'pastɔr| *m* vicar; pastor, minister
Pate |'pa:tə| (-n, -n) *m* godfather; ~**nkind** *nt*
godchild
Patent |pa'tent| (-(e)s, -e) *nt* patent; (*MIL*)
commission; **p~** *adj* clever; ~**amt** *nt* patent
office
Patentante *f* godmother
patentieren |paten'ti:rən| *vt* to patent
Patentinhaber *m* patentee
pathetisch |pa'te:tɪʃ| *adj* emotional;
bombastic
Pathologe |pato'lo:gə| (-n, -n) *m* pathologist
pathologisch *adj* pathological
Pathos |'pa:tɔs| (-) *nt* emotiveness,
emotionalism
Patient(in) |patsi'ent(ɪn)| *m(f)* patient
Patin |'pa:tɪn| *f* godmother
Patriot |patri'o:t| (-en, -en) *m* patriot;
p~isch *adj* patriotic; ~**ismus** |-'tɪsmʊs| *m*
patriotism
Patrone |pa'tro:nə| *f* cartridge
Patrouille |pa'troljə| *f* patrol
patrouillieren |patrol'ji:rən| *vi* to patrol
patsch |patʃ| *excl* splash; **P~e** (*umg*) *f*
(*Bedrängnis*) mess, jam; ~**en** *vi* to smack, to
slap; (*im Wasser*) to splash; ~**nass** ▲ *adj*
soaking wet
patzig |'patsɪç| (*umg*) *adj* cheeky, saucy
Pauke |'paukə| *f* kettledrum; **auf die ~ hauen**
to live it up
pauken *vt* (*intensiv lernen*) to swot up (*inf*)
♦ *vi* to swot (*inf*), cram (*inf*)
pausbäckig |'pausbɛkɪç| *adj* chubby-

cheeked
pauschal |pau'ʃa:l| *adj* (*Kosten*) inclusive;
(*Urteil*) sweeping; **P~e** *f* flat rate; **P~gebühr**
f flat rate; **P~preis** *m* all-in price; **P~reise** *f*
package tour; **P~summe** *f* lump sum
Pause |'pauzə| *f* break; (*THEAT*) interval;
(*Innehalten*) pause; (*Kopie*) tracing
pausen *vt* to trace; ~**los** *adj* non-stop;
P~zeichen *nt* call sign; (*MUS*) rest
Pauspapier |'pauspapi:r| *nt* tracing paper
Pavillon |'paviljõ| (-s, -s) *m* pavilion
Pazif- |pa'tsi:f| *zW:* ~**ik** (-s) *m* Pacific;
p~istisch *adj* pacifist
Pech |pɛç| (-s, -e) *nt* pitch; (*fig*) bad luck; ~
haben to be unlucky; **p~schwarz** *adj* pitch-
black; ~**strähne** (*umg*) *m* unlucky patch;
~**vogel** (*umg*) *m* unlucky person
Pedal |pe'da:l| (-s, -e) *nt* pedal
Pedant |pe'dant| *m* pedant; ~**e'rie** *f*
pedantry; **p~isch** *adj* pedantic
Pediküre |pedi'ky:rə| *f* (*Fußpflege*) pedicure
Pegel |'pe:gəl| (-s, -) *m* water gauge; ~**stand**
m water level
peilen |'pailən| *vt* to get a fix on
Pein |pain| (-) *f* agony, pain; **p~igen** *vt* to
torture; (*plagen*) to torment; **p~lich** *adj*
(*unangenehm*) embarrassing, awkward,
painful; (*genau*) painstaking
Peitsche |'paitʃə| *f* whip; **p~n** *vt* to whip;
(*Regen*) to lash
Pelle |'pɛlə| *f* skin; **p~n** *vt* to skin, to peel
Pellkartoffeln *pl* jacket potatoes
Pelz |pɛlts| (-es, -e) *m* fur
Pendel |'pɛndəl| (-s, -) *nt* pendulum; **p~n** *vi*
(*Zug, Fähre etc*) to operate a shuttle service;
(*Mensch*) to commute; ~**verkehr** *m* shuttle
traffic; (*für Pendler*) commuter traffic
Pendler |'pɛndlər| (-s, -) *m* commuter
penetrant |pene'trant| *adj* sharp; (*Person*)
pushing
Penis |'pe:nɪs| (-, -se) *m* penis
pennen |'pɛnən| (*umg*) *vi* to kip
Penner (*umg*: *pej*) *m* (*Landstreicher*) tramp
Pension |pɛnzi'o:n| *f* (*Geld*) pension;
(*Ruhestand*) retirement; (*für Gäste*) boarding
od guesthouse; ~**är(in)** |-'nɛːr(ɪn)| (-s, -e)
m(f) pensioner; **p~ieren** *vt* to pension off;
p~iert *adj* retired; ~**ierung** *f* retirement;
~**sgast** *m* boarder, paying guest
Pensum |'pɛnzʊm| (-s, **Pensen**) *nt* quota;
(*SCH*) curriculum
per |pɛr| *präp* +*akk* by, per; (*pro*) per; (*bis*) by
Perfekt |'pɛrfɛkt| (-(e)s, -e) *nt* perfect; **p~**
adj perfect
perforieren |pɛrfo'ri:rən| *vt* to perforate
Pergament |pɛrga'mɛnt| *nt* parchment;
~**papier** *nt* greaseproof paper
Periode |peri'o:də| *f* period; **periodisch** *adj*
periodic; (*dezimal*) recurring
Perle |'pɛrlə| *f* (*auch fig*) pearl; **p~n** *vi* to
sparkle; (*Tropfen*) to trickle

Perl- |'pɛrl| zW: **~mutt (-s)** nt mother-of-pearl; **~wein** m sparkling wine

perplex |pɛr'plɛks| adj dumbfounded

Person |pɛr'zoːn| (-, **-en**) f person; **ich für meine ~** ... personally I ...

Personal |pɛrzo'naːl| (-s) nt personnel; (Bedienung) servants pl; **~ausweis** m identity card; **~computer** m personal computer; **~ien** |-iən| pl particulars; **~mangel** m undermanning; **~pronomen** nt personal pronoun

personell |pɛrzo'nɛl| adj (Veränderungen) personnel

Personen- zW: **~aufzug** m lift, elevator (US); **~kraftwagen** m private motorcar; **~schaden** m injury to persons; **~zug** m stopping train; passenger train

personifizieren |pɛrzonifi'tsiːrən| vt to personify

persönlich |pɛr'zøːnlɪç| adj personal ♦ adv in person; personally; **P~keit** f personality

Perspektive |pɛrspɛk'tiːvə| f perspective

Perücke |pe'rʏkə| f wig

pervers |pɛr'vɛrs| adj perverse

Pessimismus |pɛsi'mɪsmʊs| m pessimism

Pessimist |pɛsi'mɪst| m pessimist; **p~isch** adj pessimistic

Pest |pɛst| (-) f plague

Petersilie |petər'ziːliə| f parsley

Petroleum |pe'troːleʊm| (-s) nt paraffin, kerosene (US)

Pfad |pfaːt| (-(e)s, **-e**) m path; **~finder (-s, -)** m boy scout; **~finderin** f girl guide

Pfahl |pfaːl| (-(e)s, ⸗e) m post, stake

Pfand |pfant| (-(e)s, ⸗er) nt pledge, security; (Flaschenpfand) deposit; (im Spiel) forfeit; **~brief** m bond

pfänden |'pfɛndən| vt to seize, to distrain

Pfänderspiel nt game of forfeits

Pfandflasche f returnable bottle

Pfandschein m pawn ticket

Pfändung |'pfɛndʊŋ| f seizure, distraint

Pfanne |'pfanə| f (frying) pan

Pfannkuchen m pancake; (Berliner) doughnut

Pfarr- |'pfar| zW: **~ei** f parish; **~er (-s, -)** m priest; (evangelisch) vicar; minister; **~haus** nt vicarage; manse

Pfau |pfaʊ| (-(e)s, **-en**) m peacock; **~enauge** nt peacock butterfly

Pfeffer |'pfɛfər| (-s, -) m pepper; **~kuchen** m gingerbread; **~minz (-es, -e)** nt peppermint; **~mühle** f pepper mill; **p~n** vt to pepper; (umg: werfen) to fling; **gepfefferte Preise/Witze** steep prices/spicy jokes

Pfeife |'pfaɪfə| f whistle; (Tabakpfeife, Orgelpfeife) pipe; **p~n** (unreg) vt, vi to whistle; **~r (-s, -)** m piper

Pfeil |pfaɪl| (-(e)s, **-e**) m arrow

Pfeiler |'pfaɪlər| (-s, -) m pillar, prop; (Brückenpfeiler) pier

Pfennig |'pfɛnɪç| (-(e)s, **-e**) m pfennig (hundredth part of a mark)

Pferd |pfeːrt| (-(e)s, **-e**) nt horse

Pferde- |'pfeːrdə| zW: **~rennen** nt horse race; horse racing; **~schwanz** m (Frisur) ponytail; **~stall** m stable

Pfiff |pfɪf| (-(e)s, **-e**) m whistle

Pfifferling |'pfɪfərlɪŋ| m yellow chanterelle (mushroom); **keinen ~ wert** not worth a thing

pfiffig adj sly, sharp

Pfingsten |'pfɪŋstən| (-, -) nt Whitsun (BRIT), Pentecost

Pfirsich |'pfɪrzɪç| (-s, **-e**) m peach

Pflanz- |'pflants| zW: **~e** f plant; **p~en** vt to plant; **~enfett** nt vegetable fat; **p~lich** adj vegetable; **~ung** f plantation

Pflaster |'pflastər| (-s, -) nt plaster; (Straße) pavement; **p~n** vt to pave; **~stein** m paving stone

Pflaume |'pflaʊmə| f plum

Pflege |'pfleːgə| f care; (von Idee) cultivation; (Krankenpflege) nursing; **in ~ sein** (Kind) to be fostered out; **p~bedürftig** adj needing care; **~eltern** pl foster parents; **~heim** nt nursing home; **~kind** nt foster child; **p~leicht** adj easy-care; **~mutter** f foster mother; **p~n** vt to look after; (Kranke) to nurse; (Beziehungen) to foster; **~r (-s, -)** m orderly; male nurse; **~rin** f nurse, attendant; **~vater** m foster father

Pflicht |pflɪçt| (-, **-en**) f duty; (SPORT) compulsory section; **p~bewusst ▲** adj conscientious; **~fach** nt (SCH) compulsory subject; **~gefühl** nt sense of duty; **p~gemäß** adj dutiful ♦ adv as in duty bound; **~versicherung** f compulsory insurance

pflücken |'pflʏkən| vt to pick; (Blumen) to pick, to pluck

Pflug |pfluːk| (-(e)s, ⸗e) m plough

pflügen |'pflyːgən| vt to plough

Pforte |'pfɔrtə| f gate; door

Pförtner |'pfœrtnər| (-s, -) m porter, doorkeeper, doorman

Pfosten |'pfɔstən| (-s, -) m post

Pfote |'pfoːtə| f paw; (umg: Schrift) scrawl ·

Pfropfen (-s, -) m (Flaschenpfropfen) stopper; (Blutpfropfen) clot

pfui |pfʊi| excl ugh!

Pfund |pfʊnt| (-(e)s, **-e**) nt pound

pfuschen |'pfʊʃən| (umg) vi to be sloppy; **jdm ins Handwerk ~** to interfere in sb's business

Pfuscher |'pfʊʃər| (-s, -) (umg) m sloppy worker; (Kurpfuscher) quack; **~ei** (umg) f

sloppy work; quackery
Pfütze |'pfʏtsə| f puddle
Phänomen |feno'me:n| (-s, -e) nt
phenomenon; **p~al** |-'na:l| adj phenomenal
Phantasie etc △ |fanta'zi:| = **Fantasie** etc
phantastisch △ |fan'tastıʃ| adj = **fantastisch**
Phase |'fa:zə| f phase
Philologie |filolo'gi:| f philology
Philosoph |filo'zo:f| (-en, -en) m
philosopher; **~ie** |-'fi:| f philosophy; **p~isch**
adj philosophical
phlegmatisch |flɛ'gma:tıʃ| adj lethargic
Phonetik |fo'ne:tık| f phonetics sg
phonetisch adj phonetic
Phosphor |'fɔsfɔr| (-s) m phosphorus
Photo etc |'fo:to| (-s, -s) nt = **Foto** etc
Phrase |'fra:zə| f phrase; (pej) hollow phrase
pH-Wert |pe:'ha:vɛːrt| m pH-value
Physik |fy'zi:k| f physics sg; **p~alisch**
|-'ka:lıʃ| adj of physics; **~er(in)** |'fy:zıkər(ın)|
(-s, -) m(f) physicist
Physiologie |fyziolo'gi:| f physiology
physisch |'fy:zıʃ| adj physical
Pianist(in) |pia'nıst(ın)| m(f) pianist
Pickel |'pıkəl| (-s, -) m pimple; (Werkzeug)
pickaxe; (Bergpickel) ice axe; **p~ig** adj
pimply, spotty
picken |'pıkən| vi to pick, to peck
Picknick |'pıknık| (-s, -e od -s) nt picnic; **~
machen** to have a picnic
piepen |'pi:pən| vi to chirp
piepsen |'pi:psən| vi to chirp
Piepser (umg) m pager, paging device
Pier |pi:ər| (-s, -s od -e) m od f pier
Pietät |pie'tɛːt| f piety, reverence; **p~los** adj
impious, irreverent
Pigment |pıg'mɛnt| nt pigment
Pik |pi:k| (-s, -s) nt (KARTEN) spades
pikant |pi'kant| adj spicy, piquant;
(anzüglich) suggestive
Pilger |'pılgər| (-s, -) m pilgrim; **~fahrt** f
pilgrimage
Pille |'pılə| f pill
Pilot |pi'lo:t| (-en, -en) m pilot
Pilz |pılts| (-es, -e) m fungus; (essbar)
mushroom; (giftig) toadstool; **~krankheit** f
fungal disease
Pinguin |'pınguiːn| (-s, -e) m penguin
Pinie |'pi:niə| f pine
pinkeln |'pınkəln| (umg) vi to pee
Pinnwand |'pınvant| f noticeboard
Pinsel |'pınzəl| (-s, -) m paintbrush
Pinzette |pın'tsɛtə| f tweezers pl
Pionier |pio'ni:r| (-s, -e) m pioneer; (MIL)
sapper, engineer
Pirat |pi'ra:t| (-en, -en) m pirate
Piste |'pıstə| f (SKI) run, piste; (AVIAT) runway
Pistole |pıs'to:lə| f pistol
Pizza |'pıtsa| (-, -s) f pizza
Pkw |pe:ka:'ve:| (-(s), -(s)) m abk = **Perso-**

nenkraftwagen
plädieren |plɛ'di:rən| vi to plead
Plädoyer |plɛdoa'je:| (-s, -s) nt speech for
the defence; (fig) plea
Plage |'pla:gə| f plague; (Mühe) nuisance;
~geist m pest, nuisance; **p~n** vt to torment
♦ vr to toil, to slave
Plakat |pla'ka:t| (-(e)s, -e) nt placard; poster
Plan |pla:n| (-(e)s, ⁼e) m plan; (Karte) map
Plane f tarpaulin
planen vt to plan; (Mord etc) to plot
Planer (-s, -) m planner
Planet |pla'ne:t| (-en, -en) m planet
planieren |pla'ni:rən| vt to plane, to level
Planke |'plankə| f plank
plan- |'pla:n| zW: **~los** adj (Vorgehen)
unsystematic; (Umherlaufen) aimless;
~mäßig adj according to plan; systematic;
(EISENB) scheduled
Plansoll (-s) nt output target
Plantage |plan'ta:ʒə| f plantation
Plan(t)schbecken |'plan(t)ʃbɛkən| nt
paddling pool
plan(t)schen |'plan(t)ʃən| vi to splash
Planung f planning
Planwirtschaft f planned economy
plappern |'plapərn| vi to chatter
plärren |'plɛrən| vi (Mensch) to cry, to whine;
(Radio) to blare
Plasma |'plasma| (-s, **Plasmen**) nt plasma
Plastik¹ |'plastık| f sculpture
Plastik² |'plastık| (-s) nt (Kunststoff) plastic;
~beutel m plastic bag, carrier bag; **~folie** f
plastic film
plastisch |'plastıʃ| adj plastic; **stell dir das ~
vor!** just picture it!
Platane |pla'ta:nə| f plane (tree)
Platin |'pla:ti:n| (-s) nt platinum
platonisch |pla'to:nıʃ| adj platonic
platsch |platʃ| excl splash; **~en** vi to splash
plätschern |'plɛtʃərn| vi to babble
platschnass ▲ adj drenched
platt |plat| adj flat; (umg: überrascht)
flabbergasted; (fig: geistlos) flat, boring;
~deutsch adj low German; **P~e** f
(Speisenplatte, PHOT, TECH) plate;
(Steinplatte) flag; (Kachel) tile; (Schallplatte)
record; **P~enspieler** m record player;
P~enteller m turntable
Platz |plats| (-es, ⁼e) m place; (Sitzplatz) seat;
(Raum) space, room; (in Stadt) square;
(Sportplatz) playing field; **~ nehmen** to take
a seat; **jdm ~ machen** to make room for sb;
~angst f claustrophobia; **~anweiser(in)**
(-s, -) m(f) usher(ette)
Plätzchen |'plɛtsçən| nt spot; (Gebäck)
biscuit
platzen vi to burst; (Bombe) to explode; **vor
Wut ~** (umg) to be bursting with anger
platzieren ▲ |pla'tsi:rən| vt to place ♦ vr
(SPORT) to be placed; (TENNIS) to be seeded

Platz- *zW:* **~karte** *f* seat reservation;
~mangel *m* lack of space; **~patrone** *f*
blank cartridge; **~regen** *m* downpour;
~reservierung |-rezεrvi:roŋ] *f* seat
reservation; **~wunde** *f* cut
Plauderei [plaodə'raı] *f* chat, conversation;
(*RAD*) talk
plaudern |'plaodərn] *vi* to chat, to talk
plausibel [plao'zi:bəl] *adj* plausible
plazieren △ |pla'tsi:rən] *vt, vr* = **platzieren**
Pleite ['plaıtə] *f* bankruptcy; (*umg: Reinfall*)
flop; **~ machen** to go bust; **p~** (*umg*) *adj*
broke
Plenum ['ple:nom] **(-s)** *nt* plenum
Plombe ['plɔmbə] *f* lead seal; (*Zahnplombe*)
filling
plombieren [plɔm'bi:rən] *vt* to seal; (*Zahn*)
to fill
plötzlich ['plœtslıç] *adj* sudden ♦ *adv*
suddenly
plump [plump] *adj* clumsy; (*Hände*) coarse;
(*Körper*) shapeless; **~sen** (*umg*) *vi* to plump
down, to fall
Plunder ['plondər] **(-s)** *m* rubbish
plündern ['plʏndərn] *vt* to plunder; (*Stadt*)
to sack ♦ *vi* to plunder; **Plünderung** *f*
plundering, sack, pillage
Plural ['plu:ra:l] **(-s, -e)** *m* plural; **p~istisch**
adj pluralistic
Plus [plos] **(-, -)** *nt* plus; (*FIN*) profit; (*Vorteil*)
advantage; **p~** *adv* plus
Plüsch [ply:ʃ] **(-(e)s, -e)** *m* plush
Plus- [plos] *zW:* **~pol** *m* (*ELEK*) positive pole;
~punkt *m* point; (*fig*) point in sb's favour
Plutonium [plu'to:niom] **(-s)** *nt* plutonium
PLZ *abk* = **Postleitzahl**
Po [po:] **(-s, -s)** (*umg*) *m* bottom, bum
Pöbel ['pø:bal] **(-s)** *m* mob, rabble; **~ei** *f*
vulgarity; **p~haft** *adj* low, vulgar
pochen ['pɔxən] *vi* to knock; (*Herz*) to
pound; **auf etw** *akk* **~** (*fig*) to insist on sth
Pocken ['pɔkən] *pl* smallpox *sg*
Podium ['po:diom] *nt* podium;
~sdiskussion *f* panel discussion
Poesie [poe'zi:] *f* poetry
Poet [po'e:t] **(-en, -en)** *m* poet; **p~isch** *adj*
poetic
Pointe [po'ɛ:tə] *f* point
Pokal [po'ka:l] **(-s, -e)** *m* goblet; (*SPORT*) cup;
~spiel *nt* cup tie
pökeln ['pø:kəln] *vt* to pickle, to salt
Poker ['po:kər] **(-s)** *nt od m* poker
Pol [po:l] **(-s, -e)** *m* pole; **p~ar** *adj* polar;
~arkreis *m* Arctic circle
Pole ['po:lə] **(-n, -n)** *m* Pole
polemisch [po:le:mıʃ] *adj* polemical
Polen ['po:lən] **(-s)** *nt* Poland
Police [po'li:s(ə)] *f* insurance policy
Polier [po'li:r] **(-s, -e)** *m* foreman

polieren *vt* to polish
Poliklinik [poli'kli:nık] *f* outpatients
(department) *sg*
Polin *f* Pole
Politik [poli'ti:k] *f* politics *sg*; (*eine bestimmte*)
policy; **~er(in)** |poli'ti:kər(ın)] **(-s, -)** *m(f)*
politician
politisch [po'li:tıʃ] *adj* political
Politur |poli'tu:r] *f* polish
Polizei [poli'tsaı] *f* police; **~beamte(r)** *m*
police officer; **p~lich** *adj* police; **sich p~lich
melden** to register with the police; **~revier**
nt police station; **~staat** *m* police state;
~streife *f* police patrol; **~stunde** *f* closing
time; **~wache** *f* police station
Polizist(in) [poli'tsıst(ın)] **(-en, -en)** *m(f)*
policeman(-woman)
Pollen ['pɔlən] **(-s, -)** *m* pollen; **~flug** *m*
pollen count
polnisch ['pɔlnıʃ] *adj* Polish
Polohemd ['po:lohεmt] *nt* polo shirt
Polster ['pɔlstər] **(-s, -)** *nt* cushion;
(*Polsterung*) upholstery; (*in Kleidung*)
padding; (*fig: Geld*) reserves *pl*; **~er (-s, -)** *m*
upholsterer; **~möbel** *pl* upholstered
furniture *sg*; **p~n** *vt* to upholster; to pad
Polterabend ['pɔltərɑ:bənt] *m* party on eve
of wedding
poltern *vi* (*Krach machen*) to crash;
(*schimpfen*) to rant
Polyp [po'ly:p] **(-en, -en)** *m* polyp; (*umg*)
cop; **~en** *pl* (*MED*) adenoids
Pomade [po'ma:də] *f* pomade
Pommes frites [pɔm'frıt] *pl* chips, French
fried potatoes
Pomp [pɔmp] **(-(e)s)** *m* pomp; **p~ös**
|pɔm'pø:s] *adj* (*Auftritt, Fest, Haus*)
ostentatious, showy
Pony ['pɔni] **(-s, -s)** *nt* (*Pferd*) pony ♦ *m*
(*Frisur*) fringe
Popmusik ['pɔpmuzi:k] *f* pop music
Popo [po'po:] **(-s, -s)** (*umg*) *m* bottom, bum
poppig ['pɔpıç] *adj* (*Farbe etc*) gaudy
populär [popu'lε:r] *adj* popular
Popularität |populari'tε:t] *f* popularity
Pore ['po:rə] *f* pore
Pornografie ▲ |pɔrnogra'fi:] *f*
pornography; **pornografisch** ▲
|pɔrno'gra:fıʃ] *adj* pornographic
porös |po'rø:s] *adj* porous
Porree ['pɔre] **(-s, -s)** *m* leek
Portal [pɔr'ta:l] **(-s, -e)** *nt* portal
Portefeuille [pɔrt(ə)'fø:j] *nt* (*POL, FIN*) portfolio
Portemonnaie [pɔrtmo'nε:] **(-s, -s)** *nt* purse
Portier [pɔrti'e:] **(-s, -s)** *m* porter
Portion [pɔrtsi'o:n] *f* portion, helping; (*umg: Anteil*) amount
Portmonee |pɔrtmo'ne:] **(-s, -s)** *nt* =
Portemonnaie

Porto ['pɔrto] (-s, -s) nt postage; **p~frei** adj
post-free, (postage) prepaid

Portrait [pɔr'trɛː] (-s, -s) nt = **Porträt**;
p~ieren vt = **porträtieren**

Porträt [pɔr'trɛː] (-s, -s) nt portrait; **p~ieren**
vt to paint, to portray

Portugal ['pɔrtugal] (-s) nt Portugal;
Portugiese [pɔrtu'giːzə] (-n, -n) m
Portuguese; **Portu'giesin** f Portuguese;
portu'giesisch adj Portuguese

Porzellan [pɔrtsɛ'laːn] (-s, -e) nt china,
porcelain; (Geschirr) china

Posaune [po'zaunə] f trombone

Pose ['poːzə] f pose

Position [pozitsi'oːn] f position

positiv ['poːzitiːf] adj positive; **P~** (-s, -e) nt
(PHOT) positive

possessiv [pɔsɛ'siːf] adj possessive;
P~pronomen (-s, -e) nt possessive
pronoun

possierlich [pɔ'siːrlɪç] adj funny

Post [pɔst] (-, -en) f post (office); (Briefe)
mail; **~amt** nt post office; **~anweisung** f
postal order, money order; **~bote** m
postman; **~en** (-s, -) m post, position;
(COMM) item; (auf Liste) entry; (MIL) sentry;
(Streikposten) picket; **~er** (-s, -(s)) nt poster;
~fach nt post office box; **~karte** f postcard;
p~lagernd adv poste restante (BRIT),
general delivery (US); **~leitzahl** f postal
code; **~scheckkonto** nt postal giro
account; **~sparbuch** nt post office savings
book; **~sparkasse** f post office savings
bank; **~stempel** nt postmark; **p~wendend**
adv by return of post; **~wertzeichen** nt
postage stamp

potent [po'tɛnt] adj potent

Potential △ [potɛntsi'aːl] (-s, -e) nt =
Potenzial

potentiell △ adj = potenziell

Potenz [po'tɛnts] f power; (eines Mannes)
potency

Potenzial ▲ [potɛntsi'aːl] (-s, -e) nt
potential

potenziell ▲ adj potential

Pracht [praxt] (-) f splendour, magnificence;
prächtig ['prɛçtɪç] adj splendid

Prachtstück nt showpiece

prachtvoll adj splendid, magnificent

Prädikat [prɛdi'kaːt] (-(e)s, -e) nt title;
(GRAM) predicate; (Zensur) distinction

prägen ['prɛːgən] vt to stamp; (Münze) to
mint; (Ausdruck) to coin; (Charakter) to form

prägnant [prɛ'gnant] adj precise, terse

Prägung ['prɛːgʊŋ] f minting, forming;
(Eigenart) character, stamp

prahlen ['praːlən] vi to boast, to brag;
Prahle'rei f boasting

Praktik ['praktɪk] f practice; **p~abel** [-'kaːbəl]
adj practicable; **~ant(in)** [-'kant(ɪn)] m(f)
trainee; **~um** (-s, Praktika od Praktiken) nt

practical training

praktisch ['praktɪʃ] adj practical, handy; **~er**
Arzt general practitioner

praktizieren [prakti'tsiːrən] vt, vi to practise

Praline [pra'liːnə] f chocolate

prall [pral] adj firmly rounded; (Segel) taut;
(Arme) plump; (Sonne) blazing; **~en** vi to
bounce, to rebound; (Sonne) to blaze

Prämie ['prɛːmiə] f premium; (Belohnung)
award, prize; **p~ren** vt to give an award to

Präparat [prɛpa'raːt] (-(e)s, -e) nt (BIOL)
preparation; (MED) medicine

Präposition [prɛpozitsi'oːn] f preposition

Prärie [prɛ'riː] f prairie

Präsens ['prɛːzɛns] (-) nt present tense

präsentieren [prɛzɛn'tiːrən] vt to present

Präservativ [prɛzɛrva'tiːf] (-s, -e) nt
contraceptive

Präsident(in) [prɛzi'dɛnt(ɪn)] m(f)
president; **~schaft** f presidency

Präsidium [prɛ'ziːdiʊm] nt presidency,
chair(manship); (Polizeipräsidium) police
headquarters pl

prasseln ['prasəln] vi (Feuer) to crackle;
(Hagel) to drum; (Wörter) to rain down

Praxis ['praksɪs] (-, Praxen) f practice;
(Behandlungsraum) surgery; (von Anwalt)
office

Präzedenzfall [prɛtsɛ'dɛnts-] m precedent

präzis [prɛ'tsiːs] adj precise; **P~ion**
[prɛtsizi'oːn] f precision

predigen ['preːdɪgən] vt, vi to preach;
Prediger (-s, -) m preacher

Predigt ['preːdɪçt] (-, -en) f sermon

Preis [prais] (-es, -e) m price; (Siegespreis)
prize; **um keinen ~** at no price;
p~bewusst ▲ adj price-conscious

Preiselbeere f cranberry

preis- ['prais] zW: **~en** (unreg) vi to praise;
~geben (unreg) vt to abandon; (opfern) to
sacrifice; (zeigen) to expose; **~gekrönt** adj
prizewinning; **P~gericht** nt jury; **~günstig**
adj inexpensive; **P~lage** f price range; **~lich**
adj (Lage, Unterschied) price, in price;
P~liste f price list; **P~richter** m judge (in a
competition); **P~schild** nt price tag;
P~träger(in) m(f) prizewinner; **~wert** adj
inexpensive

Prell- [prɛl] zW: **~bock** m buffers pl; **p~en** vt
to bump; (fig) to cheat, to swindle; **~ung** f
bruise

Premiere [prəmi'eːrə] f premiere

Premierminister [prəmi'eːmɪnɪstər] m
prime minister, premier

Presse ['prɛsə] f press; **~agentur** f press
agency; **~freiheit** f freedom of the press;
p~n vt to press

Pressluft ▲ ['prɛslʊft] f compressed air;
~bohrer ▲ m pneumatic drill

Prestige [prɛs'tiːʒə] (-s) nt prestige

prickeln ['prɪkəln] vt, vi to tingle; to tickle

Priester ['priːstər] (**-s, -**) *m* priest
prima *adj inv* first-class, excellent
primär [priˈmɛːr] *adj* primary
Primel ['priːməl] (**-, -n**) *f* primrose
primitiv [primiˈtiːf] *adj* primitive
Prinz [prɪnts] (**-en, -en**) *m* prince; **~essin** *f*
   princess
Prinzip [prɪnˈtsiːp] (**-s, -ien**) *nt* principle;
   p~iell [-iˈɛl] *adj, adv* on principle; **p~ienlos**
   adj unprincipled
Priorität [prioriˈtɛːt] *f* priority
Prise ['priːzə] *f* pinch
Prisma ['prɪsma] (**-s, Prismen**) *nt* prism
privat [priˈvaːt] *adj* private; **P~besitz** *m*
   private property; **P~fernsehen** *nt*
   commercial television; **P~patient(in)** *m(f)*
   private patient; **P~schule** *f* public school
Privileg [priviˈleːk] (**-(e)s, -ien**) *nt* privilege
Pro [proː] (**-**) *nt* pro
pro *präp +akk* per
Probe ['proːbə] *f* test; (*Teststück*) sample;
   (*THEAT*) rehearsal; **jdn auf die ~ stellen** to
   put sb to the test; **~exemplar** *nt* specimen
   copy; **~fahrt** *f* test drive; **p~n** *vt* to try;
   (*THEAT*) to rehearse; **p~weise** *adv* on
   approval; **~zeit** *f* probation period
probieren [proˈbiːrən] *vt* to try; (*Wein,
   Speise*) to taste, to sample ♦ *vi* to try; to taste
Problem [proˈbleːm] (**-s, -e**) *nt* problem;
   ~atik [-ˈmaːtik] *f* problem; **p~atisch**
   [-ˈmaːtɪʃ] *adj* problematic; **p~los** *adj*
   problem-free
Produkt [proˈdʊkt] (**-(e)s, -e**) *nt* product;
   (*AGR*) produce *no pl*; **~ion** [prodʊktsiˈoːn] *f*
   production; output; **p~iv** [-ˈtiːf] *adj*
   productive; **~ivität** [-iviˈtɛːt] *f* productivity
Produzent [produˈtsɛnt] *m* manufacturer;
   (*Film*) producer
produzieren [produˈtsiːrən] *vt* to produce
Professor [proˈfɛsɔr] *m* professor
Profi ['proːfi] (**-s, -s**) *m* (*umg, SPORT*) pro
Profil [proˈfiːl] (**-s, -e**) *nt* profile; (*fig*) image
Profit [proˈfiːt] (**-(e)s, -e**) *m* profit; **p~ieren**
   vi: **p~ieren (von**) to profit (from)
Prognose [proˈɡnoːzə] *f* prediction, prognosis
Programm [proˈɡram] (**-s, -e**) *nt*
   programme; (*COMPUT*) program; **p~ieren**
   [-ˈmiːrən] *vt* to programme; (*COMPUT*) to
   program; **~ierer(in)** (**-s, -**) *m(f)* programmer
progressiv [progrɛˈsiːf] *adj* progressive
Projekt [proˈjɛkt] (**-(e)s, -e**) *nt* project; **~or**
   [proˈjɛktɔr] *m* projector
proklamieren [proklaˈmiːrən] *vt* to proclaim
Prokurist(in) [prokuˈrɪst(ɪn)] *m(f)* ≈
   company secretary
Prolet [proˈleːt] (**-en, -en**) *m* prole, pleb;
   ~arier [-ˈtaːriər] (**-s, -**) *m* proletarian
Prolog [proˈloːk] (**-(e)s, -e**) *m* prologue
Promenade [proməˈnaːdə] *f* promenade

Promille [proˈmɪlə] (**-(s)**, **-**) *nt* alcohol level
prominent [promiˈnɛnt] *adj* prominent
Prominenz [promiˈnɛnts] *f* VIPs *pl*
Promotion [promotsiˈoːn] *f* doctorate, Ph.D.
promovieren [promoˈviːrən] *vi* to do a
   doctorate *od* Ph.D.
prompt [prɔmpt] *adj* prompt
Pronomen [proˈnoːmɛn] (**-s, -**) *nt* pronoun
Propaganda [propaˈɡanda] (**-**) *f* propaganda
Propeller [proˈpɛlər] (**-s, -**) *m* propeller
Prophet [proˈfeːt] (**-en, -en**) *m* prophet
prophezeien [profeˈtsaɪən] *vt* to prophesy;
   Prophezeiung *f* prophecy
Proportion [proportsiˈoːn] *f* proportion;
   p~al [-ˈnaːl] *adj* proportional
proportioniert [proportsioˈniːrt] *adj*: **gut/
   schlecht ~** well-/badly-proportioned
Prosa ['proːza] (**-**) *f* prose; **p~isch** [proˈzaːɪʃ]
   adj prosaic
prosit ['proːzɪt] *excl* cheers
Prospekt [proˈspɛkt] (**-(e)s, -e**) *m* leaflet,
   brochure
prost [proːst] *excl* cheers
Prostituierte [prostituˈiːrtə] *f* prostitute
Prostitution [prostitutsiˈoːn] *f* prostitution
Protest [proˈtɛst] (**-(e)s, -e**) *m* protest;
   ~ant(in) [protɛsˈtant(ɪn)] *m(f)* Protestant;
   p~antisch [protɛsˈtantɪʃ] *adj* Protestant;
   p~ieren [protɛsˈtiːrən] *vi* to protest
Prothese [proˈteːzə] *f* artificial limb;
   (*Zahnprothese*) dentures *pl*
Protokoll [protoˈkɔl] (**-s, -e**) *nt* register; (*von
   Sitzung*) minutes *pl*; (*diplomatisch*) protocol;
   (*Polizeiprotokoll*) statement; **p~ieren**
   [-ˈliːrən] *vt* to take down in the minutes
protzen ['prɔtsən] *vi* to show off
Proviant [proviˈant] (**-s, -e**) *m* provisions *pl*,
   supplies *pl*
Provinz [proˈvɪnts] (**-, -en**) *f* province;
   p~i'ell *adj* provincial
Provision [proviziˈoːn] *f* (*COMM*) commission
provisorisch [proviˈzoːrɪʃ] *adj* provisional
Provokation [provokatsiˈoːn] *f* provocation
provozieren [provoˈtsiːrən] *vt* to provoke
Prozedur [protseˈduːr] *f* procedure; (*pej*)
   carry-on
Prozent [proˈtsɛnt] (**-(e)s, -e**) *nt* per cent,
   percentage; **~satz** *m* percentage; **p~ual**
   [-uˈaːl] *adj* percentage *cpd*; as a percentage
Prozess ▲ [proˈtsɛs] (**-es, -e**) *m* trial, case
Prozession [protsɛsiˈoːn] *f* procession
prüde ['pryːdə] *adj* prudish; **P~rie** [-ˈriː] *f*
   prudery
Prüf- ['pryːf] *zW:* **p~en** *vt* to examine, to test;
   (*nachprüfen*) to check; **~er** (**-s, -**) *m*
   examiner; **~ling** *m* examinee; **~ung** *f*
   examination; checking; **~ungsaus-
   schuss ▲** *m* examining board
Prügel ['pryːɡəl] (**-s, -**) *m* cudgel ♦ *pl*

(*Schläge*) beating; **~ei** |-'laɪ| *f* fight; **p~n** *vt*
to beat ♦ *vr* to fight; **~strafe** *f* corporal
punishment
Prunk |pruŋk| (-(e)s) *m* pomp, show; **p~voll**
adj splendid, magnificent
PS |peː'|ɛs| *abk* (= *Pferdestärke*) H.P.
Psych- |'psyç| *zW*: **~iater** |-iˈaːtər| (**-s**, **-**) *m*
psychiatrist; **p~iatrisch** *adj* (*MED*)
psychiatric; **p~isch** *adj* psychological;
~oanalyse |-oˌanaˈlyːze| *f* psychoanalysis;
~ologe (**-n**, **-n**) *m* psychologist; **~olo'gie** *f*
psychology; **p~ologisch** *adj* psychological;
~otherapeut(in) (**-en**, **-en**) *m(f)*
psychotherapist
Pubertät |pubɛr'tɛːt| *f* puberty
Publikum |'puːblikʊm| (**-s**) *nt* audience;
(*SPORT*) crowd
publizieren |publiˈtsiːrən| *vt* to publish, to
publicize
Pudding |'pʊdɪŋ| (**-s**, **-e** *od* **-s**) *m* blancmange
Pudel |'puːdəl| (**-s**) *m* poodle
Puder |'puːdər| (**-s**, **-**) *m* powder; **~dose** *f*
powder compact; **p~n** *vt* to powder;
~zucker *m* icing sugar
Puff[1] |pʊf| (**-s**, **-e**) *m* (*Wäschepuff*) linen
basket; (*Sitzpuff*) pouf
Puff[2] |pʊf| (**-s**, **-e**) (*umg*) *m* (*Stoß*) push
Puff[3] |pʊf| (**-s**, **-**) (*umg*) *m od nt* (*Bordell*)
brothel
Puffer (**-s**, **-**) *m* buffer
Pullover |pʊˈloːvər| (**-s**, **-**) *m* pullover, jumper
Puls |pʊls| (**-es**, **-e**) *m* pulse; **~ader** *f* artery;
p~ieren *vi* to throb, to pulsate
Pult |pʊlt| (**-(e)s**, **-e**) *nt* desk
Pulver |'pʊlfər| (**-s**, **-**) *nt* powder; **p~ig** *adj*
powdery; **~schnee** *m* powdery snow
pummelig |'pʊməlɪç| *adj* chubby
Pumpe |'pʊmpə| *f* pump; **p~n** *vt* to pump;
(*umg*) to lend; to borrow
Punkt |pʊŋkt| (**-(e)s**, **-e**) *m* point; (*bei*
Muster) dot; (*Satzzeichen*) full stop; **p~ieren**
|-'tiːrən| *vt* to dot; (*MED*) to aspirate
pünktlich |'pʏŋktlɪç| *adj* punctual; **P~keit** *f*
punctuality
Punktsieg *m* victory on points
Punktzahl *f* score
Punsch |pʊnʃ| (**-(e)s**, **-e**) *m* punch
Pupille |puˈpɪlə| *f* pupil
Puppe |'pʊpə| *f* doll; (*Marionette*) puppet;
(*Insektenpuppe*) pupa, chrysalis
Puppen- *zW*: **~spieler** *m* puppeteer;
~stube *f* doll's house; **~theater** *nt* puppet
theatre
pur |puːr| *adj* pure; (*völlig*) sheer; (*Whisky*) neat
Püree |pyˈreː| (**-s**, **-s**) *nt* mashed potatoes *pl*
Purzelbaum |'pʊrtsəlbaʊm| *m* somersault
purzeln |'pʊrtsəln| *vi* to tumble
Puste |'puːstə| (**-**) (*umg*) *f* puff; (*fig*) steam;
p~n *vi* to puff, to blow
Pute |'puːtə| *f* turkey hen; **~r** (**-s**, **-**) *m* turkey
cock

Putsch |pʊtʃ| (**-(e)s**, **-e**) *m* revolt, putsch
Putz |pʊts| (**-es**) *m* (*Mörtel*) plaster,
roughcast
putzen *vt* to clean; (*Nase*) to wipe, to blow
♦ *vr* to clean o.s.; to dress o.s. up
Putz- *zW*: **~frau** *f* charwoman; **p~ig** *adj*
quaint, funny; **~lappen** *m* cloth
Puzzle |'pasəl| (**-s**, **-s**) *nt* jigsaw
PVC (**-s**) *nt abk* PVC
Pyjama |piˈdʒaːma| (**-s**, **-s**) *m* pyjamas *pl*
Pyramide |pyraˈmiːdə| *f* pyramid
Pyrenäen |pyreˈnɛːən| *pl* Pyrenees

Q, q

Quacksalber |'kvakzalbər| (**-s**, **-**) *m* quack
(doctor)
Quader |'kvaːdər| (**-s**, **-**) *m* square stone;
(*MATH*) cuboid
Quadrat |kvaˈdraːt| (**-(e)s**, **-e**) *nt* square;
q~isch *adj* square; **~meter** *m* square metre
quaken |'kvaːkən| *vi* to croak; (*Ente*) to quack
quäken |'kvɛːkən| *vi* to screech
Qual |kvaːl| (**-**, **-en**) *f* pain, agony; (*seelisch*)
anguish
quälen |'kvɛːlən| *vt* to torment ♦ *vr* to
struggle; (*geistig*) to torment o.s.
Quälerei |kvɛːləˈraɪ| *f* torture, torment
Qualifikation |kvalifikatsiˈoːn| *f* qualification
qualifizieren |kvalifiˈtsiːrən| *vt* to qualify;
(*einstufen*) to label ♦ *vr* to qualify
Qualität |kvaliˈtɛːt| *f* quality; **~sware** *f*
article of high quality
Qualle |'kvalə| *f* jellyfish
Qualm |kvalm| (**-(e)s**) *m* thick smoke; **q~en**
vt, vi to smoke
qualvoll |'kvaːlfɔl| *adj* excruciating, painful,
agonizing
Quant- |'kvant| *zW*: **~ität** |-iˈtɛːt| *f* quantity;
q~itativ |-itaˈtiːf| *adj* quantitative; **~um** (**-s**)
nt quantity, amount
Quarantäne |karanˈtɛːnə| *f* quarantine
Quark |kvark| (**-s**) *m* curd cheese
Quartal |kvarˈtaːl| (**-s**, **-e**) *nt* quarter (year)
Quartier |kvarˈtiːr| (**-s**, **-e**) *nt*
accommodation; (*MIL*) quarters *pl*;
(*Stadtquartier*) district
Quarz |kvarts| (**-es**, **-e**) *m* quartz
quasseln |'kvasəln| (*umg*) *vi* to natter
Quatsch |kvatʃ| (**-es**) *m* rubbish; **q~en** *vi* to
chat, to natter
Quecksilber |'kvɛkzɪlbər| *nt* mercury
Quelle |'kvɛlə| *f* spring; (*eines Flusses*) source;
q~n (*unreg*) *vi* (*hervorquellen*) to pour *od*
gush forth; (*schwellen*) to swell
quer |kveːr| *adv* crossways, diagonally;
(*rechtwinklig*) at right angles; **~ auf dem**
Bett across the bed; **Q~balken** *m*
crossbeam; **Q~flöte** *f* flute; **Q~format** *nt*
(*PHOT*) oblong format; **Q~schnitt** *m* cross-

section; **~schnittsgelähmt** adj paralysed below the waist; **Q~straße** f intersecting road

quetschen ['kvɛtʃən] vt to squash, to crush; (MED) to bruise

Quetschung f bruise, contusion

quieken ['kviːkən] vi to squeak

quietschen ['kviːtʃən] vi to squeak

Quintessenz ['kvɪntɛsɛnts] f quintessence

Quirl [kvɪrl] (-(e)s, -e) m whisk

quitt [kvɪt] adj quits, even

Quitte f quince

quittieren [kvɪˈtiːrən] vt to give a receipt for; (Dienst) to leave

Quittung f receipt

Quiz [kvɪs] (-, -) nt quiz

quoll etc [kvɔl] vb siehe **quellen**

Quote ['kvoːtə] f number, rate

R, r

Rabatt [raˈbat] (-(e)s, -e) m discount

Rabattmarke f trading stamp

Rabe ['raːbə] (-n, -n) m raven

rabiat [rabiˈaːt] adj furious

Rache ['raxə] (-) f revenge, vengeance

Rachen (-s, -) m throat

rächen ['rɛçən] vt to avenge, to revenge ♦ vr to take (one's) revenge; **das wird sich ~** you'll pay for that

Rad [raːt] (-(e)s, ⸚er) nt wheel; (Fahrrad) bike; **~ fahren** to cycle

Radar ['raːdaːr] (-s) m od nt radar; **~falle** f speed trap; **~kontrolle** f radar-controlled speed trap

Radau [raˈdaʊ] (-s) (umg) m row

radeln ['raːdəln] (umg) vi to cycle

Radfahr- zW: **r~en** vi siehe **Rad**; **~er(in)** m(f) cyclist; **~weg** m cycle track od path

Radier- [raˈdiːr] zW: **r~en** vt to rub out, to erase; (KUNST) to etch; **~gummi** m rubber, eraser; **~ung** f etching

Radieschen [raˈdiːsçən] nt radish

radikal [radiˈkaːl] adj radical

Radio ['raːdio] (-s, -s) nt radio, wireless; **r~aktiv** adj radioactive; **~aktivität** f radioactivity; **~apparat** m radio, wireless set

Radius ['raːdius] (-, Radien) m radius

Rad- zW: **~kappe** f (AUT) hub cap; **~ler(in)** (umg) m(f) cyclist; **~rennen** nt cycle race; cycle racing; **~sport** m cycling; **~weg** m cycleway

raffen ['rafən] vt to snatch, to pick up; (Stoff) to gather (up); (Geld) to pile up, to rake in

raffiniert adj crafty, cunning

ragen ['raːgən] vi to tower, to rise

Rahm [raːm] (-s) m cream

Rahmen (-s, -) m frame(work); **im ~ des Möglichen** within the bounds of possibility; **r~** vt to frame

räkeln ['rɛːkln] vr = **rekeln**

Rakete [raˈkeːtə] f rocket; **~nstützpunkt** m missile base

rammen ['ramən] vt to ram

Rampe ['rampə] f ramp; **~nlicht** nt (THEAT) footlights pl

ramponieren [rampoˈniːrən] (umg) vt to damage

Ramsch [ramʃ] (-(e)s, -e) m junk

ran [ran] (umg) adv = **heran**

Rand [rant] (-(e)s, ⸚er) m edge; (von Brille, Tasse etc) rim; (Hutrand) brim; (auf Papier) margin; (Schmutzrand, unter Augen) ring; (fig) verge, brink; **außer ~ und Band** wild; **am ~e bemerkt** mentioned in passing

randalieren [randaˈliːrən] vi to (go on the) rampage

Rang [raŋ] (-(e)s, ⸚e) m rank; (Stand) standing; (Wert) quality; (THEAT) circle

Rangier- [rãˈʒiːr] zW: **~bahnhof** m marshalling yard; **r~en** vt, vr to shunt, to switch (US) ♦ vi to rank, to be classed; **~gleis** nt siding

Ranke ['raŋkə] f tendril, shoot

ranzig ['rantsiç] adj rancid

Rappen ['rapən] m (FIN) rappen, centime

rar [raːr] adj rare; **sich ~ machen** (umg) to keep o.s. to o.s.; **R~i'tät** f rarity; (Sammelobjekt) curio

rasant [raˈzant] adj quick, rapid

rasch [raʃ] adj quick

rascheln vi to rustle

Rasen ['raːzən] (-s, -) m lawn; grass

rasen vi to rave; (schnell) to race; **~d** adj furious; **~de Kopfschmerzen** a splitting headache

Rasenmäher (-s, -) m lawnmower

Rasier- [raˈziːr] zW: **~apparat** m shaver; **~creme** f shaving cream; **r~en** vt, vr to shave; **~klinge** f razor blade; **~messer** nt razor; **~pinsel** m shaving brush; **~schaum** m shaving foam; **~seife** f shaving soap od stick; **~wasser** nt shaving lotion

Rasse ['rasə] f race; (Tierrasse) breed; **~hund** m thoroughbred dog

rasseln ['rasəln] vi to clatter

Rassen- zW: **~hass** ▲ m race od racial hatred; **~trennung** f racial segregation

Rassismus [raˈsɪsmʊs] m racism

Rast [rast] (-, -en) f rest; **r~en** vi to rest; **~hof** m (AUT) service station; **r~los** adj tireless; (unruhig) restless; **~platz** m (AUT) layby; **~stätte** f (AUT) service station

Rasur [raˈzuːr] f shaving

Rat [raːt] (-(e)s, **-schläge**) m advice no pl; **ein ~** a piece of advice; **keinen ~ wissen** not to know what to do; *siehe* zurate

Rate *f* instalment

raten [*unreg*] *vt, vi* to guess; (*empfehlen*): **jdm ~ to** advise sb

Ratenzahlung *f* hire purchase

Ratgeber (**-s, -**) *m* adviser

Rathaus *nt* town hall

ratifizieren [ratifi'tsi:rən] *vt* to ratify

Ration [ratsi'o:n] *f* ration; **r~al** [-'na:l] *adj* rational; **r~ali'sieren** *vt* to rationalize; **r~ell** [-'nɛl] *adj* efficient; **r~ieren** [-'ni:rən] *vt* to ration

Rat- *zW*: **r~los** *adj* at a loss, helpless; **r~sam** *adj* advisable; **~schlag** *m* (piece of) advice

Rätsel ['rɛ:tsəl] (**-s, -**) *nt* puzzle; (*Worträtsel*) riddle; **r~haft** *adj* mysterious; **es ist mir r~haft** it's a mystery to me

Ratte ['ratə] *f* rat; **~nfänger** (**-s, -**) *m* ratcatcher

rattern ['ratərn] *vi* to rattle, to clatter

rau ▲ [rau] *adj* rough, coarse; (*Wetter*) harsh

Raub [raup] (**-(e)s**) *m* robbery; (*Beute*) loot, booty; **~bau** *m* ruthless exploitation; **r~en** ['raubən] *vt* to rob; (*Mensch*) to kidnap, to abduct

Räuber ['rɔybər] (**-s, -**) *m* robber

Raub- *zW*: **~mord** *m* robbery with murder; **~tier** *nt* predator; **~überfall** *m* robbery with violence; **~vogel** *m* bird of prey

Rauch [raux] (**-(e)s**) *m* smoke; **r~en** *vt, vi* to smoke; **~er(in)** (**-s, -**) *m(f)* smoker; **~erabteil** *nt* (*EISENB*) smoker; **räuchern** *vt* to smoke, to cure; **~fleisch** *nt* smoked meat; **r~ig** *adj* smoky

rauf [rauf] (*umg*) *adv* = **herauf; hinauf**

raufen *vt* (*Haare*) to pull out ♦ *vi, vr* to fight; **Raufe'rei** *f* brawl, fight

rauh *etc* △ = **rau** *etc*

Raum [raum] (**-(e)s**) *m* space; (*Zimmer, Platz*) room; (*Gebiet*) area

räumen ['rɔymən] *vt* to clear; (*Wohnung, Platz*) to vacate; (*wegbringen*) to shift, to move; (*in Schrank etc*) to put away

Raum- *zW*: **~fähre** *f* space shuttle; **~fahrt** *f* space travel; **~inhalt** *m* cubic capacity, volume

räumlich ['rɔymlɪç] *adj* spatial; **R~keiten** *pl* premises

Raum- *zW*: **~pflegerin** *f* cleaner; **~schiff** *nt* spaceship; **~schifffahrt** ▲ *f* space travel

Räumung ['rɔymuŋ] *f* vacating, evacuation; clearing (away)

Räumungs- *zW*: **~arbeiten** *pl* clearance operations; **~verkauf** *m* clearance sale; (*bei Geschäftsaufgabe*) closing down sale

raunen ['raunən] *vt, vi* to whisper

Raupe ['raupə] *f* caterpillar; (*Raupenkette*) (caterpillar) track

Raureif ['raurai̯f] ▲ *m* hoarfrost

raus [raus] (*umg*) *adv* = **heraus; hinaus**

Rausch [rauʃ] (**-(e)s**) *m* intoxication

rauschen *vi* (*Wasser*) to rush; (*Baum*) to rustle; (*Radio etc*) to hiss; (*Mensch*) to sweep, to sail; **~d** *adj* (*Beifall*) thunderous; (*Fest*) sumptuous

Rauschgift *nt* drug; **~süchtige(r)** *f(m)* drug addict

räuspern ['rɔyspərn] *vr* to clear one's throat

Razzia ['ratsia] (**-, Razzien**) *f* raid

Reagenzglas [rea'gɛntsgla:s] *nt* test tube

reagieren [rea'gi:rən] *vi*: **~ (auf** +*akk***)** to react (to)

Reakt- *zW*: **~ion** [reaktsi'o:n] *f* reaction; **r~io'när** *adj* reactionary; **~or** [re'aktɔr] *m* reactor

real [re'a:l] *adj* real, material

reali'sieren *vt* (*verwirklichen: Pläne*) to carry out

Realismus [rea'lɪsmus] *m* realism

rea'listisch *adj* realistic

Realschule *f* secondary school

Rebe ['re:bə] *f* vine

rebellieren [rebɛ'li:rən] *vi* to rebel; **Rebelli'on** *f* rebellion; **re'bellisch** *adj* rebellious

Rebhuhn ['rɛphu:n] *nt* (*KOCH, ZOOL*) partridge

Rechen ['rɛçən] (**-s, -**) *m* rake

Rechen- *zW*: **~fehler** *m* miscalculation; **~maschine** *f* calculating machine; **~schaft** *f* account; **für etw ~schaft ablegen** to account for sth; **~schieber** *m* slide rule

Rech- ['rɛç] *zW*: **r~nen** *vt, vi* to calculate; **jdn/etw r~nen zu** to count sb/sth among; **r~nen mit** to reckon with; **r~nen auf** +*akk* to count on; **~nen** *nt* arithmetic; **~ner** (**-s, -**) *m* calculator; (*COMPUT*) computer; **~nung** *f* calculation(s); (*COMM*) bill, check (*US*); **jdm/etw ~nung tragen** to take sb/sth into account; **~nungsbetrag** *m* total amount of a bill/invoice; **~nungsjahr** *nt* financial year; **~nungsprüfer** *m* auditor

Recht [rɛçt] (**-(e)s, -e**) *nt* right; (*JUR*) law; **mit ~** rightly, justly; **~ haben** to be right; **jdm ~ geben** to agree with sb; **von ~s wegen** by rights

recht *adj* right ♦ *adv* (*vor Adjektiv*) really, quite; **das ist mir ~** that suits me; **jetzt erst ~** now more than ever

Rechte *f* right (hand); (*POL*) Right; **r~(r, s)** *adj* right; (*POL*) right-wing; **ein ~r** a right-winger; **~(s)** *nt* right thing; **etwas/nichts ~s** something/nothing proper

recht- *zW*: **~eckig** *adj* rectangular; **~fertigen** *vt insep* to justify ♦ *vr insep* to justify o.s.; **R~fertigung** *f* justification; **~haberisch** (*pej*) *adj* (*Mensch*) opinionated; **~lich** *adj* (*gesetzlich: Gleichstellung, Anspruch*) legal; **~los** *adj* with no rights; **~mäßig** *adj* legal, lawful

rechts [rɛçts] *adv* on/to the right; **R~anwalt** *m* lawyer, barrister; **R~anwältin** *f* lawyer, barrister

Rechtschreibung *f* spelling
Rechts- *zW:* **~fall** *m* (law) case; **~händer**
(**-s**, **-**) *m* right-handed person; **r~kräftig** *adj*
valid, legal; **~kurve** *f* right-hand bend;
r~verbindlich *adj* legally binding;
~verkehr *m* driving on the right; **r~widrig**
adj illegal; **~wissenschaft** *f* jurisprudence
rechtwinklig *adj* right-angled
rechtzeitig *adj* timely ♦ *adv* in time
Reck |rɛk| (**-(e)s**, **-e**) *nt* horizontal bar; **r~en**
vt, *vr* to stretch
recyceln |ri:'saikəln| *vt* to recycle;
Recycling |ri:'saiklıŋ| *nt* recycling
Redakteur |redak'tøːr| *m* editor
Redaktion |redaktsi'oːn| *f* editing; (*Leute*)
editorial staff; (*Büro*) editorial office(s)
Rede |'reːdə| *f* speech; (*Gespräch*) talk; **jdn**
zur ~ stellen to take sb to task; **~freiheit** *f*
freedom of speech; **r~gewandt** *adj*
eloquent; **r~n** *vi* to talk, to speak ♦ *vt* to say;
(*Unsinn etc*) to talk; **~nsart** *f* set phrase
redlich |'reːtlıç| *adj* honest
Redner (**-s**, **-**) *m* speaker, orator
redselig |'reːtzeːlıç| *adj* talkative, loquacious
reduzieren |redu'tsiːrən| *vt* to reduce
Reede |'reːdə| *f* protected anchorage; **~r** (**-s**,
-) *m* shipowner; **~'rei** *f* shipping line *od* firm
reell |re'ɛl| *adj* fair, honest; (*MATH*) real
Refer- *zW:* **~at** |refe'raːt| (**-(e)s**, **-e**) *nt* report;
(*Vortrag*) paper; (*Gebiet*) section; **~ent**
|refe'rɛnt| *m* speaker; (*Berichterstatter*)
reporter; (*Sachbearbeiter*) expert; **r~ieren**
|refe'riːrən| *vi*: **r~ieren über** +*akk* to speak
od talk on
reflektieren |reflek'tiːrən| *vt* (*Licht*) to reflect
Reflex |re'flɛks| (**-es**, **-e**) *m* reflex; **r~iv**
|-'ksi:f| *adj* (*GRAM*) reflexive
Reform |re'fɔrm| (**-**, **-en**) *f* reform; **~ati'on** *f*
reformation; **~ationstag** *m* Reformation
Day; **~haus** *nt* health food shop; **r~ieren**
|-'miːrən| *vt* to reform
Regal |re'gaːl| (**-s**, **-e**) *nt* (book)shelves *pl*,
bookcase; stand, rack
rege |'reːgə| *adj* (*lebhaft: Treiben*) lively;
(*wach, lebendig: Geist*) keen
Regel |'reːgəl| (**-**, **-n**) *f* rule; (*MED*) period;
r~mäßig *adj* regular; **~mäßigkeit** *f*
regularity; **r~n** *vt* to regulate, to control;
(*Angelegenheit*) to settle ♦ *vr*: **sich von**
selbst r~n to take care of itself; **r~recht** *adj*
regular, proper, thorough; **~ung** *f*
regulation; settlement; **r~widrig** *adj*
irregular, against the rules
Regen |'reːgən| (**-s**, **-**) *m* rain; **~bogen** *m*
rainbow; **~bogenpresse** *f* tabloids *pl*
regenerierbar |regene'riːrbaːr| *adj*
renewable
Regen- *zW:* **~mantel** *m* raincoat, mac
(kintosh); **~schauer** *m* shower (of rain);

~schirm *m* umbrella; **~wald** *m* (*GEOG*)
rainforest; **~wurm** *m* earthworm; **~zeit** *f*
rainy season
Regie |re'ʒi:| *f* (*Film etc*) direction; (*THEAT*)
production
Regier- |re'giːr| *zW:* **r~en** *vt*, *vi* to govern, to
rule; **~ung** *f* government; (*Monarchie*) reign;
~ungssitz *m* seat of government;
~ungswechsel *m* change of government;
~ungszeit *f* period in government; (*von*
König) reign
Regiment |regi'mɛnt| (**-s**, **-er**) *nt* regiment
Region |regi'o:n| *f* region
Regisseur |reʒi'søːr| *m* director; (*THEAT*)
(stage) producer
Register |re'gıstər| (**-s**, **-**) *nt* register; (*in*
Buch) table of contents, index
registrieren |regis'triːrən| *vt* to register
Regler |'reːglər| (**-s**, **-**) *m* regulator, governor
reglos |'reːkloːs| *adj* motionless
regnen |'reːgnən| *vi unpers* to rain
regnerisch *adj* rainy
regulär |regu'lɛːr| *adj* regular
regulieren |regu'liːrən| *vt* to regulate;
(*COMM*) to settle
Regung |'reːgʊŋ| *f* motion; (*Gefühl*) feeling,
impulse; **r~slos** *adj* motionless
Reh |re:| (**-(e)s**, **-e**) *nt* deer, roe; **~bock** *m*
roebuck; **~kitz** *nt* fawn
Reib- |'raıb| *zW:* **~e** *f* grater; **~eisen** *nt*
grater; **r~en** (*unreg*) *vt* to rub; (*KOCH*) to
grate; **~fläche** *f* rough surface; **~ung** *f*
friction; **r~ungslos** *adj* smooth
Reich (**-(e)s**, **-e**) *nt* empire, kingdom; (*fig*)
realm; **das Dritte ~** the Third Reich
reich |raıç| *adj* rich
reichen *vi* to reach; (*genügen*) to be enough
od sufficient ♦ *vt* to hold out; (*geben*) to
pass, to hand; (*anbieten*) to offer; **jdm ~** to
be enough *od* sufficient for sb
reich- *zW:* **~haltig** *adj* ample, rich; **~lich** *adj*
ample, plenty of; **R~tum** (**-s**) *m* wealth;
R~weite *f* range
Reif (**-(e)s**, **-e**) *m* (*Ring*) ring, hoop
reif |raıf| *adj* ripe; (*Mensch, Urteil*) mature
Reife (**-**) *f* ripeness; maturity; **r~n** *vi* to
mature; to ripen
Reifen (**-s**, **-**) *m* ring, hoop; (*Fahrzeugreifen*)
tyre; **~druck** *m* tyre pressure; **~panne** *f*
puncture
Reihe |'raıə| *f* row; (*von Tagen etc, umg:*
Anzahl) series *sg*; **der ~ nach** in turn; **er ist**
an der ~ it's his turn; **an die ~ kommen** to
have one's turn
Reihen- *zW:* **~folge** *f* sequence;
alphabetische ~folge alphabetical order;
~haus *nt* terraced house
reihum |raı'lʊm| *adv*: **es geht/wir machen**
das ~ we take turns

Spelling reform: ▲ *new spelling* △ *old spelling (to be phased out)*

Reim |raɪm| (-(e)s, -e) *m* rhyme; **r~en** *vt* to rhyme

rein¹ |raɪn| (*umg*) *adv* = **herein**; **hinein**

rein² |raɪn| *adj* pure; (*sauber*) clean ♦ *adv* purely; **etw ins R~e schreiben** to make a fair copy of sth; **etw ins R~e bringen** to clear up sth; **R~fall** (*umg*) *m* let-down; **R~gewinn** *m* net profit; **R~heit** *f* purity; cleanness; **~igen** *vt* to clean; (*Wasser*) to purify; **R~igung** *f* cleaning; purification; (*Geschäft*) cleaner's; **chemische R~igung** dry cleaning; dry cleaner's; **R~igungsmittel** *nt* cleansing agent; **~rassig** *adj* pedigree; **R~schrift** *f* fair copy

Reis |raɪs| (-es, -e) *m* rice

Reise |'raɪzə| *f* journey; (*Schiffsreise*) voyage; **~n** *pl* (*Herumreisen*) travels; **gute ~!** have a good journey; **~apotheke** *f* first-aid kit; **~büro** *nt* travel agency; **r~fertig** *adj* ready to start; **~führer** *m* guide(book); (*Mensch*) travel guide; **~gepäck** *nt* luggage; **~gesellschaft** *f* party of travellers; **~kosten** *pl* travelling expenses; **~leiter** *m* courier; **~lektüre** *f* reading matter for the journey; **r~n** *vi* to travel; **r~n nach** to go to; **~nde(r)** *f(m)* traveller; **~pass** ▲ *m* passport; **~proviant** *m* food and drink for the journey; **~route** *f* route, itinerary; **~ruf** *m* personal message; **~scheck** *m* traveller's cheque; **~veranstalter** *m* tour operator; **~versicherung** *f* travel insurance; **~ziel** *nt* destination

Reißbrett *nt* drawing board

reißen |'raɪsən| (*unreg*) *vt* to tear; (*ziehen*) to pull, to drag; (*Witz*) to crack ♦ *vi* to tear, to drag; **etw an sich ~** to snatch sth up; (*fig*) to take over sth; **sich um etw ~** to scramble for sth; **~d** *adj* (*Fluss*) raging; (*WIRTS: Verkauf*) rapid

Reiß- *zW*: **~verschluss** ▲ *m* zip(per), zip fastener; **~zwecke** *m* drawing pin (*BRIT*), thumbtack (*US*)

Reit- |'raɪt| *zW*: **r~en** (*unreg*) *vt, vi* to ride; **~er** (-s, -) *m* rider; (*MIL*) cavalryman, trooper; **~erin** *f* rider; **~hose** *f* riding breeches *pl*; **~pferd** *nt* saddle horse; **~stiefel** *m* riding boot; **~weg** *n* bridle path; **~zeug** *nt* riding outfit

Reiz |raɪts| (-es, -e) *m* stimulus; (*angenehm*) charm; (*Verlockung*) attraction; **r~bar** *adj* irritable; **~barkeit** *f* irritability; **r~en** *vt* to stimulate; (*unangenehm*) to irritate; (*verlocken*) to appeal to, to attract; **r~end** *adj* charming; **r~voll** *adj* attractive

rekeln |'re:kəln| *vr* to stretch out; (*lümmeln*) to lounge *od* loll about

Reklamation |reklamatsi'o:n| *f* complaint

Reklame |re'kla:mə| *f* advertising; advertisement; **~ machen für etw** to advertise sth

rekonstruieren |rekɔnstru'i:rən| *vt* to reconstruct

Rekord |re'kɔrt| (-(e)s, -e) *m* record; **~leistung** *f* record performance

Rektor |'rɛktɔr| *m* (*UNIV*) rector, vice-chancellor; (*SCH*) headteacher (*BRIT*), principal (*US*); **~at** |-'rat| (-(e)s, -e) *nt* rectorate, vice-chancellorship; headship; (*Zimmer*) rector's *etc* office

Relais |rə'lɛ:| (-, -) *nt* relay

relativ |rela'ti:f| *adj* relative; **R~ität** |relativi'tɛ:t| *f* relativity

relevant |rele'vant| *adj* relevant

Relief |reli'ɛf| (-s, -s) *nt* relief

Religion |religi'o:n| *f* religion

religiös |religi'ø:s| *adj* religious

Reling |'re:lɪŋ| (-, -s) *f* (*NAUT*) rail

Remoulade |remu'la:də| *f* remoulade

Rendezvous |rãde'vu:| (-, -) *nt* rendezvous

Renn- |'rɛn| *zW*: **~bahn** *f* racecourse; (*AUT*) circuit, race track; **r~en** (*unreg*) *vt, vi* to run, to race; **~en** (-s, -) *nt* running; (*Wettbewerb*) race; **~fahrer** *m* racing driver; **~pferd** *nt* racehorse; **~wagen** *m* racing car

renommiert |reno'mi:rt| *adj* renowned

renovieren |reno'vi:rən| *vt* to renovate; **Renovierung** *f* renovation

rentabel |rɛn'ta:bəl| *adj* profitable, lucrative

Rentabilität |rɛntabili'tɛ:t| *f* profitability

Rente |'rɛntə| *f* pension

Rentenversicherung *f* pension scheme

rentieren |rɛn'ti:rən| *vr* to pay, to be profitable

Rentner(in) |'rɛntnər(ɪn)| (-s, -) *m(f)* pensioner

Reparatur |repara'tu:r| *f* repairing; repair; **~werkstatt** *f* repair shop; (*AUT*) garage

reparieren |repa'ri:rən| *vt* to repair

Reportage |repɔr'ta:ʒə| *f* (on-the-spot) report; (*TV, RAD*) live commentary *od* coverage

Reporter |re'pɔrtər| (-s, -) *m* reporter, commentator

repräsentativ |reprɛzɛnta'ti:f| *adj* (*stellvertretend, typisch: Menge, Gruppe*) representative; (*beeindruckend: Haus, Auto etc*) impressive

repräsentieren |reprɛzɛn'ti:rən| *vt* (*Staat, Firma*) to represent; (*darstellen: Wert*) to constitute ♦ *vi* (*gesellschaftlich*) to perform official duties

Repressalie |reprɛ'sa:liə| *f* reprisal

Reprivatisierung |reprivati'zi:rʊŋ| *f* denationalization

Reproduktion |reprodʊktsi'o:n| *f* reproduction

reproduzieren |reprodu'tsi:rən| *vt* to reproduce

Reptil |rɛp'ti:l| (-s, -ien) *nt* reptile

Republik |repu'bli:k| *f* republic; **r~anisch** *adj* republican

Reservat |rezɛr'va:t| (-(e)s, -e) *nt* reservation

Reserve |re'zɛrvə| *f* reserve; **~rad** *nt* (*AUT*)

spare wheel; **~spieler** m reserve; **~tank** m reserve tank

reservieren |rɛzɛr'viːrən| vt to reserve

Reservoir |rɛzɛrvo'aːr| (-s, -e) nt reservoir

Residenz |rezi'dɛnts| f residence, seat

resignieren |rezi'gniːrən| vi to resign

resolut |rezo'luːt| adj resolute

Resonanz |rezo'nants| f resonance; (fig) response

Resozialisierung |rezotsiali'ziːruŋ| f rehabilitation

Respekt |rɛ'spɛkt| (-(e)s) m respect; **r~ieren** |-'tiːrən| vt to respect; **r~los** adj disrespectful; **r~voll** adj respectful

Ressort |rɛ'soːr| (-s, -s) nt department

Rest |rɛst| (-(e)s, -e) m remainder, rest; (Überrest) remains pl

Restaurant |rɛsto'rãː| (-s, -s) nt restaurant

restaurieren |rɛstau'riːrən| vt to restore

Rest- zW: **~betrag** m remainder, outstanding sum; **r~lich** adj remaining; **r~los** adj complete

Resultat |rezʊl'taːt| (-(e)s, -e) nt result

Retorte |re'tɔrtə| f retort

Retouren |re'tuːrən| pl (COMM) returns

retten |'rɛtən| vt to save, to rescue

Retter(in) m(f) rescuer

Rettich |'rɛtɪç| (-s, -e) m radish

Rettung f rescue; (Hilfe) help; **seine letzte ~** his last hope

Rettungs- zW: **~boot** nt lifeboat; **~dienst** m rescue service; **r~los** adj hopeless; **~ring** m lifebelt, life preserver (US); **~wagen** m ambulance

retuschieren |retu'ʃiːrən| vt (PHOT) to retouch

Reue |'rɔyə| (-) f remorse; (Bedauern) regret; **r~n** vt: **es reut ihn** he regrets (it) od is sorry (about it)

Revanche |re'vãːʃə| f revenge; (SPORT) return match

revanchieren |revã'ʃiːrən| vr (sich rächen) to get one's own back, to have one's revenge; (erwidern) to reciprocate, to return the compliment

Revier |re'viːr| (-s, -e) nt district; (Jagdrevier) preserve; (Polizeirevier) police station; beat

Revolte |re'vɔltə| f revolt

revol'tieren vi (gegen jdn/etw) to rebel

Revolution |revolutsi'oːn| f revolution; **~är** |-'nɛːr| (-s, -e) m revolutionary; **r~ieren** |-'niːrən| vt to revolutionize

Rezept |re'tsɛpt| (-(e)s, -e) nt recipe; (MED) prescription; **r~frei** adj available without prescription; **~ion** f reception; **r~pflichtig** adj available only on prescription

R-Gespräch |'ɛrgəʃprɛːç| nt reverse charge call (BRIT), collect call (US)

Rhabarber |ra'barbər| (-s) m rhubarb

Rhein |raɪn| (-s) m Rhine; **r~isch** adj Rhenish

Rheinland-Pfalz nt (GEOG) Rheinland-Pfalz, Rhineland-Palatinate

Rhesusfaktor |'reːzusfaktər| m rhesus factor

rhetorisch |re'toːrɪʃ| adj rhetorical

Rheuma |'rɔymal| (-s) nt rheumatism; **r~tisch** |-'maːtɪʃ| adj rheumatic

rhythmisch |'rʏtmɪʃ| adj rhythmical

Rhythmus |'rʏtmʊs| m rhythm

richt- |'rɪçt| zW: **~en** vt to direct; (Waffe) to aim; (einstellen) to adjust; (instandsetzen) to repair; (zurechtmachen) to prepare; (bestrafen) to pass judgement on ♦ vr: **sich ~en nach** to go by; **~en an** +akk to direct at; (fig) to direct to; **~en auf** +akk to aim at; **R~er(in)** (-s, -) m(f) judge; **~erlich** adj judicial; **R~geschwindigkeit** f recommended speed

richtig adj right, correct; (echt) proper ♦ adv (umg: sehr) really; **bin ich hier ~?** am I in the right place?; **der/die R~e** the right one/person; **das R~e** the right thing; **~ stellen** to correct; **R~keit** f correctness

Richt- zW: **~linie** f guideline; **~preis** m recommended price

Richtung f direction; tendency, orientation

rieb etc |riːp| vb siehe **reiben**

riechen |'riːçən| (unreg) vt, vi to smell; **an etw** dat **~** to smell sth; **nach etw ~** to smell of sth; **ich kann das/ihn nicht ~** (umg) I can't stand it/him

rief etc |riːf| vb siehe **rufen**

Riegel |'riːgəl| (-s, -) m bolt; (Schokolade usw) bar

Riemen |'riːmən| (-s, -) m strap; (Gürtel, TECH) belt; (NAUT) oar

Riese |'riːzə| (-n, -n) m giant

rieseln vi to trickle; (Schnee) to fall gently

Riesen- zW: **~erfolg** m enormous success; **r~groß** adj colossal, gigantic, huge; **~rad** nt big wheel

riesig |'riːzɪç| adj enormous, huge, vast

riet etc |riːt| vb siehe **raten**

Riff |rɪf| (-(e)s, -e) nt reef

Rille |'rɪlə| f groove

Rind |rɪnt| (-(e)s, -er) nt ox; cow; cattle pl; (KOCH) beef

Rinde |'rɪndə| f rind; (Baumrinde) bark; (Brotrinde) crust

Rind- |'rɪnt| zW: **~fleisch** nt beef; **~vieh** nt cattle pl; (umg) blockhead, stupid oaf

Ring |rɪŋ| (-(e)s, -e) m ring; **~buch** nt ring binder; **r~en** (unreg) vi to wrestle; **~en** (-s) nt wrestling; **~finger** m ring finger; **~kampf** m wrestling bout; **~richter** m referee; **r~s** adv: **r~s um** round; **r~sherum** adv round about; **~straße** f ring road; **r~sum** adv (rundherum) round about; (überall) all round; **r~sumher** = **ringsum**

Rinn- |'rɪn| zW: **~e** f gutter, drain; **r~en** (unreg) vi to run, to trickle; **~stein** m gutter

Rippchen |'rɪpçən| nt small rib; cutlet

Rippe |'rɪpə| f rib

Risiko |'riːziko| (**-s, -s** od **Risiken**) nt risk

riskant |rɪs'kant| adj risky, hazardous

riskieren |rɪs'kiːrən| vt to risk

Riss ▲ |rɪs| (**-es, -e**) m tear; (in Mauer, Tasse etc) crack; (in Haut) scratch; (TECH) design

rissig |'rɪsɪç| adj torn; cracked; scratched

Ritt |rɪt| (**-(e)s, -e**) m ride

ritt etc vb siehe **reiten**

Ritter (**-s, -**) m knight; **r~lich** adj chivalrous

Ritze |'rɪtsə| f crack, chink

Rivale |ri'vaːlə| (**-n, -n**) m rival

Rivalität |rivali'tɛːt| f rivalry

Robbe |'rɔbə| f seal

Roboter |'rɔbɔtər| (**-s, -**) m robot

robust |ro'bʊst| adj (kräftig: Mensch, Gesundheit) robust

roch etc vb siehe **riechen**

Rock |rɔk| (**-(e)s, ⁼e**) m skirt; (Jackett) jacket; (Uniformrock) tunic

Rodel |'roːdəl| (**-s, -**) m toboggan; **~bahn** f toboggan run; **r~n** vi to toboggan

Rogen |'roːgən| (**-s, -**) m roe, spawn

Roggen |'rɔgən| (**-s, -**) m rye; **~brot** nt (KOCH) rye bread

roh |ro| adj raw; (Mensch) coarse, crude; **R~bau** m shell of a building; **R~material** nt raw material; **R~öl** nt crude oil

Rohr |roːr| (**-(e)s, -e**) nt pipe, tube; (BOT) cane; (Schilf) reed; (Gewehrrohr) barrel; **~bruch** m burst pipe

Röhre |'røːrə| f tube, pipe; (RAD etc) valve; (Backröhre) oven

Rohr- zW: **~leitung** f pipeline; **~zucker** m cane sugar

Rohstoff m raw material

Rokoko |'rɔkoko| (**-s**) nt rococo

Rollbahn |'rɔlbaːn| f (AVIAT) runway

Rolle |'rɔlə| f roll; (THEAT, soziologisch) role; (Garnrolle etc) reel, spool; (Walze) roller; (Wäscherolle) mangle; **keine ~ spielen** not to matter; **eine (wichtige) ~ spielen bei** to play a (major) part od role in; **r~n** vt, vi to roll; (AVIAT) to taxi; **~r** (**-s, -**) m scooter; (Welle) roller

Roll- zW: **~kragen** m rollneck, polo neck; **~mops** m pickled herring; **~schuh** m roller skate; **~stuhl** m wheelchair; **~stuhlfahrer(in)** m(f) wheelchair user; **~treppe** f escalator

Rom |roːm| (**-s**) nt Rome

Roman |ro'maːn| (**-s, -e**) m novel; **~tik** f romanticism; **~tiker** |ro'mantɪkər| (**-s, -**) m romanticist; **r~tisch** |ro'mantɪʃ| adj romantic; **~ze** |ro'mantsə| f romance

Römer |'røːmər| (**-s, -**) m wineglass; (Mensch) Roman

römisch |'røːmɪʃ| adj Roman; **~-katholisch**

adj (REL) Roman Catholic

röntgen |'rœntgən| vt to X-ray; **R~bild** nt X-ray; **R~strahlen** pl X-rays

rosa |'roːza| adj inv pink, rose(-coloured)

Rose |'roːzə| f rose

Rosen- zW: **~kohl** m Brussels sprouts pl; **~kranz** m rosary; **~montag** m Monday before Ash Wednesday

rosig |'roːzɪç| adj rosy

Rosine |ro'ziːnə| f raisin, currant

Ross ▲ |rɔs| (**-es, -e**) nt horse, steed; **~kastanie** ▲ f horse chestnut

Rost |rɔst| (**-(e)s, -e**) m rust; (Gitter) grill, gridiron; (Bettrost) springs pl; **~braten** m roast(ed) meat, roast; **r~en** vi to rust

rösten |'rœstən| vt to roast; to toast; to grill

Rost- zW: **r~frei** adj rust-free; rustproof; stainless; **r~ig** adj rusty; **~schutz** m rustproofing

rot |roːt| adj red; **in den ~en Zahlen** in the red

Röte |'røːtə| (**-**) f redness; **~ln** pl German measles sg; **r~n** vt, vr to redden

rothaarig adj red-haired

rotieren |ro'tiːrən| vi to rotate

Rot- zW: **~kehlchen** nt robin; **~stift** m red pencil; **~wein** m red wine

Rouge |ruːʒ| nt blusher

Roulade |ru'laːdə| f (KOCH) beef olive

Route |'ruːtə| f route

Routine |ru'tiːnə| f experience; routine

Rübe |'ryːbə| f turnip; **Gelbe ~** carrot; **Rote ~** beetroot (BRIT), beet (US)

rüber |'ryːbər| (umg) adv = **herüber**; **hinüber**

Rubrik |ru'briːk| f heading; (Spalte) column

Ruck |rʊk| (**-(e)s, -e**) m jerk, jolt

Rück- |'rʏk| zW: **~antwort** f reply, answer; **r~bezüglich** adj reflexive

Rücken |'rʏkən| (**-s, -**) m back; (Bergrücken) ridge

rücken vt, vi to move

Rücken- zW: **~mark** nt spinal cord; **~schwimmen** nt backstroke

Rück- zW: **~erstattung** f return, restitution; **~fahrkarte** f return (ticket); **~fahrt** f return journey; **~fall** m relapse; **r~fällig** adj relapsing; **r~fällig werden** to relapse; **~flug** m return flight; **~frage** f question; **r~fragen** vi to check, to inquire (further); **~gabe** f return; **~gaberecht** nt right of return; **~gang** m decline, fall; **r~gängig** adj: **etw r~gängig machen** to cancel sth; **~grat** (**-(e)s, -e**) nt spine, backbone; **~halt** m (Unterstützung) backing, support; **~kehr** (**-, -en**) f return; **~licht** nt back light; **r~lings** adv from behind; backwards; **~nahme** f taking back; **~porto** nt return postage; **~reise** f return journey; (NAUT) home voyage; **~reiseverkehr** m homebound traffic; **~ruf** m recall

Rucksack |'rʊkzak| m rucksack; **~tourist(in)**

m(f) backpacker

Rück- *zW:* **~schau** *f* reflection; **~schlag** *m* (*plötzliche Verschlechterung*) setback; **~schluss** ▲ *m* conclusion; **~schritt** *m* retrogression; **r~schrittlich** *adj* reactionary; retrograde; **~seite** *f* back; (*von Münze etc*) reverse; **~sicht** *f* consideration; **~sicht nehmen auf** *+akk* to show consideration for; **r~sichtslos** *adj* inconsiderate; (*Fahren*) reckless; (*unbarmherzig*) ruthless; **r~sichtsvoll** *adj* considerate; **~sitz** *m* back seat; **~spiegel** *m* (*AUT*) rear-view mirror; **~spiel** *nt* return match; **~sprache** *f* further discussion *od* talk; **~stand** *m* arrears *pl*; **r~ständig** *adj* backward, out-of-date; (*Zahlungen*) in arrears; **~strahler** (**-s, -**) *m* rear reflector; **~tritt** *m* resignation; **~trittbremse** *f* pedal brake; **~vergütung** *f* repayment; (*COMM*) refund; **~versicherung** *f* reinsurance; **r~wärtig** *adj* rear; **r~wärts** *adv* backward(s), back; **~wärtsgang** *m* (*AUT*) reverse gear; **~weg** *m* return journey, way back; **r~wirkend** *adj* retroactive; **~wirkung** *f* reaction; retrospective effect; **~zahlung** *f* repayment; **~zug** *m* retreat

Rudel ['ru:dəl] (**-s, -**) *nt* pack; herd
Ruder ['ru:dər] (**-s, -**) *nt* oar; (*Steuer*) rudder; **~boot** *nt* rowing boat; **r~n** *vt, vi* to row
Ruf [ru:f] (**-(e)s, -e**) *m* call, cry; (*Ansehen*) reputation; **r~en** (*unreg*) *vt, vi* to call; to cry; **~name** *m* usual (first) name; **~nummer** *f* (tele)phone number; **~säule** *f* (*an Autobahn*) emergency telephone; **~zeichen** *nt* (*RAD*) call sign; (*TEL*) ringing tone
rügen ['ry:gən] *vt* to rebuke
Ruhe ['ru:ə] (**-**) *f* rest; (*Ungestörtheit*) peace, quiet; (*Gelassenheit, Stille*) calm; (*Schweigen*) silence; **jdn in ~ lassen** to leave sb alone; **sich zur ~ setzen** to retire; **~!** be quiet!, silence!; **r~n** *vi* to rest; **~pause** *f* break; **~stand** *m* retirement; **~stätte** *f*: **letzte ~stätte** final resting place; **~störung** *f* breach of the peace; **~tag** *m* (*von Geschäft*) closing day
ruhig ['ru:ɪç] *adj* quiet; (*bewegungslos*) still; (*Hand*) steady; (*gelassen, friedlich*) calm; (*Gewissen*) clear; **kommen Sie ~ herein** just come on in; **tu das ~** feel free to do that
Ruhm [ru:m] (**-(e)s**) *m* fame, glory
rühmen ['ry:mən] *vt* to praise ♦ *vr* to boast
Rühr- [ry:r] *zW:* **~ei** *nt* scrambled egg; **r~en** *vt, vr* (*auch fig*) to move, to stir ♦ *vi:* **r~en von** to come *od* stem from; **r~en an** *+akk* to touch; (*fig*) to touch on; **r~end** *adj* touching, moving; **r~selig** *adj* sentimental, emotional; **~ung** *f* emotion
Ruin [ru'i:n] (**-s, -e**) *m* ruin; **~e** *f* ruin; **r~ieren** [-'ni:rən] *vt* to ruin

rülpsen ['rʏlpsən] *vi* to burp, to belch
Rum [rom] (**-s, -s**) *m* rum
Rumän- [ru'mɛ:n] *zW:* **~ien** (**-s**) *nt* Ro(u)mania; **r~isch** *adj* Ro(u)manian
Rummel ['roməl] (**-s**) (*umg*) *m* hubbub; (*Jahrmarkt*) fair; **~platz** *m* fairground, fair
Rumpf [rompf] (**-(e)s, ⁼e**) *m* trunk, torso; (*AVIAT*) fuselage; (*NAUT*) hull
rümpfen ['rʏmpfən] *vt* (*Nase*) to turn up
rund [ront] *adj* round ♦ *adv* (*etwa*) around; **~ um etw** round sth; **R~brief** *m* circular; **R~e** ['rondə] *f* round; (*in Rennen*) lap; (*Gesellschaft*) circle; **R~fahrt** *f* (round) trip
Rundfunk ['rontfoŋk] (**-(e)s**) *m* broadcasting; **im ~** on the radio; **~gerät** *nt* wireless set; **~sendung** *f* broadcast, radio programme
Rund- *zW:* **r~heraus** *adv* straight out, bluntly; **r~herum** *adv* round about; all round; **r~lich** *adj* plump, rounded; **~reise** *f* round trip; **r~schreiben** *nt* (*COMM*) circular; **~(wander)weg** *m* circular path *od* route
runter ['rontər] (*umg*) *adv* = **herunter; hinunter**
Runzel ['rontsəl] (**-, -n**) *f* wrinkle; **r~ig** *adj* wrinkled; **r~n** *vt* to wrinkle; **die Stirn r~n** to frown
rupfen ['ropfən] *vt* to pluck
ruppig ['ropɪç] *adj* rough, gruff
Rüsche ['ry:ʃə] *f* frill
Ruß [ru:s] (**-es**) *m* soot
Russe ['rosə] (**-n, -n**) *m* Russian
Rüssel ['rʏsəl] (**-s, -**) *m* snout; (*Elefantenrüssel*) trunk
rußig ['ru:sɪç] *adj* sooty
Russin ['rosɪn] *f* Russian
russisch *adj* Russian
Russland ▲ ['roslant] (**-s**) *nt* Russia
rüsten ['rʏstən] *vt* to prepare ♦ *vi* to prepare; (*MIL*) to arm ♦ *vr* to prepare (o.s.); to arm o.s.
rüstig ['rʏstɪç] *adj* sprightly, vigorous
Rüstung ['rʏstoŋ] *f* preparation; arming; (*Ritterrüstung*) armour; (*Waffen etc*) armaments *pl*; **~skontrolle** *f* arms control
Rute ['ru:tə] *f* rod
Rutsch [rotʃ] (**-(e)s, -e**) *m* slide; (*Erdrutsch*) landslide; **~bahn** *f* slide; **r~en** *vi* to slide; (*ausrutschen*) to slip; **r~ig** *adj* slippery
rütteln ['rʏtəln] *vt, vi* to shake, to jolt

S, s

S. *abk* (= *Seite*) p.; = **Schilling**
s. *abk* (= *siehe*) see
Saal [za:l] (**-(e)s, Säle**) *m* hall; room
Saarland ['za:rlant] *nt*: **das ~** the Saar(land)

Saat |zaːt| f (-, -en) f seed; (Pflanzen) crop; (Säen) sowing

Säbel |'zɛːbəl| (-s, -) m sabre, sword

Sabotage |zabo'taːʒə| f sabotage

Sach- |'zax| zW: ~**bearbeiter** m specialist; **s~dienlich** adj relevant, helpful; ~**e** f thing; (Angelegenheit) affair, business; (Frage) matter; (Pflicht) task; **zur ~e** to the point; **s~kundig** adj expert; **s~lich** adj matter-of-fact; objective; (Irrtum, Angabe) factual

sächlich |'zɛxlɪç| adj neuter

Sachschaden m material damage

Sachsen |'zaksən| (-s) nt Saxony

sächsisch |'zɛksɪʃ| adj Saxon

sacht(e) |'zaxt(ə)| adv softly, gently

Sachverständige(r) f(m) expert

Sack |zak| (-(e)s, ⁼e) m sack; ~**gasse** f cul-de-sac, dead-end street (US)

Sadismus |za'dɪsmʊs| m sadism

Sadist |za'dɪst| m sadist

säen |'zɛːən| vt, vi to sow

Safersex, Safer Sex m safe sex

Saft |zaft| (-(e)s, ⁼e) m juice; (BOT) sap; **s~ig** adj juicy; **s~los** adj dry

Sage |'zaːgə| f saga

Säge |'zɛːgə| f saw; ~**mehl** nt sawdust

sagen |'zaːgən| vt, vi to say; (mitteilen): **jdm ~** to tell sb; ► **Sie ihm, dass ...** tell him ...

sägen vt, vi to saw

sagenhaft adj legendary; (umg) great, smashing

sah etc |zaː| vb siehe sehen

Sahne |'zaːnə| (-) f cream

Saison |zɛ'zõː| (-, -s) f season

Saite |'zaɪtə| f string

Sakko |'zako| (-s, -s) m od nt jacket

Sakrament |zakra'mɛnt| nt sacrament

Sakristei |zakrɪs'taɪ| f sacristy

Salat |za'laːt| (-(e)s, -e) m salad; (Kopfsalat) lettuce; ~**soße** f salad dressing

Salbe |'zalbə| f ointment

Salbei |'zalbaɪ| (-s od -) m od f sage

Saldo |'zaldo| (-s, Salden) m balance

Salmiak |zalmi'ak| (-s) m sal ammoniac; ~**geist** m liquid ammonia

Salmonellenvergiftung |zalmo'nɛlən-| f salmonella (poisoning)

salopp |za'lɔp| adj casual

Salpeter |zal'peːtər| (-s) m saltpetre; ~**säure** f nitric acid

Salz |zalts| (-es, -e) nt salt; **s~en** (unreg) vt to salt; **s~ig** adj salty; ~**kartoffeln** pl boiled potatoes; ~**säure** f hydrochloric acid; ~**streuer** m salt cellar; ~**wasser** nt (Meerwasser) salt water

Samen |'zaːmən| (-s, -) m seed; (ANAT) sperm

Sammel- |'zaməl| zW: ~**band** m anthology; ~**fahrschein** m multi-journey ticket; (für mehrere Personen) group ticket

sammeln |'zaməln| vt to collect ► vr to

assemble, to gather; (konzentrieren) to concentrate

Sammlung |'zamlʊŋ| f collection; assembly, gathering; concentration

Samstag |'zamstaːk| m Saturday; **s~s** adv (on) Saturdays

Samt |zamt| (-(e)s, -e) m velvet

samt präp +dat (along) with, together with; ~ **und sonders** each and every one (of them)

sämtlich |'zɛmtlɪç| adj all (the), entire

Sand |zant| (-(e)s, -e) m sand

Sandale |zan'daːlə| f sandal

Sand- zW: ~**bank** f sandbank; **s~ig** |'zandɪç| adj sandy; ~**kasten** m sandpit; ~**kuchen** m Madeira cake; ~**papier** nt sandpaper; ~**stein** m sandstone; **s~strahlen** vt, vi insep to sandblast; ~**strand** m sandy beach

sandte etc |'zantə| vb siehe senden

sanft |zanft| adj soft, gentle; ~**mütig** adj gentle, meek

sang etc |zaŋ| vb siehe singen

Sänger(in) |'zɛŋər(ɪn)| (-s, -) m(f) singer

Sani- zW: **s~eren** |za'niːrən| vt to redevelop; (Betrieb) to make financially sound ► vr to line one's pockets; to become financially sound; **s~tär** |zani'tɛːr| adj sanitary; **s~täre Anlagen** sanitation sg; ~**täter** |zani'tɛːtər| (-s, -) m first-aid attendant; (MIL) (medical) orderly

sanktionieren |zaŋktsio'niːrən| vt to sanction

Sardelle |zar'dɛlə| f anchovy

Sardine |zar'diːnə| f sardine

Sarg |zark| (-(e)s, ⁼e) m coffin

Sarkasmus |zar'kasmʊs| m sarcasm

saß etc |zaːs| vb siehe sitzen

Satan |'zaːtan| (-s, -e) m Satan; devil

Satellit |zate'liːt| (-en, -en) m satellite; ~**enfernsehen** nt satellite television

Satire |za'tiːrə| f satire; **satirisch** adj satirical

satt |zat| adj full; (Farbe) rich, deep; **jdn/etw ~ sein** od **haben** to be fed up with sb/sth; **sich ~ hören/sehen an** +dat to hear/see enough of; **sich ~ essen** to eat one's fill; ~ **machen** to be filling

Sattel |'zatəl| (-s, ⁼) m saddle; (Berg) ridge; **s~n** vt to saddle; ~**schlepper** m articulated lorry

sättigen |'zɛtɪgən| vt to satisfy; (CHEM) to saturate

Satz |zats| (-es, ⁼e) m (GRAM) sentence; (Nebensatz, Adverbialsatz) clause; (Theorem) theorem; (MUS) movement; (TENNIS, Briefmarken etc) set; (Kaffee) grounds pl; (COMM) rate; (Sprung) jump; ~**teil** m part of a sentence; ~**ung** f (Statut) statute, rule; ~**zeichen** nt punctuation mark

Sau |zaʊ| (-, Säue) f sow; (umg) dirty pig

sauber |'zaʊbər| adj clean; (ironisch) fine; ~ **halten** to keep clean; **S~keit** f cleanness; (einer Person) cleanliness

säuberlich |'zɔybərlɪç| adv neatly

säubern vt to clean; (POL etc) to purge; **Säuberung** f cleaning; purge

Sauce |'zo:sə| f sauce, gravy

sauer |'zauɐ| adj sour; (CHEM) acid; (umg) cross; **saurer Regen** acid rain; **S~braten** m braised beef marinated in vinegar

Sauerei |zauə'rai| (umg) f rotten state of affairs, scandal; (Schmutz etc) mess; (Unanständigkeit) obscenity

Sauerkraut nt sauerkraut, pickled cabbage

säuerlich |'zɔyɐlɪç| adj (Geschmack) sour; (missvergnügt: Gesicht) dour

Sauer- zW: **~milch** f sour milk; **~rahm** m (KOCH) sour cream; **~stoff** m oxygen; **~teig** m leaven

saufen |'zaufən| (unreg) (umg) vt, vi to drink, to booze; **Säufer** |'zɔyfɐ| (-s, -) (umg) m boozer

saugen |'zaugən| (unreg) vt, vi to suck

säugen |'zɔygən| vt to suckle

Sauger |'zaugɐ| (-s, -) m dummy, comforter (US); (auf Flasche) teat

Säugetier |'zɔygə-| nt mammal

Säugling m infant, baby

Säule |'zɔylə| f column, pillar

Saum |zaum| (-(e)s, Säume) m hem; (Naht) seam

säumen |'zɔymən| vt to hem; to seam ♦ vi to delay, to hesitate

Sauna |'zauna| (-, -s) f sauna

Säure |'zɔyrə| f acid

sausen |'zauzən| vi to blow; (umg: eilen) to rush; (Ohren) to buzz; **etw ~ lassen** (umg) not to bother with sth

Saxofon, Saxophon |zakso'fo:n| (-s, -e) nt saxophone

SB abk = **Selbstbedienung**

S-Bahn f abk (= Schnellbahn) high speed railway; (= Stadtbahn) suburban railway

schaben |'ʃa:bən| vt to scrape

schäbig |'ʃɛ:bɪç| adj shabby

Schablone |ʃa'blo:nə| f stencil; (Muster) pattern; (fig) convention

Schach |ʃax| (-s, -s) nt chess; (Stellung) check; **~brett** nt chessboard; **~figur** f chessman; **'s~'matt** adj checkmate; **~spiel** nt game of chess

Schacht |ʃaxt| (-(e)s, ⁼e) m shaft

Schachtel (-, -n) f box

schade |'ʃa:də| adj a pity od shame ♦ excl: (wie) **~!** (what a) pity od shame; **sich** dat **zu ~ sein für etw** to consider o.s. too good for sth

Schädel |'ʃɛ:dəl| (-s, -) m skull; **~bruch** m fractured skull

Schaden |'ʃa:dən| (-s, ⁼) m damage; (Verletzung) injury; (Nachteil) disadvantage; **s~** vi +dat to hurt; **einer Sache s~** to damage sth; **~ersatz** m compensation,

damages pl; **~freude** f malicious glee; **s~froh** adj (Mensch, Lachen) gloating; **~sfall** m: **im ~sfall** in the event of a claim

schadhaft |'ʃa:thaft| adj faulty, damaged

schäd- |'ʃɛ:t| zW: **~igen** vt to damage; (Person) to do harm to, to harm; **~lich** adj: **~lich (für)** harmful (to); **S~lichkeit** f harmfulness; **S~ling** m pest

Schadstoff |'ʃa:tʃtɔf| m harmful substance; **s~arm** adj: **s~arm sein** to contain a low level of harmful substances

Schaf |ʃa:f| (-(e)s, -e) nt sheep

Schäfer |'ʃɛ:fɐ| (-s, -e) m shepherd; **~hund** m Alsatian (dog) (BRIT), German shepherd (dog) (US)

Schaffen |'ʃafən| (-s) nt (creative) activity

schaffen¹ |'ʃafən| (unreg) vt to create; (Platz) to make

schaffen² |'ʃafən| vt (erreichen) to manage, to do; (erledigen) to finish; (Prüfung) to pass; (transportieren) to take ♦ vi (umg: arbeiten) to work; **sich** dat **etw ~** to get o.s. sth; **sich an etw** dat **zu ~ machen** to busy o.s. with sth

Schaffner(in) |'ʃafnɐ(m)| (-s, -) m(f) (Busschaffner) conductor(-tress); (EISENB) guard

Schaft |ʃaft| (-(e)s, ⁼e) m shaft; (von Gewehr) stock; (von Stiefel) leg; (BOT) stalk; tree trunk

Schal |ʃa:l| (-s, -e od -s) m scarf

schal adj flat; (fig) insipid

Schälchen |'ʃɛ:lçən| nt cup, bowl

Schale |'ʃa:lə| f skin; (abgeschält) peel; (Nussschale, Muschelschale, Eischale) shell; (Geschirr) dish, bowl

schälen |'ʃɛ:lən| vt to peel; to shell ♦ vr to peel

Schall |ʃal| (-(e)s, -e) m sound; **~dämpfer** (-s, -) m (AUT) silencer; **s~dicht** adj soundproof; **s~en** vi to (re)sound; **s~end** adj resounding, loud; **~mauer** f sound barrier; **~platte** f (gramophone) record

Schalt- |'ʃalt| zW: **~bild** nt circuit diagram; **~brett** nt switchboard; **s~en** vt to switch, to turn ♦ vi (AUT) to change (gear); (umg: begreifen) to catch on; **~er** (-s, -) m counter; (an Gerät) switch; **~erbeamte(r)** m counter clerk; **~erstunden** pl hours of business; **~hebel** m switch; (AUT) gear lever; **~jahr** nt leap year; **~ung** f switching; (ELEK) circuit; (AUT) gear change

Scham |ʃa:m| (-) f shame; (~gefühl) modesty; (Organe) private parts pl

schämen |'ʃɛ:mən| vr to be ashamed

schamlos adj shameless

Schande |'ʃandə| (-) f disgrace

schändlich |'ʃɛntlɪç| adj disgraceful, shameful

Schändung |'ʃɛndʊŋ| f violation, defilement

Schanze |'ʃantsə| f (Sprungschanze) ski jump

Spelling reform: ▲ new spelling △ old spelling (to be phased out)

Schar [ʃaːr] (-, -en) f band, company; (*Vögel*) flock; (*Menge*) crowd; **in ~en** in droves; **s~en** vr to assemble, to rally

scharf [ʃarf] adj sharp; (*Essen*) hot, spicy; (*Munition*) live; **~ nachdenken** to think hard; **auf etw** akk **~ sein** (*umg*) to be keen on sth

Schärfe [ˈʃɛrfə] f sharpness; (*Strenge*) rigour; **s~n** vt to sharpen

Scharf- zW: **s~machen** (*umg*) vt to stir up; **~richter** m executioner; **~schütze** m marksman, sharpshooter; **s~sinnig** adj astute, shrewd

Scharlach [ˈʃarlax] (-s, -e) m (~*fieber*) scarlet fever

Scharnier [ʃarˈniːr] (-s, -e) nt hinge

scharren [ˈʃarən] vt, vi to scrape, to scratch

Schaschlik [ˈʃaʃlɪk] (-s, -s) m od nt (shish) kebab

Schatten [ˈʃatən] (-s, -) m shadow; **~riss** ▲ m silhouette; **~seite** f shady side, dark side

schattieren [ʃaˈtiːrən] vt, vi to shade

schattig [ˈʃatɪç] adj shady

Schatulle [ʃaˈtʊlə] f casket; (*Geldschatulle*) coffer

Schatz [ʃats] (-es, ⁻e) m treasure; (*Person*) darling

schätz- [ʃɛts] zW: **~bar** adj assessable; **S~chen** nt darling, love; **~en** vt (*abschätzen*) to estimate; (*Gegenstand*) to value; (*würdigen*) to value, to esteem; (*vermuten*) to reckon; **S~ung** f estimate; estimation; valuation; **nach meiner S~ung ...** I reckon that ...

Schau [ʃaʊ] (-) f show; (*Ausstellung*) display, exhibition; **etw zur ~ stellen** to make a show of sth, to show sth off; **~bild** nt diagram

Schauder [ˈʃaʊdər] (-s, -s) m shudder; (*wegen Kälte*) shiver; **s~haft** adj horrible; **s~n** vi to shudder; to shiver

schauen [ˈʃaʊən] vi to look

Schauer [ˈʃaʊər] (-s, -) m (*Regenschauer*) shower; (*Schreck*) shudder; **~geschichte** f horror story; **s~lich** adj horrific, spine-chilling

Schaufel [ˈʃaʊfəl] (-, -n) f shovel; (*NAUT*) paddle; (*TECH*) scoop; **s~n** vt to shovel, to scoop

Schau- zW: **~fenster** nt shop window; **~fensterbummel** m window shopping (expedition); **~kasten** m showcase

Schaukel [ˈʃaʊkəl] (-, -n) f swing; **s~n** vi to swing, to rock; **~pferd** nt rocking horse; **~stuhl** m rocking chair

Schaulustige(r) [ˈʃaʊlʊstɪgə(r)] f(m) onlooker

Schaum [ʃaʊm] (-(e)s, Schäume) m foam; (*Seifenschaum*) lather; **~bad** nt bubble bath

schäumen [ˈʃɔʏmən] vi to foam

Schaum- zW: **~festiger** (-s, -) m mousse;

~gummi m foam (rubber); **s~ig** adj frothy, foamy; **~stoff** m foam material; **~wein** m sparkling wine

Schauplatz m scene

schaurig [ˈʃaʊrɪç] adj horrific, dreadful

Schauspiel nt spectacle; (*THEAT*) play; **~er(in)** m(f) actor (actress); **s~ern** vi insep to act; **~haus** nt theatre

Scheck [ʃɛk] (-s, -s) m cheque; **~gebühr** f encashment fee; **~heft** m cheque book; **~karte** f cheque card

scheffeln [ˈʃɛfəln] vt to amass

Scheibe [ˈʃaɪbə] f disc; (*Brot etc*) slice; (*Glasscheibe*) pane; (*MIL*) target

Scheiben- zW: **~bremse** f (*AUT*) disc brake; **~wischer** m (*AUT*) windscreen wiper

Scheide [ˈʃaɪdə] f sheath; (*Grenze*) boundary; (*ANAT*) vagina; **s~n** (*unreg*) vt to separate; (*Ehe*) to dissolve ♦ vi to depart; to part; **sich s~n lassen** to get a divorce

Scheidung f (*Ehescheidung*) divorce

Schein [ʃaɪn] (-(e)s, -e) m light; (*Anschein*) appearance; (*Geld*) (bank)note; (*Bescheinigung*) certificate; **zum ~** in pretence; **s~bar** adj apparent; **s~en** (*unreg*) vi to shine; (*Anschein haben*) to seem; **s~heilig** adj hypocritical; **~werfer** (-s, -) m floodlight; spotlight; (*Suchscheinwerfer*) searchlight; (*AUT*) headlamp

Scheiß- [ʃaɪs] (*umg*) in zW bloody

Scheiße [ˈʃaɪsə] (-) (*umg*) f shit

Scheitel [ˈʃaɪtəl] (-s, -) m top; (*Haarscheitel*) parting; **s~n** vt to part

scheitern [ˈʃaɪtərn] vi to fail

Schelle [ˈʃɛlə] f small bell; **s~n** vi to ring

Schellfisch [ˈʃɛlfɪʃ] m haddock

Schelm [ʃɛlm] (-(e)s, -e) m rogue; **s~isch** adj mischievous, roguish

Schelte [ˈʃɛltə] f scolding; **s~n** (*unreg*) vt to scold

Schema [ˈʃeːma] (-s, -s od -ta) nt scheme, plan; (*Darstellung*) schema; **nach ~** quite mechanically; **s~tisch** [ʃeˈmaːtɪʃ] adj schematic; (*pej*) mechanical

Schemel [ˈʃeːməl] (-s, -) m (foot)stool

Schenkel [ˈʃɛŋkəl] (-s, -) m thigh

schenken [ˈʃɛŋkən] vt (*auch fig*) to give; (*Getränk*) to pour; **sich** dat **etw ~** (*umg*) to skip sth; **das ist geschenkt!** (*billig*) that's a giveaway!; (*nichts wert*) that's worthless!

Scherbe [ˈʃɛrbə] f broken piece, fragment; (*archäologisch*) potsherd

Schere [ˈʃeːrə] f scissors pl; (*groß*) shears pl; **s~n** (*unreg*) vt to cut; (*Schaf*) to shear; (*kümmern*) to bother ♦ vr to care; **scher dich zum Teufel!** get lost!; **~'rei** (*umg*) f bother, trouble

Scherz [ʃɛrts] (-es, -e) m joke; fun; **~frage** f conundrum; **s~haft** adj joking, jocular

Scheu [ʃɔʏ] (-) f shyness; (*Angst*) fear; (*Ehrfurcht*) awe; **s~** adj shy; **s~en** vr: **sich**

s~en vor +dat to be afraid of, to shrink from ♦ vt to shun ♦ vi (Pferd) to shy

scheuern |'ʃɔʏərn| vt to scour, to scrub

Scheune |'ʃɔʏnə| f barn

Scheusal |'ʃɔʏzaːl| (-s, -e) nt monster

scheußlich |'ʃɔʏslɪç| adj dreadful, frightful

Schi |ʃiː| m = **Ski**

Schicht |ʃɪçt| (-, -en) f layer; (Klasse) class, level; (in Fabrik etc) shift; **~arbeit** f shift work; **s~en** vt to layer, to stack

schick |ʃɪk| adj stylish, chic

schicken vt to send ♦ vr: **sich ~ (in** +akk) to resign o.s. (to) ♦ vb unpers (anständig sein) to be fitting

schicklich adj proper, fitting

Schicksal (-s, -e) nt fate; **~sschlag** m great misfortune, blow

Schieb- |'ʃiːb| zW: **~edach** nt (AUT) sun roof; **s~en** (unreg) vt (auch Drogen) to push; (Schuld) to put ♦ vi to push; **~etür** f sliding door; **~ung** f fiddle

Schieds- |'ʃiːts| zW: **~gericht** nt court of arbitration; **~richter** m referee; umpire; (Schlichter) arbitrator

schief |ʃiːf| adj crooked; (Ebene) sloping; (Turm) leaning; (Winkel) oblique; (Blick) funny; (Vergleich) distorted ♦ adv crooked(ly); (ansehen) askance; **etw ~ stellen** to slope sth; **~ gehen** (umg) to go wrong

Schiefer |'ʃiːfər| (-s, -) m slate

schielen |'ʃiːlən| vi to squint; **nach etw ~** (fig) to eye sth

schien etc |ʃiːn| vb siehe **scheinen**

Schienbein nt shinbone

Schiene |'ʃiːnə| f rail; (MED) splint; **s~n** vt to put in splints

schier |ʃiːr| adj (fig) sheer ♦ adv nearly, almost

Schieß- |'ʃiːs| zW: **~bude** f shooting gallery; **s~en** (unreg) vt to shoot; (Ball) to kick; (Geschoss) to fire ♦ vi to shoot; (Salat etc) to run to seed; **s~en auf** +akk to shoot at; **~e'rei** f shooting incident, shoot-out; **~pulver** nt gunpowder; **~scharte** f embrasure

Schiff |ʃɪf| (-(e)s, -e) nt ship, vessel; (Kirchenschiff) nave; **s~bar** adj (Fluss) navigable; **~bruch** m shipwreck; **s~brüchig** adj shipwrecked; **~chen** nt small boat; (Weben) shuttle; (Mütze) forage cap; **~er** (-s, -) m bargeman, boatman; **~fahrt** ▲ f shipping; (Reise) voyage

Schikane |ʃiˈkaːnə| f harassment; dirty trick; **mit allen ~n** with all the trimmings

schikanieren |ʃikaˈniːrən| vt to harass, to torment

Schikoree |'ʃikore| (-s) m od f = **Chicorée**

Schild¹ |ʃɪlt| (-(e)s, -e) nt shield; **etw im ~e führen** to be up to sth

Schild² |ʃɪlt| (-(e)s, -er) nt sign; nameplate; (Etikett) label

Schilddrüse f thyroid gland

schildern |'ʃɪldərn| vt to depict, to portray

Schildkröte f tortoise; (Wasserschildkröte) turtle

Schilf |ʃɪlf| (-(e)s, -e) nt (Pflanze) reed; (Material) reeds pl, rushes pl; **~rohr** nt (Pflanze) reed

schillern |'ʃɪlərn| vi to shimmer; **~d** adj iridescent

Schilling |'ʃɪlɪŋ| m schilling

Schimmel |'ʃɪməl| (-s, -) m mould; (Pferd) white horse; **s~ig** adj mouldy; **s~n** vi to get mouldy

Schimmer |'ʃɪmər| (-s) m (Lichtsein) glimmer; (Glanz) shimmer; **s~n** vi to glimmer, to shimmer

Schimpanse |ʃɪmˈpanzə| (-n, -n) m chimpanzee

schimpfen |'ʃɪmpfən| vt to scold ♦ vi to curse, to complain; to scold

Schimpfwort nt term of abuse

schinden |'ʃɪndən| (unreg) vt to maltreat, to drive too hard ♦ vr: **sich ~ (mit)** to sweat and strain (at), to toil away (at); **Eindruck ~** (umg) to create an impression

Schinde'rei f grind, drudgery

Schinken |'ʃɪŋkən| (-s, -) m ham

Schirm |ʃɪrm| (-(e)s, -e) m (Regenschirm) umbrella; (Sonnenschirm) parasol, sunshade; (Wandschirm, Bildschirm) screen; (Lampenschirm) (lamp)shade; (Mützenschirm) peak; (Pilzschirm) cap; **~mütze** f peaked cap; **~ständer** m umbrella stand

schizophren |ʃitsoˈfreːn| adj schizophrenic

Schlacht |ʃlaxt| (-, -en) f battle; **s~en** vt to slaughter, to kill; **~er** (-s, -) m butcher; **~feld** nt battlefield; **~hof** m slaughterhouse, abattoir; **~schiff** nt battleship; **~vieh** nt animals kept for meat; beef cattle

Schlaf |ʃlaːf| (-(e)s) m sleep; **~anzug** m pyjamas pl

Schläfe f (ANAT) temple

schlafen |'ʃlaːfən| (unreg) vi to sleep; **~ gehen** to go to bed; **S~szeit** f bedtime

schlaff |ʃlaf| adj slack; (energielos) limp; (erschöpft) exhausted

Schlaf- zW: **~gelegenheit** f sleeping accommodation; **~lied** nt lullaby; **s~los** adj sleepless; **~losigkeit** f sleeplessness, insomnia; **~mittel** nt sleeping pill

schläfrig |'ʃlɛːfrɪç| adj sleepy

Schlaf- zW: **~saal** m dormitory; **~sack** m sleeping bag; **~tablette** f sleeping pill; **~wagen** m sleeping car, sleeper; **s~wandeln** vi insep to sleepwalk; **~zimmer** nt bedroom

---

Spelling reform: ▲ *new spelling* △ *old spelling (to be phased out)*

Schlag [ʃlaːk] (-(e)s, ⁓e) m (auch fig) blow; (auch MED) stroke; (Pulsschlag, Herzschlag) beat; (ELEK) shock; (Blitzschlag) bolt, stroke; (Autotür) car door; (umg: Portion) helping; (Art) kind, type; **Schläge** pl (Tracht Prügel) beating sg; **mit einem ⁓** all at once; **~ auf ~** in rapid succession; **~ader** f artery; **~anfall** m stroke; **s~artig** adj sudden, without warning; **~baum** m barrier

Schlägel [ʃlɛːgl] (-s, -) m (drum)stick; (Hammer) mallet, hammer

schlagen [ʃlaːgən] (unreg) vt, vi to strike, to hit; (wiederholt ~, besiegen) to beat; (Glocke) to ring; (Stunde) to strike; (Sahne) to whip; (Schlacht) to fight ♦ vⁱ to fight; **nach jdm ~** (fig) to take after sb; **sich gut ~** (fig) to do well

Schlager [ʃlaːgər] (-s, -) m (auch fig) hit

Schläger [ʃlɛːgər] m brawler; (SPORT) bat; (TENNIS etc) racket; (GOLF) club; hockey stick; (Waffe) rapier; **Schläge'rei** f fight, punch-up

Schlagersänger(in) m(f) pop singer

Schlag- zW: **s~fertig** adj quick-witted; **~fertigkeit** f ready wit, quickness of repartee; **~loch** nt pothole; **~obers** (ÖSTERR) nt = **Schlagsahne**; **~sahne** f (whipped) cream; **~seite** f (NAUT) list; **~wort** nt slogan, catch phrase; **~zeile** f headline; **~zeug** nt percussion; drums pl; **~zeuger** (-s, -) m drummer

Schlamassel [ʃlaˈmasl] (-s, -) (umg) m mess

Schlamm [ʃlam] (-(e)s, ⁓e) m mud; **s~ig** adj muddy

Schlamp- zW: **~e** (umg) f slut; **s~en** (umg) vi to be sloppy; **~e'rei** (umg) f disorder, untidiness; sloppy work; **s~ig** (umg) adj (Mensch, Arbeit) sloppy, messy

Schlange [ʃlaŋə] f snake; (Menschenschlange) queue (BRIT), line-up (US); **~ stehen** to (form a) queue, to line up

schlängeln [ʃlɛŋəln] vr (Schlange) to wind; (Weg) to wind, twist; (Fluss) to meander

Schlangen- zW: **~biss** ▲ m snake bite; **~gift** nt snake venom; **~linie** f wavy line

schlank [ʃlaŋk] adj slim, slender; **S~heit** f slimness, slenderness; **S~heitskur** f diet

schlapp [ʃlap] adj limp; (locker) slack; **S~e** (umg) f setback

Schlaraffenland [ʃlaˈrafənlant] nt land of milk and honey

schlau [ʃlau] adj crafty, cunning

Schlauch [ʃlaux] (-(e)s, Schläuche) m hose; (in Reifen) inner tube; (umg: Anstrengung) grind; **~boot** nt rubber dinghy; **s~en** (umg) vt to tell on, to exhaust

Schläue [ʃlɔyə] (-) f cunning

Schlaufe [ʃlaufə] f loop; (Aufhänger) hanger

Schlauheit f cunning

schlecht [ʃlɛçt] adj bad ♦ adv badly; **~**

---

gelaunt in a bad mood; **~ und recht** after a fashion; **jdm ist ~** sb feels sick od bad; **jdm geht es ~** sb is in a bad way; **~ machen** to run down; **S~igkeit** f badness; bad deed

schlecken [ʃlɛkən] vt, vi to lick

Schlegel [ʃleːgl] (-s, -) m siehe **Schlägel** (KOCH) leg

schleichen [ʃlaiçən] (unreg) vi to creep, to crawl; **~d** adj gradual; creeping

Schleichwerbung f (COMM) plug

Schleier [ʃlaiər] (-s, -) m veil; **s~haft** (umg) adj: **jdm s~haft sein** to be a mystery to sb

Schleif- [ʃlaif] zW: **~e** f loop; (Band) bow; **s~en¹** vt, vi to drag; **s~en²** (unreg) vt to grind; (Edelstein) to cut; **~stein** m grindstone

Schleim [ʃlaim] (-(e)s, ⁓e) m slime; (MED) mucus; (KOCH) gruel; **~haut** f (ANAT) mucous membrane; **s~ig** adj slimy

Schlemm- [ʃlɛm] zW: **s~en** vi to feast; **~er** (-s, -) m gourmet; **~e'rei** f gluttony, feasting

schlendern [ʃlɛndərn] vi to stroll

schlenkern [ʃlɛŋkərn] vt, vi to swing, to dangle

Schlepp- [ʃlɛp] zW: **~e** f train; **s~en** vt to drag; (Auto, Schiff) to tow; (tragen) to lug; **s~end** adj dragging, slow; **~er** (-s, -) m tractor; (Schiff) tug

Schlesien [ʃleːziən] (-s) nt (GEOG) Silesia

Schleuder [ʃlɔydər] (-, -n) f catapult; (Wäscheschleuder) spin-drier; (Butterschleuder etc) centrifuge; **~gefahr** f risk of skidding; **„Achtung ~gefahr"** "slippery road ahead"; **s~n** vt to hurl; (Wäsche) to spin-dry ♦ vi (AUT) to skid; **~preis** m give-away price; **~sitz** m (AVIAT) ejector seat; (fig) hot seat; **~ware** f cheap od cut-price goods pl

schleunigst [ʃlɔynɪçst] adv straight away

Schleuse [ʃlɔyzə] f lock; (Schleusentor) sluice

schlicht [ʃlɪçt] adj simple, plain; **~en** vt (glätten) to smooth, to dress; (Streit) to settle; **S~er** (-s, -) m mediator, arbitrator; **S~ung** f settlement; arbitration

Schlick [ʃlɪk] (-(e)s, ⁓e) m mud; (Ölschlick) slick

schlief etc [ʃliːf] vb siehe **schlafen**

Schließ- [ʃliːs] zW: **s~en** (unreg) vt to close, to shut; (beenden) to close; (Freundschaft, Bündnis, Ehe) to enter into; (folgern): **s~en (aus)** to infer (from) ♦ vi, vr to close, to shut; **etw in sich s~en** to include sth; **~fach** nt locker; **s~lich** adv finally; **s~lich doch** after all

Schliff [ʃlɪf] (-(e)s, ⁓e) m cut(ting); (fig) polish

schlimm [ʃlɪm] adj bad; **~er** adj worse; **~ste(r, s)** adj worst; **~stenfalls** adv at (the) worst

Schlinge [ʃlɪŋə] f loop; (bes Henkersschlinge) noose; (Falle) snare; (MED) sling; **~l** (-s, -) m rascal; **s~n** (unreg) vt to wind; (essen) to bolt, to gobble ♦ vi (essen) to bolt one's food, to gobble

schlingern vi to roll

Schlips [ʃlɪps] (-es, -e) m tie

Schlitten ['ʃlɪtən] (-s, -) m sledge, sleigh;
~fahren (-s) nt tobogganing

schlittern ['ʃlɪtərn] vi to slide

Schlittschuh ['ʃlɪtʃuː] m skate; **~ laufen** to
skate; **~bahn** f skating rink; **~läufer(in)**
m(f) skater

Schlitz [ʃlɪts] (-es, -e) m slit; (für Münze)
slot; (Hosenschlitz) flies pl; **s~äugig** adj
slant-eyed

Schloss ▲ [ʃlɔs] (-es, ⁼er) nt lock; (an
Schmuck etc) clasp; (Bau) castle; chateau

schloss etc ▲ vb siehe **schließen**

Schlosser ['ʃlɔsər] (-s, -) m (Autoschlosser)
fitter; (für Schlüssel etc) locksmith

Schlosserei [-'raɪ] f metal (working) shop

Schlot [ʃloːt] (-(e)s, -e) m chimney; (NAUT)
funnel

schlottern ['ʃlɔtərn] vi to shake, to tremble;
(Kleidung) to be baggy

Schlucht [ʃluxt] (-, -en) f gorge, ravine

schluchzen ['ʃluxtsən] vi to sob

Schluck [ʃluk] (-(e)s, -e) m swallow; (Menge)
drop; **~auf (-s, -s)** m hiccups pl; **s~en** vt, vi
to swallow

schludern ['ʃluːdərn] vi to skimp, to do
sloppy work

schlug etc [ʃluːk] vb siehe **schlagen**

Schlummer ['ʃlʊmər] (-s) m slumber; **s~n**
vi to slumber

Schlund [ʃlʊnt] (-(e)s, ⁼e) m gullet; (fig) jaw

schlüpfen ['ʃlʏpfən] vi to slip; (Vogel etc) to
hatch (out)

Schlüpfer ['ʃlʏpfər] (-s, -) m panties pl,
knickers pl

schlüpfrig ['ʃlʏpfrɪç] adj slippery; (fig) lewd;
S~keit f slipperiness; (fig) lewdness

schlurfen ['ʃlʊrfən] vi to shuffle

schlürfen ['ʃlʏrfən] vt, vi to slurp

Schluss ▲ [ʃlʊs] (-es, ⁼e) m end;
(Schlussfolgerung) conclusion; **am ~** at the
end; **~ machen mit** to finish with

Schlüssel ['ʃlʏsəl] (-s, -) m (auch fig) key;
(Schraubenschlüssel) spanner, wrench; (MUS)
clef; **~bein** nt collarbone; **~blume** f
cowslip, primrose; **~bund** m bunch of keys;
~dienst m key cutting service; **~loch** nt
keyhole; **~position** f key position; **~wort** nt
keyword

schlüssig ['ʃlʏsɪç] adj conclusive

Schluss- ▲ zW: **~licht** ▲ nt taillight; (fig)
tailender; **~strich** ▲ m (fig) final stroke;
~verkauf ▲ m clearance sale

schmächtig ['ʃmɛçtɪç] adj slight

schmackhaft ['ʃmakhaft] adj tasty

schmal [ʃmaːl] adj narrow; (Person, Buch etc)
slender, slim; (karg) meagre

schmälern ['ʃmɛːlərn] vt to diminish; (fig) to
belittle

Schmalfilm m cine film

Schmalz [ʃmalts] (-es, -e) nt dripping, lard;
(fig) sentiment, schmaltz; **s~ig** adj (fig)
schmaltzy

schmarotzen [ʃma'rɔtsən] vi to sponge;
(BOT) to be parasitic; **Schmarotzer (-s, -)**
m parasite; sponger

Schmarren ['ʃmarən] (-s, -) m (ÖSTERR)
small piece of pancake; (fig) rubbish, tripe

schmatzen ['ʃmatsən] vi to smack one's lips;
to eat noisily

schmecken ['ʃmɛkən] vt, vi to taste; **es
schmeckt ihm** he likes it

Schmeichel- ['ʃmaɪçəl] zW: **~ei** [-'laɪ] f
flattery; **s~haft** adj flattering; **s~n** vi to
flatter

schmeißen ['ʃmaɪsən] (unreg) (umg) vt to
throw, to chuck

Schmeißfliege f bluebottle

Schmelz [ʃmɛlts] (-es, -e) m enamel;
(Glasur) glaze; (von Stimme) melodiousness;
s~en (unreg) vi to melt; (Erz) to smelt ♦ vi
to melt; **~punkt** m melting point;
~wasser nt melted snow

Schmerz [ʃmɛrts] (-es, -en) m pain; (Trauer)
grief; **s~empfindlich** adj sensitive to pain;
s~en vt, vi to hurt; **~ensgeld** nt
compensation; **s~haft** adj painful; **s~lich**
adj painful; **s~los** adj painless; **~mittel** nt
painkiller; **~tablette** f painkiller

Schmetterling ['ʃmɛtərlɪŋ] m butterfly

schmettern ['ʃmɛtərn] vt (werfen) to hurl;
(TENNIS: Ball) to smash; (singen) to belt out
(inf)

Schmied [ʃmiːt] (-(e)s, -e) m blacksmith; **~e**
['ʃmiːdə] f smithy, forge; **~eeisen** nt
wrought iron; **s~en** vt to forge; (Pläne) to
devise, to concoct

schmiegen ['ʃmiːgən] vt to press, to nestle
♦ vr: **sich ~ (an +akk)** to cuddle up (to), to
nestle (up to)

Schmier- ['ʃmiːr] zW: **~e** f grease; (THEAT)
greasepaint, make-up; **s~en** vt to smear;
(ölen) to lubricate, to grease; (bestechen) to
bribe; (schreiben) to scrawl ♦ vi (schreiben) to
scrawl; **~fett** nt grease; **~geld** nt bribe;
s~ig adj greasy; **~seife** f soft soap

Schminke ['ʃmɪŋkə] f make-up; **s~n** vt, vr to
make up

schmirgeln ['ʃmɪrgəln] vt to sand (down)

Schmirgelpapier nt emery paper

schmollen ['ʃmɔlən] vi to sulk, to pout

Schmorbraten m stewed od braised meat

schmoren ['ʃmoːrən] vt to stew, to braise

Schmuck [ʃmʊk] (-(e)s, -e) m jewellery;
(Verzierung) decoration

schmücken ['ʃmʏkən] vt to decorate

Spelling reform: ▲ *new spelling* △ *old spelling (to be phased out)*

schmucklos → schon

150

Schmuck- zW: **s~los** adj unadorned, plain;
~sachen pl jewels, jewellery sg
Schmuggel ['ʃmʊgəl] (-s) m smuggling;
s~n vt, vi to smuggle
Schmuggler (-s, -) m smuggler
schmunzeln ['ʃmʊntsəln] vi to smile
benignly
schmusen ['ʃmu:zən] (umg) vi (zärtlich sein)
to cuddle, to canoodle (inf)
Schmutz [ʃmʊts] (-es) m dirt, filth; **~fink** m
filthy creature; **~fleck** m stain; **s~ig** adj dirty
Schnabel ['ʃna:bəl] (-s, ⁓) m beak, bill;
(Ausguss) spout
Schnalle ['ʃnalə] f buckle, clasp; **s~n** vt to
buckle
Schnapp- ['ʃnap] zW: **s~en** vt to grab, to
catch ♦ vi to snap; **~schloss** ▲ nt spring
lock; **~schuss** ▲ m (PHOT) snapshot
Schnaps [ʃnaps] (-es, ⁓e) m spirits pl;
schnapps
schnarchen ['ʃnarçən] vi to snore
schnattern ['ʃnatərn] vi (Gänse) to gabble;
(Ente) to quack
schnauben ['ʃnaubən] vi to snort ♦ vr to
blow one's nose
schnaufen ['ʃnaufən] vi to puff, to pant
Schnauze f snout, muzzle; (Ausguß) spout;
(umg) gob
schnäuzen ▲ ['ʃnɔytsn] vr to blow one's
nose
Schnecke ['ʃnɛkə] f snail; **~nhaus** nt snail's
shell
Schnee [ʃne:] (-s) m snow; (Eischnee) beaten
egg white; **~ball** m snowball; **~flocke** f
snowflake; **s~frei** adj free of snow;
~gestöber nt snowstorm; **~glöckchen** nt
snowdrop; **~grenze** f snow line; **~kette** f
(AUT) snow chain; **~mann** m snowman;
~pflug m snowplough; **~regen** m sleet;
~schmelze f thaw; **~wehe** f snowdrift
Schneide ['ʃnaidə] f edge; (Klinge) blade;
s~n (unreg) vt to cut; (kreuzen) to cross, to
intersect with ♦ vr to cut o.s.; to cross, to
intersect; **s~nd** adj cutting; **~r** (-s, -) m
tailor; **~rei** f (Geschäft) tailor's; **~rin** f
dressmaker; **s~rn** vt to make ♦ vi to be a
tailor; **~zahn** m incisor
schneien ['ʃnaiən] vi unpers to snow
Schneise ['ʃnaizə] f clearing
schnell [ʃnɛl] adj quick, fast ♦ adv quick,
quickly, fast; **S~hefter** (-s, -) m loose-leaf
binder; **S~igkeit** f speed; **S~imbiss** m
(Lokal) snack bar; **S~kochtopf** m
(Dampfkochtopf) pressure cooker;
S~reinigung f dry cleaner's; **~stens** adv as
quickly as possible, **S~straße** f expressway;
S~zug m fast od express train
schneuzen △ ['ʃnɔytsən] vr = **schnäuzen**
schnippeln ['ʃnɪpəln] (umg) vt: ~ (an +dat)
to snip (at)
schnippisch ['ʃnɪpɪʃ] adj sharp-tongued

Schnitt (-(e)s, -e) m cut(ting); (~punkt)
intersection; (Querschnitt) (cross) section;
(Durchschnitt) average; (~muster) pattern;
(an Buch) edge; (umg: Gewinn) profit
schnitt etc vb siehe **schneiden**
Schnitt- zW: **~blumen** pl cut flowers; **~e** f
slice; (belegt) sandwich; **~fläche** f section;
~lauch m chive; **~punkt** m (point of)
intersection; **~stelle** f (COMPUT) interface;
~wunde f cut
Schnitz- ['ʃnɪts] zW: **~arbeit** f wood carving;
~el (-s, -) nt chip; (KOCH) escalope; **s~en** vt
to carve; **~er** (-s, -) m carver; (umg) blunder;
~e'rei f carving; carved woodwork
schnodderig ['ʃnɔdərɪç] (umg) adj snotty
Schnorchel ['ʃnɔrçəl] (-s, -) m snorkel
Schnörkel ['ʃnœrkəl] (-s, -) m flourish;
(ARCHIT) scroll
schnorren ['ʃnɔrən] vt, vi to cadge
schnüffeln ['ʃnyfəln] vi to sniff
Schnüffler (-s, -) m snooper
Schnuller ['ʃnʊlər] (-s, -) m dummy,
comforter (US)
Schnupfen ['ʃnʊpfən] (-s, -) m cold
schnuppern ['ʃnʊpərn] vi to sniff
Schnur [ʃnu:r] (-, ⁓e) f string, cord; (ELEK) flex
schnüren ['ʃny:rən] vt to tie
schnurgerade adj straight (as a die)
Schnurrbart ['ʃnʊrba:rt] m moustache
schnurren ['ʃnʊrən] vi to purr; (Kreisel) to
hum
Schnürschuh m lace-up (shoe)
Schnürsenkel m shoelace
schnurstracks adv straight (away)
Schock [ʃɔk] (-(e)s, -e) m shock; **s~ieren**
[ʃɔ'ki:rən] vt to shock, to outrage
Schöffe ['ʃœfə] (-n, -n) m lay magistrate;
Schöffin f lay magistrate
Schokolade [ʃoko'la:də] f chocolate
Scholle ['ʃɔlə] f clod; (Eisscholle) ice floe;
(Fisch) plaice

SCHLÜSSELWORT

schon [ʃo:n] adv 1 (bereits) already; **er ist
schon da** he's there already, he's already
there; **ist er schon da?** is he there yet?;
warst du schon einmal da? have you ever
been there?; **ich war schon einmal da** I've
been there before; **das war schon immer
so** that has always been the case; **schon
oft** often; **hast du schon gehört?** have you
heard?
2 (bestimmt) all right; **du wirst schon
sehen** you'll see (all right); **das wird
schon noch gut** that'll be OK
3 (bloß) just; **allein schon das Gefühl** ...
just the very feeling ...; **schon der Gedanke**
the very thought; **wenn ich das schon
höre** I can't bear to hear that
4 (einschränkend): **ja schon, aber** ... yes
(well), but ...

5: schon möglich possible; **schon gut!**
OK!; **du weißt schon** you know; **komm
schon!** come on!

schön [ʃøːn] *adj* beautiful; *(nett)* nice; **~e
Grüße** best wishes; **~e Ferien** have a nice
holiday; **~en Dank** (many) thanks; **sich ~
machen** to make o.s. look nice

schonen [ˈʃoːnən] *vt* to look after ♦ *vr* to take
it easy; **~d** *adj* careful, gentle

Schön- *zW:* **~heit** *f* beauty; **~heitsfehler** *m*
blemish, flaw; **~heitsoperation** *f* cosmetic
surgery

Schonkost (-) *f* light diet; *(Spezialdiät)*
special diet

Schon- *zW:* **~ung** *f* good care; *(Nachsicht)*
consideration; *(Forst)* plantation of young
trees; **s~ungslos** *adj* unsparing, harsh;
~zeit *f* close season

Schöpf- [ˈʃœpf] *zW:* **s~en** *vt* to scoop, to
ladle; *(Mut)* to summon up; *(Luft)* to
breathe in; **~er** (-s, -) *m* creator; **s~erisch**
adj creative; **~kelle** *f* ladle; **~ung** *f* creation

Schorf [ʃɔrf] (-(e)s, -e) *m* scab

Schornstein [ˈʃɔrnʃtain] *m* chimney;
(NAUT) funnel; **~feger** (-s, -) *m* chimney
sweep

Schoß [ʃoːs] (-es, ⸚e) *m* lap; *(Rockschoß)* coat
tail

schoss *etc* ▲ *vb siehe* **schießen**

Schoßhund *m* pet dog, lapdog

Schote [ˈʃoːtə] *f* pod

Schotte [ˈʃɔtə] *m* Scot, Scotsman

Schotter [ˈʃɔtər] (-s) *m* broken stone, road
metal; *(EISENB)* ballast

Schott- [ʃɔt] *zW:* **~in** *f* Scot, Scotswoman;
s~isch *adj* Scottish, Scots; **~land** *nt*
Scotland

schraffieren [ʃraˈfiːrən] *vt* to hatch

schräg [ʃrɛːk] *adj* slanting, not straight; **etw
~ stellen** to put sth at an angle; **~
gegenüber** diagonally opposite; **S~e**
[ˈʃrɛːgə] *f* slant; **S~strich** *m* oblique stroke

Schramme [ˈʃramə] *f* scratch; **s~n** *vt* to
scratch

Schrank [ʃraŋk] (-(e)s, ⸚e) *m* cupboard;
(Kleiderschrank) wardrobe; **~e** *f* barrier;
~koffer *m* trunk

Schraube [ˈʃraubə] *f* screw; **s~n** *vt* to screw;
~nschlüssel *m* spanner; **~nzieher** (-s, -) *m*
screwdriver

Schraubstock [ˈʃraupʃtɔk] *m* (TECH) vice

Schreck [ʃrɛk] (-(e)s, -e) *m* terror; fright;
~en (-s, -) *m* terror; fright; **s~en** *vt* to
frighten, to scare; **~gespenst** *nt* spectre,
nightmare; **s~haft** *adj* jumpy, easily
frightened; **s~lich** *adj* terrible, dreadful

Schrei [ʃrai] (-(e)s, -e) *m* scream; *(Ruf)* shout

Schreib- [ˈʃraib] *zW:* **~block** *m* writing pad;

s~en *(unreg)* *vt, vi* to write; *(buchstabieren)*
to spell; **~en** (-s, -) *nt* letter,
communication; **s~faul** *adj* bad about
writing letters; **~kraft** *f* typist; **~maschine** *f*
typewriter; **~papier** *nt* notepaper; **~tisch** *m*
desk; **~ung** *f* spelling; **~waren** *pl* stationery
sg; **~weise** *f* spelling; way of writing;
~zentrale *f* typing pool; **~zeug** *nt* writing
materials *pl*

schreien [ˈʃraiən] *(unreg)* *vt, vi* to scream;
(rufen) to shout; **~d** *adj* (fig) glaring; *(Farbe)*
loud

Schrein [ʃrain] (-(e)s, -e) *m* shrine

Schreiner [ˈʃrainər] (-s, -) *m* joiner;
(Zimmermann) carpenter; *(Möbelschreiner)*
cabinetmaker; **~ei** [-ˈrai] *f* joiner's workshop

schreiten [ˈʃraitən] *(unreg)* *vi* to stride

schrieb *etc* [ʃriːp] *vb siehe* **schreiben**

Schrift [ʃrift] (-, -en) *f* writing; handwriting;
(~art) script; *(Gedrucktes)* pamphlet, work;
~deutsch *nt* written German; **~führer** *m*
secretary; **s~lich** *adj* written ♦ *adv* in
writing; **~sprache** *f* written language;
~steller(in) (-s, -) *m(f)* writer; **~stück** *nt*
document; **~wechsel** *m* correspondence

schrill [ʃril] *adj* shrill

Schritt [ʃrit] (-(e)s, -e) *m* step; *(Gangart)*
walk; *(Tempo)* pace; *(von Hose)* crutch; **~
fahren** to drive at walking pace; **~macher**
(-s, -) *m* pacemaker; **~tempo** ▲ *nt:* **im
~tempo** at a walking pace

schroff [ʃrɔf] *adj* steep; *(zackig)* jagged; *(fig)*
brusque

schröpfen [ˈʃrœpfən] *vt* (fig) to fleece

Schrot [ʃroːt] (-(e)s, -e) *m od nt* (Blei) (small)
shot; *(Getreide)* coarsely ground grain,
groats *pl*; **~flinte** *f* shotgun

Schrott [ʃrɔt] (-(e)s, -e) *m* scrap metal;
~haufen *m* scrap heap; **s~reif** *adj* ready for
the scrap heap

schrubben [ˈʃrubən] *vt* to scrub

Schrubber (-s, -) *m* scrubbing brush

schrumpfen [ˈʃrumpfən] *vi* to shrink; *(Apfel)*
to shrivel

Schub- [ˈʃuːb] *zW:* **~fach** *nt* drawer;
~karren *m* wheelbarrow; **~lade** *f* drawer

Schubs [ʃuːps] (-es, -e) *(umg)* *m* shove (inf),
push

schüchtern [ˈʃʏçtərn] *adj* shy; **S~heit** *f*
shyness

Schuft [ʃuft] (-(e)s, -e) *m* scoundrel

schuften *(umg)* *vi* to graft, to slave away

Schuh [ʃuː] (-(e)s, -e) *m* shoe; **~band** *nt*
shoelace; **~creme** *f* shoe polish; **~größe** *f*
shoe size; **~löffel** *m* shoehorn; **~macher**
(-s, -) *m* shoemaker

Schul- *zW:* **~arbeit** *f* homework (no pl);
~aufgaben *pl* homework *sg*; **~besuch** *m*
school attendance; **~buch** *nt* school book

Schuld [ʃʊlt] (-, -en) f guilt; (FIN) debt; (Verschulden) fault; ~ **haben (an** +dat) to be to blame (for); **er hat ~** it's his fault; **jdm ~ geben** to blame sb; siehe **zuschulden**; **s~** adj: **s~ sein (an** +dat) to be to blame (for); **er ist s~** it's his fault; **s~en** [ˈʃʊldən] vt to owe; **s~enfrei** adj free from debt; **~gefühl** nt feeling of guilt; **s~ig** adj guilty; (gebührend) due; **s~ig an etw dat sein** to be guilty of sth; **jdm etw s~ig sein** to owe sb sth; **jdm etw s~ig bleiben** not to provide sb with sth; **s~los** adj innocent, without guilt; **~ner (-s, -)** m debtor; **~schein** m promissory note, IOU

Schule [ˈʃuːlə] f school; **s~n** vt to train, to school

Schüler(in) [ˈʃyːlər(ɪn)] (-s, -) m(f) pupil; **~austausch** m school od student exchange; **~ausweis** m (school) student card

Schul- zW: **~ferien** pl school holidays; **s~frei** adj: **~freier Tag** holiday; **s~frei sein** to be a holiday; **~hof** m playground; **~jahr** nt school year; **~kind** nt schoolchild; **s~pflichtig** adj of school age; **~schiff** nt (NAUT) training ship; **~stunde** f period, lesson; **~tasche** f school bag

Schulter [ˈʃʊltər] (-, -n) f shoulder; **~blatt** nt shoulder blade; **s~n** vt to shoulder

Schulung f education, schooling

Schulzeugnis nt school report

Schund [ʃʊnt] (-(e)s) m trash, garbage

Schuppe [ˈʃʊpə] f scale; **~n** pl (Haarschuppen) dandruff sg

Schuppen (-s, -) m shed

schuppig [ˈʃʊpɪç] adj scaly

Schur [ʃuːr] (-, -en) f shearing

schüren [ˈʃyːrən] vt to rake; (fig) to stir up

schürfen [ˈʃʏrfən] vt, vi to scrape, to scratch; (MIN) to prospect

Schurke [ˈʃʊrkə] (-n, -n) m rogue

Schurwolle f: „reine ~" "pure new wool"

Schürze [ˈʃʏrtsə] f apron

Schuss ▲ [ʃʊs] (-es, ²e) m shot; (WEBEN) woof; **~bereich** ▲ m effective range

Schüssel [ˈʃʏsəl] (-, -n) f bowl

Schuss- ▲ zW: **~linie** ▲ f line of fire; **~verletzung** ▲ f bullet wound; **~waffe** ▲ f firearm

Schuster [ˈʃuːstər] (-s, -) m cobbler, shoemaker

Schutt [ʃʊt] (-(e)s) m rubbish; (Bauschutt) rubble

Schüttelfrost m shivering

schütteln [ˈʃʏtəln] vt, vr to shake

schütten [ˈʃʏtən] vt to pour; (Zucker, Kies etc) to tip; (verschütten) to spill ♦ vi unpers to pour (down)

Schutthalde f dump

Schutthaufen m heap of rubble

Schutz [ʃʊts] (-es) m protection; (Unterschlupf) shelter; **jdn in ~ nehmen** to stand up for sb; **~anzug** m overalls pl; **~blech** nt mudguard

Schütze [ˈʃʏtsə] (-n, -n) m gunman; (Gewehrschütze) rifleman; (Scharfschütze, Sportschütze) marksman; (ASTROL) Sagittarius

schützen [ˈʃʏtsən] vt to protect; **~ vor** +dat od **gegen** to protect from

Schützenfest nt fair featuring shooting matches

Schutz- zW: **~engel** m guardian angel; **~gebiet** nt protectorate; (Naturschutzgebiet) reserve; (Naturschutzgebiet) reserve; **~hütte** f shelter, refuge; **~impfung** f immunisation

Schützling [ˈʃʏtslɪŋ] m protégé(e); (bes Kind) charge

Schutz- zW: **s~los** adj defenceless; **~mann** m policeman; **~patron** m patron saint

Schwaben [ˈʃvaːbən] nt Swabia; **schwäbisch** adj Swabian

schwach [ʃvax] adj weak, feeble

Schwäche [ˈʃvɛçə] f weakness; **s~n** vt to weaken

Schwachheit f weakness

schwächlich adj weakly, delicate

Schwächling m weakling

Schwach- zW: **~sinn** m imbecility; **s~sinnig** adj mentally deficient; (Idee) idiotic; **~strom** m weak current

Schwächung [ˈʃvɛçʊŋ] f weakening

Schwager [ˈʃvaːɡər] (-s, ²) m brother-in-law; **Schwägerin** [ˈʃvɛːɡərɪn] f sister-in-law

Schwalbe [ˈʃvalbə] f swallow

Schwall [ʃval] (-(e)s, -e) m surge; (Worte) flood, torrent

Schwamm [ʃvam] (-(e)s, ²e) m sponge; (Pilz) fungus

schwamm etc vb siehe **schwimmen**

schwammig adj spongy; (Gesicht) puffy

Schwan [ʃvaːn] (-(e)s, ²e) m swan

schwanger [ˈʃvaŋər] adj pregnant; **S~schaft** f pregnancy

schwanken vi to sway; (taumeln) to stagger, to reel; (Preise, Zahlen) to fluctuate; (zögern) to hesitate, to vacillate

Schwankung f fluctuation

Schwanz [ʃvants] (-es, ²e) m tail

schwänzen [ˈʃvɛntsən] (umg) vt to skip, to cut ♦ vi to play truant

Schwarm [ʃvarm] (-(e)s, ²e) m swarm; (umg) heart-throb, idol

schwärm- [ˈʃvɛrm] zW: **~en** vi to swarm; **~en für** to be mad od wild about; **S~erei** [-əˈraɪ] f enthusiasm; **~erisch** adj impassioned, effusive

Schwarte [ˈʃvartə] f hard skin; (Speckschwarte) rind

schwarz [ʃvarts] adj black; **~es Brett** notice board; **ins S~e treffen** (auch fig) to hit the bull's eye; **in den ~en Zahlen** in the black; **~ sehen** (umg) to see the gloomy side of things; **S~arbeit** f illicit work, moonlighting;

S~brot nt black bread; **S~e(r)** f(m) black (man/woman)

Schwärze |ˈʃvɛrtsə| f blackness; (Farbe) blacking; (Druckerschwärze) printer's ink; **s~n** vt to blacken

Schwarz- zW: **s~fahren** (unreg) vi to travel without paying; to drive without a licence; **~handel** m black market (trade); **~markt** m black market; **s~sehen** (unreg) (umg) vi (TV) to watch TV without a licence; **~wald** m Black Forest; **s~weiß**, **s~-weiß** adj black and white

schwatzen |ˈʃvatsən| vi to chatter

schwätzen |ˈʃvɛtsən| vi to chatter

Schwätzer |ˈʃvɛtsər| (**-s**, **-**) m gasbag

schwatzhaft adj talkative, gossipy

Schwebe |ˈʃveːbə| f: **in der ~** (fig) in abeyance; **~bahn** f overhead railway; **s~n** vi to drift, to float; (hoch) to soar

Schwed- |ˈʃveːd| zW: **~e** m Swede; **~en** nt Sweden; **~in** f Swede; **s~isch** adj Swedish

Schwefel |ˈʃveːfəl| (**-s**) m sulphur; **s~ig** adj sulphurous; **~säure** f sulphuric acid

Schweig- |ˈʃvaig| zW: **~egeld** nt hush money; **~en** (**-s**) nt silence; **s~en** (unreg) vi to be silent; to stop talking; **~epflicht** f pledge of secrecy; (von Anwalt) requirement of confidentiality; **s~sam** |ˈʃvaikzaːm| adj silent, taciturn; **~samkeit** f taciturnity, quietness

Schwein |ʃvain| (**-(e)s**, **-e**) nt pig; (umg) (good) luck

Schweine- zW: **~fleisch** nt pork; **~'rei** f mess; (Gemeinheit) dirty trick; **~stall** m pigsty

schweinisch adj filthy

Schweinsleder nt pigskin

Schweiß |ʃvais| (**-es**) m sweat, perspiration; **s~en** vt, vi to weld; **~er** (**-s**, **-**) m welder; **~füße** pl sweaty feet; **~naht** f weld

Schweiz |ʃvaits| f Switzerland; **~er(in)** m(f) Swiss; **s~erisch** adj Swiss

schwelgen |ˈʃvɛlgən| vi to indulge

Schwelle |ˈʃvɛlə| f (auch fig) threshold; doorstep; (EISENB) sleeper (BRIT), tie (US)

schwellen (unreg) vi to swell

Schwellung f swelling

Schwemme |ˈʃvɛmə| f (WIRTS: Überangebot) surplus

Schwenk- |ˈʃvɛŋk| zW: **s~bar** adj swivel-mounted; **s~en** vt to swing; (Fahne) to wave; (abspülen) to rinse ♦ vi to turn, to swivel; (MIL) to wheel; **~ung** f turn; wheel

schwer |ʃveːr| adj heavy; (schwierig) difficult, hard; (schlimm) serious, bad ♦ adv (sehr) very (much); (verletzt etc) seriously, badly; **~erziehbar** difficult (to bring up); **jdm ~ fallen** to be difficult for sb; **jdm/sich etw ~ machen** to make sth difficult for sb/o.s.; **~**

nehmen to take to heart; **sich** dat od akk **~ tun** to have difficulties; **~ verdaulich** indigestible, heavy; **~ wiegend** weighty, important; **S~arbeiter** m manual worker, labourer; **S~behinderte(r)** f(m) seriously handicapped person; **S~e** f weight, heaviness; (PHYS) gravity; **~elos** adj weightless; (Kammer) zero-G; **~fällig** adj ponderous; **S~gewicht** nt heavyweight; (fig) emphasis; **~hörig** adj hard of hearing; **S~industrie** f heavy industry; **S~kraft** f gravity; **S~kranke(r)** f(m) person who is seriously ill; **~lich** adv hardly; **~mütig** adj melancholy; **S~punkt** m centre of gravity; (fig) emphasis, crucial point

Schwert |ʃveːrt| (**-(e)s**, **-er**) nt sword; **~lilie** f iris

schwer- zW: **S~verbrecher(in)** m(f) criminal, serious offender; **S~verletzte(r)** f(m) serious casualty; (bei Unfall usw auch) seriously injured person

Schwester |ˈʃvɛstər| (**-**, **-n**) f sister; (MED) nurse; **s~lich** adj sisterly

Schwieger- |ˈʃviːgər| zW: **~eltern** pl parents-in-law; **~mutter** f mother-in-law; **~sohn** m son-in-law; **~tochter** f daughter-in-law; **~vater** m father-in-law

schwierig |ˈʃviːrɪç| adj difficult, hard; **S~keit** f difficulty

Schwimm- |ˈʃvɪm| zW: **~bad** nt swimming baths pl; **~becken** nt swimming pool; **s~en** (unreg) vi to swim; (treiben, nicht sinken) to float; (fig: unsicher sein) to be all at sea; **~er** (**-s**, **-**) m swimmer; (Angeln) float; **~erin** f (female) swimmer; **~lehrer** m swimming instructor; **~weste** f life jacket

Schwindel |ˈʃvɪndəl| (**-s**) m giddiness; dizzy spell; (Betrug) swindle, fraud; (Zeug) stuff; **s~frei** adj: **s~frei sein** to have a good head for heights; **s~n** (umg) vi (lügen) to fib; **jdm s~t es** sb feels dizzy

schwinden |ˈʃvɪndən| (unreg) vi to disappear; (sich verringern) to decrease; (Kräfte) to decline

Schwindler |ˈʃvɪndlər| m swindler; (Lügner) liar

schwindlig adj dizzy; **mir ist ~** I feel dizzy

Schwing- |ˈʃvɪŋ| zW: **s~en** (unreg) vt to swing; (Waffe etc) to brandish ♦ vi to swing; (vibrieren) to vibrate; (klingen) to sound; **~tür** f swing door(s); **~ung** f vibration; (PHYS) oscillation

Schwips |ʃvɪps| (**-es**, **-e**) m: **einen ~ haben** to be tipsy

schwirren |ˈʃvɪrən| vi to buzz

schwitzen |ˈʃvɪtsən| vi to sweat, to perspire

schwören |ˈʃvøːrən| (unreg) vt, vi to swear

schwul |ʃvuːl| (umg) adj gay, queer

schwül |ʃvyːl| adj sultry, close; **S~e** (**-**) f sultriness

---

Spelling reform: ▲ *new spelling* △ *old spelling (to be phased out)*

Schwule(r) (umg) f(m) gay (man/woman)
Schwung [ʃvʊŋ] (-(e)s, ²e) m swing;
(Triebkraft) momentum; (fig: Energie) verve,
energy; (umg: Menge) batch; **s~haft** adj
brisk, lively; **s~voll** adj vigorous
Schwur [ʃvuːr] (-(e)s, ²e) m oath; **~gericht**
nt court with a jury
sechs [zɛks] num six; **~hundert** num six
hundred; **~te(r, s)** adj sixth; **S~tel** (-s, -) nt
sixth
sechzehn ['zɛçtseːn] num sixteen
sechzig ['zɛçtsɪç] num sixty
See¹ [zeː] (-, -n) f sea
See² [zeː] (-s, -n) m lake
See- [zeː] zW: **~bad** nt seaside resort; **~hund**
m seal; **~igel** ['zeːliːgəl] m sea urchin;
s~krank adj seasick; **~krankheit** f
seasickness; **~lachs** m rock salmon
Seele ['zeːlə] f soul; **s~nruhig** adv calmly
Seeleute ['zeːlɔʏtə] pl seamen
Seel- zW: **s~isch** adj mental; **~sorge** f
pastoral duties pl; **~sorger** (-s, -) m
clergyman
See- [zeː] zW: **~macht** f naval power; **~mann** (pl
-leute) m seaman, sailor; **~meile** f nautical
mile; **~möwe** f (ZOOL) seagull; **~not** f
distress; **~räuber** m pirate; **~rose** f water
lily; **~stern** m starfish; **s~tüchtig** adj
seaworthy; **~weg** m sea route; **auf dem
~weg** by sea; **~zunge** f sole
Segel ['zeːgəl] (-s, -) nt sail; **~boot** nt yacht;
~fliegen (-s) nt gliding; **~flieger** m glider
pilot; **~flugzeug** nt glider; **s~n** vt, vi to sail;
~schiff nt sailing vessel; **~sport** m sailing;
~tuch nt canvas
Segen ['zeːgən] (-s, -) m blessing
Segler ['zeːglər] (-s, -) m sailor, yachtsman
segnen ['zeːgnən] vt to bless
Seh- ['zeː] zW: **s~behindert** adj partially
sighted; **s~en** (unreg) vt, vi to see; (in
bestimmte Richtung) to look; **mal s~en(, ob
...**) let's see (if ...); **siehe Seite 5** see page
5; **s~enswert** adj worth seeing;
~enswürdigkeiten pl sights (of a town);
~fehler m sight defect
Sehne ['zeːnə] f sinew; (an Bogen) string
sehnen vr: **sich ~ nach** to long od yearn for
sehnig adj sinewy
Sehn- zW: **s~lich** adj ardent; **~sucht** f
longing; **s~süchtig** adj longing
sehr [zeːr] adv very; (mit Verben) a lot, (very)
much; **zu ~** too much; **zu ~ geehrte(r) ...**
dear ...
seicht [zaɪçt] adj (auch fig) shallow
Seide ['zaɪdə] f silk; **s~n** adj silk; **~npapier** nt
tissue paper
seidig ['zaɪdɪç] adj silky
Seife ['zaɪfə] f soap
Seifen- zW: **~lauge** f soapsuds pl; **~schale** f
soap dish; **~schaum** m lather
seihen ['zaɪən] vt to strain, to filter

Seil [zaɪl] (-(e)s, -e) nt rope; cable; **~bahn** f
cable railway; **~hüpfen** (-s) nt skipping;
~springen (-s) nt skipping; **~tänzer(in)**
m(f) tightrope walker

sein [zaɪn] (pt war, pp gewesen) vi 1 to be;
ich bin I am; **du bist** you are; **er/sie/es ist**
he/she/it is; **wir sind/ihr seid/sie sind** we/
you/they are; **wir waren** we were; **wir sind
gewesen** we have been
2: **seien Sie nicht böse** don't be angry; **sei
so gut und ...** be so kind as to ...; **das
wäre gut** that would od that'd be a good
thing; **wenn ich Sie wäre** if I were you;
das wärs that's all, that's it; **morgen
bin ich in Rom** tomorrow I'll od I will od I
shall be in Rome; **waren Sie mal in Rom?**
have you ever been to Rome?
3: **wie ist das zu verstehen?** how is that
to be understood?; **er ist nicht zu ersetzen**
he cannot be replaced; **mit ihr ist nicht zu
reden** you can't talk to her
4: **mir ist kalt** I'm cold; **was ist?** what's the
matter?, what is it?; **ist was?** is something
the matter?; **es sei denn, dass ...** unless ...;
wie dem auch sei be that as it may; **wie
wäre es mit ...?** how od what about ...?;
lass das sein! stop that!

sein(e) ['zaɪn(ə)] adj his; its; **~e(r, s)** pron his;
its; **~er** (gen von **er**) pron of him; **~erseits**
adv for his part; **~erzeit** adv in those days,
formerly; **~esgleichen** pron people like
him; **~etwegen** adv (für ihn) for his sake;
(wegen ihm) on his account; (von ihm aus)
as far as he is concerned; **~etwillen** adv:
um ~etwillen = seinetwegen; **~ige** pron:
der/die/das ~ige od **S~ige** his

seit [zaɪt] präp +dat since ♦ konj since; **er ist ~
einer Woche hier** he has been here for a
week; **~ langem** for a long time; **~dem**
[zaɪt'deːm] adv, konj since
Seite ['zaɪtə] f side; (Buchseite) page; (MIL)
flank
Seiten- zW: **~ansicht** f side view; **~hieb** m
(fig) passing shot, dig; **s~s** präp +gen on the
part of; **~schiff** nt aisle; **~sprung** m
extramarital escapade; **~stechen** nt (a)
stitch; **~straße** f side road; **~streifen** m
verge; (der Autobahn) hard shoulder
seither [zaɪt'heːr] adv, konj since (then)
seit- zW: **~lich** adj on one od the side; side
cpd; **~wärts** adv sidewards
Sekretär [zekre'tɛːr] m secretary; (Möbel)
bureau
Sekretariat [zekretari'aːt] (-(e)s, -e) nt
secretary's office, secretariat
Sekretärin f secretary
Sekt [zɛkt] (-(e)s, -e) m champagne
Sekte ['zɛktə] f sect

Sekunde |zeˈkʊndə| f second
selber |ˈzɛlbər| = **selbst**
Selbst |zɛlpst| (-) nt self

SCHLÜSSELWORT

selbst |zɛlpst| pron 1: **ich/er/wir selbst** I
myself/he himself/we ourselves; **sie ist die
Tugend selbst** she's virtue itself; **er braut
sein Bier selbst** he brews his own beer;
wie gehts? – gut, und selbst? how are
things? – fine, and yourself?
2 (ohne Hilfe) alone, on my/his/one's etc
own; **von selbst** by itself; **er kam von
selbst** he came of his own accord; **selbst
gemacht** home-made
♦ adv even; **selbst wenn** even if; **selbst
Gott** even God (himself)

selbständig etc △ |ˈzɛlpʃtɛndɪç| = **selbst-
ständig** etc
Selbst- zW: **~auslöser** m (PHOT) delayed-
action shutter release; **~bedienung** f self-
service; **~befriedigung** f masturbation;
~beherrschung f self-control;
~bestimmung f (POL) self-determination;
~beteiligung f (VERSICHERUNG: bei Kosten)
(voluntary) excess; **s~bewusst ▲** adj
(self-)confident; **~bewusstsein ▲** nt self-
confidence; **~erhaltung** f self-preservation;
~erkenntnis f self-knowledge; **s~gefällig**
adj smug, self-satisfied; **~gespräch** nt
conversation with o.s.; **~kostenpreis** m
cost price; **s~los** adj unselfish, selfless;
~mord m suicide; **~mörder(in)** m(f)
suicide; **s~mörderisch** adj suicidal;
s~sicher adj self-assured; **s~ständig ▲**
|ˈzɛlpʃtɛndɪç| adj independent;
~ständigkeit ▲ f independence;
s~süchtig adj (Mensch) selfish;
~versorger (-s, -) m (im Urlaub etc) self-
caterer; **s~verständlich** |ˈzɛlpstfɛrʃtɛntlɪç|
adj obvious ♦ adv naturally; **ich halte das
für s~verständlich** I take that for granted;
~verteidigung f self-defence; **~vertrauen**
nt self-confidence; **~verwaltung** f
autonomy, self-government

selig |ˈzeːlɪç| adj happy, blissful; (REL) blessed;
(tot) late; **S~keit** f bliss
Sellerie |ˈzɛləriː| (-s, -(s) od -, -) m od f celery
selten |ˈzɛltən| adj rare ♦ adv seldom, rarely;
S~heit f rarity
Selterswasser |ˈzɛltərsvasər| nt soda water
seltsam |ˈzɛltzaːm| adj strange, curious;
S~keit f strangeness
Semester |zeˈmɛstər| (-s, -) nt semester;
~ferien pl vacation sg
Semi- |ˈzeːmi| in zW semi-; **~kolon** |-ˈkoːlɔn|
(-s, -s) nt semicolon
Seminar |zemiˈnaːr| (-s, -e) nt seminary;

(Kurs) seminar; (UNIV: Ort) department
building
Semmel |ˈzɛməl| (-, -n) f roll
Senat |zeˈnaːt| (-(e)s, -e) m senate, council
Sende- |ˈzɛndə| zW: **~bereich** m
transmission range; **~folge** f (Serie) series;
s~n (unreg) vt to send; (RAD, TV) to
transmit, to broadcast ♦ vi to transmit, to
broadcast; **~r** (-s, -) m station; (Anlage)
transmitter; **~reihe** f series (of broadcasts)
Sendung |ˈzɛndʊn| f consignment;
(Aufgabe) mission; (RAD, TV) transmission;
(Programm) programme
Senf |zɛnf| (-(e)s, -e) m mustard
senil |zeˈniːl| (pej) adj senile
Senior(in) |ˈzeːniɔr(ɪn)| (-s, -en) m(f)
(Mensch im Rentenalter) (old age) pensioner
Seniorenheim |zeniˈoːrənhaim| nt old
people's home
Senk- |ˈzɛnk| zW: **~blei** nt plumb; **~e** f
depression; **s~en** vt to lower ♦ vr to sink, to
drop gradually; **s~recht** adj vertical,
perpendicular; **~rechte** f perpendicular;
~rechtstarter m (AVIAT) vertical take-off
plane; (fig) high-flyer
Sensation |zɛnzatsiˈoːn| f sensation; **s~ell**
|-ˈnɛl| adj sensational
sensibel |zɛnˈziːbəl| adj sensitive
sentimental |zɛntimɛnˈtaːl| adj sentimental;
S~i'tät f sentimentality
separat |zepaˈraːt| adj separate
September |zɛpˈtɛmbər| (-(s), -) m
September
Serie |ˈzeːriə| f series
serien- zW: **~mäßig** adj standard;
S~mörder(in) m(f) serial killer; **~weise**
adv in series
seriös |zeriˈøːs| adj serious, bona fide
Service¹ |zɛrˈviːs| (-(s), -) nt (Geschirr) set,
service
Service² (-, -s) m service
servieren |zɛrˈviːrən| vt, vi to serve
Serviererin |zɛrˈviːrərɪn| f waitress
Serviette |zɛrviˈɛta| f napkin, serviette
Servo- |ˈzɛrvo| zW: **~bremse** f (AUT) servo(-
assisted) brake; **~lenkung** f (AUT) power
steering
Sessel |ˈzɛsəl| (-s, -) m armchair; **~lift** m
chairlift
sesshaft ▲ |ˈzɛshaft| adj settled; (ansässig)
resident
setzen |ˈzɛtsən| vt to put, to set; (Baum etc)
to plant; (Segel, TYP) to set ♦ vr to settle;
(Person) to sit down ♦ vi (springen) to leap;
(wetten) to bet
Setz- |ˈzɛts| zW: **~er (-s, -)** m (TYP)
compositor; **~ling** m young plant
Seuche |ˈzɔʏçə| f epidemic; **~ngebiet** nt
infected area

Spelling reform: ▲ *new spelling* △ *old spelling (to be phased out)*

seufzen |'zɔyftsən| vt, vi to sigh
Seufzer |'zɔyftsər| (-s, -) m sigh
Sex |zɛks| (-(es)) m sex; **~ualität** |-uali'tɛt| f
sex, sexuality; **~ualkunde** |zɛksu'aːl-| f (SCH)
sex education; **s~uell** |-u'ɛl| adj sexual
sezieren |ze'tsiːrən| vt to dissect
Shampoo |ʃam'puː| (-s, -s) nt shampoo
Sibirien |zi'biːriən| nt Siberia

┌─ SCHLÜSSELWORT ──────────────┐

sich |zɪç| pron 1 (akk): **er/sie/es ... sich** he/
she/it ... himself/herself/itself; **sie** pl/**man**
... **sich** they/one ... themselves/oneself; **Sie**
... **sich** you ... yourself/yourselves pl; **sich
wiederholen** to repeat oneself/itself
2 (dat): **er/sie/es ... sich** he/she/it ... to
himself/herself/itself; **sie** pl/**man ... sich**
they/one ... to themselves/oneself; **Sie ...
sich** you ... to yourself/yourselves pl; **sie
hat sich einen Pullover gekauft** she
bought herself a jumper; **sich die Haare
waschen** to wash one's hair
3 (mit Präposition): **haben Sie Ihren
Ausweis bei sich?** do you have your pass
on you?; **er hat nichts bei sich** he's got
nothing on him; **sie bleiben gern unter
sich** they keep themselves to themselves
4 (einander) each other, one another; **sie
bekämpfen sich** they fight each other od
one another
5: **dieses Auto fährt sich gut** this car
drives well; **hier sitzt es sich gut** it's good
to sit here

└──────────────────────────────┘

Sichel |'zɪçəl| (-, -n) f sickle; (Mondsichel)
crescent
sicher |'zɪçər| adj safe; (gewiss) certain;
(zuverlässig) secure, reliable; (selbstsicher)
confident; **vor jdm/etw ~ sein** to be safe
from sb/sth; **ich bin nicht ~** I'm not sure od
certain; **~ nicht** surely not; **aber ~!** of
course!; **~gehen** (unreg) vi to make sure
Sicherheit |'zɪçərhait| f safety; (auch FIN)
security; (Gewissheit) certainty;
(Selbstsicherheit) confidence
Sicherheits- zW: **~abstand** m safe
distance; **~glas** nt safety glass; **~gurt** m
safety belt; **s~halber** adv for safety; to be
on the safe side; **~nadel** f safety pin;
~schloss ▲ nt safety lock; **~vorkehrung** f
safety precaution
sicher- zW: **~lich** adv certainly, surely; **~n** vt
to secure; (schützen) to protect; (Waffe) to
put the safety catch on; **jdm etw ~n** to
secure sth for sb; **sich** dat **etw ~n** to secure
sth (for o.s.); **~stellen** vt to impound;
S~ung f (Sichern) securing; (Vorrichtung)
safety device; (an Waffen) safety catch; (ELEK)
fuse; **S~ungskopie** f back-up copy
Sicht |zɪçt| (-) f sight; (Aussicht) view; **auf** od
nach ~ (FIN) at sight; **auf lange ~** on a

long-term basis; **s~bar** adj visible; **s~en** vt
to sight; (auswählen) to sort out; **s~lich** adj
evident, obvious; **~verhältnisse** pl visibility
sg; **~vermerk** m visa; **~weite** f visibility
sickern |'zɪkərn| vi to trickle, to seep
Sie |ziː| (nom, akk) pron you
sie |ziː| pron (sg: nom) she, it; (: akk) her, it;
(pl: nom) they; (: akk) them
Sieb |ziːp| (-(e)s, -e) nt sieve; (KOCH) strainer;
s~en¹ |'ziːbən| vt to sift; (Flüssigkeit) to strain
sieben² num seven; **~hundert** num seven
hundred; **S~sachen** pl belongings
siebte(r, s) |'ziːptə(r, s)| adj seventh; **S~l**
(-s, -) nt seventh
siebzehn |'ziːptseːn| num seventeen
siebzig |'ziːptsɪç| num seventy
siedeln |'ziːdəln| vi to settle
sieden |'ziːdən| vt, vi to boil, to simmer
Siedepunkt m boiling point
Siedler (-s, -) m settler
Siedlung f settlement; (Häusersiedlung)
housing estate
Sieg |ziːk| (-(e)s, -e) m victory
Siegel |'ziːgəl| (-s, -) nt seal; **~ring** m signet
ring
Sieg- zW: **s~en** vi to be victorious; (SPORT) to
win; **~er** (-s, -) m victor; (SPORT etc) winner;
s~reich adj victorious
siehe etc |'ziːə| vb siehe **sehen**
siezen |'ziːtsən| vt to address as "Sie"
Signal |zɪ'gnaːl| (-s, -e) nt signal
Silbe |'zɪlbə| f syllable
Silber |'zɪlbər| (-s) nt silver; **~hochzeit** f
silver wedding (anniversary); **s~n** adj silver;
~papier nt silver paper
Silhouette |zilu'etə| f silhouette
Silvester |zɪl'vestər| (-s, -) nt New Year's Eve,
Hogmanay (SCOTTISH); **~abend** m =
Silvester
simpel |'zɪmpəl| adj simple
Sims |zɪms| (-es, -e) nt od m (Kaminsims)
mantelpiece; (Fenstersims) (window)sill
simulieren |zimu'liːrən| vt to simulate;
(vortäuschen) to feign ♦ vi to feign illness
simultan |zimul'taːn| adj simultaneous
Sinfonie |zɪnfo'niː| f symphony
singen |'zɪŋən| (unreg) vt, vi to sing
Singular |'zɪŋgulaːr| m singular
Singvogel |'zɪŋfoːgəl| m songbird
sinken |'zɪŋkən| (unreg) vi to sink; (Preise etc)
to fall, to go down
Sinn |zɪn| (-(e)s, -e) m mind; (Wahr-
nehmungssinn) sense; (Bedeutung) sense,
meaning; **~ für etw** sense of sth; **von ~en
sein** to be out of one's mind; **es hat keinen
~** there's no point; **~bild** nt symbol; **s~en**
(unreg) vi to ponder; **auf etw** akk **s~en** to
contemplate sth; **~estäuschung** f illusion;
s~gemäß adj faithful; (Wiedergabe) in one's
own words; **s~ig** adj clever; **s~lich** adj
sensual, sensuous; (Wahrnehmung) sensory;

~**lichkeit** f sensuality; **s~los** adj senseless; meaningless; ~**losigkeit** f senselessness; meaninglessness; **s~voll** adj meaningful; (*vernünftig*) sensible

Sintflut ['zɪntfluːt] f Flood

Sippe ['zɪpə] f clan, kin

Sippschaft ['zɪpʃaft] (*pej*) f relations pl, tribe; (*Bande*) gang

Sirene [zi're:nə] f siren

Sirup ['ziːrʊp] (**-s, -e**) m syrup

Sitt- ['zɪt] zW: ~**e** f custom; ~**en** pl (~*lichkeit*) morals; ~**enpolizei** f vice squad; **s~sam** adj modest, demure

Situation [zituatsi'o:n] f situation

Sitz [zɪts] (**-es, -e**) m seat; **der Anzug hat einen guten ~** the suit is a good fit; **s~en** (*unreg*) vi to sit; (*Bemerkung, Schlag*) to strike home, to tell; (*Gelerntes*) to have sunk in; **s~en bleiben** to remain seated; (*SCH*) to have to repeat a year; **auf etw** dat **s~en bleiben** to be lumbered with sth; **s~en lassen** (*SCH*) to make (sb) repeat a year; (*Mädchen*) to jilt; (*Wartenden*) to stand up; **etw auf sich** dat **s~en lassen** to take sth lying down; **s~end** adj (*Tätigkeit*) sedentary; ~**gelegenheit** f place to sit down; ~**platz** m seat; ~**streik** m sit-down strike; ~**ung** f meeting

Sizilien [zi'tsi:liən] nt Sicily

Skala ['ska:la] (**-, Skalen**) f scale

Skalpell [skal'pɛl] (**-s, -e**) nt scalpel

Skandal [skan'da:l] (**-s, -e**) m scandal; **s~ös** [-'lø:s] adj scandalous

Skandinav- [skandi'na:v] zW: ~**ien** nt Scandinavia; ~**ier(in)** m(f) Scandinavian; **s~isch** adj Scandinavian

Skelett [ske'lɛt] (**-(e)s, -e**) nt skeleton

Skepsis ['skɛpsɪs] (**-**) f scepticism

skeptisch ['skɛptɪʃ] adj sceptical

Ski [ʃi:] (**-, -er**) m ski; ~ **laufen** od **fahren** to ski; ~**fahrer** m skier; ~**gebiet** nt ski(ing) area; ~**läufer** m skier; ~**lehrer** m ski instructor; ~**lift** m ski-lift; ~**springen** nt ski-jumping; ~**stock** m ski-pole

Skizze ['skɪtsə] f sketch

skizzieren [skɪ'tsi:rən] vt, vi to sketch

Sklave ['skla:və] (**-n, -n**) m slave; ~**'rei** f slavery; **Sklavin** f slave

Skonto ['skɔnto] (**-s, -s**) m od nt discount

Skorpion [skɔrpi'o:n] (**-s, -e**) m scorpion; (*ASTROL*) Scorpio

Skrupel ['skru:pəl] (**-s, -**) m scruple; **s~los** adj unscrupulous

Skulptur [skʊlp'tu:r] f (*Gegenstand*) sculpture

S-Kurve ['ɛskʊrvə] f S-bend

Slip [slɪp] (**-s, -s**) m (under)pants; ~**einlage** f panty liner

Slowakei [slova'kaɪ] f: **die ~** Slovakia

Slowenien [slo've:niən] nt Slovenia

Smaragd [sma'rakt] (**-(e)s, -e**) m emerald

Smoking ['smo:kɪŋ] (**-s, -s**) m dinner jacket

┌─────────────────┐
│ *SCHLÜSSELWORT* │
└─────────────────┘

so [zo:] adv **1** (*so sehr*) so; **so groß/schön** etc so big/nice etc; **so groß/schön wie ...** as big/nice as ...; **so viel (wie)** as much as; **rede nicht so viel** don't talk so much; **so weit sein** to be ready; **so weit wie** od **als möglich** as far as possible; **ich bin so weit zufrieden** by and large I'm quite satisfied; **so wenig (wie)** as little (as); **das hat ihn so geärgert, daß ...** that annoyed him so much that ...; **so einer wie ich** somebody like me; **na so was!** well, well!

2 (*auf diese Weise*) like this; **mach es nicht so** don't do it like that; **so oder so** in one way or the other; **und so weiter** and so on; **... oder so was** ... or something like that; **das ist gut so** that's fine; **so gennant** so-called

3 (*umg: umsonst*): **ich habe es so bekommen** I got it for nothing

♦ *konj*: **so dass, sodass** so that; **so wie es jetzt ist** as things are at the moment

♦ *excl*: **so?** really?; **so, das wärs** so, that's it then

---

s. o. abk = **siehe oben**

Söckchen ['zœkçən] nt ankle socks

Socke ['zɔkə] f sock

Sockel ['zɔkəl] (**-s, -**) m pedestal, base

sodass [zo'das] konj so that

Sodawasser ['zo:davasər] nt soda water

Sodbrennen ['zo:tbrɛnən] (**-s, -**) nt heartburn

soeben [zo'je:bən] adv just (now)

Sofa ['zo:fa] (**-s, -s**) nt sofa

sofern [zo'fɛrn] konj if, provided (that)

sofort [zo'fɔrt] adv immediately, at once; ~**ig** adj immediate

Sog [zo:k] (**-(e)s, -e**) m (*Strömung*) undertow

sogar [zo'ga:r] adv even

sogleich [zo'glaɪç] adv straight away, at once

Sohle ['zo:lə] f sole; (*Talsohle etc*) bottom; (*MIN*) level

Sohn [zo:n] (**-(e)s, ²e**) m son

Solar- [zo'la:r] in zW solar; ~**zelle** f solar cell

solch [zɔlç] pron such; **ein ~e(r, s) ...** such a ...

Soldat [zɔl'da:t] (**-en, -en**) m soldier

Söldner ['zœldnər] (**-s, -**) m mercenary

solidarisch [zoli'da:rɪʃ] adj in od with solidarity; **sich ~ erklären** to declare one's solidarity

Solidari'tät f solidarity

solid(e) [zo'li:d(ə)] adj solid; (*Leben, Person*) respectable

Solist(in) [zo'lɪst(ɪn)] *m(f)* soloist
Soll [zɔl] (**-(s), -(s)**) *nt* (*FIN*) debit (side);
(*Arbeitsmenge*) quota, target

SCHLÜSSELWORT
---

sollen ['zɔlən] (*pt* **sollte**, *pp* **gesollt** *od* (*als
Hilfsverb*) **sollen**) *Hilfsverb* **1** (*Pflicht, Befehl*)
to be supposed to; **du hättest nicht gehen
sollen** you shouldn't have gone; **du
oughtn't to have gone; soll ich?** shall I?;
soll ich dir helfen? shall I help you?; **sag
ihm, er soll warten** tell him he's to wait;
was soll ich machen? what should I do?
2 (*Vermutung*): **sie soll verheiratet sein**
she's said to be married; **was soll das
heißen?** what's that supposed to mean?;
man sollte glauben, dass ... you would
think that ...; **sollte das passieren, ...** if
that should happen ...
♦ *vt, vi*: **was soll das?** what's all this?; **das
sollst du nicht** you shouldn't do that; **was
solls?** what the hell!

Solo ['zo:lo] (**-s, -s** *od* **Soli**) *nt* solo
somit [zo'mɪt] *konj* and so, therefore
Sommer ['zɔmər] (**-s, -**) *m* summer; **s~lich**
adj summery; summer; **~reifen** *m* normal
tyre; **~schlussverkauf** ▲ *m* summer sale;
~sprossen *pl* freckles
Sonde ['zɔndə] *f* probe
Sonder- ['zɔndər] *in zW* special; **~angebot**
nt special offer; **s~bar** *adj* strange, odd;
~fahrt *f* special trip; **~fall** *m* special case;
s~lich *adj* particular; (*außergewöhnlich*)
remarkable; (*eigenartig*) peculiar; **~marke** *f*
special issue stamp; **s~n** *konj* but ♦ *vt* to
separate; **nicht nur ..., s~n auch** not only
..., but also; **~preis** *m* special reduced price;
~zug *m* special train
Sonnabend ['zɔnˌaːbənt] *m* Saturday
Sonne ['zɔnə] *f* sun; **s~n** *vr* to sun o.s.
Sonnen- *zW*: **~aufgang** *m* sunrise;
s~baden *vi* to sunbathe; **~brand** *m*
sunburn; **~brille** *f* sunglasses *pl*; **~creme** *f*
suntan lotion; **~energie** *f* solar energy, solar
power; **~finsternis** *f* solar eclipse;
~kollektor *m* solar panel; **~schein** *m*
sunshine; **~schirm** *m* parasol, sunshade;
~schutzfaktor *m* protection factor; **~stich**
m sunstroke; **~uhr** *f* sundial; **~untergang**
m sunset; **~wende** *f* solstice
sonnig ['zɔnɪç] *adj* sunny
Sonntag ['zɔntaːk] *m* Sunday
sonst [zɔnst] *adv* otherwise; (*mit pron, in
Fragen*) else; (*zu anderer Zeit*) at other times,
normally ♦ *konj* otherwise; **~ noch etwas?**
anything else?; **~ nichts** nothing else; **~
jemand** anybody (at all); **~ wo** somewhere
else; **~ woher** from somewhere else; **~
wohin** somewhere else; **~ig** *adj* other
sooft [zo'ɔft] *konj* whenever

Sopran [zo'praːn] (**-s, -e**) *m* soprano
Sorge ['zɔrgə] *f* care, worry
sorgen *vi*: **für jdn ~** to look after sb ♦ *vr*:
sich ~ (um) to worry (about); **für etw ~** to
take care of *od* see to sth; **~frei** *adj* carefree;
~voll *adj* troubled, worried
Sorgerecht *nt* custody (of a child)
Sorg- [zɔrk] *zW*: **~falt** (**-**) *f* care(fulness);
s~fältig *adj* careful; **s~los** *adj* careless;
(*ohne ~en*) carefree; **s~sam** *adj* careful
Sorte ['zɔrtə] *f* sort; (*Warensorte*) brand; **~n** *pl*
(*FIN*) foreign currency *sg*
sortieren [zɔr'tiːrən] *vt* to sort (out)
Sortiment [zɔrti'mɛnt] *nt* assortment
sosehr [zo'zeːr] *konj* as much as
Soße ['zoːsə] *f* sauce; (*Bratensoße*) gravy
soufflieren [zu'fliːrən] *vt, vi* to prompt
Souterrain [zuˈtɛˈrɛ̃ː] (**-s, -e**) *nt* basement
souverän [zuvəˈrɛːn] *adj* sovereign;
(*überlegen*) superior
so- *zW*: **~viel** [zo'fiːl] *konj*: **~viel ich weiß** as
far as I know; *siehe* **so**; **~weit** [zo'vait] *konj*
as far as; *siehe* **so**; **~wenig** [zo'veːnɪç] *konj*
little as; *siehe* **so**; **~wie** [zo'viː] *konj* (*~bald*)
as soon as; (*ebenso*) as well as; **~wieso**
[zovi'zo:] *adv* anyway
sowjetisch [zɔ'vjɛtɪʃ] *adj* Soviet
Sowjetunion *f* Soviet Union
sowohl [zo'vo:l] *konj*: **~ ... als** *od* **wie auch**
both ... and
sozial [zotsiˈaːl] *adj* social; **S~abgaben** *pl*
national insurance contributions;
S~arbeiter(in) *m(f)* social worker;
S~demokrat *m* social democrat;
~demokratisch *adj* social democratic;
S~hilfe *f* income support (*BRIT*), welfare
(aid) (*US*); **~isieren** *vt* to socialize;
S~ismus [-'lɪsmʊs] *m* socialism; **S~ist**
[-'lɪst] *m* socialist; **~istisch** *adj* socialist;
S~politik *f* social welfare policy;
S~produkt *nt* (net) national product;
S~staat *m* welfare state; **S~versicherung**
f national insurance (*BRIT*), social security
(*US*); **S~wohnung** *f* council flat
soziologisch [zotsioˈloːgɪʃ] *adj* sociological
sozusagen [zotsu'zaːgən] *adv* so to speak
Spachtel ['ʃpaxtəl] (**-s, -**) *m* spatula
spähen ['ʃpeːən] *vi* to peep, to peek
Spalier [ʃpaˈliːr] (**-s, -e**) *nt* (*Gerüst*) trellis;
(*Leute*) guard of honour
Spalt [ʃpalt] (**-(e)s, -e**) *m* crack; (*Türspalt*)
chink; (*fig: Kluft*) split; **~e** *f* crack, fissure;
(*Gletscherspalte*) crevasse; (*in Text*) column;
s~en *vt, vr* (*auch fig*) to split; **~ung** *f*
splitting
Span [ʃpaːn] (**-(e)s, ⁼e**) *m* shaving
Spanferkel *nt* sucking pig
Spange ['ʃpaŋə] *f* clasp; (*Haarspange*) hair
slide; (*Schnalle*) buckle
Spanien ['ʃpaːniən] *nt* Spain; **Spanier(in)**
m(f) Spaniard; **spanisch** *adj* Spanish

Spann- |'ʃpan| zW: **~beton** m prestressed concrete; **~betttuch** ▲ nt fitted sheet; **~e** f (Zeitspanne) space; (Differenz) gap; **s~en** vt (straffen) to tighten, to tauten; (befestigen) to brace ♦ vi to be tight; **s~end** adj exciting, gripping; **~ung** f tension; (ELEK) voltage; (fig) suspense; (unangenehm) tension

Spar- |'ʃpaːr| zW: **~buch** nt savings book; **~büchse** f money box; **s~en** vt, vi to save; **sich** dat **etw s~en** to save o.s. sth; (Bemerkung) to keep sth to o.s.; **mit etw s~en** to be sparing with sth; **an etw** dat **s~en** to economize on sth; **~er** (-s, -) m saver

Spargel |'ʃpargǝl| (-s, -) m asparagus

Sparkasse f savings bank

Sparkonto nt savings account

spärlich |'ʃpɛːrlɪç| adj meagre; (Bekleidung) scanty

Spar- zW: **~preis** m economy price; **s~sam** adj economical, thrifty; **~samkeit** f thrift, economizing; **~schwein** nt piggy bank

Sparte |'ʃpartə| f field; line of business; (PRESSE) column

Spaß |ʃpaːs| (-es, ̈e) m joke; (Freude) fun; **jdm ~ machen** to be fun (for sb); **viel ~!** have fun!; **s~en** vi to joke; **mit ihm ist nicht zu s~en** you can't take liberties with him; **s~haft** adj funny, droll; **s~ig** adj funny, droll

spät |ʃpɛːt| adj, adv late; **wie ~ ist es?** what's the time?

Spaten |'ʃpaːtən| (-s, -) m spade

später adj, adv later

spätestens adv at the latest

Spätvorstellung f late show

Spatz |ʃpats| (-en, -en) m sparrow

spazier- |ʃpa'tsiːr| zW: **~en** vi to stroll, to walk; **~en fahren** to go for a drive; **~en gehen** to go for a walk; **S~gang** m walk; **S~stock** m walking stick; **S~weg** m path, walk

Specht |ʃpɛçt| (-(e)s, -e) m woodpecker

Speck |ʃpɛk| (-(e)s, -e) m bacon

Spediteur |ʃpedi'tøːr| m carrier; (Möbelspediteur) furniture remover

Spedition |ʃpedi'tsi'oːn| f carriage; (Speditionsfirma) road haulage contractor; removal firm

Speer |ʃpeːr| (-(e)s, -e) m spear; (SPORT) javelin

Speiche |'ʃpaiçə| f spoke

Speichel |'ʃpaiçəl| (-s) m saliva, spit(tle)

Speicher |'ʃpaiçər| (-s, -) m storehouse; (Dachspeicher) attic, loft; (Kornspeicher) granary; (Wasserspeicher) tank; (TECH) store; (COMPUT) memory; **s~n** vi (COMPUT) to store; (COMPUT) to save

speien |'ʃpaiən| (unreg) vt, vi to spit; (erbrechen) to vomit; (Vulkan) to spew

Speise |'ʃpaizə| f food; **~eis** |-|ais| nt ice-cream; **~kammer** f larder, pantry; **~karte** f menu; **s~n** vt to feed; to eat ♦ vi to dine; **~röhre** f gullet, oesophagus; **~saal** m dining room; **~wagen** m dining car

Speku- |ʃpeku| zW: **~lant** m speculator; **~lation** |-latsi'oːn| f speculation; **s~lieren** |-'liːrən| vi (fig) to speculate; **auf etw** akk **s~lieren** to have hopes of sth

Spelunke |ʃpe'lʊŋkə| f dive

Spende |'ʃpɛndə| f donation; **s~n** vt to donate, to give; **~r** (-s, -) m donor, donator

spendieren |ʃpɛn'diːrən| vt to pay for, to buy; **jdm etw ~** to treat sb to sth, to stand sb sth

Sperling |'ʃpɛrlɪŋ| m sparrow

Sperma |'ʃpɛrma| (-s, **Spermen**) nt sperm

Sperr- |'ʃpɛr| zW: **~e** f barrier; (Verbot) ban; **s~en** vt to block; (SPORT) to suspend; to bar; (vom Ball) to obstruct; (einschließen) to lock; (verbieten) to ban ♦ vr to baulk, to jib(e); **~gebiet** nt prohibited area; **~holz** nt plywood; **s~ig** adj bulky; **~müll** m bulky refuse; **~sitz** m (THEAT) stalls pl; **~stunde** f closing time

Spesen |'ʃpeːzən| pl expenses

Spezial- |ʃpetsi'aːl| in zW special; **~gebiet** nt specialist field; **s~i'sieren** vr to specialize; **~i'sierung** f specialization; **~ist** |-'lɪst| m specialist; **~i'tät** f speciality

speziell |ʃpetsi'ɛl| adj special

spezifisch |ʃpe'tsiːfɪʃ| adj specific

Sphäre |'sfɛːrə| f sphere

Spiegel |'ʃpiːgəl| (-s, -) m mirror; (Wasserspiegel) level; (MIL) tab; **~bild** nt reflection; **s~bildlich** adj reversed; **~ei** nt fried egg; **s~n** vt to mirror, to reflect ♦ vr to be reflected ♦ vi to gleam; (widerspiegeln) to be reflective; **~ung** f reflection

Spiel |ʃpiːl| (-(e)s, -e) nt game; (Schauspiel) play; (Tätigkeit) play(ing); (KARTEN) deck; (TECH) (free) play; **s~en** vt, vi to play; (um Geld) to gamble; (THEAT) to perform, to act; **s~end** adv easily; **~er** (-s, -) m player; (um Geld) gambler; **~e'rei** f trifling pastime; **~feld** nt pitch, field; **~film** m feature film; **~kasino** nt casino; **~plan** m (THEAT) programme; **~platz** m playground; **~raum** m room to manoeuvre, scope; **~regel** f rule; **~sachen** pl toys; **~uhr** f musical box; **~verderber** (-s, -) m spoilsport; **~waren** pl toys; **~zeug** nt toy(s)

Spieß |ʃpiːs| (-es, -e) m spear; (Bratspieß) spit; **~bürger** m bourgeois; **~er** (-s, -) (umg) m bourgeois; **s~ig** (pej) adj (petit) bourgeois

Spinat |ʃpi'naːt| (-(e)s, -e) m spinach

Spind [ʃpɪnt] (-(e)s, -e) m od nt locker
Spinn- [ˈʃpɪn] zW: **~e** f spider; **s~en** (unreg) vt, vi to spin; (umg) to talk rubbish; (verrückt sein) to be crazy od mad; **~erei** f spinning mill; **~rad** nt spinning wheel; **~webe** f cobweb
Spion [ʃpiˈoːn] (-s, -e) m spy; (in Tür) spyhole; **~age** [ʃpioˈnaːʒə] f espionage; **s~ieren** [ʃpioˈniːrən] vi to spy; **~in** f (female) spy
Spirale [ʃpiˈraːlə] f spiral
Spirituosen [ʃpirituˈoːzən] pl spirits
Spiritus [ˈʃpiːritus] (-, -se) m (methylated) spirit
Spital [ʃpiˈtaːl] (-s, ̈er) nt hospital
spitz [ʃpɪts] adj pointed; (Winkel) acute; (fig: Zunge) sharp; (: Bemerkung) caustic
Spitze f point, tip; (Bergspitze) peak; (Bemerkung) taunt, dig; (erster Platz) lead, top; (meist pl: Gewebe) lace
Spitzel (-s, -) m police informer
spitzen vt to sharpen
Spitzenmarke f brand leader
spitzfindig adj (over)subtle
Spitzname m nickname
Splitter [ˈʃplɪtɐ] (-s, -) m splinter
sponsern [ˈʃpɔnzɐn] vt to sponsor
spontan [ʃpɔnˈtaːn] adj spontaneous
Sport [ʃpɔrt] (-(e)s, -e) m sport; (fig) hobby; **~lehrer(in)** m(f) games od P.E. teacher; **~ler(in)** (-s, -) m(f) sportsman(-woman); **s~lich** adj sporting; (Mensch) sporty; **~platz** m playing od sports field; **~schuh** m (Turnschuh) training shoe, trainer; **~stadion** nt sports stadium; **~verein** m sports club; **~wagen** m sports car
Spott [ʃpɔt] (-(e)s) m mockery, ridicule; **s~billig** adj dirt-cheap; **s~en** vi to mock; **s~en** (über +akk) to mock (at), to ridicule
spöttisch [ˈʃpœtɪʃ] adj mocking
sprach etc [ʃpraːx] vb siehe **sprechen**
Sprach- [ˈʃpraːx] zW: **s~begabt** adj good at languages; **~e** f language; **~enschule** f language school; **~fehler** m speech defect; **~führer** m phrasebook; **~gefühl** nt feeling for language; **~kenntnisse** pl linguistic proficiency sg; **~kurs** m language course; **~labor** nt language laboratory; **s~lich** adj linguistic; **s~los** adj speechless
sprang etc [ʃpraŋ] vb siehe **springen**
Spray [spreː] (-s, -s) m od nt spray
Sprech- [ˈʃprɛç] zW: **~anlage** f intercom; **s~en** (unreg) vi to speak, to talk ♦ vt to say; (Sprache) to speak; (Person) to speak to; **mit jdm s~en** to speak to sb; **das spricht für ihn** that's a point in his favour; **~er(in)** (-s, -) m(f) speaker; (für Gruppe) spokesman(-woman); (RAD, TV) announcer; **~stunde** f consultation (hour); (doctor's) surgery; **~stundenhilfe** f (doctor's) receptionist; **~zimmer** nt consulting room, surgery,

office (US)
spreizen [ˈʃpraɪtsən] vt (Beine) to open, to spread; (Finger, Flügel) to spread
Spreng- [ˈʃprɛŋ] zW: **s~en** vt to sprinkle; (mit ~stoff) to blow up; (Gestein) to blast; (Versammlung) to break up; **~stoff** m explosive(s)
sprichst etc [ʃprɪçst] vb siehe **sprechen**
Sprichwort nt proverb; **sprichwörtlich** adj proverbial
Spring- [ˈʃprɪŋ] zW: **~brunnen** m fountain; **s~en** (unreg) vi to jump; (Glas) to crack; (mit Kopfsprung) to dive; **~er** (-s, -) m jumper; (Schach) knight
Sprit [ʃprɪt] (-(e)s, -e) (umg) m juice, gas
Spritz- [ˈʃprɪts] zW: **~e** f syringe; injection; (an Schlauch) nozzle; **s~en** vt to spray; (MED) to inject ♦ vi to splash; (herausspritzen) to spurt; (MED) to give injections; **~pistole** f spray gun; **~tour** f (umg) spin
spröde [ˈʃprøːdə] adj brittle; (Person) reserved, coy
Sprosse [ˈʃprɔsə] f rung
Sprössling ▲ [ˈʃprœslɪŋ] (umg) m (Kind) offspring (pl inv)
Spruch [ʃprʊx] (-(e)s, ̈e) m saying, maxim; (JUR) judgement
Sprudel [ˈʃpruːdəl] (-s, -) m mineral water; lemonade; **s~n** vi to bubble; (umg) to spurt (KOCH) sparkling od fizzy mineral water
Sprüh- [ˈʃpryː] zW: **~dose** f aerosol (can); **s~en** vi to spray; (fig) to sparkle ♦ vt to spray; **~regen** m drizzle
Sprung [ʃprʊŋ] (-(e)s, ̈e) m jump; (Riss) crack; **~brett** nt springboard; **s~haft** adj erratic; (Aufstieg) rapid; **~schanze** f ski jump
Spucke [ˈʃpʊkə] (-) f spit; **s~n** vt, vi to spit
Spuk [ʃpuːk] (-(e)s, -e) m haunting; (fig) nightmare; **s~en** vi (Geist) to walk; **hier s~t es** this place is haunted
Spülbecken [ˈʃpyːlbɛkən] nt (in Küche) sink
Spule [ˈʃpuːlə] f spool; (ELEK) coil
Spül- [ˈʃpyːl] zW: **~e** f (kitchen) sink; **s~en** vt, vi to rinse; (Geschirr) to wash up; (Toilette) to flush; **~maschine** f dishwasher; **~mittel** nt washing-up liquid; **~stein** m sink; **~ung** f rinsing; flush; (MED) irrigation
Spur [ʃpuːr] (-, -en) f trace; (Fußspur, Radspur, Tonbandspur) track; (Fährte) trail; (Fahrspur) lane
spürbar adj noticeable, perceptible
spüren [ˈʃpyːrən] vt to feel
spurlos adv without (a) trace
Spurt [ʃpʊrt] (-(e)s, -s od -e) m spurt; **s~en** vi to spurt
sputen [ˈʃpuːtən] vr to make haste
St. abk = **Stück**; (= Sankt) St.
Staat [ʃtaːt] (-(e)s, -en) m state; (Prunk) show; (Kleidung) finery; **s~enlos** adj

stateless; **s~lich** adj state(-); state-run

Staats- zW: **~angehörige(r)** f(m) national; **~angehörigkeit** f nationality; **~anwalt** m public prosecutor; **~bürger** m citizen; **~dienst** m civil service; **~examen** nt (UNIV) state exam(ination); **s~feindlich** adj subversive; **~mann** (pl **-männer**) m statesman; **~oberhaupt** nt head of state

Stab [ʃtaːp] (-(e)s, ˁe) m rod; (Gitterstab) bar; (Menschen) staff; **~hochsprung** m pole vault

stabil [ʃtaˈbiːl] adj stable; (Möbel) sturdy; **~i'sieren** vt to stabilize

Stachel [ˈʃtaxəl] (-s, -n) m spike; (von Tier) spine; (von Insekten) sting; **~beere** f gooseberry; **~draht** m barbed wire; **s~ig** adj prickly; **~schwein** nt porcupine

Stadion [ˈʃtaːdiɔn] (-s, **Stadien**) nt stadium

Stadium [ˈʃtaːdiʊm] nt stage, phase

Stadt [ʃtat] (-, ˁe) f town; **~autobahn** f urban motorway; **~bahn** f suburban railway; **~bücherei** f municipal library

Städt- [ˈʃtɛːt] zW: **~ebau** m town planning; **~epartnerschaft** f town twinning; **~er(in)** (-s, -) m(f) town dweller; **s~isch** adj municipal; (nicht ländlich) urban

Stadt- zW: **~kern** m town centre, city centre; **~mauer** f city wall(s); **~mitte** f town centre; **~plan** m street map; **~rand** m outskirts pl; **~rat** m (Behörde) town council, city council; **~rundfahrt** f tour of a/the city; **~teil** m district, part of town; **~zentrum** nt town centre

Staffel [ˈʃtafəl] (-, -n) f rung; (SPORT) relay (team); (AVIAT) squadron; **~lauf** m (SPORT) relay (race); **s~n** vt to graduate

Stahl [ʃtaːl] (-(e)s, ˁe) m steel

stahl etc vb siehe **stehlen**

stak etc [ʃtaːk] vb siehe **stecken**

Stall [ʃtal] (-(e)s, ˁe) m stable; (Kaninchen-stall) hutch; (Schweinestall) sty; (Hühnerstall) henhouse

Stamm [ʃtam] (-(e)s, ˁe) m (Baumstamm) trunk; (Menschenstamm) tribe; (GRAM) stem; **~baum** m family tree; (von Tier) pedigree; **s~eln** vt, vi to stammer; **s~en** vi: **s~en von** od **aus** to come from; **~gast** m regular (customer)

stämmig [ˈʃtɛmɪç] adj sturdy; (Mensch) stocky

Stammtisch [ˈʃtamtɪʃ] m table for the regulars

stampfen [ˈʃtampfən] vt, vi to stamp; (stapfen) to tramp; (mit Werkzeug) to pound

Stand [ʃtant] (-(e)s, ˁe) m position; (Wasserstand, Benzinstand etc) level; (Stehen) standing position; (Zustand) state; (Spielstand) score; (Messestand etc) stand; (Klasse) class; (Beruf) profession; siehe

instande; **zustande**

stand etc vb siehe **stehen**

Standard [ˈʃtandart] (-s, -s) m standard

Ständer [ˈʃtɛndar] (-s, -) m stand

Standes- [ˈʃtandəs] zW: **~amt** nt registry office; **~beamte(r)** m registrar; **s~gemäß** adj, adv according to one's social position; **~unterschied** m social difference

Stand- zW: **s~haft** adj steadfast; **s~halten** (unreg) vi: (**jdm/etw**) **s~halten** to stand firm (against sb/sth), to resist (sb/sth)

ständig [ˈʃtɛndɪç] adj permanent; (ununterbrochen) constant, continual

Stand- zW: **~licht** nt sidelights pl, parking lights pl (US); **~ort** m location; (MIL) garrison; **~punkt** m standpoint; **~spur** f hard shoulder

Stange [ˈʃtaŋə] f stick; (Stab) pole, bar; rod; (Zigaretten) carton; **von der ~** (COMM) off the peg; **eine ~ Geld** (umg) quite a packet

Stängel [ˈʃtɛŋl] (-s, -) m stalk

Stapel [ˈʃtaːpəl] (-s, -) m pile; (NAUT) stocks pl; **~lauf** m launch; **s~n** vt to pile (up)

Star¹ [ʃtaːr] (-(e)s, -e) m starling; (MED) cataract

Star² [ʃtaːr] (-s, -s) m (Filmstar etc) star

starb etc [ʃtarp] vb siehe **sterben**

stark [ʃtark] adj strong; (heftig, groß) heavy; (Maßangabe) thick

Stärke [ˈʃtɛrkə] f strength; heaviness; thickness; (KOCH: Wäschestärke) starch; **s~n** vt to strengthen; (Wäsche) to starch

Starkstrom m heavy current

Stärkung [ˈʃtɛrkʊŋ] f strengthening; (Essen) refreshment

starr [ʃtar] adj stiff; (unnachgiebig) rigid; (Blick) staring; **~en** vi to stare; **~en vor** od **von** to be covered in; (Waffen) to be bristling with; **S~heit** f rigidity; **~köpfig** adj stubborn; **S~sinn** m obstinacy

Start [ʃtart] (-(e)s, -e) m start; (AVIAT) takeoff; **~automatik** f (AUT) automatic choke; **~bahn** f runway; **s~en** vt to start ♦ vi to start; to take off; **~er** (-s, -) m starter; **~erlaubnis** f takeoff clearance; **~hilfekabel** nt jump leads pl

Station [ʃtatsiˈoːn] f station; hospital ward; **s~är** [ʃtatsioˈnɛːr] adj (MED) in-patient attr; **s~ieren** [-ˈniːrən] vt to station

Statist [ʃtaˈtɪst] m extra, supernumerary

Statistik f statistics sg; **~er** (-s, -) m statistician

statistisch adj statistical

Stativ [ʃtaˈtiːf] (-s, -e) nt tripod

statt [ʃtat] konj instead of ♦ präp (+gen od dat) instead of

Stätte [ˈʃtɛtə] f place

statt- zW: **~finden** (unreg) vi to take place; **~haft** adj admissible; **~lich** adj imposing, handsome

Statue |'ʃtaːtuə| f statue

Status |'ʃtaːtʊs| (-, -) m status

Stau |ʃtaʊ| (-(e)s, -e) m blockage; (*Verkehrsstau*) (traffic) jam

Staub |ʃtaʊp| (-(e)s) m dust; ~ **saugen** to vacuum, to hoover ®; **s~en** |'ʃtaʊbən| vi to be dusty; **s~ig** adj dusty; **s~saugen** vi to vacuum, to hoover; ~**sauger** m vacuum cleaner; ~**tuch** nt duster

Staudamm m dam

Staude |'ʃtaʊdə| f shrub

stauen |'ʃtaʊən| vt (*Wasser*) to dam up; (*Blut*) to stop the flow of ♦ vr (*Wasser*) to become dammed up; (*MED: Verkehr*) to become congested; (*Menschen*) to collect; (*Gefühle*) to build up

staunen |'ʃtaʊnən| vi to be astonished; **S~** (-s) nt amazement

Stausee |'ʃtaʊzeː| (-s, -n) m reservoir, man-made lake

Stauung |'ʃtaʊʊŋ| f (*von Wasser*) damming-up; (*von Blut, Verkehr*) congestion

Std. abk (= *Stunde*) hr.

Steak |ʃteːk| nt steak

Stech- |'ʃtɛç| zW: **s~en** (*unreg*) vt (*mit Nadel etc*) to prick; (*mit Messer*) to stab; (*mit Finger*) to poke; (*Biene etc*) to sting; (*Mücke*) to bite; (*Sonne*) to burn; (*KARTEN*) to take; (*KUNST*) to engrave; (*Torf, Spargel*) to cut; **in See s~en** to put to sea; ~**en** (-s, -) nt (*SPORT*) play-off; jump-off; **s~end** adj piercing, stabbing; (*Geruch*) pungent; ~**palme** f holly; ~**uhr** f time clock

Steck- |'ʃtɛk| zW: ~**brief** m "wanted" poster; ~**dose** f (wall) socket; **s~en** vt to put, to insert; (*Nadel*) to stick; (*Pflanzen*) to plant; (*beim Nähen*) to pin ♦ vi (*auch unreg*) to be; (*festsitzen*) to be stuck; (*Nadeln*) to stick; **s~en bleiben** to get stuck; **s~en lassen** to leave in; ~**enpferd** nt hobby-horse; ~**er** (-s, -) m plug; ~**nadel** f pin

Steg |ʃteːk| (-(e)s, -e) m small bridge; (*Anlegesteg*) landing stage; ~**reif** m: **aus dem ~reif** just like that

stehen |'ʃteːən| (*unreg*) vi to stand; (*sich befinden*) to be; (*in Zeitung*) to say; (*stillstehen*) to have stopped ♦ vi unpers: **es steht schlecht um jdn/etw** things are bad for sb/sth; **zu jdm/etw ~** to stand by sb/sth; **jdm ~** to suit sb; **wie stehts?** how are things?; (*SPORT*) what's the score?; ~ **bleiben** to remain standing; (*Uhr*) to stop; (*Fehler*) to stay as it is; ~ **lassen** to leave; (*Bart*) to grow

Stehlampe |'ʃteːlampə| f standard lamp

stehlen |'ʃteːlən| (*unreg*) vt to steal

Stehplatz |'ʃteːplats| m standing place

steif |ʃtaɪf| adj stiff; **S~heit** f stiffness

Steig- |'ʃtaɪk| zW: ~**bügel** m stirrup; **s~en** |'ʃtaɪgən| (*unreg*) vi to rise; (*klettern*) to

climb; **s~en in** +akk/**auf** +akk to get in/on; **s~ern** vt to raise; (*GRAM*) to compare ♦ vi (*Auktion*) to bid ♦ vr to increase; ~**erung** f raising; (*GRAM*) comparison; ~**ung** f incline, gradient, rise

steil |ʃtaɪl| adj steep; **S~küste** f steep coast; (*Klippen*) cliffs pl

Stein |ʃtaɪn| (-(e)s, -e) m stone; (*in Uhr*) jewel; ~**bock** m (*ASTROL*) Capricorn; ~**bruch** m quarry; **s~ern** adj (made of) stone; (*fig*) stony; ~**gut** nt stoneware; **s~ig** |'ʃtaɪnɪç| adj stony; **s~igen** vt to stone; ~**kohle** f mineral coal; ~**zeit** f Stone Age

Stelle |'ʃtɛlə| f place; (*Arbeit*) post, job; (*Amt*) office; **an Ihrer/meiner ~** in your/my place; *siehe* **anstelle**

stellen vt to put; (*Uhr etc*) to set; (*zur Verfügung ~*) to supply; (*fassen: Dieb*) to apprehend ♦ vr (*sich aufstellen*) to stand; (*sich einfinden*) to present o.s.; (*bei Polizei*) to give o.s. up; (*vorgeben*) to pretend (to be); **sich zu etw ~** to have an opinion of sth

Stellen- zW: ~**angebot** nt offer of a post; (*in Zeitung*) "vacancies"; ~**anzeige** f job advertisement; ~**gesuch** nt application for a post; ~**vermittlung** f employment agency

Stell- zW: ~**ung** f position; (*MIL*) line; ~**ung nehmen zu** to comment on; ~**ungnahme** f comment; **s~vertretend** adj deputy, acting; ~**vertreter** m deputy

Stelze |'ʃtɛltsə| f stilt

stemmen |'ʃtɛmən| vt to lift (up); (*drücken*) to press; **sich ~ gegen** (*fig*) to resist, to oppose

Stempel |'ʃtɛmpəl| (-s, -) m stamp; (*BOT*) pistil; ~**kissen** nt ink pad; **s~n** vt to stamp; (*Briefmarke*) to cancel; **s~n gehen** (*umg*) to be od go on the dole

Stengel |'ʃtɛŋəl| (-s, -) m = **Stängel**

Steno- |ʃteno| zW: ~**gramm** |-'gram| nt shorthand report; ~**grafie** ▲ |-gra'fiː| f shorthand; **s~grafieren** ▲ |-gra'fiːrən| vt, vi to write (in) shorthand; ~**typist(in)** |-ty'pɪst(ɪn)| m(f) shorthand typist

Stepp- |'ʃtɛp| zW: ~**decke** f quilt; ~**e** f prairie; steppe; **s~en** vt to stitch ♦ vi to tap-dance

Sterb- |'ʃtɛrb| zW: ~**efall** m death; ~**ehilfe** f euthanasia; **s~en** (*unreg*) vi to die; **s~lich** |'ʃtɛrplɪç| adj mortal; ~**lichkeit** f mortality; ~**lichkeitsziffer** f death rate

stereo- |'ʃteːreo| in zW stereo(-); **S~anlage** f stereo (system); ~**typ** |ʃtereo'tyːp| adj stereotype

steril |ʃteˈriːl| adj sterile; ~**i'sieren** vt to sterilize; **S~i'sierung** f sterilization

Stern |ʃtɛrn| (-(e)s, -e) m star; ~**bild** nt constellation; ~**schnuppe** f meteor, falling star; ~**stunde** f historic moment; ~**zeichen** nt sign of the zodiac

stet |ʃteːt| adj steady; ~**ig** adj constant, continual; ~**s** adv continually, always

Steuer¹ |ˈʃtɔyər| (-s, -) nt (NAUT) helm; (-ruder) rudder; (AUT) steering wheel

Steuer² |ˈʃtɔyər| (-, -n) f tax; ~**berater(in)** m(f) tax consultant

Steuerbord nt (NAUT, AVIAT) starboard

Steuer- |ˈʃtɔyər| zW: ~**erklärung** f tax return; **s~frei** adj tax-free; ~**freibetrag** m tax allowance; ~**klasse** f tax group; ~**knüppel** m control column; (AVIAT, COMPUT) joystick; ~**mann** (pl -männer od -leute) m helmsman; **s~n** vt, vi to steer; (Flugzeug) to pilot; (Entwicklung, Tonstärke) to control; **s~pflichtig** |-pflɪçtɪç| adj taxable; ~**rad** nt steering wheel; ~**ung** f (auch AUT) steering; piloting; control; (Vorrichtung) controls pl; ~**zahler** (-s, -) m taxpayer

Steward |ˈstjuːərt| (-s, -s) m steward; ~**ess** ▲ |ˈstjuːərdɛs| (-, -en) f stewardess; air hostess

Stich |ʃtɪç| (-(e)s, -e) m (Insektenstich) sting; (Messerstich) stab; (beim Nähen) stitch; (Färbung) tinge; (KARTEN) trick; (ART) engraving; **jdn im ~ lassen** to leave sb in the lurch; **s~eln** vi (fig) to jibe; **s~haltig** adj sound, tenable; ~**probe** f spot check; ~**wahl** f final ballot; ~**wort** nt cue; (in Wörterbuch) headword; (für Vortrag) note

sticken |ˈʃtɪkən| vt, vi to embroider

Sticke·rei f embroidery

stickig adj stuffy, close

Stickstoff m nitrogen

Stief- |ˈʃtiːf| in zW step

Stiefel |ˈʃtiːfəl| (-s, -) m boot

Stief- zW: ~**kind** nt stepchild; (fig) Cinderella; ~**mutter** f stepmother; ~**mütterchen** nt pansy; **s~mütterlich** adj (fig): **jdn/etw s~mütterlich behandeln** to pay little attention to sb/sth; ~**vater** m stepfather

stiehlst etc |ʃtiːlst| vb siehe **stehlen**

Stiel |ʃtiːl| (-(e)s, -e) m handle; (BOT) stalk

Stier |ʃtiːr| (-(e)s, -e) m bull; (ASTROL) Taurus

stieren vi to stare

Stierkampf m bullfight

Stierkämpfer m bullfighter

Stift |ʃtɪft| (-(e)s, -e) m peg; (Nagel) tack; (Farbstift) crayon; (Bleistift) pencil ♦ nt (charitable) foundation; (ECCL) religious institution; **s~en** vt to found; (Unruhe) to cause; (spenden) to contribute; ~**er(in)** (-s, -) m(f) founder; ~**ung** f donation; (Organisation) foundation; ~**zahn** m post crown

Stil |ʃtiːl| (-(e)s, -e) m style

still |ʃtɪl| adj quiet; (unbewegt) still; (heimlich) secret; **S~er Ozean** Pacific; ~ **halten** to keep still; ~ **stehen** to stand still; **S~e** f stillness, quietness; **in aller S~e** quietly; ~**en** vt to stop; (befriedigen) to satisfy; (Säugling) to breast-feed; ~**legen** ▲ vt to close down;

~**schweigen** (unreg) vi to be silent; **S~schweigen** nt silence; ~**schweigend** adj silent; (Einverständnis) tacit ♦ adv silently; tacitly; **S~stand** m standstill

Stimm- |ˈʃtɪm| zW: ~**bänder** pl vocal cords; **s~berechtigt** adj entitled to vote; ~**e** f voice; (Wahlstimme) vote; **s~en** vt (MUS) to tune ♦ vi to be right; **das s~te ihn traurig** that made him feel sad; **s~en für/gegen** to vote for/against; **s~t so!** that's right; ~**enmehrheit** f majority (of votes); ~**enthaltung** f abstention; ~**gabel** f tuning fork; ~**recht** nt right to vote; ~**ung** f mood; atmosphere; **s~ungsvoll** adj enjoyable; full of atmosphere; ~**zettel** m ballot paper

stinken |ˈʃtɪŋkən| (unreg) vi to stink

Stipendium |ʃtiˈpɛndiʊm| nt grant

stirbst etc |ʃtɪrpst| vb siehe **sterben**

Stirn |ʃtɪrn| (-, -en) f forehead, brow; (Frechheit) impudence; ~**band** nt headband; ~**höhle** f sinus

stöbern |ˈʃtøːbərn| vi to rummage

stochern |ˈʃtɔxərn| vi to poke (about)

Stock¹ |ʃtɔk| (-(e)s, ⁼e) m stick; (BOT) stock

Stock² |ʃtɔk| (-(e)s, - od Stockwerke) m storey

stocken vi to stop, to pause; ~**d** adj halting

Stockung f stoppage

Stockwerk nt storey, floor

Stoff |ʃtɔf| (-(e)s, -e) m (Gewebe) material, cloth; (Materie) matter; (von Buch etc) subject (matter); **s~lich** adj material; ~**tier** nt soft toy; ~**wechsel** m metabolism

stöhnen |ˈʃtøːnən| vi to groan

Stollen |ˈʃtɔlən| (-s, -) m (MIN) gallery; (KOCH) cake eaten at Christmas; (von Schuhen) stud

stolpern |ˈʃtɔlpərn| vi to stumble, to trip

Stolz |ʃtɔlts| (-es) m pride; **s~** adj proud; **s~ieren** |ʃtɔlˈtsiːrən| vi to strut

stopfen |ˈʃtɔpfən| vt (hineinstopfen) to stuff; (voll ~) to fill (up); (nähen) to darn ♦ vi (MED) to cause constipation

Stopfgarn nt darning thread

Stoppel |ˈʃtɔpəl| (-, -n) f stubble

Stopp- |ˈʃtɔp| zW: **s~en** vt to stop; (mit Uhr) to time ♦ vi to stop; ~**schild** nt stop sign; ~**uhr** f stopwatch

Stöpsel |ˈʃtœpsəl| (-s, -) m plug; (für Flaschen) stopper

Storch |ʃtɔrç| (-(e)s, ⁼e) m stork

Stör- |ˈʃtøːr| zW: **s~en** vt to disturb; (behindern, RADIO) to interfere with ♦ vr: **sich an etw dat s~en** to let sth bother one; **s~end** adj disturbing, annoying; ~**enfried** (-(e)s, -e) m troublemaker

stornieren |ʃtɔrˈniːrən| vt (Auftrag) to cancel; (Buchung) to reverse

Stornogebühr |ˈʃtɔrno-| f cancellation fee

---

störrisch ['ʃtœrɪʃ] adj stubborn, perverse

Störung f disturbance; interference

Stoß [ʃtoːs] (-es, ⁼e) m (Schub) push; (Schlag) blow; knock; (mit Schwert) thrust; (mit Fuß) kick; (Erdstoß) shock; (Haufen) pile; **~dämpfer** (-s, -) m shock absorber; **s~en** (unreg) vt (mit Druck) to shove, to push; (mit Schlag) to knock, to bump; (mit Fuß) to kick; (Schwert etc) to thrust; (anstoßen: Kopf etc) to bump ♦ vr to get a knock ♦ vi: **s~en an** od **auf** +akk to bump into; (finden) to come across; (angrenzen) to be next to; **sich s~en an** +dat (fig) to take exception to; **~stange** f (AUT) bumper

stottern ['ʃtɔtərn] vt, vi to stutter

Str. abk (= Straße) St.

Straf- ['ʃtraːf] zW: **~anstalt** f penal institution; **~arbeit** f (SCH) punishment; lines pl; **s~bar** adj punishable; **~e** f punishment; (JUR) penalty; (Gefängnisstrafe) sentence; (Geldstrafe) fine; **s~en** vt to punish

straff [ʃtraf] adj tight; (streng) strict; (Stil etc) concise; (Haltung) erect; **~en** vt to tighten, to tauten

Strafgefangene(r) f(m) prisoner, convict

Strafgesetzbuch nt penal code

sträflich ['ʃtrɛːflɪç] adj criminal

Sträfling m convict

Straf- zW: **~porto** nt excess postage (charge); **~predigt** f telling-off; **~raum** m (SPORT) penalty area; **~recht** nt criminal law; **~stoß** m (SPORT) penalty (kick); **~tat** f punishable act; **~zettel** m ticket

Strahl [ʃtraːl] (-s, -en) m ray, beam; (Wasserstrahl) jet; **s~en** vi to radiate; (fig) to beam; **~ung** f radiation

Strähne ['ʃtrɛːnə] f strand

stramm [ʃtram] adj tight; (Haltung) erect; (Mensch) robust

strampeln ['ʃtrampəln] vi to kick (about), to fidget

Strand [ʃtrant] (-(e)s, ⁼e) m shore; (mit Sand) beach; **~bad** nt open-air swimming pool, lido; **s~en** ['ʃtrandən] vi to run aground; (fig: Mensch) to fail; **~gut** nt flotsam; **~korb** m beach chair

Strang [ʃtraŋ] (-(e)s, ⁼e) m cord, rope; (Bündel) skein

Strapaz- zW: **~e** [ʃtra'paːtsə] f strain, exertion; **s~ieren** [ʃtrapa'tsiːrən] vt (Material) to treat roughly, to punish; (Mensch, Kräfte) to wear out, to exhaust; **s~ierfähig** adj hard-wearing; **s~iös** [ʃtrapatsi'øːs] adj exhausting, tough

Straße ['ʃtraːsə] f street, road

Straßen- zW: **~bahn** f tram, streetcar (US); **~glätte** f slippery road surface; **~karte** f road map; **~kehrer** (-s, -) m roadsweeper; **~sperre** f roadblock; **~verkehr** m (road) traffic; **~verkehrsordnung** f highway code

Strateg- [ʃtra'teːg] zW: **~e** (-n, -n) m strategist; **~ie** [ʃtrateˈgiː] f strategy; **s~isch** adj strategic

sträuben ['ʃtrɔybən] vt to ruffle ♦ vr to bristle; (Mensch): **sich (gegen etw) ~** to resist (sth)

Strauch [ʃtraux] (-(e)s, Sträucher) m bush, shrub

Strauß¹ [ʃtraus] (-es, Sträuße) m bunch; bouquet

Strauß² [ʃtraus] (-es, -e) m ostrich

Streb- [ˈʃtreːb] zW: **s~en** vi to strive, to endeavour; **s~en nach** to strive for; **~er** (-s, -) (pej) m pusher, climber; (SCH) swot (BRIT)

Strecke ['ʃtrɛkə] f stretch; (Entfernung) distance; (EISENB, MATH) line; **s~n** vt to stretch; (Waffen) to lay down; (KOCH) to eke out ♦ vr to stretch (o.s.)

Streich [ʃtraiç] (-(e)s, -e) m trick, prank; (Hieb) blow; **s~eln** vt to stroke; **s~en** (unreg) vt (berühren) to stroke; (auftragen) to spread; (anmalen) to paint; (durchstreichen) to delete; (nicht genehmigen) to cancel ♦ vi (berühren) to brush; (schleichen) to prowl; **~holz** nt match; **~instrument** nt string instrument

Streif- [ˈʃtraif] zW: **~e** f patrol; **s~en** vt (leicht berühren) to brush against, to graze; (Blick) to skim over; (Thema, Problem) to touch on; (abstreifen) to take off ♦ vi (gehen) to roam; **~en** (-s, -) m (Linie) stripe; (Stück) strip; (Film) film; **~enwagen** m patrol car; **~schuss** ▲ m graze, grazing shot; **~zug** m scouting trip

Streik [ʃtraik] (-(e)s, -s) m strike; **~brecher** (-s, -) m blackleg, strikebreaker; **s~en** vi to strike; **~posten** m (strike) picket

Streit [ʃtrait] (-(e)s, -e) m argument; dispute; **s~en** (unreg) vi, vr to argue; to dispute; **~frage** f point at issue; **s~ig** adj: **jdm etw s~ig machen** to dispute sb's right to sth; **~igkeiten** pl quarrel sg, dispute sg; **~kräfte** pl (MIL) armed forces

streng [ʃtrɛŋ] adj severe; (Lehrer, Maßnahme) strict; (Geruch etc) sharp; **~ genommen** strictly speaking; **S~e** (-) f severity, strictness, sharpness; **~gläubig** adj orthodox, strict; **~stens** adv strictly

Stress ▲ [ʃtrɛs] (-es, -e) m stress

stressen vt to put under stress

streuen ['ʃtrɔyən] vt to strew, to scatter, to spread

Strich [ʃtrɪç] (-(e)s, -e) m (Linie) line; (Federstrich, Pinselstrich) stroke; (von Geweben) nap; (von Fell) pile; **auf den ~ gehen** (umg) to walk the streets; **jdm gegen den ~ gehen** to rub sb up the wrong way; **einen ~ machen durch** to cross out; (fig) to foil; **~kode** m (auf Waren) bar code; **~mädchen** nt streetwalker; **s~weise** adv here and there

Strick [ʃtrɪk] (-(e)s, -e) m rope; **s~en** vt, vi to

knit; **~jacke** f cardigan; **~leiter** f rope
ladder; **~nadel** f knitting needle; **~waren** pl
knitwear sg
strikt [strɪkt] adj strict
strittig ['ʃtrɪtɪç] adj disputed, in dispute
Stroh [ʃtro:] (-(e)s) nt straw; **~blume** f
everlasting flower; **~dach** nt thatched roof;
~halm m (drinking) straw
Strom [ʃtro:m] (-(e)s, ⁓e) m river; (fig)
stream; (ELEK) current; **s~abwärts** adv
downstream; **s~aufwärts** adv upstream;
~ausfall m power failure
strömen ['ʃtrø:mən] vi to stream, to pour
Strom- zW: **~kreis** m circuit;
s~linienförmig adj streamlined; **~sperre** f
power cut
Strömung ['ʃtrø:mʊŋ] f current
Strophe ['ʃtro:fə] f verse
strotzen ['ʃtrɔtsən] vi: **~ vor** od **von** to
abound in, to be full of
Strudel ['ʃtru:dəl] (-s, -) m whirlpool, vortex;
(KOCH) strudel
Struktur [ʃtrʊk'tu:r] f structure
Strumpf [ʃtrʊmpf] (-(e)s, ⁓e) m stocking;
~band nt garter; **~hose** f (pair of) tights
Stube ['ʃtu:bə] f room
Stuben- zW: **~arrest** m confinement to
one's room; (MIL) confinement to quarters;
~hocker (umg) m stay-at-home; **s~rein** adj
house-trained
Stuck [ʃtʊk] (-(e)s) m stucco
Stück [ʃtyk] (-(e)s, -e) nt piece; (etwas) bit;
(THEAT) play; **~chen** nt little piece; **~lohn** m
piecework wages pl; **s~weise** adv bit by
bit, piecemeal; (COMM) individually
Student(in) [ʃtu'dɛnt(ɪn)] m(f) student;
s~isch adj student, academic
Studie ['ʃtu:diə] f study
Studienfahrt f study trip
studieren [ʃtu'di:rən] vt, vi to study
Studio ['ʃtu:dio] (-s, -s) nt studio
Studium ['ʃtu:diʊm] nt studies pl
Stufe ['ʃtu:fə] f step; (Entwicklungsstufe) stage;
s~nweise adv gradually
Stuhl [ʃtu:l] (-(e)s, ⁓e) m chair; **~gang** m
bowel movement
stülpen ['ʃtʏlpən] vt (umdrehen) to turn
upside down; (bedecken) to put
stumm [ʃtʊm] adj silent; (MED) dumb
Stummel ['ʃtʊməl] (-s, -) m stump;
(Zigarettenstummel) stub
Stummfilm m silent film
Stümper ['ʃtʏmpər] (-s, -) m incompetent,
duffer; **s~haft** adj bungling, incompetent;
s~n vi to bungle
Stumpf [ʃtʊmpf] (-(e)s, ⁓e) m stump; **s~** adj
blunt; (teilnahmslos, glanzlos) dull; (Winkel)
obtuse; **~sinn** m tediousness; **s~sinnig** adj
dull

Stunde ['ʃtʊndə] f hour; (SCH) lesson
stunden vt: **jdm etw ~** to give sb time to
pay sth; **S~geschwindigkeit** f average
speed per hour; **S~kilometer** pl kilometres
per hour; **~lang** adj for hours; **S~lohn** m
hourly wage; **S~plan** m timetable; **~weise**
adj by the hour; every hour
stündlich ['ʃtʏntlɪç] adj hourly
Stups [ʃtʊps] (-es, -e) (umg) m push; **~nase**
f snub nose
stur [ʃtu:r] adj obstinate, pigheaded
Sturm [ʃtʊrm] (-(e)s, ⁓e) m storm, gale; (MIL
etc) attack, assault
stürm- ['ʃtʏrm] zW: **~en** vi (Wind) to blow
hard, to rage; (rennen) to storm ♦ vt (MIL,
fig) to storm ♦ vb unpers: **es ~t** there's a gale
blowing; **S~er** (-s, -) m (SPORT) forward,
striker; **~isch** adj stormy
Sturmwarnung f gale warning
Sturz [ʃtʊrts] (-es, ⁓e) m fall; (POL) overthrow
stürzen ['ʃtʏrtsən] vt (werfen) to hurl; (POL)
to overthrow; (umkehren) to overturn ♦ vr to
rush; (hineinstürzen) to plunge ♦ vi to fall;
(AVIAT) to dive; (rennen) to dash
Sturzflug m nose dive
Sturzhelm m crash helmet
Stute ['ʃtu:tə] f mare
Stützbalken m brace, joist
Stütze ['ʃtʏtsə] f support; help
stutzen ['ʃtʊtsən] vt to trim; (Ohr, Schwanz)
to dock; (Flügel) to clip ♦ vi to hesitate; to
become suspicious
stützen vt (auch fig) to support; (Ellbogen
etc) to prop up
stutzig adj perplexed, puzzled; (misstrauisch)
suspicious
Stützpunkt m point of support; (von Hebel)
fulcrum; (MIL, fig) base
Styropor ® [ʃtyro'po:r] (-s) nt polystyrene
s. u. abk = **siehe unten**
Subjekt [zʊp'jɛkt] (-(e)s, -e) nt subject; **s~iv**
[-'ti:f] adj subjective; **~ivi'tät** f subjectivity
Subsidiarität f subsidiarity
Substantiv [zʊpstan'ti:f] (-s, -e) nt noun
Substanz [zʊp'stants] f substance
subtil [zʊp'ti:l] adj subtle
subtrahieren [zʊptra'hi:rən] vt to subtract
subtropisch ['zʊptro:pɪʃ] adj subtropical
Subvention [zʊpvɛntsi'o:n] f subsidy;
s~ieren vt to subsidize
Such- ['zu:x] zW: **~aktion** f search; **~e** f
search; **s~en** vt to look (for), to seek;
(versuchen) to try ♦ vi to seek, to search; **~er**
(-s, -) m seeker, searcher; (PHOT) viewfinder
Sucht [zʊxt] (-, ⁓e) f mania; (MED) addiction,
craving
süchtig ['zʏçtɪç] adj addicted; **S~e(r)** f(m)
addict
Süd- ['zy:t] zW: **~en** ['zy:dən] (-s) m south;

~früchte pl Mediterranean fruit sg; **s~lich** adj southern; **s~lich von** (to the) south of; **~pol** m South Pole; **s~wärts** adv southwards
süffig ['zyfɪç] adj (Wein) pleasant to the taste
süffisant [zyfi'zant] adj smug
suggerieren [zʊgeˈriːrən] vt to suggest
Sühne ['zyːnə] f atonement, expiation; **s~n** vt to atone for, to expiate
Sultan |ˈzʊltan| (-s, -e) m sultan; **~ine** |zʊltaˈniːnə| f sultana
Sülze ['zʏltsə] f brawn
Summe ['zʊmə] f sum, total
summen vt, vi to buzz; (Lied) to hum
Sumpf |zʊmpf| (-(e)s, ⁼e) m swamp, marsh; **s~ig** adj marshy
Sünde ['zʏndə] f sin; **~nbock** (umg) m scapegoat; **~r(in)** (-s, -) m(f) sinner;
sündigen vi to sin
Super |ˈzuːpər| (-s) nt (Benzin) four star (petrol) (BRIT), premium (US); **~lativ** |-latiːf| (-s, -e) m superlative; **~macht** f superpower; **~markt** m supermarket
Suppe ['zʊpə] f soup; **~nteller** m soup plate
süß |zyːs| adj sweet; **S~e** (-) f sweetness; **~en** vt to sweeten; **S~igkeit** f sweetness; (Bonbon etc) sweet (BRIT), candy (US); **~lich** adj sweetish; (fig) sugary; **~sauer** adj (Gurke) pickled; (Sauce etc) sweet-and-sour; **S~speise** f pudding, sweet; **S~stoff** m sweetener; **S~waren** pl confectionery sg; **S~wasser** nt fresh water
Symbol |zym'boːl| (-s, -e) nt symbol; **s~isch** adj symbolic(al)
Symmetrie |zymeˈtriː| f symmetry
symmetrisch [zyˈmeːtrɪʃ] adj symmetrical
Sympathie |zympaˈtiː| f liking, sympathy; **sympathisch** [zymˈpaːtɪʃ] adj likeable; **er ist mir sympathisch** I like him; **sympathi'sieren** vi to sympathize
Symphonie |zymfoˈniː| f (MUS) symphony
Symptom |zympˈtoːm| (-s, -e) nt symptom; **s~atisch** |zymptoˈmaːtɪʃ| adj symptomatic
Synagoge |zynaˈgoːgə| f synagogue
synchron |zynˈkroːn| adj synchronous; **~i'sieren** vt to synchronize; (Film) to dub
Synonym |zynoˈnyːm| (-s, -e) nt synonym; **s~** adj synonymous
Synthese |zynˈteːzə| f synthesis
synthetisch adj synthetic
System |zysˈteːm| (-s, -e) nt system; **s~atisch** adj systematic; **s~ati'sieren** vt to systematize
Szene ['stseːnə] f scene; **~rie** |stsenəˈriː| f scenery

T, t

t abk (= Tonne) t
Tabak ['taːbak] (-s, -e) m tobacco
Tabell- |taˈbɛl| zW: **t~arisch** |tabeˈlaːrɪʃ] adj

tabular; **~e** f table
Tablett [taˈblɛt] nt tray; **~e** f tablet, pill
Tabu |taˈbuː| nt taboo; **t~** adj taboo
Tachometer [taxoˈmeːtər] (-s, -) m (AUT) speedometer
Tadel |ˈtaːdəl] (-s, -) m censure; scolding; (Fehler) fault, blemish; **t~los** adj faultless, irreproachable; **t~n** vt to scold
Tafel ['taːfəl] (-, -n) f (auch MATH) table; (Anschlagtafel) board; (Wandtafel) blackboard; (Schiefertafel) slate; (Gedenktafel) plaque; (Illustration) plate; (Schalttafel) panel; (Schokolade etc) bar
Tag |taːk| (-(e)s, -e) m day; daylight; **unter/ über ~e** (MIN) underground/on the surface; **an den ~ kommen** to come to light; **guten ~!** good morning/afternoon!; siehe zutage; **t~aus** adv: **t~aus, t~ein** day in, day out; **~dienst** m day duty
Tage- |ˈtaːgə| zW: **~buch** [ˈtaːgəbuːx] nt diary, journal; **~geld** nt daily allowance; **t~lang** adv for days; **t~n** vi to sit, to meet ♦ vb unpers: **es tagt** dawn is breaking
Tages- zW: **~ablauf** m course of the day; **~anbruch** m dawn; **~fahrt** f day trip; **~karte** f menu of the day; (Fahrkarte) day ticket; **~licht** nt daylight; **~ordnung** f agenda; **~zeit** f time of day; **~zeitung** f daily (paper)
täglich ['tɛːklɪç] adj, adv daily
tagsüber ['taːkslʏbər] adv during the day
Tagung f conference
Taille ['taljə] f waist
Takt |takt| (-(e)s, -e) m tact; (MUS) time; **~gefühl** nt tact
Taktik f tactics pl; **taktisch** adj tactical
Takt- zW: **t~los** adj tactless; **~losigkeit** f tactlessness; **~stock** m (conductor's) baton; **t~voll** adj tactful
Tal |taːl| (-(e)s, ⁼er) nt valley
Talent |taˈlɛnt| (-(e)s, -e) nt talent; **t~iert** |talɛnˈtiːrt| adj talented, gifted
Talisman ['taːlɪsman] (-s, -e) m talisman
Talsohle f bottom of a valley
Talsperre f dam
Tampon ['tampɔn] (-s, -s) m tampon
Tandem ['tandɛm] (-s, -s) nt tandem
Tang |taŋ| (-(e)s, -e) m seaweed
Tank |taŋk| (-s, -s) m tank; **~anzeige** f fuel gauge; **t~en** vi to fill up with petrol (BRIT) od gas (US); (AVIAT) to (re)fuel; **~er** (-s, -) m tanker; **~schiff** nt tanker; **~stelle** f petrol (BRIT) od gas (US) station; **~wart** m petrol pump (BRIT) od gas station (US) attendant
Tanne ['tanə] f fir
Tannen- zW: **~baum** m fir tree; **~zapfen** m fir cone
Tante ['tantə] f aunt
Tanz |tants| (-es, ⁼e) m dance; **t~en** vt, vi to dance
Tänzer(in) |ˈtɛntsər(ɪn)| (-s, -) m(f) dancer

Tanzfläche f (dance) floor

Tanzschule f dancing school

Tapete |ta'pe:tə| f wallpaper; **~nwechsel** m (fig) change of scenery

tapezieren |tape'tsi:rən| vt to (wall)paper; **Tapezierer** |tape'tsi:rər| (-s, -) m (interior) decorator

tapfer |'tapfər| adj brave; **T~keit** f courage, bravery

Tarif |ta'ri:f| (-s, -e) m tariff, (scale of) fares od charges; **~lohn** m standard wage rate; **~verhandlungen** pl wage negotiations; **~zone** f fare zone

Tarn- |'tarn| zW: **t~en** vt to camouflage; (Person, Absicht) to disguise; **~ung** f camouflaging; disguising

Tasche |'tafə| f pocket; handbag

Taschen- in zW pocket; **~buch** nt paperback; **~dieb** m pickpocket; **~geld** nt pocket money; **~lampe** f (electric) torch, flashlight (US); **~messer** nt penknife; **~tuch** nt handkerchief

Tasse |'tasə| f cup

Tastatur |tasta'tu:r| f keyboard

Taste |'tastə| f push-button control; (an Schreibmaschine) key; **t~n** vt to feel, to touch ♦ vi to feel, to grope ♦ vr to feel one's way

Tat |ta:t| (-, -en) f act, deed, action; **in der ~** indeed, as a matter of fact; **t~** etc vb siehe **tun**; **~bestand** m facts pl of the case; **t~enlos** adj inactive

Tät- |'tɛ:t| zW: **~er(in)** (-s, -) m(f) perpetrator, culprit; **t~ig** adj active; **in einer Firma t~ig sein** to work for a firm; **~igkeit** f activity; (Beruf) occupation; **t~lich** adj violent; **~lichkeit** f violence; **~lichkeiten** pl (Schläge) blows

tätowieren |teto'vi:rən| vt to tattoo

Tatsache f fact

tatsächlich adj actual ♦ adv really

Tau¹ |tau| (-(e)s, -e) nt rope

Tau² |tau| (-(e)s) m dew

taub |taup| adj deaf; (Nuss) hollow

Taube |'taubə| f dove; pigeon; **~nschlag** m dovecote; **hier geht es zu wie in einem ~nschlag** it's a hive of activity here

taub- zW: **T~heit** f deafness; **~stumm** adj deaf-and-dumb

Tauch- |'taux| zW: **t~en** vt to dip ♦ vi to dive; (NAUT) to submerge; **~er** (-s, -) m diver; **~eranzug** m diving suit; **~erbrille** f diving goggles pl; **~sieder** (-s, -) m immersion coil (for boiling water)

tauen |'tauən| vt, vi to thaw ♦ vb unpers: **es taut** it's thawing

Tauf- |'tauf| zW: **~becken** nt font; **~e** f baptism; **t~en** vt to christen, to baptize; **~pate** m godfather; **~patin** f godmother; **~schein** m certificate of baptism

taug- |taug| zW: **~en** vi to be of use; **~en für** to do for, to be good for; **nicht ~en** to be no good od useless; **T~enichts** (-es, -e) m good-for-nothing; **~lich** |'tauklɪç| adj suitable; (MIL) fit (for service)

Taumel |'taumal| (-s) m dizziness; (fig) frenzy; **t~n** vi to reel, to stagger

Tausch |tauʃ| (-(e)s, -e) m exchange; **t~en** vt to exchange, to swap

täuschen |'tɔyʃən| vt to deceive ♦ vi to be deceptive ♦ vr to be wrong; **~d** adj deceptive

Tauschhandel m barter

Täuschung f deception; (optisch) illusion

tausend |'tauzənt| num (a) thousand

Tauwetter nt thaw

Taxi |'taksi| (-(s), -(s)) nt taxi; **~fahrer** m taxi driver; **~stand** m taxi rank

Tech- |'tɛç| zW: **~nik** f technology; (Methode, Kunstfertigkeit) technique; **~niker** (-s, -) m technician; **t~nisch** adj technical; **~nolo'gie** f technology; **t~no'logisch** adj technological

Tee |te:| (-s, -s) m tea; **~beutel** m tea bag; **~kanne** f teapot; **~löffel** m teaspoon

Teer |te:r| (-(e)s, -e) m tar; **t~en** vt to tar

Teesieb nt tea strainer

Teich |taɪç| (-(e)s, -e) m pond

Teig |taɪk| (-(e)s, -e) m dough; **t~ig** |'taɪgɪç| adj doughy; **~waren** pl pasta sg

Teil |taɪl| (-(e)s, -e) m od nt part; (Anteil) share; (Bestandteil) component; **zum ~** partly; **t~bar** adj divisible; **~betrag** m instalment; **~chen** nt (atomic) particle; **t~en** vt, vr to divide; (mit jdm) to share; **t~haben** (unreg) vi: **t~haben an** +dat to share in; **~haber** (-s, -) m partner; **~kaskoversicherung** f third party, fire and theft insurance; **t~möbliert** adj partially furnished; **~nahme** f participation; (Mitleid) sympathy; **t~nahmslos** adj disinterested, apathetic; **t~nehmen** (unreg) vi: **t~nehmen an** +dat to take part in; **~nehmer** (-s, -) m participant; **t~s** adv partly; **~ung** f division; **t~weise** adv partially, in part; **~zahlung** f payment by instalments; **~zeitarbeit** f part-time work

Teint |tɛ̃:| (-s, -s) m complexion

Telearbeit |'te:le|arbaɪt| f teleworking

Telefax |'te:lefaks| nt fax

Telefon |tele'fo:n| (-s, -e) nt telephone; **~anruf** m (tele)phone call; **~at** |telefo'na:t| (-(e)s, -e) nt (tele)phone call; **~buch** nt telephone directory; **~hörer** m (telephone) receiver; **t~ieren** vi to telephone; **t~isch** |-ɪʃ| adj telephone; (Benachrichtigung) by telephone; **~ist(in)** |telefo'nɪst(ɪn)| m(f) telephonist; **~karte** f phonecard; **~nummer** f (tele)phone number; **~zelle** f telephone kiosk, callbox; **~zentrale** f telephone exchange

Telegraf [tele'graːf] (**-en, -en**) *m* telegraph; **~enmast** *m* telegraph pole; **~ie** [-'fiː] *f* telegraphy; **t~ieren** [-'fiːrən] *vt, vi* to telegraph, to wire

Telegramm [tele'gram] (**-s, -e**) *nt* telegram, cable; **~adresse** *f* telegraphic address

Tele- *zW:* **~objektiv** ['teːlɛ|ɔpjɛktiːf] *nt* telephoto lens; **t~pathisch** [tele'paːtɪʃ] *adj* telepathic; **~skop** [tele'skoːp] (**-s, -e**) *nt* telescope

Teller ['tɛlɐr] (**-s, -**) *m* plate; **~gericht** *nt* (*KOCH*) one-course meal

Tempel ['tɛmpəl] (**-s, -**) *m* temple

Temperament [tɛmpera'mɛnt] *nt* temperament; (*Schwung*) vivacity, liveliness; **t~voll** *adj* high-spirited, lively

Temperatur [tɛmpera'tuːr] *f* temperature

Tempo¹ ['tɛmpo] (**-s, Tempi**) *nt* (*MUS*) tempo

Tempo² ['tɛmpo] (**-s, -s**) *nt* speed, pace; **~!** get a move on!; **~limit** [-lɪmɪt] (**-s, -s**) *nt* speed limit; **~taschentuch** ® *nt* tissue

Tendenz [tɛn'dɛnts] *f* tendency; (*Absicht*) intention; (*Neigung*) [-i'øːs] *adj* biased, tendentious

tendieren [tɛn'diːrən] *vi:* **~ zu** to show a tendency to, to incline towards

Tennis ['tɛnɪs] (**-**) *nt* tennis; **~ball** *m* tennis ball; **~platz** *m* tennis court; **~schläger** *m* tennis racket; **~schuh** *m* tennis shoe; **~spieler(in)** *m(f)* tennis player

Tenor [te'noːr] (**-s, -̈e**) *m* tenor

Teppich ['tɛpɪç] (**-s, -e**) *m* carpet; **~boden** *m* wall-to-wall carpeting

Termin [tɛr'miːn] (**-s, -e**) *m* (*Zeitpunkt*) date; (*Frist*) time limit, deadline; (*Arzttermin etc*) appointment; **~kalender** *m* diary, appointments book; **~planer** *m* personal organizer

Terrasse [tɛ'rasə] *f* terrace

Terrine [tɛ'riːnə] *f* tureen

territorial [tɛritori'aːl] *adj* territorial

Territorium [tɛri'toːrium] *nt* territory

Terror ['tɛrɔr] (**-s**) *m* terror; reign of terror; **t~isieren** [tɛrori'ziːrən] *vt* to terrorize; **~ismus** [-'rɪsmʊs] *m* terrorism; **~ist** [-'rɪst] *m* terrorist

Tesafilm ['teːzafɪlm] ® *m* Sellotape ® (*BRIT*), Scotch tape ® (*US*)

Tessin [tɛ'siːn] *nt:* **das ~** Ticino

Test [tɛst] (**-s, -s**) *m* test

Testament [tɛsta'mɛnt] *nt* will, testament; (*REL*) Testament; **t~arisch** [-'taːrɪʃ] *adj* testamentary; **~svollstrecker** *m* executor (of a will)

testen *vt* to test

Tetanus ['teːtanʊs] (**-**) *m* tetanus; **~impfung** *f* (anti-)tetanus injection

teuer ['tɔyɐr] *adj* dear, expensive; **T~ung** *f* increase in prices; **T~ungszulage** *f* cost of living bonus

Teufel ['tɔyfəl] (**-s, -**) *m* devil; **teuflisch**

['tɔyflɪʃ] *adj* fiendish, diabolical

Text [tɛkst] (**-(e)s, -e**) *m* text; (*Liedertext*) words *pl*; **t~en** *vi* to write the words

textil [tɛks'tiːl] *adj* textile; **T~ien** *pl* textiles; **T~industrie** *f* textile industry; **T~waren** *pl* textiles

Textverarbeitung *f* word processing

Theater [te'aːtɐr] (**-s, -**) *nt* theatre; (*umg*) fuss; **~ spielen** (*auch fig*) to playact; **~besucher** *m* playgoer; **~kasse** *f* box office; **~stück** *nt* (stage) play

Theke ['teːkə] *f* (*Schanktisch*) bar; (*Ladentisch*) counter

Thema ['teːma] (**-s, Themen** *od* **-ta**) *nt* theme, topic, subject

Themse ['tɛmzə] *f* Thames

Theo- [teo] *zW:* **~loge** [-'loːgə] (**-n, -n**) *m* theologian; **~logie** [-lo'giː] *f* theology; **t~logisch** [-'loːgɪʃ] *adj* theological; **~retiker** [-'reːtikɐr] (**-s, -**) *m* theorist; **t~retisch** [-'reːtɪʃ] *adj* theoretical; **~rie** [-'riː] *f* theory

Thera- [tera] *zW:* **~peut** [-'pɔyt] (**-en, -en**) *m* therapist; **t~peutisch** [-'pɔytɪʃ] *adj* therapeutic; **~pie** [-'piː] *f* therapy

Therm- *zW:* **~albad** [tɛr'maːlbaːt] *nt* thermal bath; thermal spa; **~odrucker** [tɛrmo-] *m* thermal printer; **~ometer** [tɛrmo'meːtɐr] (**-s, -**) *nt* thermometer; **~osflasche** ® ['tɛrmɔsflaʃə] *f* Thermos ® flask

These ['teːzə] *f* thesis

Thrombose [trɔm'boːzə] *f* thrombosis

Thron [troːn] (**-(e)s, -e**) *m* throne; **t~en** *vi* to sit enthroned; (*fig*) to sit in state; **~folge** *f* succession (to the throne); **~folger(in)** (**-s, -**) *m(f)* heir to the throne

Thunfisch ['tuːnfɪʃ] *m* tuna

Thüringen ['tyːrɪŋən] (**-s**) *nt* Thuringia

Thymian ['tyːmiaːn] (**-s, -e**) *m* thyme

Tick [tɪk] (**-(e)s, -s**) *m* tic; (*Eigenart*) quirk; (*Fimmel*) craze

ticken *vi* to tick

tief [tiːf] *adj* deep; (*~sinnig*) profound; (*Ausschnitt, Preis, Ton*) low; **~ greifend** far-reaching; **~ schürfend** profound; **T~** (**-s, -s**) *nt* (*MET*) depression; **T~druck** *m* low pressure; **T~e** *f* depth; **T~ebene** *f* plain; **T~enschärfe** *f* (*PHOT*) depth of focus; **T~garage** *f* underground garage; **~gekühlt** *adj* frozen; **T~kühlfach** *nt* deepfreeze compartment; **T~kühlkost** *f* (deep-)frozen food; **T~kühltruhe** *f* deep-freeze, freezer; **T~punkt** *m* low point; (*fig*) low ebb; **T~schlag** *m* (*BOXEN, fig*) blow below the belt; **T~see** *f* deep sea; **~sinnig** *adj* profound; melancholy; **T~stand** *m* low level; **T~stwert** *m* minimum *od* lowest value

Tier [tiːr] (**-(e)s, -e**) *nt* animal; **~arzt** *m* vet(erinary surgeon); **~garten** *m* zoo(logical gardens *pl*); **~heim** *nt* cat/dog home; **t~isch** *adj* animal; (*auch fig*) brutish; (*fig: Ernst etc*) deadly; **~kreis** *m* zodiac; **~kunde**

f zoology; **t~liebend** adj fond of animals;
~park m zoo; **~quälerei** [-kvɛːlə'raɪ] f
cruelty to animals; **~schutzverein** m
society for the prevention of cruelty to
animals

Tiger(in) ['tiːɡər(ɪn)] (-s, -) m(f) tiger(-gress)

tilgen ['tɪlɡən] vt to erase; (Sünden) to
expiate; (Schulden) to pay off

Tinte ['tɪntə] f ink

Tintenfisch m cuttlefish

Tipp ▲ [tɪp] m tip; **t~en** vt, vi to tap, to
touch; (umg: schreiben) to type; (im Lotto
etc) to bet (on); **auf jdn t~en** (umg: raten)
to tip sb, to put one's money on sb (fig)

Tipp- ['tɪp] zW: **~fehler** (umg) m typing error;
t~topp (umg) adj tip-top; **~zettel** m
(pools) coupon

Tirol [ti'roːl] nt the Tyrol; **~er(in)** m(f)
Tyrolean; **t~isch** adj Tyrolean

Tisch [tɪʃ] (-(e)s, -e) m table; **bei ~** at table;
vor/nach ~ before/after eating; **unter den ~
fallen** (fig) to be dropped; **~decke** f
tablecloth; **~ler** (-s, -) m carpenter, joiner;
~le'rei f joiner's workshop; (Arbeit)
carpentry, joinery; **t~lern** vi to do carpentry
etc; **~rede** f after-dinner speech; **~tennis** nt
table tennis; **~tuch** nt tablecloth

Titel ['tiːtəl] (-s, -) m title; **~bild** nt cover
(picture); (von Buch) frontispiece; **~rolle** f
title role; **~seite** f cover; (Buchtitelseite) title
page; **~verteidiger** m defending champion,
title holder

Toast [toːst] (-(e)s, -s od -e) m toast; **~brot**
nt bread for toasting; **~er** (-s, -) m toaster

tob- ['toːb] zW: **~en** vi to rage; (Kinder) to
romp about; **~süchtig** adj maniacal

Tochter ['tɔxtər] (-, -̈) f daughter;
~gesellschaft f subsidiary (company)

Tod [toːt] (-(e)s, -e) m death; **t~ernst** adj
deadly serious ♦ adv in dead earnest

Todes- ['toːdəs] zW: **~angst** [-aŋst] f mortal
fear; **~anzeige** f obituary (notice); **~fall** m
death; **~strafe** f death penalty; **~ursache** f
cause of death; **~urteil** nt death sentence;
~verachtung f utter disgust

todkrank adj dangerously ill

tödlich ['tøːtlɪç] adj deadly, fatal

tod- zW: **~müde** adj dead tired; **~schick**
(umg) adj smart, classy; **~sicher** (umg) adj
absolutely od dead certain; **T~sünde** f
deadly sin

Toilette [toa'lɛtə] f toilet, lavatory;
(Frisiertisch) dressing table

Toiletten- zW: **~artikel** pl toiletries, toilet
articles; **~papier** nt toilet paper; **~tisch** m
dressing table

toi, toi, toi ['tɔy'tɔy'tɔy] excl touch wood

tolerant [tole'rant] adj tolerant

Toleranz [tole'rants] f tolerance

tolerieren [tole'riːrən] vt to tolerate

toll [tɔl] adj mad; (Treiben) wild; (umg)
terrific; **~en** vi to romp; **T~kirsche** f deadly
nightshade; **~kühn** adj daring; **T~wut** f
rabies

Tomate [to'maːtə] f tomato; **~nmark** nt
tomato purée

Ton¹ [toːn] (-(e)s, -e) m (Erde) clay

Ton² [toːn] (-(e)s, -̈e) m (Laut) sound; (MUS)
note; (Redeweise) tone; (Farbton, Nuance)
shade; (Betonung) stress; **t~angebend** adj
leading; **~art** f (musical) key; **~band** nt
tape; **~bandgerät** nt tape recorder

tönen ['tøːnən] vi to sound ♦ vt to shade;
(Haare) to tint

tönern ['tøːnərn] adj clay

Ton- zW: **~fall** m intonation; **~film** m sound
film; **~leiter** f (MUS) scale; **t~los** adj soundless

Tonne ['tɔnə] f barrel; (Maß) ton

Ton- zW: **~taube** f clay pigeon; **~waren** pl
pottery sg, earthenware pl

Topf [tɔpf] (-(e)s, -̈e) m pot; **~blume** f pot
plant

Töpfer ['tœpfər] (-s, -) m potter; **~ei** [-'raɪ] f
piece of pottery; potter's workshop;
~scheibe f potter's wheel

topografisch ▲ [topo'graːfɪʃ] adj
topographic

Tor¹ [toːr] (-en, -en) m fool

Tor² [toːr] (-(e)s, -e) m gate; (SPORT) goal;
~bogen m archway

Torf [tɔrf] (-(e)s) m peat

Torheit f foolishness; foolish deed

töricht ['tøːrɪçt] adj foolish

torkeln ['tɔrkəln] vi to stagger, to reel

Torte ['tɔrtə] f cake; (Obsttorte) flan, tart

Tortur [tɔr'tuːr] f ordeal

Torwart (-(e)s, -e) m goalkeeper

tosen ['toːzən] vi to roar

tot [toːt] adj dead; **~ geboren** stillborn; **sich ~
stellen** to pretend to be dead

total [to'taːl] adj total; **~itär** [totali'tɛːr] adj
totalitarian; **T~schaden** m (AUT) complete
write-off

Tote(r) f(m) dead person

töten ['tøːtən] vt, vi to kill

Toten- zW: **~bett** nt death bed; **t~blass** ▲
adj deathly pale, white as a sheet; **~kopf** m
skull; **~schein** m death certificate; **~stille** f
deathly silence

tot- zW: **~fahren** (unreg) vt to run over;
~lachen (umg) vr to laugh one's head off

Toto ['toːto] (-s, -s) m od nt pools pl;
~schein m pools coupon

tot- zW: **T~schlag** m manslaughter;
~schlagen (unreg) vt (auch fig) to kill;
~schweigen (unreg) vt to hush up

Tötung ['tøːtʊŋ] f killing

Toupet [tu'peː] (-s, -s) nt toupee

Spelling reform: ▲ *new spelling* △ *old spelling (to be phased out)*

toupieren [tuˈpiːrən] vt to backcomb

Tour [tuːr] (-, -en) f tour, trip; (Umdrehung) revolution; (Verhaltensart) way; **in einer ~** incessantly; **~enzähler** m rev counter; **~ismus** [tuˈrɪsmʊs] m tourism; **~ist** [tuˈrɪst] m tourist; **~istenklasse** f tourist class; **~nee** [torˈneː] (-, -n) f (THEAT etc) tour; **auf ~nee gehen** to go on tour

Trab [traːp] (-(e)s) m trot

Trabantenstadt f satellite town

traben [ˈtraːbən] vi to trot

Tracht [traxt] (-, -en) f (Kleidung) costume, dress; **eine ~ Prügel** a sound thrashing; **t~en** vi: **t~en (nach)** to strive (for); **jdm nach dem Leben t~en** to seek to kill sb; **danach t~en, etw zu tun** to strive od endeavour to do sth

trächtig [ˈtrɛçtɪç] adj (Tier) pregnant

Tradition [traditsiˈoːn] f tradition; **t~ell** [-ˈnɛl] adj traditional

traf etc [traːf] vb siehe **treffen**

Tragbahre f stretcher

tragbar adj (Gerät) portable; (Kleidung) wearable; (erträglich) bearable

träge [ˈtrɛːgə] adj sluggish, slow; (PHYS) inert

tragen [ˈtraːgən] (unreg) vt to carry; (Kleidung, Brille) to wear; (Namen, Früchte) to bear; (erdulden) to endure ♦ vi (schwanger sein) to be pregnant; (Eis) to hold; **sich mit einem Gedanken ~** to have an idea in mind; **zum T~ kom:men** to have an effect

Träger [ˈtrɛːgər] (-s, -) m carrier; wearer; bearer; (Ordensträger) holder; (an Kleidung) (shoulder) strap; (Körperschaft etc) sponsor

Tragetasche f carrier bag

Tragfläche f (AVIAT) wing

Tragflügelboot nt hydrofoil

Trägheit [ˈtrɛːkhait] f laziness; (PHYS) inertia

Tragik [ˈtraːgɪk] f tragedy; **tragisch** adj tragic

Tragödie [traˈgøːdiə] f tragedy

Tragweite f range; (fig) scope

Train- [trɛːn] zW: **~er** (-s, -) m (SPORT) trainer, coach; (Fußball) manager; **t~ieren** [trɛˈniːrən] vt, vi to train; (Mensch) to train, to coach; (Übung) to practise; **~ing** (-s, -s) nt training; **~ingsanzug** m track suit

Traktor [ˈtraktɔr] m tractor; (von Drucker) tractor feed

trällern [ˈtrɛlərn] vt, vi to trill, to sing

Tram [tram] (-, -s) f tram

trampeln [ˈtrampəln] vt, vi to trample, to stamp

trampen [ˈtrɛmpən] vi to hitch-hike

Tramper(in) [ˈtrɛmpər(ɪn)] (-s, -) m(f) hitch-hiker

Tran [traːn] (-(e)s, -e) m train oil, blubber

tranchieren [trãˈʃiːrən] vt to carve

Träne [ˈtrɛːnə] f tear; **t~n** vi to water; **~ngas** nt teargas

trank etc [trank] vb siehe **trinken**

tränken [ˈtrɛŋkən] vt (Tiere) to water

transchieren [tranˈʃiːrən] vt to carve

Trans- zW: **~formator** [transfɔrˈmaːtɔr] m transformer; **t~istor** [tranˈzɪstɔr] m transistor; **~itverkehr** [tranˈziːtfɛrkeːr] m transit traffic; **~itvisum** nt transit visa; **t~parent** adj transparent; **~parent** (-(e)s, -e) nt (Bild) transparency; (Spruchband) banner; **~plantation** [transplantatsiˈoːn] f transplantation; (Hauttransplantation) graft(ing)

Transport [transˈpɔrt] (-(e)s, -e) m transport; **t~ieren** [transpɔrˈtiːrən] vt to transport; **~kosten** pl transport charges, carriage sg; **~mittel** nt means sg of transportation; **~unternehmen** nt carrier

Traube [ˈtraubə] f grape; bunch (of grapes); **~nzucker** m glucose

trauen [ˈtrauən] vi: **jdm/etw ~** to trust sb/sth ♦ vr to dare ♦ vt to marry

Trauer [ˈtrauər] (-) f sorrow; (für Verstorbenen) mourning; **~fall** m death, bereavement; **~feier** f funeral service; **~kleidung** f mourning; **t~n** vi to mourn; **um jdn t~n** to mourn (for) sb; **~rand** m black border; **~spiel** nt tragedy

traulich [ˈtraulɪç] adj cosy, intimate

Traum [traum] (-(e)s, Träume) m dream

Trauma (-s, -men) nt trauma

träum- [ˈtrɔym] zW: **~en** vt, vi to dream; **T~er** (-s, -) m dreamer; **T~e'rei** f dreaming; **~erisch** adj dreamy

traumhaft adj dreamlike; (fig) wonderful

traurig [ˈtraurɪç] adj sad; **T~keit** f sadness

Trau- [ˈtrau] zW: **~ring** m wedding ring; **~schein** m marriage certificate; **~ung** f wedding ceremony; **~zeuge** m witness (to a marriage); **~zeugin** f witness (to a marriage)

treffen [ˈtrɛfən] (unreg) vt to strike, to hit; (Bemerkung) to hurt; (begegnen) to meet; (Entscheidung etc) to make; (Maßnahmen) to take ♦ vi to hit ♦ vr to meet; **er hat es gut getroffen** he did well; **~ auf** +akk to come across, to meet with; **es traf sich, dass ...** it so happened that ...; **es trifft sich gut** it's convenient; **wie es so trifft** as these things happen; **T~** (-s, -) nt meeting; **~d** adj pertinent, apposite

Treffer (-s, -) m hit; (Tor) goal; (Los) winner

Treffpunkt m meeting place

Treib- [ˈtraib] zW: **~eis** nt drift ice; **t~en** (unreg) vt to drive; (Studien etc) to pursue; (Sport) to do, to go in for ♦ vi (Schiff etc) to drift; (Pflanzen) to sprout; (KOCH: aufgehen) to rise; (Tee, Kaffee) to be diuretic; **~haus** nt greenhouse; **~hauseffekt** m greenhouse effect; **~hausgas** nt greenhouse gas; **~stoff** m fuel

trenn- [ˈtrɛn] zW: **~bar** adj separable; **~en** vt to separate; (teilen) to divide ♦ vr to separate; **sich ~en von** to part with; **T~ung** f separation; **T~wand** f partition (wall)

Trepp- ['trɛp] zW: **t~ab** adv downstairs;
　t~auf adv upstairs; **~e** f stair(case);
　~engeländer nt banister; **~enhaus** nt
　staircase
Tresor [tre'zo:r] (**-s**, **-e**) m safe
Tretboot nt pedalo, pedal boat
treten ['tre:tən] (unreg) vi to step; (Tränen,
　Schweiß) to appear ♦ vt (mit Fußtritt) to kick;
　(niedertreten) to tread, to trample; **~ nach** to
　kick at; **~ in** +akk to step in(to); **in**
　Verbindung ~ to get in contact; **in**
　Erscheinung ~ to appear
treu [trɔy] adj faithful, true; **T~e** (-) f loyalty,
　faithfulness; **T~händer** (**-s**, -) m trustee;
　T~handanstalt f trustee organization;
　T~handgesellschaft f trust company;
　~herzig adj innocent; **~los** adj faithless
Tribüne [tri'by:nə] f grandstand;
　(Rednertribüne) platform
Trichter ['trɪçtər] (**-s**, -) m funnel; (in Boden)
　crater
Trick [trɪk] (**-s**, **-e** od **-s**) m trick; **~film** m
　cartoon
Trieb [tri:p] (**-(e)s**, **-e**) m urge, drive;
　(Neigung) inclination; (an Baum etc) shoot;
　t~ etc vb siehe **treiben**; **~kraft** f (fig) drive;
　~täter m sex offender; **~werk** nt engine
triefen ['tri:fən] vi to drip
triffst etc [trɪfst] vb siehe **treffen**
triftig ['trɪftɪç] adj good, convincing
Trikot [tri'ko:] (**-s**, **-s**) nt vest; (SPORT) shirt
Trimester [tri'mɛstər] (**-s**, -) nt term
trimmen ['trɪmən] vr to do keep fit exercises
trink- ['trɪŋk] zW: **~bar** adj drinkable; **~en**
　(unreg) vt, vi to drink; **T~er** (**-s**, -) m drinker;
　T~geld nt tip; **T~halle** f refreshment kiosk;
　T~wasser nt drinking water
Tripper ['trɪpər] (**-s**, -) m gonorrhoea
Tritt [trɪt] (**-(e)s**, **-e**) m step; (Fußtritt) kick;
　~brett nt (EISENB) step; (AUT) running board
Triumph [tri'ʊmf] (**-(e)s**, **-e**) m triumph;
　~bogen m triumphal arch; **t~ieren**
　[triʊm'fi:rən] vi to triumph; (jubeln) to exult
trocken ['trɔkən] adj dry; **T~element** nt dry
　cell; **T~haube** f hair dryer; **T~heit** f
　dryness; **~legen** vt (Sumpf) to drain; (Kind)
　to put a clean nappy on; **T~milch** f dried
　milk; **T~rasur** f dry shave, electric shave
trocknen ['trɔknən] vt, vi to dry
Trödel ['trø:dəl] (**-s**) (umg) m junk; **~markt**
　m flea market; **t~n** (umg) vi to dawdle
Trommel ['trɔməl] (-, **-n**) f drum; **~fell** nt
　eardrum; **t~n** vt, vi to drum
Trompete [trɔm'pe:tə] f trumpet; **~r** (**-s**, -)
　m trumpeter
Tropen ['tro:pən] pl tropics; **~helm** m sun
　helmet
tröpfeln ['trœpfəln] vi to drop, to trickle
Tropfen ['trɔpfən] (**-s**, -) m drop; **t~** vt, vi to

drip ♦ vb unpers: **es tropft** a few raindrops
　are falling; **t~weise** adv in drops
Tropfsteinhöhle f stalactite cave
tropisch ['tro:pɪʃ] adj tropical
Trost [tro:st] (**-es**) m consolation, comfort
trösten ['trø:stən] vt to console, to comfort
trost- zW: **~los** adj bleak; (Verhältnisse)
　wretched; **T~preis** m consolation prize;
　~reich adj comforting
Trott [trɔt] (**-(e)s**, **-e**) m trot; (Routine)
　routine; **~el** (**-s**, -) (umg) m fool, dope; **t~en**
　vi to trot
Trotz [trɔts] (**-es**) m pigheadedness; **etw aus**
　~ tun to do sth just to show them; **jdm**
　zum ~ in defiance of sb; **t~** präp (+gen od
　dat) in spite of; **t~dem** adv nevertheless, all
　the same ♦ konj although; **t~en** vi (+dat) to
　defy; (der Kälte, Klima etc) to withstand; (der
　Gefahr) to brave; (t~ig sein) to be awkward;
　t~ig adj defiant, pig-headed; **~kopf** m
　obstinate child
trüb [try:p] adj dull; (Flüssigkeit, Glas) cloudy;
　(fig) gloomy
Trubel ['tru:bəl] (**-s**) m hurly-burly
trüb- zW: **~en** ['try:bən] vt to cloud ♦ vr to
　become clouded; **T~heit** f dullness;
　cloudiness; gloom; **T~sal** (-, **-e**) f distress;
　~selig adj sad, melancholy; **T~sinn** m
　depression; **~sinnig** adj depressed, gloomy
Trüffel ['trʏfəl] (-, **-n**) f truffle
trug etc [tru:k] vb siehe **tragen**
trügen ['try:gən] (unreg) vt to deceive ♦ vi to
　be deceptive
trügerisch adj deceptive
Trugschluss ▲ ['tru:gʃlʊs] m false conclusion
Truhe ['tru:ə] f chest
Trümmer ['trʏmər] pl wreckage sg;
　(Bautrümmer) ruins; **~haufen** m heap of
　rubble
Trumpf [trʊmpf] (**-(e)s**, **-e**) m (auch fig)
　trump; **t~en** vt, vi to trump
Trunk [trʊŋk] (**-(e)s**, **-e**) m drink; **t~en** adj
　intoxicated; **~enheit** f intoxication; **~enheit**
　am Steuer drunken driving; **~sucht** f
　alcoholism
Trupp [trʊp] (**-s**, **-s**) m troop; **~e** f troop;
　(Waffengattung) corps; (Schauspieltruppe)
　troupe; **~en** pl (MIL) troops;
　~enübungsplatz m training area
Truthahn ['tru:tha:n] m turkey
Tschech- ['tʃɛç] zW: **~e** m Czech; **~ien** (**-s**)
　nt the Czech Republic; **~in** f Czech; **t~isch**
　adj Czech; **~oslowakei** [-oslova'kaɪ]
　f: **die ~oslowakei** Czechoslovakia;
　t~oslowakisch [-oslo'va:kɪʃ] adj
　Czechoslovak(ian)
tschüs(s) [tʃʏs] excl cheerio
T-Shirt ['ti:ʃə:t] nt T-shirt
Tube ['tu:bə] f tube

Tuberkulose [tubɛrkuˈloːzə] f tuberculosis

Tuch [tuːx] (-(e)s, ⁻er) nt cloth; (Halstuch) scarf; (Kopftuch) headscarf; (Handtuch) towel

tüchtig [ˈtʏçtɪç] adj efficient, (cap)able; (umg: kräftig) good, sound; **T~keit** f efficiency, ability

Tücke [ˈtʏkə] f (Arglist) malice; (Trick) trick; (Schwierigkeit) difficulty, problem

tückisch [ˈtʏkɪʃ] adj treacherous; (böswillig) malicious

Tugend [ˈtuːgənt] (-, -en) f virtue; **t~haft** adj virtuous

Tülle f spout

Tulpe [ˈtʊlpə] f tulip

Tumor [ˈtuːmɔr] (-s, -e) m tumour

Tümpel [ˈtʏmpəl] (-s, -) m pool, pond

Tumult [tuˈmʊlt] (-(e)s, -e) m tumult

tun [tuːn] (unreg) vt (machen) to do; (legen) to put ♦ vi to act ♦ vr: **es tut sich etwas/viel** something/a lot is happening; **jdm etw ~** (antun) to do sth to sb; **etw tut es auch** sth will do; **das tut nichts** that doesn't matter; **das tut nichts zur Sache** that's neither here nor there; **so ~, als ob** to act as if

tünchen [ˈtʏnçən] vt to whitewash

Tunfisch [ˈtuːnfɪʃ] m = Thunfisch

Tunke [ˈtʊnkə] f sauce; **t~n** vt to dip, to dunk

tunlichst [ˈtuːnlɪçst] adv if at all possible; ~ **bald** as soon as possible

Tunnel [ˈtʊnəl] (-s, -s od -) m tunnel

Tupfen [ˈtʊpfən] (-s, -) m dot, spot; **t~** vt, vi to dab; (mit Farbe) to dot

Tür [tyːr] (-, -en) f door

Turbine [tʊrˈbiːnə] f turbine

Türk- [tʏrk] zW: **~e** m Turk; **~ei** [tʏrˈkaɪ] f: **die ~ei** Turkey; **~in** f Turk

Türkis [tʏrˈkiːs] (-es, -e) m turquoise; **t~** adj turquoise

türkisch [ˈtʏrkɪʃ] adj Turkish

Türklinke f doorknob, door handle

Turm [tʊrm] (-(e)s, ⁻e) m tower; (Kirchturm) steeple; (Sprungturm) diving platform; (SCHACH) castle, rook

türmen [ˈtʏrmən] vr to tower up ♦ vt to heap up ♦ vi (umg) to scarper, to bolt

Turn- [tʊrn] zW: **t~en** vi to do gymnastic exercises ♦ vt to perform; **~en** (-s) nt gymnastics; (SCH) physical education, P.E.; **~er(in)** (-s, -) m(f) gymnast; **~halle** f gym(nasium); **~hose** f gym shorts pl

Turnier [tʊrˈniːr] (-s, -e) nt tournament

Turn- zW: **~schuh** m gym shoe; **~verein** m gymnastics club; **~zeug** nt gym things pl

Tusche [ˈtʊʃə] f Indian ink

tuscheln [ˈtʊʃəln] vt, vi to whisper

Tuschkasten m paintbox

Tüte [ˈtyːtə] f bag

tuten [ˈtuːtən] vi (AUT) to hoot (BRIT), to honk (US)

TÜV [tʏf] (-s, -s) m abk (= Technischer Überwachungs-Verein) ≈ MOT

Typ [tyːp] (-s, -en) m type; **~e** f (TYP) type

Typhus [ˈtyːfʊs] (-) m typhoid (fever)

typisch [ˈtyːpɪʃ] adj: ~ (für) typical (of)

Tyrann [tyˈran] (-en, -en) m tyrant; **~ei** [-ˈnaɪ] f tyranny; **t~isch** adj tyrannical; **t~i'sieren** vt to tyrannize

U, u

u. a. abk = unter anderem

U-Bahn [ˈuːbaːn] f underground, tube

übel [ˈyːbəl] adj bad; (moralisch) bad, wicked; **jdm ist ~** sb feels sick; **~ gelaunt** bad-tempered; **jdm eine Bemerkung etc ~ nehmen** to be offended at sb's remark etc; **Ü~** (-s, -) nt evil; (Krankheit) disease; **Ü~keit** f nausea

üben [ˈyːbən] vt, vi to exercise, to practise

SCHLÜSSELWORT

über [ˈyːbər] präp +dat 1 (räumlich) over, above; **zwei Grad über null** two degrees above zero

2 (zeitlich) over; **über der Arbeit einschlafen** to fall asleep over one's work
♦ präp +akk 1 (räumlich) over; (hoch über auch) above; (quer über auch) across
2 (zeitlich) over; **über Weihnachten** over Christmas; **über kurz oder lang** sooner or later

3 (mit Zahlen): **Kinder über 12 Jahren** children over od above 12 years of age; **ein Scheck über 200 Mark** a cheque for 200 marks

4 (auf dem Wege) via; **nach Köln über Aachen** to Cologne via Aachen; **ich habe es über die Auskunft erfahren** I found out from information

5 (betreffend) about; **ein Buch über ...** a book about od on ...; **über jdn/etw lachen** to laugh about od at sb/sth

6: **Macht über jdn haben** to have power over sb; **sie liebt ihn über alles** she loves him more than anything
♦ adv over; **über und über** over and over; **den ganzen Tag über** all day long; **jdm in etw** dat **über sein** to be superior to sb in sth

überall [yːbərˈal] adv everywhere; **~'hin** adv everywhere

überanstrengen [yːbərˈʔanʃtrɛŋən] vt insep to overexert ♦ vr insep to overexert o.s.

überarbeiten [yːbərˈʔarbaɪtən] vt insep to revise, to rework ♦ vr insep to overwork (o.s.)

überaus [ˈyːbərˈʔaʊs] adv exceedingly

überbelichten [ˈyːbərbəlɪçtən] vt (PHOT) to overexpose

über'bieten (unreg) vt insep to outbid; (übertreffen) to surpass; (Rekord) to break

Überbleibsel |'y:bərblaıpsəl| (-s, -) nt residue, remainder

Überblick |'y:bərblık| m view; (fig: Darstellung) survey, overview; (Fähigkeit): ~ (über +akk) grasp (of), overall view (of); **ü~en** |-'blıkən| vt insep to survey

überbring- |y:bər'brıŋ| zW: **~en** (unreg) vt insep to deliver, to hand over; **Ü~er (-s, -)** m bearer

überbrücken |y:bər'brʏkən| vt insep to bridge (over)

überbuchen |'y:bərbu:xən| vt insep to overbook

über'dauern vt insep to outlast

über'denken (unreg) vt insep to think over

überdies |y:bər'di:s| adv besides

überdimensional |'y:bərdimenziona:l| adj oversize

Überdruss ▲ |'y:bərdrʊs| (-es) m weariness; **bis zum ~** ad nauseam

überdurchschnittlich |'y:bərdʊrçʃnıtlıç| adj above-average ♦ adv exceptionally

übereifrig |'y:bərlaıfrıç| adj over-keen

übereilt |y:bər'laılt| adj (over)hasty, premature

überein- |y:bər'laın| zW: **~ander** |y:bərlaı'nandər| adv one upon the other; (sprechen) about each other; **~kommen** (unreg) vi to agree; **Ü~kunft (-, -künfte)** f agreement; **~stimmen** vi to agree; **Ü~stimmung** f agreement

überempfindlich |'y:bərlempfıntlıç| adj hypersensitive

über'fahren |y:bər'fa:rən| (unreg) vt insep (AUT) to run over; (fig) to walk all over

Überfahrt |'y:bərfa:rt| f crossing

Überfall |'y:bərfal| m (Banküberfall, MIL) raid; (auf jdn) assault; **ü~en** |-'falən| (unreg) vt insep to attack; (Bank) to raid; (besuchen) to drop in on, to descend on

überfällig |'y:bərfɛlıç| adj overdue

über'fliegen (unreg) vt insep to fly over, to overfly; (Buch) to skim through

Überfluss ▲ |'y:bərflʊs| m: **~ (an +dat)** (super)abundance (of), excess (of)

überflüssig |'y:bərflʏsıç| adj superfluous

über'fordern vt insep to demand too much of; (Kräfte etc) to overtax

über'führen vt insep (Leiche etc) to transport; (Täter) to have convicted

Über'führung f transport; conviction; (Brücke) bridge, overpass

über'füllt adj (Schulen, Straßen) overcrowded; (Kurs) oversubscribed

Übergabe |'y:bərga:bə| f handing over; (MIL) surrender

Übergang |'y:bərgaŋ| m crossing; (Wandel, Überleitung) transition

Übergangs- zW: **~lösung** f provisional solution, stopgap; **~zeit** f transitional period

über'geben (unreg) vt insep to hand over; (MIL) to surrender ♦ vr insep to be sick

übergehen |'y:bərge:ən| (unreg) vi (Besitz) to pass; (zum Feind etc) to go over, to defect; **~ in +akk** to turn into; **über'gehen** (unreg) vt insep to pass over, to omit

Übergewicht |'y:bərgəvıçt| nt excess weight; (fig) preponderance

überglücklich |'y:bərglʏklıç| adj overjoyed

Übergröße |'y:bərgrø:sə| f oversize

überhaupt |y:bər'haʊpt| adv at all; (im Allgemeinen) in general; (besonders) especially; **~ nicht/keine** not/none at all

überheblich |y:bər'he:plıç| adj arrogant; **Ü~keit** f arrogance

über'holen vt insep to overtake; (TECH) to overhaul

über'holt adj out-of-date, obsolete

Überholverbot |y:bər'ho:lferbo:t| nt restriction on overtaking

über'hören vt insep not to hear; (absichtlich) to ignore

überirdisch |'y:bərlırdıʃ| adj supernatural, unearthly

über'laden (unreg) vt insep to overload ♦ adj (fig) cluttered

über'lassen (unreg) vt insep: **jdm etw ~** to leave sth to sb ♦ vr insep: **sich einer Sache dat ~** to give o.s. over to sth

über'lasten vt insep to overload; (Mensch) to overtax

überlaufen |'y:bərlaʊfən| (unreg) vi (Flüssigkeit) to flow over; (zum Feind etc) to go over, to defect; **~ sein** to be inundated od besieged; **über'laufen** (unreg) vt insep (Schauer etc) to come over

über'leben vt insep to survive; **Über'lebende(r)** f(m) survivor

über'legen vt insep to consider ♦ adj superior; **ich muss es mir ~** I'll have to think about it; **Über'legenheit** f superiority

Über'legung f consideration, deliberation

über'liefern vt insep to hand down, to transmit

Überlieferung f tradition

überlisten |y:bər'lıstən| vt insep to outwit

überm |'y:bərm| = **über dem**

Übermacht |'y:bərmaxt| f superior force, superiority; **übermächtig** |'y:bərmɛçtıç| adj superior (in strength); (Gefühl etc) overwhelming

übermäßig |'y:bərmɛ:sıç| adj excessive

Übermensch |'y:bərmɛnʃ| m superman; **ü~lich** adj superhuman

übermitteln |y:bər'mıtəln| vt insep to convey

übermorgen |'y:bərmɔrgən| adv the day

after tomorrow

Übermüdung |y:bər'my:dʊŋ| f fatigue, overtiredness

Übermut |'y:bərmu:t| m exuberance

übermütig |'y:bərmy:tıç| adj exuberant, high-spirited; ~ **werden** to get overconfident

übernächste(r, s) |'y:bərnɛ:çstə(r, s)| adj (Jahr) next but one

übernacht- |y:bər'naxt| zW: **~en** vi insep: (bei jdm) ~en to spend the night (at sb's place); **Ü~ung** f overnight stay; **Ü~ung mit Frühstück** bed and breakfast; **Ü~ungsmöglichkeit** f overnight accommodation no pl

Übernahme |'y:bərna:mə| f taking over od on, acceptance

über'nehmen (unreg) vt insep to take on, to accept; (Amt, Geschäft) to take over ♦ vr insep to take on too much

über'prüfen vt insep to examine, to check

überqueren |y:bər'kve:rən| vt insep to cross

überragen |y:bər'ra:gən| vt insep to tower above; (fig) to surpass

überraschen |y:bər'raʃən| vt insep to surprise

Überraschung f surprise

überreden |y:bər're:dən| vt insep to persuade

überreichen |y:bər'raıçən| vt insep to present, to hand over

'Überrest m remains, remnants

überrumpeln |y:bər'rʊmpəln| vt insep to take by surprise

überrunden |y:bər'rʊndən| vt insep to lap

übers |'y:bərs| = **über das**

Überschall- |'y:bərʃal| zW: **~flugzeug** nt supersonic jet; **~geschwindigkeit** f supersonic speed

über'schätzen vt insep to overestimate

'überschäumen vi (Bier) to foam over, bubble over; (Temperament) to boil over

Überschlag |'y:bərʃla:k| m (FIN) estimate; (SPORT) somersault; **ü~en** |-'ʃla:gən| (unreg) vt insep (berechnen) to estimate; (auslassen: Seite) to omit ♦ vr insep to somersault; (Stimme) to crack; (AVIAT) to loop the loop; **'ü~en** (unreg) vt (Beine) to cross ♦ vi (Wellen) to break; (Funken) to flash

überschnappen |'y:bərʃnapən| vi (Stimme) to crack; (umg: Mensch) to flip one's lid

über'schneiden (unreg) vr insep (auch fig) to overlap; (Linien) to intersect

über'schreiben (unreg) vt insep to provide with a heading; **jdm etw ~** to transfer od make over sth to sb

über'schreiten (unreg) vt insep to cross over; (fig) to exceed; (verletzen) to transgress

Überschrift |'y:bərʃrıft| f heading, title

Überschuss ▲ |'y:bərʃʊs| m: **~ (an** +dat) surplus (of); **überschüssig** |'y:bərʃysıç| adj

surplus, excess

über'schütten vt insep: **jdn/etw mit etw ~** to pour sth over sb/sth; **jdn mit etw ~** (fig) to shower sb with sth

überschwänglich |'y:bərʃvɛŋlıç| adj effusive

überschwemmen |y:bər'ʃvɛmən| vt insep to flood

Überschwemmung f flood

Übersee |'y:bərze:| f: **nach/in ~** overseas; **ü~isch** adj overseas

über'sehen vt insep to look (out) over; (fig: Folgen) to see, to get an overall view of; (: nicht beachten) to overlook

über'senden (unreg) vt insep to send, to forward

übersetz- zW: **~en** |y:bər'zɛtsən| vt insep to translate; **'übersetzen** vt to cross; **Ü~er(in)** |-'zɛtsər(ın)| (-s, -) m(f) translator; **Ü~ung** |-'zɛtsʊŋ| f translation; (TECH) gear ratio

Übersicht |'y:bərzıçt| f overall view; (Darstellung) survey; **ü~lich** adj clear; (Gelände) open; **~lichkeit** f clarity, lucidity

übersiedeln |y:bər'zi:dəln| vi sep to move; **'übersiedeln** vi to move

über'spannt adj eccentric; (Idee) wild, crazy

überspitzt |y:bər'ʃpıtst| adj exaggerated

über'springen (unreg) vt insep to jump over; (fig) to skip

überstehen |y:bər'ʃte:ən| (unreg) vt insep to overcome, to get over; (Winter etc) to survive, to get through; **'überstehen** (unreg) vi to project

über'steigen (unreg) vt insep to climb over; (fig) to exceed

über'stimmen vt insep to outvote

Überstunden |'y:bərʃtʊndən| pl overtime sg

über'stürzen vt insep to rush ♦ vr insep to follow (one another) in rapid succession

überstürzt adj (over)hasty

Übertrag |'y:bərtra:k| (-(e)s, -träge) m (COMM) amount brought forward; **ü~bar** |-'tra:kba:r| adj transferable; (MED) infectious; **ü~en** |-'tra:gən| (unreg) vt insep to transfer; (RAD) to broadcast; (übersetzen) to render; (Krankheit) to transmit ♦ vr insep to spread ♦ adj figurative; **ü~en auf** +akk to transfer to; **jdm etw ü~en auf** to assign sth to sb; **sich ü~en auf** +akk to spread to; **~ung** |-'tra:gʊŋ| f transfer(ence); (RAD) broadcast; rendering; transmission

über'treffen (unreg) vt insep to surpass

über'treiben (unreg) vt insep to exaggerate; **Übertreibung** f exaggeration

übertreten |y:bər'tre:tən| (unreg) vt insep to cross; (Gebot etc) to break; **'übertreten** (unreg) vi (über Linie, Gebiet) to step (over); (SPORT) to overstep; (zu anderem Glauben) to be converted; **~ (in** +akk) (POL) to go over (to)

Über'tretung f violation, transgression

übertrieben |y:bər'tri:bən| adj exaggerated,

excessive
übervölkert [yːbər'fœlkərt] *adj*
overpopulated
übervoll ['yːbərfɔl] *adj* overfull
übervorteilen [yːbər'fɔrtaɪlən] *vt insep* to
dupe, to cheat
über'wachen *vt insep* to supervise;
(*Verdächtigen*) to keep under surveillance;
Überwachung *f* supervision; surveillance
überwältigen [yːbər'vɛltɪgən] *vt insep* to
overpower; **~d** *adj* overwhelming
überweisen [yːbər'vaɪzən] (*unreg*) *vt insep*
to transfer
Überweisung *f* transfer; **~sauftrag** *m*
(credit) transfer order
über'wiegen (*unreg*) *vi insep* to
predominate; **~d** *adj* predominant
über'winden (*unreg*) *vt insep* to overcome
♦ *vr insep* to make an effort, to bring o.s. (to
do sth)
Überwindung *f* effort, strength of mind
Überzahl ['yːbərtsaːl] *f* superiority, superior
numbers *pl*; **in der ~ sein** to be numerically
superior
überzählig ['yːbərtsɛːlɪç] *adj* surplus
über'zeugen *vt insep* to convince; **~d** *adj*
convincing
Überzeugung *f* conviction
überziehen [yːbər'tsiːən] (*unreg*) *vt* to put
on; **über'ziehen** (*unreg*) *vt insep* to cover;
(*Konto*) to overdraw
Überziehungskredit *m* overdraft provision
Überzug ['yːbərtsuːk] *m* cover; (*Belag*)
coating
üblich ['yːplɪç] *adj* usual
U-Boot ['uːboːt] *nt* submarine
übrig ['yːbrɪç] *adj* remaining; **für jdn etwas ~
haben** (*umg*) to be fond of sb; **die Ü~en** the
others; **das Ü~e** the rest; **im Ü~en** besides;
~ bleiben to remain, to be left (over); **~
lassen** to leave (over); **~ens** ['yːbrɪgəns]
adv besides; (*nebenbei bemerkt*) by the
way
Übung ['yːbʊŋ] *f* practice; (*Turnübung,
Aufgabe etc*) exercise; **~ macht den Meister**
practice makes perfect
Ufer ['uːfər] (**-s, -**) *nt* bank; (*Meeresufer*) shore
Uhr [uːr] (**-, -en**) *f* clock; (*Armbanduhr*) watch;
wie viel ~ ist es? what time is it?; **1 ~ 1**
o'clock; **20 ~ 8** o'clock, **20.00** (twenty
hundred) hours; **~(arm)band** *nt* watch
strap; **~band** *nt* watch strap; **~macher** (**-s,
-**) *m* watchmaker; **~werk** *nt* clockwork;
works of a watch; **~zeiger** *m* hand;
~zeigersinn *m*: **im ~zeigersinn** clockwise;
entgegen dem ~zeigersinn anticlockwise;
~zeit *f* time (of day)
Uhu ['uːhu] (**-s, -s**) *m* eagle owl
UKW [uːkaː'veː] *abk* (= *Ultrakurzwelle*) VHF

ulkig ['ʊlkɪç] *adj* funny
Ulme ['ʊlmə] *f* elm
Ultimatum [ʊlti'maːtʊm] (**-s, Ultimaten**) *nt*
ultimatum
Ultra- ['ʊltra] *zW*: **~schall** *m* (*PHYS*)
ultrasound; **u~violett** *adj* ultraviolet

SCHLÜSSELWORT

um [ʊm] *präp +akk* **1** (*um herum*) (a)round;
um Weihnachten around Christmas; **er
schlug um sich** he hit about him
2 (*mit Zeitangabe*) at; **um acht (Uhr)** at
eight (o'clock)
3 (*mit Größenangabe*) by; **etw um 4 cm
kürzen** to shorten sth by 4 cm; **um 10%
teurer** 10% more expensive; **um vieles
besser** better by far; **um so besser** so
much the better
4: **der Kampf um den Titel** the battle for
the title; **um Geld spielen** to play for
money; **Stunde um Stunde** hour after
hour; **Auge um Auge** an eye for an eye
♦ *präp +gen*: **um ... willen** for the sake of
...; **um Gottes willen** for goodness *od*
(*stärker*) God's sake
♦ *konj*: **um ... zu** (in order) to ...; **zu klug,
um zu ...** too clever to ...; **siehe umso**
♦ *adv* **1** (*ungefähr*) about; **um (die) 30
Leute** about *od* around 30 people
2 (*vorbei*): **die 2 Stunden sind um** the
two hours are up

umändern ['ʊmɛndərn] *vt* to alter
Umänderung *f* alteration
umarbeiten ['ʊmarbaɪtən] *vt* to remodel;
(*Buch etc*) to revise, to rework
umarmen [ʊm'armən] *vt insep* to embrace
Umbau ['ʊmbaʊ] (**-(e)s, -e** *od* **-ten**) *m*
reconstruction, alteration(s); **u~en** *vt* to
rebuild, to reconstruct
umbilden ['ʊmbɪldən] *vt* to reorganize; (*POL*:
Kabinett) to reshuffle
umbinden ['ʊmbɪndən] (*unreg*) *vt* (*Krawatte
etc*) to put on
umblättern ['ʊmblɛtərn] *vt* to turn over
umblicken ['ʊmblɪkən] *vr* to look around
umbringen ['ʊmbrɪŋən] (*unreg*) *vt* to kill
umbuchen ['ʊmbuːxən] *vi* to change one's
reservation/flight *etc* ♦ *vt* to change
umdenken ['ʊmdɛŋkən] (*unreg*) *vi* to adjust
one's views
umdrehen ['ʊmdreːən] *vt* to turn (round);
(*Hals*) to wring ♦ *vr* to turn (round)
Um'drehung *f* revolution; rotation
umeinander [ʊmaɪ'nandər] *adv* round one
another; (*füreinander*) for one another
umfahren ['ʊmfaːrən] (*unreg*) *vt* to run over;
um'fahren (*unreg*) *vt insep* to drive round;
to sail round

Spelling reform: ▲ *new spelling* △ *old spelling (to be phased out)*

umfallen ['ʊmfalən] (unreg) vi to fall down od over

Umfang ['ʊmfaŋ] m extent; (von Buch) size; (Reichweite) range; (Fläche) area; (MATH) circumference; **u~reich** adj extensive; (Buch etc) voluminous

um'fassen vt insep to embrace; (umgeben) to surround; (enthalten) to include; **~d** adj comprehensive, extensive

umformen ['ʊmfɔrmən] vi to transform

Umfrage ['ʊmfraːgə] f poll

umfüllen ['ʊmfʏlən] vt to transfer; (Wein) to decant

umfunktionieren ['ʊmfʊŋktsioniːrən] vt to convert, to transform

Umgang ['ʊmgaŋ] m company; (mit jdm) dealings pl; (Behandlung) way of behaving

umgänglich ['ʊmgɛŋlɪç] adj sociable

Umgangs- zW: **~formen** pl manners; **~sprache** f colloquial language

umgeben [ʊm'geːbən] (unreg) vt insep to surround

Umgebung f surroundings pl; (Milieu) environment; (Personen) people in one's circle

umgehen ['ʊmgeːən] (unreg) vi to go (a)round; **im Schlosse ~** to haunt the castle; **mit jdm grob etc ~** to treat sb roughly etc; **mit Geld sparsam ~** to be careful with one's money; **um'gehen** vt insep to bypass; (MIL) to outflank; (Gesetz etc) to circumvent; (vermeiden) to avoid; **'~d** adj immediate

Um'gehung f bypassing; outflanking; circumvention; avoidance; **~sstraße** f bypass

umgekehrt ['ʊmgəkeːrt] adj reverse(d); (gegenteilig) opposite ♦ adv the other way around; **und ~** and vice versa

umgraben ['ʊmgraːbən] (unreg) vt to dig up

Umhang ['ʊmhaŋ] m wrap, cape

umhauen ['ʊmhaʊən] vt to fell; (fig) to bowl over

umher [ʊm'heːr] adv about, around; **~gehen** (unreg) vi to walk about; **~ziehen** (unreg) vi to wander from place to place

umhinkönnen [ʊm'hɪnkœnən] (unreg) vi: **ich kann nicht umhin, das zu tun** I can't help doing it

umhören ['ʊmhøːrən] vr to ask around

Umkehr ['ʊmkeːr] (-) f turning back; (Änderung) change; **u~en** vi to turn back ♦ vt to turn round, to reverse; (Tasche etc) to turn inside out; (Gefäß etc) to turn upside down

umkippen ['ʊmkɪpən] vt to tip over ♦ vi to overturn; (umg: Mensch) to keel over; (fig: Meinung ändern) to change one's mind

Umkleide- ['ʊmklaɪdə] zW: **~kabine** f (im Schwimmbad) (changing) cubicle; **~raum** m changing od dressing room

umkommen ['ʊmkɔmən] (unreg) vi to die,

to perish; (Lebensmittel) to go bad

Umkreis ['ʊmkraɪs] m neighbourhood; **im ~ von** within a radius of

Umlage ['ʊmlaːgə] f share of the costs

Umlauf ['ʊmlaʊf] m (Geldumlauf) circulation; (von Gestirn) revolution; **~bahn** f orbit

Umlaut ['ʊmlaʊt] m umlaut

umlegen ['ʊmleːgən] vt to put on; (verlegen) to move, to shift; (Kosten) to share out; (umkippen) to tip over; (umg: töten) to bump off

umleiten ['ʊmlaɪtən] vt to divert

Umleitung f diversion

umliegend ['ʊmliːgənt] adj surrounding

um'randen vt insep to border, to edge

umrechnen ['ʊmrɛçnən] vt to convert

Umrechnung f conversion; **~skurs** m rate of exchange

um'reißen (unreg) vt insep to outline, to sketch

Umriss ▲ ['ʊmrɪs] m outline

umrühren ['ʊmryːrən] vt, vi to stir

ums [ʊms] = **um das**

Umsatz ['ʊmzats] m turnover; **~steuer** f sales tax

umschalten ['ʊmʃaltən] vt to switch

umschauen vr to look round

Umschlag ['ʊmʃlaːk] m cover; (Buchumschlag auch) jacket; (MED) compress; (Briefumschlag) envelope; (Wechsel) change; (von Hose) turn-up; **u~en** [-gən] (unreg) vi to change; (NAUT) to capsize ♦ vt to knock over; (Ärmel) to turn up; (Seite) to turn over; (Waren) to transfer; **~platz** m (COMM) distribution centre

umschreiben ['ʊmʃraɪbən] (unreg) vt (neu schreiben) to rewrite; (übertragen) to transfer; **~ auf** +akk to transfer to; **um'schreiben** (unreg) vt insep to paraphrase; (abgrenzen) to define

umschulen ['ʊmʃuːlən] vt to retrain; (Kind) to send to another school

Umschweife ['ʊmʃvaɪfə] pl: **ohne ~** without beating about the bush, straight out

Umschwung ['ʊmʃvʊŋ] m change (around), revolution

umsehen ['ʊmzeːən] (unreg) vr to look around od about; (suchen): **sich ~ (nach)** to look out (for)

umseitig ['ʊmzaɪtɪç] adv overleaf

umsichtig ['ʊmzɪçtɪç] adj cautious, prudent

umso ['ʊmzo] konj: **~ besser/schlimmer** so much the better/worse

umsonst [ʊm'zɔnst] adv in vain; (gratis) for nothing

umspringen ['ʊmʃprɪŋən] (unreg) vi to change; (Wind auch) to veer; **mit jdm ~ to** treat sb badly

Umstand ['ʊmʃtant] m circumstance; **Umstände** pl (fig: Schwierigkeiten) fuss; **in anderen Umständen sein** to be pregnant;

Umstände machen to go to a lot of trouble; **unter Umständen** possibly

umständlich ['ʊmʃtɛntlɪç] adj (Methode) cumbersome, complicated; (Ausdrucksweise, Erklärung) long-winded; (Mensch) ponderous

Umstandskleid nt maternity dress

Umstehende(n) ['ʊmʃteːəndə(n)] pl bystanders

umsteigen ['ʊmʃtaɪgən] (unreg) vi (EISENB) to change

umstellen ['ʊmʃtɛlən] vt (an anderen Ort) to change round, to rearrange; (TECH) to convert ♦ vr to adapt (o.s.); **sich auf etw** akk ~ to adapt to sth; **um'stellen** vt insep to surround

Umstellung ['ʊmʃtɛlʊŋ] f change; (Umgewöhnung) adjustment; (TECH) conversion

umstimmen ['ʊmʃtɪmən] vt (MUS) to retune; **jdn** ~ to make sb change his mind

umstoßen ['ʊmʃtoːsən] (unreg) vt to overturn; (Plan etc) to change, to upset

umstritten [ʊm'ʃtrɪtən] adj disputed

Umsturz ['ʊmʃtʊrts] m overthrow

umstürzen ['ʊmʃtʏrtsən] vt (umwerfen) to overturn ♦ vi to collapse, to fall down; (Wagen) to overturn

Umtausch ['ʊmtaʊʃ] m exchange; **u~en** vt to exchange

Umverpackung ['ʊmfɛrpakʊŋ] f packaging

umwandeln ['ʊmvandəln] vt to change, to convert; (ELEK) to transform

umwechseln ['ʊmvɛksəln] vt to change

Umweg ['ʊmveːk] m detour, roundabout way

Umwelt ['ʊmvɛlt] f environment; **u~freundlich** adj not harmful to the environment, environment-friendly; **u~schädlich** adj ecologically harmful; **~schutz** m environmental protection; **~schützer** m environmentalist; **~verschmutzung** f environmental pollution

umwenden ['ʊmvɛndən] (unreg) vt, vr to turn (round)

umwerfen ['ʊmvɛrfən] (unreg) vt to upset, to overturn; (fig: erschüttern) to upset, to throw; **~d** (umg) adj fantastic

umziehen ['ʊmtsiːən] (unreg) vt, vr to change ♦ vi to move

Umzug ['ʊmtsuːk] m procession; (Wohnungsumzug) move, removal

unab- ['ʊnʔap] zW: **~änderlich** adj irreversible, unalterable; **~hängig** adj independent; **U~hängigkeit** f independence; **~kömmlich** adj indispensable; **zur Zeit ~kömmlich** not free at the moment; **~lässig** adj incessant, constant; **~sehbar** adj immeasurable;

(Folgen) unforeseeable; (Kosten) incalculable; **~sichtlich** adj unintentional; **~'wendbar** adj inevitable

unachtsam ['ʊnʔaxtzaːm] adj careless; **U~keit** f carelessness

unan- ['ʊnʔan] zW: **~'fechtbar** adj indisputable; **~gebracht** adj uncalled-for; **~gemessen** adj inadequate; **~genehm** adj unpleasant; **U~nehmlichkeit** f inconvenience; **U~nehmlichkeiten** pl (Ärger) trouble sg; **~sehnlich** adj unsightly; **~ständig** adj indecent, improper

unappetitlich ['ʊnʔapetiːtlɪç] adj unsavoury

Unart ['ʊnʔaːrt] f bad manners pl; (Angewohnheit) bad habit; **u~ig** adj naughty, badly behaved

unauf- ['ʊnʔaʊf] zW: **~fällig** adj unobtrusive; (Kleidung) inconspicuous; **~'findbar** adj not to be found; **~gefordert** adj unasked ♦ adv spontaneously; **~haltsam** adj irresistible; **~'hörlich** adj incessant, continuous; **~merksam** adj inattentive; **~richtig** adj insincere

unaus- ['ʊnʔaʊs] zW: **~geglichen** adj unbalanced; **~'sprechlich** adj inexpressible; **~'stehlich** adj intolerable

unbarmherzig ['ʊnbarmhɛrtsɪç] adj pitiless, merciless

unbeabsichtigt ['ʊnbəʔapzɪçtɪçt] adj unintentional

unbeachtet ['ʊnbəʔaxtət] adj unnoticed, ignored

unbedenklich ['ʊnbədɛŋklɪç] adj (Plan) unobjectionable

unbedeutend ['ʊnbədɔʏtənt] adj insignificant, unimportant; (Fehler) slight

unbedingt ['ʊnbədɪŋt] adj unconditional ♦ adv absolutely; **musst du ~ gehen?** do you really have to go?

unbefangen ['ʊnbəfaŋən] adj impartial, unprejudiced; (ohne Hemmungen) uninhibited; **U~heit** f impartiality; uninhibitedness

unbefriedigend ['ʊnbəfriːdɪgənd] adj unsatisfactory

unbefriedigt ['ʊnbəfriːdɪçt] adj unsatisfied, dissatisfied

unbefugt ['ʊnbəfuːkt] adj unauthorized

unbegreiflich [ʊnbə'graɪflɪç] adj inconceivable

unbegrenzt ['ʊnbəgrɛntst] adj unlimited

unbegründet ['ʊnbəgrʏndət] adj unfounded

Unbehagen ['ʊnbəhaːgən] nt discomfort; **unbehaglich** ['ʊnbəhaːklɪç] adj uncomfortable; (Gefühl) uneasy

unbeholfen ['ʊnbəhɔlfən] adj awkward, clumsy

unbekannt ['ʊnbəkant] adj unknown

unbekümmert ['ʊnbəkʏmərt] adj unconcerned

unbeliebt ['ʊnbəliːpt] adj unpopular

unbequem ['ʊnbəkveːm] adj (Stuhl) uncomfortable; (Mensch) bothersome; (Regelung) inconvenient

unberechenbar [ʊnbə'rɛçənbaːr] adj incalculable; (Mensch, Verhalten) unpredictable

unberechtigt ['ʊnbərɛçtɪçt] adj unjustified; (nicht erlaubt) unauthorized

unberührt ['ʊnbərʏːrt] adj untouched, intact; **sie ist noch ~** she is still a virgin

unbescheiden ['ʊnbəʃaɪdən] adj presumptuous

unbeschreiblich [ʊnbə'ʃraɪplɪç] adj indescribable

unbeständig ['ʊnbəʃtɛndɪç] adj (Mensch) inconstant; (Wetter) unsettled; (Lage) unstable

unbestechlich [ʊnbə'ʃtɛçlɪç] adj incorruptible

unbestimmt ['ʊnbəʃtɪmt] adj indefinite; (Zukunft auch) uncertain

unbeteiligt [ʊnbə'taɪlɪçt] adj unconcerned, indifferent

unbeweglich ['ʊnbəveːklɪç] adj immovable

unbewohnt ['ʊnbəvoːnt] adj uninhabited; (Wohnung) unoccupied

unbewusst ▲ ['ʊnbəvʊst] adj unconscious

unbezahlt ['ʊnbətsaːlt] adj (Rechnung) outstanding, unsettled; (Urlaub) unpaid

unbrauchbar ['ʊnbrauxbaːr] adj (Arbeit) useless; (Gerät auch) unusable

und [ʊnt] konj and; **~ so weiter** and so on

Undank ['ʊndaŋk] m ingratitude; **u~bar** adj ungrateful

undefinierbar [ʊndefi'niːrbaːr] adj indefinable

undenkbar [ʊn'dɛŋkbaːr] adj inconceivable

undeutlich ['ʊndɔʏtlɪç] adj indistinct

undicht ['ʊndɪçt] adj leaky

Unding ['ʊndɪŋ] nt absurdity

undurch- ['ʊndʊrç] zW: **~führbar** [-'fyːrbaːr] adj impracticable; **~lässig** [-'lɛsɪç] adj waterproof, impermeable; **~sichtig** [-'zɪçtɪç] adj opaque; (fig) obscure

uneben ['ʊnˈeːbən] adj uneven

unecht ['ʊnˈɛçt] adj (Schmuck) fake; (vorgetäuscht: Freundlichkeit) false

unehelich ['ʊnˈeːəlɪç] adj illegitimate

uneinig ['ʊnˈaɪnɪç] adj divided; **~ sein** to disagree; **U~keit** f discord, dissension

uneins ['ʊnˈaɪns] adj at variance, at odds

unempfindlich ['ʊnˈɛmpfɪntlɪç] adj insensitive; (Stoff) practical

unendlich [ʊn'ɛntlɪç] adj infinite

unent- ['ʊnˈɛnt] zW: **~behrlich** [-'beːrlɪç] adj indispensable; **~geltlich** [-gɛltlɪç] adj free (of charge); **~schieden** [-'ʃiːdən] adj undecided; **~schieden enden** (SPORT) to end in a draw; **~schlossen** [-'ʃlɔsən] adj undecided; irresolute; **~wegt** [-'veːkt] adj unswerving; (unaufhörlich) incessant

uner- ['ʊnˈer] zW: **~bittlich** [-'bɪtlɪç] adj unyielding, inexorable; **~fahren** [-'faːrən] adj inexperienced; **~freulich** [-'frɔʏlɪç] adj unpleasant; **~gründlich** adj unfathomable; **~hört** [-'høːrt] adj unheard-of; (Bitte) outrageous; **~lässlich** ▲ [-'lɛslɪç] adj indispensable; **~laubt** adj unauthorized; **~messlich** ▲ adj immeasurable, immense; **~reichbar** adj (Ziel) unattainable; (Ort) inaccessible; (telefonisch) unobtainable; **~schöpflich** [-'ʃœpflɪç] adj inexhaustible; **~schwinglich** [-'ʃvɪŋlɪç] adj (Preis) exorbitant; too expensive; **~träglich** [-'trɛːklɪç] adj unbearable; (Frechheit) insufferable; **~wartet** adj unexpected; **~wünscht** adj undesirable, unwelcome

unfähig ['ʊnfɛːɪç] adj incapable, incompetent; **zu etw ~ sein** to be incapable of sth; **U~keit** f incapacity; incompetence

unfair ['ʊnfɛːr] adj unfair

Unfall ['ʊnfal] m accident; **~flucht** f hit-and-run (driving); **~schaden** m damages pl; **~station** f emergency ward; **~stelle** f scene of the accident; **~versicherung** f accident insurance

unfassbar ▲ [ʊn'fasbaːr] adj inconceivable

unfehlbar [ʊn'feːlbaːr] adj infallible ♦ adv inevitably; **U~keit** f infallibility

unförmig ['ʊnfœrmɪç] adj (formlos) shapeless

unfrei ['ʊnfraɪ] adj not free, unfree; (Paket) unfranked; **~willig** adj involuntary, against one's will

unfreundlich ['ʊnfrɔʏntlɪç] adj unfriendly; **U~keit** f unfriendliness

Unfriede(n) ['ʊnfriːdə(n)] m dissension, strife

unfruchtbar ['ʊnfrʊxtbaːr] adj infertile; (Gespräche) unfruitful; **U~keit** f infertility; unfruitfulness

Unfug ['ʊnfuːk] (-s) m (Benehmen) mischief; (Unsinn) nonsense; **grober ~** (JUR) gross misconduct; malicious damage

Ungar(in) ['ʊŋɡar(ɪn)] m(f) Hungarian; **u~isch** adj Hungarian; **~n** nt Hungary

ungeachtet ['ʊngəˈaxtət] präp +gen notwithstanding

ungeahnt ['ʊngəˈaːnt] adj unsuspected, undreamt-of

ungebeten ['ʊngəbeːtən] adj uninvited

ungebildet ['ʊngəbɪldət] adj uneducated; uncultured

ungedeckt ['ʊngədɛkt] adj (Scheck) uncovered

Ungeduld ['ʊngədʊlt] f impatience; **u~ig** [-dɪç] adj impatient

ungeeignet ['ʊngəˈaɪɡnət] adj unsuitable

ungefähr ['ʊngəfɛːr] adj rough, approximate; **das kommt nicht von ~** that's hardly surprising

ungefährlich ['ʊngəfɛːrlɪç] adj not dangerous, harmless

ungehalten ['ʊngəhaltən] adj indignant

ungeheuer ['ʊngəhɔʏər] adj huge ♦ adv (umg) enormously; **U~** (-s, -) nt monster; **~lich** [-'hɔʏrlɪç] adj monstrous

ungehörig ['ʊngəhøːrɪç] adj impertinent, improper

ungehorsam ['ʊngəhoːrzaːm] adj disobedient; **U~** m disobedience

ungeklärt ['ʊngəklɛːrt] adj not cleared up; (Rätsel) unsolved

ungeladen ['ʊngəlaːdən] adj not loaded; (Gast) uninvited

ungelegen ['ʊngəleːgən] adj inconvenient

ungelernt ['ʊngəlɛrnt] adj unskilled

ungelogen ['ʊngəloːgən] adv really, honestly

ungemein ['ʊngəmaɪn] adj uncommon

ungemütlich ['ʊngəmyːtlɪç] adj uncomfortable; (Person) disagreeable

ungenau ['ʊngənaʊ] adj inaccurate; **U~igkeit** f inaccuracy

ungenießbar ['ʊngəniːsbaːr] adj inedible; undrinkable; (umg) unbearable

ungenügend ['ʊngənyːgənt] adj insufficient, inadequate

ungepflegt ['ʊngəpfleːkt] adj (Garten etc) untended; (Person) unkempt; (Hände) neglected

ungerade ['ʊngəraːdə] adj uneven, odd

ungerecht ['ʊngərɛçt] adj unjust; **~fertigt** adj unjustified; **U~igkeit** f injustice, unfairness

ungern ['ʊngɛrn] adv unwillingly, reluctantly

ungeschehen ['ʊngəʃeːən] adj: **~ machen** to undo

Ungeschicklichkeit ['ʊngəʃɪklɪçkaɪt] f clumsiness

ungeschickt adj awkward, clumsy

ungeschminkt ['ʊngəʃmɪŋkt] adj without make-up; (fig) unvarnished

ungesetzlich ['ʊngəzɛtslɪç] adj illegal

ungestört ['ʊngəʃtøːrt] adj undisturbed

ungestraft ['ʊngəʃtraːft] adv with impunity

ungestüm ['ʊngəʃtyːm] adj impetuous; tempestuous

ungesund ['ʊngəzʊnt] adj unhealthy

ungetrübt ['ʊngətryːpt] adj clear; (fig) untroubled; (Freude) unalloyed

Ungetüm ['ʊngətyːm] (-(e)s, -e) nt monster

ungewiss ▲ ['ʊngəvɪs] adj uncertain; **U~heit** ▲ f uncertainty

ungewöhnlich ['ʊngəvøːnlɪç] adj unusual

ungewohnt ['ʊngəvoːnt] adj unaccustomed

Ungeziefer ['ʊngətsiːfər] (-s) nt vermin

ungezogen ['ʊngətsoːgən] adj rude, impertinent; **U~heit** f rudeness, impertinence

ungezwungen ['ʊngətsvʊŋən] adj natural, unconstrained

unglaublich [ʊn'glaʊplɪç] adj incredible

ungleich ['ʊnglaɪç] adj dissimilar; unequal ♦ adv incomparably; **~artig** adj different; **U~heit** f dissimilarity; inequality; **~mäßig** adj irregular, uneven

Unglück ['ʊnglvk] (-(e)s, -e) nt misfortune; (Pech) bad luck; (Unglücksfall) calamity, disaster; (Verkehrsunglück) accident; **u~lich** adj unhappy; (erfolglos) unlucky; (unerfreulich) unfortunate; **u~licherweise** [-'vaɪzə] adv unfortunately; **~sfall** m accident, calamity

ungültig ['ʊngʏltɪç] adj invalid; **U~keit** f invalidity

ungünstig ['ʊngʏnstɪç] adj unfavourable

ungut ['ʊnguːt] adj (Gefühl) uneasy; **nichts für ~** no offence

unhaltbar ['ʊnhaltbaːr] adj untenable

Unheil ['ʊnhaɪl] nt evil; (Unglück) misfortune; **~ anrichten** to cause mischief; **u~bar** adj incurable

unheimlich ['ʊnhaɪmlɪç] adj weird, uncanny ♦ adv (umg) tremendously

unhöflich ['ʊnhøːflɪç] adj impolite; **U~keit** f impoliteness

unhygienisch ['ʊnhygieːnɪʃ] adj unhygienic

Uni ['ʊni] (-, -s) (umg) f university

Uniform [uni'fɔrm] f uniform; **u~iert** [-'miːrt] adj uniformed

uninteressant ['ʊnɪnterɛsant] adj uninteresting

Uni- zW: **~versität** [univerzi'tɛːt] f university; **~versum** [uni'vɛrzʊm] (-s) nt universe

unkenntlich ['ʊnkɛntlɪç] adj unrecognizable

Unkenntnis ['ʊnkɛntnɪs] f ignorance

unklar ['ʊnklaːr] adj unclear; **im U~en sein über** +akk to be in the dark about; **U~heit** f unclarity; (Unentschiedenheit) uncertainty

unklug ['ʊnkluːk] adj unwise

Unkosten ['ʊnkɔstən] pl expense(s); **~beitrag** m contribution to costs od expenses

Unkraut ['ʊnkraʊt] nt weed; weeds pl

unkündbar ['ʊnkʏntbaːr] adj (Stelle) permanent; (Vertrag) binding

unlauter ['ʊnlaʊtər] adj unfair

unleserlich ['ʊnleːzərlɪç] adj illegible

unlogisch ['ʊnloːgɪʃ] adj illogical

unlösbar [ʊn'løːsbaːr] adj insoluble

Unlust ['ʊnlʊst] f lack of enthusiasm

Unmenge ['ʊnmɛŋə] f tremendous number, hundreds pl

Unmensch ['ʊnmɛnʃ] m ogre, brute; **u~lich** adj inhuman, brutal; (ungeheuer) awful

unmerklich [ʊn'mɛrklɪç] adj imperceptible

unmissverständlich ▲ ['ʊnmɪsfɛrʃtɛntlɪç] adj unmistakable

Spelling reform: ▲ new spelling △ old spelling (to be phased out)

unmittelbar ['ʊnmɪtəlbaːr] *adj* immediate
unmodern ['ʊnmodɛrn] *adj* old-fashioned
unmöglich ['ʊnmøːklɪç] *adj* impossible;
U~keit *f* impossibility
unmoralisch ['ʊnmoraːlɪʃ] *adj* immoral
Unmut ['ʊnmuːt] *m* ill humour
unnachgiebig ['ʊnnaːxgiːbɪç] *adj* unyielding
unnahbar [ʊn'naːbaːr] *adj* unapproachable
unnötig ['ʊnnøːtɪç] *adj* unnecessary
unnütz ['ʊnnʏts] *adj* useless
unordentlich ['ʊnɔrdəntlɪç] *adj* untidy
Unordnung ['ʊnɔrdnʊŋ] *f* disorder
unparteiisch ['ʊnpartaɪɪʃ] *adj* impartial;
U~e(r) *f(m)* umpire; (*FUSSBALL*) referee
unpassend ['ʊnpasənt] *adj* inappropriate;
(*Zeit*) inopportune
unpässlich ▲ ['ʊnpɛslɪç] *adj* unwell
unpersönlich ['ʊnpɛrzøːnlɪç] *adj* impersonal
unpolitisch ['ʊnpoliːtɪʃ] *adj* apolitical
unpraktisch ['ʊnpraktɪʃ] *adj* unpractical
unpünktlich ['ʊnpʏŋktlɪç] *adj* unpunctual
unrationell ['ʊnratsɪɔnɛl] *adj* inefficient
unrealistisch ['ʊnrealɪstɪʃ] *adj* unrealistic
unrecht ['ʊnrɛçt] *adj* wrong; U~ *nt* wrong;
zu U~ wrongly; U~ haben to be wrong;
~mäßig *adj* unlawful, illegal
unregelmäßig ['ʊnreːgəlmɛːsɪç] *adj*
irregular; U~keit *f* irregularity
unreif ['ʊnraɪf] *adj* (*Obst*) unripe; (*fig*)
immature
unrentabel ['ʊnrɛntaːbəl] *adj* unprofitable
unrichtig ['ʊnrɪçtɪç] *adj* incorrect, wrong
Unruhe ['ʊnruːə] *f* unrest; ~stifter *m*
troublemaker
unruhig ['ʊnruːɪç] *adj* restless
uns [ʊns] (*akk, dat von* wir) *pron* us;
ourselves
unsachlich ['ʊnzaxlɪç] *adj* not to the point,
irrelevant
unsagbar [ʊn'zaːkbaːr] *adj* indescribable
unsanft ['ʊnzanft] *adj* rough
unsauber ['ʊnzaʊbər] *adj* unclean, dirty; (*fig*)
crooked; (*MUS*) fuzzy
unschädlich ['ʊnʃɛːtlɪç] *adj* harmless; jdn/
etw ~ machen to render sb/sth harmless
unscharf ['ʊnʃarf] *adj* indistinct; (*Bild etc*)
out of focus, blurred
unscheinbar ['ʊnʃaɪnbaːr] *adj* insignificant;
(*Aussehen, Haus etc*) unprepossessing
unschlagbar [ʊn'ʃlaːkbaːr] *adj* invincible
unschön ['ʊnʃøːn] *adj* (*hässlich: Anblick*)
ugly, unattractive; (*unfreundlich: Benehmen*)
unpleasant, ugly
Unschuld ['ʊnʃʊlt] *f* innocence; u~ig [-dɪç]
adj innocent
unselbst(st)ändig ['ʊnzɛlpʃtɛndɪç] *adj*
dependent, over-reliant on others
unser(e) ['ʊnzər(ə)] *adj* our; ~e(r, s) *pron*
ours; ~einer *pron* people like us; ~eins *pron*
= unsereiner; ~erseits *adv* on our part;
~twegen *adv* (*für uns*) for our sake; (*wegen*

uns) on our account; ~twillen *adv*: um
~twillen = unsertwegen
unsicher ['ʊnzɪçər] *adj* uncertain; (*Mensch*)
insecure; U~heit *f* uncertainty; insecurity
unsichtbar ['ʊnzɪçtbaːr] *adj* invisible
Unsinn ['ʊnzɪn] *m* nonsense; u~ig *adj*
nonsensical
Unsitte ['ʊnzɪtə] *f* deplorable habit
unsozial ['ʊnzotsiaːl] *adj* (*Verhalten*)
antisocial
unsportlich ['ʊnʃpɔrtlɪç] *adj* not sporty;
unfit; (*Verhalten*) unsporting
unsre ['ʊnzrə] = **unsere**
unsterblich ['ʊnʃtɛrplɪç] *adj* immortal
Unstimmigkeit ['ʊnʃtɪmɪçkaɪt] *f*
inconsistency; (*Streit*) disagreement
unsympathisch ['ʊnzʏmpaːtɪʃ] *adj*
unpleasant; er ist mir ~ I don't like him
untätig ['ʊntɛːtɪç] *adj* idle
untauglich ['ʊntaʊklɪç] *adj* unsuitable; (*MIL*)
unfit
unteilbar [ʊn'taɪlbaːr] *adj* indivisible
unten ['ʊntən] *adv* below; (*im Haus*)
downstairs; (*an der Treppe etc*) at the
bottom; nach ~ down; ~ am Berg *etc* at the
bottom of the mountain *etc*; ich bin bei
ihm ~ durch (*umg*) he's through with me

SCHLÜSSELWORT

unter ['ʊntər] *präp +dat* 1 (*räumlich, mit
Zahlen*) under; (*drunter*) underneath,
below; unter 18 Jahren under 18 years
2 (*zwischen*) among(st); sie waren unter
sich they were by themselves; einer unter
ihnen one of them; unter anderem
among other things
♦ *präp +akk* under, below

Unterarm ['ʊntərarm] *m* forearm
unter- *zW*: ~belichten *vt* (*PHOT*) to
underexpose; U~bewusstsein ▲ *nt*
subconscious; ~bezahlt *adj* underpaid
unterbieten [ʊntər'biːtən] (*unreg*) *vt insep*
(*COMM*) to undercut; (*Rekord*) to lower
unterbrechen [ʊntər'brɛçən] (*unreg*) *vt*
insep to interrupt
Unterbrechung *f* interruption
unterbringen ['ʊntərbrɪŋən] (*unreg*) *vt* (*in
Koffer*) to stow; (*in Zeitung*) to place; (*Person:
in Hotel etc*) to accommodate, to put up
unterdessen [ʊntər'dɛsən] *adv* meanwhile
Unterdruck ['ʊntərdrʊk] *m* low pressure
unterdrücken [ʊntər'drʏkən] *vt insep* to
suppress; (*Leute*) to oppress
untere(r, s) ['ʊntərə(r, s)] *adj* lower
untereinander [ʊntəraɪ'nandər] *adv* with
each other; among themselves *etc*
unterentwickelt ['ʊntərɛntvɪkəlt] *adj*
underdeveloped
unterernährt ['ʊntərɛrnɛːrt] *adj*
undernourished, underfed

Unterernährung f malnutrition

Unter'führung f subway, underpass

Untergang ['ʊntərgaŋ] m (down)fall, decline; (NAUT) sinking; (von Gestirn) setting

unter'geben adj subordinate

untergehen ['ʊntərgeːən] (unreg) vi to go down; (Sonne auch) to set; (Staat) to fall; (Volk) to perish; (Welt) to come to an end; (im Lärm) to be drowned

Untergeschoss ▲ ['ʊntərgəʃɔs] nt basement

'Untergewicht nt underweight

unter'gliedern vt insep to subdivide

Untergrund ['ʊntərgrʊnt] m foundation; (POL) underground; **~bahn** f underground, tube, subway (US)

unterhalb ['ʊntərhalp] präp +gen below ♦ adv below; **~ von** below

Unterhalt ['ʊntərhalt] m maintenance; **u~en** (unreg) vt insep to maintain; (belustigen) to entertain ♦ vr insep to talk; (sich belustigen) to enjoy o.s.; **u~sam** adj (Abend, Person) entertaining, amusing; **~ung** f maintenance; (Belustigung) entertainment, amusement; (Gespräch) talk

Unterhändler ['ʊntərhɛntlər] m negotiator

Unter- zW: **~hemd** nt vest, undershirt (US); **~hose** f underpants pl; **~kiefer** m lower jaw

unterkommen ['ʊntərkɔmən] (unreg) vi to find shelter; to find work; **das ist mir noch nie untergekommen** I've never met with that

unterkühlt [ʊntər'kyːlt] adj (Körper) affected by hypothermia

Unterkunft ['ʊntərkʊnft] (-, **-künfte**) f accommodation

Unterlage ['ʊntərlaːgə] f foundation; (Beleg) document; (Schreibunterlage etc) pad

unter'lassen (unreg) vt insep (versäumen) to fail to do; (sich enthalten) to refrain from

unterlaufen [ʊntər'laʊfən] (unreg) vi insep to happen ♦ adj: **mit Blut ~** suffused with blood; (Augen) bloodshot

unterlegen ['ʊntərleːgən] vt to lay od put under; **unter'legen** adj inferior; (besiegt) defeated

Unterleib ['ʊntərlaɪp] m abdomen

unter'liegen (unreg) vi insep (+dat) to be defeated od overcome (by); (unterworfen sein) to be subject to)

Untermiete ['ʊntərmiːtə] f: **zur ~ wohnen** to be a subtenant od lodger; **~r(in)** m(f) subtenant, lodger

unter'nehmen (unreg) vt insep to undertake; **Unter'nehmen (-s, -)** nt undertaking, enterprise (auch COMM)

Unternehmer [ʊntər'neːmər] (-s, -) m entrepreneur, businessman

'unterordnen ['ʊntərɔrdnən] vr +dat to

submit o.s. (to), to give o.s. second place to

Unterredung [ʊntər'reːdʊŋ] f discussion, talk

Unterricht ['ʊntərrɪçt] (-(e)s, -e) m instruction, lessons pl; **u~en** [ʊntər'rɪçtən] vt insep to instruct; (SCH) to teach ♦ vr insep: **sich u~en (über** +akk) to inform o.s. (about), to obtain information (about); **~sfach** nt subject (on school etc curriculum)

Unterrock ['ʊntərrɔk] m petticoat, slip

unter'sagen vt insep to forbid; **jdm etw ~** to forbid sb to do sth

Untersatz ['ʊntərzats] m coaster, saucer

unter'schätzen vt insep to underestimate

unter'scheiden (unreg) vt insep to distinguish ♦ vr insep to differ

Unter'scheidung f (Unterschied) distinction; (Unterscheiden) differentiation

Unterschied ['ʊntərʃiːt] (-(e)s, -e) m difference, distinction; **im ~ zu** as distinct from; **u~lich** adj varying, differing; (diskriminierend) discriminatory

unterschiedslos adv indiscriminately

unter'schlagen (unreg) vt insep to embezzle; (verheimlichen) to suppress

Unter'schlagung f embezzlement

Unterschlupf ['ʊntərʃlʊpf] (-(e)s, **-schlüpfe**) m refuge

unter'schreiben (unreg) vt insep to sign

Unterschrift ['ʊntərʃrɪft] f signature

Unterseeboot ['ʊntərzeːboːt] nt submarine

Untersetzer ['ʊntərzetsər] m tablemat; (für Gläser) coaster

untersetzt [ʊntər'zetst] adj stocky

unterste(r, s) ['ʊntərstə(r, s)] adj lowest, bottom

unterstehen [ʊntər'ʃteːən] (unreg) vi insep (+dat) to be under ♦ vr insep to dare; **'unterstehen** (unreg) vi to shelter

unterstellen [ʊntər'ʃtelən] vt insep to subordinate; (fig) to impute ♦ vt (Auto) to garage, to park ♦ vr to take shelter

unter'streichen (unreg) vt insep (auch fig) to underline

Unterstufe ['ʊntərʃtuːfə] f lower grade

unter'stützen vt insep to support

Unter'stützung f support, assistance

unter'suchen vt insep (MED) to examine; (Polizei) to investigate

Unter'suchung f examination; investigation, inquiry; **~sausschuss** ▲ m committee of inquiry; **~shaft** f imprisonment on remand

Untertasse ['ʊntərtasə] f saucer

untertauchen ['ʊntərtaʊxən] vi to dive; (fig) to disappear, to go underground

Unterteil ['ʊntərtaɪl] nt od m lower part, bottom; **u~en** [ʊntər'taɪlən] vt insep to divide up

Untertitel ['ʊntərtiːtəl] m subtitle

Spelling reform: ▲ *new spelling* △ *old spelling (to be phased out)*

Unterwäsche ['ʊntərvɛʃə] f underwear
unterwegs [ʊntər've:ks] adv on the way
unter'werfen (unreg) vt insep to subject; (Volk) to subjugate ♦ vr insep (+dat) to submit (to)
unter'zeichnen vt insep to sign
unter'ziehen (unreg) vt insep to subject ♦ vr insep (+dat) to undergo; (einer Prüfung) to take
untragbar [ʊn'tra:kba:r] adj unbearable, intolerable
untreu ['ʊntrɔy] adj unfaithful; **U~e** f unfaithfulness
untröstlich [ʊn'trø:stlɪç] adj inconsolable
unüberlegt [ʊn|y:bərle:kt] adj ill-considered ♦ adv without thinking
unübersichtlich adj (Gelände) broken; (Kurve) blind
unumgänglich [ʊn|ʊm'gɛŋlɪç] adj indispensable, vital; absolutely necessary
ununterbrochen ['ʊn|ʊntərbrɔxən] adj uninterrupted
unver- ['ʊnfɛr] zW: **~änderlich** [-'ɛndərlɪç] adj unchangeable; **~antwortlich** [-'antvɔrtlɪç] adj irresponsible; (unentschuldbar) inexcusable; **~besserlich** adj incorrigible; **~bindlich** adj not binding; (Antwort) curt ♦ adv (COMM) without obligation; **~bleit** adj (Benzin usw) unleaded; **ich fahre ~bleit** I use unleaded; **~blümt** [-'bly:mt] adj plain, blunt ♦ adv plainly, bluntly; **~daulich** adj indigestible; **~einbar** adj incompatible; **~fänglich** [-'fɛŋlɪç] adj harmless; **~froren** adj impudent; **~gesslich** ▲ adj (Tag, Erlebnis) unforgettable; **~hofft** [-'hɔft] adj unexpected; **~meidlich** [-'maɪtlɪç] adj unavoidable; **~mutet** adj unexpected; **~nünftig** [-'nynftɪç] adj foolish; **~schämt** adj impudent; **U~schämtheit** f impudence, insolence; **~sehrt** adj uninjured; **~söhnlich** [-'zø:nlɪç] adj irreconcilable; **~ständlich** [-'ʃtɛntlɪç] adj unintelligible; **~träglich** adj quarrelsome; (Meinungen, MED) incompatible; **~zeihlich** adj unpardonable; **~züglich** [-'tsy:klɪç] adj immediate
unvollkommen ['ʊnfɔlkɔmən] adj imperfect
ınvollständig adj incomplete
unvor- ['ʊnfo:r] zW: **~bereitet** adj unprepared; **~eingenommen** adj unbiased; **~hergesehen** [-he:rgeze:ən] adj unforeseen; **~sichtig** [-zɪçtɪç] adj careless, imprudent; **~stellbar** [-'ʃtɛlba:r] adj inconceivable; **~teilhaft** adj disadvantageous
unwahr ['ʊnva:r] adj untrue; **~scheinlich** adj improbable, unlikely ♦ adv (umg) incredibly
unweigerlich [ʊn'vaɪgərlɪç] adj

unquestioning ♦ adv without fail
Unwesen ['ʊnve:zən] nt nuisance; (Unfug) mischief; **sein ~ treiben** to wreak havoc
unwesentlich adj inessential, unimportant; **~ besser** marginally better
Unwetter ['ʊnvɛtər] nt thunderstorm
unwichtig ['ʊnvɪçtɪç] adj unimportant
unwider- ['ʊnvi:dər] zW: **~legbar** adj irrefutable; **~ruflich** adj irrevocable; **~stehlich** adj irresistible
unwill- ['ʊnvɪl] zW: **U~e(n)** m indignation; **~ig** adj indignant; (widerwillig) reluctant; **~kürlich** [-ky:rlɪç] adj involuntary ♦ adv instinctively; (lachen) involuntarily
unwirklich ['ʊnvɪrklɪç] adj unreal
unwirksam ['ʊnvɪrkza:m] adj (Mittel, Methode) ineffective
unwirtschaftlich ['ʊnvɪrtʃaftlɪç] adj uneconomical
unwissen- ['ʊnvɪsən] zW: **~d** adj ignorant; **U~heit** f ignorance; **~tlich** adv unknowingly, unwittingly
unwohl ['ʊnvo:l] adj unwell, ill; **U~sein (-s)** nt indisposition
unwürdig ['ʊnvʏrdɪç] adj unworthy
unzählig [ʊn'tsɛ:lɪç] adj innumerable, countless
unzer- [ʊntsɛr] zW: **~brechlich** adj unbreakable; **~störbar** adj indestructible; **~trennlich** adj inseparable
Unzucht ['ʊntsʊxt] f sexual offence
unzüchtig ['ʊntsʏçtɪç] adj immoral; lewd
unzu- ['ʊntsu] zW: **~frieden** adj dissatisfied; **U~friedenheit** f discontent; **~länglich** adj inadequate; **~lässig** adj inadmissible; **~rechnungsfähig** adj irresponsible; **~treffend** adj incorrect; **~verlässig** adj unreliable
unzweideutig ['ʊntsvaɪdɔytɪç] adj unambiguous
üppig ['ʏpɪç] adj (Frau) curvaceous; (Busen) full, ample; (Essen) sumptuous; (Vegetation) luxuriant, lush
Ur- ['u:r] in zW original
uralt ['u:r|alt] adj ancient, very old
Uran [u'ra:n] (-s) nt uranium
Ur- zW: **~aufführung** f first performance; **~einwohner** m original inhabitant; **~enkel(in)** m(f) great-grandchild, great-grandson(-daughter); **~großeltern** pl great-grandparents; **~heber (-s, -)** m originator; (Autor) author; **~heberrecht** nt copyright
Urin [u'ri:n] (-s, -e) m urine
Urkunde ['u:rkʊndə] f document, deed
Urlaub ['u:rlaʊp] (-(e)s, -e) m holiday(s pl) (BRIT), vacation (US); (MIL etc) leave; **~er** [-'laʊbər] (-s, -) m holiday-maker (BRIT), vacationer (US); **~sort** m holiday resort; **~szeit** f holiday season
Urne ['ʊrnə] f urn

Ursache [ˈuːrzaxə] f cause; **keine ~** that's all right

Ursprung [ˈuːrʃprʊŋ] m origin, source; *(von Fluss)* source

ursprünglich [ˈuːrʃprʏŋlɪç] adj original ♦ adv originally

Ursprungsland nt country of origin

Urteil [ˈʊrtaɪl] **(-s, -e)** nt opinion; *(JUR)* sentence, judgement; **u~en** vi to judge; **~sspruch** m sentence, verdict

Urwald m jungle

Urzeit f prehistoric times pl

USA [uːˈʔɛsˈlaː] pl abk (= *Vereinigte Staaten von Amerika*) USA

usw. abk (= *und so weiter*) etc

Utensilien [utɛnˈziːliən] pl utensils

Utopie [utoˈpiː] f pipe dream

utopisch [uˈtoːpɪʃ] adj utopian

V, v

vag(e) [vaːk, ˈvaːgə] adj vague

Vagina [vaˈgiːna] **(-, Vaginen)** f vagina

Vakuum [ˈvaːkuʊm] **(-s, Vakua** od **Vakuen)** nt vacuum

Vampir [vamˈpiːr] **(-s, -e)** m vampire

Vanille [vaˈnɪljə] **(-)** f vanilla

Variation [variatsiˈoːn] f variation

variieren [variˈiːrən] vt, vi to vary

Vase [ˈvaːzə] f vase

Vater [ˈfaːtər] **(-s, ⁼)** m father; **~land** nt native country; Fatherland

väterlich [ˈfɛːtərlɪç] adj fatherly

Vaterschaft f paternity

Vaterunser **(-s, -)** nt Lord's prayer

Vati [ˈfaːti] m daddy

v. Chr. abk (= *vor Christus*) B.C.

Vegetarier(in) [vegeˈtaːriər(ɪn)] **(-s, -)** m(f) vegetarian

vegetarisch [vegeˈtaːrɪʃ] adj vegetarian

Veilchen [ˈfaɪlçən] nt violet

Vene [ˈveːnə] f vein

Ventil [vɛnˈtiːl] **(-s, -e)** nt valve

Ventilator [vɛntiˈlaːtɔr] m ventilator

verab- [fɛrˈʔap] zW: **~reden** vt to agree, to arrange ♦ vr: **sich mit jdm ~reden** to arrange to meet sb; **mit jdm ~redet sein** to have arranged to meet sb; **V~redung** f arrangement; *(Treffen)* appointment; **~scheuen** vt to detest, to abhor; **~schieden** vt *(Gäste)* to say goodbye to; *(entlassen)* to discharge; *(Gesetz)* to pass ♦ vr to take one's leave; **V~schiedung** f leave-taking; discharge; passing

ver- [fɛr] zW: **~achten** vt to despise; **~ächtlich** [-ˈʔɛçtlɪç] adj contemptuous; (*~achtenswert*) contemptible; **jdn ~ächtlich machen** to run sb down; **V~achtung** f

contempt

verallgemeinern [fɛrʔalgəˈmaɪnərn] vt to generalize; **Verallgemeinerung** f generalization

veralten [fɛrˈʔaltən] vi to become obsolete od out-of-date

Veranda [veˈranda] **(-, Veranden)** f veranda

veränder- [fɛrˈʔɛndər] zW: **~lich** adj changeable; **~n** vt, vr to change, to alter; **V~ung** f change, alteration

veran- [fɛrˈʔan] zW: **~lagt** adj with a … nature; **V~lagung** f disposition; **~lassen** vt to cause; **Maßnahmen ~lassen** to take measures; **sich ~lasst sehen** to feel prompted; **~schaulichen** vt to illustrate; **~schlagen** vt to estimate; **~stalten** vt to organize, to arrange; **V~stalter (-s, -)** m organizer; **V~staltung** f *(Veranstalten)* organizing; *(Konzert etc)* event, function

verantwort- [fɛrˈʔantvɔrt] zW: **~en** vt to answer for ♦ vr to justify o.s.; **~lich** adj responsible; **V~ung** f responsibility; **~ungsbewusst** ▲ adj responsible; **~ungslos** adj irresponsible

verarbeiten [fɛrˈʔarbaɪtən] vt to process; *(geistig)* to assimilate; **etw zu etw ~** make sth into sth; **Verarbeitung** f processing; assimilation

verärgern [fɛrˈʔɛrgərn] vt to annoy

verausgaben [fɛrˈʔaʊsgaːbən] vr to run out of money; *(fig)* to exhaust o.s.

Verb [vɛrp] **(-s, -en)** nt verb

Verband [fɛrˈbant] **(-(e)s, ⁼e)** m *(MED)* bandage, dressing; *(Bund)* association, society; *(MIL)* unit; **~skasten** m medicine chest, first-aid box; **~szeug** nt bandage

verbannen [fɛrˈbanən] vt to banish

verbergen [fɛrˈbɛrgən] *(unreg)* vt, vr: **(sich) ~ (vor** +dat**)** to hide (from)

verbessern [fɛrˈbɛsərn] vt, vr to improve; *(berichtigen)* to correct (o.s.)

Verbesserung f improvement; correction

verbeugen [fɛrˈbɔygən] vr to bow

Verbeugung f bow

verbiegen *(unreg)* vi to bend

verbieten *(unreg)* vt to forbid; **jdm etw ~** to forbid sb to do sth

verbilligen [fɛrˈbɪlɪgən] vt to reduce the cost of; *(Preis)* to reduce

verbinden *(unreg)* vt to connect; *(kombinieren)* to combine; *(MED)* to bandage ♦ vr *(auch CHEM)* to combine, to join; **jdm die Augen ~** to blindfold sb

verbindlich [fɛrˈbɪntlɪç] adj binding; *(freundlich)* friendly

Verbindung f connection; *(Zusammensetzung)* combination; *(CHEM)* compound; *(UNIV)* club

verbissen [fɛrˈbɪsən] adj *(Kampf)* bitter;

Spelling reform: ▲ *new spelling* △ *old spelling (to be phased out)*

(*Gesichtsausdruck*) grim
ver'bitten (*unreg*) *vt*: **sich** *dat* **etw ~** not to tolerate sth, not to stand for sth
Verbleib [fɛr'blaɪp] (-(e)s) *m* whereabouts; **v~en** (*unreg*) *vi* to remain
verbleit [fɛr'blaɪt] *adj* (*Benzin*) leaded
verblüffen [fɛr'blʏfən] *vt* to stagger, to amaze; **Verblüffung** *f* stupefaction
ver'blühen *vi* to wither, to fade
ver'bluten *vi* to bleed to death
verborgen [fɛr'bɔrgən] *adj* hidden
Verbot [fɛr'boːt] (-(e)s, -e) *nt* prohibition, ban; **v~en** *adj* forbidden; **Rauchen v~en!** no smoking; **~sschild** *nt* prohibitory sign
Verbrauch [fɛr'braʊx] (-(e)s) *m* consumption; **v~en** *vt* to use up; **~er** (-s, -) *m* consumer; **v~t** *adj* used up, finished; (*Luft*) stale; (*Mensch*) worn-out
Verbrechen [fɛr'brɛçən] (-s, -) *nt* crime
Verbrecher [fɛr'brɛçər] (-s, -) *m* criminal; **v~isch** *adj* criminal
ver'breiten *vt, vr* to spread; **sich über etw** *akk* **~** to expound on sth
verbreitern [fɛr'braɪtərn] *vt* to broaden
Verbreitung *f* spread(ing), propagation
verbrenn- [fɛr'brɛn] *zW*: **~bar** *adj* combustible; **~en** (*unreg*) *vt* to burn; (*Leiche*) to cremate; **V~ung** *f* burning; (*in Motor*) combustion; (*von Leiche*) cremation; **V~ungsmotor** *m* internal combustion engine
verbringen [fɛr'brɪŋən] (*unreg*) *vt* to spend
ver'brühen *vt* to scald
verbuchen [fɛr'buːxən] *vt* (*FIN*) to register; (*Erfolg*) to enjoy; (*Misserfolg*) to suffer
verbunden [fɛr'bʊndən] *adj* connected; **jdm ~ sein** to be obliged *od* indebted to sb; **„falsch ~"** (*TEL*) "wrong number"
verbünden [fɛr'bʏndən] *vr* to ally o.s.; **Verbündete(r)** *f(m)* ally
ver'bürgen *vr*: **sich ~ für** to vouch for
ver'büßen *vt*: **eine Strafe ~** to serve a sentence
Verdacht [fɛr'daxt] (-(e)s) *m* suspicion
verdächtig [fɛr'dɛçtɪç] *adj* suspicious, suspect; **~en** [fɛr'dɛçtɪgən] *vt* to suspect
verdammen [fɛr'damən] *vt* to damn, to condemn; **verdammt!** damn!
verdammt (*umg*) *adj, adv* damned; **~ noch mal!** damn!, dammit!
ver'dampfen *vi* to vaporize, to evaporate
ver'danken *vt*: **jdm etw ~** to owe sb sth
verdau- [fɛr'daʊ] *zW*: **~en** *vt* (*auch fig*) to digest; **~lich** *adj* digestible; **das ist schwer ~lich** that is hard to digest; **V~ung** *f* digestion
Verdeck [fɛr'dɛk] (-(e)s, -e) *nt* (*AUT*) hood; (*NAUT*) deck; **v~en** *vt* to cover (up); (*verbergen*) to hide
Verderb- [fɛr'dɛrp] *zW*: **~en** [-'dɛrbən] (-s) *nt* ruin; **v~en** (*unreg*) *vt* to spoil; (*schädigen*) to

ruin; (*moralisch*) to corrupt ♦ *vi* (*Essen*) to spoil, to rot; (*Mensch*) to go to the bad; **es mit jdm v~en** to get into sb's bad books; **v~lich** *adj* (*Einfluss*) pernicious; (*Lebensmittel*) perishable
verdeutlichen [fɛr'dɔytlɪçən] *vt* to make clear
ver'dichten *vt, vr* to condense
ver'dienen *vt* to earn; (*moralisch*) to deserve
Ver'dienst (-(e)s, -e) *m* earnings *pl* ♦ *nt* merit; (*Leistung*): **~ (um)** service (to)
verdient [fɛr'diːnt] *adj* well-earned; (*Person*) deserving of esteem; **sich um etw ~ machen** to do a lot for sth
verdoppeln [fɛr'dɔpəln] *vt* to double
verdorben [fɛr'dɔrbən] *adj* spoilt; (*geschädigt*) ruined; (*moralisch*) corrupt
verdrängen [fɛr'drɛŋən] *vt* to oust, to displace (*auch PHYS*); (*PSYCH*) to repress
ver'drehen *vt* (*auch fig*) to twist; (*Augen*) to roll; **jdm den Kopf ~** (*fig*) to turn sb's head
verdrießlich [fɛr'driːslɪç] *adj* peevish, annoyed
Verdruss [fɛr'drʊs] (-es, -e) *m* annoyance, worry
verdummen [fɛr'dʊmən] *vt* to make stupid ♦ *vi* to grow stupid
verdunkeln [fɛr'dʊŋkəln] *vt* to darken; (*fig*) to obscure ♦ *vr* to darken
Verdunk(e)lung *f* blackout; (*fig*) obscuring
verdünnen [fɛr'dʏnən] *vt* to dilute
verdunsten [fɛr'dʊnstən] *vi* to evaporate
verdursten [fɛr'dʊrstən] *vi* to die of thirst
verdutzt [fɛr'dʊtst] *adj* nonplussed, taken aback
verehr- [fɛr'eːr] *zW*: **~en** *vt* to venerate, to worship (*auch REL*) **jdm etw ~en** to present sb with sth; **V~er(in)** (-s, -) *m(f)* admirer, worshipper (*auch REL*); **~t** *adj* esteemed; **V~ung** *f* respect; (*REL*) worship
Verein [fɛr'aɪn] (-(e)s, -e) *m* club, association; **v~bar** *adj* compatible; **v~baren** *vt* to agree upon; **~barung** *f* agreement; **v~en** *vt* (*Menschen, Länder*) to unite; (*Prinzipien*) to reconcile; **mit v~ten Kräften** having pooled resources, having joined forces; **~te Nationen** United Nations; **v~fachen** *vt* to simplify; **v~heitlichen** [-haɪtlɪçən] *vt* to standardize; **v~igen** *vt, vr* to unite; **~igung** *f* union; (*Verein*) association; **v~t** *adj* united; **v~zelt** *adj* isolated
ver'eitern *vi* to suppurate, to fester
verengen [fɛr'ɛŋən] *vr* to narrow
vererb- [fɛr'ɛrb] *zW*: **~en** *vt* to bequeath; (*BIOL*) to transmit ♦ *vr* to be hereditary; **V~ung** *f* bequeathing; (*BIOL*) transmission; (*Lehre*) heredity
verewigen [fɛr'eːvɪgən] *vt* to immortalize ♦ *vr* (*umg*) to immortalize o.s.
ver'fahren (*unreg*) *vi* to act ♦ *vr* to get lost ♦ *adj* tangled; **~ mit** to deal with;

Ver'fahren (-s, -) nt procedure; (TECH) process; (JUR) proceedings pl

Verfall |fɛr'fal| (-(e)s) m decline; (von Haus) dilapidation; (FIN) expiry; **v~en**(unreg) vi to decline; (Haus) to be falling down; (FIN) to lapse; **v~en in** +akk to lapse into; **v~en auf** +akk to hit upon; **einem Laster v~en sein** to be addicted to a vice; **~sdatum** nt expiry date; (der Haltbarkeit) sell-by date

ver'färben vr to change colour

verfassen |fɛr'fasən| vt (Rede) to prepare, work out

Verfasser(in) |fɛr'fasər(ɪn)| (-s, -) m(f) author, writer

Verfassung f (auch POL) constitution

Verfassungs- zW: **~gericht** nt constitutional court; **v~widrig** adj unconstitutional

ver'faulen vi to rot

ver'fehlen vt to miss; **etw für verfehlt halten** to regard sth as mistaken

verfeinern |fɛr'faɪnərn| vt to refine

ver'filmen vt to film

verflixt |fɛr'flɪkst| (umg) adj damned, damn

ver'fluchen vt to curse

verfolg- |fɛr'fɔlg| zW: **~en** vt to pursue; (gerichtlich) to prosecute; (grausam, bes POL) to persecute; **V~er** (-s, -) m pursuer; **V~ung** f pursuit; prosecution; persecution

verfrüht |fɛr'fry:t| adj premature

verfüg- |fɛr'fy:g| zW: **~bar** adj available; **~en** vt to direct, to order ♦ vr to proceed ♦ vi: **~en über** +akk to have at one's disposal; **V~ung** f direction, order; **zur V~ung** at one's disposal; **jdm zur V~ung stehen** to be available to sb

verführ- |fɛr'fy:r| zW: **~en** vt to tempt; (sexuell) to seduce; **V~er** m tempter; seducer; **~erisch** adj seductive; **V~ung** f seduction; (Versuchung) temptation

ver'gammeln (umg) vi to go to seed; (Nahrung) to go off

vergangen |fɛr'gaŋən| adj past; **V~heit** f past

vergänglich |fɛr'gɛŋlɪç| adj transitory

vergasen |fɛr'ga:zən| vt (töten) to gas

Vergaser (-s, -) m (AUT) carburettor

vergaß etc |fɛr'ga:s| vb siehe **vergessen**

vergeb- |fɛr'ge:b| zW: **~en** (unreg) vt (verzeihen) to forgive; (weggeben) to give away; **jdm etw ~en** to forgive sb (for) sth; **~ens** adv in vain; **~lich** |fɛr'ge:plɪç| adv in vain ♦ adj vain, futile; **V~ung** f forgiveness

ver'gehen (unreg) vi to pass by od away ♦ vr to commit an offence; **jdm vergeht etw** sb loses sth; **sich an jdm ~** to (sexually) assault sb; **Ver'gehen** (-s, -) nt offence

ver'gelten (unreg) vt: **jdm etw ~** to pay sb back for sth, to repay sb for sth

Ver'geltung f retaliation, reprisal

vergessen |fɛr'gesən| (unreg) vt to forget; **V~heit** f oblivion

vergesslich ▲ |fɛr'geslɪç| adj forgetful; **V~keit** ▲ f forgetfulness

vergeuden |fɛr'gɔʏdən| vt to squander, to waste

vergewaltigen |fɛrgə'valtɪgən| vt to rape; (fig) to violate

Vergewaltigung f rape

vergewissern |fɛrgə'vɪsərn| vr to make sure

ver'gießen (unreg) vt to shed

vergiften |fɛr'gɪftən| vt to poison

Vergiftung f poisoning

Vergissmeinnicht ▲ |fɛr'gɪsmaɪnnɪçt| (-(e)s, -e) nt forget-me-not

vergisst etc ▲ |fɛr'gɪst| vb siehe **vergessen**

Vergleich |fɛr'glaɪç| (-(e)s, -e) m comparison; (JUR) settlement; **im ~ mit** od **zu** compared with od to; **v~bar** adj comparable; **v~en** (unreg) vt to compare ♦ vr to reach a settlement

vergnügen |fɛr'gny:gən| vr to enjoy od amuse o.s.; **V~** (-s, -) nt pleasure; **viel V~!** enjoy yourself!

vergnügt |fɛr'gny:kt| adj cheerful

Vergnügung f pleasure, amusement; **~spark** m amusement park

vergolden |fɛr'gɔldən| vt to gild

ver'graben vt to bury

ver'greifen (unreg) vr: **sich an jdm ~** to lay hands on sb; **sich an etw ~** to misappropriate sth; **sich im Ton ~** to say the wrong thing

vergriffen |fɛr'grɪfən| adj (Buch) out of print; (Ware) out of stock

vergrößern |fɛr'grø:sərn| vt to enlarge; (mengenmäßig) to increase; (Lupe) to magnify

Vergrößerung f enlargement; increase; magnification; **~sglas** nt magnifying glass

Vergünstigung |fɛr'gʏnstɪgʊŋ| f concession, privilege

Vergütung f compensation

verhaften |fɛr'haftən| vt to arrest

Verhaftung f arrest

ver'halten (unreg) vr to be, to stand; (sich benehmen) to behave ♦ vt to hold od keep back; (Schritt) to check; **sich ~ (zu)** (MATH) to be in proportion (to); **Ver'halten** (-s) nt behaviour

Verhältnis |fɛr'hɛltnɪs| (-ses, -se) nt relationship; (MATH) proportion, ratio; **~se** pl (Umstände) conditions; **über seine ~se leben** to live beyond one's means; **v~mäßig** adj relative, comparative ♦ adv relatively, comparatively

verhandeln |fɛr'handəln| vi to negotiate; (JUR) to hold proceedings ♦ vt to discuss;

(*JUR*) to hear; **über etw** *akk* ~ to negotiate sth *od* about sth

Verhandlung *f* negotiation; (*JUR*) proceedings *pl*; ~**sbasis** *f* (*FIN*) basis for negotiations

ver'hängen *vt* (*fig*) to impose, to inflict

Verhängnis |fɛr'hɛŋnɪs| (**-ses, -se**) *nt* fate, doom; **jdm zum ~ werden** to be sb's undoing; **v~voll** *adj* fatal, disastrous

verharmlosen |fɛr'harmlo:zən| *vt* to make light of, to play down

verhärten |fɛr'hɛrtən| *vr* to harden

verhasst ▲ |fɛr'hast| *adj* odious, hateful

verhauen |fɛr'hauən| (*unreg*) (*umg*) *vt* (*verprügeln*) to beat up

verheerend |fɛr'he:rənt| *adj* disastrous, devastating

verheimlichen |fɛr'haimlɪçən| *vt*: **jdm etw ~** to keep sth secret from sb

verheiratet |fɛr'haira:tət| *adj* married

ver'helfen (*unreg*) *vi*: **jdm ~ zu** to help sb get

ver'hindern *vt* to prevent; **verhindert sein** to be unable to make it

verhöhnen |fɛr'hø:nən| *vt* to mock, to sneer at

Verhör |fɛr'hø:r| (**-(e)s, -e**) *nt* interrogation; (*gerichtlich*) (cross-)examination; **v~en** *vt* to interrogate; to (cross-)examine ♦ *vr* to misunderstand, to mishear

ver'hungern *vi* to starve, to die of hunger

ver'hüten *vt* to prevent, to avert

Ver'hütung *f* prevention; ~**smittel** *nt* contraceptive

verirren |fɛr'ɪrən| *vr* to go astray

ver'jagen *vt* to drive away *od* out

verkalken |fɛr'kalkən| *vi* to calcify; (*umg*) to become senile

Verkauf |fɛr'kauf| *m* sale; **v~en** *vt* to sell

Verkäufer(in) |fɛr'kɔyfər(ɪn)| (**-s, -**) *m(f)* seller; salesman(-woman); (*in Laden*) shop assistant

verkaufsoffen *adj*: ~**er Samstag** *Saturday when the shops stay open all day*

Verkehr |fɛr'ke:r| (**-s, -e**) *m* traffic; (*Umgang, bes sexuell*) intercourse; (*Umlauf*) circulation; **v~en** *vi* (*Fahrzeug*) to ply, to run ♦ *vt, vr* to turn, to transform; **v~en mit** to associate with; **bei jdm v~en** (*besuchen*) to visit sb regularly

Verkehrs- *zW*: ~**ampel** *f* traffic lights *pl*; ~**aufkommen** *nt* volume of traffic; ~**beruhigung** *f* traffic calming; ~**delikt** *nt* traffic offence; ~**funk** *m* radio traffic service; **v~günstig** *adj* convenient; ~**mittel** *nt* means of transport; ~**schild** *nt* road sign; ~**stau** *m* traffic jam, stoppage; ~**unfall** *m* traffic accident; ~**verein** *m* tourist information office; ~**zeichen** *nt* traffic sign

verkehrt *adj* wrong; (*umgekehrt*) the wrong way round

ver'kennen (*unreg*) *vt* to misjudge, not to appreciate

ver'klagen *vt* to take to court

verkleiden |fɛr'klaidən| *vr* to disguise (o.s.); (*sich kostümieren*) to get dressed up ♦ *vt* (*Wand*) to cover

Verkleidung *f* disguise; (*ARCHIT*) wainscoting

verkleinern |fɛr'klainərn| *vt* to make smaller, to reduce in size

ver'kneifen (*umg*) *vt*: **sich** *dat* **etw ~** (*Lachen*) to stifle sth; (*Schmerz*) to hide sth; (*sich versagen*) to do without sth

verknüpfen |fɛr'knʏpfən| *vt* to tie (up), to knot; (*fig*) to connect

ver'kommen (*unreg*) *vi* to deteriorate, to decay; (*Mensch*) to go downhill, to come down in the world ♦ *adj* (*moralisch*) dissolute, depraved

verkörpern |fɛr'kœrpərn| *vt* to embody, to personify

verkraften |fɛr'kraftən| *vt* to cope with

ver'kriechen (*unreg*) *vr* to creep away, to creep into a corner

verkrüppelt |fɛr'krʏpəlt| *adj* crippled

ver'kühlen *vr* to get a chill

ver'kümmern *vi* to waste away

verkünden |fɛr'kʏndən| *vt* to proclaim; (*Urteil*) to pronounce

verkürzen |fɛr'kʏrtsən| *vt* to shorten; (*Wort*) to abbreviate; **sich** *dat* **die Zeit ~** to while away the time

Verkürzung *f* shortening; abbreviation

verladen |fɛr'la:dən| (*unreg*) *vt* (*Waren, Vieh*) to load; (*Truppen*) to embark, entrain, enplane

Verlag |fɛr'la:k| (**-(e)s, -e**) *m* publishing firm

verlangen |fɛr'laŋən| *vt* to demand; to desire ♦ *vi*: ~ **nach** to ask for, to desire; **Sie Herrn X** ask for Mr X; **V~ (-s, -)** *nt*: **V~ (nach)** desire (for); **auf jds V~ (hin)** at sb's request

verlängern |fɛr'lɛŋərn| *vt* to extend; (*länger machen*) to lengthen

Verlängerung *f* extension; (*SPORT*) extra time; ~**sschnur** *f* extension cable

verlangsamen |fɛr'laŋza:mən| *vt, vr* to decelerate, to slow down

Verlass ▲ |fɛr'las| *m*: **auf ihn/das ist kein ~** he/it cannot be relied upon

ver'lassen (*unreg*) *vt* to leave ♦ *vr*: **sich ~ auf** +*akk* to depend on ♦ *adj* desolate; (*Mensch*) abandoned

verlässlich ▲ |fɛr'lɛslɪç| *adj* reliable

Verlauf |fɛr'lauf| *m* course; **v~en** (*unreg*) *vi* (*zeitlich*) to pass; (*Farben*) to run ♦ *vr* to get lost; (*Menschenmenge*) to disperse

ver'lauten *vi*: **etw ~ lassen** to disclose sth; **wie verlautet** as reported

ver'legen *vt* to move; (*verlieren*) to mislay; (*Buch*) to publish ♦ *vr*: **sich auf etw** *akk* ~ to take up *od* to sth ♦ *adj* embarrassed; **nicht**

~ **um** never at a loss for; **Ver'legenheit** *f*
embarrassment; (*Situation*) difficulty, scrape
Verleger |fɛr'leːɡər| (**-s, -**) *m* publisher
Verleih |fɛr'laɪ| (**-(e)s, -e**) *m* hire service;
v~en (*unreg*) *vt* to lend; (*Kraft, Anschein*) to
confer, to bestow; (*Preis, Medaille*) to award;
~ung *f* lending; bestowal; award
ver'leiten *vt* to lead astray; ~ **zu** to talk into,
to tempt into
ver'lernen *vt* to forget, to unlearn
ver'lesen (*unreg*) *vt* to read out; (*aussondern*) to sort out ♦ *vr* to make a mistake in
reading
verletz- |fɛr'lɛts| *zW:* **~en** *vt* (*auch fig*) to
injure, to hurt; (*Gesetz etc*) to violate; **~end**
adj (*fig: Worte*) hurtful; **~lich** *adj* vulnerable,
sensitive; **V~te(r)** *f(m)* injured person;
V~ung *f* injury; (*Verstoß*) violation,
infringement
verleugnen |fɛr'lɔygnən| *vt* (*Herkunft,
Glauben*) to belie; (*Menschen*) to disown
verleumden |fɛr'lɔymdən| *vt* to slander;
Verleumdung *f* slander, libel
ver'lieben *vr:* **sich ~ (in** +*akk*) to fall in love
(with)
verliebt |fɛr'liːpt| *adj* in love
verlieren |fɛr'liːrən| (*unreg*) *vt, vi* to lose ♦ *vr*
to get lost
Verlierer *m* loser
verlob- |fɛr'loːb| *zW:* **~en** *vr:* **sich ~en (mit)**
to get engaged (to); **V~te(r)** |fɛr'loːptə(r)|
f(m) fiancé *m*, fiancée *f*; **V~ung** *f*
engagement
ver'locken *vt* to entice, to lure
Ver'lockung *f* temptation, attraction
verlogen |fɛr'loːɡən| *adj* untruthful
verlor *etc vb siehe* **verlieren**
verloren |fɛr'loːrən| *adj* lost; (*Eier*) poached
♦ *vb siehe* **verlieren**; **etw ~ geben** to give
sth up for lost; ~ **gehen** to get lost
verlosen |fɛr'loːzən| *vt* to raffle, to draw lots
for; **Verlosung** *f* raffle, lottery
Verlust |fɛr'lʊst| (**-(e)s, -e**) *m* loss; (*MIL*)
casualty
ver'machen *vt* to bequeath, to leave
Vermächtnis |fɛr'mɛçtnɪs| (**-ses, -se**) *nt*
legacy
Vermählung |fɛr'mɛːlʊŋ| *f* wedding, marriage
vermarkten |fɛr'marktən| *vt* (*COMM: Artikel*)
to market
vermehren |fɛr'meːrən| *vt, vr* to multiply;
(*Menge*) to increase
Vermehrung *f* multiplying; increase
ver'meiden (*unreg*) *vt* to avoid
vermeintlich |fɛr'maɪntlɪç| *adj* supposed
Vermerk |fɛr'mɛrk| (**-(e)s, -e**) *m* note; (*in
Ausweis*) endorsement; **v~en** *vt* to note
ver'messen (*unreg*) *vt* to survey ♦ *adj*
presumptuous, bold; **Ver'messenheit** *f*

presumptuousness; recklessness
Ver'messung *f* survey(ing)
vermiet- |fɛr'miːt| *zW:* **ver'mieten** *vt* to let,
to rent (out); (*Auto*) to hire out, to rent;
Ver'mieter(in) (**-s, -**) *m(f)* landlord(-lady);
Ver'mietung *f* letting, renting (out); (*von
Autos*) hiring (out)
vermindern |fɛr'mɪndərn| *vt, vr* to lessen, to
decrease; (*Preise*) to reduce
Verminderung *f* reduction
ver'mischen *vt, vr* to mix, to blend
vermissen |fɛr'mɪsən| *vt* to miss
vermitt- |fɛr'mɪt| *zW:* **~eln** *vi* to mediate ♦ *vt*
(*Gespräch*) to connect; **jdm etw ~eln** to
help sb to obtain sth; **V~ler** (**-s, -**) *m*
(*Schlichter*) agent, mediator; **V~lung** *f*
procurement; (*Stellenvermittlung*) agency;
(*TEL*) exchange; (*Schlichtung*) mediation;
V~lungsgebühr *f* commission
ver'mögen (*unreg*) *vt* to be capable of; ~ **zu**
to be able to; **Ver'mögen** (**-s, -**) *nt* wealth;
(*Fähigkeit*) ability; **ein V~ kosten** to cost a
fortune; **ver'mögend** *adj* wealthy
vermuten |fɛr'muːtən| *vt* to suppose, to
guess; (*argwöhnen*) to suspect
vermutlich |fɛr'muːtlɪç| *adj* supposed, presumed ♦ *adv*
probably
Vermutung *f* supposition; suspicion
vernachlässigen |fɛr'naːxlɛsɪɡən| *vt* to
neglect
ver'nehmen (*unreg*) *vt* to perceive, to hear;
(*erfahren*) to learn; (*JUR*) to (cross-)examine;
dem V~ nach from what I/we *etc* hear
Vernehmung *f* (cross-)examination
verneigen |fɛr'naɪɡən| *vr* to bow
verneinen |fɛr'naɪnən| *vt* (*Frage*) to answer
in the negative; (*ablehnen*) to deny; (*GRAM*)
to negate; **~d** *adj* negative
Verneinung *f* negation
vernichten |fɛr'nɪçtən| *vt* to annihilate, to
destroy; **~d** *adj* (*fig*) crushing; (*Blick*)
withering; (*Kritik*) scathing
Vernunft |fɛr'nʊnft| (**-**) *f* reason,
understanding
vernünftig |fɛr'nʏnftɪç| *adj* sensible,
reasonable
veröffentlichen |fɛr'|œfəntlɪçən| *vt* to
publish; **Veröffentlichung** *f* publication
verordnen |fɛr'|ɔrdnən| *vt* (*MED*) to
prescribe
Verordnung *f* order, decree; (*MED*)
prescription
ver'pachten *vt* to lease (out)
ver'packen *vt* to pack
Ver'packung *f* packing, wrapping;
~smaterial *nt* packing, wrapping
ver'passen *vt* to miss; **jdm eine Ohrfeige ~**
(*umg*) to give sb a clip round the ear
verpfänden |fɛr'pfɛndən| *vt* (*Besitz*) to

mortgage
ver'pflanzen vt to transplant
ver'pflegen vt to feed, to cater for
Ver'pflegung f feeding, catering; (*Kost*) food; (*in Hotel*) board
verpflichten |fɛr'pflɪçtən| vt to oblige, to bind; (*anstellen*) to engage ♦ vr to undertake; (*MIL*) to sign on ♦ vi to carry obligations; **jdm zu Dank verpflichtet sein** to be obliged to sb
Verpflichtung f obligation, duty
verpönt |fɛr'pøːnt| adj disapproved (of), taboo
ver'prügeln (*umg*) vt to beat up, to do over
Verputz |fɛr'pʊts| m plaster, roughcast; **v~en** vt to plaster; (*umg: Essen*) to put away
Verrat |fɛr'raːt| (-**(e)s**) m treachery; (*POL*) treason; **v~en** (*unreg*) vt to betray; (*Geheimnis*) to divulge ♦ vr to give o.s. away
Verräter |fɛr'rɛːtər| (-**s**, -) m traitor(-tress); **v~isch** adj treacherous
ver'rechnen vt: ~ **mit** to set off against ♦ vr to miscalculate
Verrechnungsscheck |fɛr'rɛçnʊŋsʃɛk| m crossed cheque
verregnet |fɛr'reːgnət| adj spoilt by rain, rainy
ver'reisen vi to go away (on a journey)
verrenken |fɛr'rɛŋkən| vt to contort; (*MED*) to dislocate; **sich** dat **den Knöchel ~** to sprain one's ankle
ver'richten vt to do, to perform
verriegeln |fɛr'riːgəln| vt to bolt up, to lock
verringern |fɛr'rɪŋərn| vt to reduce ♦ vr to diminish
Verringerung f reduction; lessening
ver'rinnen (*unreg*) vi to run out od away; (*Zeit*) to elapse
ver'rosten vi to rust
verrotten |fɛr'rɔtən| vi to rot
ver'rücken vt to move, to shift
verrückt |fɛr'rʏkt| adj crazy, mad; **V~e(r)** f(m) lunatic; **V~heit** f madness, lunacy
Verruf |fɛr'ruːf| m: **in ~ geraten/bringen** to fall/bring into disrepute; **v~en** adj notorious, disreputable
Vers |fɛrs| (-**es**, -**e**) m verse
ver'sagen vt: **jdm/sich etw ~** to deny sb/o.s. sth ♦ vi to fail; **Ver'sagen** (-**s**) nt failure
ver'salzen (*unreg*) vt to put too much salt in; (*fig*) to spoil
ver'sammeln vt, vr to assemble, to gather
Ver'sammlung f meeting, gathering
Versand |fɛr'zant| (-**(e)s**) m forwarding; dispatch; (*~abteilung*) dispatch department; **~haus** nt mail-order firm
versäumen |fɛr'zɔʏmən| vt to miss; (*unterlassen*) to neglect, to fail
ver'schaffen vt: **jdm/sich etw ~** to get od procure sth for sb/o.s.
verschämt |fɛr'ʃɛːmt| adj bashful

verschandeln |fɛr'ʃandəln| (*umg*) vt to spoil
verschärfen |fɛr'ʃɛrfən| vt to intensify; (*Lage*) to aggravate ♦ vr to intensify; to become aggravated
ver'schätzen vr to be out in one's reckoning
ver'schenken vt to give away
verscheuchen |fɛr'ʃɔʏçən| vt (*Tiere*) to chase off od away
ver'schicken vt to send off
ver'schieben (*unreg*) vt to shift; (*EISENB*) to shunt; (*Termin*) to postpone
verschieden |fɛr'ʃiːdən| adj different; (*pl: mehrere*) various; **sie sind ~ groß** they are of different sizes; **~tlich** adv several times
verschimmeln |fɛr'ʃɪməln| vi (*Nahrungsmittel*) to go mouldy
verschlafen |fɛr'ʃlaːfən| (*unreg*) vt to sleep through; (*fig: versäumen*) to miss ♦ vi, vr to oversleep ♦ adj sleepy
Verschlag |fɛr'ʃlaːk| m shed; **v~en** |-gən| (*unreg*) vt to board up ♦ adj cunning; **jdm den Atem v~en** to take sb's breath away; **an einen Ort v~en werden** to wind up in a place
verschlechtern |fɛr'ʃlɛçtərn| vt to make worse ♦ vr to deteriorate, to get worse; **Verschlechterung** f deterioration
Verschleiß |fɛr'ʃlaɪs| (-**es**, -**e**) m wear and tear; **v~en** (*unreg*) vt to wear out
ver'schleppen vt to carry off, to abduct; (*Krankheit*) to protract; (*zeitlich*) to drag out
ver'schleudern vt to squander; (*COMM*) to sell dirt-cheap
verschließbar adj lockable
verschließen |fɛr'ʃliːsən| (*unreg*) vt to close; to lock ♦ vr: **sich einer Sache** dat **~** to close one's mind to sth
verschlimmern |fɛr'ʃlɪmərn| vt to make worse, to aggravate ♦ vr to get worse, to deteriorate
verschlingen |fɛr'ʃlɪŋən| (*unreg*) vt to devour, to swallow up; (*Fäden*) to twist
verschlossen |fɛr'ʃlɔsən| adj locked; (*fig*) reserved; **V~heit** f reserve
ver'schlucken vt to swallow ♦ vr to choke
Verschluss △ |fɛr'ʃlʊs| m lock; (*von Kleid etc*) fastener; (*PHOT*) shutter; (*Stöpsel*) plug
verschlüsseln |fɛr'ʃlʏsəln| vt to encode
verschmieren |fɛr'ʃmiːrən| vt (*verstreichen: Gips, Mörtel*) to apply, spread on; (*schmutzig machen: Wand etc*) to smear
verschmutzen |fɛr'ʃmʊtsən| vt to soil; (*Umwelt*) to pollute
verschneit |fɛr'ʃnaɪt| adj snowed up, covered in snow
verschollen |fɛr'ʃɔlən| adj lost, missing
ver'schonen vt: **jdn mit etw ~** to spare sb sth
verschönern |fɛr'ʃøːnərn| vt to decorate; (*verbessern*) to improve
ver'schreiben (*unreg*) vt (*MED*) to prescribe ♦ vr to make a mistake (in writing); **sich**

einer Sache *dat* ~ to devote o.s. to sth
verschreibungspflichtig *adj*
(*Medikament*) available on prescription only
verschrotten |fɛrˈʃrɔtən| *vt* to scrap
verschuld- |fɛrˈʃʊld| *zW*: **~en** *vt* to be guilty of; **V~en (-s)** *nt* fault, guilt; **~et** *adj* in debt; **V~ung** *f* fault; (*Geld*) debts *pl*
ver'schütten *vt* to spill; (*zuschütten*) to fill; (*unter Trümmer*) to bury
ver'schweigen (*unreg*) *vt* to keep secret; **jdm etw** ~ to keep sth from sb
verschwend- |fɛrˈʃvɛnd| *zW*: **~en** *vt* to squander; **V~er (-s, -)** *m* spendthrift; **~erisch** *adj* wasteful, extravagant; **V~ung** *f* waste; extravagance
verschwiegen |fɛrˈʃviːgən| *adj* discreet; (*Ort*) secluded; **V~heit** *f* discretion; seclusion
ver'schwimmen (*unreg*) *vi* to grow hazy, to become blurred
ver'schwinden (*unreg*) *vi* to disappear, to vanish; **V~ (-s)** *nt* disappearance
verschwitzt |fɛrˈʃvɪtst| *adj* (*Mensch*) sweaty
verschwommen |fɛrˈʃvɔmən| *adj* hazy, vague
verschwör- |fɛrˈʃvøːr| *zW*: **~en** (*unreg*) *vr* to plot, to conspire; **V~ung** *f* conspiracy, plot
ver'sehen (*unreg*) *vt* to supply, to provide; (*Pflicht*) to carry out; (*Amt*) to fill; (*Haushalt*) to keep ♦ *vr* (*fig*) to make a mistake; **ehe er (es) sich ~ hatte ...** before he knew it ...; **V~ (-s, -)** *nt* oversight; **aus V~** by mistake; **~tlich** *adv* by mistake
Versehrte(r) |fɛrˈzeːrtə(r)| *f(m)* disabled person
ver'senden (*unreg*) *vt* to forward, to dispatch
ver'senken *vt* to sink ♦ *vr*: **sich ~ in** +*akk* to become engrossed in
versessen |fɛrˈzɛsən| *adj*: ~ **auf** +*akk* mad about
ver'setzen *vt* to transfer; (*verpfänden*) to pawn; (*umg*) to stand up ♦ *vr*: **sich in jdn od in jds Lage** ~ to put o.s. in sb's place; **jdm einen Tritt/Schlag** ~ to kick/hit sb; **etw mit etw** ~ to mix sth with sth; **jdn in gute Laune** ~ to put sb in a good mood
Ver'setzung *f* transfer
verseuchen |fɛrˈzɔʏçən| *vt* to contaminate
versichern |fɛrˈzɪçərn| *vt* to assure; (*mit Geld*) to insure
Versicherung *f* assurance; insurance
Versicherungs- *zW*: **~gesellschaft** *f* insurance company; **~karte** *f* insurance card; **die grüne ~karte** the green card; **~police** *f* insurance policy
ver'sinken (*unreg*) *vi* to sink
versöhnen |fɛrˈzøːnən| *vt* to reconcile ♦ *vr* to become reconciled

Versöhnung *f* reconciliation
ver'sorgen *vt* to provide, to supply; (*Familie etc*) to look after
Ver'sorgung *f* provision; (*Unterhalt*) maintenance; (*Altersversorgung etc*) benefit, assistance
ver'späten |fɛrˈʃpeːtən| *vr* to be late
verspätet *adj* (*Zug, Abflug, Ankunft*) late; (*Glückwünsche*) belated
Verspätung *f* delay; ~ **haben** to be late
ver'sperren *vt* to bar, to obstruct
verspielt |fɛrˈʃpiːlt| *adj* (*Kind, Tier*) playful
ver'spotten *vt* to ridicule, to scoff at
ver'sprechen (*unreg*) *vt* to promise; **sich** *dat* **etw von etw** ~ to expect sth from sth; **Ver'sprechen (-s, -)** *nt* promise
verstaatlichen |fɛrˈʃtaːtlɪçən| *vt* to nationalize
Verstand |fɛrˈʃtant| *m* intelligence; mind; **den** ~ **verlieren** to go out of one's mind; **über jds** ~ **gehen** to go beyond sb
verständig |fɛrˈʃtɛndɪç| *adj* sensible; **~en** |fɛrˈʃtɛndɪgən| *vt* to inform ♦ *vr* to communicate; (*sich einigen*) to come to an understanding; **V~ung** *f* communication; (*Benachrichtigung*) informing; (*Einigung*) agreement
verständ- |fɛrˈʃtɛnt| *zW*: **~lich** *adj* understandable, comprehensible; **V~lichkeit** *f* clarity, intelligibility; **V~nis (-ses, -se)** *nt* understanding; **~nislos** *adj* uncomprehending; **~nisvoll** *adj* understanding, sympathetic
verstärk- |fɛrˈʃtɛrk| *zW*: **~en** *vt* to strengthen; (*Ton*) to amplify; (*erhöhen*) to intensify ♦ *vr* to intensify; **V~er (-s, -)** *m* amplifier; **V~ung** *f* strengthening; (*Hilfe*) reinforcements *pl*; (*von Ton*) amplification
verstauchen |fɛrˈʃtaʊxən| *vt* to sprain
verstauen |fɛrˈʃtaʊən| *vt* to stow away
Versteck |fɛrˈʃtɛk| **(-(e)s, -e)** *nt* hiding (place); **v~en** *vt, vr* to hide; **v~t** *adj* hidden
ver'stehen (*unreg*) *vt* to understand ♦ *vr* to get on; **das versteht sich (von selbst)** that goes without saying
versteigern |fɛrˈʃtaɪgərn| *vt* to auction; **Versteigerung** *f* auction
verstell- |fɛrˈʃtɛl| *zW*: **~bar** *adj* adjustable, variable; **~en** *vt* to move, to shift; (*Uhr*) to adjust; (*versperren*) to block; (*fig*) to disguise ♦ *vr* to pretend, to put on an act; **V~ung** *f* pretence
versteuern |fɛrˈʃtɔʏərn| *vt* to pay tax on
verstimmt |fɛrˈʃtɪmt| *adj* out of tune; (*fig*) cross, put out; (*Magen*) upset
ver'stopfen *vt* to block, to stop up; (*MED*) to constipate
Ver'stopfung *f* obstruction; (*MED*) constipation

Spelling reform: ▲ *new spelling* △ *old spelling (to be phased out)*

verstorben |fɛrˈʃtɔrbən| adj deceased, late

verstört |fɛrˈʃtøːrt| adj (Mensch) distraught

Verstoß |fɛrˈʃtoːs| m: ~ **(gegen)** infringement (of), violation (of); **v~en** (unreg) vt to disown, to reject ♦ vi: **v~en gegen** to offend against

ver'streichen (unreg) vt to spread ♦ vi to elapse

ver'streuen vt to scatter (about)

verstümmeln |fɛrˈʃtʏməln| vt to maim, to mutilate (auch fig)

verstummen |fɛrˈʃtʊmən| vi to go silent; (Lärm) to die away

Versuch |fɛrˈzuːx| (-(e)s, -e) m attempt; (SCI) experiment; **v~en** vt to try; (verlocken) to tempt ♦ vr: **sich an etw** dat **v~en** to try one's hand at sth; **~skaninchen** nt (fig) guinea-pig; **~ung** f temptation

vertagen |fɛrˈtaːgən| vt, vi to adjourn

ver'tauschen vt to exchange; (versehentlich) to mix up

verteidig- |fɛrˈtaɪdɪg| zW: **~en** vt to defend; **V~er** (-s, -) m defender; (JUR) defence counsel; **V~ung** f defence

ver'teilen vt to distribute; (Rollen) to assign; (Salbe) to spread

Verteilung f distribution, allotment

vertiefen |fɛrˈtiːfən| vt to deepen ♦ vr: **sich in etw** akk ~ to become engrossed od absorbed in sth

Vertiefung f depression

vertikal |vɛrtiˈkaːl| adj vertical

vertilgen |fɛrˈtɪlgən| vt to exterminate; (umg) to eat up, to consume

vertonen |fɛrˈtoːnən| vt to set to music

Vertrag |fɛrˈtraːk| (-(e)s, ⁼e) m contract, agreement; (POL) treaty; **v~en** |-gən| (unreg) vt to tolerate, to stand ♦ vr to get along; (sich aussöhnen) to become reconciled; **v~lich** adj contractual

verträglich |fɛrˈtrɛːklɪç| adj good-natured, sociable; (Speisen) easily digested; (MED) easily tolerated; **V~keit** f sociability; good nature; digestibility

Vertrags- zW: **~bruch** m breach of contract; **~händler** m appointed retailer; **~partner** m party to a contract; **~werkstatt** f appointed repair shop; **v~widrig** adj contrary to contract

vertrauen |fɛrˈtraʊən| vi: **jdm** ~ to trust sb; ~ **auf** +akk to rely on; **V~** (-s) nt confidence; **V~ erweckend** inspiring trust; **~svoll** adj trustful; **~swürdig** adj trustworthy

vertraulich |fɛrˈtraʊlɪç| adj familiar; (geheim) confidential

vertraut |fɛrˈtraʊt| adj familiar; **V~heit** f familiarity

ver'treiben (unreg) vt to drive away; (aus Land) to expel; (COMM) to sell; (Zeit) to pass

vertret- |fɛrˈtreːt| zW: **~en** (unreg) vt to

represent; (Ansicht) to hold, to advocate; **sich** dat **die Beine ~en** to stretch one's legs; **V~er** (-s, -) m representative; (Verfechter) advocate; **V~ung** f representation; advocacy

Vertrieb |fɛrˈtriːp| (-(e)s, -e) m marketing (department)

ver'trocknen vi to dry up

ver'trösten vt to put off

vertun |fɛrˈtuːn| (unreg) vt to waste ♦ vr (umg) to make a mistake

vertuschen |fɛrˈtʊʃən| vt to hush od cover up

verübeln |fɛrˈyːbəln| vt: **jdm etw** ~ to be cross od offended with sb on account of sth

verüben |fɛrˈyːbən| vt to commit

verun- |fɛrˈʊn| zW: **~glimpfen** vt to disparage; **~glücken** vi to have an accident; **tödlich ~glücken** to be killed in an accident; **~reinigen** vt to soil; (Umwelt) to pollute; **~sichern** vt to rattle; **~treuen** |-trɔyən| vt to embezzle

verur- |fɛrˈuːr| zW: **~sachen** vt to cause; **~teilen** |-taɪlən| vt to condemn; **V~teilung** f condemnation; (JUR) sentence

verviel- |fɛrˈfiːl| zW: **~fachen** vt to multiply; **~fältigen** |-fɛltɪgən| vt to duplicate, to copy; **V~fältigung** f duplication, copying

vervollkommnen |fɛrˈfɔlkɔmnən| vt to perfect

vervollständigen |fɛrˈfɔlʃtɛndɪgən| vt to complete

ver'wackeln vt (Foto) to blur

ver'wählen vr (TEL) to dial the wrong number

verwahren |fɛrˈvaːrən| vt to keep, to lock away ♦ vr to protest

verwalt- |fɛrˈvalt| zW: **~en** vt to manage; to administer; **V~er** (-s, -) m manager; (Vermögensverwalter) trustee; **V~ung** f administration; management

ver'wandeln vt to change, to transform ♦ vr to change; to be transformed; **Ver'wandlung** f change, transformation

verwandt |fɛrˈvant| adj: ~ **(mit)** related (to); **V~e(r)** f(m) relative, relation; **V~schaft** f relationship; (Menschen) relations pl

ver'warnen vt to caution

Ver'warnung f caution

ver'wechseln vt: ~ **mit** to confuse with; to mistake for; **zum V~ ähnlich** as like as two peas

Ver'wechslung f confusion, mixing up

Verwehung |fɛrˈveːʊŋ| f snowdrift; sand drift

verweichlicht |fɛrˈvaɪçlɪçt| adj effeminate, soft

ver'weigern vt: **jdm etw** ~ to refuse sb sth; **den Gehorsam/die Aussage** ~ to refuse to obey/testify

Ver'weigerung f refusal

Verweis |fɛrˈvaɪs| (-es, -e) m reprimand,

rebuke; (*Hinweis*) reference; **v~en** (*unreg*) *vt* to refer; **jdn von der Schule v~en** to expel sb (from school); **jdn des Landes v~en** to deport *od* expel sb

ver'welken *vi* to fade

verwend- |fɛr'vɛnd| *zW:* **~bar** |-'vɛntba:r| *adj* usable; **ver'wenden** (*unreg*) *vt* to use; (*Mühe, Zeit, Arbeit*) to spend ♦ *vr* to intercede; **Ver'wendung** *f* use

ver'werfen (*unreg*) *vt* to reject

verwerflich |fɛr'vɛrflɪç| *adj* reprehensible

ver'werten *vt* to utilize

Ver'wertung *f* utilization

verwesen |fɛr've:zən| *vi* to decay

ver'wickeln *vt* to tangle (up); (*fig*) to involve ♦ *vr* to get tangled (up); **jdn in etw** *akk* **~** to involve sb in sth; **sich in etw** *akk* **~** to get involved in sth

verwickelt |fɛr'vɪkəlt| *adj* (*Situation, Fall*) difficult, complicated

verwildern |fɛr'vɪldərn| *vi* to run wild

verwirklichen |fɛr'vɪrklɪçən| *vt* to realize, to put into effect

Verwirklichung *f* realization

verwirren |fɛr'vɪrən| *vt* to tangle (up); (*fig*) to confuse

Verwirrung *f* confusion

verwittern |fɛr'vɪtərn| *vi* to weather

verwitwet |fɛr'vɪtvət| *adj* widowed

verwöhnen |fɛr'vø:nən| *vt* to spoil

verworren |fɛr'vɔrən| *adj* confused

verwundbar |fɛr'vʊntba:r| *adj* vulnerable

verwunden |fɛr'vʊndən| *vt* to wound

verwunder- |fɛr'vʊndər| *zW:* **~lich** *adj* surprising; **V~ung** *f* astonishment

Verwundete(r) *f(m)* injured person

Verwundung *f* wound, injury

ver'wünschen *vt* to curse

verwüsten |fɛr'vy:stən| *vt* to devastate

verzagen |fɛr'tsa:gən| *vi* to despair

ver'zählen *vr* to miscount

verzehren |fɛr'tse:rən| *vt* to consume

ver'zeichnen *vt* to list; (*Niederlage, Verlust*) to register

Verzeichnis |fɛr'tsaɪçnɪs| (**-ses, -se**) *nt* list, catalogue; (*in Buch*) index

verzeih- |fɛr'tsaɪ| *zW:* **~en** (*unreg*) *vt, vi* to forgive; **jdm etw ~en** to forgive sb for sth; **~lich** *adj* pardonable; **V~ung** *f* forgiveness, pardon; **V~ung!** sorry!, excuse me!

verzichten |fɛr'tsɪçtən| *vi:* **~ auf** +*akk* to forgo, to give up

ver'ziehen (*unreg*) *vi* to move ♦ *vt* to put out of shape; (*Kind*) to spoil; (*Pflanzen*) to thin out ♦ *vr* to go out of shape; (*Gesicht*) to contort; (*verschwinden*) to disappear; **das Gesicht ~** to pull a face

verzieren |fɛr'tsi:rən| *vt* to decorate, to ornament

Verzierung *f* decoration

verzinsen |fɛr'tsɪnzən| *vt* to pay interest on

ver'zögern *vt* to delay

Ver'zögerung *f* delay, time lag; **~staktik** *f* delaying tactics *pl*

verzollen |fɛr'tsɔlən| *vt* to pay duty on

Verzug |fɛr'tsu:k| *m* delay

verzweif- |fɛr'tsvaɪf| *zW:* **~eln** *vi* to despair; **~elt** *adj* desperate; **V~lung** *f* despair

Veto |'ve:to| (**-s, -s**) *nt* veto

Vetter |'fɛtər| (**-s, -n**) *m* cousin

vgl. *abk* (= *vergleiche*) cf.

v. H. *abk* (= *vom Hundert*) p.c.

vibrieren |vi'bri:rən| *vi* to vibrate

Video |'vi:deo| *nt* video; **~gerät** *nt* video recorder; **~rekorder** *m* video recorder

Vieh |fi:| (**-(e)s**) *nt* cattle *pl*; **v~isch** *adj* bestial

viel |fi:l| *adj* a lot of, much ♦ *adv* a lot, much; **~ sagend** significant; **~ versprechend** promising; **~e** *pron pl* a lot of, many; **~ zuwenig** much too little; **~erlei** *adj* a great variety of; **~es** *pron* a lot; **~fach** *adj, adv* many times; **auf ~fachen Wunsch** at the request of many people; **V~falt** (**-**) *f* variety; **~fältig** *adj* varied, many-sided

vielleicht |fi'laɪçt| *adv* perhaps

viel- *zW:* **~mal(s)** *adv* many times; **danke ~mals** many thanks; **~mehr** *adv* rather, on the contrary; **~seitig** *adj* many-sided

vier |fi:r| *num* four; **V~eck** (**-(e)s, -e**) *nt* four-sided figure; (*gleichseitig*) square; **~eckig** *adj* four-sided; square; **V~taktmotor** *m* four-stroke engine; **~te(r, s)** |'fi:rtə(r, s)| *adj* fourth; **V~tel** |'fɪrtəl| (**-s, -**) *nt* quarter; **V~teljahr** *nt* quarter; **~teljährlich** *adj* quarterly; **~teln** *vt* to divide into four; (*Kuchen usw*) to divide into quarters; **V~telstunde** *f* quarter of an hour; **~zehn** |'fɪrtse:n| *num* fourteen; **in ~zehn Tagen** in a fortnight; **~zehntägig** *adj* fortnightly; **~zig** |'fɪrtsɪç| *num* forty

Villa |'vɪla| (**-, Villen**) *f* villa

violett |vio'lɛt| *adj* violet

Violin- |vio'li:n| *zW:* **~e** *f* violin; **~schlüssel** *m* treble clef

virtuell |vɪrtu'ɛl| *adj* (*COMPUT*) virtual; **~e Realität** virtual reality

Virus |'vi:rʊs| (**-, Viren**) *m od nt* (*auch COMPUT*) virus

Visa |'vi:za| *pl von* **Visum**

vis-a-vis ▲, vis-à-vis |viza'vi:| *adv* opposite

Visen |'vi:zən| *pl von* **Visum**

Visier |vi'zi:r| (**-s, -e**) *nt* gunsight; (*am Helm*) visor

Visite |vi'zi:tə| *f* (*MED*) visit; **~nkarte** *f* visiting card

Visum |'vi:zʊm| (**-s, Visa** *od* **Visen**) *nt* visa

vital |vi'ta:l| *adj* lively, full of life, vital

Vitamin |vita'mi:n| (**-s, -e**) *nt* vitamin

Vogel |'fo:gəl| (-s, ⁀) *m* bird; **einen ~ haben** (*umg*) to have bats in the belfry; **jdm den ~ zeigen** (*umg*) to tap one's forehead (*meaning that one thinks sb stupid*); **~bauer** *nt* birdcage; **~perspektive** *f* bird's-eye view; **~scheuche** *f* scarecrow

Vokabel |vo'ka:bəl| (-, -n) *f* word

Vokabular |vokabu'la:r| (-s, -e) *nt* vocabulary

Vokal |vo'ka:l| (-s, -e) *m* vowel

Volk |fɔlk| (-(e)s, ⁀er) *nt* people; nation

Völker- |'fœlkar| *zW:* **~recht** *nt* international law; **~rechtlich** *adj* according to international law; **~verständigung** *f* international understanding

Volks- *zW:* **~entscheid** *m* referendum; **~fest** *nt* fair; **~hochschule** *f* adult education classes *pl*; **~lied** *nt* folksong; **~republik** *f* people's republic; **~schule** *f* elementary school; **~tanz** *m* folk dance; **~vertreter(in)** *m(f)* people's representative; **~wirtschaft** *f* economics *sg*

voll |fɔl| *adj* full; **etw ~ machen** to fill sth up; **~ tanken** to fill up; **~ und ganz** completely; **jdn für ~ nehmen** (*umg*) to take sb seriously; **~auf** *adv* amply; **V~bart** *m* full beard; **V~beschäftigung** *f* full employment; **~bringen** (*unreg*) *vt insep* to accomplish; **~'enden** *vt insep* to finish, to complete; **~'endet** *adj* (~*kommen*) completed; **~ends** |'fɔlɛnts| *adv* completely; **V~'endung** *f* completion

Volleyball |'vɔliba| *m* volleyball

Vollgas *nt:* **mit ~ at** full throttle; **~ geben** to step on it

völlig |'fœlıç| *adj* complete ♦ *adv* completely

voll- *zW:* **~jährig** *adj* of age; **V~kasko-versicherung** |'fɔlkaskofɛrzıçərʊŋ| *f* fully comprehensive insurance; **~'kommen** *adj* perfect; **V~'kommenheit** *f* perfection; **V~kornbrot** *nt* wholemeal bread; **V~macht** (-, -en) *f* authority, full powers *pl*; **V~milch** *f* (*KOCH*) full-cream milk; **V~mond** *m* full moon; **V~pension** *f* full board; **~ständig** |'fɔlʃtɛndıç| *adj* complete; **~'strecken** *vt insep* to execute; **~tanken** △ *vt, vi siehe* **voll**; **V~waschmittel** *nt* detergent; **V~wertkost** *f* wholefood; **~zählig** |'fɔltsɛ:lıç| *adj* complete; in full number; **~'ziehen** (*unreg*) *vt insep* to carry out ♦ *vr insep* to happen; **V~'zug** *m* execution

Volumen |vo'lu:mən| (-s, *- od* **Volumina**) *nt* volume

vom |fɔm| = **von dem**

von |fɔn| *präp +dat* **1** (*Ausgangspunkt*) from; **von ... bis** from ... to; **von morgens bis abends** from morning till night; **von ... nach ...** from ... to ...; **von ... an** from ...;

von ... aus from ...; **von dort aus** from there; **etw von sich aus tun** to do sth of one's own accord; **von mir aus** (*umg*) if you like, I don't mind; **von wo/wann ...?** where/when ... from?

2 (*Ursache, im Passiv*) by; **ein Gedicht von Schiller** a poem by Schiller; **von etw müde** tired from sth

3 (*als Genitiv*) of; **ein Freund von mir** a friend of mine; **nett von dir** nice of you; **jeweils zwei von zehn** two out of every ten

4 (*über*) about; **er erzählte vom Urlaub** he talked about his holiday

5: von wegen! (*umg*) no way!

voneinander *adv* from each other

vor |fo:r| *präp +dat* **1** (*räumlich*) in front of; **vor der Kirche links abbiegen** turn left before the church

2 (*zeitlich*) before; **ich war vor ihm da** I was there before him; **vor 2 Tagen** 2 days ago; **5 (Minuten) vor 4** 5 (minutes) to 4; **vor kurzem** a little while ago

3 (*Ursache*) with; **vor Wut/Liebe** with rage/love; **vor Hunger sterben** to die of hunger; **vor lauter Arbeit** because of work

4: vor allem, vor allen Dingen most of all

♦ *präp +akk* (*räumlich*) in front of

♦ *adv:* **vor und zurück** backwards and forwards

Vorabend |'fo:r|a:bənt| *m* evening before, eve

voran |fo'ran| *adv* before, ahead; **mach ~!** get on with it!; **~gehen** (*unreg*) *vi* to go ahead; **einer Sache** *dat* **~gehen** to precede sth; **~kommen** (*unreg*) *vi* to come along, to make progress

Voranschlag |'fo:r|anʃla:k| *m* estimate

Vorarbeiter |'fo:r|arbaitar| *m* foreman

voraus |fo'raus| *adv* ahead; (*zeitlich*) in advance; **jdm ~ sein** to be ahead of sb; **im V~** in advance; **~gehen** (*unreg*) *vi* to go (on) ahead; (*fig*) to precede; **~haben** (*unreg*) *vt:* **jdm etw ~haben** to have the edge on sb in sth; **V~sage** *f* prediction; **~sagen** *vt* to predict; **~sehen** (*unreg*) *vt* to foresee; **~setzen** *vt* to assume; **~gesetzt, dass ...** provided that ...; **V~setzung** *f* requirement, prerequisite; **V~sicht** *f* foresight; **aller V~sicht nach** in all probability; **~sichtlich** *adv* probably

Vorbehalt |'fo:rbahalt| (-(e)s, -e) *m* reservation, proviso; **v~en** (*unreg*) *vt:* **sich/ jdm etw v~en** to reserve sth (for o.s.)/for sb; **v~los** *adj* unconditional ♦ *adv* unconditionally

vorbei |fɔr'bai| *adv* by, past; **das ist ~** that's

over; **~gehen** (unreg) vi to pass by, to go past; **~kommen** (unreg) vi: **bei jdm ~kommen** to drop in od call in on sb

vor- zW: **~belastet** ['fo:rbəlastət] adj (fig) handicapped; **~bereiten** vt to prepare; **V~bereitung** f preparation; **V~bestellung** f advance order; (von Platz, Tisch etc) advance booking; **~bestraft** ['fo:rbəʃtra:ft] adj previously convicted, with a record

vorbeugen ['fo:rbɔygən] vt, vr to lean forward ♦ vi +dat to prevent; **~d** adj preventive

Vorbeugung f prevention; **zur ~ gegen** for the prevention of

Vorbild ['fo:rbɪlt] nt model; **sich** dat **jdn zum ~ nehmen** to model o.s. on sb; **v~lich** adj model, ideal

vorbringen ['fo:rbrɪŋən] (unreg) vt to advance, to state

Vorder- ['fɔrdər] zW: **~achse** f front axle; **v~e(r, s)** adj front; **~grund** m foreground; **~mann** (pl **-männer**) m man in front; **jdn auf ~mann bringen** (umg) to get sb to shape up; **~seite** f front (side); **v~ste(r, s)** adj front

vordrängen ['fo:rdrɛŋən] vr to push to the front

voreilig ['fo:railɪç] adj hasty, rash

voreinander [fo:rai'nandər] adv (räumlich) in front of each other

voreingenommen ['fo:raiŋənɔmən] adj biased; **V~heit** f bias

vorenthalten ['fo:rɛnthaltən] (unreg) vt: **jdm etw ~** to withhold sth from sb

vorerst ['fo:r|e:rst] adv for the moment od present

Vorfahr ['fo:rfa:r] (**-en, -en**) m ancestor

vorfahren (unreg) vi to drive (on) ahead; (vors Haus etc) to drive up

Vorfahrt f (AUT) right of way; **~ gewähren!** give way!

Vorfahrts- zW: **~regel** f right of way; **~schild** nt give way sign; **~straße** f major road

Vorfall ['fo:rfal] m incident; **v~en** (unreg) vi to occur

vorfinden ['fo:rfɪndən] (unreg) vt to find

Vorfreude ['fo:rfrɔydə] f (joyful) anticipation

vorführen ['fo:rfy:rən] vt to show, to display; **dem Gericht ~** to bring before the court

Vorgabe ['fo:rga:bə] f (SPORT) start, handicap ♦ in zW (COMPUT) default

Vorgang ['fo:rgaŋ] m course of events; (bes SCI) process

Vorgänger(in) ['fo:rgɛŋər(ɪn)] (**-s, -**) m(f) predecessor

vorgeben ['fo:rge:bən] (unreg) vt to pretend, to use as a pretext; (SPORT) to give an advantage od a start of

vorgefertigt ['fo:rgəfɛrtɪçt] adj prefabricated

vorgehen ['fo:rge:ən] (unreg) vi (voraus) to go (on) ahead; (nach vorn) to go up front; (handeln) to act, to proceed; (Uhr) to be fast; (Vorrang haben) to take precedence; (passieren) to go on

Vorgehen (**-s**) nt action

Vorgeschichte ['fo:rgəʃɪçtə] f past history

Vorgeschmack ['fo:rgəʃmak] m foretaste

Vorgesetzte(r) ['fo:rgəzɛtstə(r)] f(m) superior

vorgestern ['fo:rgɛstərn] adv the day before yesterday

vorhaben ['fo:rha:bən] (unreg) vt to intend; **hast du schon was vor?** have you got anything on?; **V~** (**-s, -**) nt intention

vorhalten ['fo:rhaltən] (unreg) vt to hold od put up ♦ vi to last; **jdm etw ~** (fig) to reproach sb for sth

vorhanden [fo:r'handən] adj existing; (erhältlich) available

Vorhang ['fo:rhaŋ] m curtain

Vorhängeschloss ▲ ['fo:rhɛŋəʃlɔs] nt padlock

vorher [fo:r'he:r] adv before(hand); **~bestimmen** vt (Schicksal) to preordain; **~gehen** (unreg) vi to precede; **~ig** adj previous

Vorherrschaft ['fo:rhɛrʃaft] f predominance, supremacy

vorherrschen ['fo:rhɛrʃən] vi to predominate

vorher- ['fo:r'he:r] zW: **V~sage** f forecast; **~sagen** vt to forecast, to predict; **~sehbar** adj predictable; **~sehen** (unreg) vt to foresee

vorhin [fo:r'hɪn] adv not long ago, just now; **V~ein** ▲ adv: **im V~ein** beforehand

vorig ['fo:rɪç] adj previous, last

Vorkämpfer(in) ['fo:rkɛmpfər(ɪn)] m(f) pioneer

Vorkaufsrecht ['fo:rkaufsrɛçt] nt option to buy

Vorkehrung ['fo:rke:rʊŋ] f precaution

vorkommen ['fo:rkɔmən] (unreg) vi to come forward; (geschehen, sich finden) to occur; (scheinen) to seem (to be); **sich** dat **dumm** etc **~** to feel stupid etc; **V~** (**-s, -**) nt occurrence

Vorkriegs- ['fo:rkri:ks] in zW prewar

Vorladung ['fo:rla:dʊŋ] f summons sg

Vorlage ['fo:rla:gə] f model, pattern; (Gesetzesvorlage) bill; (SPORT) pass

vorlassen ['fo:rlasən] (unreg) vt to admit; (vorgehen lassen) to allow to go in front

vorläufig ['fo:rlɔyfɪç] adj temporary, provisional

vorlaut ['fo:rlaut] adj impertinent, cheeky

vorlesen ['fo:rle:zən] (unreg) vt to read (out)

Spelling reform: ▲ *new spelling* △ *old spelling (to be phased out)*

Vorlesung f (UNIV) lecture
vorletzte(r, s) |'fo:rlɛtstə(r, s)| adj last but one
vorlieb [fo:r'li:p] adv: ~ **nehmen mit** to make do with
Vorliebe [fo:'rli:bə] f preference, partiality
vorliegen |'fo:rli:gən| (unreg) vi to be (here); **etw liegt jdm vor** sb has sth; **~d** adj present, at issue
vormachen |'fo:rmaxən| vt: **jdm etw ~** to show sb how to do sth; (fig) to fool sb; to have sb on
Vormachtstellung |'fo:rmaxtʃtɛlʊŋ| f supremacy, hegemony
Vormarsch |'fo:rmarʃ| m advance
vormerken |'fo:rmɛrkən| vt to book
Vormittag |'fo:rmita:k| m morning; **v~s** adv in the morning, before noon
vorn [fɔrn] adv in front; **von ~ anfangen** to start at the beginning; **nach ~** to the front
Vorname |'fo:rna:mə| m first name, Christian name
vorne |'fɔrnə| adv = **vorn**
vornehm |'fo:rne:m| adj distinguished; refined; elegant
vornehmen (unreg) vt (fig) to carry out; **sich** dat **etw ~** to start on sth; (beschließen) to decide to do sth; **sich** dat **jdn ~** to tell sb off
vornherein |'fɔrnhɛraɪn| adv: **von ~** from the start
Vorort |'fo:rʔɔrt| m suburb
Vorrang |'fo:rraŋ| m precedence, priority; **v~ig** adj of prime importance, primary
Vorrat |'fo:rra:t| m stock, supply
vorrätig |'fo:rrɛtɪç| adj in stock
Vorratskammer f pantry
Vorrecht |'fo:rrɛçt| nt privilege
Vorrichtung |'fo:rrɪçtʊŋ| f device, contrivance
vorrücken |'fo:rrʏkən| vi to advance ♦ vt to move forward
Vorsaison |'fo:rzɛzɔ̃ː| f early season
Vorsatz |'fo:rzats| m intention; (JUR) intent; **einen ~ fassen** to make a resolution
vorsätzlich |'fo:rzɛtslɪç| adj intentional; (JUR) premeditated ♦ adv intentionally
Vorschau |'fo:rʃaʊ| f (RAD, TV) (programme) preview; (Film) trailer
Vorschlag |'fo:rʃla:k| m suggestion, proposal; **v~en** (unreg) vt to suggest, to propose
vorschreiben |'fo:rʃraɪbən| (unreg) vt to prescribe, to specify
Vorschrift |'fo:rʃrɪft| f regulation(s); rule(s); (Anweisungen) instruction(s); **Dienst nach ~** work-to-rule; **v~smäßig** adj as per regulations/instructions
Vorschuss ▲ |'fo:rʃʊs| m advance
vorsehen |'fo:rze:ən| (unreg) vt to provide for, to plan ♦ vr to take care, to be careful

♦ vi to be visible
Vorsehung f providence
Vorsicht |'fo:rzɪçt| f caution, care; **~!** look out!, take care!; (auf Schildern) caution!, danger!; **~, Stufe!** mind the step!; **v~ig** adj cautious, careful; **v~shalber** adv just in case
Vorsilbe |'fo:rzɪlbə| f prefix
vorsingen |'fo:rzɪŋən| vt (vor Zuhörern) to sing (to); (in Prüfung, für Theater etc) to audition (for) ♦ vi to sing
Vorsitz |'fo:rzɪts| m chair(manship); **~ende(r)** f(m) chairman(-woman)
Vorsorge |'fo:rzɔrgə| f precaution(s), provision(s); **v~n** vi: **v~n für** to make provision(s) for; **~untersuchung** f check-up
vorsorglich |'fo:rzɔrklɪç| adv as a precaution
Vorspeise |'fo:rʃpaɪzə| f hors d'oeuvre, appetizer
Vorspiel |'fo:rʃpi:l| nt prelude
vorspielen vt: **jdm etw ~** (MUS) to play sth for od to sb ♦ vi (zur Prüfung etc) to play for od to sb
vorsprechen |'fo:rʃprɛçən| (unreg) vt to say out loud, to recite ♦ vi: **bei jdm ~** to call on sb
Vorsprung |'fo:rʃprʊŋ| m projection, ledge; (fig) advantage, start
Vorstadt |'fo:rʃtat| f suburbs pl
Vorstand |'fo:rʃtant| m executive committee; (COMM) board (of directors); (Person) director, head
vorstehen |'fo:rʃte:ən| (unreg) vi to project; **einer Sache** dat **~** (fig) to be the head of sth
vorstell- |'fo:rʃtɛl| zW: **~bar** adj conceivable; **~en** vt to put forward; (bekannt machen) to introduce; (darstellen) to represent; **~en vor** +akk to put in front of; **sich** dat **etw ~en** to imagine sth; **V~ung** f (Bekanntmachen) introduction; (THEAT etc) performance; (Gedanke) idea, thought
vorstoßen |'fo:rʃto:sən| (unreg) vi (ins Unbekannte) to venture (forth)
Vorstrafe |'fo:rʃtra:fə| f previous conviction
Vortag |'fo:rta:k| m: **am ~ einer Sache** gen on the day before sth
vortäuschen |'fo:rtɔʏʃən| vt to feign, to pretend
Vorteil |'fo:rtaɪl| (**-s, -e**) m: **~ (gegenüber)** advantage (over); **im ~ sein** to have the advantage; **v~haft** adj advantageous
Vortrag |'fo:rtra:k| (**-(e)s, Vorträge**) m talk, lecture; **v~en** |-gən| (unreg) vt to carry forward; (fig) to recite; (Rede) to deliver; (Lied) to perform; (Meinung etc) to express
vortreten |'fo:rtre:tən| (unreg) vi to step forward; (Augen etc) to protrude
vorüber |fo'ry:bər| adv past, over; **~gehen** (unreg) vi to pass (by); **~gehen an** +dat (fig) to pass over; **~gehend** adj temporary, passing

Vorurteil ['fo:rǀʊrtaɪl] nt prejudice
Vorverkauf ['fo:rfɛrkaʊf] m advance booking
Vorwahl ['fo:rvaːl] f preliminary election; (TEL) dialling code
Vorwand ['fo:rvant] (-(e)s, Vorwände) m pretext
vorwärts ['fo:rvɛrts] adv forward; **V~gang** m (AUT etc) forward gear; ~ **gehen** to progress; ~ **kommen** to get on, to make progress
Vorwäsche f prewash
vorweg [fo:r'vɛk] adv in advance; ~**nehmen** (unreg) vt to anticipate
vorweisen ['fo:rvaɪzən] (unreg) vt to show, to produce
vorwerfen ['fo:rvɛrfən] (unreg) vt: **jdm etw** ~ to reproach sb for sth, to accuse sb of sth; **sich** dat **nichts vorzuwerfen haben** to have nothing to reproach o.s. with
vorwiegend ['fo:rvi:gənt] adj predominant ♦ adv predominantly
vorwitzig ['fo:rvɪtsɪç] adj (Mensch, Bemerkung) cheeky
Vorwort ['fo:rvɔrt] (-(e)s, -e) nt preface
Vorwurf ['fo:rvʊrf] m reproach; **jdm/sich Vorwürfe machen** to reproach sb/o.s.; **v~svoll** adj reproachful
vorzeigen ['fo:rtsaɪgən] vt to show, to produce
vorzeitig ['fo:rtsaɪtɪç] adj premature
vorziehen ['fo:rtsi:ən] (unreg) vt to pull forward; (Gardinen) to draw; (lieber haben) to prefer
Vorzimmer ['fo:rtsɪmər] nt (Büro) outer office
Vorzug ['fo:rtsu:k] m preference; (gute Eigenschaft) merit, good quality; (Vorteil) advantage
vorzüglich [fo:r'tsy:klɪç] adj excellent
Vorzugspreis m special discount price
vulgär [vʊl'gɛːr] adj vulgar
Vulkan [vʊl'kaːn] (-s, -e) m volcano

W, w

Waage ['vaːgə] f scales pl; (ASTROL) Libra; **w~recht** adj horizontal
Wabe ['vaːbə] f honeycomb
wach [vax] adj awake; (fig) alert; **W~e** f guard, watch; **W~e halten** to keep watch; **W~e stehen** to stand guard; ~**en** vi to be awake; (Wache halten) to guard
Wachs [vaks] (-es, -e) nt wax
wachsam ['vaxzaːm] adj watchful, vigilant, alert
wachsen (unreg) vi to grow
Wachstuch ['vakstuːx] nt oilcloth

Wachstum ['vakstuːm] (-s) nt growth
Wächter ['vɛçtər] (-s, -) m guard, warden, keeper; (Parkplatzwächter) attendant
wackel- ['vakəl] zW: ~**ig** adj shaky, wobbly; **W~kontakt** m loose connection; ~**n** vi to shake; (fig: Position) to be shaky
wacker ['vakər] adj valiant, stout ♦ adv well, bravely
Wade ['vaːdə] f (ANAT) calf
Waffe ['vafə] f weapon
Waffel ['vafəl] (-, -n) f waffle; wafer
Waffen- zW: ~**schein** m gun licence; ~**stillstand** m armistice, truce
Wagemut ['vaːgəmuːt] m daring
wagen ['vaːgən] vt to venture, to dare
Wagen ['vaːgən] (-s, -) m vehicle; (Auto) car; (EISENB) carriage; (Pferdewagen) cart; ~**heber** (-s, -) m jack
Waggon [va'gɔ̃:] (-s, -s) m carriage; (Güterwaggon) goods van, freight truck (US)
Wagnis ['vaːknɪs] (-ses, -se) nt risk
Wagon [va'gõ:, va'goːn] (-s, -s) m = Waggon
Wahl [vaːl] (-, -en) f choice; (POL) election; **zweite** ~ (COMM) seconds pl
wähl- ['vɛːl] zW: ~**bar** adj eligible; ~**en** vt, vi to choose; (POL) to elect, to vote (for); (TEL) to dial; **W~er(in)** (-s, -) m(f) voter; ~**erisch** adj fastidious, particular
Wahl- zW: ~**fach** nt optional subject; ~**gang** m ballot; ~**kabine** f polling booth; ~**kampf** m election campaign; ~**kreis** m constituency; ~**lokal** nt polling station; **w~los** adv at random; ~**recht** nt franchise; ~**spruch** m motto; ~**urne** f ballot box
Wahn [vaːn] (-(e)s) m delusion; folly; ~**sinn** m madness; **w~sinnig** adj insane, mad ♦ adv (umg) incredibly
wahr [vaːr] adj true
wahren vt to maintain, to keep
während ['vɛːrənt] präp +gen during ♦ konj while; ~**dessen** adv meanwhile
wahr- zW: ~**haben** (unreg) vt: **etw nicht ~haben wollen** to refuse to admit sth; ~**haft** adv (tatsächlich) truly; ~**haftig** [vaːr'haftɪç] adj true, real ♦ adv really; **W~heit** f truth; ~**nehmen** (unreg) vt to perceive, to observe; **W~nehmung** f perception; ~**sagen** vi to prophesy, to tell fortunes; **W~sager(in)** (-s, -) m(f) fortune teller; ~**scheinlich** [vaːr'ʃaɪnlɪç] adj probable ♦ adv probably; **W~'scheinlichkeit** f probability; **aller W~scheinlichkeit nach** in all probability
Währung ['vɛːrʊŋ] f currency
Wahrzeichen nt symbol
Waise ['vaɪzə] f orphan; ~**nhaus** nt orphanage
Wald [valt] (-(e)s, ⁼er) m wood(s); (groß)

forest; **~brand** m forest fire; **~sterben** nt
trees dying due to pollution
Wales [weːlz] (-) nt Wales
Wal(fisch) ['vaːl(fɪʃ)] (-(e)s, -e) m whale
Waliser [va'liːzər] (-s, -) m Welshman;
Waliserin [va'liːzərɪn] f Welshwoman;
walisisch [va'liːzɪʃ] adj Welsh
Walkman ['wɔːkman] ® (-s, Walkmen) m
Walkman ®, personal stereo
Wall [val] (-(e)s, ⸚e) m embankment;
(Bollwerk) rampart
Wallfahr- zW: **~er(in)** m(f) pilgrim; **~t** f
pilgrimage
Walnuss ▲ ['valnʊs] f walnut
Walross ▲ ['valrɔs] nt walrus
Walze ['valtsə] f (Gerät) cylinder; (Fahrzeug)
roller; **w~n** vt to roll (out)
wälzen ['vɛltsən] vt to roll (over); (Bücher) to
hunt through; (Probleme) to deliberate on
♦ vr to wallow; (vor Schmerzen) to roll
about; (im Bett) to toss and turn
Walzer ['valtsər] (-s, -) m waltz
Wand [vant] (-, ⸚e) f wall; (Trennwand)
partition; (Bergwand) precipice
Wandel ['vandəl] (-s) m change; **w~bar** adj
changeable, variable; **w~n** vt, vr to change
♦ vi (gehen) to walk
Wander- ['vandər] zW: **~er** (-s, -) m hiker,
rambler; **~karte** f map of country walks;
w~n vi to hike; (Blick) to wander;
(Gedanken) to stray; **~schaft** f travelling;
~ung f walk, hike; **~weg** m trail, walk
Wandlung f change, transformation
Wange ['vaŋə] f cheek
wanken ['vankən] vi to stagger; (fig) to
waver
wann [van] adv when
Wanne ['vanə] f tub
Wanze ['vantsə] f bug
Wappen ['vapən] (-s, -) nt coat of arms,
crest; **~kunde** f heraldry
war etc [vaːr] vb siehe **sein**
Ware ['vaːrə] f ware
Waren- zW: **~haus** nt department store;
~lager nt stock, store; **~muster** nt trade
sample; **~probe** f sample; **~sendung** f
trade sample (sent by post); **~zeichen** nt:
(eingetragenes) **~zeichen** (registered)
trademark
warf etc [varf] vb siehe **werfen**
warm [varm] adj warm; (Essen) hot
Wärm- ['vɛrm] zW: **~e** f warmth; **w~en** vt, vr
to warm (up), to heat (up); **~flasche** f hot-
water bottle
Warn- ['varn] zW: **~blinkanlage** f (AUT)
hazard warning lights pl; **~dreieck** nt
warning triangle; **w~en** vt to warn; **~ung** f
warning
warten ['vartən] vi: **~** (**auf** +akk) to wait
(for); **auf sich ~ lassen** to take a long time
Wärter(in) ['vɛrtər(ɪn)] (-s, -) m(f) attendant

Warte- ['vartə] zW: **~saal** m (EISENB) waiting
room; **~zimmer** nt waiting room
Wartung f servicing; service; **~ und
Instandhaltung** maintenance
warum [va'rʊm] adv why
Warze ['vartsə] f wart
was [vas] pron what; (umg: etwas)
something; **~ für (ein) ...** what sort of ...
waschbar adj washable
Waschbecken nt washbasin
Wäsche ['vɛʃə] f wash(ing); (Bettwäsche)
linen; (Unterwäsche) underclothing
waschecht adj colourfast; (fig) genuine
Wäsche- zW: **~klammer** f clothes peg
(BRIT), clothespin (US); **~leine** f washing line
(BRIT)
waschen ['vaʃən] (unreg) vt, vi to wash ♦ vr
to (have a) wash; **sich** dat **die Hände ~** to
wash one's hands
Wäsche'rei f laundry
Wasch- zW: **~gelegenheit** f washing
facilities; **~küche** f laundry room; **~lappen**
m face flannel, washcloth (US); (umg) sissy;
~maschine f washing machine; **~mittel** nt
detergent, washing powder; **~pulver** nt
detergent, washing powder; **~raum** m
washroom; **~salon** m Launderette ®
Wasser ['vasər] (-s, -) nt water; **~ball** m
water polo; **w~dicht** adj waterproof; **~fall**
m waterfall; **~farbe** f watercolour; **~hahn** m
tap, faucet (US); **~kraftwerk** nt
hydroelectric power station; **~leitung** f
water pipe; **~mann** n (ASTROL) Aquarius
wässern ['vɛsərn] vt, vi to water
Wasser- zW: **w~scheu** adj afraid of (the)
water; **~ski** ['vasərʃiː] nt water-skiing;
~stoff m hydrogen; **~waage** f spirit level;
~zeichen nt watermark
wässrig ▲ ['vɛsrɪç] adj watery
Watt [vat] (-(e)s, -en) nt mud flats pl
Watte f cotton wool, absorbent cotton (US)
WC ['veː'tseː] (-s, -s) nt abk (= water closet)
W.C.
Web- ['veːb] zW: **w~en** (unreg) vt to weave;
~er (-s, -) m weaver; **~e'rei** f (Betrieb).
weaving mill; **~stuhl** m loom
Wechsel ['vɛksəl] (-s, -) m change; (COMM)
bill of exchange; **~geld** nt change; **w~haft**
adj (Wetter) variable; **~jahre** pl change of
life sg; **~kurs** m rate of exchange; **w~n** vt
to change; (Blicke) to exchange ♦ vi to
change; to vary; (Geldwechseln) to have
change; **~strom** m alternating current;
~stube f bureau de change; **~wirkung** f
interaction
Weck- ['vɛk] zW: **~dienst** m alarm call
service; **w~en** vt to wake (up); to call; **~er**
(-s, -) m alarm clock
wedeln ['veːdəln] vi (mit Schwanz) to wag;
(mit Fächer etc) to wave
weder ['veːdər] konj neither; **~ ... noch ...**

neither … nor …

Weg |veːk| (-(e)s, -e) *m* way; (*Pfad*) path;
(*Route*) route; **sich auf den ~ machen** to be
on one's way; **jdm aus dem ~ gehen** to
keep out of sb's way; *siehe* **zuwege**

weg |vɛk| *adv* away, off; **über etw** *akk* **~
sein** to be over sth; **er war schon ~** he had
already left; **Finger ~!** hands off!

wegbleiben (*unreg*) *vi* to stay away

wegen |'veːgən| *präp* +*gen* (*umg*: +*dat*)
because of

weg- |'vɛk| *zW*: **~fallen** (*unreg*) *vi* to be left
out; (*Ferien, Bezahlung*) to be cancelled;
(*aufhören*) to cease; **~gehen** (*unreg*) *vi* to go
away; to leave; **~lassen** (*unreg*) *vt* to leave
out; **~laufen** (*unreg*) *vi* to run away *od* off;
~legen *vt* to put aside; **~machen** (*umg*) *vt*
to get rid of; **~müssen** (*unreg*) (*umg*) *vi* to
have to go; **~nehmen** (*unreg*) *vt* to take
away; **~tun** (*unreg*) *vt* to put away;
W~weiser |'veːkˌ| (-s, -) *m* road sign,
signpost; **~werfen** (*unreg*) *vt* to throw away

weh |veː| *adj* sore; **~(e)** *excl*: **~(e), wenn du
… woe betide you if …; **o ~!** oh dear!; **~e!**
just you dare!

wehen *vt, vi* to blow; (*Fahnen*) to flutter

weh- *zW*: **~leidig** *adj* whiny, whining;
~mütig *adj* melancholy

Wehr |veːr| (-, -en) *f*: **sich zur ~ setzen** to
defend o.s.; **~dienst** *m* military service;
~dienstverweigerer *m* ≈ conscientious
objector; **w~en** *vr* to defend o.s.; **w~los** *adj*
defenceless; **~pflicht** *f* compulsory military
service; **w~pflichtig** *adj* liable for military
service

wehtun |'veːtuːn| (*unreg*) *vt* to hurt, to be
sore; **jdm/sich ~** to hurt sb/o.s.

Weib |vaɪp| (-(e)s, -er) *nt* woman, female;
wife; **~chen** *nt* female; **w~lich** *adj* feminine

weich |vaɪç| *adj* soft; **W~e** *f* (*EISENB*) points
pl; **~en** (*unreg*) *vi* to yield, to give way;
W~heit *f* softness; **~lich** *adj* soft, namby-
pamby

Weide |'vaɪdə| *f* (*Baum*) willow; (*Gras*)
pasture; **w~n** *vi* to graze ♦ *vr*: **sich an etw**
dat **w~n** to delight in sth

weigern |'vaɪɡərn| *vr* to refuse

Weigerung |'vaɪɡərʊŋ| *f* refusal

Weihe |'vaɪə| *f* consecration; (*Priesterweihe*)
ordination; **w~n** *vt* to consecrate; to ordain

Weihnacht- *zW*: **~en** (-) *nt* Christmas;
w~lich *adj* Christmas *cpd*

Weihnachts- *zW*: **~abend** *m* Christmas Eve;
~lied *nt* Christmas carol; **~mann** *m* Father
Christmas, Santa Claus; **~markt** *m*
Christmas fair; **~tag** *m* Christmas Day;
zweiter ~tag Boxing Day

Weihwasser *nt* holy water

weil |vaɪl| *konj* because

Weile |'vaɪlə| (-) *f* while, short time

Wein |vaɪn| (-(e)s, -e) *m* wine; (*Pflanze*) vine;
~bau *m* cultivation of vines; **~berg** *m*
vineyard; **~bergschnecke** *f* snail; **~brand**
m brandy

weinen *vt, vi* to cry; **das ist zum W~** it's
enough to make you cry *od* weep

Wein- *zW*: **~glas** *nt* wine glass; **~karte** *f*
wine list; **~lese** *f* vintage; **~probe** *f* wine-
tasting; **~rebe** *f* vine; **w~rot** *adj* burgundy,
claret, wine-red; **~stock** *m* vine; **~stube** *f*
wine bar; **~traube** *f* grape

weise |'vaɪzə| *adj* wise

Weise *f* manner, way; (*Lied*) tune; **auf diese
~** in this way

weisen (*unreg*) *vt* to show

Weisheit |'vaɪshaɪt| *f* wisdom; **~szahn** *m*
wisdom tooth

weiß |vaɪs| *adj* white ♦ *vb siehe* **wissen**;
W~bier *nt* weissbier (*light, fizzy beer made
using top-fermentation yeast*); **W~brot** *nt*
white bread; **~en** *vt* to whitewash; **W~glut**
f (*TECH*) incandescence; **jdn bis zur W~glut
bringen** (*fig*) to make sb see red; **W~kohl**
m (white) cabbage; **W~wein** *m* white wine;
W~wurst *f* veal sausage

weit |vaɪt| *adj* wide; (*Begriff*) broad; (*Reise,
Wurf*) long ♦ *adv* far; **wie ~ ist es …?** how
far is it …?; **in ~er Ferne** in the far distance;
~ blickend far-seeing; **~ reichend** long-
range; (*fig*) far-reaching; **~ verbreitet**
widespread; **das geht zu ~** that's going too
far; **~aus** *adv* by far; **W~e** *f* width; (*Raum*)
space; (*von Entfernung*) distance; **~en** *vt, vr*
to widen

weiter |'vaɪtər| *adj* wider; broader; farther
(away); (*zusätzlich*) further ♦ *adv* further;
ohne ~es without further ado; just like that;
~ nichts/niemand nothing/nobody else;
~arbeiten *vi* to go on working; **~bilden** *vr*
to continue one's education; **~empfehlen**
(*unreg*) *vt* to recommend (to others);
W~fahrt *f* continuation of the journey;
~führen *vi* (*Straße*) to lead on (to) ♦ *vt*
(*fortsetzen*) to continue, carry on; **~gehen**
(*unreg*) *vi* to go on; **~hin** *adv*: **etw ~hin
tun** to go on doing sth; **~kommen**
(*unreg*) *vi* (*fig*: *mit Arbeit*) to make progress;
~leiten *vt* to pass on; **~machen** *vt, vi* to
continue

weit- *zW*: **~gehend** *adj* considerable ♦ *adv*
largely; **~läufig** *adj* (*Gebäude*) spacious;
(*Erklärung*) lengthy; (*Verwandter*) distant;
~reichend △ *adj siehe* **weit**; **~schweifig**
adj long-winded; **~sichtig** *adj* (*MED*) long-
sighted; (*fig*) far-sighted; **W~sprung** *m* long
jump; **~verbreitet** △ *adj siehe* **weit**

Weizen |'vaɪtsən| (-s, -) *m* wheat

Spelling reform: ▲ *new spelling* △ *old spelling (to be phased out)*

welche(r, s) *interrogativ pron* which; **welcher von beiden?** which (one) of the two?; **welchen hast du genommen?** which (one) did you take?; **welche eine ...!** what a ...!; **welche Freude!** what joy!
♦ *indef pron* some; (*in Fragen*) any; **ich habe welche** I have some; **haben Sie welche?** do you have any?
♦ *relativ pron* (*bei Menschen*) who; (*bei Sachen*) which, that; **welche(r, s) auch immer** whoever/whichever/whatever

welk [vɛlk] *adj* withered; **~en** *vi* to wither
Welle ['vɛlə] *f* wave; (*TECH*) shaft
Wellen- *zW:* **~bereich** *m* waveband; **~länge** *f* (*auch fig*) wavelength; **~linie** *f* wavy line; **~sittich** *m* budgerigar
Welt [vɛlt] *f* (-, -en) *f* world; **~all** *nt* universe; **~anschauung** *f* philosophy of life; **w~berühmt** *adj* world-famous; **~krieg** *m* world war; **w~lich** *adj* worldly; (*nicht kirchlich*) secular; **~macht** *f* world power; **~meister** *m* world champion; **~raum** *m* space; **~reise** *f* trip round the world; **~stadt** *f* metropolis; **w~weit** *adj* world-wide
wem [ve:m] (*dat von* **wer**) *pron* to whom
wen [ve:n] (*akk von* **wer**) *pron* whom
Wende ['vɛndə] *f* turn; (*Veränderung*) change; **~kreis** *m* (*GEOG*) tropic; (*AUT*) turning circle; **~ltreppe** *f* spiral staircase; **w~n** (*unreg*) *vt, vi, vr* to turn; **sich an jdn w~n** to go/come to sb
wendig ['vɛndɪç] *adj* (*Auto etc*) manoeuvrable; (*fig*) agile
Wendung *f* turn; (*Redewendung*) idiom
wenig ['ve:nɪç] *adj, adv* little; **~e** *pron pl* few *pl*; **~er** *adj* less; (*mit pl*) fewer ♦ *adv* less; **~ste(r, s)** *adj* least; **am ~sten** least; **~stens** *adv* at least

wenn [vɛn] *konj* **1** (*falls, bei Wünschen*) if; **wenn auch ..., selbst wenn ...** even if ...; **wenn ich doch ...** if only I ...
2 (*zeitlich*) when; **immer wenn** whenever

wennschon ['vɛnʃoːn] *adv:* **na ~** so what?; **~, dennschon!** in for a penny, in for a pound
wer [ve:r] *pron* who
Werbe- ['vɛrbə] *zW:* **~fernsehen** *nt* commercial television; **~geschenk** *nt* gift (*from company*); (*zu Gekauftem*) free gift; **w~n** (*unreg*) *vt* to win; (*Mitglied*) to recruit ♦ *vi* to advertise; **um jdn/etw w~n** to try to win sb/sth; **für jdn/etw w~n** to promote sb/sth
Werbung *f* advertising; (*von Mitgliedern*) recruitment; **~ um** **jdn/etw** promotion of

sb/sth
Werdegang ['ve:rdəgaŋ] *m* (*Laufbahn*) development; (*beruflich*) career

werden ['ve:rdən] (*pt* **wurde**, *pp* **geworden** *od* (*bei Passiv*) **worden**) *vi* to become; **was ist aus ihm/aus der Sache geworden?** what became of him/it?; **es ist nichts/gut geworden** it came to nothing/turned out well; **es wird Nacht/Tag** it's getting dark/light; **mir wird kalt** I'm getting cold; **mir wird schlecht** I feel ill; **Erster werden** to come *od* be first; **das muss anders werden** that'll have to change; **rot/zu Eis werden** to turn red/to ice; **was willst du (mal) werden?** what do you want to be?; **die Fotos sind gut geworden** the photos have come out nicely
♦ *als Hilfsverb* **1** (*bei Futur*): **er wird es tun** he will *od* he'll do it; **er wird das nicht tun** he will not *od* he won't do it; **es wird gleich regnen** it's going to rain
2 (*bei Konjunktiv*): **ich würde ...** I would ...; **er würde gern ...** he would *od* he'd like to ...; **ich würde lieber ...** I would *od* I'd rather ...
3 (*bei Vermutung*): **sie wird in der Küche sein** she will be in the kitchen
4 (*bei Passiv*): **gebraucht werden** to be used; **er ist erschossen worden** he has *od* he's been shot; **mir wurde gesagt, dass ...** I was told that ...

werfen ['vɛrfən] (*unreg*) *vt* to throw
Werft [vɛrft] (-, -en) *f* shipyard, dockyard
Werk [vɛrk] (-(e)s, -e) *nt* work; (*Tätigkeit*) job; (*Fabrik, Mechanismus*) works *pl*; **ans ~ gehen** to set to work; **~statt** (-, -stätten) *f* workshop; (*AUT*) garage; **~tag** *m* working day; **w~tags** *adv* on working days; **w~tätig** *adj* working; **~zeug** *nt* tool
Wermut ['ve:rmu:t] (-(e)s) *m* wormwood; (*Wein*) vermouth
Wert [ve:rt] (-(e)s, -e) *m* worth; (*FIN*) value; **~ legen auf** +*akk* to attach importance to; **es hat doch keinen ~** it's useless; **w~** *adj* worth; (*geschätzt*) dear; worthy; **das ist nichts/viel w~** it's not worth anything/it's worth a lot; **das ist es/er mir w~** it's/he's worth that to me; **~angabe** *f* declaration of value; **~brief** *m* registered letter (*containing sth of value*); **w~en** *vt* to rate; **~gegenstände** *mpl* valuables; **w~los** *adj* worthless; **~papier** *nt* security; **w~voll** *adj* valuable
Wesen ['ve:zən] (-s, -) *nt* (*Geschöpf*) being; (*Natur, Charakter*) nature; **w~tlich** *adj* significant; (*beträchtlich*) considerable
weshalb [vɛs'halp] *adv* why
Wespe ['vɛspə] *f* wasp

wessen ['vɛsən] (gen von **wer**) pron whose
Weste ['vɛstə] f waistcoat, vest (US);
(Wollweste) cardigan
West- zW: **~en** (-s) m west; **~europa** nt
Western Europe; **w~lich** adj western ♦ adv
to the west
weswegen [vɛs've:gən] adv why
wett [vɛt] adj even; **W~bewerb** m
competition; **W~e** f bet, wager; **~en** vt, vi to
bet
Wetter ['vɛtər] (-s, -) nt weather; **~bericht** m
weather report; **~dienst** m meteorological
service; **~lage** f (weather) situation;
~vorhersage f weather forecast; **~warte** f
weather station
Wett- zW: **~kampf** m contest; **~lauf** m race;
w~machen vt to make good
wichtig ['vɪçtɪç] adj important; **W~keit** f
importance
wickeln ['vɪkəln] vt to wind; (Haare) to set;
(Kind) to change; **jdn/etw in etw** akk **~** to
wrap sb/sth in sth
Wickelraum m mothers' (and babies') room
Widder ['vɪdər] (-s, -) m ram; (ASTROL) Aries
wider ['vi:dər] präp +akk against; **~'fahren**
(unreg) vt to happen; **~'legen** vt to refute
widerlich ['vi:dərlɪç] adj disgusting, repulsive
wider- ['vi:dər] zW: **~rechtlich** adj unlawful;
W~rede f contradiction; **~'rufen** (unreg) vt
insep to retract; (Anordnung) to revoke;
(Befehl) to countermand; **~'setzen** vr insep:
sich jdm/etw ~setzen to oppose sb/sth
widerspenstig ['vi:dərʃpɛnstɪç] adj wilful
wider- ['vi:dər] zW: **~spiegeln** vt
(Entwicklung, Erscheinung) to mirror, reflect
♦ vr to be reflected; **~'sprechen** (unreg) vi
insep: **jdm ~sprechen** to contradict sb
Widerspruch ['vi:dərʃprʊx] m contradiction;
w~slos adv without arguing
Widerstand ['vi:dərʃtant] m resistance
Widerstands- zW: **~bewegung** f resistance
(movement); **w~fähig** adj resistant, tough;
w~los adj unresisting
wider'stehen (unreg) vi insep: **jdm/etw ~**
to withstand sb/sth
wider- ['vi:dər] zW: **~wärtig** adj nasty,
horrid; **W~wille** m: **W~wille (gegen)**
aversion (to); **~willig** adj unwilling,
reluctant
widmen ['vɪtmən] vt to dedicate; to devote
♦ vr to devote o.s.
widrig ['vi:drɪç] adj (Umstände) adverse

SCHLÜSSELWORT

---

wie [vi:] adv how; **wie groß/schnell?** how
big/fast?; **wie wärs?** how about it?; **wie ist
er?** what's he like?; **wie gut du das kannst!**
you're very good at it; **wie bitte?** pardon?;
(entrüstet) I beg your pardon!; **und wie!**

and how!; **wie viel** how much; **wie viel
Menschen** how many people; **wie weit** to
what extent
♦ konj **1** (bei Vergleichen): **so schön wie** ...
as beautiful as ...; **wie ich schon sagte** as I
said; **wie du** like you; **singen wie ein** ... to
sing like a ...; **wie (zum Beispiel)** such as
(for example)
2 (zeitlich): **wie er das hörte, ging er**
when he heard that he left; **er hörte, wie
der Regen fiel** he heard the rain falling

---

wieder ['vi:dər] adv again; **~ da sein** to be
back (again); **~ auf bereiten** to recycle; **~
auf nehmen** to resume; **~ erkennen** to
recognize; **~ gutmachen** to make up for;
(Fehler) to put right; **~ herstellen** (Ruhe,
Frieden etc) to restore; **~ vereinigen** to
reunite; (POL) to reunify; **gehst du schon ~?**
are you off again?; **~ ein(e)** ... another ...;
W~aufbau m rebuilding; **W~gabe** f
reproduction; **~geben** (unreg) vt
(zurückgeben) to return; (Erzählung etc) to
repeat; (Gefühle etc) to convey;
W~'gutmachung f reparation;
~'herstellen vt (Gesundheit, Gebäude) to
restore; **~'holen** vt insep to repeat;
W~'holung f repetition; **W~hören** nt: **auf
W~hören** (TEL) goodbye; **W~kehr** (-) f
return; (von Vorfall) repetition, recurrence; **~
sehen** ▲ (unreg) vt to see again; **auf
W~sehen** goodbye; **~um** adv again;
(andererseits) on the other hand;
W~vereinigung f (POL) reunification; **~
verwerten** ▲ vt sep to recycle; **W~wahl** f
re-election
Wiege ['vi:gə] f cradle; **w~n¹** vt (schaukeln)
to rock
wiegen² (unreg) vt, vi (Gewicht) to weigh
Wien [vi:n] nt Vienna
Wiese ['vi:zə] f meadow
Wiesel ['vi:zəl] (-s, -) nt weasel
wieso [vi:'zo:] adv why
wievielmal [vi:'fi:lma:l] adv how often
wievielte(r, s) adj: **zum ~n Mal?** how
many times?; **den W~n haben wir?** what's
the date?; **an ~r Stelle?** in what place?; **der
~ Besucher war er?** how many visitors
were there before him?
wild [vɪlt] adj wild; **W~** (-(e)s) nt game;
W~e(r) ['vɪldə(r)] f(m) savage; **~ern** vi to
poach; **~'fremd** (umg) adj quite strange od
unknown; **W~heit** f wildness; **W~leder** nt
suede; **W~nis** (-, -se) f wilderness;
W~schwein nt wild boar
will etc [vɪl] vb siehe **wollen**
Wille ['vɪlə] (-ns, -n) m will; **w~n** präp +gen:
um ... w~n for the sake of ...; **w~nsstark**
adj strong-willed

---

will- zW: **~ig** adj willing; **W~kommen** [vɪlˈkɔmən] (-s, -) nt welcome; **~kommen** adj welcome; jdn **~kommen heißen** to welcome sb; **~kürlich** adj arbitrary; (Bewegung) voluntary

wimmeln [ˈvɪməln] vi: **~ (von)** to swarm (with)

wimmern [ˈvɪmərn] vi to whimper

Wimper [ˈvɪmpər] (-, -n) f eyelash

Wimperntusche f mascara

Wind [vɪnt] (-(e)s, -e) m wind; **~beutel** m cream puff; (fig) rake; **~e** f (TECH) winch, windlass; (BOT) bindweed; **~el** [ˈvɪndəl] (-, -n) f nappy, diaper (US); **w~en** vi unpers to be windy ♦ vt (unreg) to wind; (Kranz) to weave; (entwinden) to twist ♦ vr (unreg) to wind; (Person) to writhe; **~energie** f wind energy; **w~ig** [ˈvɪndɪç] adj windy; (fig) dubious; **~jacke** f windcheater; **~mühle** f windmill; **~pocken** pl chickenpox sg; **~schutzscheibe** f (AUT) windscreen (BRIT), windshield (US); **~stärke** f wind force; **w~still** adj (Tag) still, windless; (Platz) sheltered; **~stille** f calm; **~stoß** m gust of wind

Wink [vɪŋk] (-(e)s, -e) m (mit Hand) wave; (mit Kopf) nod; (Hinweis) hint

Winkel [ˈvɪŋkəl] (-s, -) m (MATH) angle; (Gerät) set square; (in Raum) corner

winken [ˈvɪŋkən] vt, vi to wave

winseln [ˈvɪnzəln] vi to whine

Winter [ˈvɪntər] (-s, -) m winter; **w~fest** adj (Pflanze) hardy; **~garten** m conservatory; **w~lich** adj wintry; **~reifen** m winter tyre; **~sport** m winter sports pl

Winzer [ˈvɪntsər] (-s, -) m vine grower

winzig [ˈvɪntsɪç] adj tiny

Wipfel [ˈvɪpfəl] (-s, -) m treetop

wir [viːr] pron we; **~ alle** all of us, we all

Wirbel [ˈvɪrbəl] (-s, -) m whirl, swirl; (Trubel) hurly-burly; (Aufsehen) fuss; (ANAT) vertebra; **w~n** vi to whirl, to swirl; **~säule** f spine

wird |vɪrt| vb siehe **werden**

wirfst etc [vɪrfst] vb siehe **werfen**

wirken [ˈvɪrkən] vi to have an effect; (erfolgreich sein) to work; (scheinen) to seem ♦ vt (Wunder) to work

wirklich [ˈvɪrklɪç] adj real ♦ adv really; **W~keit** f reality

wirksam [ˈvɪrkzaːm] adj effective

Wirkstoff m (biologisch, chemisch, pflanzlich) active substance

Wirkung [ˈvɪrkʊŋ] f effect; **w~slos** adj ineffective; **w~slos bleiben** to have no effect; **w~svoll** adj effective

wirr |vɪr| adj confused, wild; **W~warr** (-s) m disorder, chaos

wirst |vɪrst| vb siehe **werden**

Wirt(in) [vɪrt(ɪn)] (-(e)s, -e) m(f) landlord (lady); **~schaft** f (Gaststätte) pub; (Haushalt) housekeeping; (eines Landes) economy; (umg: Durcheinander) mess;

w~schaftlich adj economical; (POL) economic

Wirtschafts- zW: **~krise** f economic crisis; **~politik** f economic policy; **~prüfer** m chartered accountant; **~wunder** nt economic miracle

Wirtshaus nt inn

wischen [ˈvɪʃən] vt to wipe

Wischer (-s, -) m (AUT) wiper

Wissbegier(de) ▲ [ˈvɪsbəɡiːr(də)] f thirst for knowledge; **wissbegierig** ▲ adj inquisitive, eager for knowledge

wissen [ˈvɪsən] (unreg) vt to know; **was weiß ich!** I don't know!; **W~** (-s) nt knowledge; **W~schaft** f science; **W~schaftler(in)** (-s, -) m(f) scientist; **~schaftlich** adj scientific; **~swert** adj worth knowing

wittern [ˈvɪtərn] vt to scent; (fig) to suspect

Witterung f weather; (Geruch) scent

Witwe [ˈvɪtvə] f widow; **~r** (-s, -) m widower

Witz [vɪts] (-es, -e) m joke; **~bold** (-(e)s, -e) m joker, wit; **w~ig** adj funny

wo [voː] adv where; (umg: irgendwo) somewhere; **im Augenblick, ~ ...** the moment (that) ...; **die Zeit, ~ ...** the time when ...; **~anders** [voːˈandərs] adv elsewhere; **~bei** [-ˈbaɪ] adv (relativ) by/with which; (interrogativ) what ... in/by/with

Woche [ˈvɔxə] f week

Wochen- zW: **~ende** nt weekend; **w~lang** adj, adv for weeks; **~markt** m weekly market; **~schau** f newsreel

wöchentlich [ˈvœçəntlɪç] adj, adv weekly

wodurch [voˈdʊrç] adv (relativ) through which; (interrogativ) what ... through

wofür [voˈfyːr] adv (relativ) for which; (interrogativ) what ... for

wog etc [voːk] vb siehe **wiegen**

wo- [voː] zW: **w~gegen** adv (relativ) against which; (interrogativ) what ... against; **~her** |-ˈheːr| adv where ... from; **~hin** |-ˈhɪn| adv where ... to

---

SCHLÜSSELWORT

---

wohl [voːl] adv **1**: **sich wohl fühlen** (zufrieden) to feel happy; (gesundheitlich) to feel well; **jdm wohl tun** to do sb good; **wohl oder übel** whether one likes it or not
2 (wahrscheinlich) probably; (gewiss) certainly; (vielleicht) perhaps; **sie ist wohl zu Hause** she's probably at home; **das ist doch wohl nicht dein Ernst!** surely you're not serious!; **das mag wohl sein** that may well be; **ob das wohl stimmt?** I wonder if that's true; **er weiß das sehr wohl** he knows that perfectly well

---

Wohl [voːl] (-(e)s) nt welfare; **zum ~!** cheers!; **w~auf** adv well; **~behagen** nt comfort; **~fahrt** f welfare; **~fahrtsstaat** m

welfare state; **w~habend** *adj* wealthy;
w~ig *adj* contented, comfortable;
w~schmeckend *adj* delicious; **~stand** *m*
prosperity; **~standsgesellschaft** *f* affluent
society; **~tat** *f* relief; act of charity;
~täter(in) *m(f)* benefactor; **w~tätig** *adj*
charitable; **~tätigkeits-** *zW* charity,
charitable; **w~verdient** *adj* well-earned,
well-deserved; **w~weislich** *adv* prudently;
~wollen (-s) *nt* good will; **w~wollend** *adj*
benevolent
wohn- |'vo:n] *zW*: **~en** *vi* to live;
W~gemeinschaft *f* (*Menschen*) people
sharing a flat; **~haft** *adj* resident; **W~heim**
nt (*für Studenten*) hall of residence; (*für
Senioren*) home; (*bes für Arbeiter*) hostel;
~lich *adj* comfortable; **W~mobil (-s, -e)** *nt*
camper; **W~ort** *m* domicile; **W~sitz** *m*
place of residence; **W~ung** *f* house;
(*Etagenwohnung*) flat, apartment (*US*);
W~wagen *m* caravan; **W~zimmer** *nt*
living room
wölben |'vœlbən] *vt*, *vr* to curve
Wolf |vɔlf] **(-(e)s, ⸚e)** *m* wolf
Wolke |'vɔlkə] *f* cloud; **~nkratzer** *m*
skyscraper
wolkig |'vɔlkɪç] *adj* cloudy
Wolle |'vɔlə] *f* wool; **w~n¹** *adj* woollen

---

wollen² |'vɔlən] (*pt* **wollte**, *pp* **gewollt** *od*
(*als Hilfsverb*) **wollen**) *vt*, *vi* to want; **ich
will nach Hause** I want to go home; **er
will nicht** he doesn't want to; **er wollte
das nicht** he didn't want it; **wenn du
willst** if you like; **ich will, dass du mir
zuhörst** I want you to listen to me
♦ *Hilfsverb*: **er will ein Haus kaufen** he
wants to buy a house; **ich wollte, ich
wäre ...** I wish I were ...; **etw gerade
tun wollen** to be going to do sth

---

wollüstig |'vɔlʏstɪç] *adj* lusty, sensual
wo- *zW*: **~mit** *adv* (*relativ*) with which;
(*interrogativ*) what ... with; **~möglich** *adv*
probably, I suppose; **~nach** *adv* (*relativ*)
after/for which; (*interrogativ*) what ... for/
after; **~ran** *adv* (*relativ*) on/at which;
(*interrogativ*) what ... on/at; **~rauf** *adv*
(*relativ*) on which; (*interrogativ*) what ... on;
~raus *adv* (*relativ*) from/out of which;
(*interrogativ*) what ... from/out of; **~rin** *adv*
(*relativ*) in which; (*interrogativ*) what ... in
Wort |vɔrt] **(-(e)s, ⸚er** *od* **-e)** *nt* word; **jdn
beim ~ nehmen** to take sb at his word; **mit
anderen ~en** in other words; **w~brüchig**
adj not true to one's word
Wörterbuch |'vœrtərbu:x] *nt* dictionary
Wort- *zW*: **~führer** *m* spokesman; **w~karg**

adj taciturn; **~laut** *m* wording
wörtlich |'vœrtlɪç] *adj* literal
Wort- *zW*: **w~los** *adj* mute; **w~reich** *adj*
wordy, verbose; **~schatz** *m* vocabulary;
~spiel *nt* play on words, pun
wo- *zW*: **~rüber** *adv* (*relativ*) over/about
which; (*interrogativ*) what ... over/about;
~rum *adv* (*relativ*) about/round which;
(*interrogativ*) what ... about/round; **~runter**
adv (*relativ*) under which; (*interrogativ*) what
... under; **~von** *adv* (*relativ*) from which;
(*interrogativ*) what ... from; **~vor** *adv*
(*relativ*) in front of/before which;
(*interrogativ*) in front of/before what; of
what; **~zu** *adv* (*relativ*) to/for which;
(*interrogativ*) what ... for/to; (*warum*) why
Wrack |vrak] **(-(e)s, -s)** *nt* wreck
Wucher |'vu:xər] **(-s)** *m* profiteering; **~er (-s,
-)** *m* profiteer; **w~isch** *adj* profiteering;
w~n *vi* (*Pflanzen*) to grow wild; **~ung** *f*
(*MED*) growth, tumour
Wuchs |vu:ks] **(-es)** *m* (*Wachstum*) growth;
(*Statur*) build
Wucht |vʊxt] **(-)** *f* force
wühlen |'vy:lən] *vi* to scrabble; (*Tier*) to
root; (*Maulwurf*) to burrow; (*umg: arbeiten*)
to slave away ♦ *vt* to dig
Wulst |vʊlst] **(-es, ⸚e)** *m* bulge; (*an Wunde*)
swelling
wund |vʊnt] *adj* sore, raw; **W~e** *f* wound
Wunder |'vʊndər] **(-s, -)** *nt* miracle; **es ist
kein ~** it's no wonder; **w~bar** *adj*
wonderful, marvellous; **~kerze** *f* sparkler;
~kind *nt* infant prodigy; **w~lich** *adj* odd,
peculiar; **w~n** *vr* to be surprised ♦ *vt* to
surprise; **sich w~n über** *+akk* to be
surprised at; **w~schön** *adj* beautiful;
w~voll *adj* wonderful
Wundstarrkrampf |'vʊntʃtarkrampf] *m*
tetanus, lockjaw
Wunsch |vʊnʃ] **(-(e)s, ⸚e)** *m* wish
wünschen |'vʏnʃən] *vt* to wish; **sich** *dat*
etw ~ to want sth, to wish for sth; **~swert**
adj desirable
wurde *etc* |'vʊrdə] *vb siehe* **werden**
Würde |'vʏrdə] *f* dignity; (*Stellung*) honour;
w~voll *adj* dignified
würdig |'vʏrdɪç] *adj* worthy; (*würdevoll*)
dignified; **~en** *vt* to appreciate
Wurf |vʊrf] **(-s, ⸚e)** *m* throw; (*Junge*) litter
Würfel |'vʏrfəl] **(-s, -)** *m* dice; (*MATH*) cube;
~becher *m* (dice) cup; **w~n** *vi* to play dice
♦ *vt* to dice; **~zucker** *m* lump sugar
würgen |'vʏrgən] *vt*, *vi* to choke
Wurm |vʊrm] **(-(e)s, ⸚er)** *m* worm;
w~stichig *adj* worm-ridden
Wurst |vʊrst] **(-, ⸚e)** *f* sausage; **das ist mir ~**
(*umg*) I don't care, I don't give a damn
Würstchen |'vʏrstçən] *nt* sausage

Würze ['vʏrtsə] f seasoning, spice
Wurzel ['vʊrtsəl] (-, -n) f root
würzen ['vʏrtsən] vt to season, to spice
würzig adj spicy
wusch etc |vʊʃ| vb siehe **waschen**
wusste etc ▲ |'vʊstə| vb siehe **wissen**
wüst [vyːst] adj untidy, messy; (ausschweifend) wild; (öde) waste; (umg: heftig) terrible; **W~e** f desert
Wut |vuːt| (-) f rage, fury; **~anfall** m fit of rage
wüten ['vyːtən] vi to rage; **~d** adj furious, mad

X, x

X-Beine ['ɪksbaɪnə] pl knock-knees
x-beliebig |ɪksbə'liːbɪç| adj any (whatever)
xerokopieren [kseroko'piːrən] vt to xerox, to photocopy
x-mal ['ɪksmaːl] adv any number of times, n times
Xylofon, Xylophon [ksylo'foːn] (-s, -e) nt xylophone

Y, y

Yacht (-, -en) f siehe **Jacht**
Ypsilon ['ʏpsilɔn] (-(s), -s) nt the letter Y

Z, z

Zacke ['tsakə] f point; (Bergzacke) jagged peak; (Gabelzacke) prong; (Kammzacke) tooth
zackig ['tsakɪç] adj jagged; (umg) smart; (Tempo) brisk
zaghaft ['tsaːkhaft] adj timid
zäh [tseː] adj tough; (Mensch) tenacious; (Flüssigkeit) thick; (schleppend) sluggish; **Z~igkeit** f toughness; tenacity
Zahl |tsaːl| (-, -en) f number; **z~bar** adj payable; **z~en** vt, vi to pay; **z~en bitte!** the bill please!
zählen ['tseːlən] vt, vi to count; **~ auf** +akk to count on; **~ zu** to be numbered among
Zahlenschloss ▲ nt combination lock
Zähler ['tseːlər] (-s, -) m (TECH) meter; (MATH) numerator
Zahl- zW: **z~los** adj countless; **z~reich** adj numerous; **~tag** m payday; **~ung** f payment; **~ungsanweisung** f giro transfer order; **z~ungsfähig** adj solvent; **~wort** nt numeral
zahm |tsaːm| adj tame
zähmen ['tseːmən] vt to tame; (fig) to curb
Zahn |tsaːn| (-(e)s, ⁼e) m tooth; **~arzt** m dentist; **~ärztin** f (female) dentist; **~bürste** f toothbrush; **~fleisch** nt gums pl; **~pasta** f toothpaste; **~rad** nt cog(wheel); **~schmerzen** pl toothache sg; **~stein** m tartar; **~stocher** (-s, -) m toothpick
Zange ['tsaŋə] f pliers pl; (Zuckerzange etc) tongs pl; (Beißzange, ZOOL) pincers pl; (MED) forceps pl
zanken ['tsaŋkən] vi, vr to quarrel
zänkisch ['tsɛŋkɪʃ] adj quarrelsome
Zäpfchen ['tsɛpfçən] nt (ANAT) uvula; (MED) suppository
Zapfen ['tsapfən] (-s, -) m plug; (BOT) cone; (Eiszapfen) icicle
zappeln ['tsapəln] vi to wriggle; to fidget
zart [tsaɾt] adj (weich, leise) soft; (Fleisch) tender; (fein, schwächlich) delicate; **Z~heit** f softness; tenderness; delicacy
zärtlich ['tseːɾtlɪç] adj tender, affectionate
Zauber ['tsaʊbər] (-s, -) m magic; (~bann) spell; **~ei** [-'raɪ] f magic; **~er** (-s, -) m magician; conjuror; **z~haft** adj magical, enchanting; **~künstler** m conjuror; **~kunststück** nt conjuring trick; **z~n** vi to conjure, to practise magic
zaudern ['tsaʊdərn] vi to hesitate
Zaum |tsaʊm| (-(e)s, Zäume) m bridle; **etw im ~ halten** to keep sth in check
Zaun |tsaʊn| (-(e)s, Zäune) m fence
z. B. abk (= zum Beispiel) e.g.
Zebra ['tseːbra] nt zebra; **~streifen** m zebra crossing
Zeche ['tsɛçə] f (Rechnung) bill; (Bergbau) mine
Zeh |tseː| (-s, -en) m toe
Zehe |tseːə| f toe; (Knoblauchzehe) clove
zehn [tseːn] num ten; **~te(r, s)** adj tenth; **Z~tel** (-s, -) nt tenth (part)
Zeich- ['tsaɪç] zW: **~en** (-s, -) nt sign; **z~nen** vt to draw; (kennzeichnen) to mark; (unterzeichnen) to sign ♦ vi to draw; to sign; **~ner** (-s, -) m artist; **technischer ~ner** draughtsman; **~nung** f drawing; (Markierung) markings pl
Zeige- ['tsaɪgə] zW: **~finger** m index finger; **z~n** vt to show ♦ vi to point ♦ vr to show o.s.; **z~n auf** +akk to point to; to point at; **es wird sich z~n** time will tell; **es zeigte sich, dass ...** it turned out that ...; **~r** (-s, -) m pointer; (Uhrzeiger) hand
Zeile ['tsaɪlə] f line; (Häuserzeile) row
Zeit |tsaɪt| (-, -en) f time; (GRAM) tense; **sich dat ~ lassen** to take one's time; **von ~ zu ~** from time to time; siehe **zurzeit**; **~alter** nt age; **~ansage** f (TEL) speaking clock; **~arbeit** f (COMM) temporary job; **z~gemäß** adj in keeping with the times; **~genosse** m contemporary; **z~ig** adj early; **z~lich** adj temporal; **~lupe** f slow motion; **z~raubend** adj time-consuming; **~raum** m period; **~rechnung** f time, era; **nach/vor unserer ~rechnung** A.D./B.C.; **~schrift** f

periodical; **~ung** f newspaper; **~vertreib** m pastime, diversion; **z~weilig** adj temporary; **z~weise** adv for a time; **~wort** nt verb

Zelle |'tselə| f cell; (*Telefonzelle*) callbox

Zellstoff m cellulose

Zelt |tselt| (-(e)s, -e) nt tent; **z~en** vi to camp; **~platz** m camp site

Zement |tse'mɛnt| (-(e)s, -e) m cement; **z~ieren** vt to cement

zensieren |tsɛn'ziːrən| vt to censor; (*SCH*) to mark

Zensur |tsɛn'zuːr| f censorship; (*SCH*) mark

Zentimeter |tsɛnti'meːtər| m od nt centimetre

Zentner |'tsɛntnər| (-s, -) m hundredweight

zentral |tsɛn'traːl| adj central; **Z~e** f central office; (*TEL*) exchange; **Z~heizung** f central heating

Zentrum |'tsɛntrum| (-s, Zentren) nt centre

zerbrechen |tsɛr'brɛçən| (*unreg*) vt, vi to break

zerbrechlich adj fragile

zer'drücken vt to squash, to crush; (*Kartoffeln*) to mash

Zeremonie |tseremo'niː| f ceremony

Zerfall |tsɛr'fal| m decay; **z~en** (*unreg*) vi to disintegrate, to decay; (*sich gliedern*): **z~en (in** +akk) to fall (into)

zer'gehen (*unreg*) vi to melt, to dissolve

zerkleinern |tsɛr'klainərn| vt to reduce to small pieces

zerlegbar |tsɛr'leːkbaːr| adj able to be dismantled

zerlegen |tsɛr'leːgən| vt to take to pieces; (*Fleisch*) to carve; (*Satz*) to analyse

zermürben |tsɛr'myrbən| vt to wear down

zerquetschen |tsɛr'kvetʃən| vt to squash

zer'reißen (*unreg*) vt to tear to pieces ♦ vi to tear, to rip

zerren |'tsɛrən| vt to drag ♦ vi: **~ (an** +dat) to tug (at)

zer'rinnen (*unreg*) vi to melt away

zerrissen |tsɛr'risən| adj torn, tattered; **Z~heit** f tattered state; (*POL*) disunion, discord; (*innere Z~heit*) disintegration

Zerrung f (*MED*) pulled muscle

zerrütten |tsɛr'rytən| vt to wreck, to destroy

zer'schlagen (*unreg*) vt to shatter, to smash ♦ vr to fall through

zer'schneiden (*unreg*) vt to cut up

zer'setzen vt, vr to decompose, to dissolve

zer'springen (*unreg*) vi to shatter, to burst

Zerstäuber |tsɛr'ʃtɔybər| (-s, -) m atomizer

zerstören |tsɛr'ʃtøːrən| vt to destroy

Zerstörung f destruction

zerstreu- |tsɛr'ʃtrɔy| zW: **~en** vt to disperse, to scatter; (*unterhalten*) to divert; (*Zweifel etc*) to dispel ♦ vr to disperse, to scatter; to be dispelled; **~t** adj scattered; (*Mensch*)

absent-minded; **Z~theit** f absent-mindedness; **Z~ung** f dispersion; (*Ablenkung*) diversion

zerstückeln |tsɛr'ʃtykəln| vt to cut into pieces

zer'teilen vt to divide into parts

Zertifikat |tsɛrtifi'kaːt| (-(e)s, -e) nt certificate

zer'treten (*unreg*) vt to crush underfoot

zertrümmern |tsɛr'trymərn| vt to shatter; (*Gebäude etc*) to demolish

Zettel |'tsɛtəl| (-s, -) m piece of paper, slip; (*Notizzettel*) note; (*Formular*) form

Zeug |tsɔyk| (-(e)s, -e) (*umg*) nt stuff ; (*Ausrüstung*) gear; **dummes ~** (stupid) nonsense; **das ~ haben zu** to have the makings of; **sich ins ~ legen** to put one's shoulder to the wheel

Zeuge |'tsɔygə| (-n, -n) m witness; **z~n** vi to bear witness, to testify ♦ vt (*Kind*) to father; **es zeugt von ...** it testifies to ...; **~naussage** f evidence; **Zeugin** |'tsɔygɪn| f witness

Zeugnis |'tsɔygnɪs| (-ses, -se) nt certificate; (*SCH*) report; (*Referenz*) reference; (*Aussage*) evidence, testimony; **~ geben von** to be evidence of, to testify to

z. H(d). abk (= zu Händen) attn.

Zickzack |'tsɪktsak| (-(e)s, -e) m zigzag

Ziege |'tsiːgə| f goat

Ziegel |'tsiːgəl| (-s, -) m brick; (*Dachziegel*) tile

ziehen |'tsiːən| (*unreg*) vt to draw; (*zerren*) to pull; (*SCHACH etc*) to move; (*züchten*) to rear ♦ vi to draw; (*umziehen, wandern*) to move; (*Rauch, Wolke etc*) to drift; (*reißen*) to pull ♦ vb unpers: **es zieht** there is a draught, it's draughty ♦ vr (*Gummi*) to stretch; (*Grenze etc*) to run; (*Gespräche etc*) to be drawn out; **etw nach sich ~** to lead to sth, to entail sth

Ziehung |'tsiːʊŋ| f (*Losziehung*) drawing

Ziel |tsiːl| (-(e)s, -e) nt (*einer Reise*) destination; (*SPORT*) finish; (*MIL*) target; (*Absicht*) goal; **z~bewusst** ▲ adj decisive; **z~en** vi: **z~en (auf** +akk) to aim (at); **z~los** adj aimless; **~scheibe** f target; **z~strebig** adj purposeful

ziemlich |'tsiːmlɪç| adj quite a; fair ♦ adv rather; quite a bit

zieren |'tsiːrən| vr to act coy

zierlich |'tsiːrlɪç| adj dainty

Ziffer |'tsɪfər| (-, -n) f figure, digit; **~blatt** nt dial, clock-face

zig |tsɪk| (*umg*) adj umpteen

Zigarette |tsiga'rɛtə| f cigarette

Zigaretten- zW: **~automat** m cigarette machine; **~schachtel** f cigarette packet; **~spitze** f cigarette holder

Zigarre |tsi'garə| f cigar

Spelling reform: ▲ new spelling △ old spelling (to be phased out)

Zigeuner(in) [tsi'gɔynər(ın)] (-s, -) m(f) gipsy

Zimmer ['tsɪmər] (-s, -) nt room; **~lautstärke** f reasonable volume; **~mädchen** nt chambermaid; **~mann** m carpenter; **z~n** vt to make (from wood); **~nachweis** m accommodation office; **~pflanze** f indoor plant; **~service** m room service

zimperlich ['tsɪmpərlıç] adj squeamish; (pingelig) fussy, finicky

Zimt [tsɪmt] (-(e)s, -e) m cinnamon

Zink [tsɪŋk] (-(e)s) nt zinc

Zinn [tsɪn] (-(e)s) nt (Element) tin; (in ~waren) pewter; **~soldat** m tin soldier

Zins [tsɪns] (-es, -en) m interest; **~eszins** m compound interest; **~fuß** m rate of interest; **z~los** adj interest-free; **~satz** m rate of interest

Zipfel ['tsɪpfəl] (-s, -) m corner; (spitz) tip; (Hemdzipfel) tail; (Wurstzipfel) end

zirka ['tsɪrka] adv (round) about

Zirkel ['tsɪrkəl] (-s, -) m circle; (MATH) pair of compasses

Zirkus ['tsɪrkʊs] (-, -se) m circus

zischen ['tsɪʃən] vi to hiss

Zitat [tsi'ta:t] (-(e)s, -e) nt quotation, quote

zitieren [tsi'ti:rən] vt to quote

Zitrone [tsi'tro:nə] f lemon; **~nlimonade** f lemonade; **~nsaft** m lemon juice

zittern ['tsɪtərn] vi to tremble

zivil [tsi'vi:l] adj civil; (Preis) moderate; **Z~** (-s) nt plain clothes pl; (MIL) civilian clothing; **Z~courage** f courage of one's convictions; **Z~dienst** m community service; **Z~isation** [tsivilizatsi'o:n] f civilization; **Z~isationskrankheit** f disease peculiar to civilization; **~i'sieren** vt to civilize

Zivilist [tsivi'lɪst] m civilian

zögern ['tsø:gərn] vi to hesitate

Zoll [tsɔl] (-(e)s, ⁼e) m customs pl; (Abgabe) duty; **~abfertigung** f customs clearance; **~amt** nt customs office; **~beamte(r)** m customs official; **~erklärung** f customs declaration; **z~frei** adj duty-free; **~kontrolle** f customs check; **z~pflichtig** adj liable to duty, dutiable

Zone ['tso:nə] f zone

Zoo [tso:] (-s, -s) m zoo; **~loge** [tsoo'lo:gə] (-n, -n) m zoologist; **~lo'gie** f zoology; **z~'logisch** adj zoological

Zopf [tsɔpf] (-(e)s, ⁼e) m plait; pigtail; **alter ~** antiquated custom

Zorn [tsɔrn] (-(e)s) m anger; **z~ig** adj angry

zottig ['tsɔtıç] adj shaggy

z. T. abk = **zum Teil**

zu [tsu:] präp +dat 1 (örtlich) to; **zum Bahnhof/Arzt gehen** to go to the station/doctor; **zur Schule/Kirche gehen** to go to school/church; **sollen wir zu euch gehen?** shall we go to your place?; **sie sah zu ihm hin** she looked towards him; **zum Fenster herein** through the window; **zu meiner Linken** to od on my left

2 (zeitlich) at; **zu Ostern** at Easter; **bis zum 1. Mai** until May 1st; (nicht später als) by May 1st; **zu meiner Zeit** in my time

3 (Zusatz) with; **Wein zum Essen trinken** to drink wine with one's meal; **sich zu jdm setzen** to sit down beside sb; **setz dich doch zu uns** (come and) sit with us; **Anmerkungen zu etw** notes on sth

4 (Zweck) for; **Wasser zum Waschen** water for washing; **Papier zum Schreiben** paper to write on; **etw zum Geburtstag bekommen** to get sth for one's birthday

5 (Veränderung) into; **zu etw werden** to turn into sth; **jdn zu etw machen** to make sb (into) sth; **zu Asche verbrennen** to burn to ashes

6 (mit Zahlen): **3 zu 2** (SPORT) 3-2; **das Stück zu 2 Mark** at 2 marks each; **zum ersten Mal** for the first time

7: **zu meiner Freude** etc to my joy etc; **zum Glück** luckily; **zu Fuß** on foot; **es ist zum Weinen** it's enough to make you cry

♦ konj to; **etw zu essen** sth to eat; **um besser sehen zu können** in order to see better; **ohne es zu wissen** without knowing it; **noch zu bezahlende Rechnungen** bills that are still to be paid

♦ adv 1 (allzu) too; **zu sehr** too much; **zu viel** too much; **zu wenig** too little

2 (örtlich) toward(s); **er kam auf mich zu** he came up to me

3 (geschlossen) shut, closed; **die Geschäfte haben zu** the shops are closed; **„auf/zu"** (Wasserhahn etc) "on/off"

4 (umg: los): **nur zu!** just keep on!; **mach zu!** hurry up!

zualler- [tsu'|alər] zW: **~erst** [-'|e:rst] adv first of all; **~letzt** [-'letst] adv last of all

Zubehör ['tsu:bəhø:r] (-(e)s, -e) nt accessories pl

zubereiten ['tsu:bəraıtən] vt to prepare

zubilligen ['tsu:bılıgən] vt to grant

zubinden ['tsu:bındən] (unreg) vt to tie up

zubringen ['tsu:brıŋən] (unreg) vt (Zeit) to spend

Zubringer (-s, -) m (Straße) approach od slip road

Zucchini [tsu'ki:ni:] pl (BOT, KOCH) courgette (BRIT), zucchini (US)

Zucht [tsʊxt] (-, -en) f (von Tieren) breeding; (von Pflanzen) cultivation; (Rasse) breed; (Erziehung) raising; (Disziplin) discipline

züchten ['tsʏçtən] vt (Tiere) to breed; (Pflanzen) to cultivate, to grow; **Züchter** (-s, -) m breeder; grower

Zuchthaus nt prison, penitentiary (US)
züchtigen |'tsʏçtɪgən| vt to chastise
Züchtung f (Zuchtart, Sorte: von Tier) breed; (: von Pflanze) variety
zucken |'tsʊkən| vi to jerk, to twitch; (Strahl etc) to flicker ♦ vt (Schultern) to shrug
Zucker |'tsʊkər| (-s, -) m sugar; (MED) diabetes; **~guss** ▲ m icing; **z~krank** adj diabetic; **~krankheit** f (MED) diabetes; **z~n** vt to sugar; **~rohr** nt sugar cane; **~rübe** f sugar beet
Zuckung |'tsʊkʊŋ| f convulsion, spasm; (leicht) twitch
zudecken |'tsu:dɛkən| vt to cover (up)
zudem |tsu'de:m| adv in addition (to this)
zudringlich |'tsu:drɪŋlɪç| adj forward, pushing, obtrusive
zudrücken |'tsu:drʏkən| vt to close; **ein Auge ~** to turn a blind eye
zueinander |tsuǀaɪ'nandər| adv to one other; (in Verbindung) together
zuerkennen |'tsu:ǀɛrkɛnən| (unreg) vt to award; **jdm etw ~** to award sth to sb, to award sb sth
zuerst |tsu'ǀe:rst| adv first; (zu Anfang) at first; **~ einmal** first of all
Zufahrt |'tsu:fa:rt| f approach; **~sstraße** f approach road; (von Autobahn etc) slip road
Zufall |'tsu:fal| m chance; (Ereignis) coincidence; **durch ~** by accident; **so ein ~** what a coincidence; **z~en** vi to close, to shut; (Anteil, Aufgabe) to fall
zufällig |'tsu:fɛlɪç| adj chance ♦ adv by chance; (in Frage) by any chance
Zuflucht |'tsu:flʊxt| f recourse; (Ort) refuge
zufolge |tsu'fɔlgə| präp (+dat od gen) judging by; (laut) according to
zufrieden |tsu'fri:dən| adj content(ed), satisfied; **~ geben** to be content od satisfied (with); **~ stellen** to satisfy
zufrieren |'tsu:fri:rən| (unreg) vi to freeze up od over
zufügen |'tsu:fy:gən| vt to add; (Leid etc): **(jdm) etw ~** to cause (sb) sth
Zufuhr |'tsu:fu:r| (-, -en) f (Herbeibringen) supplying; (MET) influx
Zug |tsu:k| (-(e)s, ⁻e) m (EISENB) train; (Luftzug) draught; (Ziehen) pull(ing); (Gesichtszug) feature; (SCHACH etc) move; (Schriftzug) stroke; (Atemzug) breath; (Charakterzug) trait; (an Zigarette) puff, pull, drag; (Schluck) gulp; (Menschengruppe) procession; (von Vögeln) flight; (MIL) platoon; **etw in vollen Zügen genießen** to enjoy sth to the full
Zu- |'tsu:| zW: **~gabe** f extra; (in Konzert etc) encore; **~gang** m access, approach; **z~gänglich** adj accessible; (Mensch) approachable

zugeben |'tsu:ge:bən| (unreg) vt (beifügen) to add, to throw in; (zugestehen) to admit; (erlauben) to permit
zugehen |'tsu:ge:ən| (unreg) vi (schließen) to shut; **es geht dort seltsam zu** there are strange goings-on there; **auf jdn/etw ~** to walk towards sb/sth; **dem Ende ~** to be finishing
Zugehörigkeit |'tsu:gəhørɪçkaɪt| f: **~ (zu)** membership (of), belonging (to)
Zügel |'tsy:gəl| (-s, -) m rein(s); (fig) curb; **z~n** vt to curb; (Pferd) to rein in
zuge- |'tsu:gə| zW: **Z~ständnis (-ses, -se)** nt concession; **~stehen** (unreg) vt to admit; (Rechte) to concede
Zugführer m (EISENB) guard
zugig |'tsu:gɪç| adj draughty
zügig |'tsy:gɪç| adj speedy, swift
zugreifen |'tsu:graɪfən| (unreg) vi to seize od grab at; (helfen) to help; (beim Essen) to help o.s.
Zugrestaurant nt dining car
zugrunde, zu Grunde |tsu'grʊndə| adv: **~ gehen** to collapse; (Mensch) to perish; **einer Sache** dat **etw ~ legen** to base sth on sth; **einer Sache** dat **~ liegen** to be based on sth; **~ richten** to ruin, to destroy
zugunsten, zu Gunsten |tsu'gʊnstən| präp (+gen od dat) in favour of
zugute |tsu'gu:tə| adv: **jdm etw ~ halten** to concede sth to sb; **jdm ~ kommen** to be of assistance to sb
Zugvogel m migratory bird
zuhalten |'tsu:haltən| (unreg) vt to keep closed ♦ vi: **auf jdn/etw ~** to make a beeline for sb/sth
Zuhälter |'tsu:hɛltər| (-s, -) m pimp
zuhause |tsu'hauzə| adv (österreichisch, schweizerisch) at home
Zuhause |tsu'hauzə| (-) nt home
zuhören |'tsu:hø:rən| vi to listen
Zuhörer (-s, -) m listener
zukleben |'tsu:kle:bən| vt to paste up
zukommen |'tsu:kɔmən| (unreg) vi to come up; **auf jdn ~** to come up to sb; **jdm etw ~ lassen** to give sb sth; **etw auf sich ~ lassen** to wait and see; **jdm ~ (sich gehören)** to be fitting for sb
Zukunft |'tsu:kʊnft| (-, Zukünfte) f future; **zukünftig** |'tsu:kʏnftɪç| adj future ♦ adv in future; **mein zukünftiger Mann** my husband-to-be
Zulage |'tsu:la:gə| f bonus
zulassen |'tsu:lasən| (unreg) vt (hereinlassen) to admit; (erlauben) to permit; (Auto) to license; (umg: nicht öffnen) to (keep) shut
zulässig |'tsu:lɛsɪç| adj permissible, permitted
Zulassung f (amtlich) authorization; (von Kfz) licensing
zulaufen |'tsu:laufən| (unreg) vi (subj:

Mensch): ~ **auf jdn/etw** to run up to sb/sth;
(: *Straße*): ~ **auf** to lead towards
zuleide, zu Leide |tsu'laɪdə| *adv*: **jdm etw**
~ **tun** to hurt *od* harm sb
zuletzt |tsu'lɛtst| *adv* finally, at last
zuliebe |tsu'liːbə| *adv*: **jdm** ~ to please sb
zum |tsʊm| = **zu dem**; ~ **dritten Mal** for the
third time; ~ **Scherz** as a joke; ~ **Trinken** for
drinking
zumachen ['tsuːmaxən] *vt* to shut;
(*Kleidung*) to do up, to fasten ♦ *vi* to shut;
(*umg*) to hurry up
zu- *zW*: ~**mal** |tsu'maːl| *konj* especially (as);
~**meist** |tsu'maɪst| *adv* mostly; ~**mindest**
|tsu'mɪndəst| *adv* at least
zumutbar ['tsuːmuːtbaːr] *adj* reasonable
zumute, zu Mute |tsu'muːtə| *adv*: **wie ist**
ihm ~? how does he feel?
zumuten ['tsuːmuːtən] *vt*: {**jdm**} **etw** ~ to
expect *od* ask sth (of sb)
Zumutung ['tsuːmuːtʊŋ] *f* unreasonable
expectation *od* demand, impertinence
zunächst |tsu'nɛːçst| *adv* first of all; ~
einmal to start with
Zunahme ['tsuːnaːmə] *f* increase
Zuname ['tsuːnaːmə] *m* surname
Zünd- [tsʏnd] *zW*: **z~en** *vi* (*Feuer*) to light, to
ignite; (*Motor*) to fire; (*begeistern*): **bei jdm**
z~en to fire sb (with enthusiasm); **z~end**
adj fiery; ~**er** (**-s**, **-**) *m* fuse; (*MIL*.) detonator;
~**holz** [-ts-] *nt* match; ~**kerze** *f* (*AUT*)
spark(ing) plug; ~**schloss** ▲ *nt* ignition
lock; ~**schlüssel** *m* ignition key; ~**schnur** *f*
fuse wire; ~**stoff** *m* (*fig*) inflammatory stuff;
~**ung** *f* ignition
zunehmen ['tsuːneːmən] (*unreg*) *vi* to
increase, to grow; (*Mensch*) to put on
weight
Zuneigung ['tsuːnaɪɡʊŋ] *f* affection
Zunft |tsʊnft| (**-**, **-̈e**) *f* guild
zünftig ['tsʏnftɪç] *adj* proper, real;
(*Handwerk*) decent
Zunge ['tsʊŋə] *f* tongue
zunichte |tsu'nɪçtə| *adv*: ~ **machen** to ruin,
to destroy; ~ **werden** to come to nothing
zunutze, zu Nutze |tsu'nʊtsə| *adv*: **sich**
dat **etw** ~ **machen** to make use of sth
zuoberst |tsu'joːbərst| *adv* at the top
zupfen ['tsʊpfən] *vt* to pull, to pick, to pluck;
(*Gitarre*) to pluck
zur |tsuːr| = **zu der**
zurate, zu Rate |tsu'raːtə| *adv*: **jdn** ~
ziehen to consult sb
zurechnungsfähig ['tsuːrɛçnʊŋsfɛːɪç] *adj*
responsible, accountable
zurecht- |tsu'rɛçt| *zW*: ~**finden** (*unreg*) *vr* to
find one's way (about); ~**kommen** (*unreg*)
vi to (be able to) cope, to manage; ~**legen**
vt to get ready; (*Ausrede etc*) to have ready;
~**machen** *vt* to prepare ♦ *vr* to get ready;
~**weisen** (*unreg*) *vt* to reprimand

zureden ['tsuːreːdən] *vi*: **jdm** ~ to persuade
od urge sb
zurück |tsu'rʏk| *adv* back; ~**behalten**
(*unreg*) *vt* to keep back; ~**bekommen**
(*unreg*) *vt* to get back; ~**bleiben** (*unreg*) *vi*
(*Mensch*) to remain behind; (*nicht*
nachkommen) to fall behind, to lag;
(*Schaden*) to remain; ~**bringen** (*unreg*) *vt* to
bring back; (*vor Schreck*) to recoil, to start ♦ *vt* to
drive back; ~**finden** (*unreg*) *vi* to find one's
way back; ~**fordern** *vt* to demand back;
~**führen** *vt* to lead back; **etw auf etw** *akk*
~**führen** to trace sth back to sth; ~**geben**
(*unreg*) *vt* to give back; (*antworten*) to retort
with; ~**geblieben** *adj* retarded; ~**gehen**
(*unreg*) *vi* to go back; (*fallen*) to go down, to
fall; (*zeitlich*): ~**gehen** (**auf** +*akk*) to date
back (to); ~**gezogen** *adj* retired,
withdrawn; ~**halten** (*unreg*) *vt* to hold back;
(*Mensch*) to restrain; (*hindern*) to prevent
♦ *vr* (*reserviert sein*) to be reserved; (*im*
Essen) to hold back; ~**haltend** *adj* reserved;
Z~haltung *f* reserve; ~**kehren** *vi* to return;
~**kommen** (*unreg*) *vi* to come back; **auf**
etw *akk* ~**kommen** to return to sth;
~**lassen** (*unreg*) *vt* to leave behind; ~**legen**
vt to put back; (*Geld*) to put by; (*reservieren*)
to keep back; (*Strecke*) to cover; ~**nehmen**
(*unreg*) *vt* to take back; ~**stellen** *vt* to put
back, to replace; (*aufschieben*) to put off, to
postpone; (*Interessen*) to defer; (*Ware*) to
keep; ~**treten** (*unreg*) *vi* to step back; (*vom*
Amt) to retire; **gegenüber etw** *od* **hinter**
etw *dat* ~**treten** to diminish in importance
in view of sth; ~**weisen** (*unreg*) *vt* to turn
down; (*Mensch*) to reject; ~**zahlen** *vt* to
repay, to pay back; ~**ziehen** (*unreg*) *vt* to
pull back; (*Angebot*) to withdraw ♦ *vr* to
retire
Zuruf ['tsuːruːf] *m* shout, cry
zurzeit |tsur'tsaɪt| *adv* at the moment
Zusage ['tsuːzaːɡə] *f* promise; (*Annahme*)
consent; **z~n** *vt* to promise ♦ *vi* to accept;
jdm z~n (*gefallen*) to agree with *od* please
sb
zusammen |tsu'zamən| *adv* together;
Z~arbeit *f* cooperation; ~**arbeiten** *vi* to
cooperate; ~**beißen** (*unreg*) *vt* (*Zähne*) to
clench; ~**brechen** (*unreg*) *vi* to collapse;
(*Mensch auch*) to break down; ~**bringen**
(*unreg*) *vt* to bring *od* get together; (*Geld*) to
get; (*Sätze*) to put together; **Z~bruch** *m*
collapse; ~**fassen** *vt* to summarize;
(*vereinigen*) to unite; **Z~fassung** *f* summary,
résumé; ~**fügen** *vt* to join (together), to
unite; ~**halten** (*unreg*) *vi* to stick together;
Z~hang *m* connection; **im/aus dem**
Z~hang in/out of context; ~**hängen**
(*unreg*) *vi* to be connected *od* linked;
~**kommen** (*unreg*) *vi* to meet, to assemble;

(*sich ereignen*) to occur at once *od* together; **~legen** *vt* to put together; (*stapeln*) to pile up; (*falten*) to fold; (*verbinden*) to combine, to unite; (*Termine, Fest*) to amalgamate; (*Geld*) to collect; **~nehmen** (*unreg*) *vt* to summon up ♦ *vr* to pull o.s. together; **alles ~genommen** all in all; **~passen** *vi* to go well together, to match; **~schließen** (*unreg*) *vt, vr* to join (together); **Z~schluss** ▲ *m* amalgamation; **~schreiben** (*unreg*) *vt* to write as one word; (*Bericht*) to put together; **Z~sein** (**-s**) *nt* get-together; **~setzen** *vt* to put together ♦ *vr* (*Stoff*) to be composed of; (*Menschen*) to get together; **Z~setzung** *f* composition; **~stellen** *vt* to put together; to compile; **Z~stoß** *m* collision; **~stoßen** (*unreg*) *vi* to collide; **~treffen** (*unreg*) *vi* to coincide; (*Menschen*) to meet; **Z~treffen** *nt* coincidence; meeting; **~zählen** *vt* to add up; **~ziehen** (*unreg*) *vt* (*verengern*) to draw together; (*vereinigen*) to bring together; (*addieren*) to add up ♦ *vr* to shrink; (*sich bilden*) to form, to develop

zusätzlich ▲ |'tsu:zɛtslɪç| *adj* additional ♦ *adv* in addition

zuschauen |'tsu:ʃaʊən| *vi* to watch, to look on; **Zuschauer(in)** (**-s, -**) *m(f)* spectator ♦ *pl* (THEAT) audience *sg*

zuschicken |'tsu:ʃɪkən| *vt:* (**jdm etw**) **~** to send *od* to forward (sth to sb)

Zuschlag |'tsu:ʃla:k| *m* extra charge, surcharge; **z~en** (*unreg*) *vt* (*Tür*) to slam; (*Ball*) to hit; (*bei Auktion*) to knock down; (*Steine etc*) to knock into shape ♦ *vi* (*Fenster, Tür*) to shut; (*Mensch*) to hit, to punch; **~karte** *f* (EISENB) surcharge ticket; **z~pflichtig** *adj* subject to surcharge

zuschneiden |'tsu:ʃnaɪdən| (*unreg*) *vt* to cut out; to cut to size

zuschrauben |'tsu:ʃraʊbən| *vt* to screw down *od* up

zuschreiben |'tsu:ʃraɪbən| (*unreg*) *vt* (*fig*) to ascribe, to attribute; (COMM) to credit

Zuschrift |'tsu:ʃrɪft| *f* letter, reply

zuschulden, **zu Schulden** |tsu'ʃʊldən| *adv:* **sich** *dat* **etw ~ kommen lassen** to make o.s. guilty of sth

Zuschuss |'tsu:ʃʊs| *m* subsidy, allowance

zusehen |'tsu:ze:ən| (*unreg*) *vi* to watch; (*dafür sorgen*) to take care; **jdm/etw ~** to watch sb/sth; **~ds** *adv* visibly

zusenden |'tsu:zɛndən| (*unreg*) *vt* to forward, to send on

zusichern |'tsu:zɪçərn| *vt:* **jdm etw ~** to assure sb of sth

zuspielen |'tsu:ʃpi:lən| *vt, vi* to pass

zuspitzen |'tsu:ʃpɪtsən| *vt* to sharpen ♦ *vr* (*Lage*) to become critical

zusprechen |'tsu:ʃprɛçən| (*unreg*) *vt*

(*zuerkennen*) to award ♦ *vi* to speak; **jdm etw ~** to award sb sth *od* sth to sb; **jdm Trost ~** to comfort sb; **dem Essen/Alkohol ~** to eat/drink a lot

Zustand |'tsu:ʃtant| *m* state, condition

zustande, **zu Stande** |tsu'ʃtandə| *adv:* **~ bringen** to bring about; **~ kommen** to come about

zuständig |'tsu:ʃtɛndɪç| *adj* responsible; **Z~keit** *f* competence, responsibility

zustehen |'tsu:ʃte:ən| (*unreg*) *vi:* **jdm ~** to be sb's right

zustellen |'tsu:ʃtɛlən| *vt* (*verstellen*) to block; (*Post etc*) to send

Zustellung *f* delivery

zustimmen |'tsu:ʃtɪmən| *vi* to agree

Zustimmung *f* agreement, consent

zustoßen |'tsu:ʃto:sən| (*unreg*) *vi* (*fig*) to happen

zutage, **zu Tage** |tsu'ta:gə| *adv:* **~ bringen** to bring to light; **~ treten** to come to light

Zutaten |'tsu:ta:tən| *pl* ingredients

zuteilen |'tsu:taɪlən| *vt* (*Arbeit, Rolle*) to designate, assign; (*Aktien, Wohnung*) to allocate

zutiefst |tsu'ti:fst| *adv* deeply

zutragen |'tsu:tra:gən| (*unreg*) *vt* to bring; (*Klatsch*) to tell ♦ *vr* to happen

zutrau- |'tsu:trau| *zW:* **Z~en** (**-s**) *nt:* **Z~en** (**zu**) trust (in); **~en** *vt:* **jdm etw ~en** to credit sb with sth; **~lich** *adj* trusting, friendly

zutreffen |'tsu:trɛfən| (*unreg*) *vi* to be correct; to apply; **~d** *adj* (*richtig*) accurate; **Z~des bitte unterstreichen** please underline where applicable

Zutritt |'tsu:trɪt| *m* access, admittance

Zutun |'tsu:tu:n| (**-s**) *nt* assistance

zuverlässig |'tsu:fɛrlɛsɪç| *adj* reliable; **Z~keit** *f* reliability

zuversichtlich |'tsu:fɛrzɪçtlɪç| *adj* confident

zuvor |tsu'fo:r| *adv* before, previously; **~kommen** (*unreg*) *vi* +*dat* to anticipate; **jdm ~kommen** to beat sb to it; **~kommend** *adj* obliging, courteous

Zuwachs |'tsu:vaks| (**-es**) *m* increase, growth; (*umg*) addition; **z~en** (*unreg*) *vi* to become overgrown; (*Wunde*) to heal (up)

zuwege, **zu Wege** |tsu've:gə| *adv:* **etw ~ bringen** to accomplish sth

zuweilen |tsu'vaɪlən| *adv* at times, now and then

zuweisen |'tsu:vaɪzən| (*unreg*) *vt* to assign, to allocate

zuwenden |'tsu:vɛndən| (*unreg*) *vt* (+*dat*) to turn (towards) ♦ *vr:* **sich jdm/etw ~** to devote o.s. to sb/sth; to turn to sb/sth

zuwider |tsu'vi:dər| *adv:* **etw ist jdm ~** loathes sth, sb finds sth repugnant; **~handeln** *vi:* **einer Sache** *dat* **~handeln** to

act contrary to sth; **einem Gesetz
~handeln** to contravene a law
zuziehen ['tsuːtsiːən] (*unreg*) *vt* (*schließen:
Vorhang*) to draw, to close; (*herbeirufen:
Experten*) to call in ♦ *vi* to move in, to come;
sich *dat* **etw ~** (*Krankheit*) to catch sth;
(*Zorn*) to incur sth
zuzüglich ['tsuːtsyːklɪç] *präp +gen* plus, with
the addition of
Zwang [tsvaŋ] (-(e)s, ⸚e) *m* compulsion,
coercion
zwängen ['tsvɛŋən] *vt, vr* to squeeze
zwanglos *adj* informal
Zwangs- *zW:* **~arbeit** *f* forced labour;
(*Strafe*) hard labour; **~lage** *f* predicament,
tight corner; **z~läufig** *adj* necessary,
inevitable
zwanzig ['tsvantsɪç] *num* twenty
zwar [tsvaːr] *adv* to be sure, indeed; **das ist ~
..., aber ...** that may be ... but ...; **und ~
am Sonntag** on Sunday to be precise; **und
~ so schnell, dass ...** in fact so quickly
that ...
Zweck [tsvɛk] (-(e)s, -e) *m* purpose, aim; **es
hat keinen ~** there's no point; **z~dienlich**
adj practical; expedient
Zwecke *f* hobnail; (*Heftzwecke*) drawing pin,
thumbtack (*US*)
Zweck- *zW:* **z~los** *adj* pointless; **z~mäßig**
adj suitable, appropriate; **z~s** *präp +gen* for
the purpose of
zwei [tsvaɪ] *num* two; **Z~bettzimmer** *nt*
twin room; **~deutig** *adj* ambiguous;
(*unanständig*) suggestive; **~erlei** *adj:* **~erlei
Stoff** two different kinds of material; **~erlei
Meinung** of differing opinions; **~fach** *adj*
double
Zweifel ['tsvaɪfəl] (-s, -) *m* doubt; **z~haft** *adj*
doubtful, dubious; **z~los** *adj* doubtless; **z~n**
vi: (**an etw** *dat*) **z~n** to doubt (sth)
Zweig [tsvaɪk] (-(e)s, -e) *m* branch; **~stelle** *f*
branch (office)
zwei- *zW:* **~hundert** *num* two hundred;
Z~kampf *m* duel; **~mal** *adv* twice;
~sprachig *adj* bilingual; **~spurig** *adj* (*AUT*)
two-lane; **~stimmig** *adj* for two voices
zweit [tsvaɪt] *adv:* **zu ~** together; (*bei
mehreren Paaren*) in twos
zweitbeste(r, s) *adj* second best

zweite(r, s) *adj* second
zweiteilig ['tsvaɪtaɪlɪç] *adj* (*Gruppe*) two-
piece; (*Fernsehfilm*) two-part; (*Kleidung*) two-
piece
zweit- *zW:* **~ens** *adv* secondly; **~größte(r, s)**
adj second largest; **~klassig** *adj* second-
class; **~letzte(r, s)** *adj* last but one,
penultimate; **~rangig** *adj* second-rate
Zwerchfell ['tsvɛrçfɛl] *nt* diaphragm
Zwerg [tsvɛrk] (-(e)s, -e) *m* dwarf
Zwetsch(g)e ['tsvɛtʃ(g)ə] *f* plum
Zwieback ['tsviːbak] (-(e)s, -e) *m* rusk
Zwiebel ['tsviːbəl] (-, -n) *f* onion;
(*Blumenzwiebel*) bulb
Zwie- ['tsviː] *zW:* **z~lichtig** *adj* shady,
dubious; **z~spältig** *adj* (*Gefühle*) conflicting;
(*Charakter*) contradictory; **~tracht** *f* discord,
dissension
Zwilling ['tsvɪlɪŋ] (-s, -e) *m* twin; **~e** *pl*
(*ASTROL*) Gemini
zwingen ['tsvɪŋən] (*unreg*) *vt* to force; **~d**
adj (*Grund etc*) compelling
zwinkern ['tsvɪŋkərn] *vi* to blink;
(*absichtlich*) to wink
Zwirn [tsvɪrn] (-(e)s, -e) *m* thread
zwischen ['tsvɪʃən] *präp* (+*akk od dat*)
between; **Z~bemerkung** *f* (incidental)
remark; **Z~ding** *nt* cross; **~durch** *adv* in
between; (*räumlich*) here and there;
Z~ergebnis *nt* intermediate result; **Z~fall**
m incident; **Z~frage** *f* question; **Z~handel**
m middlemen *pl*; middleman's trade;
Z~landung *f* (*AVIAT*) stopover;
~menschlich *adj* interpersonal; **Z~raum** *m*
space; **Z~ruf** *m* interjection; **Z~stecker** *m*
adaptor (plug); **Z~zeit** *f* interval; **in der
Z~zeit** in the interim, meanwhile
zwitschern ['tsvɪtʃərn] *vt, vi* to twitter, to
chirp
zwo [tsvoː] *num* two
zwölf [tsvœlf] *num* twelve
Zyklus ['tsyːklʊs] (-, Zyklen) *m* cycle
Zylinder [tsiˈlɪndər] (-s, -) *m* cylinder; (*Hut*)
top hat
Zyniker ['tsyːnikər] (-s, -) *m* cynic
zynisch ['tsyːnɪʃ] *adj* cynical
Zypern ['tsyːpərn] *nt* Cyprus
Zyste ['tsystə] *f* cyst
zzt. *abk* = **zurzeit**

ENGLISH – GERMAN
ENGLISCH – DEUTSCH

A, a

A [eɪ] n (MUS) A nt; **~ road** Hauptverkehrsstraße f

a [eɪ, ə] (before vowel or silent h: an) indef art
1 ein; eine; **a woman** eine Frau; **a book** ein Buch; **an eagle** ein Adler; **she's a doctor** sie ist Ärztin
2 (instead of the number "one") ein, eine; **a year ago** vor einem Jahr; **a hundred/thousand** etc **pounds** (ein)hundert/(ein)tausend etc Pfund
3 (in expressing ratios, prices etc) pro; **3 a day/week** 3 pro Tag/Woche, 3 am Tag/in der Woche; **10 km an hour** 10 km pro Stunde/in der Stunde

A.A. n abbr = **Alcoholics Anonymous**; (BRIT) = **Automobile Association**
A.A.A. (US) n abbr = **American Automobile Association**
aback [ə'bæk] adv: **to be taken ~** verblüfft sein
abandon [ə'bændən] vt (give up) aufgeben; (desert) verlassen ♦ n Hingabe f
abate [ə'beɪt] vi nachlassen, sich legen
abattoir ['æbətwɑːᵊ] (BRIT) n Schlachthaus nt
abbey ['æbɪ] n Abtei f
abbot ['æbət] n Abt m
abbreviate [ə'briːvɪeɪt] vt abkürzen; **abbreviation** [əbriːvɪ'eɪʃən] n Abkürzung f
abdicate ['æbdɪkeɪt] vt aufgeben ♦ vi abdanken
abdomen ['æbdəmən] n Unterleib m
abduct [æb'dʌkt] vt entführen
aberration [æbə'reɪʃən] n (geistige) Verwirrung f
abet [ə'bet] vt see **aid**
abeyance [ə'beɪəns] n: **in ~** in der Schwebe; (disuse) außer Kraft
abide [ə'baɪd] vt vertragen; leiden; **~ by** vt sich halten an +acc
ability [ə'bɪlɪtɪ] n (power) Fähigkeit f; (skill) Geschicklichkeit f
abject ['æbdʒekt] adj (liar) übel; (poverty) größte(r, s); (apology) zerknirscht
ablaze [ə'bleɪz] adj in Flammen
able ['eɪbl] adj geschickt, fähig; **to be ~ to do sth** etw tun können; **~-bodied** ['eɪbl'bɒdɪd] adj kräftig; (seaman) Voll-; **ably** ['eɪblɪ] adv geschickt

abnormal [æb'nɔːməl] adj regelwidrig, abnorm
aboard [ə'bɔːd] adv, prep an Bord +gen
abode [ə'bəʊd] n: **of no fixed ~** ohne festen Wohnsitz
abolish [ə'bɒlɪʃ] vt abschaffen; **abolition** [æbə'lɪʃən] n Abschaffung f
abominable [ə'bɒmɪnəbl] adj scheußlich
aborigine [æbə'rɪdʒɪnɪ] n Ureinwohner m
abort [ə'bɔːt] vt abtreiben; fehlgebären; **~ion** [ə'bɔːʃən] n Abtreibung f; (miscarriage) Fehlgeburt f; **~ive** adj misslungen
abound [ə'baʊnd] vi im Überfluss vorhanden sein; **to ~ in** Überfluss haben an +dat

about [ə'baʊt] adv 1 (approximately) etwa, ungefähr; **a hundred/thousand** etc etwa hundert/tausend etc; **at about 2 o'clock** etwa um 2 Uhr; **I've just about finished** ich bin gerade fertig
2 (referring to place) herum, umher; **to leave things lying about** Sachen herumliegen lassen; **to run/walk** etc **about** herumrennen/gehen etc
3: **to be about to do sth** im Begriff sein, etw zu tun; **he was about to go to bed** er wollte gerade ins Bett gehen
♦ prep 1 (relating to) über +acc; **a book about London** ein Buch über London; **what is it about?** worum geht es?; (book etc) wovon handelt es?; **we talked about it** wir haben darüber geredet; **what or how about doing this?** wollen wir das machen?
2 (referring to place) um (... herum); **to walk about the town** in der Stadt herumgehen; **her clothes were scattered about the room** ihre Kleider waren über das ganze Zimmer verstreut

about-turn [ə'baʊt'tɜːn] n Kehrtwendung f
above [ə'bʌv] adv oben ♦ prep über; **~ all** vor allem; **~ board** adj offen, ehrlich
abrasive [ə'breɪzɪv] adj Abschleif-; (personality) zermürbend, aufreibend
abreast [ə'brest] adv nebeneinander; **to keep ~ of** Schritt halten mit
abroad [ə'brɔːd] adv (be) im Ausland; (go) ins Ausland

abrupt |ə'brʌpt| adj (sudden) abrupt, jäh; (curt) schroff; **~ly** adv abrupt

abscess |'æbsɪs| n Geschwür nt

abscond |əb'skɔnd| vi flüchten, sich davonmachen

abseil |'æbseɪl| vi (also: ~ **down**) sich abseilen

absence |'æbsəns| n Abwesenheit f

absent |'æbsənt| adj abwesend, nicht da; (lost in thought) geistesabwesend; **~-minded** adj zerstreut

absolute |'æbsəlu:t| adj absolut; (power) unumschränkt; (rubbish) vollkommen, rein; **~ly** |æbsə'lu:tlɪ| adv absolut, vollkommen; **~ly!** ganz bestimmt!

absolve |əb'zɔlv| vt entbinden; freisprechen

absorb |əb'zɔ:b| vt aufsaugen, absorbieren; (fig) ganz in Anspruch nehmen, fesseln; **to be ~ed in a book** in ein Buch vertieft sein; **~ent cotton** (US) n Verbandwatte f; **~ing** adj aufsaugend; (fig) packend; **absorption** |əb'sɔ:pʃən| n Aufsaugung f, Absorption f; (fig) Versunkenheit f

abstain |əb'steɪn| vi (in vote) sich enthalten; **to ~ from** (keep from) sich enthalten +gen

abstemious |əb'sti:mɪəs| adj enthaltsam

abstinence |'æbstɪnəns| n Enthaltsamkeit f

abstract |'æbstrækt| adj abstrakt

absurd |əb'sə:d| adj absurd

abundance |ə'bʌndəns| n: ~ **(of)** Überfluss m (an +dat); **abundant** |ə'bʌndənt| adj reichlich

abuse |n ə'bju:s, vb ə'bju:z| n (rude language) Beschimpfung f; (ill usage) Missbrauch m; (bad practice) (Amts)missbrauch m ♦ vt (misuse) missbrauchen; **abusive** |ə'bju:sɪv| adj beleidigend, Schimpf-

abysmal |ə'bɪzməl| adj scheußlich; (ignorance) bodenlos

abyss |ə'bɪs| n Abgrund m

AC abbr (= alternating current) Wechselstrom m

academic |ækə'demɪk| adj akademisch; (theoretical) theoretisch ♦ n Akademiker(in) m(f)

academy |ə'kædəmɪ| n (school) Hochschule f; (society) Akademie f

accelerate |æk'seləreɪt| vi schneller werden; (AUT) Gas geben ♦ vt beschleunigen; **acceleration** |æksələ'reɪʃən| n Beschleunigung f; **accelerator** |æk'seləreɪtə³| n Gas(pedal) nt

accent |'æksent| n Akzent m, Tonfall m; (mark) Akzent m; (stress) Betonung f

accept |ək'sept| vt (take) annehmen; (agree to) akzeptieren; **~able** adj annehmbar; **~ance** n Annahme f

access |'ækses| n Zugang m; **~ible** |æk'sesəbl| adj (easy to approach) zugänglich; (within reach) (leicht) erreichbar

accessory |æk'sesərɪ| n Zubehörteil nt; **toilet accessories** Toilettenartikel pl

accident |'æksɪdənt| n Unfall m; (coincidence) Zufall m; **by ~** zufällig; **~al** |æksɪ'dentl| adj unbeabsichtigt; **~ally** |æksɪ'dentəlɪ| adv zufällig; **~ insurance** n Unfallversicherung f; **~-prone** adj: **to be ~-prone** zu Unfällen neigen

acclaim |ə'kleɪm| vt zujubeln +dat ♦ n Beifall m

acclimatize |ə'klaɪmətaɪz| vt: **to become ~d (to)** sich gewöhnen (an +acc), sich akklimatisieren (in +dat)

accommodate |ə'kɔmədeɪt| vt unterbringen; (hold) Platz haben für; (oblige) (aus)helfen +dat

accommodating |ə'kɔmədeɪtɪŋ| adj entgegenkommend

accommodation |əkɔmə'deɪʃən| (US **~s**) n Unterkunft f

accompany |ə'kʌmpənɪ| vt begleiten

accomplice |ə'kʌmplɪs| n Helfershelfer m, Komplize m

accomplish |ə'kʌmplɪʃ| vt (fulfil) durchführen; (finish) vollenden; (aim) erreichen; **~ed** adj vollendet, ausgezeichnet; **~ment** n (skill) Fähigkeit f; (completion) Vollendung f; (feat) Leistung f

accord |ə'kɔ:d| n Übereinstimmung f ♦ vt gewähren; **of one's own ~** freiwillig; **~ing to** nach, laut +gen; **~ance** n: **in ~ance with** in Übereinstimmung mit; **~ingly** adv danach, dementsprechend

accordion |ə'kɔ:dɪən| n Akkordeon nt

accost |ə'kɔst| vt ansprechen

account |ə'kaunt| n (bill) Rechnung f; (narrative) Bericht m; (report) (in bank) Konto nt; (importance) Geltung f; **~s** npl (FIN) Bücher pl; **on ~** auf Rechnung; **of no ~** ohne Bedeutung; **on no ~** keinesfalls; **on ~ of** wegen; **to take into ~** berücksichtigen; **~ for** vt fus (expenditure) Rechenschaft ablegen für; **how do you ~ for that?** wie erklären Sie (sich) das?; **~able** adj verantwortlich; **~ancy** |ə'kauntənsɪ| n Buchhaltung f; **~ant** |ə'kauntənt| n Wirtschaftsprüfer(in) m(f); **~ number** n Kontonummer f

accumulate |ə'kju:mjuleɪt| vt ansammeln ♦ vi sich ansammeln

accuracy |'ækjurəsɪ| n Genauigkeit f

accurate |'ækjurɪt| adj genau; **~ly** adv genau, richtig

accusation |ækju'zeɪʃən| n Anklage f, Beschuldigung f

accuse |ə'kju:z| vt anklagen, beschuldigen; **~d** n Angeklagte(r) f(m)

accustom |ə'kʌstəm| vt: **to ~ sb (to sth)** jdn (an etw acc) gewöhnen; **~ed** adj gewohnt

ace |eɪs| n Ass nt; (inf) Ass nt, Kanone f

ache |eɪk| n Schmerz m ♦ vi (be sore) schmerzen, wehtun

achieve |ə'tʃiːv| vt zustande or zu Stande bringen; (aim) erreichen; **~ment** n Leistung f; (act) Erreichen nt

acid ['æsɪd] n Säure f ♦ adj sauer, scharf; ~ **rain** n saure(r) Regen m

acknowledge |ək'nɔlɪdʒ| vt (receipt) bestätigen; (admit) zugeben; **~ment** n Anerkennung f; (letter) Empfangsbestätigung f

acne ['æknɪ] n Akne f

acorn ['eɪkɔːn] n Eichel f

acoustic |ə'kuːstɪk| adj akustisch; **~s** npl Akustik f

acquaint |ə'kweɪnt| vt vertraut machen; **to be ~ed with sb** mit jdm bekannt sein; **~ance** (person) Bekannte(r) f(m); (knowledge) Kenntnis f

acquire |ə'kwaɪəʳ| vt erwerben; **acquisition** |ækwɪ'zɪʃən| n Errungenschaft f; (act) Erwerb m

acquit |ə'kwɪt| vt (free) freisprechen; **to ~ o.s. well** sich bewähren; **~tal** n Freispruch m

acre ['eɪkəʳ] n Morgen m

acrid ['ækrɪd] adj (smell, taste) bitter; (smoke) beißend

acrobat ['ækrəbæt] n Akrobat m

across |ə'krɔs| prep über +acc ♦ adv hinüber, herüber; **he lives ~ the river** er wohnt auf der anderen Seite des Flusses; **ten metres ~** zehn Meter breit; **he lives ~ from us** er wohnt uns gegenüber; **to run/swim ~** hinüberlaufen/schwimmen

acrylic |ə'krɪlɪk| adj Acryl-

act |ækt| n (deed) Tat f; (JUR) Gesetz nt; (THEAT) Akt m; (: turn) Nummer f ♦ vi (take action) handeln; (behave) sich verhalten; (pretend) vorgeben; (THEAT) spielen ♦ vt (in play) spielen; **to ~ as** fungieren als; **~ing** adj stellvertretend ♦ n Schauspielkunst f; (performance) Aufführung f

action ['ækʃən] n (deed) Tat f; Handlung f; (motion) Bewegung f; (way of working) Funktionieren nt; (battle) Einsatz m, Gefecht nt; (lawsuit) Klage f, Prozess m; **out of ~** (person) nicht einsatzfähig; (thing) außer Betrieb; **to take ~** etwas unternehmen; **~ replay** n (TV) Wiederholung f

activate ['æktɪveɪt] vt (mechanism) betätigen; (CHEM, PHYS) aktivieren

active ['æktɪv] adj (brisk) rege, tatkräftig; (working) aktiv; (GRAM) aktiv, Tätigkeits-; **~ly** adv aktiv; (dislike) offen

activity |æk'tɪvɪtɪ| n Aktivität f; (doings) Unternehmungen pl; (occupation) Tätigkeit f; **~ holiday** n Aktivurlaub m

actor ['æktəʳ] n Schauspieler m

actress ['æktrɪs] n Schauspielerin f

actual ['æktjuəl] adj wirklich; **~ly** adv tatsächlich; **~ly no** eigentlich nicht

acumen ['ækjumən] n Scharfsinn m

acute |ə'kjuːt| adj (severe) heftig, akut; (keen) scharfsinnig

ad |æd| n abbr = **advertisement**

A.D. adv abbr (= Anno Domini) n. Chr.

adamant ['ædəmənt] adj eisern; hartnäckig

adapt |ə'dæpt| vt anpassen ♦ vi: **to ~ (to)** sich anpassen (an +acc); **~able** adj anpassungsfähig; **~ation** |ædæp'teɪʃən| n (THEAT etc) Bearbeitung f; (adjustment) Anpassung f; **~er, ~or** n (ELEC) Zwischenstecker m

add |æd| vt (join) hinzufügen; (numbers: also: ~ **up**) addieren; **~ up** vi (make sense) stimmen; **~ up to** vt fus ausmachen

adder ['ædəʳ] n Kreuzotter f, Natter f

addict ['ædɪkt] n Süchtige(r) f(m); **~ed** |ə'dɪktɪd| adj: **~ed to** -süchtig; **~ion** |ə'dɪkʃən| n Sucht f; **~ive** |ə'dɪktɪv| adj: **to be ~ive** süchtig machen

addition |ə'dɪʃən| n Anhang m, Addition f; (MATH) Addition f, Zusammenzählen nt; **in ~** zusätzlich, außerdem; **~al** adj zusätzlich, weiter

additive ['ædɪtɪv] n Zusatz m

address |ə'dres| n Adresse f; (speech) Ansprache f ♦ vt (letter) adressieren; (speak to) ansprechen; (make speech to) eine Ansprache halten an +acc

adept ['ædept] adj geschickt; **to be ~ at** gut sein in +dat

adequate ['ædɪkwɪt] adj angemessen

adhere |əd'hɪəʳ| vi: **to ~ to** haften an +dat; (fig) festhalten an +dat

adhesive |əd'hiːzɪv| adj klebend; Kleb(e)- ♦ n Klebstoff m; **~ tape** n (BRIT) Klebestreifen m; (US) Heftpflaster nt

ad hoc |æd'hɔk| adj (decision, committee) Ad-hoc- ♦ adv ad hoc

adjacent |ə'dʒeɪsənt| adj benachbart; **~ to** angrenzend an +acc

adjective ['ædʒektɪv] n Adjektiv nt, Eigenschaftswort nt

adjoining |ə'dʒɔɪnɪŋ| adj benachbart, Neben-

adjourn |ə'dʒɜːn| vt vertagen ♦ vi abbrechen

adjudicate |ə'dʒuːdɪkeɪt| vi entscheiden, ein Urteil fällen

adjust |ə'dʒʌst| vt (alter) anpassen; (put right) regulieren, richtig stellen ♦ vi sich anpassen; **~able** adj verstellbar

ad-lib |æd'lɪb| vt, vi improvisieren ♦ adv: **ad lib** aus dem Stegreif

administer |əd'mɪnɪstəʳ| vt (manage) verwalten; (dispense) ausüben; (justice) sprechen; (medicine) geben; **administration** |ədmɪnɪs'treɪʃən| n Verwaltung f; (POL) Regierung f; **administrative** |əd'mɪnɪstrətɪv| adj Verwaltungs-; **administrator** |əd'mɪnɪstreɪtəʳ| n Verwaltungsbeamte(r) f(m)

Admiralty ['ædmərəltɪ] (BRIT) n Admiralität f

admiration [ædmə'reɪʃən] n Bewunderung f
admire [əd'maɪər] vt (respect) bewundern; (love) verehren; **~r** n Bewunderer m
admission [əd'mɪʃən] n (entrance) Einlass m; (fee) Eintritt(spreis) m; (confession) Geständnis nt; **~ charge** n Eintritt(spreis) m
admit [əd'mɪt] vt (let in) einlassen; (confess) gestehen; (accept) anerkennen; **~tance** n Zulassung f; **~tedly** adv zugegebenermaßen
admonish [əd'mɒnɪʃ] vt ermahnen
ad nauseam [æd'nɔːsɪæm] adv (repeat, talk) endlos
ado [ə'duː] n: **without more ~** ohne weitere Umstände
adolescence [ædəu'lesns] n Jugendalter nt; **adolescent** [ædəu'lesnt] adj jugendlich ♦ n Jugendliche(r) f(m)
adopt [ə'dɒpt] vt (child) adoptieren; (idea) übernehmen; **~ion** [ə'dɒpʃən] n Adoption f; Übernahme f
adore [ə'dɔːr] vt anbeten; verehren
adorn [ə'dɔːn] vt schmücken
Adriatic [eɪdrɪ'ætɪk] n: **the ~ (Sea)** die Adria
adrift [ə'drɪft] adv Wind und Wellen preisgegeben
adult ['ædʌlt] n Erwachsene(r) f(m)
adultery [ə'dʌltərɪ] n Ehebruch m
advance [əd'vɑːns] n (progress) Vorrücken nt; (money) Vorschuss m ♦ vt (move forward) vorrücken; (money) vorschießen; (argument) vorbringen ♦ vi vorwärts gehen; **in ~** im Voraus; **~ booking** n Vorverkauf m; **~d** adj (ahead) vorgerückt; (modern) fortgeschritten; (study) für Fortgeschrittene
advantage [əd'vɑːntɪdʒ] n Vorteil m; **to have an ~ over sb** jdm gegenüber im Vorteil sein; **to take ~ of** (misuse) ausnutzen; (profit from) Nutzen ziehen aus; **~ous** [ædvən'teɪdʒəs] adj vorteilhaft
advent ['ædvənt] n Ankunft f; **A~** Advent m
adventure [əd'ventʃər] n Abenteuer nt; **adventurous** adj abenteuerlich, waghalsig
adverb ['ædvɜːb] n Adverb nt, Umstandswort nt
adversary ['ædvəsərɪ] n Gegner m
adverse ['ædvɜːs] adj widrig; **adversity** [əd'vɜːsɪtɪ] n Widrigkeit f, Missgeschick nt
advert ['ædvɜːt] n Anzeige f; **~ise** ['ædvətaɪz] vt werben für ♦ vi annoncieren; **to ~ise for sth** etw (per Anzeige) suchen; **~isement** [əd'vɜːtɪsmənt] n Anzeige f, Inserat nt; **~iser** n (in newspaper etc) Inserent m; **~ising** n Werbung f
advice [əd'vaɪs] n Rat(schlag) m
advisable [əd'vaɪzəbl] adj ratsam
advise [əd'vaɪz] vt: **to ~ (sb)** (jdm) raten; **~dly** [əd'vaɪzɪdlɪ] adv (deliberately) bewusst; **~r** n Berater m; **advisory** [əd'vaɪzərɪ] adj beratend, Beratungs-
advocate [vb 'ædvəkeɪt, n 'ædvəkət] vt vertreten ♦ n Befürworter(in) f(m)

Aegean [iː'dʒiːən] n: **the ~ (Sea)** die Ägäis
aerial ['ɛərɪəl] n Antenne f ♦ adj Luft-
aerobics [ɛə'rəubɪks] n Aerobic nt
aerodynamic ['ɛərəudaɪ'næmɪk] adj aerodynamisch
aeroplane ['ɛərəpleɪn] n Flugzeug nt
aerosol ['ɛərəsɔl] n Aerosol nt; Sprühdose f
aesthetic [iːs'θetɪk] adj ästhetisch
afar [ə'fɑːr] adv: **from ~** aus der Ferne
affable ['æfəbl] adj umgänglich
affair [ə'fɛər] n (concern) Angelegenheit f; (event) Ereignis nt; (love ~) Verhältnis nt; **~s** npl (business) Geschäfte pl
affect [ə'fekt] vt (influence) (ein)wirken auf +acc; (move deeply) bewegen; **this change doesn't ~ us** diese Änderung betrifft uns nicht; **~ed** adj affektiert, gekünstelt
affection [ə'fekʃən] n Zuneigung f; **~ate** adj liebevoll
affiliated [ə'fɪlɪeɪtɪd] adj angeschlossen
affinity [ə'fɪnɪtɪ] n (attraction) gegenseitige Anziehung f; (relationship) Verwandtschaft f
affirmative [ə'fɜːmətɪv] adj bestätigend
afflict [ə'flɪkt] vt quälen, heimsuchen
affluence ['æfluəns] n (wealth) Wohlstand m; **affluent** adj wohlhabend, Wohlstands-
afford [ə'fɔːd] vt sich dat leisten; (yield) bieten, einbringen
afield [ə'fiːld] adv: **far ~** weit fort
afloat [ə'fləut] adj: **to be ~** schwimmen
afoot [ə'fut] adv im Gang
afraid [ə'freɪd] adj ängstlich; **to be ~ of** Angst haben vor +dat; **to be ~ to do sth** sich scheuen, etw zu tun; **I am ~ I have ...** ich habe leider ...; **I'm ~ so/not** leider/leider nicht; **I am ~ that ...** ich fürchte(, dass) ...
afresh [ə'freʃ] adv von neuem
Africa ['æfrɪkə] n Afrika nt; **~n** adj afrikanisch ♦ n Afrikaner(in) f(m)
after ['ɑːftər] prep nach; (following, seeking) hinter ... dat ... her; (in imitation) nach, im Stil von ♦ adv: **soon ~** bald danach ♦ conj nachdem; **what are you ~?** was wollen Sie?; **~ he left** nachdem er gegangen war; **~ you!** nach Ihnen!; **~ all** letzten Endes; **~ having shaved** als er sich rasiert hatte; **~effects** npl Nachwirkungen pl; **~math** n Auswirkungen pl; **~noon** n Nachmittag m; **~s** (inf) n (dessert) Nachtisch m; **~-sales service** (BRIT) n Kundendienst m; **~shave (lotion)** n Rasierwasser nt; **~sun** n Aftersunlotion f; **~thought** n nachträgliche(r) Einfall m; **~wards** adv danach, nachher
again [ə'gen] adv wieder, noch einmal; (besides) außerdem, ferner; **~ and ~** immer wieder
against [ə'genst] prep gegen
age [eɪdʒ] n (of person) Alter nt; (in history) Zeitalter nt ♦ vi altern, alt werden ♦ vt älter machen; **to come of ~** mündig werden; **20**

years of ~ 20 Jahre alt; **it's been** ~**s since**
... es ist ewig her, seit ...
aged[1] |eɪdʒd| adj ... Jahre alt, -jährig
aged[2] |eɪdʒɪd| adj (elderly) betagt ♦ npl: **the**
~ die Alten pl
age group n Altersgruppe f
age limit n Altersgrenze f
agency |'eɪdʒənsɪ| n Agentur f; Vermittlung
f; (CHEM) Wirkung f; **through** or **by the** ~
of ... mithilfe or mit Hilfe von ...
agenda |ə'dʒɛndə| n Tagesordnung f
agent |'eɪdʒənt| n (COMM) Vertreter m; (spy)
Agent m
aggravate |'ægrəveɪt| vt (make worse)
verschlimmern; (irritate) reizen
aggregate |'ægrɪgɪt| n Summe f
aggression |ə'greʃən| n Aggression f;
aggressive |ə'gresɪv| adj aggressiv
aghast |ə'gɑːst| adj entsetzt
agile |'ædʒaɪl| adj flink, agil; (mind) rege
agitate |'ædʒɪteɪt| vt rütteln; **to ~ for** sich
stark machen für
AGM n abbr (= annual general meeting) JHV f
ago |ə'gəu| adv: **two days** ~ vor zwei Tagen;
not long ~ vor kurzem; **it's so long** ~ es ist
schon so lange her
agog |ə'gɒg| adj gespannt
agonizing |'ægənaɪzɪŋ| adj quälend
agony |'ægənɪ| n Qual f; **to be in** ~ Qualen
leiden
agree |ə'griː| vt (date) vereinbaren ♦ vi (have
same opinion, correspond) übereinstimmen;
(consent) zustimmen; (be in harmony) sich
vertragen; **to ~ to sth** einer Sache dat
zustimmen; **to ~ that** ... (admit) zugeben,
dass ...; **to ~ to do sth** sich bereit erklären,
etw zu tun; **garlic doesn't ~ with me**
Knoblauch vertrage ich nicht; **I ~**
einverstanden, ich stimme zu; **to ~ on sth**
sich auf etw acc einigen; ~**able** adj
(pleasing) liebenswürdig; (willing to consent)
einverstanden; ~**d** adj vereinbart; ~**ment** n
(~ing) Übereinstimmung f; (contract)
Vereinbarung f, Vertrag m; **to be in** ~**ment**
übereinstimmen
agricultural |ægrɪ'kʌltʃərəl| adj
landwirtschaftlich, Landwirtschafts-
agriculture |'ægrɪkʌltʃə'| n Landwirtschaft f
aground |ə'graund| adv: **to run** ~ auf Grund
laufen
ahead |ə'hɛd| adv vorwärts; **to be** ~ voraus
sein; ~ **of time** der Zeit voraus; **go right** or
straight ~ gehen Sie geradeaus; fahren Sie
geradeaus
aid |eɪd| n (assistance) Hilfe f, Unterstützung f;
(person) Hilfe f; (thing) Hilfsmittel nt ♦ vt
unterstützen, helfen +dat; **in ~ of** zugunsten
or zu Gunsten +gen; **to ~ and abet sb** jdm
Beihilfe leisten
aide |eɪd| n (person) Gehilfe m; (MIL) Adjutant
m

AIDS |eɪdz| n abbr (= acquired immune
deficiency syndrome) Aids nt; ~~**related**
aidsbedingt
ailing |'eɪlɪŋ| adj kränkelnd
ailment |'eɪlmənt| n Leiden nt
aim |eɪm| vt (gun, camera) richten ♦ vi (with
gun: also: **take** ~) zielen; (intend)
beabsichtigen ♦ n (intention) Absicht f, Ziel
nt; (pointing) Zielen nt, Richten nt; **to ~ at**
sth auf etw dat richten; (fig) etw anstreben;
to ~ to do sth vorhaben, etw zu tun; ~**less**
adj ziellos; ~**lessly** adv ziellos
ain't |eɪnt| (inf) = **am not; are not; is not;**
has not; have not
air |eə'| n Luft f; (manner) Miene f, Anschein
m; (MUS) Melodie f ♦ vt lüften; (fig) an die
Öffentlichkeit bringen ♦ cpd Luft-; **by** ~
(travel) auf dem Luftweg; **to be on the** ~
(RADIO, TV: programme) gesendet werden;
~**bed** (BRIT) n Luftmatratze f; ~~
conditioned adj mit Klimaanlage; ~~
conditioning n Klimaanlage f; ~**craft** n
Flugzeug nt, Maschine f; ~**craft carrier** n
Flugzeugträger m; ~**field** n Flugplatz m; ~
force n Luftwaffe f; ~ **freshener** n
Raumspray nt; ~**gun** n Luftgewehr nt; ~
hostess (BRIT) n Stewardess f; ~**letter**
(BRIT) n Luftpostbrief m; ~**lift** n Luftbrücke f;
~**line** n Luftverkehrsgesellschaft f; ~**liner** n
Verkehrsflugzeug nt; ~**lock** n Luftblase f;
~**mail** n: **by** ~**mail** mit Luftpost; ~ **miles**
npl ≈ Flugkilometer m; ~**plane** (US) n
Flugzeug nt; ~**port** n Flughafen m, Flugplatz
m; ~ **raid** n Luftangriff m; ~**sick** adj
luftkrank; ~**space** n Luftraum m; ~**strip** n
Landestreifen m; ~**terminal** n Terminal nt;
~**tight** adj luftdicht; ~ **traffic controller** n
Fluglotse m; ~**y** adj luftig; (manner)
leichtfertig
aisle |aɪl| n Gang m; ~ **seat** n Sitz m am
Gang
ajar |ə'dʒɑː'| adv angelehnt; einen Spalt offen
alarm |ə'lɑːm| n (warning) Alarm m; (bell etc)
Alarmanlage f; (anxiety) Sorge f ♦ vt
erschrecken; ~ **call** n (in hotel etc) Weckruf
m; ~ **clock** n Wecker m
Albania |æl'beɪnɪə| n Albanien nt
albeit |ɔːl'biːɪt| conj obgleich
album |'ælbəm| n Album nt
alcohol |'ælkəhɒl| n Alkohol m; ~~**free** adj
alkoholfrei; ~**ic** adj (drink)
alkoholisch ♦ n Alkoholiker(in) m(f); ~**ism** n
Alkoholismus m
alert |ə'lɜːt| adj wachsam ♦ n Alarm m ♦ vt
alarmieren; **to be on the** ~ wachsam sein
Algeria |æl'dʒɪərɪə| n Algerien nt
alias |'eɪlɪəs| adv alias ♦ n Deckname m
alibi |'ælɪbaɪ| n Alibi nt
alien |'eɪlɪən| n Ausländer m ♦ adj (foreign)
ausländisch; (strange) fremd; ~ **to** fremd
+dat; ~**ate** vt entfremden

alight |ə'laɪt| *adj* brennend; *(of building)* in Flammen ♦ *vi (descend)* aussteigen; *(bird)* sich setzen

align |ə'laɪn| *vt* ausrichten

alike |ə'laɪk| *adj* gleich, ähnlich ♦ *adv* gleich, ebenso; **to look ~** sich *dat* ähnlich sehen

alimony |'ælɪmənɪ| *n* Unterhalt *m*, Alimente *pl*

alive |ə'laɪv| *adj (living)* lebend; *(lively)* lebendig, aufgeweckt; **~ (with)** *(full of)* voll (von), wimmelnd (von)

KEYWORD

all |ɔːl| *adj* alle(r, s); **all day/night** den ganzen Tag/die ganze Nacht; **all men are equal** alle Menschen sind gleich; **all five came** alle fünf kamen; **all the books/food** die ganzen Bücher/das ganze Essen; **all the time** die ganze Zeit (über); **all his life** sein ganzes Leben (lang)
♦ *pron* 1 alles; **I ate it all, I ate all of it** ich habe alles gegessen; **all of us/the boys went** wir gingen alle/alle Jungen gingen; **we all sat down** wir setzten uns alle
2 *(in phrases)*: **above all** vor allem; **after all** schließlich; **at all: not at all** *(in answer to question)* überhaupt nicht; *(in answer to thanks)* gern geschehen; **I'm not at all tired** ich bin überhaupt nicht müde; **anything at all will do** es ist egal, welche(r, s); **all in all** alles in allem
♦ *adv* ganz; **all alone** ganz allein; **it's not as hard as all that** so schwer ist es nun auch wieder nicht; **all the more/the better** umso mehr/besser; **all but** fast; **the score is 2 all** es steht 2 zu 2

allay |ə'leɪ| *vt (fears)* beschwichtigen

all clear *n* Entwarnung *f*

allegation |ælɪ'geɪʃən| *n* Behauptung *f*

allege |ə'ledʒ| *vt (declare)* behaupten; *(falsely)* vorgeben; **~dly** *adv* angeblich

allegiance |ə'liːdʒəns| *n* Treue *f*

allergic |ə'lɜːdʒɪk| *adj*: **~ (to)** allergisch (gegen)

allergy |'ælədʒɪ| *n* Allergie *f*

alleviate |ə'liːvɪeɪt| *vt* lindern

alley |'ælɪ| *n* Gasse *f*, Durchgang *m*

alliance |ə'laɪəns| *n* Bund *m*, Allianz *f*

allied |'ælaɪd| *adj* vereinigt; *(powers)* alliiert; **~ (to)** verwandt (mit)

all: **~-in** *(BRIT) adj, adv (charge)* alles inbegriffen, Gesamt-; **~-in wrestling** *n* Freistilringen *nt*; **~-night** *adj (café, cinema)* die ganze Nacht geöffnet, Nacht-

allocate |'æləkeɪt| *vt* zuteilen

allot |ə'lɒt| *vt* zuteilen; **~ment** *n (share)* Anteil *m*; *(plot)* Schrebergarten *m*

all-out |'ɔːlaʊt| *adj* total; **all out** *adv* mit voller Kraft

allow |ə'laʊ| *vt (permit)* erlauben, gestatten;

(grant) bewilligen; *(deduct)* abziehen; *(concede)*: **to ~ that ...** annehmen, dass ...; **to ~ sb sth** jdm etw erlauben, jdm etw gestatten; **to ~ sb to do sth** jdm erlauben or gestatten, etw zu tun; **~ for** *vt fus* berücksichtigen, einplanen; **~ance** *n* Beihilfe *f*; **to make ~ances for** berücksichtigen

alloy |'ælɔɪ| *n* Metalllegierung *f*

all: **~ right** *adv (well)* gut; *(correct)* richtig; *(as answer)* okay; **~-round** *adj (sportsman)* allseitig, Allround-; *(view)* Rundum-; **~-time** *adj (record, high)* ... aller Zeiten, Höchst-

allude |ə'luːd| *vi*: **to ~ to** hinweisen auf +*acc*, anspielen auf +*acc*

alluring |ə'ljʊərɪŋ| *adj* verlockend

ally |*n* 'ælaɪ, *vb* ə'laɪ| *n* Verbündete(r) *f(m)*; *(POL)* Alliierte(r) *f(m)* ♦ *vr*: **to ~ o.s. with** sich verbünden mit

almighty |ɔːl'maɪtɪ| *adj* allmächtig

almond |'ɑːmənd| *n* Mandel *f*

almost |'ɔːlməʊst| *adv* fast, beinahe

alms |ɑːmz| *npl* Almosen *nt*

alone |ə'ləʊn| *adj, adv* allein; **to leave sth ~** etw sein lassen; **let ~ ...** geschweige denn ...

along |ə'lɒŋ| *prep* entlang, längs ♦ *adv* *(onward)* vorwärts, weiter; **~ with** zusammen mit; **he was limping ~** er humpelte einher; **all ~** *(all the time)* die ganze Zeit; **~side** *adv (walk)* nebenher; *(come)* nebendran; *(be)* daneben ♦ *prep (walk, compared with)* neben +*dat*; *(come)* neben +*acc*; *(be)* entlang, neben +*dat*; *(of ship)* längsseits +*gen*

aloof |ə'luːf| *adj* zurückhaltend ♦ *adv* fern; **to stand ~** abseits stehen

aloud |ə'laʊd| *adv* laut

alphabet |'ælfəbet| *n* Alphabet *nt*; **~ical** |ælfə'betɪkl| *adj* alphabetisch

alpine |'ælpaɪn| *adj* alpin, Alpen-

Alps |ælps| *npl*: **the ~** die Alpen *pl*

already |ɔːl'redɪ| *adv* schon, bereits

alright |'ɔːl'raɪt| *(BRIT) adv* = **all right**

Alsatian |æl'seɪʃən| *n (dog)* Schäferhund *m*

also |'ɔːlsəʊ| *adv* auch, außerdem

altar |'ɔːltər| *n* Altar *m*

alter |'ɔːltər| *vt* ändern; *(dress)* umändern; **~ation** |ɔːltə'reɪʃən| *n* Änderung *f*; Umänderung *f*; *(to building)* Umbau *m*

alternate |*adj* ɔl'tɜːnɪt, *vb* 'ɔltəːneɪt| *adj* abwechselnd ♦ *vi* abwechseln; **on ~ days** jeden zweiten Tag

alternating |'ɔːltəːneɪtɪŋ| *adj*: **~ current** Wechselstrom *m*; **alternative** |ɒl'tɜːnətɪv| *adj* andere(r, s) ♦ *n* Alternative *f*; **alternative medicine** Alternativmedizin *f*; **alternatively** *adv* im anderen Falle; **alternatively one could ...** oder man könnte ...; **alternator** |'ɔːltəːneɪtər| *n (AUT)* Lichtmaschine *f*

although |ɔːl'ðəʊ| *conj* obwohl

altitude |'æltɪtjuːd| *n* Höhe *f*

alto [ˈæltəʊ] n Alt m
altogether [ɔːltəˈgeðəʳ] adv (on the whole) im Ganzen genommen; (entirely) ganz und gar
aluminium [æljuˈmɪnɪəm] (BRIT) n Aluminium nt
aluminum [əˈluːmɪnəm] (US) n Aluminium nt
always [ˈɔːlweɪz] adv immer
Alzheimer's (disease) [ˈæltshaɪməz-] n (MED) Alzheimerkrankheit f
AM n abbr (= Assembly Member) Mitglied nt der walisischen Versammlung
am [æm] see be
a.m. adv abbr (= ante meridiem) vormittags
amalgamate [əˈmælgəmeɪt] vi (combine) sich vereinigen ♦ vt (mix) amalgamieren
amass [əˈmæs] vt anhäufen
amateur [ˈæmətəʳ] n Amateur m; (pej) Amateur m, Stümper m; **~ish** (pej) adj dilettantisch, stümperhaft
amaze [əˈmeɪz] vt erstaunen; **to be ~d (at)** erstaunt sein (über); **~ment** n höchste(s) Erstaunen nt; **amazing** adj höchst erstaunlich
Amazon [ˈæməzən] n (GEOG) Amazonas m
ambassador [æmˈbæsədəʳ] n Botschafter m
amber [ˈæmbəʳ] n Bernstein m; **at ~** (BRIT: AUT) auf Gelb, gelb
ambiguous [æmˈbɪgjuəs] adj zweideutig; (not clear) unklar
ambition [æmˈbɪʃən] n Ehrgeiz m; **ambitious** adj ehrgeizig
amble [ˈæmbl] vi (usu: ~ along) schlendern
ambulance [ˈæmbjʊləns] n Krankenwagen m; **~ man** (irreg) n Sanitäter m
ambush [ˈæmbʊʃ] n Hinterhalt m ♦ vt (aus dem Hinterhalt) überfallen
amenable [əˈmiːnəbl] adj gefügig; **~ (to)** (reason) zugänglich (+dat); (flattery) empfänglich (für)
amend [əˈmend] vt (law etc) abändern, ergänzen; **to make ~s for sth** etw wieder gutmachen; **~ment** n Abänderung f
amenities [əˈmiːnɪtɪz] npl Einrichtungen pl
America [əˈmerɪkə] n Amerika nt; **~n** adj amerikanisch ♦ n Amerikaner(in) m(f)
amiable [ˈeɪmɪəbl] adj liebenswürdig
amicable [ˈæmɪkəbl] adj freundschaftlich; (settlement) gütlich
amid(st) [əˈmɪd(st)] prep mitten in or unter +dat
amiss [əˈmɪs] adv: **to take sth ~** etw übel nehmen; **there's something ~** da stimmt irgendetwas nicht
ammonia [əˈməʊnɪə] n Ammoniak nt
ammunition [æmjʊˈnɪʃən] n Munition f
amnesia [æmˈniːzɪə] n Gedächtnisverlust m
amnesty [ˈæmnɪstɪ] n Amnestie f
amok [əˈmɔk] adv: **to run ~** Amok laufen
among(st) [əˈmʌŋ(st)] prep unter

amoral [æˈmɔrəl] adj unmoralisch
amorous [ˈæmərəs] adj verliebt
amount [əˈmaʊnt] n (of money) Betrag m; (of water, sand) Menge f ♦ vi: **to ~ to** (total) sich belaufen auf +acc; **a great ~ of time/ energy** ein großer Aufwand an Zeit/Energie (dat); **this ~s to treachery** das kommt Verrat gleich; **he won't ~ to much** aus ihm wird nie was
amp(ere) [æmp(eəʳ)] n Ampere nt
amphibian [æmˈfɪbɪən] n Amphibie f
ample [ˈæmpl] adj (portion) reichlich; (dress) weit, groß; **~ time** genügend Zeit
amplifier [ˈæmplɪfaɪəʳ] n Verstärker m
amuse [əˈmjuːz] vt (entertain) unterhalten; (make smile) belustigen; **~ment** n (feeling) Unterhaltung f; (recreation) Zeitvertreib m; **~ment arcade** n Spielhalle f; **~ment park** n Vergnügungspark m
an [æn, ən] see a
anaemia [əˈniːmɪə] n Anämie f; **anaemic** adj blutarm
anaesthetic [ænɪsˈθetɪk] n Betäubungsmittel nt; **under ~** unter Narkose; **anaesthetist** [æˈniːsθɪtɪst] n Anästhesist(in) m(f)
analgesic [ænælˈdʒiːsɪk] n schmerzlindernde(s) Mittel nt
analog(ue) [ˈænəlɔg] adj Analog-
analogy [əˈnælədʒɪ] n Analogie f
analyse [ˈænəlaɪz] (BRIT) vt analysieren
analyses [əˈnæləsiːz] (BRIT) npl of analysis
analysis [əˈnæləsɪs] (pl analyses) n Analyse f
analyst [ˈænəlɪst] n Analytiker(in) m(f)
analytic(al) [ænəˈlɪtɪk(l)] adj analytisch
analyze [ˈænəlaɪz] (US) vt = analyse
anarchy [ˈænəkɪ] n Anarchie f
anatomy [əˈnætəmɪ] n (structure) anatomische(r) Aufbau m; (study) Anatomie f
ancestor [ˈænsɪstəʳ] n Vorfahr m
anchor [ˈæŋkəʳ] n Anker m ♦ vi (also: **to drop ~**) ankern, vor Anker gehen ♦ vt verankern; **to weigh ~** den Anker lichten
anchovy [ˈæntʃəvɪ] n Sardelle f
ancient [ˈeɪnʃənt] adj alt; (car etc) uralt
ancillary [ænˈsɪlərɪ] adj Hilfs-
and [ænd] conj und; **~ so on** und so weiter; **try ~ come** versuche zu kommen; **better ~ better** immer besser
Andes [ˈændiːz] npl: **the ~** die Anden pl
anemia etc [əˈniːmɪə] (US) n = anaemia etc
anesthetic etc [ænɪsˈθetɪk] (US) n = anaesthetic etc
anew [əˈnjuː] adv von neuem
angel [ˈeɪndʒəl] n Engel m
anger [ˈæŋgəʳ] n Zorn m ♦ vt ärgern
angina [ænˈdʒaɪnə] n Angina f
angle [ˈæŋgl] n Winkel m; (point of view) Standpunkt m
angler [ˈæŋgləʳ] n Angler m
Anglican [ˈæŋglɪkən] adj anglikanisch ♦ n

Anglikaner(in) *m(f)*

angling ['æŋlɪŋ] *n* Angeln *nt*

angrily ['æŋgrɪlɪ] *adv* ärgerlich, böse

angry ['æŋgrɪ] *adj* ärgerlich, ungehalten, böse; *(wound)* entzündet; **to be ~ with sb** auf jdn böse sein; **to be ~ at sth** über etw *acc* verärgert sein

anguish ['æŋgwɪʃ] *n* Qual *f*

angular ['æŋgjʊlə'] *adj* eckig, winkelförmig; *(face)* kantig

animal ['ænɪməl] *n* Tier *nt*; *(living creature)* Lebewesen *nt* ♦ *adj* tierisch

animate [*vb* 'ænɪmeɪt, *adj* 'ænɪmɪt] *vt* beleben ♦ *adj* lebhaft; **~d** *adj* lebendig; *(film)* Zeichentrick-

animosity [ænɪ'mɔsɪtɪ] *n* Feindseligkeit *f*, Abneigung *f*

aniseed ['ænɪsiːd] *n* Anis *m*

ankle ['æŋkl] *n* (Fuß)knöchel *m*; **~ sock** *n* Söckchen *nt*

annex [*n* 'ænɛks, *vb* ə'nɛks] *n* (BRIT: *also:* **~e**) Anbau *m* ♦ *vt* anfügen; *(POL)* annektieren, angliedern

annihilate [ə'naɪəleɪt] *vt* vernichten

anniversary [ænɪ'vɜːsərɪ] *n* Jahrestag *m*

announce [ə'naʊns] *vt* ankündigen, anzeigen; **~ment** *n* Ankündigung *f*; *(official)* Bekanntmachung *f*; **~r** *n* Ansager(in) *m(f)*

annoy [ə'nɔɪ] *vt* ärgern; **don't get ~ed!** reg dich nicht auf!; **~ance** *n* Ärgernis *nt*, Störung *f*; **~ing** *adj* ärgerlich; *(person)* lästig

annual ['ænjʊəl] *adj* jährlich; *(salary)* Jahres- ♦ *n* *(plant)* einjährige Pflanze *f*; *(book)* Jahrbuch *nt*; **~ly** *adv* jährlich

annul [ə'nʌl] *vt* aufheben, annullieren

annum ['ænəm] *n see* **per**

anonymous [ə'nɔnɪməs] *adj* anonym

anorak ['ænəræk] *n* Anorak *m*, Windjacke *f*

anorexia [ænə'rɛksɪə] *n* (MED) Magersucht *f*

another [ə'nʌðə'] *adj*, *pron* *(different)* ein(e) andere(r, s); *(additional)* noch eine(r, s); *see also* **one**

answer ['ɑːnsə'] *n* Antwort *f* ♦ *vi* antworten; *(on phone)* sich melden ♦ *vt* *(person)* antworten *+dat*; *(letter, question)* beantworten; *(telephone)* gehen an *+acc*, abnehmen; *(door)* öffnen; **in ~ to your letter** in Beantwortung Ihres Schreibens; **to ~ the phone** ans Telefon gehen; **to ~ the bell** *or* **the door** aufmachen; **~ back** *vi* frech sein; **~ for** *vt fus*: **to ~ for sth** verantwortlich sein; **~able** *adj*: **to be ~able to sb for sth** jdm gegenüber für etw verantwortlich sein; **~ing machine** *n* Anrufbeantworter *m*

ant [ænt] *n* Ameise *f*

antagonism [æn'tægənɪzəm] *n* Antagonismus *m*

antagonize [æn'tægənaɪz] *vt* reizen

Antarctic [ænt'ɑːktɪk] *adj* antarktisch ♦ *n*: **the ~** die Antarktis

antelope ['æntɪləʊp] *n* Antilope *f*

antenatal ['æntɪ'neɪtl] *adj* vor der Geburt; **~ clinic** *n* Sprechstunde *f* für werdende Mütter

antenna [æn'tɛnə] *n* (BIOL) Fühler *m*; (RAD) Antenne *f*

antennae [æn'tɛniː] *npl of* **antenna**

anthem ['ænθəm] *n* Hymne *f*; **national ~** Nationalhymne *f*

anthology [æn'θɔlədʒɪ] *n* Gedichtsammlung *f*, Anthologie *f*

anti- ['æntɪ] *prefix* Gegen-, Anti-

anti-aircraft ['æntɪ'ɛəkrɑːft] *adj* Flugabwehr-

antibiotic ['æntɪbaɪ'ɔtɪk] *n* Antibiotikum *nt*

antibody ['æntɪbɔdɪ] *n* Antikörper *m*

anticipate [æn'tɪsɪpeɪt] *vt* *(expect: trouble, question)* erwarten, rechnen mit; *(look forward to)* sich freuen auf *+acc*; *(do first)* vorwegnehmen; *(foresee)* ahnen, vorhersehen; **anticipation** [æntɪsɪ'peɪʃən] *n* Erwartung *f*; *(foreshadowing)* Vorwegnahme *f*

anticlimax ['æntɪ'klaɪmæks] *n* Ernüchterung *f*

anticlockwise ['æntɪ'klɔkwaɪz] *adv* entgegen dem Uhrzeigersinn

antics ['æntɪks] *npl* Possen *pl*

anti-: **~cyclone** *n* Hoch *nt*, Hochdruckgebiet *nt*; **~depressant** *n* Antidepressivum *nt*; **~dote** *n* Gegenmittel *nt*; **~freeze** *n* Frostschutzmittel *nt*; **~histamine** *n* Antihistamin

antiquated ['æntɪkweɪtɪd] *adj* antiquiert

antique [æn'tiːk] *n* Antiquität *f* ♦ *adj* antik; *(old-fashioned)* altmodisch; **~ shop** *n* Antiquitätenladen *m*; **antiquity** [æn'tɪkwɪtɪ] *n* Altertum *nt*

antiseptic [æntɪ'sɛptɪk] *n* Antiseptikum *nt* ♦ *adj* antiseptisch

antisocial ['æntɪ'səʊʃəl] *adj* *(person)* ungesellig; *(law)* unsozial

antlers ['æntləz] *npl* Geweih *nt*

anus ['eɪnəs] *n* After *m*

anvil ['ænvɪl] *n* Amboss *m*

anxiety [æŋ'zaɪətɪ] *n* Angst *f*; *(worry)* Sorge *f*; **anxious** ['æŋkʃəs] *adj* ängstlich; *(worried)* besorgt; **to be anxious to do sth** etw unbedingt tun wollen

---

KEYWORD

any ['ɛnɪ] *adj* **1** *(in questions etc)*: **have you any butter?** haben Sie (etwas) Butter?; **have you any children?** haben Sie Kinder?; **if there are any tickets left** falls noch Karten da sind

2 *(with negative)*: **I haven't any money/books** ich habe kein Geld/keine Bücher

3 *(no matter which)* jede(r, s) (beliebige); **any colour (at all)** jede beliebige Farbe; **choose any book you like** nehmen Sie ein beliebiges Buch

4 *(in phrases)*: **in any case** in jedem Fall;

any day now jeden Tag; **at any moment** jeden Moment; **at any rate** auf jeden Fall
♦ *pron* **1** (*in questions etc*): **have you got any?** haben Sie welche?; **can any of you sing?** kann (irgend)einer von euch singen? **2** (*with negative*): **I haven't any** (**of them**) ich habe keinen/keines (davon) **3** (*no matter which one(s)*): **take any of those books** (**you like**) nehmen Sie irgendeines dieser Bücher
♦ *adv* **1** (*in questions etc*): **do you want any more soup/sandwiches?** möchten Sie noch Suppe/Brote?; **are you feeling any better?** fühlen Sie sich etwas besser? **2** (*with negative*): **I can't hear him any more** ich kann ihn nicht mehr hören

anybody ['ɛnɪbɔdɪ] *pron* (*no matter who*) jede(r); (*in questions etc*) (irgend)jemand, (irgend)eine(r); (*with negative*): **I can't see ~** ich kann niemanden sehen
anyhow ['ɛnɪhaʊ] *adv* (*at any rate*): **I shall go ~** ich gehe sowieso; (*haphazardly*): **do it ~** machen Sie es, wie Sie wollen
anyone ['ɛnɪwʌn] *pron* = **anybody**

KEYWORD

anything ['ɛnɪθɪŋ] *pron* **1** (*in questions etc*) (irgend)etwas; **can you see anything?** können Sie etwas sehen? **2** (*with negative*): **I can't see anything** ich kann nichts sehen **3** (*no matter what*): **you can say anything you like** Sie können sagen, was Sie wollen; **anything will do** irgendetwas(, wird genügen), irgendeine(r, s) (wird genügen); **he'll eat anything** er isst alles

anyway ['ɛnɪweɪ] *adv* (*at any rate*) auf jeden Fall; (*besides*): **~, I couldn't come even if I wanted to** jedenfalls könnte ich nicht kommen, selbst wenn ich wollte; **why are you phoning, ~?** warum rufst du überhaupt an?
anywhere ['ɛnɪwɛəʳ] *adv* (*in questions etc*) irgendwo; (: *with direction*) irgendwohin; (*no matter where*) überall; (: *with direction*) überallhin; (*with negative*): **I can't see him ~** ich kann ihn nirgendwo *or* nirgends sehen; **can you see him ~?** siehst du ihn irgendwo?; **put the books down ~** leg die Bücher irgendwohin
apart [ə'pɑːt] *adv* (*parted*) auseinander; (*away*) beiseite, abseits; **10 miles ~** 10 Meilen auseinander; **to take ~** auseinander nehmen; **~ from** *prep* außer
apartheid [ə'pɑːteɪt] *n* Apartheid *f*
apartment [ə'pɑːtmənt] (*US*) *n* Wohnung *f*; **~ building** *n* Wohnhaus *nt*
apathy ['æpəθɪ] *n* Teilnahmslosigkeit *f*, Apathie *f*
ape |eɪp| *n* (Menschen)affe *m* ♦ *vt* nachahmen

aperitif [ə'pɛrɪtiːf] *n* Aperitif *m*
aperture ['æpətʃjʊəʳ] *n* Öffnung *f*; (*PHOT*) Blende *f*
APEX ['eɪpɛks] *n abbr* (*AVIAT*: = *advance purchase excursion*) APEX (*im Voraus reservierte(r) Fahrkarte/Flugschein zu reduzierten Preisen*)
apex ['eɪpɛks] *n* Spitze *f*
apiece [ə'piːs] *adv* pro Stück; (*per person*) pro Kopf
apologetic [əpɔlə'dʒɛtɪk] *adj* entschuldigend; **to be ~** sich sehr entschuldigen
apologize [ə'pɔlədʒaɪz] *vi*: **to ~ (for sth to sb)** sich (für etw bei jdm) entschuldigen; **apology** *n* Entschuldigung *f*
apostle [ə'pɔsl] *n* Apostel *m*
apostrophe [ə'pɔstrəfɪ] *n* Apostroph *m*
appal [ə'pɔːl] *vt* erschrecken; **~ling** *adj* schrecklich
apparatus [æpə'reɪtəs] *n* Gerät *nt*
apparel [ə'pærəl] (*US*) *n* Kleidung *f*
apparent [ə'pærənt] *adj* offenbar; **~ly** *adv* anscheinend
apparition [æpə'rɪʃən] *n* (*ghost*) Erscheinung *f*, Geist *m*
appeal [ə'piːl] *vi* dringend ersuchen; (*JUR*) Berufung einlegen ♦ *n* Aufruf *m*; (*JUR*) Berufung *f*; **to ~ for** dringend bitten um; **to ~ to** sich wenden an +*acc*; (*to public*) appellieren an +*acc*; **it doesn't ~ to me** es gefällt mir nicht; **~ing** *adj* ansprechend
appear [ə'pɪəʳ] *vi* (*come into sight*) erscheinen; (*be seen*) auftauchen; (*seem*) scheinen; **it would ~ that ...** anscheinend ...; **~ance** *n* (*coming into sight*) Erscheinen *nt*; (*outward show*) Äußere(s) *nt*
appease [ə'piːz] *vt* beschwichtigen
appendices [ə'pɛndɪsiːz] *npl of* **appendix**
appendicitis [əpɛndɪ'saɪtɪs] *n* Blinddarmentzündung *f*
appendix [ə'pɛndɪks] (*pl* **appendices**) *n* (*in book*) Anhang *m*; (*MED*) Blinddarm *m*
appetite ['æpɪtaɪt] *n* Appetit *m*; (*fig*) Lust *f*
appetizer ['æpɪtaɪzəʳ] *n* Appetitanreger *m*; **appetizing** ['æpɪtaɪzɪŋ] *adj* appetit-anregend
applaud [ə'plɔːd] *vi* Beifall klatschen, applaudieren ♦ *vt* Beifall klatschen +*dat*; **applause** [ə'plɔːz] *n* Beifall *m*, Applaus *m*
apple |'æpl| *n* Apfel *m*; **~ tree** *n* Apfelbaum *m*
appliance [ə'plaɪəns] *n* Gerät *nt*
applicable [ə'plɪkəbl] *adj* anwendbar; (*in forms*) zutreffend
applicant ['æplɪkənt] *n* Bewerber(in) *m(f)*
application [æplɪ'keɪʃən] *n* (*request*) Antrag *m*; (*for job*) Bewerbung *f*; (*putting into practice*) Anwendung *f*; (*hard work*) Fleiß *m*; **~ form** *n* Bewerbungsformular *nt*

applied [ə'plaɪd] adj angewandt
apply [ə'plaɪ] vi (be suitable) zutreffen; (ask):
to ~ {to} sich wenden (an +acc); (request:)
to ~ for sich melden für +acc ♦ vt (place on)
auflegen; (cream) auftragen; (put into
practice) anwenden; **to ~ for sth** sich um
etw bewerben; **to ~ o.s. to sth** sich bei etw
anstrengen
appoint [ə'pɔɪnt] vt (to office) ernennen,
berufen; (settle) festsetzen; **~ment** n
(meeting) Verabredung f; (at hairdresser etc)
Bestellung f; (in business) Termin m; (choice
for a position) Ernennung f; (UNIV) Berufung
f
appraisal [ə'preɪzl] n Beurteilung f
appreciable [ə'priːʃəbl] adj (perceptible)
merklich; (able to be estimated) abschätzbar
appreciate [ə'priːʃeɪt] vt (value) zu schätzen
wissen; (understand) einsehen ♦ vi (increase
in value) im Wert steigen; **appreciation**
[əpriːʃɪ'eɪʃən] n Wertschätzung f; (COMM)
Wertzuwachs m; **appreciative** [ə'priːʃɪətɪv]
adj (showing thanks) dankbar; (showing
liking) anerkennend
apprehend [æprɪ'hend] vt (arrest)
festnehmen; (understand) erfassen
apprehension [æprɪ'henʃən] n Angst f
apprehensive [æprɪ'hensɪv] adj furchtsam
apprentice [ə'prentɪs] n Lehrling m; **~ship** n
Lehrzeit f
approach [ə'prəʊtʃ] vi sich nähern ♦ vt
herantreten an +acc; (problem) herangehen
an +acc ♦ n Annäherung f; (to problem)
Ansatz m; (path) Zugang m, Zufahrt f;
~able adj zugänglich
appropriate [adj ə'prəʊprɪɪt, vb ə'prəʊprɪeɪt]
adj angemessen; (remark) angebracht ♦ vt
(take for o.s.) sich aneignen; (set apart)
bereitstellen
approval [ə'pruːvəl] n (show of satisfaction)
Beifall m; (permission) Billigung f; **on ~**
(COMM) bei Gefallen
approve [ə'pruːv] vt, vi billigen; **I don't ~ of
it/him** ich halte nichts davon/von ihm; **~d
school** (BRIT) n Erziehungsheim nt
approximate [adj ə'prɔksɪmɪt, vb
ə'prɔksɪmeɪt] adj annähernd, ungefähr ♦ vi
nahe kommen +dat; **~ly** adv rund, ungefähr
apricot ['eɪprɪkɔt] n Aprikose f
April ['eɪprəl] n April m; **~ Fools' Day** n der
erste April
apron ['eɪprən] n Schürze f
apt [æpt] adj (suitable) passend; (able)
begabt; (likely): **to be ~ to do sth** dazu
neigen, etw zu tun
aptitude ['æptɪtjuːd] n Begabung f
aqualung ['ækwəlʌŋ] n Unterwasser-
atmungsgerät nt
aquarium [ə'kweərɪəm] n Aquarium nt
Aquarius [ə'kweərɪəs] n Wassermann m
aquatic [ə'kwætɪk] adj Wasser-

Arab ['ærəb] n Araber(in) m(f)
Arabia [ə'reɪbɪə] n Arabien nt; **~n** adj
arabisch
Arabic ['ærəbɪk] adj arabisch ♦ n Arabisch nt
arable ['ærəbl] adj bebaubar, Kultur-
arbitrary ['ɑːbɪtrərɪ] adj willkürlich
arbitration [ɑːbɪ'treɪʃən] n Schlichtung f
arc [ɑːk] n Bogen m
arcade [ɑː'keɪd] n Säulengang m; (with video
games) Spielhalle f
arch [ɑːtʃ] n Bogen m ♦ vt überwölben; (back)
krumm machen
archaeologist [ɑːkɪ'ɔlədʒɪst] n Archäologe
m
archaeology [ɑːkɪ'ɔlədʒɪ] n Archäologie f
archaic [ɑː'keɪɪk] adj altertümlich
archbishop [ɑːtʃ'bɪʃəp] n Erzbischof m
archenemy [ɑːtʃ'enəmɪ] n Erzfeind m
archeology etc [ɑːkɪ'ɔlədʒɪ] (US) =
archaeology etc
archery ['ɑːtʃərɪ] n Bogenschießen nt
architect ['ɑːkɪtekt] n Architekt(in) m(f);
~ural [ɑːkɪ'tektʃərəl] adj architektonisch;
~ure n Architektur f
archives ['ɑːkaɪvz] npl Archiv nt
archway ['ɑːtʃweɪ] n Bogen m
Arctic ['ɑːktɪk] adj arktisch ♦ n: **the ~** die
Arktis
ardent ['ɑːdənt] adj glühend
arduous ['ɑːdjuəs] adj mühsam
are [ɑːʳ] see **be**
area ['eərɪə] n Fläche f; (of land) Gebiet nt;
(part of sth) Teil m, Abschnitt m
arena [ə'riːnə] n Arena f
aren't [ɑːnt] = **are not**
Argentina [ɑːdʒən'tiːnə] n Argentinien nt;
Argentinian [ɑːdʒən'tɪnɪən] adj
argentinisch ♦ n Argentinier(in) m(f)
arguably ['ɑːgjuəblɪ] adv wohl
argue ['ɑːgjuː] vi diskutieren; (angrily)
streiten; **argument** n (theory) Argument nt;
(reasoning) Argumentation f; (row)
Auseinandersetzung f, Streit m; **to have an
argument** sich streiten; **argumentative**
[ɑːgju'mentətɪv] adj streitlustig
aria ['ɑːrɪə] n Arie f
Aries ['eərɪz] n Widder m
arise [ə'raɪz] (pt arose, pp arisen) vi
aufsteigen; (get up) aufstehen; (difficulties etc)
entstehen; (case) vorkommen; **to ~ from sth**
herrühren von etw; **~n** [ə'rɪzn] pp of **arise**
aristocracy [ærɪ'stɔkrəsɪ] n Adel m,
Aristokratie f; **aristocrat** ['ærɪstəkræt] n
Adlige(r) f(m), Aristokrat(in) m(f)
arithmetic [ə'rɪθmətɪk] n Rechnen nt,
Arithmetik f
arm [ɑːm] n Arm m; (branch of military service)
Zweig m ♦ vt bewaffnen; **~s** npl (weapons)
Waffen pl
armaments ['ɑːməmənts] npl Ausrüstung f
armchair ['ɑːmtʃeəʳ] n Lehnstuhl m

armed [ɑːmd] adj (forces) Streit-, bewaffnet; **~ robbery** n bewaffnete(r) Raubüberfall m

armistice ['ɑːmɪstɪs] n Waffenstillstand m

armour ['ɑːməʳ] (US **armor**) n (knight's) Rüstung f; (MIL) Panzerplatte f; **~ed car** n Panzerwagen m

armpit ['ɑːmpɪt] n Achselhöhle f

armrest ['ɑːmrɛst] n Armlehne f

army ['ɑːmɪ] n Armee f, Heer nt; (host) Heer nt

aroma [ə'rəumə] n Duft m, Aroma nt; **~therapy** [ərəumə'θerəpɪ] n Aromatherapie f; **~tic** [ærə'mætɪk] adj aromatisch, würzig

arose [ə'rəuz] pt of **arise**

around [ə'raund] adv ringsherum; (almost) ungefähr ♦ prep um … herum; **is he ~?** ist er hier?

arrange [ə'reɪndʒ] vt (time, meeting) festsetzen; (holidays) festlegen; (flowers, hair, objects) anordnen; **I ~d to meet him** ich habe mit ihm ausgemacht, ihn zu treffen; **it's all ~d** es ist alles arrangiert; **~ment** n (order) Reihenfolge f; (agreement) Vereinbarung f; **~ments** npl (plans) Pläne pl

array [ə'reɪ] n (collection) Ansammlung f

arrears [ə'rɪəz] npl (of debts) Rückstand m; (of work) Unerledigte(s) nt; **in ~** im Rückstand

arrest [ə'rest] vt (person) verhaften; (stop) aufhalten ♦ n Verhaftung f; **under ~** in Haft

arrival [ə'raɪvl] n Ankunft f

arrive [ə'raɪv] vi ankommen; **to ~ at** ankommen in +dat, ankommen bei

arrogance ['ærəgəns] n Überheblichkeit f, Arroganz f; **arrogant** ['ærəgənt] adj überheblich, arrogant

arrow ['ærəu] n Pfeil m

arse [ɑːs] (inf!) n Arsch m (!)

arsenal ['ɑːsɪnl] n Waffenlager nt, Zeughaus nt

arsenic ['ɑːsnɪk] n Arsen nt

arson ['ɑːsn] n Brandstiftung f

art [ɑːt] n Kunst f; **A~s** npl (UNIV) Geisteswissenschaften pl

artery ['ɑːtərɪ] n Schlagader f, Arterie f

art gallery n Kunstgalerie f

arthritis [ɑː'θraɪtɪs] n Arthritis f

artichoke ['ɑːtɪtʃəuk] n Artischocke f; **Jerusalem ~** Erdartischocke f

article ['ɑːtɪkl] n (PRESS, GRAM) Artikel m; (thing) Gegenstand m, Artikel m; (clause) Abschnitt m, Paragraf m; **~ of clothing** Kleidungsstück nt

articulate [adj ɑː'tɪkjulɪt, vb ɑː'tɪkjuleɪt] adj (able to express o.s.) redegewandt; (speaking clearly) deutlich, verständlich ♦ vt (connect) zusammenfügen, gliedern; **to be ~** sich gut ausdrücken können; **~d vehicle** n Sattelschlepper m

artificial [ɑːtɪ'fɪʃl] adj künstlich, Kunst-; **~ respiration** n künstliche Atmung f

artisan ['ɑːtɪzæn] n gelernte(r) Hand-werker m

artist ['ɑːtɪst] n Künstler(in) m(f); **~ic** [ɑː'tɪstɪk] adj künstlerisch; **~ry** n künstlerische(s) Können nt

art school n Kunsthochschule f

as [æz] conj 1 (referring to time) als; **as the years went by** mit den Jahren; **he came in as I was leaving** als er hereinkam, ging ich gerade; **as from tomorrow** ab morgen

2 (in comparisons): **as big as** so groß wie; **twice as big as** zweimal so groß wie; **as much/many as** so viel/so viele wie; **as soon as** sobald

3 (since, because) da; **he left early as he had to be home by 10** er ging früher, da er um 10 zu Hause sein musste

4 (referring to manner, way) wie; **do as you wish** mach was du willst; **as she said** wie sie sagte

5 (concerning): **as for or to that** was das betrifft or angeht

6: **as if or though** als ob

♦ prep als; see also **long**; **he works as a driver** er arbeitet als Fahrer; see also **such**; **he gave it to me as a present** er hat es mir als Geschenk gegeben; see also **well**

a.s.a.p. abbr = **as soon as possible**

asbestos [æz'bestəs] n Asbest m

ascend [ə'send] vi aufsteigen ♦ vt besteigen; **ascent** n Aufstieg m; Besteigung f

ascertain [æsə'teɪn] vt feststellen

ascribe [ə'skraɪb] vt: **to ~ sth to sth/sth to sb** etw einer Sache/jdm etw zuschreiben

ash [æʃ] n Asche f; (tree) Esche f

ashamed [ə'ʃeɪmd] adj beschämt; **to be ~ of sth** sich für etw schämen

ashen ['æʃən] adj (pale) aschfahl

ashore [ə'ʃɔːʳ] adv an Land

ashtray ['æʃtreɪ] n Aschenbecher m

Ash Wednesday n Aschermittwoch m

Asia ['eɪʃə] n Asien nt; **~n** adj asiatisch ♦ n Asiat(in) m(f)

aside [ə'saɪd] adv beiseite

ask [ɑːsk] vt fragen; (permission) bitten um; **~ him his name** frage ihn nach seinem Namen; **he ~ed to see you** er wollte dich sehen; **to ~ sb to do sth** jdn bitten, etw zu tun; **to ~ sb about sth** jdn nach etw fragen; **to ~ (sb) a question** (jdn) etwas fragen; **to ~ sb out to dinner** jdn zum Essen einladen; **~ after** vt fus fragen nach; **~ for** vt fus bitten um

askance [ə'skɑːns] adv: **to look ~ at sb** jdn schief ansehen

asking price ['ɑːskɪŋ-] n Verkaufspreis m

asleep [ə'sliːp] adj: **to be ~** schlafen; **to fall ~** einschlafen

asparagus [əs'pærəgəs] n Spargel m

aspect |'æspɛkt| n Aspekt m
aspersions |əs'pəːʃənz| npl: **to cast ~ on sb/sth** sich abfällig über jdn/etw äußern
asphyxiation |æsfıksı'eıʃən| n Erstickung f
aspirations |æspə'reıʃənz| npl: **to have ~ towards sth** etw anstreben
aspire |əs'paıər| vi: **to ~ to** streben nach
aspirin |'æsprın| n Aspirin nt ®
ass |æs| n (also fig) Esel m; (US: inf!) Arsch m (!)
assailant |ə'seılənt| n Angreifer m
assassin |ə'sæsın| n Attentäter(in) m(f); **~ate** vt ermorden; **~ation** |əsæsı'neıʃən| n (geglückte(s)) Attentat nt
assault |ə'sɔːlt| n Angriff m ♦ vt überfallen; (woman) herfallen über +acc
assemble |ə'sɛmbl| vt versammeln; (parts) zusammensetzen ♦ vi sich versammeln; **assembly** n (meeting) Versammlung f; (construction) Zusammensetzung f, Montage f; **assembly line** n Fließband nt
assent |ə'sɛnt| n Zustimmung f
assert |ə'sɜːt| vt erklären; **~ion** n Behauptung f
assess |ə'sɛs| vt schätzen; **~ment** n Bewertung f, Einschätzung f; **~or** n Steuerberater m
asset |'æsɛt| n Vorteil m, Wert m; **~s** npl (FIN) Vermögen nt; (estate) Nachlass m
assign |ə'saın| vt zuweisen; **~ment** n Aufgabe f, Auftrag m
assimilate |ə'sımıleıt| vt sich aneignen, aufnehmen
assist |ə'sıst| vt beistehen +dat; **~ance** n Unterstützung f, Hilfe f; **~ant** n Assistent(in) m(f), Mitarbeiter(in) m(f); (BRIT: also: **shop ~ant**) Verkäufer(in) m(f)
associate |n ə'səuʃııt, vb ə'səuʃıeıt| n (partner) Kollege m, Teilhaber m; (member) außerordentliche(s) Mitglied n ♦ vt verbinden ♦ vi (keep company) verkehren; **association** |əsəuʃı'eıʃən| n Verband m, Verein m; (PSYCH) Assoziation f; (link) Verbindung f
assorted |ə'sɔːtıd| adj gemischt
assortment |ə'sɔːtmənt| n Sammlung f; (COMM): **~ (of)** Sortiment nt (von), Auswahl f (an +dat)
assume |ə'sjuːm| vt (take for granted) annehmen; (put on) annehmen, sich geben; **~d name** n Deckname m
assumption |ə'sʌmpʃən| n Annahme f
assurance |ə'ʃuərəns| n (firm statement) Versicherung f; (confidence) Selbstsicherheit f; (insurance) (Lebens)versicherung f
assure |ə'ʃuər| vt (make sure) sicherstellen; (convince) versichern +dat; (life) versichern
asterisk |'æstərısk| n Sternchen nt
asthma |'æsmə| n Asthma nt
astonish |ə'stɒnıʃ| vt erstaunen; **~ment** n Erstaunen nt

astound |ə'staund| vt verblüffen
astray |ə'streı| adv in die Irre; auf Abwege; **to go ~** (go wrong) sich vertun; **to lead ~** irreführen
astride |ə'straıd| adv rittlings ♦ prep rittlings auf
astrologer |əs'trɒlədʒər| n Astrologe m, Astrologin f; **astrology** n Astrologie f
astronaut |'æstrənɔːt| n Astronaut(in) m(f)
astronomer |əs'trɒnəmər| n Astronom m
astronomical |æstrə'nɒmıkl| adj astronomisch; (success) riesig
astronomy |əs'trɒnəmı| n Astronomie f
astute |əs'tjuːt| adj scharfsinnig; schlau, gerissen
asylum |ə'saıləm| n (home) Heim nt; (refuge) Asyl nt

KEYWORD
---

at |æt| prep **1** (referring to position, direction) an +dat, bei +dat; (with place) in +dat; **at the top** an der Spitze; **at home/school** zu Hause, zuhause (österreichisch, schweizerisch)/in der Schule; **at the baker's** beim Bäcker; **to look at sth** auf etw acc blicken; **to throw sth at sb** etw nach jdm werfen
2 (referring to time): **at 4 o'clock** um 4 Uhr; **at night** bei Nacht; **at Christmas** zu Weihnachten; **at times** manchmal
3 (referring to rates, speed etc): **at £1 a kilo** zu £1 pro Kilo; **two at a time** zwei auf einmal; **at 50 km/h** mit 50 km/h
4 (referring to manner): **at a stroke** mit einem Schlag; **at peace** in Frieden
5 (referring to activity): **to be at work** bei der Arbeit sein; **to play at cowboys** Cowboy spielen; **to be good at sth** gut in etw dat sein
6 (referring to cause): **shocked/surprised/annoyed at sth** schockiert/überrascht/verärgert über etw acc; **I went at his suggestion** ich ging auf seinen Vorschlag hin

---

ate |eıt| pt of **eat**
atheist |'eıθııst| n Atheist(in) m(f)
Athens |'æθınz| n Athen nt
athlete |'æθliːt| n Athlet m, Sportler m
athletic |æθ'lɛtık| adj sportlich, athletisch; **~s** n Leichtathletik f
Atlantic |ət'læntık| adj atlantisch ♦ n: **the ~ (Ocean)** der Atlantik
atlas |'ætləs| n Atlas m
ATM abbr (= automated teller machine) Geldautomat m
atmosphere |'ætməsfıər| n Atmosphäre f
atom |'ætəm| n Atom nt; (fig) bisschen nt; **~ic** |ə'tɒmık| adj atomar, Atom-; **~(ic) bomb** n Atombombe f
atomizer |'ætəmaızər| n Zerstäuber m

atone [əˈtəun] *vi* sühnen; **to ~ for sth** etw sühnen

atrocious [əˈtrəuʃəs] *adj* grässlich

atrocity [əˈtrɒsɪtɪ] *n* Scheußlichkeit *f*; *(deed)* Gräueltat *f*

attach [əˈtætʃ] *vt (fasten)* befestigen; **to be ~ed to sb/sth** an jdm/etw hängen; **to ~ importance** *etc* **to sth** Wichtigkeit *etc* auf etw *acc* legen, einer Sache *dat* Wichtigkeit *etc* beimessen

attaché case [əˈtæʃeɪ-] *n* Aktenkoffer *m*

attachment [əˈtætʃmənt] *n (tool)* Zubehörteil *nt*; *(love):* **~ (to sb)** Zuneigung *f* (zu jdm)

attack [əˈtæk] *vt* angreifen ♦ *n* Angriff *m*; *(MED)* Anfall *m*; **~er** *n* Angreifer(in) *m(f)*

attain [əˈteɪn] *vt* erreichen; **~ments** *npl* Kenntnisse *pl*

attempt [əˈtempt] *n* Versuch *m* ♦ *vt* versuchen; **~ed murder** Mordversuch *m*

attend [əˈtend] *vt (go to)* teilnehmen (an +*dat*); *(lectures)* besuchen; **to ~ to** *(needs)* nachkommen +*dat*; *(person)* sich kümmern um; **~ance** *n (presence)* Anwesenheit *f*; *(people present)* Besucherzahl *f*; **good ~ance** gute Teilnahme; **~ant** *n (companion)* Begleiter(in) *m(f)*; Gesellschafter(in) *m(f)*; *(in car park etc)* Wächter(in) *m(f)*; *(servant)* Bedienstete(r) *mf* ♦ *adj* begleitend; *(fig)* damit verbunden

attention [əˈtenʃən] *n* Aufmerksamkeit *f*; *(care)* Fürsorge *f*; *(for machine etc)* Pflege *f* ♦ *excl (MIL)* Achtung!; **for the ~ of** ... zu Händen (von) ...

attentive [əˈtentɪv] *adj* aufmerksam

attic [ˈætɪk] *n* Dachstube *f*, Mansarde *f*

attitude [ˈætɪtjuːd] *n (mental)* Einstellung *f*

attorney [əˈtɜːnɪ] *n (solicitor)* Rechtsanwalt *m*; **A~ General** *n* Justizminister *m*

attract [əˈtrækt] *vt* anziehen; *(attention)* erregen; **~ion** *n* Anziehungskraft *f*; *(thing)* Attraktion *f*; **~ive** *adj* attraktiv

attribute [*n* ˈætrɪbjuːt, *vb* əˈtrɪbjuːt] *n* Eigenschaft *f*, Attribut *nt* ♦ *vt* zuschreiben

attrition [əˈtrɪʃən] *n:* **war of ~** Zermürbungskrieg *m*

aubergine [ˈəubəʒiːn] *n* Aubergine *f*

auburn [ˈɔːbən] *adj* kastanienbraun

auction [ˈɔːkʃən] *n (also:* **sale by ~)** Versteigerung *f*, Auktion *f* ♦ *vt* versteigern; **~eer** [ɔːkʃəˈnɪəʳ] *n* Versteigerer *m*

audacity [ɔːˈdæsɪtɪ] *n (boldness)* Wagemut *m*; *(impudence)* Unverfrorenheit *f*

audible [ˈɔːdɪbl] *adj* hörbar

audience [ˈɔːdɪəns] *n* Zuhörer *pl*, Zuschauer *pl*; *(with queen)* Audienz *f*

audiotypist [ˈɔːdɪəʊtaɪpɪst] *n* Phonotypistin *f*, Fonotypistin *f*

audiovisual [ˈɔːdɪəʊˈvɪzjʊəl] *adj* audiovisuell

audit [ˈɔːdɪt] *vt* prüfen

audition [ɔːˈdɪʃən] *n* Probe *f*

auditor [ˈɔːdɪtəʳ] *n (accountant)* Rechnungsprüfer(in) *m(f)*, Buchprüfer *m*

auditorium [ɔːdɪˈtɔːrɪəm] *n* Zuschauerraum *m*

augment [ɔːgˈment] *vt* vermehren

augur [ˈɔːgəʳ] *vi* bedeuten, voraussagen; **this ~s well** das ist ein gutes Omen

August [ˈɔːgəst] *n* August *m*

aunt [ɑːnt] *n* Tante *f*; **~ie** *n* Tantchen *nt*; **~y** *n* = **auntie**

au pair [ˈəuˈpeəʳ] *n (also:* **~ girl)** Aupairmädchen *nt*, Au-pair-Mädchen *nt*

aura [ˈɔːrə] *n* Nimbus *m*

auspicious [ɔːsˈpɪʃəs] *adj* günstig; verheißungsvoll

austere [ɒsˈtɪəʳ] *adj* streng; *(room)* nüchtern; **austerity** [ɒsˈtɛrɪtɪ] *n* Strenge *f*; *(POL)* wirtschaftliche Einschränkung *f*

Australia [ɒsˈtreɪlɪə] *n* Australien *nt*; **~n** *adj* australisch ♦ *n* Australier(in) *m(f)*

Austria [ˈɒstrɪə] *n* Österreich *nt*; **~n** *adj* österreichisch ♦ *n* Österreicher(in) *m(f)*

authentic [ɔːˈθentɪk] *adj* echt, authentisch

author [ˈɔːθəʳ] *n* Autor *m*, Schriftsteller *m*; *(beginner)* Urheber *m*, Schöpfer *m*

authoritarian [ɔːθɒrɪˈtɛərɪən] *adj* autoritär

authoritative [ɔːˈθɒrɪtətɪv] *adj (account)* maßgeblich; *(manner)* herrisch

authority [ɔːˈθɒrɪtɪ] *n (power)* Autorität *f*; *(expert)* Autorität *f*, Fachmann *m*; **the authorities** *npl (ruling body)* die Behörden *pl*

authorize [ˈɔːθəraɪz] *vt* bevollmächtigen; *(permit)* genehmigen

auto [ˈɔːtəu] *(US) n* Auto *nt*, Wagen *m*

autobiography [ɔːtəbaɪˈɒgrəfɪ] *n* Autobiografie *f*

autograph [ˈɔːtəɡrɑːf] *n (of celebrity)* Autogramm *nt* ♦ *vt* mit Autogramm versehen

automatic [ɔːtəˈmætɪk] *adj* automatisch ♦ *n* *(gun)* Selbstladepistole *f*; *(car)* Automatik *m*; **~ally** *adv* automatisch

automation [ɔːtəˈmeɪʃən] *n* Automatisierung *f*

automobile [ˈɔːtəməbiːl] *(US) n* Auto(mobil) *nt*

autonomous [ɔːˈtɒnəməs] *adj* autonom; **autonomy** *n* Autonomie *f*

autumn [ˈɔːtəm] *n* Herbst *m*

auxiliary [ɔːgˈzɪlɪərɪ] *adj* Hilfs-

Av. *abbr* = **avenue**

avail [əˈveɪl] *vt:* **to ~ o.s. of sth** sich einer Sache *gen* bedienen ♦ *n:* **to no ~** nutzlos

availability [əveɪləˈbɪlɪtɪ] *n* Erhältlichkeit *f*, Vorhandensein *nt*

available [əˈveɪləbl] *adj* erhältlich; zur Verfügung stehend; *(person)* erreichbar, abkömmlich

avalanche [ˈævəlɑːnʃ] *n* Lawine *f*

avenge [əˈvendʒ] *vt* rächen, sühnen

avenue |'ævənjuː| n Allee f
average |'ævərɪdʒ| n Durchschnitt m ♦ adj
durchschnittlich, Durchschnitts- ♦ vt (figures)
den Durchschnitt nehmen von; (perform)
durchschnittlich leisten; (in car etc) im
Schnitt fahren; **on ~** durchschnittlich, im
Durchschnitt; **~ out** vi: **to ~ out at** im
Durchschnitt betragen
averse |ə'vɜːs| adj: **to be ~ to doing sth**
eine Abneigung dagegen haben, etw zu
tun
avert |ə'vɜːt| vt (turn away) abkehren;
(prevent) abwehren
aviary |'eɪvɪərɪ| n Vogelhaus nt
aviation |eɪvɪ'eɪʃən| n Luftfahrt f, Flugwesen
nt
avid |'ævɪd| adj: **~ (for)** gierig (auf +acc)
avocado |ævə'kɑːdəʊ| n (BRIT: also: **~ pear**)
Avocado(birne) f
avoid |ə'vɔɪd| vt vermeiden
await |ə'weɪt| vt erwarten, entgegensehen
+dat
awake |ə'weɪk| (pt **awoke**, pp **awoken** or
awaked) adj wach ♦ vt (auf)wecken ♦ vi
aufwachen; **to be ~** wach sein; **~ning** n
Erwachen nt
award |ə'wɔːd| n (prize) Preis m ♦ vt: **to ~
(sb sth)** (jdm etw) zuerkennen
aware |ə'weər| adj bewusst; **to be ~** sich
bewusst sein; **~ness** n Bewusstsein nt
awash |ə'wɒʃ| adj überflutet
away |ə'weɪ| adv weg, fort; **two hours ~ by
car** zwei Autostunden entfernt; **the holiday
was two weeks ~** es war noch zwei
Wochen bis zum Urlaub; **two kilometres ~**
zwei Kilometer entfernt; **~ match** n (SPORT)
Auswärtsspiel nt
awe |ɔː| n Ehrfurcht f; **~-inspiring** adj
Ehrfurcht gebietend; **~some** adj Ehrfurcht
gebietend
awful |'ɔːfəl| adj (very bad) furchtbar; **~ly** adv
furchtbar, sehr
awhile |ə'waɪl| adv eine Weile
awkward |'ɔːkwəd| adj (clumsy) ungeschickt,
linkisch; (embarrassing) peinlich
awning |'ɔːnɪŋ| n Markise f
awoke |ə'wəʊk| pt of **awake**; **~n** pp of
awake
awry |ə'raɪ| adv schief; **to go ~** (plans) schief
gehen
axe |æks| (US **ax**) n Axt f, Beil nt ♦ vt (end
suddenly) streichen
axes[1] |'æksɪz| npl of **axe**
axes[2] |'æksiːz| npl of **axis**
axis |'æksɪs| (pl **axes**) n Achse f
axle |'æksl| n Achse f
ay(e) |aɪ| excl (yes) ja
azalea |ə'zeɪlɪə| n Azalee f

B, b

B |biː| n (MUS) H nt; **~ road** (BRIT) Landstraße
f
B.A. n abbr = **Bachelor of Arts**
babble |'bæbl| vi schwätzen
baby |'beɪbɪ| n Baby nt; **~ carriage** (US) n
Kinderwagen m; **~ food** n Babynahrung f;
~-sit vi Kinder hüten, babysitten; **~-sitter**
n Babysitter m; **~-sitting** n Babysitten nt,
Babysitting nt; **~ wipe** n Ölpflegetuch
nt
bachelor |'bætʃələr| n Junggeselle m; **B~ of
Arts** Bakkalaureus m der philosophischen
Fakultät; **B~ of Science** Bakkalaureus m der
Naturwissenschaften
back |bæk| n (of person, horse) Rücken m; (of
house) Rückseite f; (of train) Ende nt;
(FOOTBALL) Verteidiger m ♦ vt (support)
unterstützen; (wager) wetten auf +acc; (car)
rückwärts fahren ♦ vi (go backwards)
rückwärts gehen or fahren ♦ adj hintere(r, s)
♦ adv zurück; (to the rear) nach hinten; **~
down** vi zurückstecken; (inf) kneifen; **~ out** vi sich
zurückziehen; (inf) kneifen; **~ up** vt
(support) unterstützen; (car) zurücksetzen;
(COMPUT) eine Sicherungskopie machen
von; **~ache** n Rückenschmerzen pl;
~bencher (BRIT) n Parlamentarier(in) m(f);
~bone n Rückgrat nt; (support) Rückhalt m;
~cloth n Hintergrund m; **~date** vt
rückdatieren; (wager) wetten auf +acc; (car)
(~ground) Hintergrund m; **~fire** vi (plan)
fehlschlagen; (TECH) fehlzünden; **~ground** n
Hintergrund m; (person's education)
Vorbildung f; **family ~ground**
Familienverhältnisse pl; **~hand** n (TENNIS:
also: **~hand stroke**) Rückhand f; **~hander**
(BRIT) n (bribe) Schmiergeld nt; **~ing** n
(support) Unterstützung f; **~lash** n (fig)
Gegenschlag m; **~log** n (of work) Rückstand
m; **~ number** n (PRESS) alte Nummer f;
~pack n Rucksack m; **~packer** n
Rucksacktourist(in) m(f); **~ pain** n
Rückenschmerzen pl; **~ pay** n (Gehalts- or
Lohn)nachzahlung f; **~ payments** npl
Zahlungsrückstände pl; **~ seat** n (AUT)
Rücksitz m; **~side** (inf) n Hintern m; **~stage**
adv hinter den Kulissen; **~stroke** n
Rückenschwimmen nt; **~up** adj (COMPUT)
Sicherungs- ♦ n (COMPUT) Sicherungskopie f;
~ward adj (less developed) zurückgeblieben;
(primitive) rückständig; **~wards** adv
rückwärts; **~water** n (fig) Kaff nt; **~yard** n
Hinterhof m
bacon |'beɪkən| n Schinkenspeck m
bacteria |bæk'tɪərɪə| npl Bakterien pl
bad |bæd| adj schlecht, schlimm; **to go ~**
schlecht werden
bade |bæd| pt of **bid**

badge |bædʒ| n Abzeichen nt
badger |'bædʒəʳ| n Dachs m
badly |'bædlı| adv schlecht, schlimm; ~
wounded schwer verwundet; **he needs it ~**
er braucht es dringend; **to be ~ off (for
money)** dringend Geld nötig haben
badminton |'bædmıntən| n Federball m,
Badminton nt
bad-tempered |'bæd'tempəd| adj schlecht
gelaunt
baffle |'bæfl| vt (puzzle) verblüffen
bag |bæg| n (sack) Beutel m; (paper) Tüte f;
(handbag) Tasche f; (suitcase) Koffer m; (inf:
old woman) alte Schachtel f ♦ vt (put in sack)
in einen Sack stecken; (hunting) erlegen; **~s
of** (inf: lots of) eine Menge +acc; **~gage**
|'bægıdʒ| n Gepäck nt; **~gage allowance** n
Freigepäck nt; **~gage reclaim** n Gepäck-
ausgabe f; **~gy** |'bægı| adj bauschig,
sackartig
bagpipes |'bægpaıps| npl Dudelsack m
bail |beıl| n (money) Kaution f ♦ vt (prisoner:
usu: grant ~ to) gegen Kaution freilassen;
(boat: also: ~ out) ausschöpfen; **on ~**
(prisoner) gegen Kaution freigelassen; **to ~
sb out** die Kaution für jdn stellen; see also
bale
bailiff |'beılıf| n Gerichtsvollzieher(in) m(f)
bait |beıt| n Köder m ♦ vt mit einem Köder
versehen; (fig) ködern
bake |beık| vt, vi backen; **~d beans**
gebackene Bohnen pl; **~d potatoes** npl in
der Schale gebackene Kartoffeln pl; **~r** n
Bäcker m; **~ry** n Bäckerei f; **baking** n
Backen nt; **baking powder** n Backpulver nt
balance |'bæləns| n (scales) Waage f;
(equilibrium) Gleichgewicht nt; (FIN: state of
account) Saldo m; (difference) Bilanz f;
(amount remaining) Restbetrag m ♦ vt
(weigh) wägen; (make equal) ausgleichen; **~
of trade/payments** Handels-/
Zahlungsbilanz f; **~d** adj ausgeglichen; **~
sheet** n Bilanz f, Rechnungsabschluss m
balcony |'bælkənı| n Balkon m
bald |bɔːld| adj kahl; (statement) knapp
bale |beıl| n Ballen m; **~ out** vi (from a plane)
abspringen
ball |bɔːl| n Ball m; **~ bearing** n Kugellager
nt
ballet |'bæleı| n Ballett nt; **~ dancer** n
Balletttänzer(in) m(f); **~ shoe** n Ballettschuh m
balloon |bə'luːn| n (Luft)ballon m
ballot |'bælət| n (geheime) Abstimmung f
ballpoint (pen) |'bɔːlpɔınt-| n
Kugelschreiber m
ballroom |'bɔːlrum| n Tanzsaal m
Baltic |'bɔːltık| n: **the ~ (Sea)** die Ostsee
bamboo |bæm'buː| n Bambus m
ban |bæn| n Verbot nt ♦ vt verbieten
banana |bə'nɑːnə| n Banane f
band |bænd| n Band nt; (group) Gruppe f;

(of criminals) Bande f; (MUS) Kapelle f, Band
f; **~ together** vi sich zusammentun
bandage |'bændıdʒ| n Verband m; (elastic)
Bandage f ♦ vt (cut) verbinden; (broken limb)
bandagieren
Bandaid |'bændeıd| (® US) n Heftpflaster nt
bandit |'bændıt| n Bandit m, Räuber m
bandwagon |'bændwægən| n: **to jump on
the ~** (fig) auf den fahrenden Zug
aufspringen
bandy |'bændı| vt wechseln; **~-legged** adj
o-beinig, O-beinig
bang |bæŋ| n (explosion) Knall m; (blow) Hieb
m ♦ vt, vi knallen
Bangladesh |bæŋglə'deʃ| n Bangladesch nt
bangle |'bæŋgl| n Armspange f
bangs |bæŋz| (US) npl (fringe) Pony m
banish |'bænıʃ| vt verbannen
banister(s) |'bænıstə(z)| n(pl)
(Treppen)geländer nt
bank |bæŋk| n (raised ground) Erdwall m; (of
lake etc) Ufer nt; (FIN) Bank f ♦ vt (tilt: AVIAT)
in die Kurve bringen; (money) einzahlen; **~
on** vt fus: **to ~ on sth** mit etw rechnen; **~
account** n Bankkonto nt; **~ card** n
Scheckkarte f; **~er** n Bankier m; **~er's card**
(BRIT) n = **bank card**; **B~ holiday** (BRIT) n
gesetzliche(r) Feiertag m; **~ing** n Bankwesen
nt; **~note** n Banknote f; **~ rate** n Banksatz
m
bankrupt |'bæŋkrʌpt| adj: **to be ~** bankrott
sein; **to go ~** Bankrott machen; **~cy** n
Bankrott m
bank statement n Kontoauszug m
banned |bænd| adj: **he was ~ from driving**
(BRIT) ihm wurde Fahrverbot erteilt
banner |'bænəʳ| n Banner nt
banns |bænz| npl Aufgebot nt
baptism |'bæptızəm| n Taufe f
baptize |bæp'taız| vt taufen
bar |bɑːʳ| n (rod) Stange f; (obstacle)
Hindernis nt; (of chocolate) Tafel f; (of soap)
Stück nt; (for food, drink) Buffet nt, Bar f;
(pub) Wirtschaft f; (MUS) Takt(strich) m ♦ vt
(fasten) verriegeln; (hinder) versperren;
(exclude) ausschließen; **behind ~s** hinter
Gittern; **the B~: to be called to the B~** als
Anwalt zugelassen werden; **~ none** ohne
Ausnahme
barbaric |bɑː'bærık| adj primitiv, unkultiviert
barbecue |'bɑːbıkjuː| n Barbecue nt
barbed wire |'bɑːbd-| n Stacheldraht m
barber |'bɑːbəʳ| n Herrenfriseur m
bar code n (COMM) Registrierkode f
bare |beəʳ| adj nackt; (trees, country) kahl;
(mere) bloß ♦ vt entblößen; **~back** adv
ungesattelt; **~faced** adj unverfroren; **~foot**
adj, adv barfuß; **~ly** adv kaum, knapp
bargain |'bɑːgın| n (sth cheap) günstiger
Kauf; (agreement: written) Kaufvertrag m;
(: oral) Geschäft nt; **into the ~** obendrein; **~**

for *vt*: **he got more than he ~ed for** er
erlebte sein blaues Wunder
barge |bɑːdʒ| *n* Lastkahn *m*; **~ in** *vi*
hereinplatzen; **~ into** *vt* rennen gegen
bark |bɑːk| *n* (*of tree*) Rinde *f*; ⟨*of dog*⟩ Bellen
nt ♦ *vi* ⟨*dog*⟩ bellen
barley |'bɑːlɪ| *n* Gerste *f*; **~ sugar** *n*
Malzbonbon *nt*
bar: **~maid** *n* Bardame *f*; **~man** (*irreg*) *n*
Barkellner *m*; **~ meal** *n* einfaches Essen in
einem Pub
barn |bɑːn| *n* Scheune *f*
barometer |bə'rɒmɪtəʳ| *n* Barometer *nt*
baron |'bærən| *n* Baron *m*; **~ess** *n* Baronin *f*
barracks |'bærəks| *npl* Kaserne *f*
barrage |'bærɑːʒ| *n* (*gunfire*) Sperrfeuer *nt*;
(*dam*) Staudamm *m*; Talsperre *f*
barrel |'bærəl| *n* Fass *nt*; (*of gun*) Lauf *m*
barren |'bærən| *adj* unfruchtbar
barricade |bærɪ'keɪd| *n* Barrikade *f* ♦ *vt*
verbarrikadieren
barrier |'bærɪəʳ| *n* (*obstruction*) Hindernis *nt*;
(*fence*) Schranke *f*
barring |'bɑːrɪŋ| *prep* außer im Falle +*gen*
barrister |'bærɪstəʳ| (*BRIT*) *n* Rechtsanwalt *m*
barrow |'bærəʊ| *n* (*cart*) Schubkarren *m*
bartender |'bɑːtɛndəʳ| (*US*) *n* Barmann or
-kellner *m*
barter |'bɑːtəʳ| *vt* handeln
base |beɪs| *n* (*bottom*) Boden *m*, Basis *f*; (*MIL*)
Stützpunkt *m* ♦ *vt* gründen; (*opinion,*
theory): **to be ~d on** basieren auf +*dat* ♦ *adj*
(*low*) gemein; **I'm ~d in London** ich wohne
in London; **~ball** |'beɪsbɔːl| *n* Baseball *m*;
~ment |'beɪsmənt| *n* Kellergeschoss *nt*
bases[1] |'beɪsɪz| *npl of* **base**
bases[2] |'beɪsiːz| *npl of* **basis**
bash |bæʃ| (*inf*) *vt* (heftig) schlagen
bashful |'bæʃful| *adj* schüchtern
basic |'beɪsɪk| *adj* grundlegend; **~s** *npl*: **the**
~s das Wesentliche *sg*; **~ally** *adv* im
Grunde
basil |'bæzl| *n* Basilikum *nt*
basin |'beɪsn| *n* (*dish*) Schüssel *f*; (*for*
washing, also valley) Becken *nt*; (*dock*)
(Trocken)becken *nt*
basis |'beɪsɪs| (*pl* **bases**) *n* Basis *f*, Grundlage
f
bask |bɑːsk| *vi*: **to ~ in the sun** sich sonnen
basket |'bɑːskɪt| *n* Korb *m*; **~ball** *n* Basketball
m
bass |beɪs| *n* (*MUS, also instrument*) Bass *m*;
(*voice*) Bassstimme *f*; **~ drum** *n* große
Trommel
bassoon |bə'suːn| *n* Fagott *nt*
bastard |'bɑːstəd| *n* Bastard *m*; (*inf!*)
Arschloch *nt* (!)
bat |bæt| *n* (*SPORT*) Schlagholz *nt*; Schläger
m; (*ZOOL*) Fledermaus *f* ♦ *vt*: **he didn't ~ an**
eyelid er hat nicht mit der Wimper gezuckt
batch |bætʃ| *n* (*of letters*) Stoß *m*; (*of samples*)

Satz *m*
bated |'beɪtɪd| *adj*: **with ~ breath** mit
angehaltenem Atem
bath |bɑːθ| *n* Bad *nt*; (*~ tub*) Badewanne *f*
♦ *vt* baden; **to have a ~** baden; *see also*
baths
bathe |beɪð| *vt*, *vi* baden; **~r** *n* Badende(r)
f(m)
bathing |'beɪðɪŋ| *n* Baden *nt*; **~ cap** *n*
Badekappe *f*; **~ costume** *n* Badeanzug *m*; **~**
suit (*US*) *n* Badeanzug *m*; **~ trunks** (*BRIT*)
npl Badehose *f*
bath: **~robe** *n* Bademantel *m*; **~room** *n*
Bad(ezimmer) *nt*; **~s** *npl* (Schwimm)bad *nt*;
~ towel *n* Badetuch *nt*
baton |'bætən| *n* (*of police*) Gummiknüppel
m; (*MUS*) Taktstock *m*
batter |'bætəʳ| *vt* verprügeln ♦ *n* Schlagteig
m; (*for cake*) Biskuitteig *m*; **~ed** *adj* (*hat,*
pan) verbeult
battery |'bætərɪ| *n* (*ELEC*) Batterie *f*; (*MIL*)
Geschützbatterie *f*
battery farming *n* (Hühner- *etc*)batterien *pl*
battle |'bætl| *n* Schlacht *f*; (*small*) Gefecht *nt*
♦ *vi* kämpfen; **~field** *n* Schlachtfeld *nt*;
~ship *n* Schlachtschiff *nt*
Bavaria |bə'veərɪə| *n* Bayern *nt*; **~n** *adj*
bay(e)risch ♦ *n* (*person*) Bayer(in) *m(f)*
bawdy |'bɔːdɪ| *adj* unflätig
bawl |bɔːl| *vi* brüllen
bay |beɪ| *n* (*of sea*) Bucht *f* ♦ *vi* bellen; **to**
keep at ~ unter Kontrolle halten; **~**
window *n* Erkerfenster *nt*
bazaar |bə'zɑːʳ| *n* Basar *m*
B. & B. *abbr* = **bed and breakfast**
BBC *n abbr* (= *British Broadcasting*
Corporation) BBC *f* or *m*
B.C. *adv abbr* (= *before Christ*) v. Chr.

KEYWORD

be |biː| (*pt* **was, were,** *pp* **been**) *aux vb* **1**
(*with present participle: forming continuous*
tenses): **what are you doing?** was machst
du (gerade)?; **it is raining** es regnet; **I've**
been waiting for you for hours ich warte
schon seit Stunden auf dich
2 (*with pp: forming passives*): **to be killed**
getötet werden; **the thief was nowhere to**
be seen der Dieb war nirgendwo zu sehen
3 (*in tag questions*): **it was fun, wasn't it?**
es hat Spaß gemacht, nicht wahr?
4 (*+to +infin*): **the house is to be sold** das
Haus soll verkauft werden; **he's not to open**
it er darf es nicht öffnen
♦ *vb +complement* **1** (*usu*) sein; **I'm tired** ich
bin müde; **I'm hot/cold** mir ist heiß/kalt;
he's a doctor or ist Arzt; **2 and 2 are 4** 2
und 2 ist or sind 4; **she's tall/pretty** sie ist
groß/hübsch; **be careful/quiet** sei
vorsichtig/ruhig
2 (*of health*): **how are you?** wie geht es

dir?; **he's very ill** er ist sehr krank; **I'm fine now** jetzt geht es mir gut
3 (*of age*): **how old are you?** wie alt bist du?; **I'm sixteen (years old)** ich bin sechzehn (Jahre alt)
4 (*cost*): **how much was the meal?** was *or* wie viel hat das Essen gekostet?; **that'll be £5.75, please** das macht £5.75, bitte
♦ *vi* **1** (*exist, occur etc*) sein; **is there a God?** gibt es einen Gott?; **be that as it may** wie dem auch sei; **so be it** also gut
2 (*referring to place*) sein; **I won't be here tomorrow** ich werde morgen nicht hier sein
3 (*referring to movement*): **where have you been?** wo bist du gewesen?; **I've been in the garden** ich war im Garten
♦ *impers vb* **1** (*referring to time, distance, weather*) sein; **it's 5 o'clock** es ist 5 Uhr; **it's 10 km to the village** es sind 10 km bis zum Dorf; **it's too hot/cold** es ist zu heiß/kalt
2 (*emphatic*): **it's me** ich bins; **it's the postman** es ist der Briefträger

beach |biːtʃ| *n* Strand *m* ♦ *vt* (*ship*) auf den Strand setzen
beacon |ˈbiːkən| *n* (*signal*) Leuchtfeuer *nt*; (*traffic ~*) Bake *f*
bead |biːd| *n* Perle *f*; (*drop*) Tropfen *m*
beak |biːk| *n* Schnabel *m*
beaker |ˈbiːkəʳ| *n* Becher *m*
beam |biːm| *n* (*of wood*) Balken *m*; (*of light*) Strahl *m*; (*smile*) strahlende(s) Lächeln *nt* ♦ *vi* strahlen
bean |biːn| *n* Bohne *f*; (*also:* **baked ~s**) gebackene Bohnen *pl*; **~ sprouts** *npl* Sojasprossen *pl*
bear |bɛəʳ| (*pt* **bore**, *pp* **borne**) *n* Bär *m* ♦ *vt* (*weight, crops*) tragen; (*tolerate*) ertragen; (*young*) gebären ♦ *vi*: **to ~ it** schlagen; **to ~ right/left** sich rechts/links halten; **~ out** *vt* (*suspicions etc*) bestätigen; **~ up** *vi* sich halten
beard |biəd| *n* Bart *m*; **~ed** *adj* bärtig
bearer |ˈbɛərəʳ| *n* Träger *m*
bearing |ˈbɛərɪŋ| *n* (*posture*) Haltung *f*; (*relevance*) Relevanz *f*; (*relation*) Bedeutung *f*; (*TECH*) Kugellager *nt*; **~s** *npl* (*direction*) Orientierung *f*; (*also:* **ball ~s**) (Kugel)lager *nt*
beast |biːst| *n* Tier *nt*, Vieh *nt*; (*person*) Biest *nt*
beat |biːt| (*pt* **beat**, *pp* **beaten**) *n* (*stroke*) Schlag *m*; (*pulsation*) (Herz)schlag *m*; (*police round*) Runde *f*; Revier *nt*; (*MUS*) Takt *m*; Beat *m* ♦ *vt, vi* schlagen; **to ~ it** abhauen; **off the ~en track** abgelegen; **~ off** *vt* abschlagen; **~ up** *vt* zusammenschlagen; **~en up** *pp* of **beat**; **~ing** *n* Prügel *pl*
beautiful |ˈbjuːtɪful| *adj* schön; **~ly** *adv* ausgezeichnet
beauty |ˈbjuːtɪ| *n* Schönheit *f*; **~ salon** *n* Schönheitssalon *m*; **~ spot** *n* Schönheitsfleck

m; (*BRIT: TOURISM*) (besonders) schöne(r) Ort *m*
beaver |ˈbiːvəʳ| *n* Biber *m*
became |bɪˈkeɪm| *pt* of **become**
because |bɪˈkɒz| *conj* weil ♦ *prep*: **~ of** wegen +*gen*, wegen +*dat* (*inf*)
beck |bɛk| *n*: **to be at the ~ and call of sb** nach jds Pfeife tanzen
beckon |ˈbɛkən| *vt, vi*: **to ~ to sb** jdm ein Zeichen geben
become |bɪˈkʌm| (*irreg: like* **come**) *vi* werden ♦ *vt* werden; (*clothes*) stehen +*dat*
becoming |bɪˈkʌmɪŋ| *adj* (*suitable*) schicklich; (*clothes*) kleidsam
bed |bɛd| *n* Bett *nt*; (*of river*) Flussbett *nt*; (*foundation*) Schicht *f*; (*in garden*) Beet *nt*; **to go to ~** zu Bett gehen; **~ and breakfast** *n* Übernachtung *f* mit Frühstück; **~clothes** *npl* Bettwäsche *f*; **~ding** *n* Bettzeug *nt*
bedlam |ˈbɛdləm| *n* (*uproar*) tolle(s) Durcheinander *nt*
bed linen *n* Bettwäsche *f*
bedraggled |bɪˈdrægld| *adj* ramponiert
bed-: **~ridden** *adj* bettlägerig; **~room** *n* Schlafzimmer *nt*; **~side** *n*: **at the ~side** am Bett; **~sit(ter)** (*BRIT*) *n* Einzimmerwohnung *f*, möbliertes Zimmer *nt*; **~spread** *n* Tagesdecke *f*; **~time** *n* Schlafenszeit *f*
bee |biː| *n* Biene *f*
beech |biːtʃ| *n* Buche *f*
beef |biːf| *n* Rindfleisch *nt*; **roast ~** Roastbeef *nt*; **~burger** *n* Hamburger *m*
beehive |ˈbiːhaɪv| *n* Bienenstock *m*
beeline |ˈbiːlaɪn| *n*: **to make a ~ for** schnurstracks zugehen auf +*acc*
been |biːn| *pp* of **be**
beer |biəʳ| *n* Bier *nt*
beet |biːt| *n* (*vegetable*) Rübe *f*; (*US: also:* **red ~**) Rote Bete *f or* Rübe *f*
beetle |ˈbiːtl| *n* Käfer *m*
beetroot |ˈbiːtruːt| (*BRIT*) *n* Rote Bete *f*
before |bɪˈfɔːʳ| *prep* vor ♦ *conj* bevor ♦ *adv* (*of time*) zuvor; früher; **the week ~** die Woche zuvor *or* vorher; **I've done it ~** das hab ich schon mal getan; **~ going** bevor er/sie *etc* geht/ging; **~ she goes** bevor sie geht; **~hand** *adv* im Voraus
beg |bɛg| *vt, vi* (*implore*) dringend bitten; (*alms*) betteln
began |bɪˈgæn| *pt* of **begin**
beggar |ˈbɛgəʳ| *n* Bettler(in) *m(f)*
begin |bɪˈgɪn| (*pt* **began**, *pp* **begun**) *vt, vi* anfangen, beginnen; (*found*) gründen; **to ~ doing** *or* **to do sth** anfangen *or* beginnen, etw zu tun; **to ~ with** zunächst (einmal); **~ner** *n* Anfänger *m*; **~ning** *n* Anfang *m*
begun |bɪˈgʌn| *pp* of **begin**
behalf |bɪˈhɑːf| *n*: **on ~ of** im Namen +*gen*; **on my ~** für mich
behave |bɪˈheɪv| *vi* sich benehmen; **behaviour** |bɪˈheɪvjəʳ| (*US* **behavior**) *n*

Benehmen nt

beheld |bɪˈheld| pt, pp of **behold**

behind |bɪˈhaɪnd| prep hinter ♦ adv (late) im Rückstand; (in the rear) hinten ♦ n (inf) Hinterteil nt; ~ **the scenes** (fig) hinter den Kulissen

behold |bɪˈhəuld| (irreg: like **hold**) vt erblicken

beige |beɪʒ| adj beige

Beijing |ˈbeɪˈdʒɪŋ| n Peking nt

being |ˈbiːɪŋ| n (existence) (Da)sein nt; (person) Wesen nt; **to come into ~** entstehen

Belarus |belaˈrus| n Weißrußland nt

belated |bɪˈleɪtɪd| adj verspätet

belch |beltʃ| vi rülpsen ♦ vt (smoke) ausspeien

belfry |ˈbelfrɪ| n Glockenturm m

Belgian |ˈbeldʒən| adj belgisch ♦ n Belgier(in) m(f)

Belgium |ˈbeldʒəm| n Belgien nt

belie |bɪˈlaɪ| vt Lügen strafen +acc

belief |bɪˈliːf| n Glaube m; (conviction) Überzeugung f; ~ **in sb/sth** Glaube an jdn/ etw

believe |bɪˈliːv| vt glauben +dat; (think) glauben, meinen, denken ♦ vi (have faith) glauben; **to ~ in sth** an etw acc glauben; **~r** n Gläubige(r) f(m)

belittle |bɪˈlɪtl| vt herabsetzen

bell |bel| n Glocke f

belligerent |bɪˈlɪdʒərənt| adj (person) streitsüchtig; (country) Krieg führend

bellow |ˈbeləu| vt, vi brüllen

bellows |ˈbeləuz| npl (TECH) Gebläse nt; (for fire) Blasebalg m

belly |ˈbelɪ| n Bauch m

belong |bɪˈlɒŋ| vi gehören; **to ~ to sb** jdm gehören; **to ~ to a club** etc einem Klub etc angehören; **~ings** npl Habe f

beloved |bɪˈlʌvɪd| adj innig geliebt ♦ n Geliebte(r) f(m)

below |bɪˈləu| prep unter ♦ adv unten

belt |belt| n (band) Riemen m; (round waist) Gürtel m ♦ vt (fasten) mit Riemen befestigen; (inf: beat) schlagen; **~way** (US) n (AUT: ring road) Umgehungsstraße f

bemused |bɪˈmjuːzd| adj verwirrt

bench |bentʃ| n (seat) Bank f; (workshop) Werkbank f; (judge's seat) Richterbank f; (judges) Richter pl

bend |bend| (pt, pp bent) vt (curve) biegen; (stoop) beugen ♦ vi sich biegen; sich beugen ♦ n Biegung f; (BRIT: in road) Kurve f; **~ down or over** vi sich bücken

beneath |bɪˈniːθ| prep unter ♦ adv darunter

benefactor |ˈbenɪfæktər| n Wohltäter(in) m(f)

beneficial |benɪˈfɪʃəl| adj vorteilhaft; (to health) heilsam

benefit |ˈbenɪfɪt| n (advantage) Nutzen m ♦ vt fördern ♦ vi: **to ~ (from)** Nutzen ziehen (aus)

Benelux |ˈbenɪlʌks| n Beneluxstaaten pl

benevolent |bɪˈnevələnt| adj wohlwollend

benign |bɪˈnaɪn| adj (person) gütig; (climate) mild

bent |bent| pt, pp of **bend** ♦ n (inclination) Neigung f ♦ adj (inf: dishonest) unehrlich; **to be ~ on** versessen sein auf +acc

bequest |bɪˈkwest| n Vermächtnis nt

bereaved |bɪˈriːvd| npl: **the ~** die Hinterbliebenen pl

beret |ˈbereɪ| n Baskenmütze f

Berlin |bəːˈlɪn| n Berlin nt

berm |bəːm| (US) n (AUT) Seitenstreifen m

berry |ˈberɪ| n Beere f

berserk |bəˈsəːk| adj: **to go ~** wild werden

berth |bəːθ| n (for ship) Ankerplatz m; (in ship) Koje f; (in train) Bett nt ♦ vt am Kai festmachen ♦ vi anlegen

beseech |bɪˈsiːtʃ| (pt, pp **besought**) vt anflehen

beset |bɪˈset| (pt, pp **beset**) vt bedrängen

beside |bɪˈsaɪd| prep neben, bei; (except) außer; **to be ~ o.s. (with)** außer sich sein (vor +dat); **that's ~ the point** das tut nichts zur Sache

besides |bɪˈsaɪdz| prep außer, neben ♦ adv außerdem

besiege |bɪˈsiːdʒ| vt (MIL) belagern; (surround) umlagern, bedrängen

besought |bɪˈsɔːt| pt, pp of **beseech**

best |best| adj beste(r, s) ♦ adv am besten; **the ~ part of** (quantity) das meiste +gen; **at ~** höchstens; **to make the ~ of it** das Beste daraus machen; **to do one's ~** sein Bestes tun; **to the ~ of my knowledge** meines Wissens; **to the ~ of my ability** so gut ich kann; **for the ~** zum Besten; **~-before date** n Mindesthaltbarkeitsdatum nt; **~ man** n Trauzeuge m

bestow |bɪˈstəu| vt verleihen

bet |bet| (pt, pp bet or betted) n Wette f ♦ vt, vi wetten

betray |bɪˈtreɪ| vt verraten

better |ˈbetər| adj, adv besser ♦ vt verbessern ♦ n: **to get the ~ of sb** jdn überwinden; **he thought ~ of it** er hat sich eines Besseren besonnen; **you had ~ leave** Sie gehen jetzt wohl besser; **to get ~** (MED) gesund werden; **~ off** adj (richer) wohlhabender

betting |ˈbetɪŋ| n Wetten nt; **~ shop** (BRIT) n Wettbüro nt

between |bɪˈtwiːn| prep zwischen; (among) unter ♦ adv dazwischen

beverage |ˈbevərɪdʒ| n Getränk nt

bevy |ˈbevɪ| n Schar f

beware |bɪˈweər| vt, vi sich hüten vor +dat; **"~ of the dog"** „Vorsicht, bissiger Hund!"

bewildered |bɪˈwɪldəd| adj verwirrt

beyond |bɪˈjɒnd| prep (place) jenseits +gen; (time) über ... hinaus; (out of reach) außerhalb +gen ♦ adv darüber hinaus; ~

doubt ohne Zweifel; **~ repair** nicht mehr zu reparieren

bias ['baɪəs] n (slant) Neigung f; (prejudice) Vorurteil nt; **~(s)ed** adj voreingenommen

bib |bɪb| n Latz m

Bible ['baɪbl] n Bibel f

bicarbonate of soda |baɪ'kɑːbənɪt-| n Natron nt

bicker ['bɪkə'] vi zanken

bicycle ['baɪsɪkl] n Fahrrad nt

bid |bɪd| (pt **bade** or **bid**, pp **bid(den)**) (offer) Gebot nt; (attempt) Versuch m ♦ vt, vi (offer) bieten; **to ~ farewell** Lebewohl sagen; **~der** n (person) Steigerer m; **the highest ~der** der Meistbietende; **~ding** n (command) Geheiß nt

bide |baɪd| vt: **to ~ one's time** abwarten

bifocals |baɪ'fəuklz| npl Bifokalbrille f

big |bɪg| adj groß; **~ dipper** [-'dɪpə'] n Achterbahn f; **~headed** ['bɪg'hedɪd] adj eingebildet

bigot ['bɪgət] n Frömmler m; **~ed** adj bigott; **~ry** n Bigotterie f

big top n Zirkuszelt nt

bike |baɪk| n Rad nt

bikini [bɪ'kiːnɪ] n Bikini m

bile |baɪl| n (BIOL) Galle f

bilingual [baɪ'lɪŋgwəl] adj zweisprachig

bill |bɪl| n (account) Rechnung f; (POL) Gesetzentwurf m; (US: FIN) Geldschein m; **to fit** or **fill the ~** (fig) der/die/das Richtige sein; **"post no ~s"** „Plakate ankleben verboten"; **~board** ['bɪlbɔːd] n Reklameschild nt

billet ['bɪlɪt] n Quartier nt

billfold ['bɪlfəuld] (US) n Geldscheintasche f

billiards ['bɪljədz] n Billard nt

billion ['bɪljən] n (BRIT) Billion f; (US) Milliarde f

bimbo ['bɪmbəu] (inf: pej) n Puppe f, Häschen nt

bin |bɪn| n Kasten m; (dustbin) (Abfall)eimer m

bind |baɪnd| (pt, pp **bound**) vt (tie) binden; (tie together) zusammenbinden; (oblige) verpflichten; **~ing** n (Buch)einband m ♦ adj verbindlich

binge |bɪndʒ| (inf) n Sauferei f

bingo ['bɪŋgəu] n Bingo nt

binoculars [bɪ'nɔkjuləz] npl Fernglas nt

bio... |baɪəu| prefix: **~chemistry** n Biochemie f; **~degradable** adj biologisch abbaubar; **~graphy** n Biografie f; **~logical** [baɪə'lɔdʒɪkl] adj biologisch; **~logy** |baɪ'ɔlədʒɪ| n Biologie f

birch |bɜːtʃ| n Birke f

bird |bɜːd| n Vogel m; (BRIT: inf: girl) Mädchen nt; **~'s-eye view** n Vogelschau f; **~ watcher** n Vogelbeobachter(in) m(f); **~ watching** n Vogelbeobachten nt

Biro ['baɪərəu] ® n Kugelschreiber m

birth [bɜːθ] n Geburt f; **to give ~ to** zur Welt bringen; **~ certificate** n Geburtsurkunde f; **~ control** n Geburtenkontrolle f; **~day** n Geburtstag m; **~day card** n Geburtstagskarte f; **~place** n Geburtsort m; **~ rate** n Geburtenrate f

biscuit ['bɪskɪt] n Keks m

bisect [baɪ'sekt] vt halbieren

bishop ['bɪʃəp] n Bischof m

bit |bɪt| pt of **bite** ♦ n bisschen, Stückchen nt; (horse's) Gebiss nt; (COMPUT) Bit nt; **a ~ tired** etwas müde

bitch |bɪtʃ| n (dog) Hündin f; (unpleasant woman) Weibsstück nt

bite |baɪt| (pt **bit**, pp **bitten**) vt, vi beißen ♦ n Biss m; (mouthful) Bissen m; **to ~ one's nails** Nägel kauen; **let's have a ~ to eat** lass uns etwas essen

bitten ['bɪtn] pp of **bite**

bitter ['bɪtə'] adj bitter; (memory etc) schmerzlich; (person) verbittert ♦ n (BRIT: beer) dunkle(s) Bier nt; **~ness** n Bitterkeit f

blab |blæb| vi klatschen ♦ vt (also: ~ **out**) ausplaudern

black |blæk| adj schwarz; (night) finster ♦ vt schwärzen; (shoes) wichsen; (eye) blau schlagen; (BRIT: INDUSTRY) boykottieren; **to give sb a ~ eye** jdm ein blaues Auge schlagen; **in the ~** (bank account) in den schwarzen Zahlen; **~ and blue** adj grün und blau; **~berry** n Brombeere f; **~bird** n Amsel f; **~board** n (Wand)tafel f; **~ coffee** n schwarze(r) Kaffee m; **~currant** n schwarze Johannisbeere f; **~en** vt schwärzen; (fig) verunglimpfen; **B~ Forest** n Schwarzwald m; **~ ice** n Glatteis nt; **~leg** (BRIT) n Streikbrecher(in) m(f); **~list** n schwarze Liste f; **~mail** n Erpressung f ♦ vt erpressen; **~ market** n Schwarzmarkt m; **~out** n Verdunklung f; (MED): **to have a ~out** bewusstlos werden; **~ pudding** n ≈ Blutwurst f; **B~ Sea** n: **the B~ Sea** das Schwarze Meer; **~ sheep** n schwarze(s) Schaf nt; **~smith** n Schmied m; **~ spot** n (AUT) Gefahrenstelle f; (for unemployment etc) schwer betroffene(s) Gebiet nt

bladder ['blædə'] n Blase f

blade |bleɪd| n (of weapon) Klinge f; (of grass) Halm m; (of oar) Ruderblatt nt

blame |bleɪm| n Tadel m, Schuld f ♦ vt Vorwürfe machen +dat; **to ~ sb for sth** jdm die Schuld an etw dat geben; **he is to ~** er ist daran schuld

bland [blænd] adj mild

blank |blæŋk| adj leer, unbeschrieben; (look) verdutzt; (verse) Blank- ♦ n (space) Lücke f; Zwischenraum m; (cartridge) Platzpatrone f; **~ cheque** n Blankoscheck m; (fig) Freibrief m

blanket ['blæŋkɪt] n (Woll)decke f

blare [blɛəʳ] vi (radio) plärren; (horn) tuten; (MUS) schmettern

blasé ['blɑːzeɪ] adj blasiert

blast [blɑːst] n Explosion f; (of wind) Windstoß m ♦ vt (blow up) sprengen; ~! (inf) verflixt!; ~off n (SPACE) (Raketen)abschuss m

blatant ['bleɪtənt] adj offenkundig

blaze [bleɪz] n (fire) lodernde(s) Feuer nt ♦ vi lodern ♦ vt: to ~ a trail Bahn brechen

blazer ['bleɪzəʳ] n Blazer m

bleach [bliːtʃ] n (also: household ~) Bleichmittel nt ♦ vt bleichen; ~ed adj gebleicht

bleachers ['bliːtʃəz] (US) npl (SPORT) unüberdachte Tribüne f

bleak [bliːk] adj kahl, rau; (future) trostlos

bleary-eyed ['blɪərˈaɪd] adj triefäugig; (on waking up) mit verschlafenen Augen

bleat [bliːt] vi blöken; (fig: complain) meckern

bled [bled] pt, pp of **bleed**

bleed [bliːd] (pt, pp **bled**) vi bluten ♦ vt (draw blood) zur Ader lassen; to ~ to death verbluten

bleeper ['bliːpəʳ] n (of doctor etc) Funkrufempfänger m

blemish ['blemɪʃ] n Makel m ♦ vt verunstalten

blend [blend] n Mischung f ♦ vt mischen ♦ vi sich mischen; ~er n Mixer m, Mixgerät nt

bless [bles] (pt, pp **blessed**) vt segnen; (give thanks) preisen; (make happy) glücklich machen; ~ you! Gesundheit!; ~ing n Segen m; (at table) Tischgebet nt; (happiness) Wohltat f; Segen m; (good wish) Glück m

blew [bluː] pt of **blow**

blimey ['blaɪmɪ] (BRIT: inf) excl verflucht

blind [blaɪnd] adj blind; (corner) unübersichtlich ♦ n (for window) Rouleau nt ♦ vt blenden; ~ alley n Sackgasse f; ~fold n Augenbinde f ♦ adj, adv mit verbundenen Augen ♦ vt: to ~fold sb jdm die Augen verbinden; ~ly adv blind; (fig) blindlings; ~ness n Blindheit f; ~ spot n (AUT) tote(r) Winkel m; (fig) schwache(r) Punkt m

blink [blɪŋk] vi blinzeln; ~ers npl Scheuklappen pl

bliss [blɪs] n (Glück)seligkeit f

blister ['blɪstəʳ] n Blase f ♦ vi Blasen werfen

blitz [blɪts] n Luftkrieg m

blizzard ['blɪzəd] n Schneesturm m

bloated ['bləʊtɪd] adj aufgedunsen; (inf: full) nudelsatt

blob [blɔb] n Klümpchen nt

bloc [blɔk] n (POL) Block m

block [blɔk] n (of wood) Block m, Klotz m; (of houses) Häuserblock m ♦ vt hemmen; ~ade [blɔˈkeɪd] n Blockade f ♦ vt blockieren; ~age n Verstopfung f; ~buster n Knüller m; ~ letters npl Blockbuchstaben pl; ~ of flats (BRIT) n Häuserblock m

bloke [bləʊk] (BRIT: inf) n Kerl m, Typ m

blond(e) [blɔnd] adj blond ♦ n Blondine f

blood [blʌd] n Blut nt; ~ donor n Blutspender m; ~ group n Blutgruppe f; ~ poisoning n Blutvergiftung f; ~ pressure n Blutdruck m; ~shed n Blutvergießen nt; ~shot adj blutunterlaufen; ~ sports npl Jagdsport, Hahnenkampf etc; ~stained adj blutbefleckt; ~stream n Blut nt, Blutkreislauf m; ~ test n Blutprobe f; ~thirsty adj blutrünstig; ~ vessel n Blutgefäß nt; ~y adj blutig; (BRIT: inf) verdammt; ~y-minded (BRIT: inf) adj stur

bloom [bluːm] n Blüte f; (freshness) Glanz m ♦ vi blühen

blossom ['blɔsəm] n Blüte f ♦ vi blühen

blot [blɔt] n Klecks m ♦ vt beklecksen; (ink) (ab)löschen; ~ out vt auslöschen

blotchy ['blɔtʃɪ] adj fleckig

blotting paper ['blɔtɪŋ-] n Löschpapier nt

blouse [blaʊz] n Bluse f

blow [bləʊ] (pt **blew**, pp **blown**) n Schlag m ♦ vt blasen ♦ vi (wind) wehen; to ~ one's nose sich dat die Nase putzen; ~ away vt wegblasen; ~ down vt umwehen; ~ off vt wegwehen ♦ vi wegfliegen; ~ out vi ausgehen; ~ over vi vorübergehen; ~ up vi explodieren ♦ vt sprengen; ~-dry n: to have a ~-dry sich föhnen lassen ♦ vt föhnen; ~lamp (BRIT) n Lötlampe f; ~n pp of **blow**; ~-out n (AUT) geplatzte(r) Reifen m; ~torch n = **blowlamp**

blue [bluː] adj blau; (inf: unhappy) niedergeschlagen; (obscene) pornografisch; (joke) anzüglich ♦ n: out of the ~ (fig) aus heiterem Himmel; to have the ~s traurig sein; ~bell n Glockenblume f; ~bottle n Schmeißfliege f; ~ film n Pornofilm m; ~print n (fig) Entwurf m

bluff [blʌf] vi bluffen, täuschen ♦ n (deception) Bluff m; to call sb's ~ es darauf ankommen lassen

blunder ['blʌndəʳ] n grobe(r) Fehler m, Schnitzer m ♦ vi einen groben Fehler machen

blunt [blʌnt] adj (knife) stumpf; (talk) unverblümt ♦ vt abstumpfen

blur [bləːʳ] n Fleck m ♦ vt verschwommen machen

blurb [bləːb] n Waschzettel m

blush [blʌʃ] vi erröten

blustery ['blʌstərɪ] adj stürmisch

boar [bɔːʳ] n Keiler m, Eber m

board [bɔːd] n (of wood) Brett nt; (of card) Pappe f; (committee) Ausschuss m; (of firm) Aufsichtsrat m; (SCH) Direktorium nt ♦ vt (train) einsteigen in +acc; (ship) an Bord gehen +gen; on ~ (AVIAT, NAUT) an Bord; ~ and lodging n Unterkunft f und Verpflegung; full/half ~ (BRIT) Voll-/Halbpension f; to go by the ~ flachfallen, über Bord gehen; ~ up *vt* mit Brettern vernageln; **~er** *n* Kostgänger *m*; (*SCH*) Internatsschüler(in) *m(f)*; **~ game** *n* Brettspiel *nt*; **~ing card** *n* (*AVIAT, NAUT*) Bordkarte *f*; **~ing house** *n* Pension *f*; **~ing school** *n* Internat *nt*; **~ room** *n* Sitzungszimmer *nt*

boast |bəust| *vi* prahlen ♦ *vt* sich rühmen +*gen* ♦ *n* Großtuerei *f*; Prahlerei *f*; **to ~ about** *or* **of sth** mit etw prahlen

boat |bəut| *n* Boot *nt*; (*ship*) Schiff *nt*; **~er** *n* (*hat*) Kreissäge *f*; **~swain** *n* = **bosun**; **~ train** *n* Zug *m* mit Fährenanschluss

bob |bɔb| *vi* sich auf und nieder bewegen; **~ up** *vi* auftauchen

bobbin |'bɔbɪn| *n* Spule *f*

bobby |'bɔbɪ| (*BRIT: inf*) *n* Bobby *m*

bobsleigh |'bɔbsleɪ| *n* Bob *m*

bode |bəud| *vi*: **to ~ well/ill** ein gutes/ schlechtes Zeichen sein

bodily |'bɔdɪlɪ| *adj, adv* körperlich

body |'bɔdɪ| *n* Körper *m*; (*dead*) Leiche *f*; (*group*) Mannschaft *f*; (*AUT*) Karosserie *f*; (*trunk*) Rumpf *m*; **~ building** *n* Bodybuilding *nt*; **~guard** *n* Leibwache *f*; **~work** *n* Karosserie *f*

bog |bɔg| *n* Sumpf *m* ♦ *vt*: **to get ~ged down** sich festfahren

boggle |'bɔgl| *vi* stutzen; **the mind ~s** es ist kaum auszumalen

bog-standard *adj* stinknormal (*inf*)

bogus |'bəugəs| *adj* unecht, Schein-

boil |bɔɪl| *vt, vi* kochen ♦ *n* (*MED*) Geschwür *nt*; **to come to the** (*BRIT*) *or* **a** (*US*) **~** zu kochen anfangen; **to ~ down to** (*fig*) hinauslaufen auf +*acc*; **~ over** *vi* überkochen; **~ed egg** *n* (weich) gekochte(s) Ei *nt*; **~ed potatoes** *npl* Salzkartoffeln *pl*; **~er** *n* Boiler *m*; **~er suit** (*BRIT*) *n* Arbeitsanzug *m*; **~ing point** *n* Siedepunkt *m*

boisterous |'bɔɪstərəs| *adj* ungestüm

bold |bəuld| *adj* (*fearless*) unerschrocken; (*handwriting*) fest und klar

bollard |'bɔləd| *n* (*NAUT*) Poller *m*; (*BRIT: AUT*) Pfosten *m*

bolt |bəult| *n* Bolzen *m*; (*lock*) Riegel *m* ♦ *adv*: **~ upright** kerzengerade ♦ *vt* verriegeln; (*swallow*) verschlingen ♦ *vi* (*horse*) durchgehen

bomb |bɔm| *n* Bombe *f* ♦ *vt* bombardieren; **~ard** |bɔm'baːd| *vt* bombardieren; **~ardment** |bɔm'baːdmənt| *n* Beschießung *f*; **~ disposal** *n*: **~ disposal unit** *n* Bombenräumkommando *nt*; **~er** *n* Bomber *m*; (*terrorist*) Bombenattentäter(in) *m(f)*; **~ing** *n* Bomben *nt*; **~shell** *n* (*fig*) Bombe *f*

bona fide |'bəunə'faɪdɪ| *adj* echt

bond |bɔnd| *n* (*link*) Band *nt*; (*FIN*) Schuldverschreibung *f*

bondage |'bɔndɪdʒ| *n* Sklaverei *f*

bone |bəun| *n* Knochen *m*; (*of fish*) Gräte *f*; (*piece of ~*) Knochensplitter *m* ♦ *vt* die

Knochen herausnehmen +*dat*; (*fish*) entgräten; **~ dry** *adj* (*inf*) knochentrocken; **~ idle** *adj* stinkfaul; **~ marrow** *n* (*ANAT*) Knochenmark *nt*

bonfire |'bɔnfaɪə[r]| *n* Feuer *nt* im Freien

bonnet |'bɔnɪt| *n* Haube *f*; (*for baby*) Häubchen *nt*; (*BRIT: AUT*) Motorhaube *f*

bonus |'bəunəs| *n* Bonus *m*; (*annual ~*) Prämie *f*

bony |'bəunɪ| *adj* knochig, knochendürr

boo |buː| *vt* auspfeifen

booby trap |'buːbɪ-| *n* Falle *f*

book |buk| *n* Buch *nt* ♦ *vt* (*ticket etc*) vorbestellen; (*person*) vormerken; **~s** *npl* (*COMM*) Bücher *pl*; **~case** *n* Bücherregal *nt*, Bücherschrank *m*; **~ing office** (*BRIT*) *n* (*RAIL*) Fahrkartenschalter *m*; (*THEAT*) Vorverkaufsstelle *f*; **~-keeping** *n* Buchhaltung *f*; **~let** *n* Broschüre *f*; **~maker** *n* Buchmacher *m*; **~seller** *n* Buchhändler *m*; **~shelf** *n* Bücherbord *nt*; **~shop** |'bukʃɔp|, **~store** *n* Buchhandlung *f*

boom |buːm| *n* (*noise*) Dröhnen *nt*; (*busy period*) Hochkonjunktur *f* ♦ *vi* dröhnen

boon |buːn| *n* Wohltat *f*, Segen *m*

boost |buːst| *n* Auftrieb *m*; (*fig*) Reklame *f* ♦ *vt* Auftrieb geben; **~er** *n* (*MED*) Wiederholungsimpfung *f*

boot |buːt| *n* Stiefel *m*; (*BRIT: AUT*) Kofferraum *m* ♦ *vt* (*kick*) einen Fußtritt geben; (*COMPUT*) laden; **to ~** (*in addition*) obendrein

booth |buːð| *n* (*at fair*) Bude *f*; (*telephone ~*) Zelle *f*; (*voting ~*) Kabine *f*

booze |buːz| (*inf*) *n* Alkohol *m*, Schnaps *m* ♦ *vi* saufen

border |'bɔːdə[r]| *n* Grenze *f*; (*edge*) Kante *f*; (*in garden*) (Blumen)rabatte *f* ♦ *adj* Grenz-; **the B~s** Grenzregion zwischen England und Schottland; **~ on** *vt* grenzen an +*acc*; **~line** *n* Grenze *f*; **~line case** *n* Grenzfall *m*

bore |bɔː[r]| *pt of* **bear** ♦ *vt* bohren; (*weary*) langweilen ♦ *n* (*person*) Langweiler *m*; (*thing*) langweilige Sache *f*; (*of gun*) Kaliber *nt*; **I am ~d** ich langweile mich; **~dom** *n* Langeweile *f*

boring |'bɔːrɪŋ| *adj* langweilig

born |bɔːn| *adj*: **to be ~** geboren werden

borne |bɔːn| *pp of* **bear**

borough |'bʌrə| *n* Stadt(gemeinde) *f*, Stadtbezirk *m*

borrow |'bɔrəu| *vt* borgen

Bosnia (and) Herzegovina |'bɔznɪə (ənd) haːtsəgau'viːnə| *n* Bosnien und Herzegowina *nt*; **Bosnian** *n* Bosnier(in) *m(f)* ♦ *adj* bosnisch

bosom |'buzəm| *n* Busen *m*

boss |bɔs| *n* Chef *m*, Boss *m* ♦ *vt*: **to ~ around** *or* **about** herumkommandieren; **~y** *adj* herrisch

bosun |'bəusn| *n* Bootsmann *m*

botany |'bɔtənɪ| *n* Botanik *f*

botch [bɔtʃ] vt (also: ~ up) verpfuschen
both [bəuθ] adj beide(s) ♦ pron beide(s)
♦ adv: ~ X and Y sowohl X wie or als auch
Y; ~ (of) the books beide Bücher; ~ of us
went, we ~ went wir gingen beide
bother [ˈbɔðəʳ] vt (pester) quälen ♦ vi (fuss)
sich aufregen ♦ n Mühe f, Umstand m; to ~
doing sth sich dat die Mühe machen, etw
zu tun; what a ~! wie ärgerlich!
bottle [ˈbɔtl] n Flasche f ♦ vt (in Flaschen)
abfüllen; ~ up vt aufstauen; ~ bank n
Altglascontainer m; ~d beer n Flaschenbier
nt; ~d water n in Flaschen abgefülltes
Wasser; ~neck n (also fig) Engpass m; ~
opener n Flaschenöffner m
bottom [ˈbɔtəm] n Boden m; (of person)
Hintern m; (riverbed) Flussbett nt ♦ adj
unterste(r, s)
bough [bau] n Zweig m, Ast m
bought [bɔːt] pt, pp of **buy**
boulder [ˈbəuldəʳ] n Felsbrocken m
bounce [bauns] vi (person) herumhüpfen;
(ball) hochspringen; (cheque) platzen ♦ vt
(auf)springen lassen ♦ n (rebound) Aufprall
m; ~r n Rausschmeißer m
bound [baund] pt, pp of **bind** ♦ n Grenze f;
(leap) Sprung m ♦ vi (spring, leap)
(auf)springen ♦ adj (obliged) gebunden,
verpflichtet; out of ~s Zutritt verboten; to
be ~ to do sth verpflichtet sein, etw zu tun;
it's ~ to happen es muss so kommen; to be
~ for ... nach ... fahren
boundary [ˈbaundrɪ] n Grenze f
bouquet [ˈbukeɪ] n Strauß m; (of wine) Blume f
bourgeois [ˈbuəʒwɑː] adj kleinbürgerlich,
bourgeois ♦ n Spießbürger(in) m(f)
bout [baut] n (of illness) Anfall m; (of contest)
Kampf m
bow¹ [bəu] n (ribbon) Schleife f; (weapon,
MUS) Bogen m
bow² [bau] n (with head, body) Verbeugung
f; (of ship) Bug m ♦ vi sich verbeugen;
(submit): to ~ to sich beugen +dat
bowels [ˈbauəlz] npl (ANAT) Darm m
bowl [bəul] n (basin) Schüssel f; (of pipe)
(Pfeifen)kopf m; (wooden ball) (Holz)kugel f
♦ vt, vi (die Kugel) rollen
bow-legged [ˈbəuˈlegɪd] adj o-beinig,
O-beinig
bowler [ˈbəuləʳ] n Werfer m; (BRIT: also: ~
hat) Melone f
bowling [ˈbəulɪŋ] n Kegeln nt; ~ alley n
Kegelbahn f; ~ green n Rasen m zum
Bowlingspiel
bowls n (game) Bowlsspiel nt
bow tie [bəu-] n Fliege f
box [bɔks] n (also: cardboard ~) Schachtel f;
(bigger) Kasten m; (THEAT) Loge f ♦ vt
einpacken ♦ vi boxen; ~er n Boxer m; ~er
shorts (BRIT) npl Boxer-Shorts pl; ~ing n
(SPORT) Boxen nt; B~ing Day (BRIT) n

zweite(r) Weihnachtsfeiertag m; ~ing
gloves npl Boxhandschuhe pl; ~ing ring n
Boxring m; ~ office n (Theater)kasse f;
~room n Rumpelkammer f
boy [bɔɪ] n junge m
boycott [ˈbɔɪkɔt] n Boykott m ♦ vt
boykottieren
boyfriend [ˈbɔɪfrend] n Freund m
boyish [ˈbɔɪʃ] adj jungenhaft
B.R. n abbr = **British Rail**
bra [brɑː] n BH m
brace [breɪs] n (TECH) Stütze f; (MED)
Klammer f ♦ vt stützen; ~s npl (BRIT)
Hosenträger pl; to ~ o.s. for sth (fig) sich
auf etw acc gefasst machen
bracelet [ˈbreɪslɪt] n Armband nt
bracing [ˈbreɪsɪŋ] adj kräftigend
bracken [ˈbrækən] n Farnkraut nt
bracket [ˈbrækɪt] n Halter m, Klammer f; (in
punctuation) Klammer f; (group) Gruppe f
♦ vt einklammern; (fig) in dieselbe Gruppe
einordnen
brag [bræg] vi sich rühmen
braid [breɪd] n (hair) Flechte f; (trim) Borte f
Braille [breɪl] n Blindenschrift f
brain [breɪn] n (ANAT) Gehirn nt; (intellect)
Intelligenz f, Verstand m; (person) kluge(r)
Kopf m; ~s npl (intelligence) Verstand m;
~child n Erfindung f; ~wash vt eine
Gehirnwäsche vornehmen bei; ~wave n
Geistesblitz m; ~y adj gescheit
braise [breɪz] vt schmoren
brake [breɪk] n Bremse f ♦ vt, vi bremsen; ~
fluid n Bremsflüssigkeit f; ~ light n
Bremslicht nt
bramble [ˈbræmbl] n Brombeere f
bran [bræn] n Kleie f; (food)
Frühstücksflocken pl
branch [brɑːntʃ] n Ast m; (division) Zweig m
♦ vi (also: ~ out: road) sich verzweigen
brand [brænd] n (COMM) Marke f, Sorte f;
(on cattle) Brandmal nt ♦ vt brandmarken;
(COMM) ein Warenzeichen geben +dat
brandish [ˈbrændɪʃ] vt (drohend) schwingen
brand-new [ˈbrændˈnjuː] adj funkelnagelneu
brandy [ˈbrændɪ] n Weinbrand m, Kognak m
brash [bræʃ] adj unverschämt
brass [brɑːs] n Messing nt; the ~ (MUS) das
Blech; ~ band n Blaskapelle f
brassière [ˈbræsɪəʳ] n Büstenhalter m
brat [bræt] n Gör nt
bravado [brəˈvɑːdəu] n Tollkühnheit f
brave [breɪv] adj tapfer ♦ vt die Stirn bieten
+dat; ~ry [ˈbreɪvərɪ] n Tapferkeit f
brawl [brɔːl] n Rauferei f
brawn [brɔːn] n (ANAT) Muskeln pl;
(strength) Muskelkraft f
bray [breɪ] vi schreien
brazen [ˈbreɪzn] adj (shameless) unverschämt
♦ vt: to ~ it out sich mit Lügen und
Betrügen durchsetzen

brazier [ˈbreɪzɪəʳ] n (of workmen) offene(r) Kohlenofen m

Brazil [brəˈzɪl] n Brasilien nt; **~ian** adj brasilianisch ♦ n Brasilianer(in) m(f.)

breach [briːtʃ] n (gap) Lücke f; (MIL) Durchbruch m; (of discipline) Verstoß m (gegen die Disziplin); (of faith) Vertrauensbruch m ♦ vt durchbrechen; **~ of contract** Vertragsbruch m; **~ of the peace** öffentliche Ruhestörung f

bread [brɛd] n Brot nt; **~ and butter** Butterbrot nt; **~bin** n Brotkasten m; **~ box** (US) n Brotkasten m; **~crumbs** npl Brotkrumen pl; (COOK) Paniermehl nt; **~line** n: **to be on the ~line** sich gerade so durchschlagen

breadth [brɛtθ] n Breite f

breadwinner [ˈbrɛdwɪnəʳ] n Ernährer m

break [breɪk] (pt broke, pp broken) vt (destroy) (ab- or zer)brechen; (promise) brechen, nicht einhalten ♦ vi (fall apart) auseinander brechen; (collapse) zusammenbrechen; (dawn) anbrechen ♦ n (gap) Lücke f; (chance) Chance f, Gelegenheit f; (fracture) Bruch m; (rest) Pause f; **~ down** vt (figures, data) aufschlüsseln; (undermine) überwinden ♦ vi (car) eine Panne haben; (person) zusammenbrechen; **~ even** vi die Kosten decken; **~ free** vi sich losreißen; **~ in** vt (horse) zureiten ♦ vi (burglar) einbrechen; **~ into** vt fus (house) einbrechen in +acc; **~ loose** vi sich losreißen; **~ off** vi abbrechen; **~ open** vt (door etc) aufbrechen; **~ out** vi ausbrechen; **to ~ out in spots** Pickel bekommen; **~ up** vi zerbrechen; (fig) sich zerstreuen; (BRIT: SCH) in die Ferien gehen ♦ vt brechen; **~age** n Bruch m, Beschädigung f; **~down** n (TECH) Panne f; (MED: also: nervous **~down**) Zusammenbruch m; **~down van** (BRIT) n Abschleppwagen m; **~er** n Brecher m

breakfast [ˈbrɛkfəst] n Frühstück nt

break: **~-in** n Einbruch m; **~ing** n: **~ing and entering** (JUR) Einbruch m; **~through** n Durchbruch m; **~water** n Wellenbrecher m

breast [brɛst] n Brust f; **~feed** (irreg: like feed) vt, vi stillen; **~-stroke** n Brustschwimmen nt

breath [brɛθ] n Atem m; **out of ~** außer Atem; **under one's ~** flüsternd

Breathalyzer [ˈbrɛθəlaɪzəʳ] ® n Röhrchen nt

breathe [briːð] vt, vi atmen; **~ in** vt, vi einatmen; **~ out** vt, vi ausatmen; **~r** n Verschnaufpause f; **breathing** n Atmung f

breathless [ˈbrɛθlɪs] adj atemlos

breathtaking [ˈbrɛθteɪkɪŋ] adj atemberaubend

bred [brɛd] pt, pp of breed

breed [briːd] (pt, pp bred) vi sich vermehren ♦ vt züchten ♦ n (race) Rasse f, Zucht f; **~ing**

n Züchtung f; (upbringing) Erziehung f

breeze [briːz] n Brise f; **breezy** adj windig; (manner) munter

brevity [ˈbrɛvɪtɪ] n Kürze f

brew [bruː] vt (beer) brauen ♦ vi (storm) sich zusammenziehen; **~ery** n Brauerei f

bribe [braɪb] n Bestechungsgeld nt, Bestechungsgeschenk nt ♦ vt bestechen; **~ry** [ˈbraɪbərɪ] n Bestechung f

bric-a-brac [ˈbrɪkəbræk] n Nippes pl

brick [brɪk] n Backstein m; **~layer** n Maurer m; **~works** n Ziegelei f

bridal [ˈbraɪdl] adj Braut-

bride [braɪd] n Braut f; **~groom** n Bräutigam m; **~smaid** n Brautjungfer f

bridge [brɪdʒ] n Brücke f; (NAUT) Kommandobrücke f; (CARDS) Bridge nt; (ANAT) Nasenrücken m ♦ vt eine Brücke schlagen über +acc; (fig) überbrücken

bridle [ˈbraɪdl] n Zaum m ♦ vt (fig) zügeln; (horse) aufzäumen; **~ path** n Reitweg m

brief [briːf] adj kurz ♦ n (JUR) Akten pl ♦ vt instruieren; **~s** npl (underwear) Schlüpfer m, Slip m; **~case** n Aktentasche f; **~ing** n (genaue) Anweisung f; **~ly** adv kurz

brigadier [brɪɡəˈdɪəʳ] n Brigadegeneral m

bright [braɪt] adj hell; (cheerful) heiter; (idea) klug; **~en (up)** [ˈbraɪtn-] vt aufhellen; (person) aufheitern ♦ vi sich aufheitern

brilliance [ˈbrɪljəns] n Glanz m; (of person) Scharfsinn m

brilliant [ˈbrɪljənt] adj glänzend

brim [brɪm] n Rand m

brine [braɪn] n Salzwasser nt

bring [brɪŋ] (pt, pp brought) vt bringen; **~ about** vt zustande or zu Stande bringen; **~ back** vt zurückbringen; **~ down** vt (price) senken; **~ forward** vt (meeting) vorverlegen; (COMM) übertragen; **~ in** vt hereinbringen; (harvest) einbringen; **~ off** vt davontragen; (success) erzielen; **~ out** vt (object) herausbringen; **~ round** or **to** vt wieder zu sich bringen; **~ up** vt aufziehen; (question) zur Sprache bringen

brink [brɪŋk] n Rand m

brisk [brɪsk] adj lebhaft

bristle [ˈbrɪsl] n Borste f ♦ vi sich sträuben; **bristling with** strotzend vor +dat

Britain [ˈbrɪtən] n (also: **Great ~**) Großbritannien nt

British [ˈbrɪtɪʃ] adj britisch ♦ npl: **the ~** die Briten pl; **~ Isles** npl: **the ~ Isles** die Britischen Inseln pl; **~ Rail** n die Britischen Eisenbahnen

Briton [ˈbrɪtən] n Brite m, Britin f

Brittany [ˈbrɪtənɪ] n die Bretagne

brittle [ˈbrɪtl] adj spröde

broach [brəʊtʃ] vt (subject) anschneiden

broad [brɔːd] adj breit; (hint) deutlich; (general) allgemein; (accent) stark; **in ~ daylight** am helllichten Tag; **~cast**

(*pt, pp* **broadcast**) *n* Rundfunkübertragung *f*
♦ *vt, vi* übertragen, senden; **~en** *vt* erweitern
♦ *vi* sich erweitern; **~ly** *adv* allgemein
gesagt; **~-minded** *adj* tolerant

broccoli [ˈbrɔkəlɪ] *n* Brokkoli *pl*

brochure [ˈbrəʊʃjuəʳ] *n* Broschüre *f*

broil [brɔɪl] *vt* (*grill*) grillen

broke [brəʊk] *pt of* **break** ♦ *adj* (*inf*) pleite

broken [ˈbrəʊkn] *pp of* **break** ♦ *adj*: **~ leg**
gebrochenes Bein; **in ~ English** in
gebrochenem Englisch; **~-hearted** *adj*
untröstlich

broker [ˈbrəʊkəʳ] *n* Makler *m*

brolly [ˈbrɔlɪ] (*BRIT: inf*) *n* Schirm *m*

bronchitis [brɔŋˈkaɪtɪs] *n* Bronchitis *f*

bronze [brɔnz] *n* Bronze *f*

brooch [brəʊtʃ] *n* Brosche *f*

brood [bruːd] *n* Brut *f* ♦ *vi* brüten

brook [brʊk] *n* Bach *m*

broom [brʊm] *n* Besen *m*

Bros. *abbr* = **Brothers**

broth [brɔθ] *n* Suppe *f*, Fleischbrühe *f*

brothel [ˈbrɔθl] *n* Bordell *nt*

brother [ˈbrʌðəʳ] *n* Bruder *m*; **~-in-law** *n*
Schwager *m*

brought [brɔːt] *pt, pp of* **bring**

brow [braʊ] *n* (*eyebrow*) (Augen)braue *f*;
(*forehead*) Stirn *f*; (*of hill*) Bergkuppe *f*

brown [braʊn] *adj* braun ♦ *n* Braun *nt* ♦ *vt*
bräunen; **~ bread** *n* Mischbrot *nt*; **B~ie** *n*
Wichtel *m*; **~ paper** *n* Packpapier *nt*; **~
sugar** *n* braune(r) Zucker *m*

browse [braʊz] *vi* (*in books*) blättern; (*in
shop*) schmökern, herumschauen; **~r** *n*
(*INTERNET*) Browser *m*

bruise [bruːz] *n* Bluterguss *m*, blaue(r) Fleck
m ♦ *vt* einen blauen Fleck geben ♦ *vi* einen
blauen Fleck bekommen

brunt [brʌnt] *n* volle Wucht *f*

brush [brʌʃ] *n* Bürste *f*; (*for sweeping*)
Handbesen *m*; (*for painting*) Pinsel *m*; (*fight*)
kurze(r) Kampf *m*; (*MIL*) Scharmützel *nt*;
(*fig*) Auseinandersetzung *f* ♦ *vt* (*clean*)
bürsten; (*sweep*) fegen; (*usu: ~ past, ~
against*) streifen; **~ aside** *vt* abtun; **~ up** *vt*
(*knowledge*) auffrischen; **~wood** *n* Gestrüpp
nt

brusque [bruːsk] *adj* schroff

Brussels [ˈbrʌslz] *n* Brüssel *nt*; **~ sprout** *n*
Rosenkohl *m*

brutal [ˈbruːtl] *adj* brutal

brute [bruːt] *n* (*person*) Scheusal *m* ♦ *adj*: **by
~ force** mit roher Kraft

B.Sc. *n abbr* = **Bachelor of Science**

BSE *n abbr* (= *bovine spongiform encepha-
lopathy*) BSE *f*

bubble [ˈbʌbl] *n* (Luft)blase *f* ♦ *vi* sprudeln;
(*with joy*) übersprudeln; **~ bath** *n*
Schaumbad *nt*; **~ gum** *n* Kaugummi *m or nt*

buck [bʌk] *n* Bock *m*; (*US: inf*) Dollar *m* ♦ *vi*
bocken; **to pass the ~ (to sb)** die

Verantwortung (auf jdn) abschieben; **~ up**
(*inf*) *vi* sich zusammenreißen

bucket [ˈbʌkɪt] *n* Eimer *m*

buckle [ˈbʌkl] *n* Schnalle *f* ♦ *vt* (*an- or
zusammen*)schnallen ♦ *vi* (*bend*) sich
verziehen

bud [bʌd] *n* Knospe *f* ♦ *vi* knospen, keimen

Buddhism [ˈbʊdɪzəm] *n* Buddhismus *m*;
Buddhist *adj* buddhistisch ♦ *n*
Buddhist(in) *m(f)*

budding [ˈbʌdɪŋ] *adj* angehend

buddy [ˈbʌdɪ] (*inf*) *n* Kumpel *m*

budge [bʌdʒ] *vt, vi* (sich) von der Stelle
rühren

budgerigar [ˈbʌdʒərɪgɑːʳ] *n* Wellensittich *m*

budget [ˈbʌdʒɪt] *n* Budget *nt*; (*POL*) Haushalt
m ♦ *vi*: **to ~ for sth** etw einplanen

budgie [ˈbʌdʒɪ] *n* = **budgerigar**

buff [bʌf] *adj* (*colour*) lederfarben ♦ *n*
(*enthusiast*) Fan *m*

buffalo [ˈbʌfələʊ] (*pl ~ or ~es*) *n* (*BRIT*) Büffel
m; (*US: bison*) Bison *m*

buffer [ˈbʌfəʳ] *n* Puffer *m*; (*COMPUT*)
Pufferspeicher *m*; **~ zone** *n* Pufferzone *f*

buffet¹ [ˈbʌfɪt] *n* (*blow*) Schlag *m* ♦ *vt*
(herum)stoßen

buffet² [ˈbʊfeɪ] (*BRIT*) *n* (*bar*) Imbissraum *m*,
Erfrischungsraum *m*; (*food*) (kaltes) Büfett
nt; **~ car** (*BRIT*) *n* Speisewagen *m*

bug [bʌg] *n* (*also fig*) Wanze *f* ♦ *vt* verwanzen
das Zimmer ist verwanzt

bugle [ˈbjuːgl] *n* Jagdhorn *nt*; (*MIL: MUS*)
Bügelhorn *n*

build [bɪld] (*pt, pp* **built**) *vt* bauen ♦ *n*
Körperbau *m*; **~ up** *vt* aufbauen; **~er** *n*
Bauunternehmer *m*; **~ing** *n* Gebäude *nt*;
~ing society (*BRIT*) *n* Bausparkasse *f*

built [bɪlt] *pt, pp of* **build**; **~-in** *adj* (*cupboard*)
eingebaut; **~-up area** *n* Wohngebiet *nt*

bulb [bʌlb] *n* (*BOT*) (Blumen)zwiebel *f*; (*ELEC*)
Glühlampe *f*, Birne *f*

Bulgaria [bʌlˈgɛərɪə] *n* Bulgarien *nt*; **~n** *adj*
bulgarisch ♦ *n* Bulgare *m*, Bulgarin *f*; (*LING*)
Bulgarisch *nt*

bulge [bʌldʒ] *n* Wölbung *f* ♦ *vi* sich wölben

bulk [bʌlk] *n* Größe *f*, Masse *f*; (*greater part*)
Großteil *m*; **in ~** (*COMM*) en gros; **the ~ of**
der größte Teil *+gen*; **~head** *n* Schott *nt*; **~y**
adj (sehr) umfangreich; (*goods*) sperrig

bull [bʊl] *n* Bulle *m*; (*cattle*) Stier *m*; **~dog** *n*
Bulldogge *f*

bulldozer [ˈbʊldəʊzəʳ] *n* Planierraupe *f*

bullet [ˈbʊlɪt] *n* Kugel *f*

bulletin [ˈbʊlɪtɪn] *n* Bulletin *nt*,
Bekanntmachung *f*

bulletproof [ˈbʊlɪtpruːf] *adj* kugelsicher

bullfight [ˈbʊlfaɪt] *n* Stierkampf *m*; **~er** *n*
Stierkämpfer *m*; **~ing** *n* Stierkampf *m*

bullion [ˈbʊljən] *n* Barren *m*

bullock [ˈbʊlək] *n* Ochse *m*

bullring [ˈbʊlrɪŋ] *n* Stierkampfarena *f*

bull's-eye ['bulzaɪ] n Zentrum nt
bully ['bulɪ] n Raufbold m ♦ vt einschüchtern
bum [bʌm] n (inf: backside) Hintern m; (tramp) Landstreicher m
bumblebee ['bʌmblbiː] n Hummel f
bump [bʌmp] n (blow) Stoß m; (swelling) Beule f ♦ vt, vi stoßen, prallen; **~ into** vt fus stoßen gegen ♦ vt (person) treffen; **~er** n (AUT) Stoßstange f ♦ adj (edition) dick; (harvest) Rekord-
bumpy ['bʌmpɪ] adj holprig
bun [bʌn] n Korinthenbrötchen nt
bunch [bʌntʃ] n (of flowers) Strauß m; (of keys) Bund m; (of people) Haufen m; **~es** npl (in hair) Zöpfe pl
bundle ['bʌndl] n Bündel nt ♦ vt (also: **~ up**) bündeln
bungalow ['bʌŋɡələu] n einstöckige(s) Haus nt, Bungalow m
bungle ['bʌŋɡl] vt verpfuschen
bunion ['bʌnjən] n entzündete(r) Fußballen m
bunk [bʌŋk] n Schlafkoje f; **~ beds** npl Etagenbett nt
bunker ['bʌŋkə'] n (coal store) Kohlenbunker m; (GOLF) Sandloch nt
bunny ['bʌnɪ] n (also: **~ rabbit**) Häschen nt
bunting ['bʌntɪŋ] n Fahnentuch nt
buoy [bɔɪ] n Boje f; (lifebuoy) Rettungsboje f; **~ant** adj (floating) schwimmend; (fig) heiter
burden ['bə:dn] n (weight) Ladung f, Last f; (fig) Bürde f ♦ vt belasten
bureau ['bjuərəu] (pl **~x**) n (BRIT: writing desk) Sekretär m; (US: chest of drawers) Kommode f; (for information etc) Büro nt
bureaucracy [bjuə'rɔkrəsɪ] n Bürokratie f
bureaucrat ['bjuərəkræt] n Bürokrat(in) m(f)
bureaux ['bjuərəuz] npl of **bureau**
burglar ['bə:glə'] n Einbrecher m; **~ alarm** n Einbruchssicherung f; **~y** n Einbruch m
burial ['berɪəl] n Beerdigung f
burly ['bə:lɪ] adj stämmig
Burma ['bə:mə] n Birma nt
burn [bə:n] (pt, pp **burned** or **burnt**) vt verbrennen ♦ vi brennen ♦ n Brandwunde f; **~ down** vt, vi abbrennen; **~er** n Brenner m; **~ing** adj brennend
burrow ['bʌrəu] n (of fox) Bau m; (of rabbit) Höhle f ♦ vt eingraben
bursar ['bə:sə'] n Kassenverwalter m, Quästor m; **~y** (BRIT) n Stipendium nt
burst [bə:st] (pt, pp **burst**) vt zerbrechen ♦ vi platzen ♦ n Explosion f; (outbreak) Ausbruch m; (in pipe) Bruch(stelle f) m; **to ~ into flames** in Flammen aufgehen; **to ~ into tears** in Tränen ausbrechen; **to ~ out laughing** in Gelächter ausbrechen; **~ into** vt fus (room etc) platzen in +acc; **~ open** vi aufbrechen
bury ['berɪ] vt vergraben; (in grave) beerdigen
bus [bʌs] n (Auto)bus m, Omnibus m

bush [buʃ] n Busch m; **to beat about the ~** wie die Katze um den heißen Brei herumgehen; **~y** ['buʃɪ] adj buschig
busily ['bɪzɪlɪ] adv geschäftig
business ['bɪznɪs] n Geschäft nt; (concern) Angelegenheit f; **it's none of your ~** es geht dich nichts an; **to mean ~** es ernst meinen; **to be away on ~** geschäftlich verreist sein; **it's my ~ to ...** es ist meine Sache, zu ...; **~like** adj geschäftsmäßig; **~man** (irreg) n Geschäftsmann m; **~ trip** n Geschäftsreise f; **~woman** (irreg) n Geschäftsfrau f
busker ['bʌskə'] (BRIT) n Straßenmusikant m
bus: **~ shelter** n Wartehäuschen nt; **~ station** n Busbahnhof m; **~ stop** n Bushaltestelle f
bust [bʌst] n Büste f ♦ adj (broken) kaputt(gegangen); (business) pleite; **to go ~** Pleite machen
bustle ['bʌsl] n Getriebe nt ♦ vi hasten
bustling ['bʌslɪŋ] adj geschäftig
busy ['bɪzɪ] adj beschäftigt; (road) belebt ♦ vt: **to ~ o.s.** sich beschäftigen; **~body** n Übereifrige(r) mf; **~ signal** (US) n (TEL) Besetztzeichen nt

but [bʌt] conj **1** (yet) aber; **not X but Y** nicht X sondern Y

2 (however): **I'd love to come, but I'm busy** ich würde gern kommen, bin aber beschäftigt

3 (showing disagreement, surprise etc): **but that's fantastic!** (aber) das ist ja fantastisch!
♦ prep (apart from, except): **nothing but trouble** nichts als Ärger; **no-one but him can do it** niemand außer ihm kann es machen; **but for you/your help** ohne dich/ deine Hilfe; **anything but that** alles, nur das nicht

♦ adv (just, only): **she's but a child** sie ist noch ein Kind; **had I but known** wenn ich es nur gewusst hätte; **I can but try** ich kann es immerhin versuchen; **all but finished** so gut wie fertig

butcher ['butʃə'] n Metzger m; (murderer) Schlächter m ♦ vt schlachten; (kill) abschlachten; **~'s (shop)** n Metzgerei f
butler ['bʌtlə'] n Butler m
butt [bʌt] n (cask) große(s) Fass nt; (BRIT: fig: target) Zielscheibe f; (of gun) Kolben m; (of cigarette) Stummel m ♦ vt (mit dem Kopf) stoßen; **~ in** vi sich einmischen
butter ['bʌtə'] n Butter f ♦ vt buttern; **~ bean** n Wachsbohne f; **~cup** n Butterblume f
butterfly ['bʌtəflaɪ] n Schmetterling m; (SWIMMING: also: **~ stroke**) Butterflystil m
buttocks ['bʌtəks] npl Gesäß nt

button ['bʌtn] n Knopf m ♦ vt, vi (also: ~ **up**) zuknöpfen

buttress ['bʌtrɪs] n Strebepfeiler m; Stützbogen m

buxom ['bʌksəm] adj drall

buy [baɪ] (pt, pp **bought**) vt kaufen ♦ n Kauf m; **to ~ sb a drink** jdm einen Drink spendieren; **~er** n Käufer(in) m(f)

buzz [bʌz] n Summen nt ♦ vi summen; **~er** ['bʌzəʳ] n Summer m; **~ word** n Modewort nt

KEYWORD

by [baɪ] prep 1 (referring to cause, agent) von, durch; **killed by lightning** vom Blitz getötet; **a painting by Picasso** ein Gemälde von Picasso

2 (referring to method, manner): **by bus/car/train** mit dem Bus/Auto/Zug; **to pay by cheque** per Scheck bezahlen; **by moonlight** bei Mondschein; **by saving hard, he** ... indem er eisern sparte, ... er ...

3 (via, through) über +acc; **he came in by the back door** er kam durch die Hintertür herein

4 (close to, past) bei, an +dat; **a holiday by the sea** ein Urlaub am Meer; **she rushed by me** sie eilte an mir vorbei

5 (not later than): **by 4 o'clock** bis 4 Uhr; **by this time tomorrow** morgen um diese Zeit; **by the time I got here it was too late** als ich hier ankam, war es zu spät

6 (during): **by day** bei Tag

7 (amount): **by the kilo/metre** kiloweise/meterweise; **paid by the hour** stundenweise bezahlt

8 (MATH, measure): **to divide by 3** durch 3 teilen; **to multiply by 3** mit 3 malnehmen; **a room 3 metres by 4** ein Zimmer 3 mal 4 Meter; **it's broader by a metre** es ist (um) einen Meter breiter

9 (according to) nach; **it's all right by me** von mir aus gern

10: **(all) by oneself** etc ganz allein

11: **by the way** übrigens

♦ adv 1 see go; pass etc

2: **by and by** irgendwann; (with past tenses) nach einiger Zeit; **by and large** (on the whole) im Großen und Ganzen

bye(-bye) ['baɪ('baɪ)] excl (auf) Wiedersehen

by(e)-law ['baɪlɔː] n Verordnung f

by-election ['baɪɪlekʃən] (BRIT) n Nachwahl f

bygone ['baɪgɒn] adj vergangen ♦ n: **let ~s be ~s** lass(t) das Vergangene vergangen sein

bypass ['baɪpɑːs] n Umgehungsstraße f ♦ vt umgehen

by-product ['baɪprɒdʌkt] n Nebenprodukt nt

bystander ['baɪstændəʳ] n Zuschauer m

byte [baɪt] n (COMPUT) Byte nt

byword ['baɪwɜːd] n Inbegriff m

C, c

C [siː] n (MUS) C nt

C. abbr (= centigrade) C

C.A. abbr = **chartered accountant**

cab [kæb] n Taxi nt; (of train) Führerstand m; (of truck) Führersitz m

cabaret ['kæbəreɪ] n Kabarett nt

cabbage ['kæbɪdʒ] n Kohl(kopf) m

cabin ['kæbɪn] n Hütte f; (NAUT) Kajüte f; (AVIAT) Kabine f; **~ crew** n (AVIAT) Flugbegleitpersonal nt; **~ cruiser** n Motorjacht f

cabinet ['kæbɪnɪt] n Schrank m; (for china) Vitrine f; (POL) Kabinett nt; **~-maker** n Kunsttischler m

cable ['keɪbl] n Drahtseil nt, Tau nt; (TEL) (Leitungs)kabel nt; (telegram) Kabel nt ♦ vt kabeln, telegrafieren; **~ car** n Seilbahn f; **~ television** n Kabelfernsehen nt

cache [kæʃ] n geheime(s) (Waffen)lager nt; geheime(s) (Proviant)lager nt

cackle ['kækl] vi gackern

cacti ['kæktaɪ] npl of cactus

cactus ['kæktəs] (pl **cacti**) n Kaktus m, Kaktee f

caddie ['kædɪ] n (GOLF) Golfjunge m; **caddy** ['kædɪ] n = **caddie**

cadet [kə'det] n Kadett m

cadge [kædʒ] vt schmarotzen

Caesarean [sɪ'zɛərɪən] adj: **~ (section)** Kaiserschnitt m

café ['kæfeɪ] n Café nt, Restaurant nt

cafeteria [kæfɪ'tɪərɪə] n Selbstbedienungsrestaurant nt

caffein(e) ['kæfiːn] n Koffein nt

cage [keɪdʒ] n Käfig m ♦ vt einsperren

cagey ['keɪdʒɪ] adj geheimnistuerisch, zurückhaltend

cagoule [kə'guːl] n Windhemd nt

Cairo ['kaɪərəu] n Kairo nt

cajole [kə'dʒəul] vt überreden

cake [keɪk] n Kuchen m; (of soap) Stück nt; **~d** adj verkrustet

calamity [kə'læmɪtɪ] n Unglück nt, (Schicksals)schlag m

calcium ['kælsɪəm] n Kalzium nt

calculate ['kælkjuleɪt] vt berechnen, kalkulieren; **calculating** adj berechnend; **calculation** [kælkju'leɪʃən] n Berechnung f; **calculator** n Rechner m

calendar ['kælɪndəʳ] n Kalender m; **~ month** n Kalendermonat m

calf [kɑːf] (pl **calves**) n Kalb nt; (also: ~skin) Kalbsleder nt; (ANAT) Wade f

calibre ['kælɪbəʳ] (US **caliber**) n Kaliber nt

call [kɔːl] vt rufen; (name) nennen; (meeting) einberufen; (awaken) wecken; (TEL) anrufen ♦ vi (shout) rufen; (visit: also: ~ **in**, ~ **round**) vorbeikommen ♦ n (shout) Ruf m; (TEL)

235   **callous → capital**

Anruf *m*; **to be ~ed** heißen; **on ~** in
Bereitschaft; **~ back** *vi (return)*
wiederkommen; *(TEL)* zurückrufen; **~ for** *vt
fus (demand)* erfordern, verlangen; *(fetch)*
abholen; **~ off** *vt (cancel)* absagen; **~ on** *vt
fus (visit)* besuchen; *(turn to)* bitten; **~ out** *vi*
rufen; **~ up** *vt (MIL)* einberufen; **~box** *(BRIT)*
n Telefonzelle *f*; **~ centre** Callcenter *nt*; **~er**
n Besucher(in) *m(f)*; *(TEL)* Anrufer *m*; **~ girl**
n Callgirl[1] *nt*; **~-in** *n (US) n (phone-in)* Phone-in
nt; **~ing** *n (vocation)* Berufung *f*; **~ing card**
(US) n Visitenkarte *f*

callous [ˈkæləs] *adj* herzlos
calm [kɑːm] *n* Ruhe *f*; *(NAUT)* Flaute *f* ♦ *vt*
beruhigen ♦ *adj* ruhig; *(person)* gelassen; **~
down** *vi* sich beruhigen ♦ *vt* beruhigen
Calor gas [ˈkælə-] ® *n* Propangas *nt*
calorie [ˈkæləri] *n* Kalorie *f*
calves [kɑːvz] *npl* of **calf**
Cambodia [kæmˈbəudiə] *n* Kambodscha
nt
camcorder [ˈkæmkɔːdəʳ] *n* Camcorder *m*
came [keim] *pt* of **come**
cameo [ˈkæmiəu] *n* Kamee *f*
camera [ˈkæmərə] *n* Fotoapparat *m*; *(CINE,
TV)* Kamera *f*; **in ~** unter Ausschluss der
Öffentlichkeit; **~man** *(irreg) n* Kameramann
m
camouflage [ˈkæməflɑːʒ] *n* Tarnung *f* ♦ *vt*
tarnen
camp [kæmp] *n* Lager *nt* ♦ *vi* zelten, campen
♦ *adj* affektiert
campaign [kæmˈpein] *n* Kampagne *f*; *(MIL)*
Feldzug *m* ♦ *vi (MIL)* Krieg führen; *(fig)*
werben, Propaganda machen; *(POL)* den
Wahlkampf führen
camp: ~ bed [ˈkæmpˈbed] *(BRIT) n*
Campingbett *nt*; **~er** [ˈkæmpəʳ] *n*
Camper(in) *m(f)*; *(vehicle)* Campingwagen
m; **~ing** [ˈkæmpɪŋ] *n*: **to go ~ing** zelten,
Camping machen; **~ing gas** *(US) n*
Campinggas *nt*; **~site** [ˈkæmpsait] *n*
Campingplatz *m*
campus [ˈkæmpəs] *n* Universitätsgelände *nt*,
Campus *m*
can[1] [kæn] *n* Büchse *f*, Dose *f*; *(for water)*
Kanne *f* ♦ *vt* konservieren, in Büchsen
einmachen

⸺ KEYWORD ⸺

can[2] [kæn] *(negative* **cannot, can't,** *conditional* **could)** *aux vb* **1** *(be able to, know
how to)* können; **I can see you tomorrow,
if you like** ich könnte Sie morgen sehen,
wenn Sie wollen; **I can swim** ich kann
schwimmen; **can you speak German?**
sprechen Sie Deutsch?
2 *(may)* können, dürfen; **could I have a
word with you?** könnte ich Sie kurz
sprechen?

Canada [ˈkænədə] *n* Kanada *nt*; **Canadian**
[kəˈneidiən] *adj* kanadisch ♦ *n* Kanadier(in)
m(f)
canal [kəˈnæl] *n* Kanal *m*
canapé [ˈkænəpei] *n* Cocktail- or
Appetithappen *m*
canary [kəˈneəri] *n* Kanarienvogel *m*
cancel [ˈkænsəl] *vt* absagen; *(delete)*
durchstreichen; *(train)* streichen; **~lation**
[kænsəˈleiʃən] *n* Absage *f*; Streichung *f*
cancer [ˈkænsəʳ] *n (ASTROL: C~)* Krebs *m*
candid [ˈkændid] *adj* offen, ehrlich
candidate [ˈkændideit] *n* Kandidat(in) *m(f)*
candle [ˈkændl] *n* Kerze *f*; **~light** *n*
Kerzenlicht *nt*; **~stick** *n (also: ~ holder)*
Kerzenhalter *m*
candour [ˈkændəʳ] *(US* **candor)** *n* Offenheit
f
candy [ˈkændi] *n* Kandis(zucker) *m*; *(US)*
Bonbons *pl*; **~floss** *(BRIT) n* Zuckerwatte *f*
cane [kein] *n (BOT)* Rohr *nt*; *(stick)* Stock *m*
♦ *vt (BRIT: beat)* schlagen
canine [ˈkeinain] *adj* Hunde-
canister [ˈkænistəʳ] *n* Blechdose *f*
cannabis [ˈkænəbis] *n* Hanf *m*, Haschisch *nt*
canned [kænd] *adj* Büchsen-, eingemacht
cannon [ˈkænən] *(pl ~ or ~s) n* Kanone *f*
cannot [ˈkænɔt] = **can not**
canny [ˈkæni] *adj* schlau
canoe [kəˈnuː] *n* Kanu *nt*; **~ing** *n* Kanusport
m, Kanufahren *nt*
canon [ˈkænən] *n (clergyman)* Domherr *m*;
(standard) Grundsatz *m*
can-opener [ˈkænəupnəʳ] *n* Büchsenöffner *m*
canopy [ˈkænəpi] *n* Baldachin *m*
can't [kænt] = **can not**
cantankerous [kænˈtæŋkərəs] *adj* zänkisch,
mürrisch
canteen [kænˈtiːn] *n* Kantine *f*; *(BRIT: of
cutlery)* Besteckkasten *m*
canter [ˈkæntəʳ] *n* Kanter *m* ♦ *vi* in kurzem
Galopp reiten
canvas [ˈkænvəs] *n* Segeltuch *nt*; *(sail)* Segel
nt; *(for painting)* Leinwand *f*; **under ~**
(camping) in Zelten
canvass [ˈkænvəs] *vi* um Stimmen werben;
~ing *n* Wahlwerbung *f*
canyon [ˈkænjən] *n* Felsenschlucht *f*
cap [kæp] *n* Mütze *f*; *(of pen)* Kappe *f*; *(of
bottle)* Deckel *m* ♦ *vt (surpass)* übertreffen;
(SPORT) aufstellen; *(put limit on)* einen
Höchstsatz festlegen für
capability [keipəˈbiliti] *n* Fähigkeit *f*
capable [ˈkeipəbl] *adj* fähig
capacity [kəˈpæsiti] *n* Fassungsvermögen *nt*;
(ability) Fähigkeit *f*; *(position)* Eigenschaft *f*
cape [keip] *n (garment)* Cape *nt*, Umhang *m*;
(GEOG) Kap *nt*
caper [ˈkeipəʳ] *n (COOK: usu: ~s)* Kaper *f*;
(prank) Kapriole *f*
capital [ˈkæpitl] *n (~ city)* Hauptstadt *f*; *(FIN)*

Kapital *nt*; (~ *letter*) Großbuchstabe *m*; ~
gains tax *n* Kapitalertragssteuer *f*; **~ism** *n*
Kapitalismus *m*; **~ist** *adj* kapitalistisch ♦ *n*
Kapitalist(in) *m(f)*; **~ize** *vi*: **to ~ize on**
Kapital schlagen aus; ~ **punishment** *n*
Todesstrafe *f*

Capricorn |'kæprɪkɔːn| *n* Steinbock *m*

capsize |kæp'saɪz| *vt*, *vi* kentern

capsule |'kæpsjuːl| *n* Kapsel *f*

captain |'kæptɪn| *n* Kapitän *m*; (MIL)
Hauptmann *m* ♦ *vt* anführen

caption |'kæpʃən| *n* (*heading*) Überschrift *f*;
(*to picture*) Unterschrift *f*

captivate |'kæptɪveɪt| *vt* fesseln

captive |'kæptɪv| *n* Gefangene(r) *f(m)* ♦ *adj*
gefangen (gehalten); **captivity** |kæp'tɪvɪtɪ|
n Gefangenschaft *f*

capture |'kæptʃə*| *vt* gefangen nehmen;
(*place*) erobern; (*attention*) erregen ♦ *n*
Gefangennahme *f*; (*data* ~) Erfassung *f*

car |kɑː*| *n* Auto *nt*, Wagen *m*; (RAIL) Wagen
m

caramel |'kærəməl| *n* Karamelle *f*,
Karamelbonbon *m* or *nt*; (*burnt sugar*)
Karamel *m*

carat |'kærət| *n* Karat *nt*

caravan |'kærəvæn| *n* (BRIT) Wohnwagen *m*;
(*in desert*) Karawane *f*; **~ning** *n* Caravaning
nt, Urlaub *m* im Wohnwagen; ~ **site** (BRIT) *n*
Campingplatz *m* für Wohnwagen

carbohydrate |kɑːbəu'haɪdreɪt| *n*
Kohlenhydrat *nt*

carbon |'kɑːbən| *n* Kohlenstoff *m*; ~ **copy** *n*
Durchschlag *m*; ~ **dioxide** *n* Kohlendioxyd
nt; ~ **monoxide** *n* Kohlenmonoxyd *nt*; ~
paper *n* Kohlepapier *nt*

car boot sale *n* auf einem Parkplatz
stattfindender Flohmarkt mit dem Kofferraum
als Auslage

carburettor |kɑːbju'retə*| (US **carburetor**) *n*
Vergaser *m*

carcass |'kɑːkəs| *n* Kadaver *m*

card |kɑːd| *n* Karte *f*; **~board** *n* Pappe *f*; ~
game *n* Kartenspiel *nt*

cardiac |'kɑːdɪæk| *adj* Herz-

cardigan |'kɑːdɪɡən| *n* Strickjacke *f*

cardinal |'kɑːdɪnl| *adj*: ~ **number**
Kardinalzahl *f* ♦ *n* (REL) Kardinal *m*

card index *n* Kartei *f*; (*in library*) Katalog *m*

cardphone *n* Kartentelefon *nt*

care |keə*| *n* (*of teeth, car etc*) Pflege *f*; (*of
children*) Fürsorge *f*; (*carefulness*) Sorgfalt *f*;
(*worry*) Sorge *f* ♦ *vi*: **to ~ about** sich
kümmern um; ~ **of** bei; **in sb's ~** in jds
Obhut; **I don't ~** das ist mir egal; **I couldn't
~ less** es ist mir doch völlig egal; **to take ~**
aufpassen; **to take ~ of** sorgen für; **to take
~ to do sth** sich bemühen, etw zu tun; ~
for *vt* sorgen für; (*like*) mögen

career |kə'rɪə*| *n* Karriere *f*, Laufbahn *f* ♦ *vi*
(*also*: ~ **along**) rasen; ~ **woman** (*irreg*) *n*

Karrierefrau *f*

care: **~free** *adj* sorgenfrei; **~ful** *adj* sorgfältig;
(**be**) **~ful!** pass auf!; **~fully** *adv* vorsichtig;
(*methodically*) sorgfältig; **~less** *adj*
nachlässig; **~lessness** *n* Nachlässigkeit *f*; **~r**
n (MED) Betreuer(in) *m(f)*

caress |kə'res| *n* Liebkosung *f* ♦ *vt* liebkosen

caretaker |'keəteɪkə*| *n* Hausmeister *m*

car ferry *n* Autofähre *f*

cargo |'kɑːɡəu| (*pl* **~es**) *n* Schiffsladung *f*

car hire *n* Autovermietung *f*

Caribbean |kærɪ'biːən| *n*: **the ~ (Sea)** die
Karibik

caricature |'kærɪkətjuə*| *n* Karikatur *f*

caring |'keərɪŋ| *adj* (*society, organization*)
sozial eingestellt; (*person*) liebevoll

carnage |'kɑːnɪdʒ| *n* Blutbad *nt*

carnation |kɑː'neɪʃən| *n* Nelke *f*

carnival |'kɑːnɪvl| *n* Karneval *m*, Fasching *m*;
(US: *fun fair*) Kirmes *f*

carnivorous |kɑː'nɪvərəs| *adj* Fleisch
fressend

carol |'kærəl| *n*: **(Christmas)** ~ (Weih-
nachts)lied *nt*

carp |kɑːp| *n* (*fish*) Karpfen *m*

car park (BRIT) *n* Parkplatz *m*; (*covered*)
Parkhaus *nt*

carpenter |'kɑːpɪntə*| *n* Zimmermann *m*;
carpentry |'kɑːpɪntrɪ| *n* Zimmerei *f*

carpet |'kɑːpɪt| *n* Teppich *m* ♦ *vt* mit einem
Teppich auslegen; ~ **bombing** *n*
Flächenbombardierung *f*; ~ **slippers** *npl*
Pantoffeln *pl*; ~ **sweeper** |'kɑːpɪtswiːpə*| *n*
Teppichkehrer *m*

car phone *n* (TEL) Autotelefon *nt*

car rental (US) *n* Autovermietung *f*

carriage |'kærɪdʒ| *n* Kutsche *f*; (RAIL, *of
typewriter*) Wagen *m*; (*of goods*) Beförderung
f; (*bearing*) Haltung *f*; ~ **return** *n* (*on
typewriter*) Rücklauftaste *f*; **~way** (BRIT) *n*
(*part of road*) Fahrbahn *f*

carrier |'kærɪə*| *n* Träger(in) *m(f)*; (COMM)
Spediteur *m*; ~ **bag** (BRIT) *n* Tragetasche *f*

carrot |'kærət| *n* Möhre *f*, Karotte *f*

carry |'kærɪ| *vt*, *vi* tragen; **to get carried
away** (*fig*) sich nicht mehr bremsen können;
~ **on** *vi* (*continue*) weitermachen; (*inf*:
complain) Theater machen; ~ **out** *vt* (*orders*)
ausführen; (*investigation*) durchführen; **~cot**
(BRIT) *n* Babytragetasche *f*; **~-on** (*inf*) *n*
(*fuss*) Theater *nt*

cart |kɑːt| *n* Wagen *m*, Karren *m* ♦ *vt*
schleppen

cartilage |'kɑːtɪlɪdʒ| *n* Knorpel *m*

carton |'kɑːtən| *n* Karton *m*; (*of milk*) Tüte *f*

cartoon |kɑː'tuːn| *n* (PRESS) Karikatur *f*;
(*comic strip*) Comics *pl*; (CINE)
(Zeichen)trickfilm *m*

cartridge |'kɑːtrɪdʒ| *n* Patrone *f*

carve |kɑːv| *vt* (*wood*) schnitzen; (*stone*)
meißeln; (*meat*) (vor)schneiden; ~ **up** *vt*

aufschneiden; **carving** ['kɑːvɪŋ] n
Schnitzerei f; **carving knife** n
Tran(s)chiermesser nt

car wash n Autowäsche f

cascade |kæsˈkeɪd| n Wasserfall m ♦ vi
kaskadenartig herabfallen

case |keɪs| n (box) Kasten m; (BRIT: also:
suit~) Koffer m; (JUR, matter) Fall m; **in ~**
falls, im Falle; **in any ~** jedenfalls, auf jeden
Fall

cash |kæʃ| n (Bar)geld nt ♦ vt einlösen; **~ on
delivery** per Nachnahme; **~ book** n
Kassenbuch nt; **~ card** n Scheckkarte f; **~
desk** (BRIT) n Kasse f; **~ dispenser** n
Geldautomat m

cashew |kæˈʃuː| n (also: **~ nut**) Cashewnuss f

cash flow n Cashflow m

cashier |kæˈʃɪər| n Kassierer(in) m(f)

cashmere ['kæʃmɪər] n Kaschmirwolle f

cash register n Registrierkasse f

casing ['keɪsɪŋ] n Gehäuse nt

casino |kəˈsiːnəu| n Kasino nt

casket ['kɑːskɪt] n Kästchen nt; (US: coffin)
Sarg m

casserole ['kæsərəul] n Kasserolle f; (food)
Auflauf m

cassette |kæˈset| n Kassette f; **~ player** n
Kassettengerät nt

cast |kɑːst| (pt, pp **cast**) vt werfen; (horns)
verlieren; (metal) gießen; (THEAT) besetzen;
(vote) abgeben ♦ n (THEAT) Besetzung f;
(also: **plaster ~**) Gipsverband m; **~ off** vi
(NAUT) losmachen

castaway ['kɑːstəweɪ] n Schiffbrüchige(r)
f(m)

caste |kɑːst| n Kaste f

caster sugar ['kɑːstə-] (BRIT) n Raffinade f

casting vote ['kɑːstɪŋ-] (BRIT) n
entscheidende Stimme f

cast iron n Gusseisen nt

castle ['kɑːsl] n Burg f; Schloss nt; (CHESS)
Turm m

castor ['kɑːstər] n (wheel) Laufrolle f

castor oil n Rizinusöl nt

castrate |kæsˈtreɪt| vt kastrieren

casual ['kæʒjul] adj (attitude) nachlässig;
(dress) leger; (meeting) zufällig; (work)
Gelegenheits-; **~ly** adv (dress) zwanglos,
leger; (remark) beiläufig

casualty ['kæʒjultɪ] n Verletzte(r) f(m);
(dead) Tote(r) f(m); (also: **~ department**)
Unfallstation f

cat |kæt| n Katze f

catalogue ['kætəlɔg] (US **catalog**) n Katalog
m ♦ vt katalogisieren

catalyst ['kætəlɪst] n Katalysator m

catalytic converter [kætəˈlɪtɪk kənˈvɜːtər] n
Katalysator m

catapult ['kætəpʌlt] n Schleuder f

cataract ['kætərækt] n (MED) graue(r) Star m

catarrh |kəˈtɑːr| n Katarr(h) m

catastrophe |kəˈtæstrəfi| n Katastrophe f

catch |kætʃ| (pt, pp **caught**) vt fangen;
(arrest) fassen; (train) erreichen; (person: by
surprise) ertappen; (also: **~ up**) einholen ♦ vi
(fire) in Gang kommen; (in branches etc)
hängen bleiben ♦ n (fish etc) Fang m; (trick)
Haken m; (of lock) Sperrhaken m; **to ~ an
illness** sich dat eine Krankheit holen; **to ~
fire** Feuer fangen; **~ on** vi (understand)
begreifen; (grow popular) ankommen; **~ up**
vi (fig) aufholen; **~ing** ['kætʃɪŋ] adj
ansteckend; **~ment area** ['kætʃmənt-] (BRIT)
n Einzugsgebiet nt; **~ phrase** n Slogan m;
~y ['kætʃɪ] adj (tune) eingängig

categoric(al) |kætɪˈgɔrɪk(l)| adj kategorisch

category ['kætɪgərɪ] n Kategorie f

cater ['keɪtər] vi versorgen; **~ for** (BRIT) vt fus
(party) ausrichten; (needs) eingestellt sein
auf +acc; **~er** n Lieferant(in) m(f) von
Speisen und Getränken; **~ing** n Gastronomie
f

caterpillar ['kætəpɪlər] n Raupe f; **~ track** ®
n Gleiskette f

cathedral |kəˈθiːdrəl| n Kathedrale f, Dom m

Catholic ['kæθəlɪk] adj (REL) katholisch ♦ n
Katholik(in) m(f); **c~** adj (tastes etc) vielseitig

CAT scan |kæt-| n Computertomographie f

Catseye ['kætsˌaɪ] (BRIT: ®) n (AUT)
Katzenauge nt

cattle |kætl| npl Vieh nt

catty ['kætɪ] adj gehässig

caucus ['kɔːkəs] n (POL) Gremium nt; (US:
meeting) Sitzung f

caught |kɔːt| pt, pp of **catch**

cauliflower ['kɔlɪflauər] n Blumenkohl m

cause |kɔːz| n Ursache f; (purpose) Sache f
♦ vt verursachen

causeway ['kɔːzweɪ] n Damm m

caustic ['kɔːstɪk] adj ätzend; (fig) bissig

caution ['kɔːʃən] n Vorsicht f; (warning)
Verwarnung f ♦ vt verwarnen; **cautious**
['kɔːʃəs] adj vorsichtig

cavalry ['kævəlrɪ] n Kavallerie f

cave |keɪv| n Höhle f; **~ in** vi einstürzen;
~man (irreg) n Höhlenmensch m

cavern ['kævən] n Höhle f

caviar(e) ['kævɪɑːr] n Kaviar m

cavity ['kævɪtɪ] n Loch nt

cavort |kəˈvɔːt| vi umherspringen

C.B. n abbr (= Citizens' Band (Radio)) CB

C.B.I. n abbr (= Confederation of British
Industry) ≈ BDI m

cc n abbr = **carbon copy**; **cubic centimetres**

CD n abbr (= compact disc) CD f

CDI n abbr (= Compact Disc Interactive) CD-I f

CD player n CD-Spieler m

CD-ROM |siːdiːˈrɔm| n abbr (= compact disc
read-only memory) CD-Rom f

cease |siːs| vi aufhören ♦ vt beenden; **~fire** n
Feuereinstellung f; **~less** adj unaufhörlich

cedar ['siːdər] n Zeder f

ceiling [ˈsiːlɪŋ] n Decke f; (fig) Höchstgrenze f

celebrate [ˈsɛlɪbreɪt] vt, vi feiern; **~d** adj gefeiert: **celebration** [sɛlɪˈbreɪʃən] n Feier f

celebrity [sɪˈlɛbrɪtɪ] n gefeierte Persönlichkeit f

celery [ˈsɛlərɪ] n Sellerie m or f

celibacy [ˈsɛlɪbəsɪ] n Zölibat nt or m

cell [sɛl] n Zelle f; (ELEC) Element nt

cellar [ˈsɛləʳ] n Keller m

cello [ˈtʃɛləu] n Cello nt

Cellophane [ˈsɛləfeɪn] ® n Cellophan nt ®

cellphone [ˈsɛlfəun] n Funktelefon nt

cellular [ˈsɛljuləʳ] adj zellular

cellulose [ˈsɛljuləus] n Zellulose f

Celt [kɛlt, sɛlt] n Kelte m, Keltin f; **~ic** [ˈkɛltɪk, ˈsɛltɪk] adj keltisch

cement [səˈmɛnt] n Zement m ♦ vt zementieren; **~ mixer** n Betonmischmaschine f

cemetery [ˈsɛmɪtrɪ] n Friedhof m

censor [ˈsɛnsəʳ] n Zensor m ♦ vt zensieren; **~ship** n Zensur f

censure [ˈsɛnʃəʳ] vt rügen

census [ˈsɛnsəs] n Volkszählung f

cent [sɛnt] n (US: coin) Cent m; see also **per cent**

centenary [sɛnˈtiːnərɪ] n Jahrhundertfeier f

center [ˈsɛntəʳ] (US) n = **centre**

centigrade [ˈsɛntɪgreɪd] adj Celsius

centimetre [ˈsɛntɪmiːtəʳ] (US **centimeter**) n Zentimeter nt

centipede [ˈsɛntɪpiːd] n Tausendfüßler m

central [ˈsɛntrəl] adj zentral; **C~ America** n Mittelamerika nt; **~ heating** n Zentralheizung f; **~ize** vt zentralisieren; **~ reservation** (BRIT) n (AUT) Mittelstreifen m

centre [ˈsɛntəʳ] (US **center**) n Zentrum nt ♦ vt zentrieren; **~-forward** n (SPORT) Mittelstürmer m; **~-half** n (SPORT) Stopper m

century [ˈsɛntjurɪ] n Jahrhundert nt

ceramic [sɪˈræmɪk] adj keramisch; **~s** npl Keramiken pl

cereal [ˈsiːrɪəl] n (grain) Getreide nt; (at breakfast) Getreideflocken pl

cerebral [ˈsɛrɪbrəl] adj zerebral; (intellectual) geistig

ceremony [ˈsɛrɪmənɪ] n Zeremonie f; **to stand on ~** förmlich sein

certain [ˈsəːtən] adj sicher; (particular) gewiß; **for ~** ganz bestimmt; **~ly** adv sicher, bestimmt; **~ty** n Gewißheit f

certificate [səˈtɪfɪkɪt] n Bescheinigung f; (SCH etc) Zeugnis nt

certified mail [ˈsəːtɪfaɪd-] (US) n Einschreiben nt

certified public accountant [ˈsəːtɪfaɪd-] (US) n geprüfte(r) Buchhalter m

certify [ˈsəːtɪfaɪ] vt bescheinigen

cervical [ˈsəːvɪkl] adj (smear, cancer) Gebärmutterhals-

cervix [ˈsəːvɪks] n Gebärmutterhals m

cf. abbr (= compare) vgl.

CFC n abbr (= chlorofluorocarbon) FCKW m

ch. abbr (= chapter) Kap.

chafe [tʃeɪf] vt scheuern

chaffinch [ˈtʃæfɪntʃ] n Buchfink m

chain [tʃeɪn] n Kette f ♦ vt (also: ~ up) anketten; **~ reaction** n Kettenreaktion f; **~ smoke** vi kettenrauchen; **~ store** n Kettenladen m

chair [tʃɛəʳ] n Stuhl m; (armchair) Sessel m; (UNIV) Lehrstuhl m ♦ vt (meeting) den Vorsitz führen bei; **~lift** n Sessellift m; **~man** (irreg) n Vorsitzende(r) m

chalet [ˈʃæleɪ] n Chalet nt

chalk [tʃɔːk] n Kreide f

challenge [ˈtʃælɪndʒ] n Herausforderung f ♦ vt herausfordern; (contest) bestreiten; **challenging** adj (tone) herausfordernd; (work) anspruchsvoll

chamber [ˈtʃeɪmbəʳ] n Kammer f; **~ of commerce** Handelskammer f; **~maid** n Zimmermädchen nt; **~ music** n Kammermusik f

chamois [ˈʃæmwɑː] n Gämse f

champagne [ʃæmˈpeɪn] n Champagner m, Sekt m

champion [ˈtʃæmpɪən] n (SPORT) Meister(in) m(f); (of cause) Verfechter(in) m(f); **~ship** n Meisterschaft f

chance [tʃɑːns] n (luck) Zufall m; (possibility) Möglichkeit f; (opportunity) Gelegenheit f, Chance f; (risk) Risiko nt ♦ adj zufällig ♦ vt: **to ~ it** es darauf ankommen lassen; **by ~** zufällig; **to take a ~** ein Risiko eingehen

chancellor [ˈtʃɑːnsələʳ] n Kanzler m; **C~ of the Exchequer** (BRIT) n Schatzkanzler m

chandelier [ʃændəˈlɪəʳ] n Kronleuchter m

change [tʃeɪndʒ] vt ändern; (replace, COMM: money) wechseln; (exchange) umtauschen; (transform) verwandeln ♦ vi sich ändern; (~ trains) umsteigen; (~ clothes) sich umziehen ♦ n Veränderung f; (money returned) Wechselgeld nt; (coins) Kleingeld nt; **to ~ one's mind** es sich dat anders überlegen; **to ~ into sth** (be transformed) sich in etw acc verwandeln; **for a ~** zur Abwechslung; **~able** adj (weather) wechselhaft; **~ machine** n Geldwechselautomat m; **~over** n Umstellung f

changing [ˈtʃeɪndʒɪŋ] adj veränderlich; **~ room** (BRIT) n Umkleideraum m

channel [ˈtʃænl] n (stream) Bachbett nt; (NAUT) Straße f; (TV) Kanal m; (fig) Weg m ♦ vt (efforts) lenken; **the (English) C~** der Ärmelkanal; **~-hopping** n (TV) ständiges Umschalten; **C~ Islands** npl: **the C~ Islands** die Kanalinseln pl; **C~ Tunnel** n: **the C~ Tunnel** der Kanaltunnel

chant [tʃɑːnt] n Gesang m; (of fans) Sprechchor m ♦ vt intonieren

chaos ['keɪɔs] n Chaos nt

chap [tʃæp] (inf) n Kerl m

chapel ['tʃæpl] n Kapelle f

chaperon ['ʃæpərəun] n Anstandsdame f

chaplain ['tʃæplɪn] n Kaplan m

chapped [tʃæpt] adj (skin, lips) spröde

chapter ['tʃæptəʳ] n Kapitel nt

char [tʃɑːʳ] vt (burn) verkohlen

character ['kærɪktəʳ] n Charakter m, Wesen nt; (in novel, film) Figur f; **~istic** [kærɪktə'rɪstɪk] adj: **~istic (of sb/sth)** (für jdn/etw) charakteristisch ♦ n Kennzeichen nt; **~ize** vt charakterisieren, kennzeichnen

charade [ʃə'rɑːd] n Scharade f

charcoal ['tʃɑːkəul] n Holzkohle f

charge [tʃɑːdʒ] n (cost) Preis m; (JUR) Anklage f; (explosive) Ladung f; (attack) Angriff m ♦ vt (gun, battery) laden; (price) verlangen; (JUR) anklagen; (MIL) angreifen ♦ vi (rush) (an)stürmen; **bank ~s** Bankgebühren pl; **free of ~** kostenlos; **to reverse the ~s** (TEL) ein R-Gespräch führen; **to be in ~ of** verantwortlich sein für; **to take ~** (die Verantwortung) übernehmen; **to ~ sth (up) to sb's account** jdm etw in Rechnung stellen; **~ card** n Kundenkarte f

charitable ['tʃærɪtəbl] adj wohltätig; (lenient) nachsichtig

charity ['tʃærɪtɪ] n (institution) Hilfswerk nt; (attitude) Nächstenliebe f

charm [tʃɑːm] n (also: **have a ~**) plaudern ♦ n Talisman m ♦ vt bezaubern; **~ing** adj reizend

chart [tʃɑːt] n Tabelle f; (NAUT) Seekarte f ♦ vt (course) abstecken

charter ['tʃɑːtəʳ] vt chartern ♦ n Schutzbrief m; **~ed accountant** n Wirtschaftsprüfer(in) m(f); **~ flight** n Charterflug m

chase [tʃeɪs] vt jagen, verfolgen ♦ n Jagd f

chasm ['kæzəm] n Kluft f

chassis ['ʃæsɪ] n Fahrgestell nt

chat [tʃæt] vi (also: **have a ~**) plaudern ♦ n Plauderei f; **~ show** (BRIT) n Talkshow f

chatter ['tʃætəʳ] vi schwatzen; (teeth) klappern ♦ n Geschwätz nt; **~box** n Quasselstrippe f

chatty ['tʃætɪ] adj geschwätzig

chauffeur ['ʃəufəʳ] n Chauffeur m

chauvinist ['ʃəuvɪnɪst] n (male ~) Chauvi m (inf)

cheap [tʃiːp] adj, adv billig; **~ day return** n Tagesrückfahrkarte f (zu einem günstigeren Tarif); **~ly** adv billig

cheat [tʃiːt] vt, vi betrügen; (SCH) mogeln ♦ n Betrüger(in) m(f)

check [tʃɛk] vt (examine) prüfen; (make sure) nachsehen; (control) kontrollieren; (restrain) zügeln; (stop) anhalten ♦ n (examination, restraint) Kontrolle f; (bill) Rechnung f;

(pattern) Karo(muster) nt; (US) = **cheque** ♦ adj (pattern, cloth) kariert; **~ in** vi (in hotel, airport) einchecken ♦ vt (luggage) abfertigen lassen; **~ out** vi (of hotel) abreisen; **~ up** vi nachschauen; **~ up on** vt kontrollieren; **~ered** (US) adj = **chequered**; **~ers** (US) n (draughts) Damespiel nt; **~-in (desk)** n Abfertigung f; **~ing account** (US) n (current account) Girokonto nt; **~mate** n Schachmatt nt; **~out** n Kasse f; **~point** n Kontrollpunkt m; **~ room** (US) n (left-luggage office) Gepäckaufbewahrung f; **~up** n (Nach)prüfung f; (MED) (ärztliche) Untersuchung f

cheek [tʃiːk] n Backe f; (fig) Frechheit f; **~bone** n Backenknochen m; **~y** adj frech

cheep [tʃiːp] vi piepsen

cheer [tʃɪəʳ] n (usu pl) Hurra- or Beifallsruf m ♦ vt zujubeln; (encourage) aufmuntern ♦ vi jauchzen; **~s!** Prost!; **~ up** vi bessere Laune bekommen ♦ vt aufmuntern; **~ up!** nun lach doch mal!; **~ful** adj fröhlich

cheerio [tʃɪərɪ'au] (BRIT) excl tschüss!

cheese [tʃiːz] n Käse m; **~board** n (gemischte) Käseplatte f

cheetah ['tʃiːtə] n Gepard m

chef [ʃef] n Küchenchef m

chemical ['kemɪkl] adj chemisch ♦ n Chemikalie f

chemist ['kemɪst] n (BRIT: pharmacist) Apotheker m, Drogist m; (scientist) Chemiker m; **~ry** n Chemie f; **~'s (shop)** (BRIT) n Apotheke f; Drogerie f

cheque [tʃek] (BRIT) n Scheck m; **~book** n Scheckbuch nt; **~ card** n Scheckkarte f

chequered ['tʃekəd] adj (fig) bewegt

cherish ['tʃerɪʃ] vt (person) lieben; (hope) hegen

cherry ['tʃerɪ] n Kirsche f

chess [tʃes] n Schach nt; **~board** n Schachbrett nt; **~man** (irreg) n Schachfigur f

chest [tʃest] n (ANAT) Brust f; (box) Kiste f; **~ of drawers** n Kommode f

chestnut ['tʃesnʌt] n Kastanie f

chew [tʃuː] vt, vi kauen; **~ing gum** n Kaugummi m

chic [ʃiːk] adj schick, elegant

chick [tʃɪk] n Küken nt; (US: inf: girl) Biene f

chicken ['tʃɪkɪn] n Huhn nt; (food) Hähnchen nt; **~ out** (inf) vi kneifen

chickenpox ['tʃɪkɪnpɔks] n Windpocken pl

chicory ['tʃɪkərɪ] n (in coffee) Zichorie f; (plant) Chicorée f, Schikoree f

chief [tʃiːf] n (of tribe) Häuptling m; (COMM) Chef m ♦ adj Haupt-; **~ executive** n Geschäftsführer(in) m(f); **~ly** adv hauptsächlich

chilblain ['tʃɪlbleɪn] n Frostbeule f

child [tʃaɪld] (pl **~ren**) n Kind nt; **~birth** n Entbindung f; **~hood** n Kindheit f; **~ish** adj kindisch; **~like** adj kindlich; **~ minder** (BRIT) n Tagesmutter f; **~ren** ['tʃɪldrən] npl of child; ~ **seat** *n* Kindersitz *m*

Chile ['tʃɪlɪ] *n* Chile *nt*; **~an** *adj* chilenisch

chill [tʃɪl] *n* Kühle *f*; (*MED*) Erkältung *f* ♦ *vt*
(*CULIN*) kühlen

chilli ['tʃɪlɪ] *n* Peperoni *pl*; (*meal, spice*) Chili *m*

chilly ['tʃɪlɪ] *adj* kühl, frostig

chime [tʃaɪm] *n* Geläut *nt* ♦ *vi* ertönen

chimney ['tʃɪmnɪ] *n* Schornstein *m*; ~
sweep *n* Schornsteinfeger(in) *m(f)*

chimpanzee [tʃɪmpæn'ziː] *n* Schimpanse *m*

chin [tʃɪn] *n* Kinn *nt*

China ['tʃaɪnə] *n* China *nt*

china ['tʃaɪnə] *n* Porzellan *nt*

Chinese [tʃaɪ'niːz] *adj* chinesisch ♦ *n* (*inv*)
Chinese *m*, Chinesin *f*; (*LING*) Chinesisch *nt*

chink [tʃɪŋk] *n* (*opening*) Ritze *f*; (*noise*)
Klirren *nt*

chip [tʃɪp] *n* (*of wood etc*) Splitter *m*; (*in poker
etc; US: crisp*) Chip *m* ♦ *vt* absplittern; **~s** *npl*
(*BRIT: COOK*) Pommes frites *pl*; **~ in** *vi*
Zwischenbemerkungen machen

chiropodist [kɪ'rɔpədɪst] (*BRIT*) *n*
Fußpfleger(in) *m(f)*

chirp [tʃəːp] *vi* zwitschern

chisel ['tʃɪzl] *n* Meißel *m*

chit [tʃɪt] *n* Notiz *f*

chivalrous ['ʃɪvəlrəs] *adj* ritterlich; **chivalry**
['ʃɪvəlrɪ] *n* Ritterlichkeit *f*

chives [tʃaɪvz] *npl* Schnittlauch *m*

chlorine ['klɔːriːn] *n* Chlor *nt*

chock-a-block ['tʃɔkə'blɔk] *adj* voll
gepfropft

chock-full [tʃɔk'ful] *adj* voll gepfropft

chocolate ['tʃɔklɪt] *n* Schokolade *f*

choice [tʃɔɪs] *n* Wahl *f*; (*of goods*) Auswahl *f*
♦ *adj* Qualitäts-

choir ['kwaɪəʳ] *n* Chor *m*; **~boy** *n* Chorknabe
m

choke [tʃəuk] *vi* ersticken ♦ *vt* erdrosseln;
(*block*) (ab)drosseln ♦ *n* (*AUT*) Starterklappe *f*

cholera ['kɔlərə] *n* Cholera *f*

cholesterol [kə'lestərɔl] *n* Cholesterin *nt*

choose [tʃuːz] (*pt* chose, *pp* chosen) *vt*
wählen; **choosy** ['tʃuːzɪ] *adj* wählerisch

chop [tʃɔp] *vt* (*wood*) spalten; (*COOK: also: ~
up*) (zer)hacken ♦ *n* Hieb *m*; (*COOK*) Kotelett
nt; **~s** *npl* (*jaws*) Lefzen *pl*

chopper ['tʃɔpəʳ] *n* (*helicopter*) Hubschrauber
m

choppy ['tʃɔpɪ] *adj* (*sea*) bewegt

chopsticks ['tʃɔpstɪks] *npl* (*Ess*)stäbchen *pl*

choral ['kɔːrəl] *adj* Chor-

chord [kɔːd] *n* Akkord *m*

chore [tʃɔːʳ] *n* Pflicht *f*; **~s** *npl* (*housework*)
Hausarbeit *f*

choreographer [kɔrɪ'ɔgrəfəʳ] *n*
Choreograf(in) *m(f)*

chorister ['kɔrɪstəʳ] *n* Chorsänger(in) *m(f)*

chortle ['tʃɔːtl] *vi* glucksen

chorus ['kɔːrəs] *n* Chor *m*; (*in song*) Refrain *m*

chose [tʃəuz] *pt of* choose

chosen ['tʃəuzn] *pp of* choose

chowder ['tʃaudəʳ] (*US*) *n* sämige Fischsuppe
f

Christ [kraɪst] *n* Christus *m*

christen ['krɪsn] *vt* taufen; **~ing** *n* Taufe *f*

Christian ['krɪstɪən] *adj* christlich ♦ *n*
Christ(in) *m(f)*; **~ity** [krɪstɪ'ænɪtɪ] *n*
Christentum *nt*; ~ **name** *n* Vorname *m*

Christmas ['krɪsməs] *n* Weihnachten *pl*;
Happy *or* Merry ~! frohe *or* fröhliche
Weihnachten!; ~ **card** *n* Weihnachtskarte *f*;
~ **Day** *n* der erste Weihnachtstag; ~ **Eve** *n*
Heiligabend *m*; ~ **tree** *n* Weihnachtsbaum *m*

chrome [krəum] *n* Verchromung *f*

chromium ['krəumɪəm] *n* Chrom *nt*

chronic ['krɔnɪk] *adj* chronisch

chronicle ['krɔnɪkl] *n* Chronik *f*

chronological [krɔnə'lɔdʒɪkl] *adj*
chronologisch

chubby ['tʃʌbɪ] *adj* rundlich

chuck [tʃʌk] *vt* werfen; (*BRIT: also: ~ up*)
hinwerfen; **~ out** *n* (*person*) rauswerfen;
(*old clothes etc*) wegwerfen

chuckle ['tʃʌkl] *vi* in sich hineinlachen

chug [tʃʌg] *vi* tuckern

chunk [tʃʌŋk] *n* Klumpen *m*; (*of food*)
Brocken *m*

church [tʃəːtʃ] *n* Kirche *f*; **~yard** *n* Kirchhof *m*

churn [tʃəːn] *n* (*for butter*) Butterfass *nt*; (*for
milk*) Milchkanne *f*; ~ **out** (*inf*) *vt*
produzieren

chute [ʃuːt] *n* Rutsche *f*; (*rubbish ~*)
Müllschlucker *m*

chutney ['tʃʌtnɪ] *n* Chutney *nt*

CIA (*US*) *n abbr* (= *Central Intelligence Agency*)
CIA *m*

CID (*BRIT*) *n abbr* (= *Criminal Investigation
Department*) ≈ Kripo *f*

cider ['saɪdəʳ] *n* Apfelwein *m*

cigar [sɪ'gɑːʳ] *n* Zigarre *f*

cigarette [sɪgə'ret] *n* Zigarette *f*; ~ **case** *n*
Zigarettenetui *nt*; ~ **end** *n* Zigarettenstummel *m*

Cinderella [sɪndə'relə] *n* Aschenbrödel *nt*

cinders ['sɪndəz] *npl* Asche *f*

cine camera ['sɪnɪ-] (*BRIT*) *n* Filmkamera *f*

cine film (*BRIT*) *n* Schmalfilm *m*

cinema ['sɪnəmə] *n* Kino *nt*

cinnamon ['sɪnəmən] *n* Zimt *m*

circle ['səːkl] *n* Kreis *m*; (*in cinema etc*) Rang
m ♦ *vi* kreisen ♦ *vt* (*surround*) umgeben;
(*move round*) kreisen um

circuit ['səːkɪt] *n* (*track*) Rennbahn *f*; (*lap*)
Runde *f*; (*ELEC*) Stromkreis *m*

circular ['səːkjuləʳ] *adj* rund ♦ *n*
Rundschreiben *nt*

circulate ['səːkjuleɪt] *vi* zirkulieren ♦ *vt* in
Umlauf setzen; **circulation** [səːkju'leɪʃən] *n*
(*of blood*) Kreislauf *m*; (*of newspaper*)
Auflage *f*; (*of money*) Umlauf *m*

circumcise ['səːkəmsaɪz] *vt* beschneiden

circumference |səˈkʌmfərəns| n
(Kreis)umfang m

circumspect |ˈsɜːkəmspɛkt| adj umsichtig

circumstances |ˈsɜːkəmstənsɪz| npl
Umstände pl; (financial) Verhältnisse pl

circumvent |sɜːkəmˈvɛnt| vt umgehen

circus |ˈsɜːkəs| n Zirkus m

CIS n abbr (= Commonwealth of Independent
States) GUS f

cistern |ˈsɪstən| n Zisterne f; (of W.C.)
Spülkasten m

cite |saɪt| vt zitieren, anführen

citizen |ˈsɪtɪzn| n Bürger(in) m(f); **~ship** n
Staatsbürgerschaft f

citrus fruit |ˈsɪtrəs-| n Zitrusfrucht f

city |ˈsɪtɪ| n Großstadt f; **the C~** die City, das
Finanzzentrum Londons

city technology college n ≈ Technische
Fachschule f

civic |ˈsɪvɪk| adj (of town) städtisch; (of citizen)
Bürger-; **~ centre** (BRIT) n Stadtverwaltung f

civil |ˈsɪvl| adj bürgerlich; (not military) zivil;
(polite) höflich; **~ engineer** n Bauingenieur
m; **~ian** |sɪˈvɪlɪən| n Zivilperson f ♦ adj zivil,
Zivil-

civilization |sɪvɪlaɪˈzeɪʃən| n Zivilisation f

civilized |ˈsɪvɪlaɪzd| adj zivilisiert

civil: ~ law n Zivilrecht nt; **~ servant** n
Staatsbeamte(r) m; **C~ Service** n
Staatsdienst m; **~ war** n Bürgerkrieg m

clad |klæd| adj: **~ in** gehüllt in +acc

claim |kleɪm| vt beanspruchen; (have opinion)
behaupten ♦ vi (for insurance) Ansprüche
geltend machen ♦ n (demand) Forderung f;
(right) Anspruch m; (pretension) Behauptung
f; **~ant** n Antragsteller(in) m(f)

clairvoyant |klɛəˈvɔɪənt| n Hellseher(in) m(f)

clam |klæm| n Venusmuschel f

clamber |ˈklæmbəʳ| vi kraxeln

clammy |ˈklæmɪ| adj klamm

clamour |ˈklæməʳ| vi: **to ~ for sth** nach etw
verlangen

clamp |klæmp| n Schraubzwinge f ♦ vt
einspannen; (AUT: wheel) krallen; **~ down
on** vt fus Maßnahmen ergreifen gegen

clan |klæn| n Clan m

clandestine |klænˈdɛstɪn| adj geheim

clang |klæŋ| vi scheppern

clap |klæp| vi klatschen ♦ vt Beifall klatschen
+dat ♦ n (of hands) Klatschen nt; (of
thunder) Donnerschlag m; **~ping** n
Klatschen nt

claret |ˈklærət| n rote(r) Bordeaux(wein) m

clarify |ˈklærɪfaɪ| vt klären, erklären

clarinet |klærɪˈnɛt| n Klarinette f

clarity |ˈklærɪtɪ| n Klarheit f

clash |klæʃ| n (fig) Konflikt m ♦ vi
zusammenprallen; (colours) sich beißen;
(argue) sich streiten

clasp |klɑːsp| n Griff m; (on jewels, bag)
Verschluss m ♦ vt umklammern

class |klɑːs| n Klasse f ♦ vt einordnen; **~-
conscious** adj klassenbewusst

classic |ˈklæsɪk| n Klassiker m ♦ adj klassisch;
~al adj klassisch

classified |ˈklæsɪfaɪd| adj (information)
Geheim-; **~ advertisement** n Kleinanzeige
f

classify |ˈklæsɪfaɪ| vt klassifizieren

classmate |ˈklɑːsmeɪt| n Klassenkamerad(in)
m(f)

classroom |ˈklɑːsrum| n Klassenzimmer nt

clatter |ˈklætəʳ| vi klappern; (feet) trappeln

clause |klɔːz| n (JUR) Klausel f; (GRAM) Satz
m

claustrophobia |klɔːstrəˈfəubɪə| n
Platzangst f

claw |klɔː| n Kralle f ♦ vt (zer)kratzen

clay |kleɪ| n Lehm m; (for pots) Ton m

clean |kliːn| adj sauber ♦ vt putzen; (clothes)
reinigen; **~ out** vt gründlich putzen; **~ up** vt
aufräumen; **~-cut** adj (person) adrett; (clear)
klar; **~er** n (person) Putzfrau f; **~er's** n (also:
dry ~er's) Reinigung f; **~ing** n Putzen nt;
(clothes) Reinigung f; **~liness** |ˈklɛnlɪnɪs| n
Reinlichkeit f

cleanse |klɛnz| vt reinigen; **~r** n (for face)
Reinigungsmilch f

clean-shaven |ˈkliːnˈʃeɪvn| adj glatt rasiert

cleansing department |ˈklɛnzɪŋ-| (BRIT) n
Stadtreinigung f

clear |klɪəʳ| adj klar; (road) frei ♦ vt (road etc)
freimachen; (obstacle) beseitigen; (JUR:
suspect) freisprechen ♦ vi klar werden; (fog)
sich lichten ♦ adv: **~ of** von ... entfernt; **to ~
the table** den Tisch abräumen; **~ up** vt
aufräumen; (solve) aufklären; **~ance**
|ˈklɪərəns| n (removal) Räumung f; (free
space) Lichtung f; (permission) Freigabe f; **~-
cut** adj (case) eindeutig; **~ing** n Lichtung f;
~ing bank (BRIT) n Clearingbank f; **~ly** adv
klar; (obviously) eindeutig; **~way** (BRIT) n
(Straße f mit) Halteverbot nt

cleaver |ˈkliːvəʳ| n Hackbeil f

cleft |klɛft| n (in rock) Spalte f

clementine |ˈklɛməntaɪn| n (fruit)
Klementine f

clench |klɛntʃ| vt (teeth) zusammenbeißen;
(fist) ballen

clergy |ˈklɜːdʒɪ| n Geistliche(n) pl; **~man**
(irreg) n Geistliche(r) m

clerical |ˈklɛrɪkl| adj (office) Schreib-, Büro-;
(REL) geistlich

clerk |klɑːk, (US) klɜːrk| n (in office)
Büroangestellte(r) mf; (US: sales person)
Verkäufer(in) m(f)

clever |ˈklɛvəʳ| adj klug; (crafty) schlau

cliché |ˈkliːʃeɪ| n Klischee nt

click |klɪk| vt (tongue) schnalzen mit; (heels)
zusammenklappen

client |ˈklaɪənt| n Klient(in) m(f); **~ele**
|kliːɑːnˈtɛl| n Kundschaft f

cliff [klɪf] n Klippe f
climate ['klaɪmɪt] n Klima nt
climax ['klaɪmæks] n Höhepunkt m
climb [klaɪm] vt besteigen ♦ vi steigen,
klettern ♦ n Aufstieg m; **~-down** n Abstieg
m; **~er** n Bergsteiger(in) m(f); **~ing** n
Bergsteigen nt
clinch [klɪntʃ] vt (decide) entscheiden; (deal)
festmachen
cling [klɪŋ] (pt, pp **clung**) vi (clothes) eng
anliegen; **to ~ to** sich festklammern an +dat
clinic ['klɪnɪk] n Klinik f; **~al** adj klinisch
clink [klɪŋk] vi klimpern
clip [klɪp] n Spange f; (also: **paper ~**)
Klammer f ♦ vt (papers) heften; (hair, hedge)
stutzen; **~pers** npl (for hedge) Heckenschere
f; (for hair) Haarschneidemaschine f; **~ping**
n Ausschnitt m
cloak [kləʊk] n Umhang m ♦ vt hüllen;
~room n (for coats) Garderobe f; (BRIT:
W.C.) Toilette f
clock [klɒk] n Uhr f; **~ in** or **on** vi stempeln;
~ off or **out** vi stempeln; **~wise** adv im
Uhrzeigersinn; **~work** n Uhrwerk nt ♦ adj
zum Aufziehen
clog [klɒg] n Holzschuh m ♦ vt verstopfen
cloister ['klɒɪstər] n Kreuzgang m
clone [kləʊn] n Klon m
close[1] [kləʊs] adj (near) in der Nähe; (friend,
connection, print) eng; (relative) nahe;
(result) knapp; (examination) eingehend;
(weather) schwül; (room) stickig ♦ adv nahe,
dicht; **~ by** in der Nähe; **~ at hand** in der
Nähe; **to have a ~ shave** (fig) mit knapper
Not davonkommen
close[2] [kləʊz] vt (shut) schließen; (end)
beenden ♦ vi (shop etc) schließen; (door etc)
sich schließen ♦ n Ende nt; **~ down** vi
schließen; **~d** adj (shop etc) geschlossen; **~d
shop** n Gewerkschaftszwang m
close-knit ['kləʊs'nɪt] adj eng zusammen-
gewachsen
closely ['kləʊslɪ] adv eng; (carefully) genau
closet ['klɒzɪt] n Schrank m
close-up ['kləʊsʌp] n Nahaufnahme f
closure ['kləʊʒər] n Schließung f
clot [klɒt] n (of blood) Blutgerinnsel nt; (fool)
Blödmann m ♦ vi gerinnen
cloth [klɒθ] n (material) Tuch nt; (rag)
Lappen m
clothe [kləʊð] vt kleiden
clothes [kləʊðz] npl Kleider pl; **~ brush** n
Kleiderbürste f; **~ line** n Wäscheleine f; **~
peg**, **~ pin** (US) n Wäscheklammer f
clothing ['kləʊðɪŋ] n Kleidung f
clotted cream ['klɒtɪd-] (BRIT) n Sahne aus
erhitzter Milch
cloud [klaʊd] n Wolke f; **~burst** n
Wolkenbruch m; **~y** adj bewölkt; (liquid)
trüb
clout [klaʊt] vt hauen

clove [kləʊv] n Gewürznelke f; **~ of garlic**
Knoblauchzehe f
clover ['kləʊvər] n Klee m
clown [klaʊn] n Clown m ♦ vi (also: **~ about**,
~ around) kaspern
cloying ['klɒɪŋ] adj (taste, smell) übersüß
club [klʌb] n (weapon) Knüppel m; (society)
Klub m; (also: **golf ~**) Golfschläger m ♦ vt
prügeln ♦ vi: **to ~ together**
zusammenlegen; **~s** npl (CARDS) Kreuz nt; **~
car** (US) n (RAIL) Speisewagen m; **~ class** n
(AVIAT) Club-Klasse f; **~house** n Klubhaus nt
cluck [klʌk] vi glucken
clue [kluː] n Anhaltspunkt m; (in crosswords)
Frage f; **I haven't a ~** (ich hab') keine
Ahnung
clump [klʌmp] n Gruppe f
clumsy ['klʌmzɪ] adj (person) unbeholfen;
(shape) unförmig
clung [klʌŋ] pt, pp of **cling**
cluster ['klʌstər] n (of trees etc) Gruppe f ♦ vi
sich drängen, sich scharen
clutch [klʌtʃ] n Griff m; (AUT) Kupplung f ♦ vt
sich festklammern an +dat
clutter ['klʌtər] vt voll propfen; (desk)
übersäen
CND n abbr = **Campaign for Nuclear
Disarmament**
Co. abbr = **county**; **company**
c/o abbr (= care of) c/o
coach [kəʊtʃ] n (bus) Reisebus m; (horse-
drawn) Kutsche f; (RAIL) (Personen)wagen
m; (trainer) Trainer m ♦ vt (SCH)
Nachhilfeunterricht geben +dat; (SPORT)
trainieren; **~ trip** n Busfahrt f
coal [kəʊl] n Kohle f; **~ face** n Streb m
coalition [kəʊə'lɪʃən] n Koalition f
coalman ['kəʊlmən] (irreg) n Kohlenhändler
m
coal mine n Kohlenbergwerk nt
coarse [kɔːs] adj grob; (fig) ordinär
coast [kəʊst] n Küste f ♦ vi dahinrollen; (AUT)
im Leerlauf fahren; **~al** adj Küsten-; **~guard**
n Küstenwache f; **~line** n Küste(nlinie) f
coat [kəʊt] n Mantel m; (on animals) Fell nt;
(of paint) Schicht f ♦ vt überstreichen;
~hanger n Kleiderbügel m; **~ing** n Überzug
m; (of paint) Schicht f; **~ of arms** n
Wappen nt
coax [kəʊks] vt beschwatzen
cob [kɒb] n see **corn**
cobbler ['kɒblər] n Schuster m
cobbles ['kɒblz] npl Pflastersteine pl
cobweb ['kɒbweb] n Spinnennetz nt
cocaine [kə'keɪn] n Kokain nt
cock [kɒk] n Hahn m ♦ vt (gun) entsichern;
~erel ['kɒkərl] n junge(r) Hahn m; **~eyed**
adj (fig) verrückt
cockle ['kɒkl] n Herzmuschel f
cockney ['kɒknɪ] n echte(r) Londoner m
cockpit ['kɒkpɪt] n (AVIAT) Pilotenkanzel f

cockroach [ˈkɔkrəutʃ] n Küchenschabe f
cocktail [ˈkɔkteɪl] n Cocktail m; ~ **cabinet** n
Hausbar f; ~ **party** n Cocktailparty f
cocoa [ˈkəukəu] n Kakao m
coconut [ˈkəukənʌt] n Kokosnuss f
cocoon [kəˈkuːn] n Kokon m
cod [kɔd] n Kabeljau m
C.O.D. abbr = **cash on delivery**
code [kəud] n Kode m; (JUR) Kodex m
cod-liver oil [ˈkɔdlɪvə-] n Lebertran m
coercion [kəuˈəːʃən] n Zwang m
coffee [ˈkɔfɪ] n Kaffee m; ~ **bar** (BRIT) n Café
nt; ~ **bean** n Kaffeebohne f; ~ **break** n
Kaffeepause f; ~**pot** n Kaffeekanne f; ~
table n Couchtisch m
coffin [ˈkɔfɪn] n Sarg m
cog [kɔg] n (Rad)zahn m
cognac [ˈkɔnjæk] n Kognak m
coherent [kəuˈhɪərənt] adj zusammenhängend; (person) verständlich
coil [kɔɪl] n Rolle f; (ELEC) Spule f;
(contraceptive) Spirale f ♦ vt aufwickeln
coin [kɔɪn] n Münze f ♦ vt prägen; ~**age**
[ˈkɔɪnɪdʒ] n (word) Prägung f; ~ **box** (BRIT)
n Münzfernsprecher m
coincide [kəuɪnˈsaɪd] vi (happen together)
zusammenfallen; (agree) übereinstimmen;
~**nce** [kəuˈɪnsɪdəns] n Zufall m
coinphone [ˈkɔɪnfəun] n Münzfernsprecher
m
Coke [kəuk] ® n (drink) Coca-Cola f ®
coke [kəuk] n Koks m
colander [ˈkɔləndəʳ] n Durchschlag m
cold [kəuld] adj kalt ♦ n Kälte f; (MED)
Erkältung f; **I'm** ~ mir ist kalt; **to catch** ~
sich erkälten; **in** ~ **blood** kaltblütig; **to give**
sb the ~ **shoulder** jdm die kalte Schulter
zeigen; ~**ly** adv kalt; ~**-shoulder** vt die
kalte Schulter zeigen +dat; ~ **sore** n
Erkältungsbläschen nt
coleslaw [ˈkəulslɔː] n Krautsalat m
colic [ˈkɔlɪk] n Kolik f
collaborate [kəˈlæbəreɪt] vi zusammenarbeiten
collapse [kəˈlæps] vi (people) zusammenbrechen; (things) einstürzen ♦ n Zusammenbruch m; Einsturz m; **collapsible** adj
zusammenklappbar, Klapp-
collar [ˈkɔləʳ] n Kragen m; ~**bone** n
Schlüsselbein nt
collateral [kɔˈlætərl] n (zusätzliche)
Sicherheit f
colleague [ˈkɔliːg] n Kollege m, Kollegin f
collect [kəˈlekt] vt sammeln; (BRIT: call and
pick up) abholen ♦ vi sich sammeln ♦ adv: **to**
call ~ (US: TEL) ein R-Gespräch führen; ~**ion**
[kəˈlekʃən] n Sammlung f; (REL) Kollekte f;
(of post) Leerung f; ~**ive** [kəˈlektɪv] adj
gemeinsam; (POL) kollektiv; ~**or** [kəˈlektəʳ] n
Sammler m; (tax ~or) (Steuer)einnehmer m
college [ˈkɔlɪdʒ] n (UNIV) College nt; (TECH)

Fach-, Berufsschule f
collide [kəˈlaɪd] vi zusammenstoßen
collie [ˈkɔlɪ] n Collie m
colliery [ˈkɔlɪərɪ] (BRIT) n Zeche f
collision [kəˈlɪʒən] n Zusammenstoß m
colloquial [kəˈləukwɪəl] adj
umgangssprachlich
colon [ˈkəulən] n Doppelpunkt m; (MED)
Dickdarm m
colonel [ˈkəːnl] n Oberst m
colonial [kəˈləunɪəl] adj Kolonial-
colonize [ˈkɔlənaɪz] vt kolonisieren
colony [ˈkɔlənɪ] n Kolonie f
colour [ˈkʌləʳ] (US color) n Farbe f ♦ vt (also
fig) färben ♦ vi sich verfärben; ~**s** npl (of
club) Fahne f; ~ **bar** n Rassenschranke f; ~**-**
blind adj farbenblind; ~**ed** adj farbig; ~
film n Farbfilm m; ~**ful** adj bunt;
(personality) schillernd; ~**ing** n (complexion)
Gesichtsfarbe f; (substance) Farbstoff m; ~
scheme n Farbgebung f; ~ **television** n
Farbfernsehen nt
colt [kəult] n Fohlen nt
column [ˈkɔləm] n Säule f; (MIL) Kolonne f;
(of print) Spalte f; ~**ist** [ˈkɔləmnɪst] n
Kolumnist m
coma [ˈkəumə] n Koma nt
comb [kəum] n Kamm m ♦ vt kämmen;
(search) durchkämmen
combat [ˈkɔmbæt] n Kampf m ♦ vt
bekämpfen
combination [kɔmbɪˈneɪʃən] n Kombination
f
combine [vb kəmˈbaɪn, n ˈkɔmbaɪn] vt
verbinden ♦ vi sich vereinigen ♦ n (COMM)
Konzern m; ~ (**harvester**) n Mähdrescher
m
combustion [kəmˈbʌstʃən] n Verbrennung f
come [kʌm] (pt came, pp come) vi kommen;
to ~ undone aufgehen; ~ **about** vi
geschehen; ~ **across** vt fus (find) stoßen auf
+acc; ~ **away** vi (person) weggehen;
(handle etc) abgehen; ~ **back** vi
zurückkommen; ~ **by** vt fus (find): **to ~ by**
sth zu etw kommen; ~ **down** vi (price)
fallen; ~ **forward** vi (volunteer) sich melden;
~ **from** vt fus (result) kommen von; **where**
do you ~ from? wo kommen Sie her?; **I ~**
from London ich komme aus London; ~ **in**
vi hereinkommen; (train) einfahren; ~ **in for**
vt fus abkriegen; ~ **into** vt fus (inherit)
erben; ~ **off** vi (handle) abgehen; (succeed)
klappen; ~ **on** vi (progress) vorankommen; ~
on! komm!; (hurry) beeil dich!; ~ **out** vi
herauskommen; ~ **round** (MED) wieder zu
sich kommen; ~ **to** vi (MED) wieder zu sich
kommen ♦ vt fus (bill) sich belaufen auf
+acc; ~ **up** vi hochkommen; (sun) aufgehen;
(problem) auftauchen; ~ **up against** vt fus
(resistance, difficulties) stoßen auf +acc; ~
upon vt fus stoßen auf +acc; ~ **up with** vt

fus sich einfallen lassen
comedian |kə'mi:dɪən| *n* Komiker *m*;
  comedienne |kəmi:dɪ'ɛn| *n* Komikerin *f*
comedown |'kʌmdaun| *n* Abstieg *m*
comedy |'kɒmɪdɪ| *n* Komödie *f*
comet |'kɒmɪt| *n* Komet *m*
comeuppance |kʌm'ʌpəns| *n*: **to get one's**
  ~ seine Quittung bekommen
comfort |'kʌmfət| *n* Komfort *m*; *(consolation)*
  Trost *m* ♦ *vt* trösten; **~able** *adj* bequem;
  ~ably *adv (sit etc)* bequem; *(live)*
  angenehm; **~ station** *(US) n* öffentliche
  Toilette *f*
comic |'kɒmɪk| *n* Comic(heft) *nt*; *(comedian)*
  Komiker *m* ♦ *adj (also:* **~al**) komisch; **~ strip**
  n Comicstrip *m*
coming |'kʌmɪŋ| *n* Kommen *nt*; **~(s) and**
  going(s) *n(pl)* Kommen und Gehen *nt*
comma |'kɒmə| *n* Komma *nt*
command |kə'mɑ:nd| *n* Befehl *m*; *(control)*
  Führung *f*; *(MIL)* Kommando *nt*; *(mastery)*
  Beherrschung *f* ♦ *vt* befehlen +*dat*; *(MIL)*
  kommandieren; *(be able to get)* verfügen
  über +*acc*; **~eer** |kɒmən'dɪər| *vt* requirieren;
  ~er *n* Kommandant *m*; **~ment** *n (REL)*
  Gebot *nt*
commando |kə'mɑ:ndəu| *n* Kommando-
  truppe *f*; *(person)* Mitglied *nt* einer
  Kommandotruppe
commemorate |kə'meməreɪt| *vt* gedenken
  +*gen*
commence |kə'mɛns| *vt, vi* beginnen
commend |kə'mɛnd| *vt (recommend)*
  empfehlen; *(praise)* loben
commensurate |kə'mɛnʃərɪt| *adj*: **~ with**
  sth einer Sache *dat* entsprechend
comment |'kɒmɛnt| *n* Bemerkung *f* ♦ *vi*: **to**
  ~ (on) sich äußern (zu); **~ary** *n* Kommentar
  m; **~ator** *n* Kommentator *m*; *(TV)*
  Reporter(in) *m(f)*
commerce |'kɒmə:s| *n* Handel *m*
commercial |kə'mə:ʃəl| *adj* kommerziell,
  geschäftlich; *(training)* kaufmännisch ♦ *n*
  (TV) Fernsehwerbung *f*; **~ break** *n*
  Werbespot *m*; **~ize** *vt* kommerzialisieren
commiserate |kə'mɪzəreɪt| *vi*: **to ~ with**
  Mitleid haben mit
commission |kə'mɪʃən| *n (act)* Auftrag *m*;
  (fee) Provision *f*; *(body)* Kommission *f* ♦ *vt*
  beauftragen; *(MIL)* zum Offizier ernennen;
  (work of art) in Auftrag geben; **out of ~**
  außer Betrieb; **~er** *n (POLICE)* Polizeipräsident
  m
commit |kə'mɪt| *vt (crime)* begehen; *(entrust)*
  anvertrauen; **to ~ o.s.** sich festlegen; **~ment**
  n Verpflichtung *f*
committee |kə'mɪtɪ| *n* Ausschuss *m*
commodity |kə'mɒdɪtɪ| *n* Ware *f*
common |'kɒmən| *adj (cause)* gemeinsam;
  (pej) gewöhnlich; *(widespread)* üblich, häufig
  ♦ *n* Gemeindeland *nt*; **C~s** *npl (BRIT):* **the**

C~s das Unterhaus; **~er** *n* Bürgerliche(r) *mf*;
~ law *n* Gewohnheitsrecht *nt*; **~ly** *adv*
gewöhnlich; **C~ Market** *n* Gemeinsame(r)
Markt *m*; **~place** *adj* alltäglich; **~ room** *n*
Gemeinschaftsraum *m*; **~ sense** *n*
gesunde(r) Menschenverstand *m*;
C~wealth *n*: **the C~wealth** das
Commonwealth
commotion |kə'məuʃən| *n* Aufsehen *nt*
communal |'kɒmju:nl| *adj* Gemeinde-;
  Gemeinschafts-
commune [*n* 'kɒmju:n, *vb* kə'mju:n] *n*
  Kommune *f* ♦ *vi*: **to ~ with** sich mitteilen
  +*dat*
communicate |kə'mju:nɪkeɪt| *vt (transmit)*
  übertragen ♦ *vi (be in touch)* in Verbindung
  stehen; *(make self understood)* sich
  verständigen; **communication**
  |kəmju:nɪ'keɪʃən| *n (message)* Mitteilung *f*;
  (making understood) Kommunikation *f*;
  communication cord *(BRIT) n* Notbremse
  f
communion |kə'mju:nɪən| *n (also:* **Holy C~)**
  Abendmahl *nt*, Kommunion *f*
communism |'kɒmjunɪzəm| *n*
  Kommunismus *m*; **communist** |'kɒmjunɪst|
  n Kommunist(in) *m(f)* ♦ *adj* kommunistisch
community |kə'mju:nɪtɪ| *n* Gemeinschaft *f*;
  ~ centre *n* Gemeinschaftszentrum *nt*; **~**
  chest *(US) n* Wohltätigkeitsfonds *m*; **~**
  home *(BRIT) n* Erziehungsheim *nt*
commutation ticket |kɒmju'teɪʃən-| *(US) n*
  Zeitkarte *f*
commute |kə'mju:t| *vi* pendeln ♦ *vt*
  umwandeln; **~r** *n* Pendler *m*
compact [*adj* kəm'pækt, *n* 'kɒmpækt] *adj*
  kompakt ♦ *n (for make-up)* Puderdose *f*; **~**
  disc *n* Compactdisc *f*, Compact Disc *f*; **~**
  disc player *n* CD-Spieler *m*
companion |kəm'pænjən| *n* Begleiter(in)
  m(f); **~ship** *n* Gesellschaft *f*
company |'kʌmpənɪ| *n* Gesellschaft *f*;
  (COMM) Firma *f*, Gesellschaft *f*; **to keep sb ~**
  jdm Gesellschaft leisten; **~ secretary** *(BRIT)*
  n ≈ Prokurist(in) *m(f)*
comparable |'kɒmpərəbl| *adj* vergleichbar
comparative |kəm'pærətɪv| *adj (relative)*
  relativ; **~ly** *adv* verhältnismäßig
compare |kəm'pɛər| *vt* vergleichen ♦ *vi*
  sich vergleichen lassen; **comparison**
  |kəm'pærɪsn| *n* Vergleich *m*; **in comparison**
  (with) im Vergleich (mit *or* zu)
compartment |kəm'pɑ:tmənt| *n (RAIL)*
  Abteil *nt*; *(in drawer)* Fach *nt*
compass |'kʌmpəs| *n* Kompass *m*; **~es** *npl*
  (MATH etc: also: **pair of ~es**) Zirkel *m*
compassion |kəm'pæʃən| *n* Mitleid *nt*; **~ate**
  adj mitfühlend
compatible |kəm'pætɪbl| *adj* vereinbar;
  (COMPUT) kompatibel
compel |kəm'pɛl| *vt* zwingen

compensate ['kɔmpənseɪt] vt entschädigen
♦ vi: **to ~ for** Ersatz leisten für;
compensation [kɔmpən'seɪʃən] n
Entschädigung f

compère ['kɔmpɛəʳ] n Conférencier m

compete [kəm'piːt] vi (take part)
teilnehmen; (vie with) konkurrieren

competent ['kɔmpɪtənt] adj kompetent

competition [kɔmpɪ'tɪʃən] n (contest)
Wettbewerb m; (COMM, rivalry) Konkurrenz
f; **competitive** [kəm'pɛtɪtɪv] adj
Konkurrenz-; (COMM) konkurrenzfähig;
competitor [kəm'pɛtɪtəʳ] n (COMM)
Konkurrent(in) m(f); (participant)
Teilnehmer(in) m(f)

compile [kəm'paɪl] vt zusammenstellen

complacency [kəm'pleɪsnsɪ] n
Selbstzufriedenheit f

complacent [kəm'pleɪsnt] adj
selbstzufrieden

complain [kəm'pleɪn] vi sich beklagen;
(formally) sich beschweren; **~t** n Klage f;
(formal ~t) Beschwerde f; (MED) Leiden nt

complement [n 'kɔmplɪmənt, vb
'kɔmplɪment] n Ergänzung f; (ship's crew
etc) Bemannung f ♦ vt ergänzen; **~ary**
[kɔmplɪ'mentərɪ] adj (sich) ergänzend

complete [kəm'pliːt] adj (full) vollkommen,
ganz; (finished) fertig ♦ vt vervollständigen;
(finish) beenden; (fill in: form) ausfüllen; **~ly**
adv ganz; **completion** [kəm'pliːʃən] n
Fertigstellung f; (of contract etc) Abschluss m

complex ['kɔmplɛks] adj kompliziert

complexion [kəm'plekʃən] n Gesichtsfarbe
f; (fig) Aspekt m

complexity [kəm'plɛksɪtɪ] n Kompliziertheit f

compliance [kəm'plaɪəns] n Fügsamkeit f,
Einwilligung f; **in ~ with sth** einer Sache dat
gemäß

complicate ['kɔmplɪkeɪt] vt komplizieren;
~d adj kompliziert; **complication**
[kɔmplɪ'keɪʃən] n Komplikation f

compliment [n 'kɔmplɪmənt, vb
'kɔmplɪment] n Kompliment nt ♦ vt ein
Kompliment machen +dat; **~s** npl
(greetings) Grüße pl; **to pay sb a ~** jdm ein
Kompliment machen; **~ary** [kɔmplɪ'mentərɪ]
adj schmeichelhaft; (free) Frei-, Gratis-

comply [kəm'plaɪ] vi: **to ~ with** erfüllen
+acc; entsprechen +dat

component [kəm'pəunənt] adj Teil- ♦ n
Bestandteil m

compose [kəm'pəuz] vt (music)
komponieren; (poetry) verfassen; **to ~ o.s.**
sich sammeln; **~d** adj gefasst; **~r** n
Komponist(in) m(f); **composition**
[kɔmpə'zɪʃən] n (MUS) Komposition f; (SCH)
Aufsatz m; (structure) Zusammensetzung f,
Aufbau m

compost ['kɔmpɔst] n Kompost m

composure [kəm'pəuʒəʳ] n Fassung f

compound ['kɔmpaund] n (CHEM)
Verbindung f; (enclosure) Lager nt; (LING)
Kompositum nt ♦ adj zusammengesetzt;
(fracture) kompliziert; **~ interest** n
Zinseszins m

comprehend [kɔmprɪ'hend] vt begreifen;
comprehension n Verständnis nt

comprehensive [kɔmprɪ'hensɪv] adj
umfassend ♦ n = **comprehensive school**; **~
insurance** n Vollkasko nt; **~ school** (BRIT) n
Gesamtschule f

compress [vb kəm'pres, n 'kɔmpres] vt
komprimieren ♦ n (MED) Kompresse f

comprise [kəm'praɪz] vt (also: **be ~d of**)
umfassen, bestehen aus

compromise ['kɔmprəmaɪz] n Kompromiss
m ♦ vt kompromittieren ♦ vi einen
Kompromiss schließen

compulsion [kəm'pʌlʃən] n Zwang m;
compulsive [kəm'pʌlsɪv] adj zwanghaft;
compulsory [kəm'pʌlsərɪ] adj obligatorisch

computer [kəm'pjuːtəʳ] n Computer m,
Rechner m; **~ game** n Computerspiel nt; **~-
generated** adj computergeneriert; **~ize** vt
(information) computerisieren; (company,
accounts) auf Computer umstellen; **~
programmer** n Programmierer(in) m(f); **~
programming** n Programmieren nt; **~
science** n Informatik f; **computing**
[kəm'pjuːtɪŋ] n (science) Informatik f; (work)
Computerei f

comrade ['kɔmrɪd] n Kamerad m; (POL)
Genosse m

con [kɔn] vt hereinlegen ♦ n Schwindel nt

concave ['kɔnkeɪv] adj konkav

conceal [kən'siːl] vt (secret) verschweigen;
(hide) verbergen

concede [kən'siːd] vt (grant) gewähren;
(point) zugeben ♦ vi (admit defeat)
nachgeben

conceit [kən'siːt] n Einbildung f; **~ed** adj
eingebildet

conceivable [kən'siːvəbl] adj vorstellbar

conceive [kən'siːv] vt (idea) ausdenken;
(imagine) sich vorstellen; (baby) empfangen
♦ vi empfangen

concentrate ['kɔnsəntreɪt] vi sich
konzentrieren ♦ vt konzentrieren; **to ~ on
sth** sich auf etw acc konzentrieren;
concentration [kɔnsən'treɪʃən] n
Konzentration f; **concentration camp** n
Konzentrationslager nt, KZ nt

concept ['kɔnsept] n Begriff m

conception [kən'sepʃən] n (idea) Vorstellung
f; (BIOL) Empfängnis f

concern [kən'sɜːn] n (affair) Angelegenheit
f; (COMM) Unternehmen nt; (worry) Sorge f
♦ vt (interest) angehen; (be about) handeln
von; (have connection with) betreffen; **to be
~ed (about)** sich Sorgen machen (um);
~ing prep hinsichtlich +gen

concert ['kɔnsət] n Konzert nt
concerted [kən'sə:tɪd] adj gemeinsam
concert hall n Konzerthalle f
concertina [kɔnsə'ti:nə] n Handharmonika f
concerto [kən'tʃɑ:təu] n Konzert nt
concession [kən'seʃən] n (yielding) Zugeständnis nt; **tax ~** Steuerkonzession f
conciliation [kənsɪlɪ'eɪʃən] n Versöhnung f; (official) Schlichtung f
concise [kən'saɪs] adj präzis
conclude [kən'klu:d] vt (end) beenden; (treaty) (ab)schließen; (decide) schließen, folgern; **conclusion** [kən'klu:ʒən] n (Ab)schluss m; (deduction) Schluss m; **conclusive** [kən'klu:sɪv] adj schlüssig
concoct [kən'kɔkt] vt zusammenbrauen; **~ion** [kən'kɔkʃən] n Gebräu nt
concourse ['kɔŋkɔ:s] n (Bahnhofs)halle f, Vorplatz m
concrete ['kɔŋkri:t] n Beton m ♦ adj konkret
concur [kən'kə:ʳ] vi übereinstimmen
concurrently [kən'kʌrntlɪ] adv gleichzeitig
concussion [kən'kʌʃən] n (Gehirn)erschütterung f
condemn [kən'dem] vt (JUR) verurteilen; (building) abbruchreif erklären
condensation [kɔndən'seɪʃən] n Kondensation f
condense [kən'dens] vi (CHEM) kondensieren ♦ vt (fig) zusammendrängen; **~d milk** n Kondensmilch f
condescending [kɔndɪ'sendɪŋ] adj herablassend
condition [kən'dɪʃən] n (state) Zustand m; (presupposition) Bedingung f ♦ vt (hair etc) behandeln; (accustom) gewöhnen; **~s** npl (circumstances) Verhältnisse pl; **on ~ that ...** unter der Bedingung, dass ...; **~al** adj bedingt; **~er** n (for hair) Spülung f; (for fabrics) Weichspüler m
condolences [kən'dəulənsɪz] npl Beileid nt
condom ['kɔndəm] n Kondom nt or m
condominium [kɔndə'mɪnɪəm] n (US) Eigentumswohnung f; (block) Eigentumsblock m
condone [kən'dəun] vt gutheißen
conducive [kən'dju:sɪv] adj: **~ to** dienlich +dat
conduct [n 'kɔndʌkt, vb kən'dʌkt] n (behaviour) Verhalten nt; (management) Führung f ♦ vt führen; (MUS) dirigieren; **~ed tour** n Führung f; **~or** [kən'dʌktəʳ] n (of orchestra) Dirigent m; (in bus, US: on train) Schaffner m; (ELEC) Leiter m; **~ress** [kən'dʌktrɪs] n (in bus) Schaffnerin f
cone [kəun] n (MATH) Kegel m; (for ice cream) (Waffel)tüte f; (BOT) Tannenzapfen m
confectioner's (shop) [kən'fekʃənəz-] n Konditorei f
confectionery [kən'fekʃənrɪ] n Süßig-

keiten pl
confederation [kənfedə'reɪʃən] n Bund m
confer [kən'fə:ʳ] vt (degree) verleihen ♦ vi (discuss) konferieren, verhandeln; **~ence** ['kɔnfərəns] n Konferenz f
confess [kən'fes] vt, vi gestehen; (ECCL) beichten; **~ion** [kən'feʃən] n Geständnis nt; (ECCL) Beichte f; **~ional** n Beichtstuhl m
confide [kən'faɪd] vi: **to ~ in** (sich) anvertrauen +dat
confidence ['kɔnfɪdns] n Vertrauen nt; (assurance) Selbstvertrauen nt; (secret) Geheimnis nt; **in ~** (speak, write) vertraulich; **~ trick** n Schwindel m
confident ['kɔnfɪdənt] adj (sure) überzeugt; (self-assured) selbstsicher
confidential [kɔnfɪ'denʃəl] adj vertraulich
confine [kən'faɪn] vt (limit) beschränken; (lock up) einsperren; **~d** adj (space) eng; **~ment** n (in prison) Haft f; (MED) Wochenbett nt; **~s** ['kɔnfaɪnz] npl Grenzen pl
confirm [kən'fə:m] vt bestätigen; **~ation** [kɔnfə'meɪʃən] n Bestätigung f; (REL) Konfirmation f; **~ed** adj unverbesserlich; (bachelor) eingefleischt
confiscate ['kɔnfɪskeɪt] vt beschlagnahmen
conflict [n 'kɔnflɪkt, vb kən'flɪkt] n Konflikt m ♦ vi im Widerspruch stehen; **~ing** [kən'flɪktɪŋ] adj widersprüchlich
conform [kən'fɔ:m] vi: **to ~ (to)** (things) entsprechen +dat; (people) sich anpassen +dat; (to rules) sich richten (nach)
confound [kən'faund] vt verblüffen; (confuse) durcheinander bringen
confront [kən'frʌnt] vt (enemy) entgegentreten +dat; (problems) sich stellen +dat; **to ~ sb with sth** jdn mit etw konfrontieren; **~ation** [kɔnfrən'teɪʃən] n Konfrontation f
confuse [kən'fju:z] vt verwirren; (sth with sth) verwechseln; **~d** adj verwirrt; **confusing** adj verwirrend; **confusion** [kən'fju:ʒən] n (perplexity) Verwirrung f; (mixing up) Verwechslung f; (tumult) Aufruhr m
congeal [kən'dʒi:l] vi (freeze) gefrieren; (clot) gerinnen
congenial [kən'dʒi:nɪəl] adj angenehm
congested [kən'dʒestɪd] adj überfüllt
congestion [kən'dʒestʃən] n Stau m
conglomerate [kən'glɔmərɪt] n (COMM, GEOL) Konglomerat nt
conglomeration [kənglɔmə'reɪʃən] n Anhäufung f
congratulate [kən'grætjuleɪt] vt: **to ~ sb (on sth)** jdn (zu etw) beglückwünschen; **congratulations** [kəngrætju'leɪʃənz] npl Glückwünsche pl; **congratulations!** gratuliere!, herzlichen Glückwunsch!
congregate ['kɔŋgrɪgeɪt] vi sich

versammeln; **congregation** |kɔŋgrı'geıʃən| n Gemeinde f

congress |'kɔŋgres| n Kongress m; **C~man** (irreg: US) n Mitglied nt des amerikanischen Repräsentantenhauses

conifer |'kɔnıfəʳ| n Nadelbaum m

conjunction |kən'dʒʌŋkʃən| n Verbindung f; (GRAM) Konjunktion f

conjunctivitis |kəndʒʌŋktı'vaıtıs| n Bindehautentzündung f

conjure |'kʌndʒəʳ| vi zaubern; ~ **up** vt heraufbeschwören; **~r** n Zauberkünstler(in) m(f)

conk out |kɔŋk-| (inf) vi den Geist aufgeben

con man (irreg) n Schwindler m

connect |kə'nekt| vt verbinden; (ELEC) anschließen; **to be ~ed with** eine Beziehung haben zu; (be related to) verwandt sein mit; **~ion** |kə'nekʃən| n Verbindung f; (relation) Zusammenhang m; (ELEC, TEL, RAIL) Anschluss m

connive |kə'naıv| vi: **to ~ at** stillschweigend dulden

connoisseur |kɔnı'səːʳ| n Kenner m

conquer |'kɔŋkəʳ| vt (feelings) überwinden; (enemy) besiegen; (country) erobern; **~or** n Eroberer m

conquest |'kɔŋkwest| n Eroberung f

cons |kɔnz| npl see **convenience**; **pro**

conscience |'kɔnʃəns| n Gewissen nt

conscientious |kɔnʃı'enʃəs| adj gewissenhaft

conscious |'kɔnʃəs| adj bewusst; (MED) bei Bewusstsein; **~ness** n Bewusstsein nt

conscript |'kɔnskrıpt| n Wehrpflichtige(r) m; **~ion** |kən'skrıpʃən| n Wehrpflicht f

consecutive |kən'sekjutıv| adj aufeinander folgend

consensus |kən'sensəs| n allgemeine Übereinstimmung f

consent |kən'sent| n Zustimmung f ♦ vi zustimmen

consequence |'kɔnsıkwəns| n (importance) Bedeutung f; (effect) Folge f

consequently |'kɔnsıkwəntlı| adv folglich

conservation |kɔnsə'veıʃən| n Erhaltung f; (nature ~) Umweltschutz m

conservative |kən'səːvətıv| adj konservativ; **C~** (BRIT) adj konservativ ♦ n Konservative(r) mf

conservatory |kən'səːvətrı| n (room) Wintergarten m

conserve |kən'səːv| vt erhalten

consider |kən'sıdəʳ| vt überlegen; (take into account) in Betracht ziehen; (regard as) halten für; **to ~ doing sth** daran denken, etw zu tun; **~able** |kən'sıdərəbl| adj beträchtlich; **~ably** adv beträchtlich; **~ate** |kən'sıdərıt| adj rücksichtsvoll; **~ation** |kɔnsıdə'reıʃən| n Rücksicht(nahme) f; (thought) Erwägung f; **~ing** |kən'sıdərıŋ|

prep in Anbetracht +gen

consign |kən'saın| vt übergeben; **~ment** n Sendung f

consist |kən'sıst| vi: **to ~ of** bestehen aus

consistency |kən'sıstənsı| n (of material) Konsistenz f; (of argument, person) Konsequenz f

consistent |kən'sıstənt| adj (person) konsequent; (argument) folgerichtig

consolation |kɔnsə'leıʃən| n Trost m

console[1] |kən'səul| vt trösten

console[2] |'kɔnsəul| n Kontrollpult nt

consolidate |kən'sɔlıdeıt| vt festigen

consommé |kən'sɔmeı| n Fleischbrühe f

consonant |'kɔnsənənt| n Konsonant m, Mitlaut m

conspicuous |kən'spıkjuəs| adj (prominent) auffällig; (visible) deutlich sichtbar

conspiracy |kən'spırəsı| n Verschwörung f

conspire |kən'spaıəʳ| vi sich verschwören

constable |'kʌnstəbl| (BRIT) n Polizist(in) m(f); **chief ~** Polizeipräsident m; **constabulary** |kən'stæbjulərı| n Polizei f

constant |'kɔnstənt| adj (continuous) ständig; (unchanging) konstant; **~ly** adv ständig

constellation |kɔnstə'leıʃən| n Sternbild nt

consternation |kɔnstə'neıʃən| n Bestürzung f

constipated |'kɔnstıpeıtıd| adj verstopft; **constipation** |kɔnstı'peıʃən| n Verstopfung f

constituency |kən'stıtjuənsı| n Wahlkreis m

constituent |kən'stıtjuənt| n (person) Wähler m; (part) Bestandteil m

constitute |'kɔnstıtjuːt| vt (make up) bilden; (amount to) darstellen

constitution |kɔnstı'tjuːʃən| n Verfassung f; **~al** adj Verfassungs-

constraint |kən'streınt| n Zwang m; (shyness) Befangenheit f

construct |kən'strʌkt| vt bauen; **~ion** |kən'strʌkʃən| n Konstruktion f; (building) Bau m; **~ive** adj konstruktiv

construe |kən'struː| vt deuten

consul |'kɔnsl| n Konsul m; **~ate** n Konsulat nt

consult |kən'sʌlt| vt um Rat fragen; (doctor) konsultieren; (book) nachschlagen in +dat; **~ant** n (MED) Facharzt m; (other specialist) Gutachter m; **~ation** |kɔnsəl'teıʃən| n Beratung f; (MED) Konsultation f; **~ing room** n Sprechzimmer nt

consume |kən'sjuːm| vt verbrauchen; (food) konsumieren; **~r** n Verbraucher m; **~r goods** npl Konsumgüter pl; **~rism** n Konsum m; **~r society** n Konsumgesellschaft f

consummate |'kɔnsʌmeıt| vt (marriage) vollziehen

consumption |kən'sʌmpʃən| n Verbrauch

m; (of food) Konsum *m*
cont. *abbr (= continued)* Forts.
contact ['kɒntækt] *n (touch)* Berührung *f; (connection)* Verbindung *f; (person)* Kontakt *m* ♦ *vt* sich in Verbindung setzen mit; **~ lenses** *npl* Kontaktlinsen *pl*
contagious [kən'teɪdʒəs] *adj* ansteckend
contain [kən'teɪn] *vt* enthalten; **to ~ o.s.** sich zügeln; **~er** *n* Behälter *m; (transport)* Container *m*
contaminate [kən'tæmɪneɪt] *vt* verunreinigen
cont'd *abbr (= continued)* Forts.
contemplate ['kɒntəmpleɪt] *vt (look at)* (nachdenklich) betrachten; *(think about)* überdenken; *(plan)* vorhaben
contemporary [kən'tempərərɪ] *adj* zeitgenössisch ♦ *n* Zeitgenosse *m*
contempt [kən'tempt] *n* Verachtung *f;* **~ of court** *(JUR)* Missachtung *f* des Gerichts; **~ible** *adj* verachtenswert; **~uous** *adj* verächtlich
contend [kən'tend] *vt (argue)* behaupten ♦ *vi* kämpfen; **~er** *n (for post)* Bewerber(in) *m(f); (SPORT)* Wettkämpfer(in) *m(f)*
content [*adj, vb* kən'tent, *n* 'kɒntent] *adj* zufrieden ♦ *vt* befriedigen ♦ *n (also:* **~s)** Inhalt *m;* **~ed** *adj* zufrieden
contention [kən'tenʃən] *n (dispute)* Streit *m; (argument)* Behauptung *f*
contentment [kən'tentmənt] *n* Zufriedenheit *f*
contest [*n* 'kɒntest, *vb* kən'test] *n* (Wett)kampf *m* ♦ *vt (dispute)* bestreiten; *(JUR)* anfechten; *(POL)* kandidieren in +*dat;* **~ant** [kən'testənt] *n* Bewerber(in) *m(f)*
context ['kɒntekst] *n* Zusammenhang *m*
continent ['kɒntɪnənt] *n* Kontinent *m;* **the C~** *(BRIT)* das europäische Festland; **~al** [kɒntɪ'nentl] *adj* kontinental; **~al breakfast** *n* kleines Frühstück *nt;* **~al quilt** *(BRIT)* n Federbett *nt*
contingency [kən'tɪndʒənsɪ] *n* Möglichkeit *f*
contingent [kən'tɪndʒənt] *n* Kontingent *nt*
continual [kən'tɪnjuəl] *adj (endless)* fortwährend; *(repeated)* immer wiederkehrend; **~ly** *adv* immer wieder
continuation [kəntɪnju'eɪʃən] *n* Fortsetzung *f*
continue [kən'tɪnjuː] *vi (person)* weitermachen; *(thing)* weitergehen ♦ *vt* fortsetzen
continuity [kɒntɪ'njuːɪtɪ] *n* Kontinuität *f*
continuous [kən'tɪnjuəs] *adj* ununterbrochen; **~ stationery** *n* Endlospapier *nt*
contort [kən'tɔːt] *vt* verdrehen; **~ion** [kən'tɔːʃən] *n* Verzerrung *f*
contour ['kɒntuər] *n* Umriss *m; (also:* **~ line)** Höhenlinie *f*
contraband ['kɒntrəbænd] *n* Schmuggel-

ware *f*
contraception [kɒntrə'sepʃən] *n* Empfängnisverhütung *f*
contraceptive [kɒntrə'septɪv] *n* empfängnisverhütende(s) Mittel *nt* ♦ *adj* empfängnisverhütend
contract [*n* 'kɒntrækt, *vb* kən'trækt] *n* Vertrag *m* ♦ *vi (muscle, metal)* sich zusammenziehen ♦ *vt* zusammenziehen; **to ~ to do sth** *(COMM)* sich vertraglich verpflichten, etw zu tun; **~ion** [kən'trækʃən] *n (shortening)* Verkürzung *f;* **~or** [kən'træktər] *n* Unternehmer *m*
contradict [kɒntrə'dɪkt] *vt* widersprechen +*dat;* **~ion** [kɒntrə'dɪkʃən] *n* Widerspruch *m*
contraflow ['kɒntrəfləʊ] *n (AUT)* Gegenverkehr *m*
contraption [kən'træpʃən] *(inf) n* Apparat *m*
contrary¹ ['kɒntrərɪ] *adj (opposite)* entgegengesetzt ♦ *n* Gegenteil *nt;* **on the ~** im Gegenteil
contrary² [kən'treərɪ] *adj (obstinate)* widerspenstig
contrast [*n* 'kɒntrɑːst, *vb* kən'trɑːst] *n* Kontrast *m* ♦ *vt* entgegensetzen; **~ing** [kən'trɑːstɪŋ] *adj* Kontrast-
contravene [kɒntrə'viːn] *vt* verstoßen gegen
contribute [kən'trɪbjuːt] *vt, vi:* **to ~ to** beitragen zu; **contribution** [kɒntrɪ'bjuːʃən] *n* Beitrag *m;* **contributor** [kən'trɪbjutər] *n* Beitragende(r) *f(m)*
contrive [kən'traɪv] *vt* ersinnen ♦ *vi:* **to ~ to do sth** es schaffen, etw zu tun
control [kən'trəʊl] *vt (direct, test)* kontrollieren ♦ *n* Kontrolle *f;* **~s** *npl (of vehicle)* Steuerung *f; (of engine)* Schalttafel *f;* **to be in ~ of** *(business, office)* leiten; *(group of children)* beaufsichtigen; **out of ~** außer Kontrolle; **under ~** unter Kontrolle; **~led substance** *n* verschreibungspflichtiges Medikament; **~ panel** *n* Schalttafel *f;* **~ room** *n* Kontrollraum *m;* **~ tower** *n (AVIAT)* Kontrollturm *m*
controversial [kɒntrə'vɜːʃl] *adj* umstritten; **controversy** ['kɒntrəvɜːsɪ] *n* Kontroverse *f*
conurbation [kɒnə'beɪʃən] *n* Ballungsgebiet *nt*
convalesce [kɒnvə'les] *vi* genesen; **~nce** [kɒnvə'lesns] *n* Genesung *f*
convector [kən'vektər] *n* Heizlüfter *m*
convene [kən'viːn] *vt* zusammenrufen ♦ *vi* sich versammeln
convenience [kən'viːnɪəns] *n* Annehmlichkeit *f;* **all modern ~s** *or (BRIT)* **mod cons** mit allem Komfort; **at your ~** wann es Ihnen passt
convenient [kən'viːnɪənt] *adj* günstig
convent ['kɒnvənt] *n* Kloster *nt*
convention [kən'venʃən] *n* Versammlung *f; (custom)* Konvention *f;* **~al** *adj* konventionell

convent school n Klosterschule f
converge |kən'vɜːdʒ| vi zusammenlaufen
conversant |kən'vɜːsnt| adj: **to be ~ with** bewandert sein in +dat
conversation |kɔnvə'seɪʃən| n Gespräch nt; **~al** adj Unterhaltungs-
converse [n 'kɔnvɜːs, vb kən'vɜːs] n Gegenteil nt ♦ vi sich unterhalten
conversion |kən'vɜːʃən| n Umwandlung f; (REL) Bekehrung f
convert |vb kən'vɜːt, n 'kɔnvɜːt| vt (change) umwandeln; (REL) bekehren ♦ n Bekehrte(r) mf; Konvertit(in) m(f); **~ible** n (AUT) Kabriolett nt ♦ adj umwandelbar; (FIN) konvertierbar
convex |'kɔnveks| adj konvex
convey |kən'veɪ| vt (carry) befördern; (feelings) vermitteln; **~or belt** n Fließband nt
convict [vb kən'vɪkt, n 'kɔnvɪkt] vt verurteilen ♦ n Häftling m; **~ion** |kən'vɪkʃən| n (verdict) Verurteilung f; (belief) Überzeugung f
convince |kən'vɪns| vt überzeugen; **~d** adj: **~d that** überzeugt davon, dass; **convincing** adj überzeugend
convoluted |'kɔnvəluːtɪd| adj verwickelt; (style) gewunden
convoy |'kɔnvɔɪ| n (of vehicles) Kolonne f; (protected) Konvoi m
convulse |kən'vʌls| vt zusammenzucken lassen; **to be ~d with laughter** sich vor Lachen krümmen; **convulsion** |kən'vʌlʃən| n (esp MED) Zuckung f, Krampf m
coo |kuː| vi gurren
cook |kuk| vt, vi kochen ♦ n Koch m, Köchin f; **~ book** n Kochbuch nt; **~er** n Herd m; **~ery** n Kochkunst f; **~ery book** (BRIT) n = **cook book**; **~ie** (US) n Plätzchen nt; **~ing** n Kochen nt
cool |kuːl| adj kühl ♦ vt, vi (ab)kühlen; **~ down** vt, vi (fig) (sich) beruhigen; **~ness** n Kühle f; (of temperament) kühle(r) Kopf m
coop |kuːp| n Hühnerstall m ♦ vt: **~ up** (fig) einpferchen
cooperate |kəʊ'ɔpəreɪt| vi zusammenarbeiten; **cooperation** |kəʊɔpə'reɪʃən| n Zusammenarbeit f
cooperative |kəʊ'ɔpərətɪv| adj hilfsbereit; (COMM) genossenschaftlich ♦ n (of farmers) Genossenschaft f; (~ store) Konsumladen m
coordinate [vb kəʊ'ɔːdɪneɪt, n kəʊ'ɔːdɪnət] vt koordinieren ♦ n (MATH) Koordinate f; **~s** npl (clothes) Kombinationen pl; **coordination** |kəʊɔːdɪ'neɪʃən| n Koordination f
cop |kɔp| (inf) n Polyp m, Bulle m
cope |kəʊp| vi: **to ~ with** fertig werden mit
copious |'kəʊpɪəs| adj reichhaltig
copper |'kɔpəʳ| n (metal) Kupfer nt; (inf: policeman) Polyp m, Bulle m; **~s** npl (money) Kleingeld nt

copse |kɔps| n Unterholz nt
copy |'kɔpɪ| n (imitation) Kopie f; (of book etc) Exemplar nt; (of newspaper) Nummer f ♦ vt kopieren, abschreiben; **~right** n Copyright nt
coral |'kɔrəl| n Koralle f; **~ reef** n Korallenriff nt
cord |kɔːd| n Schnur f; (ELEC) Kabel nt
cordial |'kɔːdɪəl| adj herzlich ♦ n Fruchtsaft m
cordon |'kɔːdn| n Absperrkette f; **~ off** vt abriegeln
corduroy |'kɔːdərɔɪ| n Kord(samt) m
core |kɔːʳ| n Kern m ♦ vt entkernen
cork |kɔːk| n (bark) Korkrinde f; (stopper) Korken m; **~screw** n Korkenzieher m
corn |kɔːn| n (BRIT: wheat) Getreide nt, Korn nt; (US: maize) Mais m; (on foot) Hühnerauge nt; **~ on the cob** Maiskolben m
corned beef |'kɔːnd-| n Cornedbeef nt, Corned Beef nt
corner |'kɔːnəʳ| n Ecke f; (on road) Kurve f ♦ vt in die Enge treiben; (market) monopolisieren ♦ vi (AUT) in die Kurve gehen; **~stone** n Eckstein m
cornet |'kɔːnɪt| n (MUS) Kornett nt; (BRIT: of ice cream) Eistüte f
corn: ~flakes |'kɔːnfleɪks| npl Cornflakes pl ®; **~flour** |'kɔːnflaʊəʳ| (BRIT) n Maizena nt ®; **~starch** |'kɔːnstɑːtʃ| (US) n Maizena nt ®
corny |'kɔːnɪ| adj (joke) blöd
coronary |'kɔrənərɪ| n (also: ~ thrombosis) Herzinfarkt m
coronation |kɔrə'neɪʃən| n Krönung f
coroner |'kɔrənəʳ| n Untersuchungsrichter m
corporal |'kɔːpərl| n Obergefreite(r) m ♦ adj: **~ punishment** Prügelstrafe f
corporate |'kɔːpərɪt| adj gemeinschaftlich, korporativ
corporation |kɔːpə'reɪʃən| n (of town) Gemeinde f; (COMM) Körperschaft f, Aktiengesellschaft f
corps |kɔːʳ| (pl ~) n (Armee)korps nt
corpse |kɔːps| n Leiche f
corral |kə'rɑːl| n Pferch m, Korral m
correct |kə'rekt| adj (accurate) richtig; (proper) korrekt ♦ vt korrigieren; **~ion** |kə'rekʃən| n Berichtigung f
correlation |kɔrɪ'leɪʃən| n Wechselbeziehung f
correspond |kɔrɪs'pɔnd| vi (agree) übereinstimmen; (exchange letters) korrespondieren; **~ence** n (similarity) Entsprechung f; (letters) Briefwechsel m, Korrespondenz f; **~ence course** n Fernkurs m; **~ent** n (PRESS) Berichterstatter m
corridor |'kɔrɪdɔːʳ| n Gang m
corroborate |kə'rɔbəreɪt| vt bestätigen
corrode |kə'rəʊd| vt zerfressen ♦ vi rosten
corrosion |kə'rəʊʒən| n Korrosion f
corrugated |'kɔrəgeɪtɪd| adj gewellt; **~ iron** n Wellblech nt

corrupt [kə'rʌpt] adj korrupt ♦ vt verderben; (bribe) bestechen; **~ion** [kə'rʌpʃən] n Verdorbenheit f; (bribery) Bestechung f

corset ['kɔːsɪt] n Korsett nt

Corsica ['kɔːsɪkə] n Korsika nt

cosmetics [kɔz'metɪks] npl Kosmetika pl

cosmic ['kɔzmɪk] adj kosmisch

cosmonaut ['kɔzmənɔːt] n Kosmonaut(in) m(f)

cosmopolitan [kɔzmə'pɔlɪtn] adj international; (city) Welt-

cosmos ['kɔzmɔs] n Kosmos m

cost [kɔst] (pt, pp cost) n Kosten pl, Preis m ♦ vt, vi kosten; **~s** npl (JUR) Kosten pl; **how much does it ~?** wie viel kostet das?; **at all ~s** um jeden Preis

co-star ['kəustɑːᵣ] n zweite(r) or weitere(in) Hauptdarsteller(r) m(f)

cost: **~-effective** adj rentabel; **~ly** ['kɔstlɪ] adj kostspielig; **~-of-living** ['kɔstəv'lɪvɪŋ] adj (index) Lebenshaltungskosten-; **~ price** (BRIT) n Selbstkostenpreis m

costume ['kɔstjuːm] n Kostüm nt; (fancy dress) Maskenkostüm nt; (BRIT: also: **swimming ~**) Badeanzug m; **~ jewellery** n Modeschmuck m

cosy ['kəuzɪ] (BRIT) adj behaglich; (atmosphere) gemütlich

cot [kɔt] n (BRIT: child's) Kinderbett(chen) nt; (US: camp bed) Feldbett nt

cottage ['kɔtɪdʒ] n kleine(s) Haus nt; **~ cheese** n Hüttenkäse m; **~ industry** n Heimindustrie f; **~ pie** n Auflauf mit Hackfleisch und Kartoffelbrei

cotton ['kɔtn] n Baumwolle f; (thread) Garn nt; **~ on to** (inf) vt kapieren; **~ candy** (US) n Zuckerwatte f; **~ wool** (BRIT) n Watte f

couch [kautʃ] n Couch f

couchette [kuː'ʃet] n (on train, boat) Liegewagenplatz m

cough [kɔf] vi husten ♦ n Husten m; **~ drop** n Hustenbonbon nt

could [kud] pt of can²

couldn't ['kudnt] = could not

council ['kaunsl] n (of town) Stadtrat m; **~ estate** (BRIT) n Siedlung f des sozialen Wohnungsbaus; **~ house** (BRIT) n Haus nt des sozialen Wohnungsbaus; **~lor** ['kaunslər] n Stadtrat m/-rätin f

counsel ['kaunsl] n (barrister) Anwalt m; (advice) Rat(schlag) m ♦ vt beraten; **~lor** ['kaunslər] n Berater m

count [kaunt] vt, vi zählen ♦ n (reckoning) Abrechnung f; (nobleman) Graf m; **~ on** vt zählen auf +acc

countenance ['kauntɪnəns] n (old) Antlitz nt ♦ vt (tolerate) gutheißen

counter ['kauntəʳ] n (in shop) Ladentisch m; (in café) Theke f; (in bank, post office) Schalter m ♦ vt entgegnen

counteract ['kauntər'ækt] vt entgegen-

wirken +dat

counterfeit ['kauntəfɪt] n Fälschung f ♦ vt fälschen ♦ adj gefälscht

counterfoil ['kauntəfɔɪl] n (Kontroll)abschnitt m

counterpart ['kauntəpɑːt] n (object) Gegenstück nt; (person) Gegenüber nt

counterproductive ['kauntəprə'dʌktɪv] adj destruktiv

countersign ['kauntəsaɪn] vt gegenzeichnen

countess ['kauntɪs] n Gräfin f

countless ['kauntlɪs] adj zahllos, unzählig

country ['kʌntrɪ] n Land nt; **~ dancing** (BRIT) n Volkstanz m; **~ house** n Landhaus nt; **~man** (irreg) n (national) Landsmann m; (rural) Bauer m; **~side** n Landschaft f

county ['kauntɪ] n Landkreis m; (BRIT) Grafschaft f

coup [kuː] (pl **~s**) n Coup m; (also: **~ d'état**) Staatsstreich m, Putsch m

couple ['kʌpl] n Paar nt ♦ vt koppeln; **a ~ of** ein paar

coupon ['kuːpɔn] n Gutschein m

coups [kuː] npl of **coup**

courage ['kʌrɪdʒ] n Mut m; **~ous** [kə'reɪdʒəs] adj mutig

courgette [kuə'ʒet] (BRIT) n Zucchini f or pl

courier ['kurɪəʳ] n (for holiday) Reiseleiter m; (messenger) Kurier m

course [kɔːs] n (race) Bahn f; (of stream) Lauf m; (golf ~) Platz m; (NAUT, SCH) Kurs m; (in meal) Gang m; **of ~** natürlich

court [kɔːt] n (royal) Hof m; (JUR) Gericht nt ♦ vt (woman) gehen mit; (danger) herausfordern; **to take to ~** vor Gericht bringen

courteous ['kɜːtɪəs] adj höflich

courtesy ['kɜːtəsɪ] n Höflichkeit f; **courtesy bus, courtesy coach** n gebührenfreier Bus m

court: **~ house** (US) n Gerichtsgebäude nt; **~ier** ['kɔːtɪəʳ] n Höfling m; **~ martial** ['kɔːt'mɑːʃəl] (pl **~s martial**) n Kriegsgericht nt ♦ vt vor ein Kriegsgericht stellen; **~room** n Gerichtssaal m; **~s martial** npl of **court martial**; **~yard** ['kɔːtjɑːd] n Hof m

cousin ['kʌzn] n Cousin m, Vetter m; Kusine f

cove [kəuv] n kleine Bucht f

covenant ['kʌvənənt] n (ECCL) Bund m; (JUR) Verpflichtung f

cover ['kʌvəʳ] vt (spread over) bedecken; (shield) abschirmen; (include) sich erstrecken über +acc; (protect) decken; (distance) zurücklegen; (report on) berichten über +acc ♦ n (lid) Deckel m; (for bed) Decke f; (MIL) Bedeckung f; (of book) Einband m; (of magazine) Umschlag m; (insurance) Versicherung f; **to take ~** (from rain) sich unterstellen; (MIL) in Deckung gehen; **under ~** (indoors) drinnen; **under ~ of** im Schutze +gen; **under separate ~** (COMM) mit

getrennter Post; **to ~ up for sb** jdn decken;
~age n (PRESS: reports) Berichterstattung f;
(distribution) Verbreitung f; **~ charge** n
Bedienungsgeld nt; **~ing** n Bedeckung f;
~ing letter, **~ letter** (US) n Begleitbrief m;
~ note n (INSURANCE) vorläufige(r)
Versicherungsschein m
covert |ˈkʌvət| adj geheim
cover-up |ˈkʌvərʌp| n Vertuschung f
cow |kau| n Kuh f ♦ vt einschüchtern
coward |ˈkauəd| n Feigling m; **~ice** |ˈkauədɪs|
n Feigheit f; **~ly** adj feige
cower |ˈkauəʳ| vi kauern
coy |kɔɪ| adj schüchtern
coyote |kɔɪˈəutɪ| n Präriewolf m
cozy |ˈkəuzɪ| (US) adj = **cosy**
CPA (US) n abbr = **certified public
accountant**
crab |kræb| n Krebs m
crab apple n Holzapfel m
crack |kræk| n Riss m, Sprung m; (noise) Knall
m; (drug) Crack nt ♦ vt (break) springen
lassen; (joke) reißen; (nut, safe) knacken;
(whip) knallen lassen ♦ vi springen ♦ adj
erstklassig; (troops) Elite-; **~ down** vi: **to ~
down (on)** hart durchgreifen (bei); **~ up** vi
(fig) zusammenbrechen
cracked |krækt| adj (glass, plate, ice)
gesprungen; (rib, bone) gebrochen,
angeknackst (umg); (broken) gebrochen;
(surface, walls) rissig; (inf: mad)
übergeschnappt
cracker |ˈkrækəʳ| n (firework) Knallkörper m,
Kracher m; (biscuit) Keks m; (Christmas ~)
Knallbonbon m
crackle |ˈkrækl| vi knistern; (fire) prasseln
cradle |ˈkreɪdl| n Wiege f
craft |krɑːft| n (skill) (Hand- or
Kunst)fertigkeit f; (trade) Handwerk nt;
(NAUT) Schiff nt; **~sman** (irreg) n
Handwerker m; **~smanship** n (quality)
handwerkliche Ausführung f; (ability)
handwerkliche(s) Können nt
crafty |ˈkrɑːftɪ| adj schlau
crag |kræg| n Klippe f
cram |kræm| vt voll stopfen ♦ vi (learn)
pauken; **to ~ sth into sth** etw in etw acc
stopfen
cramp |kræmp| n Krampf m ♦ vt (limit)
einengen; (hinder) hemmen; **~ed** adj
(position) verkrampft; (space) eng
crampon |ˈkræmpən| n Steigeisen nt
cranberry |ˈkrænbərɪ| n Preiselbeere f
crane |kreɪn| n (machine) Kran m; (bird)
Kranich m
crank |kræŋk| n (lever) Kurbel f; (person)
Spinner m; **~shaft** n Kurbelwelle f
cranny |ˈkrænɪ| n see **nook**
crash |kræʃ| n (noise) Krachen nt; (with cars)
Zusammenstoß m; (with plane) Absturz m;
(COMM) Zusammenbruch m ♦ vt (plane)

abstürzen mit ♦ vi (cars) zusammenstoßen;
(plane) abstürzen; (economy)
zusammenbrechen; (noise) knallen; **~
course** n Schnellkurs m; **~ helmet** n
Sturzhelm m; **~ landing** n Bruchlandung
f
crass |kræs| adj krass
crate |kreɪt| n (also fig) Kiste f
crater |ˈkreɪtəʳ| n Krater m
cravat(e) |krəˈvæt| n Halstuch nt
crave |kreɪv| vt verlangen nach
crawl |krɔːl| vi kriechen; (baby) krabbeln ♦ n
Kriechen nt; (swim) Kraul nt
crayfish |ˈkreɪfɪʃ| n inv (freshwater) Krebs m;
(saltwater) Languste f
crayon |ˈkreɪən| n Buntstift m
craze |kreɪz| n Fimmel m
crazy |ˈkreɪzɪ| adj verrückt
creak |kriːk| vi knarren
cream |kriːm| n (from milk) Rahm m, Sahne
f; (polish, cosmetic) Creme f; (fig: people)
Elite f ♦ adj cremefarbig; **~ cake** n
Sahnetorte f; **~ cheese** n Rahmquark m; **~y**
adj sahnig
crease |kriːs| n Falte f ♦ vt falten; (wrinkle)
zerknittern ♦ vi (wrinkle up) knittern; **~d** adj
zerknittert, faltig
create |kriːˈeɪt| vt erschaffen; (cause)
verursachen; **creation** |kriːˈeɪʃən| n
Schöpfung f; **creative** adj kreativ; **creator**
n Schöpfer m
creature |ˈkriːtʃəʳ| n Geschöpf nt
crèche |kreʃ| n Krippe f
credence |ˈkriːdns| n: **to lend** or **give ~ to
sth** etw dat Glauben schenken
credentials |krɪˈdenʃlz| npl Beglaubigungs-
schreiben nt
credibility |kredɪˈbɪlɪtɪ| n Glaubwürdigkeit f
credible |ˈkredɪbl| adj (person) glaubwürdig;
(story) glaubhaft
credit |ˈkredɪt| n (also COMM) Kredit m ♦ vt
Glauben schenken +dat; (COMM)
gutschreiben; **~s** npl (of film) Mitwirkende
pl; **~able** adj rühmlich; **~ card** n Kreditkarte
f; **~or** n Gläubiger m
creed |kriːd| n Glaubensbekenntnis nt
creek |kriːk| n (inlet) kleine Bucht f; (US:
river) kleine(r) Wasserlauf m
creep |kriːp| (pt, pp crept) vi kriechen; **~er** n
Kletterpflanze f; **~y** adj (frightening) gruselig
cremate |krɪˈmeɪt| vt einäschern; **cremation**
|krɪˈmeɪʃən| n Einäscherung f; **cremato-
rium** |kreməˈtɔːrɪəm| n Krematorium nt
crêpe |kreɪp| n Krepp m; **~ bandage** (BRIT) n
Elastikbinde f
crept |krept| pt, pp of **creep**
crescent |ˈkresnt| n (of moon) Halbmond m
cress |kres| n Kresse f
crest |krest| n (of cock) Kamm m; (of wave)
Wellenkamm m; (coat of arms) Wappen nt
crestfallen |ˈkrestfɔːlən| adj nieder-

geschlagen

Crete |kriːt| n Kreta nt

crevice |ˈkrevɪs| n Riss m

crew |kruː| n Besatzung f, Mannschaft f; **~-cut** n Bürstenschnitt m; **~ neck** n runde(r) Ausschnitt m

crib |krɪb| n (bed) Krippe f ♦ vt (inf) spicken

crick |krɪk| n Muskelkrampf m

cricket |ˈkrɪkɪt| n (insect) Grille f; (game) Kricket nt

crime |kraɪm| n Verbrechen nt

criminal |ˈkrɪmɪnl| n Verbrecher m ♦ adj kriminell; (act) strafbar

crimson |ˈkrɪmzn| adj leuchtend rot

cringe |krɪndʒ| vi sich ducken

crinkle |ˈkrɪŋkl| vt zerknittern

cripple |ˈkrɪpl| n Krüppel m ♦ vt lahm legen; (MED) verkrüppeln

crises |ˈkraɪsiːz| npl of **crisis**

crisis |ˈkraɪsɪs| (pl **crises**) n Krise f

crisp |krɪsp| adj knusprig; **~s** (BRIT) npl Chips pl

crisscross |ˈkrɪskrɒs| adj gekreuzt, Kreuz-

criteria |kraɪˈtɪərɪə| npl of **criterion**

criterion |kraɪˈtɪərɪən| (pl **criteria**) n Kriterium nt

critic |ˈkrɪtɪk| n Kritiker(in) m(f); **~al** adj kritisch; **~ally** adv kritisch; (ill) gefährlich; **~ism** |ˈkrɪtɪsɪzəm| n Kritik f; **~ize** |ˈkrɪtɪsaɪz| vt kritisieren

croak |krəuk| vi krächzen; (frog) quaken

Croatia |krəuˈeɪʃə| n Kroatien nt

crochet |ˈkrəuʃeɪ| n Häkelei f

crockery |ˈkrɒkəri| n Geschirr nt

crocodile |ˈkrɒkədaɪl| n Krokodil nt

crocus |ˈkrəukəs| n Krokus m

croft |krɒft| (BRIT) n kleine(s) Pachtgut nt

crony |ˈkrəuni| (inf) n Kumpel m

crook |kruk| n (criminal) Gauner m; (stick) Hirtenstab m

crooked |ˈkrukɪd| adj krumm

crop |krɒp| n (harvest) Ernte f; (riding ~) Reitpeitsche f ♦ vt ernten; **~ up** vi passieren

croquet |ˈkrəukeɪ| n Krocket nt

croquette |krəˈket| n Krokette f

cross |krɒs| n Kreuz nt ♦ vt (road) überqueren; (legs) übereinander legen; kreuzen ♦ adj (annoyed) böse; **~ out** vt streichen; **~ over** vi hinübergehen; **~bar** n Querstange f; **~-country (race)** n Geländelauf m; **~-examine** vt ins Kreuzverhör nehmen; **~-eyed** adj: **to be ~-eyed** schielen; **~fire** n Kreuzfeuer nt; **~ing** n (~roads) (Straßen)kreuzung f; (of ship) Überfahrt f; (for pedestrians) Fußgängerüberweg m; **~ing guard** (US) n Schülerlotse m; **~ purposes** npl: **to be at ~ purposes** aneinander vorbeireden; **~reference** n Querverweis m; **~roads** n Straßenkreuzung f; (fig) Scheideweg m; **~ section** n Querschnitt m; **~walk** (US) n

Fußgängerüberweg m; **~wind** n Seitenwind m; **~word (puzzle)** n Kreuzworträtsel nt

crotch |krɒtʃ| n Zwickel m; (ANAT) Unterleib nt

crouch |krautʃ| vi hocken

crow |krəu| n (bird) Krähe f; (of cock) Krähen nt ♦ vi krähen

crowbar |ˈkrəubaːʳ| n Stemmeisen nt

crowd |kraud| n Menge f ♦ vt (fill) überfüllen ♦ vi drängen; **~ed** adj überfüllt

crown |kraun| n Krone f; (of head, hat) Kopf m ♦ vt krönen; **~ jewels** npl Kronjuwelen pl; **~ prince** n Kronprinz m

crow's-feet |ˈkrəuzfiːt| npl Krähenfüße pl

crucial |ˈkruːʃl| adj entscheidend

crucifix |ˈkruːsɪfɪks| n Kruzifix nt; **~ion** |kruːsɪˈfɪkʃən| n Kreuzigung f

crude |kruːd| adj (raw) roh; (humour, behaviour) grob; (basic) primitiv; **~ (oil)** n Rohöl nt

cruel |ˈkruəl| adj grausam; **~ty** n Grausamkeit f

cruise |kruːz| n Kreuzfahrt f ♦ vi kreuzen; **~r** (MIL) Kreuzer m

crumb |krʌm| n Krume f

crumble |ˈkrʌmbl| vt, vi zerbröckeln; **crumbly** adj krümelig

crumpet |ˈkrʌmpɪt| n Tee(pfann)kuchen m

crumple |ˈkrʌmpl| vt zerknittern

crunch |krʌntʃ| n: **the ~** (fig) der Knackpunkt ♦ vt knirschen; **~y** adj knusprig

crusade |kruːˈseɪd| n Kreuzzug m

crush |krʌʃ| n Gedränge nt ♦ vt zerdrücken; (rebellion) unterdrücken

crust |krʌst| n Kruste f

crutch |krʌtʃ| n Krücke f

crux |krʌks| n springende(r) Punkt m

cry |kraɪ| vi (shout) schreien; (weep) weinen ♦ n (call) Schrei m; **~ off** vi (plötzlich) absagen

crypt |krɪpt| n Krypta f

cryptic |ˈkrɪptɪk| adj hintergründig

crystal |ˈkrɪstl| n Kristall m; (glass) Kristallglas nt; (mineral) Bergkristall m; **~-clear** adj kristallklar

crystallize |ˈkrɪstəlaɪz| vt, vi kristallisieren; (fig) klären

CSA n abbr (= Child Support Agency) Amt zur Regelung von Unterhaltszahlungen für Kinder

CTC (BRIT) n abbr = **city technology college**

cub |kʌb| n Junge(s) nt; (also: **C~ scout**) Wölfling m

Cuba |ˈkjuːbə| n Kuba nt; **~n** adj kubanisch ♦ n Kubaner(in) m(f)

cubbyhole |ˈkʌbɪhəul| n Eckchen nt

cube |kjuːb| n Würfel m ♦ vt (MATH) hoch drei nehmen

cubic |ˈkjuːbɪk| adj würfelförmig; (centimetre etc) Kubik-; **~ capacity** n Fassungsvermögen nt

cubicle |ˈkjuːbɪkl| n Kabine f

cuckoo ['kuku:] n Kuckuck m; **~ clock** n Kuckucksuhr f

cucumber ['kju:kʌmbəʳ] n Gurke f

cuddle ['kʌdl] vt, vi herzen, drücken (inf)

cue [kju:] n (THEAT) Stichwort nt; (snooker ~) Billardstock m

cuff [kʌf] n (BRIT: of shirt, coat etc) Manschette f; Aufschlag m; (US) = turn-up; **off the ~** aus dem Handgelenk; **~link** n Manschettenknopf m

cuisine [kwɪ'zi:n] n Kochkunst f, Küche f

cul-de-sac ['kʌldəsæk] n Sackgasse f

culinary ['kʌlɪnərɪ] adj Koch-

cull [kʌl] vt (select) auswählen

culminate ['kʌlmɪneɪt] vi gipfeln; **culmination** [kʌlmɪ'neɪʃən] n Höhepunkt m

culottes [kju:'lɔts] npl Hosenrock m

culpable ['kʌlpəbl] adj schuldig

culprit ['kʌlprɪt] n Täter m

cult [kʌlt] n Kult m

cultivate ['kʌltɪveɪt] vt (AGR) bebauen; (mind) bilden; **cultivation** [kʌltɪ'veɪʃən] n (AGR) Bebauung f; (of person) Bildung f

cultural ['kʌltʃərəl] adj kulturell, Kultur-

culture ['kʌltʃəʳ] n Kultur f; **~d** adj gebildet

cumbersome ['kʌmbəsəm] adj (object) sperrig

cumulative ['kju:mjulətɪv] adj gehäuft

cunning ['kʌnɪŋ] n Verschlagenheit f ♦ adj schlau

cup [kʌp] n Tasse f; (prize) Pokal m

cupboard ['kʌbəd] n Schrank m

cup tie (BRIT) n Pokalspiel nt

curate ['kjuərɪt] n (Catholic) Kurat m; (Protestant) Vikar m

curator [kjuə'reɪtəʳ] n Kustos m

curb [kə:b] vt zügeln ♦ n (on spending etc) Einschränkung f; (US) Bordstein m

curdle ['kə:dl] vi gerinnen

cure [kjuəʳ] n Heilmittel nt; (process) Heilverfahren nt ♦ vt heilen

curfew ['kə:fju:] n Ausgangssperre f; Sperrstunde f

curio ['kjuərɪəu] n Kuriosität f

curiosity [kjuərɪ'ɔsɪtɪ] n Neugier f

curious ['kjuərɪəs] adj neugierig; (strange) seltsam

curl [kə:l] n Locke f ♦ vt locken ♦ vi sich locken; **~ up** vi sich zusammenrollen; (person) sich ankuscheln; **~er** n Lockenwickler m; **~y** ['kə:lɪ] adj lockig

currant ['kʌrnt] n Korinthe f

currency ['kʌrnsɪ] n Währung f; **to gain ~** an Popularität gewinnen

current ['kʌrnt] n Strömung f ♦ adj (expression) gängig, üblich; (issue) neueste; **~ account** (BRIT) n Girokonto nt; **~ affairs** npl Zeitgeschehen nt; **~ly** adv zurzeit

curricula [kə'rɪkjulə] npl of **curriculum**

curriculum [kə'rɪkjuləm] (pl **~s** or **curricula**) n Lehrplan m; **~ vitae** [-'vi:taɪ] n Lebens-

lauf m

curry ['kʌrɪ] n Currygericht nt ♦ vt: **to ~ favour with** sich einschmeicheln bei; **~ powder** n Curry(pulver) nt

curse [kə:s] vi (swear): **to ~ (at)** fluchen (auf or über +acc) ♦ vt (insult) verwünschen ♦ n Fluch m

cursor ['kə:səʳ] n (COMPUT) Cursor m

cursory ['kə:sərɪ] adj flüchtig

curt [kə:t] adj schroff

curtail [kə:'teɪl] vt abkürzen; (rights) einschränken

curtain ['kə:tn] n Vorhang m

curts(e)y ['kə:tsɪ] n Knicks m ♦ vi knicksen

curve [kə:v] n Kurve f; (of body, vase etc) Rundung f ♦ vi sich biegen; (hips, breasts) sich runden; (road) einen Bogen machen

cushion ['kuʃən] n Kissen nt ♦ vt dämpfen

custard ['kʌstəd] n Vanillesoße f

custodian [kʌs'təudɪən] n Kustos m, Verwalter(in) m(f)

custody ['kʌstədɪ] n Aufsicht f; (police ~) Haft f; **to take into ~** verhaften

custom ['kʌstəm] n (tradition) Brauch m; (COMM) Kundschaft f; **~ary** adj üblich

customer ['kʌstəməʳ] n Kunde m, Kundin f

customized ['kʌstəmaɪzd] adj (car etc) mit Spezialausrüstung

custom-made ['kʌstəm'meɪd] adj speziell angefertigt

customs ['kʌstəmz] npl Zoll m; **~ duty** n Zollabgabe f; **~ officer** n Zollbeamte(r) m, Zollbeamtin f

cut [kʌt] (pt, pp **cut**) vt schneiden; (wages) kürzen; (prices) heruntersetzen ♦ vi schneiden; (intersect) sich schneiden ♦ n Schnitt m; (wound) Schnittwunde f; (in income etc) Kürzung f; (share) Anteil m; **to ~ a tooth** zahnen; **~ down** vt (tree) fällen; (reduce) einschränken; **~ off** vt (also fig) abschneiden; (allowance) sperren; **~ out** vt (shape) ausschneiden; (delete) streichen; **~ up** vt (meat) aufschneiden; **~back** n Kürzung f

cute [kju:t] adj niedlich

cuticle ['kju:tɪkl] n Nagelhaut f

cutlery ['kʌtlərɪ] n Besteck nt

cutlet ['kʌtlɪt] n (pork) Kotelett nt; (veal) Schnitzel nt

cut: **~out** n (cardboard ~out) Ausschneidemodell nt; **~-price**, **~-rate** (US) adj verbilligt; **~throat** n Verbrechertyp m ♦ adj mörderisch

cutting ['kʌtɪŋ] adj schneidend ♦ n (BRIT: PRESS) Ausschnitt m; (: RAIL) Durchstich m

CV n abbr = **curriculum vitae**

cwt abbr = **hundredweight(s)**

cyanide ['saɪənaɪd] n Zyankali nt

cybercafé ['saɪbəkæfeɪ] n Internetcafé nt, Cybercafé nt

cyberspace ['saɪbəspeɪs] n Cyberspace m

cycle ['saɪkl] n Fahrrad nt; (series) Reihe f ♦ vi
Rad fahren; ~ **hire** n Fahrradverleih m; ~
lane, ~ **path** n (Fahr)radweg m; **cycling** n
Radfahren nt; **cyclist** n Radfahrer(in) m(f)

cyclone ['saɪkləʊn] n Zyklon m

cygnet ['sɪgnɪt] n junge(r) Schwan m

cylinder ['sɪlɪndəʳ] n Zylinder m; (TECH)
Walze f; ~ **head gasket** n
Zylinderkopfdichtung f

cymbals ['sɪmblz] npl Becken nt

cynic ['sɪnɪk] n Zyniker(in) m(f); ~**al** adj
zynisch; ~**ism** ['sɪnɪsɪzəm] n Zynismus m

cypress ['saɪprɪs] n Zypresse f

Cyprus ['saɪprəs] n Zypern nt

cyst [sɪst] n Zyste f

cystitis [sɪs'taɪtɪs] n Blasenentzündung f

czar [zɑːʳ] n Zar m

Czech [tʃek] adj tschechisch ♦ n Tscheche m,
Tschechin f

Czechoslovakia [tʃekəslə'vækɪə] (HIST)
n die Tschechoslowakei; ~**n** adj
tschechoslowakisch ♦ n Tschechoslowake m,
Tchechoslowakin f

D, d

D [diː] n (MUS) D nt

dab |dæb| vt (wound, paint) betupfen ♦ n
(little bit) bisschen nt; (of paint) Tupfer m

dabble ['dæbl] vi: **to ~ in sth** in etw dat
machen

dad |dæd| n Papa m, Vati m; ~**dy** ['dædɪ] n
Papa m, Vati m; ~**dy-long-legs** n
Weberknecht m

daffodil ['dæfədɪl] n Osterglocke f

daft [dɑːft] (inf) adj blöd(e), doof

dagger ['dægəʳ] n Dolch m

daily ['deɪlɪ] adj täglich ♦ n (PRESS)
Tageszeitung f; (BRIT: cleaner) Haushaltshilfe
f ♦ adv täglich

dainty ['deɪntɪ] adj zierlich

dairy ['dɛərɪ] n (shop) Milchgeschäft nt; (on
farm) Molkerei f ♦ adj Milch-; ~ **farm** n Hof
m mit Milchwirtschaft; ~ **produce** n
Molkereiprodukte pl; ~ **products** npl
Milchprodukte pl, Molkereiprodukte pl; ~
store (US) n Milchgeschäft nt

dais ['deɪɪs] n Podium nt

daisy ['deɪzɪ] n Gänseblümchen nt

dale [deɪl] n Tal nt

dam [dæm] n (Stau)damm m ♦ vt stauen

damage ['dæmɪdʒ] n Schaden m ♦ vt
beschädigen; ~**s** npl (JUR) Schaden(s)ersatz
m

damn |dæm| vt verdammen ♦ n (inf): **I don't
give a ~** das ist mir total egal ♦ adj (inf: also:
~**ed**) verdammt; ~ **it!** verflucht!; ~**ing** adj
vernichtend

damp [dæmp] adj feucht ♦ n Feuchtigkeit f
♦ vt (also: ~**en**) befeuchten; (discourage)

dämpfen

damson ['dæmzən] n Damaszenerpflaume f

dance [dɑːns] n Tanz m ♦ vi tanzen; ~ **hall** n
Tanzlokal nt; ~**r** n Tänzer(in) m(f); **dancing**
n Tanzen nt

dandelion ['dændɪlaɪən] n Löwenzahn m

dandruff ['dændrəf] n (Kopf)schuppen pl

Dane [deɪn] n Däne m, Dänin f

danger ['deɪndʒəʳ] n Gefahr f; ~! (sign)
Achtung!; **to be in ~ of doing sth** Gefahr
laufen, etw zu tun; ~**ous** adj gefährlich

dangle ['dæŋgl] vi baumeln ♦ vt
herabhängen lassen

Danish ['deɪnɪʃ] adj dänisch ♦ n Dänisch nt

dare [dɛəʳ] vt herausfordern ♦ vi: **to ~ (to) do
sth** es wagen, etw zu tun; **I ~ say** ich würde
sagen; **daring** ['dɛərɪŋ] adj (audacious)
verwegen; (bold) wagemutig; (dress)
gewagt ♦ n Mut m

dark [dɑːk] adj dunkel; (fig) düster, trübe;
(deep colour) dunkel- ♦ n Dunkelheit f; **to be
left in the ~ about** im Dunkeln sein über
+acc; **after ~** nach Anbruch der Dunkelheit;
~**en** vt, vi verdunkeln; ~ **glasses** npl
Sonnenbrille f; ~**ness** n Finsternis nt;
~**room** n Dunkelkammer f

darling ['dɑːlɪŋ] n Liebling m ♦ adj lieb

darn [dɑːn] vt stopfen

dart |dɑːt| n (weapon) Pfeil m; (in sewing)
Abnäher m ♦ vi sausen; ~**s** n (game)
Pfeilwerfen nt; ~**board** n Zielscheibe f

dash [dæʃ] n Sprung m; (mark)
(Gedanken)strich m; (small amount)
bisschen nt ♦ vt (hopes) zunichte machen
♦ vi stürzen; ~ **away** vi davonstürzen; ~ **off**
vi davonstürzen

dashboard ['dæʃbɔːd] n Armaturenbrett nt

dashing ['dæʃɪŋ] adj schneidig

data ['deɪtə] npl Einzelheiten pl, Daten pl;
~**base** n Datenbank f; ~ **processing** n
Datenverarbeitung f

date |deɪt| n Datum nt; (for meeting etc)
Termin m; (with person) Verabredung f;
(fruit) Dattel f ♦ vt (letter etc) datieren;
(person) gehen mit; ~ **of birth**
Geburtsdatum nt; **to ~** bis heute; **out of ~**
überholt; **up to ~** (clothes) modisch; (report)
up-to-date; (with news) auf dem Laufenden;
~**d** adj altmodisch; ~ **rape** n Vergewaltigung
f nach einem Rendezvous

daub [dɔːb] vt beschmieren; (paint)
schmieren

daughter ['dɔːtəʳ] n Tochter f; ~**-in-law** n
Schwiegertochter f

daunting ['dɔːntɪŋ] adj entmutigend

dawdle ['dɔːdl] vi trödeln

dawn [dɔːn] n Morgendämmerung f ♦ vi
dämmern; (fig): **it ~ed on him that ...** es
dämmerte ihm, dass ...

day |deɪ| n Tag m; **the ~ before/after** am Tag
zuvor/danach; **the ~ after tomorrow**

255   **daze → deduce**

übermorgen; **the ~ before yesterday**
vorgestern; **by ~** am Tage; **~break** n
Tagesanbruch m; **~dream** vi mit offenen
Augen träumen; **~light** n Tageslicht nt; **~
return** (BRIT) n Tagesrückfahrkarte f; **~time**
n Tageszeit f; **~to-~** adj alltäglich
daze [deɪz] vt betäuben ♦ n Betäubung f; **in a
~** benommen
dazzle ['dæzl] vt blenden
DC abbr (= direct current) Gleichstrom m
D-day ['diːdeɪ] n (HIST) Tag der Invasion durch
die Alliierten (6.6.44); (fig) der Tag X
deacon ['diːkən] n Diakon m
dead [dɛd] adj tot; (without feeling) gefühllos
♦ adv ganz; (exactly) genau ♦ npl: **the ~** die
Toten pl; **to shoot sb ~** jdn erschießen; **~
tired** todmüde; **to stop ~** abrupt stehen
bleiben; **~en** vt (pain) abtöten; (sound)
ersticken; **~ end** n Sackgasse f; **~ heat** n
tote(s) Rennen nt; **~line** n Stichtag m;
~lock n Stillstand m; **~ loss** (inf) n: **to be a
~ loss** ein hoffnungsloser Fall sein; **~ly** adj
tödlich; **~pan** adj undurchdringlich; **D~ Sea**
n: **the D~ Sea** das Tote Meer
deaf [dɛf] adj taub; **~en** vt taub machen;
~ening adj (noise) ohrenbetäubend; (noise)
lautstark; **~-mute** n Taubstumme(r) mf;
~ness n Taubheit f
deal [diːl] (pt, pp dealt) n Geschäft nt ♦ vt
austeilen; (CARDS) geben; **a great ~ of** sehr
viel; **~ in** vt fus handeln mit; **~ with** vt fus
(person) behandeln; (subject) sich befassen
mit; (problem) in Angriff nehmen; **~er** n
(COMM) Händler m; (CARDS) Kartengeber m;
~ings npl (FIN) Geschäfte pl; (relations)
Beziehungen pl
dean [diːn] n (Protestant) Superintendent m;
(Catholic) Dechant m; (UNIV) Dekan m
dear [dɪə'] adj lieb; (expensive) teuer ♦ n
Liebling m ♦ excl: **~ me!** du liebe Zeit!; **D~
Sir** Sehr geehrter Herr!; **D~ John** Lieber
John!; **~ly** adv (love) herzlich; (pay) teuer
death [dɛθ] n Tod m; (statistic) Todesfall m; **~
certificate** n Totenschein m; **~ly** adj
totenähnlich, Toten-; **~ penalty** n
Todesstrafe f; **~ rate** n Sterblichkeitsziffer f
debar [dɪ'bɑː'] vt ausschließen
debase [dɪ'beɪs] vt entwerten
debatable [dɪ'beɪtəbl] adj anfechtbar
debate [dɪ'beɪt] n Debatte f ♦ vt debattieren,
diskutieren; (consider) überlegen
debilitating [dɪ'bɪlɪteɪtɪŋ] adj schwächend
debit ['dɛbɪt] n Schuldposten m ♦ vt belasten
debris ['deɪbriː] n Trümmer pl
debt [dɛt] n Schuld f; **to be in ~** verschuldet
sein; **~or** n Schuldner m
debunk [dɪ'bʌŋk] vt entlarven
decade ['dɛkeɪd] n Jahrzehnt nt
decadence ['dɛkədəns] n Dekadenz f
decaff ['diːkæf] (inf) n koffeinfreier Kaffee
decaffeinated [dɪ'kæfɪneɪtɪd] adj koffeinfrei

decanter [dɪ'kæntə'] n Karaffe f
decay [dɪ'keɪ] n Verfall m; (tooth ~) Karies m
♦ vi verfallen; (teeth, meat etc) faulen; (leaves
etc) verrotten
deceased [dɪ'siːst] adj verstorben
deceit [dɪ'siːt] n Betrug m; **~ful** adj falsch
deceive [dɪ'siːv] vt täuschen
December [dɪ'sɛmbə'] n Dezember m
decency ['diːsənsɪ] n Anstand m
decent ['diːsənt] adj (respectable) anständig;
(pleasant) annehmbar
deception [dɪ'sɛpʃən] n Betrug m
deceptive [dɪ'sɛptɪv] adj irreführend
decibel ['dɛsɪbɛl] n Dezibel nt
decide [dɪ'saɪd] vt entscheiden ♦ vi sich
entscheiden; **to ~ on sth** etw beschließen;
~d adj entschieden; **~dly** [dɪ'saɪdɪdlɪ] adv
entschieden
deciduous [dɪ'sɪdjuəs] adj Laub-
decimal ['dɛsɪməl] adj dezimal ♦ n
Dezimalzahl f; **~ point** n Komma nt
decipher [dɪ'saɪfə'] vt entziffern
decision [dɪ'sɪʒən] n Entscheidung f,
Entschluss m
decisive [dɪ'saɪsɪv] adj entscheidend; (person)
entschlossen
deck [dɛk] n (NAUT) Deck nt; (of cards) Pack
m; **~chair** n Liegestuhl m
declaration [dɛklə'reɪʃən] n Erklärung f
declare [dɪ'klɛə'] vt erklären; (CUSTOMS)
verzollen
decline [dɪ'klaɪn] n (decay) Verfall m;
(lessening) Rückgang m ♦ vt (invitation)
ablehnen ♦ vi (say no) ablehnen; (of
strength) nachlassen
decode [diː'kəud] vt entschlüsseln; **~r** n (TV)
Decoder m
decompose [diːkəm'pəuz] vi (sich)
zersetzen
décor ['deɪkɔː'] n Ausstattung f
decorate ['dɛkəreɪt] vt (room: paper)
tapezieren; (: paint) streichen; (adorn)
(aus)schmücken; (cake) verzieren; (honour)
auszeichnen; **decoration** [dɛkə'reɪʃən] n (of
house) (Wand)dekoration f; (medal) Orden
m; **decorator** ['dɛkəreɪtə'] n Maler m,
Anstreicher m
decorum [dɪ'kɔːrəm] n Anstand m
decoy ['diːkɔɪ] n Lockvogel m
decrease [n 'diːkriːs, vb diː'kriːs] n Abnahme
f ♦ vt vermindern ♦ vi abnehmen
decree [dɪ'kriː] n Erlass m; **~ nisi** n
vorläufige(s) Scheidungsurteil nt
decrepit [dɪ'krɛpɪt] adj hinfällig
dedicate ['dɛdɪkeɪt] vt widmen; **~d** adj
hingebungsvoll, engagiert; (COMPUT)
dediziert; **dedication** [dɛdɪ'keɪʃən] n
(devotion) Ergebenheit f; (in book) Widmung
f
deduce [dɪ'djuːs] vt: **to ~ sth (from sth)**
etw (aus etw) ableiten, etw (aus etw)

schließen

deduct [dɪ'dʌkt] vt abziehen; **~ion**
|dɪ'dʌkʃən| n (of money) Abzug m;
(conclusion) (Schluss)folgerung f

deed |di:d| n Tat f; (document) Urkunde f

deem |di:m| vt: **to ~ sb/sth (to be) sth** jdn/
etw für etw halten

deep |di:p| adj tief ♦ adv: **the spectators
stood 20 ~** die Zuschauer standen in 20
Reihen hintereinander; **to be 4m ~** 4 Meter
tief sein; **~en** vt vertiefen ♦ vi (darkness)
tiefer werden; **~ end** n: **the ~ end** (of
swimming pool) das Tiefe; **~-freeze** n
Tiefkühlung f; **~-fry** vt frittieren; **~ly** adv
tief; **~-sea diving** n Tiefseetauchen nt; **~-
seated** adj tief sitzend

deer |dɪəʳ| n Reh nt; **~skin** n Hirsch-/
Rehleder nt

deface |dɪ'feɪs| vt entstellen

defamation [defə'meɪʃən] n Verleumdung f

default |dɪ'fɔ:lt| n Versäumnis nt; (COMPUT)
Standardwert m ♦ vi versäumen; **by ~** durch
Nichterscheinen

defeat |dɪ'fi:t| n Niederlage f ♦ vt schlagen;
~ist adj defätistisch ♦ Defätist m

defect [n 'di:fekt, vb dɪ'fekt] n Fehler m ♦ vi
überlaufen; **~ive** |dɪ'fektɪv| adj fehlerhaft

defence |dɪ'fens| n Verteidigung f; **~less** adj
wehrlos

defend |dɪ'fend| vt verteidigen; **~ant** n
Angeklagte(r) m; **~er** n Verteidiger m

defense |dɪ'fens| (US) n = **defence**

defensive |dɪ'fensɪv| adj defensiv ♦ n: **on the
~** in der Defensive

defer |dɪ'fɜ:ʳ| vt verschieben

deference ['defərəns] n Rücksichtnahme f

defiance |dɪ'faɪəns| n Trotz m,
Unnachgiebigkeit f; **in ~ of sth** einer
Sache dat zum Trotz

defiant |dɪ'faɪənt| adj trotzig, unnachgiebig

deficiency |dɪ'fɪʃənsɪ| n (lack) Mangel m;
(weakness) Schwäche f

deficient |dɪ'fɪʃənt| adj mangelhaft

deficit ['defɪsɪt] n Defizit nt

defile [vb dɪ'faɪl, n 'di:faɪl] vt beschmutzen
♦ n Hohlweg m

define |dɪ'faɪn| vt bestimmen; (explain)
definieren

definite ['defɪnɪt] adj (fixed) definitiv; (clear)
eindeutig; **~ly** adv bestimmt

definition [defɪ'nɪʃən] n Definition f

deflate |di:'fleɪt| vt die Luft ablassen aus

deflect |dɪ'flekt| vt ablenken

deformity |dɪ'fɔ:mɪtɪ| n Missbildung f

defraud |dɪ'frɔ:d| vt betrügen

defrost |di:'frɔst| vt (fridge) abtauen; (food)
auftauen; **~er** n (US) n (demister) Gebläse nt

deft |deft| adj geschickt

defunct |dɪ'fʌŋkt| adj verstorben

defuse |di:'fju:z| vt entschärfen

defy |dɪ'faɪ| vt (disobey) sich widersetzen

+dat; (orders, death) trotzen +dat;
(challenge) herausfordern

degenerate |vb dɪ'dʒenəreɪt, adj dɪ'dʒenərɪt|
vi degenerieren ♦ adj degeneriert

degrading |dɪ'greɪdɪŋ| adj erniedrigend

degree |dɪ'gri:| n Grad m; (UNIV)
Universitätsabschluss m; **by ~s** allmählich; **to
some ~** zu einem gewissen Grad

dehydrated |di:haɪ'dreɪtɪd| adj (person)
ausgetrocknet

de-ice ['di:'aɪs] vt enteisen

deign |deɪn| vi sich herablassen

deity ['di:ɪtɪ] n Gottheit f

dejected |dɪ'dʒektɪd| adj niedergeschlagen

delay |dɪ'leɪ| vt (hold back) aufschieben ♦ vi
(linger) sich aufhalten ♦ n Aufschub m,
Verzögerung f; (of train etc) Verspätung f; **to
be ~ed** (train) Verspätung haben; **without ~**
unverzüglich

delectable |dɪ'lektəbl| adj köstlich; (fig)
reizend

delegate [n 'delɪgɪt, vb 'delɪgeɪt] n
Delegierte(r) mf ♦ vt delegieren

delete |dɪ'li:t| vt (aus)streichen

deliberate [adj dɪ'lɪbərɪt, vb dɪ'lɪbəreɪt] adj
(intentional) absichtlich; (slow) bedächtig
♦ vi (consider) überlegen; (debate) sich
beraten; **~ly** adv absichtlich

delicacy ['delɪkəsɪ] n Zartheit f; (weakness)
Anfälligkeit f; (food) Delikatesse f

delicate ['delɪkɪt] adj (fine) fein; (fragile) zart;
(situation) heikel; (MED) empfindlich

delicatessen [delɪkə'tesn] n Feinkostgeschäft
nt

delicious |dɪ'lɪʃəs| adj lecker

delight |dɪ'laɪt| n Wonne f ♦ vt entzücken; **to
take ~ in sth** Freude an etw dat haben; **~ed**
adj: **~ed (at or with sth)** entzückt (über
+acc etw); **~ed to do sth** etw sehr gern tun;
~ful adj entzückend, herrlich

delinquency |dɪ'lɪŋkwənsɪ| n Kriminalität f

delinquent |dɪ'lɪŋkwənt| n Straffällige(r) mf
♦ adj straffällig

delirious |dɪ'lɪrɪəs| adj im Fieberwahn

deliver |dɪ'lɪvəʳ| vt (goods) (ab)liefern;
(letter) zustellen; (speech) halten; **~y** n
(Ab)lieferung f; (of letter) Zustellung f; (of
speech) Vortragsweise f; (MED) Entbindung
f; **to take ~y of** in Empfang nehmen

delude |dɪ'lu:d| vt täuschen

deluge |'delju:dʒ| n Überschwemmung f;
(fig) Flut f ♦ vt (fig) überfluten

delusion |dɪ'lu:ʒən| n (Selbst)täuschung f

de luxe |də'lʌks| adj Luxus-

delve |delv| vi: **to ~ into** sich vertiefen in
+acc

demand |dɪ'mɑ:nd| vt verlangen ♦ n
(request) Verlangen nt; (COMM) Nachfrage f;
in ~ gefragt; **on ~** auf Verlangen; **~ing** adj
anspruchsvoll

demean |dɪ'mi:n| vt: **to ~ o.s.** sich

erniedrigen
demeanour |dɪ'miːnər| (*US* **demeanor**) *n*
Benehmen *nt*
demented |dɪ'mentɪd| *adj* wahnsinnig
demister |diː'mɪstər| *n* (*AUT*) Gebläse *nt*
demo ['deməu| (*inf*) *n abbr* (= *demonstration*)
Demo *f*
democracy |dɪ'mɔkrəsɪ| *n* Demokratie *f*
democrat ['deməkræt| *n* Demokrat *m*;
democratic |demə'krætɪk| *adj* demokratisch
demolish |dɪ'mɔlɪʃ| *vt* abreißen; (*fig*)
vernichten
demolition |demə'lɪʃən| *n* Abbruch *m*
demon ['diːmən| *n* Dämon *m*
demonstrate ['demənstreɪt| *vt, vi*
demonstrieren; **demonstration**
|demən'streɪʃən| *n* Demonstration *f*;
demonstrator ['demənstreɪtər| *n* (*POL*)
Demonstrant(in) *m(f)*
demote |dɪ'məut| *vt* degradieren
demure |dɪ'mjuər| *adj* ernst
den |den| *n* (*of animal*) Höhle *f*; (*study*) Bude
f
denatured alcohol |diː'neɪtʃəd-| (*US*) *n*
ungenießbar gemachte(r) Alkohol *m*
denial |dɪ'naɪəl| *n* Leugnung *f*; **official ~**
Dementi *nt*
denim ['denɪm| *adj* Denim-; **~s** *npl*
Denimjeans *pl*
Denmark ['denmɑːk| *n* Dänemark *nt*
denomination |dɪnɔmɪ'neɪʃən| *n* (*ECCL*)
Bekenntnis *nt*; (*type*) Klasse *f*; (*FIN*) Wert *m*
denote |dɪ'nəut| *vt* bedeuten
denounce |dɪ'nauns| *vt* brandmarken
dense |dens| *adj* dicht; (*stupid*) schwer von
Begriff; **~ly** *adv* dicht; **density** ['densɪtɪ| *n*
Dichte *f*; **single/double density disk**
Diskette *f* mit einfacher/doppelter Dichte
dent |dent| *n* Delle *f* ♦ *vt* (*also:* **make a ~ in**)
einbeulen
dental ['dentl| *adj* Zahn-; **~ surgeon** *n* =
dentist
dentist ['dentɪst| *n* Zahnarzt(-ärztin) *m(f)*
dentures ['dentʃəz| *npl* Gebiss *nt*
deny |dɪ'naɪ| *vt* leugnen; (*officially*)
dementieren; (*help*) abschlagen
deodorant |diː'əudərənt| *n* Deodorant *nt*
depart |dɪ'pɑːt| *vi* abfahren; **to ~ from** (*fig:
differ from*) abweichen von
department |dɪ'pɑːtmənt| *n* (*COMM*)
Abteilung *f*; (*UNIV*) Seminar *nt*; (*POL*)
Ministerium *nt*; **~ store** *n* Warenhaus *nt*
departure |dɪ'pɑːtʃər| *n* (*of person*) Abreise *f*;
(*of train*) Abfahrt *f*; (*of plane*) Abflug *m*; **new
~** Neuerung *f*; **~ lounge** *n* (*at airport*)
Abflughalle *f*
depend |dɪ'pend| *vi*: **to ~ on** abhängen von;
(*rely on*) angewiesen sein auf +*acc*; **it ~s** es
kommt darauf an; **~ing on the result ...**
abhängend vom Resultat ...; **~able** *adj*
zuverlässig; **~ant** *n* Angehörige(r) *f(m)*;

~ence *n* Abhängigkeit *f*; **~ent** *adj* abhängig
♦ *n* = **dependant**; **~ent on** abhängig von
depict |dɪ'pɪkt| *vt* schildern
depleted |dɪ'pliːtɪd| *adj* aufgebraucht
deplorable |dɪ'plɔːrəbl| *adj* bedauerlich
deploy |dɪ'plɔɪ| *vt* einsetzen
depopulation |'diːpɔpjuˈleɪʃən| *n*
Entvölkerung *f*
deport |dɪ'pɔːt| *vt* deportieren; **~ation**
|diːpɔːˈteɪʃən| *n* Abschiebung *f*
deportment |dɪ'pɔːtmənt| *n* Betragen *nt*
deposit |dɪ'pɔzɪt| *n* (*in bank*) Guthaben *nt*;
(*down payment*) Anzahlung *f*; (*security*)
Kaution *f*; (*CHEM*) Niederschlag *m* ♦ *vt* (*in
bank*) deponieren; (*put down*) niederlegen;
~ account *n* Sparkonto *nt*
depot ['depəu| *n* Depot *nt*
depraved |dɪ'preɪvd| *adj* verkommen
depreciate |dɪ'priːʃɪeɪt| *vi* im Wert sinken;
depreciation |dɪpriːʃɪ'eɪʃən| *n*
Wertminderung *f*
depress |dɪ'pres| *vt* (*press down*)
niederdrücken; (*in mood*) deprimieren; **~ed**
adj deprimiert; **~ion** |dɪ'preʃən| *n* (*mood*)
Depression *f*; (*in trade*) Wirtschaftskrise *f*;
(*hollow*) Vertiefung *f*; (*MET*)
Tief(druckgebiet) *nt*
deprivation |depri'veɪʃən| *n* Not *f*
deprive |dɪ'praɪv| *vt*: **to ~ sb of sth** jdn
einer Sache *gen* berauben; **~d** *adj* (*child*)
sozial benachteiligt; (*area*) unterentwickelt
depth |depθ| *n* Tiefe *f*; **in the ~s of despair**
in tiefster Verzweiflung
deputation |depjuˈteɪʃən| *n* Abordnung *f*
deputize ['depjutaɪz| *vi*: **to ~ (for sb)** (jdn)
vertreten
deputy ['depjutɪ| *adj* stellvertretend ♦ *n*
(Stell)vertreter *m*; **~ head** (*BRIT: SCH*) *n*
Konrektor(in) *m(f)*
derail |dɪ'reɪl| *vt*: **to be ~ed** entgleisen;
~ment *n* Entgleisung *f*
deranged |dɪ'reɪndʒd| *adj* verrückt
derby ['dɑːrbɪ| (*US*) *n* Melone *f*
derelict ['derɪlɪkt| *adj* verlassen
deride |dɪ'raɪd| *vt* auslachen
derisory |dɪ'raɪsərɪ| *adj* spöttisch
derivative |dɪ'rɪvətɪv| *n* Derivat *nt* ♦ *adj*
abgeleitet
derive |dɪ'raɪv| *vt* (*get*) gewinnen; (*deduce*)
ableiten ♦ *vi* (*come from*) abstammen
dermatitis |dəːmə'taɪtɪs| *n* Hautentzündung
f
derogatory |dɪ'rɔgətərɪ| *adj* geringschätzig
derrick ['derɪk| *n* Drehkran *m*
descend |dɪ'send| *vt, vi* hinuntersteigen; **to ~
from** abstammen von; **~ant** *n* Nachkomme
m; **descent** |dɪ'sent| *n* (*coming down*)
Abstieg *m*; (*origin*) Abstammung *f*
describe |dɪs'kraɪb| *vt* beschreiben
description |dɪs'krɪpʃən| *n* Beschreibung *f*;
(*sort*) Art *f*

descriptive |dɪˈskrɪptɪv| adj beschreibend;
(word) anschaulich

desecrate |ˈdɛsɪkreɪt| vt schänden

desert |n ˈdɛzət, vb dɪˈzɜːt| n Wüste f ♦ vt
verlassen; (temporarily) im Stich lassen ♦ vi
(MIL) desertieren; **~s** npl (what one deserves):
to get one's just ~s seinen gerechten Lohn
bekommen; **~er** n Deserteur m; **~ion**
|dɪˈzɜːʃən| n (of wife) Verlassen nt; (MIL)
Fahnenflucht f; **~ island** n einsame Insel f

deserve |dɪˈzɜːv| vt verdienen; **deserving**
adj verdienstvoll

design |dɪˈzaɪn| n (plan) Entwurf m;
(planning) Design nt ♦ vt entwerfen

designate |vb ˈdɛzɪgneɪt, adj ˈdɛzɪgnɪt| vt
bestimmen ♦ adj designiert

designer |dɪˈzaɪnəʳ| n Designer(in) m(f);
(TECH) Konstrukteur(in) m(f); (fashion ~)
Modeschöpfer(in) m(f)

desirable |dɪˈzaɪərəbl| adj wünschenswert

desire |dɪˈzaɪəʳ| n Wunsch m, Verlangen nt
♦ vt (lust) begehren; (ask for) wollen

desk |dɛsk| n Schreibtisch m; (BRIT: in shop,
restaurant) Kasse f; **~top publishing** n
Desktop-Publishing nt

desolate |ˈdɛsəlɪt| adj öde; (sad) trostlos;
desolation |dɛsəˈleɪʃən| n Trostlosigkeit f

despair |dɪsˈpɛəʳ| n Verzweiflung f ♦ vi: **to ~
(of)** verzweifeln (an +dat)

despatch |dɪsˈpætʃ| n, vt = **dispatch**

desperate |ˈdɛspərɪt| adj verzweifelt; **~ly** adv
verzweifelt; **desperation** |dɛspəˈreɪʃən| n
Verzweiflung f

despicable |dɪsˈpɪkəbl| adj abscheulich

despise |dɪsˈpaɪz| vt verachten

despite |dɪsˈpaɪt| prep trotz +gen

despondent |dɪsˈpɔndənt| adj mutlos

dessert |dɪˈzɜːt| n Nachtisch m; **~spoon** n
Dessertlöffel m

destination |dɛstɪˈneɪʃən| n (of person)
(Reise)ziel nt; (of goods) Bestimmungsort m

destiny |ˈdɛstɪnɪ| n Schicksal nt

destitute |ˈdɛstɪtjuːt| adj Not leidend

destroy |dɪsˈtrɔɪ| vt zerstören; **~er** n (NAUT)
Zerstörer m

destruction |dɪsˈtrʌkʃən| n Zerstörung f

destructive |dɪsˈtrʌktɪv| adj zerstörend

detach |dɪˈtætʃ| vt loslösen; **~able** adj
abtrennbar; **~ed** adj (attitude) distanziert;
(house) Einzel-; **~ment** n (fig) Abstand m;
(MIL) Sonderkommando nt

detail |ˈdiːteɪl| n Einzelheit f, Detail nt ♦ vt
(relate) ausführlich berichten; (appoint)
abkommandieren; **in ~** im Detail; **~ed** adj
detailliert

detain |dɪˈteɪn| vt aufhalten; (imprison) in
Haft halten

detect |dɪˈtɛkt| vt entdecken; **~ion** |dɪˈtɛkʃən|
n Aufdeckung f; **~ive** n Detektiv m; **~ive
story** n Kriminalgeschichte f, Krimi m

détente |deɪˈtɑːnt| n Entspannung f

detention |dɪˈtɛnʃən| n Haft f; (SCH)
Nachsitzen nt

deter |dɪˈtɜːʳ| vt abschrecken

detergent |dɪˈtɜːdʒənt| n Waschmittel nt

deteriorate |dɪˈtɪərɪəreɪt| vi sich
verschlechtern; **deterioration**
|dɪtɪərɪəˈreɪʃən| n Verschlechterung f

determination |dɪtɜːmɪˈneɪʃən| n
Entschlossenheit f

determine |dɪˈtɜːmɪn| vt bestimmen; **~d** adj
entschlossen

deterrent |dɪˈtɛrənt| n Abschreckungsmittel
nt

detest |dɪˈtɛst| vt verabscheuen

detonate |ˈdɛtəncɪt| vt explodieren lassen
♦ vi detonieren

detour |ˈdiːtuəʳ| n Umweg m; (US: AUT:
diversion) Umleitung f ♦ vt (: traffic)
umleiten

detract |dɪˈtrækt| vi: **to ~ from** schmälern

detriment |ˈdɛtrɪmənt| n: **to the ~ of** zum
Schaden +gen; **~al** |dɛtrɪˈmɛntl| adj
schädlich

devaluation |dɪvæljuˈeɪʃən| n Abwertung f

devastate |ˈdɛvəsteɪt| vt verwüsten; (fig:
shock): **to be ~d by** niedergeschmettert sein
von; **devastating** adj verheerend

develop |dɪˈvɛləp| vt entwickeln; (resources)
erschließen ♦ vi sich entwickeln; **~ing
country** n Entwicklungsland nt; **~ment** n
Entwicklung f

deviate |ˈdiːvɪeɪt| vi abweichen

device |dɪˈvaɪs| n Gerät nt

devil |ˈdɛvl| n Teufel m

devious |ˈdiːvɪəs| adj (means) krumm;
(person) verschlagen

devise |dɪˈvaɪz| vt entwickeln

devoid |dɪˈvɔɪd| adj: **~ of** ohne

devolution |diːvəˈluːʃən| n (POL)
Dezentralisierung f

devote |dɪˈvəʊt| vt: **to ~ sth (to sth)** etw
(einer Sache dat) widmen; **~d** adj ergeben;
~e |dɛvəʊˈtiː| n Anhänger(in) m(f), Verehrer(in)
m(f); **devotion** |dɪˈvəʊʃən| n (piety)
Andacht f; (loyalty) Ergebenheit f, Hingabe f

devour |dɪˈvaʊəʳ| vt verschlingen

devout |dɪˈvaʊt| adj andächtig

dew |djuː| n Tau m

dexterity |dɛksˈtɛrɪtɪ| n Geschicklichkeit f

DHSS (BRIT) n abbr = **Department of Health
and Social Security**

diabetes |daɪəˈbiːtiːz| n Zuckerkrankheit f

diabetic |daɪəˈbɛtɪk| adj zuckerkrank; (food)
Diabetiker-; ♦ n Diabetiker m

diabolical |daɪəˈbɔlɪkl| (inf) adj (weather,
behaviour) saumäßig

diagnose |daɪəgˈnəʊz| vt diagnostizieren

diagnoses |daɪəgˈnəʊsiːz| npl of **diagnosis**

diagnosis |daɪəgˈnəʊsɪs| n Diagnose f

diagonal |daɪˈægənl| adj diagonal ♦ n
Diagonale f

diagram ['daɪəgræm] n Diagramm nt, Schaubild nt
dial ['daɪəl] n (TEL) Wählscheibe f; (of clock) Zifferblatt nt ♦ vt wählen
dialect ['daɪəlekt] n Dialekt m
dialling code ['daɪəlɪŋ-] n Vorwahl f
dialling tone n Amtszeichen nt
dialogue ['daɪəlɔg] n Dialog m
dial tone (US) n = dialling tone
diameter [daɪ'æmɪtəʳ] n Durchmesser m
diamond ['daɪəmənd] n Diamant m; ~s npl (CARDS) Karo nt
diaper ['daɪəpəʳ] (US) n Windel f
diaphragm ['daɪəfræm] n Zwerchfell nt
diarrhoea [daɪə'rɪːə] (US **diarrhea**) n Durchfall m
diary ['daɪərɪ] n Taschenkalender m; (account) Tagebuch nt
dice [daɪs] n Würfel pl ♦ vt in Würfel schneiden
dictate [dɪk'teɪt] vt diktieren; ~s ['dɪkteɪts] npl Gebote pl; **dictation** [dɪk'teɪʃən] n Diktat nt
dictator [dɪk'teɪtəʳ] n Diktator m
dictionary ['dɪkʃənrɪ] n Wörterbuch nt
did [dɪd] pt of do
didn't ['dɪdnt] = did not
die [daɪ] vi sterben; **to be dying for sth** etw unbedingt haben wollen; **to be dying to do sth** darauf brennen, etw zu tun; ~ **away** vi schwächer werden; ~ **down** vi nachlassen; ~ **out** vi aussterben
diesel ['diːzl] n (car) Diesel m; ~ **engine** n Dieselmotor m; ~ **oil** n Dieselkraftstoff m
diet ['daɪət] n Nahrung f; (special food) Diät f; (slimming) Abmagerungskur f ♦ vi (also: **be on a** ~) eine Abmagerungskur machen
differ ['dɪfəʳ] vi sich unterscheiden; (disagree) anderer Meinung sein; ~**ence** n Unterschied m; ~**ent** adj anders; (two things) verschieden; ~**entiate** [dɪfə'renʃɪeɪt] vt, vi unterscheiden; ~**ently** adv anders; (from one another) unterschiedlich
difficult ['dɪfɪkəlt] adj schwierig; ~**y** n Schwierigkeit f
diffident ['dɪfɪdənt] adj schüchtern
diffuse [adj dɪ'fjuːs, vb dɪ'fjuːz] adj langatmig ♦ vt verbreiten
dig [dɪg] (pt, pp **dug**) vt graben ♦ n (prod) Stoß m; (remark) Spitze f; (archaeological) Ausgrabung f; ~ **in** vi (MIL) sich eingraben; ~ **into** vt fus (savings) angreifen; ~ **up** vt ausgraben; (fig) aufgabeln
digest [vb daɪ'dʒest, n 'daɪdʒest] vt verdauen ♦ n Auslese f; ~**ion** [dɪ'dʒestʃən] n Verdauung f
digit ['dɪdʒɪt] n Ziffer f; (ANAT) Finger m; ~**al** adj digital, Digital-; ~**al TV** n digitales Fernsehen nt
dignified ['dɪgnɪfaɪd] adj würdevoll
dignity ['dɪgnɪtɪ] n Würde f
digress [daɪ'gres] vi abschweifen

digs [dɪgz] (BRIT: inf) npl Bude f
dilapidated [dɪ'læpɪdeɪtɪd] adj baufällig
dilate [daɪ'leɪt] vt weiten ♦ vi sich weiten
dilemma [daɪ'lemə] n Dilemma nt
diligent ['dɪlɪdʒənt] adj fleißig
dilute [daɪ'luːt] vt verdünnen
dim [dɪm] adj trübe; (stupid) schwer von Begriff ♦ vt verdunkeln; **to ~ one's headlights** (esp US) abblenden
dime [daɪm] (US) n Zehncentstück nt
dimension [daɪ'menʃən] n Dimension f
diminish [dɪ'mɪnɪʃ] vt, vi verringern
diminutive [dɪ'mɪnjʊtɪv] adj winzig ♦ n Verkleinerungsform f
dimmer ['dɪməʳ] (US) n (AUT) Abblendschalter m; ~s npl Abblendlicht nt; (sidelights) Begrenzungsleuchten pl
dimple ['dɪmpl] n Grübchen nt
din [dɪn] n Getöse nt
dine [daɪn] vi speisen; ~r n Tischgast m; (RAIL) Speisewagen m
dinghy ['dɪŋgɪ] n Dingi nt; **rubber ~** Schlauchboot nt
dingy ['dɪndʒɪ] adj armselig
dining car (BRIT) n Speisewagen m
dining room ['daɪnɪŋ-] n Esszimmer nt; (in hotel) Speisezimmer nt
dinner ['dɪnəʳ] n (lunch) Mittagessen nt; (evening) Abendessen nt; (public) Festessen nt; ~ **jacket** n Smoking m; ~ **party** n Tischgesellschaft f; ~ **time** n Tischzeit f
dinosaur ['daɪnəsɔːʳ] n Dinosaurier m
dint [dɪnt] n: **by ~ of** durch
diocese ['daɪəsɪs] n Diözese f
dip [dɪp] n (hollow) Senkung f; (bathe) kurze(s) Baden nt ♦ vt eintauchen; (BRIT: AUT) abblenden ♦ vi (slope) sich senken, abfallen
diploma [dɪ'pləʊmə] n Diplom nt
diplomacy [dɪ'pləʊməsɪ] n Diplomatie f
diplomat ['dɪpləmæt] n Diplomat(in) m(f); ~**ic** [dɪplə'mætɪk] adj diplomatisch
dip stick n Ölmessstab m
dipswitch ['dɪpswɪtʃ] (BRIT) n (AUT) Abblendschalter m
dire [daɪəʳ] adj schrecklich
direct [daɪ'rekt] adj direkt ♦ vt leiten; (film) die Regie führen +gen; (aim) richten; (order) anweisen; **can you ~ me to ...?** können Sie mir sagen, wo ich zu ... komme?; ~ **debit** n (BRIT) Einzugsauftrag m; (transaction) automatische Abbuchung f
direction [dɪ'rekʃən] n Richtung f; (CINE) Regie f; Leitung f; ~**s** npl (for use) Gebrauchsanleitung f; (orders) Anweisungen pl; **sense of ~** Orientierungssinn m
directly [dɪ'rektlɪ] adv direkt; (at once) sofort
director [dɪ'rektəʳ] n Direktor m; (of film) Regisseur m
directory [dɪ'rektərɪ] n (TEL) Telefonbuch nt; ~ **enquiries**, ~ **assistance** (US) n

(Fernsprech)auskunft f

dirt [dəːt] n Schmutz m, Dreck m; **~-cheap** adj spottbillig; **~y** adj schmutzig ♦ vt beschmutzen; **~y trick** n gemeine(r) Trick m

disability [dɪsə'bɪlɪ] n Körperbehinderung f

disabled [dɪs'eɪbld] adj körperbehindert

disadvantage [dɪsəd'vɑːntɪdʒ] n Nachteil m

disagree [dɪsə'griː] vi nicht übereinstimmen; (quarrel) (sich) streiten; (food): **to ~ with sb** jdm nicht bekommen; **~able** adj unangenehm; **~ment** n (between persons) Streit m; (between things) Widerspruch m

disallow ['dɪsə'laʊ] vt nicht zulassen

disappear [dɪsə'pɪə'] vi verschwinden; **~ance** n Verschwinden nt

disappoint [dɪsə'pɔɪnt] vt enttäuschen; **~ed** adj enttäuscht; **~ment** n Enttäuschung f

disapproval [dɪsə'pruːvəl] n Missbilligung f

disapprove [dɪsə'pruːv] vi: **to ~ of** missbilligen

disarm [dɪs'ɑːm] vt entwaffnen; (POL) abrüsten; **~ament** n Abrüstung f

disarray [dɪsə'reɪ] n: **to be in ~** (army) in Auflösung (begriffen) sein; (clothes) in unordentlichem Zustand sein

disaster [dɪ'zɑːstə'] n Katastrophe f; **disastrous** [dɪ'zɑːstrəs] adj verhängnisvoll

disband [dɪs'bænd] vt auflösen ♦ vi auseinander gehen

disbelief ['dɪsbə'liːf] n Ungläubigkeit f

disc [dɪsk] n Scheibe f; (record) (Schall)platte f; (COMPUT) = **disk**

discard [dɪs'kɑːd] vt ablegen

discern [dɪ'sɜːn] vt erkennen; **~ing** adj scharfsinnig

discharge [vb dɪs'tʃɑːdʒ, n 'dɪstʃɑːdʒ] vt (ship) entladen; (duties) nachkommen +dat; (dismiss) entlassen; (gun) abschießen; (JUR) freisprechen ♦ n (of ship, ELEC) Entladung f; (dismissal) Entlassung f; (MED) Ausfluss m

disciple [dɪ'saɪpl] n Jünger m

discipline ['dɪsɪplɪn] n Disziplin f ♦ vt (train) schulen; (punish) bestrafen

disc jockey n Diskjockey m

disclaim [dɪs'kleɪm] vt nicht anerkennen

disclose [dɪs'kləʊz] vt enthüllen; **disclosure** [dɪs'kləʊʒə'] n Enthüllung f

disco ['dɪskəʊ] n abbr = **discotheque** =

discoloured [dɪs'kʌləd] (US **discolored**) adj verfärbt

discomfort [dɪs'kʌmfət] n Unbehagen nt

disconcert [dɪskən'sɜːt] vt aus der Fassung bringen

disconnect [dɪskə'nekt] vt abtrennen

discontent [dɪskən'tent] n Unzufriedenheit f; **~ed** adj unzufrieden

discontinue [dɪskən'tɪnjuː] vt einstellen

discord ['dɪskɔːd] n Zwietracht f; (noise) Dissonanz f

discotheque ['dɪskəʊtek] n Diskothek f

discount [n 'dɪskaʊnt, vb dɪs'kaʊnt] n Rabatt

m ♦ vt außer Acht lassen

discourage [dɪs'kʌrɪdʒ] vt entmutigen; (prevent) abraten

discourteous [dɪs'kɜːtɪəs] adj unhöflich

discover [dɪs'kʌvə'] vt entdecken; **~y** n Entdeckung f

discredit [dɪs'kredɪt] vt in Verruf bringen

discreet [dɪs'kriːt] adj diskret

discrepancy [dɪs'krepənsɪ] n Diskrepanz f

discriminate [dɪs'krɪmɪneɪt] vi unterscheiden; **to ~ against** diskriminieren; **discriminating** adj anspruchsvoll; **discrimination** [dɪskrɪmɪ'neɪʃən] n Urteilsvermögen nt; (pej) Diskriminierung f

discuss [dɪs'kʌs] vt diskutieren, besprechen; **~ion** [dɪs'kʌʃən] n Diskussion f, Besprechung f

disdain [dɪs'deɪn] n Verachtung f

disease [dɪ'ziːz] n Krankheit f

disembark [dɪsɪm'bɑːk] vi von Bord gehen

disenchanted ['dɪsɪn'tʃɑːntɪd] adj desillusioniert

disengage [dɪsɪn'geɪdʒ] vt (AUT) auskuppeln

disentangle [dɪsɪn'tæŋgl] vt entwirren

disfigure [dɪs'fɪgə'] vt entstellen

disgrace [dɪs'greɪs] n Schande f ♦ vt Schande bringen über +acc; **~ful** adj unerhört

disgruntled [dɪs'grʌntld] adj verärgert

disguise [dɪs'gaɪz] vt verkleiden; (feelings) verhehlen ♦ n Verkleidung f; **in ~** verkleidet, maskiert

disgust [dɪs'gʌst] n Abscheu f ♦ vt anwidern; **~ed** adj angeekelt; (at sb's behaviour) empört; **~ing** adj widerlich

dish [dɪʃ] n Schüssel f; (food) Gericht nt; **to do or wash the ~es** abwaschen; **~ up** vt auftischen; **~ cloth** n Spüllappen m

dishearten [dɪs'hɑːtn] vt entmutigen

dishevelled [dɪ'ʃevəld] adj (hair) zerzaust; (clothing) ungepflegt

dishonest [dɪs'ɔnɪst] adj unehrlich

dishonour [dɪs'ɔnə'] (US **dishonor**) n Unehre f; **~able** adj unehrenhaft

dishtowel ['dɪʃtaʊəl] n Geschirrtuch nt

dishwasher ['dɪʃwɔʃə'] n Geschirr-spülmaschine f

disillusion [dɪsɪ'luːʒən] vt enttäuschen, desillusionieren

disincentive [dɪsɪn'sentɪv] n Entmutigung f

disinfect [dɪsɪn'fekt] vt desinfizieren; **~ant** n Desinfektionsmittel nt

disintegrate [dɪs'ɪntɪgreɪt] vi sich auflösen

disinterested [dɪs'ɪntrəstɪd] adj uneigennützig; (inf) uninteressiert

disjointed [dɪs'dʒɔɪntɪd] adj unzusammenhängend

disk [dɪsk] n (COMPUT) Diskette f; **single/ double sided ~** einseitige/beidseitige Diskette; **~ drive** n Diskettenlaufwerk nt; **~ette** [dɪs'ket] (US) n = **disk**

dislike [dɪs'laɪk] n Abneigung f ♦ vt nicht

leiden können

dislocate |'dɪsləkeɪt| vt auskugeln

dislodge |dɪs'lɔdʒ| vt verschieben; (MIL) aus der Stellung werfen

disloyal |dɪs'lɔɪəl| adj treulos

dismal |'dɪzml| adj trostlos, trübe

dismantle |dɪs'mæntl| vt demontieren

dismay |dɪs'meɪ| n Bestürzung f ♦ vt bestürzen

dismiss |dɪs'mɪs| vt (employee) entlassen; (idea) von sich weisen; (send away) wegschicken; (JUR) abweisen; **~al** n Entlassung f

dismount |dɪs'maunt| vi absteigen

disobedience |dɪsə'biːdɪəns| n Ungehorsam m; **disobedient** adj ungehorsam

disobey |dɪsə'beɪ| vt nicht gehorchen +dat

disorder |dɪs'ɔːdər| n (confusion) Verwirrung f; (commotion) Aufruhr m; (MED) Erkrankung f

disorderly |dɪs'ɔːdəlɪ| adj (untidy) unordentlich; (unruly) ordnungswidrig

disorganized |dɪs'ɔːgənaɪzd| adj unordentlich

disorientated |dɪs'ɔːrɪenteɪtɪd| adj (person: after journey) verwirrt

disown |dɪs'əun| vt (child) verstoßen

disparaging |dɪs'pærɪdʒɪŋ| adj geringschätzig

dispassionate |dɪs'pæʃənət| adj objektiv

dispatch |dɪs'pætʃ| vt (of goods) abschicken, abfertigen ♦ n Absendung f; (esp MIL) Meldung f

dispel |dɪs'pel| vt zerstreuen

dispensary |dɪs'pensərɪ| n Apotheke f

dispense |dɪs'pens| vt verteilen, austeilen; **~ with** vt fus verzichten auf +acc; **~r** n (container) Spender m; **dispensing** adj: **dispensing chemist** (BRIT) Apotheker m

dispersal |dɪs'pɜːsl| n Zerstreuung f

disperse |dɪs'pɜːs| vt zerstreuen ♦ vi sich verteilen

dispirited |dɪs'pɪrɪtɪd| adj niedergeschlagen

displace |dɪs'pleɪs| vt verschieben; **~d person** n Verschleppte(r) mf

display |dɪs'pleɪ| n (of goods) Auslage f; (of feeling) Zurschaustellung f ♦ vt zeigen; (ostentatiously) vorführen; (goods) ausstellen

displease |dɪs'pliːz| vt missfallen +dat

displeasure |dɪs'pleʒər| n Missfallen nt

disposable |dɪs'pəuzəbl| adj Wegwerf-; **~ nappy** n Papierwindel f

disposal |dɪs'pəuzl| n (of property) Verkauf m; (throwing away) Beseitigung f; **to be at one's ~** einem zur Verfügung stehen

dispose |dɪs'pəuz| vi: **to ~ of** loswerden; **~d** adj geneigt

disposition |dɪspə'zɪʃən| n Wesen nt

disproportionate |dɪsprə'pɔːʃənət| adj unverhältnismäßig

disprove |dɪs'pruːv| vt widerlegen

dispute |dɪs'pjuːt| n Streit m; (also: **industrial ~**) Arbeitskampf m ♦ vt bestreiten

disqualify |dɪs'kwɔlɪfaɪ| vt disqualifizieren

disquiet |dɪs'kwaɪət| n Unruhe f

disregard |dɪsrɪ'gɑːd| vt nicht (be)achten

disrepair |'dɪsrɪ'peər| n: **to fall into ~** verfallen

disreputable |dɪs'repjutəbl| adj verrufen

disrespectful |dɪsrɪ'spektful| adj respektlos

disrupt |dɪs'rʌpt| vt stören; (service) unterbrechen; **~ion** |dɪs'rʌpʃən| n Störung f; Unterbrechung f

dissatisfaction |dɪssætɪs'fækʃən| n Unzufriedenheit f; **dissatisfied** |dɪs'sætɪsfaɪd| adj unzufrieden

dissect |dɪ'sekt| vt zerlegen, sezieren

dissent |dɪ'sent| n abweichende Meinung f

dissertation |dɪsə'teɪʃən| n wissenschaftliche Arbeit f; (Ph.D.) Doktorarbeit f

disservice |dɪs'sɜːvɪs| n: **to do sb a ~** jdm einen schlechten Dienst erweisen

dissident |'dɪsɪdnt| adj anders denkend ♦ n Dissident m

dissimilar |dɪ'sɪmɪlər| adj: **~ (to sb/sth)** (jdm/etw) unähnlich

dissipate |'dɪsɪpeɪt| vt (waste) verschwenden; (scatter) zerstreuen

dissociate |dɪ'səuʃɪeɪt| vt trennen

dissolve |dɪ'zɔlv| vt auflösen ♦ vi sich auflösen

dissuade |dɪ'sweɪd| vt: **to ~ sb from doing sth** jdn davon abbringen, etw zu tun

distance |'dɪstns| n Entfernung f; **in the ~** in der Ferne; **distant** adj entfernt, fern; (with time) fern

distaste |dɪs'teɪst| n Abneigung f; **~ful** adj widerlich

distended |dɪs'tendɪd| adj (stomach) aufgebläht

distil |dɪs'tɪl| vt destillieren; **~lery** n Brennerei f

distinct |dɪs'tɪŋkt| adj (separate) getrennt; (clear) klar, deutlich; **as ~ from** im Unterschied zu; **~ion** |dɪs'tɪŋkʃən| n Unterscheidung f; (eminence) Auszeichnung f; **~ive** adj bezeichnend

distinguish |dɪs'tɪŋgwɪʃ| vt unterscheiden; **~ed** adj (eminent) berühmt; **~ing** adj bezeichnend

distort |dɪs'tɔːt| vt verdrehen; (misrepresent) entstellen; **~ion** |dɪs'tɔːʃən| n Verzerrung f

distract |dɪs'trækt| vt ablenken; **~ing** adj verwirrend; **~ion** |dɪs'trækʃən| n (distress) Raserei f; (diversion) Zerstreuung f

distraught |dɪs'trɔːt| adj bestürzt

distress |dɪs'tres| n Not f; (suffering) Qual f ♦ vt quälen; **~ing** adj erschütternd; **~ signal** n Notsignal nt

distribute |dɪs'trɪbjuːt| vt verteilen; **distribution** |dɪstrɪ'bjuːʃən| n Verteilung f; **distributor** n Verteiler m

district |'dıstrıkt| n (of country) Kreis m; (of town) Bezirk m; ~ **attorney** (US) n Oberstaatsanwalt m; ~ **nurse** n Kreiskrankenschwester f

distrust |dıs'trʌst| n Misstrauen nt ♦ vt misstrauen +dat

disturb |dıs'tə:b| vt stören; (agitate) erregen; ~**ance** n Störung f; ~**ed** adj beunruhigt; **emotionally ~ed** emotional gestört; ~**ing** adj beunruhigend

disuse |dıs'ju:s| n: **to fall into** ~ außer Gebrauch kommen; ~**d** |dıs'ju:zd| adj außer Gebrauch; (mine, railway line) stillgelegt

ditch |dıtʃ| n Graben m ♦ vt (person) loswerden; (plan) fallen lassen

dither |'dıðər| vi verdattert sein

ditto |'dıtəu| adv dito, ebenfalls

divan |dı'væn| n Liegesofa nt

dive |daıv| n (into water) Kopfsprung m; (AVIAT) Sturzflug m ♦ vi tauchen; ~**r** n Taucher m

diverge |daı'və:dʒ| vi auseinander gehen

diverse |daı'və:s| adj verschieden

diversion |daı'və:ʃən| n Ablenkung f; (BRIT: AUT) Umleitung f

diversity |daı'və:sıtı| n Vielfalt f

divert |daı'və:t| vt ablenken; (traffic) umleiten

divide |dı'vaıd| vt teilen ♦ vi sich teilen; ~**d highway** (US) n Schnellstraße f

divine |dı'vaın| adj göttlich

diving |'daıvıŋ| n (SPORT) Turmspringen nt; (underwater ~) Tauchen nt; ~ **board** n Sprungbrett nt

divinity |dı'vınıtı| n Gottheit f; (subject) Religion f

division |dı'vıʒən| n Teilung f; (MIL) Division f; (part) Abteilung f; (in opinion) Uneinigkeit f; (BRIT: POL) (Abstimmung f durch) Hammelsprung f

divorce |dı'vɔ:s| n (Ehe)scheidung f ♦ vt scheiden; ~**d** adj geschieden; ~**e** |dıvɔ:'si:| n Geschiedene(r) f(m)

divulge |daı'vʌldʒ| vt preisgeben

DIY (BRIT) n abbr = **do-it-yourself**

dizzy |'dızı| adj schwindlig

DJ n abbr = **disc jockey**

DNA fingerprinting n genetische Fingerabdrücke pl

do |du:| (pt **did**, pp **done**) n (inf: party etc) Fete f

♦ aux vb 1 (in negative constructions and questions): **I don't understand** ich verstehe nicht; **didn't you know?** wusstest du das nicht?; **what do you think?** was meinen Sie?

2 (for emphasis, in polite phrases): **she does seem rather tired** sie scheint wirklich sehr müde zu sein; **do sit down/help yourself** setzen Sie sich doch hin/greifen Sie doch zu

3 (used to avoid repeating vb): **she swims better than I do** sie schwimmt besser als ich; **she lives in Glasgow – so do I** sie wohnt in Glasgow – ich auch

4 (in tag questions): **you like him, don't you?** du magst ihn doch, oder?

♦ vt 1 (carry out, perform etc) tun, machen; **what are you doing tonight?** was machst du heute Abend?; **I've got nothing to do** ich habe nichts zu tun; **to do one's hair/ nails** sich die Haare/Nägel machen

2 (AUT etc) fahren

♦ vi 1 (act, behave): **do as I do** mach es wie ich

2 (get on, fare): **he's doing well/badly at school** er ist gut/schlecht in der Schule; **how do you do?** guten Tag

3 (be suitable) gehen; (be sufficient) reichen; **to make do (with)** auskommen mit

do away with vt (kill) umbringen; (abolish: law etc) abschaffen

do up vt (laces, dress, buttons) zumachen; (room, house) renovieren

do with vt (need) brauchen; (be connected) zu tun haben mit

do without vt, vi auskommen ohne

docile |'dəusaıl| adj gefügig

dock |dɔk| n Dock nt; (JUR) Anklagebank f; ~**er** n Hafenarbeiter m; ~**yard** n Werft f

doctor |'dɔktər| n Arzt m, Ärztin f; (UNIV) Doktor m ♦ vt (fig) fälschen; (drink etc) etw beimischen +dat; **D~ of Philosophy** n Doktor m der Philosophie

document |'dɔkjumənt| n Dokument nt; ~**ary** |dɔkju'mentərı| n Dokumentarbericht m; (film) Dokumentarfilm m ♦ adj dokumentarisch; ~**ation** |dɔkjumən'teıʃən| n dokumentarische(r) Nachweis m

dodge |dɔdʒ| n Kniff m ♦ vt ausweichen +dat

Dodgems |'dɔdʒəmz| ® (BRIT) npl Autoskooter m

doe |dəu| n (roe deer) Ricke f; (red deer) Hirschkuh f; (rabbit) Weibchen nt

does |dʌz| vb see **do**; ~**n't** = **does not**

dog |dɔg| n Hund m; ~ **collar** n Hundehalsband nt; (ECCL) Kragen m des Geistlichen; ~**-eared** adj mit Eselsohren

dogged |'dɔgıd| adj hartnäckig

dogsbody |'dɔgzbɔdı| n Mädchen nt für alles

doings |'du:ıŋz| npl (activities) Treiben nt

do-it-yourself |'du:ıtjɔ:'self| n Do-it-yourself nt

doldrums |'dɔldrəmz| npl: **to be in the** ~ (business) Flaute haben; (person) deprimiert sein

dole |dəul| (BRIT) n Stempelgeld nt; **to be on the** ~ stempeln gehen; ~ **out** vt ausgeben, austeilen

doleful |'dəulful| adj traurig

doll |dɔl| n Puppe f ♦ vt: **to ~ o.s. up** sich

aufdonnern
dollar ['dɔlər] n Dollar m
dolphin ['dɔlfin] n Delfin m, Delphin m
dome [dəum] n Kuppel f
domestic [də'mestik] adj häuslich; (within country) Innen-, Binnen-; (animal) Haus-; **~ated** adj (person) häuslich; (animal) zahm
dominant ['dɔminənt] adj vorherrschend
dominate ['dɔmineit] vt beherrschen
domineering [dɔmi'niəriŋ] adj herrisch
dominion [də'miniən] n (rule) Regierungsgewalt f; (land) Staatsgebiet nt mit Selbstverwaltung
domino ['dɔminəu] (pl **-es**) n Dominostein m; **~es** n (game) Domino(spiel) nt
don [dɔn] (BRIT) n akademische(r) Lehrer m
donate [də'neit] vt (blood, money) spenden; (lot of money) stiften; **donation** [də'neiʃən] n Spende f
done [dʌn] pp of **do**
donkey ['dɔŋki] n Esel m
donor ['dəunər] n Spender m; **~ card** n Organspenderausweis m
don't [dəunt] = **do not**
doodle ['duːdl] vi kritzeln
doom [duːm] n böse(s) Geschick nt; (downfall) Verderben nt ♦ vt: **to be ~ed** zum Untergang verurteilt sein; **~sday** n der Jüngste Tag
door [dɔːr] n Tür f; **~bell** n Türklingel f; **~ handle** n Türklinke f; **~man** (irreg) n Türsteher m; **~mat** n Fußmatte f; **~step** n Türstufe f; **~way** n Türöffnung f
dope [dəup] n (drug) Aufputschmittel nt ♦ vt (horse) dopen
dopey ['dəupi] (inf) adj bekloppt
dormant ['dɔːmənt] adj latent
dormitory ['dɔːmitri] n Schlafsaal m
dormouse ['dɔːmaus] (pl **-mice**) n Haselmaus f
DOS [dɔs] n abbr (= disk operating system) DOS nt
dosage ['dəusidʒ] n Dosierung f
dose [dəus] n Dosis f
dosh [dɔʃ] (inf) n (money) Moos nt, Knete f
doss house ['dɔs-] (BRIT) n Bleibe f
dot [dɔt] n Punkt m; **~ted with** übersät mit; **on the ~** pünktlich
dote [dəut]: **to ~ on** vt fus vernarrt sein in +acc
dotted line ['dɔtid-] n punktierte Linie f
double ['dʌbl] adj, adv doppelt ♦ n Doppelgänger m ♦ vt verdoppeln ♦ vi sich verdoppeln; **~s** npl (TENNIS) Doppel nt; **on** or **at the ~** im Laufschritt; **~ bass** n Kontrabass m; **~ bed** n Doppelbett nt; **~ bend** (BRIT) n S-Kurve f; **~-breasted** adj zweireihig; **~-cross** vt hintergehen; **~-decker** n Doppeldecker m; **~ glazing** (BRIT) n Doppelverglasung f; **~ room** n Doppelzimmer nt

doubly ['dʌbli] adv doppelt
doubt [daut] n Zweifel m ♦ vt bezweifeln; **~ful** adj zweifelhaft; **~less** adv ohne Zweifel
dough [dəu] n Teig m; **~nut** n Berliner m
douse [dauz] vt (drench) mit Wasser begießen, durchtränken; (extinguish) ausmachen
dove [dʌv] n Taube f
dovetail ['dʌvteil] vi (plans) übereinstimmen
dowdy ['daudi] adj unmodern
down [daun] n (fluff) Flaum m; (hill) Hügel m ♦ adv unten; (motion) herunter; hinunter ♦ prep: **to go ~ the street** die Straße hinuntergehen ♦ vt niederschlagen; **~ with X!** nieder mit X!; **~-and-out** n Tramp m; **~-at-heel** adj schäbig; **~cast** adj niedergeschlagen; **~fall** n Sturz m; **~hearted** adj niedergeschlagen; **~hill** adv bergab; **~ payment** n Anzahlung f; **~pour** n Platzregen m; **~right** adj ausgesprochen; **~size** vi (ECON: company) sich verkleinern
Down's syndrome [daunz-] n (MED) Down-Syndrom nt
down: **~stairs** adv unten; (motion) nach unten; **~stream** adv flussabwärts; **~-to-earth** adj praktisch; **~town** adv in der Innenstadt; (motion) in die Innenstadt; **~ under** (BRIT: inf) adv in/nach Australien/ Neuseeland; **~ward** adj Abwärts-, nach unten ♦ adv abwärts, nach unten; **~wards** adv abwärts, nach unten
dowry ['dauri] n Mitgift f
doz. abbr (= dozen) Dtzd.
doze [dəuz] vi dösen; **~ off** vi einnicken
dozen ['dʌzn] n Dutzend nt; **a ~ books** ein Dutzend Bücher; **~s of** dutzende or Dutzende von

Dr. abbr = **doctor; drive**
drab [dræb] adj düster, eintönig
draft [drɑːft] n Entwurf m; (FIN) Wechsel m; (US: MIL) Einberufung f ♦ vt skizzieren; see also **draught**
draftsman ['drɑːftsmən] (US: irreg) n = **draughtsman**
drag [dræg] vt schleppen; (river) mit einem Schleppnetz absuchen ♦ vi sich (dahin)schleppen ♦ n (bore) etwas Blödes; **in ~** als Tunte; **a man in ~** eine Tunte; **~ on** vi sich in die Länge ziehen; **~ and drop** vt (COMPUT) Drag & Drop
dragon ['drægn] n Drache m; **~fly** ['drægənflai] n Libelle f
drain [drein] n Abfluss m; (fig: burden) Belastung f ♦ vt ableiten; (exhaust) erschöpfen ♦ vi (of water) abfließen; **~age** n Kanalisation f; **~ing board** (US **~board**) n Ablaufbrett nt; **~pipe** n Abflussrohr nt
dram [dræm] n Schluck m
drama ['drɑːmə] n Drama nt; **~tic** [drə'mætik] adj dramatisch; **~tist** ['dræmətist] n Dramatiker m; **~tize**

['dræmətaɪz] vt (events) dramatisieren; (for TV etc) bearbeiten

drank [dræŋk] pt of **drink**

drape [dreɪp] vt drapieren; **~s** (US) npl vorhänge pi

drastic ['dræstɪk] adj drastisch

draught [drɑːft] (US **draft**) n Zug m; (NAUT) Tiefgang m; **~s** n Damespiel nt; **on ~** (beer) vom Fass; **~ beer** n Bier nt vom Fass; **~board** (BRIT) n Zeichenbrett nt

draughtsman ['drɑːftsmən] (irreg) n technische(r) Zeichner m

draw [drɔː] (pt **drew**, pp **drawn**) vt ziehen; (crowd) anlocken; (picture) zeichnen; (money) abheben; (water) schöpfen ♦ vi (SPORT) unentschieden spielen ♦ n (SPORT) Unentschieden nt; (lottery) Ziehung f; **~ near** vi näher rücken; **~ out** vi (train) ausfahren; (lengthen) sich hinziehen; **~ up** vi (stop) halten ♦ vt (document) aufsetzen

drawback ['drɔːbæk] n Nachteil m

drawbridge ['drɔːbrɪdʒ] n Zugbrücke f

drawer [drɔːʳ] n Schublade f

drawing ['drɔːɪŋ] n Zeichnung f; Zeichnen nt; **~ board** n Reißbrett nt; **~ pin** (BRIT) n Reißzwecke f; **~ room** n Salon m

drawl [drɔːl] n schleppende Sprechweise f

drawn [drɔːn] pp of **draw**

dread [dred] n Furcht f ♦ vt fürchten; **~ful** adj furchtbar

dream [driːm] (pt, pp **dreamed** or **dreamt**) n Traum m ♦ vt träumen ♦ vi: **to ~ (about)** träumen (von); **~er** n Träumer m; **~t** [dremt] pt, pp of **dream**; **~y** adj verträumt

dreary ['drɪərɪ] adj trostlos, öde

dredge [dredʒ] vt ausbaggern

dregs [dregz] npl Bodensatz m; (fig) Abschaum m

drench [drentʃ] vt durchnässen

dress [dres] n Kleidung f; (garment) Kleid nt ♦ vt anziehen; (MED) verbinden; **to get ~ed** sich anziehen; **~ up** vi sich fein machen; **~ circle** (BRIT) n erste(r) Rang m; **~er** n (furniture) Anrichte f; (MED) Verband m; (COOK) Soße f; **~ing gown** (BRIT) n Morgenrock m; **~ing room** n (THEAT) Garderobe f; (SPORT) Umkleideraum m; **~ing table** n Toilettentisch m; **~maker** n Schneiderin f; **~ rehearsal** n Generalprobe f

drew [druː] pt of **draw**

dribble ['drɪbl] vi sabbern ♦ vt (ball) dribbeln

dried [draɪd] adj getrocknet; (fruit) Dörr-, gedörrte(r, s); **~ milk** n Milchpulver nt

drier ['draɪəʳ] n = **dryer**

drift [drɪft] n Strömung f; (snowdrift) Schneewehe f; (fig) Richtung f ♦ vi sich treiben lassen; **~wood** n Treibholz nt

drill [drɪl] n Bohrer m; (MIL) Drill m ♦ vt bohren; (MIL) ausbilden ♦ vi: **to ~ (for)** bohren (nach)

drink [drɪŋk] (pt **drank**, pp **drunk**) n Getränk nt; (spirits) Drink m ♦ vt, vi trinken; **to have a ~** etwas trinken; **~er** n Trinker m; **~ing water** n Trinkwasser nt

drip [drɪp] n Tropfen m ♦ vi tropfen; **~-dry** adj bügelfrei; **~ping** n Bratenfett nt

drive [draɪv] (pt **drove**, pp **driven**) n Fahrt f; (road) Einfahrt f; (campaign) Aktion f; (energy) Schwung m; (SPORT) Schlag m; (also: **disk ~**) Diskettenlaufwerk nt ♦ vt (car) fahren; (animals, people, objects) treiben; (power) antreiben ♦ vi fahren; **left-/right-hand ~** Links-/Rechtssteuerung f; **to ~ sb mad** jdn verrückt machen; **~-by shooting** n Schusswaffenangriff aus einem vorbeifahrenden Wagen

drivel ['drɪvl] n Faselei f

driven ['drɪvn] pp of **drive**

driver ['draɪvəʳ] n Fahrer m; **~'s license** (US) n Führerschein m

driveway ['draɪvweɪ] n Auffahrt f; (longer) Zufahrtsstraße f

driving ['draɪvɪŋ] adj (rain) stürmisch; **~ instructor** n Fahrlehrer m; **~ lesson** n Fahrstunde f; **~ licence** (BRIT) n Führerschein m; **~ school** n Fahrschule f; **~ test** n Fahrprüfung f

drizzle ['drɪzl] n Nieselregen m ♦ vi nieseln

droll [drəʊl] adj drollig

drone [drəʊn] n (sound) Brummen nt; (bee) Drohne f

drool [druːl] vi sabbern

droop [druːp] vi (schlaff) herabhängen

drop [drɒp] n (of liquid) Tropfen m; (fall) Fall m ♦ vt fallen lassen; (lower) senken; (abandon) fallen lassen ♦ vi (fall) herunterfallen; **~s** npl (MED) Tropfen pl; **~ off** vi (sleep) einschlafen ♦ vt (passenger) absetzen; **~ out** vi (withdraw) ausscheiden; **~-out** n Aussteiger m; **~per** n Pipette f; **~pings** npl Kot m

drought [draut] n Dürre f

drove [drəʊv] pt of **drive**

drown [draun] vt ertränken; (sound) übertönen ♦ vi ertrinken

drowsy ['drauzɪ] adj schläfrig

drudgery ['drʌdʒərɪ] n Plackerei f

drug [drʌg] n (MED) Arznei f; (narcotic) Rauschgift nt ♦ vt betäuben; **~ addict** n Rauschgiftsüchtige(r) f(m); **~gist** (US) n Drogist(in) m(f); **~store** (US) n Drogerie f

drum [drʌm] n Trommel f ♦ vi trommeln; **~s** npl (MUS) Schlagzeug nt; **~mer** n Trommler m

drunk [drʌŋk] pp of **drink** ♦ adj betrunken ♦ n (also: **~ard**) Trinker(in) m(f); **~en** adj betrunken

dry [draɪ] adj trocken ♦ vt (ab)trocknen ♦ vi trocknen; **~ up** vi austrocknen ♦ vt (dishes) abtrocknen; **~ cleaner's** n chemische Reinigung f; **~ cleaning** n chemische Reinigung f; **~er** n Trockner m; (US: spin-

dryer) (Wäsche)schleuder *f*; **~ goods store** (*US*) *n* Kurzwarengeschäft *nt*; **~ness** *n* Trockenheit *f*; **~ rot** *n* Hausschwamm *m*

DSS (*BRIT*) *n abbr* (= *Department of Social Security*) ≈ Sozialministerium *nt*

DTP *n abbr* (= *desktop publishing*) DTP *nt*

dual ['djuəl] *adj* doppelt; **~ carriageway** (*BRIT*) *n* zweispurige Fahrbahn *f*; **~ nationality** *n* doppelte Staatsangehörigkeit *f*; **~-purpose** *adj* Mehrzweck-

dubbed [dʌbd] *adj* (*film*) synchronisiert

dubious ['djuːbɪəs] *adj* zweifelhaft

duchess ['dʌtʃɪs] *n* Herzogin *f*

duck [dʌk] *n* Ente *f* ♦ *vi* sich ducken; **~ling** *n* Entchen *nt*

duct [dʌkt] *n* Röhre *f*

dud [dʌd] *n* Niete *f* ♦ *adj* (*cheque*) ungedeckt

due [djuː] *adj* fällig; (*fitting*) angemessen ♦ *n* Gebühr *f*; (*right*) Recht *nt* ♦ *adv* (*south etc*) genau; **~s** *npl* (*for club*) Beitrag *m*; (*NAUT*) Gebühren *pl*; **~ to** wegen +*gen*

duel ['djuəl] *n* Duell *nt*

duet |djuˈɛt| *n* Duett *nt*

duffel ['dʌfl] *adj*: **~ bag** Matchbeutel *m*, Matchsack *m*

dug [dʌg] *pt, pp of* **dig**

duke |djuːk| *n* Herzog *m*

dull [dʌl] *adj* (*colour, weather*) trübe; (*stupid*) schwer von Begriff; (*boring*) langweilig ♦ *vt* abstumpfen

duly ['djuːlɪ] *adv* ordnungsgemäß

dumb [dʌm] *adj* stumm; (*inf: stupid*) doof, blöde; **~founded** [dʌmˈfaundɪd] *adj* verblüfft

dummy ['dʌmɪ] *n* Schneiderpuppe *f*; (*substitute*) Attrappe *f*; (*BRIT: for baby*) Schnuller *m* ♦ *adj* Schein-

dump [dʌmp] *n* Abfallhaufen *m*; (*MIL*) Stapelplatz *m*; (*inf: place*) Nest *nt* ♦ *vt* abladen, auskippen; **~ing** *n* (*COMM*) Schleuderexport *m*; (*of rubbish*) Schuttabladen *nt*

dumpling ['dʌmplɪŋ] *n* Kloß *m*, Knödel *m*

dumpy ['dʌmpɪ] *adj* pummelig

dunce [dʌns] *n* Dummkopf *m*

dune [djuːn] *n* Düne *f*

dung [dʌŋ] *n* Dünger *m*

dungarees [dʌŋɡəˈriːz] *npl* Latzhose *f*

dungeon ['dʌndʒən] *n* Kerker *m*

dupe [djuːp] *n* Gefoppte(r) *m* ♦ *vt* hintergehen, anführen

duplex ['djuːplɛks] (*US*) *n* zweistöckige Wohnung *f*

duplicate [*n* 'djuːplɪkət, *vb* 'djuːplɪkeɪt] *n* Duplikat *nt* ♦ *vt* verdoppeln; (*make copies*) kopieren; **in ~** in doppelter Ausführung

duplicity [djuːˈplɪsɪtɪ] *n* Doppelspiel *nt*

durable ['djuərəbl] *adj* haltbar

duration [djuəˈreɪʃən] *n* Dauer *f*

duress [djuəˈrɛs] *n*: **under ~** unter Zwang

during ['djuərɪŋ] *prep* während +*gen*

dusk [dʌsk] *n* Abenddämmerung *f*

dust [dʌst] *n* Staub *m* ♦ *vt* abstauben; (*sprinkle*) bestäuben; **~bin** (*BRIT*) *n* Mülleimer *m*, **~er** *n* Staubtuch *nt*; **~ jacket** *n* Schutzumschlag *m*; **~man** (*BRIT: irreg*) *n* Müllmann *m*; **~y** *adj* staubig

Dutch [dʌtʃ] *adj* holländisch, niederländisch ♦ *n* (*LING*) Holländisch *nt*, Niederländisch *nt*; **the ~** *npl* (*people*) die Holländer *pl*, die Niederländer *pl*; **to go ~** getrennte Kasse machen; **~man/woman** (*irreg*) *n* Holländer(in) *m(f)*, Niederländer(in) *m(f)*

dutiful ['djuːtɪful] *adj* pflichtbewusst

duty ['djuːtɪ] *n* Pflicht *f*; (*job*) Aufgabe *f*; (*tax*) Einfuhrzoll *m*; **on ~** im Dienst; **~ chemist's** *n* Apotheke *f* im Bereitschaftsdienst; **~-free** *adj* zollfrei

duvet ['duːveɪ] (*BRIT*) *n* Daunendecke *f*

DVD *n abbr* (= *digital versatile disc*) DVD *f*

dwarf [dwɔːf] (*pl* **dwarves**) *n* Zwerg *m* ♦ *vt* überragen

dwell [dwɛl] (*pt, pp* **dwelt**) *vi* wohnen; **~ on** *vt fus* verweilen bei; **~ing** *n* Wohnung *f*

dwelt [dwɛlt] *pt, pp of* **dwell**

dwindle ['dwɪndl] *vi* schwinden

dye [daɪ] *n* Farbstoff *m* ♦ *vt* färben

dying ['daɪɪŋ] *adj* (*person*) sterbend; (*moments*) letzt

dyke [daɪk] (*BRIT*) *n* (*channel*) Kanal *m*; (*barrier*) Deich *m*, Damm *m*

dynamic [daɪˈnæmɪk] *adj* dynamisch

dynamite ['daɪnəmaɪt] *n* Dynamit *nt*

dynamo ['daɪnəməu] *n* Dynamo *m*

dyslexia [dɪsˈlɛksɪə] *n* Legasthenie *f*

E, e

E |iː| *n* (*MUS*) E *nt*

each [iːtʃ] *adj* jeder/jede/jedes ♦ *pron* (*ein*) jeder/(eine) jede/(ein) jedes; **~ other** einander, sich; **they have two books ~** sie haben je 2 Bücher

eager ['iːgər] *adj* eifrig

eagle ['iːgl] *n* Adler *m*

ear [ɪər] *n* Ohr *nt*; (*of corn*) Ähre *f*; **~ache** *n* Ohrenschmerzen *pl*; **~drum** *n* Trommelfell *nt*

earl [əːl] *n* Graf *m*

earlier ['əːlɪər] *adj, adv* früher; **I can't come any ~** ich kann nicht früher *or* eher kommen

early ['əːlɪ] *adj, adv* früh; **~ retirement** *n* vorzeitige Pensionierung

earmark ['ɪəmɑːk] *vt* vorsehen

earn [əːn] *vt* verdienen

earnest ['əːnɪst] *adj* ernst; **in ~** im Ernst

earnings ['əːnɪŋz] *npl* Verdienst *m*

ear: **~phones** ['ɪəfəunz] *npl* Kopfhörer *pl*; **~ring** ['ɪərɪŋ] *n* Ohrring *m*; **~shot** ['ɪəʃɔt] *n* Hörweite *f*

earth [əːθ] *n* Erde *f*; (*BRIT: ELEC*) Erdung *f* ♦ *vt* erden; **~enware** *n* Steingut *nt*; **~quake** *n* Erdbeben *nt*; **~y** *adj* roh

earwig [ˈɪəwɪg] n Ohrwurm m
ease [iːz] n (simplicity) Leichtigkeit f; (social) Ungezwungenheit f ♦ vt (pain) lindern; (burden) erleichtern; **at ~** ungezwungen; (MIL) rührt euch!; **~ off** or **up** vi nachlassen
easel [ˈiːzl] n Staffelei f
easily [ˈiːzɪlɪ] adv leicht
east [iːst] n Osten m ♦ adj östlich ♦ adv nach Osten
Easter [ˈiːstər] n Ostern nt; **~ egg** n Osterei nt
east: **~erly** adj östlich, Ost-; **~ern** adj östlich; **~ward(s)** adv ostwärts
easy [ˈiːzɪ] adj (task) einfach; (life) bequem; (manner) ungezwungen, natürlich ♦ adv leicht; **~ chair** n Sessel m; **~-going** adj gelassen; (lax) lässig
eat [iːt] (pt **ate**, pp **eaten**) vt essen; (animals) fressen; (destroy) (zer)fressen ♦ vi essen; fressen; **~ away** vt zerfressen; **~ into** vt fus zerfressen; **~en** pp of **eat**
eau de Cologne [ˈəʊdəkəˈləʊn] n Kölnischwasser nt
eaves [iːvz] npl Dachrand m
eavesdrop [ˈiːvzdrɒp] vi lauschen; **to ~ on sb** jdn belauschen
ebb [ɛb] n Ebbe f ♦ vi (fig: also: **~ away**) (ab)ebben
ebony [ˈɛbənɪ] n Ebenholz nt
EC n abbr (= European Community) EG f
ECB n abbr (= European Central Bank) EZB f
eccentric [ɪkˈsɛntrɪk] adj exzentrisch ♦ n Exzentriker(in) m(f)
ecclesiastical [ɪkliːzɪˈæstɪkl] adj kirchlich
echo [ˈɛkəʊ] (pl **~es**) n Echo nt ♦ vt zurückwerfen; (fig) nachbeten ♦ vi widerhallen
eclipse [ɪˈklɪps] n Finsternis f ♦ vt verfinstern
ecology [ɪˈkɒlədʒɪ] n Ökologie f
e-commerce [ˈiːkɒmɜːs] n (COMPUT) Onlinehandel m
economic [iːkəˈnɒmɪk] adj wirtschaftlich; **~al** adj wirtschaftlich; (person) sparsam; **~ refugee** n Wirtschaftsflüchtling m; **~s** n Volkswirtschaft f
economist [ɪˈkɒnəmɪst] n Volkswirt(schaftler) m
economize [ɪˈkɒnəmaɪz] vi sparen
economy [ɪˈkɒnəmɪ] n (thrift) Sparsamkeit f; (of country) Wirtschaft f; **~ class** n Touristenklasse f
ecstasy [ˈɛkstəsɪ] n Ekstase f; (drug) Ecstasy nt; **ecstatic** [ɛksˈtætɪk] adj hingerissen
ECU [ˈeɪkjuː] n abbr (= European Currency Unit) ECU m
eczema [ˈɛksɪmə] n Ekzem nt
edge [ɛdʒ] n Rand m; (of knife) Schneide f ♦ vt (SEWING) einfassen; **on ~** (fig) = edgy; **to ~ away from** langsam abrücken von; **~ways** adv: **he couldn't get a word in ~ways** er kam überhaupt nicht zu Wort
edgy [ˈɛdʒɪ] adj nervös

edible [ˈɛdɪbl] adj essbar
edict [ˈiːdɪkt] n Erlass m
edit [ˈɛdɪt] vt redigieren; **~ion** [ɪˈdɪʃən] n Ausgabe f; **~or** n (of newspaper) Redakteur m; (of book) Lektor m
editorial [ɛdɪˈtɔːrɪəl] adj Redaktions- ♦ n Leitartikel m
educate [ˈɛdjukeɪt] vt erziehen, (aus)bilden; **~d** adj gebildet; **education** [ɛdjuˈkeɪʃən] n (teaching) Unterricht m; (system) Schulwesen nt; (schooling) Erziehung f; Bildung f; **educational** adj pädagogisch
eel [iːl] n Aal m
eerie [ˈɪərɪ] adj unheimlich
effect [ɪˈfɛkt] n Wirkung f ♦ vt bewirken; **~s** npl (sound, visual) Effekte pl; **in ~** in der Tat; **to take ~** (law) in Kraft treten; (drug) wirken; **~ive** adj wirksam, effektiv; **~ively** adv wirksam, effektiv
effeminate [ɪˈfɛmɪnɪt] adj weibisch
effervescent [ɛfəˈvɛsnt] adj (also fig) sprudelnd
efficiency [ɪˈfɪʃənsɪ] n Leistungsfähigkeit f
efficient [ɪˈfɪʃənt] adj tüchtig; (TECH) leistungsfähig; (method) wirksam
effigy [ˈɛfɪdʒɪ] n Abbild nt
effort [ˈɛfət] n Anstrengung f; **~less** adj mühelos
effusive [ɪˈfjuːsɪv] adj überschwänglich
e.g. adv abbr (= exempli gratia) z. B.
egalitarian [ɪgælɪˈtɛərɪən] adj Gleichheits-, egalitär
egg [ɛg] n Ei nt; **~ on** vt anstacheln; **~cup** n Eierbecher m; **~plant** (esp US) n Aubergine f; **~shell** n Eierschale f
ego [ˈiːgəʊ] n Ich nt, Selbst nt; **~tism** [ˈeɡəʊtɪzəm] n Ichbezogenheit f; **~tist** [ˈɛgəʊtɪst] n Egozentriker m
Egypt [ˈiːdʒɪpt] n Ägypten nt; **~ian** [ɪˈdʒɪpʃən] adj ägyptisch ♦ n Ägypter(in) m(f)
eiderdown [ˈaɪdədaʊn] n Daunendecke f
eight [eɪt] num acht; **~een** num achtzehn; **~h** [eɪtθ] adj achte(r, s) ♦ n Achtel nt; **~y** num achtzig
Eire [ˈɛərə] n Irland nt
either [ˈaɪðər] conj: **~ ... or** entweder ... oder ♦ pron: **~ of the two** eine(r, s) von beiden ♦ adj: **on ~ side** auf beiden Seiten ♦ adv: **I don't ~** ich auch nicht; **I don't want ~** ich will keins von beiden
eject [ɪˈdʒɛkt] vt ausstoßen, vertreiben
eke [iːk] vt: **to ~ out** strecken
elaborate [adj ɪˈlæbərɪt, vb ɪˈlæbəreɪt] adj sorgfältig ausgearbeitet, ausführlich ♦ vt sorgfältig ausarbeiten ♦ vi ausführlich darstellen
elapse [ɪˈlæps] vi vergehen
elastic [ɪˈlæstɪk] n Gummiband nt ♦ adj elastisch; **~ band** (BRIT) n Gummiband nt
elated [ɪˈleɪtɪd] adj froh
elation [ɪˈleɪʃən] n gehobene Stimmung f

elbow ['ɛlbəu] *n* Ellbogen *m*

elder ['ɛldəʳ] *adj* älter ♦ *n* Ältere(r) *f(m)*; **~ly** *adj* ältere(r, s) ♦ *npl*: **the ~ly** die Älteren *pl*; **eldest** ['ɛldɪst] *adj* älteste(r, s) ♦ *n* Älteste(r) *f(m)*

elect [ɪ'lɛkt] *vt* wählen ♦ *adj* zukünftig; **~ion** [ɪ'lɛkʃən] *n* Wahl *f*; **~ioneering** [ɪlɛkʃə'nɪərɪŋ] *n* Wahlpropaganda *f*; **~or** *n* Wähler *m*; **~oral** *adj* Wahl-; **~orate** *n* Wähler *pl*, Wählerschaft *f*

electric [ɪ'lɛktrɪk] *adj* elektrisch, Elektro-; **~al** *adj* elektrisch; **~ blanket** *n* Heizdecke *f*; **~ chair** *n* elektrische(r) Stuhl *m*; **~ fire** *n* elektrische(r) Heizofen *m*

electrician [ɪlɛk'trɪʃən] *n* Elektriker *m*

electricity [ɪlɛk'trɪsɪtɪ] *n* Elektrizität *f*

electrify [ɪ'lɛktrɪfaɪ] *vt* elektrifizieren; *(fig)* elektrisieren

electrocute [ɪ'lɛktrəkjuːt] *vt* durch elektrischen Strom töten

electronic [ɪlɛk'trɔnɪk] *adj* elektronisch, Elektronen-; **~ mail** *n* elektronische(r) Briefkasten *m*; **~s** *n* Elektronik *f*

elegance ['ɛlɪgəns] *n* Eleganz *f*; **elegant** ['ɛlɪgənt] *adj* elegant

element ['ɛlɪmənt] *n* Element *nt*; **~ary** [ɛlɪ'mɛntərɪ] *adj* einfach; *(primary)* Grund-

elephant ['ɛlɪfənt] *n* Elefant *m*

elevate ['ɛlɪveɪt] *vt* emporheben; **elevation** [ɛlɪ'veɪʃən] *n* *(height)* Erhebung *f*; *(ARCHIT)* (Quer)schnitt *m*; **elevator** *(US)* *n* Fahrstuhl *m*, Aufzug *m*

eleven [ɪ'lɛvn] *num* elf *f*; **~ses** *(BRIT)* *npl* ≈ zweite(s) Frühstück *nt*; **~th** *adj* elfte(r, s)

elicit [ɪ'lɪsɪt] *vt* herausbekommen

eligible ['ɛlɪdʒəbl] *adj* wählbar; **to be ~ for a pension** pensionsberechtigt sein

eliminate [ɪ'lɪmɪneɪt] *vt* ausschalten

elite [eɪ'liːt] *n* Elite *f*

elm [ɛlm] *n* Ulme *f*

elocution [ɛlə'kjuːʃən] *n* Sprecherziehung *f*

elongated ['iːlɔŋgeɪtɪd] *adj* verlängert

elope [ɪ'ləup] *vi* entlaufen

eloquence ['ɛləkwəns] *n* Beredsamkeit *f*; **eloquent** *adj* redegewandt

else [ɛls] *adv* sonst; **who ~?** wer sonst?; **somebody ~** jemand anders; **or ~** sonst; **~where** *adv* anderswo, woanders

elude [ɪ'luːd] *vt* entgehen +*dat*

elusive [ɪ'luːsɪv] *adj* schwer fassbar

emaciated [ɪ'meɪsɪeɪtɪd] *adj* abgezehrt

E-mail ['iːmeɪl] *n abbr* (= *electronic mail*) E-Mail *f*

emancipation [ɪmænsɪ'peɪʃən] *n* Emanzipation *f*; Freilassung *f*

embankment [ɪm'bæŋkmənt] *n* *(of river)* Uferböschung *f*; *(of road)* Straßendamm *m*

embargo [ɪm'baːgəu] *(pl* **~es**) *n* Embargo *nt*

embark [ɪm'baːk] *vi* sich einschiffen; **~ on** *vt fus* unternehmen; **~ation** [ɛmbaː'keɪʃən] *n* Einschiffung *f*

embarrass [ɪm'bærəs] *vt* in Verlegenheit bringen; **~ed** *adj* verlegen; **~ing** *adj* peinlich; **~ment** *n* Verlegenheit *f*

embassy ['ɛmbəsɪ] *n* Botschaft *f*

embed [ɪm'bɛd] *vt* einbetten

embellish [ɪm'bɛlɪʃ] *vt* verschönern

embers ['ɛmbəz] *npl* Glut(asche) *f*

embezzle [ɪm'bɛzl] *vt* unterschlagen; **~ment** *n* Unterschlagung *f*

embitter [ɪm'bɪtəʳ] *vt* verbittern

embody [ɪm'bɔdɪ] *vt* *(ideas)* verkörpern; *(new features)* (in sich) vereinigen

embossed [ɪm'bɔst] *adj* geprägt

embrace [ɪm'breɪs] *vt* umarmen; *(include)* einschließen ♦ *vi* sich umarmen ♦ *n* Umarmung *f*

embroider [ɪm'brɔɪdəʳ] *vt* (be)sticken; *(story)* ausschmücken; **~y** *n* Stickerei *f*

emerald ['ɛmərəld] *n* Smaragd *m*

emerge [ɪ'məːdʒ] *vi* auftauchen; *(truth)* herauskommen; **~nce** *n* Erscheinen *nt*

emergency [ɪ'məːdʒənsɪ] *n* Notfall *m*; **~ cord** *(US)* *n* Notbremse *f*; **~ exit** *n* Notausgang *m*; **~ landing** *n* Notlandung *f*; **~ services** *npl* Notdienste *pl*

emery board ['ɛmərɪ-] *n* Papiernagelfeile *f*

emigrant ['ɛmɪgrənt] *n* Auswanderer *m*

emigrate ['ɛmɪgreɪt] *vi* auswandern; **emigration** [ɛmɪ'greɪʃən] *n* Auswanderung *f*

eminence ['ɛmɪnəns] *n* hohe(r) Rang *m*

eminent ['ɛmɪnənt] *adj* bedeutend

emission [ɪ'mɪʃən] *n* Ausströmen *nt*; **~s** *npl* Emissionen *fpl*

emit [ɪ'mɪt] *vt* von sich *dat* geben

emotion [ɪ'məuʃən] *n* Emotion *f*, Gefühl *nt*; **~al** *adj* *(person)* emotional; *(scene)* ergreifend

emotive [ɪ'məutɪv] *adj* gefühlsbetont

emperor ['ɛmpərəʳ] *n* Kaiser *m*

emphases ['ɛmfəsiːz] *npl of* **emphasis**

emphasis ['ɛmfəsɪs] *n* *(LING)* Betonung *f*; *(fig)* Nachdruck *m*; **emphasize** ['ɛmfəsaɪz] *vt* betonen

emphatic [ɛm'fætɪk] *adj* nachdrücklich; **~ally** *adv* nachdrücklich

empire ['ɛmpaɪəʳ] *n* Reich *nt*

empirical [ɛm'pɪrɪkl] *adj* empirisch

employ [ɪm'plɔɪ] *vt* *(hire)* anstellen; *(use)* verwenden; **~ee** [ɪmplɔɪ'iː] *n* Angestellte(r) *f(m)*; **~er** *n* Arbeitgeber(in) *m(f)*; **~ment** *n* Beschäftigung *f*; **~ment agency** *n* Stellenvermittlung *f*

empower [ɪm'pauəʳ] *vt*: **to ~ sb to do sth** jdn ermächtigen, etw zu tun

empress ['ɛmprɪs] *n* Kaiserin *f*

emptiness ['ɛmptɪnɪs] *n* Leere *f*

empty ['ɛmptɪ] *adj* leer ♦ *n* *(bottle)* Leergut *nt* ♦ *vt* *(contents)* leeren; *(container)* ausleeren ♦ *vi* *(water)* abfließen; *(river)* münden; *(house)* sich leeren; **~-handed** *adj* mit leeren Händen

EMU ['iːmjuː] *n abbr* (= *European monetary union*) EWU *f*

emulate ['emjuleɪt] *vt* nacheifern +*dat*

emulsion [ɪ'mʌlʃən] *n* Emulsion *f*

enable [ɪ'neɪbl] *vt*: **to ~ sb to do sth** es jdm ermöglichen, etw zu tun

enact [ɪ'nækt] *vt* (*law*) erlassen; (*play*) aufführen; (*role*) spielen

enamel [ɪ'næməl] *n* Email *nt*; (*of teeth*) (Zahn)schmelz *m*

encased [ɪn'keɪst] *adj*: **~ in** (*enclosed*) eingeschlossen in +*dat*; (*covered*) verkleidet mit

enchant [ɪn'tʃɑːnt] *vt* bezaubern; **~ing** *adj* entzückend

encircle [ɪn'sɜːkl] *vt* umringen

encl. *abbr* (= *enclosed*) Anl.

enclose [ɪn'kləʊz] *vt* einschließen; **to ~ sth** (**in** *or* **with a letter**) etw (einem Brief) beilegen; **~d** (*in letter*) beiliegend, anbei; **enclosure** [ɪn'kləʊʒəʳ] *n* Einfriedung *f*; (*in letter*) Anlage *f*

encompass [ɪn'kʌmpəs] *vt* (*include*) umfassen

encore [ɒŋ'kɔːʳ] *n* Zugabe *f*

encounter [ɪn'kaʊntəʳ] *n* Begegnung *f*; (*MIL*) Zusammenstoß *m* ♦ *vt* treffen; (*resistance*) stoßen auf +*acc*

encourage [ɪn'kʌrɪdʒ] *vt* ermutigen; **~ment** *n* Ermutigung *f*, Förderung *f*; **encouraging** *adj* ermutigend, viel versprechend

encroach [ɪn'krəʊtʃ] *vi*: **to ~ (up)on** eindringen in +*acc*; (*time*) in Anspruch nehmen

encrusted [ɪn'krʌstɪd] *adj*: **~ with** besetzt mit

encyclop(a)edia [ensaɪkləʊ'piːdɪə] *n* Konversationslexikon *nt*

end [end] *n* Ende *nt*, Schluss *m*; (*purpose*) Zweck *m* ♦ *vt* (*also*: **bring to an ~, put an ~ to**) beenden ♦ *vi* zu Ende gehen; **in the ~** zum Schluss; **on ~** (*object*) hochkant; **to stand on ~** (*hair*) zu Berge stehen; **for hours on ~** stundenlang; **~ up** *vi* landen

endanger [ɪn'deɪndʒəʳ] *vt* gefährden; **~ed species** *n* eine vom Aussterben bedrohte Art

endearing [ɪn'dɪərɪŋ] *adj* gewinnend

endeavour [ɪn'devəʳ] (*US* **endeavor**) *n* Bestrebung *f* ♦ *vi* sich bemühen

ending ['endɪŋ] *n* Ende *nt*

endless ['endlɪs] *adj* endlos

endorse [ɪn'dɔːs] *vt* unterzeichnen; (*approve*) unterstützen; **~ment** *n* (*AUT*) Eintrag *m*

endow [ɪn'daʊ] *vt*: **to ~ sb with sth** jdm etw verleihen; (*with money*) jdm etw stiften

endurance [ɪn'djʊərəns] *n* Ausdauer *f*

endure [ɪn'djʊəʳ] *vt* ertragen ♦ *vi* (*last*) (fort)dauern

enemy ['enəmɪ] *n* Feind *m* ♦ *adj* feindlich

energetic [enə'dʒetɪk] *adj* tatkräftig

energy ['enədʒɪ] *n* Energie *f*

enforce [ɪn'fɔːs] *vt* durchsetzen

engage [ɪn'geɪdʒ] *vt* (*employ*) einstellen; (*in conversation*) verwickeln; (*TECH*) einschalten ♦ *vi* (*TECH*) ineinander greifen; (*clutch*) fassen; **to ~ in** sich beteiligen an +*dat*; **~d** *adj* verlobt; (*BRIT*: *TEL, toilet*) besetzt; (: *busy*) beschäftigt; **to get ~d** sich verloben; **~d tone** (*BRIT*) *n* (*TEL*) Besetztzeichen *nt*; **~ment** *n* (*appointment*) Verabredung *f*; (*to marry*) Verlobung *f*; (*MIL*) Gefecht *nt*; **~ment ring** *n* Verlobungsring *m*; **engaging** *adj* gewinnend

engender [ɪn'dʒendəʳ] *vt* hervorrufen

engine ['endʒɪn] *n* (*AUT*) Motor *m*; (*RAIL*) Lokomotive *f*; **~ driver** *n* Lok(omotiv)führer(in) *m(f)*

engineer [endʒɪ'nɪəʳ] *n* Ingenieur *m*; (*US*: *RAIL*) Lok(omotiv)führer(in) *m(f)*; **~ing** [endʒɪ'nɪərɪŋ] *n* Technik *f*

England ['ɪŋɡlənd] *n* England *nt*

English ['ɪŋɡlɪʃ] *adj* englisch ♦ *n* (*LING*) Englisch *nt*; **the ~** *npl* (*people*) die Engländer *pl*; **~ Channel** *n*: **the ~ Channel** der Ärmelkanal *m*; **~man/woman** (*irreg*) *n* Engländer(in) *m(f)*

engraving [ɪn'ɡreɪvɪŋ] *n* Stich *m*

engrossed [ɪn'ɡrəʊst] *adj* vertieft

engulf [ɪn'ɡʌlf] *vt* verschlingen

enhance [ɪn'hɑːns] *vt* steigern, heben

enigma [ɪ'nɪɡmə] *n* Rätsel *nt*; **~tic** [enɪɡ'mætɪk] *adj* rätselhaft

enjoy [ɪn'dʒɔɪ] *vt* genießen; (*privilege*) besitzen; **to ~ o.s.** sich amüsieren; **~able** *adj* erfreulich; **~ment** *n* Genuss *m*, Freude *f*

enlarge [ɪn'lɑːdʒ] *vt* erweitern; (*PHOT*) vergrößern ♦ *vi*: **to ~ on sth** etw weiter ausführen; **~ment** *n* Vergrößerung *f*

enlighten [ɪn'laɪtn] *vt* aufklären; **~ment** *n*: **the E~ment** (*HIST*) die Aufklärung

enlist [ɪn'lɪst] *vt* gewinnen ♦ *vi* (*MIL*) sich melden

enmity ['enmɪtɪ] *n* Feindschaft *f*

enormity [ɪ'nɔːmɪtɪ] *n* Ungeheuerlichkeit *f*

enormous [ɪ'nɔːməs] *adj* ungeheuer

enough [ɪ'nʌf] *adj, adv* genug; **funnily ~** komischerweise

enquire [ɪn'kwaɪəʳ] *vt, vi* = **inquire**

enrage [ɪn'reɪdʒ] *vt* wütend machen

enrich [ɪn'rɪtʃ] *vt* bereichern

enrol [ɪn'rəʊl] *vt* einschreiben ♦ *vi* (*register*) sich anmelden; **~ment** *n* (*for course*) Anmeldung *f*

en route [ɒn'ruːt] *adv* unterwegs

ensign ['ensaɪn, 'ensən] *n* (*NAUT*) Flagge *f*; (*MIL*) Fähnrich *m*

enslave [ɪn'sleɪv] *vt* versklaven

ensue [ɪn'sjuː] *vi* folgen, sich ergeben

en suite [ɒnswiːt] *adj*: **room with ~ bathroom** Zimmer *nt* mit eigenem Bad

ensure [ɪn'ʃʊəʳ] *vt* garantieren

entail |ɪnˈteɪl| vt mit sich bringen
entangle |ɪnˈtæŋgl| vt verwirren, verstricken;
~**d** adj: **to become ~d (in)** (in net, rope etc)
sich verfangen (in +dat)
enter |ˈentə^r| vt eintreten in +dat, betreten;
(club) beitreten +dat; (in book) eintragen
♦ vi hereinkommen, hineingehen; ~ **for** vt
fus sich beteiligen an +dat; ~ **into** vt fus
(agreement) eingehen; (plans) eine Rolle
spielen bei; ~ **(up)on** vt fus beginnen
enterprise |ˈentəpraɪz| n (in person) Initiative
f; (COMM) Unternehmen nt; **enterprising**
|ˈentəpraɪzɪŋ| adj unternehmungslustig
entertain |entəˈteɪn| vt (guest) bewirten;
(amuse) unterhalten; ~**er** n
Unterhaltungskünstler(in) m(f); ~**ing** adj
unterhaltsam; ~**ment** n Unterhaltung f
enthralled |ɪnˈθrɔːld| adj gefesselt
enthusiasm |ɪnˈθuːzɪæzəm| n Begeisterung f
enthusiast |ɪnˈθuːzɪæst| n Enthusiast m; ~**ic**
|ɪnθuːzɪˈæstɪk| adj begeistert
entice |ɪnˈtaɪs| vt verleiten, locken
entire |ɪnˈtaɪə^r| adj ganz; ~**ly** adv ganz,
völlig; ~**ty** |ɪnˈtaɪərəti| n: **in its ~ty** in seiner
Gesamtheit
entitle |ɪnˈtaɪtl| vt (allow) berechtigen;
(name) betiteln; ~**d** adj (book) mit dem
Titel; **to be ~d to sth** das Recht auf etw acc
haben; **to be ~d to do sth** das Recht haben,
etw zu tun
entity |ˈentɪti| n Ding nt, Wesen nt
entourage |ɒntuˈrɑːʒ| n Gefolge nt
entrails |ˈentreɪlz| npl Eingeweide pl
entrance |n ˈentrns, vb ɪnˈtrɑːns| n Eingang
m; (entering) Eintritt m ♦ vt hinreißen; ~
examination n Aufnahmeprüfung f; ~ **fee**
n Eintrittsgeld nt; ~ **ramp** (US) n (AUT)
Einfahrt f
entrant |ˈentrnt| n (for exam) Kandidat m; (in
race) Teilnehmer m
entreat |enˈtriːt| vt anflehen
entrenched |enˈtrentʃt| adj (fig) verwurzelt
entrepreneur |ɒntrəprəˈnəː^r| n
Unternehmer(in) m(f)
entrust |ɪnˈtrʌst| vt: **to ~ sb with sth** or **sth**
to sb jdm etw anvertrauen
entry |ˈentrɪ| n Eingang m; (THEAT) Auftritt m;
(in account) Eintragung f; (in dictionary)
Eintrag m; "**no ~**" „Eintritt verboten"; (for
cars) „Einfahrt verboten"; ~ **form** n
Anmeldeformular nt; ~ **phone** n
Sprechanlage f
enumerate |ɪˈnjuːməreɪt| vt aufzählen
enunciate |ɪˈnʌnsɪeɪt| vt aussprechen
envelop |ɪnˈveləp| vt einhüllen
envelope |ˈenvələʊp| n Umschlag m
enviable |ˈenvɪəbl| adj beneidenswert
envious |ˈenvɪəs| adj neidisch
environment |ɪnˈvaɪərnmənt| n Umgebung
f; (ECOLOGY) Umwelt f; ~**al** |ɪnvaɪərnˈmentl|
adj Umwelt-; ~-**friendly** adj

umweltfreundlich
envisage |ɪnˈvɪzɪdʒ| vt sich dat vorstellen
envoy |ˈenvɔɪ| n Gesandte(r) mf
envy |ˈenvɪ| n Neid m ♦ vt: **to ~ sb sth** jdn
um etw beneiden
enzyme |ˈenzaɪm| n Enzym nt
epic |ˈepɪk| n Epos nt ♦ adj episch
epidemic |epɪˈdemɪk| n Epidemie f
epilepsy |ˈepɪlepsɪ| n Epilepsie f; **epileptic**
|epɪˈleptɪk| adj epileptisch ♦ n
Epileptiker(in) m(f)
episode |ˈepɪsəʊd| n (incident) Vorfall m;
(story) Episode f
epitaph |ˈepɪtɑːf| n Grabinschrift f
epithet |ˈepɪθet| n Beiname m
epitome |ɪˈpɪtəmɪ| n Inbegriff m
epitomize |ɪˈpɪtəmaɪz| vt verkörpern
equable |ˈekwəbl| adj ausgeglichen
equal |ˈiːkwl| adj gleich ♦ n Gleichgestellte(r)
mf ♦ vt gleichkommen +dat; ~ **to the task**
der Aufgabe gewachsen; ~**ity** |iːˈkwɔlɪti| n
Gleichheit f; (equal rights)
Gleichberechtigung f; ~**ize** vt gleichmachen
♦ vi (SPORT) ausgleichen; ~**izer** n (SPORT)
Ausgleich(streffer) m; ~**ly** adv gleich
equanimity |ekwəˈnɪmɪtɪ| n Gleichmut m
equate |ɪˈkweɪt| vt gleichsetzen
equation |ɪˈkweɪʒən| n Gleichung f
equator |ɪˈkweɪtə^r| n Äquator m
equestrian |ɪˈkwestrɪən| adj Reit-
equilibrium |iːkwɪˈlɪbrɪəm| n Gleichgewicht
nt
equinox |ˈiːkwɪnɔks| n Tagundnachtgleiche f
equip |ɪˈkwɪp| vt ausrüsten; **to be well ~ped**
gut ausgerüstet sein; ~**ment** n Ausrüstung f;
(TECH) Gerät nt
equitable |ˈekwɪtəbl| adj gerecht, billig
equities |ˈekwɪtɪz| (BRIT) npl (FIN)
Stammaktien pl
equivalent |ɪˈkwɪvələnt| adj gleichwertig,
entsprechend ♦ n Äquivalent nt; (in money)
Gegenwert m; ~ **to** gleichwertig +dat,
entsprechend +dat
equivocal |ɪˈkwɪvəkl| adj zweideutig
era |ˈɪərə| n Epoche f, Ära f
eradicate |ɪˈrædɪkeɪt| vt ausrotten
erase |ɪˈreɪz| vt ausradieren; (tape) löschen;
~**r** n Radiergummi m
erect |ɪˈrekt| adj aufrecht ♦ vt errichten; ~**ion**
|ɪˈrekʃn| n Errichtung f; (ANAT) Erektion f
ERM n abbr (= Exchange Rate Mechanism)
Wechselkursmechanismus m
erode |ɪˈrəʊd| vt zerfressen; (land)
auswaschen
erotic |ɪˈrɔtɪk| adj erotisch
err |əː^r| vi sich irren
errand |ˈerənd| n Besorgung f
erratic |ɪˈrætɪk| adj unberechenbar
erroneous |ɪˈrəʊnɪəs| adj irrig
error |ˈerə^r| n Fehler m
erupt |ɪˈrʌpt| vi ausbrechen; ~**ion** |ɪˈrʌpʃən| n

Ausbruch m

escalate [ˈɛskəleɪt] vi sich steigern

escalator [ˈɛskəleɪtəʳ] n Rolltreppe f

escape [ɪsˈkeɪp] n Flucht f; (of gas)
Entweichen nt ♦ vi entkommen; (prisoners)
fliehen; (leak) entweichen ♦ vt entkommen
+dat; **escapism** n Flucht f (vor der
Wirklichkeit)

escort [n ˈeskɔːt, vb ɪsˈkɔːt] n (person
accompanying) Begleiter m; (guard) Eskorte f
♦ vt (lady) begleiten; (MIL) eskortieren

Eskimo [ˈeskɪməu] n Eskimo(frau) m(f)

especially [ɪsˈpeʃlɪ] adv besonders

espionage [ˈespɪɔnɑːʒ] n Spionage f

esplanade [esplaˈneɪd] n Promenade f

Esquire [ɪsˈkwaɪəʳ] n: J. Brown ~ Herrn
J. Brown

essay [ˈeseɪ] n Aufsatz m; (LITER) Essay m

essence [ˈesns] n (quality) Wesen nt;
(extract) Essenz f

essential [ɪˈsenʃl] adj (necessary)
unentbehrlich; (basic) wesentlich ♦ n
Allernötigste(s) nt; ~**ly** adv eigentlich

establish [ɪsˈtæblɪʃ] vt (set up) gründen;
(prove) nachweisen; ~**ed** adj anerkannt;
(belief, laws etc) herrschend; ~**ment** n
(setting up) Einrichtung f

estate [ɪsˈteɪt] n Gut nt; (BRIT: housing ~)
Siedlung f; (will) Nachlass m; ~ **agent** (BRIT)
n Grundstücksmakler m; ~ **car** (BRIT) n
Kombiwagen m

esteem [ɪsˈtiːm] n Wertschätzung f

esthetic [ɪsˈθetɪk] (US) adj = **aesthetic**

estimate [n ˈestɪmət, vb ˈestɪmeɪt] n
Schätzung f; (of price) (Kosten)voranschlag
m ♦ vt schätzen; **estimation** [estɪˈmeɪʃən] n
Einschätzung f; (esteem) Achtung f

estranged [ɪsˈtreɪndʒd] adj entfremdet

estuary [ˈestjuərɪ] n Mündung f

etc abbr (= et cetera) usw.

etching [ˈetʃɪŋ] n Kupferstich m

eternal [ɪˈtəːnl] adj ewig

eternity [ɪˈtəːnɪtɪ] n Ewigkeit f

ether [ˈiːθəʳ] n Äther m

ethical [ˈeθɪkl] adj ethisch

ethics [ˈeθɪks] n Ethik f ♦ npl Moral f

Ethiopia [iːθɪˈəupɪə] n Äthiopien nt

ethnic [ˈeθnɪk] adj Volks-, ethnisch; ~
minority n ethnische Minderheit f

ethos [ˈiːθɔs] n Gesinnung f

etiquette [ˈetɪket] n Etikette f

EU abbr (= European Union) EU f

euphemism [ˈjuːfəmɪzəm] n Euphemismus
m

euro [ˈjuərəu] n Euro m

Eurocheque [ˈjuərəutʃek] n Euroscheck m

Euroland [ˈjuərəlænd] n Eurozone f, Euroland
nt

Europe [ˈjuərəp] n Europa nt; ~**an**
[juərəˈpiːən] adj europäisch ♦ n
Europäer(in) m(f); ~**an Community** n: the

~**an Community** die Europäische
Gemeinschaft

Euro-sceptic [ˈjuərəuskeptɪk] n Kritiker der
~~Europäischen Gemeinschaft~~

evacuate [ɪˈvækjueɪt] vt (place) räumen;
(people) evakuieren; **evacuation**
[ɪvækjuˈeɪʃən] n Räumung f; Evakuierung f

evade [ɪˈveɪd] vt (escape) entkommen +dat;
(avoid) meiden; (duty) sich entziehen +dat

evaluate [ɪˈvæljueɪt] vt bewerten;
(information) auswerten

evaporate [ɪˈvæpəreɪt] vi verdampfen
♦ vt verdampfen lassen; ~**d milk** n
Kondensmilch f

evasion [ɪˈveɪʒən] n Umgehung f

evasive [ɪˈveɪsɪv] adj ausweichend

eve [iːv] n: on the ~ of am Vorabend +gen

even [ˈiːvn] adj eben; gleichmäßig; (score etc)
unentschieden; (number) gerade ♦ adv: ~
you sogar du; to get ~ with sb jdm
heimzahlen; ~ if selbst wenn; ~ so dennoch;
~ though obwohl; ~ more sogar noch
mehr; ~ out vi sich ausgleichen

evening [ˈiːvnɪŋ] n Abend m; in the ~
abends, am Abend; ~ **class** n Abendschule
f; ~ **dress** n (man's) Gesellschaftsanzug m;
(woman's) Abendkleid nt

event [ɪˈvent] n (happening) Ereignis nt;
(SPORT) Disziplin f; in the ~ of im Falle
+gen; ~**ful** adj ereignisreich

eventual [ɪˈventʃuəl] adj (final) schließlich;
~**ity** [ɪventʃuˈælɪtɪ] n Möglichkeit f; ~**ly** adv
am Ende; (given time) schließlich

ever [ˈevəʳ] adv (always) immer; (at any time)
je(mals) ♦ conj seit; ~ **since** seitdem; **have
you ~ seen it?** haben Sie es je gesehen?;
~**green** n Immergrün nt; ~**lasting** adj
immer während

every [ˈevrɪ] adj jede(r, s); ~ **other/third day**
jeden zweiten/dritten Tag; ~ **one of them**
alle; **I have ~ confidence in him** ich habe
uneingeschränktes Vertrauen in ihn; **we
wish you ~ success** wir wünschen Ihnen
viel Erfolg; **he's ~ bit as clever as his
brother** er ist genauso klug wie sein Bruder;
~ **now and then** ab und zu; ~**body** pron =
everyone; ~**day** adj (daily) täglich;
(commonplace) alltäglich, Alltags-; ~**one**
pron jeder, alle pl; ~**thing** pron alles;
~**where** adv überall(hin); (wherever) wohin;
~**where you go** wohin du auch gehst

evict [ɪˈvɪkt] vt ausweisen; ~**ion** [ɪˈvɪkʃən] n
Ausweisung f

evidence [ˈevɪdns] n (sign) Spur f; (proof)
Beweis m; (testimony) Aussage f

evident [ˈevɪdnt] adj augenscheinlich; ~**ly**
adv offensichtlich

evil [ˈiːvl] adj böse ♦ n Böse nt

evocative [ɪˈvɔkətɪv] adj: to be ~ of sth an
etw acc erinnern

evoke [ɪˈvəuk] vt hervorrufen

evolution |iːvəˈluːʃən| n Entwicklung f; (of life) Evolution f

evolve |ɪˈvɒlv| vt entwickeln ♦ vi sich entwickeln

ewe |juː| n Mutterschaf nt

ex- |ɛks| prefix Ex-, Alt-, ehemalig

exacerbate |ɛksˈæsəbeɪt| vt verschlimmern

exact |ɪgˈzækt| adj genau ♦ vt (demand) verlangen; **~ing** adj anspruchsvoll; **~ly** adv genau

exaggerate |ɪgˈzædʒəreɪt| vt, vi übertreiben; **exaggeration** |ɪgzædʒəˈreɪʃən| n Übertreibung f

exalted |ɪgˈzɔːltɪd| adj (position, style) hoch; (person) exaltiert

exam |ɪgˈzæm| n abbr (SCH) = examination

examination |ɪgzæmɪˈneɪʃən| n Untersuchung f; (SCH) Prüfung f, Examen nt; (customs) Kontrolle f

examine |ɪgˈzæmɪn| vt untersuchen; (SCH) prüfen; (consider) erwägen; **~r** n Prüfer m

example |ɪgˈzaːmpl| n Beispiel nt; **for ~** zum Beispiel

exasperate |ɪgˈzaːspəreɪt| vt zur Verzweiflung bringen; **exasperating** adj ärgerlich, zum Verzweifeln bringend; **exasperation** |ɪgzaːspəˈreɪʃən| n Verzweiflung f

excavate |ˈɛkskəveɪt| vt ausgraben; **excavation** |ɛkskəˈveɪʃən| n Ausgrabung f

exceed |ɪkˈsiːd| vt überschreiten; (hopes) übertreffen; **~ingly** adv äußerst

excel |ɪkˈsɛl| vi sich auszeichnen; **~lence** |ˈɛksələns| n Vortrefflichkeit f; **E~lency** n; **His E~lency** Seine Exzellenz f; **~lent** |ˈɛksələnt| adj ausgezeichnet

except |ɪkˈsɛpt| prep (also: ~ for, ~ing) außer +dat ♦ vt ausnehmen; **~ion** |ɪkˈsɛpʃən| n Ausnahme f; **to take ~ion to** Anstoß nehmen an +dat; **~ional** |ɪkˈsɛpʃənl| adj außergewöhnlich

excerpt |ˈɛksɜːpt| n Auszug m

excess |ɪkˈsɛs| n Übermaß nt; **an ~ of** ein Übermaß an +dat; **~ baggage** n Mehrgepäck nt; **~ fare** n Nachlösegebühr f; **~ive** adj übermäßig

exchange |ɪksˈtʃeɪndʒ| n Austausch m; (also: **telephone ~**) Zentrale f ♦ vt (goods) tauschen; (greetings) austauschen; (money, blows) wechseln; **~ rate** n Wechselkurs m

Exchequer |ɪksˈtʃɛkəˈ| (BRIT) n: **the ~** das Schatzamt

excise |ˈɛksaɪz| n Verbrauchssteuer f

excite |ɪkˈsaɪt| vt erregen; **to get ~d** sich aufregen; **~ment** n Aufregung f; **exciting** adj spannend

exclaim |ɪksˈkleɪm| vi ausrufen

exclamation |ɛkskləˈmeɪʃən| n Ausruf m; **~ mark** n Ausrufezeichen nt

exclude |ɪksˈkluːd| vt ausschließen

exclusion |ɪksˈkluːʒən| n Ausschluss m; **~**

zone n Sperrzone f

exclusive |ɪksˈkluːsɪv| adj (select) exklusiv; (sole) ausschließlich, Allein-; **~ of** exklusive +gen; **~ly** adv nur, ausschließlich

excommunicate |ɛkskəˈmjuːnɪkeɪt| vt exkommunizieren

excrement |ˈɛkskrəmənt| n Kot m

excruciating |ɪksˈkruːʃɪeɪtɪŋ| adj qualvoll

excursion |ɪksˈkəːʃən| n Ausflug m

excusable |ɪksˈkjuːzəbl| adj entschuldbar

excuse |n ɪksˈkjuːs, vb ɪksˈkjuːz| n Entschuldigung f ♦ vt entschuldigen; **~ me!** entschuldigen Sie!

ex-directory |ˈɛksdɪˈrɛktərɪ| (BRIT) adj: **to be ~** nicht im Telefonbuch stehen

execute |ˈɛksɪkjuːt| vt (carry out) ausführen; (kill) hinrichten; **execution** |ɛksɪˈkjuːʃən| n Ausführung f; (killing) Hinrichtung f; **executioner** |ɛksɪˈkjuːʃnəˈ| n Scharfrichter m

executive |ɪgˈzɛkjutɪv| n (COMM) Geschäftsführer m; (POL) Exekutive f ♦ adj Exekutiv-, ausführend

executor |ɪgˈzɛkjutəˈ| n Testamentsvollstrecker m

exemplary |ɪgˈzɛmplərɪ| adj musterhaft

exemplify |ɪgˈzɛmplɪfaɪ| vt veranschaulichen

exempt |ɪgˈzɛmpt| adj befreit ♦ vt befreien; **~ion** |ɪgˈzɛmpʃən| n Befreiung f

exercise |ˈɛksəsaɪz| n Übung f ♦ vt (power) ausüben; (muscle, patience) üben; (dog) ausführen ♦ vi Sport treiben; **~ bike** n Heimtrainer m; **~ book** n (Schul)heft nt

exert |ɪgˈzəːt| vt (influence) ausüben; **to ~ o.s.** sich anstrengen; **~ion** |ɪgˈzəːʃən| n Anstrengung f

exhale |ɛksˈheɪl| vt, vi ausatmen

exhaust |ɪgˈzɔːst| n (fumes) Abgase pl; (pipe) Auspuffrohr nt ♦ vt erschöpfen; **~ed** adj erschöpft; **~ion** |ɪgˈzɔːstʃən| n Erschöpfung f; **~ive** adj erschöpfend

exhibit |ɪgˈzɪbɪt| n (JUR) Beweisstück nt; (ART) Ausstellungsstück nt ♦ vt ausstellen; **~ion** |ɛksɪˈbɪʃən| n (ART) Ausstellung f; (of temper etc) Zurschaustellung f; **~ionist** |ɛksɪˈbɪʃənɪst| n Exhibitionist m

exhilarating |ɪgˈzɪləreɪtɪŋ| adj erhebend

ex-husband n Ehemann m

exile |ˈɛksaɪl| n Exil nt; (person) Verbannte(r) f(m) ♦ vt verbannen

exist |ɪgˈzɪst| vi existieren; **~ence** n Existenz f; **~ing** adj bestehend

exit |ˈɛksɪt| n Ausgang m; (THEAT) Abgang m ♦ vi (THEAT) abtreten; (COMPUT) aus einem Programm herausgehen; **~ poll** n bei Wahlen unmittelbar nach Verlassen der Wahllokale durchgeführte Umfrage; **~ ramp** (US) n (AUT) Ausfahrt f

exodus |ˈɛksədəs| n Auszug m

exonerate |ɪgˈzɒnəreɪt| vt entlasten

exorbitant |ɪgˈzɔːbɪtnt| adj übermäßig;

(*price*) Fantasie-
exotic [ɪɡ'zɒtɪk] *adj* exotisch
expand [ɪks'pænd] *vt* ausdehnen ♦ *vi* sich ausdehnen

expanse [ɪks'pæns] *n* Fläche *f*
expansion [ɪks'pænʃən] *n* Erweiterung *f*
expatriate [eks'pætrɪət] *n* Ausländer(in) *m(f)*
expect [ɪks'pɛkt] *vt* erwarten; (*suppose*) annehmen ♦ *vi*: **to be ~ing** ein Kind erwarten; **~ancy** *n* Erwartung *f*; **~ant mother** *n* werdende Mutter *f*; **~ation** [ɛkspɛk'teɪʃən] *n* Hoffnung *f*
expedient [ɪks'piːdɪənt] *adj* zweckdienlich ♦ *n* (Hilfs)mittel *nt*
expedition [ɛkspə'dɪʃən] *n* Expedition *f*
expel [ɪks'pɛl] *vt* ausweisen; (*student*) (ver)weisen
expend [ɪks'pɛnd] *vt* (*effort*) aufwenden; **~iture** *n* Ausgaben *pl*
expense [ɪks'pɛns] *n* Kosten *pl*; **~s** *npl* (COMM) Spesen *pl*; **at the ~ of** auf Kosten von; **~ account** *n* Spesenkonto *nt*; **expensive** [ɪks'pɛnsɪv] *adj* teuer
experience [ɪks'pɪərɪəns] *n* (*incident*) Erlebnis *nt*; (*practice*) Erfahrung *f* ♦ *vt* erleben; **~d** *adj* erfahren
experiment [ɪks'pɛrɪmənt] *n* Versuch *m*, Experiment *nt* ♦ *vi* experimentieren; **~al** [ɪkspɛrɪ'mɛntl] *adj* experimentell
expert ['ɛkspɜːt] *n* Fachmann *m*; (*official*) Sachverständige(r) *m* ♦ *adj* erfahren; **~ise** [ɛkspɜː'tiːz] *n* Sachkenntnis *f*
expire [ɪks'paɪər] *vi* (*end*) ablaufen; (*ticket*) verfallen; (*die*) sterben; **expiry** *n* Ablauf *m*
explain [ɪks'pleɪn] *vt* erklären
explanation [ɛksplə'neɪʃən] *n* Erklärung *f*; **explanatory** [ɪks'plænətrɪ] *adj* erklärend
explicit [ɪks'plɪsɪt] *adj* ausdrücklich
explode [ɪks'pləʊd] *vi* explodieren ♦ *vt* (*bomb*) sprengen
exploit [*n* 'ɛksplɔɪt, *vb* ɪks'plɔɪt] *n* (Helden)tat *f* ♦ *vt* ausbeuten; **~ation** [ɛksplɔɪ'teɪʃən] *n* Ausbeutung *f*
exploration [ɛksplə'reɪʃən] *n* Erforschung *f*
exploratory [ɪks'plɔrətrɪ] *adj* Probe-
explore [ɪks'plɔːr] *vt* (*travel*) erforschen; (*search*) untersuchen; **~r** *n* Erforscher(in) *m(f)*
explosion [ɪks'pləʊʒən] *n* Explosion *f*; (*fig*) Ausbruch *m*
explosive [ɪks'pləʊsɪv] *adj* explosiv, Spreng- ♦ *n* Sprengstoff *m*
export [*vb* ɛks'pɔːt, *n* 'ɛkspɔːt] *vt* exportieren ♦ *n* Export *m* ♦ *cpd* (*trade*) Export-; **~er** [ɛks'pɔːtər] *n* Exporteur *m*
expose [ɪks'pəʊz] *vt* (*to danger etc*) aussetzen; (*impostor*) entlarven; **to ~ sb to sth** jdn einer Sache *dat* aussetzen; **~d** *adj* (*position*) exponiert; **exposure** [ɪks'pəʊʒər] *n* (MED) Unterkühlung *f*; (PHOT) Belichtung *f*; **exposure meter** *n* Belichtungsmesser *m*

express [ɪks'prɛs] *adj* ausdrücklich; (*speedy*) Express-, Eil- ♦ *n* (RAIL) Schnellzug *m* ♦ *adv* (*send*) per Express ♦ *vt* ausdrücken; **to ~ o.s.** sich ausdrücken; **~ion** [ɪks'prɛʃən] *n* Ausdruck *m*; **~ive** *adj* ausdrucksvoll; **~ly** *adv* ausdrücklich; **~way** (US) *n* (*urban motorway*) Schnellstraße *f*
expulsion [ɪks'pʌlʃən] *n* Ausweisung *f*
exquisite [ɛks'kwɪzɪt] *adj* erlesen
extend [ɪks'tɛnd] *vt* (*visit etc*) verlängern; (*building*) ausbauen; (*hand*) ausstrecken; (*welcome*) bieten ♦ *vi* (*land*) sich erstrecken
extension [ɪks'tɛnʃən] *n* Erweiterung *f*; (*of building*) Anbau *m*; (TEL) Apparat *m*
extensive [ɪks'tɛnsɪv] *adj* (*knowledge*) umfassend; (*use*) weitgehend, weit gehend
extent [ɪks'tɛnt] *n* Ausdehnung *f*; (*fig*) Ausmaß *nt*; **to a certain ~** bis zu einem gewissen Grade; **to such an ~ that ...** dermaßen, dass ...; **to what ~?** inwieweit?
extenuating [ɪks'tɛnjueɪtɪŋ] *adj* mildernd
exterior [ɛks'tɪərɪər] *adj* äußere(r, s), Außen- ♦ *n* Äußere(s) *nt*
exterminate [ɪks'tɜːmɪneɪt] *vt* ausrotten
external [ɛks'tɜːnl] *adj* äußere(r, s), Außen-
extinct [ɪks'tɪŋkt] *adj* ausgestorben; **~ion** [ɪks'tɪŋkʃən] *n* Aussterben *nt*
extinguish [ɪks'tɪŋgwɪʃ] *vt* (aus)löschen
extort [ɪks'tɔːt] *vt* erpressen; **~ion** [ɪks'tɔːʃən] *n* Erpressung *f*; **~ionate** [ɪks'tɔːʃnɪt] *adj* überhöht, erpresserisch
extra ['ɛkstrə] *adj* zusätzlich ♦ *adv* besonders ♦ *n* (*for car etc*) Extra *nt*; (*charge*) Zuschlag *m*; (THEAT) Statist *m* ♦ *prefix* außer...
extract [*vb* ɪks'trækt, *n* 'ɛkstrækt] *vt* (heraus)ziehen ♦ *n* (*from book etc*) Auszug *m*; (COOK) Extrakt *m*
extracurricular ['ɛkstrəkə'rɪkjʊlər] *adj* außerhalb des Stundenplans
extradite ['ɛkstrədaɪt] *vt* ausliefern
extramarital ['ɛkstrə'mærɪtl] *adj* außerehelich
extramural ['ɛkstrə'mjʊərl] *adj* (*course*) Volkshochschul-
extraordinary [ɪks'trɔːdnrɪ] *adj* außerordentlich; (*amazing*) erstaunlich
extravagance [ɪks'trævəgəns] *n* Verschwendung *f*; (*lack of restraint*) Zügellosigkeit *f*; (*an ~*) Extravaganz *f*
extravagant [ɪks'trævəgənt] *adj* extravagant
extreme [ɪks'triːm] *adj* (*edge*) äußerste(r, s), hinterste(r, s); (*cold*) äußerste(r, s); (*behaviour*) außergewöhnlich, übertrieben ♦ *n* Extrem *nt*; **~ly** *adv* äußerst, höchst; **extremist** *n* Extremist(in) *m(f)*
extremity [ɪks'trɛmɪtɪ] *n* (*end*) Spitze *f*, äußerste(s) Ende *nt*; (*hardship*) bitterste Not *f*; (ANAT) Hand *f*; Fuß *m*
extricate ['ɛkstrɪkeɪt] *vt* losmachen, befreien
extrovert ['ɛkstrəvɜːt] *n* extrovertierte(r) Mensch *m*

exuberant [ɪgˈzjuːbərnt] *adj* ausgelassen
exude [ɪgˈzjuːd] *vt* absondern
eye [aɪ] *n* Auge *nt*; (*of needle*) Öhr *nt* ♦ *vt*
betrachten; (*up and down*) mustern; **to keep
an ~ on** aufpassen auf *+acc*; **~ball** *n*
Augapfel *m*; **~bath** *n* Augenbad *nt*; **~brow**
n Augenbraue *f*; **~brow pencil** *n*
Augenbrauenstift *m*; **~drops** *npl*
Augentropfen *pl*; **~lash** *n* Augenwimper *f*;
~lid *n* Augenlid *nt*; **~liner** *n* Eyeliner *nt*; **~-
opener** *n*: **that was an ~-opener** das hat
mir/ihm *etc* die Augen geöffnet; **~shadow**
n Lidschatten *m*; **~sight** *n* Sehkraft *f*; **~sore**
n Schandfleck *m*; **~ witness** *n* Augenzeuge
m

F, f

F [ɛf] *n* (*MUS*) F *nt*
F. *abbr* (= *Fahrenheit*) F
fable [ˈfeɪbl] *n* Fabel *f*
fabric [ˈfæbrɪk] *n* Stoff *m*; (*fig*) Gefüge *nt*
fabrication [fæbrɪˈkeɪʃən] *n* Erfindung *f*
fabulous [ˈfæbjuləs] *adj* sagenhaft
face [feɪs] *n* Gesicht *nt*; (*surface*) Oberfläche *f*;
(*of clock*) Zifferblatt *nt* ♦ *vt* (*point towards*)
liegen nach; (*situation, difficulty*) sich stellen
+dat; **~ down** (*person*) mit dem Gesicht
nach unten; (*card*) mit der Vorderseite nach
unten; **to make** *or* **pull a ~** das Gesicht
verziehen; **in the ~ of** angesichts *+gen*; **on
the ~ of it** so, wie es aussieht; **~ to ~** Auge
in Auge; **to ~ up to sth** einer Sache *dat* ins
Auge sehen; **~ cloth** (*BRIT*) *n* Waschlappen
m; **~ cream** *n* Gesichtscreme *f*; **~ lift** *n*
Facelifting *nt*; **~ powder** *n* (Gesichts)puder
m
facet [ˈfæsɪt] *n* Aspekt *m*; (*of gem*) Facette *f*,
Fassette *f*
facetious [fəˈsiːʃəs] *adj* witzig
face value *n* Nennwert *m*; **to take sth at
(its) ~** (*fig*) etw für bare Münze nehmen
facial [ˈfeɪʃl] *adj* Gesichts-
facile [ˈfæsaɪl] *adj* (*easy*) leicht
facilitate [fəˈsɪlɪteɪt] *vt* erleichtern
facilities [fəˈsɪlɪtɪz] *npl* Einrichtungen *pl*;
credit ~ Kreditmöglichkeiten *pl*
facing [ˈfeɪsɪŋ] *adj* zugekehrt ♦ *prep*
gegenüber
facsimile [fækˈsɪmɪlɪ] *n* Faksimile *nt*;
(*machine*) Telekopierer *m*
fact [fækt] *n* Tatsache *f*; **in ~** in der Tat
faction [ˈfækʃən] *n* Splittergruppe *f*
factor [ˈfæktəʳ] *n* Faktor *m*
factory [ˈfæktərɪ] *n* Fabrik *f*
factual [ˈfæktjuəl] *adj* sachlich
faculty [ˈfækəltɪ] *n* Fähigkeit *f*; (*UNIV*) Fakultät
f; (*US: teaching staff*) Lehrpersonal *nt*
fad [fæd] *n* Tick *m*; (*fashion*) Masche *f*
fade [feɪd] *vi* (*lose colour*) verblassen; (*dim*)

nachlassen; (*sound, memory*) schwächer
werden; (*wilt*) verwelken
fag [fæg] (*inf*) *n* (*cigarette*) Kippe *f*
fail [feɪl] *vt* (*exam*) nicht bestehen; (*student*)
durchfallen lassen; (*courage*) verlassen;
(*memory*) im Stich lassen ♦ *vi* (*supplies*) zu
Ende gehen; (*student*) durchfallen; (*eyesight*)
nachlassen; (*light*) schwächer werden; (*crop*)
fehlschlagen; (*remedy*) nicht wirken; **to ~ to
do sth** (*neglect*) es unterlassen, etw zu tun;
(*be unable*) es nicht schaffen, etw zu tun;
without ~ unbedingt; **~ing** *n* Schwäche *f*
♦ *prep* mangels *+gen*; **~ure** [ˈfeɪljəʳ] *n*
(*person*) Versager *m*; (*act*) Versagen *nt*;
(*TECH*) Defekt *m*
faint [feɪnt] *adj* schwach ♦ *n* Ohnmacht *f* ♦ *vi*
ohnmächtig werden
fair [fɛəʳ] *adj* (*just*) gerecht, fair; (*hair*) blond;
(*skin*) hell; (*weather*) schön; (*not very good*)
mittelmäßig; (*sizeable*) ansehnlich ♦ *adv*
(*play*) fair ♦ *n* (*COMM*) Messe *f*; (*BRIT:
funfair*) Jahrmarkt *m*; **~ly** *adv* (*honestly*)
gerecht, fair; (*rather*) ziemlich; **~ness** *n*
Fairness *f*
fairy [ˈfɛərɪ] *n* Fee *f*; **~ tale** *n* Märchen *nt*
faith [feɪθ] *n* Glaube *m*; (*trust*) Vertrauen *nt*;
(*sect*) Bekenntnis *nt*; **~ful** *adj* treu; **~fully**
adv treu; **yours ~fully** (*BRIT*)
hochachtungsvoll
fake [feɪk] *n* (*thing*) Fälschung *f*; (*person*)
Schwindler *m* ♦ *adj* vorgetäuscht ♦ *vt* fälschen
falcon [ˈfɔːlkən] *n* Falke *m*
fall [fɔːl] (*pt* **fell**, *pp* **fallen**) *n* Fall *m*, Sturz *m*;
(*decrease*) Fallen *nt*; (*of snow*) (Schnee)fall *m*;
(*US: autumn*) Herbst *m* ♦ *vi* (*also fig*) fallen;
(*night*) hereinbrechen; **~s** *npl* (*waterfall*)
Fälle *pl*; **to ~ flat** platt hinfallen; (*joke*) nicht
ankommen; **~ back** *vi* zurückweichen; **~
back on** *vt fus* zurückgreifen auf *+acc*; **~
behind** *vi* zurückbleiben; **~ down** *vi*
(*person*) hinfallen; (*building*) einstürzen; **~
for** *vt fus* (*trick*) hereinfallen auf *+acc*;
(*person*) sich verknallen in *+acc*; **~ in** *vi*
(*roof*) einstürzen; **~ off** *vi* herunterfallen;
(*diminish*) sich vermindern; **~ out** *vi* sich
streiten; (*MIL*) wegtreten; **~ through** *vi*
(*plan*) ins Wasser fallen
fallacy [ˈfæləsɪ] *n* Trugschluss *m*
fallen [ˈfɔːlən] *pp of* **fall**
fallible [ˈfæləbl] *adj* fehlbar
fallout [ˈfɔːlaʊt] *n* radioaktive(r) Niederschlag
m; **~ shelter** *n* Atombunker *m*
fallow [ˈfæləu] *adj* brach(liegend)
false [fɔːls] *adj* falsch; (*artificial*) künstlich;
under ~ pretences unter Vorspiegelung
falscher Tatsachen; **~ alarm** *n* Fehlalarm *m*;
~ teeth (*BRIT*) *npl* Gebiss *nt*
falter [ˈfɔːltəʳ] *vi* schwanken; (*in speech*)
stocken
fame [feɪm] *n* Ruhm *m*
familiar [fəˈmɪlɪəʳ] *adj* bekannt; (*intimate*)

familiär; **to be ~ with** vertraut sein mit; **~ize** vt vertraut machen

family ['fæmɪlɪ] n Familie f; (*relations*) Verwandtschaft f; **~ business** n Familienunternehmen nt; **~ doctor** n Hausarzt m

famine ['fæmɪn] n Hungersnot f

famished ['fæmɪʃt] adj ausgehungert

famous ['feɪməs] adj berühmt

fan [fæn] n (*folding*) Fächer m; (ELEC) Ventilator m; (*admirer*) Fan m ♦ vt fächeln; **~ out** vi sich (fächerförmig) ausbreiten

fanatic [fə'nætɪk] n Fanatiker(in) m(f)

fan belt n Keilriemen m

fanciful ['fænsɪfʊl] adj (*odd*) seltsam; (*imaginative*) fantasievoll

fancy ['fænsɪ] n (*liking*) Neigung f; (*imagination*) Einbildung f ♦ adj schick ♦ vt (*like*) gern haben; wollen; (*imagine*) sich einbilden; **he fancies her** er mag sie; **~ dress** n Maskenkostüm nt; **~-dress ball** n Maskenball m

fang [fæŋ] n Fangzahn m; (*of snake*) Giftzahn m

fantastic [fæn'tæstɪk] adj fantastisch

fantasy ['fæntəsɪ] n Fantasie f

far [faːʳ] adj weit ♦ adv weit entfernt; (*very much*) weitaus; **by ~** bei weitem; **so ~** so weit; bis jetzt; **go as ~ as the station** gehen Sie bis zum Bahnhof; **as ~ as I know** soweit or soviel ich weiß; **~away** adj weit entfernt

farce [faːs] n Farce f; **farcical** ['faːsɪkl] adj lächerlich

fare [fɛəʳ] n Fahrpreis m; Fahrgeld nt; (*food*) Kost f; **half/full ~** halber/voller Fahrpreis m

Far East n: **the ~** der Ferne Osten

farewell [fɛə'wɛl] n Abschied(sgruß) m ♦ excl lebe wohl!

farm [faːm] n Bauernhof m, Farm f ♦ vt bewirtschaften; **~er** n Bauer m, Landwirt m; **~hand** n Landarbeiter m; **~house** n Bauernhaus nt; **~ing** n Landwirtschaft f; **~land** n Ackerland nt; **~yard** n Hof m

far-reaching ['faː'riːtʃɪŋ] adj (*reform, effect*) weitreichend, weit reichend

fart [faːt] (*inf!*) n Furz m ♦ vi furzen

farther ['faːðəʳ] adv weiter; **farthest** ['faːðɪst] adj fernste(r, s) ♦ adv am weitesten

fascinate ['fæsɪneɪt] vt faszinieren; **fascinating** adj faszinierend; **fascination** [fæsɪ'neɪʃən] n Faszination f

fascism ['fæʃɪzəm] n Faschismus m

fashion ['fæʃən] n (*of clothes*) Mode f; (*manner*) Art f (und Weise f) ♦ vt machen; **in ~** in Mode; **out of ~** unmodisch; **~able** adj (*clothes*) modisch; (*place*) elegant; **~ show** n Mode(n)schau f

fast [faːst] adj schnell; (*firm*) fest ♦ adv schnell; fest ♦ n Fasten nt ♦ vi fasten; **to be ~** (*clock*) vorgehen

fasten ['faːsn] vt (*attach*) befestigen; (*with rope*) zuschnüren; (*seat belt*) festmachen; (*coat*) zumachen ♦ vi sich schließen lassen; **~er** n Verschluss m; **~ing** n Verschluss m

fast food n Fastfood nt, Fast Food nt

fastidious [fæs'tɪdɪəs] adj wählerisch

fat [fæt] adj dick ♦ n Fett nt

fatal ['feɪtl] adj tödlich; (*disastrous*) verhängnisvoll; **~ity** [fə'tælɪtɪ] n (*road death etc*) Todesopfer nt; **~ly** adv tödlich

fate [feɪt] n Schicksal nt; **~ful** adj (*prophetic*) schicksalsschwer; (*important*) schicksalhaft

father ['faːðəʳ] n Vater m; (REL) Pater m; **~-in-law** n Schwiegervater m; **~ly** adj väterlich

fathom ['fæðəm] n Klafter m ♦ vt ausloten; (*fig*) ergründen

fatigue [fə'tiːg] n Ermüdung f

fatten ['fætn] vt dick machen; (*animals*) mästen ♦ vi dick werden

fatty ['fætɪ] adj fettig ♦ n (*inf*) Dickerchen nt

fatuous ['fætjʊəs] adj albern, affig

faucet ['fɔːsɪt] (US) n Wasserhahn m

fault [fɔːlt] n (*defect*) Defekt m; (ELEC) Störung f; (*blame*) Schuld f; (GEOG) Verwerfung f; **it's your ~** du bist daran schuld; **to find ~ with (sth/sb)** etwas auszusetzen haben an (etw/jdm); **at ~** im Unrecht; **~less** adj tadellos; **~y** adj fehlerhaft, defekt

fauna ['fɔːnə] n Fauna f

favour ['feɪvəʳ] (US **favor**) n (*approval*) Wohlwollen nt; (*kindness*) Gefallen m ♦ vt (*prefer*) vorziehen; **in ~ of** für; zugunsten or zu Gunsten +gen; **to find ~ with sb** bei jdm Anklang finden; **~able** ['feɪvrəbl] adj günstig; **~ite** ['feɪvrɪt] adj Lieblings- ♦ n (*child*) Liebling m; (SPORT) Favorit m

fawn [fɔːn] adj rehbraun ♦ n (*animal*) (Reh)kitz nt ♦ vi: **to ~ (up)on** (*fig*) katzbuckeln vor +dat

fax [fæks] n (*document*) Fax nt; (*machine*) Telefax nt ♦ vt: **to ~ sth to sb** jdm etw faxen

FBI (US) n abbr (= *Federal Bureau of Investigation*) FBI nt

fear [fɪəʳ] n Furcht f ♦ vt fürchten; **~ful** adj (*timid*) furchtsam; (*terrible*) fürchterlich; **~less** adj furchtlos

feasible ['fiːzəbl] adj durchführbar

feast [fiːst] n Festmahl nt; (REL: also: **~ day**) Feiertag m ♦ vi: **to ~ (on)** sich gütlich tun (an +dat)

feat [fiːt] n Leistung f

feather ['fɛðəʳ] n Feder f

feature ['fiːtʃəʳ] n (Gesichts)zug m; (*important part*) Grundzug m; (CINE, PRESS) Feature nt ♦ vt (*advertising etc*) groß herausbringen ♦ vi vorkommen; **featuring X** mit X; **~ film** n Spielfilm m

February ['fɛbruərɪ] n Februar m

fed [fɛd] pt, pp of **feed**

federal ['fedərəl] adj Bundes-
federation [fedə'reɪʃən] n (society) Verband m; (of states) Staatenbund m
fed up adj: **to be ~ with sth** etw satt haben; **I'm ~** ich habe die Nase voll
fee [fi:] n Gebühr f
feeble ['fi:bl] adj (person) schwach; (excuse) lahm
feed [fi:d] (pt, pp **fed**) n (for animals) Futter nt ♦ vt füttern; (support) ernähren; (data) eingeben; **to ~ on** fressen; **~back** n (information) Feed-back nt, Feedback nt; **~ing bottle** (BRIT) n Flasche f
feel [fi:l] (pt, pp **felt**) n: **it has a soft ~** es fühlt sich weich an ♦ vt (sense) fühlen; (touch) anfassen; (think) meinen ♦ vi (person) sich fühlen; (thing) sich anfühlen; **to get the ~ of sth** sich an etw acc gewöhnen; **I ~ cold** mir ist kalt; **I ~ like a cup of tea** ich habe Lust auf eine Tasse Tee; **~ about** or **around** vi herumsuchen; **~er** n Fühler m; **~ing** n Gefühl nt; (opinion) Meinung f
feet [fi:t] npl of **foot**
feign [feɪn] vt vortäuschen
feline ['fi:laɪn] adj katzenartig
fell [fel] pt of **fall** ♦ vt (tree) fällen
fellow ['feləu] n (man) Kerl m; **~ citizen** n Mitbürger(in) m(f); **~ countryman** (irreg) n Landsmann m; **~ men** npl Mitmenschen pl; **~ship** n (group) Körperschaft f; (friendliness) Kameradschaft f; (scholarship) Forschungsstipendium nt; **~ student** n Kommilitone m, Kommilitonin f
felony ['feləni] n schwere(s) Verbrechen nt
felt [felt] pt, pp of **feel** ♦ n Filz m; **~-tip pen** n Filzstift m
female ['fi:meɪl] n (of animals) Weibchen nt ♦ adj weiblich
feminine ['feminin] adj (LING) weiblich; (qualities) fraulich
feminist ['feminist] n Feminist(in) m(f)
fence [fens] n Zaun m ♦ vt (also: **~ in**) einzäunen ♦ vi fechten; **fencing** ['fensiŋ] n Zaun m; (SPORT) Fechten nt
fend [fend] vi: **to ~ for o.s.** sich (allein) durchschlagen; **~ off** vt abwehren
fender ['fendər] n Kaminvorsetzer m; (US: AUT) Kotflügel m
ferment [vb fə'ment, n 'fə:ment] vi (CHEM) gären ♦ n (unrest) Unruhe f
fern [fə:n] n Farn m
ferocious [fə'rəuʃəs] adj wild, grausam
ferret ['ferit] n Frettchen nt ♦ vt: **to ~ out** aufspüren
ferry ['feri] n Fähre f ♦ vt übersetzen
fertile ['fə:taɪl] adj fruchtbar
fertilize ['fə:tɪlaɪz] vt (AGR) düngen; (BIOL) befruchten; **~r** n (Kunst)dünger m
fervent ['fə:vənt] adj (admirer) glühend; (hope) innig
fervour ['fə:vər] (US **fervor**) n Leidenschaft f

fester ['festər] vi eitern
festival ['festɪvl] n (REL etc) Fest nt; (ART, MUS) Festspiele pl
festive ['festiv] adj festlich; **the ~ season** (Christmas) die Festzeit; **festivities** [fes'tɪvɪtɪz] npl Feierlichkeiten pl
festoon [fes'tu:n] vt: **to ~ with** schmücken mit
fetch [fetʃ] vt holen; (in sale) einbringen
fetching ['fetʃiŋ] adj reizend
fête [feɪt] n Fest nt
fetus ['fi:təs] (esp US) n = **foetus**
feud [fju:d] n Fehde f
feudal ['fju:dl] adj Feudal-
fever ['fi:vər] n Fieber nt; **~ish** adj (MED) fiebrig; (fig) fieberhaft
few [fju:] adj wenig; **a ~** einige; **~er** adj weniger; **~est** adj wenigste(r, s)
fiancé [fɪ'ɑ:nseɪ] n Verlobte(r) m; **~e** n Verlobte f
fib [fib] n Flunkerei f ♦ vi flunkern
fibre ['faɪbər] (US **fiber**) n Faser f; **~glass** n Glaswolle f
fickle ['fikl] adj unbeständig
fiction ['fɪkʃən] n (novels) Romanliteratur f; (story) Erdichtung f; **~al** adj erfunden
fictitious [fik'tɪʃəs] adj erfunden, fingiert
fiddle ['fidl] n Geige f; (trick) Schwindelei f ♦ vt (BRIT: accounts) frisieren; **~ with** vt fus herumfummeln an +dat
fidelity [fɪ'delɪtɪ] n Treue f
fidget ['fidʒɪt] vi zappeln
field [fi:ld] n Feld nt; (range) Gebiet nt; **~ marshal** n Feldmarschall m; **~work** n Feldforschung f
fiend [fi:nd] n Teufel m
fierce [fɪəs] adj wild
fiery ['faɪərɪ] adj (person) hitzig
fifteen [fif'ti:n] num fünfzehn
fifth [fifθ] adj fünfte(r, s) ♦ n Fünftel nt
fifty ['fifti] num fünfzig; **~~** adj, adv halbe-halbe, fifty-fifty (inf)
fig [fig] n Feige f
fight [fait] (pt, pp **fought**) n Kampf m; (brawl) Schlägerei f; (argument) Streit m ♦ vt kämpfen gegen; sich schlagen mit; (fig) bekämpfen ♦ vi kämpfen; sich schlagen; streiten; **~er** n Kämpfer(in) m(f); (plane) Jagdflugzeug nt; **~ing** n Kämpfen nt; (war) Kampfhandlungen pl
figment ['figmənt] n: **~ of the imagination** reine Einbildung f
figurative ['figjurətɪv] adj bildlich
figure ['figər] n (of person) Figur f; (person) Gestalt f; (number) Ziffer f ♦ vt (US: imagine) glauben ♦ vi (appear) erscheinen; **~ out** vt herausbekommen; **~head** n (NAUT, fig) Galionsfigur f; **~ of speech** n Redensart f
file [fail] n (tool) Feile f; (dossier) Akte f; (folder) Aktenordner m; (COMPUT) Datei f; (row) Reihe f ♦ vt (metal, nails) feilen;

(papers) abheften; (claim) einreichen ♦ vi: to ~ in/out hintereinander hereinkommen/hinausgehen; to ~ past vorbeimarschieren; **filing** ['faɪlɪŋ] n Ablage f; **filing cabinet** n Aktenschrank m

fill [fɪl] vt füllen; (occupy) ausfüllen; (satisfy) sättigen ♦ n: to eat one's ~ sich richtig satt essen; ~ in vt (hole) (aus)füllen; (form) ausfüllen; ~ up vt (container) auffüllen; (form) ausfüllen ♦ vi (AUT) tanken

fillet ['fɪlɪt] n Filet nt; ~ **steak** n Filetsteak nt

filling ['fɪlɪŋ] n (COOK) Füllung f; (for tooth) (Zahn)plombe f; ~ **station** n Tankstelle f

film [fɪlm] n Film m ♦ vt (scene) filmen; ~ **star** n Filmstar m

filter ['fɪltə'] n Filter m ♦ vt filtern; ~ **lane** (BRIT) n Abbiegespur f; ~**-tipped** adj Filter-

filth [fɪlθ] n Dreck m; ~**y** adj dreckig; (weather) scheußlich.

fin [fɪn] n Flosse f

final ['faɪnl] adj letzte(r, s); End-; (conclusive) endgültig ♦ n (FOOTBALL etc) Endspiel nt; ~**s** npl (UNIV) Abschlussexamen nt; (SPORT) Schlussrunde f

finale [fɪ'nɑ:lɪ] n (MUS) Finale nt

final: ~**ist** n (SPORT) Schlussrundenteilnehmer m; ~**ize** vt endgültige Form geben +dat; abschließen; ~**ly** adv (lastly) zuletzt; (eventually) endlich; (irrevocably) endgültig

finance [faɪ'næns] n Finanzwesen nt ♦ vt finanzieren; ~**s** npl (funds) Finanzen pl; **financial** [faɪ'nænʃəl] adj Finanz-; finanziell

find [faɪnd] (pt, pp found) vt finden ♦ n Fund m; to ~ **sb guilty** jdn für schuldig erklären; ~ **out** vt herausfinden; ~**ings** npl (JUR) Ermittlungsergebnis nt; (of report) Befund m

fine [faɪn] adj fein; (good) gut; (weather) schön ♦ adv (well) gut; (small) klein ♦ n (JUR) Geldstrafe f ♦ vt (JUR) mit einer Geldstrafe belegen; ~ **arts** npl schöne(n) Künste pl

finger ['fɪŋgə'] n Finger m ♦ vt befühlen; ~**nail** n Fingernagel m; ~**print** n Fingerabdruck m; ~**tip** n Fingerspitze f

finicky ['fɪnɪkɪ] adj pingelig

finish ['fɪnɪʃ] n Ende nt; (SPORT) Ziel nt; (of object) Verarbeitung f; (of paint) Oberflächenwirkung f ♦ vt beenden; (book) zu Ende lesen ♦ vi aufhören; (SPORT) aus Ziel kommen; to be ~**ed with sth** fertig sein mit etw; to ~ **doing sth** mit etw fertig werden; ~ **off** vt (complete) fertig machen; (kill) den Gnadenstoß geben +dat; (knock out) erledigen (umg); ~ **up** vt (food) aufessen; (drink) austrinken ♦ vi (end up) enden; ~**ing line** n Ziellinie f; ~**ing school** n Mädchenpensionat nt

finite ['faɪnaɪt] adj endlich, begrenzt

Finland ['fɪnlənd] n Finnland nt

Finn [fɪn] n Finne m, Finnin f; ~**ish** adj

finnisch ♦ n (LING) Finnisch nt

fir [fɜː'] n Tanne f

fire ['faɪə'] n Feuer nt; (in house etc) Brand m ♦ vt (gun) abfeuern; (imagination) entzünden; (dismiss) hinauswerfen ♦ vi (AUT) zünden; **to be on** ~ brennen; ~ **alarm** n Feueralarm m; ~**arm** n Schusswaffe f; ~ **brigade** (BRIT) n Feuerwehr f; ~ **department** (US) n Feuerwehr f; ~ **engine** n Feuerwehrauto nt; ~ **escape** n Feuerleiter f; ~ **extinguisher** n Löschgerät nt; ~**man** (irreg) n Feuerwehrmann m; ~**place** n Kamin m; ~**side** n Kamin m; ~ **station** n Feuerwehrwache f; ~**wood** n Brennholz nt; ~**works** npl Feuerwerk nt; **firing squad** n Exekutionskommando nt

firm [fɜːm] adj fest ♦ n Firma f; ~**ly** ['fɜːmlɪ] adv (grasp, speak) fest; (push, tug) energisch; (decide) endgültig

first [fɜːst] adj erste(r, s) ♦ adv zuerst; (arrive) als Erste(r); (happen) zum ersten Mal ♦ n (person: in race) Erste(r) mf; (UNIV) Eins f; (AUT) erste(r) Gang m; **at** ~ zuerst; ~ **of all** zuallererst; ~ **aid** n erste Hilfe f; ~**aid kit** n Verbandskasten m; ~**-class** adj erstklassig; (travel) erster Klasse; ~**-hand** adj aus erster Hand; ~ **lady** (US) n First Lady f; ~**ly** adv erstens; ~ **name** n Vorname m; ~**-rate** adj erstklassig

fiscal ['fɪskl] adj Finanz-

fish [fɪʃ] n inv Fisch m ♦ vi fischen; angeln; **to go ~ing** angeln gehen; (in sea) fischen gehen; ~**erman** (irreg) n Fischer m; ~ **farm** n Fischzucht f; ~ **fingers** (BRIT) npl Fischstäbchen pl; ~**ing boat** n Fischerboot nt; ~**ing line** n Angelschnur f; ~**ing rod** n Angel(rute) f; ~**ing tackle** n (for sport) Angelgeräte pl; ~**monger's (shop)** n Fischhändler m; ~ **slice** n Fischvorlegemesser nt; ~ **sticks** (US) npl = fish fingers

fishy ['fɪʃɪ] (inf) adj (suspicious) faul

fission ['fɪʃən] n Spaltung f

fissure ['fɪʃə'] n Riss m

fist [fɪst] n Faust f

fit [fɪt] adj (MED) gesund; (SPORT) in Form, fit; (suitable) geeignet ♦ vt passen +dat; (insert, attach) einsetzen ♦ vi passen; (in space, gap) hineinpassen ♦ n (of clothes) Sitz m; (MED, of anger) Anfall m; (of laughter) Krampf m; **by ~s and starts** (move) ruckweise; (work) unregelmäßig; ~ **in** vi hineinpassen; (fig: person) passen; ~ **out** vt (also: ~ **up**) ausstatten; ~**ful** adj (sleep) unruhig; ~**ment** n Einrichtungsgegenstand m; ~**ness** n (suitability) Eignung f; (MED) Gesundheit f; (SPORT) Fitness f; ~**ted carpet** n Teppichboden m; ~**ted kitchen** n Einbauküche f; ~**ter** n (TECH) Monteur m; ~**ting** adj passend ♦ n (of dress) Anprobe f; (piece of equipment) (Ersatz)teil nt; ~**tings**

npl *(equipment)* Zubehör *nt*; **~ting room** *n* Anproberaum *m*

five |faɪv| *num* fünf; **~r** *(inf) n (BRIT)* Fünfpfundnote *f*; *(US)* Fünfdollarnote *f*

fix |fɪks| *vt* befestigen; *(settle)* festsetzen; *(repair)* reparieren ♦ *n:* **in a ~** in der Klemme; **~ up** *vt (meeting)* arrangieren; **to ~ sb up with sth** jdm etw *acc* verschaffen; **~ation** |fɪk'seɪʃən| *n* Fixierung *f*; **~ed** |fɪkst| *adj* fest; **~ture** |'fɪkstʃə'| *n* Installationsteil *m*; *(SPORT)* Spiel *nt*

fizzy |'fɪzɪ| *adj* Sprudel-, sprudelnd

flabbergasted |'flæbəgɑːstɪd| *(inf) adj* platt

flabby |'flæbɪ| *adj* wabbelig

flag |flæg| *n* Fahne *f* ♦ *vi (strength)* nachlassen; *(spirit)* erlahmen; **~ down** *vt* anhalten; **~pole** |'flægpəʊl| *n* Fahnenstange *f*

flair |fleə'| *n* Talent *nt*

flak |flæk| *n* Flakfeuer *nt*

flake |fleɪk| *n (of snow)* Flocke *f*; *(of rust)* Schuppe *f* ♦ *vi (also: ~ off)* abblättern

flamboyant |flæm'bɔɪənt| *adj* extravagant

flame |fleɪm| *n* Flamme *f*

flamingo |flə'mɪŋgəʊ| *n* Flamingo *m*

flammable |'flæməbl| *adj* brennbar

flan |flæn| *(BRIT) n* Obsttorte *f*

flank |flæŋk| *n* Flanke *f* ♦ *vt* flankieren

flannel |'flænl| *n* Flanell *m*; *(BRIT: also:* **face ~**) Waschlappen *m*; *(: inf)* Geschwafel *nt*; **~s** *npl (trousers)* Flanellhose *f*

flap |flæp| *n* Klappe *f*; *(inf: crisis)* (helle) Aufregung *f* ♦ *vt (wings)* schlagen mit ♦ *vi* flattern

flare |fleə'| *n (signal)* Leuchtsignal *nt*; *(in skirt etc)* Weite *f*; **~ up** *vi* aufflammen; *(fig)* aufbrausen; *(revolt)* (plötzlich) ausbrechen

flash |flæʃ| *n* Blitz *m*; *(also:* **news ~**) Kurzmeldung *f*; *(PHOT)* Blitzlicht *nt* ♦ *vt* aufleuchten lassen ♦ *vi* aufleuchten; **in a ~** im Nu; **~ by** *or* **past** *vi* vorbeirasen; **~back** *n* Rückblende *f*; **~bulb** *n* Blitzlichtbirne *f*; **~cube** *n* Blitzwürfel *m*; **~light** *n* Blitzlicht *nt*

flashy |'flæʃɪ| *(pej) adj* knallig

flask |flɑːsk| *n (CHEM)* Kolben *m*; *(also:* **vacuum ~**) Thermosflasche *f* ®

flat |flæt| *adj* flach; *(dull)* matt; *(MUS)* erniedrigt; *(beer)* schal; *(tyre)* platt ♦ *n (BRIT: rooms)* Wohnung *f*; *(MUS)* b *nt*; *(AUT)* Platte(r) *m*; **to work ~ out** auf Hochtouren arbeiten; **~ly** *adv* glatt; **~-screen** *adj (TV, COMPUT)* mit flachem Bildschirm; **~ten** *vt (also:* **~ten out**) ebnen

flatter |'flætə'| *vt* schmeicheln +*dat*; **~ing** *adj* schmeichelhaft; **~y** *n* Schmeichelei *f*

flatulence |'flætjʊləns| *n* Blähungen *pl*

flaunt |flɔːnt| *vt* prunken mit

flavour |'fleɪvə'| *(US* **flavor**) *n* Geschmack *m* ♦ *vt* würzen; **~ed** *adj:* **strawberry-~ed** mit Erdbeergeschmack; **~ing** *n* Würze *f*

flaw |flɔː| *n* Fehler *m*; **~less** *adj* einwandfrei

flax |flæks| *n* Flachs *m*; **~en** *adj* flachsfarben

flea |fliː| *n* Floh *m*

fleck |flek| *n (mark)* Fleck *m*; *(pattern)* Tupfen *m*

fled |fled| *pt, pp of* **flee**

flee |fliː| *(pt, pp* **fled**) *vi* fliehen ♦ *vt* fliehen vor +*dat*; *(country)* fliehen aus

fleece |fliːs| *n* Vlies *nt* ♦ *vt (inf)* schröpfen

fleet |fliːt| *n* Flotte *f*

fleeting |'fliːtɪŋ| *adj* flüchtig

Flemish |'flemɪʃ| *adj* flämisch

flesh |fleʃ| *n* Fleisch *nt*; **~ wound** *n* Fleischwunde *f*

flew |fluː| *pt of* **fly**

flex |fleks| *n* Kabel *nt* ♦ *vt* beugen; **~ibility** |fleksɪ'bɪlɪtɪ| *n* Biegsamkeit *f*; *(fig)* Flexibilität *f*; **~ible** *adj* biegsam; *(plans)* flexibel

flick |flɪk| *n* leichte(r) Schlag *m* ♦ *vt* leicht schlagen; **~ through** *vt fus* durchblättern

flicker |'flɪkə'| *n* Flackern *nt* ♦ *vi* flackern

flier |'flaɪə'| *n* Flieger *m*

flight |flaɪt| *n* Flug *m*; *(fleeing)* Flucht *f*; *(also:* **~ of steps**) Treppe *f*; **to take ~** die Flucht ergreifen; **~ attendant** *(US) n* Steward(ess) *m(f)*; **~ deck** *n* Flugdeck *nt*

flimsy |'flɪmzɪ| *adj (thin)* hauchdünn; *(excuse)* fadenscheinig

flinch |flɪntʃ| *vi:* **to ~ (away from)** zurückschrecken (vor +*dat*)

fling |flɪŋ| *(pt, pp* **flung**) *vt* schleudern

flint |flɪnt| *n* Feuerstein *m*

flip |flɪp| *vt* werfen

flippant |'flɪpənt| *adj* schnippisch

flipper |'flɪpə'| *n* Flosse *f*

flirt |flɜːt| *vi* flirten ♦ *n:* **he/she is a ~** er/sie flirtet gern

flit |flɪt| *vi* flitzen

float |fləʊt| *n (FISHING)* Schwimmer *m*; *(esp in procession)* Plattformwagen *m* ♦ *vi* schwimmen; *(in air)* schweben ♦ *vt (COMM)* gründen; *(currency)* floaten

flock |flɒk| *n (of sheep, REL)* Herde *f*; *(of birds)* Schwarm *m*

flog |flɒg| *vt* prügeln; *(inf: sell)* verkaufen

flood |flʌd| *n* Überschwemmung *f*; *(fig)* Flut *f* ♦ *vt* überschwemmen; **~ing** *n* Überschwemmung *f*; **~light** *n* Flutlicht *nt*

floor |flɔː'| *n (of room)* (Fuß)boden *m*; *(storey)* Stock *m* ♦ *vt (person)* zu Boden schlagen; **ground ~** *(BRIT)* Erdgeschoss *nt*; **first ~** *(BRIT)* erste(r) Stock *m*; *(US)* Erdgeschoss *nt*; **~board** *n* Diele *f*; **~ show** *n* Kabarettvorstellung *f*

flop |flɒp| *n* Plumps *m*; *(failure)* Reinfall *m* ♦ *vi (fail)* durchfallen

floppy |'flɒpɪ| *adj* hängend; **~ (disk)** *n (COMPUT)* Diskette *f*

flora |'flɔːrə| *n* Flora *f*; **~l** *adj* Blumen-

florist |'flɒrɪst| *n* Blumenhändler(in) *m(f)*; **~'s (shop)** *n* Blumengeschäft *nt*

flotation |fləʊ'teɪʃən| *n (FIN)* Auflegung *f*

flounce |flaʊns| *n* Volant *m*

flounder |ˈflaundəʳ| vi (fig) ins Schleudern
kommen ♦ n (ZOOL) Flunder f

flour |ˈflauəʳ| n Mehl nt

flourish |ˈflʌrɪʃ| vi blühen; gedeihen ♦ n
(waving) Schwingen nt; (of trumpets) Tusch
m, Fanfare f

flout |flaut| vt missachten

flow |fləu| n Fließen nt; (of sea) Flut f ♦ vi
fließen; ~ **chart** n Flussdiagramm nt

flower |ˈflauəʳ| n Blume f ♦ vi blühen; ~ **bed**
n Blumenbeet nt; ~**pot** n Blumentopf m; ~**y**
adj (style) blumenreich

flown |fləun| pp of **fly**

flu |fluː| n Grippe f

fluctuate |ˈflʌktjueɪt| vi schwanken;
fluctuation |flʌktjuˈeɪʃən| n Schwankung f

fluency |ˈfluːənsɪ| n Flüssigkeit f

fluent |ˈfluːənt| adj fließend; ~**ly** adv fließend

fluff |flʌf| n Fussel f; ~**y** adj flaumig

fluid |ˈfluːɪd| n Flüssigkeit f ♦ adj flüssig; (fig:
plans) veränderbar

fluke |fluːk| (inf) n Dusel m

flung |flʌŋ| pt, pp of **fling**

fluoride |ˈfluəraɪd| n Fluorid nt; ~
toothpaste n Fluorzahnpasta f

flurry |ˈflʌrɪ| n (of snow) Gestöber nt; (of
activity) Aufregung f

flush |flʌʃ| n Erröten nt; (of excitement)
Glühen nt ♦ vt (aus)spülen ♦ vi erröten ♦ adj
glatt; ~ **out** vt aufstöbern; ~**ed** adj rot

flustered |ˈflʌstəd| adj verwirrt

flute |fluːt| n Querflöte f

flutter |ˈflʌtəʳ| n Flattern nt ♦ vi flattern

flux |flʌks| n: **in a state of ~** im Fluss

fly |flaɪ| (pt **flew**, pp **flown**) n (insect) Fliege
f; (on trousers: also: **flies**) (Hosen)schlitz m
♦ vt fliegen ♦ vi fliegen; (flee) fliehen; (flag)
wehen; ~ **away** or **off** vi (bird, insect)
wegfliegen; ~**drive** n: ~**drive holiday** Fly
& Drive-Urlaub m; ~**ing** n Fliegen nt ♦ adj:
with ~ing colours mit fliegenden Fahnen;
~**ing start** gute(r) Start m; ~**ing visit**
Stippvisite f; ~**ing saucer** n fliegende
Untertasse f; ~**over** (BRIT) n Überführung f;
~**sheet** n (for tent) Regendach nt

foal |fəul| n Fohlen nt

foam |fəum| n Schaum m ♦ vi schäumen; ~
rubber n Schaumgummi m

fob |fɔb| vt: **to ~ sb off with sth** jdm etw
andrehen; (with promise) jdn mit etw
abspeisen

focal |ˈfəukl| adj Brenn-; ~ **point** n (of room,
activity) Mittelpunkt m

focus |ˈfəukəs| (pl ~**es**) n Brennpunkt m ♦ vt
(attention) konzentrieren; (camera) scharf
einstellen ♦ vi: **to ~ (on)** sich konzentrieren
(auf +acc); **in ~** scharf eingestellt; **out of ~**
unscharf

fodder |ˈfɔdəʳ| n Futter nt

foe |fəu| n Feind m

foetus |ˈfiːtəs| (US **fetus**) n Fötus m

fog |fɔg| n Nebel m; ~**gy** adj neblig; ~ **lamp**
(BRIT), ~ **light** (US) n (AUT) Nebel-
scheinwerfer m

foil |fɔɪl| vt vereiteln ♦ n (metal. also fig) Folie
f; (FENCING) Florett nt

fold |fəuld| n (bend, crease) Falte f; (AGR)
Pferch m ♦ vt falten; ~ **up** vt (map etc)
zusammenfalten ♦ vi (business) eingehen;
~**er** n Schnellhefter m; ~**ing** adj (chair etc)
Klapp-

foliage |ˈfəulɪdʒ| n Laubwerk nt

folk |fəuk| npl Leute pl ♦ adj Volks-; ~**s** npl
(family) Leute pl; ~**lore** |ˈfəuklɔːʳ| n (study)
Volkskunde f; (tradition) Folklore f; ~ **song**
n Volkslied nt; (modern) Folksong m

follow |ˈfɔləu| vt folgen +dat; (fashion)
mitmachen ♦ vi folgen; ~ **up** vt verfolgen;
~**er** n Anhänger(in) m(f); ~**ing** adj folgend
♦ n (people) Gefolgschaft f; ~-**on call** n
weiteres Gespräch in einer Telefonzelle um
Guthaben zu verbrauchen

folly |ˈfɔlɪ| n Torheit f

fond |fɔnd| adj: **to be ~ of** gern haben

fondle |ˈfɔndl| vt streicheln

font |fɔnt| n Taufbecken nt

food |fuːd| n Essen nt; (fodder) Futter nt; ~
mixer n Küchenmixer m; ~ **poisoning** n
Lebensmittelvergiftung f; ~ **processor** n
Küchenmaschine f; ~**stuffs** npl Lebensmittel
pl

fool |fuːl| n Narr m, Närrin f ♦ vt (deceive)
hereinlegen ♦ vi (also: ~ **around**)
(herum)albern; ~**hardy** adj tollkühn; ~**ish**
adj albern; ~**proof** adj idiotensicher

foot |fut| n (pl **feet**) n Fuß m ♦ vt (bill)
bezahlen; **on ~** zu Fuß

footage |ˈfutɪdʒ| n (CINE) Filmmaterial nt

football |ˈfutbɔːl| n Fußball m; (game: BRIT)
Fußball m; (: US) Football m; ~ **player** n
(BRIT: also: ~**er**) Fußballspieler m, Fußballer
m; (US) Footballer m

foot: ~**brake** n Fußbremse f; ~**bridge** n
Fußgängerbrücke f; ~**hills** npl Ausläufer pl;
~**hold** n Halt m; ~**ing** n Halt m; (fig)
Verhältnis nt; ~**lights** npl Rampenlicht nt;
~**man** (irreg) n Bedienstete(r) m; ~**note** n
Fußnote f; ~**path** n Fußweg m; ~**print** n
Fußabdruck m; ~**sore** adj fußkrank; ~**step** n
Schritt m; ~**wear** n Schuhzeug nt

KEYWORD
---

for |fɔːʳ| prep 1 für; **is this for me?** ist das
für mich?; **the train for London** der Zug
nach London; **he went for the paper** er
ging die Zeitung holen; **give it to me –
what for?** gib es mir – warum?

2 (because of) wegen; **for this reason** aus
diesem Grunde

3 (referring to distance): **there are
roadworks for 5 km** die Baustelle ist 5 km
lang; **we walked for miles** wir sind

meilenweit gegangen
4 (*referring to time*) seit; (: *with future sense*)
für; **he was away for 2 years** er war zwei
Jahre lang weg
5 (*+infin clauses*): **it is not for me to
decide** das kann ich nicht entscheiden; **for
this to be possible** ... damit dies möglich
wird/wurde ...
6 (*in spite of*) trotz +*gen* or (*inf*) *dat*; **for all
his complaints** obwohl er sich ständig
beschwert
♦ *conj* denn

forage ['fɒrɪdʒ] *n* (Vieh)futter *nt*
foray ['fɒreɪ] *n* Raubzug *m*
forbad(e) [fə'bæd] *pt of* **forbid**
forbid [fə'bɪd] (*pt* forbad(e), *pp* forbidden)
vt verbieten; **~ding** *adj* einschüchternd
force [fɔːs] *n* Kraft *f*; (*compulsion*) Zwang *m*
♦ *vt* zwingen; (*lock*) aufbrechen; **the F~s** *npl*
(BRIT) die Streitkräfte; **in ~** (*rule*) gültig;
(*group*) in großer Stärke; **~d** *adj* (*smile*)
gezwungen; (*landing*) Not-; **~-feed** *vt*
zwangsernähren; **~ful** *adj* (*speech*) kraftvoll;
(*personality*) resolut
forceps ['fɔːseps] *npl* Zange *f*
forcibly ['fɔːsəblɪ] *adv* zwangsweise
ford [fɔːd] *n* Furt *f* ♦ *vt* durchwaten
fore [fɔːʳ] *n*: **to the ~** in den Vordergrund;
~arm ['fɔːraːm] *n* Unterarm *m*; **~boding**
[fɔː'bəudɪŋ] *n* Vorahnung *f*; **~cast** ['fɔːkaːst]
(*irreg: like* cast) *n* Vorhersage *f* ♦ *vt*
voraussagen; **~court** ['fɔːkɔːt] *n* (*of garage*)
Vorplatz *m*; **~fathers** ['fɔːfaːðəz] *npl*
Vorfahren *pl*; **~finger** ['fɔːfɪŋgəʳ] *n*
Zeigefinger *m*; **~front** ['fɔːfrʌnt] *n* Spitze *f*
forego [fɔː'gəu] (*irreg: like* go) *vt* verzichten
auf +*acc*
fore-: **~gone** ['fɔːgɒn] *adj*: **it's a ~gone
conclusion** es steht von vornherein fest;
~ground ['fɔːgraund] *n* Vordergrund *m*;
~head ['fɒrɪd] *n* Stirn *f*
foreign ['fɒrɪn] *adj* Auslands-; (*accent*)
ausländisch; (*trade*) Außen-; (*body*) Fremd-;
~er *n* Ausländer(in) *m(f)*; **~ exchange** *n*
Devisen *pl*; **F~ Office** (BRIT) *n*
Außenministerium *nt*; **F~ Secretary** (BRIT)
n Außenminister *m*
fore ['fɔː-]: **~leg** *n* Vorderbein *nt*; **~man**
(*irreg*) *n* Vorarbeiter *m*; **~most** *adj* erste(r, s)
♦ *adv*: **first and ~most** vor allem
forensic [fə'rensɪk] *adj* gerichtsmedizinisch
fore ['fɔː-]: **~runner** *n* Vorläufer *m*; **~see**
[fɔː'siː] (*irreg: like* see) *vt* vorhersehen;
~seeable *adj* absehbar; **~shadow**
[fɔː'ʃædəu] *vt* andeuten; **~sight** ['fɔːsaɪt] *n*
Voraussicht *f*
forest ['fɒrɪst] *n* Wald *m*
forestall [fɔː'stɔːl] *vt* zuvorkommen +*dat*
forestry ['fɒrɪstrɪ] *n* Forstwirtschaft *f*
foretaste ['fɔːteɪst] *n* Vorgeschmack *m*

foretell [fɔː'tel] (*irreg: like* tell) *vt*
vorhersagen
forever [fə'revəʳ] *adv* für immer
foreword ['fɔːwəːd] *n* Vorwort *nt*
forfeit ['fɔːfɪt] *n* Einbuße *f* ♦ *vt* verwirken
forgave [fə'geɪv] *pt of* **forgive**
forge [fɔːdʒ] *n* Schmiede *f* ♦ *vt* fälschen;
(*iron*) schmieden; **~ ahead** *vi* Fortschritte
machen; **~d** *adj* gefälscht; **~d banknotes**
Blüten *pl* (*inf*); **~r** *n* Fälscher *m*; **~ry** *n*
Fälschung *f*
forget [fə'get] (*pt* forgot, *pp* forgotten) *vt, vi*
vergessen; **~ful** *adj* vergesslich; **~-me-not** *n*
Vergissmeinnicht *nt*
forgive [fə'gɪv] (*pt* forgave, *pp* forgiven) *vt*
verzeihen; **to ~ sb (for sth)** jdm (etw)
verzeihen; **~ness** *n* Verzeihung *f*
forgot [fə'gɒt] *pt of* **forget**; **~ten** *pp of*
forget
fork [fɔːk] *n* Gabel *f*; (*in road*) Gabelung *f* ♦ *vi*
(*road*) sich gabeln; **~ out** (*inf*) *vt* (*pay*)
blechen; **~-lift truck** *n* Gabelstapler *m*
forlorn [fə'lɔːn] *adj* (*person*) verlassen; (*hope*)
vergeblich
form [fɔːm] *n* Form *f*; (*type*) Art *f*; (*figure*)
Gestalt *f*; (SCH) Klasse *f*; (*bench*)
(Schul)bank *f*; (*document*) Formular *nt* ♦ *vt*
formen; (*be part of*) bilden
formal ['fɔːməl] *adj* formell; (*occasion*)
offiziell; **~ly** *adv* (*ceremoniously*) formell;
(*officially*) offiziell
format ['fɔːmæt] *n* Format *nt* ♦ *vt* (COMPUT)
formatieren
formation [fɔː'meɪʃən] *n* Bildung *f*; (AVIAT)
Formation *f*
formative ['fɔːmətɪv] *adj* (*years*) formend
former ['fɔːməʳ] *adj* früher; (*opposite of
latter*) erstere(r, s); **~ly** *adv* früher
formidable ['fɔːmɪdəbl] *adj* furchtbar
formula ['fɔːmjulə] (*pl* -e *or* -s) *n* Formel *f*;
~te ['fɔːmjuleɪt] *vt* formulieren
fort [fɔːt] *n* Feste *f*, Fort *nt*
forte ['fɔːtɪ] *n* Stärke *f*, starke Seite *f*
forth [fɔːθ] *adv*: **and so ~** und so weiter;
~coming *adj* kommend; (*character*)
entgegenkommend; **~right** *adj* offen;
~with *adv* umgehend
fortify ['fɔːtɪfaɪ] *vt* (ver)stärken; (*protect*)
befestigen
fortitude ['fɔːtɪtjuːd] *n* Seelenstärke *f*
fortnight ['fɔːtnaɪt] (BRIT) *n* vierzehn Tage *pl*;
~ly (BRIT) *adj* zweiwöchentlich ♦ *adv* alle
vierzehn Tage
fortress ['fɔːtrɪs] *n* Festung *f*
fortunate ['fɔːtʃənɪt] *adj* glücklich; **~ly** *adv*
glücklicherweise, zum Glück
fortune ['fɔːtʃən] *n* Glück *nt*; (*money*)
Vermögen *nt*; **~-teller** *n* Wahrsager(in)
m(f)
forty ['fɔːtɪ] *num* vierzig
forum ['fɔːrəm] *n* Forum *nt*

forward ['fɔːwəd] *adj* vordere(r, s); (*movement*) Vorwärts-; (*person*) vorlaut; (*planning*) Voraus- ♦ *adv* vorwärts ♦ *n* (*SPORT*) Stürmer *m* ♦ *vt* (*send*) schicken; (*help*) fördern; **~s** *adv* vorwärts

fossil ['fɔsl] *n* Fossil *nt*, Versteinerung *f*

foster ['fɔstə^r] *vt* (*talent*) fördern; **~ child** *n* Pflegekind *nt*; **~ mother** *n* Pflegemutter *f*

fought [fɔːt] *pt, pp of* **fight**

foul [faul] *adj* schmutzig; (*language*) gemein; (*weather*) schlecht ♦ *n* (*SPORT*) Foul *nt* ♦ *vt* (*mechanism*) blockieren; (*SPORT*) foulen; **~ play** *n* (*SPORT*) Foulspiel *nt*; (*LAW*) Verbrechen *nt*

found [faund] *pt, pp of* **find** ♦ *vt* gründen; **~ation** [faun'deɪʃən] *n* (*act*) Gründung *f*; (*fig*) Fundament *nt*; (*also*: **~ation cream**) Grundierungscreme *f*; **~ations** *npl* (*of house*) Fundament *nt*; **~er** ['faundə^r] *n* Gründer(in) *m(f)* ♦ *vi* sinken

foundry ['faundrɪ] *n* Gießerei *f*

fountain ['fauntɪn] *n* (*Spring*)brunnen *m*; **~ pen** *n* Füllfederhalter *m*

four [fɔː^r] *num* vier; **on all ~s** auf allen vieren; **~-poster** *n* Himmelbett *nt*; **~some** *n* Quartett *nt*; **~teen** *num* vierzehn; **~teenth** *adj* vierzehnte(r, s); **~th** *adj* vierte(r, s)

fowl [faul] *n* Huhn *nt*; (*food*) Geflügel *nt*

fox [fɔks] *n* Fuchs *m* ♦ *vt* täuschen

foyer ['fɔɪeɪ] *n* Foyer *nt*, Vorhalle *f*

fraction ['frækʃən] *n* (*MATH*) Bruch *m*; (*part*) Bruchteil *m*

fracture ['fræktʃə^r] *n* (*MED*) Bruch *m* ♦ *vt* brechen

fragile ['frædʒaɪl] *adj* zerbrechlich

fragment ['frægmənt] *n* Bruchstück *nt*; (*small part*) Splitter *m*

fragrance ['freɪgrəns] *n* Duft *m*; **fragrant** ['freɪgrənt] *adj* duftend

frail [freɪl] *adj* schwach, gebrechlich

frame [freɪm] *n* Rahmen *m*; (*of spectacles*: *also*: **~s**) Gestell *nt*; (*body*) Gestalt *f* ♦ *vt* einrahmen; **to ~ sb** (*inf*: *incriminate*) jdm etwas anhängen; **~ of mind** Verfassung *f*; **~work** *n* Rahmen *m*; (*of society*) Gefüge *nt*

France [frɑːns] *n* Frankreich *nt*

franchise ['fræntʃaɪz] *n* (*POL*) (aktives) Wahlrecht *nt*; (*COMM*) Lizenz *f*

frank [fræŋk] *adj* offen ♦ *vt* (*letter*) frankieren; **~ly** *adv* offen gesagt

frantic ['fræntɪk] *adj* verzweifelt

fraternal [frə'təːnl] *adj* brüderlich

fraternity [frə'təːnɪtɪ] *n* (*club*) Vereinigung *f*; (*spirit*) Brüderlichkeit *f*; (*US: SCH*) Studentenverbindung *f*

fraternize ['frætənaɪz] *vi* fraternisieren

fraud [frɔːd] *n* (*trickery*) Betrug *m*; (*person*) Schwindler(in) *m(f)*; **~ulent** ['frɔːdjulənt] *adj* betrügerisch

fraught [frɔːt] *adj*: **~ with** voller +*gen*

fray [freɪ] *vt, vi* ausfransen; **tempers were**

~ed die Gemüter waren erhitzt

freak [friːk] *n* Monstrosität *f* ♦ *cpd* (*storm etc*) anormal

freckle ['frekl] *n* Sommersprosse *f*

free [friː] *adj* frei; (*loose*) lose; (*liberal*) freigebig ♦ *vt* (*set ~*) befreien; (*unblock*) freimachen; **~ (of charge)** gratis, umsonst; **for ~** gratis, umsonst; **~dom** ['friːdəm] *n* Freiheit *f*; **F~fone** ® *n*: **call F~fone 0800 ...** rufen Sie gebührenfrei 0800 ... an; **~-for-all** *n* (*fight*) allgemeine(s) Handgemenge *nt*; **~ gift** *n* Geschenk *nt*; **~ kick** *n* Freistoß *m*; **~lance** *adj* frei; (*artist*) freischaffend; **~ly** *adv* frei; (*admit*) offen; **F~post** ® *n* ≈ Gebühr zahlt Empfänger; **~range** *adj* (*hen*) Farmhof-; (*eggs*) Land-; **~ trade** *n* Freihandel *m*; **~way** *n* (*US*) Autobahn *f*; **~wheel** *vi* im Freilauf fahren; **~ will** *n*: **of one's own ~ will** aus freien Stücken

freeze [friːz] (*pt* **froze**, *pp* **frozen**) *vi* gefrieren; (*feel cold*) frieren ♦ *vt* (*also fig*) einfrieren ♦ *n* (*fig, FIN*) Stopp *m*; **~r** *n* Tiefkühltruhe *f*; (*in fridge*) Gefrierfach *nt*; **freezing** *adj* eisig; (*freezing cold*) eiskalt; **freezing point** *n* Gefrierpunkt *m*

freight [freɪt] *n* Fracht *f*; **~ train** *n* Güterzug *m*

French [frentʃ] *adj* französisch ♦ *n* (*LING*) Französisch *nt*; **the ~** *npl* (*people*) die Franzosen *pl*; **~ bean** *n* grüne Bohne *f*; **~ fried potatoes** *npl* Pommes frites *pl*; **~ fries** (*US*) *npl* Pommes frites *pl*; **~ horn** *n* (*MUS*) (Wald)horn *nt*; **~ kiss** *n* Zungenkuss *m*; **~ loaf** *n* Baguette *f*; **~man/woman** (*irreg*) *n* Franzose *m*/Französin *f*; **~ window** *n* Verandatür *f*

frenzy ['frenzɪ] *n* Raserei *f*

frequency ['friːkwənsɪ] *n* Häufigkeit *f*; (*PHYS*) Frequenz *f*

frequent [*adj* 'friːkwənt, *vb* frɪ'kwent] *adj* häufig ♦ *vt* (*regelmäßig*) besuchen; **~ly** *adv* (*often*) häufig, oft

fresh [freʃ] *adj* frisch; **~en** *vi* (*also*: **~en up**) (sich) auffrischen; (*person*) sich frisch machen; **~er** (*inf*: *BRIT*) *n* (*UNIV*) Erstsemester *nt*; **~ly** *adv* gerade; **~man** (*irreg*) (*US*) *n* = **fresher**; **~ness** *n* Frische *f*; **~water** *adj* (*fish*) Süßwasser-

fret [fret] *vi* sich *dat* Sorgen machen

friar ['fraɪə^r] *n* Klosterbruder *m*

friction ['frɪkʃən] *n* (*also fig*) Reibung *f*

Friday ['fraɪdɪ] *n* Freitag *m*

fridge [frɪdʒ] (*BRIT*) *n* Kühlschrank *m*

fried [fraɪd] *adj* gebraten

friend [frend] *n* Freund(in) *m(f)*; **~ly** *adj* freundlich; (*relations*) freundschaftlich; **~ly fire** *n* Beschuss *m* durch die eigene Seite; **~ship** *n* Freundschaft *f*

frieze [friːz] *n* Fries *m*

frigate ['frɪgɪt] *n* Fregatte *f*

fright [fraɪt] *n* Schrecken *m*; **to take ~** es mit

der Angst zu tun bekommen; **~en** vt
erschrecken; **to be ~ened** Angst haben;
~ening adj schrecklich; **~ful** (inf) adj
furchtbar

frigid |'frɪdʒɪd| adj frigide

frill |frɪl| n Rüsche f

fringe |frɪndʒ| n Besatz m; (BRIT: of hair)
Pony m; (fig) Peripherie f; **~ benefits** npl
zusätzliche Leistungen pl

Frisbee |'frɪzbɪ| ® n Frisbee nt ®

frisk |frɪsk| vt durchsuchen

frisky |'frɪskɪ| adj lebendig, ausgelassen

fritter |'frɪtə'| vt: **to ~ away** vergeuden

frivolous |'frɪvələs| adj frivol

frizzy |'frɪzɪ| adj kraus

fro |frəu| adv see **to**

frock |frɔk| n Kleid nt

frog |frɔg| n Frosch m; **~man** (irreg) n
Froschmann m

frolic |'frɔlɪk| vi ausgelassen sein

KEYWORD
---

from |frɔm| prep 1 (indicating starting place)
von; (indicating origin etc) aus +dat; **a
letter/telephone call from my sister** ein
Brief/Anruf von meiner Schwester; **where
do you come from?** woher kommen Sie?;
to drink from the bottle aus der Flasche
trinken

2 (indicating time) von ... an; (: past) seit;
from one o'clock to or **until** or **till two**
von ein Uhr bis zwei; **from January (on)**
ab Januar

3 (indicating distance) von ... (entfernt)

4 (indicating price, number etc) ab +dat;
**from £10 ab £10; there were from 20
to 30 people there** es waren zwischen 20
und 30 Leute da

5 (indicating difference): **he can't tell red
from green** er kann nicht zwischen Rot und
Grün unterscheiden; **to be different from
sb/sth** anders sein als jd/etw

6 (because of, based on): **from what he
says** aus dem, was er sagt; **weak from
hunger** schwach vor Hunger

front |frʌnt| n Vorderseite f; (of house)
Fassade f; (promenade: also: **sea ~**)
Strandpromenade f; (MIL, POL, MET) Front f;
(fig: appearances) Fassade f ♦ adj (forward)
vordere(r, s), Vorder-; (first) vorderste(r, s);
in ~ vorne; **in ~ of** vor; **~age** |'frʌntɪdʒ| n
Vorderfront f; **~ door** n Haustür f; **~ier**
|'frʌntɪə'| n Grenze f; **~ page** n Titelseite f;
~ room (BRIT) n Wohnzimmer nt; **~-wheel
drive** n Vorderradantrieb m

frost |frɔst| n Frost m; **~bite** n Erfrierung f;
~ed adj (glass) Milch-; **~y** adj frostig

froth |frɔθ| n Schaum m

frown |fraun| n Stirnrunzeln nt ♦ vi die Stirn
runzeln

froze |frəuz| pt of **freeze**

frozen |'frəuzn| pp of **freeze**

frugal |'fru:gl| adj sparsam, bescheiden

fruit |fru:t| n inv (as collective) Obst nt;
(particular) Frucht f; **~ful** adj fruchtbar;
~ion |fru:'ɪʃən| n: **to come to ~ion** in
Erfüllung gehen; **~ juice** n Fruchtsaft m; **~
machine** n (BRIT) Spielautomat m; **~ salad**
n Obstsalat m

frustrate |frʌs'treɪt| vt vereiteln; **~d** adj
gehemmt; (PSYCH) frustriert

fry |fraɪ| (pt, pp **fried**) vt braten ♦ npl: **small
~** kleine Fische pl; **~ing pan** n Bratpfanne f

ft. abbr = **foot; feet**

fuddy-duddy |'fʌdɪdʌdɪ| n altmodische(r)
Kauz m

fudge |fʌdʒ| n Fondant m

fuel |'fjuəl| n Treibstoff m; (for heating)
Brennstoff m; (for lighter) Benzin nt; **~ oil** n
(diesel ~) Heizöl nt; **~ tank** n Tank m

fugitive |'fju:dʒɪtɪv| n Flüchtling m

fulfil |ful'fɪl| vt (duty) erfüllen; (promise)
einhalten; **~ment** n Erfüllung f

full |ful| adj (box, bottle, price) voll; (person:
satisfied) satt; (member, power, employment)
Voll-; (complete) vollständig, Voll-; (speed)
höchste(r, s); (skirt) weit ♦ adv: **~ well** sehr
wohl; **in ~** vollständig; **a ~ two hours** volle
zwei Stunden; **~-length** adj (lifesize)
lebensgroß; **a ~-length photograph** eine
Ganzaufnahme; **~ moon** n Vollmond m; **~-
scale** adj (attack) General-; (drawing) in
Originalgröße; **~ stop** n Punkt m; **~-time**
adj (job) Ganztags- ♦ adv (work) ganztags
♦ n (SPORT) Spielschluss nt; **~y** adv völlig; **~y
fledged** adj (also fig) flügge; **~y licensed**
adj (hotel, restaurant) mit voller
Schankkonzession or -erlaubnis

fumble |'fʌmbl| vi: **to ~ (with)**
herumfummeln (an +dat)

fume |fju:m| vi qualmen; (fig) kochen (inf);
~s npl (of fuel, car) Abgase pl

fumigate |'fju:mɪgeɪt| vt ausräuchern

fun |fʌn| n Spaß m; **to make ~ of** sich lustig
machen über +acc

function |'fʌŋkʃən| n Funktion f; (occasion)
Veranstaltung f ♦ vi funktionieren; **~al** adj
funktionell

fund |fʌnd| n (money) Geldmittel pl, Fonds
m; (store) Vorrat m; **~s** npl (resources) Mittel
pl

fundamental |fʌndə'mentl| adj
fundamental, grundlegend

funeral |'fju:nərəl| n Beerdigung f; **~
parlour** n Leichenhalle f; **~ service** n
Trauergottesdienst m

funfair |'fʌnfeə'| (BRIT) n Jahrmarkt m

fungi |'fʌŋgaɪ| npl of **fungus**

fungus |'fʌŋgəs| n Pilz m

funnel |'fʌnl| n Trichter m; (NAUT)
Schornstein m

funny ['fʌnɪ] *adj* komisch
fur |fɜː^r| *n* Pelz *m*; ~ **coat** *n* Pelzmantel *m*
furious ['fjʊərɪəs] *adj* wütend; *(attempt)* heftig
furlong ['fɜːlɒŋ] *n* = 201.17 m
furnace ['fɜːnɪs] *n* (Brenn)ofen *m*
furnish ['fɜːnɪʃ] *vt* einrichten; *(supply)* versehen; **~ings** *npl* Einrichtung *f*
furniture ['fɜːnɪtʃə^r] *n* Möbel *pl*; **piece of ~** Möbelstück *nt*
furrow ['fʌrəʊ] *n* Furche *f*
furry ['fɜːrɪ] *adj (tongue)* pelzig; *(animal)* Pelz-
further ['fɜːðə^r] *adj* weitere(r, s) ♦ *adv* weiter ♦ *vt* fördern; **~ education** *n* Weiterbildung *f*; Erwachsenenbildung *f*; **~more** *adv* ferner
furthest ['fɜːðɪst] *superl of* **far**
furtive ['fɜːtɪv] *adj* verstohlen
fury ['fjʊərɪ] *n* Wut *f*, Zorn *m*
fuse [fjuːz] *(US* fuze) *n (ELEC)* Sicherung *f*; *(of bomb)* Zünder *m* ♦ *vt* verschmelzen ♦ *vi (BRIT: ELEC)* durchbrennen; **~ box** *n* Sicherungskasten *m*
fuselage ['fjuːzəlɑːʒ] *n* Flugzeugrumpf *m*
fusion ['fjuːʒən] *n* Verschmelzung *f*
fuss [fʌs] *n* Theater *nt*; **~y** *adj* kleinlich
futile ['fjuːtaɪl] *adj* zwecklos, sinnlos; **futility** [fjuːˈtɪlɪtɪ] *n* Zwecklosigkeit *f*
future ['fjuːtʃə^r] *adj* zukünftig ♦ *n* Zukunft *f*; **in (the)** ~ in Zukunft
fuze [fjuːz] *(US)* = **fuse**
fuzzy ['fʌzɪ] *adj (indistinct)* verschwommen; *(hair)* kraus

G, g

G |dʒiː| *n (MUS)* G *nt*
G8 *n abbr* (= Group of Eight) G8 *f*
gabble ['gæbl] *vi* plappern
gable ['geɪbl] *n* Giebel *m*
gadget ['gædʒɪt] *n* Vorrichtung *f*
Gaelic ['geɪlɪk] *adj* gälisch ♦ *n (LING)* Gälisch *nt*
gaffe [gæf] *n* Fauxpas *m*
gag [gæg] *n* Knebel *m*; *(THEAT)* Gag *m* ♦ *vt* knebeln
gaiety ['geɪɪtɪ] *n* Fröhlichkeit *f*
gain [geɪn] *vt (obtain)* erhalten; *(win)* gewinnen ♦ *vi (clock)* vorgehen ♦ *n* Gewinn *m*; **to ~ in sth** an etw *dat* gewinnen; **~ on** *vt fus* einholen
gait [geɪt] *n* Gang *m*
gal. *abbr* = **gallon**
gala ['gɑːlə] *n* Fest *nt*
galaxy ['gæləksɪ] *n* Sternsystem *nt*
gale [geɪl] *n* Sturm *m*
gallant ['gælənt] *adj* tapfer; *(polite)* galant
gallbladder ['gɔːlblædə^r] *n* Gallenblase *f*
gallery ['gælərɪ] *n (also:* **art ~)** Galerie *f*
galley ['gælɪ] *n (ship's kitchen)* Kombüse *f*; *(ship)* Galeere *f*

gallon ['gæln] *n* Gallone *f*
gallop ['gæləp] *n* Galopp *m* ♦ *vi* galoppieren
gallows ['gæləuz] *n* Galgen *m*
gallstone ['gɔːlstəun] *n* Gallenstein *m*
galore [gə'lɔː^r] *adv* in Hülle und Fülle
galvanize ['gælvənaɪz] *vt (metal)* galvanisieren; *(fig)* elektrisieren
gambit ['gæmbɪt] *n (fig):* **opening ~** (einleitende(r)) Schachzug *m*
gamble ['gæmbl] *vi* (um Geld) spielen ♦ *vt (risk)* aufs Spiel setzen ♦ *n* Risiko *nt*; **~r** *n* Spieler(in) *m(f)*; **gambling** *n* Glücksspiel *nt*
game [geɪm] *n* Spiel *nt*; *(hunting)* Wild *nt* ♦ *adj:* ~ **(for)** bereit (zu); **~keeper** *n* Wildhüter *m*; **~s console** *n (COMPUT)* Gameboy *m* ®, Konsole *f*
gammon ['gæmən] *n* geräucherte(r) Schinken *m*
gamut ['gæmət] *n* Tonskala *f*
gang [gæŋ] *n (of criminals, youths)* Bande *f*; *(of workmen)* Kolonne *f* ♦ *vi:* **to ~ up on sb** sich gegen jdn verschwören
gangrene ['gæŋgriːn] *n* Brand *m*
gangster ['gæŋstə^r] *n* Gangster *m*
gangway ['gæŋweɪ] *n (NAUT)* Laufplanke *f*; *(aisle)* Gang *m*
gaol [dʒeɪl] *(BRIT)* *n, vt* = **jail**
gap [gæp] *n* Lücke *f*
gape [geɪp] *vi* glotzen; **gaping** ['geɪpɪŋ] *adj (wound)* klaffend; *(hole)* gähnend
garage ['gærɑːʒ] *n* Garage *f*; *(for repair)* (Auto)reparaturwerkstatt *f*; *(for petrol)* Tankstelle *f*
garbage ['gɑːbɪdʒ] *n* Abfall *m*; **~ can** *(US)* *n* Mülltonne *f*
garbled ['gɑːbld] *adj (story)* verdreht
garden ['gɑːdn] *n* Garten *m*; **~s** *npl (public park)* Park *m*; *(private)* Gartenanlagen *pl*; **~er** *n* Gärtner(in) *m(f)*; **~ing** *n* Gärtnern *nt*
gargle ['gɑːgl] *vi* gurgeln
gargoyle ['gɑːgɔɪl] *n* Wasserspeier *m*
garish ['gɛərɪʃ] *adj* grell
garland ['gɑːlənd] *n* Girlande *f*
garlic ['gɑːlɪk] *n* Knoblauch *m*
garment ['gɑːmənt] *n* Kleidungsstück *nt*
garnish ['gɑːnɪʃ] *vt (food)* garnieren
garrison ['gærɪsn] *n* Garnison *f*
garter ['gɑːtə^r] *n* Strumpfband *nt*; *(US)* Strumpfhalter *m*
gas [gæs] *n* Gas *nt*; *(esp US: petrol)* Benzin *nt* ♦ *vt* vergasen; **~ cooker** *(BRIT)* *n* Gasherd *m*; **~ cylinder** *n* Gasflasche *f*; **~ fire** *n* Gasofen *m*
gash [gæʃ] *n* klaffende Wunde *f* ♦ *vt* tief verwunden
gasket ['gæskɪt] *n* Dichtungsring *m*
gas mask *n* Gasmaske *f*
gas meter *n* Gaszähler *m*
gasoline ['gæsəliːn] *(US)* *n* Benzin *nt*
gasp [gɑːsp] *vi* keuchen; *(in surprise)* tief Luft holen ♦ *n* Keuchen *nt*

gas: ~ **ring** n Gasring m; ~ **station** (US) n Tankstelle f; ~ **tap** n Gashahn m

gastric ['gæstrɪk] adj Magen-

gate |geɪt| n Tor nt; (barrier) Schranke f

gateau ['gætəu] (pl ~x) n Torte f

gatecrash ['geɪtkræʃ] (BRIT) vt (party) platzen in +acc

gateway ['geɪtweɪ] n Toreingang m

gather ['gæðə'] vt (people) versammeln; (things) sammeln; (understand) annehmen ♦ vi (assemble) sich versammeln; **to ~ speed** schneller werden; **to ~ (from)** schließen (aus); **~ing** n Versammlung f

gauche |gəuʃ| adj linkisch

gaudy |'gɔːdɪ| adj schreiend

gauge |geɪdʒ| n (instrument) Messgerät nt; (RAIL) Spurweite f; (dial) Anzeiger m; (measure) Maß nt ♦ vt (ab)messen; (fig) abschätzen

gaunt |gɔːnt| adj hager

gauze |gɔːz| n Gaze f

gave |geɪv| pt of **give**

gay |geɪ| adj (homosexual) schwul; (lively) lustig

gaze |geɪz| n Blick m ♦ vi starren; **to ~ at sth** etw dat anstarren

gazelle |gə'zel| n Gazelle f

gazumping |gə'zʌmpɪŋ| (BRIT) n Hausverkauf an höher Bietenden trotz Zusage an anderen

GB n abbr = **Great Britain**

GCE (BRIT) n abbr = **General Certificate of Education**

GCSE (BRIT) n abbr = **General Certificate of Secondary Education**

gear |gɪə'| n Getriebe nt; (equipment) Ausrüstung f; (AUT) Gang m ♦ vt (fig: adapt): **to be ~ed to** ausgerichtet sein auf +acc; **top** ~ höchste(r) Gang m; **high** ~ (US) höchste(r) Gang m; **low** ~ niedrige(r) Gang m; **in** ~ eingekuppelt; ~ **box** n Getriebe(gehäuse) nt; ~ **lever** n Schalthebel m; ~ **shift** (US) n Schalthebel m

geese |giːs| npl of **goose**

gel |dʒel| n Gel nt

gelatin(e) ['dʒelətiːn] n Gelatine f

gem |dʒem| n Edelstein m; (fig) Juwel nt

Gemini ['dʒemɪnaɪ] n Zwillinge pl

gender ['dʒendə'] n (GRAM) Geschlecht nt

gene |dʒiːn| n Gen nt

general ['dʒenərl] n General m ♦ adj allgemein; ~ **delivery** (US) n Ausgabe (schalter m) f postlagernder Sendungen; ~ **election** n allgemeine Wahlen pl; **~ize** vi verallgemeinern; ~ **knowledge** n Allgemeinwissen nt; **~ly** adv allgemein, im Allgemeinen; ~ **practitioner** n praktische(r) Arzt m, praktische Ärztin f

generate ['dʒenəreɪt] vt erzeugen

generation |dʒenə'reɪʃən| n Generation f; (act) Erzeugung f

generator ['dʒenəreɪtə'] n Generator m

generosity |dʒenə'rɒsɪtɪ| n Großzügigkeit f

generous ['dʒenərəs] adj großzügig

genetic |dʒɪ'netɪk| adj genetisch; **~ally** adv genetisch; **~ally modified** genmanipuliert; ~ **engineering** n Gentechnik f; ~ **fingerprinting** |-'fɪŋɡəprɪntɪŋ| n genetische Fingerabdrücke pl

genetics |dʒɪ'netɪks| n Genetik f

Geneva |dʒɪ'niːvə| n Genf nt

genial ['dʒiːnɪəl] adj freundlich, jovial

genitals ['dʒenɪtlz] npl Genitalien pl

genius ['dʒiːnɪəs] n Genie nt

genocide ['dʒenəusaɪd] n Völkermord m

gent |dʒent| n abbr = **gentleman**

genteel |dʒen'tiːl| adj (polite) wohlanständig; (affected) affektiert

gentle ['dʒentl] adj sanft, zart

gentleman ['dʒentlmən] (irreg) n Herr m; (polite) Gentleman m

gentleness ['dʒentlnɪs] n Zartheit f, Milde f

gently ['dʒentlɪ] adv zart, sanft

gentry ['dʒentrɪ] n Landadel m

gents |dʒents| n: **G~** (lavatory) Herren pl

genuine ['dʒenjuɪn] adj echt

geographic(al) |dʒɪə'græfɪk(l)| adj geografisch

geography |dʒɪ'ɒɡrəfɪ| n Geografie f

geological |dʒɪə'lɒdʒɪkl| adj geologisch

geology |dʒɪ'ɒlədʒɪ| n Geologie f

geometric(al) |dʒɪə'metrɪk(l)| adj geometrisch

geometry |dʒɪ'ɒmətrɪ| n Geometrie f

geranium |dʒɪ'reɪnɪəm| n Geranie f

geriatric |dʒerɪ'ætrɪk| adj Alten- ♦ n Greis(in) m(f)

germ |dʒɜːm| n Keim m; (MED) Bazillus m

German ['dʒɜːmən] adj deutsch ♦ n Deutsche(r) f(m); (LING) Deutsch nt; ~ **measles** n Röteln pl; **~y** n Deutschland nt

germination |dʒɜːmɪ'neɪʃən| n Keimen nt

gesticulate |dʒes'tɪkjuleɪt| vi gestikulieren

gesture ['dʒestjə'] n Geste f

KEYWORD

get |get| (pt, pp **got**, pp **gotten** (US)) vi 1 (become, be) werden; **to get old/tired** alt/müde werden; **to get married** heiraten
2 (go) (an)kommen, gehen
3 (begin): **to get to know sb** jdn kennen lernen; **let's get going** or **started!** fangen wir an!
4 (modal aux vb): **you've got to do it** du musst es tun
♦ vt 1: **to get sth done** (do) etw machen; (have done) etw machen lassen; **to get sth going** or **to go** etw in Gang bringen or bekommen; **to get sb to do sth** jdn dazu bringen, etw zu tun
2 (obtain: money, permission, results) erhalten; (find: job, flat) finden; (fetch: person, object) holen; **to get sth for sb** jdm

etw besorgen; **get me Mr Jones, please**
(TEL) verbinden Sie mich bitte mit Mr Jones
3 (receive: present, letter) bekommen,
kriegen; (acquire: reputation etc) erwerben
4 (catch) bekommen, kriegen; (hit: target
etc) treffen, erwischen; **get him!** (to dog)
fass!
5 (take, move) bringen; **to get sth to sb**
jdm etw bringen
6 (understand) verstehen; (hear)
mitbekommen; **I've got it!** ich habs!
7 (have, possess): **to have got sth** etw
haben
get about vi herumkommen; (news) sich
verbreiten
get along vi (people) (gut) zurechtkommen; (depart) sich acc auf den Weg
machen
get at vt (facts) herausbekommen; **to get
at sb** (nag) an jdm herumnörgeln
get away vi (leave) sich acc davonmachen;
(escape): **to get away from sth** von etw dat
entkommen; **to get away with sth** mit etw
davonkommen
get back vi (return) zurückkommen ♦ vt
zurückbekommen
get by vi (pass) vorbeikommen; (manage)
zurechtkommen
get down vi (her)untergehen ♦ vt (depress)
fertig machen; **to get down to** in Angriff
nehmen; (find time to do) kommen zu
get in vi (train) ankommen; (arrive home)
heimkommen
get into vt (enter) hinein-/hereinkommen in
+acc; (: car, train etc) einsteigen in +acc;
(clothes) anziehen
get off vi (from train etc) aussteigen; (from
horse) absteigen ♦ vt aussteigen aus;
absteigen von
get on vi (progress) vorankommen; (be
friends) auskommen; (age) alt werden; (onto
train etc) einsteigen; (onto horse) aufsteigen
♦ vt einsteigen in +acc; auf etw acc
aufsteigen
get out vi (of house) herauskommen; (of
vehicle) aussteigen ♦ vt (take out)
herausholen
get out of vt (duty etc) herumkommen um
get over vt (illness) sich acc erholen von;
(surprise) verkraften; (news) fassen; (loss)
sich abfinden mit
get round vt herumkommen; (fig: person)
herumkriegen
get through to vt (TEL) durchkommen zu
get together vi zusammenkommen
get up vi aufstehen ♦ vt hinaufbringen; (go
up) hinaufgehen; (organize) auf die Beine
stellen
get up to vt (reach) erreichen; (prank etc)
anstellen

getaway ['gɛtəweɪ] n Flucht f
get-up ['gɛtʌp] (inf) n Aufzug m
geyser ['giːzəʳ] n Geiser m; (heater)
Durchlauferhitzer m
ghastly ['gɑːstlɪ] adj grässlich
gherkin ['gɜːkɪn] n Gewürzgurke f
ghetto ['gɛtəu] n G(h)etto nt; **~ blaster** n
(große(r)) Radiorekorder m
ghost [gəust] n Gespenst nt
giant ['dʒaɪənt] n Riese m ♦ adj riesig, Riesen-
gibberish ['dʒɪbərɪʃ] n dumme(s) Geschwätz nt
gibe [dʒaɪb] n spöttische Bemerkung f
giblets ['dʒɪblɪts] npl Geflügelinnereien pl
giddiness ['gɪdɪnɪs] n Schwindelgefühl nt
giddy ['gɪdɪ] adj schwindlig
gift [gɪft] n Geschenk nt; (ability) Begabung f;
~ed adj begabt; **~ shop** n Geschenkeladen
m; **~ token, ~ voucher** n Geschenkgutschein
m
gigantic [dʒaɪˈgæntɪk] adj riesenhaft
giggle ['gɪgl] vi kichern ♦ n Gekicher nt
gild [gɪld] vt vergolden
gill [dʒɪl] n (1/4 pint) Viertelpinte f
gills [gɪlz] npl (of fish) Kiemen pl
gilt [gɪlt] n Vergoldung f ♦ adj vergoldet; **~-
edged** adj mündelsicher
gimmick ['gɪmɪk] n Gag m
gin [dʒɪn] n Gin m
ginger ['dʒɪndʒəʳ] n Ingwer m; **~ ale** n
Ingwerbier m; **~ beer** n Ingwerbier nt;
~bread n Pfefferkuchen m; **~-haired** adj
rothaarig
gingerly ['dʒɪndʒəlɪ] adv behutsam
gipsy ['dʒɪpsɪ] n Zigeuner(in) m(f)
giraffe [dʒɪˈrɑːf] n Giraffe f
girder ['gɜːdəʳ] n Eisenträger m
girdle ['gɜːdl] n Hüftgürtel m
girl [gɜːl] n Mädchen nt; **an English ~** eine
(junge) Engländerin; **~friend** n Freundin f;
~ish adj mädchenhaft
giro ['dʒaɪrəu] n (bank ~) Giro nt; (post office
~) Postscheckverkehr m
girth [gɜːθ] n (measure) Umfang m; (strap)
Sattelgurt m
gist [dʒɪst] n Wesentliche(s) nt
give [gɪv] (pt gave, pp given) vt geben ♦ vi
(break) nachgeben; **~ away** vt verschenken;
(betray) verraten; **~ back** vt zurückgeben; **~
in** vi nachgeben ♦ vt (hand in) abgeben; **~
off** vt abgeben; **~ out** vt verteilen;
(announce) bekannt geben; **~ up** vt, vi
aufgeben; **to ~ o.s. up** sich stellen; (after
siege) sich ergeben; **~ way** vi (BRIT: traffic)
Vorfahrt lassen; (to feelings): **to ~ way to**
nachgeben +dat
glacier ['glæsɪəʳ] n Gletscher m
glad [glæd] adj froh; **~ly** ['glædlɪ] adv gern(e)
glamorous ['glæmərəs] adj reizvoll
glamour ['glæməʳ] n Glanz m
glance [glɑːns] n Blick m ♦ vi: **to ~ (at)**
(hin)blicken (auf +acc); **~ off** vt fus (fly off)

abprallen von; **glancing** |'glɑːnsɪŋ| adj (blow) Streif-

gland |glænd| n Drüse f

glare |glɛəʳ| n (light) grelle(s) Licht nt; (stare) wilde(r) Blick m ♦ vi grell scheinen; (angrily): **to ~ at** böse ansehen; **glaring** |'glɛərɪŋ| adj (injustice) schreiend; (mistake) krass

glass |glɑːs| n Glas nt; (mirror: also: **looking ~**) Spiegel m; **~es** npl (spectacles) Brille f; **~house** n Gewächshaus nt; **~ware** n Glaswaren pl; **~y** adj glasig

glaze |gleɪz| vt verglasen; (finish with a ~) glasieren ♦ n Glasur f; **~d** adj (eye) glasig; (pot) glasiert; **glazier** |'gleɪzɪəʳ| n Glaser m

gleam |gliːm| n Schimmer m ♦ vi schimmern

glean |gliːn| vt (fig) ausfindig machen

glen |glɛn| n Bergtal nt

glib |glɪb| adj oberflächlich

glide |glaɪd| vi gleiten; **~r** n (AVIAT) Segelflugzeug nt; **gliding** |'glaɪdɪŋ| n Segelfliegen nt

glimmer |'glɪməʳ| n Schimmer m

glimpse |glɪmps| n flüchtige(r) Blick m ♦ vt flüchtig erblicken

glint |glɪnt| n Glitzern nt ♦ vi glitzern

glisten |'glɪsn| vi glänzen

glitter |'glɪtəʳ| vi funkeln ♦ n Funkeln nt

gloat |gləut| vi: **to ~ over** sich weiden an +dat

global |'gləubl| adj: **~ warming** globale(r) Temperaturanstieg m

globe |gləub| n Erdball m; (sphere) Globus m

gloom |gluːm| n (darkness) Dunkel nt; (depression) düstere Stimmung f; **~y** adj düster

glorify |'glɔːrɪfaɪ| vt verherrlichen

glorious |'glɔːrɪəs| adj glorreich

glory |'glɔːrɪ| n Ruhm m

gloss |glɔs| n (shine) Glanz m; **~ over** vt fus übertünchen

glossary |'glɔsərɪ| n Glossar nt

glossy |'glɔsɪ| adj (surface) glänzend

glove |glʌv| n Handschuh m; **~ compartment** n (AUT) Handschuhfach nt

glow |gləu| vi glühen ♦ n Glühen nt

glower |'glauəʳ| vi: **to ~ at** finster anblicken

glucose |'gluːkəus| n Traubenzucker m

glue |gluː| n Klebstoff m ♦ vt kleben

glum |glʌm| adj bedrückt

glut |glʌt| n Überfluss m

glutton |'glʌtn| n Vielfraß m; **a ~ for work** ein Arbeitstier nt

glycerin(e) |'glɪsəriːn| n Glyzerin nt

GM abbr = **genetically modified**

gnarled |nɑːld| adj knorrig

gnat |næt| n Stechmücke f

gnaw |nɔː| vt nagen an +dat

gnome |nəum| n Gnom m

go |gəu| (pt **went**, pp **gone**, pl **~es**) vi gehen; (travel) reisen, fahren; (depart: train) (ab)fahren; (be sold) verkauft werden; (work) gehen, funktionieren; (fit, suit) passen; (become) werden; (break etc) nachgeben ♦ n (energy) Schwung m; (attempt) Versuch m; **he's ~ing to do it** er wird es tun; **to ~ for a walk** spazieren gehen; **to ~ dancing** tanzen gehen; **how did it ~?** wie wars?; **to ~ with** (be suitable) passen zu; **to have a ~ at sth** etw versuchen; **to be on the ~** auf Trab sein; **whose ~ is it?** wer ist dran?; **~ about** vi (rumour) umgehen ♦ vt fus: **how do I ~ about this?** wie packe ich das an?; **~ after** vt fus (pursue: person) nachgehen +dat; **~ ahead** vi (proceed) weitergehen; **~ along** vi dahingehen, dahinfahren ♦ vt entlanggehen, entlangfahren; **to ~ along with** (support) zustimmen +dat; **~ away** vi (depart) weggehen; **~ back** vi (return) zurückgehen; **~ back on** vt fus (promise) nicht halten; **~ by** vi (years, time) vergehen ♦ vt fus sich richten nach; **~ down** vi (sun) untergehen ♦ vt fus hinuntergehen, hinunterfahren; **~ for** vt fus (fetch) holen (gehen); (like) mögen; (attack) sich stürzen auf +acc; **~ in** vi hineingehen; **~ in for** vt fus (competition) teilnehmen an; **~ into** vt fus (enter) hineingehen in +acc; (study) sich befassen mit; **~ off** vi (depart) weggehen; (lights) ausgehen; (milk etc) sauer werden; (explode) losgehen ♦ vt fus (dislike) nicht mehr mögen; **~ on** vi (continue) weitergehen; (inf: complain) meckern; (lights) angehen; **to ~ on with sth** mit etw weitermachen; **~ out** vi (fire, light) ausgehen; (of house) hinausgehen; **~ over** vi (ship) kentern ♦ vt fus (examine, check) durchgehen; **~ past** vi: **to ~ past sth** an etw +dat vorbeigehen; **~ round** vi (visit): **to ~ round (to sb's)** (bei jdm) vorbeigehen; **~ through** vt fus (town etc) durchgehen, durchfahren; **~ up** vi (price) steigen; **~ with** vt fus (suit) zu etw passen; **~ without** vt fus sich behelfen ohne; (food) entbehren

goad |gəud| vt anstacheln

go-ahead |'gəuəhɛd| adj zielstrebig; (progressive) fortschrittlich ♦ n grüne(s) Licht nt

goal |gəul| n Ziel nt; (SPORT) Tor nt; **~keeper** n Torwart m; **~ post** n Torpfosten m

goat |gəut| n Ziege f

gobble |'gɔbl| vt (also: **~ down**, **~ up**) hinunterschlingen

go-between |'gəubɪtwiːn| n Mittelsmann m

god |gɔd| n Gott m; **G~** n Gott m; **~child** n Patenkind nt; **~daughter** n Patentochter f; **~dess** n Göttin f; **~father** n Pate m; **~forsaken** adj gottverlassen; **~mother** n Patin f; **~send** n Geschenk nt des Himmels; **~son** n Patensohn m

goggles |'gɔglz| npl Schutzbrille f

going |'gəuɪŋ| n (HORSE-RACING) Bahn f ♦ adj (rate) gängig; (concern) gut gehend; **it's hard ~** es ist schwierig

gold [gəʊld] n Gold nt ♦ adj golden; **~en** adj golden, Gold-; **~fish** n Goldfisch m; **~ mine** n Goldgrube f; **~plated** adj vergoldet; **~smith** n Goldschmied(in) m(f)

golf [gɒlf] n Golf nt; **~ ball** n Golfball m; (on typewriter) Kugelkopf m; **~ club** n (society) Golfklub m; (stick) Golfschläger m; **~ course** n Golfplatz m; **~er** n Golfspieler(in) m(f)

gondola ['gɒndələ] n Gondel f

gone [gɒn] pp of **go**

gong [gɒŋ] n Gong m

good [gʊd] n (benefit) Wohl nt; (moral excellence) Güte f ♦ adj gut; **~s** npl (merchandise etc) Waren pl, Güter pl; **a ~ deal (of)** ziemlich viel; **a ~ many** ziemlich viele; **~ morning!** guten Morgen!; **~ afternoon!** guten Tag!; **~ evening!** guten Abend!; **~ night!** gute Nacht!; **would you be ~ enough to …?** könnten Sie bitte …?

goodbye ['gʊd'baɪ] excl auf Wiedersehen!

good: G~ Friday n Karfreitag m; **~-looking** adj gut aussehend; **~-natured** adj gutmütig; (joke) harmlos; **~ness** n Güte f; (virtue) Tugend f; **~s train** (BRIT) n Güterzug m; **~will** n (favour) Wohlwollen nt; (COMM) Firmenansehen nt

goose [guːs] n (pl **geese**) n Gans f

gooseberry ['gʊzbərɪ] n Stachelbeere f

gooseflesh ['guːsfleʃ] n Gänsehaut f

goose pimples npl Gänsehaut f

gore [gɔːʳ] vt aufspießen ♦ n Blut nt

gorge [gɔːdʒ] n Schlucht f ♦ vt: **to ~ o.s.** (sich voll) fressen

gorgeous ['gɔːdʒəs] adj prächtig

gorilla [gə'rɪlə] n Gorilla m

gorse [gɔːs] n Stechginster m

gory ['gɔːrɪ] adj blutig

go-slow ['gəʊ'sləʊ] (BRIT) n Bummelstreik m

gospel ['gɒspl] n Evangelium nt

gossip ['gɒsɪp] n Klatsch m; (person) Klatschbase f ♦ vi klatschen

got [gɒt] pt, pp of **get**

gotten ['gɒtn] (US) pp of **get**

gout [gaʊt] n Gicht f

govern ['gʌvn] vt regieren; verwalten

governess ['gʌvənɪs] n Gouvernante f

government ['gʌvnmənt] n Regierung f

governor ['gʌvənəʳ] n Gouverneur m

gown [gaʊn] n Gewand nt; (UNIV) Robe f

G.P. n abbr = **general practitioner**

grab [græb] vt packen

grace [greɪs] n Anmut f; (blessing) Gnade f; (prayer) Tischgebet nt ♦ vt (adorn) zieren; (honour) auszeichnen; **5 days' ~** 5 Tage Aufschub; **~ful** adj anmutig

gracious ['greɪʃəs] adj gnädig; (kind) freundlich

grade [greɪd] n Grad m; (slope) Gefälle f ♦ vt (classify) einstufen; **~ crossing** (US) n Bahnübergang m; **~ school** (US) n Grundschule f

gradient ['greɪdɪənt] n Steigung f; Gefälle nt

gradual ['grædjʊəl] adj allmählich; **~ly** adv allmählich

graduate [n 'grædjuɪt, vb 'grædjueɪt] n: **to be a ~** das Staatsexamen haben ♦ vi das Staatsexamen machen; **graduation** [grædjʊ'eɪʃən] n Abschlussfeier f

graffiti [grə'fiːtɪ] npl Graffiti pl

graft [grɑːft] n (hard work) Schufterei f; (MED) Verpflanzung f ♦ vt pfropfen; (fig) aufpfropfen; (MED) verpflanzen

grain [greɪn] n Korn nt; (in wood) Maserung f

gram [græm] n Gramm nt

grammar ['græməʳ] n Grammatik f; **~ school** (BRIT) n Gymnasium nt; **grammatical** [grə'mætɪkl] adj grammat(ikal)isch

gramme [græm] n = **gram**

granary ['grænərɪ] n Kornspeicher m

grand [grænd] adj großartig; **~child** (pl **~children**) n Enkelkind nt, Enkel(in) m(f); **~dad** n Opa m; **~daughter** n Enkelin f; **~eur** ['grændjəʳ] n Erhabenheit f; **~father** n Großvater m; **~iose** ['grændɪəʊs] adj (imposing) großartig; (pompous) schwülstig; **~ma** n Oma f; **~mother** n Großmutter f; **~pa** n = **granddad**; **~parents** npl Großeltern pl; **~ piano** n Flügel m; **~son** n Enkel m; **~stand** n Haupttribüne f

granite ['grænɪt] n Granit m

granny ['grænɪ] n Oma f

grant [grɑːnt] vt gewähren ♦ n Unterstützung f; (UNIV) Stipendium nt; **to take sth for ~ed** etw als selbstverständlich (an)nehmen

granulated sugar ['grænjʊleɪtɪd-] n Zuckerraffinade f

granule ['grænjuːl] n Körnchen nt

grape [greɪp] n (Wein)traube f

grapefruit ['greɪpfruːt] n Pampelmuse f, Grapefruit f

graph [grɑːf] n Schaubild nt; **~ic** ['græfɪk] adj (descriptive) anschaulich; (drawing) grafisch; **~ics** npl Grafik f

grapple ['græpl] vi: **to ~ with** kämpfen mit

grasp [grɑːsp] vt ergreifen; (understand) begreifen ♦ n Griff m; (of subject) Beherrschung f; **~ing** adj habgierig

grass [grɑːs] n Gras nt; **~hopper** n Heuschrecke f; **~land** n Weideland nt; **~roots** adj an der Basis; **~ snake** n Ringelnatter f

grate [greɪt] n Kamin m ♦ vi (sound) knirschen ♦ vt (cheese etc) reiben; **to ~ on the nerves** auf die Nerven gehen

grateful ['greɪtful] adj dankbar

grater ['greɪtəʳ] n Reibe f

gratify ['grætɪfaɪ] vt befriedigen; **~ing** adj erfreulich

grating ['greɪtɪŋ] n (iron bars) Gitter nt ♦ adj (noise) knirschend

gratitude ['grætɪtjuːd] n Dankbarkeit f

gratuity [grə'tjuːɪtɪ] n Gratifikation f

grave [greɪv] n Grab nt ♦ adj (serious) ernst

gravel ['grævl] n Kies m

gravestone ['greɪvstəʊn] n Grabstein m
graveyard ['greɪvjɑːd] n Friedhof m
gravity ['grævɪtɪ] n Schwerkraft f;
(seriousness) Schwere f
gravy ['greɪvɪ] n (Braten)soße f
gray [greɪ] adj = **grey**
graze [greɪz] vi grasen ♦ vt (touch) streifen;
(MED) abschürfen ♦ n Abschürfung f
grease [griːs] n (fat) Fett nt; (lubricant)
Schmiere f ♦ vt (ab)schmieren; **~proof**
(BRIT) adj (paper) Butterbrot-; **greasy**
['griːsɪ] adj fettig
great [greɪt] adj groß; (inf: good) prima; **G~
Britain** n Großbritannien nt; **~-
grandfather** n Urgroßvater m; **~-
grandmother** n Urgroßmutter f; **~ly** adv
sehr
Greece [griːs] n Griechenland nt
greed [griːd] n (also: **~iness**) Gier f;
(meanness) Geiz m; **~(iness) for** Gier nach;
~y adj gierig
Greek [griːk] adj griechisch ♦ n Grieche m,
Griechin f; (LING) Griechisch nt
green [griːn] adj grün ♦ n (village ~)
Dorfwiese f; **~ belt** n Grüngürtel m; **~ card**
n (AUT) grüne Versicherungskarte f; **~ery** n
Grün nt; grüne(s) Laub nt; **~gage** n
Reneklode f, Reineclaude f; **~grocer** (BRIT) n
Obst- und Gemüsehändler m; **~house** n
Gewächshaus nt; **~house effect** n
Treibhauseffekt m; **~house gas** n
Treibhausgas nt
Greenland ['griːnlənd] n Grönland nt
greet [griːt] vt grüßen; **~ing** n Gruß m;
~ing(s) card n Glückwunschkarte f
gregarious [grə'gɛərɪəs] adj gesellig
grenade [grə'neɪd] n Granate f
grew [gruː] pt of **grow**
grey [greɪ] adj grau; **~-haired** adj grauhaarig;
~hound n Windhund m
grid [grɪd] n Gitter nt; (ELEC) Leitungsnetz nt;
(on map) Gitternetz nt
gridlock ['grɪdlɒk] n (AUT: traffic jam)
totale(r) Stau m; **~ed** adj: **to be ~ed** (roads)
total verstopft sein; (talks etc) festgefahren sein
grief [griːf] n Gram m, Kummer m
grievance ['griːvəns] n Beschwerde f
grieve [griːv] vi sich grämen ♦ vt betrüben
grievous ['griːvəs] adj: **~ bodily harm** (JUR)
schwere Körperverletzung f
grill [grɪl] n Grill m ♦ vt (BRIT) grillen;
(question) in die Mangel nehmen
grille [grɪl] n (AUT) (Kühler)gitter nt
grim [grɪm] adj grimmig; (situation) düster
grimace [grɪ'meɪs] n Grimasse f ♦ vi
Grimassen schneiden
grime [graɪm] n Schmutz m; **grimy** ['graɪmɪ]
adj schmutzig
grin [grɪn] n Grinsen nt ♦ vi grinsen
grind [graɪnd] (pt, pp **ground**) vt mahlen;
(US: meat) durch den Fleischwolf drehen;

(sharpen) schleifen; (teeth) knirschen mit ♦ n
(bore) Plackerei f
grip [grɪp] n Griff m; (suitcase) Handkoffer m
♦ vt packen; **~ping** adj (exciting) spannend
grisly ['grɪzlɪ] adj grässlich
gristle ['grɪsl] n Knorpel m
grit [grɪt] n Splitt m; (courage) Mut m ♦ vt
(teeth) zusammenbeißen; (road) (mit Splitt
be)streuen
groan [grəʊn] n Stöhnen nt ♦ vi stöhnen
grocer ['grəʊsər] n Lebensmittelhändler m;
~ies npl Lebensmittel pl; **~'s (shop)** n
Lebensmittelgeschäft nt
groggy ['grɒgɪ] adj benommen
groin [grɔɪn] n Leistengegend f
groom [gruːm] n (also: **bridegroom**)
Bräutigam m; (for horses) Pferdeknecht m
♦ vt (horse) striegeln; **(well-)ed** adj gepflegt
groove [gruːv] n Rille f, Furche f
grope [grəʊp] vi tasten; **~ for** vt fus suchen
nach
gross [grəʊs] adj (coarse) dick, plump; (bad)
grob, schwer; (COMM) brutto; **~ly** adv höchst
grotesque [grə'tɛsk] adj grotesk
grotto ['grɒtəʊ] n Grotte f
ground [graʊnd] pt, pp of **grind** ♦ n Boden
m; (land) Grundbesitz m; (reason) Grund m;
(US: also: **~ wire**) Endleitung f ♦ vi (run
ashore) stranden, auflaufen; **~s** npl (dregs)
Bodensatz m; (around house)
(Garten)anlagen pl; **on the ~** am Boden; **to
the ~** zu Boden; **to gain/lose ~** Boden
gewinnen/verlieren; **(well-)ground** (US) n =
groundsheet; **~ing** n (instruction)
Anfangsunterricht m; **~less** adj grundlos;
~sheet (BRIT) n Zeltboden m; **~ staff** n
Bodenpersonal nt; **~work** n Grundlage f
group [gruːp] n Gruppe f ♦ vt (also: **~
together**) gruppieren ♦ vi sich gruppieren
grouse [graʊs] n inv (bird) schottische(s)
Moorhuhn nt
grove [grəʊv] n Gehölz nt, Hain m
grovel ['grɒvl] vi (fig) kriechen
grow [grəʊ] (pt **grew**, pp **grown**) vi
wachsen; (become) werden ♦ vt (raise)
anbauen; **~ up** vi aufwachsen; **~er** n
Züchter m; **~ing** adj zunehmend
growl [graʊl] vi knurren
grown [grəʊn] pp of **grow**; **~-up** n
Erwachsene(r) mf
growth [grəʊθ] n Wachstum nt; (increase)
Zunahme f; (of beard etc) Wuchs m
grub [grʌb] n Made f, Larve f; (inf: food)
Futter nt; **~by** ['grʌbɪ] adj schmutzig
grudge [grʌdʒ] n Groll m ♦ vt: **to ~ sb sth**
jdm etw missgönnen; **to bear sb a ~** einen
Groll gegen jdn hegen
gruelling ['gruːəlɪŋ] adj (climb, race) mörderisch
gruesome ['gruːsəm] adj grauenhaft
gruff [grʌf] adj barsch
grumble ['grʌmbl] vi murren

grumpy ['grʌmpɪ] adj verdrießlich
grunt |grʌnt| vi grunzen ♦ n Grunzen nt
G-string |'dʒiːstrɪŋ| n Minislip m
guarantee |gærən'tiː| n Garantie f ♦ vt garantieren
guard |gɑːd| n (sentry) Wache f; (BRIT: RAIL) Zugbegleiter m ♦ vt bewachen; **~ed** adj vorsichtig; **~ian** n Vormund m; (keeper) Hüter m; **~'s van** (BRIT) n (RAIL) Dienstwagen m
guerrilla |gə'rɪlə| n Guerilla(kämpfer) m; **~ warfare** n Guerillakrieg m
guess |ges| vt, vi (er)raten, schätzen ♦ n Vermutung f; **~work** n Raterei f
guest |gest| n Gast m; **~ house** n Pension f; **~ room** n Gastzimmer nt
guffaw |gʌ'fɔː| vi schallend lachen
guidance ['gaɪdəns] n (control) Leitung f; (advice) Beratung f
guide |gaɪd| n Führer m; (also: girl ~) Pfadfinderin f ♦ vt führen; **~book** n Reiseführer m; **~ dog** n Blindenhund m; **~lines** npl Richtlinien pl
guild |gɪld| n (HIST) Gilde f
guillotine ['gɪlətiːn] n Guillotine f
guilt |gɪlt| n Schuld f; **~y** adj schuldig
guinea pig |'gɪnɪ-| n Meerschweinchen nt; (fig) Versuchskaninchen nt
guise |gaɪz| n: **in the ~ of** in der Form +gen
guitar |gɪ'tɑː| n Gitarre f
gulf |gʌlf| n Golf m; (fig) Abgrund m
gull |gʌl| n Möwe f
gullet ['gʌlɪt] n Schlund m
gullible ['gʌlɪbl] adj leichtgläubig
gully ['gʌlɪ] n (Wasser)rinne f
gulp |gʌlp| vt (also: **~ down**) hinunterschlucken ♦ vi (gasp) schlucken
gum |gʌm| n (around teeth) Zahnfleisch nt; (glue) Klebstoff m; (also: **chewing ~**) Kaugummi m ♦ vt gummieren; **~boots** (BRIT) npl Gummistiefel pl
gun |gʌn| n Schusswaffe f; **~boat** n Kanonenboot m; **~fire** n Geschützfeuer nt; **~man** (irreg) n bewaffnete(r) Verbrecher m; **~point** n: **at ~point** mit Waffengewalt; **~powder** n Schießpulver nt; **~shot** n Schuss m
gurgle ['gɜːgl] vi gluckern
gush |gʌʃ| vi (rush out) hervorströmen; (fig) schwärmen
gust |gʌst| n Windstoß m, Bö f
gusto ['gʌstəu] n Genuss m, Lust f
gut |gʌt| n (ANAT) Gedärme pl; (string) Darm m; **~s** npl (fig) Schneid m
gutter ['gʌtər] n Dachrinne f; (in street) Gosse f
guttural ['gʌtərl] adj guttural, Kehl-
guy |gaɪ| n (also: **~rope**) Halteseil nt; (man) Typ m, Kerl m
guzzle ['gʌzl] vt, vi (drink) saufen; (eat) fressen

gym [dʒɪm] n (also: **~nasium**) Turnhalle f; (also: **~nastics**) Turnen nt; **~nast** ['dʒɪmnæst] n Turner(in) m(f); **~nastics** |dʒɪm'næstɪks| n Turnen nt, Gymnastik f; **~ shoes** npl Turnschuhe pl
gynaecologist |gaɪnɪ'kɔlədʒɪst| (US **gynecologist**) n Frauenarzt(-ärztin) m(f)
gypsy ['dʒɪpsɪ] n = **gipsy**
gyrate |dʒaɪ'reɪt| vi kreisen

H, h

haberdashery |hæbə'dæʃərɪ| (BRIT) n Kurzwaren pl
habit ['hæbɪt] n (An)gewohnheit f; (monk's) Habit nt or m
habitable ['hæbɪtəbl] adj bewohnbar
habitat ['hæbɪtæt] n Lebensraum m
habitual [hə'bɪtjuəl] adj gewohnheitsmäßig; **~ly** adv gewöhnlich
hack |hæk| vt hacken ♦ n Hieb m; (writer) Schreiberling m
hacker ['hækər] n (COMPUT) Hacker m
hackneyed ['hæknɪd] adj abgedroschen
had |hæd| pt, pp of **have**
haddock ['hædək] (pl **~** or **~s**) n Schellfisch m
hadn't ['hædnt] = **had not**
haemorrhage ['hemərɪdʒ] (US **hemorrhage**) n Blutung f
haemorrhoids ['hemərɔɪdz] (US **hemorrhoids**) npl Hämorr(ho)iden pl
haggard ['hægəd] adj abgekämpft
haggle ['hægl] vi feilschen
Hague [heɪg] n: **The ~** Den Haag nt
hail |heɪl| n Hagel m ♦ vt umjubeln ♦ vi hageln; **~stone** n Hagelkorn nt
hair |heər| n Haar nt, Haare pl; (one ~) Haar nt; **~brush** n Haarbürste f; **~cut** n Haarschnitt m; **to get a ~cut** sich dat die Haare schneiden lassen; **~do** n Frisur f; **~dresser** n Friseur m, Friseuse f; **~dresser's** n Friseursalon m; **~ dryer** n Trockenhaube f; (hand-held) Föhn m, Fön m ®; **~ gel** n Haargel nt; **~grip** n Klemme f; **~net** n Haarnetz nt; **~pin** n Haarnadel f; **~pin bend** (US **~pin curve**) n Haarnadelkurve f; **~-raising** adj haarsträubend; **~ removing cream** n Enthaarungscreme nt; **~ spray** n Haarspray nt; **~style** n Frisur f; **~y** adj haarig
hake [heɪk] n Seehecht m
half |hɑːf| (pl **halves**) n Hälfte f ♦ adj halb ♦ adv halb, zur Hälfte; **~ an hour** eine halbe Stunde; **two and a ~** zweieinhalb; **to cut sth in ~** etw halbieren; **~ a dozen** ein halbes Dutzend, sechs; **~ board** n Halbpension f; **~-caste** n Mischling m; **~ fare** n halbe(r) Fahrpreis m; **~-hearted** adj lustlos; **~-hour** n halbe Stunde f; **~-price** n: **(at) ~-price**

zum halben Preis; **~ term** (BRIT) n (SCH)
Ferien pl in der Mitte des Trimesters; **~~time**
n Halbzeit f; **~way** adv halbwegs, auf
halbem Wege

halibut ['hælɪbət] n inv Heilbutt m

hall [hɔːl] n Saal m; (entrance ~) Hausflur m;
(building) Halle f; **~ of residence** (BRIT)
Studentenwohnheim nt

hallmark ['hɔːlmɑːk] n Stempel m

hallo [hə'ləu] excl = **hello**

Hallowe'en ['hæləu'iːn] n Tag m vor
Allerheiligen

hallucination [həluːsɪ'neɪʃən] n
Halluzination f

hallway ['hɔːlweɪ] n Korridor m

halo ['heɪləu] n Heiligenschein m

halt [hɔːlt] n Halt m ♦ vt, vi anhalten

halve [hɑːv] vt halbieren

halves [hɑːvz] pl of **half**

ham [hæm] n Schinken m

hamburger ['hæmbɜːgəʳ] n Hamburger m

hamlet ['hæmlɪt] n Weiler m

hammer ['hæməʳ] n Hammer m ♦ vt, vi
hämmern

hammock ['hæmək] n Hängematte f

hamper ['hæmpəʳ] vt (be)hindern ♦ n
Picknickkorb m

hamster ['hæmstəʳ] n Hamster m

hand [hænd] n Hand f; (of clock) (Uhr)zeiger
m; (worker) Arbeiter m ♦ vt (pass) geben; **to
give sb a ~** jdm helfen; **at ~** nahe; **to ~** zur
Hand; **in ~** (under control) unter Kontrolle;
(being done) im Gange; (extra) übrig; **on ~**
zur Verfügung; **on the one ~ ..., on the
other ~, ...** einerseits ..., andererseits ...; **~
in** vt abgeben; (forms) einreichen; **~ out** vt
austeilen; **~ over** vt (deliver) übergeben;
(surrender) abgeben; (: prisoner) ausliefern;
~bag n Handtasche f; **~book** n Handbuch
nt; **~brake** n Handbremse f; **~cuffs** npl
Handschellen pl; **~ful** n Hand f voll; (inf:
person) Plage f

handicap ['hændɪkæp] n Handikap nt ♦ vt
benachteiligen; **mentally/physically ~ped**
geistig/körperlich behindert

handicraft ['hændɪkrɑːft] n Kunsthandwerk
nt

handiwork ['hændɪwɜːk] n Arbeit f; (fig)
Werk nt

handkerchief ['hæŋkətʃɪf] n Taschentuch nt

handle ['hændl] n (of door etc) Klinke f; (of
cup etc) Henkel m; (for winding) Kurbel f ♦ vt
(touch) anfassen; (deal with: things) sich
befassen mit; (: people) umgehen mit;
~bar(s) n(pl) Lenkstange f

hand: **~ luggage** n Handgepäck nt; **~made**
adj handgefertigt; **~out** n (distribution)
Verteilung f; (charity) Geldzuwendung f;
(leaflet) Flugblatt nt; **~rail** n Geländer nt;
(on ship) Reling f; **~set** n (TEL) Hörer m;
please replace the ~set bitte legen Sie auf;

~shake n Händedruck f

handsome ['hænsəm] adj gut aussehend

handwriting ['hændraɪtɪŋ] n Handschrift f

handy ['hændɪ] adj praktisch; (shops) leicht
erreichbar; **~man** ['hændɪmæn] (irreg) n
Bastler m

hang [hæŋ] (pt, pp hung) vt aufhängen; (pt,
pp hanged: criminal) hängen ♦ vi hängen
♦ n: **to get the ~ of sth** (inf) den richtigen
Dreh bei etw herauskriegen; **~ about**, **~
around** vi sich herumtreiben; **~ on** vi (wait)
warten; **~ up** vi (TEL) auflegen

hangar ['hæŋəʳ] n Hangar m

hanger ['hæŋəʳ] n Kleiderbügel m

hanger-on [hæŋər'ɒn] n Anhänger(in) m(f)

hang: **~-gliding** n Drachenfliegen nt;
~over n Kater m; **~-up** n Komplex m

hanker ['hæŋkəʳ] vi: **to ~ for** or **after** sich
sehnen nach

hankie ['hæŋkɪ] n abbr = **handkerchief**

hanky ['hæŋkɪ] n abbr = **handkerchief**

haphazard [hæp'hæzəd] adj zufällig

happen ['hæpən] vi sich ereignen, passieren;
as it ~s I'm going there today
zufällig(erweise) gehe ich heute (dort)hin;
~ing n Ereignis nt

happily ['hæpɪlɪ] adv glücklich; (fortunately)
glücklicherweise

happiness ['hæpɪnɪs] n Glück nt

happy ['hæpɪ] adj glücklich; **~ birthday!** alles
Gute zum Geburtstag!; **~-go-lucky** adj
sorglos; **~ hour** n Happy Hour f

harass ['hærəs] vt plagen; **~ment** n
Belästigung f

harbour ['hɑːbəʳ] (US **harbor**) n Hafen m
♦ vt (hope etc) hegen; (criminal etc)
Unterschlupf gewähren

hard [hɑːd] adj (firm) hart; (difficult) schwer;
(harsh) hart(herzig) ♦ adv hart; (try)
sehr; (push, hit) fest; **no ~ feelings!** ich
nehme es dir nicht übel; **~ of hearing**
schwerhörig; **to be ~ done by** übel dran
sein; **~back** n kartonierte Ausgabe f; **~ cash**
n Bargeld nt; **~ disk** n (COMPUT) Festplatte
f; **~en** vt erhärten; (fig) verhärten ♦ vi hart
werden; (fig) sich verhärten; **~-headed** adj
nüchtern; **~ labour** n Zwangsarbeit f

hardly ['hɑːdlɪ] adv kaum

hard: **~ship** n Not f; **~ shoulder** (BRIT) n
(AUT) Seitenstreifen m; **~ up** adj knapp bei
Kasse; **~ware** n Eisenwaren pl; (COMPUT)
Hardware f; **~ware shop** n
Eisenwarenhandlung f; **~-wearing** adj
strapazierfähig; **~-working** adj fleißig

hardy ['hɑːdɪ] adj widerstandsfähig

hare [hɛəʳ] n Hase m; **~-brained** adj
schwachsinnig

harm [hɑːm] n Schaden m ♦ vt schaden +dat;
out of ~'s way in Sicherheit; **~ful** adj
schädlich; **~less** adj harmlos

harmonica [hɑː'mɒnɪkə] n Mundharmonika f

harmonious |hɑːˈməʊnɪəs| adj harmonisch
harmonize |ˈhɑːmənaɪz| vt abstimmen ♦ vi
harmonieren
harmony |ˈhɑːmənɪ| n Harmonie f
harness |ˈhɑːnɪs| n Geschirr nt ♦ vt (horse)
anschirren; (fig) nutzbar machen
harp |hɑːp| n Harfe f ♦ vi: to ~ on about sth
auf etw dat herumreiten
harpoon |hɑːˈpuːn| n Harpune f
harrowing |ˈhærəʊɪŋ| adj nervenaufreibend
harsh |hɑːʃ| adj (rough) rau; (severe) streng;
~ness n Härte f
harvest |ˈhɑːvɪst| n Ernte f ♦ vt, vi ernten
has |hæz| vb see have
hash |hæʃ| vt klein hacken ♦ n (mess)
Kuddelmuddel m
hashish |ˈhæʃɪʃ| n Haschisch nt
hasn't |ˈhæznt| = has not
hassle |ˈhæsl| (inf) n Theater nt
haste |heɪst| n Eile f; ~n |ˈheɪsn| vt
beschleunigen ♦ vi eilen; **hasty** adj hastig;
(rash) vorschnell
hat |hæt| n Hut m
hatch |hætʃ| n (NAUT: also: ~way) Luke f; (in
house) Durchreiche f ♦ vi (young)
ausschlüpfen ♦ vt (brood) ausbrüten; (plot)
aushecken; ~back |ˈhætʃbæk| n (AUT) (Auto
nt mit) Heckklappe f
hatchet |ˈhætʃɪt| n Beil nt
hate |heɪt| vt hassen ♦ n Hass m; ~ful adj
verhasst
hatred |ˈheɪtrɪd| n Hass m
haughty |ˈhɔːtɪ| adj hochnäsig, überheblich
haul |hɔːl| vt ziehen ♦ n (catch) Fang m;
~age n Spedition f; ~ier (US ~er) n
Spediteur m
haunch |hɔːntʃ| n Lende f
haunt |hɔːnt| vt (ghost) spuken in +dat;
(memory) verfolgen; (pub) häufig besuchen
♦ n Lieblingsplatz m; **the castle is ~ed** in
dem Schloss spukt es

| KEYWORD |
---

have |hæv| (pt, pp **had**) aux vb **1** haben; (esp
with vbs of motion) sein; **to have arrived/
slept** angekommen sein/geschlafen haben;
to have been gewesen sein; **having eaten**
or **when he had eaten, he left** nachdem er
gegessen hatte, ging er
2 (in tag questions): **you've done it,
haven't you?** du hast es doch gemacht,
oder nicht?
3 (in short answers and questions): **you've
made a mistake – so I have/no I haven't**
du hast einen Fehler gemacht – ja, stimmt/
nein; **we haven't paid – yes we have!** wir
haben nicht bezahlt – doch; **I've been there
before, have you?** ich war schon einmal da,
du auch?

♦ modal aux vb (be obliged): **to have (got)
to do sth** etw tun müssen; **you haven't to**

tell her du darfst es ihr nicht erzählen
♦ vt **1** (possess) haben; **he has (got) blue
eyes** er hat blaue Augen; **I have (got) an
idea** ich habe eine Idee
2 (referring to meals etc): **to have
breakfast/a cigarette** frühstücken/eine
Zigarette rauchen
3 (receive, obtain etc) haben; **may I have
your address?** kann ich Ihre Adresse
haben?; **to have a baby** ein Kind
bekommen
4 (maintain, allow): **he will have it that he
is right** er besteht darauf, dass er Recht hat;
I won't have it das lasse ich mir nicht
bieten
5: **to have sth done** etw machen lassen; **to
have sb do sth** jdn etw machen lassen; **he
soon had them all laughing** er brachte sie
alle zum Lachen
6 (experience, suffer): **she had her bag
stolen** man hat ihr die Tasche gestohlen; **he
had his arm broken** er hat sich den Arm
gebrochen
7 (+noun: take, hold etc): **to have a walk/
rest** spazieren gehen/sich ausruhen; **to
have a meeting/party** eine Besprechung/
Party haben
have out vt: **to have it out with sb**
(settle problem) etw mit jdm bereden

---

haven |ˈheɪvn| n Zufluchtsort m
haven't |ˈhævnt| = have not
havoc |ˈhævək| n Verwüstung f
hawk |hɔːk| n Habicht m
hay |heɪ| n Heu nt; ~ **fever** n Heuschnupfen
m; ~**stack** n Heuhaufen m
haywire |ˈheɪwaɪər| (inf) adj durcheinander
hazard |ˈhæzəd| n Risiko nt ♦ vt aufs Spiel
setzen; ~**ous** adj gefährlich; ~ **(warning)
lights** npl (AUT) Warnblinklicht nt
haze |heɪz| n Dunst m
hazelnut |ˈheɪzlnʌt| n Haselnuss f
hazy |ˈheɪzɪ| adj (misty) dunstig; (vague)
verschwommen
he |hiː| pron er
head |hed| n Kopf m; (leader) Leiter m ♦ vt
(an)führen, leiten; (ball) köpfen; ~s (or
tails) Kopf (oder Zahl); ~ **first** mit dem
Kopf nach unten; ~ **over heels** kopfüber; ~
for vt fus zugehen auf +acc; ~**ache** n
Kopfschmerzen pl; ~**dress** n Kopfschmuck
m; ~**ing** n Überschrift f; ~**lamp** (BRIT) n
Scheinwerfer m; ~**land** n Landspitze f;
~**light** n Scheinwerfer m; ~**line** n
Schlagzeile f; ~**long** adv kopfüber;
~**master** n (of primary school) Rektor m; (of
secondary school) Direktor m; ~**mistress** n
Rektorin f; Direktorin f; ~ **office** n Zentrale
f; ~**-on** adj Frontal-; ~**phones** npl
Kopfhörer pl; ~**quarters** npl Zentrale f;
(MIL) Hauptquartier nt; ~**rest** n Kopfstütze

f; **~room** n (of bridges etc) lichte Höhe f; **~scarf** n Kopftuch nt; **~strong** adj eigenwillig; **~teacher** (BRIT) n Schulleiter(in) m(f); (of secondary school also) Direktor(in) m; **~ waiter** n Oberkellner m; **~way** n Fortschritte pl; **~wind** n Gegenwind m; **~y** adj berauschend

heal [hiːl] vt heilen ♦ vi verheilen

health [hɛlθ] n Gesundheit f; **~ food** n Reformkost f; **H~ Service** (BRIT) n: **the H~ Service** das Gesundheitswesen; **~y** adj gesund

heap [hiːp] n Haufen m ♦ vt häufen

hear [hɪəʳ] (pt, pp heard) vt hören; (listen to) anhören ♦ vi hören; **~d** [həːd] pt, pp of **hear**; **~ing** n Gehör nt; (JUR) Verhandlung f; **~ing aid** n Hörapparat m; **~say** n Hörensagen nt

hearse [həːs] n Leichenwagen m

heart [haːt] n Herz nt; **~s** npl (CARDS) Herz nt; **by ~** auswendig; **~ attack** n Herzanfall m; **~beat** n Herzschlag m; **~breaking** adj herzzerbrechend; **~broken** adj untröstlich; **~burn** n Sodbrennen nt; **~ failure** n Herzschlag m; **~felt** adj aufrichtig

hearth [haːθ] n Herd m

heartily [ˈhaːtɪlɪ] adv herzlich; (eat) herzhaft

heartless [ˈhaːtlɪs] adj herzlos

hearty [ˈhaːtɪ] adj kräftig; (friendly) freundlich

heat [hiːt] n Hitze f; (of food, water etc) Wärme f; (SPORT: also: **qualifying ~**) Ausscheidungsrunde f ♦ vt (house) heizen; (substance) heiß machen, erhitzen; **~ up** vi warm werden ♦ vt aufwärmen; **~ed** adj erhitzt; (fig) hitzig; **~er** n (Heiz)ofen m

heath [hiːθ] (BRIT) n Heide f

heathen [ˈhiːðn] n Heide m/Heidin f ♦ adj heidnisch, Heiden-

heather [ˈhɛðəʳ] n Heidekraut nt

heat: **~ing** n Heizung f; **~-seeking** adj Wärme suchend; **~stroke** n Hitzschlag m; **~ wave** n Hitzewelle f

heave [hiːv] vt hochheben; (sigh) ausstoßen ♦ vi wogen ♦ n Heben nt

heaven [ˈhɛvn] n Himmel m; **~ly** adj himmlisch

heavily [ˈhɛvɪlɪ] adv schwer

heavy [ˈhɛvɪ] adj schwer; **~ goods vehicle** n Lastkraftwagen m; **~weight** n (SPORT) Schwergewicht nt

Hebrew [ˈhiːbruː] adj hebräisch ♦ n (LING) Hebräisch nt

Hebrides [ˈhɛbrɪdiːz] npl Hebriden pl

heckle [ˈhɛkl] vt unterbrechen

hectic [ˈhɛktɪk] adj hektisch

he'd [hiːd] = **he had; he would**

hedge [hɛdʒ] n Hecke f ♦ vt einzäunen ♦ vi (fig) ausweichen; **to ~ one's bets** sich absichern

hedgehog [ˈhɛdʒhɒg] n Igel m

heed [hiːd] vt (also: **take ~ of**) beachten ♦ n

Beachtung f; **~less** adj achtlos

heel [hiːl] n Ferse f; (of shoe) Absatz m ♦ vt mit Absätzen versehen

hefty [ˈhɛftɪ] adj (person) stämmig; (portion) reichlich

heifer [ˈhɛfəʳ] n Färse f

height [haɪt] n (of person) Größe f; (of object) Höhe f; **~en** vt erhöhen

heir [ɛəʳ] n Erbe m; **~ess** [ˈɛəres] n Erbin f; **~loom** n Erbstück nt

held [hɛld] pt, pp of **hold**

helicopter [ˈhɛlɪkɒptəʳ] n Hubschrauber m

heliport [ˈhɛlɪpɔːt] n Hubschrauberlandeplatz m

hell [hɛl] n Hölle f ♦ excl verdammt!

he'll [hiːl] = **he will; he shall**

hellish [ˈhɛlɪʃ] adj höllisch, verteufelt

hello [həˈləu] excl hallo

helm [hɛlm] n Ruder nt, Steuer nt

helmet [ˈhɛlmɪt] n Helm m

help [hɛlp] n Hilfe f ♦ vt helfen +dat; **I can't ~ it** ich kann nichts dafür; **~ yourself** bedienen Sie sich; **~er** n Helfer m; **~ful** adj hilfreich; **~ing** n Portion f; **~less** adj hilflos

hem [hɛm] n Saum m ♦ vt säumen; **~ in** vt einengen

hemorrhage [ˈhɛmərɪdʒ] (US) n = **haemorrhage**

hemorrhoids [ˈhɛmərɔɪdz] (US) npl = **haemorrhoids**

hen [hɛn] n Henne f

hence [hɛns] adv von jetzt an; (therefore) daher; **~forth** adv von nun an; (from then on) von da an

henchman [ˈhɛntʃmən] (irreg) n Gefolgsmann m

her [həːʳ] pron (acc) sie; (dat) ihr ♦ adj ihr; see also **me; my**

herald [ˈhɛrəld] n (Vor)bote m ♦ vt verkünden

heraldry [ˈhɛrəldrɪ] n Wappenkunde f

herb [həːb] n Kraut nt

herd [həːd] n Herde f

here [hɪəʳ] adv hier; (to this place) hierher; **~after** [hɪərˈɑːftəʳ] adv hernach, künftig ♦ n Jenseits nt; **~by** [hɪəˈbaɪ] adv hiermit

hereditary [hɪˈrɛdɪtrɪ] adj erblich

heredity [hɪˈrɛdɪtɪ] n Vererbung f

heritage [ˈhɛrɪtɪdʒ] n Erbe nt

hermit [ˈhəːmɪt] n Einsiedler m

hernia [ˈhəːnɪə] n Bruch m

hero [ˈhɪərəu] (pl **~es**) n Held m; **~ic** [hɪˈrəuɪk] adj heroisch

heroin [ˈhɛrəuɪn] n Heroin nt

heroine [ˈhɛrəuɪn] n Heldin f

heroism [ˈhɛrəuɪzəm] n Heldentum nt

heron [ˈhɛrən] n Reiher m

herring [ˈhɛrɪŋ] n Hering m

hers [həːz] pron ihre(r, s); see also **mine²**

herself [həːˈsɛlf] pron sich (selbst); (emphatic) selbst; see also **oneself**

he's |hiːz| = he is; he has

hesitant |'hezɪtənt| adj zögernd

hesitate |'hezɪteɪt| vi zögern; **hesitation** |hezɪ'teɪʃən| n Zögern nt

heterosexual |'hetərəu'seksjuəl| adj heterosexuell ♦ n Heterosexuelle(r) mf

hew |hjuː| (pt hewed, pp hewn) vt hauen, hacken

hexagonal |hɛk'sægənl| adj sechseckig

heyday |'heɪdeɪ| n Blüte f, Höhepunkt m

HGV n abbr = **heavy goods vehicle**

hi |haɪ| excl he, hallo

hibernate |'haɪbəneɪt| vi Winterschlaf m halten; **hibernation** |haɪbə'neɪʃən| n Winterschlaf m

hiccough |'hɪkʌp| vi den Schluckauf haben; **~s** npl Schluckauf m

hiccup |'hɪkʌp| = **hiccough**

hid |hɪd| pt of **hide**; **~den** |'hɪdn| pp of **hide**

hide |haɪd| (pt hid, pp hidden) n (skin) Haut f, Fell nt ♦ vt verstecken ♦ vi sich verstecken; **~-and-seek** n Versteckspiel nt; **~away** n Versteck nt

hideous |'hɪdɪəs| adj abscheulich

hiding |'haɪdɪŋ| n (beating) Tracht f Prügel; **to be in ~** (concealed) sich versteckt halten; **~ place** n Versteck nt

hi-fi |'haɪfaɪ| n Hi-Fi nt ♦ adj Hi-Fi-

high |haɪ| adj hoch; (wind) stark ♦ adv hoch; **it is 20m ~** es ist 20 Meter hoch; **~brow** adj (betont) intellektuell; **~chair** n Hochstuhl m; **~er education** n Hochschulbildung f; **~-handed** adj eigenmächtig; **~-heeled** adj hochhackig; **~ jump** n (SPORT) Hochsprung m; **H~lands** npl: **the H~lands** das schottische Hochland; **~light** n (fig) Höhepunkt m ♦ vt hervorheben; **~ly** adv höchst; **~ly strung** adj überempfindlich; **~ness** n Höhe f; **Her H~ness** Ihre Hoheit f; **~-pitched** adj hoch; **~-rise block** n Hochhaus nt; **~ school** (US) n Oberschule f; **~ season** (BRIT) n Hochsaison f; **~ street** (BRIT) n Hauptstraße f

highway |'haɪweɪ| n Landstraße f; **H~ Code** (BRIT) n Straßenverkehrsordnung f

hijack |'haɪdʒæk| vt entführen; **~er** n Entführer(in) m(f)

hike |haɪk| vi wandern ♦ n Wanderung f; **~r** n Wanderer m; **hiking** n Wandern nt

hilarious |hɪ'lɛərɪəs| adj lustig

hill |hɪl| n Berg m; **~side** n (Berg)hang m; **~ walking** n Bergwandern nt; **~y** adj hügelig

hilt |hɪlt| n Heft nt; **(up) to the ~** ganz und gar

him |hɪm| pron (acc) ihn; (dat) ihm; see also **me**; **~self** pron sich (selbst) (selbst); (emphatic) selbst; see also **oneself**

hind |haɪnd| adj hinter, Hinter-

hinder |'hɪndə'| vt (stop) hindern; (delay) behindern; **hindrance** n (delay) Behinderung f; (obstacle) Hindernis nt

hindsight |'haɪndsaɪt| n: **with ~** im nachhinein

Hindu |'hɪnduː| n Hindu m

hinge |hɪndʒ| n Scharnier nt; (on door) Türangel f ♦ vi (fig): **to ~ on** abhängen von

hint |hɪnt| n Tipp m; (trace) Anflug m ♦ vt: **to ~ that** andeuten, dass ♦ vi: **to ~ at** andeuten

hip |hɪp| n Hüfte f

hippie |'hɪpɪ| n Hippie m

hippo |'hɪpəu| (inf) n Nilpferd nt

hippopotami |hɪpə'pɒtəmaɪ| npl of **hippopotamus**

hippopotamus |hɪpə'pɒtəməs| (pl **~es** or **hippopotami**) n Nilpferd nt

hire |'haɪə'| vt (worker) anstellen; (BRIT: car) mieten ♦ n Miete f; **for ~** (taxi) frei; **~(d) car** (BRIT) n Mietwagen m, Leihwagen m; **~ purchase** (BRIT) n Teilzahlungskauf m

his |hɪz| adj sein ♦ pron seine(r, s); see also **my; mine²**

hiss |hɪs| vi zischen ♦ n Zischen nt

historian |hɪ'stɔːrɪən| n Historiker m

historic |hɪ'stɒrɪk| adj historisch; **~al** adj historisch, geschichtlich

history |'hɪstərɪ| n Geschichte f

hit |hɪt| (pt, pp hit) vt schlagen; (injure) treffen ♦ n (blow) Schlag m; (success) Erfolg m; (MUS) Hit m; **to ~ it off with sb** prima mit jdm auskommen; **~-and-run driver** n jemand, der Fahrerflucht begeht

hitch |hɪtʃ| vt festbinden; (also: **~ up**) hochziehen ♦ n (difficulty) Haken m; **to ~ a lift** trampen; **~hike** vi trampen; **~hiker** n Tramper m; **~hiking** n Trampen nt

hi-tech |'haɪ'tɛk| adj Hightech- ♦ n Spitzentechnologie f

hitherto |hɪðə'tuː| adv bislang

hit man (inf) (irreg) n Killer m

HIV n abbr: **~-negative/-positive** HIV-negativ/-positiv

hive |haɪv| n Bienenkorb m

HMS abbr = **His/Her Majesty's Ship**

hoard |hɔːd| n Schatz m ♦ vt horten, hamstern

hoarding |'hɔːdɪŋ| n Bretterzaun m; (BRIT: for posters) Reklamewand f

hoarse |hɔːs| adj heiser, rau

hoax |həuks| n Streich m

hob |hɒb| n Kochmulde f

hobble |'hɒbl| vi humpeln

hobby |'hɒbɪ| n Hobby nt

hobby-horse |'hɒbɪhɔːs| n (fig) Steckenpferd nt

hobo |'həubəu| (US) n Tippelbruder m

hockey |'hɒkɪ| n Hockey nt

hoe |həu| n Hacke f ♦ vt hacken

hog |hɒg| n Schlachtschwein nt ♦ vt mit Beschlag belegen; **to go the whole ~** aufs Ganze gehen

hoist |hɔɪst| n Winde f ♦ vt hochziehen

husky [ˈhʌskɪ] adj (voice) rau ♦ n Eskimohund m

hustle [ˈhʌsl] vt (push) stoßen; (hurry) antreiben ♦ n: ~ **and bustle** Geschäftigkeit f

hut [hʌt] n Hütte f

hutch [hʌtʃ] n (Kaninchen)stall m

hyacinth [ˈhaɪəsɪnθ] n Hyazinthe f

hydrant [ˈhaɪdrənt] n (also: fire ~) Hydrant m

hydraulic [haɪˈdrɔːlɪk] adj hydraulisch

hydroelectric [ˈhaɪdrəʊˈlɛktrɪk] adj (energy) durch Wasserkraft erzeugt; ~ **power station** n Wasserkraftwerk nt

hydrofoil [ˈhaɪdrəfɔɪl] n Tragflügelboot nt

hydrogen [ˈhaɪdrədʒən] n Wasserstoff m

hyena [haɪˈiːnə] n Hyäne f

hygiene [ˈhaɪdʒiːn] n Hygiene f; **hygienic** [haɪˈdʒiːnɪk] adj hygienisch

hymn [hɪm] n Kirchenlied nt

hype [haɪp] (inf) n Publicity f

hypermarket [ˈhaɪpəmɑːkɪt] (BRIT) n Hypermarkt m

hypertext [ˈhaɪpətɛkst] n Hypertext m

hyphen [ˈhaɪfn] n Bindestrich m

hypnosis [hɪpˈnəʊsɪs] n Hypnose f

hypnotize [ˈhɪpnətaɪz] vt hypnotisieren

hypocrisy [hɪˈpɔkrɪsɪ] n Heuchelei f

hypocrite [ˈhɪpəkrɪt] n Heuchler m; **hypocritical** [hɪpəˈkrɪtɪkl] adj scheinheilig, heuchlerisch

hypothermia [haɪpəˈθɜːmɪə] n Unterkühlung f

hypotheses [haɪˈpɔθɪsiːz] npl of **hypothesis**

hypothesis [haɪˈpɔθɪsɪs] (pl **hypotheses**) n Hypothese f

hypothetic(al) [haɪpəʊˈθɛtɪk(l)] adj hypothetisch

hysterical [hɪˈstɛrɪkl] adj hysterisch

hysterics [hɪˈstɛrɪks] npl hysterische(r) Anfall m

I, i

I [aɪ] pron ich

ice [aɪs] n Eis nt ♦ vt (COOK) mit Zuckerguss überziehen ♦ vi (also: ~ **up**) vereisen; ~ **axe** n Eispickel m; **~berg** n Eisberg m; **~box** (US) n Kühlschrank m; ~ **cream** n Eis nt; ~ **cube** n Eiswürfel m; **~d** [aɪst] adj (cake) mit Zuckerguss überzogen, glasiert; (tea, coffee) Eis-; ~ **hockey** n Eishockey nt

Iceland [ˈaɪslənd] n Island nt

ice: ~ **lolly** (BRIT) n Eis nt am Stiel; ~ **rink** n (Kunst)eisbahn f; ~ **skating** n Schlittschuhlaufen nt

icicle [ˈaɪsɪkl] n Eiszapfen m

icing [ˈaɪsɪŋ] n (on cake) Zuckerguss m; (on window) Vereisung f; ~ **sugar** (BRIT) n Puderzucker m

icon [ˈaɪkɔn] n Ikone f

icy [ˈaɪsɪ] adj (slippery) vereist; (cold) eisig

I'd [aɪd] = **I would**; **I had**

idea [aɪˈdɪə] n Idee f

ideal [aɪˈdɪəl] n Ideal nt ♦ adj ideal

identical [aɪˈdɛntɪkl] adj identisch; (twins) eineiig

identification [aɪdɛntɪfɪˈkeɪʃən] n Identifizierung f; **means of ~** Ausweispapiere pl

identify [aɪˈdɛntɪfaɪ] vt identifizieren; (regard as the same) gleichsetzen

Identikit [aɪˈdɛntɪkɪt] ® n: ~ **picture** Phantombild nt

identity [aɪˈdɛntɪtɪ] n Identität f; ~ **card** n Personalausweis m

ideology [aɪdɪˈɔlədʒɪ] n Ideologie f

idiom [ˈɪdɪəm] n (expression) Redewendung f; (dialect) Idiom nt; **~atic** [ɪdɪəˈmætɪk] adj idiomatisch

idiosyncrasy [ɪdɪəʊˈsɪŋkrəsɪ] n Eigenart f

idiot [ˈɪdɪət] n Idiot(in) m(f); **~ic** [ɪdɪˈɔtɪk] adj idiotisch

idle [ˈaɪdl] adj (doing nothing) untätig; (lazy) faul; (useless) nutzlos; (machine) still(stehend); (threat, talk) leer ♦ vi (machine) leer laufen ♦ vt: **to ~ away the time** die Zeit vertrödeln; **~ness** n Müßiggang m; Faulheit f

idol [ˈaɪdl] n Idol m; **~ize** vt vergöttern

i.e. abbr (= id est) d. h.

```
KEYWORD
```

if [ɪf] conj 1 wenn; (in case also) falls; **if I were you** wenn ich Sie wäre

2 (although): (even) **if** (selbst or auch) wenn

3 (whether) ob

4: **if so/not** wenn ja/nicht; **if only ...** wenn ... doch nur ...; **if only I could** wenn ich doch nur könnte; see also **as**

ignite [ɪgˈnaɪt] vt (an)zünden ♦ vi sich entzünden; **ignition** [ɪgˈnɪʃən] n Zündung f; **to switch on/off the ignition** den Motor anlassen/abstellen; **ignition key** n (AUT) Zündschlüssel m

ignorance [ˈɪgnərəns] n Unwissenheit f

ignorant [ˈɪgnərənt] adj unwissend; **to be ~ of** nicht wissen

ignore [ɪgˈnɔːʳ] vt ignorieren

I'll [aɪl] = **I will**; **I shall**

ill [ɪl] adj krank ♦ n Übel nt ♦ adv schlecht; **~-advised** adj unklug; **~-at-ease** adj unbehaglich

illegal [ɪˈliːgl] adj illegal

illegible [ɪˈlɛdʒɪbl] adj unleserlich

illegitimate [ɪlɪˈdʒɪtɪmət] adj unehelich

ill-fated [ɪlˈfeɪtɪd] adj unselig

ill feeling n Verstimmung f

illicit [ɪˈlɪsɪt] adj verboten

illiterate [ɪˈlɪtərət] adj ungebildet

ill-mannered [ɪlˈmænəd] adj ungehobelt

illness ['ɪlnɪs] n Krankheit f

illogical [ɪ'lɒdʒɪkl] adj unlogisch

ill-treat [ɪl'triːt] vt misshandeln

illuminate [ɪ'luːmɪneɪt] vt beleuchten; **illumination** [ɪluːmɪ'neɪʃən] n Beleuchtung f; **illuminations** pl (decorative lights) festliche Beleuchtung f

illusion [ɪ'luːʒən] n Illusion f; **to be under the ~ that** ... sich dat einbilden, dass ...

illustrate ['ɪlʌstreɪt] vt (book) illustrieren; (explain) veranschaulichen; **illustration** [ɪlə'streɪʃən] n Illustration f; (explanation) Veranschaulichung f

illustrious [ɪ'lʌstrɪəs] adj berühmt

I'm [aɪm] = **I am**

image ['ɪmɪdʒ] n Bild nt; (public ~) Image nt; **~ry** n Symbolik f

imaginary [ɪ'mædʒɪnərɪ] adj eingebildet; (world) Fantasie-

imagination [ɪmædʒɪ'neɪʃən] n Einbildung f; (creative) Fantasie f

imaginative [ɪ'mædʒɪnətɪv] adj fantasiereich, einfallsreich

imagine [ɪ'mædʒɪn] vt sich vorstellen; (wrongly) sich einbilden

imbalance [ɪm'bæləns] n Unausgeglichenheit f

imbecile ['ɪmbəsiːl] n Schwachsinnige(r) mf

imitate ['ɪmɪteɪt] vt imitieren; **imitation** [ɪmɪ'teɪʃən] n Imitation f

immaculate [ɪ'mækjʊlət] adj makellos; (dress) tadellos; (ECCL) unbefleckt

immaterial [ɪmə'tɪərɪəl] adj unwesentlich; **it is ~ whether** ... es ist unwichtig, ob ...

immature [ɪmə'tjʊəʳ] adj unreif

immediate [ɪ'miːdɪət] adj (instant) sofortig; (near) unmittelbar; (relatives) nächste(r, s); (needs) dringlich; **~ly** adv sofort; **~ly next to** direkt neben

immense [ɪ'mens] adj unermesslich

immerse [ɪ'mɜːs] vt eintauchen; **to be ~d in** (fig) vertieft sein in +acc

immersion heater [ɪ'mɜːʃən-] (BRIT) n Boiler m

immigrant ['ɪmɪgrənt] n Einwanderer m

immigrate ['ɪmɪgreɪt] vi einwandern; **immigration** [ɪmɪ'greɪʃən] n Einwanderung f

imminent ['ɪmɪnənt] adj bevorstehend

immobile [ɪ'məʊbaɪl] adj unbeweglich; **immobilize** [ɪ'məʊbɪlaɪz] vt lähmen

immoral [ɪ'mɒrl] adj unmoralisch; **~ity** [ɪmə'rælɪtɪ] n Unsittlichkeit f

immortal [ɪ'mɔːtl] adj unsterblich

immune [ɪ'mjuːn] adj (secure) sicher; (MED) immun; **~ from** sicher vor +dat; **immunity** n (MED, JUR) Immunität f; (fig) Freiheit f; **immunize** ['ɪmjʊnaɪz] vt immunisieren

impact ['ɪmpækt] n Aufprall m; (fig) Wirkung f

impair [ɪm'peəʳ] vt beeinträchtigen

impart [ɪm'pɑːt] vt mitteilen; (knowledge) vermitteln; (exude) abgeben

impartial [ɪm'pɑːʃl] adj unparteiisch

impassable [ɪm'pɑːsəbl] adj unpassierbar

impassive [ɪm'pæsɪv] adj gelassen

impatience [ɪm'peɪʃəns] n Ungeduld f; **impatient** adj ungeduldig; **impatiently** adv ungeduldig

impeccable [ɪm'pekəbl] adj tadellos

impede [ɪm'piːd] vt (be)hindern; **impediment** [ɪm'pedɪmənt] n Hindernis nt; **speech impediment** Sprachfehler m

impending [ɪm'pendɪŋ] adj bevorstehend

impenetrable [ɪm'penɪtrəbl] adj (also fig) undurchdringlich

imperative [ɪm'perətɪv] adj (necessary) unbedingt erforderlich

imperceptible [ɪmpə'septɪbl] adj nicht wahrnehmbar

imperfect [ɪm'pɜːfɪkt] adj (faulty) fehlerhaft; **~ion** [ɪmpə'fekʃən] n Unvollkommenheit f; (fault) Fehler m

imperial [ɪm'pɪərɪəl] adj kaiserlich

impersonal [ɪm'pɜːsənl] adj unpersönlich

impersonate [ɪm'pɜːsəneɪt] vt sich ausgeben als; (for fun) imitieren

impertinent [ɪm'pɜːtɪnənt] adj unverschämt, frech

impervious [ɪm'pɜːvɪəs] adj (fig): **~ (to)** unempfänglich (für)

impetuous [ɪm'petjʊəs] adj ungestüm

impetus ['ɪmpɪtəs] n Triebkraft f; (fig) Auftrieb m

impinge [ɪm'pɪndʒ]: **~ on** vt beeinträchtigen

implacable [ɪm'plækəbl] adj unerbittlich

implement [n 'ɪmplɪmənt, vb 'ɪmplɪment] n Werkzeug nt ♦ vt ausführen

implicate ['ɪmplɪkeɪt] vt verwickeln; **implication** [ɪmplɪ'keɪʃən] n (effect) Auswirkung f; (in crime) Verwicklung f

implicit [ɪm'plɪsɪt] adj (suggested) unausgesprochen; (utter) vorbehaltlos

implore [ɪm'plɔːʳ] vt anflehen

imply [ɪm'plaɪ] vt (hint) andeuten; (be evidence for) schließen lassen auf +acc

impolite [ɪmpə'laɪt] adj unhöflich

import [vb ɪm'pɔːt, n 'ɪmpɔːt] vt einführen ♦ n Einfuhr f; (meaning) Bedeutung f

importance [ɪm'pɔːtns] n Bedeutung f

important [ɪm'pɔːtənt] adj wichtig; **it's not ~** es ist unwichtig

importer [ɪm'pɔːtəʳ] n Importeur m

impose [ɪm'pəʊz] vt, vi: **to ~ (on)** auferlegen (+dat); (penalty, sanctions) verhängen (gegen); **to ~ (o.s.) on sb** sich jdm aufdrängen

imposing [ɪm'pəʊzɪŋ] adj eindrucksvoll

imposition [ɪmpə'zɪʃən] n (of burden, fine) Auferlegung f; **to be an ~ (on person)** eine Zumutung sein

impossible [ɪmˈpɔsɪbl] adj unmöglich
impostor [ɪmˈpɔstə^r] n Hochstapler m
impotent [ˈɪmpətnt] adj machtlos; (sexually) impotent
impound [ɪmˈpaund] vt beschlagnahmen
impoverished [ɪmˈpɔvərɪʃt] adj verarmt
impracticable [ɪmˈpræktɪkəbl] adj undurchführbar
impractical [ɪmˈpræktɪkl] adj unpraktisch
imprecise [ɪmprɪˈsaɪs] adj ungenau
impregnable [ɪmˈpregnəbl] adj (castle) uneinnehmbar
impregnate [ˈɪmpregneɪt] vt (saturate) sättigen; (fertilize) befruchten
impress [ɪmˈpres] vt (influence) beeindrucken; (imprint) (auf)drücken; **to ~ sth on sb** jdm etw einschärfen; **~ed** adj beeindruckt; **~ion** [ɪmˈpreʃən] n Eindruck m; (on wax, footprint) Abdruck m; (of book) Auflage f; (take-off) Nachahmung f; **I was under the ~ion** ich hatte den Eindruck; **~ionable** adj leicht zu beeindrucken; **~ive** adj eindrucksvoll
imprint [ˈɪmprɪnt] n Abdruck m
imprison [ɪmˈprɪzn] vt ins Gefängnis schicken; **~ment** n Inhaftierung f
improbable [ɪmˈprɔbəbl] adj unwahrscheinlich
impromptu [ɪmˈprɔmptjuː] adj, adv aus dem Stegreif, improvisiert
improper [ɪmˈprɔpə^r] adj (indecent) unanständig; (unsuitable) unpassend
improve [ɪmˈpruːv] vt verbessern ♦ vi besser werden; **~ment** n (Ver)besserung f
improvise [ˈɪmprəvaɪz] vt, vi improvisieren
imprudent [ɪmˈpruːdnt] adj unklug
impudent [ˈɪmpjudnt] adj unverschämt
impulse [ˈɪmpʌls] n Impuls m; **to act on ~** spontan handeln; **impulsive** [ɪmˈpʌlsɪv] adj impulsiv
impure [ɪmˈpjuə^r] adj (dirty) verunreinigt; (bad) unsauber; **impurity** [ɪmˈpjuərɪtɪ] n Unreinheit f; (TECH) Verunreinigung f

KEYWORD

in [ɪn] prep 1 (indicating place, position) in +dat; (with motion) in +acc; **in here/there** hier/dort; **in London** in London; **in the United States** in den Vereinigten Staaten
2 (indicating time: during) in +dat; **in summer** im Sommer; **in 1988** (im Jahre) 1988; **in the afternoon** nachmittags, am Nachmittag
3 (indicating time: in the space of) innerhalb von; **I'll see you in 2 weeks** or **in 2 weeks' time** ich sehe Sie in zwei Wochen
4 (indicating manner, circumstances, state etc) in +dat; **in the sun/rain** in der Sonne/im Regen; **in English/French** auf Englisch/Französisch; **in a loud/soft voice** mit lauter/leiser Stimme
5 (with ratios, numbers): **1 in 10** jeder Zehnte; **20 pence in the pound** 20 Pence pro Pfund; **they lined up in twos** sie stellten sich in Zweierreihe auf
6 (referring to people, works): **the disease is common in children** die Krankheit ist bei Kindern häufig; **in Dickens** bei Dickens; **we have a loyal friend in him** er ist uns ein treuer Freund
7 (indicating profession etc): **to be in teaching/the army** Lehrer(in)/beim Militär sein; **to be in publishing** im Verlagswesen arbeiten
8 (with present participle): **in saying this, I ...** wenn ich das sage, ... ich; **in accepting this view, he ...** weil er diese Meinung akzeptierte, ... er
♦ adv: **to be in** (person: at home, work) da sein; (train, ship, plane) angekommen sein; (in fashion) in sein; **to ask sb in** jdn hereinbitten; **to run/limp etc in** hereingerannt/gehumpelt etc kommen
♦ n: **the ins and outs** (of proposal, situation etc) die Feinheiten pl

in. abbr = inch
inability [ɪnəˈbɪlɪtɪ] n Unfähigkeit f
inaccessible [ɪnəkˈsesɪbl] adj unzugänglich
inaccurate [ɪnˈækjurət] adj ungenau; (wrong) unrichtig
inactivity [ɪnækˈtɪvɪtɪ] n Untätigkeit f
inadequate [ɪnˈædɪkwət] adj unzulänglich
inadvertently [ɪnədˈvɜːtntlɪ] adv unabsichtlich
inadvisable [ɪnədˈvaɪzəbl] adj nicht ratsam
inane [ɪˈneɪn] adj dumm, albern
inanimate [ɪnˈænɪmət] adj leblos
inappropriate [ɪnəˈprəuprɪət] adj (clothing) ungeeignet; (remark) unangebracht
inarticulate [ɪnɑːˈtɪkjulət] adj unklar
inasmuch as [ɪnəzˈmʌtʃ-] adv da; (in so far as) so weit
inaudible [ɪnˈɔːdɪbl] adj unhörbar
inaugural [ɪˈnɔːgjurəl] adj Eröffnungs-
inaugurate [ɪˈnɔːgjureɪt] vt (open) einweihen; (admit to office) (feierlich) einführen
inauguration [ɪnɔːgjuˈreɪʃən] n Eröffnung f; (feierliche) Amtseinführung f
inborn [ɪnˈbɔːn] adj angeboren
inbred [ɪnˈbred] adj angeboren
Inc. abbr = incorporated
incalculable [ɪnˈkælkjuləbl] adj (consequences) unabsehbar
incapable [ɪnˈkeɪpəbl] adj: **~ (of doing sth)** unfähig(, etw zu tun)
incapacitate [ɪnkəˈpæsɪteɪt] vt untauglich machen
incapacity [ɪnkəˈpæsɪtɪ] n Unfähigkeit f
incarcerate [ɪnˈkɑːsəreɪt] vt einkerkern
incarnation [ɪnkɑːˈneɪʃən] n (ECCL) Menschwerdung f; (fig) Inbegriff m

incendiary |ɪnˈsendɪərɪ| adj Brand-

incense |n ˈɪnsens, vb ɪnˈsens| n Weihrauch m ♦ vt erzürnen

incentive |ɪnˈsentɪv| n Anreiz m

incessant |ɪnˈsesnt| adj unaufhörlich; **~ly** adv unaufhörlich

incest |ˈɪnsest| n Inzest m

inch |ɪntʃ| n Zoll m ♦ vi: **to ~ forward** sich Stückchen für Stückchen vorwärts bewegen; **to be within an ~ of** kurz davor sein; **he didn't give an ~** er gab keinen Zentimeter nach

incidence |ˈɪnsɪdns| n Auftreten nt; (of crime) Quote f

incident |ˈɪnsɪdnt| n Vorfall m; (disturbance) Zwischenfall m

incidental |ɪnsɪˈdentl| adj (music) Begleit-; (unimportant) nebensächlich; (remark) beiläufig; **~ly** adv übrigens

incinerator |ɪnˈsɪnəreɪtəʳ| n Verbrennungsofen m

incision |ɪnˈsɪʒən| n Einschnitt m

incisive |ɪnˈsaɪsɪv| adj (style) treffend; (person) scharfsinnig

incite |ɪnˈsaɪt| vt anstacheln

inclination |ɪnklɪˈneɪʃən| n Neigung f

incline |n ˈɪnklaɪn, vb ɪnˈklaɪn| n Abhang m ♦ vt neigen; (fig) veranlassen ♦ vi sich neigen; **to be ~d to do sth** dazu neigen, etw zu tun

include |ɪnˈkluːd| vt einschließen; (on list, in group) aufnehmen; **including** prep: **including X** X inbegriffen; **inclusion** |ɪnˈkluːʒən| n Aufnahme f; **inclusive** |ɪnˈkluːsɪv| adj einschließlich, (COMM) inklusive; **inclusive of** einschließlich +gen

incoherent |ɪnkəʊˈhɪərənt| adj zusammenhanglos

income |ˈɪnkʌm| n Einkommen nt; (from business) Einkünfte pl; **~ tax** n Lohnsteuer f; (of self-employed) Einkommenssteuer f

incoming |ˈɪnkʌmɪŋ| adj: **~ flight** eintreffende Maschine f

incomparable |ɪnˈkɒmpərəbl| adj unvergleichlich

incompatible |ɪnkəmˈpætɪbl| adj unvereinbar; (people) unverträglich

incompetence |ɪnˈkɒmpɪtns| n Unfähigkeit f; **incompetent** adj unfähig

incomplete |ɪnkəmˈpliːt| adj unvollständig

incomprehensible |ɪnkɒmprɪˈhensɪbl| adj unverständlich

inconceivable |ɪnkənˈsiːvəbl| adj unvorstellbar

incongruous |ɪnˈkɒŋgruəs| adj seltsam; (remark) unangebracht

inconsiderate |ɪnkənˈsɪdərət| adj rücksichtslos

inconsistency |ɪnkənˈsɪstənsɪ| n Widersprüchlichkeit f; (state) Unbeständigkeit f

inconsistent |ɪnkənˈsɪstnt| adj (action, speech) widersprüchlich; (person, work) unbeständig; **~ with** nicht übereinstimmend mit

inconspicuous |ɪnkənˈspɪkjuəs| adj unauffällig

incontinent |ɪnˈkɒntɪnənt| adj (MED) nicht fähig, Stuhl und Harn zurückzuhalten

inconvenience |ɪnkənˈviːnjəns| n Unbequemlichkeit f; (trouble to others) Unannehmlichkeiten pl

inconvenient |ɪnkənˈviːnjənt| adj ungelegen; (journey) unbequem

incorporate |ɪnˈkɔːpəreɪt| vt (include) aufnehmen; (contain) enthalten; **~d** adj: **~d company** (US) eingetragene Aktiengesellschaft f

incorrect |ɪnkəˈrekt| adj unrichtig

incorrigible |ɪnˈkɒrɪdʒɪbl| adj unverbesserlich

incorruptible |ɪnkəˈrʌptɪbl| adj unzerstörbar; (person) unbestechlich

increase |n ˈɪnkriːs, vb ɪnˈkriːs| n Zunahme f; (pay ~) Gehaltserhöhung f; (in size) Vergrößerung f ♦ vt erhöhen; (wealth, rage) vermehren; (business) erweitern ♦ vi zunehmen; (prices) steigen; (in size) größer werden; (in number) sich vermehren; **increasing** adj (number) steigend; **increasingly** |ɪnˈkriːsɪŋlɪ| adv zunehmend

incredible |ɪnˈkredɪbl| adj unglaublich

incredulous |ɪnˈkredjuləs| adj ungläubig

increment |ˈɪnkrɪmənt| n Zulage f

incriminate |ɪnˈkrɪmɪneɪt| vt belasten

incubation |ɪnkjuˈbeɪʃən| n Ausbrüten nt

incubator |ˈɪnkjubeɪtəʳ| n Brutkasten m

incumbent |ɪnˈkʌmbənt| adj: **it is ~ on him to ...** es obliegt ihm, ...

incur |ɪnˈkəːʳ| vt sich zuziehen; (debts) machen

incurable |ɪnˈkjuərəbl| adj unheilbar

indebted |ɪnˈdetɪd| adj (obliged): **~ (to sb)** (jdm) verpflichtet

indecent |ɪnˈdiːsnt| adj unanständig; **~ assault** (BRIT) n Notzucht f; **~ exposure** n Exhibitionismus m

indecisive |ɪndɪˈsaɪsɪv| adj (battle) nicht entscheidend; (person) unentschlossen

indeed |ɪnˈdiːd| adv tatsächlich, in der Tat; **yes ~!** allerdings!

indefinite |ɪnˈdefɪnɪt| adj unbestimmt; **~ly** adv auf unbestimmte Zeit; (wait) unbegrenzt lange

indelible |ɪnˈdelɪbl| adj unauslöschlich

indemnity |ɪnˈdemnɪtɪ| n (insurance) Versicherung f; (compensation) Entschädigung f

independence |ɪndɪˈpendns| n Unabhängigkeit f; **independent** adj unabhängig

indestructible |ɪndɪsˈtrʌktəbl| adj

unzerstörbar

indeterminate |ˌɪndɪˈtəːmɪnɪt| *adj* unbestimmt

index |ˈɪndɛks| (*pl* **~es** *or* **indices**) *n* Index *m*; **~ card** *n* Karteikarte *f*; **~ finger** *n* Zeigefinger *m*; **~linked** (*US* **~ed**) *adj* (*salaries*) dem Inflationsrate *dat* angeglichen; (*pensions*) dynamisch

India |ˈɪndɪə| *n* Indien *nt*; **~n** *adj* indisch ♦ *n* Inder(in) *m(f)*; **American ~n** Indianer(in) *m(f)*; **~n Ocean** *n*: **the ~n Ocean** der Indische Ozean

indicate |ˈɪndɪkeɪt| *vt* anzeigen; (*hint*) andeuten; **indication** |ˌɪndɪˈkeɪʃən| *n* Anzeichen *nt*; (*information*) Angabe *f*; **indicative** |ɪnˈdɪkətɪv| *adj*: **indicative of** bezeichnend für; **indicator** *n* (An)zeichen *nt*; (*AUT*) Richtungsanzeiger *m*

indict |ɪnˈdaɪt| *vt* anklagen; **~ment** *n* Anklage *f*

indifference |ɪnˈdɪfrəns| *n* Gleichgültigkeit *f*; Unwichtigkeit *f*; **indifferent** *adj* gleichgültig; (*mediocre*) mäßig

indigenous |ɪnˈdɪdʒɪnəs| *adj* einheimisch

indigestion |ˌɪndɪˈdʒɛstʃən| *n* Verdauungsstörung *f*

indignant |ɪnˈdɪgnənt| *adj*: **to be ~ about sth** über etw *acc* empört sein

indignation |ˌɪndɪgˈneɪʃən| *n* Entrüstung *f*

indignity |ɪnˈdɪgnɪtɪ| *n* Demütigung *f*

indirect |ˌɪndɪˈrɛkt| *adj* indirekt

indiscreet |ˌɪndɪsˈkriːt| *adj* (*insensitive*) taktlos; (*telling secrets*) indiskret; **indiscretion** |ˌɪndɪsˈkreʃən| *n* Taktlosigkeit *f*; Indiskretion *f*

indiscriminate |ˌɪndɪsˈkrɪmɪnət| *adj* wahllos; kritiklos

indispensable |ˌɪndɪsˈpɛnsəbl| *adj* unentbehrlich

indisposed |ˌɪndɪsˈpəʊzd| *adj* unpässlich

indisputable |ˌɪndɪsˈpjuːtəbl| *adj* unbestreitbar; (*evidence*) unanfechtbar

indistinct |ˌɪndɪsˈtɪŋkt| *adj* undeutlich

individual |ˌɪndɪˈvɪdjuəl| *n* Individuum *nt* ♦ *adj* individuell; (*case*) Einzel-; (*of, for one person*) eigen, individuell; (*characteristic*) eigentümlich; **~ly** *adv* einzeln, individuell

indivisible |ˌɪndɪˈvɪzɪbl| *adj* unteilbar

indoctrinate |ɪnˈdɔktrɪneɪt| *vt* indoktrinieren

Indonesia |ˌɪndəˈniːzɪə| *n* Indonesien *nt*

indoor |ˈɪndɔːʳ| *adj* Haus-; Zimmer-; Innen-; (*SPORT*) Hallen-; **~s** |ɪnˈdɔːz| *adv* drinnen, im Haus

induce |ɪnˈdjuːs| *vt* dazu bewegen; (*reaction*) herbeiführen

induction course |ɪnˈdʌkʃən-| (*BRIT*) *n* Einführungskurs *m*

indulge |ɪnˈdʌldʒ| *vt* (*give way*) nachgeben +*dat*; (*gratify*) frönen +*dat* ♦ *vi*: **to ~ (in)** frönen (+*dat*); **~nce** *n* Nachsicht *f*; (*enjoyment*) Genuss *m*; **~nt** *adj* nachsichtig;

(*pej*) nachgiebig

industrial |ɪnˈdʌstrɪəl| *adj* Industrie-, industriell; (*dispute, injury*) Arbeits-; **~ action** *n* Arbeitskampfmaßnahmen *pl*; **~ estate** (*BRIT*) *n* Industriegebiet *nt*; **~ist** *n* Industrielle(r) *mf*; **~ize** *vt* industrialisieren; **~ park** (*US*) *n* Industriegebiet *nt*

industrious |ɪnˈdʌstrɪəs| *adj* fleißig

industry |ˈɪndəstrɪ| *n* Industrie *f*; (*diligence*) Fleiß *m*

inebriated |ɪˈniːbrɪeɪtɪd| *adj* betrunken

inedible |ɪnˈɛdɪbl| *adj* ungenießbar

ineffective |ˌɪnɪˈfɛktɪv| *adj* unwirksam; (*person*) untauglich

ineffectual |ˌɪnɪˈfɛktʃuəl| *adj* = **ineffective**

inefficiency |ˌɪnɪˈfɪʃənsɪ| *n* Ineffizienz *f*

inefficient |ˌɪnɪˈfɪʃənt| *adj* ineffizient; (*ineffective*) unwirksam

inept |ɪˈnɛpt| *adj* (*remark*) unpassend; (*person*) ungeeignet

inequality |ˌɪnɪˈkwɔlɪtɪ| *n* Ungleichheit *f*

inert |ɪˈnəːt| *adj* träge; (*CHEM*) inaktiv; (*motionless*) unbeweglich

inescapable |ˌɪnɪˈskeɪpəbl| *adj* unvermeidbar

inevitable |ɪnˈɛvɪtəbl| *adj* unvermeidlich; **inevitably** *adv* zwangsläufig

inexcusable |ˌɪnɪksˈkjuːzəbl| *adj* unverzeihlich

inexhaustible |ˌɪnɪgˈzɔːstɪbl| *adj* unerschöpflich

inexpensive |ˌɪnɪkˈspɛnsɪv| *adj* preiswert

inexperience |ˌɪnɪkˈspɪərɪəns| *n* Unerfahrenheit *f*; **~d** *adj* unerfahren

inexplicable |ˌɪnɪksˈplɪkəbl| *adj* unerklärlich

inextricably |ˌɪnɪksˈtrɪkəblɪ| *adv* untrennbar

infallible |ɪnˈfælɪbl| *adj* unfehlbar

infamous |ˈɪnfəməs| *adj* (*deed*) schändlich; (*person*) niederträchtig

infancy |ˈɪnfənsɪ| *n* frühe Kindheit *f*; (*fig*) Anfangsstadium *nt*

infant |ˈɪnfənt| *n* kleine(s) Kind *nt*, Säugling *m*; **~ile** |ˈɪnfəntaɪl| *adj* kindisch, infantil; **~ school** (*BRIT*) *n* Vorschule *f*

infatuated |ɪnˈfætjueɪtɪd| *adj* vernarrt; **to become ~ with** sich vernarren in +*acc*; **infatuation** |ɪnˌfætjuˈeɪʃən| *n*: **infatuation (with)** Vernarrtheit *f* (in +*acc*)

infect |ɪnˈfɛkt| *vt* anstecken (*also fig*); **~ed with** (*illness*) infiziert mit; **~ion** |ɪnˈfɛkʃən| *n* Infektion *f*; **~ious** |ɪnˈfɛkʃəs| *adj* ansteckend

infer |ɪnˈfəːʳ| *vt* schließen

inferior |ɪnˈfɪərɪəʳ| *adj* (*rank*) untergeordnet; (*quality*) minderwertig ♦ *n* Untergebene(r) *m*; **~ity** |ɪnˌfɪərɪˈɔrɪtɪ| *n* Minderwertigkeit *f*; (*in rank*) untergeordnete Stellung *f*; **~ity complex** *n* Minderwertigkeitskomplex *m*

infernal |ɪnˈfəːnl| *adj* höllisch

infertile |ɪnˈfəːtaɪl| *adj* unfruchtbar; **infertility** |ˌɪnfəˈtɪlɪtɪ| *n* Unfruchtbarkeit *f*

infested |ɪnˈfɛstɪd| *adj*: **to be ~ with** wimmeln von

infidelity |ˌɪnfɪˈdelɪtɪ| n Untreue f
infighting |ˈɪnfaɪtɪŋ| n Nahkampf m
infiltrate |ˈɪnfɪltreɪt| vt infiltrieren; (spies)
einschleusen ♦ vi (MIL, liquid) einsickern
(POL): **to ~ (into)** unterwandern (+acc)
infinite |ˈɪnfɪnɪt| adj unendlich
infinitive |ɪnˈfɪnɪtɪv| n Infinitiv m
infinity |ɪnˈfɪnɪtɪ| n Unendlichkeit f
infirm |ɪnˈfɜːm| adj gebrechlich; **~ary** n
Krankenhaus nt
inflamed |ɪnˈfleɪmd| adj entzündet
inflammable |ɪnˈflæməbl| (BRIT) adj
feuergefährlich
inflammation |ɪnfləˈmeɪʃən| n Entzündung f
inflatable |ɪnˈfleɪtəbl| adj aufblasbar
inflate |ɪnˈfleɪt| vt aufblasen; (tyre)
aufpumpen; (prices) hoch treiben; **inflation**
|ɪnˈfleɪʃən| n Inflation f; **inflationary**
|ɪnˈfleɪʃənərɪ| adj (increase) inflationistisch;
(situation) inflationär
inflexible |ɪnˈfleksɪbl| adj (person) nicht
flexibel; (opinion) starr; (thing) unbiegsam
inflict |ɪnˈflɪkt| vt: **to ~ sth on sb** jdm etw
zufügen; (wound) jdm etw beibringen
influence |ˈɪnfluəns| n Einfluss m ♦ vt
beeinflussen
influential |ɪnfluˈenʃl| adj einflussreich
influenza |ɪnfluˈenzə| n Grippe f
influx |ˈɪnflʌks| n (of people) Zustrom m; (of
ideas) Eindringen nt
infomercial |ˈɪnfəʊməːʃl| n Werbeinfor-
mationssendung f
inform |ɪnˈfɔːm| vt informieren ♦ vi: **to ~ on**
sb jdn denunzieren; **to keep sb ~ed** jdn auf
dem Laufenden halten
informal |ɪnˈfɔːml| adj zwanglos; **~ity**
|ɪnfɔːˈmælɪtɪ| n Ungezwungenheit f
informant |ɪnˈfɔːmənt| n Informant(in) m(f)
information |ɪnfəˈmeɪʃən| n Auskunft f,
Information f; **a piece of ~** eine Auskunft,
eine Information; **~ desk** n
Auskunftsschalter m; **~ office** n
Informationsbüro nt
informative |ɪnˈfɔːmətɪv| adj informativ;
(person) mitteilsam
informer |ɪnˈfɔːmər| n Denunziant(in) m(f)
infra-red |ɪnfrəˈred| adj infrarot
infrequent |ɪnˈfriːkwənt| adj selten
infringe |ɪnˈfrɪndʒ| vt (law) verstoßen gegen;
~ upon vt verletzen; **~ment** n Verstoß m,
Verletzung f
infuriating |ɪnˈfjʊərɪeɪtɪŋ| adj ärgerlich
ingenuity |ɪndʒɪˈnjuːɪtɪ| n Genialität f
ingenuous |ɪnˈdʒenjuəs| adj aufrichtig;
(naive) naiv
ingot |ˈɪŋgət| n Barren m
ingrained |ɪnˈgreɪnd| adj tief sitzend
ingratiate |ɪnˈgreɪʃɪeɪt| vt: **to ~ o.s. with sb**
sich bei jdm einschmeicheln
ingratitude |ɪnˈgrætɪtjuːd| n Undankbarkeit f
ingredient |ɪnˈgriːdɪənt| n Bestandteil m;

(COOK) Zutat f
inhabit |ɪnˈhæbɪt| vt bewohnen; **~ant** n
Bewohner(in) m(f); (of island, town)
Einwohner(in) m(f)
inhale |ɪnˈheɪl| vt einatmen; (MED, cigarettes)
inhalieren
inherent |ɪnˈhɪərənt| adj: **~ (in)**
innewohnend (+dat)
inherit |ɪnˈherɪt| vt erben; **~ance** n Erbe nt,
Erbschaft f
inhibit |ɪnˈhɪbɪt| vt hemmen; **to ~ sb from**
doing sth jdn daran hindern, etw zu tun;
~ion |ɪnhɪˈbɪʃən| n Hemmung f
inhospitable |ɪnhɔsˈpɪtəbl| adj (person)
ungastlich; (country) unwirtlich
inhuman |ɪnˈhjuːmən| adj unmenschlich
initial |ɪˈnɪʃl| adj anfänglich, Anfangs- ♦ n
Initiale f ♦ vt abzeichnen; (POL) paraphieren;
~ly adv anfangs
initiate |ɪˈnɪʃɪeɪt| vt einführen; (negotiations)
einleiten; **to ~ proceedings against sb**
(JUR) gerichtliche Schritte gegen jdn
einleiten; **initiation** |ɪnɪʃɪˈeɪʃən| n
Einführung f, Einleitung f
initiative |ɪˈnɪʃətɪv| n Initiative f
inject |ɪnˈdʒekt| vt einspritzen; (fig) einflößen;
~ion |ɪnˈdʒekʃən| n Spritze f
injunction |ɪnˈdʒʌŋkʃən| n Verfügung f
injure |ˈɪndʒər| vt verletzen; **~d** adj (person,
arm) verletzt; **injury** |ˈɪndʒərɪ| n Verletzung
f; **to play injury time** (SPORT) nachspielen
injustice |ɪnˈdʒʌstɪs| n Ungerechtigkeit f
ink |ɪŋk| n Tinte f
inkling |ˈɪŋklɪŋ| n (dunkle) Ahnung f
inlaid |ˈɪnleɪd| adj eingelegt, Einlege-
inland |adj ˈɪnlənd, adv ɪnˈlænd| adj Binnen-;
(domestic) Inlands- ♦ adv landeinwärts; **~**
revenue (BRIT) n Fiskus m
in-laws |ˈɪnlɔːz| npl (parents-in-law)
Schwiegereltern pl; (others) angeheiratete
Verwandte pl
inlet |ˈɪnlet| n Einlass m; (bay) kleine Bucht f
inmate |ˈɪnmeɪt| n Insasse m
inn |ɪn| n Gasthaus nt, Wirtshaus nt
innate |ɪˈneɪt| adj angeboren
inner |ˈɪnər| adj inner, Innen-; (fig) verborgen;
~ city n Innenstadt f; **~ tube** n (of tyre)
Schlauch m
innings |ˈɪnɪŋz| n (CRICKET) Innenrunde f
innocence |ˈɪnəsns| n Unschuld f;
(ignorance) Unkenntnis f
innocent |ˈɪnəsnt| adj unschuldig
innocuous |ɪˈnɔkjuəs| adj harmlos
innovation |ɪnəʊˈveɪʃən| n Neuerung f
innuendo |ɪnjuˈendəʊ| n (versteckte)
Anspielung f
innumerable |ɪˈnjuːmrəbl| adj unzählig
inoculation |ɪnɔkjuˈleɪʃən| n Impfung f
inopportune |ɪnˈɔpətjuːn| adj (remark)
unangebracht; (visit) ungelegen
inordinately |ɪˈnɔːdɪnətlɪ| adv unmäßig

inpatient |'ɪnpeɪʃənt| n stationäre(r) Patient m/stationäre Patientin f

input |'ɪnpʊt| n (COMPUT) Eingabe f; (power ~) Energiezufuhr f; (of energy, work) Aufwand m

inquest |'ɪnkwest| n gerichtliche Untersuchung f

inquire |ɪn'kwaɪəʳ| vi sich erkundigen ♦ vt (price) sich erkundigen nach; **~ into** vt untersuchen; **inquiry** |ɪn'kwaɪərɪ| n (question) Erkundigung f; (investigation) Untersuchung f; **inquiries** Auskunft f; **inquiry office** (BRIT) n Auskunft(sbüro nt) f

inquisitive |ɪn'kwɪzɪtɪv| adj neugierig

ins. abbr = **inches**

insane |ɪn'seɪn| adj wahnsinnig; (MED) geisteskrank; **insanity** |ɪn'sænɪtɪ| n Wahnsinn m

insatiable |ɪn'seɪʃəbl| adj unersättlich

inscribe |ɪn'skraɪb| vt eingravieren; **inscription** |ɪn'skrɪpʃən| n (on stone) Inschrift f; (in book) Widmung f

inscrutable |ɪn'skruːtəbl| adj unergründlich

insect |'ɪnsekt| n Insekt nt; **~icide** |ɪn'sektɪsaɪd| n Insektenvertilgungsmittel nt; **~ repellent** n Insektenbekämpfungsmittel nt

insecure |ɪnsɪ'kjuəʳ| adj (person) unsicher; (thing) nicht fest or sicher; **insecurity** |ɪnsɪ'kjuərɪtɪ| n Unsicherheit f

insemination |ɪnsemɪ'neɪʃən| n: **artificial ~** künstliche Befruchtung f

insensible |ɪn'sensɪbl| adj (unconscious) bewusstlos

insensitive |ɪn'sensɪtɪv| adj (to pain) unempfindlich; (unfeeling) gefühllos

inseparable |ɪn'sepərəbl| adj (people) unzertrennlich; (word) untrennbar

insert |vb ɪn'səːt, n 'ɪnsəːt| vt einfügen; (coin) einwerfen; (stick into) hineinstecken; (advertisement) aufgeben ♦ n (in book) Einlage f; (in magazine) Beilage f; **~ion** |ɪn'səːʃən| n Einfügung f; (PRESS) Inserat nt

in-service |'ɪn'səːvɪs| adj (training) berufsbegleitend

inshore |'ɪn'ʃɔːʳ| adj Küsten- ♦ adv an der Küste

inside |'ɪn'saɪd| n Innenseite f, Innere(s) nt ♦ adj innere(r, s), Innen- ♦ adv (place) innen; (direction) nach innen, hinein ♦ prep (place) in +dat; (direction) in +acc ... hinein; (time) innerhalb +gen; **~s** npl (inf) Eingeweide nt; **~ 10 minutes** unter 10 Minuten; **~ information** n interne Informationen pl; **~ lane** n (AUT: in Britain) linke Spur; **~ out** adv linksherum; (know) in- und auswendig

insider dealing, insider trading |ɪn'saɪdəʳ-| n (STOCK EXCHANGE) Insiderhandel m

insidious |ɪn'sɪdɪəs| adj heimtückisch

insight |'ɪnsaɪt| n Einsicht f; **~ into** Einblick m

in +acc

insignificant |ɪnsɪg'nɪfɪknt| adj unbedeutend

insincere |ɪnsɪn'sɪəʳ| adj unaufrichtig

insinuate |ɪn'sɪnjueɪt| vt (hint) andeuten

insipid |ɪn'sɪpɪd| adj fad(e)

insist |ɪn'sɪst| vi: **to ~ (on)** bestehen (auf +acc); **~ence** n Bestehen nt; **~ent** adj hartnäckig; (urgent) dringend

insole |'ɪnsəul| n Einlegesohle f

insolence |'ɪnsələns| n Frechheit f

insolent |'ɪnsələnt| adj frech

insoluble |ɪn'sɔljubl| adj unlösbar; (CHEM) unlöslich

insolvent |ɪn'sɔlvənt| adj zahlungsunfähig

insomnia |ɪn'sɔmnɪə| n Schlaflosigkeit f

inspect |ɪn'spekt| vt prüfen; (officially) inspizieren; **~ion** |ɪn'spekʃən| n Inspektion f; **~or** n (official) Inspektor m; (police) Polizeikommissar m; (BRIT: on buses, trains) Kontrolleur m

inspiration |ɪnspə'reɪʃən| n Inspiration f

inspire |ɪn'spaɪəʳ| vt (person) inspirieren; **to ~ sth in sb** (respect) jdm etw einflößen; (hope) etw in jdm wecken

instability |ɪnstə'bɪlɪtɪ| n Unbeständigkeit f, Labilität f

install |ɪn'stɔːl| vt (put in) installieren; (telephone) anschließen; (establish) einsetzen; **~ation** |ɪnstə'leɪʃən| n (of person) (Amts)einsetzung f; (of machinery) Installierung f; (machines etc) Anlage f

instalment |ɪn'stɔːlmənt| (US **installment**) n Rate f; (of story) Fortsetzung f; **to pay in ~s** in Raten zahlen

instance |'ɪnstəns| n Fall m; (example) Beispiel nt; **for ~** zum Beispiel; **in the first ~** zunächst

instant |'ɪnstənt| n Augenblick m ♦ adj augenblicklich, sofortig; **~aneous** |ɪnstən'teɪnɪəs| adj unmittelbar; **~ coffee** n Pulverkaffee m; **~ly** adv sofort

instead |ɪn'sted| adv stattdessen; **~ of** prep anstatt +gen

instep |'ɪnstep| n Spann m; (of shoe) Blatt m

instil |ɪn'stɪl| vt (fig): **to ~ sth in sb** jdm etw beibringen

instinct |'ɪnstɪŋkt| n Instinkt m; **~ive** |ɪn'stɪŋktɪv| adj instinktiv

institute |'ɪnstɪtjuːt| n Institut nt ♦ vt einführen; (search) einleiten

institution |ɪnstɪ'tjuːʃən| n Institution f; (home) Anstalt f

instruct |ɪn'strʌkt| vt anweisen; (officially) instruieren; **~ion** |ɪn'strʌkʃən| n Unterricht m; **~ions** npl (orders) Anweisungen pl; (for use) Gebrauchsanweisung f; **~or** n Lehrer m

instrument |'ɪnstrumənt| n Instrument nt; **~al** |ɪnstru'mentl| adj (MUS) Instrumental-; (helpful): **~al (in)** behilflich (bei); **~ panel** n Armaturenbrett nt

insubordinate [ɪnsə'bɔːdənɪt] adj aufsässig, widersetzlich

insufferable [ɪn'sʌfrəbl] adj unerträglich

insufficient [ɪnsə'fɪʃənt] adj ungenügend

insular ['ɪnsjulə] adj (fig) engstirnig

insulate ['ɪnsjuleɪt] vt (ELEC) isolieren; (fig): **to ~ (from)** abschirmen (vor +dat); **insulating tape** n Isolierband nt; **insulation** [ɪnsju'leɪʃən] n Isolierung f

insulin ['ɪnsjulɪn] n Insulin nt

insult [n 'ɪnsʌlt, vb ɪn'sʌlt] n Beleidigung f ♦ vt beleidigen

insurance [ɪn'ʃuərəns] n Versicherung f; **fire/ life ~** Feuer-/Lebensversicherung; **~ agent** n Versicherungsvertreter m; **~ policy** n Versicherungspolice f

insure [ɪn'ʃuə] vt versichern

intact [ɪn'tækt] adj unversehrt

intake ['ɪnteɪk] n (place) Einlassöffnung f; (act) Aufnahme f; (BRIT: SCH): **an ~ of 200 a year** ein Neuzugang von 200 im Jahr

intangible [ɪn'tændʒɪbl] adj nicht greifbar

integral ['ɪntɪgrəl] adj (essential) wesentlich; (complete) vollständig; (MATH) Integral-

integrate ['ɪntɪgreɪt] vt integrieren ♦ vi sich integrieren

integrity [ɪn'tegrɪtɪ] n (honesty) Redlichkeit f, Integrität f

intellect ['ɪntəlekt] n Intellekt m; **~ual** [ɪntə'lektjuəl] adj geistig, intellektuell ♦ n Intellektuelle(r) mf

intelligence [ɪn'telɪdʒəns] n (understanding) Intelligenz f; (news) Information f; (MIL) Geheimdienst m; **~ service** n Nachrichtendienst m, Geheimdienst m

intelligent [ɪn'telɪdʒənt] adj intelligent; **~ly** adv klug; (write, speak) verständlich

intelligentsia [ɪntelɪ'dʒentsɪə] n Intelligenz f

intelligible [ɪn'telɪdʒɪbl] adj verständlich

intend [ɪn'tend] vt beabsichtigen; **that was ~ed for you** das war für dich gedacht

intense [ɪn'tens] adj stark, intensiv; (person) ernsthaft; **~ly** adv äußerst; (study) intensiv

intensify [ɪn'tensɪfaɪ] vt verstärken, intensivieren

intensity [ɪn'tensɪtɪ] n Intensität f

intensive [ɪn'tensɪv] adj intensiv; **~ care unit** n Intensivstation f

intent [ɪn'tent] n Absicht f ♦ adj: **to be ~ on doing sth** fest entschlossen sein, etw zu tun; **to all ~s and purposes** praktisch

intention [ɪn'tenʃən] n Absicht f; **~al** adj absichtlich

intently [ɪn'tentlɪ] adv konzentriert

interact [ɪntər'ækt] vi aufeinander einwirken; **~ion** [ɪntər'ækʃən] n Wechselwirkung f; **~ive** adj (COMPUT) interaktiv

intercept [ɪntə'sept] vt abfangen

interchange [n 'ɪntətʃeɪndʒ, vb ɪntə'tʃeɪndʒ] n (exchange) Austausch m; (on roads) Verkehrskreuz nt ♦ vt austauschen; **~able**

[ɪntə'tʃeɪndʒəbl] adj austauschbar

intercom ['ɪntəkɔm] n (Gegen)sprechanlage f

intercourse ['ɪntəkɔːs] n (exchange) Beziehungen pl; (sexual) Geschlechtsverkehr m

interest ['ɪntrɪst] n Interesse nt; (FIN) Zinsen pl; (COMM: share) Anteil m; (group) Interessengruppe f ♦ vt interessieren; **~ed** adj (having claims) beteiligt; (attentive) interessiert; **to be ~ed in** sich interessieren für; **~ing** adj interessant; **~ rate** n Zinssatz m

interface ['ɪntəfeɪs] n (COMPUT) Schnittstelle f, Interface nt

interfere [ɪntə'fɪə] vi: **to ~ (with)** (meddle) sich einmischen (in +acc); (disrupt) stören +acc; **~nce** [ɪntə'fɪərəns] n Einmischung f; (TV) Störung f

interim ['ɪntərɪm] n: **in the ~** inzwischen

interior [ɪn'tɪərɪə] n Innere(s) nt ♦ adj innere(r, s), Innen-; **~ designer** n Innenarchitekt(in) m(f)

interjection [ɪntə'dʒekʃən] n Ausruf m

interlock [ɪntə'lɔk] vi ineinander greifen

interlude ['ɪntəluːd] n Pause f

intermediary [ɪntə'miːdɪərɪ] n Vermittler m

intermediate [ɪntə'miːdɪət] adj Zwischen-, Mittel-

interminable [ɪn'təːmɪnəbl] adj endlos

intermission [ɪntə'mɪʃən] n Pause f

intermittent [ɪntə'mɪtnt] adj periodisch, stoßweise

intern [vb ɪn'təːn, n 'ɪntəːn] vt internieren ♦ n (US) Assistenzarzt m/-ärztin f

internal [ɪn'təːnl] adj (inside) innere(r, s); (domestic) Inlands-; **~ly** adv innen; (MED) innerlich; **"not to be taken ~ly"** „nur zur äußerlichen Anwendung"; **I~ Revenue Service** (US) n Finanzamt nt

international [ɪntə'næʃənl] adj international ♦ n (SPORT) Nationalspieler(in) m(f); (: match) internationale(s) Spiel nt

Internet ['ɪntənet] n: **the ~** das Internet; **~ café** n Internet-Café nt

interplay ['ɪntəpleɪ] n Wechselspiel nt

interpret [ɪn'təːprɪt] vt (explain) auslegen, interpretieren; (translate) dolmetschen; **~er** n Dolmetscher(in) m(f)

interrelated [ɪntərɪ'leɪtɪd] adj untereinander zusammenhängend

interrogate [ɪn'terəgeɪt] vt verhören; **interrogation** [ɪnterə'geɪʃən] n Verhör nt

interrupt [ɪntə'rʌpt] vt unterbrechen; **~ion** [ɪntə'rʌpʃən] n Unterbrechung f

intersect [ɪntə'sekt] vt (durch)schneiden ♦ vi sich schneiden; **~ion** [ɪntə'sekʃən] n (of roads) Kreuzung f; (of lines) Schnittpunkt m

intersperse [ɪntə'spəːs] vt: **to ~ sth with sth** etw mit etw durchsetzen

intertwine [ɪntə'twaɪn] vt verflechten ♦ vi

sich verflechten

interval |ˈɪntəvl| n Abstand m; (BRIT: SCH, THEAT, SPORT) Pause f; **at ~s** in Abständen

intervene |ɪntəˈviːn| vi dazwischenliegen; (act): **to ~ (in)** einschreiten (gegen); **intervention** |ɪntəˈvɛnʃən| n Eingreifen nt, Intervention f

interview |ˈɪntəvjuː| n (PRESS etc) Interview nt; (for job) Vorstellungsgespräch nt ♦ vt interviewen; **~er** n Interviewer m

intestine |ɪnˈtɛstɪn| n: **large/small ~** Dick-/Dünndarm m

intimacy |ˈɪntɪməsɪ| n Intimität f

intimate |adj ˈɪntɪmət, vb ˈɪntɪmeɪt| adj (inmost) innerste(r, s); (knowledge) eingehend; (familiar) vertraut; (friends) eng ♦ vt andeuten

intimidate |ɪnˈtɪmɪdeɪt| vt einschüchtern

into |ˈɪntu| prep (motion) in +acc ... hinein; **5 ~ 25** 25 durch 5

intolerable |ɪnˈtɔlərəbl| adj unerträglich

intolerant |ɪnˈtɔlərnt| adj: **~ of** unduldsam gegen(über)

intoxicate |ɪnˈtɔksɪkeɪt| vt berauschen; **~d** adj betrunken; **intoxication** |ɪntɔksɪˈkeɪʃən| n Rausch m

intractable |ɪnˈtræktəbl| adj schwer zu handhaben; (problem) schwer lösbar

intranet |ˈɪntrənet| n (COMPUT) Intranet nt

intransitive |ɪnˈtrænsɪtɪv| adj intransitiv

intravenous |ɪntrəˈviːnəs| adj intravenös

in-tray |ˈɪntreɪ| n Eingangskorb m

intrepid |ɪnˈtrepɪd| adj unerschrocken

intricate |ˈɪntrɪkət| adj kompliziert

intrigue |ɪnˈtriːg| n Intrige f ♦ vt faszinieren ♦ vi intrigieren

intrinsic |ɪnˈtrɪnsɪk| adj innere(r, s); (difference) wesentlich

introduce |ɪntrəˈdjuːs| vt (person) vorstellen; (sth new) einführen; (subject) anschneiden; **to ~ sb to sb** jdm jdn vorstellen; **to ~ sb to sth** jdn in etw acc einführen; **introduction** |ɪntrəˈdʌkʃən| n Einführung f; (to book) Einleitung f; **introductory** |ɪntrəˈdʌktərɪ| adj Einführungs-, Vor-

introspective |ɪntrəˈspektɪv| adj nach innen gekehrt

introvert |ˈɪntrəuvəːt| n Introvertierte(r) mf ♦ adj introvertiert

intrude |ɪnˈtruːd| vi: **to ~ (on sb/sth)** (jdn/etw) stören; **~r** n Eindringling m

intrusion |ɪnˈtruːʒən| n Störung f

intrusive |ɪnˈtruːsɪv| adj aufdringlich

intuition |ɪntjuˈɪʃən| n Intuition f

inundate |ˈɪnʌndeɪt| vt (also fig) überschwemmen

invade |ɪnˈveɪd| vt einfallen in +acc; **~r** n Eindringling m

invalid¹ |ˈɪnvəlɪd| n (disabled) Invalide m ♦ adj (ill) krank; (disabled) invalide

invalid² |ɪnˈvælɪd| adj (not valid) ungültig

invaluable |ɪnˈvæljuəbl| adj unschätzbar

invariable |ɪnˈveərɪəbl| adj unveränderlich; **invariably** adv ausnahmslos

invent |ɪnˈvent| vt erfinden; **~ion** |ɪnˈvenʃən| n Erfindung f; **~ive** adj erfinderisch; **~or** n Erfinder m

inventory |ˈɪnvəntrɪ| n Inventar nt

inverse |ɪnˈvəːs| n Umkehrung f ♦ adj umgekehrt

invert |ɪnˈvəːt| vt umdrehen; **~ed commas** (BRIT) npl Anführungsstriche pl

invest |ɪnˈvest| vt investieren

investigate |ɪnˈvestɪgeɪt| vt untersuchen; **investigation** |ɪnvestɪˈgeɪʃən| n Untersuchung f; **investigator** |ɪnˈvestɪgeɪtəʳ| n Untersuchungsbeamte(r) m

investiture |ɪnˈvestɪtʃəʳ| n Amtseinsetzung f

investment |ɪnˈvestmənt| n Investition f

investor |ɪnˈvestəʳ| n (Geld)anleger m

invigilate |ɪnˈvɪdʒɪleɪt| vi (in exam) Aufsicht führen ♦ vt Aufsicht führen bei; **invigilator** n Aufsicht f

invigorating |ɪnˈvɪgəreɪtɪŋ| adj stärkend

invincible |ɪnˈvɪnsɪbl| adj unbesiegbar

invisible |ɪnˈvɪzɪbl| adj unsichtbar

invitation |ɪnvɪˈteɪʃən| n Einladung f

invite |ɪnˈvaɪt| vt einladen

invoice |ˈɪnvɔɪs| n Rechnung f ♦ vt (goods): **to ~ sb for sth** jdm etw acc in Rechnung stellen

invoke |ɪnˈvəuk| vt anrufen

involuntary |ɪnˈvɔləntrɪ| adj unabsichtlich

involve |ɪnˈvɔlv| vt (entangle) verwickeln; (entail) mit sich bringen; **~d** adj verwickelt; **~ment** n Verwicklung f

inward |ˈɪnwəd| adj innere(r, s); (curve) Innen- ♦ adv nach innen; **~ly** adv im Innern; **~s** adv nach innen

I/O abbr (COMPUT: = input/output) I/O

iodine |ˈaɪəudiːn| n Jod nt

ioniser |ˈaɪənaɪzəʳ| n Ionisator m

iota |aɪˈəutə| n (fig) bisschen nt

IOU n abbr (= I owe you) Schuldschein m

IQ n abbr (= intelligence quotient) IQ m

Iran |ɪˈrɑːn| n Iran m; **~ian** |ɪˈreɪnɪən| adj iranisch ♦ n Iraner(in) m(f); (LING) Iranisch nt

Iraq |ɪˈrɑːk| n Irak m; **~i** adj irakisch ♦ n Iraker(in) m(f)

irate |aɪˈreɪt| adj zornig

Ireland |ˈaɪələnd| n Irland nt

iris |ˈaɪrɪs| n (pl **~es**) Iris f

Irish |ˈaɪrɪʃ| adj irisch ♦ npl: **the ~** die Iren pl, die Irländer pl; **~man** (irreg) n Ire m, Irländer m; **~ Sea** n: **the ~ Sea** die Irische See f; **~woman** (irreg) n Irin f, Irländerin f

irksome |ˈəːksəm| adj lästig

iron |ˈaɪən| n Eisen nt; (for ironing) Bügeleisen nt ♦ adj eisern ♦ vt bügeln; **~ out** vt (also fig) ausbügeln; **I~ Curtain** n (HIST) Eiserne(r) Vorhang m

ironic(al) |aɪˈrɔnɪk(l)| adj ironisch;

(*coincidence etc*) witzig

iron: ~ing *n* Bügeln *nt*; (*laundry*)
Bügelwäsche *f*; **~ing board** *n* Bügelbrett
nt; **~monger's (shop)** *n* Eisen- und
Haushaltswarenhandlung *f*

irony ['aɪrənɪ] *n* Ironie *f*

irrational [ɪ'ræʃənl] *adj* irrational

irreconcilable [ɪrekən'saɪləbl] *adj*
unvereinbar

irrefutable [ɪrɪ'fjuːtəbl] *adj* unwiderlegbar

irregular [ɪ'regjulə*r*] *adj* unregelmäßig;
(*shape*) ungleich(mäßig); (*fig*) unüblich;
(: *behaviour*) ungehörig

irrelevant [ɪ'reləvənt] *adj* belanglos,
irrelevant

irreparable [ɪ'repərəbl] *adj* nicht wieder
gutzumachen

irreplaceable [ɪrɪ'pleɪsəbl] *adj* unersetzlich

irresistible [ɪrɪ'zɪstɪbl] *adj* unwiderstehlich

irrespective [ɪrɪ'spektɪv]: **~ of** *prep*
ungeachtet +*gen*

irresponsible [ɪrɪ'spɒnsɪbl] *adj*
verantwortungslos

irreverent [ɪ'revərnt] *adj* respektlos

irrevocable [ɪ'revəkəbl] *adj* unwiderrufbar

irrigate ['ɪrɪgeɪt] *vt* bewässern

irritable ['ɪrɪtəbl] *adj* reizbar

irritate ['ɪrɪteɪt] *vt* irritieren, reizen (*also MED*);
irritating *adj* ärgerlich, irritierend; **he is**
irritating er kann einem auf die Nerven
gehen; **irritation** [ɪrɪ'teɪʃən] *n* (*anger*) Ärger
m; (*MED*) Reizung *f*

IRS *n abbr* = **Internal Revenue Service**

is [ɪz] *vb see* **be**

Islam ['ɪzlɑːm] *n* Islam *m*; **~ic** [ɪz'læmɪk] *adj*
islamisch

island ['aɪlənd] *n* Insel *f*; **~er** *n*
Inselbewohner(in) *m(f)*

isle [aɪl] *n* (kleine) Insel *f*

isn't ['ɪznt] = **is not**

isolate ['aɪsəleɪt] *vt* isolieren; **~d** *adj* isoliert;
(*case*) Einzel-; **isolation** [aɪsə'leɪʃən] *n*
Isolierung *f*

Israel ['ɪzreɪl] *n* Israel *nt*; **~i** [ɪz'reɪlɪ] *adj*
israelisch ♦ *n* Israeli *mf*

issue ['ɪʃjuː] *n* (*matter*) Frage *f*; (*outcome*)
Ausgang *m*; (*of newspaper, shares*) Ausgabe
f; (*offspring*) Nachkommenschaft *f* ♦ *vt*
ausgeben; (*warrant*) erlassen; (*documents*)
ausstellen; (*orders*) erteilen; (*books*)
herausgeben; (*verdict*) aussprechen; **to be at**
~ zur Debatte stehen; **to take ~ with**
sb over sth jdm in etw *dat*
widersprechen

KEYWORD
---

it [ɪt] *pron* **1** (*specific: subject*) er/sie/es;
(: *direct object*) ihn/sie/es; (: *indirect object*)
ihm/ihr/ihm; **about/from/in/of it** darüber/
davon/darin/davon

2 (*impers*) es; **it's raining** es regnet; **it's**

Friday tomorrow morgen ist Freitag; **who**
is it? – it's me wer ist da? – ich (bins)

Italian [ɪ'tæljən] *adj* italienisch ♦ *n*
Italiener(in) *m(f)*; (*LING*) Italienisch *nt*

italic [ɪ'tælɪk] *adj* kursiv; **~s** *npl* Kursivschrift *f*

Italy ['ɪtəlɪ] *n* Italien *nt*

itch [ɪtʃ] *n* Juckreiz *m*; (*fig*) Lust *f* ♦ *vi* jucken;
to be ~ing to do sth darauf brennen, etw
zu tun; **~y** *adj* juckend

it'd ['ɪtd] = **it would**; **it had**

item ['aɪtəm] *n* Gegenstand *m*; (*on list*)
Posten *m*; (*in programme*) Nummer *f*; (*in*
agenda) (Programm)punkt *m*; (*in*
newspaper) (Zeitungs)notiz *f*; **~ize** *vt*
verzeichnen

itinerant [ɪ'tɪnərənt] *adj* (*person*)
umherreisend

itinerary [aɪ'tɪnərərɪ] *n* Reiseroute *f*

it'll ['ɪtl] = **it will**; **it shall**

its [ɪts] *adj* (*masculine, neuter*) sein; (*feminine*)
ihr

it's [ɪts] = **it is**; **it has**

itself [ɪt'self] *pron* sich (selbst); (*emphatic*)
selbst

ITV (*BRIT*) *n abbr* = **Independent Television**

I.U.D. *n abbr* (= *intra-uterine device*) Pessar *nt*

I've [aɪv] = **I have**

ivory ['aɪvərɪ] *n* Elfenbein *nt*

ivy ['aɪvɪ] *n* Efeu *nt*

J, j

jab [dʒæb] *vt* (hinein)stechen ♦ *n* Stich *m*,
Stoß *m*; (*inf*) Spritze *f*

jack [dʒæk] *n* (*AUT*) (Wagen)heber *m*; (*CARDS*)
Bube *m*; **~ up** *vt* aufbocken

jackal ['dʒækl] *n* (*ZOOL*) Schakal *m*

jackdaw ['dʒækdɔː] *n* Dohle *f*

jacket ['dʒækɪt] *n* Jacke *f*; (*of book*)
Schutzumschlag *m*; (*TECH*) Ummantelung *f*;
~ potatoes *npl* in der Schale gebackene
Kartoffeln *pl*

jackknife ['dʒæknaɪf] *vi* (*truck*) sich
zusammenschieben

jack plug *n* (*ELEC*) Buchsenstecker *m*

jackpot ['dʒækpɒt] *n* Haupttreffer *m*

jaded ['dʒeɪdɪd] *adj* ermattet

jagged ['dʒægɪd] *adj* zackig

jail [dʒeɪl] *n* Gefängnis *nt* ♦ *vt* einsperren; **~er**
n Gefängniswärter *m*

jam [dʒæm] *n* Marmelade *f*; (*also:* **traffic ~**)
(Verkehrs)stau *m*; (*inf: trouble*) Klemme *f* ♦ *vt*
(*wedge*) einklemmen; (*cram*) hineinzwängen;
(*obstruct*) blockieren ♦ *vi* sich verklemmen;
to ~ sth into sth etw in etw *acc*
hineinstopfen

Jamaica [dʒə'meɪkə] *n* Jamaika *nt*

jam jar *n* Marmeladenglas *nt*

jammed [dʒæmd] *adj*: **it's ~** es klemmt

jam-packed |dʒæmˈpækt| adj überfüllt, proppenvoll

jangle |ˈdʒæŋgl| vt, vi klimpern

janitor |ˈdʒænɪtəʳ| n Hausmeister m

January |ˈdʒænjuərɪ| n Januar m

Japan |dʒəˈpæn| n Japan nt; **~ese** |dʒæpəˈniːz| adj japanisch ♦ n inv Japaner(in) m(f); (LING) Japanisch nt

jar |dʒɑːʳ| n Glas nt ♦ vi kreischen; (colours etc) nicht harmonieren

jargon |ˈdʒɑːgən| n Fachsprache f, Jargon m

jaundice |ˈdʒɔːndɪs| n Gelbsucht f; **~d** adj (fig) missgünstig

jaunt |dʒɔːnt| n Spritztour f

javelin |ˈdʒævlɪn| n Speer m

jaw |dʒɔː| n Kiefer m

jay |dʒeɪ| n (ZOOL) Eichelhäher m

jaywalker |ˈdʒeɪwɔːkəʳ| n unvorsichtige(r) Fußgänger m

jazz |dʒæz| n Jazz m; **~ up** vt (MUS) verjazzen; (enliven) aufpolieren

jealous |ˈdʒeləs| adj (envious) missgünstig; (husband) eifersüchtig; **~y** n Missgunst f; Eifersucht f

jeans |dʒiːnz| npl Jeans pl

Jeep |dʒiːp| ® n Jeep m ®

jeer |dʒɪəʳ| vi: **to ~ (at sb)** (über jdn) höhnisch lachen, (jdn) verspotten

Jehovah's Witness |dʒɪˈhəʊvəz-| n Zeuge m/Zeugin f Jehovas

jelly |ˈdʒelɪ| n Gelee nt; (dessert) Grütze f; **~fish** n Qualle f

jeopardize |ˈdʒepədaɪz| vt gefährden

jeopardy |ˈdʒepədɪ| n: **to be in ~** in Gefahr sein

jerk |dʒɜːk| n Ruck m, (inf: idiot) Trottel m ♦ vt ruckartig bewegen ♦ vi sich ruckartig bewegen

jerky |ˈdʒɜːkɪ| adj (movement) ruckartig, (ride) rüttelnd

jersey |ˈdʒɜːzɪ| n Pullover m

jest |dʒest| n Scherz m ♦ vi spaßen; **in ~** im Spaß

Jesus |ˈdʒiːzəs| n Jesus m

jet |dʒet| n (stream: of water etc) Strahl m; (spout) Düse f; (AVIAT) Düsenflugzeug nt; **~-black** adj rabenschwarz; **~ engine** n Düsenmotor m; **~ lag** n Jetlag m

jettison |ˈdʒetɪsn| vt über Bord werfen

jetty |ˈdʒetɪ| n Landesteg m, Mole f

Jew |dʒuː| n Jude m

jewel |ˈdʒuːəl| n (also fig) Juwel nt; **~ler** (US **~er**) n Juwelier m; **~ler's (shop)** n Juwelier m; **~lery** (US **~ry**) n Schmuck m

Jewess |ˈdʒuːɪs| n Jüdin f

Jewish |ˈdʒuːɪʃ| adj jüdisch

jibe |dʒaɪb| n spöttische Bemerkung f

jiffy |ˈdʒɪfɪ| (inf) n: **in a ~** sofort

jigsaw |ˈdʒɪgsɔː| n (also: **~ puzzle**) Puzzle(spiel) nt

jilt |dʒɪlt| vt den Laufpass geben +dat

jingle |ˈdʒɪŋgl| n (advertisement) Werbesong m ♦ vi klimpern; (bells) bimmeln ♦ vt klimpern mit; bimmeln lassen

jinx |dʒɪŋks| n: **there's a ~ on it** es ist verhext

jitters |ˈdʒɪtəz| (inf) npl: **to get the ~** einen Bammel kriegen

job |dʒɔb| n (piece of work) Arbeit f; (position) Stellung f; (duty) Aufgabe f; (difficulty) Mühe f; **it's a good ~ he …** es ist ein Glück, dass er …; **just the ~** genau das Richtige; **J~centre** (BRIT) n Arbeitsamt nt; **~less** adj arbeitslos

jockey |ˈdʒɔkɪ| n Jockei m, Jockey m ♦ vi: **to ~ for position** sich in eine gute Position drängeln

jocular |ˈdʒɔkjuləʳ| adj scherzhaft

jog |dʒɔg| vt (an)stoßen ♦ vi (run) joggen; **to ~ along** vor sich acc hinwursteln; (work) seinen Gang gehen; **~ging** n Jogging nt

join |dʒɔɪn| vt (club) beitreten +dat; (person) sich anschließen +dat; (fasten): **to ~ (sth to sth)** (etw mit etw) verbinden ♦ vi (unite) sich vereinigen ♦ n Verbindungsstelle f, Naht f; **~ in** vt, vi: **to ~ in (sth)** (bei etw) mitmachen; **~ up** vi (MIL) zur Armee gehen

joiner |ˈdʒɔɪnəʳ| n Schreiner m; **~y** n Schreinerei f

joint |dʒɔɪnt| n (TECH) Fuge f; (of bones) Gelenk nt; (of meat) Braten m; (inf: place) Lokal n ♦ adj gemeinsam; **~ account** n (with bank etc) gemeinsame(s) Konto nt; **~ly** adv gemeinsam

joke |dʒəʊk| n Witz m ♦ vi Witze machen; **to play a ~ on sb** jdm einen Streich spielen; **~r** n Witzbold m; (CARDS) Joker m

jolly |ˈdʒɔlɪ| adj lustig ♦ adv (inf) ganz schön

jolt |dʒəʊlt| n (shock) Schock m; (jerk) Stoß m ♦ vt (push) stoßen; (shake) durchschütteln; (fig) aufrütteln ♦ vi holpern

Jordan |ˈdʒɔːdən| n Jordanien nt

jostle |ˈdʒɔsl| vt anrempeln

jot |dʒɔt| n: **not one ~** kein Jota nt; **~ down** vt notieren; **~ter** (BRIT) n Notizblock m

journal |ˈdʒɜːnl| n (diary) Tagebuch nt; (magazine) Zeitschrift f; **~ism** n Journalismus m; **~ist** n Journalist(in) m(f)

journey |ˈdʒɜːnɪ| n Reise f

jovial |ˈdʒəʊvɪəl| adj jovial

joy |dʒɔɪ| n Freude f; **~ful** adj freudig; **~ous** adj freudig; **~ ride** n Schwarzfahrt f; **~rider** n Autodieb, der den Wagen nur für eine Spritztour stiehlt; **~stick** n Steuerknüppel m; (COMPUT) Joystick m

J.P. n abbr = **Justice of the Peace**

Jr abbr = **junior**

jubilant |ˈdʒuːbɪlnt| adj triumphierend

jubilee |ˈdʒuːbɪliː| n Jubiläum nt

judge |dʒʌdʒ| n Richter m; (fig) Kenner m ♦ vt (JUR: person) die Verhandlung führen über +acc; (case) verhandeln; (assess) beurteilen; (estimate) einschätzen; **~ment** n (JUR) Urteil

nt; (ECCL) Gericht nt; (ability)
Urteilsvermögen nt

judicial |dʒuːˈdɪʃl| adj gerichtlich, Justiz-

judiciary |dʒuːˈdɪʃɪərɪ| n Gerichtsbehörden
pl; (judges) Richterstand m

judicious |dʒuːˈdɪʃəs| adj weise

judo |ˈdʒuːdəu| n Judo nt

jug |dʒʌg| n Krug m

juggernaut |ˈdʒʌgənɔːt| (BRIT) n (huge truck)
Schwertransporter m

juggle |ˈdʒʌgl| vt, vi jonglieren; **~r** n Jongleur
m

Jugoslav etc |ˈjuːgəuˈslɑːv| = **Yugoslav** etc

juice |dʒuːs| n Saft m; **juicy** |ˈdʒuːsɪ| adj (also
fig) saftig

jukebox |ˈdʒuːkbɔks| n Musikautomat m

July |dʒuːˈlaɪ| n Juli m

jumble |ˈdʒʌmbl| n Durcheinander nt ♦ vt
(also: ~ **up**) durcheinander werfen; (facts)
durcheinander bringen; ~ **sale** (BRIT) n
Basar m, Flohmarkt m

jumbo (jet) |ˈdʒʌmbəu-| n Jumbo(jet) m

jump |dʒʌmp| vi springen; (nervously)
zusammenzucken ♦ vt überspringen ♦ n
Sprung m; **to ~ the queue** (BRIT) sich
vordrängeln

jumper |ˈdʒʌmpər| n (BRIT: pullover) Pullover
m; (US: dress) Trägerkleid nt

jump leads (BRIT), **jumper cables** (US)
npl Überbrückungskabel nt

jumpy |ˈdʒʌmpɪ| adj nervös

Jun. abbr = **junior**

junction |ˈdʒʌŋkʃən| n (BRIT: of roads)
(Straßen)kreuzung f; (RAIL) Knotenpunkt m

juncture |ˈdʒʌŋktʃər| n: **at this ~** in diesem
Augenblick

June |dʒuːn| n Juni m

jungle |ˈdʒʌŋgl| n Dschungel m

junior |ˈdʒuːnɪər| adj (younger) jünger; (after
name) junior; (SPORT) Junioren-; (lower
position) untergeordnet; (for young people)
Junioren- ♦ n Jüngere(r) mf; ~ **school** (BRIT)
n Grundschule f

junk |dʒʌŋk| n (rubbish) Plunder m; (ship)
Dschunke f; ~ **bond** n (COMM) niedrig
eingestuftes Wertpapier mit hohen
Ertragschancen bei erhöhtem Risiko; ~ **food**
n Junk food nt; ~ **mail** n Reklame, die
unangefordert in den Briefkasten gesteckt wird;
~ **shop** n Ramschladen m

Junr abbr = **junior**

jurisdiction |dʒuərɪsˈdɪkʃən| n
Gerichtsbarkeit f; (range of authority)
Zuständigkeit(sbereich m) f

juror |ˈdʒuərər| n Geschworene(r) mf; (in
competition) Preisrichter m

jury |ˈdʒuərɪ| n (court) Geschworene pl;
(panel) Jury f

just |dʒʌst| adj gerecht ♦ adv (recently, now)
gerade, eben; (barely) gerade noch; (exactly)
genau, gerade; (only) nur, bloß; (a small

distance) gleich; (absolutely) einfach; ~ **as I
arrived** gerade als ich ankam; ~ **as nice**
genauso nett; ~ **as well** umso besser; ~
now soeben, gerade; ~ **try** versuch es mal;
she's ~ left sie ist gerade or (so)eben
gegangen; **he's ~ done it** er hat es gerade
or (so)eben getan; ~ **before** gerade or kurz
bevor; ~ **enough** gerade genug; **he ~
missed** er hat fast or beinahe getroffen

justice |ˈdʒʌstɪs| n (fairness) Gerechtigkeit f;
J~ of the Peace n Friedensrichter m

justifiable |dʒʌstɪˈfaɪəbl| adj berechtigt

justification |dʒʌstɪfɪˈkeɪʃən| n
Rechtfertigung f

justify |ˈdʒʌstɪfaɪ| vt rechtfertigen; (text)
justieren

justly |ˈdʒʌstlɪ| adv (say) mit Recht;
(condemn) gerecht

jut |dʒʌt| vi (also: ~ **out**) herausragen,
vorstehen

juvenile |ˈdʒuːvənaɪl| adj (young) jugendlich;
(for the young) Jugend- ♦ n Jugendliche(r) mf

juxtapose |ˈdʒʌkstəpəuz| vt nebeneinander
stellen

K, k

K |keɪ| abbr (= one thousand) Tsd.; (= kilobyte)
K

kangaroo |kæŋgəˈruː| n Känguru nt

karate |kəˈrɑːtɪ| n Karate nt

kebab |kəˈbæb| n Kebab m

keel |kiːl| n Kiel m; **on an even ~** (fig) im Lot

keen |kiːn| adj begeistert; (wind, blade,
intelligence) scharf; (sight, hearing) gut; **to
be ~ to do** or **on doing sth** etw unbedingt
tun wollen; **to be ~ on sth/sb** scharf auf
etw/jdn sein

keep |kiːp| (pt, pp **kept**) vt (retain) behalten;
(have) haben; (animals, one's word) halten;
(support) versorgen; (maintain in state)
halten; (preserve) aufbewahren; (restrain)
abhalten ♦ vi (continue in direction) sich
halten; (food) sich halten; (remain: quiet etc)
bleiben ♦ n Unterhalt m; (tower) Burgfried
m; (inf): **for ~s** für immer; **to ~ sth to o.s.**
etw für sich behalten; **it ~s happening** es
passiert immer wieder; ~ **back** vt fern
halten; (information) verschweigen; ~ **on** vi:
~ **on doing sth** etw immer weiter tun; ~
out vt nicht hereinlassen; **"~ out"** „Eintritt
verboten!"; ~ **up** vi Schritt halten ♦ vt
aufrechterhalten; (continue) weitermachen;
to ~ up with Schritt halten mit; **~er** n
Wärter(in) m(f); (goalkeeper) Torhüter(in)
m(f); **~-fit** n Keep-fit nt; **~ing** n (care)
Obhut f; **in ~ing with** in Übereinstimmung
mit; **~sake** n Andenken nt

keg |keg| n Fass nt

kennel |ˈkenl| n Hundehütte f; **~s** npl: **to put**

a dog in ~s (*for boarding*) einen Hund in Pflege geben

Kenya |'kenjə| *n* Kenia *nt*; **~n** *adj* kenianisch ♦ *n* Kenianer(in) *m(f)*

kept |kept| *pt, pp of* **keep**

kerb |kə:b| (*BRIT*) *n* Bordstein *m*

kernel |'kə:nl| *n* Kern *m*

kerosene |'kerəsi:n| *n* Kerosin *nt*

kettle |'ketl| *n* Kessel *m*; **~drum** *n* Pauke *f*

key |ki:| *n* Schlüssel *m*; (*of piano, typewriter*) Taste *f*; (*MUS*) Tonart *f* ♦ *vt* (*also:* **~ in**) eingeben; **~board** *n* Tastatur *f*; **~ed up** *adj* (*person*) überdreht; **~hole** *n* Schlüsselloch *nt*; **~hole surgery** *n* minimal invasive Chirurgie *f*, Schlüssellochchirurgie *f*; **~note** *n* Grundton *m*; **~ ring** *n* Schlüsselring *m*

khaki |'ka:ki| *n* K(h)aki *nt* ♦ *adj* k(h)aki(farben)

kick |kik| *vt* einen Fußtritt geben +*dat*, treten ♦ *vi* treten; (*baby*) strampeln; (*horse*) ausschlagen ♦ *n* (*Fuß*)tritt *m*; (*thrill*) Spaß *m*; **he does it for ~s** er macht das aus Jux; **~ off** *vi* (*SPORT*) anstoßen; **~-off** *n* (*SPORT*) Anstoß *m*

kid |kid| *n* (*inf: child*) Kind *nt*; (*goat*) Zicklein *nt*; (*leather*) Glacéleder *nt*, Glaceeleder *nt* ♦ *vi* (*inf*) Witze machen

kidnap |'kidnæp| *vt* entführen; **~per** *n* Entführer *m*; **~ping** *n* Entführung *f*

kidney |'kidni| *n* Niere *f*

kill |kil| *vt* töten, umbringen ♦ *vi* töten ♦ *n* (*hunting*) (Jagd)beute *f*; **~er** *n* Mörder(in) *m(f)*; **~ing** *n* Mord *m*; **~joy** *n* Spaßverderber(in) *m(f)*

kiln |kiln| *n* Brennofen *m*

kilo |'ki:ləu| *n* Kilo *nt*; **~byte** *n* (*COMPUT*) Kilobyte *nt*; **~gram(me)** *n* Kilogramm *nt*; **~metre** |'kiləmi:tə*r*| (*US* **~meter**) *n* Kilometer *m*; **~watt** *n* Kilowatt *nt*

kilt |kilt| *n* Schottenrock *m*

kind |kaind| *adj* freundlich ♦ *n* Art *f*; **a ~ of** eine Art von; **(two) of a ~** (zwei) von der gleichen Art; **in ~** auf dieselbe Art; (*in goods*) in Naturalien

kindergarten |'kindəga:tn| *n* Kindergarten *m*

kind-hearted |kaind'ha:tid| *adj* gutherzig

kindle |'kindl| *vt* (*set on fire*) anzünden; (*rouse*) reizen, (er)wecken

kindly |'kaindli| *adj* freundlich ♦ *adv* liebenswürdig(erweise); **would you ~ ...?** wären Sie so freundlich und ...?

kindness |'kaindnis| *n* Freundlichkeit *f*

kindred |'kindrid| *adj*: **~ spirit** Gleichgesinnte(r) *mf*

king |kiŋ| *n* König *m*; **~dom** *n* Königreich *nt*

kingfisher |'kiŋfiʃə*r*| *n* Eisvogel *m*

king-size(d) |'kiŋsaiz(d)| *adj* (*cigarette*) Kingsize

kinky |'kiŋki| (*inf*) *adj* (*person, ideas*) verrückt; (*sexual*) abartig

kiosk |'ki:ɔsk| (*BRIT*) *n* (*TEL*) Telefonhäuschen *nt*

kipper |'kipə*r*| *n* Räucherhering *m*

kiss |kis| *n* Kuss *m* ♦ *vt* küssen ♦ *vi*: **they ~ed** sie küssten sich; **~ of life** (*BRIT*) *n*: **the ~ of life** Mund-zu-Mund-Beatmung *f*

kit |kit| *n* Ausrüstung *f*; (*tools*) Werkzeug *nt*

kitchen |'kitʃin| *n* Küche *f*; **~ sink** *n* Spülbecken *nt*

kite |kait| *n* Drachen *m*

kitten |'kitn| *n* Kätzchen *nt*

kitty |'kiti| *n* (*money*) Kasse *f*

km *abbr* (= *kilometre*) km

knack |næk| *n* Dreh *m*, Trick *m*

knapsack |'næpsæk| *n* Rucksack *m*; (*MIL*) Tornister *m*

knead |ni:d| *vt* kneten

knee |ni:| *n* Knie *nt*; **~cap** *n* Kniescheibe *f*

kneel |ni:l| (*pt, pp* knelt) *vi* (*also:* **~ down**) knien

knelt |nelt| *pt, pp of* **kneel**

knew |nju:| *pt of* **know**

knickers |'nikəz| (*BRIT*) *npl* Schlüpfer *m*

knife |naif| (*pl* knives) *n* Messer *nt* ♦ *vt* erstechen

knight |nait| *n* Ritter *m*; (*chess*) Springer *m*; **~hood** *n* (*title*): **to get a ~hood** zum Ritter geschlagen werden

knit |nit| *vt* stricken ♦ *vi* stricken; (*bones*) zusammenwachsen; **~ting** *n* (*occupation*) Stricken *nt*; (*work*) Strickzeug *nt*; **~ting needle** *n* Stricknadel *f*; **~wear** *n* Strickwaren *pl*

knives |naivz| *pl of* **knife**

knob |nɔb| *n* Knauf *m*; (*on instrument*) Knopf *m*; (*BRIT: of butter etc*) kleine(s) Stück *nt*

knock |nɔk| *vt* schlagen; (*criticize*) heruntermachen ♦ *vi*: **to ~ at** *or* **on the door** an die Tür klopfen ♦ *n* Schlag *m*; (*on door*) Klopfen *nt*; **~ down** *vt* umwerfen; (*with car*) anfahren; **~ off** *vt* (*do quickly*) hinhauen; (*inf: steal*) klauen ♦ *vi* (*finish*) Feierabend machen; **~ out** *vt* ausschlagen; (*BOXING*) k. o. schlagen; **~ over** *vt* (*person, object*) umwerfen; (*with car*) anfahren; **~er** *n* (*on door*) Türklopfer *m*; **~out** *n* K.-o.-Schlag *m*; (*fig*) Sensation *f*

knot |nɔt| *n* Knoten *m* ♦ *vt* (ver)knoten

knotty |'nɔti| *adj* (*fig*) kompliziert

know |nəu| (*pt* knew, *pp* known) *vt, vi* wissen; (*be able to*) können; (*be acquainted with*) kennen; (*recognize*) erkennen; **to ~ how to do sth** wissen, wie man etw macht, etw tun können; **to ~ about** *or* **of sth/sb** etw/jdn kennen; **~-all** *n* Alleswisser *m*; **~-how** *n* Kenntnis *f*, Know-how *nt*; **~ing** *adj* (*look, smile*) wissend; **~ingly** *adv* wissend; (*intentionally*) wissentlich

knowledge |'nɔlidʒ| *n* Wissen *nt*, Kenntnis *f*; **~able** *adj* informiert

known |nəun| *pp of* **know**

knuckle [ˈnʌkl] n Fingerknöchel m

K.O. n abbr = **knockout**

Koran [kɔˈrɑːn] n Koran m

Korea [kəˈrɪə] n Korea nt

kosher [ˈkəʊʃəʳ] adj koscher

L, l

L [ɛl] abbr (BRIT: AUT) (= learner) am Auto angebrachtes Kennzeichen für Fahrschüler; = **lake**; (= large) gr.; (= left) l.

l. abbr = **litre**

lab [læb] (inf) n Labor nt

label [ˈleɪbl] n Etikett nt ♦ vt etikettieren

labor etc [ˈleɪbəʳ] (US) = **labour** etc

laboratory [ləˈbɔrətəri] n Laboratorium nt

laborious [ləˈbɔːrɪəs] adj mühsam

labour [ˈleɪbəʳ] (US labor) n Arbeit f; (workmen) Arbeitskräfte pl; (MED) Wehen pl ♦ vi: to ~ (at) sich abmühen (mit) ♦ vt breittreten (inf); in ~ (MED) in den Wehen; L~ (BRIT: party) die Labour Party; ~ed adj (movement) gequält; (style) schwerfällig; ~er n Arbeiter m; farm ~er (Land)arbeiter m

lace [leɪs] n (fabric) Spitze f; (of shoe) Schnürsenkel m; (braid) Litze f ♦ vt (also: ~ up) (zu)schnüren

lack [læk] n Mangel m ♦ vt nicht haben; sb ~s sth jdm fehlt etw nom; to be ~ing fehlen; sb is ~ing in sth es fehlt jdm an etw dat; for or through ~ of aus Mangel an +dat

lacquer [ˈlækəʳ] n Lack m

lad [læd] n Junge m

ladder [ˈlædəʳ] n Leiter f; (BRIT: in tights) Laufmasche f ♦ vt (BRIT: tights) Laufmaschen bekommen in +dat

laden [ˈleɪdn] adj beladen, voll

ladle [ˈleɪdl] n Schöpfkelle f

lady [ˈleɪdɪ] n Dame f; (title) Lady f; young ~ junge Dame; the ladies' (room) die Damentoilette; ~bird (US ~bug) n Marienkäfer m; ~like adj damenhaft, vornehm; ~ship n: your L~ship Ihre Ladyschaft

lag [læg] vi (also: ~ behind) zurückbleiben ♦ vt (pipes) verkleiden

lager [ˈlɑːgəʳ] n helle(s) Bier nt

lagging [ˈlægɪŋ] n Isolierung f

lagoon [ləˈguːn] n Lagune f

laid [leɪd] pt, pp of **lay**; ~-**back** (inf) adj cool

lain [leɪn] pp of **lie**

lair [lɛəʳ] n Lager nt

lake [leɪk] n See m

lamb [læm] n Lamm nt; (meat) Lammfleisch nt; ~ **chop** n Lammkotelett nt; ~**swool** n Lammwolle f

lame [leɪm] adj lahm; (excuse) faul

lament [ləˈmɛnt] n Klage f ♦ vt beklagen

laminated [ˈlæmɪneɪtɪd] adj beschichtet

lamp [læmp] n Lampe f; (in street) Straßenlaterne f; ~**post** n Laternenpfahl m; ~**shade** n Lampenschirm m

lance [lɑːns] n Lanze f; ~ **corporal** (BRIT) n Obergefreite(r) m

land [lænd] n Land nt ♦ vi (from ship) an Land gehen; (AVIAT, end up) landen ♦ vt (obtain) kriegen; (passengers) absetzen; (goods) abladen; (troops, space probe) landen; ~**fill site** [ˈlændfɪl-] n Mülldeponie f; ~**ing** n Landung f; (on stairs) (Treppen)absatz m; ~**ing gear** n Fahrgestell nt; ~**ing stage** (BRIT) n Landesteg m; ~**ing strip** n Landebahn f; ~**lady** n (Haus)wirtin f; ~**locked** adj landumschlossen, Binnen-; ~**lord** n (of house) Hauswirt m, Besitzer m; (of pub) Gastwirt m; (of area) Grundbesitzer m; ~**mark** n Wahrzeichen nt; (fig) Meilenstein m; ~**owner** n Grundbesitzer m; ~**scape** n Landschaft f; ~**scape gardener** n Landschaftsgärtner(in) m(f); ~**slide** n (GEOG) Erdrutsch m; (POL) überwältigende(r) Sieg m

lane [leɪn] n (in town) Gasse f; (in country) Weg m; (of motorway) Fahrbahn f, Spur f; (SPORT) Bahn f; "**get in ~**" "bitte einordnen"

language [ˈlæŋgwɪdʒ] n Sprache f; bad ~ unanständige Ausdrücke pl; ~ **laboratory** n Sprachlabor nt

languish [ˈlæŋgwɪʃ] vi schmachten

lank [læŋk] adj dürr

lanky [ˈlæŋkɪ] adj schlaksig

lantern [ˈlæntən] n Laterne f

lap [læp] n Schoß m; (SPORT) Runde f ♦ vt (also: ~ up) auflecken ♦ vi (water) plätschern

lapel [ləˈpɛl] n Revers nt or m

Lapland [ˈlæplænd] n Lappland nt

lapse [læps] n (moral) Fehltritt m ♦ vi (decline) nachlassen; (expire) ablaufen; (claims) erlöschen; to ~ **into bad habits** sich schlechte Gewohnheiten angewöhnen

laptop (computer) [ˈlæptɔp-] n Laptop(-Computer) m

lard [lɑːd] n Schweineschmalz m

larder [ˈlɑːdəʳ] n Speisekammer f

large [lɑːdʒ] adj groß; at ~ auf freiem Fuß; ~**ly** adv zum größten Teil; ~-**scale** adj groß angelegt, Groß-

lark [lɑːk] n (bird) Lerche f; (joke) Jux m; ~ **about** (inf) vi herumalbern

laryngitis [lærɪnˈdʒaɪtɪs] n Kehlkopfentzündung f

laser [ˈleɪzəʳ] n Laser m; ~ **printer** n Laserdrucker m

lash [læʃ] n Peitschenhieb m; (eyelash) Wimper f ♦ vt (rain) schlagen gegen; (whip) peitschen; (bind) festbinden; ~ **out** vi (with fists) um sich schlagen

lass |læs| n Mädchen nt

lasso |læ'suː| n Lasso nt

last |lɑːst| adj letzte(r, s) ♦ adv zuletzt; (~ time) das letzte Mal ♦ vi (continue) dauern; (remain good) sich halten; (money) ausreichen; **at ~** endlich; **~ night** gestern Abend; **~ week** letzte Woche; **~ but one** vorletzte(r, s); **~-ditch** adj (attempt) in letzter Minute; **~ing** adj dauerhaft; (shame etc) andauernd; **~ly** adv schließlich; **~-minute** adj in letzter Minute

latch |lætʃ| n Riegel m

late |leɪt| adj spät; (dead) verstorben ♦ adv spät; (after proper time) zu spät; **to be ~** zu spät kommen; **of ~** in letzter Zeit; **in ~ May** Ende Mai; **~comer** n Nachzügler(in) m(f); **~ly** adv in letzter Zeit; **~r** |'leɪtər| adj (date) später; (version) neuer ♦ adv später

lateral |'lætərəl| adj seitlich

latest |'leɪtɪst| adj (fashion) neueste(r, s) ♦ n (news) Neue(ste)(s) nt; **at the ~** spätestens

lathe |leɪð| n Drehbank f

lather |'lɑːðər| n (Seifen)schaum m ♦ vt einschäumen ♦ vi schäumen

Latin |'lætɪn| n Latein nt ♦ adj lateinisch; (Roman) römisch; **~ America** n Lateinamerika nt; **~ American** adj lateinamerikanisch

latitude |'lætɪtjuːd| n (GEOG) Breite f; (freedom) Spielraum m

latter |'lætər| adj (second of two) letztere; (coming at end) letzte(r, s), später ♦ n: **the ~** der/die/das letztere, die letzteren; **~ly** adv in letzter Zeit

lattice |'lætɪs| n Gitter nt

laudable |'lɔːdəbl| adj löblich

laugh |lɑːf| n Lachen nt ♦ vi lachen; **~ at** vt lachen über +acc; **~ off** vt lachend abtun; **~able** adj lachhaft; **~ing stock** n Zielscheibe f des Spottes; **~ter** n Gelächter nt

launch |lɔːntʃ| n (of ship) Stapellauf m; (of rocket) Abschuss m; (boat) Barkasse f; (of product) Einführung f ♦ vt (set afloat) vom Stapel lassen; (rocket) (ab)schießen; (product) auf den Markt bringen; **~(ing) pad** n Abschussrampe f

launder |'lɔːndər| vt waschen

Launderette |lɔːn'drɛt| (® BRIT) n Waschsalon m

Laundromat |'lɔːndrəmæt| (® US) n Waschsalon m

laundry |'lɔːndrɪ| n (place) Wäscherei f; (clothes) Wäsche f; **to do the ~** waschen

laureate |'lɔːrɪət| adj see **poet**

laurel |'lɒrl| n Lorbeer m

lava |'lɑːvə| n Lava f

lavatory |'lævətərɪ| n Toilette f

lavender |'lævəndər| n Lavendel m

lavish |'lævɪʃ| adj (extravagant) verschwenderisch; (generous) großzügig ♦ vt

(money): **to ~ sth on sth** etw auf etw acc verschwenden; (attention, gifts): **to ~ sth on sb** jdn mit etw überschütten

law |lɔː| n Gesetz nt; (system) Recht nt; (as studies) Jura no art; **~-abiding** adj gesetzestreu; **~ and order** n Recht nt und Ordnung f; **~ court** n Gerichtshof m; **~ful** adj gesetzlich; **~less** adj gesetzlos

lawn |lɔːn| n Rasen m; **~mower** n Rasenmäher m; **~ tennis** n Rasentennis m

law: ~ school n Rechtsakademie f; **~suit** n Prozess m; **~yer** n Rechtsanwalt m, Rechtsanwältin f

lax |læks| adj (behaviour) nachlässig; (standards) lax

laxative |'læksətɪv| n Abführmittel nt

lay |leɪ| (pt, pp **laid**) pt of **lie** ♦ adj Laien- ♦ vt (place) legen; (table) decken; (egg) legen; (trap) stellen; (money) wetten; **~ aside** vt zurücklegen; **~ by** vt (set aside) beiseite legen; **~ down** vt hinlegen; (rules) vorschreiben; (arms) strecken; **to ~ down the law** Vorschriften machen; **~ off** vt (workers) (vorübergehend) entlassen; **~ on** vt (water, gas) anschließen; (concert etc) veranstalten; **~ out** vt (her)auslegen; (money) ausgeben; (corpse) aufbahren; **~ up** vt (subj: illness) ans Bett fesseln; **~about** n Faulenzer m; **~-by** (BRIT) n Parkbucht f; (bigger) Rastplatz m

layer |'leɪər| n Schicht f

layman |'leɪmən| (irreg) n Laie m

layout |'leɪaʊt| n Anlage f; (ART) Lay-out nt, Layout nt

laze |leɪz| vi faulenzen

laziness |'leɪzɪnəs| n Faulheit f

lazy |'leɪzɪ| adj faul; (slow-moving) träge

lb. abbr = **pound** (weight)

lead¹ |lɛd| n (chemical) Blei nt; (of pencil) (Bleistift)mine f ♦ adj bleiern, Blei-

lead² |liːd| (pt, pp **led**) n (front position) Führung f; (distance, time ahead) Vorsprung f; (example) Vorbild nt; (clue) Tipp m; (of police) Spur f; (THEAT) Hauptrolle f; (dog's) Leine f ♦ vt (guide) führen; (group etc) leiten ♦ vi (be first) führen; **in the ~** (SPORT, fig) in Führung; **~ astray** vt irreführen; **~ away** vt wegführen; (prisoner) abführen; **~ back** vt zurückführen; **~ on** vt anführen; **~ on to** vt (induce) dazu bringen; **~ to** vt (street) (hin)führen nach; (result in) führen zu; **~ up to** vt (drive) führen zu; (speaker etc) hinführen auf +acc

leaded petrol |'lɛdɪd-| n verbleites Benzin nt

leaden |'lɛdn| adj (sky, sea) bleiern; (heavy: footsteps) bleischwer

leader |'liːdər| n Führer m, Leiter m; (of party) Vorsitzende(r) m; (PRESS) Leitartikel m; **~ship** n (office) Leitung f; (quality) Führerschaft f

lead-free |'lɛdfriː| adj (petrol) bleifrei

leading |'liːdɪŋ| adj führend; ~ **lady** n (THEAT) Hauptdarstellerin f; ~ **light** n (person) führende(r) Geist m

lead singer |liːd-| n Leadsänger(in) m(f)

leaf |liːf| (pl **leaves**) n Blatt nt ♦ vi: **to ~ through** durchblättern; **to turn over a new ~** einen neuen Anfang machen

leaflet |'liːflɪt| n (advertisement) Prospekt m; (pamphlet) Flugblatt nt; (for information) Merkblatt nt

league |liːg| n (union) Bund m; (SPORT) Liga f; **to be in ~ with** unter einer Decke stecken mit

leak |liːk| n undichte Stelle f; (in ship) Leck nt ♦ vt (liquid etc) durchlassen ♦ vi (pipe etc) undicht sein; (liquid etc) auslaufen; **the information was ~ed to the enemy** die Information wurde dem Feind zugespielt; **~ out** vi (liquid etc) auslaufen; (information) durchsickern; **~y** |'liːkɪ| adj undicht

lean |liːn| (pt, pp **leaned** or **leant**) adj mager ♦ vi sich neigen ♦ vt (an)lehnen; **to ~ against sth** an etw dat angelehnt sein; sich an etw acc anlehnen; **~ back** vi sich zurücklehnen; **~ forward** vi sich vorbeugen; **~ on** vt fus sich stützen auf +acc; **~ out** vi sich hinauslehnen; **~ over** vi sich hinüberbeugen; **~ing** n Neigung f ♦ adj schief; **~t** |lɛnt| pt, pp of **lean**; **~-to** n Anbau m

leap |liːp| (pt, pp **leaped** or **leapt**) n Sprung m ♦ vi springen; **~frog** n Bockspringen nt; **~t** |lɛpt| pt, pp of **leap**; **~ year** n Schaltjahr nt

learn |lɜːn| (pt, pp **learned** or **learnt**) vt, vi lernen; (find out) erfahren; **to ~ how to do sth** etw (er)lernen; **~ed** |'lɜːnɪd| adj gelehrt; **~er** n Anfänger(in) m(f); (AUT: BRIT: also: **~er driver**) Fahrschüler(in) m(f); **~ing** n Gelehrsamkeit f

lease |liːs| n (of property) Mietvertrag m ♦ vt pachten

leash |liːʃ| n Leine f

least |liːst| adj geringste(r, s) ♦ adv am wenigsten ♦ n Mindeste(s) nt; **the ~ possible effort** möglichst geringer Aufwand; **at ~** zumindest; **not in the ~!** durchaus nicht!

leather |'lɛðəʳ| n Leder nt

leave |liːv| (pt, pp **left**) vt verlassen; (~ behind) zurücklassen; (forget) vergessen; (allow to remain) lassen; (after death) hinterlassen; (entrust) **to ~ sth to sb** jdm etw überlassen ♦ vi weggehen, wegfahren; (for journey) abreisen; (bus, train) abfahren ♦ n Erlaubnis f; (MIL) Urlaub m; **to be left** (remain) übrig bleiben; **there's some milk left over** es ist noch etwas Milch übrig; **on ~** auf Urlaub; **~ behind** vt (person, object) dalassen; (forget) liegen lassen, stehen lassen; **~ out** vt auslassen; **~ of absence** n

Urlaub m

leaves |liːvz| pl of **leaf**

Lebanon |'lɛbənən| n Libanon m

lecherous |'lɛtʃərəs| adj lüstern

lecture |'lɛktʃəʳ| n Vortrag m; (UNIV) Vorlesung f ♦ vi einen Vortrag halten; (UNIV) lesen ♦ vt (scold) abkanzeln; **~r** |'lɛktʃərəʳ| n Vortragende(r) mf; (BRIT: UNIV) Dozent(in) m(f)

led |lɛd| pt, pp of **lead²**

ledge |lɛdʒ| n Leiste f; (window ~) Sims m or nt; (of mountain) (Fels)vorsprung m

ledger |'lɛdʒəʳ| n Hauptbuch nt

leech |liːtʃ| n Blutegel m

leek |liːk| n Lauch m

leer |lɪəʳ| vi: **to ~ (at sb)** (nach jdm) schielen

leeway |'liːweɪ| n (fig): **to have some ~** etwas Spielraum haben

left |lɛft| pt, pp of **leave** ♦ adj linke(r, s) ♦ n (side) linke Seite f ♦ adv links; **on the ~** links; **to the ~** nach links; **the L~** (POL) die Linke f; **~-hand drive** n mit Linkssteuerung; **~-handed** adj linkshändig; **~-hand side** n linke Seite f; **~-luggage locker** n Gepäckschließfach nt; **~-luggage (office)** (BRIT) n Gepäckaufbewahrung f; **~-overs** npl Reste pl; **~-wing** adj linke(r, s)

leg |lɛg| n Bein nt; (of meat) Keule f; (stage) Etappe f; **1st/2nd ~** (SPORT) 1./2. Etappe

legacy |'lɛgəsɪ| n Erbe nt, Erbschaft f

legal |'liːgl| adj gesetzlich; (allowed) legal; **~ holiday** (US) n gesetzliche(r) Feiertag m; **~ize** vt legalisieren; **~ly** adv gesetzlich; legal; **~ tender** n gesetzliche(s) Zahlungsmittel nt

legend |'lɛdʒənd| n Legende f; **~ary** adj legendär

leggings |'lɛgɪŋz| npl Leggings pl

legible |'lɛdʒəbl| adj leserlich

legislation |lɛdʒɪs'leɪʃən| n Gesetzgebung f; **legislative** |'lɛdʒɪslətɪv| adj gesetzgebend; **legislature** |'lɛdʒɪslətʃəʳ| n Legislative f

legitimate |lɪ'dʒɪtɪmət| adj rechtmäßig, legitim; (child) ehelich

legroom |'lɛgruːm| n Platz m für die Beine

leisure |'lɛʒəʳ| n Freizeit f; **to be at ~** Zeit haben; **~ centre** n Freizeitzentrum nt; **~ly** adj gemächlich

lemon |'lɛmən| n Zitrone f; (colour) Zitronengelb nt; **~ade** |lɛmə'neɪd| n Limonade f; **~ tea** n Zitronentee m

lend |lɛnd| (pt, pp **lent**) vt leihen; **to ~ sb sth** jdm etw leihen; **~ing library** n Leihbibliothek f

length |lɛŋθ| n Länge f; (of road, pipe etc) Strecke f; (of material) Stück nt; **at ~** (lengthily) ausführlich; (at last) schließlich; **~en** vt verlängern ♦ vi länger werden; **~ways** adv längs; **~y** adj sehr lang, langatmig

lenient |'liːnɪənt| adj nachsichtig

lens [lɛnz] n Linse f; (PHOT) Objektiv nt
Lent [lɛnt] n Fastenzeit f
lent [lɛnt] pt, pp of **lend**
lentil [ˈlɛntɪl] n Linse f
Leo [ˈliːəu] n Löwe m
leotard [ˈliːətaːd] n Trikot nt, Gymnastikanzug m
leper [ˈlɛpəʳ] n Leprakranke(r) f(m)
leprosy [ˈlɛprəsɪ] n Lepra f
lesbian [ˈlɛzbɪən] adj lesbisch ♦ n Lesbierin f
less [lɛs] adj, adv weniger ♦ n weniger ♦ pron weniger; ~ **than half** weniger als die Hälfte; ~ **than ever** weniger denn je; ~ **and** ~ immer weniger; **the** ~ **he works** je weniger er arbeitet; ~**en** [lɛsn] vi abnehmen ♦ vt verringern, verkleinern; ~**er** [ˈlɛsəʳ] adj kleiner, geringer; **to a** ~**er extent** in geringerem Maße
lesson [ˈlɛsn] n (SCH) Stunde f; (unit of study) Lektion f; (fig) Lehre f; (ECCL) Lesung f; **a maths** ~ eine Mathestunde
lest [lɛst] conj: ~ **it happen** damit es nicht passiert
let [lɛt] (pt, pp **let**) vt lassen; (BRIT: lease) vermieten; **to** ~ **sb do sth** jdn etw tun lassen; **to** ~ **sb know sth** jdn etw wissen lassen; ~'**s go!** gehen wir!; ~ **him come** soll er doch kommen; ~ **down** vt hinunterlassen; (disappoint) enttäuschen; ~ **go** vi loslassen ♦ vt (things) loslassen; (person) gehen lassen; ~ **in** vt hereinlassen; (water) durchlassen; ~ **off** vt (gun) abfeuern; (steam) ablassen; (forgive) laufen lassen; ~ **on** vi durchblicken lassen; (pretend) vorgeben; ~ **out** vt herauslassen; (scream) fahren lassen; ~ **up** vi nachlassen; (stop) aufhören
lethal [ˈliːθl] adj tödlich
lethargic [lɛˈθɑːdʒɪk] adj lethargisch
letter [ˈlɛtəʳ] n Brief m; (of alphabet) Buchstabe m; ~ **bomb** n Briefbombe f; ~**box** (BRIT) n Briefkasten m; ~**ing** n Beschriftung f; ~ **of credit** n Akkreditiv m
lettuce [ˈlɛtɪs] n (Kopf)salat m
let-up [ˈlɛtʌp] (inf) n Nachlassen nt
leukaemia [luːˈkiːmɪə] (US **leukemia**) n Leukämie f
level [ˈlɛvl] adj (ground) eben; (at same height) auf gleicher Höhe; (equal) gleich gut; (head) kühl ♦ adv auf gleicher Höhe ♦ n (instrument) Wasserwaage f; (altitude) Höhe f; (flat place) ebene Fläche f; (position on scale) Niveau nt; (amount, degree) Grad m ♦ vt (ground) einebnen; **to draw** ~ **with** gleichziehen mit; **to be** ~ **with** auf einer Höhe sein mit; **A** ~**s** (BRIT) ≈ Abitur nt; **O** ~**s** (BRIT) ≈ mittlere Reife f; **on the** ~ (fig: honest) ehrlich; **to** ~ **sth at sb** (blow) jdm etw versetzen; (remark) etw gegen jdn richten; ~ **off** or **out** vi flach or eben werden; (fig) sich ausgleichen; (plane)

horizontal fliegen ♦ vt (ground) planieren; (differences) ausgleichen; ~ **crossing** (BRIT) n Bahnübergang m; ~-**headed** adj vernünftig
lever [ˈliːvəʳ] n Hebel m; (fig) Druckmittel nt ♦ vt (hoch)stemmen; ~**age** n Hebelkraft f; (fig) Einfluss m
levy [ˈlɛvɪ] n (of taxes) Erhebung f; (tax) Abgaben pl; (MIL) Aushebung f ♦ vt erheben; (MIL) ausheben
lewd [luːd] adj unzüchtig, unanständig
liability [laɪəˈbɪlətɪ] n (obligation) Belastung f; (duty) Pflicht f; (debt) Verpflichtung f; (responsibility) Haftung f; (proneness) Anfälligkeit f
liable [ˈlaɪəbl] adj (responsible) haftbar; (prone) anfällig; **to be** ~ **for sth** etw dat unterliegen; **it's** ~ **to happen** es kann leicht vorkommen
liaise [liːˈeɪz] vi: **to** ~ (**with sb**) (mit jdm) zusammenarbeiten; **liaison** n Verbindung f
liar [ˈlaɪəʳ] n Lügner m
libel [ˈlaɪbl] n Verleumdung f ♦ vt verleumden
liberal [ˈlɪbərl] adj (generous) großzügig; (open-minded) aufgeschlossen; (POL) liberal
liberate [ˈlɪbəreɪt] vt befreien; **liberation** [lɪbəˈreɪʃən] n Befreiung f
liberty [ˈlɪbətɪ] n Freiheit f; (permission) Erlaubnis f; **to be at** ~ **to do sth** etw tun dürfen; **to take the** ~ **of doing sth** sich dat erlauben, etw zu tun
Libra [ˈliːbrə] n Waage f
librarian [laɪˈbrɛərɪən] n Bibliothekar(in) m(f)
library [ˈlaɪbrərɪ] n Bibliothek f; (lending ~) Bücherei f
Libya [ˈlɪbɪə] n Libyen nt; ~**n** adj libysch ♦ n Libyer(in) m(f)
lice [laɪs] npl of **louse**
licence [ˈlaɪsns] (US **license**) n (permit) Erlaubnis f; (also: driving ~, (US) driver's license) Führerschein m
license [ˈlaɪsns] n (US) = **licence** ♦ vt genehmigen, konzessionieren; ~**d** adj (for alcohol) konzessioniert (für den Alkoholausschank); ~ **plate** (US) n (AUT) Nummernschild nt
lichen [ˈlaɪkən] n Flechte f
lick [lɪk] vt lecken ♦ n Lecken nt; **a** ~ **of paint** ein bisschen Farbe
licorice [ˈlɪkərɪs] (US) n = **liquorice**
lid [lɪd] n Deckel m; (eyelid) Lid nt
lie [laɪ] (pt **lay**, pp **lain**) vi (rest, be situated) liegen; (put o.s. in position) sich legen; (pt, pp **lied**: tell lies) lügen ♦ n Lüge f; **to** ~ **low** (fig) untertauchen; ~ **about** vi (things) herumliegen; (people) faulenzen; ~-**down** (BRIT) n: **to have a** ~-**down** ein Nickerchen machen; ~-**in** (BRIT) n: **to have a** ~-**in** sich ausschlafen
lieu [luː] n: **in** ~ **of** anstatt +gen
lieutenant [lɛfˈtɛnənt, (US) luːˈtɛnənt] n

Leutnant m
life |laɪf| (pl **lives**) n Leben nt; ~ **assurance**
(BRIT) n = **life insurance**; ~**belt** (BRIT) n
Rettungsring m; ~**boat** n Rettungsboot nt;
~**guard** n Rettungsschwimmer m; ~
insurance n Lebensversicherung f; ~
jacket n Schwimmweste f; ~**less** adj (dead)
leblos; (dull) langweilig; ~**like** adj
lebenswahr, naturgetreu; ~**line** n
Rettungsleine f; (fig) Rettungsanker m;
~**long** adj lebenslang; ~ **preserver** (US) n =
lifebelt; ~-**saver** n Lebensretter(in) m(f); ~-
saving adj lebensrettend, Rettungs-; ~
sentence n lebenslängliche Freiheitsstrafe f;
~ **span** n Lebensspanne f; ~**style** n
Lebensstil m; ~ **support system** n (MED)
Lebenserhaltungssystem nt; ~**time** n: in his
~**time** während er lebte; **once in a ~time**
einmal im Leben
lift |lɪft| vt hochheben ♦ vi sich heben ♦ n
(BRIT: elevator) Aufzug m, Lift m; **to give sb**
a ~ jdn mitnehmen; ~-**off** n Abheben nt
(vom Boden)
ligament |'lɪgəmənt| n Band nt
light |laɪt| (pt, pp **lighted** or **lit**) n Licht nt;
(for cigarette etc): **have you got a ~?** haben
Sie Feuer? ♦ vt beleuchten; (lamp)
anmachen; (fire, cigarette) anzünden ♦ adj
(bright) hell; (pale) hell-; (not heavy, easy)
leicht; (punishment) milde; (touch) leicht; ~**s**
npl (AUT) Beleuchtung f; ~ **up** vi (lamp)
angehen; (face) aufleuchten ♦ vt (illuminate)
beleuchten; (~s) anmachen; ~ **bulb** n
Glühbirne f; ~**en** vi (brighten) hell werden;
(~ning) blitzen ♦ vt (give ~ to) erhellen;
(hair) aufhellen; (gloom) aufheitern; (make
less heavy) leichter machen; (fig) erleichtern;
~**er** n Feuerzeug nt; ~-**headed** adj
(thoughtless) leichtsinnig; (giddy)
schwindlig; ~-**hearted** adj leichtherzig,
fröhlich; ~**house** n Leuchtturm m; ~**ing** n
Beleuchtung f; ~**ly** adv leicht; (irresponsibly)
leichtfertig; **to get off ~ly** mit einem blauen
Auge davonkommen; ~**ness** n (of weight)
Leichtigkeit f; (of colour) Helle f
lightning |'laɪtnɪŋ| n Blitz m; ~ **conductor**
(US ~ **rod**) n Blitzableiter m
light: ~ **pen** n Lichtstift m; ~**weight** adj
(suit) leicht; ~**weight** n (BOXING)
Leichtgewichtler m; ~ **year** n Lichtjahr nt
like |laɪk| vt mögen, gern haben ♦ prep wie
♦ adj (similar) ähnlich; (equal) gleich ♦ n:
the ~ dergleichen; **I would** or **I'd ~** ich
möchte gern; **would you ~ a coffee?**
möchten Sie einen Kaffee?; **to be** or **look ~**
sb/sth jdm/etw ähneln; **that's just ~ him**
das ist typisch für ihn; **it is ~ this** mach es
so; **it is nothing ~ ...** es ist nicht zu
vergleichen mit ...; **what does it look ~?**
wie sieht es aus?; **what does it sound ~?**
wie hört es sich an?; **what does it taste ~?**

wie schmeckt es?; **his ~s and dislikes** was
er mag und was er nicht mag; ~**able** adj
sympathisch
likelihood |'laɪklɪhud| n Wahrscheinlichkeit f
likely |'laɪklɪ| adj wahrscheinlich; **he's ~ to**
leave er geht möglicherweise; **not ~!** wohl
kaum!
likeness |'laɪknɪs| n Ähnlichkeit f; (portrait)
Bild nt
likewise |'laɪkwaɪz| adv ebenso
liking |'laɪkɪŋ| n Zuneigung f; (taste) Vorliebe
f
lilac |'laɪlək| n Flieder m ♦ adj (colour)
fliederfarben
lily |'lɪlɪ| n Lilie f; ~ **of the valley** n
Maiglöckchen nt
limb |lɪm| n Glied nt
limber up |'lɪmbər-| vi sich auflockern; (fig)
sich vorbereiten
limbo |'lɪmbəu| n: **to be in ~** (fig) in der
Schwebe sein
lime |laɪm| n (tree) Linde f; (fruit) Limone f;
(substance) Kalk m
limelight |'laɪmlaɪt| n: **to be in the ~** (fig) im
Rampenlicht stehen
limestone |'laɪmstəun| n Kalkstein m
limit |'lɪmɪt| n Grenze f; (inf) Höhe f ♦ vt
begrenzen, einschränken; ~**ation**
|lɪmɪ'teɪʃən| n Einschränkung f; ~**ed** adj
beschränkt; **to be ~ed to** sich beschränken
auf +acc; ~**ed (liability) company** (BRIT) n
Gesellschaft f mit beschränkter Haftung
limousine |'lɪməzi:n| n Limousine f
limp |lɪmp| n Hinken nt ♦ vi hinken ♦ adj
schlaff
limpet |'lɪmpɪt| n (fig) Klette f
line |laɪn| n Linie f; (rope) Leine f; (on face)
Falte f; (row) Reihe f; (of hills) Kette f; (US:
queue) Schlange f; (company) Linie f,
Gesellschaft f; (RAIL) Strecke f; (TEL) Leitung
f; (written) Zeile f; (direction) Richtung f;
(fig: business) Branche f; (range of items)
Kollektion f ♦ vt (coat) füttern; (border)
säumen; ~**s** npl (RAIL) Gleise pl; **in ~ with** in
Übereinstimmung mit; ~ **up** vi sich
aufstellen ♦ vt aufstellen; (prepare) sorgen
für; (support) mobilisieren; (surprise) planen;
~**ar** |'lɪnɪər| adj gerade; (measure) Längen-;
~**d** adj (face) faltig; (paper) liniert
linen |'lɪnɪn| n Leinen nt; (sheets etc) Wäsche
f
liner |'laɪnər| n Überseedampfer m
linesman |'laɪnzmən| (irreg) n (SPORT)
Linienrichter m
line-up |'laɪnʌp| n Aufstellung f
linger |'lɪŋgər| vi (remain long) verweilen;
(taste) (zurück)bleiben; (delay) zögern,
verharren
lingerie |'lænʒəriː| n Damenunterwäsche f
lingering |'lɪŋgərɪŋ| adj (doubt)
zurückbleibend; (disease) langwierig; (taste)

nachhaltend; (look) lang
lingo [ˈlɪŋgəʊ] (pl **-es**) (inf) n Sprache f
linguist [ˈlɪŋgwɪst] n Sprachkundige(r) mf;
(UNIV) Sprachwissenschaftler(in) m(f); **~ic**
[lɪŋˈgwɪstɪk] adj sprachlich;
sprachwissenschaftlich; **~ics** n
Sprachwissenschaft f, Linguistik f
lining [ˈlaɪnɪŋ] n Futter nt
link [lɪŋk] n Glied nt; (connection) Verbindung
f ♦ vt verbinden; **~s** npl (GOLF) Golfplatz m;
~ up vt verbinden ♦ vi zusammenkommen;
(companies) sich zusammenschließen; **~-up**
n (TEL) Verbindung f; (of spaceships)
Kopplung f
lino [ˈlaɪnəʊ] n = **linoleum**
linoleum [lɪˈnəʊlɪəm] n Linoleum nt
linseed oil [ˈlɪnsiːd-] n Leinöl nt
lion [ˈlaɪən] n Löwe m; **~ess** n Löwin f
lip [lɪp] n Lippe f; (of jug) Schnabel m; **to pay
~ service (to)** ein Lippenbekenntnis ablegen
(zu)
liposuction [ˈlɪpəʊsʌkʃən] n Fettabsaugen nt
lip: **~-read** (irreg) vi von den Lippen ablesen; **~
salve** n Lippenbalsam m; **~stick** n
Lippenstift m
liqueur [lɪˈkjʊəʳ] n Likör m
liquid [ˈlɪkwɪd] n Flüssigkeit f ♦ adj flüssig
liquidate [ˈlɪkwɪdeɪt] vt liquidieren
liquidize [ˈlɪkwɪdaɪz] vt (COOK) (im Mixer)
pürieren; **~r** [ˈlɪkwɪdaɪzəʳ] n Mixgerät nt
liquor [ˈlɪkəʳ] n Alkohol m
liquorice [ˈlɪkərɪs] (BRIT) n Lakritze f
liquor store (US) n Spirituosengeschäft nt
Lisbon [ˈlɪzbən] n Lissabon nt
lisp [lɪsp] n Lispeln nt ♦ vt, vi lispeln
list [lɪst] n Liste f, Verzeichnis nt; (of ship)
Schlagseite f ♦ vt (write down) eine Liste
machen von; (verbally) aufzählen ♦ vi (ship)
Schlagseite haben
listen [ˈlɪsn] vi hören; **~ to** vt zuhören +dat;
~er n (Zu)hörer(in) m(f)
listless [ˈlɪstlɪs] adj lustlos
lit [lɪt] pt, pp of **light**
liter [ˈliːtəʳ] n (US) n = **litre**
literacy [ˈlɪtərəsɪ] n Fähigkeit f zu lesen und
zu schreiben
literal [ˈlɪtərəl] adj buchstäblich; (translation)
wortwörtlich; **~ly** adv buchstäblich; wörtlich
literary [ˈlɪtərərɪ] adj literarisch
literate [ˈlɪtərət] adj des Lesens und
Schreibens kundig
literature [ˈlɪtrɪtʃəʳ] n Literatur f
litigation [lɪtɪˈgeɪʃən] n Prozess m
litre [ˈliːtəʳ] (US **liter**) n Liter m
litter [ˈlɪtəʳ] n (rubbish) Abfall m; (of animals)
Wurf m ♦ vt in Unordnung bringen; **to be
~ed with** übersät sein mit; **~ bin** (BRIT) n
Abfalleimer m
little [ˈlɪtl] adj klein ♦ adv, n wenig; **a ~** ein
bisschen; **~ by ~** nach und nach
live¹ [laɪv] adj lebendig; (MIL) scharf; (ELEC)

geladen; (broadcast) live
live² [lɪv] vi leben; (dwell) wohnen ♦ vt (life)
führen; **~ down** vt: **I'll never ~ it down**
das wird man mir nie vergessen; **~ on** vi
weiterleben ♦ vt fus: **to ~ on sth** von etw
leben; **~ together** vi zusammenleben;
(share a flat) zusammenwohnen; **~ up to** vt
(standards) gerecht werden +dat; (principles)
anstreben; (hopes) entsprechen +dat
livelihood [ˈlaɪvlɪhʊd] n Lebensunterhalt m
lively [ˈlaɪvlɪ] adj lebhaft, lebendig
liven up [ˈlaɪvn-] vt beleben
liver [ˈlɪvəʳ] n (ANAT) Leber f
lives [laɪvz] pl of **life**
livestock [ˈlaɪvstɔk] n Vieh nt
livid [ˈlɪvɪd] adj bläulich; (furious)
fuchsteufelswild
living [ˈlɪvɪŋ] n (Lebens)unterhalt m ♦ adj
lebendig; (language etc) lebend; **to earn** or
make a ~ sich dat seinen Lebensunterhalt
verdienen; **~ conditions** npl
Wohnverhältnisse pl; **~ room** n
Wohnzimmer nt; **~ standards** npl
Lebensstandard m; **~ wage** n ausreichender
Lohn m
lizard [ˈlɪzəd] n Eidechse f
load [ləʊd] n (burden) Last f; (amount)
Ladung f ♦ vt (also: **~ up**) (be)laden;
(COMPUT) laden; (camera) Film einlegen in
+acc; (gun) laden; **a ~ of**, **~s of** (fig) jede
Menge; **~ed** adj beladen; (dice) präpariert;
(question) Fang-; (inf: rich) steinreich; **~ing
bay** n Ladeplatz m
loaf [ləʊf] (pl **loaves**) n Brot nt ♦ vi (also: **~
about, ~ around**) herumlungern, faulenzen
loan [ləʊn] n Leihgabe f; (FIN) Darlehen nt
♦ vt leihen; **on ~** geliehen
loath [ləʊθ] adj: **to be ~ to do sth** etw
ungern tun
loathe [ləʊð] vt verabscheuen
loaves [ləʊvz] pl of **loaf**
lobby [ˈlɔbɪ] n Vorhalle f; (POL) Lobby f ♦ vt
politisch beeinflussen (wollen)
lobster [ˈlɔbstəʳ] n Hummer m
local [ˈləʊkl] adj ortsansässig, Orts- ♦ n (pub)
Stammwirtschaft f; **the ~s** npl (people) die
Ortsansässigen pl; **~ anaesthetic** n (MED)
örtliche Betäubung f; **~ authority** n
städtische Behörden pl; **~ call** n (TEL)
Ortsgespräch nt; **~ government** n
Gemeinde-/Kreisverwaltung f; **~ity**
[ləʊˈkælɪtɪ] n Ort m; **~ly** adv örtlich, am Ort
locate [ləʊˈkeɪt] vt ausfindig machen;
(establish) errichten; **location** [ləʊˈkeɪʃən] n
Platz m, Lage f; **on location** (CINE) auf
Außenaufnahme
loch [lɔx] (SCOTTISH) n See m
lock [lɔk] n Schloss nt; (NAUT) Schleuse f; (of
hair) Locke f ♦ vt (fasten) (ver)schließen ♦ vi
(door etc) sich schließen (lassen); (wheels)
blockieren; **~ up** vt (criminal, mental patient)

einsperren; (*house*) abschließen
locker ['lɔkə^r] *n* Spind *m*
locket ['lɔkɪt] *n* Medaillon *nt*
lock ['lɔk-]: **~out** *n* Aussperrung *f*; **~smith** *n* Schlosser(in) *m(f)*; **~up** *n* (*jail*) Gefängnis *nt*; (*garage*) Garage *f*
locum ['ləukəm] *n* (*MED*) Vertreter(in) *m(f)*
lodge [lɔdʒ] *n* (*gatehouse*) Pförtnerhaus *nt*; (*freemasons'*) Loge *f* ♦ *vi* (*get stuck*) stecken (bleiben); (*in Untermiete*): **to ~ (with)** wohnen (bei) ♦ *vt* (*protest*) einreichen; **~r** *n* (Unter)mieter *m*; **lodgings** *npl* (Miet)wohnung *f*
loft [lɔft] *n* (Dach)boden *m*
lofty ['lɔftɪ] *adj* hoch(ragend); (*proud*) hochmütig
log [lɔg] *n* Klotz *m*; (*book*) = **logbook**
logbook ['lɔgbuk] *n* Bordbuch *nt*; (*for lorry*) Fahrtenschreiber *m*; (*AUT*) Kraftfahrzeugbrief *m*
loggerheads ['lɔgəhɛdz] *npl*: **to be at ~** sich in den Haaren liegen
logic ['lɔdʒɪk] *n* Logik *f*; **~al** *adj* logisch
logistics [lɔ'dʒɪstɪks] *npl* Logistik *f*
logo ['ləugəu] *n* Firmenzeichen *nt*
loin [lɔɪn] *n* Lende *f*
loiter ['lɔɪtə^r] *vi* herumstehen
loll [lɔl] *vi* (*also*: **~ about**) sich rekeln *or* räkeln
lollipop ['lɔlɪpɔp] *n* (Dauer)lutscher *m*; **~ man/lady** (*irreg: BRIT*) *n* ≈ Schülerlotse *m*
lolly ['lɔlɪ] (*inf*) *n* (*sweet*) Lutscher *m*
London ['lʌndən] *n* London *nt*; **~er** *n* Londoner(in) *m(f)*
lone [ləun] *adj* einsam
loneliness ['ləunlɪnɪs] *n* Einsamkeit *f*
lonely ['ləunlɪ] *adj* einsam
loner ['ləunə^r] *n* Einzelgänger(in) *m(f)*
long [lɔŋ] *adj* lang; (*distance*) weit ♦ *adv* lange ♦ *vi*: **to ~ for** sich sehnen nach; **before ~** bald; **as ~ as** solange; **in the ~ run** auf die Dauer; **don't be ~!** beeil dich!; **how ~ is the street?** wie lang ist die Straße?; **how ~ is the lesson?** wie lange dauert die Stunde?; **6 metres ~** 6 Meter lang; **6 months ~** 6 Monate lang; **all night ~** die ganze Nacht; **he no ~er comes** er kommt nicht mehr; **~ ago** vor langer Zeit; **~ before** lange vorher; **at ~ last** endlich; **~-distance** *adj* Fern-
longevity [lɔn'dʒɛvɪtɪ] *n* Langlebigkeit *f*
long: **~-haired** *adj* langhaarig; **~hand** *n* Langschrift *f*; **~ing** *n* Sehnsucht *f* ♦ *adj* sehnsüchtig
longitude ['lɔŋgɪtjuːd] *n* Längengrad *m*
long: **~ jump** *n* Weitsprung *m*; **~-life** *adj* (*batteries etc*) mit langer Lebensdauer; **~-lost** *adj* längst verloren geglaubt; **~-playing record** *n* Langspielplatte *f*; **~-range** *adj* Langstrecken-, Fern-; **~-sighted** *adj* weitsichtig; **~-standing** *adj* alt, seit langer Zeit bestehend; **~-suffering** *adj*

schwer geprüft; **~-term** *adj* langfristig; **~ wave** *n* Langwelle *f*; **~-winded** *adj* langatmig
loo [luː] (*BRIT: inf*) *n* Klo *nt*
look [luk] *vi* schauen; (*seem*) aussehen; (*building etc*): **to ~ on to the sea** aufs Meer gehen ♦ *n* Blick *m*; **~s** *npl* (*appearance*) Aussehen *nt*; **~ after** *vt* (*care for*) sorgen für; (*watch*) aufpassen auf +*acc*; **~ at** *vt* ansehen; (*consider*) sich überlegen; **~ back** *vi* sich umsehen; (*fig*) zurückblicken; **~ down on** *vt* (*fig*) herabsehen auf +*acc*; **~ for** *vt* (*seek*) suchen; **~ forward to** *vt* sich freuen auf +*acc*; (*in letters*): **we ~ forward to hearing from you** wir hoffen, bald von Ihnen zu hören; **~ into** *vt* untersuchen; **~ on** *vi* zusehen; **~ out** *vi* hinaussehen; (*take care*) aufpassen; **~ out for** *vt* Ausschau halten nach; (*be careful*) Acht geben auf +*acc*; **~ round** *vi* sich umsehen; **~ to** *vt* (*take care of*) Acht geben auf +*acc*; (*rely on*) sich verlassen auf +*acc*; **~ up** *vi* aufblicken; (*improve*) sich bessern ♦ *vt* (*word*) nachschlagen; (*person*) besuchen; **~ up to** *vt* aufsehen zu; **~out** *n* (*watch*) Ausschau *f*; (*person*) Wachposten *m*; (*place*) Ausguck *m*; (*prospect*) Aussichten *pl*; **to be on the ~out for sth** nach etw Ausschau halten
loom [luːm] *n* Webstuhl *m* ♦ *vi* sich abzeichnen
loony ['luːnɪ] (*inf*) *n* Verrückte(r) *mf*
loop [luːp] *n* Schlaufe *f*; **~hole** *n* (*fig*) Hintertürchen *nt*
loose [luːs] *adj* lose, locker; (*free*) frei; (*inexact*) unpräzise ♦ *vt* lösen, losbinden; **~ change** *n* Kleingeld *nt*; **~ chippings** *npl* (*on road*) Rollsplit *m*; **~ end** *n*: **to be at a ~ end** (*BRIT*) *or* **at ~ ends** (*US*) nicht wissen, was man tun soll; **~ly** *adv* locker, lose; **~n** *vt* lockern, losmachen
loot [luːt] *n* Beute *f* ♦ *vt* plündern
lop off [lɔp-] *vt* abhacken
lopsided ['lɔp'saɪdɪd] *adj* schief
lord [lɔːd] *n* (*ruler*) Herr *m*; (*BRIT: title*) Lord *m*; **the L~** (*God*) der Herr; **the (House of) L~s** das Oberhaus; **~ship** *n*: **Your L~ship** Eure Lordschaft
lorry ['lɔrɪ] (*BRIT*) *n* Lastwagen *m*; **~ driver** (*BRIT*) *n* Lastwagenfahrer(in) *m(f)*
lose [luːz] (*pt, pp* **lost**) *vt* verlieren; (*chance*) verpassen ♦ *vi* verlieren; **to ~** (*time*) (*clock*) nachgehen; **~r** *n* Verlierer *m*
loss [lɔs] *n* Verlust *m*; **at a ~** (*COMM*) mit Verlust; (*unable*) außerstande, außer Stande
lost [lɔst] *pt, pp* of **lose** ♦ *adj* verloren; **~ property** (*US* **~ and found**) *n* Fundsachen *pl*
lot [lɔt] *n* (*quantity*) Menge *f*; (*fate, at auction*) Los *nt*; (*inf: people, things*) Haufen *m*; **the ~** alles; (*people*) alle; **a ~ of** (*with sg*) viel; (*with pl*) viele; **~s of** massenhaft, viel(e);

I read a ~ ich lese viel; **to draw ~s for sth** etw verlosen
lotion ['ləʊʃən] n Lotion f
lottery ['lɒtərɪ] n Lottérie f
loud [laʊd] adj laut; (showy) schreiend ♦ adv laut; **~ly** adv laut; **~speaker** n Lautsprecher m
lounge [laʊndʒ] n (in hotel) Gesellschaftsraum m; (in house) Wohnzimmer nt ♦ vi sich herumlümmeln
louse [laʊs] (pl **lice**) n Laus f
lousy ['laʊzɪ] adj (fig) miserabel
lout [laʊt] n Lümmel m
louvre ['luːvəʳ] (US **louver**) adj (door, window) Jalousie-
lovable ['lʌvəbl] adj liebenswert
love [lʌv] n Liebe f; (person) Liebling m; (SPORT) null ♦ vt (person) lieben; (activity) gerne mögen; **to be in ~ with sb** in jdn verliebt sein; **to make ~** sich lieben; **for the ~ of** aus Liebe zu; **"15 ~"** (TENNIS) „15 null"; **to ~ to do sth** etw (sehr) gerne tun; **~ affair** n (Liebes)verhältnis nt; **~ letter** n Liebesbrief m; **~ life** n Liebesleben nt
lovely ['lʌvlɪ] adj schön
lover ['lʌvəʳ] n Liebhaber(in) m(f)
loving ['lʌvɪŋ] adj liebend, liebevoll
low [ləʊ] adj niedrig; (rank) niedere(r, s); (level, note, neckline) tief; (intelligence, density) gering; (vulgar) ordinär; (not loud) leise; (depressed) gedrückt ♦ adv (not high) niedrig; (not loudly) leise ♦ n (~ point) Tiefstand m; (MET) Tief nt; **to feel ~** sich mies fühlen; **to turn (down) ~** leiser stellen; **~ alcohol** adj alkoholarm; **~-calorie** adj kalorienarm; **~-cut** adj (dress) tief ausgeschnitten; **~er** vt herunterlassen; (eyes, gun) senken; (reduce) herabsetzen, senken ♦ vr: **to ~er o.s. to** (fig) sich herablassen zu; **~er sixth** (BRIT) n (SCH) ≈ zwölfte Klasse; **~-fat** adj fettarm, Mager-; **~lands** npl (GEOG) Flachland nt; **~ly** adj bescheiden; **~-lying** adj tief gelegen
loyal ['lɔɪəl] adj treu; **~ty** n Treue f; **~ty card** n Kundenkarte f
lozenge ['lɒzɪndʒ] n Pastille f
L.P. n abbr = **long-playing record**
L-plates ['elpleɪts] (BRIT) npl L-Schild nt (für Fahrschüler)
Ltd abbr (= limited company) ≈ GmbH
lubricant ['luːbrɪkənt] n Schmiermittel nt
lubricate ['luːbrɪkeɪt] vt schmieren
lucid ['luːsɪd] adj klar; (sane) bei klarem Verstand; (moment) licht
luck [lʌk] n Glück nt; **bad** or **hard** or **tough ~!** (so ein) Pech!; **good ~!** viel Glück!; **~ily** adv glücklicherweise, zum Glück; **~y** adj Glücks-; **to be ~y** Glück haben
lucrative ['luːkrətɪv] adj einträglich
ludicrous ['luːdɪkrəs] adj grotesk
lug [lʌg] vt schleppen

luggage ['lʌgɪdʒ] n Gepäck nt; **~ rack** n Gepäcknetz nt
lukewarm ['luːkwɔːm] adj lauwarm; (indifferent) lau
lull [lʌl] n Flaute f ♦ vt einlullen; (calm) beruhigen
lullaby ['lʌləbaɪ] n Schlaflied nt
lumbago [lʌm'beɪgəʊ] n Hexenschuss m
lumber ['lʌmbəʳ] n Plunder m; (wood) Holz nt; **~jack** n Holzfäller m
luminous ['luːmɪnəs] adj Leucht-
lump [lʌmp] n Klumpen m; (MED) Schwellung f; (in breast) Knoten m; (of sugar) Stück nt ♦ vt (also: **~ together**) zusammentun; (judge together) in einen Topf werfen; **~ sum** n Pauschalsumme f; **~y** adj klumpig
lunacy ['luːnəsɪ] n Irrsinn m
lunar ['luːnəʳ] adj Mond-
lunatic ['luːnətɪk] n Wahnsinnige(r) mf ♦ adj wahnsinnig, irr
lunch [lʌntʃ] n Mittagessen nt; **~eon** ['lʌntʃən] n Mittagessen nt; **~eon meat** n Frühstücksfleisch nt; **~eon voucher** (BRIT) n Essenmarke f; **~time** n Mittagszeit f
lung [lʌŋ] n Lunge f
lunge [lʌndʒ] vi (also: **~ forward**) (los)stürzen; **to ~ at** sich stürzen auf +acc
lurch [lɜːtʃ] vi taumeln; (NAUT) schlingern ♦ n Ruck m; (NAUT) Schlingern nt; **to leave sb in the ~** jdn im Stich lassen
lure [lʊəʳ] n Köder m; (fig) Lockung f ♦ vt (ver)locken
lurid ['lʊərɪd] adj (shocking) grausig, widerlich; (colour) grell
lurk [lɜːk] vi lauern
luscious ['lʌʃəs] adj köstlich
lush [lʌʃ] adj satt; (vegetation) üppig
lust [lʌst] n Wollust f; (greed) Gier f ♦ vi: **to ~ after** gieren nach
lustre ['lʌstəʳ] (US **luster**) n Glanz m
Luxembourg ['lʌksəmbɜːg] n Luxemburg nt
luxuriant [lʌg'zjʊərɪənt] adj üppig
luxurious [lʌg'zjʊərɪəs] adj luxuriös, Luxus-
luxury ['lʌkʃərɪ] n Luxus m ♦ cpd Luxus-
lying ['laɪɪŋ] n Lügen nt ♦ adj verlogen
lynx [lɪŋks] n Luchs m
lyric ['lɪrɪk] n Lyrik f ♦ adj lyrisch; **~s** pl (words for song) (Lied)text m; **~al** adj lyrisch, gefühlvoll

M, m

m abbr = **metre; mile; million**
M.A. n abbr = **Master of Arts**
mac [mæk] (BRIT: inf) n Regenmantel m
macaroni [mækə'rəʊnɪ] n Makkaroni pl
machine [mə'ʃiːn] n Maschine f ♦ vt (dress etc) mit der Maschine nähen; **~ gun** n Maschinengewehr nt; **~ language** n

(*COMPUT*) Maschinensprache *f*; ~**ry** *n*
Maschinerie *f*
macho ['mætʃəu] *adj* macho
mackerel ['mækrl] *n* Makrele *f*
mackintosh ['mækɪntɔʃ] (*BRIT*) *n*
Regenmantel *m*
mad [mæd] *adj* verrückt; (*dog*) tollwütig;
(*angry*) wütend; ~ **about** (*fond of*) verrückt
nach, versessen auf +*acc*
madam ['mædəm] *n* gnädige Frau *f*
madden ['mædn] *vt* verrückt machen; (*make
angry*) ärgern
made [meɪd] *pt, pp of* **make**
made-to-measure ['meɪdtə'meʒə'] (*BRIT*)
adj Maß-
mad ['mæd-]: ~**ly** *adv* wahnsinnig; ~**man**
(*irreg*) *n* Verrückte(r) *m*, Irre(r) *m*; ~**ness** *n*
Wahnsinn *m*
magazine [mægə'ziːn] *n* Zeitschrift *f*; (*in
gun*) Magazin *nt*
maggot ['mægət] *n* Made *f*
magic ['mædʒɪk] *n* Zauberei *f*, Magie *f*; (*fig*)
Zauber *m* ♦ *adj* magisch, Zauber-; ~**al** *adj*
magisch; ~**ian** [mə'dʒɪʃən] *n* Zauberer *m*
magistrate ['mædʒɪstreɪt] *n* (Friedens)richter
m
magnanimous [mæg'nænɪməs] *adj*
großmütig
magnet ['mægnɪt] *n* Magnet *m*; ~**ic**
[mæg'netɪk] *adj* magnetisch; ~**ic tape** *n*
Magnetband *nt*; ~**ism** *n* Magnetismus *m*;
(*fig*) Ausstrahlungskraft *f*
magnificent [mæg'nɪfɪsnt] *adj* großartig
magnify ['mægnɪfaɪ] *vt* vergrößern; ~**ing
glass** *n* Lupe *f*
magnitude ['mægnɪtjuːd] *n* (*size*) Größe *f*;
(*importance*) Ausmaß *nt*
magpie ['mægpaɪ] *n* Elster *f*
mahogany [mə'hɔgənɪ] *n* Mahagoni *nt*
♦ *cpd* Mahagoni-
maid [meɪd] *n* Dienstmädchen *nt*; **old ~** alte
Jungfer *f*
maiden ['meɪdn] *n* Maid *f* ♦ *adj* (*flight,
speech*) Jungfern-; ~ **name** *n* Mädchenname
m
mail [meɪl] *n* Post *f* ♦ *vt* aufgeben; ~ **box** (*US*)
n Briefkasten *m*; ~**ing list** *n* Anschreibeliste
f; ~ **order** *n* Bestellung *f* durch die Post; ~
order firm *n* Versandhaus *nt*
maim [meɪm] *vt* verstümmeln
main [meɪn] *adj* hauptsächlich, Haupt- ♦ *n*
(*pipe*) Hauptleitung *f*; **the ~s** *npl* (*ELEC*) das
Stromnetz; **in the ~** im Großen und Ganzen;
~**frame** *n* (*COMPUT*) Großrechner *m*; ~**land**
n Festland *nt*; ~**ly** *adv* hauptsächlich; ~
road *n* Hauptstraße *f*; ~**stay** *n* (*fig*)
Hauptstütze *f*; ~**stream** *n* Hauptrichtung *f*
maintain [meɪn'teɪn] *vt* (*machine, roads*)
instand or in Stand halten; (*support*)
unterhalten; (*keep up*) aufrechterhalten;
(*claim*) behaupten; (*innocence*) beteuern

maintenance ['meɪntənəns] *n* (*TECH*)
Wartung *f*; (*of family*) Unterhalt *m*
maize [meɪz] *n* Mais *m*
majestic [mə'dʒestɪk] *adj* majestätisch
majesty ['mædʒɪstɪ] *n* Majestät *f*
major ['meɪdʒə'] *n* Major *m* ♦ *adj* (*MUS*) Dur;
(*more important*) Haupt-; (*bigger*) größer
Majorca [mə'jɔːkə] *n* Mallorca *nt*
majority [mə'dʒɔrɪtɪ] *n* Mehrheit *f*; (*JUR*)
Volljährigkeit *f*
make [meɪk] (*pt, pp* **made**) *vt* machen;
(*appoint*) ernennen (zu); (*cause to do sth*)
veranlassen; (*reach*) erreichen; (*in time*)
schaffen; (*earn*) verdienen ♦ *n* Marke *f*; **to ~
sth happen** etw geschehen lassen; **to ~ it** es
schaffen; **what time do you ~ it?** wie spät
hast du es?; **to ~ do with** auskommen mit;
~ **for** *vi* gehen/fahren nach; ~ **out** *vt* (*write
out*) ausstellen; (*understand*) verstehen; ~
up *vt* machen; (*face*) schminken; (*quarrel*)
beilegen; (*story etc*) erfinden ♦ *vi* sich
versöhnen; ~ **up for** *vt* wieder gutmachen;
(*COMM*) vergüten; ~~**believe** *n* Fantasie *f*;
~**r** *n* (*COMM*) Hersteller *m*; ~**shift** *adj*
behelfsmäßig, Not-; ~~**up** *n* Schminke *f*,
Make-up *nt*; ~~**up remover** *n* Make-up-
Entferner *m*; **making** *n*: **in the making** im
Entstehen; **to have the makings of** das
Zeug haben zu
malaria [mə'leərɪə] *n* Malaria *f*
Malaysia [mə'leɪzɪə] *n* Malaysia *nt*
male [meɪl] *n* Mann *m*; (*animal*) Männchen
nt ♦ *adj* männlich
malevolent [mə'levələnt] *adj* übel wollend
malfunction [mæl'fʌŋkʃən] *n* (*MED*)
Funktionsstörung *f*; (*of machine*) Defekt *m*
malice ['mælɪs] *n* Bosheit *f*; **malicious**
[mə'lɪʃəs] *adj* böswillig, gehässig
malign [mə'laɪn] *vt* verleumden ♦ *adj* böse
malignant [mə'lɪgnənt] *adj* bösartig
mall [mɔːl] *n* (*also:* **shopping ~**)
Einkaufszentrum *nt*
malleable ['mælɪəbl] *adj* formbar
mallet ['mælɪt] *n* Holzhammer *m*
malnutrition [mælnjuː'trɪʃən] *n*
Unterernährung *f*
malpractice [mæl'præktɪs] *n* Amtsvergehen
nt
malt [mɔːlt] *n* Malz *nt*
Malta ['mɔːltə] *n* Malta *nt*; **Maltese**
[mɔːl'tiːz] *adj inv* maltesisch ♦ *n inv*
Malteser(in) *m(f)*
maltreat [mæl'triːt] *vt* misshandeln
mammal ['mæml] *n* Säugetier *nt*
mammoth ['mæməθ] *n* Mammut *nt* ♦ *adj*
Mammut-
man [mæn] (*pl* **men**) *n* Mann *m*; (*human
race*) der Mensch, die Menschen *pl* ♦ *vt*
bemannen; **an old ~** ein alter Mann, ein
Greis *m*; ~ **and wife** Mann und Frau
manage ['mænɪdʒ] *vi* zurechtkommen ♦ *vt*

(control) führen, leiten; (cope with) fertig werden mit; **~able** adj (person, animal) fügsam; (object) handlich; **~ment** n (control) Führung f, Leitung f; (directors) Management nt; **~r** n Geschäftsführer m; **~ress** |ˈmænɪdʒəˈrɛs| n Geschäftsführerin f; **~rial** |mænɪˈdʒɪərɪəl| adj (post) leitend; (problem etc) Management-; **managing** [ˈmænɪdʒɪŋ] adj: **managing director** Betriebsleiter m

mandarin [ˈmændərɪn] n (fruit) Mandarine f

mandatory [ˈmændətərɪ] adj obligatorisch

mane [meɪn] n Mähne f

maneuver [məˈnuːvəʳ] (US) = **manoeuvre**

manfully [ˈmænfəlɪ] adv mannhaft

mangle [ˈmæŋgl] vt verstümmeln ♦ n Mangel f

mango [ˈmæŋgəʊ] (pl **~es**) n Mango(pflaume) f

mangy [ˈmeɪndʒɪ] adj (dog) räudig

man [mæn]-: **~handle** vt grob behandeln; **~hole** n (Straßen)schacht m; **~hood** n Mannesalter nt; (manliness) Männlichkeit f; **~-hour** n Arbeitsstunde f; **~hunt** n Fahndung f

mania [ˈmeɪnɪə] n Manie f; **~c** [ˈmeɪnɪæk] n Wahnsinnige(r) mf

manic [ˈmænɪk] adj (behaviour, activity) hektisch

manicure [ˈmænɪkjʊəʳ] n Maniküre f; **~ set** n Necessaire nt, Nessessär nt

manifest [ˈmænɪfɛst] vt offenbaren ♦ adj offenkundig; **~ation** [mænɪfɛsˈteɪʃən] n (sign) Anzeichen nt

manifesto [mænɪˈfɛstəʊ] n Manifest nt

manipulate [məˈnɪpjʊleɪt] vt handhaben; (fig) manipulieren

man [mæn]-: **~kind** n Menschheit f; **~ly** [ˈmænlɪ] adj männlich; mannhaft; **~-made** adj (fibre) künstlich

manner [ˈmænəʳ] n Art f, Weise f; **~s** npl (behaviour) Manieren pl; **in a ~ of speaking** sozusagen; **~ism** n (of person) Angewohnheit f; (of style) Manieriertheit f

manoeuvre [məˈnuːvəʳ] (US **maneuver**) vt, vi manövrieren ♦ n (MIL) Feldzug m; (general) Manöver nt, Schachzug m

manor [ˈmænəʳ] n Landgut nt

manpower [ˈmænpaʊəʳ] n Arbeitskräfte pl

mansion [ˈmænʃən] n Villa f

manslaughter [ˈmænslɔːtəʳ] n Totschlag m

mantelpiece [ˈmæntlpiːs] n Kaminsims m

manual [ˈmænjʊəl] adj manuell, Hand- ♦ n Handbuch nt

manufacture [mænjuˈfæktʃəʳ] vt herstellen ♦ n Herstellung f; **~r** n Hersteller m

manure [məˈnjʊəʳ] n Dünger m

manuscript [ˈmænjuskrɪpt] n Manuskript nt

Manx [mæŋks] adj der Insel Man

many [ˈmɛnɪ] adj, pron viele; **a great ~** sehr viele; **~ a time** oft

map [mæp] n (Land)karte f; (of town) Stadtplan m ♦ vt eine Karte machen von; **~**

out vt (fig) ausarbeiten

maple [ˈmeɪpl] n Ahorn m

mar [mɑːʳ] vt verderben

marathon [ˈmærəθən] n (SPORT) Marathonlauf m; (fig) Marathon m

marble [ˈmɑːbl] n Marmor m; (for game) Murmel f

March [mɑːtʃ] n März m

march [mɑːtʃ] vi marschieren ♦ n Marsch m

mare [mɛəʳ] n Stute f

margarine [mɑːdʒəˈriːn] n Margarine f

margin [ˈmɑːdʒɪn] n Rand m; (extra amount) Spielraum m; (COMM) Spanne f; **~al** adj (note) Rand-; (difference etc) geringfügig; **~al (seat)** n (POL) Wahlkreis, der nur mit knapper Mehrheit gehalten wird

marigold [ˈmærɪgəʊld] n Ringelblume f

marijuana [mærɪˈwɑːnə] n Marihuana f

marina [məˈriːnə] n Jachthafen m

marinate [ˈmærɪneɪt] vt marinieren

marine [məˈriːn] adj Meeres-, See- ♦ n (MIL) Marineinfanterist m

marital [ˈmærɪtl] adj ehelich, Ehe-; **~ status** n Familienstand m

maritime [ˈmærɪtaɪm] adj See-

mark [mɑːk] n (coin) Mark f; (spot) Fleck m; (scar) Kratzer m; (sign) Zeichen nt; (target) Ziel nt; (SCH) Note f ♦ vt (make ~ on) Flecken/Kratzer machen auf +acc; (indicate) markieren; (exam) korrigieren; **to ~ time** (also fig) auf der Stelle treten; **~ out** vt bestimmen; (area) abstecken; **~ed** adj deutlich; **~er** n (in book) (Lese)zeichen nt; (on road) Schild nt

market [ˈmɑːkɪt] n Markt m; (stock ~) Börse f ♦ vt (COMM: new product) auf den Markt bringen; (sell) vertreiben; **~ garden** (BRIT) n Handelsgärtnerei f; **~ing** n Marketing nt; **~ research** n Marktforschung f; **~ value** n Marktwert m

marksman [ˈmɑːksmən] (irreg) n Scharfschütze m

marmalade [ˈmɑːməleɪd] n Orangenmarmelade f

maroon [məˈruːn] vt aussetzen ♦ adj (colour) kastanienbraun

marquee [mɑːˈkiː] n große(s) Zelt nt

marriage [ˈmærɪdʒ] n Ehe f; (wedding) Heirat f; **~ bureau** n Heiratsinstitut nt; **~ certificate** n Heiratsurkunde f

married [ˈmærɪd] adj (person) verheiratet; (couple, life) Ehe-

marrow [ˈmærəʊ] n (Knochen)mark nt; (BOT) Kürbis m

marry [ˈmærɪ] vt (join) trauen; (take as husband, wife) heiraten ♦ vi (also: **get married**) heiraten

marsh [mɑːʃ] n Sumpf m

marshal [ˈmɑːʃl] n (US) Bezirkspolizeichef m ♦ vt (an)ordnen, arrangieren

marshy [ˈmɑːʃɪ] adj sumpfig

martial law ['mɑːʃl-] n Kriegsrecht nt
martyr ['mɑːtə^r] n (also fig) Märtyrer(in) m(f)
♦ vt zum Märtyrer machen; **~dom** n
Martyrium nt
marvel ['mɑːvl] n Wunder nt ♦ vi: **to ~ (at)**
sich wundern (über +acc); **~lous** (US **~ous**)
adj wunderbar
Marxist ['mɑːksɪst] n Marxist(in) m(f)
marzipan ['mɑːzɪpæn] n Marzipan
mascara [mæs'kɑːrə] n Wimperntusche f
mascot ['mæskət] n Maskottchen nt
masculine ['mæskjulɪn] adj männlich
mash [mæʃ] n Brei m; **~ed potatoes** npl
Kartoffelbrei m or -püree nt
mask [mɑːsk] n (also fig) Maske f ♦ vt
maskieren, verdecken
mason ['meɪsn] n (stonemason) Steinmetz m;
(freemason) Freimaurer m; **~ry** n Mauerwerk
nt
masquerade [mæskə'reɪd] n Maskerade f
♦ vi: **to ~ as** sich ausgeben als
mass [mæs] n Masse f; (greater part)
Mehrheit f; (REL) Messe f ♦ vi sich sammeln;
the ~es npl (people) die Masse(n) f(pl)
massacre ['mæsəkə^r] n Blutbad nt ♦ vt
niedermetzeln, massakrieren
massage ['mæsɑːʒ] n Massage f ♦ vt
massieren
massive ['mæsɪv] adj gewaltig, massiv
mass media npl Massenmedien pl
mass production n Massenproduktion f
mast [mɑːst] n Mast m
master ['mɑːstə^r] n Herr m; (NAUT) Kapitän
m; (teacher) Lehrer m; (artist) Meister m ♦ vt
meistern; (language etc) beherrschen; **~ly**
adj meisterhaft; **~mind** n Kapazität f ♦ vt
geschickt lenken; **M~ of Arts** n Magister m
der philosophischen Fakultät; **M~ of
Science** n Magister m der
naturwissenschaftlichen Fakultät; **~piece** n
Meisterwerk nt; **~ plan** n kluge(r) Plan m;
~y n Können nt
masturbate ['mæstəbeɪt] vi masturbieren,
onanieren
mat [mæt] n Matte f; (for table) Untersetzer m
♦ adj = **matt**
match [mætʃ] n Streichholz nt; (sth
corresponding) Pendant nt; (SPORT)
Wettkampf m; (ball games) Spiel n ♦ vt (be
like, suit) passen zu; (equal) gleichkommen
+dat ♦ vi zusammenpassen; **it's a good ~
(for)** es passt gut (zu); **~box** n
Streichholzschachtel f; **~ing** adj passend
mate [meɪt] n (companion) Kamerad m;
(spouse) Lebensgefährte m; (of animal)
Weibchen nt/Männchen n; (NAUT)
Schiffsoffizier m ♦ vi (animals) sich paaren
♦ vt (animals) paaren
material [mə'tɪərɪəl] n Material nt; (for book,
cloth) Stoff m ♦ adj (important) wesentlich;
(damage) Sach-; (comforts etc) materiell; **~s**

npl (for building etc) Materialien pl; **~istic**
[mətɪərɪə'lɪstɪk] adj materialistisch; **~ize** vi
sich verwirklichen, zustande or zu Stande
kommen
maternal [mə'tɜːnl] adj mütterlich, Mutter-
maternity [mə'tɜːnɪtɪ] adj (dress) Umstands-;
(benefit) Wochen-; **~ hospital** n
Entbindungsheim nt
math [mæθ] (US) n = **maths**
mathematical [mæθə'mætɪkl] adj
mathematisch; **mathematics** n
Mathematik f; **maths** (US **math**) n Mathe f
matinée ['mætɪneɪ] n Matinee f
matrices ['meɪtrɪsiːz] npl of **matrix**
matriculation [mətrɪkjuˈleɪʃən] n
Immatrikulation f
matrimonial [mætrɪ'məunɪəl] adj ehelich,
Ehe-
matrimony ['mætrɪmənɪ] n Ehestand m
matrix ['meɪtrɪks] (pl **matrices**) n Matrize f;
(GEOL etc) Matrix f
matron ['meɪtrən] n (MED) Oberin f; (SCH)
Hausmutter f
matt [mæt] adj (paint) matt
matted ['mætɪd] adj verfilzt
matter ['mætə^r] n (substance) Materie f;
(affair) Angelegenheit f ♦ vi darauf
ankommen; **no ~ how/what** egal wie/was;
what is the ~? was ist los?; **as a ~ of
course** selbstverständlich; **as a ~ of fact**
eigentlich; **it doesn't ~** es macht nichts; **~-
of-fact** adj sachlich, nüchtern
mattress ['mætrɪs] n Matratze f
mature [mə'tjuə^r] adj reif ♦ vi reif werden;
maturity [mə'tjuərɪtɪ] n Reife f
maul [mɔːl] vt übel zurichten
maxima ['mæksɪmə] npl of **maximum**
maximum ['mæksɪməm] (pl **maxima**) adj
Höchst-, Maximal- ♦ n Maximum nt
May [meɪ] n Mai m
may [meɪ] (conditional **might**) vi (be possible)
können; (have permission) dürfen; **he ~
come** er kommt vielleicht; **~be** ['meɪbiː] adv
vielleicht
May Day n der 1. Mai
mayhem ['meɪhɛm] n Chaos nt; (US)
Körperverletzung f
mayonnaise [meɪə'neɪz] n Majonäse f,
Mayonnaise f
mayor [mɛə^r] n Bürgermeister m; **~ess** n
Bürgermeisterin f; (wife) (die) Frau f
Bürgermeister
maypole ['meɪpəul] n Maibaum m
maze [meɪz] n Irrgarten m; (fig) Wirrwarr nt
M.D. abbr = **Doctor of Medicine**

[KEYWORD]

me [miː] pron **1** (direct) mich; **it's me** ich
bins
2 (indirect) mir; **give them to me** gib sie
mir

3 (after prep: +acc) mich; (: +dat) mir; **with/ without me** mit mir/ohne mich

meadow ['mɛdəu] n Wiese f
meagre ['miːgəʳ] (US **meager**) adj dürftig, spärlich
meal [miːl] n Essen nt, Mahlzeit f; (grain) Schrotmehl nt; **to have a ~** essen (gehen); **~time** n Essenszeit f
mean [miːn] (pt, pp meant) adj (stingy) geizig; (spiteful) gemein; (average) durchschnittlich, Durchschnitts- ♦ vt (signify) bedeuten; (intend) vorhaben, beabsichtigen ♦ n (average) Durchschnitt m; **~s** npl (wherewithal) Mittel pl; (wealth) Vermögen nt; **do you ~ me?** meinst du mich?; **do you ~ it?** meinst du das ernst?; **what do you ~?** was willst du damit sagen?; **to be ~t for sb/ sth** für jdn/etw bestimmt sein; **by ~s of** durch; **by all ~s** selbstverständlich; **by no ~s** keineswegs
meander [mɪ'ændəʳ] vi sich schlängeln
meaning ['miːnɪŋ] n Bedeutung f, (of life) Sinn m; **~ful** adj bedeutungsvoll; (life) sinnvoll; **~less** adj sinnlos
meanness ['miːnnɪs] n (stinginess) Geiz m; (spitefulness) Gemeinheit f
meant [mɛnt] pt, pp of **mean**
meantime ['miːntaɪm] adv inzwischen
meanwhile ['miːnwaɪl] adv inzwischen
measles ['miːzlz] n Masern pl
measly ['miːzlɪ] (inf) adj poplig
measure ['mɛʒəʳ] vt, vi messen ♦ n Maß nt; (step) Maßnahme f; **~ments** npl Maße pl
meat [miːt] n Fleisch nt; **cold ~** Aufschnitt m; **~ ball** n Fleischkloß m; **~ pie** n Fleischpastete f; **~y** adj fleischig; (fig) gehaltvoll
Mecca ['mɛkə] n Mekka nt (also fig)
mechanic [mɪ'kænɪk] n Mechaniker m; **~al** adj mechanisch; **~s** n Mechanik f ♦ npl Technik f
mechanism ['mɛkənɪzəm] n Mechanismus m
mechanize ['mɛkənaɪz] vt mechanisieren
medal ['mɛdl] n Medaille f; (decoration) Orden m; (US **~list**) **~ist** n Medaillengewinner(in) m(f)
meddle ['mɛdl] vi: **to ~ (in)** sich einmischen (in +acc); **to ~ with sth** sich an etw dat zu schaffen machen
media ['miːdɪə] npl Medien pl
mediaeval [mɛdɪ'iːvl] adj = **medieval**
median ['miːdɪən] (US) n (also: ~ **strip**) Mittelstreifen m
mediate ['miːdɪeɪt] vi vermitteln; **mediator** n Vermittler m
Medicaid ['mɛdɪkeɪd] (® US) n medizinisches Versorgungsprogramm für sozial Schwache
medical ['mɛdɪkl] adj medizinisch; Medizin-; ärztlich ♦ n (ärztliche) Untersuchung f

Medicare ['mɛdɪkeəʳ] (US) n staatliche Krankenversicherung besonders für Ältere
medicated ['mɛdɪkeɪtɪd] adj medizinisch
medication [mɛdɪ'keɪʃən] n (drugs etc) Medikamente pl
medicinal [mɛ'dɪsɪnl] adj medizinisch, Heil-
medicine ['mɛdsɪn] n Medizin f; (drugs) Arznei f
medieval [mɛdɪ'iːvl] adj mittelalterlich
mediocre [miːdɪ'əukəʳ] adj mittelmäßig
meditate ['mɛdɪteɪt] vi: **to ~ (on sth)** (über etw acc) nachdenken;
meditation [mɛdɪ'teɪʃən] n Nachsinnen nt; Meditation f
Mediterranean [mɛdɪtə'reɪnɪən] adj Mittelmeer-; (person) südländisch; **the ~ (Sea)** das Mittelmeer
medium ['miːdɪəm] adj mittlere(r, s), Mittel-, mittel- ♦ n Mitte f; (means) Mittel nt; (person) Medium nt; **happy ~** goldener Mittelweg; **~-sized** adj mittelgroß; **~ wave** n Mittelwelle f
medley ['mɛdlɪ] n Gemisch nt
meek [miːk] adj sanft(mütig); (pej) duckmäuserisch
meet [miːt] (pt, pp met) vt (encounter) treffen, begegnen +dat; (by arrangement) sich treffen mit; (difficulties) stoßen auf +acc; (get to know) kennen lernen; (fetch) abholen; (join) zusammentreffen mit; (satisfy) entsprechen +dat ♦ vi sich treffen; (become acquainted) sich kennen lernen; **~ with** vt (problems) stoßen auf +acc; (US: people) zusammentreffen mit; **~ing** n Treffen nt; (business ~ing) Besprechung f; (of committee) Sitzung f; (assembly) Versammlung f
mega- ['mɛgə-] (inf) prefix Mega-; **~byte** n (COMPUT) Megabyte nt; **~phone** n Megafon nt, Megaphon nt
melancholy ['mɛlənkəlɪ] adj (person) melancholisch; (sight, event) traurig
mellow ['mɛləu] adj mild, weich; (fruit) reif; (fig) gesetzt ♦ vi reif werden
melodious [mɪ'ləudɪəs] adj wohlklingend
melody ['mɛlədɪ] n Melodie f
melon ['mɛlən] n Melone f
melt [mɛlt] vi schmelzen; (anger) verfliegen ♦ vt schmelzen; **~ away** vi dahinschmelzen; **~ down** vt einschmelzen; **~down** n (in nuclear reactor) Kernschmelze f; **~ing point** n Schmelzpunkt m; **~ing pot** n (fig) Schmelztiegel m
member ['mɛmbəʳ] n Mitglied nt; (of tribe, species) Angehörige(r) f(m); (ANAT) Glied nt; **M~ of Parliament** (BRIT) n Parlamentsmitglied nt; **M~ of the European Parliament** (BRIT) n Mitglied nt des Europäischen Parlaments; **~ship** n Mitgliedschaft f; **to seek ~ship of** einen Antrag auf Mitgliedschaft stellen; **~ship**

card *n* Mitgliedskarte *f*
memento [mə'mentəu] *n* Andenken *nt*
memo ['meməu] *n* Mitteilung *f*
memoirs ['memwa:z] *npl* Memoiren *pl*
memorable ['memərəbl] *adj* denkwürdig
memoranda [memə'rændə] *npl of*
memorandum
memorandum [memə'rændəm] (*pl*
memoranda) *n* Mitteilung *f*
memorial [mɪ'mɔ:rɪəl] *n* Denkmal *nt* ♦ *adj*
Gedenk-
memorize ['meməraɪz] *vt* sich einprägen
memory ['meməri] *n* Gedächtnis *nt*; (*of
computer*) Speicher *m*; (*sth recalled*)
Erinnerung *f*
men [men] *pl of* **man** ♦ *npl* (*human race*) die
Menschen *pl*
menace ['menɪs] *n* Drohung *f*; Gefahr *f* ♦ *vt*
bedrohen; **menacing** *adj* drohend
menagerie [mɪ'nædʒərɪ] *n* Tierschau *f*
mend [mend] *vt* reparieren, flicken ♦ *vi*
(ver)heilen ♦ *n* ausgebesserte Stelle *f*; **on
the ~** auf dem Wege der Besserung; **~ing** *n*
(*articles*) Flickarbeit *f*
menial ['mi:nɪəl] *adj* niedrig
meningitis [menɪn'dʒaɪtɪs] *n* Hirnhaut-
entzündung *f*, Meningitis *f*
menopause ['menəupɔ:z] *n* Wechseljahre *pl*,
Menopause *f*
menstruation [menstru'eɪʃən] *n*
Menstruation *f*
mental ['mentl] *adj* geistig, Geistes-;
(*arithmetic*) Kopf-; (*hospital*) Nerven-;
(*cruelty*) seelisch; (*inf: abnormal*) verrückt;
~ity [men'tælɪtɪ] *n* Mentalität *f*
menthol ['menθɒl] *n* Menthol *nt*
mention ['menʃən] *n* Erwähnung *f* ♦ *vt*
erwähnen; **don't ~ it!** bitte (sehr), gern
geschehen
mentor ['mentɔ:r] *n* Mentor *m*
menu ['menju:] *n* Speisekarte *f*
MEP *n abbr* = **Member of the European
Parliament**
mercenary ['mɜ:sɪnərɪ] *adj* (*person*)
geldgierig ♦ *n* Söldner *m*
merchandise ['mɜ:tʃəndaɪz] *n*
(Handels)ware *f*
merchant ['mɜ:tʃənt] *n* Kaufmann *m*; **~
bank** (*BRIT*) *n* Handelsbank *f*; **~ navy** (*US* **~
marine**) *n* Handelsmarine *f*
merciful ['mɜ:sɪful] *adj* gnädig
merciless ['mɜ:sɪlɪs] *adj* erbarmungslos
mercury ['mɜ:kjurɪ] *n* Quecksilber *nt*
mercy ['mɜ:sɪ] *n* Erbarmen *nt*; Gnade *f*; **at
the ~ of** ausgeliefert +*dat*
mere [mɪər] *adj* bloß; **~ly** *adv* bloß
merge [mɜ:dʒ] *vt* verbinden; (*COMM*)
fusionieren ♦ *vi* verschmelzen; (*roads*)
zusammenlaufen; (*COMM*) fusionieren; **~r** *n*
(*COMM*) Fusion *f*
meringue [mə'ræŋ] *n* Baiser *nt*

merit ['merɪt] *n* Verdienst *nt*; (*advantage*)
Vorzug *m* ♦ *vt* verdienen
mermaid ['mɜ:meɪd] *n* Wassernixe *f*
merry ['merɪ] *adj* fröhlich; **~-go-round** *n*
Karussell *nt*
mesh [meʃ] *n* Masche *f*
mesmerize ['mezməraɪz] *vt* hypnotisieren;
(*fig*) faszinieren
mess [mes] *n* Unordnung *f*; (*dirt*) Schmutz
m; (*trouble*) Schwierigkeiten *pl*; (*MIL*) Messe
f; **~ about** or **around** *vi* (*play the fool*)
herumalbern; (*do nothing in particular*)
herumgammeln; **~ about** or **around with**
vt fus (*tinker with*) herummurksen an +*dat*; **~
up** *vt* verpfuschen; (*make untidy*) in
Unordnung bringen
message ['mesɪdʒ] *n* Mitteilung *f*; **to get
the ~** kapieren
messenger ['mesɪndʒər] *n* Bote *m*
Messrs ['mesəz] *abbr* (*on letters*) die Herren
messy ['mesɪ] *adj* schmutzig; (*untidy*)
unordentlich
met [met] *pt, pp of* **meet**
metabolism [me'tæbəlɪzəm] *n* Stoffwechsel
m
metal ['metl] *n* Metall *nt*; **~lic** *adj* metallisch;
(*made of ~*) aus Metall
metaphor ['metəfər] *n* Metapher *f*
meteorology [mi:tɪə'rɒlədʒɪ] *n*
Meteorologie *f*
meter ['mi:tər] *n* Zähler *m*; (*US*) = **metre**
method ['meθəd] *n* Methode *f*; **~ical**
[mɪ'θɒdɪkl] *adj* methodisch; **M~ist** *adj*
methodistisch ♦ *n* Methodist(in) *m(f)*;
~ology [meθə'dɒlədʒɪ] *n* Methodik *f*
meths [meθs] (*BRIT*) *n(pl)* = **methylated
spirit(s)**
methylated spirit(s) ['meθɪleɪtɪd-] (*BRIT*) *n*
(Brenn)spiritus *m*
meticulous [mɪ'tɪkjuləs] *adj* (über)genau
metre ['mi:tər] (*US* **meter**) *n* Meter *m* or
nt
metric ['metrɪk] *adj* (*also*: **~al**) metrisch
metropolitan [metrə'pɒlɪtn] *adj der*
Großstadt; **M~ Police** (*BRIT*) *n*: **the M~
Police** die Londoner Polizei
mettle ['metl] *n* Mut *m*
mew [mju:] *vi* (*cat*) miauen
mews [mju:z] *n*: **~ cottage** ehemaliges
Kutscherhäuschen
Mexican ['meksɪkən] *adj* mexikanisch ♦ *n*
Mexikaner(in) *m(f)*
Mexico ['meksɪkəu] *n* Mexiko *nt*
miaow [mi:'au] *vi* miauen
mice [maɪs] *pl of* **mouse**
micro ['maɪkrəu] *n* (*also*: **~computer**)
Mikrocomputer *m*; **~chip** *n* Mikrochip *m*;
~cosm ['maɪkrəukɒzəm] *n* Mikrokosmos *m*;
~phone *n* Mikrofon *nt*, Mikrophon *nt*;
~scope *n* Mikroskop *nt*; **~wave** *n* (*also*:
~wave oven) Mikrowelle(nherd *nt*) *f*

mid [mɪd] adj: **in ~ afternoon** am Nachmittag; **in ~ air** in der Luft; **in ~ May** Mitte Mai

midday [mɪd'deɪ] n Mittag m

middle [mɪdl] n Mitte f; (waist) Taille f ♦ adj mittlere(r, s), Mittel-; **in the ~ of** mitten in +dat; **~-aged** adj mittleren Alters; **M~ Ages** npl: **the M~ Ages** das Mittelalter; **~-class** adj Mittelstands-; **M~ East** n: **the M~ East** der Nahe Osten; **~man** (irreg) n (COMM) Zwischenhändler m; **~ name** n zweiter Vorname m; **~ weight** n (BOXING) Mittelgewicht nt

middling [mɪdlɪŋ] adj mittelmäßig

midge [mɪdʒ] n Mücke f

midget [mɪdʒɪt] n Liliputaner(in) m(f)

midnight [mɪdnaɪt] n Mitternacht f

midriff [mɪdrɪf] n Taille f

midst [mɪdst] n: **in the ~ of** (persons) mitten unter +dat; (things) mitten in +dat

mid [mɪd-]: **~summer** n Hochsommer m; **~way** adv auf halbem Wege ♦ adj Mittel-; **~week** adv in der Mitte der Woche

midwife [mɪdwaɪf] (irreg) n Hebamme f; **~ry** [mɪdwɪfərɪ] n Geburtshilfe f

midwinter [mɪd'wɪntər] n tiefste(r) Winter m

might [maɪt] vi see may ♦ n Macht f, Kraft f; **I ~ come** ich komme vielleicht; **~y** adj, adv mächtig

migraine [mi:greɪn] n Migräne f

migrant [maɪgrənt] adj Wander-; (bird) Zug-

migrate [maɪ'greɪt] vi (ab)wandern; (birds) (fort)ziehen; **migration** [maɪ'greɪʃən] n Wanderung f, Zug m

mike [maɪk] n = microphone

Milan [mɪ'læn] n Mailand nt

mild [maɪld] adj mild; (medicine, interest) leicht; (person) sanft ♦ n (beer) leichtes dunkles Bier

mildew [mɪldju:] n (on plants) Mehltau m; (on food) Schimmel m

mildly [maɪldlɪ] adv leicht; **to put it ~** gelinde gesagt

mile [maɪl] n Meile f; **~age** n Meilenzahl f; **~ometer** n = milometer; **~stone** n (also fig) Meilenstein m

militant [mɪlɪtnt] adj militant ♦ n Militante(r) mf

military [mɪlɪtərɪ] adj militärisch, Militär-, Wehr-

militate [mɪlɪteɪt] vi: **to ~ against** entgegenwirken +dat

militia [mɪ'lɪʃə] n Miliz f

milk [mɪlk] n Milch f ♦ vt (also fig) melken; **~ chocolate** n Milchschokolade f; **~man** (irreg) n Milchmann m; **~ shake** n Milchmixgetränk nt; **~y** adj milchig; **M~y Way** n Milchstraße f

mill [mɪl] n Mühle f; (factory) Fabrik f ♦ vt mahlen ♦ vi umherlaufen

millennia [mɪ'lenɪə] npl of millennium

millennium [mɪ'lenɪəm] (pl **~s** or **millennia**) n Jahrtausend nt; **~ bug** n Jahr-2000-Problem nt

miller [mɪlər] n Müller m

milligram(me) [mɪlɪgræm] n Milligramm nt

millimetre [mɪlɪmi:tər] (US **millimeter**) n Millimeter m

million [mɪljən] n Million f; **a ~ times** tausendmal; **~aire** [mɪljə'neər] n Millionär(in) m(f)

millstone [mɪlstəun] n Mühlstein m

milometer [maɪ'lɒmɪtər] n ≈ Kilometerzähler m

mime [maɪm] n Pantomime f ♦ vt, vi mimen

mimic [mɪmɪk] n Mimiker m ♦ vt, vi nachahmen; **~ry** n Nachahmung f; (BIOL) Mimikry f

min. abbr = minutes; minimum

mince [mɪns] vt (zer)hacken ♦ n (meat) Hackfleisch nt; **~meat** n süße Pastetenfüllung f; **~ pie** n gefüllte (süße) Pastete f; **~r** n Fleischwolf m

mind [maɪnd] n Verstand m, Geist m; (opinion) Meinung f ♦ vt aufpassen auf +acc; (object to) etwas haben gegen; **on my ~** auf dem Herzen; **to my ~** meiner Meinung nach; **to be out of one's ~** wahnsinnig sein; **to bear** or **keep in ~** bedenken; **to change one's ~** sich dat anders überlegen; **to make up one's ~** sich entschließen; **I don't ~** das macht mir nichts aus; **~ you, ...** allerdings ...; **never ~!** macht nichts!; **"~ the step"** „Vorsicht Stufe"; **~ your own business** kümmern Sie sich um Ihre eigenen Angelegenheiten; **~er** n Aufpasser(in) m(f); **~ful** adj: **~ful of** achtsam auf +acc; **~less** adj sinnlos

mine¹ [maɪn] n (coalmine) Bergwerk nt; (MIL) Mine f ♦ vt abbauen; (MIL) verminen

mine² [maɪn] pron meine(r, s); **that book is ~** das Buch gehört mir; **a friend of ~** ein Freund von mir

minefield [maɪnfi:ld] n Minenfeld nt

miner [maɪnər] n Bergarbeiter m

mineral [mɪnərəl] adj mineralisch, Mineral- ♦ n Mineral nt; **~s** npl (BRIT: soft drinks) alkoholfreie Getränke pl; **~ water** n Mineralwasser nt

minesweeper [maɪnswi:pər] n Minensuchboot nt

mingle [mɪŋgl] vi: **to ~ (with)** sich mischen (unter +acc)

miniature [mɪnətʃər] adj Miniatur- ♦ n Miniatur f

minibus [mɪnɪbʌs] n Kleinbus m

minimal [mɪnɪml] adj minimal

minimize [mɪnɪmaɪz] vt auf das Mindestmaß beschränken

minimum [mɪnɪməm] (pl **minima**) n Minimum nt ♦ adj Mindest-

mining [maɪnɪŋ] n Bergbau m ♦ adj

Bergbau-, Berg-

miniskirt [ˈmɪnɪskəːt] n Minirock m

minister [ˈmɪnɪstəʳ] n (BRIT: POL) Minister m; (ECCL) Pfarrer m ♦ vi: **to ~ to sb/sb's needs** sich um jdn kümmern; **~ial** [mɪnɪsˈtɪərɪəl] adj ministeriell, Minister-

ministry [ˈmɪnɪstrɪ] n (BRIT: POL) Ministerium nt; (ECCL: office) geistliche(s) Amt nt

mink [mɪŋk] n Nerz m

minnow [ˈmɪnəu] n Elritze f

minor [ˈmaɪnəʳ] adj kleiner; (operation) leicht; (problem, poet) unbedeutend; (MUS) Moll ♦ n (BRIT: under 18) Minderjährige(r) mf

minority [maɪˈnɔrɪtɪ] n Minderheit f

mint [mɪnt] n Minze f; (sweet) Pfefferminzbonbon m ♦ vt (coins) prägen; **the (Royal (BRIT) or US (US)) M~** die Münzanstalt; **in ~ condition** in tadellosem Zustand

minus [ˈmaɪnəs] n Minuszeichen nt; (amount) Minusbetrag m ♦ prep minus, weniger

minuscule [ˈmɪnəskjuːl] adj winzig

minute[1] [maɪˈnjuːt] adj winzig; (detailed) minutiös, minuziös

minute[2] [ˈmɪnɪt] n Minute f; (moment) Augenblick m; **~s** npl (of meeting etc) Protokoll nt

miracle [ˈmɪrəkl] n Wunder nt

miraculous [mɪˈrækjuləs] adj wunderbar

mirage [ˈmɪrɑːʒ] n Fata Morgana f

mire [ˈmaɪəʳ] n Morast m

mirror [ˈmɪrəʳ] n Spiegel m ♦ vt (wider)spiegeln

mirth [məːθ] n Heiterkeit f

misadventure [mɪsədˈvɛntʃəʳ] n Missgeschick nt, Unfall m

misanthropist [mɪˈzænθrəpɪst] n Menschenfeind m

misapprehension [ˈmɪsæprɪˈhɛnʃən] n Missverständnis nt

misbehave [mɪsbɪˈheɪv] vi sich schlecht benehmen

miscalculate [mɪsˈkælkjuleɪt] vt falsch berechnen

miscarriage [ˈmɪskærɪdʒ] n (MED) Fehlgeburt f; **~ of justice** Fehlurteil nt

miscellaneous [mɪsɪˈleɪnɪəs] adj verschieden

mischief [ˈmɪstʃɪf] n Unfug m; **mischievous** [ˈmɪstʃɪvəs] adj (person) durchtrieben; (glance) verschmitzt; (rumour) bösartig

misconception [ˈmɪskənˈsɛpʃən] n fälschliche Annahme f

misconduct [mɪsˈkɔndʌkt] n Vergehen nt; **professional ~** Berufsvergehen nt

misconstrue [mɪskənˈstruː] vt missverstehen

misdemeanour [mɪsdɪˈmiːnəʳ] (US **misdemeanor**) n Vergehen nt

miser [ˈmaɪzəʳ] n Geizhals m

miserable [ˈmɪzərəbl] adj (unhappy) unglücklich; (headache, weather)

fürchterlich; (poor) elend; (contemptible) erbärmlich

miserly [ˈmaɪzəlɪ] adj geizig

misery [ˈmɪzərɪ] n Elend nt, Qual f

misfire [mɪsˈfaɪəʳ] vi (gun) versagen; (engine) fehlzünden; (plan) fehlgehen

misfit [ˈmɪsfɪt] n Außenseiter m

misfortune [mɪsˈfɔːtʃən] n Unglück nt

misgiving(s) [mɪsˈgɪvɪŋ(z)] n(pl) Bedenken pl

misguided [mɪsˈgaɪdɪd] adj fehlgeleitet; (opinions) irrig

mishandle [mɪsˈhændl] vt falsch handhaben

mishap [ˈmɪshæp] n Missgeschick nt

misinform [mɪsɪnˈfɔːm] vt falsch unterrichten

misinterpret [mɪsɪnˈtəːprɪt] vt falsch auffassen

misjudge [mɪsˈdʒʌdʒ] vt falsch beurteilen

mislay [mɪsˈleɪ] (irreg: like **lay**) vt verlegen

mislead [mɪsˈliːd] (irreg: like **lead[2]**) vt (deceive) irreführen; **~ing** adj irreführend

mismanage [mɪsˈmænɪdʒ] vt schlecht verwalten

misnomer [mɪsˈnəuməʳ] n falsche Bezeichnung f

misplace [mɪsˈpleɪs] vt verlegen

misprint [ˈmɪsprɪnt] n Druckfehler m

Miss [mɪs] n Fräulein nt

miss [mɪs] vt (fail to hit, catch) verfehlen; (not notice) verpassen; (be too late) versäumen, verpassen; (omit) auslassen; (regret the absence of) vermissen ♦ vi fehlen ♦ n (shot) Fehlschuss m; (failure) Fehlschlag m; **I ~ you** du fehlst mir; **~ out** vt auslassen

misshapen [mɪsˈʃeɪpən] adj missgestaltet

missile [ˈmɪsaɪl] n Rakete f

missing [ˈmɪsɪŋ] adj (person) vermisst; (thing) fehlend; **to be ~** fehlen

mission [ˈmɪʃən] n (work) Auftrag m; (people) Delegation f, (REL) Mission f; **~ary** n Missionar(in) m(f); **~ statement** Kurzdarstellung f der Firmenphilosophie

misspell [ˈmɪsˈspɛl] (irreg: like **spell**) vt falsch schreiben

misspent [ˈmɪsˈspɛnt] adj (youth) vergeudet

mist [mɪst] n Dunst m, Nebel m ♦ vi (also: **~ over, ~ up**) sich trüben; (BRIT: windows) sich beschlagen

mistake [mɪsˈteɪk] (irreg: like **take**) n Fehler m ♦ vt (misunderstand) missverstehen; (mix up): **to ~ (sth for sth)** (etw mit etw) verwechseln; **to make a ~** einen Fehler machen; **by ~** aus Versehen; **to ~ A for B** A mit B verwechseln; **~n** pp of mistake ♦ adj (idea) falsch; **to be ~** sich irren

mister [ˈmɪstəʳ] n (inf) Herr m; see **Mr**

mistletoe [ˈmɪsltəu] n Mistel f

mistook [mɪsˈtuk] pt of mistake

mistress [ˈmɪstrɪs] n (teacher) Lehrerin f; (in house) Herrin f; (lover) Geliebte f; see **Mrs**

mistrust |mɪs'trʌst| vt misstrauen +dat

misty |'mɪstɪ| adj neblig

misunderstand |mɪsʌndə'stænd| (irreg: like **understand**) vt, vi missverstehen, falsch verstehen; **~ing** n Missverständnis nt; (disagreement) Meinungsverschiedenheit f

misuse |n mɪs'juːs, vb mɪs'juːz| n falsche(r) Gebrauch m ♦ vt falsch gebrauchen

mitigate |'mɪtɪgeɪt| vt mildern

mitt(en) |'mɪt(n)| n Fausthandschuh m

mix |mɪks| vt (blend) (ver)mischen ♦ vi (liquids) sich (ver)mischen lassen; (people: get on) sich vertragen; (: associate) Kontakt haben ♦ n (mixture) Mischung f; **~ up** vt zusammenmischen; (confuse) verwechseln; **~ed** adj gemischt; **~ed-up** adj durcheinander; **~er** n (for food) Mixer m; **~ture** n Mischung f; **~-up** n Durcheinander nt

mm abbr (= millimetre(s)) mm

moan |məun| n Stöhnen nt; (complaint) Klage f ♦ vi stöhnen; (complain) maulen

moat |məut| n (Burg)graben m

mob |mɒb| n Mob m; (the masses) Pöbel m ♦ vt herfallen über +acc

mobile |'məubaɪl| adj beweglich; (library etc) fahrbar ♦ n (decoration) Mobile nt; **~ home** n Wohnwagen m; **~ phone** n (TEL) Mobiltelefon nt; **mobility** |məu'bɪlɪtɪ| n Beweglichkeit f; **mobilize** |'məubɪlaɪz| vt mobilisieren

mock |mɒk| vt verspotten; (defy) trotzen +dat ♦ adj Schein-; **~ery** n Spott m; (person) Gespött nt

mod |mɒd| adj see **convenience**

mode |məud| n (Art f und) Weise f

model |'mɒdl| n Modell nt; (example) Vorbild nt; (in fashion) Mannequin nt ♦ adj (railway) Modell-; (perfect) Muster-; vorbildlich ♦ vt (make) bilden; (clothes) vorführen ♦ vi als Mannequin arbeiten

modem |'məudem| n (COMPUT) Modem nt

moderate |adj, n 'mɒdərət, vb 'mɒdəreɪt| adj gemäßigt ♦ n (POL) Gemäßigte(r) mf ♦ vi sich mäßigen ♦ vt mäßigen; **moderation** |mɒdə'reɪʃən| n Mäßigung f; **in moderation** mit Maßen

modern |'mɒdən| adj modern; (history, languages) neuere(r, s); **~ize** vt modernisieren

modest |'mɒdɪst| adj bescheiden; **~y** n Bescheidenheit f

modicum |'mɒdɪkəm| n bisschen nt

modification |mɒdɪfɪ'keɪʃən| n (Ab)änderung f

modify |'mɒdɪfaɪ| vt abändern

module |'mɒdjuːl| n (component) (Bau)element nt; (SPACE) (Raum)kapsel f

mogul |'məugl| n (fig) Mogul m

mohair |'məuhɛər| n Mohär m, Mohair m

moist |mɔɪst| adj feucht; **~en** |'mɔɪsn| vt befeuchten; **~ure** |'mɔɪstʃər| n Feuchtigkeit f; **~urizer** |'mɔɪstʃəraɪzər| n Feuchtigkeitscreme f

molar |'məulər| n Backenzahn m

molasses |mə'læsɪz| n Melasse f

mold |məuld| (US) = **mould**

mole |məul| n (spot) Leberfleck m; (animal) Maulwurf m; (pier) Mole f

molest |mə'lɛst| vt belästigen

mollycoddle |'mɒlɪkɒdl| vt verhätscheln

molt |məult| (US) vi = **moult**

molten |'məultən| adj geschmolzen

mom |mɒm| (US) n = **mum**

moment |'məumənt| n Moment m, Augenblick m; (importance) Tragweite f; **at the ~** im Augenblick; **~ary** adj kurz; **~ous** |məu'mentəs| adj folgenschwer

momentum |məu'mentəm| n Schwung m; **to gather ~** in Fahrt kommen

mommy |'mɒmɪ| (US) n = **mummy**

Monaco |'mɒnəkəu| n Monaco nt

monarch |'mɒnək| n Herrscher(in) m(f); **~y** n Monarchie f

monastery |'mɒnəstərɪ| n Kloster nt

monastic |mə'næstɪk| adj klösterlich, Kloster-

Monday |'mʌndɪ| n Montag m

monetary |'mʌnɪtərɪ| adj Geld-; (of currency) Währungs-

money |'mʌnɪ| n Geld nt; **to make ~** Geld verdienen; **~ belt** n Geldgürtel nt; **~lender** n Geldverleiher m; **~ order** n Postanweisung f; **~-spinner** (inf) n Verkaufsschlager m

mongol |'mɒŋgəl| n (MED) mongoloide(s) Kind nt ♦ adj mongolisch; (MED) mongoloid

mongrel |'mʌŋgrəl| n Promenadenmischung f

monitor |'mɒnɪtər| n (SCH) Klassenordner m; (television ~) Monitor m ♦ vt (broadcasts) abhören; (control) überwachen

monk |mʌŋk| n Mönch m

monkey |'mʌŋkɪ| n Affe m; **~ nut** (BRIT) n Erdnuss f; **~ wrench** n (TECH) Engländer m, Franzose m

monochrome |'mɒnəkrəum| adj schwarz-weiß, schwarzweiß

monopolize |mə'nɒpəlaɪz| vt beherrschen

monopoly |mə'nɒpəlɪ| n Monopol nt

monosyllable |'mɒnəsɪləbl| n einsilbige(s) Wort nt

monotone |'mɒnətəun| n gleich bleibende(r) Ton(fall) m; **to speak in a ~** monoton sprechen; **monotonous** |mə'nɒtənəs| adj eintönig; **monotony** |mə'nɒtənɪ| n Eintönigkeit f, Monotonie f

monsoon |mɒn'suːn| n Monsun m

monster |'mɒnstər| n Ungeheuer nt; (person) Scheusal m

monstrosity |mɒn'strɒsɪtɪ| n Ungeheuerlichkeit f; (thing) Monstrosität f

monstrous |'mɒnstrəs| adj (shocking)

grässlich, ungeheuerlich; (*huge*) riesig
month [mʌnθ] n Monat m; **~ly** adj
monatlich, Monats- ♦ adv einmal im Monat
♦ n (*magazine*) Monatsschrift f
monument ['mɔnjumənt] n Denkmal nt;
~al [mɔnju'mentl] adj (*huge*) gewaltig;
(*ignorance*) ungeheuer
moo [muː] vi muhen
mood [muːd] n Stimmung f, Laune f; **to be
in a good/bad ~** gute/schlechte Laune
haben; **~y** adj launisch
moon [muːn] n Mond m; **~light** n Mondlicht
nt; **~lighting** n Schwarzarbeit f; **~lit** adj
mondhell
moor [muəʳ] n Heide f, Hochmoor nt ♦ vt
(*ship*) festmachen, verankern ♦ vi anlegen;
~ings npl Liegeplatz m; **~land** ['muələnd] n
Heidemoor nt
moose [muːs] n Elch m
mop [mɔp] n Mopp m ♦ vt (auf)wischen; **~
up** vt aufwischen
mope [məup] vi Trübsal blasen
moped ['məuped] n Moped nt
moral ['mɔrl] adj moralisch; (*values*) sittlich;
(*virtuous*) tugendhaft ♦ n Moral f; **~s** npl
(*ethics*) Moral f
morale [mɔ'rɑːl] n Moral f
morality [mɔ'rælɪtɪ] n Sittlichkeit f
morass [mə'ræs] n Sumpf m
morbid ['mɔːbɪd] adj krankhaft; (*jokes*)
makaber

KEYWORD

more [mɔːʳ] adj (*greater in number etc*)
mehr; (*additional*) noch mehr; **do you want
(some) more tea?** möchten Sie noch etwas
Tee?; **I have no** or **I don't have any more
money** ich habe kein Geld mehr
♦ pron (*greater amount*) mehr; (*further or
additional amount*) noch mehr; **is there any
more?** gibt es noch mehr?; (*left over*) ist
noch etwas da?; **there's no more** es ist
nichts mehr da
♦ adv mehr; **more dangerous/easily** etc
(**than**) gefährlicher/einfacher etc (als); **more
and more** immer mehr; **more and more
excited** immer aufgeregter; **more or less**
mehr oder weniger; **more than ever** mehr
denn je; **more beautiful than ever** schöner
denn je

moreover [mɔː'rəuvəʳ] adv überdies
morgue [mɔːg] n Leichenschauhaus nt
Mormon ['mɔːmən] n Mormone m,
Mormonin f
morning ['mɔːnɪŋ] n Morgen m; **in the ~**
am Morgen; **7 o'clock in the ~** 7 Uhr
morgens; **~ sickness** n (Schwanger-
schafts)übelkeit f
Morocco [mə'rɔkəu] n Marokko nt
moron ['mɔːrɔn] n Schwachsinnige(r) mf

morose [mə'rəus] adj mürrisch
morphine ['mɔːfiːn] n Morphium nt
Morse [mɔːs] n (*also:* ~ **code**) Morsealphabet
nt
morsel ['mɔːsl] n Bissen m
mortal ['mɔːtl] adj sterblich; (*deadly*) tödlich;
(*very great*) Todes- ♦ n (*human being*)
Sterbliche(r) mf; **~ity** [mɔː'tælɪtɪ] n
Sterblichkeit f; (*death rate*)
Sterblichkeitsziffer f
mortar ['mɔːtəʳ] n (*for building*) Mörtel m;
(*MIL*) Granatwerfer m
mortgage ['mɔːgɪdʒ] n Hypothek f ♦ vt
hypothekarisch belasten; **~ company** (*US*) n
≈ Bausparkasse f
mortify ['mɔːtɪfaɪ] vt beschämen
mortuary ['mɔːtjuərɪ] n Leichenhalle f
mosaic [məu'zeɪɪk] n Mosaik nt
Moscow ['mɔskəu] n Moskau nt
Moslem ['mɔzləm] = **Muslim**
mosque [mɔsk] n Moschee f
mosquito [mɔs'kiːtəu] (pl **~es**) n Moskito m
moss [mɔs] n Moos nt
most [məust] adj meiste(r, s) ♦ adv am
meisten; (*very*) höchst ♦ n das meiste, der
größte Teil; (*people*) die meisten; **~ men** die
meisten Männer; **at the (very) ~**
allerhöchstens; **to make the ~ of** das Beste
machen aus; **a ~ interesting book** ein
höchstinteressantes Buch; **~ly** adv
größtenteils
MOT (*BRIT*) n abbr (= *Ministry of Transport*):
the ~ (test) ≈ der TÜV
motel [məu'tel] n Motel nt
moth [mɔθ] n Nachtfalter m; (*wool-eating*)
Motte f; **~ball** n Mottenkugel f
mother ['mʌðəʳ] n Mutter f ♦ vt bemuttern;
~hood n Mutterschaft f; **~-in-law** n
Schwiegermutter f; **~ly** adj mütterlich; **~-of-
pearl** n Perlmutt nt; **M~'s Day** (*BRIT*) n
Muttertag m; **~-to-be** n werdende Mutter f;
~ tongue n Muttersprache f
motif [məu'tiːf] n Motiv nt
motion ['məuʃən] n Bewegung f; (*in
meeting*) Antrag m ♦ vt, vi: **to ~ (to) sb** jdm
winken, jdm zu verstehen geben; **~less** adj
regungslos; **~ picture** n Film m
motivated ['məutɪveɪtɪd] adj motiviert
motivation [məutɪ'veɪʃən] n Motivierung f
motive ['məutɪv] n Motiv nt, Beweggrund m
♦ adj treibend
motley ['mɔtlɪ] adj bunt
motor ['məutəʳ] n Motor m; (*BRIT*: inf:
vehicle) Auto nt ♦ adj Motor-; **~bike** n
Motorrad nt; **~boat** n Motorboot nt; **~car**
(*BRIT*) n Auto nt; **~cycle** n Motorrad nt;
~cyclist n Motorradfahrer(in) m(f); **~ing**
(*BRIT*) n Autofahren nt ♦ adj Auto-; **~ist** n
Autofahrer(in) m(f); **~ mechanic** n
Kraftfahrzeugmechaniker(in) m(f), Kfz-
Mechaniker(in) m(f); **~ racing** (*BRIT*) n

Autorennen nt; ~ **vehicle** n Kraftfahrzeug nt; ~**way** (BRIT) n Autobahn f

mottled ['mɔtld] adj gesprenkelt

mould |məuld| (US **mold**) n Form f; (mildew) Schimmel m ♦ vt (also: fig) formen; ~**y** adj schimmelig

moult |məult| (US **molt**) vi sich mausern

mound |maund| n (Erd)hügel m

mount |maunt| n (LITER: hill) Berg m; (horse) Pferd nt; (for jewel etc) Fassung f ♦ vt (horse) steigen auf +acc; (put in setting) fassen; (exhibition) veranstalten; (attack) unternehmen ♦ vi (also: ~ **up**) sich häufen; (on horse) aufsitzen

mountain ['mauntɪn] n Berg m ♦ cpd Berg-; ~ **bike** n Mountainbike nt; ~**eer** n Bergsteiger(in) m(f); ~**eering** [mauntɪ'nɪərɪŋ] n Bergsteigen nt; ~**ous** adj bergig; ~ **rescue team** n Bergwacht f; ~**side** n Berg(ab)hang m

mourn |mɔːn| vt betrauern, beklagen ♦ vi: to ~ (**for sb**) (um jdn) trauern; ~**er** n Trauernde(r) mf; ~**ful** adj traurig; ~**ing** n (grief) Trauer f ♦ cpd (dress) Trauer-; **in** ~**ing** (period etc) in Trauer; (dress) in Trauerkleidung f

mouse |maus| (pl **mice**) n Maus f; ~**trap** n Mausefalle f

mousse |muːs| n (COOK) Creme f; (cosmetic) Schaumfestiger m

moustache [məs'tɑːʃ] n Schnurrbart m

mousy ['mausɪ] adj (colour) mausgrau; (person) schüchtern

mouth |mauθ| n Mund m; (opening) Öffnung f; (of river) Mündung f; ~**ful** n Mund m voll; ~ **organ** n Mundharmonika f; ~**piece** n Mundstück nt; (fig) Sprachrohr nt; ~**wash** n Mundwasser nt; ~**watering** adj lecker, appetitlich

movable ['muːvəbl] adj beweglich

move |muːv| n (movement) Bewegung f; (in game) Zug m; (step) Schritt m; (of house) Umzug m ♦ vt bewegen; (people) transportieren; (in job) versetzen; (emotionally) bewegen ♦ vi sich bewegen; (vehicle, ship) fahren; (~ house) umziehen; **to get a ~ on** sich beeilen; **to ~ sb to do sth** jdn veranlassen, etw zu tun; ~ **about** or **around** vi sich hin und her bewegen; (travel) unterwegs sein; ~ **along** vi weitergehen; (cars) weiterfahren; ~ **away** vi weggehen; ~ **back** vi zurückgehen; (to the rear) zurückweichen; ~ **forward** vi vorwärts gehen, sich vorwärts bewegen ♦ vt vorschieben; (time) vorverlegen; ~ **in** vi (to house) einziehen; (troops) einrücken; ~ **on** vi weitergehen ♦ vt weitergehen lassen; ~ **out** vi (of house) ausziehen; (troops) abziehen; ~ **over** vi zur Seite rücken; ~ **up** vi aufsteigen; (in job) befördert werden ♦ vt nach oben bewegen; (in job) befördern; ~**ment**

['muːvmənt] n Bewegung f

movie ['muːvɪ] n Film m; **to go to the ~s** ins Kino gehen; ~ **camera** n Filmkamera f

moving ['muːvɪŋ] adj beweglich; (touching) ergreifend

mow |məu| (pt **mowed**, pp **mowed** or **mown**) vt mähen; ~ **down** vt (fig) niedermähen; ~**er** n (lawnmower) Rasenmäher m; ~**n** pp of **mow**

MP n abbr = **Member of Parliament**

m.p.h. abbr = **miles per hour**

Mr ['mɪstə'] (US **Mr.**) n Herr m

Mrs ['mɪsɪz] (US **Mrs.**) n Frau f

Ms |mɪz| (US **Ms.**) n (= Miss or Mrs) Frau f

M.Sc. n abbr = **Master of Science**

MSP n abbr (= Member of the Scottish Parliament) Mitglied nt des schottischen Parlaments

much |mʌtʃ| adj viel ♦ adv sehr; viel ♦ n viel, eine Menge; **how ~ is it?** wie viel kostet das?; **too ~** zu viel; **it's not ~** es ist nicht viel; **as ~ as** so sehr, so viel; **however ~ he tries** so sehr er es auch versucht

muck |mʌk| n Mist m; (fig) Schmutz m; ~ **about** or **around** (inf) vi: **to ~ about** or **around** (**with sth**) (an etw dat) herumalbern; ~ **up** vt (inf: ruin) vermasseln; (dirty) dreckig machen; ~**y** adj (dirty) dreckig

mud |mʌd| n Schlamm m

muddle ['mʌdl] n Durcheinander nt ♦ vt (also: ~ **up**) durcheinander bringen; ~ **through** vi sich durchwursteln

mud ['mʌd-]: ~**dy** adj schlammig; ~**guard** n Schutzblech nt; ~**-slinging** (inf) n Verleumdung f

muesli ['mjuːzlɪ] n Müsli nt

muffin ['mʌfɪn] n süße(s) Teilchen nt

muffle ['mʌfl] vt (sound) dämpfen; (wrap up) einhüllen; ~**d** adj gedämpft; ~**r** (US) n (AUT) Schalldämpfer m

mug |mʌg| n (cup) Becher m; (inf: face) Visage f; (: fool) Trottel m ♦ vt überfallen und ausrauben; ~**ger** n Straßenräuber m; ~**ging** n Überfall m

muggy ['mʌgɪ] adj (weather) schwül

mule |mjuːl| n Maulesel m

mull |mʌl|: ~ **over** vt nachdenken über +acc

multicoloured ['mʌltɪkʌləd] (US **multicolored**) adj mehrfarbig

multi-level ['mʌltɪlevl] (US) adj = **multistorey**

multiple ['mʌltɪpl] n Vielfache(s) nt ♦ adj mehrfach; (many) mehrere; ~ **sclerosis** n multiple Sklerose f

multiplex cinema ['mʌltɪpleks-] n Kinocenter nt

multiplication |mʌltɪplɪ'keɪʃən| n Multiplikation f; (increase) Vervielfachung f

multiply ['mʌltɪplaɪ] vt: **to ~ (by)** multiplizieren (mit) ♦ vi (BIOL) sich vermehren

multistorey [ˈmʌltɪˈstɔːrɪ] (BRIT) adj (building, car park) mehrstöckig

multitude [ˈmʌltɪtjuːd] n Menge f

mum [mʌm] n (BRIT: inf) Mutti f ♦ adj: **to keep ~ (about)** den Mund halten (über +acc)

mumble [ˈmʌmbl] vt, vi murmeln ♦ n Gemurmel nt

mummy [ˈmʌmɪ] n (dead body) Mumie f; (BRIT: inf) Mami f

mumps [mʌmps] n Mumps m

munch [mʌntʃ] vt, vi mampfen

mundane [mʌnˈdeɪn] adj banal

municipal [mjuːˈnɪsɪpl] adj städtisch, Stadt-

mural [ˈmjʊərl] n Wandgemälde nt

murder [ˈmɜːdəʳ] n Mord m ♦ vt ermorden; **~er** n Mörder m; **~ous** adj Mord-; (fig) mörderisch

murky [ˈmɜːkɪ] adj finster

murmur [ˈmɜːməʳ] n Murmeln nt; (of water, wind) Rauschen nt ♦ vt, vi murmeln

muscle [ˈmʌsl] n Muskel m; **~ in** vi mitmischen; **muscular** [ˈmʌskjʊləʳ] adj Muskel-; (strong) muskulös

museum [mjuːˈzɪəm] n Museum nt

mushroom [ˈmʌʃrʊm] n Champignon m; Pilz m ♦ vi (fig) emporschießen

music [ˈmjuːzɪk] n Musik f; (printed) Noten pl; **~al** adj (sound) melodisch; (person) musikalisch ♦ n (show) Musical nt; **~al instrument** n Musikinstrument nt; **~ centre** n Stereoanlage f; **~ hall** (BRIT) n Varietee nt, Varieté nt; **~ian** [mjuːˈzɪʃən] n Musiker(in) m(f)

Muslim [ˈmʌzlɪm] adj moslemisch ♦ n Moslem m

muslin [ˈmʌzlɪn] n Musselin m

mussel [ˈmʌsl] n Miesmuschel f

must [mʌst] vb aux müssen; (in negation) dürfen ♦ n Muss nt; **the film is a ~** den Film muss man einfach gesehen haben

mustard [ˈmʌstəd] n Senf m

muster [ˈmʌstəʳ] vt (MIL) antreten lassen; (courage) zusammennehmen

mustn't [ˈmʌsnt] = **must not**

musty [ˈmʌstɪ] adj muffig

mute [mjuːt] adj stumm ♦ n (person) Stumme(r) mf; (MUS) Dämpfer m; **~d** adj gedämpft

mutilate [ˈmjuːtɪleɪt] vt verstümmeln

mutiny [ˈmjuːtɪnɪ] n Meuterei f ♦ vi meutern

mutter [ˈmʌtəʳ] vt, vi murmeln

mutton [ˈmʌtn] n Hammelfleisch nt

mutual [ˈmjuːtʃʊəl] adj gegenseitig; beiderseitig; **~ly** adv gegenseitig; für beide Seiten

muzzle [ˈmʌzl] n (of animal) Schnauze f; (of animal) Maulkorb m; (of gun) Mündung f ♦ vt einen Maulkorb anlegen +dat

my [maɪ] adj mein; **this is ~ car** das ist mein Auto; **I've washed ~ hair** ich habe mir die Haare gewaschen

myself [maɪˈself] pron mich acc; mir dat; (emphatic) selbst; see also **oneself**

mysterious [mɪsˈtɪərɪəs] adj geheimnisvoll

mystery [ˈmɪstərɪ] n (secret) Geheimnis nt; (sth difficult) Rätsel nt

mystify [ˈmɪstɪfaɪ] vt ein Rätsel nt sein +dat; verblüffen

mystique [mɪsˈtiːk] n geheimnisvolle Natur f

myth [mɪθ] n Mythos m; (fig) Erfindung f; **~ology** [mɪˈθɒlədʒɪ] n Mythologie f

N, n

n/a abbr (= not applicable) nicht zutreffend

nab [næb] (inf) vt schnappen

naff [næf] (BRIT: inf) adj blöd

nag [næg] n (horse) Gaul m; (person) Nörgler(in) m(f) ♦ vt, vi: **to ~ (at) sb** an jdm herumnörgeln; **~ging** adj (doubt) nagend ♦ n Nörgelei f

nail [neɪl] n Nagel m ♦ vt nageln; **to ~ sb down to doing sth** jdn darauf festnageln, etw zu tun; **~brush** n Nagelbürste f; **~file** n Nagelfeile f; **~ polish** n Nagellack m; **~ polish remover** n Nagellackentferner m; **~ scissors** npl Nagelschere f; **~ varnish** (BRIT) n = **nail polish**

naïve [naɪˈiːv] adj naiv

naked [ˈneɪkɪd] adj nackt

name [neɪm] n Name m; (reputation) Ruf m ♦ vt nennen; (sth new) benennen; (appoint) ernennen; **by ~** mit Namen; **I know him only by ~** ich kenne ihn nur dem Namen nach; **what's your ~?** wie heißen Sie?; **in the ~ of** im Namen +gen; (for the sake of) um +gen ... willen; **~less** adj namenlos; **~ly** adv nämlich; **~sake** n Namensvetter m

nanny [ˈnænɪ] n Kindermädchen nt

nap [næp] n (sleep) Nickerchen nt; (on cloth) Strich m ♦ vi: **to be caught ~ping** (fig) überrumpelt werden

nape [neɪp] n Nacken m

napkin [ˈnæpkɪn] n (at table) Serviette f; (BRIT: for baby) Windel f

nappy [ˈnæpɪ] (BRIT) n (for baby) Windel f; **~ rash** n wunde Stellen pl

narcotic [nɑːˈkɒtɪk] adj betäubend ♦ n Betäubungsmittel nt

narrative [ˈnærətɪv] n Erzählung f ♦ adj erzählend

narrator [nəˈreɪtəʳ] n Erzähler(in) m(f)

narrow [ˈnærəʊ] adj eng, schmal; (limited) beschränkt ♦ vi sich verengen; **to have a ~ escape** mit knapper Not davonkommen; **to ~ sth down to sth** etw auf etw acc einschränken; **~ly** adv (miss) knapp; (escape) mit knapper Not; **~-minded** adj engstirnig

nasty [ˈnɑːstɪ] adj ekelhaft, fies; (business, wound) schlimm

nation |'neɪʃən] n Nation f, Volk nt; **~al**
|'næʃənl] adj national, National-, Landes- ♦ n
Staatsangehörige(r) mf; **~al anthem** (BRIT)
n Nationalhymne f; **~al dress** n Tracht f;
N~al Health Service (BRIT) n staatliche(r)
Gesundheitsdienst m; **N~al Insurance**
(BRIT) n Sozialversicherung f; **~alism**
|'næʃnəlɪzəm] n Nationalismus m; **~alist**
|'næʃnəlɪst] n Nationalist(in) m(f) ♦ adj
nationalistisch; **~ality** [næʃə'nælɪtɪ] n
Staatsangehörigkeit f; **~alize** |'næʃnəlaɪz] vt
verstaatlichen; **~ally** |'næʃnəlɪ] adv national,
auf Staatsebene; **~al park** (BRIT) n
Nationalpark m; **~wide** |'neɪʃənwaɪd] adj,
adv allgemein, landesweit

native |'neɪtɪv] n (born in) Einheimische(r)
mf; (original inhabitant) Eingeborene(r) mf
♦ adj einheimisch; Eingeborenen-; (belonging
by birth) heimatlich, Heimat-; (inborn)
angeboren, natürlich; **a ~ of Germany** ein
gebürtiger Deutscher; **a ~ speaker of
French** ein französischer Muttersprachler;
N~ American n Indianer(in) m(f),
Ureinwohner(in) m(f) Amerikas; **~
language** n Muttersprache f

Nativity |nə'tɪvɪtɪ] n: **the ~** Christi Geburt no
art

NATO |'neɪtəu] n abbr (= North Atlantic Treaty
Organization) NATO f

natural |'nætʃrəl] adj natürlich; Natur-;
(inborn) (an)geboren; **~ gas** n Erdgas nt;
~ist n Naturkundler(in) m(f); **~ly** adv
natürlich

nature |'neɪtʃəʳ] n Natur f; **by ~** von Natur (aus)

naught |nɔːt] n = nought

naughty |'nɔːtɪ] adj (child) unartig,
ungezogen; (action) ungehörig

nausea |'nɔːsɪə] n (sickness) Übelkeit f;
(disgust) Ekel m; **~te** |'nɔːsɪeɪt] vt anekeln

nautical |'nɔːtɪkl] adj nautisch; See-;
(expression) seemännisch

naval |'neɪvl] adj Marine-, Flotten-; **~ officer**
n Marineoffizier m

nave |neɪv] n Kirchen(haupt)schiff nt

navel |'neɪvl] n Nabel m

navigate |'nævɪgeɪt] vi navigieren;
navigation |nævɪ'geɪʃən] n Navigation f;
navigator |'nævɪgeɪtəʳ] n Steuermann m;
(AVIAT) Navigator m; (AUT) Beifahrer(in) m(f)

navvy |'nævɪ] (BRIT) n Straßenarbeiter m

navy |'neɪvɪ] n (Kriegs)marine f ♦ adj (also: ~
blue) marineblau

Nazi |'nɑːtsɪ] n Nazi m

NB abbr (= nota bene) NB

near |nɪəʳ] adj nah ♦ adv in der Nähe ♦ prep
(also: **~ to**: space) in der Nähe +gen; (also:
time) um +acc … herum ♦ vt sich nähern
+dat; **a ~ miss** knapp daneben; **~by** adj
nahe (gelegen) ♦ adv in der Nähe; **~ly** adv
fast; **I ~ly fell** ich wäre fast gefallen; **~side** n
(AUT) Beifahrerseite f ♦ adj auf der

Beifahrerseite; **~-sighted** adj kurzsichtig

neat |niːt] adj (tidy) ordentlich; (solution)
sauber; (pure) pur; **~ly** adv (tidily)
ordentlich

necessarily |'nesɪsrɪlɪ] adv unbedingt

necessary |'nesɪsrɪ] adj notwendig, nötig; **he
did all that was ~** er erledigte alles, was
nötig war; **it is ~ to/that …** man muss …

necessitate |nɪ'sesɪteɪt] vt erforderlich
machen

necessity |nɪ'sesɪtɪ] n (need) Not f;
(compulsion) Notwendigkeit f; **necessities**
npl (things needed) das Notwendigste

neck |nek] n Hals m ♦ vi (inf) knutschen; **~
and ~** Kopf an Kopf; **~lace** |'neklɪs] n
Halskette f; **~line** n Ausschnitt m;
~tie |'nektaɪ] (US) n Krawatte f

née |neɪ] adj geborene

need |niːd] n Bedürfnis nt; (lack) Mangel m;
(necessity) Notwendigkeit f; (poverty) Not f
♦ vt brauchen; **I ~ to do it** ich muss es tun;
you don't ~ to go du brauchst nicht zu
gehen

needle |'niːdl] n Nadel f ♦ vt (fig: inf) ärgern

needless |'niːdlɪs] adj unnötig; **~ to say**
natürlich

needlework |'niːdlwɜːk] n Handarbeit f

needn't |'niːdnt] = need not

needy |'niːdɪ] adj bedürftig

negative |'negətɪv] n (PHOT) Negativ nt ♦ adj
negativ; (answer) abschlägig; **~ equity** n
Differenz zwischen gefallenem Wert und
hypothekarischer Belastung eines
Wohneigentums

neglect |nɪ'glekt] vt vernachlässigen ♦ n
Vernachlässigung f; **~ed** adj vernachlässigt

negligee |'neglɪʒeɪ] n Negligee nt, Negligé nt

negligence |'neglɪdʒəns] n Nachlässigkeit f

negligible |'neglɪdʒɪbl] adj unbedeutend,
geringfügig

negotiable |nɪ'gəuʃɪəbl] adj (cheque)
übertragbar, einlösbar

negotiate |nɪ'gəuʃɪeɪt] vi verhandeln ♦ vt
(treaty) abschließen; (difficulty) überwinden;
(corner) nehmen; **negotiation**
|nɪgəuʃɪ'eɪʃən] n Verhandlung f; **negotiator**
n Unterhändler m

Negro |'niːgrəu] n Neger m

neigh |neɪ] vi wiehern

neighbour |'neɪbəʳ] (US **neighbor**) n
Nachbar(in) m(f); **~hood** n Nachbarschaft
f; Umgebung f; **~ing** adj benachbart,
angrenzend; **~ly** adj (person, attitude)
nachbarlich

neither |'naɪðəʳ] adj, pron keine(r, s) (von
beiden) ♦ conj: **he can't do it, and ~ can I**
er kann es nicht und ich auch nicht ♦ adv: **~
good nor bad** weder gut noch schlecht; **~
story is true** keine der beiden Geschichten
stimmt

neon |'niːɔn] n Neon nt; **~ light** n

Neonlampe f

nephew ['nevju:] n Neffe m

nerve [nə:v] n Nerv m; (courage) Mut m; (impudence) Frechheit f; **to have a fit of ~s** in Panik geraten; **~-racking** adj nervenaufreibend

nervous ['nə:vəs] adj (of the nerves) Nerven-; (timid) nervös, ängstlich; **~ breakdown** n Nervenzusammenbruch m; **~ness** n Nervosität f

nest [nest] n Nest nt ♦ vi nisten; **~ egg** n (fig) Notgroschen m

nestle ['nesl] vi sich kuscheln

net [net] n Netz nt ♦ adj netto, Netto- ♦ vt netto einnehmen; **the N~** (INTERNET) das Internet; **~ball** n Netzball m

Netherlands ['neðələndz] npl: **the ~** die Niederlande pl

nett [net] adj = **net**

netting ['netɪŋ] n Netz(werk) nt

nettle ['netl] n Nessel f

network ['netwə:k] n Netz nt

neurotic [njuə'rɒtɪk] adj neurotisch

neuter ['nju:təʳ] adj (BIOL) geschlechtslos; (GRAM) sächlich ♦ vt kastrieren

neutral ['nju:trəl] adj neutral ♦ n (AUT) Leerlauf m; **~ity** [nju:'trælɪtɪ] n Neutralität f; **~ize** vt (fig) ausgleichen

never ['nevəʳ] adv nie(mals); **I ~ went** ich bin gar nicht gegangen; **~ in my life** nie im Leben; **~-ending** adj endlos, **~theless** [nevəðə'les] adv trotzdem, dennoch

new [nju:] adj neu; **N~ Age** adj Newage-, New-Age-; **~born** adj neugeboren; **~comer** ['nju:kʌməʳ] n Neuankömmling m; **~-fangled** (pej) adj neumodisch; **~-found** adj neu entdeckt; **~ly** adv frisch, neu; **~ly-weds** npl Frischvermählte pl; **~ moon** n Neumond m

news [nju:z] n Nachricht f; (RAD, TV) Nachrichten pl; **a piece of ~** eine Nachricht; **~ agency** n Nachrichtenagentur f; **~agent** (BRIT) n Zeitungshändler m; **~caster** n Nachrichtensprecher(in) m(f); **~ flash** n Kurzmeldung f; **~letter** n Rundschreiben nt; **~paper** n Zeitung f; **~print** n Zeitungspapier nt; **~reader** n = **newscaster**; **~reel** n Wochenschau f; **~ stand** n Zeitungsstand m

newt [nju:t] n Wassermolch m

New Year n Neujahr nt; **~'s Day** n Neujahrstag m; **~'s Eve** n Silvester(abend m) nt

New Zealand [-'zi:lənd] n Neuseeland nt; **~er** n Neuseeländer(in) m(f)

next [nekst] adj nächste(r, s) ♦ adv (after) dann, darauf; (~ time) das nächste Mal; **the ~ day** am nächsten or folgenden Tag; **~ time** das nächste Mal; **~ year** nächstes Jahr; **~ door** adv nebenan ♦ adj (neighbour, flat) von nebenan; **~ of kin** n nächste(r)

Verwandte(r) mf; **~ to** prep neben; **~ to nothing** so gut wie nichts

NHS n abbr = **National Health Service**

nib [nɪb] n Spitze f

nibble ['nɪbl] vt knabbern an +dat

nice [naɪs] adj (person) nett; (thing) schön; (subtle) fein; **~-looking** adj gut aussehend; **~ly** adv gut, nett; **~ties** ['naɪsɪtɪz] npl Feinheiten pl

nick [nɪk] n Einkerbung f ♦ vt (inf: steal) klauen; **in the ~ of time** gerade rechtzeitig

nickel ['nɪkl] n Nickel nt; (US) Nickel m (5 cents)

nickname ['nɪkneɪm] n Spitzname m ♦ vt taufen

nicotine patch ['nɪkəti:n-] n Nikotinpflaster nt

niece [ni:s] n Nichte f

Nigeria [naɪ'dʒɪərɪə] n Nigeria nt

niggling ['nɪglɪŋ] adj pedantisch; (doubt, worry) quälend

night [naɪt] n Nacht f; (evening) Abend m; **the ~ before last** vorletzte Nacht; **at** or **by ~** (before midnight) abends; (after midnight) nachts; **~cap** n (drink) Schlummertrunk m; **~club** n Nachtlokal nt; **~dress** n Nachthemd nt; **~fall** n Einbruch m der Nacht; **~ gown** n = **nightdress**; **~ie** (inf) n Nachthemd nt

nightingale ['naɪtɪŋgeɪl] n Nachtigall f

night: **~life** ['naɪtlaɪf] n Nachtleben nt; **~ly** ['naɪtlɪ] adj, adv jeden Abend; jede Nacht; **~mare** ['naɪtmeəʳ] n Albtraum m; **~ porter** n Nachtportier m; **~ school** n Abendschule f; **~ shift** n Nachtschicht f; **~time** n Nacht f

nil [nɪl] n Null f

Nile [naɪl] n: **the ~** der Nil

nimble ['nɪmbl] adj beweglich

nine [naɪn] num neun; **~teen** num neunzehn; **~ty** num neunzig

ninth [naɪnθ] adj neunte(r, s)

nip [nɪp] vt kneifen ♦ n Kneifen nt

nipple ['nɪpl] n Brustwarze f

nippy ['nɪpɪ] (inf) adj (person) flink; (BRIT: car) flott; (: cold) frisch

nitrogen ['naɪtrədʒən] n Stickstoff m

KEYWORD

no [nəu] (pl **noes**) adv (opposite of yes) nein; **to answer no** (to question) mit Nein antworten; (to request) Nein or nein sagen; **no thank you** nein, danke
♦ adj (not any) kein(e); **I have no money/ time** ich habe kein Geld/keine Zeit; **"no smoking"** „Rauchen verboten"
♦ n Nein nt; (no vote) Neinstimme f

nobility [nəu'bɪlɪtɪ] n Adel m

noble ['nəubl] adj (rank) adlig; (splendid) nobel, edel

nobody ['nəubədɪ] *pron* niemand, keiner

nocturnal [nɔk'tɜːnl] *adj* (*tour, visit*) nächtlich; (*animal*) Nacht-

nod [nɔd] *vi* nicken ♦ *vt* nicken mit ♦ *n* Nicken *nt*; ~ **off** *vi* einnicken

noise [nɔɪz] *n* (*sound*) Geräusch *nt*; (*unpleasant, loud*) Lärm *m*; **noisy** ['nɔɪzɪ] *adj* laut; (*crowd*) lärmend

nominal ['nɔmɪnl] *adj* nominell

nominate ['nɔmɪneɪt] *vt* (*suggest*) vorschlagen; (*in election*) aufstellen; (*appoint*) ernennen; **nomination** [nɔmɪ'neɪʃən] *n* (*election*) Nominierung *f*; (*appointment*) Ernennung *f*; **nominee** [nɔmɪ'niː] *n* Kandidat(in) *m(f)*

non... [nɔn] *prefix* Nicht-, un-; ~**-alcoholic** *adj* alkoholfrei

nonchalant ['nɔnʃələnt] *adj* lässig

non-committal [nɔnkə'mɪtl] *adj* (*reserved*) zurückhaltend; (*uncommitted*) unverbindlich

nondescript ['nɔndɪskrɪpt] *adj* mittelmäßig

none [nʌn] *adj*, *pron* kein(e, er, es) ♦ *adv*: **he's ~ the worse for it** es hat ihm nicht geschadet; ~ **of you** keiner von euch; **I've ~ left** ich habe keinen mehr

nonentity [nɔ'nentɪtɪ] *n* Null *f* (*inf*)

nonetheless [nʌnðə'les] *adv* nichtsdestoweniger

non-existent [nɔnɪg'zɪstənt] *adj* nicht vorhanden

non-fiction [nɔn'fɪkʃən] *n* Sachbücher *pl*

nonplussed [nɔn'plʌst] *adj* verdutzt

nonsense ['nɔnsəns] *n* Unsinn *m*

non: ~**-smoker** *n* Nichtraucher(in) *m(f)*; ~**-smoking** *adj* Nichtraucher-; ~**-stick** *adj* (*pan, surface*) Teflon- ®; ~**-stop** *adj* Nonstop-, Non-Stop-

noodles ['nuːdlz] *npl* Nudeln *pl*

nook [nuk] *n* Winkel *m*; ~**s and crannies** Ecken und Winkel

noon [nuːn] *n* (12 Uhr) Mittag *m*

no one ['nəuwʌn] *pron* = **nobody**

noose [nuːs] *n* Schlinge *f*

nor [nɔːʳ] *conj* = **neither** ♦ *adv see* **neither**

norm [nɔːm] *n* (*convention*) Norm *f*; (*rule, requirement*) Vorschrift *f*

normal ['nɔːməl] *adj* normal; ~**ly** *adv* normal; (*usually*) normalerweise

Normandy ['nɔːməndɪ] *n* Normandie *f*

north [nɔːθ] *n* Norden *m* ♦ *adj* nördlich, Nord- ♦ *adv* nördlich, nach *or* im Norden; **N~ Africa** *n* Nordafrika *nt*; **N~ America** *n* Nordamerika *nt*; ~**-east** *n* Nordosten *m*; ~**erly** ['nɔːðəlɪ] *adj* nördlich; ~**ern** ['nɔːðən] *adj* nördlich, Nord-; **N~ern Ireland** *n* Nordirland *nt*; **N~ Pole** *n* Nordpol *m*; **N~ Sea** *n* Nordsee *f*; ~**ward(s)** ['nɔːθwəd(z)] *adv* nach Norden; ~**-west** *n* Nordwesten *m*

Norway ['nɔːweɪ] *n* Norwegen *nt*

Norwegian [nɔː'wiːdʒən] *adj* norwegisch ♦ *n* Norweger(in) *m(f)*; (*LING*) Norwegisch *nt*

nose [nəuz] *n* Nase *f* ♦ *vi*: **to ~ about** herumschnüffeln; ~**bleed** *n* Nasenbluten *nt*; ~ **dive** *n* Sturzflug *m*; ~**y** *adj* = **nosy**

nostalgia [nɔs'tældʒɪə] *n* Nostalgie *f*; **nostalgic** *adj* nostalgisch

nostril ['nɔstrɪl] *n* Nasenloch *nt*

nosy ['nəuzɪ] (*inf*) *adj* neugierig

not [nɔt] *adv* nicht; **he is ~** *or* **isn't here** er ist nicht hier; **it's too late, isn't it?** es ist zu spät, oder *or* nicht wahr?; ~ **yet/now** noch nicht/nicht jetzt; *see also* **all**; **only**

notably ['nəutəblɪ] *adv* (*especially*) besonders; (*noticeably*) bemerkenswert

notary ['nəutərɪ] *n* Notar(in) *m(f)*

notch [nɔtʃ] *n* Kerbe *f*, Einschnitt *m*

note [nəut] *n* (*MUS*) Note *f*, Ton *m*; (*short letter*) Nachricht *f*; (*POL*) Note *f*; (*comment, attention*) Notiz *f*; (*of lecture etc*) Aufzeichnung *f*; (*banknote*) Schein *m*; (*fame*) Ruf *m* ♦ *vt* (*observe*) bemerken (*also:* ~ **down**) notieren; ~**book** *n* Notizbuch *nt*; ~**d** *adj* bekannt; (*noticeable*) bemerkenswert; ~**pad** *n* Notizblock *m*; ~**paper** *n* Briefpapier *nt*

nothing ['nʌθɪŋ] *n* nichts; ~ **new/much** nichts Neues/nicht viel; **for ~** umsonst

notice ['nəutɪs] *n* (*announcement*) Bekanntmachung *f*; (*warning*) Ankündigung *f*; (*dismissal*) Kündigung *f* ♦ *vt* bemerken; **to take ~ of** beachten; **at short ~** kurzfristig; **until further ~** bis auf weiteres; **to hand in one's ~** kündigen; ~**able** *adj* merklich; ~**board** *n* Anschlagtafel *f*

notify ['nəutɪfaɪ] *vt* benachrichtigen

notion ['nəuʃən] *n* Idee *f*

notorious [nəu'tɔːrɪəs] *adj* berüchtigt

notwithstanding [nɔtwɪθ'stændɪŋ] *adv* trotzdem; ~ **this** ungeachtet dessen

nought [nɔːt] *n* Null *f*

noun [naun] *n* Substantiv *nt*

nourish ['nʌrɪʃ] *vt* nähren; ~**ing** *adj* nahrhaft; ~**ment** *n* Nahrung *f*

novel ['nɔvl] *n* Roman *m* ♦ *adj* neu(artig); ~**ist** *n* Schriftsteller(in) *m(f)*; ~**ty** *n* Neuheit *f*

November [nəu'vembəʳ] *n* November *m*

novice ['nɔvɪs] *n* Neuling *m*

now [nau] *adv* jetzt; **right ~** jetzt, gerade; **by ~** inzwischen; **just ~** gerade; ~ **and then**, ~ **and again** ab und zu, manchmal; **from ~ on** von jetzt an; ~**adays** *adv* heutzutage

nowhere ['nəuwɛəʳ] *adv* nirgends

nozzle ['nɔzl] *n* Düse *f*

nuclear ['njuːklɪəʳ] *adj* (*energy etc*) Atom-, Kern-

nuclei ['njuːklɪaɪ] *npl of* **nucleus**

nucleus ['njuːklɪəs] *n* Kern *m*

nude [njuːd] *adj* nackt ♦ *n* (*ART*) Akt *m*; **in the ~** nackt

nudge [nʌdʒ] *vt* leicht anstoßen

nudist ['njuːdɪst] *n* Nudist(in) *m(f)*

nudity ['njuːdɪtɪ] *n* Nacktheit *f*

nuisance ['njuːsns] *n* Ärgernis *nt*; **what a ~!**

wie ärgerlich!

nuke [njuːk] (inf) n Kernkraftwerk nt ♦ vt atomar vernichten

null [nʌl] adj: ~ **and void** null und nichtig

numb [nʌm] adj taub, gefühllos ♦ vt betäuben

number ['nʌmbəʳ] n Nummer f; (numeral also) Zahl f; (quantity) (An)zahl f ♦ vt nummerieren; (amount to) sein; **to be ~ed among** gezählt werden zu; **a ~ of** (several) einige; **they were ten in ~** sie waren zehn an der Zahl; ~ **plate** (BRIT) n (AUT) Nummernschild nt

numeral ['njuːmərəl] n Ziffer f

numerate ['njuːmərɪt] adj rechenkundig

numerical [njuːˈmerɪkl] adj (order) zahlenmäßig

numerous ['njuːmərəs] adj zahlreich

nun [nʌn] n Nonne f

nurse [nɜːs] n Krankenschwester f; (for children) Kindermädchen nt ♦ vt (patient) pflegen; (doubt etc) hegen

nursery ['nɜːsərɪ] n (for children) Kinderzimmer nt; (for plants) Gärtnerei f; (for trees) Baumschule f; ~ **rhyme** n Kinderreim m; ~ **school** n Kindergarten m; ~ **slope** (BRIT) n (SKI) Idiotenhügel m (inf), Anfängerhügel m

nursing ['nɜːsɪŋ] n (profession) Krankenpflege f; ~ **home** n Privatklinik f

nurture ['nɜːtʃəʳ] vt aufziehen

nut [nʌt] n Nuss f; (TECH) Schraubenmutter f; (inf) Verrückte(r) mf; **he's ~s** er ist verrückt; **~crackers** ['nʌtkrækəz] npl Nussknacker m

nutmeg ['nʌtmeg] n Muskat(nuss f) m

nutrient ['njuːtrɪənt] n Nährstoff m

nutrition [njuːˈtrɪʃən] n Nahrung f; **nutritious** [njuːˈtrɪʃəs] adj nahrhaft

nutshell ['nʌtʃel] n Nussschale f; **in a ~** (fig) kurz gesagt

nutter ['nʌtəʳ] (BRIT: inf) n Spinner(in) m(f)

nylon ['naɪlɔn] n Nylon nt ♦ adj Nylon-

O, o

oak [əuk] n Eiche f ♦ adj Eichen(holz)-

OAP n abbr = **old-age pensioner**

oar [ɔːʳ] n Ruder nt

oases [əuˈeɪsiːz] npl of **oasis**

oasis [əuˈeɪsɪs] n Oase f

oath [əuθ] n (statement) Eid m, Schwur m; (swearword) Fluch m

oatmeal ['əutmiːl] n Haferschrot m

oats [əuts] npl Hafer m

obedience [əˈbiːdɪəns] n Gehorsam m

obedient [əˈbiːdɪənt] adj gehorsam

obesity [əuˈbiːsɪtɪ] n Fettleibigkeit f

obey [əˈbeɪ] vt, vb: **to ~** (sb) (jdm) gehorchen

obituary [əˈbɪtjuərɪ] n Nachruf m

object [n ˈɔbdʒɪkt, vb əbˈdʒekt] n (thing) Gegenstand m, Objekt nt; (purpose) Ziel nt ♦ vi dagegen sein; **expense is no ~** Ausgaben spielen keine Rolle; **I ~!** ich protestiere!; **to ~ to sth** Einwände gegen etw haben; (morally) Anstoß an etw acc nehmen; **to ~ that** einwenden, dass; **~ion** [əbˈdʒekʃən] n (reason against) Einwand m, Einspruch m; (dislike) Abneigung f; **I have no ~ion to ...** ich habe nichts gegen ... einzuwenden; **~ionable** [əbˈdʒekʃənəbl] adj nicht einwandfrei; (language) anstößig

objective [əbˈdʒektɪv] n Ziel nt ♦ adj objektiv

obligation [ɔblɪˈgeɪʃən] n Verpflichtung f; **without ~** unverbindlich; **obligatory** [əˈblɪgətərɪ] adj obligatorisch

oblige [əˈblaɪdʒ] vt (compel) zwingen; (do a favour) einen Gefallen tun +dat; **to be ~d to sb for sth** jdm für etw verbunden sein

obliging [əˈblaɪdʒɪŋ] adj entgegenkommend

oblique [əˈbliːk] adj schräg, schief ♦ n Schrägstrich m

obliterate [əˈblɪtəreɪt] vt auslöschen

oblivion [əˈblɪvɪən] n Vergessenheit f

oblivious [əˈblɪvɪəs] adj nicht bewusst

oblong ['ɔblɔŋ] n Rechteck nt ♦ adj länglich

obnoxious [əbˈnɔkʃəs] adj widerlich

oboe ['əubəu] n Oboe f

obscene [əbˈsiːn] adj obszön; **obscenity** [əbˈsenɪtɪ] n Obszönität f; **obscenities** npl (oaths) Zoten pl

obscure [əbˈskjuəʳ] adj unklar; (indistinct) undeutlich; (unknown) unbekannt, obskur; (dark) düster ♦ vt verdunkeln; (view) verbergen; (confuse) verwirren; **obscurity** [əbˈskjuərɪtɪ] n Unklarheit f; (darkness) Dunkelheit f

observance [əbˈzɜːvəns] n Befolgung f

observant [əbˈzɜːvənt] adj aufmerksam

observation [ɔbzəˈveɪʃən] n (noticing) Beobachtung f; (surveillance) Überwachung f; (remark) Bemerkung f

observatory [əbˈzɜːvətrɪ] n Sternwarte f, Observatorium nt

observe [əbˈzɜːv] vt (notice) bemerken; (watch) beobachten; (customs) einhalten; **~r** n Beobachter(in) m(f)

obsess [əbˈses] vt verfolgen, quälen; **~ion** [əbˈseʃən] n Besessenheit f, Wahn m; **~ive** adj krankhaft

obsolete ['ɔbsəliːt] adj überholt, veraltet

obstacle ['ɔbstəkl] n Hindernis nt; ~ **race** n Hindernisrennen nt

obstetrics [ɔbˈstetrɪks] n Geburtshilfe f

obstinate ['ɔbstɪnɪt] adj hartnäckig, stur

obstruct [əbˈstrʌkt] vt versperren; (pipe) verstopfen; (hinder) hemmen; **~ion** [əbˈstrʌkʃən] n Versperrung f; Verstopfung f; (obstacle) Hindernis nt

obtain [əbˈteɪn] vt erhalten, bekommen; (result) erzielen

obtrusive [əbˈtruːsɪv] adj aufdringlich

obvious ['ɔbvɪəs] adj offenbar, offensichtlich;
~**ly** adv offensichtlich

occasion [ə'keɪʒən] n Gelegenheit f; (special
event) Ereignis nt; (reason) Anlass m ♦ vt
veranlassen; ~**al** adj gelegentlich; ~**ally** adv
gelegentlich

occupant ['ɔkjupənt] n Inhaber(in) m(f); (of
house) Bewohner(in) m(f)

occupation [ɔkju'peɪʃən] n (employment)
Tätigkeit f, Beruf m; (pastime) Beschäftigung
f; (of country) Besetzung f, Okkupation f;
~**al hazard** n Berufsrisiko nt

occupier ['ɔkjupaɪər] n Bewohner(in) m(f)

occupy ['ɔkjupaɪ] vt (take possession of)
besetzen; (seat) belegen; (live in) bewohnen;
(position, office) bekleiden; (position in sb's
life) einnehmen; (time) beanspruchen; **to ~
o.s. with sth** sich mit etw beschäftigen; **to
~ o.s. by doing sth** sich damit
beschäftigen, etw zu tun

occur [ə'kɜːr] vi vorkommen; **to ~ to sb** jdm
einfallen; ~**rence** n (event) Ereignis nt;
(appearing) Auftreten nt

ocean ['əuʃən] n Ozean m, Meer nt; ~**-going**
adj Hochsee-

o'clock [ə'klɔk] adv: **it is 5** ~ es ist 5 Uhr

OCR n abbr = **optical character reader**

octagonal [ɔk'tægənl] adj achteckig

October [ɔk'təubər] n Oktober m

octopus ['ɔktəpəs] n Krake f; (small)
Tintenfisch m

odd [ɔd] adj (strange) sonderbar; (not even)
ungerade; (sock etc) einzeln; (surplus) übrig;
60-~ so um die 60; **at ~ times** ab und zu;
to be the ~ one out (person) das fünfte Rad
am Wagen sein; (thing) nicht dazugehören;
~**ity** n (strangeness) Merkwürdigkeit f;
(queer person) seltsame(r) Kauz m; (thing)
Kuriosität f; ~**-job man** (irreg) n Mädchen
nt für alles; ~ **jobs** npl gelegentlich
anfallende Arbeiten; ~**ly** adv seltsam;
~**ments** npl Reste pl; ~**s** npl Chancen pl;
(betting) Gewinnchancen pl; **it makes no ~s**
es spielt keine Rolle; **at ~s** uneinig; ~**s and
ends** npl Krimskrams m

odometer [ɔ'dɔmɪtər] n (esp US) n Tacho(meter) m

odour ['əudər] (US **odor**) n Geruch m

```
KEYWORD
```

of [ɔv, əv] prep **1** von +dat; use of gen; **the
history of Germany** die Geschichte
Deutschlands; **a friend of ours** ein Freund
von uns; **a boy of 10** ein 10-jähriger Junge;
that was kind of you das war sehr
freundlich von Ihnen
2 (expressing quantity, amount, dates etc): **a
kilo of flour** ein Kilo Mehl; **how much of
this do you need?** wie viel brauchen Sie
(davon)?; **there were 3 of them** (people) sie
waren zu dritt; (objects) es gab 3 (davon); **a
cup of tea/vase of flowers** eine Tasse Tee/

Vase mit Blumen; **the 5th of July** der 5. Juli
3 (from, out of) aus; **a bridge made of
wood** eine Holzbrücke, eine Brücke aus Holz

off [ɔf] adj, adv (absent) weg, fort; (switch)
aus(geschaltet), ab(geschaltet); (BRIT: food:
bad) schlecht; (cancelled) abgesagt ♦ prep
von +dat; **to be** ~ (to leave) gehen; **to be** ~
sick krank sein; **a day** ~ ein freier Tag; **to
have an** ~ **day** einen schlechten Tag haben;
he had his coat ~ er hatte seinen Mantel
aus; **10%** ~ (COMM) 10% Rabatt; **5 km** ~
(the road) 5 km (von der Straße) entfernt;
~ **the coast** vor der Küste; **I'm** ~ **meat** (no
longer eat it) ich esse kein Fleisch mehr; (no
longer like it) ich mag kein Fleisch mehr; **on
the** ~ **chance** auf gut Glück

offal ['ɔfl] n Innereien pl

off-colour ['ɔf'kʌlər] adj nicht wohl

offence [ə'fɛns] (US **offense**) n (crime)
Vergehen nt, Straftat f; (insult) Beleidigung
f; **to take** ~ **at** gekränkt sein wegen

offend [ə'fɛnd] vt beleidigen; ~**er** n
Gesetzesübertreter m

offense [ə'fɛns] (US) n = **offence**

offensive [ə'fɛnsɪv] adj (unpleasant) übel,
abstoßend; (weapon) Kampf-; (remark)
verletzend ♦ n Angriff m

offer ['ɔfər] n Angebot f ♦ vt anbieten;
(opinion) äußern; (resistance) leisten; **on** ~
zum Verkauf angeboten; ~**ing** n Gabe f

offhand [ɔf'hænd] adj lässig ♦ adv ohne
weiteres

office ['ɔfɪs] n Büro nt; (position) Amt nt;
doctor's ~ (US) Praxis f; **to take** ~ sein Amt
antreten; (POL) die Regierung übernehmen;
~ **automation** n Büroautomatisierung f; ~
block (US ~ **building**) n Büro(hoch)haus nt;
~ **hours** npl Dienstzeit f; (US: MED)
Sprechstunde f

officer ['ɔfɪsər] n (MIL) Offizier m; (public ~)
Beamte(r) m

official [ə'fɪʃl] adj offiziell, amtlich ♦ n
Beamte(r) m; ~**dom** n Beamtentum nt

officiate [ə'fɪʃɪeɪt] vi amtieren

officious [ə'fɪʃəs] adj aufdringlich

offing ['ɔfɪŋ] n: **in the** ~ in (Aus)sicht

off: ~**-licence** (BRIT) n (shop) Wein- und
Spirituosenhandlung f; ~**-line** adj (COMPUT)
Offline- ♦ adv (COMPUT) offline; ~**-peak** adj
(charges) verbilligt; ~**-putting** (BRIT) adj
(person, remark etc) abstoßend; ~**-road
vehicle** n Geländefahrzeug nt; ~**-season**
adj außer Saison; ~ **set** (irreg: like **set**) vt
ausgleichen ♦ n (also: ~**set printing**)
Offset(druck) m; ~**shoot** n (fig: of
organization) Zweig m; (: of discussion etc)
Randergebnis nt; ~**shore** adv in einiger
Entfernung von der Küste ♦ adj küstennah,
Küsten-; ~**side** adj (SPORT) im Abseits ♦ adv
abseits ♦ n (AUT) Fahrerseite f; ~**spring** n

Nachkommenschaft f; (one) Sprössling m;
~**stage** adv hinter den Kulissen; ~-**the-cuff**
adj unvorbereitet, aus dem Stegreif; ~-**the-peg** (US ~-**the-rack**) adv von der Stange; ~-**white** adj naturweiß

Oftel [ˈɔftɛl] n Überwachungsgremium zum
Verbraucherschutz nach Privatisierung der
Telekommunikationsindustrie

often [ˈɔfn] adv oft

Ofwat [ˈɔfwɔt] n Überwachungsgremium zum
Verbraucherschutz nach Privatisierung der
Wasserindustrie

ogle [ˈəʊgl] vt liebäugeln mit

oil [ɔɪl] n Öl nt ♦ vt ölen; ~**can** n Ölkännchen
nt; ~**field** n Ölfeld nt; ~ **filter** n (AUT)
Ölfilter m; ~-**fired** adj Öl-; ~ **painting** n
Ölgemälde nt; ~ **rig** n Ölplattform f;
~**skins** npl Ölzeug nt; ~ **slick** n
Ölteppich m; ~ **tanker** n (Öl)tanker m; ~
well n Ölquelle f; ~**y** adj ölig; (dirty)
ölbeschmiert

ointment [ˈɔɪntmənt] n Salbe f

O.K. [ˈəʊˈkeɪ] excl in Ordnung, O. K., o. k.
♦ adj in Ordnung ♦ vt genehmigen

okay [ˈəʊˈkeɪ] = **O.K.**

old [əʊld] adj alt; **how ~ are you?** wie alt bist
du?; **he's 10 years ~** er ist 10 Jahre alt; ~**er
brother** ältere(r) Bruder m; ~ **age** n Alter
nt; ~-**age pensioner** (BRIT) n Rentner(in)
m(f); ~-**fashioned** adj altmodisch

olive [ˈɔlɪv] n (fruit) Olive f; (colour) Olive nt
♦ adj Oliven-; (coloured) olivenfarbig; ~ **oil** n
Olivenöl m

Olympic [əʊˈlɪmpɪk] adj olympisch; **the ~
Games, the ~s** die Olympischen Spiele

omelet(te) [ˈɔmlɪt] n Omelett nt

omen [ˈəʊmən] n Omen nt

ominous [ˈɔmɪnəs] adj bedrohlich

omission [əʊˈmɪʃən] n Auslassung f;
(neglect) Versäumnis nt

omit [əʊˈmɪt] vt auslassen; (fail to do)
versäumen

KEYWORD

on [ɔn] prep 1 (indicating position) auf +dat;
(with vb of motion) auf +acc; (on vertical
surface, part of body) an +dat/acc; **it's on
the table** es ist auf dem Tisch; **she put the
book on the table** sie legte das Buch auf
den Tisch; **on the left** links

2 (indicating means, method, condition etc):
on foot (go, be) zu Fuß; **on the train/plane**
(go) mit dem Zug/Flugzeug; (be) im Zug/
Flugzeug; **on the telephone/television** am
Telefon/im Fernsehen; **to be on drugs**
Drogen nehmen; **to be on holiday/
business** im Urlaub/auf Geschäftsreise sein

3 (referring to time): **on Friday** (am) Freitag;
on Fridays freitags; **on June 20th** am 20.
Juni; **a week on Friday** Freitag in einer
Woche; **on arrival he ...** als er ankam, ... er ...

4 (about, concerning) über +acc
♦ adv 1 (referring to dress) an; **she put her
boots/hat on** sie zog ihre Stiefel an/setzte
ihren Hut auf

2 (further, continuously) weiter; **to walk on**
weitergehen
♦ adj 1 (functioning, in operation: machine,
TV, light) an; (: tap) aufgedreht; (: brakes)
angezogen; **is the meeting still on?** findet
die Versammlung noch statt?; **there's a
good film on** es läuft ein guter Film

2: **that's not on!** (inf: of behaviour) das
liegt nicht drin!

once [wʌns] adv einmal ♦ conj wenn ...
einmal; ~ **he had left/it was done**
nachdem er gegangen war/es fertig war; **at
~** sofort; (at the same time) gleichzeitig; ~ **a
week** einmal in der Woche; ~ **more** noch
einmal; ~ **and for all** ein für alle Mal; ~
upon a time es war einmal

oncoming [ˈɔnkʌmɪŋ] adj (traffic) Gegen-,
entgegenkommend

KEYWORD

one [wʌn] num eins; (with noun, referring
back to noun) ein/eine/ein; **it is one
(o'clock)** es ist eins, es ist ein Uhr; **one
hundred and fifty** einhundertfünfzig
♦ adj 1 (sole) einzige(r, s); **the one book
which** das einzige Buch, welches

2 (same) derselbe/dieselbe/dasselbe; **they
came in the one car** sie kamen alle in dem
einen Auto

3 (indef): **one day I discovered ...** eines
Tages bemerkte ich ...
♦ pron 1 eine(r, s); **do you have a red one?**
haben Sie einen roten/eine rote/ein rotes?;
this one diese(r, s); **that one** der/die/das;
which one? welche(r, s)?; **one by one**
einzeln

2: **one another** einander; **do you two ever
see one another?** seht ihr beide euch
manchmal?

3 (impers): man; **one never knows** man
kann nie wissen; **to cut one's finger** sich in
den Finger schneiden

one: ~-**armed bandit** n einarmiger Bandit
m; ~-**day excursion** (US) n (day return)
Tagesrückfahrkarte f; ~-**man** adj Einmann-;
~-**man band** n Einmannkapelle f; (fig)
Einmannbetrieb m; ~-**off** (BRIT: inf) n
Einzelfall m

oneself [wʌnˈsɛlf] pron (reflexive: after prep)
sich; (~ personally) sich selbst or selber;
(emphatic) (sich) selbst; **to hurt ~** sich
verletzen

one: ~-**sided** adj (argument) einseitig; ~-**to-~**
adj (relationship) eins-zu-eins; ~-
upmanship n die Kunst, anderen um eine

Nasenlänge voraus zu sein; **~-way** adj
(street) Einbahn-
ongoing ['ɔngəʊɪŋ] adj momentan;
(progressing) sich entwickelnd
onion ['ʌnjən] n Zwiebel f
on-line ['ɔnlaɪn] adj (COMPUT) Online-
onlooker ['ɔnlʊkəʳ] n Zuschauer(in) m(f)
only ['əʊnlɪ] adv nur, bloß ♦ adj einzige(r, s)
♦ conj nur, bloß; **an ~ child** ein Einzelkind;
not ~ ... but also ... nicht nur ... sondern
auch ...
onset ['ɔnset] n (start) Beginn m
onshore ['ɔnʃɔːʳ] adj (wind) See-
onslaught ['ɔnslɔːt] n Angriff m
onto ['ɔntu] prep = **on to**
onus ['əʊnəs] n Last f, Pflicht f
onward(s) ['ɔnwəd(z)] adv (place) voran,
vorwärts; **from that day ~** von dem Tag an;
from today ~ ab heute
ooze [uːz] vi sickern
opaque [əʊ'peɪk] adj undurchsichtig
OPEC ['əʊpɛk] n abbr (= Organization of
Petroleum-Exporting Countries) OPEC f
open ['əʊpn] adj offen; (public) öffentlich;
(mind) aufgeschlossen ♦ vt öffnen,
aufmachen; (trial, motorway, account)
eröffnen ♦ vi (begin) anfangen; (shop)
aufmachen; (door, flower) aufgehen; (play)
Premiere haben; **in the ~ (air)** im Freien; **~
on to** vt fus sich öffnen auf +acc; **~ up** vt
(route) erschließen; (shop, prospects)
eröffnen ♦ vi öffnen; **~ing** n (hole) Öffnung
f; (beginning) Anfang m; (good chance)
Gelegenheit f; **~ing hours** npl
Öffnungszeiten pl; **~ learning centre** n
Weiterbildungseinrichtung auf Teilzeitbasis; **~ly**
adv offen; (publicly) öffentlich; **~-minded**
adj aufgeschlossen; **~-necked** adj offen; **~-
plan** adj (office) Großraum-; (flat etc) offen
angelegt
opera ['ɔpərə] n Oper f; **~ house** n
Opernhaus nt
operate ['ɔpəreɪt] vt (machine) bedienen;
(brakes, light) betätigen ♦ vi (machine)
laufen, in Betrieb sein; (person) arbeiten;
(MED): **to ~ on** operieren
operatic [ɔpə'rætɪk] adj Opern-
operating ['ɔpəreɪtɪŋ] adj: **~ table/theatre**
Operationstisch m/-saal m
operation [ɔpə'reɪʃən] n (working) Betrieb m;
(MED) Operation f; (undertaking)
Unternehmen nt; (MIL) Einsatz m; **to be in ~**
(JUR) in Kraft sein; (machine) in Betrieb sein;
to have an ~ (MED) operiert werden; **~al**
adj einsatzbereit
operative ['ɔpərətɪv] adj wirksam
operator ['ɔpəreɪtəʳ] n (of machine) Arbeiter
m; (TEL) Telefonist(in) m(f)
opinion [ə'pɪnjən] n Meinung f; **in my ~**
meiner Meinung nach; **~ated** adj
starrsinnig; **~ poll** n Meinungsumfrage f

opponent [ə'pəʊnənt] n Gegner m
opportunity [ɔpə'tjuːnɪtɪ] n Gelegenheit f,
Möglichkeit f; **to take the ~ of doing sth**
die Gelegenheit ergreifen, etw zu tun
oppose [ə'pəʊz] vt entgegentreten +dat;
(argument, idea) ablehnen; (plan)
bekämpfen; **to be ~d to sth** gegen etw
sein; **as ~d to** im Gegensatz zu; **opposing**
adj gegnerisch; (points of view)
entgegengesetzt
opposite ['ɔpəzɪt] adj (house)
gegenüberliegend; (direction)
entgegengesetzt ♦ adv gegenüber ♦ prep
gegenüber ♦ n Gegenteil nt
opposition [ɔpə'zɪʃən] n (resistance)
Widerstand m; (POL) Opposition f; (contrast)
Gegensatz m
oppress [ə'prɛs] vt unterdrücken; (heat etc)
bedrücken; **~ion** [ə'prɛʃən] n Unterdrückung
f; **~ive** adj (authority, law) repressiv; (burden,
thought) bedrückend; (heat) drückend
opt [ɔpt] vi: **to ~ for** sich entscheiden für; **to
~ to do sth** sich entscheiden, etw zu tun; **to
~ out of** sich drücken von +dat
optical ['ɔptɪkl] adj optisch; **~ character
reader** n optische(s) Lesegerät nt
optician [ɔp'tɪʃən] n Optiker m
optimist ['ɔptɪmɪst] n Optimist m; **~ic**
[ɔptɪ'mɪstɪk] adj optimistisch
optimum ['ɔptɪməm] adj optimal
option ['ɔpʃən] n Wahl f; (COMM) Option f;
to keep one's ~s open sich alle
Möglichkeiten offen halten; **~al** adj freiwillig;
(subject) wahlfrei; **~al extras** npl Extras auf
Wunsch
or [ɔːʳ] conj oder; **he could not read ~ write**
er konnte weder lesen noch schreiben; **~
else** sonst
oral ['ɔːrəl] adj mündlich ♦ n (exam)
mündliche Prüfung f
orange ['ɔrɪndʒ] n (fruit) Apfelsine f, Orange
f; (colour) Orange nt ♦ adj orange
orator ['ɔrətəʳ] n Redner(in) m(f)
orbit ['ɔːbɪt] n Umlaufbahn f
orbital (motorway) ['ɔːbɪtəl-] n
Ringautobahn f
orchard ['ɔːtʃəd] n Obstgarten m
orchestra ['ɔːkɪstrə] n Orchester nt; (US:
seating) Parkett nt; **~l** [ɔː'kɛstrəl] adj
Orchester-, orchestral
orchid ['ɔːkɪd] n Orchidee f
ordain [ɔː'deɪn] vt (ECCL) weihen
ordeal [ɔː'diːl] n Qual f
order ['ɔːdəʳ] n (sequence) Reihenfolge f;
(good arrangement) Ordnung f; (command)
Befehl m; (JUR) Anordnung f; (peace)
Ordnung f; (condition) Zustand m; (rank)
Klasse f; (COMM) Bestellung f; (ECCL,
honour) Orden m ♦ vt (also: **put in ~**)
ordnen; (command) befehlen; (COMM)
bestellen; **in ~** in der Reihenfolge; **in**

(working) ~ in gutem Zustand; **in ~ to do sth** um etw zu tun; **on ~** (COMM) auf Bestellung; **to ~ sb to do sth** jdm befehlen, etw zu tun; **to ~ sth** (command) etw acc befehlen; **~ form** n Bestellschein m; **~ly** n (MIL) Sanitäter m; (MED) Pfleger m ♦ adj (tidy) ordentlich; (well-behaved) ruhig

ordinary [ˈɔːdnrɪ] adj gewöhnlich ♦ n: **out of the ~** außergewöhnlich

Ordnance Survey [ˈɔːdnəns-] (BRIT) n amtliche(r) Kartografiedienst m

ore [ɔːʳ] n Erz nt

organ [ˈɔːgən] n (MUS) Orgel f; (BIOL, fig) Organ nt

organic [ɔːˈgænɪk] adj (food, farming etc) biodynamisch

organization [ɔːgənaɪˈzeɪʃən] n Organisation f; (make-up) Struktur f

organize [ˈɔːgənaɪz] vt organisieren; **~r** n Organisator m, Veranstalter m

orgasm [ˈɔːgæzəm] n Orgasmus m

orgy [ˈɔːdʒɪ] n Orgie f

Orient [ˈɔːrɪənt] n Orient m; **o~al** [ɔːrɪˈentl] adj orientalisch

origin [ˈɒrɪdʒɪn] n Ursprung m; (of the world) Anfang m, Entstehung f; **~al** [əˈrɪdʒɪnl] adj (first) ursprünglich; (painting) original; (idea) originell ♦ n Original nt; **~ally** adv ursprünglich; originell; **~ate** [əˈrɪdʒɪneɪt] vi entstehen ♦ vt ins Leben rufen; **to ~ate from** stammen aus

Orkney [ˈɔːknɪ] npl (also: **the ~ Islands**) die Orkneyinseln pl

ornament [ˈɔːnəmənt] n Schmuck m; (on mantelpiece) Nippesfigur f; **~al** [ɔːnəˈmentl] adj Zier-

ornate [ɔːˈneɪt] adj reich verziert

orphan [ˈɔːfn] n Waise f, Waisenkind nt ♦ vt: **to be ~ed** Waise werden; **~age** n Waisenhaus nt

orthodox [ˈɔːθədɒks] adj orthodox; **~y** n Orthodoxie f; (fig) Konventionalität f

orthopaedic [ɔːθəˈpiːdɪk] (US **orthopedic**) adj orthopädisch

ostentatious [ɒstenˈteɪʃəs] adj großtuerisch, protzig

ostracize [ˈɒstrəsaɪz] vt ausstoßen

ostrich [ˈɒstrɪtʃ] n Strauß m

other [ˈʌðəʳ] adj andere(r, s) ♦ pron andere(r, s) ♦ adv: **~ than** anders als; **the ~ (one)** der/die/das andere; **the ~ day** neulich; **~s** (~ people) andere; **~wise** adv (in a different way) anders; (or else) sonst

otter [ˈɒtəʳ] n Otter m

ouch [autʃ] excl aua

ought [ɔːt] aux vb sollen; **I ~ to do it** ich sollte es tun; **this ~ to have been corrected** das hätte korrigiert werden sollen

ounce [auns] n Unze f

our [ˈauəʳ] adj unser; see also **my**; **~s** pron unsere(r, s); see also **mine²**; **~selves** pron

uns (selbst); (emphatic) (wir) selbst; see also **oneself**

oust [aust] vt verdrängen

out [aut] adv hinaus/heraus; (not indoors) draußen; (not alight) aus; (unconscious) bewusstlos; (results) bekannt gegeben; **to eat/go ~** auswärts essen/ausgehen; **~ there** da draußen; **he is ~** (absent) er ist nicht da; **he was ~ in his calculations** seine Berechnungen waren nicht richtig; **~ loud** laut; **~ of** aus; (away from) außerhalb +gen; **to be ~ of milk** etc keine Milch etc mehr haben; **~ of order** außer Betrieb; **~-and-** adj (liar, thief etc) ausgemacht; **~back** n Hinterland nt; **~board (motor)** n Außenbordmotor m; **~break** n Ausbruch m; **~burst** n Ausbruch m; **~cast** n Ausgestoßene(r) mf; **~come** n Ergebnis nt; **~crop** n (of rock) Felsnase f; **~cry** n Protest m; **~dated** adj überholt; **~do** (irreg: like do) vt übertrumpfen; **~door** adj Außen-; (SPORT) im Freien; **~doors** adv im Freien

outer [ˈautəʳ] adj äußere(r, s); **~ space** n Weltraum m

outfit [ˈautfɪt] n Kleidung f

out: **~going** adj (character) aufgeschlossen; **~goings** (BRIT) npl Ausgaben pl; **~grow** (irreg: like grow) vt (clothes) herauswachsen aus; (habit) ablegen; **~house** n Nebengebäude nt

outing [ˈautɪŋ] n Ausflug m

outlandish [autˈlændɪʃ] adj eigenartig

out: **~law** n Geächtete(r) f(m) ♦ vt ächten; (thing) verbieten; **~lay** n Auslage f; **~let** n Auslass m, Abfluss m; (also: retail ~let) Absatzmarkt m; (US: ELEC) Steckdose f; (for emotions) Ventil n

outline [ˈautlaɪn] n Umriss m

out: **~live** vt überleben; **~look** n (also fig) Aussicht f; (attitude) Einstellung f; **~lying** adj entlegen; (district) Außen-; **~moded** adj veraltet; **~number** vt zahlenmäßig überlegen sein +dat; **~-of-date** adj (passport) abgelaufen; (clothes etc) altmodisch; (ideas etc) überholt; **~-of-the-way** adj abgelegen; **~patient** n ambulante(r) Patient m/ambulante Patientin f; **~post** n (MIL, fig) Vorposten m; **~put** n Leistung f, Produktion f; (COMPUT) Ausgabe f

outrage [ˈautreɪdʒ] n (cruel deed) Ausschreitung f; (indecency) Skandal m ♦ vt (morals) verstoßen gegen; (person) empören; **~ous** [autˈreɪdʒəs] adj unerhört

outreach worker [ˈautˈriːtʃ-] n Streetworker(in) m(f)

outright [adv autˈraɪt, adj ˈautraɪt] adv (at once) sofort; (openly) ohne Umschweife ♦ adj (denial) völlig; (sale) Total-; (winner) unbestritten

outset [ˈautset] n Beginn m

outside [autˈsaɪd] n Außenseite f ♦ adj

äußere(r, s), Außen-; (*chance*) gering ♦ *adv*
außen ♦ *prep* außerhalb *+gen*; **at the ~** (*fig*)
maximal; (*time*) spätestens; **to go ~** nach
draußen gehen; **~ lane** *n* (*AUT*) äußere Spur
f; **~ line** *n* (*TEL*) Amtsanschluss *m*; **~r** *n*
Außenseiter(in) *m(f)*

out: **~size** *adj* übergroß; **~skirts** *npl*
Stadtrand *m*; **~spoken** *adj* freimütig;
~standing *adj* hervorragend; (*debts etc*)
ausstehend; **~stay** *vt*: **to ~stay one's
welcome** länger bleiben als erwünscht;
~stretched *adj* ausgestreckt; **~strip** *vt*
übertreffen; **~ tray** *n* Ausgangskorb *m*

outward ['autwəd] *adj* äußere(r, s); (*journey*)
Hin-; (*freight*) ausgehend ♦ *adv* nach außen;
~ly *adv* äußerlich

outweigh [aut'weɪ] *vt* (*fig*) überwiegen

outwit [aut'wɪt] *vt* überlisten

oval ['əuvl] *adj* oval ♦ *n* Oval *nt*

ovary ['əuvərɪ] *n* Eierstock *m*

ovation [əu'veɪʃən] *n* Beifallssturm *m*

oven ['ʌvn] *n* Backofen *m*; **~proof** *adj*
feuerfest

over ['əuvə*] *adv* (*across*) hinüber/herüber;
(*finished*) vorbei; (*left*) übrig; (*again*) wieder,
noch einmal ♦ *prep* über ♦ *prefix* (*excessively*)
übermäßig; **~ here** hier(hin); **~ there**
dort(hin); **all ~** (*everywhere*) überall;
(*finished*) vorbei; **~ and ~** immer wieder; **~
and above** darüber hinaus; **to ask sb ~** jdn
einladen; **to bend ~** sich bücken

overall [*adj, n* 'əuvərɔ:l, *adv* əuvər'ɔ:l] *adj*
(*situation*) allgemein; (*length*) Gesamt- ♦ *n*
(*BRIT*) Kittel *m* ♦ *adv* insgesamt; **~s** *npl* (*for
man*) Overall *m*

over: **~awe** *vt* (*frighten*) einschüchtern;
(*make impression*) überwältigen; **~balance**
vi Übergewicht bekommen; **~bearing** *adj*
aufdringlich; **~board** *adv* über Bord; **~book**
vi überbuchen

overcast ['əuvəka:st] *adj* bedeckt

overcharge [əuvə'tʃa:dʒ] *vt*: **to ~ sb** von
jdm zu viel verlangen

overcoat ['əuvəkəut] *n* Mantel *m*

overcome [əuvə'kʌm] (*irreg: like* **come**) *vt*
überwinden

over: **~crowded** *adj* überfüllt; **~crowding**
n Überfüllung *f*; **~do** (*irreg: like* **do**) *vt* (*cook
too much*) verkochen; (*exaggerate*)
übertreiben; **~done** *adj* übertrieben; (*COOK*)
verbraten, verkocht; **~dose** *n* Überdosis *f*;
~draft *n* (*Konto*)überziehung *f*; **~drawn**
adj (*account*) überzogen; (*fig*) überfällig; **~due**
adj
überfällig; **~estimate** *vt* überschätzen;
~excited *adj* überreizt; (*children*) aufgeregt

overflow [*vb* əuvə'fləu, *n* 'əuvəfləu] *vi* überfließen ♦ *n*
(*excess*) Überschuss *m*; (*also:* **~ pipe**)
Überlaufrohr *nt*

overgrown [əuvə'grəun] *adj* (*garden*)
verwildert

overhaul [*vb* əuvə'hɔ:l, *n* 'əuvəhɔ:l] *vt* (*car*)

überholen; (*plans*) überprüfen ♦ *n*
Überholung *f*

overhead [*adv* əuvə'hed, *adj, n* 'əuvəhed]
adv oben ♦ *adj* Hoch-; (*wire*) oberirdisch;
(*lighting*) Decken- ♦ *n* (*US*) = **overheads**; **~s**
npl (*costs*) allgemeine Unkosten *pl*; **~
projector** *n* Overheadprojektor *m*

over: **~hear** (*irreg: like* **hear**) *vt* (mit
an)hören; **~heat** *vi* (*engine*) heiß laufen;
~joyed *adj* überglücklich; **~kill** *n* (*fig*)
Rundumschlag *m*

overland ['əuvəlænd] *adj* Überland- ♦ *adv*
(*travel*) über Land

overlap [*vb* əuvə'læp, *n* 'əuvəlæp] *vi* sich
überschneiden; (*objects*) sich teilweise
decken ♦ *n* Überschneidung *f*

over: **~leaf** *adv* umseitig; **~load** *vt*
überladen; **~look** *vt* (*view from above*)
überblicken; (*not notice*) übersehen; (*pardon*)
hinwegsehen über *+acc*

overnight [əuvə'naɪt, *adj* 'əuvənaɪt] *adv*
über Nacht ♦ *adj* (*journey*) Nacht-; **~ stay**
Übernachtung *f*; **to stay ~** übernachten

overpass ['əuvəpa:s] *n* Überführung *f*

overpower [əuvə'pauə*] *vt* überwältigen

over: **~rate** *vt* überschätzen; **~ride** (*irreg: like*
ride) *vt* (*order, decision*) aufheben;
(*objection*) übergehen; **~riding** *adj*
vorherrschend; **~rule** *vt* verwerfen; **~run**
(*irreg: like* **run**) *vt* (*country*) einfallen in; (*time
limit*) überziehen

overseas [əuvə'si:z] *adv* nach/in Übersee
♦ *adj* überseeisch, Übersee-

overseer ['əuvəsɪə*] *n* Aufseher *m*

overshadow [əuvə'ʃædəu] *vt* überschatten

overshoot [əuvə'ʃu:t] (*irreg: like* **shoot**) *vt*
(*runway*) hinausschießen über *+acc*

oversight ['əuvəsaɪt] *n* (*mistake*) Versehen *nt*

over: **~sleep** (*irreg: like* **sleep**) *vi* verschlafen;
~spill *n* (*Bevölkerungs*)überschuss *m*;
~state *vt* übertreiben; **~step** *vt*: **to ~step
the mark** zu weit gehen

overt [əu'vɜ:t] *adj* offen(kundig)

overtake [əuvə'teɪk] (*irreg: like* **take**) *vt, vi*
überholen

over: **~throw** (*irreg: like* **throw**) *vt* (*POL*)
stürzen; **~time** *n* Überstunden *pl*; **~tone** *n*
(*fig*) Note *f*

overture ['əuvətʃuə*] *n* Ouvertüre *f*

over: **~turn** *vt, vi* umkippen; **~weight** *adj* zu
dick; **~whelm** *vt* überwältigen; **~work** *n*
Überarbeitung *f* ♦ *vt* überlasten ♦ *vi* sich
überarbeiten; **~wrought** *adj* überreizt

owe [əu] *vt* schulden; **to ~ sth to sb** (*money*)
jdm etw schulden; (*favour etc*) jdm etw
verdanken; **owing to** *prep* wegen *+gen*

owl [aul] *n* Eule *f*

own [əun] *vt* besitzen ♦ *adj* eigen; **a room of
my ~** mein eigenes Zimmer; **to get one's ~
back** sich rächen; **on one's ~** allein; **~ up** *vi*:
to ~ up (to sth) (etw) zugeben; **~er** *n*

Besitzer(in) m(f); **~ership** n Besitz m

ox [ɔks] (pl **~en**) n Ochse m

oxtail [ˈɔksteɪl] n: **~ soup** Ochsenschwanzsuppe f

oxygen [ˈɔksɪdʒən] n Sauerstoff m; **~ mask** n Sauerstoffmaske f; **~ tent** n Sauerstoffzelt nt

oyster [ˈɔɪstər] n Auster f

oz. abbr = **ounce(s)**

ozone [ˈəuzaun] n Ozon nt; **~-friendly** adj (aerosol) ohne Treibgas; (fridge) FCKW-frei; **~ hole** n Ozonloch nt; **~ layer** n Ozonschicht f

P, p

p abbr = **penny**; **pence**

pa [pɑː] (inf) n Papa m

P.A. n abbr = **personal assistant**; **public address system**

p.a. abbr = **per annum**

pace [peɪs] n Schritt m; (speed) Tempo nt ♦ vi schreiten; **to keep ~ with** Schritt halten mit; **~maker** n Schrittmacher m

pacific [pəˈsɪfɪk] adj pazifisch ♦ n: **the P~ (Ocean)** der Pazifik

pacifist [ˈpæsɪfɪst] n Pazifist m

pacify [ˈpæsɪfaɪ] vt befrieden; (calm) beruhigen

pack [pæk] n (of goods) Packung f; (of hounds) Meute f; (of cards) Spiel nt; (gang) Bande f ♦ vt (case) packen; (clothes) einpacken ♦ vi packen; **to ~ sb off to ... jdn** nach ... schicken; **~ it in!** lass es gut sein!

package [ˈpækɪdʒ] n Paket nt; **~ tour** n Pauschalreise f

packed [pækt] adj abgepackt; **~ lunch** n Lunchpaket nt

packet [ˈpækɪt] n Päckchen nt

packing [ˈpækɪŋ] n (action) Packen nt; (material) Verpackung f; **~ case** n (Pack)kiste f

pact [pækt] n Pakt m, Vertrag m

pad [pæd] n (of paper) (Schreib)block m; (stuffing) Polster nt ♦ vt polstern; **~ding** n Polsterung f

paddle [ˈpædl] n Paddel nt; (US: SPORT) Schläger m ♦ vt (boat) paddeln ♦ vi (in sea) plan(t)schen; **~ steamer** n Raddampfer m

paddling pool [ˈpædlɪŋ-] (BRIT) n Plan(t)schbecken nt

paddock [ˈpædək] n Koppel f

paddy field [ˈpædɪ-] n Reisfeld nt

padlock [ˈpædlɔk] n Vorhängeschloss nt ♦ vt verschließen

paediatrics [piːdɪˈætrɪks] (US **pediatrics**) n Kinderheilkunde f

pagan [ˈpeɪgən] adj heidnisch ♦ n Heide m, Heidin f

page [peɪdʒ] n Seite f; (person) Page m ♦ vt (in hotel) ausrufen lassen

pageant [ˈpædʒənt] n Festzug m; **~ry** n Gepränge nt

pager [ˈpeɪdʒər] n (TEL) Funkrufempfänger m, Piepser m (inf)

paging device [ˈpeɪdʒɪŋ-] n (TEL) = **pager**

paid [peɪd] pt, pp of **pay** ♦ adj bezahlt; **to put ~ to** (BRIT) zunichte machen

pail [peɪl] n Eimer m

pain [peɪn] n Schmerz m; **to be in ~** Schmerzen haben; **on ~ of death** bei Todesstrafe; **to take ~s to do sth** sich dat Mühe geben, etw zu tun; **~ed** adj (expression) gequält; **~ful** adj (physically) schmerzhaft; (embarrassing) peinlich; (difficult) mühsam; **~fully** adv (fig: very) schrecklich; **~killer** n Schmerzmittel nt; **~less** adj schmerzlos; **~staking** [ˈpeɪnzteɪkɪŋ] adj gewissenhaft

paint [peɪnt] n Farbe f ♦ vt anstreichen; (picture) malen; **to ~ the door blue** die Tür blau streichen; **~brush** n Pinsel m; **~er** n Maler m; **~ing** n Malerei f; (picture) Gemälde nt; **~work** n Anstrich m; (of car) Lack m

pair [pɛər] n Paar nt; **~ of scissors** Schere f; **~ of trousers** Hose f

pajamas [pəˈdʒɑːməz] (US) npl Schlafanzug m

Pakistan [pɑːkɪˈstɑːn] n Pakistan nt; **~i** adj pakistanisch ♦ n Pakistani mf

pal [pæl] (inf) n Kumpel m

palace [ˈpæləs] n Palast m, Schloss nt

palatable [ˈpælɪtəbl] adj schmackhaft

palate [ˈpælɪt] n Gaumen m

palatial [pəˈleɪʃəl] adj palastartig

pale [peɪl] adj blass, bleich ♦ n: **to be beyond the ~** die Grenzen überschreiten

Palestine [ˈpælɪstaɪn] n Palästina nt; **Palestinian** [pælɪsˈtɪnɪən] adj palästinensisch ♦ n Palästinenser(in) m(f)

palette [ˈpælɪt] n Palette f

paling [ˈpeɪlɪŋ] n (stake) Zaunpfahl m; (fence) Lattenzaun m

pall [pɔːl] vi jeden Reiz verlieren, verblassen

pallet [ˈpælɪt] n (for goods) Palette f

pallid [ˈpælɪd] adj blass, bleich

pallor [ˈpælər] n Blässe f

palm [pɑːm] n (of hand) Handfläche f; (also: **~ tree**) Palme f ♦ vt: **to ~ sth off on sb** jdm etw andrehen; **P~ Sunday** n Palmsonntag m

palpable [ˈpælpəbl] adj (also fig) greifbar

palpitation [pælpɪˈteɪʃən] n Herzklopfen nt

paltry [ˈpɔːltrɪ] adj armselig

pamper [ˈpæmpər] vt verhätscheln

pamphlet [ˈpæmflət] n Broschüre f

pan [pæn] n Pfanne f ♦ vi (CINE) schwenken

panache [pəˈnæʃ] n Schwung m

pancake [ˈpænkeɪk] n Pfannkuchen m

pancreas [ˈpæŋkrɪəs] n Bauchspeicheldrüse

panda ['pændə] n Panda m; **~ car** (BRIT) n (Funk)streifenwagen m

pandemonium [pændɪ'məunɪəm] n Hölle f; (noise) Höllenlärm m

pander ['pændəᵊ] vi: **to ~ .to** sich richten nach

pane [peɪn] n (Fenster)scheibe f

panel ['pænl] n (of wood) Tafel f; (TV) Diskussionsrunde f; **~ling** (US **~ing**) n Täfelung f

pang [pæŋ] n: **~s of hunger** quälende(r) Hunger m; **~s of conscience** Gewissensbisse pl

panic ['pænɪk] n Panik f ♦ vi in Panik geraten; **don't ~** (nur) keine Panik; **~ky** adj (person) überängstlich; **~-stricken** adj von panischem Schrecken erfasst; (look) panisch

pansy ['pænzɪ] n Stiefmütterchen nt; (inf) Schwule(r) m

pant [pænt] vi keuchen; (dog) hecheln

panther ['pænθəᵊ] n Pant(h)er m

panties ['pæntɪz] npl (Damen)slip m

pantihose ['pæntɪhəuz] (US) n Strumpfhose f

pantomime ['pæntəmaɪm] (BRIT) n Märchenkomödie f um Weihnachten

pantry ['pæntrɪ] n Vorratskammer f

pants [pænts] npl (BRIT: woman's) Schlüpfer m; (: man's) Unterhose f; (US: trousers) Hose f

papal ['peɪpl] adj päpstlich

paper ['peɪpəᵊ] n Papier nt; (newspaper) Zeitung f; (essay) Referat nt ♦ adj Papier-, aus Papier ♦ vt (wall) tapezieren; **~s** npl (identity ~s) Ausweis(papiere pl) m; **~back** n Taschenbuch nt; **~ bag** n Tüte f; **~ clip** n Büroklammer f; **~ hankie** n Tempotaschentuch nt ®; **~weight** n Briefbeschwerer m; **~work** n Schreibarbeit f

par [pɑːᵊ] n (COMM) Nennwert m; (GOLF) Par nt; **on a ~ with** ebenbürtig +dat

parable ['pærəbl] n (REL) Gleichnis nt

parachute ['pærəʃuːt] n Fallschirm m ♦ vi (mit dem Fallschirm) abspringen

parade [pə'reɪd] n Parade f ♦ vt aufmarschieren lassen; (fig) zur Schau stellen ♦ vi paradieren, vorbeimarschieren

paradise ['pærədaɪs] n Paradies nt

paradox ['pærədɔks] n Paradox nt; **~ically** [pærə'dɔksɪklɪ] adv paradoxerweise

paraffin ['pærəfɪn] (BRIT) n Paraffin nt

paragraph ['pærəgrɑːf] n Absatz m

parallel ['pærəlel] adj parallel ♦ n Parallele f

paralyse ['pærəlaɪz] (US **paralyze**) vt (MED) lähmen, paralysieren; (fig: organization, production etc) lahm legen; **~d** adj gelähmt; **paralysis** [pə'rælɪsɪs] n Lähmung f

paralyze ['pærəlaɪz] (US) = **paralyse**

parameter [pə'ræmɪtəᵊ] n Parameter m; **~s** npl (framework, limits) Rahmen m

paramount ['pærəmaunt] adj höchste(r, s), oberste(r, s)

paranoid ['pærənɔɪd] adj (person) an Verfolgungswahn leidend, paranoid; (feeling) krankhaft

parapet ['pærəpɪt] n Brüstung f

paraphernalia [pærəfə'neɪlɪə] n Zubehör nt, Utensilien pl

paraphrase ['pærəfreɪz] vt umschreiben

paraplegic [pærə'pliːdʒɪk] n Querschnittsgelähmte(r) f(m)

parasite ['pærəsaɪt] n (also fig) Schmarotzer m, Parasit m

parasol ['pærəsɔl] n Sonnenschirm m

paratrooper ['pærətruːpəᵊ] n Fallschirmjäger m

parcel ['pɑːsl] n Paket nt ♦ vt (also: **~ up**) einpacken

parch [pɑːtʃ] vt (aus)dörren; **~ed** adj ausgetrocknet; (person) am Verdursten

parchment ['pɑːtʃmənt] n Pergament nt

pardon ['pɑːdn] n Verzeihung f ♦ vt (JUR) begnadigen; **~ me!, I beg your ~!** verzeihen Sie bitte!; **~ me?** (US) wie bitte?; **(I beg your) ~?** wie bitte?

parent ['pɛərənt] n Elternteil m; **~s** npl (mother and father) Eltern pl; **~al** [pə'rentl] adj elterlich, Eltern-

parentheses [pə'renθɪsiːz] npl of **parenthesis**

parenthesis [pə'renθɪsɪs] n Klammer f; (sentence) Parenthese f

Paris ['pærɪs] n Paris nt

parish ['pærɪʃ] n Gemeinde f

park [pɑːk] n Park m ♦ vt, vi parken

parking ['pɑːkɪŋ] n Parken nt; **"no ~"** „Parken verboten"; **~ lot** (US) n Parkplatz m; **~ meter** n Parkuhr f; **~ ticket** n Strafzettel m

parlance ['pɑːləns] n Sprachgebrauch m

parliament ['pɑːləmənt] n Parlament nt; **~ary** [pɑːlə'mentərɪ] adj parlamentarisch, Parlaments-

parlour ['pɑːləᵊ] (US **parlor**) n Salon m

parochial [pə'rəukɪəl] adj (narrow-minded) eng(stirnig)

parole [pə'rəul] n: **on ~** (prisoner) auf Bewährung

parrot ['pærət] n Papagei m

parry ['pærɪ] vt parieren, abwehren

parsley ['pɑːslɪ] n Petersilie m

parsnip ['pɑːsnɪp] n Pastinake f

parson ['pɑːsn] n Pfarrer m

part [pɑːt] n (piece) Teil m; (THEAT) Rolle f; (of machine) Teil nt ♦ adv = **partly** ♦ vt trennen; (hair) scheiteln ♦ vi (people) sich trennen; **to take ~ in** teilnehmen an +dat; **to take sth in good ~** etw nicht übel nehmen; **to take sb's ~** sich auf jds Seite acc stellen; **for my ~** ich für meinen Teil; **for the most ~** meistens, größtenteils; **in ~ exchange** (BRIT) in Zahlung; **~ with** vt fus hergeben; (renounce) aufgeben; **~ial** ['pɑːʃl] adj (*incomplete*) teilweise; (*biased*) parteiisch; **to be ~ial to** eine (besondere) Vorliebe haben für

participant |paːˈtɪsɪpənt| n Teilnehmer(in) m(f)

participate |paːˈtɪsɪpeɪt| vi: **to ~ (in)** teilnehmen (an +dat); **participation** |paːtɪsɪˈpeɪʃən| n Teilnahme f; (*sharing*) Beteiligung f

participle |ˈpaːtɪsɪpl| n Partizip nt

particle |ˈpaːtɪkl| n Teilchen nt

particular |pəˈtɪkjʊləʳ| adj bestimmt; (*exact*) genau; (*fussy*) eigen; **in ~** besonders; **~ly** adv besonders

particulars npl (*details*) Einzelheiten pl; (*of person*) Personalien pl

parting |ˈpaːtɪŋ| n (*separation*) Abschied m; (BRIT: *of hair*) Scheitel m ♦ adj Abschieds-

partition |paːˈtɪʃən| n (*wall*) Trennwand f; (*division*) Teilung f ♦ vt aufteilen

partly |ˈpaːtlɪ| adv zum Teil, teilweise

partner |ˈpaːtnəʳ| n Partner m ♦ vt der Partner sein von; **~ship** n Partnerschaft f; (COMM) Teilhaberschaft f

partridge |ˈpaːtrɪdʒ| n Rebhuhn nt

part-time |ˈpaːtˈtaɪm| adj Teilzeit- ♦ adv stundenweise

party |ˈpaːtɪ| n (POL, JUR) Partei f; (*group*) Gesellschaft f; (*celebration*) Party f ♦ adj (*dress*) Party-; (*politics*) Partei-; **~ line** n (TEL) Gemeinschaftsanschluss m

pass |paːs| vt (*on foot*) vorbeigehen an +dat; (*driving*) vorbeifahren an +dat; (*surpass*) übersteigen; (*hand on*) weitergeben; (*approve*) genehmigen; (*time*) verbringen; (*exam*) bestehen ♦ vi (*go by*) vorübergehen, vorbeifahren; (*years*) vergehen; (*be successful*) bestehen ♦ n (*in mountains, SPORT*) Pass m; (*permission*) Passierschein m; (*in exam*): **to get a ~** bestehen; **to ~ sth through sth** etw durch etw führen; **to make a ~ at sb** (inf) bei jdm Annäherungsversuche machen; **~ away** vi (*euph*) verscheiden; **~ by** vi vorbeigehen; vorbeifahren; (*years*) vergehen ♦ vt weitergeben; **~ out** vi (*faint*) ohnmächtig werden; **~ up** vt vorbeigehen lassen; **~able** adj (*road*) passierbar; (*fairly good*) passabel

passage |ˈpæsɪdʒ| n (*corridor*) Gang m; (*in book*) (Text)stelle f; (*voyage*) Überfahrt f; **~way** n Durchgang m

passbook |ˈpaːsbʊk| n Sparbuch nt

passenger |ˈpæsɪndʒəʳ| n Passagier m; (*on bus*) Fahrgast m

passer-by |paːsəˈbaɪ| n Passant(in) m(f)

passing |ˈpaːsɪŋ| adj (*car*) vorbeifahrend; (*thought, affair*) momentan ♦ n: **in ~** beiläufig; **~ place** n (AUT) Ausweichstelle f

passion |ˈpæʃən| n Leidenschaft f; **~ate** adj leidenschaftlich

(*incomplete*) teilweise; (*biased*) parteiisch; **~ smoking** n Passivrauchen nt

passive |ˈpæsɪv| adj passiv; (LING) passivisch;

Passover |ˈpaːsəʊvəʳ| n Passahfest nt

passport |ˈpaːspɔːt| n (Reise)pass m; **~ control** n Passkontrolle f; **~ office** n Passamt nt

password |ˈpaːswaːd| n Parole f, Kennwort nt, Losung f

past |paːst| prep (*motion*) an +dat … vorbei; (*position*) hinter +dat; (*later than*) nach ♦ adj (*years*) vergangen; (*president etc*) ehemalig ♦ n Vergangenheit f; **he's ~ forty** er ist über vierzig; **for the ~ few/3 days** in den letzten paar/3 Tagen; **to run ~** vorbeilaufen; **ten/ quarter ~ eight** zehn/Viertel nach acht

pasta |ˈpæstə| n Teigwaren pl

paste |peɪst| n (*fish – etc*) Paste f; (*glue*) Kleister m ♦ vt kleben

pasteurized |ˈpæstəraɪzd| adj pasteurisiert

pastime |ˈpaːstaɪm| n Zeitvertreib m

pastor |ˈpaːstəʳ| n Pfarrer m

pastry |ˈpeɪstrɪ| n Blätterteig m; **pastries** npl (*tarts etc*) Stückchen pl

pasture |ˈpaːstʃəʳ| n Weide f

pasty [n ˈpæstɪ, adj ˈpeɪstɪ] n (Fleisch)pastete f ♦ adj blässlich, käsig

pat |pæt| n leichte(r) Schlag m, Klaps m ♦ vt tätscheln

patch |pætʃ| n Fleck m ♦ vt flicken; (**to go through) a bad ~** eine Pechsträhne (haben); **~ up** vt flicken; (*quarrel*) beilegen; **~ed** adj geflickt; **~y** adj (*irregular*) ungleichmäßig

pâté |ˈpæteɪ| n Pastete f

patent |ˈpeɪtnt| n Patent nt ♦ vt patentieren lassen; (*by authorities*) patentieren ♦ adj offenkundig; **~ leather** n Lackleder nt

paternal |pəˈtɜːnl| adj väterlich

paternity |pəˈtɜːnɪtɪ| n Vaterschaft f

path |paːθ| n Pfad m; Weg m

pathetic |pəˈθetɪk| adj (*very bad*) kläglich

pathological |pæθəˈlɒdʒɪkl| adj pathologisch

pathology |pəˈθɒlədʒɪ| n Pathologie f

pathos |ˈpeɪθɒs| n Rührseligkeit f

pathway |ˈpaːθweɪ| n Weg m

patience |ˈpeɪʃns| n Geduld f; (BRIT: CARDS) Patience f

patient |ˈpeɪʃnt| n Patient(in) m(f), Kranke(r) mf ♦ adj geduldig

patio |ˈpætɪəʊ| n Terrasse f

patriotic |pætrɪˈɒtɪk| adj patriotisch

patrol |pəˈtrəʊl| n Patrouille f; (*police*) Streife f ♦ vt patrouillieren in +dat ♦ vi (*police*) die Runde machen; (MIL) patrouillieren; **~ car** n Streifenwagen m; **~man** (US: irreg) n (Streifen)polizist m

patron |ˈpeɪtrən| n (*in shop*) (Stamm)kunde m; (*in hotel*) (Stamm)gast m; (*supporter*) Förderer m; **~ of the arts** Mäzen m; **~age** |ˈpætrənɪdʒ| n Schirmherrschaft f; **~ize**

['pætrənaɪz] vt (support) unterstützen; (shop) besuchen; (treat condescendingly) von oben herab behandeln; ~ **saint** n Schutz-patron(in) m(f)

patter ['pætə^r] n (sound: of feet) Trappeln nt; (: of rain) Prasseln nt; (sales talk) Gerede nt ♦ vi (feet) trappeln; (rain) prasseln

pattern ['pætən] n Muster nt; (SEWING) Schnittmuster nt; (KNITTING) Strickanleitung f

pauper ['pɔːpə^r] n Arme(r) mf

pause [pɔːz] n Pause f ♦ vi innehalten

pave [peɪv] vt pflastern; **to ~ the way for** den Weg bahnen für

pavement ['peɪvmənt] (BRIT) n Bürgersteig m

pavilion [pə'vɪlɪən] n Pavillon m; (SPORT) Klubhaus nt

paving ['peɪvɪŋ] n Straßenpflaster nt; ~ **stone** n Pflasterstein m

paw [pɔː] n Pfote f; (of big cats) Tatze f, Pranke f ♦ vt (scrape) scharren; (handle) betatschen

pawn [pɔːn] n Pfand nt; (chess) Bauer m ♦ vt verpfänden; ~**broker** n Pfandleiher m; ~**shop** n Pfandhaus nt

pay [peɪ] (pt, pp **paid**) n Bezahlung f, Lohn m ♦ vt bezahlen ♦ vi zahlen; (be profitable) sich bezahlt machen; **to ~ attention (to)** Acht geben (auf +acc); **to ~ sb a visit** jdn besuchen; ~ **back** vt zurückzahlen; ~ **for** vt fus bezahlen; ~ **in** vt einzahlen; ~ **off** vt abzahlen ♦ vi (scheme, decision) sich bezahlt machen; ~ **up** vi bezahlen; ~**able** adj zahlbar, fällig; ~**ee** n Zahlungsempfänger m; ~ **envelope** (US) n Lohntüte f; ~**ment** n Bezahlung f; **advance ~ment** Vorauszahlung f; **monthly ~ment** monatliche Rate f; ~ **packet** (BRIT) n Lohntüte f; ~**phone** n Münzfernsprecher m; ~**roll** n Lohnliste f; ~ **slip** n Lohn-/Gehaltsstreifen m; ~ **television** n Abonnenten-Fernsehen nt

PC n abbr (= personal computer) PC m

p.c. abbr = **per cent**

pea [piː] n Erbse f

peace [piːs] n Friede(n) m; ~**able** adj friedlich; ~**ful** adj friedlich, ruhig; ~**keeping** adj Friedens-

peach [piːtʃ] n Pfirsich m

peacock ['piːkɔk] n Pfau m

peak [piːk] n Spitze f; (of mountain) Gipfel m; (fig) Höhepunkt m; ~ **hours** npl (traffic) Hauptverkehrszeit f; (telephone, electricity) Hauptbelastungszeit f; ~ **period** n Stoßzeit f, Hauptzeit f

peal [piːl] n (Glocken)läuten nt; ~**s of laughter** schallende(s) Gelächter nt

peanut ['piːnʌt] n Erdnuss f; ~ **butter** n Erdnussbutter f

pear [peə^r] n Birne f

pearl [pəːl] n Perle f

peasant ['pɛznt] n Bauer m

peat [piːt] n Torf m

pebble ['pɛbl] n Kiesel m

peck [pɛk] vt, vi picken ♦ n (with beak) Schnabelhieb m; (kiss) flüchtige(r) Kuss m; ~**ing order** n Hackordnung f; ~**ish** (BRIT: inf) adj ein bisschen hungrig

peculiar [pɪ'kjuːlɪə^r] adj (odd) seltsam; ~ **to** charakteristisch für; ~**ity** [pɪkjuːlɪ'ærɪtɪ] n (singular quality) Besonderheit f; (strangeness) Eigenartigkeit f

pedal ['pɛdl] n Pedal nt ♦ vt, vi (cycle) fahren, Rad fahren

pedantic [pɪ'dæntɪk] adj pedantisch

peddler ['pɛdlə^r] n Hausierer(in) m(f); (of drugs) Drogenhändler(in) m(f)

pedestal ['pɛdəstl] n Sockel m

pedestrian [pɪ'dɛstrɪən] n Fußgänger m ♦ adj Fußgänger-; (humdrum) langweilig; ~ **crossing** (BRIT) n Fußgängerüberweg m; ~**ized** n in eine Fußgängerzone umgewandelt; ~ **precinct** (BRIT), ~ **zone** (US) n Fußgängerzone f

pediatrics [piːdɪ'ætrɪks] (US) n = **paediatrics**

pedigree ['pɛdɪgriː] n Stammbaum m ♦ cpd (animal) reinrassig, Zucht-

pee [piː] (inf) vi pissen, pinkeln

peek [piːk] vi gucken

peel [piːl] n Schale f ♦ vt schälen ♦ vi (paint etc) abblättern; (skin) sich schälen

peep [piːp] n (BRIT: look) kurze(r) Blick m; (sound) Piepsen nt ♦ vi (BRIT: look) gucken; ~ **out** vi herausgucken; ~**hole** n Guckloch nt

peer [pɪə^r] vi starren; (peep) gucken ♦ n (nobleman) Peer m; (equal) Ebenbürtige(r) m; ~**age** n Peerswürde f

peeved [piːvd] adj (person) sauer

peg [pɛg] n (stake) Pflock m; (BRIT: also: **clothes ~**) Wäscheklammer f

Pekinese [piːkɪ'niːz] n (dog) Pekinese m

pelican ['pɛlɪkən] n Pelikan m; ~ **crossing** (BRIT) n (AUT) Ampelüberweg m

pellet ['pɛlɪt] n Kügelchen nt

pelmet ['pɛlmɪt] n Blende f

pelt [pɛlt] vt bewerfen ♦ vi (rain) schütten ♦ n Pelz m, Fell nt

pelvis ['pɛlvɪs] n Becken nt

pen [pɛn] n (fountain ~) Federhalter m; (ballpoint ~) Kuli m; (for sheep) Pferch m

penal ['piːnl] adj Straf-; ~**ize** vt (punish) bestrafen; (disadvantage) benachteiligen

penalty ['pɛnltɪ] n Strafe f; (FOOTBALL) Elfmeter m; ~ **(kick)** n Elfmeter m

penance ['pɛnəns] n Buße f

pence [pɛns] (BRIT) npl of **penny**

pencil ['pɛnsl] n Bleistift m; ~ **case** n Federmäppchen nt; ~ **sharpener** n Bleistiftspitzer m

pendant ['pɛndnt] n Anhänger m

pending ['pɛndɪŋ] prep bis (zu) ♦ adj

unentschieden, noch offen

pendulum ['pɛndjuləm] n Pendel nt

penetrate ['pɛnɪtreɪt] vt durchdringen; (enter into) eindringen in +acc; **penetration** |pɛnɪ'treɪʃən| n Durchdringen nt; Eindringen nt

penfriend ['pɛnfrɛnd] (BRIT) n Brieffreund(in) m(f)

penguin ['pɛŋgwɪn] n Pinguin m

penicillin [pɛnɪ'sɪlɪn] n Penizillin nt

peninsula [pə'nɪnsjulə] n Halbinsel f

penis ['piːnɪs] n Penis m

penitentiary |pɛnɪ'tɛnʃərɪ| (US) n Zuchthaus nt

penknife ['pɛnnaɪf] n Federmesser nt

pen name n Pseudonym nt

penniless ['pɛnɪlɪs] adj mittellos

penny ['pɛnɪ] (pl **pennies** or (BRIT) **pence**) n Penny m; (US) Centstück nt

penpal ['pɛnpæl] n Brieffreund(in) m(f)

pension ['pɛnʃən] n Rente f; **~er** (BRIT) n Rentner(in) m(f); **~ fund** n Rentenfonds m; **~ plan** n Rentenversicherung f

pensive ['pɛnsɪv] adj nachdenklich

pentathlon [pɛn'tæθlən] n Fünfkampf m

Pentecost ['pɛntɪkɔst] n Pfingsten pl or nt

penthouse ['pɛnthaus] n Dachterrassenwohnung f

pent-up ['pɛntʌp] adj (feelings) angestaut

penultimate [pɛ'nʌltɪmət] adj vorletzte(r, s)

people ['piːpl] n (nation) Volk nt ♦ npl (persons) Leute pl; (inhabitants) Bevölkerung f ♦ vt besiedeln; **several ~ came** mehrere Leute kamen; **~ say that ...** man sagt, dass ...

pepper ['pɛpər] n Pfeffer m; (vegetable) Paprika m ♦ vt (pelt) bombardieren; **~ mill** n Pfeffermühle f; **~mint** n (plant) Pfefferminze f; (sweet) Pfefferminz nt

pep talk |pɛp-| (inf) n Anstachelung f

per [pɜːr] prep pro; **~ day/person** pro Tag/ Person; **~ annum** adv pro Jahr; **~ capita** adj (income) Pro-Kopf- ♦ adv pro Kopf

perceive [pə'siːv] vt (realize) wahrnehmen; (understand) verstehen

per cent n Prozent nt; **percentage** [pə'sɛntɪdʒ] n Prozentsatz m

perception [pə'sɛpʃən] n Wahrnehmung f; (insight) Einsicht f

perceptive [pə'sɛptɪv] adj (person) aufmerksam; (analysis) tief gehend

perch [pɜːtʃ] n Stange f; (fish) Flussbarsch m ♦ vi sitzen, hocken

percolator ['pɜːkəleɪtər] n Kaffeemaschine f

percussion |pə'kʌʃən| n (MUS) Schlagzeug nt

perennial [pə'rɛnɪəl] adj wiederkehrend; (everlasting) unvergänglich

perfect [adj, n 'pɜːfɪkt, vb pə'fɛkt] adj vollkommen; (crime, solution) perfekt ♦ n (GRAM) Perfekt nt ♦ vt vervollkommnen;

~ion n Vollkommenheit f; **~ly** adv vollkommen, perfekt; (quite) ganz, einfach

perforate ['pɜːfəreɪt] vt durchlöchern; **perforation** |pɜːfə'reɪʃən| n Perforieren nt; (line of holes) Perforation f

perform |pə'fɔːm| vt (carry out) durch- or ausführen; (task) verrichten; (THEAT) spielen, geben ♦ vi (THEAT) auftreten; **~ance** n Durchführung f; (efficiency) Leistung f; (show) Vorstellung f; **~er** n Künstler(in) m(f)

perfume ['pɜːfjuːm] n Duft m; (lady's) Parfüm nt

perhaps [pə'hæps] adv vielleicht

peril ['pɛrɪl] n Gefahr f

perimeter [pə'rɪmɪtər] n Peripherie f; (of circle etc) Umfang m

period ['pɪərɪəd] n Periode f; (GRAM) Punkt m; (MED) Periode f ♦ adj (costume) historisch; **~ic** [pɪərɪ'ɔdɪk] adj periodisch; **~ical** |pɪərɪ'ɔdɪkl| n Zeitschrift f; **~ically** [pɪərɪ'ɔdɪklɪ] adv periodisch

peripheral [pə'rɪfərəl] adj Rand-, peripher ♦ n (COMPUT) Peripheriegerät nt

perish ['pɛrɪʃ] vi umkommen; (fruit) verderben; **~able** adj leicht verderblich

perjury ['pɜːdʒərɪ] n Meineid m

perk |pɜːk| (inf) n (fringe benefit) Vergünstigung f; **~ up** vi munter werden; **~y** adj keck

perm [pɜːm] n Dauerwelle f

permanent ['pɜːmənənt] adj dauernd, ständig

permeate ['pɜːmɪeɪt] vt, vi durchdringen

permissible [pə'mɪsɪbl] adj zulässig

permission [pə'mɪʃən] n Erlaubnis f

permissive [pə'mɪsɪv] adj nachgiebig; **the ~ society** die permissive Gesellschaft

permit [n 'pɜːmɪt, vb pə'mɪt] n Zulassung f ♦ vt erlauben, zulassen

perpendicular [pɜːpən'dɪkjulər] adj senkrecht

perpetrate ['pɜːpɪtreɪt] vt begehen

perpetual [pə'pɛtjuəl] adj dauernd, ständig

perpetuate [pə'pɛtjueɪt] vt verewigen, bewahren

perplex [pə'plɛks] vt verblüffen

persecute ['pɜːsɪkjuːt] vt verfolgen; **persecution** |pɜːsɪ'kjuːʃən| n Verfolgung f

perseverance [pɜːsɪ'vɪərns] n Ausdauer f

persevere [pɜːsɪ'vɪər] vi durchhalten

Persian ['pɜːʃən] adj persisch ♦ n Perser(in) m(f); **the (~) Gulf** der Persische Golf

persist [pə'sɪst] vi (in belief etc) bleiben; (rain, smell) andauern; (continue) nicht aufhören; **to ~ in** bleiben bei; **~ence** n Beharrlichkeit f; **~ent** adj beharrlich; (unending) ständig

person ['pɜːsn] n Person f; **in ~** persönlich; **~able** adj gutaussehend; **~al** adj persönlich; (private) privat; (of body) körperlich, Körper-; **~al assistant** n Assistent(in) m(f); **~al column** n private Kleinanzeigen pl; **~al**

computer n Personalcomputer m; **~ality** |pəːsəˈnælɪtɪ| n Persönlichkeit f; **~ally** adv persönlich; **~al organizer** n Terminplaner m, Zeitplaner m; (electronic) elektronisches Notizbuch nt; **~al stereo** n Walkman m ®; **~ify** |pəˈsɒnɪfaɪ| vt verkörpern

personnel |pəːsəˈnel| n Personal nt

perspective |pəˈspektɪv| n Perspektive f

Perspex |ˈpɜːspeks| ® n Acrylglas nt, Akrylglas nt

perspiration |pɜːspɪˈreɪʃən| n Transpiration f

perspire |pəˈspaɪəʳ| vi transpirieren

persuade |pəˈsweɪd| vt überreden; (convince) überzeugen

persuasion |pəˈsweɪʒən| n Überredung f; Überzeugung f

persuasive |pəˈsweɪsɪv| adj überzeugend

pert |pəːt| adj keck

pertaining |pəːˈteɪnɪŋ|: **~ to** prep betreffend +acc

pertinent |ˈpɜːtɪnənt| adj relevant

perturb |pəˈtɜːb| vt beunruhigen

pervade |pəˈveɪd| vt erfüllen

perverse |pəˈvɜːs| adj pervers; (obstinate) eigensinnig

pervert |n ˈpɜːvɜːt, vb pəˈvɜːt| n perverse(r) Mensch m ♦ vt verdrehen; (morally) verderben

pessimist |ˈpesɪmɪst| n Pessimist m; **~ic** adj pessimistisch

pest |pest| n (insect) Schädling m; (fig: person) Nervensäge f; (: thing) Plage f; **~er** |ˈpestəʳ| vt plagen; **~icide** |ˈpestɪsaɪd| n Insektenvertilgungsmittel nt

pet |pet| n (animal) Haustier nt ♦ vt liebkosen, streicheln

petal |ˈpetl| n Blütenblatt nt

peter out |ˈpiːtə-| vi allmählich zu Ende gehen

petite |pəˈtiːt| adj zierlich

petition |pəˈtɪʃən| n Bittschrift f

petrified |ˈpetrɪfaɪd| adj versteinert; (person) starr (vor Schreck)

petrify |ˈpetrɪfaɪ| vt versteinern; (person) erstarren lassen

petrol |ˈpetrəl| (BRIT) n Benzin nt, Kraftstoff m; **two-/four-star ~** = Normal-/ Superbenzin nt; **~ can** n Benzinkanister m

petroleum |pəˈtrəʊlɪəm| n Petroleum nt

petrol: **~ pump** (BRIT) n (in car) Benzinpumpe f; (at garage) Zapfsäule f; **~ station** (BRIT) n Tankstelle f; **~ tank** (BRIT) n Benzintank m

petticoat |ˈpetɪkəʊt| n Unterrock m

petty |ˈpetɪ| adj (unimportant) unbedeutend; (mean) kleinlich; **~ cash** n Portokasse f; **~ officer** n Maat m

pew |pjuː| n Kirchenbank f

pewter |ˈpjuːtəʳ| n Zinn nt

phantom |ˈfæntəm| n Phantom m;

pharmacist |ˈfɑːməsɪst| n Pharmazeut m;

(druggist) Apotheker m

pharmacy |ˈfɑːməsɪ| n Pharmazie f; (shop) Apotheke f

phase |feɪz| n Phase f ♦ vt: **to ~ sth in** etw allmählich einführen; **to ~ sth out** etw auslaufen lassen

Ph.D. n abbr = **Doctor of Philosophy**

pheasant |ˈfeznt| n Fasan m

phenomena |fəˈnɒmɪnə| npl of **phenomenon**

phenomenon |fəˈnɒmɪnən| n Phänomen nt

philanthropist |fɪˈlænθrəpɪst| n Philanthrop m, Menschenfreund m

Philippines |ˈfɪlɪpiːnz| npl: **the ~** die Philippinen pl

philosopher |fɪˈlɒsəfəʳ| n Philosoph m; **philosophical** |fɪləˈsɒfɪkl| adj philosophisch; **philosophy** |fɪˈlɒsəfɪ| n Philosophie f

phlegm |flem| n (MED) Schleim m

phobia |ˈfəʊbjə| n (irrational fear: of insects, flying, water etc) Phobie f

phone |fəʊn| n Telefon nt ♦ vt, vi telefonieren, anrufen; **to be on the ~** telefonieren; **~ back** vt, vi zurückrufen; **~ up** vt, vi anrufen; **~ bill** n Telefonrechnung f; **~ book** n Telefonbuch nt; **~ booth** n Telefonzelle f; **~ box** n Telefonzelle f; **~ call** n Telefonanruf m; **~card** n (TEL) Telefonkarte f; **~-in** n (RAD, TV) Phone-in nt; **~ number** n Telefonnummer f

phonetics |fəˈnetɪks| n Phonetik f

phoney |ˈfəʊnɪ| (inf) adj unecht ♦ n (person) Schwindler m; (thing) Fälschung f; (banknote) Blüte f

phony |ˈfəʊnɪ| adj, n = **phoney**

photo |ˈfəʊtəʊ| n Foto nt; **~copier** |ˈfəʊtəʊkɒpɪəʳ| n Kopiergerät nt; **~copy** |ˈfəʊtəʊkɒpɪ| n Fotokopie f ♦ vt fotokopieren; **~genic** |fəʊtəʊˈdʒenɪk| adj fotogen; **~graph** |ˈfəʊtəɡræf| n Fotografie f, Aufnahme f ♦ vt fotografieren; **~grapher** |fəˈtɒɡrəfəʳ| n Fotograf m; **~graphic** |fəʊtəˈɡræfɪk| adj fotografisch; **~graphy** |fəˈtɒɡrəfɪ| n Fotografie f

phrase |freɪz| n Satz m; (expression) Ausdruck m ♦ vt ausdrücken, formulieren; **~ book** n Sprachführer m

physical |ˈfɪzɪkl| adj physikalisch; (bodily) körperlich, physisch; **~ education** n Turnen nt; **~ly** adv physikalisch

physician |fɪˈzɪʃən| n Arzt m

physicist |ˈfɪzɪsɪst| n Physiker(in) m(f)

physics |ˈfɪzɪks| n Physik f

physiotherapist |fɪzɪəʊˈθerəpɪst| n Physiotherapeut(in) m(f)

physiotherapy |fɪzɪəʊˈθerəpɪ| n Heilgymnastik f, Physiotherapie f

physique |fɪˈziːk| n Körperbau m

pianist |ˈpiːənɪst| n Pianist(in) m(f)

piano |pɪˈænəʊ| n Klavier m

pick [pɪk] n (tool) Pickel m; (choice) Auswahl f
♦ vt (fruit) pflücken; (choose) aussuchen;
take your ~ such dir etwas aus; **to ~ sb's
pocket** jdn bestehlen; **~ on** vt fus (person)
herumhacken auf +dat; **~ out** vt auswählen;
~ up vi (improve) sich erholen ♦ vt (lift up)
aufheben; (learn) (schnell) mitbekommen;
(collect) abholen; (girl) (sich dat) anlachen;
(AUT: passenger) mitnehmen; (speed)
gewinnen an +dat; **to ~ o.s. up** aufstehen

picket ['pɪkɪt] n (striker) Streikposten m ♦ vt
(factory) (Streik)posten aufstellen vor +dat
♦ vi (Streik)posten stehen

pickle ['pɪkl] n (salty mixture) Pökel m; (inf)
Klemme f ♦ vt (in Essig) einlegen; einpökeln

pickpocket ['pɪkpɔkɪt] n Taschendieb m

pick-up ['pɪkʌp] n (BRIT: on record player)
Tonabnehmer m; (small truck) Lieferwagen m

picnic ['pɪknɪk] n Picknick nt ♦ vi picknicken;
~ area n Rastplatz m

pictorial [pɪk'tɔːrɪəl] adj in Bildern

picture ['pɪktʃəʳ] n (visualize) sich
dat vorstellen; **the ~s** npl (BRIT) das Kino; **~
book** n Bilderbuch nt

picturesque [pɪktʃə'rɛsk] adj malerisch

pie [paɪ] n (meat) Pastete f; (fruit) Torte f

piece [piːs] n Stück nt ♦ vt: **to ~ together**
zusammenstückeln; (fig) sich dat
zusammenreimen; **to take to ~s** in
Einzelteile zerlegen; **~meal** adv stückweise,
Stück für Stück; **~work** n Akkordarbeit f

pie chart n Kreisdiagramm nt

pier [pɪəʳ] n Pier m, Mole f

pierce [pɪəs] vt durchstechen, durchbohren
(also look); **~d** adj durchgestochen, durchbohrt

piercing ['pɪəsɪŋ] adj (cry) durchdringend

pig [pɪg] n Schwein nt

pigeon ['pɪdʒən] n Taube f; **~hole** n
(compartment) Ablegefach nt

piggy bank ['pɪgɪ-] n Sparschwein nt

pig: **~headed** ['pɪg'hɛdɪd] adj dickköpfig;
~let ['pɪglɪt] n Ferkel nt; **~skin** ['pɪgskɪn] n
Schweinsleder nt; **~sty** ['pɪgstaɪ] n
Schweinestall m; **~tail** ['pɪgteɪl] n Zopf m

pike [paɪk] n Pike f; (fish) Hecht m

pilchard ['pɪltʃəd] n Sardine f

pile [paɪl] n Haufen m; (of books, wood) Stapel
m; (in ground) Pfahl m; (on carpet) Flausch
m ♦ vt (also: **~ up**) anhäufen ♦ vi (also: **~ up**)
sich anhäufen

piles [paɪlz] npl Hämorr(ho)iden pl

pile-up ['paɪlʌp] n (AUT)
Massenzusammenstoß m

pilfering ['pɪlfərɪŋ] n Diebstahl m

pilgrim ['pɪlgrɪm] n Pilger(in) m(f); **~age** n
Wallfahrt f

pill [pɪl] n Tablette f, Pille f; **the ~** die
(Antibaby)pille

pillage ['pɪlɪdʒ] vt plündern

pillar ['pɪləʳ] n Pfeiler m, Säule f (also fig); **~
box** (BRIT) n Briefkasten m

pillion ['pɪljən] n Soziussitz m

pillow ['pɪləʊ] n Kissen nt; **~case** n
Kissenbezug m

pilot ['paɪlət] n Pilot m; (NAUT) Lotse m ♦ adj
(scheme etc) Versuchs- ♦ vt führen; (ship)
lotsen; **~ light** n Zündflamme f

pimp [pɪmp] n Zuhälter m

pimple ['pɪmpl] n Pickel m

PIN n abbr (= personal identification number)
PIN f

pin [pɪn] n Nadel f; (for sewing) Stecknadel f;
(TECH) Stift m, Bolzen m ♦ vt stecken; (keep
in one position) pressen, drücken; **to ~ sth
to sth** etw an etw acc heften; **to ~ sth on
sb** (fig) jdm etw anhängen; **~s and needles**
Kribbeln nt; **~ down** vt (fig: person): **to ~
sb down (to sth)** jdn (auf etw acc)
festnageln

pinafore ['pɪnəfɔːʳ] n Schürze f; **~ dress** n
Kleiderrock m

pinball ['pɪnbɔːl] n Flipper m

pincers ['pɪnsəz] npl Kneif- or Beißzange f;
(MED) Pinzette f

pinch [pɪntʃ] n Zwicken nt, Kneifen nt; (of
salt) Prise f ♦ vt zwicken, kneifen; (inf: steal)
klauen ♦ vi (shoe) drücken; **at a ~** notfalls,
zur Not

pincushion ['pɪnkuʃən] n Nadelkissen nt

pine [paɪn] n (also: **~ tree**) Kiefer f ♦ vi: **to ~
for** sich sehnen nach; **~ away** vi sich zu
Tode sehnen

pineapple ['paɪnæpl] n Ananas f

ping [pɪŋ] n Klingeln nt; **~-pong** ['pɪnspɔŋ] n ®
Pingpong nt

pink [pɪŋk] adj rosa inv ♦ n Rosa nt; (BOT)
Nelke f

pinnacle ['pɪnəkl] n Spitze f

PIN number n PIN-Nummer f

pinpoint ['pɪnpɔɪnt] vt festlegen

pinstripe ['pɪnstraɪp] n Nadelstreifen m

pint [paɪnt] n Pint nt; (BRIT: inf: of beer)
große(s) Bier nt

pioneer [paɪə'nɪəʳ] n Pionier m; (fig also)
Bahnbrecher m

pious ['paɪəs] adj fromm

pip [pɪp] n Kern m; **the ~s** npl (BRIT: RAD) das
Zeitzeichen

pipe [paɪp] n (smoking) Pfeife f; (tube) Rohr
nt; (in house) (Rohr)leitung f ♦ vt (durch
Rohre) leiten; (MUS) blasen; **~s** npl (also:
bagpipes) Dudelsack m; **~ down** vi (be
quiet) die Luft anhalten; **~ cleaner** n
Pfeifenreiniger m; **~ dream** n Luftschloss nt;
~line n (for oil) Pipeline f; **~r** n Pfeifer m;
(bagpipes) Dudelsackbläser m

piping ['paɪpɪŋ] adv: **~ hot** siedend heiß

pique ['piːk] n gekränkte(r) Stolz m

pirate ['paɪərət] n Pirat m, Seeräuber m; **~d**
adj: **~d version** Raubkopie f; **~ radio** (BRIT)
n Piratensender m

Pisces ['paɪsiːz] n Fische pl

piss [pɪs] (inf) vi pissen; **~ed** (inf) adj (drunk)
voll

pistol ['pɪstl] n Pistole f

piston ['pɪstən] n Kolben m

pit [pɪt] n Grube f; (THEAT) Parterre nt;
(orchestra ~) Orchestergraben m ♦ vt (mark
with scars) zerfressen; (compare): **to ~ sb
against sb** jdn an jdm messen; **the ~s** npl
(MOTOR RACING) die Boxen pl

pitch [pɪtʃ] n Wurf m; (of trader) Stand m;
(SPORT) (Spiel)feld nt; (MUS) Tonlage f;
(substance) Pech nt ♦ vt werfen; (set up)
aufschlagen ♦ vi (NAUT) rollen; **to ~ a tent**
ein Zelt aufbauen; **~-black** adj pechschwarz;
~ed battle n offene Schlacht f

piteous ['pɪtɪəs] adj kläglich, erbärmlich

pitfall ['pɪtfɔːl] n (fig) Falle f

pith [pɪθ] n Mark nt

pithy ['pɪθɪ] adj prägnant

pitiful ['pɪtɪful] adj (deserving pity)
bedauernswert; (contemptible) jämmerlich

pitiless ['pɪtɪlɪs] adj erbarmungslos

pittance ['pɪtns] n Hungerlohn m

pity ['pɪtɪ] n (sympathy) Mitleid nt ♦ vt Mitleid
haben mit; **what a ~!** wie schade!

pivot ['pɪvət] n Drehpunkt m ♦ vi: **to ~ (on)**
sich drehen (um)

pizza ['piːtsə] n Pizza f

placard ['plækɑːd] n Plakat nt, Anschlag m

placate [plə'keɪt] vt beschwichtigen

place [pleɪs] n Platz m; (spot) Stelle f; (town
etc) Ort m ♦ vt setzen, stellen, legen; (order)
aufgeben; (SPORT) platzieren; (identify)
unterbringen; **to take ~** stattfinden; **out of
~** nicht am rechten Platz; (fig: remark)
unangebracht; **in the first ~** erstens; **to
change ~s with sb** mit jdm den Platz
tauschen; **to be ~d third** (in race, exam) auf
dem dritten Platz liegen

placid ['plæsɪd] adj gelassen, ruhig

plagiarism ['pleɪdʒərɪzəm] n Plagiat nt

plague [pleɪg] n Pest f; (fig) Plage f ♦ vt
plagen

plaice [pleɪs] n Scholle f

plaid [plæd] n Plaid nt

plain [pleɪn] adj (clear) klar, deutlich; (simple)
einfach, schlicht; (not beautiful) alltäglich
♦ n Ebene f; **in ~ clothes** (police) in
Zivil(kleidung); **~ chocolate** n
Bitterschokolade f

plaintiff ['pleɪntɪf] n Kläger m

plaintive ['pleɪntɪv] adj wehleidig

plait [plæt] n Zopf m ♦ vt flechten

plan [plæn] n Plan m ♦ vt, vi planen;
according to ~ planmäßig; **to ~ to do sth**
vorhaben, etw zu tun

plane [pleɪn] n Ebene f; (AVIAT) Flugzeug nt;
(tool) Hobel m; (tree) Platane f

planet ['plænɪt] n Planet m

plank [plæŋk] n Brett nt

planning ['plænɪŋ] n Planung f; **family ~**

Familienplanung f; **~ permission** n
Baugenehmigung f

plant [plɑːnt] n Pflanze f; (TECH)
(Maschinen)anlage f; (factory) Fabrik f, Werk
nt ♦ vt pflanzen; (set firmly) stellen; **~ation**
[plæn'teɪʃən] n Plantage f

plaque [plæk] n Gedenktafel f; (on teeth)
(Zahn)belag m

plaster ['plɑːstər] n Gips m; (in house)
Verputz m; (BRIT: also: sticking ~) Pflaster
nt; (for fracture: ~ of Paris) Gipsverband m
♦ vt gipsen; (hole) zugipsen; (ceiling)
verputzen; (fig: with pictures etc) bekleben,
verkleben; **~ed** (inf) adj besoffen; **~er** n
Gipser m

plastic ['plæstɪk] n Plastik nt or f ♦ adj (made
of ~) Plastik-; (ART) plastisch, bildend; **~ bag**
n Plastiktüte f

plasticine ['plæstɪsiːn] ® n Plastilin nt

plastic surgery n plastische Chirurgie f

plate [pleɪt] n Teller m; (gold/silver ~)
vergoldete(s)/versilberte(s) Tafelgeschirr nt;
(in book) (Bild)tafel f

plateau ['plætəu] (pl **~s** or **~x**) n (GEOG)
Plateau nt, Hochebene f

plateaux ['plætəuz] npl of **plateau**

plate glass n Tafelglas nt

platform ['plætfɔːm] n (at meeting) Plattform
f, Podium nt; (RAIL) Bahnsteig m; (POL)
Parteiprogramm nt; **~ ticket** n
Bahnsteigkarte f

platinum ['plætɪnəm] n Platin nt

platoon [plə'tuːn] n (MIL) Zug m

platter ['plætər] n Platte f

plausible ['plɔːzɪbl] adj (theory, excuse,
statement) plausibel; (person) überzeugend

play [pleɪ] n (also TECH) Spiel nt; (THEAT)
(Theater)stück nt ♦ vt spielen; (another
team) spielen gegen ♦ vi spielen; **~ safe**
auf Nummer sicher or Sicher gehen; **~
down** vt herunterspielen; **~ up** vi (cause
trouble) frech werden; (bad leg etc) wehtun
♦ vt (person) plagen; **to ~ up to sb** jdm
flattieren; **~-acting** n Schauspielerei f; **~er** n
Spieler(in) m(f); **~ful** adj spielerisch;
~ground n Spielplatz m; **~group** n
Kindergarten m; **~ing card** n Spielkarte f;
~ing field n Sportplatz m; **~mate** n
Spielkamerad m; **~-off** n (SPORT)
Entscheidungsspiel nt; **~pen** n Laufstall m;
~school n = **playgroup**; **~thing** n
Spielzeug nt; **~time** n (kleine) Pause f;
~wright n ['pleɪraɪt] n Theaterschriftsteller m

plc abbr (= public limited company) ≈ AG f

plea [pliː] n Bitte f; (general appeal) Appell
m; (JUR) Plädoyer nt; **~ bargaining** n (LAW)
Aushandeln der Strafe zwischen
Staatsanwaltschaft und Verteidigung

plead [pliːd] vt (poverty) zur Entschuldigung
anführen; (JUR: sb's case) vertreten ♦ vi (beg)
dringend bitten; (JUR) plädieren; **to ~ with**

sb jdn dringend bitten
pleasant ['plɛznt] adj angenehm; **~ries** npl
(polite remarks) Nettigkeiten pl
please [pli:z] vt, vi (be agreeable to) gefallen
+dat; **~!** bitte!; **~ yourself!** wie du willst!;
~d adj zufrieden; (glad): **~d (about sth)**
erfreut (über etw acc); **~d to meet you**
angenehm; **pleasing** ['pli:zɪŋ] adj erfreulich
pleasure ['plɛʒəʳ] n Freude f ♦ cpd
Vergnügungs-; **"it's a ~"** „gern geschehen"
pleat [pli:t] n Falte f
plectrum ['plɛktrəm] n Plektron nt
pledge [plɛdʒ] n Pfand nt; (promise)
Versprechen nt ♦ vt verpfänden; (promise)
geloben, versprechen
plentiful ['plɛntɪful] adj reichlich
plenty ['plɛntɪ] n Fülle f, Überfluss m; **~ of**
eine Menge, viel
pleurisy ['pluərɪsɪ] n Rippenfellentzündung f
pliable ['plaɪəbl] adj biegsam; (person)
beeinflussbar
pliers ['plaɪəz] npl (Kneif)zange f
plight [plaɪt] n Notlage f
plimsolls ['plɪmsəlz] (BRIT) npl Turnschuhe pl
plinth [plɪnθ] n Sockel m
P.L.O. n abbr (= Palestine Liberation
Organization) PLO f
plod [plɒd] vi (work) sich abplagen; (walk)
trotten
plonk [plɒŋk] n (BRIT: inf: wine) billige(r)
Wein m ♦ vt: **to ~ sth down** etw hinknallen
plot [plɒt] n Komplott nt; (story) Handlung f;
(of land) Grundstück nt ♦ vt markieren;
(curve) zeichnen; (movements) nachzeichnen
♦ vi (plan secretly) sich verschwören
plough [plau] (US **plow**) n Pflug m ♦ vt
pflügen; **~ back** vt (COMM) wieder in das
Geschäft stecken; **~ through** vt fus (water)
durchpflügen; (book) sich kämpfen durch
plow [plau] (US) = **plough**
ploy [plɔɪ] n Masche f
pluck [plʌk] vt (fruit) pflücken; (guitar)
zupfen; (goose etc) rupfen ♦ n Mut m; **to ~
up courage** all seinen Mut zusammennehmen
plug [plʌg] n Stöpsel m; (ELEC) Stecker m;
(inf: publicity) Schleichwerbung f; (AUT)
Zündkerze f ♦ vt (zu)stopfen; (inf: advertise)
Reklame machen für; **~ in** vt (ELEC)
anschließen
plum [plʌm] n Pflaume f, Zwetsch(g)e f
plumage ['plu:mɪdʒ] n Gefieder nt
plumber ['plʌməʳ] n Klempner m,
Installateur m; **plumbing** ['plʌmɪŋ] n (craft)
Installieren nt; (fittings) Leitungen pl
plummet ['plʌmɪt] vi (ab)stürzen
plump [plʌmp] adj rundlich, füllig ♦ vt
plumpsen lassen; **to ~ for** (inf: choose) sich
entscheiden für
plunder ['plʌndəʳ] n Plünderung f; (loot)
Beute f ♦ vt plündern
plunge [plʌndʒ] n Sturz m ♦ vt stoßen ♦ vi

(sich) stürzen; **to take the ~** den Sprung
wagen; **plunging** ['plʌndʒɪŋ] adj (neckline)
offenherzig
plural ['pluərl] n Plural m, Mehrzahl f
plus [plʌs] n (also: **~ sign**) Plus(zeichen) nt
♦ prep plus, und; **ten/twenty ~** mehr als
zehn/zwanzig
plush [plʌʃ] adj (also: **~y**: inf) feudal
ply [plaɪ] vt (trade) (be)treiben; (with
questions) zusetzen +dat; (ship, taxi)
befahren ♦ vi (ship, taxi) verkehren ♦ n:
three-~ (wool) Dreifach-; **to ~ sb with
drink** jdn zum Trinken animieren; **~wood** n
Sperrholz nt
P.M. n abbr = **prime minister**
p.m. adv abbr (= post meridiem) nachmittags
pneumatic drill n Presslufthammer m
pneumonia [nju:ˈməunɪə] n
Lungenentzündung f
poach [pəutʃ] vt (COOK) pochieren; (game)
stehlen ♦ vi (steal) wildern; **~ed** adj (egg)
verloren; **~er** n Wilddieb m
P.O. Box n abbr = **Post Office Box**
pocket ['pɒkɪt] n Tasche f; (of resistance)
(Widerstands)nest nt ♦ vt einstecken; **to be
out of ~** (BRIT) draufzahlen; **~book** n
Taschenbuch nt; **~ calculator** n
Taschenrechner m; **~ knife** n Taschenmesser
nt; **~ money** n Taschengeld nt
pod [pɒd] n Hülse f; (of peas also) Schote
f
podgy ['pɒdʒɪ] adj pummelig
podiatrist [pɒˈdiːətrɪst] (US) n
Fußpfleger(in) m(f)
poem ['pəuɪm] n Gedicht nt
poet ['pəuɪt] n Dichter m, Poet m; **~ic**
[pəuˈɛtɪk] adj poetisch, dichterisch; **~
laureate** n Hofdichter m; **~ry** n Poesie f;
(poems) Gedichte pl
poignant ['pɔɪnjənt] adj (touching)
ergreifend
point [pɔɪnt] n (also in discussion, scoring)
Punkt m; (spot) Punkt m, Stelle f; (sharpened
tip) Spitze f; (moment) (Zeit)punkt m;
(purpose) Zweck m; (idea) Argument nt;
(decimal) Dezimalstelle f; (personal
characteristic) Seite f ♦ vt zeigen mit; (gun)
richten ♦ vi zeigen; **~s** npl (RAIL) Weichen pl;
to be on the ~ of doing sth drauf und dran
sein, etw zu tun; **to make a ~ of** Wert
darauf legen; **to get the ~** verstehen,
worum es geht; **to come to the ~** zur
Sache kommen; **there's no ~ (in doing sth)**
es hat keinen Sinn(, etw zu tun); **~ out** vt
hinweisen auf +acc; **~ to** vt fus zeigen auf
+acc; **~-blank** adv (at close range) aus
nächster Entfernung; (bluntly) unverblümt;
~ed adj (also fig) spitz, scharf; **~edly** adv
(fig) spitz; **~er** n Zeigestock m; (on dial)
Zeiger m; **~less** adj sinnlos; **~ of view** n
Stand- or Gesichtspunkt m

poise [pɔɪz] n Haltung f; (fig) Gelassenheit f

poison ['pɔɪzn] n (also fig) Gift nt ♦ vt vergiften; **~ing** n Vergiftung f; **~ous** adj giftig, Gift-

poke [pəʊk] vt stoßen; (put) stecken; (fire) schüren; (hole) bohren; **~ about** vi herumstochern; (nose around) herumwühlen

poker ['pəʊkəʳ] n Schürhaken m; (CARDS) Poker nt

poky ['pəʊkɪ] adj eng

Poland ['pəʊlənd] n Polen nt

polar ['pəʊləʳ] adj Polar-, polar; **~ bear** n Eisbär m

Pole [pəʊl] n Pole m, Polin f

pole [pəʊl] n Stange f, Pfosten m; (flagpole, telegraph ~) Stange f, Mast m; (ELEC, GEOG) Pol m; (SPORT: vaulting ~) Stab m; (ski ~) Stock m; **~ bean** n (US) n (runner bean) Stangenbohne f; **~ vault** n Stabhochsprung m

police [pə'liːs] n Polizei f ♦ vt kontrollieren; **~ car** n Polizeiwagen m; **~man** (irreg) n Polizist m; **~ state** n Polizeistaat m; **~ station** n (Polizei)revier nt, Wache f; **~woman** (irreg) n Polizistin f

policy ['pɒlɪsɪ] n Politik f; (insurance) (Versicherungs)police f

polio ['pəʊlɪəʊ] n (spinale) Kinderlähmung f, Polio f

Polish ['pəʊlɪʃ] adj polnisch ♦ n (LING) Polnisch nt

polish ['pɒlɪʃ] n Politur f; (for floor) Wachs nt; (for shoes) Creme f; (for nails) Lack m; (shine) Glanz m; (of furniture) Politur f; (fig) Schliff m ♦ vt polieren; (shoes) putzen; (fig) den letzten Schliff geben +dat; **~ off** vt (inf: food) wegputzen; (: drink) hinunterschütten; **~ed** adj glänzend; (manners) verfeinert

polite [pə'laɪt] adj höflich; **~ly** adv höflich; **~ness** n Höflichkeit f

political [pə'lɪtɪkl] adj politisch; **~ly** adv politisch; **~ly correct** politisch korrekt

politician [pɒlɪ'tɪʃən] n Politiker m

politics ['pɒlɪtɪks] npl Politik f

polka dot ['pɒlkə-] n Tupfen m

poll [pəʊl] n Abstimmung f; (in election) Wahl f; (votes cast) Wahlbeteiligung f; (opinion ~) Umfrage f ♦ vt (votes) erhalten

pollen ['pɒlən] n (BOT) Blütenstaub m, Pollen m

polling ['pəʊlɪŋ-]: **~ booth** (BRIT) n Wahlkabine f; **~ day** (BRIT) n Wahltag m; **~ station** (BRIT) n Wahllokal nt

pollute [pə'luːt] vt verschmutzen, verunreinigen; **~d** adj verschmutzt; **pollution** [pə'luːʃən] n Verschmutzung f

polo ['pəʊləʊ] n Polo nt; **~ neck** n (also: **~-necked sweater**) Rollkragen m; Rollkragenpullover m; **~ shirt** n Polohemd nt

polystyrene [pɒlɪ'staɪriːn] n Styropor nt

polytechnic [pɒlɪ'teknɪk] n technische Hochschule f

polythene ['pɒlɪθiːn] n Plastik nt; **~ bag** n Plastiktüte f

pomegranate ['pɒmɪɡrænɪt] n Granatapfel m

pompom ['pɒmpɒm] n Troddel f, Pompon m

pompous ['pɒmpəs] adj aufgeblasen; (language) geschwollen

pond [pɒnd] n Teich m, Weiher m

ponder ['pɒndəʳ] vt nachdenken über +acc; **~ous** adj schwerfällig

pong [pɒŋ] (BRIT: inf) n Mief m

pontiff ['pɒntɪf] n Pontifex m

pontoon [pɒn'tuːn] n Ponton m; (CARDS) 17-und-4 nt

pony ['pəʊnɪ] n Pony nt; **~tail** n Pferdeschwanz m; **~ trekking** (BRIT) n Ponyreiten nt

poodle ['puːdl] n Pudel m

pool [puːl] n (swimming ~) Schwimmbad nt; (: private) Swimmingpool m; (of liquid, blood) Lache f; (fund) (gemeinsame) Kasse f; (billiards) Poolspiel nt ♦ vt (money etc) zusammenlegen; **typing ~** Schreibzentrale f; **(football) ~s** Toto nt

poor [pʊəʳ] adj arm; (not good) schlecht ♦ npl: **the ~** die Armen pl; **~ in** (resources) arm an +dat; **~ly** adv schlecht; (dressed) ärmlich ♦ adj schlecht

pop [pɒp] n Knall m; (music) Popmusik f; (drink) Limo(nade) f; (US: inf) Pa m ♦ vt (put) stecken; (balloon) platzen lassen ♦ vi knallen; **~ in** vi kurz vorbeigehen or vorbeikommen; **~ out** vi (person) kurz rausgehen; (thing) herausspringen; **~ up** vi auftauchen; **~corn** n Puffmais m

pope [pəʊp] n Papst m

poplar ['pɒpləʳ] n Pappel f

poppy ['pɒpɪ] n Mohn m

Popsicle ['pɒpsɪkl] (® US) n (ice lolly) Eis nt am Stiel

populace ['pɒpjʊləs] n Volk nt

popular ['pɒpjʊləʳ] adj beliebt, populär; (of the people) volkstümlich; (widespread) allgemein; **~ity** [pɒpjʊ'lærɪtɪ] n Beliebtheit f, Popularität f; **~ly** adv allgemein, überall

population [pɒpjʊ'leɪʃən] n Bevölkerung f; (of town) Einwohner pl

populous ['pɒpjʊləs] adj dicht besiedelt

porcelain ['pɔːslɪn] n Porzellan nt

porch [pɔːtʃ] n Vorbau m, Veranda f

porcupine ['pɔːkjʊpaɪn] n Stachelschwein nt

pore [pɔːʳ] n Pore f ♦ vi: **to ~ over** brüten über +dat

pork [pɔːk] n Schweinefleisch nt

porn [pɔːn] n Porno m; **~ographic** [pɔːnə'ɡræfɪk] adj pornografisch; **~ography** [pɔː'nɒɡrəfɪ] n Pornografie f

porous ['pɔːrəs] adj porös; (skin) porig

porpoise ['pɔːpəs] n Tümmler m

porridge ['pɒrɪdʒ] n Haferbrei m
port [pɔːt] n Hafen m; (town) Hafenstadt f; (NAUT: left side) Backbord nt; (wine) Portwein m; **~ of call** Anlaufhafen m
portable ['pɔːtəbl] adj tragbar
porter ['pɔːtər] n Pförtner(in) m(f); (for luggage) (Gepäck)träger m
portfolio [pɔːt'fəuliəu] n (case) Mappe f; (POL) Geschäftsbereich m; (FIN) Portefeuille nt; (of artist) Kollektion f
porthole ['pɔːthəul] n Bullauge nt
portion ['pɔːʃən] n Teil m, Stück nt; (of food) Portion f
portrait ['pɔːtreɪt] n Porträt nt
portray [pɔː'treɪ] vt darstellen; **~al** n Darstellung f
Portugal ['pɔːtjugl] n Portugal nt
Portuguese [pɔːtju'giːz] adj portugiesisch ♦ n inv Portugiese m, Portugiesin f; (LING) Portugiesisch nt
pose [pəuz] n Stellung f, Pose f; (affectation) Pose f ♦ vi posieren ♦ vt stellen
posh [pɒʃ] (inf) adj (piek)fein
position [pə'zɪʃən] n Stellung f; (place) Lage f; (job) Stelle f; (attitude) Standpunkt m ♦ vt aufstellen
positive ['pɒzɪtɪv] adj positiv; (convinced) sicher; (definite) eindeutig
posse ['pɒsɪ] (US) n Aufgebot nt
possess [pə'zes] vt besitzen; **~ion** [pə'zeʃən] n Besitz m; **~ive** adj besitzergreifend, eigensüchtig
possibility [pɒsɪ'bɪlɪtɪ] n Möglichkeit f
possible ['pɒsɪbl] adj möglich; **as big as ~** so groß wie möglich, möglichst groß; **~bly** adv möglicherweise, vielleicht; **I cannot possibly come** ich kann unmöglich kommen
post [pəust] n (BRIT: letters, delivery) Post f; (pole) Pfosten m, Pfahl m; (place of duty) Posten m; (job) Stelle f ♦ vt (notice) anschlagen; (BRIT: letters) aufgeben; (: appoint) versetzen; (soldiers) aufstellen; **~age** n Postgebühr f, Porto nt; **~al** adj Post-; **~al order** n Postanweisung f; **~box** (BRIT) n Briefkasten m; **~card** n Postkarte f; **~code** (BRIT) n Postleitzahl f
postdate ['pəust'deɪt] vt (cheque) nachdatieren
poster ['pəustər] n Plakat nt, Poster nt
poste restante [pəust'restɑːnt] n Aufbewahrungsstelle f für postlagernde Sendungen
posterior [pɒs'tɪərɪər] (inf) n Hintern m
posterity [pɒs'terɪtɪ] n Nachwelt f
postgraduate ['pəust'grædjuət] n Weiterstudierende(r) mf
posthumous ['pɒstjuməs] adj post(h)um
postman ['pəustmən] (irreg) n Briefträger m
postmark ['pəustmɑːk] n Poststempel m
post-mortem [pəust'mɔːtəm] n Autopsie f

post office n Postamt nt, Post f; (organization) Post f; **Post Office Box** n Postfach nt
postpone [pəus'pəun] vt verschieben
postscript ['pəustskrɪpt] n Postskript nt; (to affair) Nachspiel nt
posture ['pɒstʃər] n Haltung f ♦ vi posieren
postwar [pəust'wɔːr] adj Nachkriegs-
postwoman ['pəustwumən] (irreg) n Briefträgerin f
posy ['pəuzɪ] n Blumenstrauß m
pot [pɒt] n Topf m; (teapot) Kanne f; (inf: marijuana) Hasch m ♦ vt (plant) eintopfen; **to go to ~** (inf: work) auf den Hund kommen
potato [pə'teɪtəu] (pl **~es**) n Kartoffel f; **~ peeler** n Kartoffelschäler m
potent ['pəutnt] adj stark; (argument) zwingend
potential [pə'tenʃl] adj potenziell, potentiell ♦ n Potenzial nt, Potential nt; **~ly** adv potenziell, potentiell
pothole ['pɒthəul] n (in road) Schlagloch nt; (BRIT: underground) Höhle f; **potholing** (BRIT) n: **to go potholing** Höhlen erforschen
potion ['pəuʃən] n Trank m
potluck [pɒt'lʌk] n: **to take ~ with sth** etw auf gut Glück nehmen
pot plant n Topfpflanze f
potter ['pɒtər] n Töpfer m ♦ vi herumhantieren; **~y** n Töpferwaren pl; (place) Töpferei f
potty ['pɒtɪ] adj (inf: mad) verrückt ♦ n Töpfchen nt
pouch [pautʃ] n Beutel m
pouf(fe) [puːf] n Sitzkissen nt
poultry ['pəultrɪ] n Geflügel nt
pounce [pauns] vi sich stürzen ♦ n Sprung m, Satz m; **to ~ on** sich stürzen auf +acc
pound [paund] n (FIN, weight) Pfund nt; (for cars, animals) Auslösestelle f ♦ vt (zer)stampfen ♦ vi klopfen, hämmern; **~ sterling** n Pfund Sterling nt
pour [pɔːr] vt gießen, schütten ♦ vi gießen; (crowds etc) strömen; **~ away** vt abgießen; **~ in** vi (people) hereinströmen; **~ off** vt abgießen; **~ out** vi (people) herausströmen ♦ vt (drink) einschenken; **~ing** adj: **~ing rain** strömende(r) Regen m
pout [paut] vi schmollen
poverty ['pɒvətɪ] n Armut f; **~-stricken** adj verarmt, sehr arm
powder ['paudər] n Pulver nt; (cosmetic) Puder m ♦ vt pulverisieren; **to ~ one's nose** sich dat die Nase pudern; **~ compact** n Puderdose f; **~ed milk** n Milchpulver nt; **~ room** n Damentoilette f; **~y** adj pulverig
power ['pauər] n (also POL) Macht f; (ability) Fähigkeit f; (strength) Stärke f; (MATH) Potenz f; (ELEC) Strom m ♦ vt betreiben, antreiben; **to be in ~** (POL etc) an der Macht

sein; ~ **cut** n Stromausfall m; **~ed** adj: **~ed
by** betrieben mit; ~ **failure** (US) n
Stromausfall m; **~ful** adj (person) mächtig;
(engine, government) stark; **~less** adj
machtlos; ~ **point** (BRIT) n elektrische(r)
Anschluss m; ~ **station** n Elektrizitätswerk
nt; ~ **struggle** n Machtkampf m
p.p. abbr (= per procurationem): ~ **J. Smith**
i. A. J. Smith
PR n abbr = **public relations**
practicable ['præktɪkəbl] adj durchführbar
practical ['præktɪkl] adj praktisch; **~ity**
[præktɪ'kælɪtɪ] n (of person) praktische
Veranlagung f; (of situation etc)
Durchführbarkeit f; ~ **joke** n Streich m; **~ly**
adv praktisch
practice ['præktɪs] n Übung f; (reality, also of
doctor, lawyer) Praxis f; (custom) Brauch m;
(in business) Usus m ♦ vt, vi (US) = **practise**;
in ~ (in reality) in der Praxis; **out of** ~ außer
Übung; **practicing** (US) adj = **practising**
practise ['præktɪs] (US **practice**) vt üben;
(profession) ausüben ♦ vi (sich) üben;
(doctor, lawyer) praktizieren; **practising** (US
practicing) adj praktizierend; (Christian etc)
aktiv
practitioner [præk'tɪʃənər] n praktische(r)
Arzt m, praktische Ärztin f
pragmatic [præg'mætɪk] adj pragmatisch
prairie ['prεərɪ] n Prärie f, Steppe f
praise [preɪz] n Lob nt ♦ vt loben; **~worthy**
adj lobenswert
pram [præm] (BRIT) n Kinderwagen m
prance [prɑːns] vi (horse) tänzeln; (person)
stolzieren
prank [præŋk] n Streich m
prawn [prɔːn] n Garnele f, Krabbe f; ~
cocktail n Krabbencocktail m
pray [preɪ] vi beten; **~er** [prεər] n Gebet nt
preach [priːtʃ] vi predigen; **~er** n Prediger m
preamble [prɪ'æmbl] n Einleitung f
precarious [prɪ'kεərɪəs] adj prekär, unsicher
precaution [prɪ'kɔːʃən] n
(Vorsichts)maßnahme f
precede [prɪ'siːd] vi vorausgehen ♦ vt
vorausgehen +dat; **~nce** ['presɪdəns] n
Vorrang m; **~nt** ['presɪdənt] n Präzedenzfall
m; **preceding** [prɪ'siːdɪŋ] adj vorhergehend
precinct ['priːsɪŋkt] n (US: district) Bezirk m;
~s npl (round building) Gelände nt; (area,
environs) Umgebung f; **pedestrian** ~
Fußgängerzone f; **shopping** ~
Geschäftsviertel nt
precious ['preʃəs] adj kostbar, wertvoll;
(affected) pretiös, preziös, geziert
precipice ['presɪpɪs] n Abgrund m
precipitate [adj prɪ'sɪpɪtɪt, vb prɪ'sɪpɪteɪt] adj
überstürzt, übereilt ♦ vt hinunterstürzen;
(events) heraufbeschwören
precise [prɪ'saɪs] adj genau, präzis; **~ly** adv
genau, präzis

precision [prɪ'sɪʒən] n Präzision f
preclude [prɪ'kluːd] vt ausschließen
precocious [prɪ'kəʊʃəs] adj frühreif
preconceived [priːkən'siːvd] adj (idea)
vorgefasst
precondition ['priːkən'dɪʃən] n
Vorbedingung f, Voraussetzung f
precursor [priː'kɜːsər] n Vorläufer m
predator ['predətər] n Raubtier m
predecessor ['priːdɪsesər] n Vorgänger m
predicament [prɪ'dɪkəmənt] n missliche
Lage f
predict [prɪ'dɪkt] vt voraussagen; **~able** adj
vorhersagbar; **~ion** [prɪ'dɪkʃən] n Voraussage
f
predominantly [prɪ'dɒmɪnəntlɪ] adv
überwiegend, hauptsächlich
predominate [prɪ'dɒmɪneɪt] vi vorherrschen;
(fig) vorherrschen, überwiegen
pre-eminent [priː'emɪnənt] adj
hervorragend, herausragend
pre-empt [priː'emt] vt (action, decision)
vorwegnehmen
preen [priːn] vt putzen; **to ~ o.s.** (person)
sich brüsten
prefab ['priːfæb] n Fertighaus nt
preface ['prefəs] n Vorwort nt
prefect ['priːfekt] n Präfekt m; (SCH)
Aufsichtsschüler(in) m(f)
prefer [prɪ'fɜːr] vt vorziehen, lieber mögen;
to ~ to do sth etw lieber tun; **~ably**
['prefrəblɪ] adv vorzugsweise, am liebsten;
~ence ['prefrəns] n Präferenz f, Vorzug m;
~ential [prefə'renʃəl] adj bevorzugt,
Vorzugs-
prefix ['priːfɪks] n Vorsilbe f, Präfix nt
pregnancy ['pregnənsɪ] n Schwangerschaft f
pregnant ['pregnənt] adj schwanger
prehistoric ['priːhɪs'tɒrɪk] adj prähistorisch,
vorgeschichtlich
prejudice ['predʒudɪs] n (bias)
Voreingenommenheit f; (opinion) Vorurteil
nt; (harm) Schaden m ♦ vt beeinträchtigen;
~d adj (person) voreingenommen
preliminary [prɪ'lɪmɪnərɪ] adj einleitend, Vor-
prelude ['prɪljuːd] n Vorspiel nt; (fig) Auftakt
m
premarital ['priː'mærɪtl] adj vorehelich
premature ['premətʃuər] adj vorzeitig,
verfrüht; (birth) Früh-
premeditated [priː'medɪteɪtɪd] adj geplant;
(murder) vorsätzlich
premenstrual syndrome [priː'menstruəl-]
n prämenstruelles Syndrom nt
premier ['premɪər] adj erste(r, s) ♦ n Premier
m
première ['premɪεər] n Premiere f;
Uraufführung f
Premier League [-liːg] n ≈ 1. Bundesliga
(höchste Spielklasse im Fußball)
premise ['premɪs] n Voraussetzung f,

Prämisse f; ~s npl (shop) Räumlichkeiten pl; (grounds) Gelände nt; **on the ~s** im Hause

premium |'priːmɪəm| n Prämie f; **to be at a ~** über pari stehen; **~ bond** (BRIT) n Prämienanleihe f

premonition |premə'nɪʃən| n Vorahnung f

preoccupation |priːɔkju'peɪʃən| n Sorge f

preoccupied |priː'ɔkjupaɪd| adj (look) geistesabwesend

prep |prep| n (SCH) Hausaufgabe f

prepaid |priː'peɪd| adj vorausbezahlt; (letter) frankiert

preparation |prepə'reɪʃən| n Vorbereitung f

preparatory |prɪ'pærətərɪ| adj Vor(bereitungs)-; **~ school** n (BRIT) private Vorbereitungsschule für die Public School; (US) private Vorbereitungsschule für die Hochschule

prepare |prɪ'peər| vt vorbereiten ♦ vi sich vorbereiten; **to ~ for/prepare sth for** sich/ etw vorbereiten auf +acc; **to be ~d to ...** bereit sein zu ...

preponderance |prɪ'pɔndərns| n Übergewicht nt

preposition |prepə'zɪʃən| n Präposition f, Verhältniswort nt

preposterous |prɪ'pɔstərəs| adj absurd

prep school n = **preparatory school**

prerequisite |priː'rekwɪzɪt| n (unerlässliche) Voraussetzung f

prerogative |prɪ'rɔgətɪv| n Vorrecht nt

Presbyterian |prezbɪ'tɪərɪən| adj presbyterianisch ♦ n Presbyterier(in) m(f)

preschool |'priː'skuːl| adj Vorschul-

prescribe |prɪ'skraɪb| vt vorschreiben; (MED) verschreiben

prescription |prɪ'skrɪpʃən| n (MED) Rezept nt

presence |'prezns| n Gegenwart f; **~ of mind** Geistesgegenwart f

present |adj, n 'preznt, vb prɪ'zent| adj (here) anwesend; (current) gegenwärtig ♦ n Gegenwart f; (gift) Geschenk nt ♦ vt vorlegen; (introduce) vorstellen; (show) zeigen; (give): **to ~ sb with sth** jdm etw überreichen; **at ~** im Augenblick; **to give sb a ~** jdm ein Geschenk machen; **~able** |prɪ'zentəbl| adj präsentabel; **~ation** |prezn'teɪʃən| n Überreichung f; **~-day** adj heutig; **~er** |prɪ'zentər| n (RAD, TV) Moderator(in) m(f); **~ly** adv bald; (at ~) im Augenblick

preservation |prezə'veɪʃən| n Erhaltung f

preservative |prɪ'zɔːvətɪv| n Konservierungsmittel nt

preserve |prɪ'zɔːv| vt erhalten; (food) einmachen ♦ n (jam) Eingemachte(s) nt; (reserve) Schutzgebiet nt

preside |prɪ'zaɪd| vi den Vorsitz haben

president |'prezɪdənt| n Präsident m; **~ial** |prezɪ'denʃl| adj Präsidenten-; (election) Präsidentschafts-; (system) Präsidial-

press |pres| n Presse f; (printing house) Druckerei f ♦ vt drücken; (iron) bügeln; (urge) (be)drängen ♦ vi (push) drücken; **to be ~ed for time** unter Zeitdruck stehen; **to ~ for sth** drängen auf etw acc; **~ on** vi vorwärts drängen; **~ agency** n Presseagentur f; **~ conference** n Pressekonferenz f; **~ed** adj (clothes) gebügelt; **~ing** adj dringend; **~ stud** (BRIT) n Druckknopf m; **~-up** (BRIT) n Liegestütz m

pressure |'preʃər| n Druck m; **~ cooker** n Schnellkochtopf m; **~ gauge** n Druckmesser m

pressurized |'preʃəraɪzd| adj Druck-

prestige |pres'tiːʒ| n Prestige nt; **prestigious** |pres'tɪdʒəs| adj Prestige-

presumably |prɪ'zjuːməblɪ| adv vermutlich

presume |prɪ'zjuːm| vt, vi annehmen; **to ~ to do sth** sich erlauben, etw zu tun; **presumption** |prɪ'zʌmpʃən| n Annahme f; **presumptuous** |prɪ'zʌmpʃəs| adj anmaßend

pretence |prɪ'tens| (US **pretense**) n Vorgabe f, Vortäuschung f; (false claim) Vorwand m

pretend |prɪ'tend| vt vorgeben, so tun als ob ... ♦ vi so tun; **to ~ to sth** Anspruch erheben auf etw acc

pretense |prɪ'tens| (US) n = **pretence**

pretension |prɪ'tenʃən| n Anspruch m; (impudent claim) Anmaßung f

pretentious |prɪ'tenʃəs| adj angeberisch

pretext |'priːtekst| n Vorwand m

pretty |'prɪtɪ| adj hübsch ♦ adv (inf) ganz schön

prevail |prɪ'veɪl| vi siegen; (custom) vorherrschen; **to ~ against** or **over** siegen über +acc; **to ~ (up)on sb to do sth** jdn dazu bewegen, etw zu tun; **~ing** adj vorherrschend

prevalent |'prevələnt| adj vorherrschend

prevent |prɪ'vent| vt (stop) verhindern, verhüten; **to ~ sb from doing sth** jdn (daran) hindern, etw zu tun; **~ative** n Vorbeugungsmittel nt; **~ion** |prɪ'venʃən| n Verhütung f; **~ive** adj vorbeugend, Schutz-

preview |'priːvjuː| n private Voraufführung f; (trailer) Vorschau f

previous |'priːvɪəs| adj früher, vorherig; **~ly** adv früher

prewar |priː'wɔːr| adj Vorkriegs-

prey |preɪ| n Beute f; **~ on** vt fus Jagd machen auf +acc; **it was ~ing on his mind** es quälte sein Gewissen

price |praɪs| n Preis m; (value) Wert m ♦ vt (label) auszeichnen; **~less** adj (also fig) unbezahlbar; **~ list** n Preisliste f

prick |prɪk| n Stich m ♦ vt, vi stechen; **to ~ up one's ears** die Ohren spitzen

prickle |'prɪkl| n Stachel m, Dorn m

prickly |'prɪklɪ| adj stachelig; (fig: person) reizbar; **~ heat** n Hitzebläschen pl

349

pride → proficient

pride |praɪd| n Stolz m; (arrogance) Hochmut m ♦ vt: **to ~ o.s. on sth** auf etw acc stolz sein

priest |priːst| n Priester m; **~hood** n Priesteramt nt

prim |prɪm| adj prüde

primarily |ˈpraɪmərɪlɪ| adv vorwiegend

primary |ˈpraɪmərɪ| adj (main) Haupt-; (SCH) Grund-; **~ school** (BRIT) n Grundschule f

prime |praɪm| adj erste(r, s); (excellent) erstklassig ♦ vt vorbereiten; (gun) laden; **in the ~ of life** in der Blüte der Jahre; **~ minister** n Premierminister m, Ministerpräsident m; **~r** |ˈpraɪmər| n Fibel f

primeval |praɪˈmiːvl| adj vorzeitlich; (forests) Ur-

primitive |ˈprɪmɪtɪv| adj primitiv

primrose |ˈprɪmrəʊz| n (gelbe) Primel f

primus (stove) |ˈpraɪməs-| (® BRIT) n Primuskocher m

prince |prɪns| n Prinz m; (ruler) Fürst m; **princess** |prɪnˈses| n Prinzessin f; Fürstin f

principal |ˈprɪnsɪpl| adj Haupt- ♦ n (SCH) (Schul)direktor m, Rektor m; (money) (Grund)kapital nt

principle |ˈprɪnsɪpl| n Grundsatz m, Prinzip nt; **in ~** im Prinzip; **on ~** aus Prinzip, prinzipiell

print |prɪnt| n Druck m; (made by feet, fingers) Abdruck m; (PHOT) Abzug m ♦ vt drucken; (name) in Druckbuchstaben schreiben; (PHOT) abziehen; **out of ~** vergriffen; **~ed matter** n Drucksache f; **~er** n Drucker m; **~ing** n Drucken nt; (of photos) Abziehen nt; **~out** n (COMPUT) Ausdruck m

prior |ˈpraɪər| adj früher ♦ n Prior m; **~ to sth** vor etw dat; **~ to going abroad, she had** … bevor sie ins Ausland ging, hatte sie …

priority |praɪˈɒrɪtɪ| n Vorrang m, Priorität f

prise |praɪz| vt: **to ~ open** aufbrechen

prison |ˈprɪzn| n Gefängnis nt ♦ adj Gefängnis-; (system etc) Strafvollzugs-; **~er** n Gefangene(r) mf

pristine |ˈprɪstiːn| adj makellos

privacy |ˈprɪvəsɪ| n Ungestörtheit f, Ruhe f; Privatleben nt

private |ˈpraɪvɪt| adj privat, Privat-; (secret) vertraulich, geheim ♦ n einfache(r) Soldat m; **"~"** (on envelope) „persönlich"; (on door) „Privat"; **in ~** privat, unter vier Augen; **~ enterprise** n Privatunternehmen nt; **~ eye** n Privatdetektiv m; **~ property** n Privatbesitz m; **~ school** n Privatschule f; **privatize** vt privatisieren

privet |ˈprɪvɪt| n Liguster m

privilege |ˈprɪvɪlɪdʒ| n Privileg nt; **~d** adj bevorzugt, privilegiert

privy |ˈprɪvɪ| adj geheim, privat; **P~ Council** n Geheime(r) Staatsrat m

prize |praɪz| n Preis m ♦ adj (example) erstklassig; (idiot) Voll- ♦ vt (hoch) schätzen;

~-giving n Preisverteilung f; **~winner** n Preisträger(in) m(f)

pro |prəʊ| n (professional) Profi m; **the ~s and cons** das Für und Wider

probability |prɒbəˈbɪlɪtɪ| n Wahrscheinlichkeit f

probable |ˈprɒbəbl| adj wahrscheinlich; **probably** adv wahrscheinlich

probation |prəˈbeɪʃən| n Probe(zeit) f; (JUR) Bewährung f; **on ~** auf Probe; auf Bewährung

probe |prəʊb| n Sonde f; (enquiry) Untersuchung f ♦ vt, vi erforschen

problem |ˈprɒbləm| n Problem nt; **~atic** |prɒbləˈmætɪk| adj problematisch

procedure |prəˈsiːdʒər| n Verfahren nt

proceed |prəˈsiːd| vi (advance) vorrücken; (start) anfangen; (carry on) fortfahren; (set about) vorgehen; **~ings** npl Verfahren nt

proceeds |ˈprəʊsiːdz| npl Erlös m

process |ˈprəʊses| n Prozess m; (method) Verfahren nt ♦ vt bearbeiten; (food) verarbeiten; (film) entwickeln; **~ing** n (PHOT) Entwickeln nt

procession |prəˈseʃən| n Prozession f, Umzug m; **funeral ~** Trauerprozession f

pro-choice |prəʊˈtʃɔɪs| adj (movement) Pro-Abtreibungs-; **~ campaigner** Abtreibungsbefürworter(in) m(f)

proclaim |prəˈkleɪm| vt verkünden

procrastinate |prəʊˈkræstɪneɪt| vi zaudern

procure |prəˈkjʊər| vt beschaffen

prod |prɒd| vt stoßen ♦ n Stoß m

prodigal |ˈprɒdɪgl| adj: **~ (with** or **of)** verschwenderisch (mit)

prodigy |ˈprɒdɪdʒɪ| n Wunder nt

produce [n ˈprɒdjuːs, vb prəˈdjuːs] n (AGR) (Boden)produkte pl, (Natur)erzeugnis nt ♦ vt herstellen, produzieren; (cause) hervorrufen; (farmer) erzeugen; (yield) liefern, bringen; (play) inszenieren; **~r** n Hersteller m, Produzent m (also CINE); Erzeuger m

product |ˈprɒdʌkt| n Produkt nt, Erzeugnis nt; **~ion** |prəˈdʌkʃən| n Produktion f, Herstellung f; (thing) Erzeugnis nt, Produkt nt; (THEAT) Inszenierung f; **~ion line** n Fließband nt; **~ive** |prəˈdʌktɪv| adj produktiv; (fertile) ertragreich, fruchtbar; **~ivity** |prɒdʌkˈtɪvɪtɪ| n Produktivität f

profane |prəˈfeɪn| adj weltlich, profan; (language etc) gotteslästerlich

profess |prəˈfes| vt bekennen; (show) zeigen; (claim to be) vorgeben

profession |prəˈfeʃən| n Beruf m; (declaration) Bekenntnis nt; **~al** n Fachmann m; (SPORT) Berufsspieler(in) m(f) ♦ adj Berufs-; (expert) fachlich; (player) professionell; **~ally** adv beruflich, fachmännisch

professor |prəˈfesər| n Professor m

proficiency |prəˈfɪʃənsɪ| n Können nt

proficient |prəˈfɪʃənt| adj fähig

profile ['prəufaɪl] n Profil nt; (fig: report) Kurzbiografie f

profit ['prɒfɪt] n Gewinn m ♦ vi: **to ~ (by or from)** profitieren (von); **~ability** [prɒfɪtə'bɪlɪtɪ] n Rentabilität f; **~able** adj einträglich, rentabel; **~eering** [prɒfɪ'tɪərɪŋ] n Profitmacherei f

profound [prə'faund] adj tief

profuse [prə'fju:s] adj überreich; **~ly** [prə'fju:slɪ] adv überschwänglich; (sweat) reichlich; **profusion** [prə'fju:ʒən] n: **profusion (of)** Überfülle f (von), Überfluss m (an +dat)

program ['prəugræm] n (COMPUT) Programm nt ♦ vt (machine) programmieren; **~me** (US ~) n Programm nt ♦ vt planen; (computer) programmieren; **~mer** (US **~er**) n Programmierer(in) m(f)

progress [n 'prəugres, vb prə'gres] n Fortschritt m ♦ vi fortschreiten, weitergehen; **in ~** im Gang; **~ion** [prə'greʃən] n Folge f; **~ive** [prə'gresɪv] adj fortschrittlich, progressiv

prohibit [prə'hɪbɪt] vt verbieten; **to ~ sb from doing sth** jdm untersagen, etw zu tun; **~ion** [prəuɪ'bɪʃən] n Verbot nt; (US) Alkoholverbot nt, Prohibition f; **~ive** adj unerschwinglich

project [n 'prɒdʒekt, vb prə'dʒekt] n Projekt nt ♦ vt vorausplanen; (film etc) projizieren; (personality, voice) zum Tragen bringen ♦ vi (stick out) hervorragen, (her)vorstehen

projectile [prə'dʒektaɪl] n Geschoss nt, Geschoß nt (österreichisch)

projection [prə'dʒekʃən] n Projektion f; (sth prominent) Vorsprung m

projector [prə'dʒektə'] n Projektor m

proletariat [prəulɪ'teərɪət] n Proletariat nt

pro-life [prəu'laɪf] adj (movement) Anti-Abtreibungs-; **~ campaigner** Abtreibungsgegner(in) m(f)

prolific [prə'lɪfɪk] adj fruchtbar; (author etc) produktiv

prologue ['prəulɒg] n Prolog m; (event) Vorspiel nt

prolong [prə'lɒŋ] vt verlängern

prom [prɒm] n abbr = **promenade**; **promenade concert**; (US: college ball) Studentenball m

promenade [prɒmə'nɑːd] n Promenade f; **~ concert** n Promenadenkonzert nt

prominence ['prɒmɪnəns] n (große) Bedeutung f

prominent ['prɒmɪnənt] adj bedeutend; (politician) prominent; (easily seen) herausragend, auffallend

promiscuous [prə'mɪskjuəs] adj lose

promise ['prɒmɪs] n Versprechen nt; (hope: ~ of sth) Aussicht f auf etw acc ♦ vt, vi versprechen; **promising** adj viel versprechend

promontory ['prɒməntrɪ] n Vorsprung m

promote [prə'məut] vt befördern; (help on) fördern, unterstützen; **~r** n (in entertainment, sport) Veranstalter m; (for charity etc) Organisator m; **promotion** [prə'məuʃən] n (in rank) Beförderung f; (furtherance) Förderung f; (COMM) **promotion (of)** Werbung f (für)

prompt [prɒmpt] adj prompt, schnell ♦ adv (punctually) genau ♦ n (COMPUT) Meldung f ♦ vt veranlassen; (THEAT) soufflieren +dat; **to ~ sb to do sth** jdn dazu veranlassen, etw zu tun; **~ly** adv sofort

prone [prəun] adj hingestreckt; **to be ~ to sth** zu etw neigen

prong [prɒŋ] n Zinke f

pronoun ['prəunaun] n Fürwort nt

pronounce [prə'nauns] vt aussprechen; (JUR) verkünden ♦ vi: **to ~ (on)** sich äußern (zu)

pronunciation [prənʌnsɪ'eɪʃən] n Aussprache f

proof [pruːf] n Beweis m; (PRINT) Korrekturfahne f; (of alcohol) Alkoholgehalt m ♦ adj sicher

prop [prɒp] n (also fig) Stütze f; (THEAT) Requisit nt ♦ vt (also: ~ **up**) (ab)stützen

propaganda [prɒpə'gændə] n Propaganda f

propel [prə'pel] vt (an)treiben; **~ler** n Propeller m; **~ling pencil** (BRIT) n Drehbleistift m

propensity [prə'pensɪtɪ] n Tendenz f

proper ['prɒpə'] adj richtig; (seemly) schicklich; **~ly** adv richtig; **~ noun** n Eigenname m

property ['prɒpətɪ] n Eigentum nt; (quality) Eigenschaft f; (land) Grundbesitz m; **~ owner** n Grundbesitzer m

prophecy ['prɒfɪsɪ] n Prophezeiung f

prophesy ['prɒfɪsaɪ] vt prophezeien

prophet ['prɒfɪt] n Prophet m

proportion [prə'pɔːʃən] n Verhältnis nt; (share) Teil m ♦ vt: **to ~ (to)** abstimmen (auf +acc); **~al** adj proportional; **~ate** adj verhältnismäßig

proposal [prə'pəuzl] n Vorschlag m; (of marriage) Heiratsantrag m

propose [prə'pəuz] vt vorschlagen; (toast) ausbringen ♦ vi (offer marriage) einen Heiratsantrag machen; **to ~ to do sth** beabsichtigen, etw zu tun

proposition [prɒpə'zɪʃən] n Angebot nt; (statement) Satz m

proprietor [prə'praɪətə'] n Besitzer m, Eigentümer m

propriety [prə'praɪətɪ] n Anstand m

pro rata [prəu'rɑːtə] adv anteilmäßig

prose [prəuz] n Prosa f

prosecute ['prɒsɪkjuːt] vt (strafrechtlich) verfolgen; **prosecution** [prɒsɪ'kjuːʃən] n (JUR) strafrechtliche Verfolgung f; (party)

Anklage f; **prosecutor** n Vertreter m der Anklage; **Public Prosecutor** Staatsanwalt m

prospect |n 'prɔspekt, vb prə'spekt| n Aussicht f ♦ vt auf Bodenschätze hin untersuchen ♦ vi: **to ~ (for)** suchen (nach); **~ing** |'prɔspektɪŋ| n (for minerals) Suche f; **~ive** |prə'spektɪv| adj (son-in-law etc) zukünftig; (customer, candidate) voraussichtlich

prospectus |prə'spektəs| n (Werbe)prospekt m

prosper |'prɔspə'| vi blühen, gedeihen; (person) erfolgreich sein; **~ity** |prɔ'sperɪtɪ| n Wohlstand m; **~ous** adj wohlhabend, reich

prostitute |'prɔstɪtjuːt| n Prostituierte f

prostrate |'prɔstreɪt| adj ausgestreckt (liegend)

protagonist |prə'tægənɪst| n Hauptperson f, Held m

protect |prə'tekt| vt (be)schützen; **~ed species** n geschützte Art; **~ion** |prə'tekʃən| n Schutz m; **~ive** adj Schutz-, (be)schützend

protégé |'prəuteʒeɪ| n Schützling m

protein |'prəutiːn| n Protein nt, Eiweiß nt

protest |n 'prəutest, vb prə'test| n Protest m ♦ vi protestieren ♦ vt (affirm) beteuern

Protestant |'prɔtɪstənt| adj protestantisch ♦ n Protestant(in) m(f)

protester |prə'testə'| n (demonstrator) Demonstrant(in) m(f)

protracted |prə'træktɪd| adj sich hinziehend

protrude |prə'truːd| vi (her)vorstehen

proud |praud| adj: **~ (of)** stolz (auf +acc)

prove |pruːv| vt beweisen ♦ vi: **to ~ (to be) correct** sich als richtig erweisen; **to ~ o.s.** sich bewähren

proverb |'prɔvəːb| n Sprichwort nt; **~ial** |prə'vəːbɪəl| adj sprichwörtlich

provide |prə'vaɪd| vt versehen; (supply) besorgen; **to ~ sb with sth** jdn mit etw versorgen; **~ for** vt fus sorgen für; (emergency) Vorkehrungen treffen für; **~d (that)** conj vorausgesetzt(, dass)

providing |prə'vaɪdɪŋ| conj vorausgesetzt(, dass)

province |'prɔvɪns| n Provinz f; (division of work) Bereich m; **provincial** |prə'vɪnʃəl| adj provinziell, Provinz-

provision |prə'vɪʒən| n Vorkehrung f; (condition) Bestimmung f; **~s** npl (food) Vorräte pl, Proviant m; **~al** adj provisorisch

proviso |prə'vaɪzəu| n Bedingung f

provocative |prə'vɔkətɪv| adj provozierend

provoke |prə'vəuk| vt provozieren; (cause) hervorrufen

prowess |'prauɪs| n überragende(s) Können nt

prowl |praul| vi herumstreichen; (animal) schleichen ♦ n: **on the ~** umherstreifend; **~er** n Herumtreiber(in) m(f)

proximity |prɔk'sɪmɪtɪ| n Nähe f

proxy |'prɔksɪ| n (Stell)vertreter m; (authority, document) Vollmacht f; **by ~** durch einen Stellvertreter

prudent |'pruːdnt| adj klug, umsichtig

prudish |'pruːdɪʃ| adj prüde

prune |pruːn| n Backpflaume f ♦ vt ausputzen; (fig) zurechtstutzen

pry |praɪ| vi: **to ~ (into)** seine Nase stecken (in +acc)

PS n abbr (= postscript) PS

pseudonym |'sjuːdənɪm| n Pseudonym nt, Deckname m

psychiatric |saɪkɪ'ætrɪk| adj psychiatrisch

psychiatrist |saɪ'kaɪətrɪst| n Psychiater m

psychic |'saɪkɪk| adj (also: **~al**) übersinnlich; (person) paranormal begabt

psychoanalyse |saɪkəu'ænəlaɪz| (US **psychoanalyze**) vt psychoanalytisch behandeln; **psychoanalyst** |saɪkəu'ænəlɪst| n Psychoanalytiker(in) m(f)

psychological |saɪkə'lɔdʒɪkl| adj psychologisch; **psychologist** |saɪ'kɔlədʒɪst| n Psychologe m, Psychologin f;

psychology |saɪ'kɔlədʒɪ| n Psychologie f

PTO abbr = **please turn over**

pub |pʌb| n abbr (= public house) Kneipe f

pubic |'pjuːbɪk| adj Scham-

public |'pʌblɪk| adj öffentlich ♦ n (also: **general ~**) Öffentlichkeit f; **in ~** in der Öffentlichkeit; **~ address system** n Lautsprecheranlage f

publican |'pʌblɪkən| n Wirt m

publication |pʌblɪ'keɪʃən| n Veröffentlichung f

public: ~ company n Aktiengesellschaft f; **~ convenience** (BRIT) n öffentliche Toiletten pl; **~ holiday** n gesetzliche(r) Feiertag m; **~ house** (BRIT) n Lokal nt, Kneipe f

publicity |pʌb'lɪsɪtɪ| n Publicity f, Werbung f

publicize |'pʌblɪsaɪz| vt bekannt machen; (advertise) Publicity machen für

publicly |'pʌblɪklɪ| adv öffentlich

public: ~ opinion n öffentliche Meinung f; **~ relations** npl Publicrelations pl, Public Relations pl; **~ school** n (BRIT) Privatschule f; (US) staatliche Schule f; **~-spirited** adj mit Gemeinschaftssinn; **~ transport** n öffentliche Verkehrsmittel pl

publish |'pʌblɪʃ| vt veröffentlichen; (event) bekannt geben; **~er** n Verleger m; **~ing** n (business) Verlagswesen nt

pub lunch n in Pubs servierter Imbiss

pucker |'pʌkə'| vt (face) verziehen; (lips) kräuseln

pudding |'pudɪŋ| n (BRIT: course) Nachtisch m; Pudding m; **black ~** ≈ Blutwurst f

puddle |'pʌdl| n Pfütze f

puff |pʌf| n (of wind etc) Stoß m; (cosmetic) Puderquaste f ♦ vt blasen, pusten; (pipe) paffen ♦ vi keuchen, schnaufen; (smoke) paffen; **to ~ out smoke** Rauch ausstoßen; **~**

pastry (*US* ~ **paste**) *n* Blätterteig *m*; ~**y** *adj* aufgedunsen

pull [pul] *n* Ruck *m*; (*influence*) Beziehung *f* ♦ *vt* ziehen; (*trigger*) abdrücken ♦ *vi* ziehen; **to ~ sb's leg** jdn auf den Arm nehmen; **to ~ to pieces** in Stücke reißen; (*fig*) verreißen; **to ~ one's punches** sich zurückhalten; **to ~ one's weight** sich in die Riemen legen; **to ~ o.s. together** sich zusammenreißen; ~ **apart** *vt* (*break*) zerreißen; (*dismantle*) auseinander nehmen; (*separate*) trennen; ~ **down** *vt* (*house*) abreißen; (*stop*) anhalten; (*RAIL*) einfahren; ~ **off** *vt* (*deal etc*) abschließen; ~ **out** *vi* (*car*) herausfahren; (*fig: partner*) aussteigen ♦ *vt* herausziehen; ~ **over** *vi* (*AUT*) an die Seite fahren; ~ **through** *vi* durchkommen; ~ **up** *vi* anhalten ♦ *vt* (*uproot*) herausreißen; (*stop*) anhalten

pulley ['puli] *n* Rolle *f*, Flaschenzug *m*

pullover ['puləuvə^r] *n* Pullover *m*

pulp [pʌlp] *n* Brei *m*; (*of fruit*) Fruchtfleisch *nt*

pulpit ['pulpit] *n* Kanzel *f*

pulsate [pʌl'seit] *vi* pulsieren

pulse [pʌls] *n* Puls *m*; ~**s** *npl* (*BOT*) Hülsenfrüchte *pl*

pummel ['pʌml] *vt* mit den Fäusten bearbeiten

pump [pʌmp] *n* Pumpe *f*; (*shoe*) leichter (Tanz)schuh *m* ♦ *vt* pumpen; ~ **up** *vt* (*tyre*) aufpumpen

pumpkin ['pʌmpkin] *n* Kürbis *m*

pun [pʌn] *n* Wortspiel *nt*

punch [pʌntʃ] *n* (*tool*) Locher *m*; (*blow*) (Faust)schlag *m*; (*drink*) Punsch *m*, Bowle *f* ♦ *vt* lochen; (*strike*) schlagen, boxen; ~ **line** *n* Pointe *f*; ~~**up** (*BRIT*: *inf*) *n* Keilerei *f*

punctual ['pʌŋktjuəl] *adj* pünktlich

punctuate ['pʌŋktjueit] *vt* mit Satzzeichen versehen; (*fig*) unterbrechen; **punctuation** [pʌŋktju'eiʃən] *n* Zeichensetzung *f*, Interpunktion *f*

puncture ['pʌŋktʃə^r] *n* Loch *nt*; (*AUT*) Reifenpanne *f* ♦ *vt* durchbohren

pundit ['pʌndit] *n* Gelehrte(r) *m*

pungent ['pʌndʒənt] *adj* scharf

punish ['pʌniʃ] *vt* bestrafen; (*in boxing etc*) übel zurichten; ~**ment** *n* Strafe *f*; (*action*) Bestrafung *f*

punk [pʌŋk] *n* (*also*: ~ **rocker**) Punker(in) *m(f)*; (*also*: ~ **rock**) Punk *m*; (*US: inf*: *hoodlum*) Ganove *m*

punt [pʌnt] *n* Stechkahn *m*

punter ['pʌntə^r] (*BRIT*) *n* (*better*) Wetter *m*

puny ['pju:ni] *adj* kümmerlich

pup [pʌp] *n* = **puppy**

pupil ['pju:pl] *n* Schüler(in) *m(f)*; (*in eye*) Pupille *f*

puppet ['pʌpit] *n* Puppe *f*; Marionette *f*

puppy ['pʌpi] *n* junge(r) Hund *m*

purchase ['pə:tʃis] *n* Kauf *m*; (*grip*) Halt *m* ♦ *vt* kaufen, erwerben; ~**r** *n* Käufer(in) *m(f)*

pure [pjuə^r] *adj* (*also fig*) rein; ~**ly** ['pjuəli] *adv* rein

purgatory ['pə:gətəri] *n* Fegefeuer *nt*

purge [pə:dʒ] *n* (*also POL*) Säuberung *f* ♦ *vt* reinigen; (*body*) entschlacken

purify ['pjuərifai] *vt* reinigen

purity ['pjuəriti] *n* Reinheit *f*

purple ['pə:pl] *adj* violett; (*face*) dunkelrot

purport [pə:'pɔ:t] *vi* vorgeben

purpose ['pə:pəs] *n* Zweck *m*, Ziel *nt*; (*of person*) Absicht *f*; **on** ~ absichtlich; ~**ful** *adj* zielbewusst, entschlossen

purr [pə:^r] *n* Schnurren *nt* ♦ *vi* schnurren

purse [pə:s] *n* Portemonnaie *nt*, Portmonee *nt*, Geldbeutel *m* ♦ *vt* (*lips*) zusammenpressen, schürzen

purser ['pə:sə^r] *n* Zahlmeister *m*

pursue [pə'sju:] *vt* verfolgen; (*study*) nachgehen +*dat*; ~**r** *n* Verfolger *m*; **pursuit** [pə'sju:t] *n* Verfolgung *f*; (*occupation*) Beschäftigung *f*

pus [pʌs] *n* Eiter *m*

push [puʃ] *n* Stoß *m*, Schub *m*; (*MIL*) Vorstoß *m* ♦ *vt* stoßen, schieben; (*button*) drücken; (*idea*) durchsetzen ♦ *vi* stoßen, schieben; ~ **aside** *vt* beiseite schieben; ~ **off** (*inf*) *vi* abschieben; ~ **on** *vi* weitermachen; ~ **through** *vt* durchdrücken; (*policy*) durchsetzen; ~ **up** *vt* (*total*) erhöhen; (*prices*) hoch treiben; ~**chair** (*BRIT*) *n* (Kinder)sportwagen *m*; ~**er** *n* (*drug dealer*) Pusher *m*; ~**over** (*inf*) *n* Kinderspiel *nt*; ~~**up** (*US*) *n* (*press-up*) Liegestütz *m*; ~**y** (*inf*) *adj* aufdringlich

puss [pus] *n* Mieze(katze) *f*; ~**y(cat)** *n* Mieze(katze) *f*

put [put] (*pt, pp* **put**) *vt* setzen, stellen, legen; (*express*) ausdrücken, sagen; (*write*) schreiben; ~ **about** *vi* (*turn back*) wenden ♦ *vt* (*spread*) verbreiten; ~ **across** *vt* (*explain*) erklären; ~ **away** *vt* weglegen; (*store*) beiseite legen; ~ **back** *vt* zurückstellen or -legen; ~ **by** *vt* zurücklegen, sparen; ~ **down** *vt* hinstellen or -legen; (*rebellion*) niederschlagen; (*animal*) einschläfern; (*in writing*) niederschreiben; ~ **forward** *vt* (*idea*) vorbringen; (*clock*) vorstellen; ~ **in** *vt* (*application, complaint*) einreichen; ~ **off** *vt* verschieben; (*discourage*): **to ~ sb off sth** jdn von etw abbringen; ~ **on** *vt* (*clothes etc*) anziehen; (*light etc*) anschalten, anmachen; (*play etc*) aufführen; (*brake*) anziehen; ~ **out** *vt* (*hand etc*) (her)ausstrecken; (*news, rumour*) verbreiten; (*light etc*) ausschalten, ausmachen; ~ **through** *vt* (*TEL*: *person*) verbinden; (: *call*) durchstellen; ~ **up** *vt* (*tent*) aufstellen; (*building*) errichten; (*price*) erhöhen; (*person*) unterbringen; ~ **up with** *vt fus* sich abfinden mit

putrid ['pju:trɪd] adj faul
putt [pʌt] vt (golf) putten ♦ n (golf) Putten nt; ~ing green n kleine(r) Golfplatz m nur zum Putten
putty ['pʌtɪ] n Kitt m; (fig) Wachs nt
put-up ['putʌp] adj: ~ job abgekartete(s) Spiel nt
puzzle ['pʌzl] n Rätsel nt; (toy) Geduldspiel nt ♦ vt verwirren ♦ vi sich den Kopf zerbrechen; ~d adj verdutzt, verblüfft; puzzling adj rätselhaft, verwirrend
pyjamas [pə'dʒɑ:məz] (BRIT) npl Schlafanzug m, Pyjama m
pylon ['paɪlən] n Mast m
pyramid ['pɪrəmɪd] n Pyramide f

Q, q

quack [kwæk] n Quaken nt; (doctor) Quacksalber m ♦ vi quaken
quad [kwɔd] n abbr = quadrangle; quadruplet
quadrangle ['kwɔdræŋgl] n (court) Hof m; (MATH) Viereck nt
quadruple [kwɔ'dru:pl] vi sich vervierfachen ♦ vt vervierfachen
quadruplets [kwɔ'dru:plɪts] npl Vierlinge pl
quagmire ['kwægmaɪər] n Morast m
quail [kweɪl] n (bird) Wachtel f ♦ vi (vor Angst) zittern
quaint [kweɪnt] adj kurios; malerisch
quake [kweɪk] vi beben, zittern ♦ n abbr = earthquake
qualification [kwɔlɪfɪ'keɪʃən] n Qualifikation f; (sth which limits) Einschränkung f
qualified ['kwɔlɪfaɪd] adj (competent) qualifiziert; (limited) bedingt
qualify ['kwɔlɪfaɪ] vt (prepare) befähigen; (limit) einschränken ♦ vi sich qualifizieren; to ~ as a doctor/lawyer sein medizinisches/juristisches Staatsexamen machen
quality ['kwɔlɪtɪ] n Qualität f; (characteristic) Eigenschaft f
quality time n intensiv genutzte Zeit
qualm [kwɑ:m] n Bedenken nt
quandary ['kwɔndrɪ] n: to be in a ~ in Verlegenheit sein
quantity ['kwɔntɪtɪ] n Menge f; ~ surveyor n Baukostenkalkulator m
quarantine ['kwɔrəntiːn] n Quarantäne f
quarrel ['kwɔrl] n Streit m ♦ vi sich streiten; ~some adj streitsüchtig
quarry ['kwɔrɪ] n Steinbruch m; (animal) Wild nt; (fig) Opfer nt
quarter ['kwɔ:tər] n Viertel nt; (of year) Quartal nt ♦ vt (divide) vierteln; (MIL) einquartieren; ~s npl (esp MIL) Quartier nt; ~ of an hour Viertelstunde f; ~ final n Viertelfinale nt; ~ly adj vierteljährlich
quartet(te) [kwɔ:'tet] n Quartett nt

quartz [kwɔ:ts] n Quarz m
quash [kwɔʃ] vt (verdict) aufheben
quaver ['kweɪvər] vi (tremble) zittern
quay [ki:] n Kai m
queasy ['kwi:zɪ] adj übel
queen [kwi:n] n Königin f; ~ mother n Königinmutter f
queer [kwɪər] adj seltsam ♦ n (inf: homosexual) Schwule(r) m
quell [kwel] vt unterdrücken
quench [kwentʃ] vt (thirst) löschen
querulous ['kwerʊləs] adj nörglerisch
query ['kwɪərɪ] n (question) (An)frage f; (question mark) Fragezeichen nt ♦ vt in Zweifel ziehen, infrage or in Frage stellen
quest [kwest] n Suche f
question ['kwestʃən] n Frage f ♦ vt (ask) (be)fragen; (suspect) verhören; (doubt) infrage or in Frage stellen, bezweifeln; beyond ~ ohne Frage; out of the ~ ausgeschlossen; ~able adj zweifelhaft; ~ mark n Fragezeichen nt
questionnaire [kwestʃə'neər] n Fragebogen m
queue [kju:] (BRIT) n Schlange f ♦ vi (also: ~ up) Schlange stehen
quibble ['kwɪbl] vi kleinlich sein
quick [kwɪk] adj schnell ♦ n (of nail) Nagelhaut f; be ~! mach schnell!; cut to the ~ (fig) tief getroffen; ~en vt (hasten) beschleunigen ♦ vi sich beschleunigen; ~ly adv schnell; ~sand n Treibsand m; ~-witted adj schlagfertig
quid [kwɪd] (BRIT: inf) n Pfund nt
quiet ['kwaɪət] adj (without noise) leise; (peaceful, calm) still, ruhig ♦ n Stille f, Ruhe f ♦ vt, vi (US) = quieten; keep ~! sei still!; ~en vi (also: ~en down) ruhig werden ♦ vt beruhigen; ~ly adv leise, ruhig; ~ness n Ruhe f, Stille f
quilt [kwɪlt] n (continental ~) Steppdecke f
quin [kwɪn] n abbr = quintuplet
quintuplets [kwɪn'tju:plɪts] npl Fünflinge pl
quip [kwɪp] n witzige Bemerkung f
quirk [kwɔ:k] n (oddity) Eigenart f
quit [kwɪt] (pt, pp quit or quitted) vt verlassen ♦ vi aufhören
quite [kwaɪt] adv (completely) ganz, völlig; (fairly) ziemlich; ~ a few of them ziemlich viele von ihnen; ~ (so)! richtig!
quits [kwɪts] adj quitt; let's call it ~ lassen wirs gut sein
quiver ['kwɪvər] vi zittern ♦ n (for arrows) Köcher m
quiz [kwɪz] n (competition) Quiz nt ♦ vt prüfen; ~zical adj fragend
quota ['kwəʊtə] n Anteil m; (COMM) Quote f
quotation [kwəʊ'teɪʃən] n Zitat nt; (price) Kostenvoranschlag m; ~ marks npl Anführungszeichen pl
quote [kwəʊt] n = quotation ♦ vi (from book) zitieren ♦ vt zitieren; (price) angeben

R, r

rabbi |'ræbaɪ| n Rabbiner m; (title) Rabbi m
rabbit |'ræbɪt| n Kaninchen nt; ~ **hole** n Kaninchenbau m; ~ **hutch** n Kaninchenstall m
rabble |'ræbl| n Pöbel m
rabies |'reɪbiːz| n Tollwut f
RAC (BRIT) n abbr = **Royal Automobile Club**
raccoon |rə'kuːn| n Waschbär m
race |reɪs| n (species) Rasse f; (competition) Rennen nt; (on foot) Rennen nt, Wettlauf m; (rush) Hetze f ♦ vt um die Wette laufen mit; (horses) laufen lassen ♦ vi (run) rennen; (in contest) am Rennen teilnehmen; ~ **car** (US) n = **racing car**; ~ **car driver** (US) n = **racing driver**; ~**course** n (for horses) Rennbahn f; ~**horse** n Rennpferd nt; ~**r** n (person) Rennfahrer(in) m(f); (car) Rennwagen m; ~**track** n (for cars etc) Rennstrecke f
racial |'reɪʃl| adj Rassen-
racing |'reɪsɪŋ| n Rennen nt; ~ **car** (BRIT) n Rennwagen m; ~ **driver** (BRIT) n Rennfahrer m
racism |'reɪsɪzəm| n Rassismus m; **racist** |'reɪsɪst| n Rassist m ♦ adj rassistisch
rack |ræk| n Ständer m, Gestell nt ♦ vt plagen; **to go to ~ and ruin** verfallen; **to ~ one's brains** sich dat den Kopf zerbrechen
racket |'rækɪt| n (din) Krach m; (scheme) (Schwindel)geschäft nt; (TENNIS) (Tennis)schläger m
racquet |'rækɪt| n (Tennis)schläger m
racy |'reɪsɪ| adj gewagt; (style) spritzig
radar |'reɪdɑːʳ| n Radar nt or m
radial |'reɪdɪəl| adj (also: US: ~-**ply**) radial
radiant |'reɪdɪənt| adj strahlend; (giving out rays) Strahlungs-
radiate |'reɪdɪeɪt| vi ausstrahlen; (roads, lines) strahlenförmig wegführen ♦ vt ausstrahlen; **radiation** |reɪdɪ'eɪʃən| n (Aus)strahlung f
radiator |'reɪdɪeɪtəʳ| n (for heating) Heizkörper m; (AUT) Kühler m
radical |'rædɪkl| adj radikal
radii |'reɪdɪaɪ| npl of **radius**
radio |'reɪdɪəʊ| n Rundfunk m, Radio nt; (set) Radio nt, Radioapparat m; **on the** ~ im Radio; ~**active** |'reɪdɪəʊ'æktɪv| adj radioaktiv; ~ **cassette** n Radiorekorder m; ~-**controlled** adj ferngesteuert; ~**logy** |reɪdɪ'ɒlədʒɪ| n Strahlenkunde f; ~ **station** n Rundfunkstation f; ~**therapy** |'reɪdɪəʊ'θerəpɪ| n Röntgentherapie f
radish |'rædɪʃ| n (big) Rettich m; (small) Radieschen nt
radius |'reɪdɪəs| n (pl **radii**) n Radius m; (area) Umkreis m
RAF n abbr = **Royal Air Force**

raffle |'ræfl| n Verlosung f, Tombola f ♦ vt verlosen
raft |rɑːft| n Floß nt
rafter |'rɑːftəʳ| n Dachsparren m
rag |ræg| n (cloth) Lumpen m, Lappen m; (inf: newspaper) Käseblatt nt; (UNIV: for charity) studentische Sammelaktion f ♦ vt (BRIT) auf den Arm nehmen; ~**s** npl (cloth) Lumpen pl; ~ **doll** n Flickenpuppe f
rage |reɪdʒ| n Wut f; (fashion) große Mode f ♦ vi wüten, toben
ragged |'rægɪd| adj (edge) gezackt; (clothes) zerlumpt
raid |reɪd| n Überfall m; (MIL) Angriff m; (by police) Razzia f ♦ vt überfallen
rail |reɪl| n (also RAIL) Schiene f; (on stair) Geländer nt; (of ship) Reling f; ~**s** npl (RAIL) Geleise pl; **by** ~ per Bahn; ~**ing(s)** n(pl) Geländer nt; ~**road** (US) n Eisenbahn f; ~**way** (BRIT) n Eisenbahn f; ~**way line** (BRIT) n (Eisen)bahnlinie f; (track) Gleis nt; ~**wayman** (irreg: BRIT) n Eisenbahner m; ~**way station** (BRIT) n Bahnhof m
rain |reɪn| n Regen m ♦ vt, vi regnen; **in the** ~ im Regen; **it's** ~**ing** es regnet; ~**bow** n Regenbogen m; ~**coat** n Regenmantel m; ~**drop** n Regentropfen m; ~**fall** n Niederschlag m; ~**forest** n Regenwald m; ~**y** adj (region, season) Regen-; (day) regnerisch, verregnet
raise |reɪz| n (esp US: increase) (Gehalts)erhöhung f ♦ vt (lift) (hoch)heben; (increase) erhöhen; (question) aufwerfen; (doubts) äußern; (funds) beschaffen; (family) großziehen; (livestock) züchten; **to ~ one's voice** die Stimme erheben
raisin |'reɪzn| n Rosine f
rake |reɪk| n Rechen m, Harke f; (person) Wüstling m ♦ vt rechen, harken; (search) (durch)suchen
rally |'rælɪ| n (POL etc) Kundgebung f; (AUT) Rallye f ♦ vt (MIL) sammeln ♦ vi Kräfte sammeln; ~ **round** vt fus (sich) scharen um; (help) zu Hilfe kommen +dat ♦ vi zu Hilfe kommen
RAM |ræm| n abbr (= random access memory) RAM m
ram |ræm| n Widder m ♦ vt (hit) rammen; (stuff) (hinein)stopfen
ramble |'ræmbl| n Wanderung f ♦ vi (talk) schwafeln; ~**r** n Wanderer m; **rambling** adj (speech) weitschweifig; (town) ausgedehnt
ramp |ræmp| n Rampe f; **on/off** ~ (US: AUT) Ein-/Ausfahrt f
rampage |ræm'peɪdʒ| n: **to be on the** ~ randalieren ♦ vi randalieren
rampant |'ræmpənt| adj wild wuchernd
rampart |'ræmpɑːt| n (Schutz)wall m
ram raid n Raubüberfall, bei dem eine Geschäftsfront mit einem Fahrzeug gerammt wird

ramshackle ['ræmʃækl] adj baufällig
ran [ræn] pt of **run**
ranch [rɑːntʃ] n Ranch f
rancid ['rænsɪd] adj ranzig
rancour ['ræŋkəʳ] (US **rancor**) n Verbitterung f, Groll m
random ['rændəm] adj ziellos, wahllos ♦ n: at ~ aufs Geratewohl; ~ **access** n (COMPUT) wahlfrei(er) Zugriff m
randy ['rændɪ] (BRIT: inf) adj geil, scharf
rang [ræŋ] pt of **ring**
range [reɪndʒ] n Reihe f; (of mountains) Kette f; (COMM) Sortiment nt; (reach) (Reich)weite f; (of gun) Schussweite f; (for shooting practice) Schießplatz m; (stove) (großer) Herd m ♦ vt (set in row) anordnen, aufstellen; (roam) durchstreifen ♦ vi: to ~ over (wander) umherstreifen in +dat; (extend) sich erstrecken auf +acc; a ~ of (selection) eine (große) Auswahl an +dat; **prices ranging from £5 to £10** Preise, die sich zwischen £5 und £10 bewegen; ~r ['reɪndʒəʳ] n Förster m
rank [ræŋk] n (row) Reihe f; (BRIT: also: **taxi** ~) (Taxi)stand m; (MIL) Rang m; (social position) Stand m ♦ vi (have ~): **to ~ among** gehören zu ♦ adj (strong-smelling) stinkend; (extreme) krass; **the ~ and file** (fig) die breite Masse
rankle ['ræŋkl] vi nagen
ransack ['rænsæk] vt (plunder) plündern; (search) durchwühlen
ransom ['rænsəm] n Lösegeld nt; **to hold sb to ~** jdn gegen Lösegeld festhalten
rant [rænt] vi hochtrabend reden
rap [ræp] n Schlag m; (music) Rap m ♦ vt klopfen
rape [reɪp] n Vergewaltigung f; (BOT) Raps m ♦ vt vergewaltigen; ~(**seed**) **oil** n Rapsöl nt
rapid ['ræpɪd] adj rasch, schnell; ~**ity** [rə'pɪdɪtɪ] n Schnelligkeit f; ~**s** npl Stromschnellen pl
rapist ['reɪpɪst] n Vergewaltiger m
rapport [ræ'pɔːʳ] n gute(s) Verhältnis nt
rapture ['ræptʃəʳ] n Entzücken nt; **rapturous** ['ræptʃərəs] adj (applause) stürmisch; (expression) verzückt
rare [rɛəʳ] adj selten, rar; (underdone) nicht durchgebraten; ~**ly** ['rɛəlɪ] adv selten
raring ['rɛərɪŋ] adj: **to be ~ to go** (inf) es kaum erwarten können, bis es losgeht
rarity ['rɛərɪtɪ] n Seltenheit f
rascal ['rɑːskl] n Schuft m
rash [ræʃ] adj übereilt; (reckless) unbesonnen ♦ n (Haut)ausschlag m
rasher ['ræʃəʳ] n Speckscheibe f
raspberry ['rɑːzbərɪ] n Himbeere f
rasping ['rɑːspɪŋ] adj (noise) kratzend; (voice) krächzend
rat [ræt] n (animal) Ratte f; (person) Halunke m

rate [reɪt] n (proportion) Rate f; (price) Tarif m; (speed) Tempo nt ♦ vt (ein)schätzen; ~**s** npl (BRIT: tax) Grundsteuer f; **to ~ as** für etw halten; ~**able value** (BRIT) n Einheitswert m (als Bemessungsgrundlage); ~**payer** (BRIT) n Steuerzahler(in) m(f)
rather ['rɑːðəʳ] adv (in preference) lieber, eher; (to some extent) ziemlich; **I would or I'd ~ go** ich würde lieber gehen; **it's ~ expensive** (quite) es ist ziemlich teuer; (too) es ist etwas zu teuer; **there's ~ a lot** es ist ziemlich viel
ratify ['rætɪfaɪ] vt (POL) ratifizieren
rating ['reɪtɪŋ] n Klasse f
ratio ['reɪʃɪəu] n Verhältnis nt; **in the ~ of 100 to 1** im Verhältnis 100 zu 1
ration ['ræʃən] n (usu pl) Ration f ♦ vt rationieren
rational ['ræʃənl] adj rational
rationale [ræʃə'nɑːl] n Grundprinzip nt
rationalize ['ræʃnəlaɪz] vt rationalisieren
rat race n Konkurrenzkampf m
rattle ['rætl] n (sound) Rasseln nt; (toy) Rassel f ♦ vi rattern, klappern ♦ vt rasseln mit; ~**snake** n Klapperschlange f
raucous ['rɔːkəs] adj heiser, rau
rave [reɪv] vi (talk wildly) fantasieren; (rage) toben ♦ n (BRIT: inf: party) Rave m, Fete f
raven ['reɪvən] n Rabe m
ravenous ['rævənəs] adj heißhungrig
ravine [rə'viːn] n Schlucht f
raving ['reɪvɪŋ] adj: ~ **lunatic** völlig Wahnsinnige(r) mf
ravishing ['rævɪʃɪŋ] adj atemberaubend
raw [rɔː] adj roh; (tender) wund (gerieben); (inexperienced) unerfahren; **to get a ~ deal** (inf) schlecht wegkommen; ~ **material** n Rohmaterial nt
ray [reɪ] n (of light) Strahl m; ~ **of hope** Hoffnungsschimmer m
raze [reɪz] vt (also: ~ **to the ground**) dem Erdboden gleichmachen
razor ['reɪzəʳ] n Rasierapparat m; ~ **blade** n Rasierklinge f
Rd abbr = **road**
RE (BRIT: SCH) abbr (= religious education) Religionsunterricht m
re [riː] prep (COMM) betreffs +gen
reach [riːtʃ] n Reichweite f; (of river) Strecke f ♦ vt (arrive at) erreichen; (give) reichen ♦ vi (stretch) sich erstrecken; **within ~** (shops etc) in erreichbarer Weite or Entfernung; **out of ~** außer Reichweite; **to ~ for** (try to get) langen nach; ~ **out** vi die Hand ausstrecken; **to ~ out for sth** nach etw greifen
react [riː'ækt] vi reagieren; ~**ion** [riː'ækʃən] n Reaktion f; ~**or** [riː'æktəʳ] n Reaktor m
read¹ [rɛd] pt, pp of **read**
read² [riːd] (pt, pp **read**) vt, vi lesen; (aloud) vorlesen; ~ **out** vt vorlesen; ~**able** adj leserlich; (worth ~ing) lesenswert; ~**er** n (person) Leser(in) m(f); ~**ership** n

Leserschaft f

readily ['rɛdɪlɪ] adv (willingly) bereitwillig; (easily) prompt

readiness ['rɛdɪnɪs] n (willingness) Bereitwilligkeit f; (being ready) Bereitschaft f; **in ~** (prepared) bereit

reading ['riːdɪŋ] n Lesen nt

readjust [riːə'dʒʌst] vt neu einstellen ♦ vi (person): **to ~ to** sich wieder anpassen an +acc

ready ['rɛdɪ] adj (prepared, willing) bereit ♦ adv: **~-cooked** vorgekocht ♦ n: **at the ~** bereit; **~-made** adj gebrauchsfertig, Fertig-; (clothes) Konfektions-; **~ money** n Bargeld nt; **~ reckoner** n Rechentabelle f; **~-to-wear** adj Konfektions-

real [rɪəl] adj wirklich; (actual) eigentlich; (not fake) echt; **in ~ terms** effektiv; **~ estate** n Grundbesitz m; **~istic** [rɪə'lɪstɪk] adj realistisch

reality [riː'ælɪtɪ] n Wirklichkeit f, Realität f; **in ~** in Wirklichkeit

realization [rɪəlaɪ'zeɪʃən] n (understanding) Erkenntnis f; (fulfilment) Verwirklichung f

realize ['rɪəlaɪz] vt (understand) begreifen; (make real) verwirklichen; **I didn't ~ ...** ich wusste nicht, ...

really ['rɪəlɪ] adv wirklich; **~?** (indicating interest) tatsächlich?; (expressing surprise) wirklich?

realm [rɛlm] n Reich nt

realtor ['rɪəltɔːʳ] (US) n Grundstücks-makler(in) m(f)

reap [riːp] vt ernten

reappear [riːə'pɪəʳ] vi wieder erscheinen

rear [rɪəʳ] adj hintere(r, s), Rück- ♦ n Rückseite f; (last part) Schluss m ♦ vt (bring up) aufziehen ♦ vi (horse) sich aufbäumen; **~guard** n Nachhut f

rearmament [riː'ɑːməmənt] n Wieder-aufrüstung f

rearrange [riːə'reɪndʒ] vt umordnen

rear-view mirror ['rɪəvjuː-] n Rückspiegel m

reason ['riːzn] n (cause) Grund m; (ability to think) Verstand m; (sensible thoughts) Vernunft f ♦ vi (think) denken; (use arguments) argumentieren; **it stands to ~ that** es ist logisch, dass; **to ~ with sb** mit jdm diskutieren; **~able** adj vernünftig; **~ably** adv vernünftig; (fairly) ziemlich; **~ed** adj (argument) durchdacht; **~ing** n Urteilen nt; (argumentation) Beweisführung f

reassurance [riːə'ʃuərəns] n Beruhigung f; (confirmation) Bestätigung f; **reassure** [riːə'ʃuəʳ] vt beruhigen; **to reassure sb of sth** jdm etw versichern

rebate ['riːbeɪt] n Rückzahlung f

rebel [n 'rɛbl, vb rɪ'bɛl] n Rebell m ♦ vi rebellieren; **~lion** rɪ'bɛljən n Rebellion f, Aufstand m; **~lious** [rɪ'bɛljəs] adj rebellisch

rebirth [riː'bɜːθ] n Wiedergeburt f

rebound [vb rɪ'baund, n 'riːbaund] vi zurückprallen ♦ n Rückprall m

rebuff [rɪ'bʌf] n Abfuhr f ♦ vt abblitzen lassen

rebuild [riː'bɪld] (irreg) vt wieder aufbauen; (fig) wieder herstellen

rebuke [rɪ'bjuːk] n Tadel m ♦ vt tadeln, rügen

rebut [rɪ'bʌt] vt widerlegen

recall [vb rɪ'kɔːl, n rɪ'kɔːl] vt (call back) zurückrufen; (remember) sich erinnern an +acc ♦ n Rückruf m

recap ['riːkæp] vt, vi wiederholen

rec'd abbr (= received) Eing.

recede [rɪ'siːd] vi zurückweichen; **receding** adj: **receding hairline** Stirnglatze f

receipt [rɪ'siːt] n (document) Quittung f; (receiving) Empfang m; **~s** npl (ECON) Einnahmen pl

receive [rɪ'siːv] vt erhalten; (visitors etc) empfangen; **~r** n (TEL) Hörer m

recent ['riːsnt] adj vor kurzem (geschehen), neuerlich; (modern) neu; **~ly** adv kürzlich, neulich

receptacle [rɪ'sɛptɪkl] n Behälter m

reception [rɪ'sɛpʃən] n Empfang m; **~ desk** n Empfang m; (in hotel) Rezeption f; **~ist** n (in hotel) Empfangschef m, Empfangsdame f; (MED) Sprechstundenhilfe f

receptive [rɪ'sɛptɪv] adj aufnahmebereit

recess [rɪ'sɛs] n (break) Ferien pl; (hollow) Nische f

recession [rɪ'sɛʃən] n Rezession f

recharge [riː'tʃɑːdʒ] vt (battery) aufladen

recipe ['rɛsɪpɪ] n Rezept nt

recipient [rɪ'sɪpɪənt] n Empfänger m

reciprocal [rɪ'sɪprəkl] adj gegenseitig; (mutual) wechselseitig

recital [rɪ'saɪtl] n Vortrag m

recite [rɪ'saɪt] vt vortragen, aufsagen

reckless ['rɛkləs] adj leichtsinnig; (driving) fahrlässig

reckon ['rɛkən] vt (count) rechnen, berechnen, errechnen; (estimate) schätzen; (think): **I ~ that ...** ich nehme an, dass ...; **~ on** vt fus rechnen mit; **~ing** n (calculation) Rechnen nt

reclaim [rɪ'kleɪm] vt (expenses) zurückverlangen; (land): **to ~ (from sth)** (etw dat) gewinnen; **reclamation** [rɛklə'meɪʃən] n (of land) Gewinnung f

recline [rɪ'klaɪn] vi sich zurücklehnen; **reclining** adj Liege-

recluse [rɪ'kluːs] n Einsiedler m

recognition [rɛkəg'nɪʃən] n (recognizing) Erkennen nt; (acknowledgement) Anerkennung f; **transformed beyond ~** völlig verändert

recognizable ['rɛkəgnaɪzəbl] adj erkennbar

recognize ['rɛkəgnaɪz] vt erkennen; (POL, approve) anerkennen; **to ~ as** anerkennen als; **to ~ by** erkennen an +dat

recoil [rɪ'kɔɪl] vi (in horror) zurückschrecken;

(*rebound*) zurückprallen; (*person*): **to ~ from
doing sth** davor zurückschrecken, etw zu
tun

recollect |rekəˈlekt| *vt* sich erinnern an +*acc*;
~ion |rekəˈlekʃən| *n* Erinnerung *f*

recommend |rekəˈmend| *vt* empfehlen;
~ation |rekəmənˈdeɪʃən| *n* Empfehlung *f*

recompense |ˈrekəmpens| *n* (*compensation*)
Entschädigung *f*; (*reward*) Belohnung *f* ♦ *vt*
entschädigen; belohnen

reconcile |ˈrekənsaɪl| *vt* (*facts*) vereinbaren;
(*people*) versöhnen; **to ~ o.s. to sth** sich mit
etw abfinden; **reconciliation**
|rekənsɪlɪˈeɪʃən| *n* Versöhnung *f*

recondition |riːkənˈdɪʃən| *vt* (*machine*)
generalüberholen

reconnoitre |rekəˈnɔɪtəʳ| (*US* **reconnoiter**)
vt erkunden ♦ *vi* aufklären

reconsider |riːkənˈsɪdəʳ| *vt* von neuem
erwägen, noch einmal überdenken ♦ *vi* es
noch einmal überdenken

reconstruct |riːkənˈstrʌkt| *vt* wieder
aufbauen; (*crime*) rekonstruieren

record |*n* ˈrekɔːd, *vb* rɪˈkɔːd| *n* Aufzeichnung
f; (*MUS*) Schallplatte *f*; (*best performance*)
Rekord *m* ♦ *vt* aufzeichnen; (*music etc*)
aufnehmen; **off the ~** (*as adj*) inoffiziell,
vertraulich; (*as adv*) im Vertrauen; **in ~ time**
in Rekordzeit; **~ card** *n* (*in file*) Karteikarte *f*;
~ed delivery (*BRIT*) *n* (*POST*) Einschreiben
nt; **~er** *n* (*TECH*) Registriergerät *nt*; (*MUS*)
Blockflöte *f*; **~ holder** *n* (*SPORT*)
Rekordinhaber *m*; **~ing** *n* (*MUS*) Aufnahme
f; **~ player** *n* Plattenspieler *m*

recount |rɪˈkaunt| *vt* (*tell*) berichten

re-count |ˈriːkaunt| *n* Nachzählung *f*

recoup |rɪˈkuːp| *vt*: **to ~ one's losses** seinen
Verlust wieder gutmachen

recourse |rɪˈkɔːs| *n*: **to have ~ to** Zuflucht
nehmen zu or bei

recover |rɪˈkʌvəʳ| *vt* (*get back*)
zurückerhalten ♦ *vi* sich erholen

re-cover |riːˈkʌvəʳ| *vt* (*quilt etc*) neu
überziehen

recovery |rɪˈkʌvərɪ| *n* Wiedererlangung *f*; (*of
health*) Erholung *f*

recreate |riːkrɪˈeɪt| *vt* wieder herstellen

recreation |rekrɪˈeɪʃən| *n* Erholung *f*; **~al** *adj*
Erholungs-; **~al drug** *n* Freizeitdroge *f*

recrimination |rɪkrɪmɪˈneɪʃən| *n*
Gegenbeschuldigung *f*

recruit |rɪˈkruːt| *n* Rekrut *m* ♦ *vt* rekrutieren;
~ment *n* Rekrutierung *f*

rectangle |ˈrektæŋgl| *n* Rechteck *nt*;
rectangular |rekˈtæŋgjuləʳ| *adj* rechteckig,
rechtwinklig

rectify |ˈrektɪfaɪ| *vt* berichtigen

rector |ˈrektəʳ| *n* (*REL*) Pfarrer *m*; (*SCH*)
Direktor(in) *m(f)*; **~y** |ˈrektərɪ| *n* Pfarrhaus *nt*

recuperate |rɪˈkjuːpəreɪt| *vi* sich erholen

recur |rɪˈkəːʳ| *vi* sich wiederholen; **~rence** *n*

Wiederholung *f*; **~rent** *adj* wiederkehrend

recycle |riːˈsaɪkl| *vt* wieder verwerten, wieder
aufbereiten; **recycling** *n* Recycling *nt*

red |red| *n* Rot *nt*; (*POL*) Rote(r) *m* ♦ *adj* rot;
in the ~ in den roten Zahlen; **~ carpet
treatment** *n* Sonderbehandlung *f*, große(r)
Bahnhof *m*; **R~ Cross** *n* Rote(s) Kreuz *nt*;
~currant *n* rote Johannisbeere *f*; **~den** *vi*
sich röten; (*blush*) erröten ♦ *vt* röten; **~dish**
adj rötlich

redecorate |riːˈdekəreɪt| *vt* neu tapezieren,
neu streichen

redeem |rɪˈdiːm| *vt* (*COMM*) einlösen; (*save*)
retten; **~ing** *adj*: **~ing feature** versöhnen-
de(s) Moment *nt*

redeploy |riːdɪˈplɔɪ| *vt* (*resources*)
umverteilen

red: ~-haired |redˈhɛəd| *adj* rothaarig; **~-
handed** |redˈhændɪd| *adv*: **to be caught ~-
handed** auf frischer Tat ertappt werden;
~head |ˈredhed| *n* Rothaarige(r) *mf*; **~-
herring** *n* Ablenkungsmanöver *nt*; **~-hot**
|redˈhɔt| *adj* rot glühend

redirect |riːdaɪˈrekt| *vt* umleiten

red light *n*: **to go through a ~** (*AUT*) bei Rot
über die Ampel fahren; **red-light district** *n*
Strichviertel *nt*

redo |riːˈduː| (*irreg: like* do) *vt* nochmals
machen

redolent |ˈredələnt| *adj*: **~ of** (*fig*) erinnernd
an +*acc*

redouble |riːˈdʌbl| *vt*: **to ~ one's efforts**
seine Anstrengungen verdoppeln

redress |rɪˈdres| *vt* wieder gutmachen

red: R~ Sea *n*: **the R~ Sea** das Rote Meer;
~skin |ˈredskɪn| *n* Rothaut *f*; **~ tape** *n*
Bürokratismus *m*

reduce |rɪˈdjuːs| *vt* (*speed, temperature*)
vermindern; (*photo*) verkleinern; **"~ speed
now"** (*AUT*) ≈ „langsam"; **to ~ the price
(to)** den Preis herabsetzen (auf +*acc*); **at a
~d price** zum ermäßigten Preis

reduction |rɪˈdʌkʃən| *n* Verminderung *f*;
Verkleinerung *f*; Herabsetzung *f*; (*amount of
money*) Nachlass *m*

redundancy |rɪˈdʌndənsɪ| *n* Überflüssigkeit
f; (*of workers*) Entlassung *f*

redundant |rɪˈdʌndnt| *adj* überflüssig;
(*workers*) ohne Arbeitsplatz; **to be made ~**
arbeitslos werden

reed |riːd| *n* Schilf *nt*; (*MUS*) Rohrblatt *nt*

reef |riːf| *n* Riff *nt*

reek |riːk| *vi*: **to ~ (of)** stinken (nach)

reel |riːl| *n* Spule *f*, Rolle *f* ♦ *vt* (*also: ~ in*)
wickeln, spulen ♦ *vi* (*stagger*) taumeln

ref |ref| (*inf*) *n abbr* (= *referee*) Schiri *m*

refectory |rɪˈfektərɪ| *n* (*UNIV*) Mensa *f*; (*SCH*)
Speisesaal *m*; (*ECCL*) Refektorium *nt*

refer |rɪˈfəːʳ| *vt*: **to ~ sb to sb/sth** jdn an
jdn/etw verweisen ♦ *vi*: **to ~ to** (*to book*)
nachschlagen in +*dat*; (*mention*) sich

beziehen auf +acc

referee |refəˈriː| n Schiedsrichter m; (BRIT: for job) Referenz f ♦ vt schiedsrichtern

reference |ˈrefrəns| n (for job) Referenz f; (in book) Verweis m; (number, code) Aktenzeichen nt; (allusion): ~ (to) Anspielung (auf +acc); with ~ to in Bezug auf +acc; ~ book n Nachschlagewerk nt; ~ number n Aktenzeichen nt

referenda |refəˈrendə| npl of **referendum**

referendum |refəˈrendəm| (pl -da) n Volksabstimmung f

refill [vb riːˈfɪl, n ˈriːfɪl] vt nachfüllen ♦ n (for pen) Ersatzmine f

refine |rɪˈfaɪn| vt (purify) raffinieren; ~d adj kultiviert; ~ment n Kultiviertheit f; ~ry n Raffinerie f

reflect |rɪˈflekt| vt (light) reflektieren; (fig) (wider)spiegeln ♦ vi (meditate): to ~ (on) nachdenken (über +acc); it ~s badly/well on him das stellt ihn in ein schlechtes/gutes Licht; ~ion |rɪˈflekʃən| n Reflexion f; (image) Spiegelbild nt; (thought) Überlegung f; on ~ion wenn man sich das recht überlegt

reflex |ˈriːfleks| adj Reflex- ♦ n Reflex m; ~ive |rɪˈfleksɪv| adj reflexiv

reform |rɪˈfɔːm| n Reform f ♦ vt (person) bessern; ~atory (US) n Besserungsanstalt f

refrain |rɪˈfreɪn| vi: to ~ from unterlassen ♦ n Refrain m

refresh |rɪˈfreʃ| vt erfrischen; ~er course (BRIT) n Wiederholungskurs m; ~ing adj erfrischend; ~ments npl Erfrischungen pl

refrigeration |rɪfrɪdʒəˈreɪʃən| n Kühlung f

refrigerator |rɪˈfrɪdʒəreɪtəʳ| n Kühlschrank m

refuel |riːˈfjuːəl| vt, vi auftanken

refuge |ˈrefjuːdʒ| n Zuflucht f; to take ~ in sich flüchten in +acc; ~e |refjuˈdʒiː| n Flüchtling m

refund [n ˈriːfʌnd, vb rɪˈfʌnd] n Rückvergütung f ♦ vt zurückerstatten

refurbish |riːˈfɜːbɪʃ| vt aufpolieren

refusal |rɪˈfjuːzəl| n (Ver)weigerung f; first ~ Vorkaufsrecht nt

refuse¹ |rɪˈfjuːz| vt abschlagen ♦ vi sich weigern

refuse² |ˈrefjuːs| n Abfall m, Müll m; ~ collection n Müllabfuhr f

refute |rɪˈfjuːt| vt widerlegen

regain |rɪˈgeɪn| vt wiedergewinnen; (consciousness) wiedererlangen

regal |ˈriːgl| adj königlich

regalia |rɪˈgeɪlɪə| npl Insignien pl

regard |rɪˈgɑːd| n Achtung f ♦ vt ansehen; to send one's ~s to sb jdn grüßen lassen; "with kindest ~s" „mit freundlichen Grüßen"; ~ing or as ~s or with ~ to bezüglich +gen, in Bezug auf +acc; ~less adj: ~less of ohne Rücksicht auf +acc ♦ adv trotzdem

regenerate |rɪˈdʒenəreɪt| vt erneuern

régime |reɪˈʒiːm| n Regime nt

regiment [n ˈredʒɪmənt, vb ˈredʒɪment] n Regiment nt ♦ vt (fig) reglementieren; ~al |redʒɪˈmentl| adj Regiments-

region |ˈriːdʒən| n Region f; in the ~ of (fig) so um; ~al adj örtlich, regional

register |ˈredʒɪstəʳ| n Register nt ♦ vt (list) registrieren; (emotion) zeigen; (write down) eintragen ♦ vi (at hotel) sich eintragen; (with police) sich melden; (make impression) wirken, ankommen; ~ed (BRIT) adj (letter) Einschreibe-, eingeschrieben; ~ed trademark n eingetragene(s) Warenzeichen nt

registrar |ˈredʒɪstrɑːʳ| n Standesbeamte(r) m

registration |redʒɪsˈtreɪʃən| n (act) Registrierung f; (AUT: also: ~ number) polizeiliche(s) Kennzeichen nt

registry |ˈredʒɪstrɪ| n Sekretariat nt; ~ office (BRIT) n Standesamt nt; to get married in a ~ office standesamtlich heiraten

regret |rɪˈgret| n Bedauern nt ♦ vt bedauern; ~fully adv mit Bedauern, ungern; ~table adj bedauerlich

regroup |riːˈgruːp| vt umgruppieren ♦ vi sich umgruppieren

regular |ˈregjʊlə| adj regelmäßig; (usual) üblich; (inf) regelrecht ♦ n (client etc) Stammkunde m; ~ity |regjʊˈlærɪtɪ| n Regelmäßigkeit f; ~ly adv regelmäßig

regulate |ˈregjʊleɪt| vt regeln, regulieren; **regulation** |regjʊˈleɪʃən| n (rule) Vorschrift f; (control) Regulierung f

rehabilitation |ˈriːəbɪlɪˈteɪʃən| n (of criminal) Resozialisierung f

rehearsal |rɪˈhɜːsəl| n Probe f

rehearse |rɪˈhɜːs| vt proben

reign |reɪn| n Herrschaft f ♦ vi herrschen

reimburse |riːɪmˈbɜːs| vt: to ~ sb for sth jdn für etw entschädigen, jdm etw zurückzahlen

rein |reɪn| n Zügel m

reincarnation |riːɪnkɑːˈneɪʃən| n Wiedergeburt f

reindeer |ˈreɪndɪəʳ| n Ren nt

reinforce |riːɪnˈfɔːs| vt verstärken; ~d concrete n Stahlbeton m; ~ment n Verstärkung f; ~ments npl (MIL) Verstärkungstruppen pl

reinstate |riːɪnˈsteɪt| vt wieder einsetzen

reissue |riːˈɪʃuː| vt neu herausgeben

reiterate |riːˈɪtəreɪt| vt wiederholen

reject [n ˈriːdʒekt, vb rɪˈdʒekt] n (COMM) Ausschuss(artikel) m ♦ vt ablehnen; ~ion |rɪˈdʒekʃən| n Zurückweisung f

rejoice |rɪˈdʒɔɪs| vi: to ~ at or over sich freuen über +acc

rejuvenate |rɪˈdʒuːvəneɪt| vt verjüngen

rekindle |riːˈkɪndl| vt wieder anfachen

relapse |rɪˈlæps| n Rückfall m

relate |rɪˈleɪt| vt (tell) erzählen; (connect)

verbinden ♦ vi: **to ~ to** zusammenhängen
mit; (form relationship) eine Beziehung
aufbauen zu; **~d** adj: **~d (to)** verwandt
(mit); **relating** prep: **relating to** bezüglich
+gen; **relation** [rɪ'leɪʃən] n Verwandte(r) mf;
(connection) Beziehung f; **relationship** n
Verhältnis nt, Beziehung f
relative ['relətɪv] n Verwandte(r) mf ♦ adj
relativ; **~ly** adv verhältnismäßig
relax [rɪ'læks] vi (slacken) sich lockern;
(muscles, person) sich entspannen ♦ vt (ease)
lockern, entspannen; **~ation** [riːlæk'seɪʃən] n
Entspannung f; **~ed** adj entspannt, locker;
~ing adj entspannend
relay [rɪ'leɪ, vb rɪ'leɪ] n (SPORT) Staffel f ♦ vt
(message) weiterleiten; (RAD, TV) übertragen
release [rɪ'liːs] n (freedom) Entlassung f;
(TECH) Auslöser m ♦ vt befreien; (prisoner)
entlassen; (report, news) verlautbaren,
bekannt geben
relegate ['reləgeɪt] vt (SPORT): **to be ~d**
absteigen
relent [rɪ'lent] vi nachgeben; **~less** adj
unnachgiebig
relevant ['reləvənt] adj wichtig, relevant; **~
to** relevant für
reliability [rɪlaɪə'bɪlɪtɪ] n Zuverlässigkeit f
reliable [rɪ'laɪəbl] adj zuverlässig; **reliably**
adv zuverlässig; **to be reliably informed
that** ... aus zuverlässiger Quelle wissen,
dass ...
reliance [rɪ'laɪəns] n: **~ (on)** Abhängigkeit f
(von)
relic ['relɪk] n (from past) Überbleibsel nt;
(REL) Reliquie f
relief [rɪ'liːf] n Erleichterung f; (help) Hilfe f;
(person) Ablösung f
relieve [rɪ'liːv] vt (ease) erleichtern; (help)
entlasten; (person) ablösen; **to ~ sb of sth**
jdm etw abnehmen; **to ~ o.s.** (euph) sich
erleichtern (euph); **~d** adj erleichtert
religion [rɪ'lɪdʒən] n Religion f; **religious**
[rɪ'lɪdʒəs] adj religiös
relinquish [rɪ'lɪŋkwɪʃ] vt aufgeben
relish ['relɪʃ] n Würze f ♦ vt genießen; **to ~
doing** gern tun
relocate [riːləu'keɪt] vt verlegen ♦ vi umziehen
reluctance [rɪ'lʌktəns] n Widerstreben nt,
Abneigung f
reluctant [rɪ'lʌktənt] adj widerwillig; **~ly** adv
ungern
rely [rɪ'laɪ] vt fus: **to ~ on** sich verlassen auf
+acc
remain [rɪ'meɪn] vi (be left) übrig bleiben;
(stay) bleiben; **~der** n Rest m; **~ing** adj
übrig (geblieben); **~s** npl Überreste pl
remake ['riːmeɪk] n (CINE) Neuverfilmung f
remand [rɪ'mɑːnd] n: **on ~** in
Untersuchungshaft ♦ vt: **to ~ in custody** in
Untersuchungshaft schicken; **~ home** (BRIT)
n Untersuchungsgefängnis nt für Jugendliche

remark [rɪ'mɑːk] n Bemerkung f ♦ vt
bemerken; **~able** adj bemerkenswert; **~ably**
adv außergewöhnlich
remarry [riː'mærɪ] vi sich wieder verheiraten
remedial [rɪ'miːdɪəl] adj Heil-; (teaching)
Hilfsschul-
remedy ['remədɪ] n Mittel nt ♦ vt (pain)
abhelfen +dat; (trouble) in Ordnung bringen
remember [rɪ'membəʳ] vt sich erinnern an
+acc; **remembrance** [rɪ'membrəns] n
Erinnerung f; (official) Gedenken nt;
Remembrance Day n ≈ Volkstrauertag
m
remind [rɪ'maɪnd] vt: **to ~ sb to do sth** jdn
daran erinnern, etw zu tun; **to ~ sb of sth**
jdn an etw acc erinnern; **she ~s me of her
mother** sie erinnert mich an ihre Mutter;
~er n Mahnung f
reminisce [remɪ'nɪs] vi in Erinnerungen
schwelgen; **~nt** [remɪ'nɪsnt] adj: **to be ~nt
of sth** an etw acc erinnern
remiss [rɪ'mɪs] adj nachlässig
remission [rɪ'mɪʃən] n Nachlass m; (of debt,
sentence) Erlass m
remit [rɪ'mɪt] vt (money): **to ~ (to)**
überweisen (an +acc); **~tance** n
Geldanweisung f
remnant ['remnənt] n Rest m; **~s** npl
(COMM) Einzelstücke pl
remorse [rɪ'mɔːs] n Gewissensbisse pl; **~ful**
adj reumütig; **~less** adj unbarmherzig
remote [rɪ'məut] adj abgelegen; (slight)
gering; **~ control** n Fernsteuerung f; **~ly**
adv entfernt
remould ['riːməuld] n (BRIT) runderneuer-
te(r) Reifen m
removable [rɪ'muːvəbl] adj entfernbar
removal [rɪ'muːvəl] n Beseitigung f; (of
furniture) Umzug m; (from office) Entlassung
f; **~ van** (BRIT) n Möbelwagen m
remove [rɪ'muːv] vt beseitigen, entfernen;
~rs npl Möbelspedition f
remuneration [rɪmjuːnə'reɪʃən] n
Vergütung f, Honorar nt
render ['rendəʳ] vt machen; (translate)
übersetzen; **~ing** n (MUS) Wiedergabe f
rendezvous ['rɒndɪvuː] n (meeting)
Rendezvous nt; (place) Treffpunkt m ♦ vi sich
treffen
renew [rɪ'njuː] vt erneuern; (contract, licence)
verlängern; (replace) ersetzen; **~able** adj
regenerierbar; **~al** n Erneuerung f;
Verlängerung f
renounce [rɪ'nauns] vt (give up) verzichten
auf +acc; (disown) verstoßen
renovate ['renəvoɪt] vt renovieren; (building)
restaurieren
renown [rɪ'naun] n Ruf m; **~ed** adj namhaft
rent [rent] n Miete f; (for land) Pacht f ♦ vt
(hold as tenant) mieten; pachten; (let)
vermieten; verpachten; (car etc) mieten;

(*firm*) vermieten; **~al** *n* Miete *f*

renunciation [rɪnʌnsɪ'eɪʃən] *n*: **~ (of)**
Verzicht *m* (auf +*acc*)

reorganize [riː'ɔːgənaɪz] *vt* umgestalten,
reorganisieren

rep [rep] *n abbr* (*COMM*) = **representative**;
(*THEAT*) = **repertory**

repair [rɪ'pɛəʳ] *n* Reparatur *f* ♦ *vt* reparieren;
(*damage*) wieder gutmachen; **in good/bad
~** in gutem/schlechtem Zustand; **~ kit** *n*
Werkzeugkasten *m*

repartee [repaː'tiː] *n* Witzeleien *pl*

repatriate [riː'pætrɪeɪt] *vt* in die Heimat
zurückschicken

repay [riː'peɪ] (*irreg*) *vt* zurückzahlen;
(*reward*) vergelten; **~ment** *n* Rückzahlung *f*;
(*fig*) Vergeltung *f*

repeal [rɪ'piːl] *vt* aufheben

repeat [rɪ'piːt] *n* (*RAD, TV*) Wiederholung(s-
sendung) *f* ♦ *vt* wiederholen; **~edly** *adv*
wiederholt

repel [rɪ'pel] *vt* (*drive back*) zurückschlagen;
(*disgust*) abstoßen; **~lent** *adj* abstoßend ♦ *n*:
insect ~lent Insektenmittel *nt*

repent [rɪ'pent] *vt, vi*: **to ~ (of)** bereuen;
~ance *n* Reue *f*

repercussion [riːpə'kʌʃən] *n* Auswirkung *f*;
to have ~s ein Nachspiel haben

repertory ['repətərɪ] *n* Repertoire *nt*

repetition [repɪ'tɪʃən] *n* Wiederholung *f*

repetitive [rɪ'petɪtɪv] *adj* sich wiederholend

replace [rɪ'pleɪs] *vt* ersetzen; (*put back*)
zurückstellen; **~ment** *n* Ersatz *m*

replay ['riːpleɪ] *n* (*of match*)
Wiederholungsspiel *nt*; (*of tape, film*)
Wiederholung *f*

replenish [rɪ'plenɪʃ] *vt* ergänzen

replica ['replɪkə] *n* Kopie *f*

reply [rɪ'plaɪ] *n* Antwort *f* ♦ *vi* antworten; **~
coupon** *n* Antwortschein *m*

report [rɪ'pɔːt] *n* Bericht *m*; (*BRIT: SCH*)
Zeugnis *nt* ♦ *vt* (*tell*) berichten; (*give
information against*) melden; (*to police*)
anzeigen ♦ *vi* (*make ~*) Bericht erstatten;
(*present o.s.*): **to ~ (to sb)** sich (bei jdm)
melden; **~ card** (*US, SCOTTISH*) *n* Zeugnis *nt*;
~edly *adv* wie verlautet; **~er** *n* Reporter *m*

reprehensible [reprɪ'hensɪbl] *adj*
tadelnswert

represent [reprɪ'zent] *vt* darstellen; (*speak
for*) vertreten; **~ation** [reprɪzen'teɪʃən] *n*
Darstellung *f*; (*being ~ed*) Vertretung *f*;
~ations *npl* (*protest*) Vorhaltungen *pl*;
~ative *n* (*person*) Vertreter *m*; (*US: POL*)
Abgeordnete(r) *mf* ♦ *adj* repräsentativ

repress [rɪ'pres] *vt* unterdrücken; **~ion**
[rɪ'preʃən] *n* Unterdrückung *f*

reprieve [rɪ'priːv] *n* (*JUR*) Begnadigung *f*;
(*fig*) Gnadenfrist *f* ♦ *vt* (*JUR*) begnadigen

reprimand ['reprɪmɑːnd] *n* Verweis *m* ♦ *vt*
einen Verweis erteilen +*dat*

reprint [*n* 'riːprɪnt, *vb* riː'prɪnt] *n* Neudruck
m ♦ *vt* wieder abdrucken

reprisal [rɪ'praɪzl] *n* Vergeltung *f*

reproach [rɪ'prəʊtʃ] *n* Vorwurf *m* ♦ *vt*
Vorwürfe machen +*dat*; **to ~ sb with sth**
jdm etw vorwerfen; **~ful** *adj* vorwurfsvoll

reproduce [riːprə'djuːs] *vt* reproduzieren ♦ *vi*
(*have offspring*) sich vermehren;
reproduction [riːprə'dʌkʃən] *n* (*ART, PHOT*)
Reproduktion *f*; (*breeding*) Fortpflanzung *f*;
reproductive [riːprə'dʌktɪv] *adj*
reproduktiv; (*breeding*) Fortpflanzungs-

reprove [rɪ'pruːv] *vt* tadeln

reptile ['reptaɪl] *n* Reptil *nt*

republic [rɪ'pʌblɪk] *n* Republik *f*

repudiate [rɪ'pjuːdɪeɪt] *vt* zurückweisen

repugnant [rɪ'pʌgnənt] *adj* widerlich

repulse [rɪ'pʌls] *vt* (*drive back*)
zurückschlagen; (*reject*) abweisen

repulsive [rɪ'pʌlsɪv] *adj* abstoßend

reputable ['repjutəbl] *adj* angesehen

reputation [repju'teɪʃən] *n* Ruf *m*

reputed [rɪ'pjuːtɪd] *adj* angeblich; **~ly**
[rɪ'pjuːtɪdlɪ] *adv* angeblich

request [rɪ'kwest] *n* Bitte *f* ♦ *vt* (*thing*)
erbitten; **to ~ sth of** or **from sb** jdn um etw
bitten; (*formally*) jdn um etw ersuchen; **~
stop** (*BRIT*) *n* Bedarfshaltestelle *f*

require [rɪ'kwaɪəʳ] *vt* (*need*) brauchen;
(*demand*) erfordern; **~ment** *n* (*condition*)
Anforderung *f*; (*need*) Bedarf *m*

requisite ['rekwɪzɪt] *adj* erforderlich

requisition [rekwɪ'zɪʃən] *n* Anforderung *f*
♦ *vt* beschlagnahmen

rescue ['reskjuː] *n* Rettung *f* ♦ *vt* retten; **~
party** *n* Rettungsmannschaft *f*; **~r** *n* Retter *m*

research [rɪ'sɜːtʃ] *n* Forschung *f* ♦ *vi* forschen
♦ *vt* erforschen; **~er** *n* Forscher *m*

resemblance [rɪ'zembləns] *n* Ähnlichkeit *f*

resemble [rɪ'zembl] *vt* ähneln +*dat*

resent [rɪ'zent] *vt* übel nehmen; **~ful** *adj*
nachtragend, empfindlich; **~ment** *n*
Verstimmung *f*, Unwille *m*

reservation [rezə'veɪʃən] *n* (*booking*)
Reservierung *f*; (*THEAT*) Vorbestellung *f*;
(*doubt*) Vorbehalt *m*; (*land*) Reservat *nt*

reserve [rɪ'zɜːv] *n* (*store*) Vorrat *m*, Reserve *f*;
(*manner*) Zurückhaltung *f*; (*game ~*)
Naturschutzgebiet *nt*; (*SPORT*)
Ersatzspieler(in) *m(f)* ♦ *vt* reservieren;
(*judgement*) sich *dat* vorbehalten; **~s** *npl*
(*MIL*) Reserve *f*; **in ~** in Reserve; **~d** *adj*
reserviert

reshuffle [riː'ʃʌfl] *n* (*POL*): **cabinet ~**
Kabinettsumbildung *f* ♦ *vt* (*POL*) umbilden

reside [rɪ'zaɪd] *vi* wohnen, ansässig sein

residence ['rezɪdəns] *n* (*house*) Wohnsitz *m*;
(*living*) Aufenthalt *m*; **~ permit** (*BRIT*) *n*
Aufenthaltserlaubnis *f*

resident ['rezɪdənt] *n* (*in house*) Bewohner *m*;
(*in area*) Einwohner *m* ♦ *adj* wohnhaft,

ansässig; **~ial** |rezɪˈdenʃəl| adj Wohn-
residue |ˈrezɪdjuː| n Rest m; (CHEM)
Rückstand m; (fig) Bodensatz m
resign |rɪˈzaɪn| vt (office) aufgeben,
zurücktreten von ♦ vi (from office)
zurücktreten; (employee) kündigen; **to be
~ed to sth, to ~ o.s. to sth** sich mit etw
abfinden; **~ation** |rezɪgˈneɪʃən| n (from job)
Kündigung f; (POL) Rücktritt m; (submission)
Resignation f; **~ed** adj resigniert
resilience |rɪˈzɪlɪəns| n Spannkraft f; (of
person) Unverwüstlichkeit f; **resilient**
|rɪˈzɪlɪənt| adj unverwüstlich
resin |ˈrezɪn| n Harz nt
resist |rɪˈzɪst| vt widerstehen +dat; **~ance** n
Widerstand m
resit [vb riːˈsɪt, n ˈriːsɪt] vt (exam)
wiederholen ♦ n Wiederholung(sprüfung) f
resolute |ˈrezəluːt| adj entschlossen, resolut;
resolution |rezəˈluːʃən| n (firmness)
Entschlossenheit f; (intention) Vorsatz m;
(decision) Beschluss m
resolve |rɪˈzɔlv| n Entschlossenheit f ♦ vt
(decide) beschließen ♦ vi sich lösen; **~d** adj
(fest) entschlossen
resonant |ˈrezənənt| adj voll
resort |rɪˈzɔːt| n (holiday place) Erholungsort
m; (help) Zuflucht f ♦ vi: **to ~ to** Zuflucht
nehmen zu; **as a last ~** als letzter Ausweg
resound |rɪˈzaund| vi: **to ~ (with)**
widerhallen (von); **~ing** adj nachhallend;
(success) groß
resource |rɪˈsɔːs| n Findigkeit f; **~s** npl
(financial) Geldmittel pl; (natural)
Bodenschätze pl; **~ful** adj findig
respect |rɪsˈpekt| n Respekt m ♦ vt achten,
respektieren; **~s** npl (regards) Grüße pl; **with
~ to** in Bezug auf +acc, hinsichtlich +gen; **in
this ~** in dieser Hinsicht; **~able** adj
anständig; (not bad) leidlich; **~ful** adj höflich
respective |rɪsˈpektɪv| adj jeweilig; **~ly** adv
beziehungsweise
respiration |respɪˈreɪʃən| n Atmung f
respite |ˈrespaɪt| n Ruhepause f
resplendent |rɪsˈplendənt| adj strahlend
respond |rɪsˈpɔnd| vi antworten; (react): **to
~ (to)** reagieren (auf +acc); **response**
|rɪsˈpɔns| n Antwort f; Reaktion f; (to advert)
Resonanz f
responsibility |rɪspɔnsɪˈbɪlɪtɪ| n
Verantwortung f
responsible |rɪsˈpɔnsɪbl| adj verantwortlich;
(reliable) verantwortungsvoll
responsive |rɪsˈpɔnsɪv| adj empfänglich
rest |rest| n Ruhe f; (break) Pause f;
(remainder) Rest m ♦ vi sich ausruhen; (be
supported) (auf)liegen ♦ vt (lean): **to ~ sth
on/against sth** etw gegen etw acc lehnen;
the ~ of them die Übrigen; **it ~s with him
to ...** es liegt bei ihm, zu ...
restaurant |ˈrestərɔŋ| n Restaurant nt; **~ car**

(BRIT) n Speisewagen m
restful |ˈrestful| adj erholsam, ruhig
rest home n Erholungsheim nt
restive |ˈrestɪv| adj unruhig
restless |ˈrestlɪs| adj unruhig
restoration |restəˈreɪʃən| n Rückgabe f; (of
building etc) Rückerstattung f
restore |rɪˈstɔːʳ| vt (order) wieder herstellen;
(customs) wieder einführen; (person to
position) wieder einsetzen; (give back)
zurückgeben; (renovate) restaurieren
restrain |rɪsˈtreɪn| vt zurückhalten; (curiosity
etc) beherrschen; (person): **to ~ sb from
doing sth** jdn davon abhalten, etw zu tun;
~ed adj (style etc) gedämpft, verhalten; **~t** n
(self-control) Zurückhaltung f
restrict |rɪsˈtrɪkt| vt einschränken; **~ion**
|rɪsˈtrɪkʃən| n Einschränkung f; **~ive** adj
einschränkend
rest room (US) n Toilette f
restructure |riːˈstrʌktʃəʳ| vt umstrukturieren
result |rɪˈzʌlt| n Resultat nt, Folge f; (of exam,
game) Ergebnis nt ♦ vi: **to ~ in sth** etw zur
Folge haben; **as a ~ of** als Folge +gen
resume |rɪˈzjuːm| vt fortsetzen; (occupy
again) wieder einnehmen ♦ vi (work etc)
wieder beginnen
résumé |ˈreɪzjuːmeɪ| n Zusammenfassung f
resumption |rɪˈzʌmpʃən| n Wiederaufnahme
f
resurgence |rɪˈsɜːdʒəns| n Wiedererwachen
nt
resurrection |rezəˈrekʃən| n Auferstehung
f
resuscitate |rɪˈsʌsɪteɪt| vt wieder beleben;
resuscitation |rɪsʌsɪˈteɪʃən| n
Wiederbelebung f
retail |ˈriːteɪl| n Einzelhandel m ♦ adj
Einzelhandels- ♦ vt im Kleinen verkaufen ♦ vi
im Einzelhandel kosten; **~er** |ˈriːteɪləʳ| n
Einzelhändler m, Kleinhändler m; **~ price** n
Ladenpreis m
retain |rɪˈteɪn| vt (keep) (zurück)behalten;
~er n (fee) (Honorar)vorschuss m
retaliate |rɪˈtælɪeɪt| vi zum Vergeltungsschlag
ausholen; **retaliation** |rɪtælɪˈeɪʃən| n
Vergeltung f
retarded |rɪˈtɑːdɪd| adj zurückgeblieben
retch |retʃ| vi würgen
retentive |rɪˈtentɪv| adj (memory) gut
reticent |ˈretɪsnt| adj schweigsam
retina |ˈretɪnə| n Netzhaut f
retire |rɪˈtaɪəʳ| vi (from work) in den
Ruhestand treten; (withdraw) sich
zurückziehen; (go to bed) schlafen gehen;
~d adj (person) pensioniert, im Ruhestand;
~ment n Ruhestand m
retiring |rɪˈtaɪərɪŋ| adj zurückhaltend
retort |rɪˈtɔːt| n (reply) Erwiderung f ♦ vi
(scharf) erwidern

retrace |riˈtreɪs| vt zurückverfolgen; **to ~ one's steps** denselben Weg zurückgehen

retract |riˈtrækt| vt (statement) zurücknehmen; (claws) einziehen ♦ vi einen Rückzieher machen; **~able** adj (aerial) ausziehbar

retrain |riːˈtreɪn| vt umschulen

retread |ˈriːtred| n (tyre) Reifen m mit erneuerter Lauffläche

retreat |riˈtriːt| n Rückzug m; (place) Zufluchtsort m ♦ vi sich zurückziehen

retribution |retriˈbjuːʃən| n Strafe f

retrieval |riˈtriːvəl| n Wiedergewinnung f

retrieve |riˈtriːv| vt wiederbekommen; (rescue) retten; **~r** n Apportierhund m

retrograde |ˈretrəgreɪd| adj (step) Rück-; (policy) rückschrittlich

retrospect |ˈretrəspekt| n: **in ~** im Rückblick, rückblickend; **~ive** |retrəˈspektɪv| adj (action) rückwirkend; (look) rückblickend

return |riˈtɜːn| n (of profits) Ertrag m; (BRIT: rail ticket etc) Rückfahrkarte f; (: plane ticket) Rückflugkarte f ♦ adj (journey, match) Rück- ♦ vi zurückkehren, zurückkommen ♦ vt zurückgeben, zurücksenden; (pay back) zurückzahlen; (elect) wählen; (verdict) aussprechen; **~s** npl (COMM) Gewinn m; (receipts) Einkünfte pl; **in ~** dafür; **by ~ of post** postwendend; **many happy ~s (of the day)!** herzlichen Glückwunsch zum Geburtstag!

reunion |riːˈjuːnɪən| n Wiedervereinigung f; (SCH etc) Treffen nt

reunite |riːjuːˈnaɪt| vt wieder vereinigen

reuse |riːˈjuːz| vt wieder verwenden, wieder verwerten

rev |rev| n abbr (AUT: = revolution) Drehzahl f ♦ vt (also: ~ up: engine) auf Touren bringen ♦ vi (also: ~ up) den Motor auf Touren bringen

revamp |riːˈvæmp| vt aufpolieren

reveal |riˈviːl| vt enthüllen; **~ing** adj aufschlussreich

revel |ˈrevl| vi: **to ~ in sth/in doing sth** seine Freude an etw dat haben/daran haben, etw zu tun

revelation |revəˈleɪʃən| n Offenbarung f

revelry |ˈrevlri| n Rummel m

revenge |riˈvendʒ| n Rache f; **to take ~ on** sich rächen an +dat

revenue |ˈrevənjuː| n Einnahmen pl

reverberate |riˈvɜːbəreɪt| vi widerhallen

revere |riˈvɪər| vt (ver)ehren; **~nce** |ˈrevərəns| n Ehrfurcht f

Reverend |ˈrevərənd| adj: **the ~ Robert Martin** ≈ Pfarrer Robert Martin

reversal |riˈvɜːsl| n Umkehrung f

reverse |riˈvɜːs| n Rückseite f; (AUT: gear) Rückwärtsgang m ♦ adj (order, direction) entgegengesetzt ♦ vt umkehren ♦ vi (BRIT: AUT) rückwärts fahren; **~-charge call** (BRIT)

n R-Gespräch nt; **reversing lights** npl (AUT) Rückfahrscheinwerfer pl

revert |riˈvɜːt| vi: **to ~ to** zurückkehren zu; (to bad state) zurückfallen in +acc

review |riˈvjuː| n (of book) Rezension f; (magazine) Zeitschrift f ♦ vt Rückschau halten auf +acc; (MIL) mustern; (book) rezensieren; (reexamine) von neuem untersuchen; **~er** n (critic) Rezensent m

revise |riˈvaɪz| vt (book) überarbeiten; (reconsider) ändern, revidieren; **revision** |riˈvɪʒən| n Prüfung f; (COMM) Revision f; (SCH) Wiederholung f

revitalize |riːˈvaɪtəlaɪz| vt neu beleben

revival |riˈvaɪvl| n Wiederbelebung f; (REL) Erweckung f; (THEAT) Wiederaufnahme f

revive |riˈvaɪv| vt wieder beleben; (fig) wieder auffrischen ♦ vi wieder erwachen; (fig) wieder aufleben

revoke |riˈvəʊk| vt aufheben

revolt |riˈvəʊlt| n Aufstand m, Revolte f ♦ vi sich auflehnen ♦ vt entsetzen; **~ing** adj widerlich

revolution |revəˈluːʃən| n (turn) Umdrehung f; (POL) Revolution f; **~ary** adj revolutionär ♦ n Revolutionär m; **~ize** vt revolutionieren

revolve |riˈvɒlv| vi kreisen; (on own axis) sich drehen

revolver |riˈvɒlvər| n Revolver m

revolving door |riˈvɒlvɪŋ-| n Drehtür f

revulsion |riˈvʌlʃən| n Ekel m

reward |riˈwɔːd| n Belohnung f ♦ vt belohnen; **~ing** adj lohnend

rewind |riːˈwaɪnd| (irreg: like wind) vt (tape etc) zurückspulen

rewire |riːˈwaɪər| vt (house) neu verkabeln

reword |riːˈwɜːd| vt anders formulieren

rewrite |riːˈraɪt| (irreg: like write) vt umarbeiten, neu schreiben

rheumatism |ˈruːmətɪzəm| n Rheumatismus m, Rheuma nt

Rhine |raɪn| n: **the ~** der Rhein

rhinoceros |raɪˈnɒsərəs| n Nashorn nt

Rhone |rəʊn| n: **the ~** die Rhone

rhubarb |ˈruːbɑːb| n Rhabarber m

rhyme |raɪm| n Reim m

rhythm |ˈrɪðm| n Rhythmus m

rib |rɪb| n Rippe f ♦ vt (mock) hänseln, aufziehen

ribbon |ˈrɪbən| n Band nt; **in ~s** (torn) in Fetzen

rice |raɪs| n Reis m; **~ pudding** n Milchreis m

rich |rɪtʃ| adj reich; (food) reichhaltig ♦ npl: **the ~** die Reichen pl; **~es** npl Reichtum m; **~ly** adv reich; (deserve) völlig

rickets |ˈrɪkɪts| n Rachitis f

rickety |ˈrɪkɪti| adj wack(e)lig

rickshaw |ˈrɪkʃɔː| n Riksha f

ricochet |ˈrɪkəʃeɪ| n Abprallen nt; (shot) Querschläger m ♦ vi abprallen

rid |rɪd| (pt, pp rid) vt befreien; **to get ~ of**

loswerden

riddle ['rɪdl] n Rätsel nt ♦ vt: **to be ~d with** völlig durchlöchert sein von

ride [raɪd] (pt **rode**, pp **ridden**) n (in vehicle) Fahrt f; (on horse) Ritt m ♦ vt (horse) reiten; (bicycle) fahren ♦ vi fahren, reiten; **to take sb for a ~** mit jdm eine Fahrt etc machen; (fig) jdn aufs Glatteis führen; **~r** n Reiter m

ridge [rɪdʒ] n Kamm m; (of roof) First m

ridicule ['rɪdɪkjuːl] n Spott m ♦ vt lächerlich machen

ridiculous [rɪ'dɪkjuləs] adj lächerlich

riding ['raɪdɪŋ] n Reiten nt; **~ school** n Reitschule f

rife [raɪf] adj weit verbreitet; **to be ~** grassieren; **to be ~ with** voll sein von

riffraff ['rɪfræf] n Pöbel m

rifle ['raɪfl] n Gewehr nt ♦ vt berauben; **~ range** n Schießstand m

rift [rɪft] n Spalte f; (fig) Bruch m

rig [rɪg] n (oil ~) Bohrinsel f ♦ vt (election etc) manipulieren; **~ out** (BRIT) vt ausstatten; **~ up** vt zusammenbasteln; **~ging** n Takelage f

right [raɪt] adj (correct, just) richtig, recht; (~ side) rechte(r, s) ♦ n Recht nt; (not left, POL) Rechte f ♦ adv (on the ~) rechts; (to the ~) nach rechts; (look, work) richtig, recht; (directly) gerade; (exactly) genau ♦ vt in Ordnung bringen, korrigieren ♦ excl gut; **on the ~** rechts; **to be in the ~** im Recht sein; **by ~s** von Rechts wegen; **to be ~** Recht haben; **~ away** sofort; **~ now** in diesem Augenblick, eben; **~ in the middle** genau in der Mitte; **~ angle** n rechte(r) Winkel m; **~eous** ['raɪtʃəs] adj rechtschaffen; **~ful** adj rechtmäßig; **~-hand** adj: **~-hand drive** mit Rechtssteuerung; **~-handed** adj rechtshändig; **~-hand man** (irreg) n rechte Hand f; **~-hand side** n rechte Seite f; **~ly** adv mit Recht; **~ of way** n Vorfahrt f; **~-wing** adj rechtsorientiert

rigid ['rɪdʒɪd] adj (stiff) starr, steif; (strict) streng; **~ity** [rɪ'dʒɪdɪtɪ] n Starrheit f; Strenge f

rigmarole ['rɪgmərəʊl] n Gewäsch nt

rigor ['rɪgəʳ] (US) n = **rigour**

rigorous ['rɪgərəs] adj streng

rigour ['rɪgəʳ] (US **rigor**) n Strenge f, Härte f

rile [raɪl] vt ärgern

rim [rɪm] n (edge) Rand m; (of wheel) Felge f

rind [raɪnd] n Rinde f

ring [rɪŋ] n (pt **rang**, pp **rung**) n Ring m; (of people) Kreis m; (arena) Manege f; (of telephone) Klingeln nt ♦ vt, vi (bell) läuten; (BRIT) anrufen; **~ back** (BRIT) vt, vi zurückrufen; **~ off** (BRIT) vi aufhängen; **~ up** (BRIT) vt anrufen; **~ binder** n Ringbuch nt; **~ing** n Klingeln nt; (of large bell) Läuten nt; (in ears) Klingen nt; **~ing tone** n (TEL) Rufzeichen nt

ringleader ['rɪŋliːdəʳ] n Anführer m,

Rädelsführer m

ringlets ['rɪŋlɪts] npl Ringellocken pl

ring road (BRIT) n Umgehungsstraße f

rink [rɪŋk] n (ice ~) Eisbahn f

rinse [rɪns] n Spülen nt ♦ vt spülen

riot ['raɪət] n Aufruhr m ♦ vi randalieren; **to run ~** (people) randalieren; (vegetation) wuchern; **~er** n Aufrührer m; **~ous** adj aufrührerisch; (noisy) lärmend

rip [rɪp] n Schlitz m, Riss m ♦ vt, vi (zer)reißen; **~cord** n Reißleine f

ripe [raɪp] adj reif; **~n** vi reifen ♦ vt reifen lassen

rip-off ['rɪpɔf] (inf) n: **it's a ~!** das ist Wucher!

ripple ['rɪpl] n kleine Welle f ♦ vt kräuseln ♦ vi sich kräuseln

rise [raɪz] (pt **rose**, pp **risen**) n (slope) Steigung f; (esp in wages: BRIT) Erhöhung f; (growth) Aufstieg m ♦ vi (sun) aufgehen; (smoke) aufsteigen; (mountain) sich erheben; (ground) ansteigen; (prices) steigen; (in revolt) sich erheben; **to give ~ to** Anlass geben zu; **to ~ to the occasion** sich der Lage gewachsen zeigen; **~n** [rɪzn] pp of **rise**; **~r** ['raɪzəʳ] n: **to be an early ~r** ein(in) Frühaufsteher(e) m(f) sein; **rising** ['raɪzɪŋ] adj (tide, prices) steigend; (sun, moon) aufgehend ♦ n (uprising) Aufstand m

risk [rɪsk] n Gefahr f, Risiko nt ♦ vt (venture) wagen; (chance loss of) riskieren, aufs Spiel setzen; **to take** or **run the ~ of doing sth** das Risiko eingehen, etw zu tun; **at ~** in Gefahr; **at one's own ~** auf eigene Gefahr; **~y** adj riskant

risqué ['riːskeɪ] adj gewagt

rissole ['rɪsəʊl] n Fleischklößchen nt

rite [raɪt] n Ritus m; **last ~s** Letzte Ölung f

ritual ['rɪtjʊəl] n Ritual nt ♦ adj ritual, Ritual-; (fig) rituell

rival ['raɪvl] n Rivale m, Konkurrent m ♦ adj rivalisierend ♦ vt rivalisieren mit; (COMM) konkurrieren mit; **~ry** n Rivalität f; Konkurrenz f

river ['rɪvəʳ] n Fluss m, Strom m ♦ cpd (port, traffic) Fluss-; **up/down ~** flussaufwärts/ -abwärts; **~bank** n Flussufer nt; **~bed** n Flussbett nt

rivet ['rɪvɪt] n Niete f ♦ vt (fasten) (ver)nieten

Riviera [rɪvɪ'eərə] n: **the ~** die Riviera

road [rəʊd] n Straße f ♦ cpd Straßen-; **major/ minor ~** Haupt-/Nebenstraße f; **~ accident** n Verkehrsunfall m; **~block** n Straßensperre f; **~hog** n Verkehrsrowdy m; **~ map** n Straßenkarte f; **~ rage** n Aggressivität f im Straßenverkehr; **~ safety** n Verkehrssicherheit f; **~side** n Straßenrand m ♦ adj an der Landstraße (gelegen); **~ sign** n Straßenschild nt; **~ user** n Verkehrsteilnehmer m; **~way** n Fahrbahn f; **~ works** npl Straßenbauarbeiten pl;

~worthy adj verkehrssicher

roam |rəum| vi (umher)streifen ♦ vt
durchstreifen

roar |rɔːʳ| n Brüllen nt, Gebrüll nt ♦ vi brüllen;
to ~ with laughter vor Lachen brüllen; **to
do a ~ing trade** ein Riesengeschäft machen

roast |rəust| n Braten m ♦ vt braten,
schmoren; **~ beef** n Roastbeef nt

rob |rɔb| vt bestehlen, berauben; (bank)
ausrauben; **to ~ sb of sth** jdm etw rauben;
~ber n Räuber m; **~bery** n Raub m

robe |rəub| n (dress) Gewand nt; (US)
Hauskleid nt; (judge's) Robe f

robin |'rɔbin| n Rotkehlchen nt

robot |'rəubɔt| n Roboter m

robust |rəu'bʌst| adj (person) robust;
(appetite, economy) gesund

rock |rɔk| n Felsen m, (BRIT: sweet)
Zuckerstange f ♦ vt, vi wiegen, schaukeln; **on
the ~s** (drink) mit Eis(würfeln); (marriage)
gescheitert; (ship) aufgelaufen; **~ and roll** n
Rock and Roll m; **~-bottom** n (fig) Tiefpunkt
m; **~ery** n Steingarten m

rocket |'rɔkit| n Rakete f

rocking chair |'rɔkiŋ-| n Schaukelstuhl m

rocking horse n Schaukelpferd nt

rocky |'rɔki| adj felsig

rod |rɔd| n (bar) Stange f; (stick) Rute f

rode |rəud| pt of ride

rodent |'rəudnt| n Nagetier nt

roe |rəu| n (also: ~ deer) Reh nt; (of fish: also:
hard ~) Rogen m; **soft ~** Milch f

rogue |rəug| n Schurke m

role |rəul| n Rolle f; **~ play** n Rollenspiel nt

roll |rəul| n Rolle f; (bread) Brötchen nt; (list)
(Namens)liste f; (of drum) Wirbel m ♦ vt
(turn) rollen, (herum)wälzen; (grass etc)
walzen ♦ vi (swing) schlingern; (sound)
rollen, grollen; **~ about** or **around** vi
herumkugeln; (ship) schlingern; (dog etc)
sich wälzen; **~ by** vi (time) verfließen; **~
over** vi sich (herum)drehen; **~ up** vi (arrive)
kommen, auftauchen ♦ vt (carpet) aufrollen;
~ call n Namensaufruf m; **~er** n Rolle f,
Walze f; (road ~er) Straßenwalze f;
~erblade ® n Rollerblade m; **~er coaster** n
Achterbahn f; **~er skates** npl Rollschuhe pl;
~er-skating n Rollschuhlaufen nt

rolling |'rəuliŋ| adj (landscape) wellig; **~ pin**
n Nudel- or Wellholz nt; **~ stock** n
Wagenmaterial nt

ROM |rɔm| n abbr (= read only memory) ROM
m

Roman |'rəumən| adj römisch ♦ n
Römer(in) m(f); **~ Catholic** adj römisch-
katholisch ♦ n Katholik(in) m(f)

romance |rə'mæns| n Romanze f; (story)
(Liebes)roman m

Romania |rəu'meiniə| n = Rumania; **~n** n =
Rumanian

Roman numeral n römische Ziffer

romantic |rə'mæntik| adj romantisch; **~ism**
|rə'mæntisizəm| n Romantik f

Rome |rəum| n Rom nt

romp |rɔmp| n Tollen n ♦ vi (also: ~ about)
herumtollen

rompers |'rɔmpəz| npl Spielanzug m

roof |ruːf| n (pl ~s) n Dach nt; (of mouth)
Gaumen m ♦ vt überdachen, überdecken;
~ing n Deckmaterial nt; **~ rack** n (AUT)
Dachgepäckträger m

rook |ruk| n (bird) Saatkrähe f; (chess) Turm
m

room |ruːm| n Zimmer nt, Raum m; (space)
Platz m; (fig) Spielraum m; **~s** npl
(accommodation) Wohnung f; **"~s to let**
(BRIT) or **for rent** (US)" „Zimmer zu
vermieten"; **single/double ~** Einzel-/
Doppelzimmer nt; **~ing house** (US) n
Mietshaus nt (mit möblierten Wohnungen);
~mate n Mitbewohner(in) m(f); **~ service**
n Zimmerbedienung f; **~y** adj geräumig

roost |ruːst| n Hühnerstange f ♦ vi auf der
Stange hocken

rooster |'ruːstəʳ| n Hahn m

root |ruːt| n (also fig) Wurzel f ♦ vi wurzeln; **~
about** vi (fig) herumwühlen; **~ for** vt fus
Stimmung machen für; **~ out** vt ausjäten;
(fig) ausrotten

rope |rəup| n Seil nt ♦ vt (tie) festschnüren; **to
know the ~s** sich auskennen; **to ~ sb in** jdn
gewinnen; **~ off** vt absperren; **~ ladder** n
Strickleiter f

rosary |'rəuzəri| n Rosenkranz m

rose |rəuz| pt of rise ♦ n Rose f ♦ adj Rosen-,
rosenrot

rosé |'rəuzei| n Rosé m

rosebud |'rəuzbʌd| n Rosenknospe f

rosebush |'rəuzbuʃ| n Rosenstock m

rosemary |'rəuzməri| n Rosmarin m

rosette |rəu'zet| n Rosette f

roster |'rɔstəʳ| n Dienstplan m

rostrum |'rɔstrəm| n Rednerbühne f

rosy |'rəuzi| adj rosig

rot |rɔt| n Fäulnis f; (nonsense) Quatsch m ♦ vi
verfaulen ♦ vt verfaulen lassen

rota |'rəutə| n Dienstliste f

rotary |'rəutəri| adj rotierend

rotate |rəu'teit| vt rotieren lassen; (take turns)
turnusmäßig wechseln ♦ vi rotieren;
rotating adj rotierend; **rotation**
|rəu'teiʃən| n Umdrehung f

rote |rəut| n: **by ~** auswendig

rotten |'rɔtn| adj faul; (fig) schlecht, gemein;
to feel ~ (ill) sich elend fühlen

rotund |rəu'tʌnd| adj rundlich

rouble |'ruːbl| (US **rubie**) n Rubel m

rough |rʌf| adj (not smooth) rau; (path)
uneben; (violent) roh, grob; (crossing)
stürmisch; (without comforts) hart,
unbequem; (unfinished, makeshift) grob;
(approximate) ungefähr ♦ n (BRIT: person)

Rowdy *m*, Rohling *m*; (*GOLF*): **in the ~** im Rau ♦ *vt*: **to ~ it** primitiv leben; **to sleep ~** im Freien schlafen; **~age** *n* Ballaststoffe *pl*; **~-and-ready** *adj* provisorisch; (*work*) zusammengehauen; **~ copy** *n* Entwurf *m*; **~ draft** *n* Entwurf *m*; **~ly** *adv* grob; (*about*) ungefähr; **~ness** *n* Rauheit *f*; (*of manner*) Ungeschliffenheit *f*

roulette [ru:'let] *n* Roulett(e) *nt*

Roumania [ru:'meɪnɪə] *n* = **Rumania**

round [raʊnd] *adj* rund; (*figures*) aufgerundet ♦ *adv* (*in a circle*) rundherum ♦ *prep* um ... herum ♦ *n* Runde *f*; (*of ammunition*) Magazin *nt* ♦ *vt* (*corner*) biegen um; **all ~** überall; **the long way ~** der Umweg; **all the year ~** das ganze Jahr über; **it's just ~ the corner** (*fig*) es ist gerade um die Ecke; **~ the clock** rund um die Uhr; **to go ~ to sb's (house)** jdn besuchen; **to go ~ the back** hintenherum gehen; **enough to go ~** genug für alle; **to go the ~s** (*story*) die Runde machen; **a ~ of applause** ein Beifall *m*; **a ~ of drinks** eine Runde Drinks; **a ~ of sandwiches** ein Sandwich *nt* or *m*, ein belegtes Brot; **~ off** *vt* abrunden; **~ up** *vt* (*end*) abschließen; (*figures*) aufrunden; (*criminals*) hochnehmen; **~about** *n* (*BRIT: traffic*) Kreisverkehr *m* ♦ (*: merry-go-~*) Karussell *nt* ♦ *adj* auf Umwegen; **~ers** *npl* (*game*) ≈ Schlagball *m*; **~ly** *adv* (*fig*) gründlich; **~-shouldered** *adj* mit abfallenden Schultern; **~ trip** *n* Rundreise *f*; **~up** *n* Zusammentreiben *nt*, Sammeln *nt*

rouse [raʊz] *vt* (*waken*) (auf)wecken; (*stir up*) erregen; **rousing** *adj* (*welcome*) stürmisch; (*speech*) zündend

route [ru:t] *n* Weg *m*, Route *f*; **~ map** (*BRIT*) *n* (*for journey*) Streckenkarte *f*

routine [ru:'ti:n] *n* Routine *f* ♦ *adj* Routine-

row[1] [rau] *n* (*noise*) Lärm *m*; (*dispute*) Streit *m* ♦ *vi* sich streiten

row[2] [rau] *n* (*line*) Reihe *f* ♦ *vt*, *vi* (*boat*) rudern; **in a ~** (*fig*) hintereinander; **~boat** ['rəubəut] (*US*) *n* Ruderboot *nt*

rowdy ['raudɪ] *adj* rüpelhaft ♦ *n* (*person*) Rowdy *m*

rowing ['rəʊɪŋ] *n* Rudern *nt*; (*SPORT*) Rudersport *m*; **~ boat** (*BRIT*) *n* Ruderboot *nt*

royal ['rɔɪəl] *adj* königlich, Königs-; **R~ Air Force** *n* Königliche Luftwaffe *f*; **~ty** ['rɔɪəltɪ] *n* (*family*) königliche Familie *f*; (*for novel etc*) Tantieme *f*

rpm *abbr* (= *revs per minute*) U/min

R.S.V.P. *abbr* (= *répondez s'il vous plaît*) u. A. w. g.

Rt. Hon. (*BRIT*) *abbr* (= *Right Honourable*) Abgeordnete(r) *mf*

rub [rʌb] *n* (*with cloth*) Polieren *nt*; (*on person*) Reiben *nt* ♦ *vt* reiben; **to ~ sb up** (*BRIT*) or **to ~ sb** (*US*) **the wrong way** jdn aufreizen; **~ off** *vi* (*also fig*): **to ~ off (on)**

abfärben (auf +*acc*); **~ out** *vt* herausreiben; (*with eraser*) ausradieren

rubber ['rʌbə*r*] *n* Gummi *m*; (*BRIT*) Radiergummi *m*; **~ band** *n* Gummiband *nt*; **~ plant** *n* Gummibaum *m*

rubbish ['rʌbɪʃ] *n* (*waste*) Abfall *m*; (*nonsense*) Blödsinn *m*, Quatsch *m*; **~ bin** (*BRIT*) *n* Mülleimer *m*; **~ dump** *n* Müllablageplatz *m*

rubble ['rʌbl] *n* (Stein)schutt *m*

ruby ['ru:bɪ] *n* Rubin *m* ♦ *adj* rubinrot

rucksack ['rʌksæk] *n* Rucksack *m*

rudder ['rʌdə*r*] *n* Steuerruder *nt*

ruddy ['rʌdɪ] *adj* (*colour*) rötlich; (*inf: bloody*) verdammt

rude [ru:d] *adj* unverschämt; (*shock*) hart; (*awakening*) unsanft; (*unrefined, rough*) grob; **~ness** *n* Unverschämtheit *f*; Grobheit *f*

rudiment ['ru:dɪmənt] *n* Grundlage *f*

rueful ['ru:ful] *adj* reuevoll

ruffian ['rʌfɪən] *n* Rohling *m*

ruffle ['rʌfl] *vt* kräuseln

rug [rʌg] *n* Brücke *f*; (*in bedroom*) Bettvorleger *m*; (*BRIT: for knees*) (Reise)decke *f*

rugby ['rʌgbɪ] *n* (*also: ~ football*) Rugby *nt*

rugged ['rʌgɪd] *adj* (*coastline*) zerklüftet; (*features*) markig

rugger ['rʌgə*r*] (*BRIT: inf*) *n* = **rugby**

ruin ['ru:ɪn] *n* Ruine *f*; (*downfall*) Ruin *m* ♦ *vt* ruinieren; **~s** *npl* (*fig*) Trümmer *pl*; **~ous** *adj* ruinierend

rule [ru:l] *n* Regel *f*; (*government*) Regierung *f*; (*for measuring*) Lineal *nt* ♦ *vt* (*govern*) herrschen über +*acc*, regieren; (*decide*) anordnen, entscheiden; (*make lines on*) linieren ♦ *vi* herrschen, regieren; entscheiden; **as a ~** in der Regel; **~ out** *vt* ausschließen; **~d** *adj* (*paper*) liniert; **~r** *n* Lineal *nt*; Herrscher *m*; **ruling** ['ru:lɪŋ] *adj* (*party*) Regierungs-; (*class*) herrschend ♦ *n* (*JUR*) Entscheid *m*

rum [rʌm] *n* Rum *m*

Rumania [ru:'meɪnɪə] *n* Rumänien *nt*; **~n** *adj* rumänisch ♦ *n* Rumäne *m*, Rumänin *f*; (*LING*) Rumänisch *nt*

rumble ['rʌmbl] *n* Rumpeln *nt*; (*of thunder*) Grollen *nt* ♦ *vi* rumpeln; grollen

rummage ['rʌmɪdʒ] *vi* durchstöbern

rumour ['ru:mə*r*] (*US* **rumor**) *n* Gerücht *nt* ♦ *vt*: **it is ~ed that** man sagt or man munkelt, dass

rump [rʌmp] *n* Hinterteil *nt*; **~ steak** *n* Rumpsteak *nt*

rumpus ['rʌmpəs] *n* Spektakel *m*

run [rʌn] (*pt* **ran**, *pp* **run**) *n* Lauf *m*; (*in car*) (Spazier)fahrt *f*; (*series*) Serie *f*, Reihe *f*; (*ski ~*) (Ski)abfahrt *f*; (*in stocking*) Laufmasche *f* ♦ *vt* (*cause to ~*) laufen lassen; (*car, train, bus*) fahren; (*race, distance*) laufen, rennen; (*manage*) leiten; (*COMPUT*) laufen lassen; (*pass: hand, eye*) gleiten lassen ♦ *vi* laufen;

(*move quickly*) laufen, rennen; (*bus, train*) fahren; (*flow*) fließen, laufen; (*colours*) (ab)färben; **there was a ~ on** (*meat, tickets*) es gab einen Ansturm auf +*acc*; **on the ~** auf der Flucht; **in the long ~** auf die Dauer; **I'll ~ you to the station** ich fahre dich zum Bahnhof; **to ~ a risk** ein Risiko eingehen; **~ about** *or* **around** *vi* (*children*) umherspringen; **~ across** *vt fus* (*find*) stoßen auf +*acc*; **~ away** *vi* weglaufen; **~ down** *vi* (*clock*) ablaufen ♦ *vt* (*production, factory*) allmählich auflösen; (*with car*) überfahren; (*talk against*) heruntermachen; **to be ~ down** erschöpft *or* abgespannt sein; **~ in** (*BRIT*) *vt* (*car*) einfahren; **~ into** *vt fus* (*meet: person*) zufällig treffen; (*trouble*) bekommen; (*collide with*) rennen gegen, fahren gegen; **~ off** *vi* fortlaufen; **~ out** *vi* (*person*) hinausrennen; (*liquid*) auslaufen; (*lease*) ablaufen; (*money*) ausgehen; **he ran out of money/petrol** ihm ging das Geld/Benzin aus; **~ over** *vt* (*in accident*) überfahren; **~ through** *vt* (*instructions*) durchgehen; **~ up** *vt* (*debt, bill*) machen; **~ up against** *vt fus* (*difficulties*) stoßen auf +*acc*; **~away** *adj* (*horse*) ausgebrochei; (*person*) flüchtig

rung |rʌŋ| *pp of* **ring** ♦ *n* Sprosse *f*
runner |'rʌnəʳ| *n* Läufer(in) *m(f)*; (*for sleigh*) Kufe *f*; **~ bean** (*BRIT*) *n* Stangenbohne *f*; **~-up** *n* Zweite(r) *mf*
running |'rʌnɪŋ| *n* (*of business*) Leitung *f*; (*of machine*) Betrieb *m* ♦ *adj* (*water*) fließend; (*commentary*) laufend; **to be in/out of the ~ for sth** im/aus dem Rennen für etw sein; **3 days ~** 3 Tage lang *or* hintereinander; **~ costs** *npl* (*of car, machine*) Unterhaltungskosten *pl*
runny |'rʌnɪ| *adj* dünn; (*nose*) laufend
run-of-the-mill |'rʌnəvðə'mɪl| *adj* gewöhnlich, alltäglich
runt |rʌnt| *n* (*animal*) Kümmerer *m*
run-up |'rʌnʌp| *n*: **the ~ to** (*election etc*) die Endphase *vor +dat*
runway |'rʌnweɪ| *n* Startbahn *f*
rupture |'rʌptʃəʳ| *n* (*MED*) Bruch *m*
rural |'ruərl| *adj* ländlich, Land-
ruse |ruːz| *n* Kniff *m*, List *f*
rush |rʌʃ| *n* Eile *f*, Hetze *f*; (*FIN*) starke Nachfrage *f* ♦ *vt* (*carry along*) auf dem schnellsten Wege schaffen *or* transportieren; (*attack*) losstürmen auf +*acc* ♦ *vi* (*hurry*) eilen, stürzen; **don't ~ me** dräng mich nicht; **~ hour** *n* Hauptverkehrszeit *f*
rusk |rʌsk| *n* Zwieback *m*
Russia |'rʌʃə| *n* Rußland *nt*; **~n** *adj* russisch ♦ *n* Russe *m*, Russin *f*; (*LING*) Russisch *nt*
rust |rʌst| *n* Rost *m* ♦ *vi* rosten
rustic |'rʌstɪk| *adj* bäuerlich, ländlich
rustle |'rʌsl| *vi* rauschen, rascheln ♦ *vt* rascheln lassen

rustproof |'rʌstpruːf| *adj* rostfrei
rusty |'rʌstɪ| *adj* rostig
rut |rʌt| *n* (*in track*) Radspur *f*; **to be in a ~** im Trott stecken
ruthless |'ruːθlɪs| *adj* rücksichtslos
rye |raɪ| *n* Roggen *m*; **~ bread** *n* Roggenbrot *nt*

S, s

sabbath |'sæbəθ| *n* Sabbat *m*
sabotage |'sæbətɑːʒ| *n* Sabotage *f* ♦ *vt* sabotieren
saccharin |'sækərɪn| *n* Sa(c)charin *nt*
sachet |'sæfeɪ| *n* (*of shampoo etc*) Briefchen *nt*, Kissen *nt*
sack |sæk| *n* Sack *m* ♦ *vt* (*inf*) hinauswerfen; (*pillage*) plündern; **to get the ~** rausfliegen; **~ing** *n* (*material*) Sackleinen *nt*; (*inf*) Rausschmiss *m*
sacrament |'sækrəmənt| *n* Sakrament *nt*
sacred |'seɪkrɪd| *adj* heilig
sacrifice |'sækrɪfaɪs| *n* Opfer *nt* ♦ *vt* (*also fig*) opfern
sacrilege |'sækrɪlɪdʒ| *n* Schändung *f*
sad |sæd| *adj* traurig; **~den** *vt* traurig machen, betrüben
saddle |'sædl| *n* Sattel *m* ♦ *vt* (*burden*): **to ~ sb with sth** jdm etw aufhalsen; **~bag** *n* Satteltasche *f*
sadistic |sə'dɪstɪk| *adj* sadistisch
sadly |'sædlɪ| *adv* traurig; (*unfortunately*) leider
sadness |'sædnɪs| *n* Traurigkeit *f*
s.a.e. *abbr* (= *stamped addressed envelope*) adressierte(r) Rückumschlag *m*
safe |seɪf| *adj* (*careful*) vorsichtig ♦ *n* Safe *m*; **~ and sound** gesund und wohl; **(just) to be on the ~ side** um ganz sicherzugehen; **~ from** (*attack*) sicher vor +*dat*; **~-conduct** *n* freie(s) Geleit *nt*; **~-deposit** *n* (*vault*) Tresorraum *m*; (*box*) Banksafe *m*; **~guard** *n* Sicherung *f* ♦ *vt* sichern, schützen; **~keeping** *n* sichere Verwahrung *f*; **~ly** *adv* sicher; (*arrive*) wohlbehalten; **~ sex** *n* geschützter Sex *m*
safety |'seɪftɪ| *n* Sicherheit *f*; **~ belt** *n* Sicherheitsgurt *m*; **~ pin** *n* Sicherheitsnadel *f*; **~ valve** *n* Sicherheitsventil *nt*
sag |sæg| *vi* (*durch*)sacken
sage |seɪdʒ| *n* (*herb*) Salbei *m*; (*person*) Weise(r) *mf*
Sagittarius |sædʒɪ'tɛərɪəs| *n* Schütze *m*
Sahara |sə'hɑːrə| *n*: **the ~ (Desert)** die (Wüste) Sahara
said |sed| *pt, pp of* **say**
sail |seɪl| *n* Segel *nt*; (*trip*) Fahrt *f* ♦ *vt* segeln ♦ *vi* segeln; (*begin voyage: person*) abfahren; (*: ship*) auslaufen; (*fig: cloud etc*)

dahinsegeln; **to go for a ~** segeln gehen;
they ~ed into Copenhagen sie liefen in
Kopenhagen ein; **~ through** vi fus, vi (fig)
(es) spielend schaffen; **~boat** (US) n
Segelboot nt; **~ing** n Segeln nt; **~ing ship**
n Segelschiff nt; **~or** n Matrose m, Seemann
m

saint |seɪnt| n Heilige(r) mf; **~ly** adj heilig,
fromm

sake |seɪk| n: **for the ~ of** um +gen willen

salad ['sæləd] n Salat m; **~ bowl** n
Salatschüssel f; **~ cream** (BRIT) n
Salatmayonnaise f, Salatmajonäse f; **~
dressing** n Salatsoße f

salary ['sælərɪ] n Gehalt nt

sale |seɪl| n Verkauf m; (reduced prices)
Schlussverkauf m; **"for ~"** "zu verkaufen";
on ~ zu verkaufen; **~room** n Verkaufsraum
m; **~s assistant** n Verkäufer(in) m(f); **~s
clerk** (US) n Verkäufer(in) m(f); **~sman**
(irreg) n Verkäufer m; (representative)
Vertreter m; **~s rep** (COMM)
Vertreter(in) m(f); **~swoman** (irreg) n
Verkäuferin f

salient ['seɪlɪənt] adj bemerkenswert

saliva [sə'laɪvə] n Speichel m

sallow ['sæləʊ] adj fahl; (face) bleich

salmon ['sæmən] n Lachs m

salon ['sælɔn] n Salon m

saloon [sə'luːn] n (BRIT: AUT) Limousine f;
(ship's lounge) Salon m; **~ car** (BRIT) n
Limousine f

salt [sɔːlt] n Salz nt ♦ vt (cure) einsalzen;
(flavour) salzen; **~cellar** n Salzfass nt;
~water adj Salzwasser-; **~y** adj salzig

salute [sə'luːt] n (MIL) Gruß m; (with guns)
Salutschüsse pl ♦ vt (MIL) salutieren

salvage ['sælvɪdʒ] n (from ship) Bergung
f; (property) Rettung f ♦ vt bergen;
retten

salvation [sæl'veɪʃən] n Rettung f; **S~ Army**
n Heilsarmee f

same [seɪm] adj, pron (similar) gleiche(r, s);
(identical) derselbe/dieselbe/dasselbe; **the ~
book** as das gleiche Buch wie; **at the ~
time** zur gleichen Zeit, gleichzeitig;
(however) zugleich, andererseits; **all or just
the ~** trotzdem; **the ~ to you!** gleichfalls!;
to do the ~ (as sb) das Gleiche tun (wie jd)

sample ['saːmpl] n Probe f ♦ vt probieren

sanctify ['sæŋktɪfaɪ] vt weihen

sanctimonious [sæŋktɪ'məʊnɪəs] adj
scheinheilig

sanction ['sæŋkʃən] n Sanktion f

sanctity ['sæŋktɪtɪ] n Heiligkeit f; (fig)
Unverletzlichkeit f

sanctuary ['sæŋktjʊərɪ] n (for fugitive) Asyl
nt; (refuge) Zufluchtsort m; (for animals)
Schutzgebiet nt

sand [sænd] n Sand m ♦ vt (furniture)
schmirgeln

sandal ['sændl] n Sandale f

sand: **~box** (US) n = **sandpit**; **~castle** n
Sandburg f; **~ dune** n (Sand)düne f;
~paper n Sandpapier nt; **~pit** n Sandkasten
m; **~stone** n Sandstein m

sandwich ['sændwɪtʃ] n Sandwich m or nt
♦ vt (also: **~ in**) einklemmen; **cheese/ham ~**
Käse-/Schinkenbrot; **~ed between**
eingeklemmt zwischen; **~ board** n
Reklametafel f; **~ course** (BRIT) n in
Theorie und Praxis abwechselnde(r)
Ausbildungsgang m

sandy ['sændɪ] adj sandig; (hair) rotblond

sane [seɪn] adj geistig gesund or normal;
(sensible) vernünftig, gescheit

sang [sæŋ] pt of **sing**

sanitary ['sænɪtərɪ] adj hygienisch; **~ towel**
n (Monats)binde f

sanitation [sænɪ'teɪʃən] n sanitäre
Einrichtungen pl; **~ department** (US) n
Stadtreinigung f

sanity ['sænɪtɪ] n geistige Gesundheit f;
(sense) Vernunft f

sank [sæŋk] pt of **sink**

Santa Claus [sæntə'klɔːz] n Nikolaus m,
Weihnachtsmann m

sap [sæp] n (of plants) Saft m ♦ vt (strength)
schwächen

sapling ['sæplɪŋ] n junge(r) Baum m

sapphire ['sæfaɪər] n Saphir m

sarcasm ['saːkæzm] n Sarkasmus m

sarcastic [saː'kæstɪk] adj sarkastisch

sardine [saː'diːn] n Sardine f

Sardinia [saː'dɪnɪə] n Sardinien nt

sardonic [saː'dɒnɪk] adj zynisch

sash [sæʃ] n Schärpe f

sat [sæt] pt, pp of **sit**

Satan ['seɪtn] n Satan m

satchel ['sætʃl] n (for school) Schulmappe f

satellite ['sætəlaɪt] n Satellit m; **~ dish** n
(TECH) Parabolantenne f, Satellitenantenne f;
~ television n Satellitenfernsehen nt

satisfaction [sætɪs'fækʃən] n Befriedigung f,
Genugtuung f; **satisfactory** [sætɪs'fæktərɪ]
adj zufrieden stellend, befriedigend;
satisfied adj befriedigt

satisfy ['sætɪsfaɪ] vt befriedigen,
zufriedenstellen; (convince) überzeugen;
(conditions) erfüllen; **~ing** adj befriedigend;
(meal) sättigend

saturate ['sætʃəreɪt] vt (durch)tränken

Saturday ['sætədɪ] n Samstag m, Sonnabend
m

sauce [sɔːs] n Soße f, Sauce f; **~pan** n
Kasserolle f

saucer ['sɔːsər] n Untertasse f

saucy ['sɔːsɪ] adj frech, keck

Saudi: **~ Arabia** n Saudi-Arabien nt; **~
(Arabian)** adj saudi-arabisch ♦ n Saudi-
Araber(in) m(f)

sauna ['sɔːnə] n Sauna f

saunter |'sɔːntə^r| vi schlendern
sausage |'sɒsɪdʒ| n Wurst f; ~ **roll** n Wurst f im Schlafrock, Wurstpastete f
sauté |'səuteɪ| adj Röst-
savage |'sævɪdʒ| adj wild ♦ n Wilde(r) mf ♦ vt (animals) zerfleischen
save |seɪv| vt retten; (money, electricity etc) sparen; (strength etc) aufsparen; (COMPUT) speichern ♦ vi (also: ~ up) sparen ♦ n (SPORT) (Ball)abwehr f ♦ prep, conj außer, ausgenommen
saving |'seɪvɪŋ| adj: the ~ grace of das Versöhnende an +dat ♦ n Sparen nt, Ersparnis f; ~s npl (money) Ersparnisse pl; ~s **account** n Sparkonto nt; ~s **bank** n Sparkasse f
saviour |'seɪvjə^r| (US **savior**) n (REL) Erlöser m
savour |'seɪvə^r| (US **savor**) vt (taste) schmecken; (fig) genießen; ~y adj pikant, würzig
saw |sɔː| (pt sawed, pp sawed or sawn) pt of see ♦ n (tool) Säge f ♦ vt, vi sägen; ~dust n Sägemehl nt; ~mill n Sägewerk nt; ~n pp of saw; ~n-off shotgun n Gewehr nt mit abgesägtem Lauf
sax |sæks| (inf) n Saxofon nt, Saxophon nt
saxophone |'sæksəfəun| n Saxofon nt, Saxophon nt
say |seɪ| (pt, pp said) n: to have a/no ~ in sth Mitspracherecht/kein Mitspracherecht bei etw haben ♦ vt, vi sagen; let him have his ~ lass ihn doch reden; to ~ yes/no Ja/Nein or ja/nein sagen; that goes without ~ing das versteht sich von selbst; that is to ~ das heißt; ~ing n Sprichwort nt
scab |skæb| n Schorf m; (pej) Streikbrecher m
scaffold |'skæfəld| n (for execution) Schafott nt; ~ing n (Bau)gerüst nt
scald |skɔːld| n Verbrühung f ♦ vt (burn) verbrühen
scale |skeɪl| n (of fish) Schuppe f; (MUS) Tonleiter f; (on map, size) Maßstab m; (gradation) Skala f ♦ vt (climb) erklimmen; ~s npl (balance) Waage f; on a large ~ (fig) im Großen, in großem Umfang; ~ of charges Gebührenordnung f; ~ down vt verkleinern; ~ model n maßstabgetreue(s) Modell nt
scallop |'skɒləp| n Kammmuschel f
scalp |skælp| n Kopfhaut f
scamper |'skæmpə^r| vi: to ~ away or off sich davonmachen
scampi |'skæmpɪ| npl Scampi pl
scan |skæn| vt (examine) genau prüfen; (quickly) überfliegen; (horizon) absuchen
scandal |'skændl| n Skandal m; (piece of gossip) Skandalgeschichte f
Scandinavia |skændɪ'neɪvɪə| n Skandinavien nt; ~n adj skandinavisch ♦ n Skandinavier(in) m(f)

scant |skænt| adj knapp; ~ily adv knapp, dürftig; ~y adj knapp, unzureichend
scapegoat |'skeɪpgəut| n Sündenbock m
scar |skɑː^r| n Narbe f ♦ vt durch Narben entstellen
scarce |skɛəs| adj selten, rar; (goods) knapp; ~ly adv kaum; **scarcity** n Mangel m
scare |skɛə^r| n Schrecken m ♦ vt erschrecken; **bomb** ~ Bombendrohung f; to ~ **sb** stiff jdn zu Tode erschrecken; to be ~d Angst haben; ~ **away** vt (animal) verscheuchen; ~ **off** vt = scare away; ~**crow** n Vogelscheuche f
scarf |skɑːf| (pl **scarves**) n Schal m; (headscarf) Kopftuch nt
scarlet |'skɑːlɪt| adj scharlachrot ♦ n Scharlachrot nt; ~ **fever** n Scharlach m
scarves |skɑːvz| npl of scarf
scary |'skɛərɪ| (inf) adj schaurig
scathing |'skeɪðɪŋ| adj scharf, vernichtend
scatter |'skætə^r| vt (sprinkle) (ver)streuen; (disperse) zerstreuen ♦ vi sich zerstreuen; ~**brained** adj flatterhaft, schusselig
scavenger |'skævəndʒə^r| n (animal) Aasfresser m
scenario |sɪ'nɑːrɪəu| n (THEAT, CINE) Szenarium nt; (fig) Szenario nt
scene |siːn| n (of happening) Ort m; (of play, incident) Szene f; (view) Anblick m; (argument) Szene f, Auftritt m; ~**ry** |'siːnərɪ| n (THEAT) Bühnenbild nt; (landscape) Landschaft f
scenic |'siːnɪk| adj landschaftlich
scent |sɛnt| n Parfüm nt; (smell) Duft m ♦ vt parfümieren
sceptical |'skɛptɪkl| (US **skeptical**) adj skeptisch
schedule |'ʃɛdjuːl, (US) 'skɛdjuːl| n (list) Liste f; (plan) Programm nt; (of work) Zeitplan m ♦ vt planen; **on** ~ pünktlich; to be ahead of/behind ~ dem Zeitplan voraus/im Rückstand sein; ~d **flight** n (not charter) Linienflug m
scheme |skiːm| n Schema nt; (dishonest) Intrige f; (plan of action) Plan m ♦ vi intrigieren ♦ vt planen; **scheming** |'skiːmɪŋ| adj intrigierend
scholar |'skɒlə^r| n Gelehrte(r) m; (holding ~ship) Stipendiat m; ~ly adj gelehrt; ~**ship** n Gelehrsamkeit f; (grant) Stipendium nt
school |skuːl| n Schule f; (UNIV) Fakultät f ♦ vt schulen; ~ **age** n schulpflichtige(s) Alter nt; ~**book** n Schulbuch nt; ~**boy** n Schüler m; ~**children** npl Schüler pl, Schulkinder pl; ~**days** npl (alte) Schulzeit f; ~**girl** n Schülerin f; ~**ing** n Schulung f, Ausbildung f; ~**master** n Lehrer m; ~**mistress** n Lehrerin f; ~**teacher** n Lehrer(in) m(f)
sciatica |saɪ'ætɪkə| n Ischias m or nt
science |'saɪəns| n Wissenschaft f; (natural ~) Naturwissenschaft f; ~ **fiction** n Science-

fiction f; **scientific** |saɪən'tɪfɪk| adj wissenschaftlich; (natural sciences) naturwissenschaftlich; **scientist** |'saɪəntɪst| n Wissenschaftler(in) m(f)

scintillating |'sɪntɪleɪtɪŋ| adj sprühend

scissors |'sɪzəz| npl Schere f; **a pair of ~** eine Schere

scoff |skɔf| vt (BRIT: inf: eat) fressen ♦ vi (mock); **to ~ (at)** spotten (über +acc)

scold |skəʊld| vt schimpfen

scone |skɒn| n weiche(s) Teegebäck nt

scoop |skuːp| n Schaufel f; (news) sensationelle Erstmeldung f; **~ out** vt herausschaufeln; **~ up** vt aufschaufeln; (liquid) aufschöpfen

scooter |'skuːtər| n Motorroller m; (child's) Roller m

scope |skəʊp| n Ausmaß nt; (opportunity) (Spiel)raum m

scorch |skɔːtʃ| n Brandstelle f ♦ vt versengen; **~ing** adj brennend

score |skɔːr| n (in game) Punktzahl f; (final ~) (Spiel)ergebnis nt; (MUS) Partitur f; (line) Kratzer m; (twenty) zwanzig, zwanzig Stück ♦ vt (goal) schießen; (points) machen; (mark) einritzen ♦ vi (keep record) Punkte zählen; **on that ~** in dieser Hinsicht; **what's the ~?** wie stehts?; **to ~ 6 out of 10** 6 von 10 Punkten erzielen; **to ~ out** vt ausstreichen; **~board** n Anschreibetafel f; **~r** n Torschütze m; (recorder) (Auf)schreiber m

scorn |skɔːn| n Verachtung f ♦ vt verhöhnen; **~ful** adj verächtlich

Scorpio |'skɔːpɪəʊ| n Skorpion m

Scot |skɒt| n Schotte m, Schottin f

Scotch |skɒtʃ| n Scotch m

scotch |skɒtʃ| vt (end) unterbinden

scot-free |'skɒt'friː| adv: **to get off ~** (unpunished) ungeschoren davonkommen

Scotland |'skɒtlənd| n Schottland nt

Scots |skɒts| adj schottisch; **~man/woman** (irreg) n Schotte m/Schottin f

Scottish |'skɒtɪʃ| adj schottisch; **~ Parliament** n schottisches Parlament nt

scoundrel |'skaʊndrl| n Schuft m

scour |'skaʊər| vt (search) absuchen; (clean) schrubben

scourge |skɜːdʒ| n (whip) Geißel f; (plague) Qual f

scout |skaʊt| n (MIL) Späher m; (also: boy ~) Pfadfinder m; **~ around** vi: **to ~ around (for)** sich umsehen (nach)

scowl |skaʊl| n finstere(r) Blick m ♦ vi finster blicken

scrabble |'skræbl| vi (also: ~ around: search) (herum)tasten; (claw): **to ~ (at)** kratzen (an +dat) ♦ n: **S~ ®** Scrabble nt ®

scraggy |'skrægɪ| adj dürr, hager

scram |skræm| (inf) vi abhauen

scramble |'skræmbl| n (climb) Kletterei f; (struggle) Kampf m ♦ vi klettern; (fight) sich

schlagen; **to ~ out/through** krabbeln aus/ durch; **to ~ for** sich um etw raufen; **~d eggs** npl Rührei nt

scrap |skræp| n (bit) Stückchen nt; (fight) Keilerei f; (also: ~ iron) Schrott m ♦ vt verwerfen ♦ vi (fight) streiten, sich prügeln; **~s** npl (leftovers) Reste pl; (waste) Abfall m; **~book** n Einklebealbum nt; **~ dealer** n Schrotthändler(in) m(f)

scrape |skreɪp| n Kratzen nt; (trouble) Klemme f ♦ vt kratzen; (car) zerkratzen; (clean) abkratzen ♦ vi (make harsh noise) kratzen; **to ~ through** gerade noch durchkommen; **~r** n Kratzer m

scrap: ~ heap n Schrotthaufen m; **on the ~ heap** (fig) zum alten Eisen; **~ iron** n Schrott m; **~ merchant** n (BRIT) n Altwarenhändler(in) m(f); **~ paper** n Schmierpapier nt

scrappy |'skræpɪ| adj zusammengestoppelt

scratch |skrætʃ| n (wound) Kratzer m, Schramme f ♦ adj: **~ team** zusammengewürfelte Mannschaft ♦ vt kratzen; (car) zerkratzen ♦ vi (sich) kratzen; **to start from ~** ganz von vorne anfangen; **to be up to ~** den Anforderungen entsprechen

scrawl |skrɔːl| n Gekritzel nt ♦ vt, vi kritzeln

scrawny |'skrɔːnɪ| adj (person, neck) dürr

scream |skriːm| n Schrei m ♦ vi schreien

scree |skriː| n Geröll(halde f) nt

screech |skriːtʃ| n Schrei m ♦ vi kreischen

screen |skriːn| n (protective) Schutzschirm m; (CINE) Leinwand f; (TV) Bildschirm m ♦ vt (shelter) (be)schirmen; (film) zeigen, vorführen; **~ing** n (MED) Untersuchung f; **~play** n Drehbuch nt; **~ saver** n Bildschirmschoner m

screw |skruː| n Schraube f ♦ vt (fasten) schrauben; (vulgar) bumsen; **~ up** vt (paper etc) zerknüllen; (inf: ruin) vermasseln (inf); **~driver** n Schraubenzieher m

scribble |'skrɪbl| n Gekritzel nt ♦ vt kritzeln

script |skrɪpt| n (handwriting) Handschrift f; (for film) Drehbuch nt; (THEAT) Manuskript nt, Text m

Scripture |'skrɪptʃər| n Heilige Schrift f

scroll |skrəʊl| n Schriftrolle f

scrounge |skraʊndʒ| (inf) vt: **to ~ sth off** or **from sb** etw bei jdm abstauben ♦ n: **on the ~** beim Schnorren

scrub |skrʌb| n (clean) Schrubben nt; (in countryside) Gestrüpp nt ♦ vt (clean) schrubben

scruff |skrʌf| n: **by the ~ of the neck** am Genick

scruffy |'skrʌfɪ| adj unordentlich, vergammelt

scrum(mage) |'skrʌm(ɪdʒ)| n Getümmel nt

scruple |'skruːpl| n Skrupel m, Bedenken pl

scrupulous |'skruːpjʊləs| adj peinlich genau, gewissenhaft

scrutinize |'skruːtınaız| vt genau prüfen; **scrutiny** |'skruːtını| n genaue Untersuchung f

scuff |skʌf| vt (shoes) abstoßen

scuffle |'skʌfl| n Handgemenge nt

sculptor |'skʌlptəˑ| n Bildhauer(in) m(f)

sculpture |'skʌlptʃəˑ| n (ART) Bildhauerei f; (statue) Skulptur f

scum |skʌm| n (also fig) Abschaum m

scurry |'skʌrı| vi huschen

scuttle |'skʌtl| n (also: coal ~) Kohleneimer m ♦ vt (ship) versenken ♦ vi (scamper): **to ~ away or off** sich davonmachen

scythe |saıð| n Sense f

SDP (BRIT) n abbr = **Social Democratic Party**

sea |siː| n Meer nt, See f; (fig) Meer nt ♦ adj Meeres-, See-; **by ~** (travel) auf dem Seeweg; **on the ~** (boat) auf dem Meer; (town) am Meer; **out to ~** aufs Meer hinaus; **out at ~** auf See; **~board** n Küste f; **~food** n Meeresfrüchte pl; **~ front** n Strandpromenade f; **~going** adj seetüchtig, Hochsee-; **~gull** n Möwe f

seal |siːl| n (animal) Robbe f, Seehund m; (stamp, impression) Siegel nt ♦ vt versiegeln; **~ off** vt (place) abriegeln

sea level n Meeresspiegel m

sea lion n Seelöwe m

seam |siːm| n Saum m; (edges joining) Naht f; (of coal) Flöz nt

seaman |'siːmən| n (irreg) n Seemann m

seaplane |'siːpleın| n Wasserflugzeug nt

seaport |'siːpɔːt| n Seehafen m

search |səːtʃ| n (for person, thing) Suche f; (of drawer, pockets, house) Durchsuchung f ♦ vi suchen ♦ vt durchsuchen; **in ~ of** auf der Suche nach; **to ~ for** suchen nach; **~ through** vt durchsuchen; **~ing** adj (look) forschend; **~light** n Scheinwerfer m; **~ party** n Suchmannschaft f; **~ warrant** n Durchsuchungsbefehl m

sea: **~shore** |'siːʃɔːˑ| n Meeresküste f; **~sick** |'siːsık| adj seekrank; **~side** |'siːsaıd| n Küste f; **~side resort** n Badeort m

season |'siːzn| n Jahreszeit f; (Christmas etc) Zeit f, Saison f ♦ vt (flavour) würzen; **~al** adj Saison-; **~ed** adj (fig) erfahren; **~ing** n Gewürz nt, Würze f; **~ ticket** n (RAIL) Zeitkarte f; (THEAT) Abonnement nt

seat |siːt| n Sitz m, Platz m; (in Parliament) Sitz m; (part of body) Gesäß nt; (of trousers) Hosenboden m ♦ vt (place) setzen; (have space for) Sitzplätze bieten für; **to be ~ed** sitzen; **~ belt** n Sicherheitsgurt m

sea: **~ water** n Meerwasser nt; **~weed** |'siːwiːd| n (See)tang m; **~worthy** |'siːwəːðı| adj seetüchtig

sec. abbr (= second(s)) Sek.

secluded |sı'kluːdıd| adj abgelegen

seclusion |sı'kluːʒən| n Zurückgezogenheit f

second |'sekənd| adj zweite(r, s) ♦ adv (in ~ position) an zweiter Stelle ♦ n Sekunde f; (person) Zweite(r) mf; (COMM: imperfect) zweite Wahl f; (SPORT) Sekundant m; (AUT: also: ~ gear) zweite(r) Gang m; (BRIT: UNIV: degree) mittlere Note bei Abschlussprüfungen ♦ vt (support) unterstützen; **~ary** adj zweitrangig; **~ary school** n höhere Schule f, Mittelschule f; **~-class** adj zweiter Klasse; **~hand** adj aus zweiter Hand; (car etc) gebraucht; **~ hand** n (on clock) Sekundenzeiger m; **~ly** adv zweitens

secondment |sı'kɒndmənt| (BRIT) n Abordnung f

second-rate |'sekənd'reıt| adj mittelmäßig

second thoughts npl: **to have ~** es sich dat anders überlegen; **on ~** (BRIT) or **second thought** (US) oder lieber (nicht)

secrecy |'siːkrəsı| n Geheimhaltung f

secret |'siːkrıt| n Geheimnis nt ♦ adj geheim, Geheim-; **in ~** geheim

secretarial |sekrı'teərıəl| adj Sekretärinnen-

secretary |'sekrətərı| n Sekretär(in) m(f); **S~ of State** (BRIT) n (POL): **S~ of State (for)** Minister(in) m(f) (für)

secretion |sı'kriːʃən| n Absonderung f

secretive |'siːkrətıv| adj geheimtuerisch

secretly |'siːkrıtlı| adv geheim

sectarian |sek'teərıən| adj (riots etc) Konfessions-, zwischen den Konfessionen

section |'sekʃən| n Teil m; (department) Abteilung f; (of document) Abschnitt m

sector |'sektəˑ| n Sektor m

secular |'sekjʊləˑ| adj weltlich, profan

secure |sı'kjʊəˑ| adj (safe) sicher; (firmly fixed) fest ♦ vt (make firm) befestigen, sichern; (obtain) sichern; **security** |sı'kjʊərıtı| n Sicherheit f; (pledge) Pfand nt; (document) Wertpapier nt; (national security) Staatssicherheit f; **security guard** n Sicherheitsbeamte(r) m, Wächter m, Wache f

sedan |sə'dæn| (US) n (AUT) Limousine f

sedate |sı'deıt| adj gesetzt ♦ vt (MED) ein Beruhigungsmittel geben +dat; **sedation** |sı'deıʃən| n (MED) Einfluss m von Beruhigungsmitteln; **sedative** |'sedıtıv| n Beruhigungsmittel nt ♦ adj beruhigend, einschläfernd

sediment |'sedımənt| n (Boden)satz m

seduce |sı'djuːs| vt verführen; **seductive** |sı'dʌktıv| adj verführerisch

see |siː| (pt saw, pp seen) vt sehen; (understand) (ein)sehen, erkennen; (visit) besuchen ♦ vi (be aware) sehen; (find out) nachsehen ♦ n (ECCL: R.C.) Bistum nt; (: Protestant) Kirchenkreis m; **to ~ sb to the door** jdn hinausbegleiten; **to ~ that** (ensure) dafür sorgen, dass; **~ you soon!** bis bald!; **~ about** vt fus sich kümmern um; **~ off** vt: **to ~ sb off** jdn zum Zug etc begleiten; **~**

through vt: **to ~ sth through** etw durchfechten; **to ~ through sb/sth** jdn/etw durchschauen; **~ to** vt fus: **to ~ to it** dafür sorgen

seed |si:d| n Samen m ♦ vt (TENNIS) platzieren; **to go to ~** (plant) schießen; (fig) herunterkommen; **~ling** n Setzling m; **~y** adj (café) übel; (person) zweifelhaft

seeing ['si:ɪŋ] conj: **~ (that)** da

seek |si:k| (pt, pp sought) vt suchen

seem |si:m| vi scheinen; **it ~s that ...** es scheint, dass ...; **~ingly** adv anscheinend

seen |si:n| pp of see

seep |si:p| vi sickern

seesaw ['si:sɔ:] n Wippe f

seethe |si:ð| vi: **to ~ with anger** vor Wut kochen

see-through ['si:θru:] adj (dress etc) durchsichtig

segment ['segmənt] n Teil m; (of circle) Ausschnitt m

segregate ['segrɪgeɪt] vt trennen

seize |si:z| vt (grasp): ~ ergreifen, packen; (power) ergreifen; (take legally) beschlagnahmen; **~ (up)on** vt fus sich stürzen auf +acc; **~ up** vi (TECH) sich festfressen; **seizure** ['si:ʒər] n (illness) Anfall m

seldom ['seldəm] adv selten

select |sɪ'lekt| adj ausgewählt ♦ vt auswählen; **~ion** |sɪ'lekʃən| n Auswahl f; **~ive** adj (person) wählerisch

self |self| (pl **selves**) pron selbst ♦ n Selbst nt, Ich nt; **the ~** das Ich; **~-assured** adj selbstbewusst; **~-catering** (BRIT) adj für Selbstversorger; **~-centred** (US **~-centered**) adj egozentrisch; **~-coloured** (US **~-colored**) adj (of one colour) einfarbig, uni; **~-confidence** n Selbstvertrauen nt, Selbstbewusstsein nt; **~-conscious** adj gehemmt, befangen; **~-contained** adj (complete) (in sich) geschlossen; (person) verschlossen; (BRIT: flat) separat; **~-control** n Selbstbeherrschung f; **~-defence** (US **~-defense**) n Selbstverteidigung f; (JUR) Notwehr f; **~-discipline** n Selbstdisziplin f; **~-employed** adj frei(schaffend); **~-evident** adj offensichtlich; **~-governing** adj selbst verwaltet; **~-indulgent** adj zügellos; **~-interest** n Eigennutz m

selfish ['selfɪʃ] adj egoistisch, selbstsüchtig; **~ness** n Egoismus m, Selbstsucht f

self: **~lessly** adv selbstlos; **~-made** adj: **~-made man** Selfmademan m; **~-pity** n Selbstmitleid nt; **~-portrait** n Selbstbildnis nt; **~-possessed** adj selbstbeherrscht; **~-preservation** n Selbsterhaltung f; **~-reliant** adj unabhängig; **~-respect** n Selbstachtung f; **~-righteous** adj selbstgerecht; **~-sacrifice** n Selbstaufopferung f; **~-satisfied** adj selbstzufrieden; **~-service** adj

Selbstbedienungs-; **~-sufficient** adj selbstgenügsam; **~-taught** adj selbst erlernt; **~-taught person** Autodidakt m

sell |sel| (pt, pp **sold**) vt verkaufen ♦ vi verkaufen; (goods) sich verkaufen; **to ~ at or for £10** für £10 verkaufen; **~ off** vt verkaufen; **~ out** vi alles verkaufen; **~-by date** n Verfalldatum nt; **~er** n Verkäufer m; **~ing price** n Verkaufspreis m

Sellotape ['seləteɪp] (® BRIT) n Tesafilm m ®

sellout ['selaut] n (of tickets): **it was a ~** es war ausverkauft

selves |selvz| npl of self

semaphore ['seməfɔ:r] n Winkzeichen pl

semblance ['sembləns] n Anschein m

semen ['si:mən] n Sperma nt

semester |sɪ'mestər| (US) n Semester nt

semi ['semi] n = **semidetached house**; **~circle** n Halbkreis m; **~colon** n Semikolon nt; **~conductor** n Halbleiter m; **~detached house** (BRIT) n halbe(s) Doppelhaus nt; **~final** n Halbfinale nt

seminary ['semɪnərɪ] n (REL) Priesterseminar nt

semiskilled |semɪ'skɪld| adj angelernt

semi-skimmed |semɪ'skɪmd| adj (milk) teilentrahmt, Halbfett-

senate ['senɪt] n Senat m; **senator** n Senator m

send |send| (pt, pp **sent**) vt senden, schicken; (inf: inspire) hinreißen; **~ away** vt wegschicken; **~ away for** vt fus anfordern; **~ back** vt zurückschicken; **~ for** vt fus holen lassen; **~ off** vt (goods) abschicken; (BRIT: SPORT: player) vom Feld schicken; **~ out** vt (invitation) aussenden; **~ up** vt hinaufsenden; (BRIT: parody) verulken; **~er** n Absender m; **~-off** n: **to give sb a good ~-off** jdn (ganz) groß verabschieden

senior ['si:nɪər] adj (older) älter; (higher rank) Ober- ♦ n (older person) Ältere(r) mf; (higher ranking) Rangälteste(r) mf; **~ citizen** n ältere(r) Mitbürger(in) m(f); **~ity** |si:nɪ'ɔrɪtɪ| n (of age) höhere(s) Alter nt; (in rank) höhere(r) Dienstgrad m

sensation |sen'seɪʃən| n Gefühl nt; (excitement) Sensation f, Aufsehen nt; **~al** adj (wonderful) wunderbar; (result) sensationell; (headlines etc) reißerisch

sense |sens| n Sinn m; (understanding) Verstand m, Vernunft f; (feeling) Gefühl nt ♦ vt fühlen, spüren; **~ of humour** Humor m; **to make ~** Sinn ergeben; **~less** adj sinnlos; (unconscious) besinnungslos

sensibility |sensɪ'bɪlɪtɪ| n Empfindsamkeit f; (feeling hurt) Empfindlichkeit f; **sensibilities** npl (feelings) Zartgefühl nt

sensible ['sensəbl] adj vernünftig

sensitive ['sensɪtɪv] adj: **~ (to)** empfindlich (gegen); **sensitivity** |sensɪ'tɪvɪtɪ| n

Empfindlichkeit f; (artistic) Feingefühl nt; (tact) Feinfühligkeit f

sensual ['sensjuəl] adj sinnlich

sensuous ['sensjuəs] adj sinnlich

sent [sent] pt, pp of **send**

sentence ['sentns] n Satz m; (JUR) Strafe f; Urteil nt ♦ vt: **to ~ sb to death/to 5 years** jdn zum Tode/zu 5 Jahren verurteilen

sentiment ['sentimənt] n Gefühl nt; (thought) Gedanke m; **~al** [senti'mentl] adj sentimental; (of feelings rather than reason) gefühlsmäßig

sentry ['sentri] n (Schild)wache f

separate [adj 'seprit, vb 'sepəreit] adj getrennt, separat ♦ vt trennen ♦ vi sich trennen; **~ly** adv getrennt; **~s** npl (clothes) Röcke, Pullover etc; **separation** [sepə'reiʃən] n Trennung f

September [sep'tembəʳ] n September m

septic ['septik] adj vereitert, septisch; **~ tank** n Klärbehälter m

sequel ['si:kwl] n Folge f

sequence ['si:kwəns] n (Reihen)folge f

sequin ['si:kwin] n Paillette f

Serbia ['sɔ:bɪə] n Serbien nt

serene [si'ri:n] adj heiter

sergeant ['sɑ:dʒənt] n Feldwebel m; (POLICE) (Polizei)wachtmeister m

serial ['sɪərɪəl] n Fortsetzungsroman m; (TV) Fernsehserie f ♦ adj (number) (fort)laufend; **~ize** vt in Fortsetzungen veröffentlichen; in Fortsetzungen senden

series ['sɪərɪz] n inv Serie f, Reihe f

serious ['sɪərɪəs] adj ernst; (injury) schwer; **~ly** adv ernst(haft); (hurt) schwer; **~ness** n Ernst m, Ernsthaftigkeit f

sermon ['sɔ:mən] n Predigt f

serrated [si'reitid] adj gezackt

servant ['sɔ:vənt] n Diener(in) m(f)

serve [sɔ:v] vt dienen +dat; (guest, customer) bedienen; (food) servieren ♦ vi dienen, nützen; (at table) servieren; (TENNIS) geben, aufschlagen; **it ~s him right** das geschieht ihm recht; **that'll ~ as a table** das geht als Tisch; **to ~ a summons (on sb)** (jdn) vor Gericht laden; **~ out** or **up** vt (food) auftragen, servieren

service ['sɔ:vis] n (help) Dienst m; (trains etc) Verbindung f; (hotel) Service m, Bedienung f; (set of dishes) Service nt; (REL) Gottesdienst m; (car) Inspektion f; (for TVs etc) Kundendienst m; (TENNIS) Aufschlag m ♦ vt (AUT, TECH) warten, überholen; **the S~s** npl (armed forces) die Streitkräfte pl; **to be of ~ to sb** jdm einen großen Dienst erweisen; **~ included/not included** Bedienung inbegriffen/nicht inbegriffen; **~able** adj brauchbar; **~ area** n (on motorway) Raststätte f; **~ charge** (BRIT) n Bedienung f; **~man** (irreg) n (soldier etc) Soldat m; **~ station** n (Groß)tankstelle f

serviette [sɔ:vi'et] n Serviette f

servile ['sɔ:vail] adj unterwürfig

session ['seʃən] n Sitzung f; (POL) Sitzungsperiode f; **to be in ~** tagen

set [set] (pt, pp **set**) n (collection of things) Satz m, Set nt; (RAD, TV) Apparat m; (TENNIS) Satz m; (group of people) Kreis m; (CINE) Szene f; (THEAT) Bühnenbild nt ♦ adj festgelegt; (ready) bereit ♦ vt (place) setzen, stellen, legen; (arrange) (an)ordnen; (table) decken; (time, price) festsetzen; (alarm, watch, task) stellen; (jewels) (ein)fassen; (exam) ausarbeiten ♦ vi (sun) untergehen; (become hard) fest werden; (bone) zusammenwachsen; **to be ~ on doing sth** etw unbedingt tun wollen; **to ~ to music** vertonen; **to ~ on fire** anstecken; **to ~ free** freilassen; **to ~ sth going** etw in Gang bringen; **to ~ sail** losfahren; **~ about** vt fus (task) anpacken; **~ aside** vt beiseite legen; **~ back** vt: **to ~ back (by)** zurückwerfen (um); **~ off** vi aufbrechen ♦ vt (explode) sprengen; (alarm) losgehen lassen; (show up well) hervorheben; **~ out** vi: **to ~ out to do sth** vorhaben, etw zu tun ♦ vt (arrange) anlegen, arrangieren; (state) darlegen; **~ up** vt (organization) aufziehen; (record) aufstellen; (monument) erstellen; **~back** n Rückschlag m; **~ meal** n Menü nt; **~ menu** n Tageskarte f

settee [se'ti:] n Sofa nt

setting ['setiŋ] n Hintergrund m

settle ['setl] vt beruhigen; (pay) begleichen, bezahlen; (agree) regeln ♦ vi sich einleben; (come to rest) sich niederlassen; (sink) sich setzen; (calm down) sich beruhigen; **to ~ for sth** sich mit etw zufrieden geben; **to ~ on sth** sich für etw entscheiden; **to ~ up with sb** mit jdm abrechnen; **~ down** vi (feel at home) sich einleben; (calm down) sich beruhigen; **~ in** vi sich eingewöhnen; **~ment** n Regelung f; (payment) Begleichung f; (colony) Siedlung f; **~r** n Siedler m

setup ['setʌp] n (situation) Lage f

seven ['sevn] num sieben; **~teen** num siebzehn; **~th** adj siebte(r, s) ♦ n Siebtel nt; **~ty** num siebzig

sever ['sevəʳ] vt abtrennen

several ['sevərl] adj mehrere, verschiedene ♦ pron mehrere; **~ of us** einige von uns

severance ['sevərəns] n: **~ pay** Abfindung f

severe [si'vɪəʳ] adj (strict) streng; (serious) schwer; (climate) rau; **severity** [si'veriti] n Strenge f; Schwere f; Rauheit f

sew [səu] (pt sewed, pp sewn) vt, vi nähen; **~ up** vt zunähen

sewage ['su:idʒ] n Abwässer pl

sewer ['su:əʳ] n (Abwasser)kanal m

sewing ['səuiŋ] n Näharbeit f; **~ machine** n Nähmaschine f

sewn [ˈsəun] pp of sew

sex [seks] n Sex m; (gender) Geschlecht nt; **to have ~ with sb** mit jdm Geschlechtsverkehr haben; **~ism** n Sexismus m; **~ist** adj sexistisch ♦ n Sexist(in) m(f); **~ual** [ˈseksjuəl] adj sexuell, geschlechtlich, Geschlechts-; **~uality** [seksjuˈælɪtɪ] n Sexualität f; **~y** adj sexy

shabby [ˈʃæbɪ] adj (also fig) schäbig

shack [ʃæk] n Hütte f

shackles [ˈʃæklz] npl (also fig) Fesseln pl, Ketten pl

shade [ʃeɪd] n Schatten m; (for lamp) Lampenschirm m; (colour) Farbton m ♦ vt abschirmen; **in the ~** im Schatten; **a ~ smaller** ein bisschen kleiner

shadow ♦ [ˈʃædəu] n Schatten m ♦ vt (follow) beschatten ♦ adj: **~ cabinet** (BRIT: POL) Schattenkabinett nt; **~y** adj schattig

shady [ˈʃeɪdɪ] adj schattig; (fig) zwielichtig

shaft [ʃɑːft] n (of spear etc) Schaft m; (in mine) Schacht m; (TECH) Welle f; (of light) Strahl m

shaggy [ˈʃægɪ] adj struppig

shake [ʃeɪk] (pt **shook**, pp **shaken**) vt schütteln, rütteln; (shock) erschüttern ♦ vi (move) schwanken; (tremble) zittern, beben ♦ n (jerk) Schütteln nt, Rütteln nt; **to ~ hands with** die Hand geben +dat; **to ~ one's head** den Kopf schütteln; **~ off** vt abschütteln; **~ up** vt aufschütteln; (fig) aufrütteln; **~n** [ˈʃeɪkn] pp of shake; **shaky** [ˈʃeɪkɪ] adj zittrig; (weak) unsicher

shall [ʃæl] vb aux: **I ~ go** ich werde gehen; **~ I open the door?** soll ich die Tür öffnen?; **I'll buy some cake, ~ I?** soll ich Kuchen kaufen?, ich kaufe Kuchen, oder?

shallow [ˈʃæləu] adj seicht

sham [ʃæm] n Schein m ♦ adj unecht, falsch

shambles [ˈʃæmblz] n Durcheinander nt

shame [ʃeɪm] n Scham f; (disgrace, pity) Schande f ♦ vt beschämen; **it is a ~ that** es ist schade, dass; **it is a ~ to do ...** es ist eine Schande, ... zu tun; **what a ~!** wie schade!; **~faced** adj beschämt; **~ful** adj schändlich; **~less** adj schamlos

shampoo [ʃæmˈpuː] n Shampoo(n) nt ♦ vt (hair) waschen; **~ and set** n Waschen nt und Legen

shamrock [ˈʃæmrɔk] n Kleeblatt nt

shandy [ˈʃændɪ] n Bier nt mit Limonade

shan't [ʃɑːnt] = shall not

shantytown [ˈʃæntɪtaun] n Bidonville f

shape [ʃeɪp] n Form f ♦ vt formen, gestalten ♦ vi (also: **~ up**) sich entwickeln; **to take ~** Gestalt annehmen; **~d** suffix: **heart-~d** herzförmig; **~less** adj formlos; **~ly** adj wohlproportioniert

share [ʃɛəʳ] n (An)teil m; (FIN) Aktie f ♦ vt teilen; **to ~ out (among/between)** verteilen (unter/zwischen); **~holder** n Aktionär(in) m(f)

shark [ʃɑːk] n Hai(fisch) m; (swindler) Gauner m

sharp [ʃɑːp] adj scharf; (pin) spitz; (person) clever; (MUS) erhöht ♦ n Kreuz nt ♦ adv zu hoch; **nine o'clock ~** Punkt neun; **~en** vt schärfen; (pencil) spitzen; **~ener** n (also: **pencil ~ener**) Anspitzer m; **~-eyed** adj scharfsichtig; **~ly** adv (turn, stop) plötzlich; (stand out, contrast) deutlich; (criticize, retort) scharf

shatter [ˈʃætəʳ] vt zerschmettern; (fig) zerstören ♦ vi zerspringen

shave [ʃeɪv] n Rasur f ♦ vt rasieren ♦ vi sich rasieren; **to have a ~** sich rasieren (lassen); **~r** n (also: **electric ~r**) Rasierapparat m

shaving [ˈʃeɪvɪŋ] n (action) Rasieren nt; **~s** npl (of wood etc) Späne pl; **~ brush** n Rasierpinsel m; **~ cream** n Rasiercreme f; **~ foam** n Rasierschaum m

shawl [ʃɔːl] n Schal m, Umhang m

she [ʃiː] pron sie ♦ adj weiblich; **~-bear** n Bärenweibchen nt

sheaf [ʃiːf] (pl **sheaves**) n Garbe f

shear [ʃɪəʳ] (pt **sheared**, pp **sheared** or **shorn**) vt scheren; **~ off** vi abbrechen; **~s** npl Heckenschere f

sheath [ʃiːθ] n Scheide f; (condom) Kondom m or nt

sheaves [ʃiːvz] npl of sheaf

shed [ʃed] (pt, pp **shed**) n Schuppen m; (for animals) Stall m ♦ vt (leaves etc) verlieren; (tears) vergießen

she'd [ʃiːd] = she had; she would

sheen [ʃiːn] n Glanz m

sheep [ʃiːp] n inv Schaf nt; **~dog** n Schäferhund m; **~ish** adj verlegen; **~skin** n Schaffell nt

sheer [ʃɪəʳ] adj bloß, rein; (steep) steil; (transparent) (hauch)dünn ♦ adv (directly) direkt

sheet [ʃiːt] n Betttuch nt, Bettlaken nt; (of paper) Blatt nt; (of metal etc) Platte f; (of ice) Fläche f

sheik(h) [ʃeɪk] n Scheich m

shelf [ʃelf] (pl **shelves**) n Brett nt, Regal nt

shell [ʃel] n Schale f; (seashell) Muschel f; (explosive) Granate f ♦ vt (peas) schälen; (fire on) beschießen

she'll [ʃiːl] = she will; she shall

shellfish [ˈʃelfɪʃ] n Schalentier nt; (as food) Meeresfrüchte pl

shell suit n Ballonseidenanzug m

shelter [ˈʃeltəʳ] n Schutz m; (air-raid ~) Bunker m ♦ vt schützen, bedecken; (refugees) aufnehmen ♦ vi sich unterstellen; **~ed** adj (life) behütet; (spot) geschützt; **~ed housing** n (for old people) Altenwohnungen pl; (for handicapped people) Behindertenwohnungen pl

shelve [ʃelv] vt aufschieben ♦ vi abfallen

shelves [ʃelvz] npl of shelf

shepherd ['ʃepəd] n Schäfer m ♦ vt treiben, führen; **~'s pie** n Auflauf aus Hackfleisch und Kartoffelbrei

sheriff ['ʃerɪf] n Sheriff m; (SCOTTISH) Friedensrichter m

sherry ['ʃerɪ] n Sherry m

she's [ʃiːz] = **she is**; **she has**

Shetland ['ʃetlənd] n (also: **the ~s, the ~ Isles**) die Shetlandinseln pl

shield [ʃiːld] n Schild m; (fig) Schirm m ♦ vt (be)schirmen; (TECH) abschirmen

shift [ʃɪft] n Verschiebung f; (work) Schicht f ♦ vt (ver)rücken, verschieben; (arm) wegnehmen ♦ vi sich verschieben; **~less** adj (person) träge; **~ work** n Schichtarbeit f; **~y** adj verschlagen

shilly-shally ['ʃɪlɪʃælɪ] vi zögern

shin [ʃɪn] n Schienbein nt

shine [ʃaɪn] (pt, pp **shone**) n Glanz m, Schein m ♦ vt polieren ♦ vi scheinen; (fig) glänzen; **to ~ a torch on sb** jdn (mit einer Lampe) anleuchten

shingle ['ʃɪŋgl] n Strandkies m; **~s** npl (MED) Gürtelrose f

shiny ['ʃaɪnɪ] adj glänzend

ship [ʃɪp] n Schiff nt ♦ vt verschiffen; **~building** n Schiffbau m; **~ment** n Schiffsladung f; **~per** n Verschiffer m; **~ping** n (act) Verschiffung f; (ships) Schiffahrt f; **~wreck** n Schiffbruch m; (destroyed ~) Wrack nt ♦ vt: **to be ~wrecked** Schiffbruch erleiden; **~yard** n Werft f

shire ['ʃaɪər] (BRIT) n Grafschaft f

shirk [ʃəːk] vt ausweichen +dat

shirt [ʃəːt] n (Ober)hemd nt; **in ~ sleeves** in Hemdsärmeln

shit [ʃɪt] (inf!) excl Scheiße (!)

shiver ['ʃɪvər] n Schauer m ♦ vi frösteln, zittern

shoal [ʃəul] n (Fisch)schwarm m

shock [ʃɔk] n Erschütterung f; (mental) Schock m; (ELEC) Schlag m ♦ vt erschüttern; (offend) schockieren; **~ absorber** n Stoßdämpfer m; **~ed** adj geschockt, schockiert, erschüttert; **~ing** adj unerhört

shod [ʃɔd] pt, pp of **shoe**

shoddy ['ʃɔdɪ] adj schäbig

shoe [ʃuː] (pt, pp **shod**) n Schuh m; (of horse) Hufeisen nt ♦ vt (horse) beschlagen; **~brush** n Schuhbürste f; **~horn** n Schuhlöffel m; **~lace** n Schnürsenkel m; **~ polish** n Schuhcreme f; **~ shop** n Schuhgeschäft nt; **~string** n (fig): **on a ~string** mit sehr wenig Geld

shone [ʃɔn] pt, pp of **shine**

shoo [ʃuː] excl sch; (to dog etc) pfui

shook [ʃuk] pt of **shake**

shoot [ʃuːt] (pt, pp **shot**) n (branch) Schössling m ♦ vt (gun) abfeuern; (goal, arrow) schießen; (person) anschießen; (kill) erschießen; (film) drehen ♦ vi (move quickly)

schießen; **to ~ (at)** schießen (auf +acc); **~ down** vt abschießen; **~ in** vi hineinschießen; **~ out** vi hinausschießen; **~ up** vi (fig) aus dem Boden schießen; **~ing** n Schießerei f; **~ing star** n Sternschnuppe f

shop [ʃɔp] n (esp BRIT) Geschäft nt, Laden m; (workshop) Werkstatt f ♦ vi (also: **go ~ping**) einkaufen gehen; **~ assistant** (BRIT) n Verkäufer(in) m(f); **~ floor** (BRIT) n Werkstatt f; **~keeper** n Geschäftsinhaber m; **~lifting** n Ladendiebstahl m; **~per** n Käufer(in) m(f); **~ping** n Einkaufen nt, Einkauf m; **~ping bag** n Einkaufstasche f; **~ping centre** (US **~ping center**) n Einkaufszentrum nt; **~soiled** adj angeschmutzt; **~ steward** (BRIT) n (INDUSTRY) Betriebsrat m; **~ window** n Schaufenster nt

shore [ʃɔːr] n Ufer nt; (of sea) Strand m ♦ vt: **to ~ up** abstützen

shorn [ʃɔːn] pp of **shear**

short [ʃɔːt] adj kurz; (person) klein; (curt) kurz angebunden; (measure) zu knapp ♦ n (also: **~ film**) Kurzfilm m ♦ adv (suddenly) plötzlich ♦ vi (ELEC) einen Kurzschluss haben; **~s** npl (clothes) Shorts pl; **to be ~ of sth** nicht genug von etw haben; **in ~** kurz gesagt; **~ of doing sth** ohne so weit zu gehen, etw zu tun; **everything ~ of ...** alles außer ...; **it is ~ for** das ist die Kurzform von; **to cut ~** abkürzen; **to fall ~ of sth** etw nicht erreichen; **to stop ~** plötzlich anhalten; **to stop ~ of** Halt machen vor; **~age** n Knappheit f, Mangel m; **~bread** n Mürbegebäck nt; **~-change** vt: **to ~-change sb** jdm zu wenig herausgeben; **~-circuit** n Kurzschluss m ♦ vi einen Kurzschluss haben ♦ vt kurzschließen; **~coming** n Mangel m; **~(crust) pastry** (BRIT) n Mürbeteig m; **~ cut** n Abkürzung f; **~en** vt (ab)kürzen; (clothes) kürzer machen; **~fall** n Defizit nt; **~hand** (BRIT) n Stenografie f; **~hand typist** (BRIT) n Stenotypistin f; **~ list** (BRIT) n (for job) engere Wahl f; **~-lived** adj kurzlebig; **~ly** adv bald; **~ notice** n: **at ~ notice** kurzfristig; **~-sighted** (BRIT) adj (also fig) kurzsichtig; **~-staffed** adj: **to be ~-staffed** zu wenig Personal haben; **~-stay** n (car park) Kurzparken nt; **~ story** n Kurzgeschichte f; **~-tempered** adj leicht aufbrausend; **~-term** adj (effect) kurzfristig; **~-wave** n (RAD) Kurzwelle f

shot [ʃɔt] pt, pp of **shoot** ♦ n (from gun) Schuss m; (person) Schütze m; (try) Versuch m; (injection) Spritze f; (PHOT) Aufnahme f; **like a ~** wie der Blitz; **~gun** n Schrotflinte f

should [ʃud] vb aux: **I ~ go now** ich sollte jetzt gehen; **he ~ be there now** er sollte eigentlich schon da sein; **I ~ go if I were you** ich würde gehen, wenn ich du wäre; **I ~**

like to ich möchte gerne
shoulder [ˈʃəʊldəʳ] n Schulter f; (BRIT: of road): **hard ~** Seitenstreifen m ♦ vt (rifle) schultern; (fig) auf sich nehmen; **~ bag** n Umhängetasche f; **~ blade** n Schulterblatt nt; **~ strap** n (of dress etc) Träger m
shouldn't [ˈʃʊdnt] = **should not**
shout [ʃaʊt] n Schrei m; (call) Ruf m ♦ vt rufen ♦ vi schreien; **~ down** vt niederbrüllen; **~ing** n Geschrei nt
shove [ʃʌv] n Schubs m, Stoß m ♦ vt schieben, stoßen, schubsen; (inf: put): **to ~ sth in(to) sth** etw in etw acc hineinschieben; **~ off** vi (NAUT) abstoßen; (fig: inf) abhauen
shovel [ˈʃʌvl] n Schaufel f ♦ vt schaufeln
show [ʃəʊ] (pt **showed**, pp **shown**) n (display) Schau f; (exhibition) Ausstellung f; (CINE, THEAT) Vorstellung f, Show f ♦ vt zeigen; (kindness) erweisen ♦ vi zu sehen sein; **to be on ~** (exhibits etc) ausgestellt sein; **to ~ sb in** jdn hereinführen; **to ~ sb out** jdn hinausbegleiten; **~ off** vi (pej) angeben ♦ vt (display) ausstellen; **~ up** vi (stand out) sich abheben; (arrive) erscheinen ♦ vt aufzeigen; (unmask) bloßstellen; **~ business** n Showbusiness nt; **~down** n Kraftprobe f
shower [ˈʃaʊəʳ] n Schauer m; (of stones) (Stein)hagel m; (~ bath) Dusche f ♦ vi duschen ♦ vt: **to ~ sb with sth** jdn mit etw überschütten; **~proof** adj Wasser abstoßend
showing [ˈʃəʊɪŋ] n Vorführung f
show jumping n Turnierreiten nt
shown [ʃəʊn] pp of **show**
show: **~-off** [ˈʃəʊɔf] n Angeber(in) m(f); **~piece** [ˈʃəʊpiːs] n Paradestück nt; **~room** [ˈʃəʊrʊm] n Ausstellungsraum m
shrank [ʃræŋk] pt of **shrink**
shred [ʃred] n Fetzen m ♦ vt zerfetzen; (COOK) raspeln; **~der** n (COOK) Gemüseschneider m; (for documents) Reißwolf m
shrewd [ʃruːd] adj clever
shriek [ʃriːk] n Schrei m ♦ vt, vi kreischen, schreien
shrill [ʃrɪl] adj schrill
shrimp [ʃrɪmp] n Krabbe f, Garnele f
shrine [ʃraɪn] n Schrein m; (fig) Gedenkstätte f
shrink [ʃrɪŋk] (pt **shrank**, pp **shrunk**) vi schrumpfen, eingehen ♦ vt einschrumpfen lassen; **to ~ from doing sth** davor zurückschrecken, etw zu tun; **~age** n Schrumpfung f; **~-wrap** vt einschweißen
shrivel [ˈʃrɪvl] vt, vi (also: ~ **up**) schrumpfen, schrumpeln
shroud [ʃraʊd] n Leichentuch nt ♦ vt: **~ed in mystery** mit einem Geheimnis umgeben
Shrove Tuesday [ˈʃrəʊv-] n Fastnachtsdienstag m
shrub [ʃrʌb] n Busch m, Strauch m; **~bery** n

Gebüsch nt
shrug [ʃrʌg] n Achselzucken nt ♦ vt, vi: **to ~ (one's shoulders)** die Achseln zucken; **~ off** vt auf die leichte Schulter nehmen
shrunk [ʃrʌŋk] pp of **shrink**
shudder [ˈʃʌdəʳ] n Schauder m ♦ vi schaudern
shuffle [ˈʃʌfl] vt (cards) mischen; **to ~ (one's feet)** schlurfen
shun [ʃʌn] vt scheuen, (ver)meiden
shunt [ʃʌnt] vt rangieren
shut [ʃʌt] (pt, pp **shut**) vt schließen, zumachen ♦ vi sich schließen (lassen); **~ down** vt, vi schließen; **~ off** vt (supply) abdrehen; **~ up** vi (keep quiet) den Mund halten ♦ vt (close) zuschließen; **~ter** n Fensterladen m; (PHOT) Verschluss m
shuttle [ˈʃʌtl] n (plane, train etc) Pendelflugzeug nt/-zug m etc; (space ~) Raumtransporter m; (also: ~ **service**) Pendelverkehr m; **~cock** [ˈʃʌtlkɔk] n Federball m; **~ diplomacy** n Pendeldiplomatie f
shy [ʃaɪ] adj schüchtern; **~ness** n Schüchternheit f
Siamese [saɪəˈmiːz] adj: **~ cat** Siamkatze f
Siberia [saɪˈbɪərɪə] n Sibirien nt
sibling [ˈsɪblɪŋ] n Geschwister nt
Sicily [ˈsɪsɪlɪ] n Sizilien nt
sick [sɪk] adj krank; (joke) makaber; **I feel ~** mir ist schlecht; **I was ~** ich habe gebrochen; **to be ~ of sb/sth** jdn/etw satt haben; **~ bay** n (Schiffs)lazarett nt; **~en** vt (disgust) krank machen ♦ vi krank werden; **~ening** adj (annoying) zum Weinen
sickle [ˈsɪkl] n Sichel f
sick: **~ leave** n: **to be on ~ leave** krankgeschrieben sein; **~ly** adj kränklich, blass; (causing nausea) widerlich; **~ness** n Krankheit f; (vomiting) Übelkeit f, Erbrechen nt; **~ note** n Arbeitsunfähigkeitsbescheinigung f; **~ pay** n Krankengeld nt
side [saɪd] n Seite f ♦ adj (door, entrance) Seiten-, Neben- ♦ vi: **to ~ with sb** jds Partei ergreifen; **by the ~ of** neben; **~ by ~** nebeneinander; **on all ~s** von allen Seiten; **to take ~s (with)** Partei nehmen (für); **from all ~s** von allen Seiten; **~board** n Sideboard nt; **~boards** (BRIT) npl Koteletten pl; **~burns** npl Koteletten pl; **~car** n Beiwagen m; **~ drum** n (MUS) kleine Trommel f; **~ effect** n Nebenwirkung f; **~light** n (AUT) Parkleuchte f; **~line** n (SPORT) Seitenlinie f; (fig: hobby) Nebenbeschäftigung f; **~long** adj Seiten-; **~ order** n Beilage f; **~saddle** adv im Damensattel; **~ show** n Nebenausstellung f; **~step** vt (fig) ausweichen; **~ street** n Seitenstraße f; **~track** vt (fig) ablenken; **~walk** (US) n Bürgersteig m; **~ways** adv seitwärts

siding ['saɪdɪŋ] n Nebengleis nt
sidle ['saɪdl] vi: **to ~ up (to)** sich heranmachen (an +acc)
siege [si:dʒ] n Belagerung f
sieve [sɪv] n Sieb nt ♦ vt sieben
sift [sɪft] vt sieben; (fig) sichten
sigh [saɪ] n Seufzer m ♦ vi seufzen
sight [saɪt] n (power of seeing) Sehvermögen nt; (look) Blick m; (fact of seeing) Anblick m; (of gun) Visier nt ♦ vt sichten; **in ~** in Sicht; **out of ~** außer Sicht; **~seeing** n Besuch m von Sehenswürdigkeiten; **to go ~seeing** Sehenswürdigkeiten besichtigen
sign [saɪn] n Zeichen nt; (notice, road ~ etc) Schild nt ♦ vt unterschreiben; **to ~ sth over to sb** jdm etw überschreiben; **~ on** vi (as unemployed) sich (arbeitslos) melden ♦ vt (employee) anstellen; **~ up** vi (MIL) sich verpflichten ♦ vt verpflichten
signal ['sɪgnl] n Signal nt ♦ vt ein Zeichen geben +dat; **~man** (irreg) n (RAIL) Stellwerkswärter m
signature ['sɪgnətʃəʳ] n Unterschrift f; **~ tune** n Erkennungsmelodie f
signet ring ['sɪgnət-] n Siegelring m
significance [sɪg'nɪfɪkəns] n Bedeutung f
significant [sɪg'nɪfɪkənt] adj (meaning sth) bedeutsam; (important) bedeutend
signify ['sɪgnɪfaɪ] vt bedeuten; (show) andeuten, zu verstehen geben
sign language n Zeichensprache f, Fingersprache f
signpost ['saɪnpəust] n Wegweiser m
silence ['saɪləns] n Stille f; (of person) Schweigen nt ♦ vt zum Schweigen bringen; **~r** n (on gun) Schalldämpfer m; (BRIT: AUT) Auspufftopf m
silent ['saɪlənt] adj still; (person) schweigsam; **to remain ~** schweigen; **~ partner** n (COMM) stille(r) Teilhaber m
silicon chip ['sɪlɪkən-] n Siliciumchip m, Siliziumchip m
silk [sɪlk] n Seide f ♦ adj seiden, Seiden-; **~y** adj seidig
silly ['sɪlɪ] adj dumm, albern
silt [sɪlt] n Schlamm m, Schlick m
silver ['sɪlvəʳ] n Silber nt ♦ adj silbern, Silber-; **~ paper** (BRIT) n Silberpapier nt; **~-plated** adj versilbert; **~smith** n Silberschmied m; **~ware** n Silber nt; **~y** adj silbern
similar ['sɪmɪləʳ] adj: **~ (to)** ähnlich (+dat); **~ity** [sɪmɪ'lærɪtɪ] n Ähnlichkeit f; **~ly** adv in ähnlicher Weise
simmer ['sɪməʳ] vi sieden ♦ vt sieden lassen
simple ['sɪmpl] adj einfach; **~(-minded)** adj einfältig
simplicity [sɪm'plɪsɪtɪ] n Einfachheit f; (of person) Einfältigkeit f
simplify ['sɪmplɪfaɪ] vt vereinfachen
simply ['sɪmplɪ] adv einfach
simulate ['sɪmjuleɪt] vt simulieren

simultaneous [sɪməl'teɪnɪəs] adj gleichzeitig
sin [sɪn] n Sünde f ♦ vi sündigen
since [sɪns] adv seither ♦ prep seit, seitdem ♦ conj (time) seit; (because) da, weil; **~ then** seitdem
sincere [sɪn'sɪəʳ] adj aufrichtig; **~ly** adv: **yours ~ly** mit freundlichen Grüßen; **sincerity** [sɪn'serɪtɪ] n Aufrichtigkeit f
sinew ['sɪnju:] n Sehne f
sinful ['sɪnful] adj sündig, sündhaft
sing [sɪŋ] (pt sang, pp sung) vt, vi singen
Singapore [sɪŋgə'pɔ:ʳ] n Singapur nt
singe [sɪndʒ] vt versengen
singer ['sɪŋəʳ] n Sänger(in) m(f)
singing ['sɪŋɪŋ] n Singen nt, Gesang m
single ['sɪŋgl] adj (one only) einzig; (bed, room) Einzel-, einzeln; (unmarried) ledig; (BRIT: ticket) einfach; (having one part only) einzeln ♦ n (BRIT: also: **~ ticket**) einfache Fahrkarte f; **in ~ file** hintereinander; **~ out** vt aussuchen, auswählen; **~ bed** n Einzelbett nt; **~-breasted** adj einreihig; **~-handed** adj allein; **~-minded** adj zielstrebig; **~ parent** n Alleinerziehende(r) f(m); **~ room** n Einzelzimmer nt; **~s** n (TENNIS) Einzel nt; **~-track road** n einspurige Straße (mit Ausweichstellen); **singly** adv einzeln, allein
singular ['sɪŋgjuləʳ] adj (odd) merkwürdig, seltsam ♦ n (GRAM) Einzahl f, Singular m
sinister ['sɪnɪstəʳ] adj (evil) böse; (ghostly) unheimlich
sink [sɪŋk] (pt sank, pp sunk) n Spülbecken nt ♦ vt (ship) versenken ♦ vi sinken; **to ~ sth into** (teeth, claws) etw schlagen in +acc; **~ in** vi (news etc) eingehen
sinner ['sɪnəʳ] n Sünder(in) m(f)
sinus ['saɪnəs] n (ANAT) Sinus m
sip [sɪp] n Schlückchen nt ♦ vt nippen an +dat
siphon ['saɪfən] n Siphon(flasche f) m; **~ off** vt absaugen; (fig) abschöpfen
sir [sɜ:ʳ] n (respect) Herr m; (knight) Sir m; **S~ John Smith** Sir John Smith; **yes ~** ja(wohl, mein Herr)
siren ['saɪərn] n Sirene f
sirloin ['sɜ:lɔɪn] n Lendenstück nt
sissy ['sɪsɪ] (inf) n Waschlappen m
sister ['sɪstəʳ] n Schwester f; (BRIT: nurse) Oberschwester f; (nun) Ordensschwester f; **~-in-law** n Schwägerin f
sit [sɪt] (pt, pp sat) vi sitzen; (hold session) tagen ♦ vt (exam) machen; **~ down** vi sich hinsetzen; **~ in on** vt fus dabei sein bei; **~ up** vi (after lying) sich aufsetzen; (straight) sich gerade setzen; (at night) aufbleiben
sitcom ['sɪtkɔm] n abbr (= situation comedy) Situationskomödie f
site [saɪt] n Platz m; (also: **building ~**) Baustelle f ♦ vt legen
sitting ['sɪtɪŋ] n (meeting) Sitzung f; **~ room** n Wohnzimmer nt
situated ['sɪtjueɪtɪd] adj: **to be ~** liegen

situation |sɪtjuˈeɪʃən| n Situation f, Lage f;
(place) Lage f; (employment) Stelle f; **"~s
vacant"** (BRIT) „Stellenangebote" pl

six |sɪks| num sechs; **~teen** num sechzehn;
~th adj sechste(r, s) ♦ n Sechstel nt; **~ty**
num sechzig

size |saɪz| n Größe f; (of project) Umfang m;
~ up vt (assess) abschätzen, einschätzen;
~able adj ziemlich groß, ansehnlich

sizzle |ˈsɪzl| vi zischen; (COOK) brutzeln

skate |skeɪt| n Schlittschuh m; (fish: pl inv)
Rochen m ♦ vi Schlittschuh laufen; **~board** n
Skateboard nt; **~boarding** n
Skateboardfahren nt; **~r** n
Schlittschuhläufer(in) m(f); **skating**
|ˈskeɪtɪŋ| n Eislauf m; **to go skating** Eis
laufen gehen; **skating rink** n Eisbahn f

skeleton |ˈskɛlɪtn| n Skelett nt; (fig) Gerüst
nt; **~ key** n Dietrich m; **~ staff** n
Notbesetzung f

skeptical |ˈskɛptɪkl| (US) adj = **sceptical**

sketch |skɛtʃ| n Skizze f; (THEAT) Sketch m
♦ vt skizzieren; **~book** n Skizzenbuch nt; **~y**
adj skizzenhaft

skewer |ˈskjuːəʳ| n Fleischspieß m

ski |skiː| n Ski m, Schi m ♦ vi Ski or Schi
laufen; **~ boot** n Skistiefel m

skid |skɪd| n (AUT) Schleudern nt ♦ vi
rutschen; (AUT) schleudern

ski: **~er** |ˈskiːəʳ| n Skiläufer(in) m(f); **~ing**
|ˈskiːɪŋ| n: **to go ~ing** Ski laufen gehen; **~-
jump** n Sprungschanze f ♦ vi Ski springen

skilful |ˈskɪlful| adj geschickt

ski-lift n Skilift m

skill |skɪl| n Können nt; **~ed** adj geschickt;
(worker) Fach-, gelernt

skim |skɪm| vt (liquid) abschöpfen; (glide
over) gleiten über +acc ♦ vi: **~ through**
(book) überfliegen; **~med milk** n
Magermilch f

skimp |skɪmp| vt (do carelessly) oberflächlich
tun; **~y** adj (dress) knapp

skin |skɪn| n Haut f; (peel) Schale f ♦ vt
abhäuten; schälen; **~ cancer** n Hautkrebs m;
~-deep adj oberflächlich; **~ diving** n
Schwimmtauchen nt; **~head** n Skinhead m;
~ny adj dünn; **~tight** adj (dress etc)
hauteng

skip |skɪp| n Sprung m ♦ vi hüpfen; (with
rope) Seil springen ♦ vt (pass over)
übergehen

ski: **~ pants** npl Skihosen pl; **~ pass** n
Skipass nt; **~ pole** n Skistock m

skipper |ˈskɪpəʳ| n Kapitän m ♦ vt führen

skipping rope |ˈskɪpɪŋ-| (BRIT) n Hüpfseil nt

skirmish |ˈskaːmɪʃ| n Scharmützel nt

skirt |skaːt| n Rock m ♦ vt herumgehen um;
(fig) umgehen; **~ing board** (BRIT) n
Fußleiste f

ski suit n Skianzug m

skit |skɪt| n Parodie f

ski tow n Schlepplift m

skittle |ˈskɪtl| n Kegel m; **~s** n (game) Kegeln
nt

skive |skaɪv| (BRIT: inf) vi schwänzen

skulk |skʌlk| vi sich herumdrücken

skull |skʌl| n Schädel m

skunk |skʌŋk| n Stinktier nt

sky |skaɪ| n Himmel m; **~light** n Oberlicht nt;
~scraper n Wolkenkratzer m

slab |slæb| n (of stone) Platte f

slack |slæk| adj (loose) locker; (business) flau;
(careless) nachlässig, lasch ♦ adj nachlässig
sein ♦ n: **to take up the ~** straff ziehen; **~s**
npl (trousers) Hose(n pl) f; **~en** vi (also: **~en
off**) locker werden; (: slow down) stocken,
nachlassen ♦ vt (: loosen) lockern

slag |slæg| (BRIT) vt: **~ off** (criticize)
(he)runtermachen

slag heap |slæg-| n Halde f

slain |sleɪn| pp of **slay**

slam |slæm| n Knall m ♦ vt (door) zuschlagen;
(throw down) knallen ♦ vi zuschlagen

slander |ˈslɑːndəʳ| n Verleumdung f ♦ vt
verleumden

slang |slæŋ| n Slang m; (jargon) Jargon m

slant |slɑːnt| n Schräge f; (fig) Tendenz f ♦ vt
schräg legen ♦ vi schräg liegen; **~ed** adj
schräg; **~ing** adj schräg

slap |slæp| n Klaps m ♦ vt einen Klaps geben
+dat ♦ adv (directly) geradewegs; **~dash** adj
salopp; **~stick** n (comedy) Klamauk m; **~-up**
(BRIT) adj (meal) erstklassig, prima

slash |slæʃ| n Schnittwunde f ♦ vt
(auf)schlitzen

slat |slæt| n Leiste f

slate |sleɪt| n (stone) Schiefer m; (roofing)
Dachziegel m ♦ vt (criticize) verreißen

slaughter |ˈslɔːtəʳ| n (of animals) Schlachten
nt; (of people) Gemetzel nt ♦ vt schlachten;
(people) niedermetzeln; **~house** n
Schlachthof m

Slav |slɑːv| adj slawisch

slave |sleɪv| n Sklave m, Sklavin f ♦ vi
schuften, sich schinden; **~ry** n Sklaverei f

slay |sleɪ| (pt slew, pp slain) vt ermorden

sleazy |ˈsliːzɪ| adj (place) schmierig

sledge |slɛdʒ| n Schlitten m

sledgehammer |ˈslɛdʒhæməʳ| n
Schmiedehammer m

sledging n Schlittenfahren nt

sleek |sliːk| adj glatt; (shape) rassig

sleep |sliːp| (pt, pp slept) n Schlaf m ♦ vi
schlafen; **to go to ~** einschlafen; **~ in** vi
ausschlafen; (oversleep) verschlafen; **~er** n
(person) Schläfer m; (BRIT: RAIL) Schlafwagen
m; (: beam) Schwelle f; **~ing bag** n
Schlafsack m; **~ing car** n Schlafwagen m;
~ing partner n = **silent partner**; **~ing pill**
n Schlaftablette f; **~less** adj (night)
schlaflos; **~walker** n Schlafwandler(in) m(f);
~y adj schläfrig

sleet [sli:t] n Schneeregen m

sleeve [sli:v] n Ärmel m; (of record) Umschlag m; **~less** adj ärmellos

sleigh [sleɪ] n Pferdeschlitten m

sleight [slaɪt] n: **~ of hand** Fingerfertigkeit f

slender ['slendəʳ] adj schlank; (fig) gering

slept [slept] pt, pp of **sleep**

slew [slu:] vi (veer) (herum)schwenken ♦ pt of **slay**

slice [slaɪs] n Scheibe f ♦ vt in Scheiben schneiden

slick [slɪk] adj (clever) raffiniert, aalglatt ♦ n Ölteppich m

slid [slɪd] pt, pp of **slide**

slide [slaɪd] (pt, pp **slid**) n Rutschbahn f; (PHOT) Dia(positiv) nt; (BRIT: for hair) (Haar)spange f ♦ vt schieben ♦ vi (slip) gleiten, rutschen; **sliding** ['slaɪdɪŋ] adj (door) Schiebe-; **sliding scale** n gleitende Skala f

slight [slaɪt] adj zierlich; (trivial) geringfügig; (small) gering ♦ n Kränkung f ♦ vt (offend) kränken; **not in the ~est** nicht im Geringsten; **~ly** adv etwas, ein bisschen

slim [slɪm] adj schlank; (book) dünn; (chance) gering ♦ vi eine Schlankheitskur machen

slime [slaɪm] n Schleim m

slimming ['slɪmɪŋ] n Schlankheitskur f

slimy ['slaɪmɪ] adj glitschig; (dirty) schlammig; (person) schmierig

sling [slɪŋ] (pt, pp **slung**) n Schlinge f; (weapon) Schleuder f ♦ vt schleudern

slip [slɪp] n (mistake) Flüchtigkeitsfehler m; (petticoat) Unterrock m; (of paper) Zettel m ♦ vt (put) stecken, schieben ♦ vi (lose balance) ausrutschen; (move) gleiten, rutschen; (decline) nachlassen; (move smoothly): **to ~ in/out** (person) hinein-/hinausschlüpfen; **to give sb the ~** jdm entwischen; **~ of the tongue** Versprecher m; **it ~ped my mind** das ist mir entfallen; **to ~ sth on/off** etw über-/abstreifen; **~ away** vi sich wegstehlen; **~ in** vt hineingleiten lassen ♦ vi (errors) sich einschleichen; **~ped disc** n Bandscheibenschaden m

slipper ['slɪpəʳ] n Hausschuh m

slippery ['slɪpərɪ] adj glatt

slip: **~ road** n (BRIT) Auffahrt f/Ausfahrt f; **~shod** adj schlampig; **~-up** n Panne f; **~way** n Auslaufbahn f

slit [slɪt] (pt, pp **slit**) n Schlitz m ♦ vt aufschlitzen

slither ['slɪðəʳ] vi schlittern; (snake) sich schlängeln

sliver ['slɪvəʳ] n (of glass, wood) Splitter m; (of cheese) Scheibchen nt

slob [slɒb] (inf) n Klotz m

slog [slɒg] vi (work hard) schuften ♦ n: **it was a ~** es war eine Plackerei

slogan ['sləugən] n Schlagwort nt; (COMM) Werbespruch m

slop [slɒp] vi (also: **~ over**) überschwappen ♦ vt verschütten

slope [sləup] n Neigung f; (of mountains) (Ab)hang m ♦ vi: **to ~ down** sich senken; **to ~ up** ansteigen; **sloping** ['sləupɪŋ] adj schräg

sloppy ['slɒpɪ] adj schlampig

slot [slɒt] n Schlitz m ♦ vt: **to ~ sth in** etw einlegen

sloth [sləuθ] n (laziness) Faulheit f

slot machine n (BRIT) Automat m; (for gambling) Spielautomat m

slouch [slautʃ] vi: **to ~ about** (laze) herumhängen (inf)

slovenly ['slʌvənlɪ] adj schlampig; (speech) salopp

slow [sləu] adj langsam ♦ adv langsam; **to be ~** (clock) nachgehen; (stupid) begriffsstutzig sein; **"~"** (road sign) „Langsam"; **in ~ motion** in Zeitlupe; **~ down** vi langsamer werden ♦ vt verlangsamen; **~ up** vi sich verlangsamen, sich verzögern ♦ vt aufhalten, langsamer machen; **~ly** adv langsam

sludge [slʌdʒ] n Schlamm m

slug [slʌg] n Nacktschnecke f; (inf: bullet) Kugel f

sluggish ['slʌgɪʃ] adj träge; (COMM) schleppend

sluice [slu:s] n Schleuse f

slum [slʌm] n (house) Elendsquartier nt

slump [slʌmp] n Rückgang m ♦ vi fallen, stürzen

slung [slʌŋ] pt, pp of **sling**

slur [slɜːʳ] n Undeutlichkeit f; (insult) Verleumdung f; **~red** [slɜːd] adj (pronunciation) undeutlich

slush [slʌʃ] n (snow) Schneematsch m; **~ fund** n Schmiergeldfonds m

slut [slʌt] n Schlampe f

sly [slaɪ] adj schlau

smack [smæk] n Klaps m ♦ vt einen Klaps geben +dat ♦ vi: **to ~ of** riechen nach; **to ~ one's lips** schmatzen, sich dat die Lippen lecken

small [smɔ:l] adj klein; **in the ~ hours** in den frühen Morgenstunden; **~ ads** (BRIT) npl Kleinanzeigen pl; **~ change** n Kleingeld nt; **~holder** (BRIT) n Kleinbauer m; **~pox** n Pocken pl; **~ talk** n Geplauder nt

smart [smɑ:t] adj (fashionable) elegant, schick; (neat) adrett; (clever) clever; (quick) scharf ♦ vi brennen, schmerzen; **~ card** n Chipkarte f; **~en up** vi sich in Schale werfen ♦ vt herausputzen

smash [smæʃ] n Zusammenstoß m; (TENNIS) Schmetterball m ♦ vt (break) zerschmettern; (destroy) vernichten ♦ vi (break) zersplittern, zerspringen; **~ing** (inf) adj toll

smattering ['smætərɪŋ] n oberflächliche Kenntnis f

smear [smɪəʳ] n Fleck m ♦ vt beschmieren

smell [smɛl] (*pt, pp* **smelt** or **smelled**) *n* Geruch *m*; (*sense*) Geruchssinn *m* ♦ *vt* riechen ♦ *vi*: **to ~ (of)** riechen (nach); (*fragrantly*) duften (nach); **~y** *adj* übel riechend

smile [smaɪl] *n* Lächeln *nt* ♦ *vi* lächeln

smiling ['smaɪlɪŋ] *adj* lächelnd

smirk [smɜːk] *n* blöde(s) Grinsen *nt*

smock [smɔk] *n* Kittel *m*

smoke [sməʊk] *n* Rauch *m* ♦ *vt* rauchen; (*food*) räuchern ♦ *vi* rauchen; (*glass*) Rauch-; **~d** *adj* (*bacon*) geräuchert; (*glass*) Rauch-; **~r** *n* Raucher(in) *m(f)*; (*RAIL*) Raucherabteil *nt*; **~ screen** *n* Rauchwand *f*

smoking ['sməʊkɪŋ] *n* Imbiss *m*: **"no ~"** „Rauchen verboten"; **~ compartment** (*BRIT*), **~ car** (*US*) *n* Raucherabteil *nt*

smoky ['sməʊkɪ] *adj* rauchig; (*room*) verraucht; (*taste*) geräuchert

smolder ['sməʊldər] (*US*) *vi* = **smoulder**

smooth [smuːð] *adj* glatt ♦ *vt* (*also:* **~ out**) glätten, glatt streichen

smother ['smʌðər] *vt* ersticken

smoulder ['sməʊldər] (*US* **smolder**) *vi* schwelen

smudge [smʌdʒ] *n* Schmutzfleck *m* ♦ *vt* beschmieren

smug [smʌg] *adj* selbstgefällig

smuggle ['smʌgl] *vt* schmuggeln; **~r** *n* Schmuggler *m*

smuggling ['smʌglɪŋ] *n* Schmuggel *m*

smutty ['smʌtɪ] *adj* schmutzig

snack [snæk] *n* Imbiss *m*; **~ bar** *n* Imbissstube *f*

snag [snæg] *n* Haken *m*

snail [sneɪl] *n* Schnecke *f*

snake [sneɪk] *n* Schlange *f*

snap [snæp] *n* Schnappen *nt*; (*photograph*) Schnappschuss *m* ♦ *adj* (*decision*) schnell ♦ *vt* (*break*) zerbrechen; (*PHOT*) knipsen ♦ *vi* (*break*) brechen; (*speak*) anfauchen; **to ~ shut** zuschnappen; **~ at** *vt fus* schnappen nach; **~ off** *vt* (*break*) abbrechen; **~ up** *vt* aufschnappen; **~shot** *n* Schnappschuss *m*

snare [snɛər] *n* Schlinge *f* ♦ *vt* mit einer Schlinge fangen

snarl [snɑːl] *n* Zähnefletschen *nt* ♦ *vi* (*dog*) knurren

snatch [snætʃ] *n* (*small amount*) Bruchteil *m* ♦ *vt* schnappen, packen

sneak [sniːk] *vi* schleichen ♦ *n* (*inf*) Petze(r) *mf*; **~ers** ['sniːkəz] (*US*) *npl* Freizeitschuhe *pl*; **~y** ['sniːkɪ] *adj* raffiniert

sneer [snɪər] *n* Hohnlächeln *nt* ♦ *vi* spötteln

sneeze [sniːz] *n* Niesen *nt* ♦ *vi* niesen

sniff [snɪf] *n* Schnüffeln *nt* ♦ *vi* schnieben; (*smell*) schnüffeln ♦ *vt* schnuppern

snigger ['snɪgər] *n* Kichern *nt* ♦ *vi* hämisch kichern

snip [snɪp] *n* Schnippel *m*, Schnipsel *m* ♦ *vt* schnippeln

sniper ['snaɪpər] *n* Heckenschütze *m*

snippet ['snɪpɪt] *n* Schnipsel *m*; (*of conversation*) Fetzen *m*

snivelling ['snɪvlɪŋ] *adj* weinerlich

snob [snɔb] *n* Snob *m*

snooker ['snuːkər] *n* Snooker *nt*

snoop [snuːp] *vi*: **to ~ about** herumschnüffeln

snooze [snuːz] *n* Nickerchen *nt* ♦ *vi* ein Nickerchen machen, dösen

snore [snɔːr] *vi* schnarchen ♦ *n* Schnarchen *nt*

snorkel ['snɔːkl] *n* Schnorchel *m*

snort [snɔːt] *n* Schnauben *nt* ♦ *vi* schnauben

snout [snaʊt] *n* Schnauze *f*

snow [snəʊ] *n* Schnee *m* ♦ *vi* schneien; **~ball** *n* Schneeball *m* ♦ *vi* eskalieren; **~bound** *adj* eingeschneit; **~drift** *n* Schneewehe *f*; **~drop** *n* Schneeglöckchen *nt*; **~fall** *n* Schneefall *m*; **~flake** *n* Schneeflocke *f*; **~man** (*irreg*) *n* Schneemann *m*; **~plough** (*US* **~plow**) *n* Schneepflug *m*; **~ shoe** *n* Schneeschuh *m*; **~storm** *n* Schneesturm *m*

snub [snʌb] *vt* schroff abfertigen ♦ *n* Verweis *m*; **~-nosed** *adj* stupsnasig

snuff [snʌf] *n* Schnupftabak *m*

snug [snʌg] *adj* gemütlich, behaglich

snuggle ['snʌgl] *vi*: **to ~ up to sb** sich an jdn kuscheln

---

KEYWORD

so [səʊ] *adv* **1** (*thus*) so; (*likewise*) auch; **so saying he walked away** indem er das sagte, ging er; **if so** wenn ja; **I didn't do it – you did so!** ich hab das nicht gemacht – hast du wohl!; **so do I, so am I** *etc* ich auch; **so it is!** tatsächlich!; **I hope/think so** hoffentlich/ich glaube schon; **so far** bis jetzt

2 (*in comparisons etc: to such a degree*) so; **so quickly/big (that)** so schnell/groß(, dass); **I'm so glad to see you** ich freue mich so, dich zu sehen

3: so many so viele; **so much work** so viel Arbeit; **I love you so much** ich liebe dich so sehr

4 (*phrases*): **10 or so** etwa 10; **so long!** (*inf*: *goodbye*) tschüss!

♦ *conj* **1** (*expressing purpose*): **so as to** um ... zu; **so (that)** damit

2 (*expressing result*) also; **so I was right after all** ich hatte also doch Recht; **so you see ...** wie du siehst ...

---

soak [səʊk] *vt* durchnässen; (*leave in liquid*) einweichen ♦ *vi* (ein)weichen; **~ in** *vi* einsickern; **~ up** *vt* aufsaugen; **~ed** *adj* völlig durchnässt; **~ing** *adj* klitschnass, patschnass

so-and-so ['səʊənsəʊ] *n* (*somebody*) Soundso *m*

soap [səʊp] *n* Seife *f*; **~flakes** *npl* Seifenflocken *pl*; **~ opera** *n* Familienserie *f* (*im Fernsehen, Radio*); **~ powder** *n*

Waschpulver *nt*; **~y** *adj* seifig, Seifen-

soar [sɔːʳ] *vi* aufsteigen; (*prices*) in die Höhe schnellen

sob [sɔb] *n* Schluchzen *nt* ♦ *vi* schluchzen

sober ['səubəʳ] *adj* (*also fig*) nüchtern; **~ up** *vi* nüchtern werden

so-called ['səu'kɔːld] *adj* so genannt

soccer ['sɔkəʳ] *n* Fußball *m*

sociable ['səuʃəbl] *adj* gesellig

social ['səuʃl] *adj* sozial; (*friendly, living with others*) gesellig ♦ *n* gesellige(r) Abend *m*; **~ club** *n* Verein *m* (für Freizeitgestaltung); **~ism** *n* Sozialismus *m*; **~ist** *n* Sozialist(in) *m(f)* ♦ *adj* sozialistisch; **~ize** *vi*: **to ~ize (with)** gesellschaftlich verkehren (mit); **~ly** *adv* gesellschaftlich, privat; **~ security** *n* Sozialversicherung *f*; **~ work** *n* Sozialarbeit *f*; **~ worker** *n* Sozialarbeiter(in) *m(f)*

society [sə'saiəti] *n* Gesellschaft *f*; (*fashionable world*) die große Welt

sociology [səusi'ɔlədʒi] *n* Soziologie *f*

sock [sɔk] *n* Socke *f*

socket ['sɔkit] *n* (*ELEC*) Steckdose *f*; (*of eye*) Augenhöhle *f*

sod [sɔd] *n* Rasenstück *nt*; (*inf!*) Saukerl *m* (!)

soda ['səudə] *n* Soda *f*; (*also:* **~ water**) Soda(wasser) *nt*; (*US: also:* **~ pop**) Limonade *f*

sodden ['sɔdn] *adj* durchweicht

sodium ['səudiəm] *n* Natrium *nt*

sofa ['səufə] *n* Sofa *nt*

soft [sɔft] *adj* weich; (*not loud*) leise; (*weak*) nachgiebig; **~ drink** *n* alkoholfreie(s) Getränk *nt*; **~en** ['sɔfn] *vt* weich machen; (*blow*) abschwächen, mildern ♦ *vi* weich werden; **~ly** *adv* sanft; leise; **~ness** *n* Weichheit *f*; (*fig*) Sanftheit *f*

software ['sɔftweəʳ] *n* (*COMPUT*) Software *f*

soggy ['sɔgi] *adj* (*ground*) sumpfig; (*bread*) aufgeweicht

soil [sɔil] *n* Erde *f* ♦ *vt* beschmutzen

solace ['sɔlis] *n* Trost *m*

solar ['səuləʳ] *adj* Sonnen-; **~ cell** *n* Solarzelle *f*; **~ energy** *n* Sonnenenergie *f*; **~ panel** *n* Sonnenkollektor *m*; **~ power** *n* Sonnenenergie *f*

sold [səuld] *pt, pp of* **sell**; **~ out** (*COMM*) ausverkauft

solder ['səuldəʳ] *vt* löten

soldier ['səuldʒəʳ] *n* Soldat *m*

sole [səul] *n* Sohle *f*; (*fish*) Seezunge *f* ♦ *adj* alleinig, Allein-; **~ly** *adv* ausschließlich

solemn ['sɔləm] *adj* feierlich

sole trader *n* (*COMM*) Einzelunternehmen *nt*

solicit [sə'lisit] *vt* (*request*) bitten um ♦ *vi* (*prostitute*) Kunden anwerben

solicitor [sə'lisitəʳ] *n* Rechtsanwalt *m*/ -anwältin *f*

solid ['sɔlid] *adj* (*hard*) fest; (*of same material, not hollow*) massiv; (*without break*) voll, ganz; (*reliable, sensible*) solide ♦ *n* Festkörper *m*; **~arity** [sɔli'dæriti] *n* Solidarität *f*; **~ify**

[sə'lidifai] *vi* fest werden

solitary ['sɔlitəri] *adj* einsam, einzeln; **~ confinement** *n* Einzelhaft *f*

solitude ['sɔlitjuːd] *n* Einsamkeit *f*

solo ['səuləu] *n* Solo *nt*; **~ist** ['səuləuist] *n* Solist(in) *m(f)*

soluble ['sɔljubl] *adj* (*substance*) löslich; (*problem*) (auf)lösbar

solution [sə'luːʃən] *n* (*also fig*) Lösung *f*; (*of mystery*) Erklärung *f*

solve [sɔlv] *vt* (auf)lösen

solvent ['sɔlvənt] *adj* (*FIN*) zahlungsfähig ♦ *n* (*CHEM*) Lösungsmittel *nt*

sombre ['sɔmbəʳ] (*US* **somber**) *adj* düster

KEYWORD

some [sʌm] *adj* **1** (*a certain amount or number of*) einige; (*a few*) ein paar; (*with singular nouns*) etwas; **some tea/biscuits** etwas Tee/ein paar Plätzchen; **I've got some money, but not much** ich habe ein bisschen Geld, aber nicht viel

2 (*certain: in contrasts*) manche(r, s); **some people say that ...** manche Leute sagen, dass ...

3 (*unspecified*) irgendein(e); **some woman was asking for you** da hat eine Frau nach Ihnen gefragt; **some day** eines Tages; **some day next week** irgendwann nächste Woche ♦ *pron* **1** (*a certain number*) einige; **have you got some?** haben Sie welche?

2 (*a certain amount*) etwas; **I've read some of the book** ich habe das Buch teilweise gelesen ♦ *adv*: **some 10 people** etwa 10 Leute

---

somebody ['sʌmbədi] *pron* = **someone**

somehow ['sʌmhau] *adv* (*in some way, for some reason*) irgendwie

someone ['sʌmwʌn] *pron* jemand; (*direct obj*) jemand(en); (*indirect obj*) jemandem

someplace ['sʌmpleis] (*US*) *adv* = **somewhere**

somersault ['sʌməsɔːlt] *n* Salto *m* ♦ *vi* einen Salto machen

something ['sʌmθiŋ] *pron* etwas

sometime ['sʌmtaim] *adv* (*irgend*)einmal

sometimes ['sʌmtaimz] *adv* manchmal

somewhat ['sʌmwɔt] *adv* etwas

somewhere ['sʌmweəʳ] *adv* irgendwo; (*to a place*) irgendwohin; **~ else** irgendwo anders

son [sʌn] *n* Sohn *m*

sonar ['səunɑːʳ] *n* Echolot *nt*

song [sɔŋ] *n* Lied *nt*

sonic boom ['sɔnik-] *n* Überschallknall *m*

son-in-law ['sʌninlɔː] *n* Schwiegersohn *m*

soon [suːn] *adv* bald; **~ afterwards** kurz danach; **~er** *adv* (*time*) früher; (*for preference*) lieber; **~er or later** früher oder später

soot [sut] *n* Ruß *m*

soothe [suːð] vt (person) beruhigen; (pain) lindern

sophisticated [səˈfɪstɪkeɪtɪd] adj (person) kultiviert; (machinery) hoch entwickelt

sophomore [ˈsɒfəmɔːʳ] (US) n College-student m im 2. Jahr

soporific [sɒpəˈrɪfɪk] adj einschläfernd

sopping [ˈsɒpɪŋ] adj patschnass

soppy [ˈsɒpɪ] (inf) adj schmalzig

soprano [səˈprɑːnəʊ] n Sopran m

sorcerer [ˈsɔːsərəʳ] n Hexenmeister m

sordid [ˈsɔːdɪd] adj erbärmlich

sore [sɔːʳ] adj schmerzend; (point) wund ♦ n Wunde f; ~ly adv (tempted) stark, sehr

sorrow [ˈsɒrəʊ] n Kummer m, Leid nt; ~ful adj sorgenvoll

sorry [ˈsɒrɪ] adj traurig, erbärmlich; ~! Entschuldigung!; to feel ~ for sb jdn bemitleiden; I feel ~ for him er tut mir Leid; ~? (pardon) wie bitte?

sort [sɔːt] n Art f, Sorte f ♦ vt (also: ~ out: papers) sortieren; (: problems) sichten, in Ordnung bringen; ~ing office n Sortierstelle f

SOS n SOS nt

so-so [ˈsəʊsəʊ] adv so(so) lala

sought [sɔːt] pt, pp of **seek**

soul [səʊl] n Seele f; (music) Soul m; ~-destroying adj trostlos; ~ful adj seelenvoll

sound [saʊnd] adj (healthy) gesund; (safe) sicher; (sensible) vernünftig; (theory) stichhaltig; (thorough) tüchtig, gehörig ♦ adv: to be ~ asleep fest schlafen ♦ n (noise) Geräusch nt, Laut m; (GEOG) Sund m ♦ vt erschallen lassen; (alarm) (Alarm) schlagen ♦ vi (make a ~) schallen, tönen; (seem) klingen; to ~ like sich anhören wie; ~ out vt erforschen; (person) auf den Zahn fühlen +dat; ~ barrier n Schallmauer f; ~bite n (RAD, TV) prägnante(s) Zitat nt; ~ effects npl Toneffekte pl; ~ly adv (sleep) fest; (beat) tüchtig; ~proof adj (room) schalldicht; ~ track n Tonstreifen m; (music) Filmmusik f

soup [suːp] n Suppe f; ~ plate n Suppenteller m; ~spoon n Suppenlöffel m

sour [saʊəʳ] adj (also fig) sauer; it's ~ grapes (fig) die Trauben hängen zu hoch

source [sɔːs] n (also fig) Quelle f

south [saʊθ] n Süden m ♦ adj Süd-, südlich ♦ adv nach Süden, südwärts; S~ Africa n Südafrika nt; S~ African adj südafrikanisch ♦ n Südafrikaner(in) m(f); S~ America n Südamerika nt; S~ American adj südamerikanisch ♦ n Südamerikaner(in) m(f); ~-east n Südosten m; ~erly [ˈsʌðəlɪ] adj südlich; ~ern [ˈsʌðən] adj südlich, Süd-; S~ Pole n Südpol m; S~ Wales n Südwales nt; ~ward(s) adv südwärts, nach Süden; ~-west n Südwesten m

souvenir [suːvəˈnɪəʳ] n Souvenir nt

sovereign [ˈsɒvrɪn] n (ruler) Herrscher(in) m(f) ♦ adj (independent) souverän

soviet [ˈsəʊvɪət] adj sowjetisch; the S~ Union die Sowjetunion

sow¹ [saʊ] n Sau f

sow² [səʊ] (pt **sowed**, pp **sown**) vt (also fig) säen

soya [ˈsɔɪə] (US **soy**) n: ~ bean Sojabohne f; ~ sauce Sojasauce f

spa [spɑː] n (place) Kurort m

space [speɪs] n Platz m, Raum m; (universe) Weltraum m, All nt; (length of time) Abstand m ♦ vt (also: ~ out) verteilen; ~craft n Raumschiff nt; ~man (irreg) n Raumfahrer m; ~ ship n Raumschiff nt

spacing [ˈspeɪsɪŋ] n Abstand m; (also: ~ out) Verteilung f

spacious [ˈspeɪʃəs] adj geräumig, weit

spade [speɪd] n Spaten m; ~s npl (CARDS) Pik nt

Spain [speɪn] n Spanien nt

span [spæn] n Spanne f; (of bridge etc) Spannweite f ♦ vt überspannen

Spaniard [ˈspænjəd] n Spanier(in) m(f)

spaniel [ˈspænjəl] n Spaniel m

Spanish [ˈspænɪʃ] adj spanisch ♦ n (LING) Spanisch nt; the ~ npl (people) die Spanier pl

spank [spæŋk] vt verhauen, versohlen

spanner [ˈspænəʳ] n (BRIT) Schraubenschlüssel m

spar [spɑːʳ] n (NAUT) Sparren m ♦ vi (BOXING) einen Sparring machen

spare [spɛəʳ] adj Ersatz- ♦ n = spare part ♦ vt (lives, feelings) verschonen; (trouble) ersparen; to ~ (surplus) übrig; ~ part n Ersatzteil nt; ~ time n Freizeit f; ~ wheel n (AUT) Reservereifen m

sparing [ˈspɛərɪŋ] adj: to be ~ with geizen mit; ~ly adv sparsam; (eat, spend etc) in Maßen

spark [spɑːk] n Funken m; ~(ing) plug n Zündkerze f

sparkle [ˈspɑːkl] n Funkeln nt; (gaiety) Schwung m ♦ vi funkeln; **sparkling** adj funkelnd; (wine) Schaum-; (mineral water) mit Kohlensäure; (conversation) spritzig, geistreich

sparrow [ˈspærəʊ] n Spatz m

sparse [spɑːs] adj spärlich

spasm [ˈspæzəm] n (MED) Krampf m; (fig) Anfall m; ~odic [spæzˈmɒdɪk] adj (fig) sprunghaft

spastic [ˈspæstɪk] (old) n Spastiker(in) m(f) ♦ adj spastisch

spat [spæt] pt, pp of **spit**

spate [speɪt] n (fig) Flut f, Schwall m; in ~ (river) angeschwollen

spatter [ˈspætəʳ] vt bespritzen, verspritzen

spatula [ˈspætjʊlə] n Spatel m

spawn [spɔːn] vi laichen ♦ n Laich m

speak [spiːk] (pt **spoke**, pp **spoken**) vt sprechen, reden; (truth) sagen; (language) sprechen ♦ vi: to ~ (to) sprechen (mit or zu);

to ~ to sb of or **about sth** mit jdm über etw acc sprechen; **~ up!** sprich lauter!; **~er** n Sprecher(in) m(f), Redner(in) m(f); (loudspeaker) Lautsprecher m; (POL): **the S~er** der Vorsitzende des Parlaments (BRIT) or des Kongresses (US)

spear [spɪəʳ] n Speer m ♦ vt aufspießen; **~head** vt (attack etc) anführen

spec [spɛk] (inf) n: **on ~** auf gut Glück

special ['spɛʃl] adj besondere(r, s); **~ist** n (TECH) Fachmann m; (MED) Facharzt m/ Fachärztin f; **~ity** [spɛʃɪ'ælɪtɪ] n Spezialität f; (study) Spezialgebiet nt; **~ize** vi: **to ~ize (in)** sich spezialisieren (auf +acc); **~ly** adv besonders; (explicitly) extra; ~ **needs** adj.: ~ **needs children** behinderte Kinder pl; **~ty** (esp US) n = **speciality**

species ['spi:ʃi:z] n Art f

specific [spə'sɪfɪk] adj spezifisch; **~ally** adv spezifisch

specification [spɛsɪfɪ'keɪʃən] n Angabe f; (stipulation) Bedingung f; **~s** npl (TECH) technische Daten pl

specify ['spɛsɪfaɪ] vt genau angeben

specimen ['spɛsɪmən] n Probe f

speck [spɛk] n Fleckchen nt

speckled ['spɛkld] adj gesprenkelt

specs [spɛks] (inf) npl Brille f

spectacle ['spɛktəkl] n Schauspiel nt; **~s** npl (glasses) Brille f

spectacular [spɛk'tækjuləʳ] adj sensationell; (success etc) spektakulär

spectator [spɛk'teɪtəʳ] n Zuschauer(in) m(f)

spectre ['spɛktəʳ] (US **specter**) n Geist m, Gespenst nt

speculate ['spɛkjuleɪt] vi spekulieren

speech [spi:tʃ] n Sprache f; (address) Rede f; (way one speaks) Sprechweise f; **~less** adj sprachlos

speed [spi:d] n Geschwindigkeit f; (gear) Gang m ♦ vi (JUR) (zu) schnell fahren; **at full** or **top** ~ mit Höchstgeschwindigkeit; ~ **up** vt beschleunigen ♦ vi schneller werden; schneller fahren; **~boat** n Schnellboot nt; **~ily** adv schleunigst; **~ing** n Geschwindigkeitsüberschreitung f; ~ **limit** n Geschwindigkeitsbegrenzung f; **~ometer** [spɪ'dɒmɪtəʳ] n Tachometer m; **~way** n (bike racing) Motorradrennstrecke f; **~y** adj schnell

spell [spɛl] (pt, pp **spelt** (BRIT) or **spelled**) n (magic) Bann m; (period of time) (eine) Zeit lang ♦ vt buchstabieren; (imply) bedeuten; **to cast a ~ on sb** jdn verzaubern; **~bound** adj (wie) gebannt; **~ing** n Rechtschreibung f

spelt [spɛlt] (BRIT) pt, pp of **spell**

spend [spɛnd] (pt, pp **spent**) vt (money) ausgeben; (time) verbringen; **~thrift** n Verschwender(in) m(f)

spent [spɛnt] pt, pp of **spend**

sperm [spə:m] n (BIOL) Samenflüssigkeit f

spew [spju:] vt (er)brechen

sphere [sfɪəʳ] n (globe) Kugel f; (fig) Sphäre f, Gebiet nt; **spherical** ['sfɛrɪkl] adj kugelförmig

spice [spaɪs] n Gewürz nt ♦ vt würzen

spick-and-span ['spɪkən'spæn] adj blitzblank

spicy ['spaɪsɪ] adj (food) stark gewürzt; (fig) pikant

spider ['spaɪdəʳ] n Spinne f

spike [spaɪk] n Dorn m, Spitze f

spill [spɪl] (pt, pp **spilt** or **spilled**) vt verschütten ♦ vi sich ergießen; ~ **over** vi überlaufen; (fig) sich ausbreiten

spilt [spɪlt] pt, pp of **spill**

spin [spɪn] (pt, pp **spun**) n (trip in car) Spazierfahrt f; (AVIAT) (Ab)trudeln nt; (on ball) Drall m ♦ vt (thread) spinnen; (like top) (herum)wirbeln ♦ vi sich drehen; ~ **out** vt in die Länge ziehen

spinach ['spɪnɪtʃ] n Spinat m

spinal ['spaɪnl] adj Rückgrat-; ~ **cord** n Rückenmark nt

spindly ['spɪndlɪ] adj spindeldürr

spin doctor n PR-Berater(in) m(f)

spin-dryer [spɪn'draɪəʳ] (BRIT) n Wäscheschleuder f

spine [spaɪn] n Rückgrat nt; (thorn) Stachel m; **~less** adj (also fig) rückgratlos

spinning ['spɪnɪŋ] n Spinnen nt; ~ **top** n Kreisel m; ~ **wheel** n Spinnrad nt

spin-off ['spɪnɔf] n Nebenprodukt nt

spinster ['spɪnstəʳ] n unverheiratete Frau f; (pej) alte Jungfer f

spiral ['spaɪərl] n Spirale f ♦ adj spiralförmig; (movement etc) in Spiralen ♦ vi sich (hoch)winden; ~ **staircase** n Wendeltreppe f

spire ['spaɪəʳ] n Turm m

spirit ['spɪrɪt] n Geist m; (humour, mood) Stimmung f; (courage) Mut m; (verve) Elan m; (alcohol) Alkohol m; **~s** npl (drink) Spirituosen pl; **in good ~s** gut aufgelegt; **~ed** adj beherzt; ~ **level** n Wasserwaage f

spiritual ['spɪrɪtjuəl] adj geistig, seelisch; (REL) geistlich ♦ n Spiritual nt

spit [spɪt] (pt, pp **spat**) n (for roasting) (Brat)spieß m; (saliva) Spucke f ♦ vi spucken; (rain) sprühen; (make a sound) zischen; (cat) fauchen

spite [spaɪt] n Gehässigkeit f ♦ vt kränken; **in ~ of** trotz; **~ful** adj gehässig

spittle ['spɪtl] n Speichel m, Spucke f

splash [splæʃ] n Spritzer m; (of colour) (Farb)fleck m ♦ vt bespritzen ♦ vi spritzen

spleen [spli:n] n (ANAT) Milz f

splendid ['splɛndɪd] adj glänzend

splendour ['splɛndəʳ] (US **splendor**) n Pracht f

splint [splɪnt] n Schiene f

splinter ['splɪntəʳ] n Splitter m ♦ vi

(zer)splittern

split |splɪt| (*pt, pp* **split**) *n* Spalte *f*; (*fig*) Spaltung *f*; (*division*) Trennung *f* ♦ *vt* spalten ♦ *vi* (*divide*) reißen; **~ up** *vi* sich trennen

splutter |ˈsplʌtəʳ| *vi* stottern

spoil |spɔɪl| (*pt, pp* **spoilt** *or* **spoiled**) *vt* (*ruin*) verderben; (*child*) verwöhnen; **~s** *npl* Beute *f*; **~sport** *n* Spielverderber *m*; **~t** *pt, pp of* **spoil**

spoke |spəuk| *pt of* **speak** ♦ *n* Speiche *f*; **~n** *pp of* **speak**

spokesman |ˈspəuksmən| (*irreg*) *n* Sprecher *m*; **spokeswoman** |ˈspəukswumən| (*irreg*) *n* Sprecherin *f*

sponge |spʌndʒ| *n* Schwamm *m* ♦ *vt* abwaschen ♦ *vi:* **to ~ on** auf Kosten +*gen* leben; **~ bag** (*BRIT*) *n* Kulturbeutel *m*; **~ cake** *n* Rührkuchen *m*

sponsor |ˈspɔnsəʳ| *n* Sponsor *m* ♦ *vt* fördern; **~ship** *n* Finanzierung *f*; (*public*) Schirmherrschaft *f*

spontaneous |spɔnˈteɪnɪəs| *adj* spontan

spooky |ˈspuːkɪ| (*inf*) *adj* gespenstisch

spool |spuːl| *n* Spule *f*, Rolle *f*

spoon |spuːn| *n* Löffel *m*; **~-feed** (*irreg*) *vt* mit dem Löffel füttern; (*fig*) hochpäppeln; **~ful** *n* Löffel *m* (voll)

sport |spɔːt| *n* Sport *m*; (*person*) feine(r) Kerl *m*; **~ing** *adj* (*fair*) sportlich, fair; **to give sb a ~ing chance** jdm eine faire Chance geben; **~ jacket** (*US*) *n* = **sports jacket**; **~s car** *n* Sportwagen *m*; **~s jacket** *n* Sportjackett *nt*; **~sman** (*irreg*) *n* Sportler *m*; **~smanship** *n* Sportlichkeit *f*; **~swear** *n* Sportkleidung *f*; **~swoman** (*irreg*) *n* Sportlerin *f*; **~y** *adj* sportlich

spot |spɔt| *n* Punkt *m*; (*dirty*) Fleck(en) *m*; (*place*) Stelle *f*; (*MED*) Pickel *m* ♦ *vt* erspähen; (*mistake*) bemerken; **on the ~** an Ort und Stelle; (*at once*) auf der Stelle; **~ check** *n* Stichprobe *f*; **~less** *adj* fleckenlos; **~light** *n* Scheinwerferlicht *nt*; (*lamp*) Scheinwerfer *m*; **~ted** *adj* gefleckt; **~ty** *adj* (*face*) pickelig

spouse |spaus| *n* Gatte *m*/Gattin *f*

spout |spaut| *n* (*of pot*) Tülle *f*; (*jet*) Wasserstrahl *m* ♦ *vi* speien

sprain |spreɪn| *n* Verrenkung *f* ♦ *vt* verrenken

sprang |spræŋ| *pt of* **spring**

sprawl |sprɔːl| *vi* sich strecken

spray |spreɪ| *n* Spray *m*; (*off sea*) Gischt *f*; (*of flowers*) Zweig *m* ♦ *vt* besprühen, sprayen

spread |spred| (*pt, pp* **spread**) *n* (*extent*) Verbreitung *f*; (*inf: meal*) Schmaus *m*; (*for bread*) Aufstrich *m* ♦ *vt* ausbreiten; (*scatter*) verbreiten; (*butter*) streichen ♦ *vi* sich ausbreiten; **~-eagled** |ˈspredɪːgld| *adj:* **to be ~-eagled** alle viere von sich strecken; **~ out** (*move apart*) sich verteilen; **~sheet** *n* Tabellenkalkulation *f*

spree |spriː| *n* (*shopping*) Einkaufsbummel *m*; **to go on a ~** einen draufmachen

sprightly |ˈspraɪtlɪ| *adj* munter, lebhaft

spring |sprɪŋ| (*pt* **sprang**, *pp* **sprung**) *n* (*leap*) Sprung *m*; (*TECH*) Feder *f*; (*season*) Frühling *m*; (*water*) Quelle *f* ♦ *vi* (*leap*) springen; **~ up** *vi* (*problem*) auftauchen; **~board** *n* Sprungbrett *nt*; **~-clean** *n* (*also:* **~-cleaning**) Frühjahrsputz *m*; **~time** *n* Frühling *m*; **~y** *adj* federnd, elastisch

sprinkle |ˈsprɪŋkl| *vt* (*salt*) streuen; (*liquid*) sprenkeln; **to ~ water on, to ~ with water** mit Wasser besprengen; **~r** |ˈsprɪŋkləʳ| *n* (*for lawn*) Sprenger *m*; (*for fire fighting*) Sprinkler *m*

sprint |sprɪnt| *n* (*race*) Sprint *m* ♦ *vi* (*run fast*) rennen; (*SPORT*) sprinten; **~er** *n* Sprinter(in) *m(f)*

sprout |spraut| *vi* sprießen

sprouts |sprauts| *npl* (*also:* **Brussels ~**) Rosenkohl *m*

spruce |spruːs| *n* Fichte *f* ♦ *adj* schmuck, adrett

sprung |sprʌŋ| *pp of* **spring**

spry |spraɪ| *adj* flink, rege

spun |spʌn| *pt, pp of* **spin**

spur |spɜːʳ| *n* Sporn *m*; (*fig*) Ansporn *m* ♦ *vt* (*also:* **~ on**) (*fig*) anspornen; **on the ~ of the moment** spontan

spurious |ˈspjuərɪəs| *adj* falsch

spurn |spɜːn| *vt* verschmähen

spurt |spɜːt| *n* (*jet*) Strahl *m*; (*acceleration*) Spurt *m* ♦ *vi* (*liquid*) schießen

spy |spaɪ| *n* Spion(in) *m(f)* ♦ *vi* spionieren ♦ *vt* erspähen; **~ing** *n* Spionage *f*

sq. *abbr* = **square**

squabble |ˈskwɔbl| *n* Zank *m* ♦ *vi* sich zanken

squad |skwɔd| *n* (*MIL*) Abteilung *f*; (*POLICE*) Kommando *nt*

squadron |ˈskwɔdrn| *n* (*cavalry*) Schwadron *f*; (*NAUT*) Geschwader *nt*; (*air force*) Staffel *f*

squalid |ˈskwɔlɪd| *adj* verkommen

squall |skwɔːl| *n* Bö(e) *f*, Windstoß *m*

squalor |ˈskwɔləʳ| *n* Verwahrlosung *f*

squander |ˈskwɔndəʳ| *vt* verschwenden

square |skwɛəʳ| *n* Quadrat *nt*; (*open space*) Platz *m*; (*instrument*) Winkel *m*; (*inf: person*) Spießer *m* ♦ *adj* viereckig; (*inf: ideas, tastes*) spießig ♦ *vt* (*arrange*) ausmachen; (*MATH*) ins Quadrat erheben ♦ *vi* (*agree*) über-einstimmen; **all ~** quitt; **a ~ meal** eine ordentliche Mahlzeit; **2 metres ~** 2 Meter im Quadrat; **1 ~ metre** 1 Quadratmeter; **~ly** *adv* fest, gerade

squash |skwɔʃ| *n* (*BRIT: drink*) Saft *m*; (*game*) Squash *nt* ♦ *vt* zerquetschen

squat |skwɔt| *adj* untersetzt ♦ *vi* hocken; **~ter** *n* Hausbesetzer *m*

squawk |skwɔːk| *vi* kreischen

squeak |skwiːk| *vi* quiek(s)en; (*spring, door etc*) quietschen

squeal |skwi:l| *vi* schrill schreien
squeamish |'skwi:mɪʃ| *adj* empfindlich
squeeze |skwi:z| *vt* pressen, drücken;
  (orange) auspressen; **~ out** *vt* ausquetschen
squelch |skweltʃ| *vi* platschen
squib |skwɪb| *n* Knallfrosch *m*
squid |skwɪd| *n* Tintenfisch *m*
squiggle |'skwɪgl| *n* Schnörkel *m*
squint |skwɪnt| *vi* schielen ♦ *n*: **to have a ~**
  schielen; **to ~ at sb/sth** nach jdm/etw
  schielen
squirm |skwɜ:m| *vi* sich winden
squirrel |'skwɪrəl| *n* Eichhörnchen *nt*
squirt |skwɜ:t| *vt, vi* spritzen
Sr *abbr (= senior)* sen.
St *abbr (= saint)* hl., St.; *(= street)* Str.
stab |stæb| *n (blow)* Stich *m*; *(inf: try)* Versuch
  m ♦ *vt* erstechen
stabilize |'steɪbəlaɪz| *vt* stabilisieren ♦ *vi* sich
  stabilisieren
stable |'steɪbl| *adj* stabil ♦ *n* Stall *m*
stack |stæk| *n* Stapel *m* ♦ *vt* stapeln
stadium |'steɪdɪəm| *n* Stadion *nt*
staff |stɑ:f| *n (stick, MIL)* Stab *m*; *(personnel)*
  Personal *nt*; *(BRIT: SCH)* Lehrkräfte *pl* ♦ *vt*
  besetzen
stag |stæg| *n* Hirsch *m*
stage |steɪdʒ| *n* Bühne *f*; *(of journey)* Etappe
  f; *(degree)* Stufe *f*; *(point)* Stadium *nt* ♦ *vt*
  (put on) aufführen; *(simulate)* inszenieren;
  (demonstration) veranstalten; **in ~s**
  etappenweise; **~coach** *n* Postkutsche *f*; **~
  door** *n* Bühneneingang *m*; **~ manager** *n*
  Intendant *m*
stagger |'stægəʳ| *vi* wanken, taumeln ♦ *vt*
  (amaze) verblüffen; *(hours)* staffeln; **~ing** *adj*
  unglaublich
stagnant |'stægnənt| *adj* stagnierend;
  (water) stehend; **stagnate** |stæg'neɪt| *vi*
  stagnieren
stag party *n* Männerabend *m* *(vom
  Bräutigam vor der Hochzeit gegeben)*
staid |steɪd| *adj* gesetzt
stain |steɪn| *n* Fleck *m* ♦ *vt* beflecken; **~ed
  glass window** buntes Glasfenster *nt*; **~less**
  adj (steel) rostfrei; **~ remover** *n*
  Fleckentferner *m*
stair |steəʳ| *n (Treppen)stufe *f*; **~s** *npl (flight
  of steps)* Treppe *f*; **~case** *n* Treppenhaus *nt*,
  Treppe *f*; **~way** *n* Treppenaufgang *m*
stake |steɪk| *n (post)* Pfahl *m*; *(money)* Einsatz
  m ♦ *vt (bet: money)* setzen; **to be at ~** auf
  dem Spiel stehen
stale |steɪl| *adj* alt; *(bread)* altbacken
stalemate |'steɪlmeɪt| *n (CHESS)* Patt *nt*; *(fig)*
  Stillstand *m*
stalk |stɔ:k| *n* Stängel *m*, Stiel *m* ♦ *vt (game)*
  jagen; **~ off** *vi* abstolzieren
stall |stɔ:l| *n (in stable)* Stand *m*, Box *f*; *(in
  market)* (Verkaufs)stand *m* ♦ *vt (AUT)*
  abwürgen ♦ *vi (AUT)* stehen bleiben; *(fig)*

Ausflüchte machen; **~s** *npl (BRIT: THEAT)*
  Parkett *nt*
stallion |'stælɪən| *n* Zuchthengst *m*
stalwart |'stɔ:lwət| *n* treue(r) Anhänger *m*
stamina |'stæmɪnə| *n* Durchhaltevermögen
  nt, Zähigkeit *f*
stammer |'stæməʳ| *n* Stottern *nt* ♦ *vt, vi*
  stottern, stammeln
stamp |stæmp| *n* Briefmarke *f*; *(for
  document)* Stempel *m* ♦ *vi* stampfen ♦ *vt
  (mark)* stempeln; *(mail)* frankieren; *(foot)*
  stampfen mit; **~ album** *n*
  Briefmarkenalbum *nt*; **~ collecting** *n*
  Briefmarkensammeln *nt*
stampede |stæm'pi:d| *n* panische Flucht *f*
stance |stæns| *n* Haltung *f*
stand |stænd| *(pt, pp stood)* *n (for objects)*
  Gestell *nt*; *(seats)* Tribüne *f* ♦ *vi* stehen; *(rise)*
  aufstehen; *(decision)* feststehen ♦ *vt* setzen,
  stellen; *(endure)* aushalten; *(person)*
  ausstehen; *(nonsense)* dulden; **to make a ~**
  Widerstand leisten; **to ~ for parliament**
  (BRIT) für das Parlament kandidieren; **~ by** *vi
  (be ready)* bereitstehen ♦ *vt fus (opinion)* treu
  bleiben +*dat*; **~ down** *vi (withdraw)*
  zurücktreten; **~ for** *vt fus (signify)* stehen für;
  (permit, tolerate) hinnehmen; **~ in for** *vt fus*
  einspringen für; **~ out** *vi (be prominent)*
  hervorstechen; **~ up** *vi (rise)* aufstehen; **~ up
  for** *vt fus* sich einsetzen für; **~ up to** *vt fus*:
  to ~ up to sth einer Sache *dat* gewachsen
  sein; **to ~ up to sb** sich jdm gegenüber
  behaupten
standard |'stændəd| *n (measure)* Norm *f*;
  (flag) Fahne *f* ♦ *adj (size etc)* Normal-; **~s** *npl
  (morals)* Maßstäbe *pl*; **~ize** *vt*
  vereinheitlichen; **~ lamp** *n (BRIT)* Stehlampe
  f; **~ of living** *n* Lebensstandard *m*
stand: ~-by *n* Reserve *f*; **to be on ~-by** in
  Bereitschaft sein; **~-by ticket** *n (AVIAT)*
  Standbyticket *nt*; **~-in** |'stændɪn| *n* Ersatz *m*
standing |'stændɪŋ| *adj (erect)* stehend;
  (permanent) ständig; *(invitation)* offen ♦ *n
  (duration)* Dauer *f*; *(reputation)* Ansehen *nt*;
  of many years' ~ langjährig; **~ order** *(BRIT)*
  n (at bank) Dauerauftrag *m*; **~ room** *n*
  Stehplatz *m*
stand: ~-offish |stænd'ɔfɪʃ| *adj*
  zurückhaltend, sehr reserviert; **~point**
  |'stændpɔɪnt| *n* Standpunkt *m*; **~still**
  |'stændstɪl| *n*: **to be at a ~still** stillstehen; **to
  come to a ~still** zum Stillstand kommen
stank |stæŋk| *pt of* **stink**
staple |'steɪpl| *n (in paper)* Heftklammer *f*;
  (article) Haupterzeugnis *nt* ♦ *adj* Grund-,
  Haupt- ♦ *vt (fest)klammern; **~r** *n*
  Heftmaschine *f*
star |stɑ:ʳ| *n* Stern *m*; *(person)* Star *m* ♦ *vi* die
  Hauptrolle spielen ♦ *vt*: **~ring ...** in der
  Hauptrolle/den Hauptrollen ...
starboard |'stɑ:bɔ:d| *n* Steuerbord *nt*

starch |stɑːtʃ| n Stärke f

stardom ['stɑːdəm] n Berühmtheit f

stare |steəᵣ| n starre(r) Blick m ♦ vi: **to ~ at** starren auf +acc, anstarren

starfish ['stɑːfɪʃ] n Seestern m

stark |stɑːk| adj öde ♦ adv: **~ naked** splitternackt

starling ['stɑːlɪŋ] n Star m

starry ['stɑːrɪ] adj Sternen-; **~-eyed** adj (innocent) blauäugig

start |stɑːt| n Anfang m; (SPORT) Start m; (lead) Vorsprung m ♦ vt in Gang setzen; (car) anlassen ♦ vi anfangen; (car) anspringen; (on journey) aufbrechen; (SPORT) starten; (with fright) zusammenfahren; **to ~ doing** or **to do sth** anfangen, etw zu tun; **~ off** vi anfangen; (begin moving) losgehen; losfahren; **~ up** vi anfangen ♦ vt beginnen; (car) anlassen; (engine) starten; **~er** n (AUT) Anlasser m; (for race) Starter m; (BRIT: COOK) Vorspeise f; **~ing point** n Ausgangspunkt m

startle ['stɑːtl] vt erschrecken; **startling** adj erschreckend

starvation [stɑːˈveɪʃən] n Verhungern nt

starve |stɑːv| vi verhungern ♦ vt verhungern lassen; **I'm starving** ich sterbe vor Hunger

state |steɪt| n (condition) Zustand m; (POL) Staat m ♦ vt erklären; (facts) angeben; **the S~s** (USA) die Staaten; **to be in a ~** durchdrehen; **~ly** adj würdevoll; **~ly home** n herrschaftliches Anwesen nt, Schloss nt; **~ment** n Aussage f; (POL) Erklärung f; **~sman** (irreg) n Staatsmann m

static ['stætɪk] n (also: **~ electricity**) Reibungselektrizität f

station ['steɪʃən] n (RAIL etc) Bahnhof m; (police etc) Wache f; (in society) Stand m ♦ vt stationieren

stationary ['steɪʃnərɪ] adj stillstehend; (car) parkend

stationer ['steɪʃənəᵣ]: **~'s** n (shop) Schreibwarengeschäft nt; **~y** n Schreibwaren pl

station master n Bahnhofsvorsteher m

station wagon n Kombiwagen m

statistics [stəˈtɪstɪks] n Statistik f

statue ['stætjuː] n Statue f

stature ['stætʃəᵣ] n Größe f

status ['steɪtəs] n Status m

statute ['stætjuːt] n Gesetz nt; **statutory** ['stætjutrɪ] adj gesetzlich

staunch [stɔːntʃ] adj standhaft

stay |steɪ| n Aufenthalt m ♦ vi bleiben; (reside) wohnen; **to ~ put** an Ort und Stelle bleiben; **to ~ the night** übernachten; **~ behind** vi zurückbleiben; **~ in** vi (at home) zu Hause bleiben; **~ on** vi (continue) länger bleiben; **~ out** vi (of house) wegbleiben; **~ up** vi (at night) aufbleiben; **~ing power** n Durchhaltevermögen nt

stead [sted] n: **in sb's ~** an jds Stelle dat; **to**

stand sb in good ~ jdm zugute kommen

steadfast ['stedfɑːst] adj standhaft, treu

steadily ['stedɪlɪ] adv stetig, regelmäßig

steady ['stedɪ] adj (firm) fest, stabil; (regular) gleichmäßig; (reliable) beständig; (hand) ruhig; (job, boyfriend) fest ♦ vt festigen; **to ~ o.s. on/against sth** sich stützen auf/gegen etw acc

steak |steɪk| n Steak nt; (fish) Filet nt

steal |stiːl| (pt **stole**, pp **stolen**) vt stehlen ♦ vi stehlen; (go quietly) sich stehlen

stealth [stelθ] n Heimlichkeit f; **~y** adj verstohlen, heimlich

steam |stiːm| n Dampf m ♦ vt (COOK) im Dampfbad erhitzen ♦ vi dampfen; **~ engine** n Dampfmaschine f; **~er** n Dampfer m; **~roller** n Dampfwalze f; **~ship** n = **steamer**; **~y** adj dampfig

steel |stiːl| n Stahl m ♦ adj Stahl-; (fig) stählern; **~works** n Stahlwerke pl

steep |stiːp| adj steil; (price) gepfeffert ♦ vt einweichen

steeple ['stiːpl] n Kirchturm m; **~chase** n Hindernisrennen nt

steer |stɪəᵣ| vt, vi steuern; (car etc) lenken; **~ing** n (AUT) Steuerung f; **~ing wheel** n Steuer- or Lenkrad nt

stem |stem| n Stiel m ♦ vt aufhalten; **~ from** vt fus abstammen von

stench [stentʃ] n Gestank m

stencil ['stensl] n Schablone f ♦ vt (auf)drucken

stenographer [steˈnɔɡrəfəᵣ] (US) n Stenograf(in) m(f)

step |step| n Schritt m; (stair) Stufe f ♦ vi treten, schreiten; **~s** npl (BRIT) = **stepladder**; **to take ~s** Schritte unternehmen; **in/out of ~ (with)** im/nicht im Gleichklang (mit); **~ down** vi (fig) abtreten; **~ off** vt fus aussteigen aus; **~ up** vt steigern

stepbrother ['stepbrʌðəᵣ] n Stiefbruder m

stepdaughter ['stepdɔːtəᵣ] n Stieftochter f

stepfather ['stepfɑːðəᵣ] n Stiefvater m

stepladder ['steplædəᵣ] n Trittleiter f

stepmother ['stepmʌðəᵣ] n Stiefmutter f

stepping stone ['stepɪŋ-] n Stein m; (fig) Sprungbrett n

stepsister ['stepsɪstəᵣ] n Stiefschwester f

stepson ['stepsʌn] n Stiefsohn m

stereo ['steriəu] n Stereoanlage f ♦ adj (also: **~phonic**) stereofonisch, stereophonisch

stereotype ['steriətaip] n (fig) Klischee nt ♦ vt stereotypieren; (fig) stereotyp machen

sterile ['sterail] adj steril; (person) unfruchtbar; **sterilize** vt sterilisieren

sterling ['stɜːlɪŋ] adj (FIN) Sterling-; (character) gediegen ♦ n (ECON) das Pfund Sterling; **a pound ~** ein Pfund Sterling

stern |stɜːn| adj streng ♦ n Heck nt, Achterschiff nt

stew |stjuː| n Eintopf m ♦ vt, vi schmoren

steward ['stjuːəd] n Steward m; **~ess** n

Stewardess f

stick |stɪk| (pt, pp **stuck**) n Stock m; (of chalk etc) Stück nt ♦ vt (stab) stechen; (fix) stecken; (put) stellen; (gum) (an)kleben; (inf: tolerate) vertragen ♦ vi (stop) stecken bleiben; (get stuck) klemmen; (hold fast) kleben, haften; ~ **out** vi (project) hervorstehen; ~ **up** vi (project) in die Höhe stehen; ~ **up for** vt fus (defend) eintreten für; ~**er** n Aufkleber m; ~**ing plaster** n Heftpflaster nt

stickler |ˈstɪklər| n: ~ **(for)** Pedant m (in +acc)

stick-up |ˈstɪkʌp| (inf) n (Raub)überfall m

sticky |ˈstɪkɪ| adj klebrig; (atmosphere) stickig

stiff |stɪf| adj steif; (difficult) hart; (paste) dick; (drink) stark; **to have a ~ neck** einen steifen Hals haben; ~**en** vt versteifen, (ver)stärken ♦ vi sich versteifen

stifle |ˈstaɪfl| vt unterdrücken; **stifling** adj drückend

stigma |ˈstɪgmə| (pl BOT, MED, REL ~**ta**; fig ~**s**) n Stigma nt

stigmata |stɪgˈmɑːtə| npl of **stigma**

stile |staɪl| n Steige f

stiletto |stɪˈletəʊ| (BRIT) n (also: ~ **heel**) Pfennigabsatz m

still |stɪl| adj still ♦ adv (immer) noch; (anyhow) immerhin; ~**born** adj tot geboren; ~ **life** n Stilleben nt

stilt |stɪlt| n Stelze f

stilted |ˈstɪltɪd| adj gestelzt

stimulate |ˈstɪmjʊleɪt| vt anregen, stimulieren

stimuli |ˈstɪmjʊlaɪ| npl of **stimulus**

stimulus |ˈstɪmjʊləs| (pl -**li**) n Anregung f, Reiz m

sting |stɪŋ| (pt, pp **stung**) n Stich m; (organ) Stachel m ♦ vi stechen; (on skin) brennen ♦ vt stechen

stingy |ˈstɪndʒɪ| adj geizig, knauserig

stink |stɪŋk| (pt **stank**, pp **stunk**) n Gestank m ♦ vi stinken; ~**ing** adj (fig) widerlich

stint |stɪnt| n (period) Betätigung f; **to do one's ~** seine Arbeit tun; (share) seinen Teil beitragen

stipulate |ˈstɪpjʊleɪt| vt festsetzen

stir |stɜːr| n Bewegung f; (COOK) Rühren nt; (sensation) Aufsehen nt ♦ vt (um)rühren ♦ vi sich rühren; ~ **up** vt (mob) aufhetzen; (mixture) umrühren; (dust) aufwirbeln

stirrup |ˈstɪrəp| n Steigbügel m

stitch |stɪtʃ| n (with needle) Stich m; (MED) Faden m; (of knitting) Masche f; (pain) Stich m ♦ vt nähen

stoat |stəʊt| n Wiesel nt

stock |stɒk| n Vorrat m; (COMM) (Waren)lager nt; (livestock) Vieh nt; (COOK) Brühe f; (FIN) Grundkapital nt ♦ adj stets vorrätig; (standard) Normal- ♦ vt (in shop) führen; ~**s** npl (FIN) Aktien pl; **in/out of ~** vorrätig/nicht vorrätig; **to take ~ of** Inventur machen von; (fig) Bilanz ziehen aus; ~**s and shares** Effekten pl; ~ **up** vi: **to ~ up (with)** Reserven anlegen (von); ~**broker** |ˈstɒkbrəʊkər| n Börsenmakler m; ~ **cube** n Brühwürfel m; ~ **exchange** n Börse f

stocking |ˈstɒkɪŋ| n Strumpf m

stock: ~ **market** n Börse f; ~ **phrase** n Standardsatz m; ~**pile** n Vorrat m ♦ vt aufstapeln; ~**taking** (BRIT) n (COMM) Inventur f, Bestandsaufnahme f

stocky |ˈstɒkɪ| adj untersetzt

stodgy |ˈstɒdʒɪ| adj pampig

stoke |stəʊk| vt schüren

stole |stəʊl| pt of **steal** ♦ n Stola f

stolen |ˈstəʊln| pp of **steal**

stomach |ˈstʌmək| n Bauch m, Magen m ♦ vt vertragen; ~**-ache** n Magen- or Bauchschmerzen pl

stone |stəʊn| n Stein m; (BRIT: weight) Gewichtseinheit = 6.35 kg ♦ vt (olive) entkernen; (kill) steinigen; ~**-cold** adj eiskalt; ~**-deaf** adj stocktaub; ~**work** n Mauerwerk nt; **stony** |ˈstəʊnɪ| adj steinig

stood |stʊd| pt, pp of **stand**

stool |stuːl| n Hocker m

stoop |stuːp| vi sich bücken

stop |stɒp| n Halt m; (bus ~) Haltestelle f; (punctuation) Punkt m ♦ vt anhalten; (bring to an end) aufhören (mit), sein lassen ♦ vi aufhören; (clock) stehen bleiben; (remain) bleiben; **to ~ doing sth** aufhören, etw zu tun; **to ~ dead** innehalten; ~ **off** vi kurz Halt machen; ~ **up** vt (hole) zustopfen, verstopfen; ~**gap** n Notlösung f; ~**lights** npl (AUT) Bremslichter pl; ~**over** n (on journey) Zwischenaufenthalt m; ~**page** |ˈstɒpɪdʒ| n (An)halten nt; (traffic) Verkehrsstockung f; (strike) Arbeitseinstellung f; ~**per** |ˈstɒpər| n Propfen m, Stöpsel m; ~ **press** n letzte Meldung f; ~**watch** |ˈstɒpwɒtʃ| n Stoppuhr f

storage |ˈstɔːrɪdʒ| n Lagerung f; ~ **heater** n (Nachtstrom)speicherofen m

store |stɔːr| n Vorrat m; (place) Lager nt, Warenhaus nt; (BRIT: large shop) Kaufhaus nt; (US) Laden m ♦ vt lagern; ~**s** npl (supplies) Vorräte pl; ~ **up** vt sich eindecken mit; ~**room** n Lagerraum m, Vorratsraum m

storey |ˈstɔːrɪ| (US **story**) n Stock m

stork |stɔːk| n Storch m

storm |stɔːm| n (also fig) Sturm m ♦ vt, vi stürmen; ~**y** adj stürmisch

story |ˈstɔːrɪ| n Geschichte f; (lie) Märchen nt; (US) = **storey**; ~**book** n Geschichtenbuch nt; ~**teller** n Geschichtenerzähler m

stout |staʊt| adj (bold) tapfer; (fat) beleibt ♦ n Starkbier nt; (also: **sweet ~**) ≈ Malzbier nt

stove |stəuv| n (Koch)herd m; (for heating) Ofen m

stow |stəu| vt verstauen; **~away** n blinde(r) Passagier m

straddle ['strædl] vt (horse, fence) rittlings sitzen auf +dat; (fig) überbrücken

straggle ['strægl] vi (people) nachhinken; **~r** n Nachzügler m; **straggly** adj (hair) zottig

straight |streɪt| adj gerade; (honest) offen, ehrlich; (drink) pur ♦ adv (direct) direkt, geradewegs; **to put** or **get sth ~** etw in Ordnung bringen; **~ away** sofort; **~ off** sofort; **~en** vt (also: **~en out**) gerade machen; (fig) klarstellen; **~-faced** adv ohne die Miene zu verziehen ♦ adj: **to be ~-faced** keine Miene verziehen; **~forward** adj einfach, unkompliziert

strain |streɪn| n Belastung f; (streak, trace) Zug m; (of music) Fetzen m ♦ vt überanstrengen; (stretch) anspannen; (muscle) zerren; (filter) (durch)seihen ♦ vi sich anstrengen; **~ed** adj (laugh) gezwungen; (relations) gespannt; **~er** n Sieb nt

strait |streɪt| n Straße f, Meerenge f; **~jacket** n Zwangsjacke f; **~-laced** adj engherzig, streng

strand [strænd] n (of hair) Strähne f; (also fig) Faden m

stranded ['strændɪd] adj (also fig) gestrandet

strange [streɪndʒ] adj fremd; (unusual) seltsam; **~r** n Fremde(r) mf

strangle ['stræŋgl] vt erwürgen; **~hold** n (fig) Umklammerung f

strap [stræp] n Riemen m; (on clothes) Träger m ♦ vt (fasten) festschnallen

strapping ['stræpɪŋ] adj stramm

strata ['strɑːtə] npl of **stratum**

strategic [strə'tiːdʒɪk] adj strategisch

strategy ['strætɪdʒɪ] n (fig) Strategie f

stratum ['strɑːtəm] (pl **-ta**) n Schicht f

straw |strɔː| n Stroh nt; (single stalk, drinking ~) Strohhalm m; **that's the last ~!** das ist der Gipfel!

strawberry ['strɔːbərɪ] n Erdbeere f

stray |streɪ| adj (animal) verirrt ♦ vi herumstreunen

streak [striːk] n Streifen m; (in character) Einschlag m; (in hair) Strähne f ♦ vt streifen ♦ vi zucken; (move quickly) flitzen; **~ of bad luck** Pechsträhne f; **~y** adj gestreift; (bacon) durchwachsen

stream [striːm] n (brook) Bach m; (fig) Strom m ♦ vt (SCH) in (Leistungs)gruppen einteilen ♦ vi strömen; **to ~ in/out** (people) hinein-/hinausströmen

streamer ['striːməʳ] n (flag) Wimpel m; (of paper) Luftschlange f

streamlined ['striːmlaɪnd] adj stromlinienförmig; (effective) rationell

street |striːt| n Straße f ♦ adj Straßen-; **~car**

(US) n Straßenbahn f; **~ lamp** n Straßenlaterne f; **~ plan** n Stadtplan m; **~wise** (inf) adj: **to be ~wise** wissen, wo es langgeht

strength [streŋθ] n (also fig) Stärke f; Kraft f; **~en** vt (ver)stärken

strenuous ['strenjuəs] adj anstrengend

stress [stres] n Druck m; (mental) Stress m; (GRAM) Betonung f ♦ vt betonen

stretch [stretʃ] n Strecke f ♦ vt ausdehnen, strecken ♦ vi sich erstrecken; (person) sich strecken; **~ out** vi sich ausstrecken ♦ vt ausstrecken

stretcher ['stretʃəʳ] n Tragbahre f

stretchy ['stretʃɪ] adj elastisch, dehnbar

strewn [struːn] adj: **~ with** übersät mit

stricken ['strɪkən] adj (person) ergriffen; (city, country) heimgesucht; **~ with** (disease) leidend unter +dat

strict |strɪkt| adj (exact) genau; (severe) streng; **~ly** adv streng, genau

stridden ['strɪdn] pp of **stride**

stride [straɪd] (pt **strode**, pp **stridden**) n lange(r) Schritt m ♦ vi schreiten

strident ['straɪdnt] adj schneidend, durchdringend

strife [straɪf] n Streit m

strike [straɪk] (pt, pp **struck**) n Streik m; (attack) Schlag m ♦ vt (hit) schlagen; (collide) stoßen gegen; (come to mind) einfallen +dat; (stand out) auffallen +dat; (find) finden ♦ vi (go on strike) streiken; (attack) zuschlagen; (clock) schlagen; **on ~** (workers) im Streik; **to ~ a match** ein Streichholz anzünden; **~ down** vt (lay low) niederschlagen; **~ out** vt (cross out) ausstreichen; **~ up** vt (music) anstimmen; (friendship) schließen; **~r** n Streikende(r) mf;

striking ['straɪkɪŋ] adj auffallend

string [strɪŋ] (pt, pp **strung**) n Schnur f; (row) Reihe f; (MUS) Saite f ♦ vt: **to ~ together** aneinander reihen ♦ vi: **to ~ out** (sich) verteilen; **the ~s** npl (MUS) die Streichinstrumente pl; **to pull ~s** (fig) Fäden ziehen; **~ bean** n grüne Bohne f; **~(ed) instrument** n (MUS) Saiteninstrument nt

stringent ['strɪndʒənt] adj streng

strip [strɪp] n Streifen m ♦ vt (uncover) abstreifen, abziehen; (clothes) ausziehen; (TECH) auseinander nehmen ♦ vi (undress) sich ausziehen; **~ cartoon** n Bildserie f

stripe [straɪp] n Streifen m; **~d** adj gestreift

strip lighting n Neonlicht nt

stripper ['strɪpəʳ] n Stripteasetänzerin f

strip-search ['strɪpsɜːtʃ] n Leibesvisitation f (bei der man sich ausziehen muss) ♦ vt: **to be ~ed** sich ausziehen müssen und durchsucht werden

stripy ['straɪpɪ] adj gestreift

strive [straɪv] (pt **strove**, pp **striven**) vi: **to ~ (for)** streben (nach)

strode [strəʊd] *pt of* stride

stroke [strəʊk] *n* Schlag *m*; (SWIMMING, ROWING) Stoß *m*; (MED) Schlaganfall *m*; (caress) Streicheln *nt* ♦ *vt* streicheln; **at a ~** mit einem Schlag

stroll [strəʊl] *n* Spaziergang *m* ♦ *vi* schlendern; **~er** (US) *n* (pushchair) Sportwagen *m*

strong [strɒŋ] *adj* stark; (firm) fest; **they are 50 ~** sie sind 50 Mann stark; **~box** *n* Kassette *f*; **~hold** *n* Hochburg *f*; **~ly** *adv* stark; **~room** *n* Tresor *m*

strove [strəʊv] *pt of* strive

struck [strʌk] *pt, pp of* strike

structure ['strʌktʃə^r] *n* Struktur *f*, Aufbau *m*; (building) Bau *m*

struggle ['strʌgl] *n* Kampf *m* ♦ *vi* (fight) kämpfen

strum [strʌm] *vt* (guitar) klimpern auf +dat

strung [strʌŋ] *pt, pp of* string

strut [strʌt] *n* Strebe *f*, Stütze *f* ♦ *vi* stolzieren

stub [stʌb] *n* Stummel *m*; (of cigarette) Kippe *f* ♦ *vt*: **to ~ one's toe** sich dat den Zeh anstoßen; **~ out** *vt* ausdrücken

stubble ['stʌbl] *n* Stoppel *f*

stubborn ['stʌbən] *adj* hartnäckig

stuck [stʌk] *pt, pp of* stick ♦ *adj* (jammed) klemmend; **~-up** *adj* hochnäsig

stud [stʌd] *n* (button) Kragenknopf *m*; (place) Gestüt *nt* ♦ *vt* (fig): **~ded with** übersät mit

student ['stjuːdənt] *n* Student(in) *m(f)*; (US) Student(in) *m(f)*, Schüler(in) *m(f)* ♦ *adj* Studenten-; **~ driver** (US) *n* Fahrschüler(in) *m(f)*

studio ['stjuːdɪəʊ] *n* Studio *nt*; (for artist) Atelier *nt*; **~ apartment** (US) *n* Appartement *nt*; **~ flat** *n* Appartement *nt*

studious ['stjuːdɪəs] *adj* lernbegierig

study ['stʌdɪ] *n* Studium *nt*; (investigation) Studium *nt*, Untersuchung *f*; (room) Arbeitszimmer *nt*; (essay etc) Studie *f* ♦ *vt* studieren; (face) erforschen; (evidence) prüfen ♦ *vi* studieren

stuff [stʌf] *n* Stoff *m*; (inf) Zeug *nt* ♦ *vt* stopfen, füllen; (animal) ausstopfen; **~ing** *n* Füllung *f*; **~y** *adj* (room) schwül; (person) spießig

stumble ['stʌmbl] *vi* stolpern; **to ~ across** (fig) zufällig stoßen auf +acc

stumbling block ['stʌmblɪŋ-] *n* Hindernis *nt*

stump [stʌmp] *n* Stumpf *m*

stun [stʌn] *vt* betäuben; (shock) niederschmettern

stung [stʌŋ] *pt, pp of* sting

stunk [stʌŋk] *pp of* stink

stunned *adj* benommen, fassungslos

stunning ['stʌnɪŋ] *adj* betäubend; (news) überwältigend, umwerfend

stunt [stʌnt] *n* Kunststück *nt*, Trick *m*

stunted ['stʌntɪd] *adj* verkümmert

stuntman ['stʌntmæn] (irreg) *n* Stuntman *m*

stupefy ['stjuːpɪfaɪ] *vt* betäuben; (by news) bestürzen

stupendous [stjuː'pɛndəs] *adj* erstaunlich, enorm

stupid ['stjuːpɪd] *adj* dumm; **~ity** [stjuː'pɪdɪtɪ] *n* Dummheit *f*

stupor ['stjuːpə^r] *n* Betäubung *f*

sturdy ['stɜːdɪ] *adj* kräftig, robust

stutter ['stʌtə^r] *n* Stottern *nt* ♦ *vi* stottern

sty [staɪ] *n* Schweinestall *m*

stye [staɪ] *n* Gerstenkorn *nt*

style [staɪl] *n* Stil *m*; (fashion) Mode *f*; **stylish** ['staɪlɪʃ] *adj* modisch; **stylist** ['staɪlɪst] *n* (hair stylist) Friseur *m*, Friseuse *f*

stylus ['staɪləs] *n* (Grammofon)nadel *f*

suave [swɑːv] *adj* zuvorkommend

sub... [sʌb] *prefix* Unter...; **~conscious** *adj* unterbewusst ♦ *n*: **the ~conscious** das Unterbewusste; **~contract** *vt* (vertraglich) untervermitteln; **~divide** *vt* unterteilen; **~dued** *adj* (lighting) gedämpft; (person) still

subject [*n, adj* 'sʌbdʒɪkt, *vb* səb'dʒɛkt] *n* (of kingdom) Untertan *m*; (citizen) Staatsangehörige(r) *mf*; (topic) Thema *nt*; (SCH) Fach *nt*; (GRAM) Subjekt *nt* ♦ *adj*: **to be ~ to** unterworfen sein +dat; (exposed) ausgesetzt sein +dat ♦ *vt* (subdue) unterwerfen; (expose) aussetzen; **~ive** [səb'dʒɛktɪv] *adj* subjektiv; **~ matter** *n* Thema *nt*

sublet [sʌb'lɛt] (irreg: like let) *vt* untervermieten

sublime [sə'blaɪm] *adj* erhaben

submachine gun ['sʌbmə'ʃiːn-] *n* Maschinenpistole *f*

submarine [sʌbmə'riːn] *n* Unterseeboot *nt*, U-Boot *nt*

submerge [səb'mɜːdʒ] *vt* untertauchen; (flood) überschwemmen ♦ *vi* untertauchen

submission [səb'mɪʃən] *n* (obedience) Gehorsam *m*; (claim) Behauptung *f*; (of plan) Unterbreitung *f*; **submissive** [səb'mɪsɪv] *adj* demütig, unterwürfig (pej)

submit [səb'mɪt] *vt* behaupten; (plan) unterbreiten ♦ *vi* sich ergeben

subnormal [sʌb'nɔːml] *adj* minderbegabt

subordinate [sə'bɔːdɪnət] *adj* untergeordnet ♦ *n* Untergebene(r) *mf*

subpoena [səb'piːnə] *n* Vorladung *f* ♦ *vt* vorladen

subscribe [səb'skraɪb] *vi*: **to ~ to** (view etc) unterstützen; (newspaper) abonnieren; **~r** *n* (to periodical) Abonnent *m*; (TEL) Telefonteilnehmer *m*

subscription [səb'skrɪpʃən] *n* Abonnement *nt*; (money subscribed) (Mitglieds)beitrag *m*

subsequent ['sʌbsɪkwənt] *adj* folgend, später; **~ly** *adv* später

subside [səb'saɪd] *vi* sich senken; **subsidence** [səb'saɪdns] *n* Senkung *f*

subsidiarity |səbsɪdɪ'ærɪtɪ| n (POL) Subsidiarität f

subsidiary |səb'sɪdɪərɪ| adj Neben- ♦ n Tochtergesellschaft f

subsidize |'sʌbsɪdaɪz| vt subventionieren

subsidy |'sʌbsɪdɪ| n Subvention f

subsistence |səb'sɪstəns| n Unterhalt m

substance |'sʌbstəns| n Substanz f

substantial |səb'stænʃl| adj (strong) fest, kräftig; (important) wesentlich; **~ly** adv erheblich

substantiate |səb'stænʃɪeɪt| vt begründen, belegen

substitute |'sʌbstɪtjuːt| n Ersatz m ♦ vt ersetzen; **substitution** |sʌbstɪ'tjuːʃən| n Ersetzung f

subterfuge |'sʌbtəfjuːdʒ| n Vorwand m; (trick) Trick m

subterranean |sʌbtə'reɪnɪən| adj unterirdisch

subtitle |'sʌbtaɪtl| n Untertitel m; **~d** adj untertitelt, mit Untertiteln versehen

subtle |'sʌtl| adj fein; **~ty** n Feinheit f

subtotal |'sʌbtəutl| n Zwischensumme f

subtract |səb'trækt| vt abziehen; **~ion** |səb'trækʃən| n Abziehen nt, Subtraktion f

suburb |'sʌbəːb| n Vorort m; **the ~s** die Außenbezirke pl; **~an** |sə'bəːbən| adj Vorort(s)-, Stadtrand-; **~ia** |sə'bəːbɪə| n Vorstadt f

subversive |səb'vəːsɪv| adj subversiv

subway |'sʌbweɪ| n (US) U-Bahn f; (BRIT) Unterführung f

succeed |sək'siːd| vi (person) erfolgreich sein, Erfolg haben; (plan etc also) gelingen ♦ vt (nach)folgen +dat; **he ~ed in doing it** es gelang ihm, es zu tun; **~ing** adj (nach)folgend

success |sək'ses| n Erfolg m; **~ful** adj erfolgreich; **to be ~ful (in doing sth)** Erfolg haben (bei etw); **~fully** adv erfolgreich

succession |sək'seʃən| n (Aufeinander)folge f; (to throne) Nachfolge f

successive |sək'sesɪv| adj aufeinander folgend

successor |sək'sesər| n Nachfolger(in) m(f)

succinct |sək'sɪŋkt| adj knapp

succulent |'sʌkjulənt| adj saftig

succumb |sə'kʌm| vi: **to ~ (to)** erliegen (+dat); (yield) nachgeben (+dat)

such |sʌtʃ| adj solche(r, s); **~ a book** so ein Buch; **~ books** solche Bücher; **~ courage** so ein Mut; **~ a long trip** so eine lange Reise; **~ a lot of** so viel(e); **~ as** wie; **a noise ~ as to** ein derartiger Lärm, dass; **as ~** an sich; **~-and-~ a time** die und die Zeit

suck |sʌk| vt saugen; (lollipop etc) lutschen

sucker |'sʌkər| (inf) n Idiot m

suction |'sʌkʃən| n Saugkraft f

sudden |'sʌdn| adj plötzlich; **all of a ~** auf einmal; **~ly** adv plötzlich

suds |sʌdz| npl Seifenlauge f; (lather) Seifenschaum m

sue |suː| vt verklagen

suede |sweɪd| n Wildleder nt

suet |'suɪt| n Nierenfett nt

Suez |'suːɪz| n: **the ~ Canal** der Suezkanal

suffer |'sʌfər| vt (er)leiden ♦ vi leiden; **~er** n Leidende(r) mf; **~ing** n Leiden nt

suffice |sə'faɪs| vi genügen

sufficient |sə'fɪʃənt| adj ausreichend; **~ly** adv ausreichend

suffix |'sʌfɪks| n Nachsilbe f

suffocate |'sʌfəkeɪt| vt, vi ersticken

suffrage |'sʌfrɪdʒ| n Wahlrecht nt

sugar |'ʃugər| n Zucker m ♦ vt zuckern; **~ beet** n Zuckerrübe f; **~ cane** n Zuckerrohr nt; **~y** adj süß

suggest |sə'dʒest| vt vorschlagen; (show) schließen lassen auf +acc; **~ion** |sə'dʒestʃən| n Vorschlag m; **~ive** adj anregend; (indecent) zweideutig

suicide |'suɪsaɪd| n Selbstmord m; **to commit ~** Selbstmord begehen

suit |suːt| n Anzug m; (CARDS) Farbe f ♦ vt passen +dat; (clothes) stehen +dat; **well ~ed** (well matched) gut zusammenpassend; **~able** adj geeignet, passend; **~ably** adv passend, angemessen

suitcase |'suːtkeɪs| n (Hand)koffer m

suite |swiːt| n (of rooms) Zimmerflucht f; (of furniture) Einrichtung f; (MUS) Suite f

suitor |'suːtər| n (JUR) Kläger(in) m(f)

sulfur |'sʌlfər| (US) n = **sulphur**

sulk |sʌlk| vi schmollen; **~y** adj schmollend

sullen |'sʌlən| adj mürrisch

sulphur |'sʌlfər| (US **sulfur**) n Schwefel m

sultana |sʌl'tɑːnə| n (fruit) Sultanine f

sultry |'sʌltrɪ| adj schwül

sum |sʌm| n Summe f; (money) Betrag m, Summe f; (arithmetic) Rechenaufgabe f; **~ up** vt, vi zusammenfassen

summarize |'sʌməraɪz| vt kurz zusammenfassen

summary |'sʌmərɪ| n Zusammenfassung f ♦ adj (justice) kurzerhand erteilt

summer |'sʌmər| n Sommer m ♦ adj Sommer-; **~house** n (in garden) Gartenhaus nt; **~time** n Sommerzeit f

summit |'sʌmɪt| n Gipfel m; **~ (conference)** n Gipfelkonferenz f

summon |'sʌmən| vt herbeirufen; (JUR) vorladen; (gather up) aufbringen; **~s** (JUR) n Vorladung f ♦ vt vorladen

sump |sʌmp| (BRIT) n (AUT) Ölwanne f

sumptuous |'sʌmptjuəs| adj prächtig

sun |sʌn| n Sonne f; **~bathe** vi sich sonnen; **~block** n Sonnenschutzcreme f; **~burn** n Sonnenbrand m; **~burnt** adj sonnenverbrannt, sonnengebräunt; **to be ~burnt** (painfully) einen Sonnenbrand haben

Sunday |'sʌndɪ| n Sonntag m; **~ school** n

Sonntagsschule f
sundial ['sʌndaɪəl] n Sonnenuhr f
sundown ['sʌndaun] n Sonnenuntergang m
sundries ['sʌndrɪz] npl (miscellaneous items)
Verschiedene(s) nt
sundry ['sʌndrɪ] adj verschieden; **all and ~**
alle
sunflower ['sʌnflauəʳ] n Sonnenblume f
sung [sʌŋ] pp of **sing**
sunglasses ['sʌnglɑːsɪz] npl Sonnenbrille f
sunk [sʌŋk] pp of **sink**
sun: **~light** ['sʌnlaɪt] n Sonnenlicht nt; **~lit**
['sʌnlɪt] adj sonnenbeschienen; **~ny** ['sʌnɪ]
adj sonnig; **~rise** n Sonnenaufgang m; **~**
roof n (AUT) Schiebedach nt; **~screen**
['sʌnskriːn] n Sonnenschutzcreme f; **~set**
['sʌnset] n Sonnenuntergang m; **~shade**
['sʌnʃeɪd] n Sonnenschirm m; **~shine**
['sʌnʃaɪn] n Sonnenschein m; **~stroke**
['sʌnstrəuk] n Hitzschlag m; **~tan** ['sʌntæn]
n (Sonnen)bräune f; **~tan oil** n Sonnenöl m
super ['suːpəʳ] (inf) adj prima, klasse
superannuation [suːpərænjuˈeɪʃən] n
Pension f
superb [suːˈpɜːb] adj ausgezeichnet,
hervorragend
supercilious [suːpəˈsɪlɪəs] adj herablassend
superficial [suːpəˈfɪʃəl] adj oberflächlich
superfluous [suˈpɜːfluəs] adj überflüssig
superhuman [suːpəˈhjuːmən] adj (effort)
übermenschlich
superimpose ['suːpərɪmˈpəuz] vt
übereinander legen
superintendent [suːpərɪnˈtendənt] n
Polizeichef m
superior [suˈpɪərɪəʳ] adj überlegen; (better)
besser ♦ n Vorgesetzte(r) mf; **~ity**
[supɪərɪˈɒrɪtɪ] n Überlegenheit f
superlative [suˈpɜːlətɪv] adj überragend
super: **~man** ['suːpəmæn] (irreg) n
Übermensch m; **~market** ['suːpəmɑːkɪt] n
Supermarkt m; **~natural** [suːpəˈnætʃərəl] adj
übernatürlich; **~power** ['suːpəpauəʳ] n
Weltmacht f
supersede [suːpəˈsiːd] vt ersetzen
supersonic ['suːpəˈsɒnɪk] adj Überschall-
superstition [suːpəˈstɪʃən] n Aberglaube m;
superstitious [suːpəˈstɪʃəs] adj
abergläubisch
supervise ['suːpəvaɪz] vt beaufsichtigen,
kontrollieren; **supervision** [suːpəˈvɪʒən] n
Aufsicht f; **supervisor** ['suːpəvaɪzəʳ] n
Aufsichtsperson f; **supervisory**
['suːpəvaɪzərɪ] adj Aufsichts-
supper ['sʌpəʳ] n Abendessen nt
supplant [səˈplɑːnt] vt (person, thing)
ersetzen
supple ['sʌpl] adj geschmeidig
supplement [n 'sʌplɪmənt, vb sʌplɪˈment] n
Ergänzung f; (in book) Nachtrag m ♦ vt
ergänzen; **~ary** [sʌplɪˈmentərɪ] adj

ergänzend; **~ary benefit** (BRIT: old) n ≈
Sozialhilfe f
supplier [səˈplaɪəʳ] n Lieferant m
supplies [səˈplaɪz] npl (food) Vorräte pl; (MIL)
Nachschub m
supply [səˈplaɪ] vt liefern ♦ n Vorrat m;
(supplying) Lieferung f; see also **supplies**; **~**
teacher (BRIT) n Aushilfslehrer(in) m(f)
support [səˈpɔːt] n Unterstützung f; (TECH)
Stütze f ♦ vt (hold up) stützen, tragen;
(provide for) ernähren; (be in favour of)
unterstützen; **~er** n Anhänger(in) m(f)
suppose [səˈpəuz] vt, vi annehmen; **to be ~d**
to do sth etw tun sollen; **~dly** [səˈpəuzɪdlɪ]
adv angeblich; **supposing** conj
angenommen; **supposition** [sʌpəˈzɪʃən] n
Voraussetzung f
suppress [səˈpres] vt unterdrücken
supremacy [suˈpreməsɪ] n Vorherrschaft f,
Oberhoheit f
supreme [suˈpriːm] adj oberste(r, s),
höchste(r, s)
surcharge ['sɜːtʃɑːdʒ] n Zuschlag m
sure [ʃuəʳ] adj sicher, gewiss; **~!** (of course)
klar!; **to make ~ of sth/that** sich einer
Sache gen vergewissern/vergewissern, dass;
~ enough (with past) tatsächlich; (with
future) ganz bestimmt; **~-footed** adj sicher
(auf den Füßen); **~ly** adv (certainly)
sicherlich, gewiss; **~ly it's wrong** das ist
doch wohl falsch
surety ['ʃuərətɪ] n Sicherheit f
surf [sɜːf] n Brandung f
surface ['sɜːfɪs] n Oberfläche f ♦ vt (roadway)
teeren ♦ vi auftauchen; **~ mail** n
gewöhnliche Post f
surfboard ['sɜːfbɔːd] n Surfbrett nt
surfeit ['sɜːfɪt] n Übermaß nt
surfing ['sɜːfɪŋ] n Surfen nt
surge [sɜːdʒ] n Woge f ♦ vi wogen
surgeon ['sɜːdʒən] n Chirurg(in) m(f)
surgery ['sɜːdʒərɪ] n (BRIT: place) Praxis f;
(: time) Sprechstunde f; (treatment)
Operation f; **to undergo ~** operiert werden;
~ hours (BRIT) npl Sprechstunden pl
surgical ['sɜːdʒɪkl] adj chirurgisch; **~ spirit**
(BRIT) n Wundbenzin nt
surly ['sɜːlɪ] adj verdrießlich, grob
surmount [sɜːˈmaunt] vt überwinden
surname ['sɜːneɪm] n Zuname m
surpass [sɜːˈpɑːs] vt übertreffen
surplus ['sɜːpləs] n Überschuss m ♦ adj
überschüssig, Über(schuss)-
surprise [səˈpraɪz] n Überraschung f ♦ vt
überraschen; **~d** adj überrascht; **surprising**
adj überraschend; **surprisingly** adv
überraschend(erweise)
surrender [səˈrendəʳ] n Kapitulation f ♦ vi
sich ergeben
surreptitious [sʌrəpˈtɪʃəs] adj heimlich; (look
also) verstohlen

surrogate |'sʌrəgɪt| n Ersatz m; ~ **mother** n Leihmutter f

surround |sə'raund| vt umgeben; ~**ing** adj (countryside) umliegend; ~**ings** npl Umgebung f; (environment) Umwelt f

surveillance |sə:'veɪləns| n Überwachung f

survey |n 'sɜ:veɪ, vb sə:'veɪ| n Übersicht f ♦ vt überblicken; (land) vermessen; ~**or** |sə'veɪə^r| n Land(ver)messer(in) m(f)

survival |sə'vaɪvl| n Überleben nt

survive |sə'vaɪv| vt, vi überleben; **survivor** |sə'vaɪvə^r| n Überlebende(r) mf

susceptible |sə'septəbl| adj: ~ (**to**) empfindlich (gegen); (charms etc) empfänglich (für)

suspect |n, adj 'sʌspekt, vb səs'pekt| n Verdächtige(r) mf ♦ adj verdächtig ♦ vt verdächtigen; (think) vermuten

suspend |səs'pend| vt verschieben; (from work) suspendieren; (hang up) aufhängen; (SPORT) sperren; ~**ed sentence** n (JUR) zur Bewährung ausgesetzte Strafe; ~**er belt** n Strumpf(halter)gürtel m; ~**ers** npl (BRIT) Strumpfhalter m; (US) Hosenträger m

suspense |səs'pens| n Spannung f

suspension |səs'penʃən| n (from work) Suspendierung f; (SPORT) Sperrung f; (AUT) Federung f; ~ **bridge** n Hängebrücke f

suspicion |səs'pɪʃən| n Misstrauen nt; Verdacht m; **suspicious** |səs'pɪʃəs| adj misstrauisch; (causing ~) verdächtig

sustain |səs'teɪn| vt (maintain) aufrechterhalten; (confirm) bestätigen; (injury) davontragen; ~**able** adj (development, growth etc) aufrechtzuerhalten; ~**ed** adj (effort) anhaltend

sustenance |'sʌstɪnəns| n Nahrung f

swab |swɒb| n (MED) Tupfer m

swagger |'swægə^r| vi stolzieren

swallow |'swɒləu| n (bird) Schwalbe f; (of food etc) Schluck m ♦ vt (ver)schlucken; ~ **up** vt verschlingen

swam |swæm| pt of swim

swamp |swɒmp| n Sumpf m ♦ vt überschwemmen

swan |swɒn| n Schwan m

swap |swɒp| n Tausch m ♦ vt: **to ~ sth (for sth)** etw (gegen etw) tauschen or eintauschen

swarm |swɔ:m| n Schwarm m ♦ vi: **to ~ or be ~ing with** wimmeln von

swarthy |'swɔ:ðɪ| adj dunkel, braun

swastika |'swɒstɪkə| n Hakenkreuz nt

swat |swɒt| vt totschlagen

sway |sweɪ| vi schwanken; (branches) schaukeln, sich wiegen ♦ vt schwenken; (influence) beeinflussen

swear |sweə^r| (pt swore, pp sworn) vi (promise) schwören; (curse) fluchen; **to ~ to sth** schwören auf etw acc; ~**word** n

Fluch m

sweat |swet| n Schweiß m ♦ vi schwitzen

sweater |'swetə^r| n Pullover m

sweatshirt |'swetʃə:t| n Sweatshirt nt

sweaty |'swetɪ| adj verschwitzt

Swede |swi:d| n Schwede m, Schwedin f

swede |swi:d| (BRIT) n Steckrübe f

Sweden |'swi:dn| n Schweden nt

Swedish |'swi:dɪʃ| adj schwedisch ♦ n (LING) Schwedisch nt

sweep |swi:p| (pt, pp swept) n (chimney ~) Schornsteinfeger m ♦ vt fegen, kehren; ~ **away** vt wegfegen; ~ **past** vi vorbeisausen; ~ **up** vt zusammenkehren; ~**ing** adj (gesture) schwungvoll; (statement) verallgemeinernd

sweet |swi:t| n (course) Nachtisch m; (candy) Bonbon m ♦ adj süß; ~**corn** n Zuckermais m; ~**en** vt süßen; (fig) versüßen; ~**heart** n Liebste(r) mf; ~**ness** n Süße f; ~ **pea** n Gartenwicke f

swell |swel| (pt swelled, pp swollen or swelled) n Seegang m ♦ adj (inf) todschick ♦ vt (numbers) vermehren ♦ vi (also: ~ up) (an)schwellen; ~**ing** n Schwellung f

sweltering |'sweltərɪŋ| adj drückend

swept |swept| pt, pp of sweep

swerve |swɜ:v| vt, vi ausscheren

swift |swɪft| n Mauersegler m ♦ adj geschwind, schnell, rasch; ~**ly** adv geschwind, schnell, rasch

swig |swɪg| n Zug m

swill |swɪl| n (for pigs) Schweinefutter nt ♦ vt spülen

swim |swɪm| (pt swam, pp swum) n: **to go for a ~** schwimmen gehen ♦ vi schwimmen ♦ vt (cross) (durch)schwimmen; ~**mer** n Schwimmer(in) m(f); ~**ming** n Schwimmen nt; ~**ming cap** n Badehaube f, Badekappe f; ~**ming costume** (BRIT) n Badeanzug m; ~**ming pool** n Schwimmbecken nt; (private) Swimmingpool m; ~**ming trunks** npl Badehose f; ~**suit** n Badeanzug m

swindle |'swɪndl| n Schwindel m, Betrug m ♦ vt betrügen

swine |swaɪn| n (also fig) Schwein nt

swing |swɪŋ| (pt, pp swung) n (child's) Schaukel f; (movement) Schwung m ♦ vt schwingen ♦ vi schwingen, schaukeln; (turn quickly) schwenken; **in full ~** in vollem Gange; ~ **bridge** n Drehbrücke f; ~ **door** (BRIT) n Schwingtür f

swingeing |'swɪndʒɪŋ| (BRIT) adj hart; (taxation, cuts) extrem

swinging door |'swɪŋɪŋ-| (US) n Schwingtür f

swipe |swaɪp| n Hieb m ♦ vt (inf: hit) hart schlagen; (: steal) klauen

swirl |swɜ:l| vi wirbeln

swish |swɪʃ| adj (inf: smart) schick ♦ vi zischen; (grass, skirts) rascheln

Swiss [swɪs] *adj* Schweizer, schweizerisch ♦ *n* Schweizer(in) *m(f)*; **the ~** *npl* (*people*) die Schweizer *pl*

switch [swɪtʃ] *n* (*ELEC*) Schalter *m*; (*change*) Wechsel *m* ♦ *vt* (*ELEC*) schalten; (*change*) wechseln ♦ *vi* wechseln; **~ off** *vt* ab- or ausschalten; **~ on** *vt* an- or einschalten; **~board** *n* Zentrale *f*; (*board*) Schaltbrett *nt*

Switzerland ['swɪtsələnd] *n* die Schweiz

swivel ['swɪvl] *vt* (*also:* **~ round**) drehen ♦ *vi* (*also:* **~ round**) sich drehen

swollen ['swəulən] *pp of* **swell**

swoon [swuːn] *vi* (*old*) in Ohnmacht fallen

swoop [swuːp] *n* Sturzflug *m*; (*esp by police*) Razzia *f* ♦ *vi* (*also:* **~ down**) stürzen

swop [swɔp] = **swap**

sword [sɔːd] *n* Schwert *nt*; **~fish** *n* Schwertfisch *m*

swore [swɔːʳ] *pt of* **swear**

sworn [swɔːn] *pp of* **swear**

swot [swɔt] *vt*, *vi* pauken

swum [swʌm] *pp of* **swim**

swung [swʌŋ] *pt*, *pp of* **swing**

sycamore ['sɪkəmɔːʳ] *n* (*US*) Platane *f*; (*BRIT*) Bergahorn *m*

syllable ['sɪləbl] *n* Silbe *f*

syllabus ['sɪləbəs] *n* Lehrplan *m*

symbol ['sɪmbl] *n* Symbol *nt*; **~ic(al)** [sɪm'bɔlɪk(l)] *adj* symbolisch

symmetry ['sɪmɪtrɪ] *n* Symmetrie *f*

sympathetic [sɪmpə'θetɪk] *adj* mitfühlend

sympathize ['sɪmpəθaɪz] *vi* mitfühlen; **~r** *n* (*POL*) Sympathisant(in) *m(f)*

sympathy ['sɪmpəθɪ] *n* Mitleid *nt*, Mitgefühl *nt*; (*condolence*) Beileid *nt*; **with our deepest ~** mit tief empfundenem Beileid

symphony ['sɪmfənɪ] *n* Sinfonie *f*

symptom ['sɪmptəm] *n* Symptom *nt*; **~atic** [sɪmptə'mætɪk] *adj* (*fig*): **~atic of** bezeichnend für

synagogue ['sɪnəgɔg] *n* Synagoge *f*

synchronize ['sɪŋkrənaɪz] *vt* synchronisieren

syndicate ['sɪndɪkɪt] *n* Konsortium *nt*

synonym ['sɪnənɪm] *n* Synonym *nt*; **synonymous** [sɪ'nɔnɪməs] *adj* gleichbedeutend

synopsis [sɪ'nɔpsɪs] *n* Zusammenfassung *f*

synthetic [sɪn'θetɪk] *adj* synthetisch; **~s** *npl* (*man-made fabrics*) Synthetik *f*

syphon ['saɪfən] = **siphon**

Syria ['sɪrɪə] *n* Syrien *nt*

syringe [sɪ'rɪndʒ] *n* Spritze *f*

syrup ['sɪrəp] *n* Sirup *m*; (*of sugar*) Melasse *f*

system ['sɪstəm] *n* System *nt*; **~atic** [sɪstə'mætɪk] *adj* systematisch; **~ disk** *n* (*COMPUT*) Systemdiskette *f*; **~s analyst** *n* Systemanalytiker(in) *m(f)*

T, t

ta [tɑː] (*BRIT: inf*) *excl* danke!

tab [tæb] *n* Aufhänger *m*; (*name* ~) Schild *nt*; **to keep ~s on** (*fig*) genau im Auge behalten

tabby ['tæbɪ] *n* (*also:* **~ cat**) getigerte Katze *f*

table ['teɪbl] *n* Tisch *m*; (*list*) Tabelle *f* ♦ *vt* (*PARL: propose*) vorlegen, einbringen; **to lay** or **set the ~** den Tisch decken; **~cloth** *n* Tischtuch *nt*; **~ d'hôte** [tɑːbl'dəut] *n* Tagesmenü *nt*; **~ lamp** *n* Tischlampe *f*; **~mat** *n* Untersatz *m*; **~ of contents** *n* Inhaltsverzeichnis *nt*; **~spoon** *n* Esslöffel *m*; **~spoonful** *n* Esslöffel *m* (voll)

tablet ['tæblɪt] *n* (*MED*) Tablette *f*

table tennis *n* Tischtennis *nt*

table wine *n* Tafelwein *m*

tabloid ['tæblɔɪd] *n* Zeitung *f* in kleinem Format; (*pej*) Boulevardzeitung *f*

tabulate ['tæbjuleɪt] *vt* tabellarisch ordnen

tacit ['tæsɪt] *adj* stillschweigend

taciturn ['tæsɪtəːn] *adj* wortkarg

tack [tæk] *n* (*small nail*) Stift *m*; (*US: thumbtack*) Reißzwecke *f*; (*stitch*) Heftstich *m*; (*NAUT*) Lavieren *nt*; (*course*) Kurs *m* ♦ *vt* (*nail*) nageln; (*stitch*) heften ♦ *vi* aufkreuzen

tackle ['tækl] *n* (*for lifting*) Flaschenzug *m*; (*NAUT*) Takelage *f*; (*SPORT*) Tackling *nt* ♦ *vt* (*deal with*) anpacken, in Angriff nehmen; (*person*) festhalten; (*player*) angehen

tacky ['tækɪ] *adj* klebrig

tact [tækt] *n* Takt *m*; **~ful** *adj* taktvoll

tactical ['tæktɪkl] *adj* taktisch

tactics ['tæktɪks] *npl* Taktik *f*

tactless ['tæktlɪs] *adj* taktlos

tadpole ['tædpəul] *n* Kaulquappe *f*

taffy ['tæfɪ] (*US*) *n* Sahnebonbon *nt*

tag [tæg] *n* (*label*) Schild *nt*, Anhänger *m*; (*maker's name*) Etikett *nt*; **~ along** *vi* mitkommen

tail [teɪl] *n* Schwanz *m*; (*of list*) Schluss *m* ♦ *vt* folgen +*dat*; **~ away** or **off** *vi* abfallen, schwinden; **~back** (*BRIT*) *n* (*AUT*) (Rück)stau *m*; **~ coat** *n* Frack *m*; **~ end** *n* Schluss *m*, Ende *nt*; **~gate** *n* (*AUT*) Heckklappe *f*

tailor ['teɪləʳ] *n* Schneider *m*; **~ing** *n* Schneidern *nt*; **~-made** *adj* maßgeschneidert; (*fig*): **~-made for sb** jdm wie auf den Leib geschnitten

tailwind ['teɪlwɪnd] *n* Rückenwind *m*

tainted ['teɪntɪd] *adj* verdorben

take [teɪk] (*pt* **took**, *pp* **taken**) *vt* nehmen; (*trip, exam, PHOT*) machen; (*capture: person*) fassen; (*: town; also COMM, FIN*) nehmen; (*carry to a place*) bringen; (*get for o.s.*) sich *dat* nehmen; (*gain, obtain*) bekommen; (*put up with*) hinnehmen; (*respond to*) aufnehmen; (*interpret*) auffassen; (*assume*) annehmen; (*contain*) Platz haben für;

(GRAM) stehen mit; **to ~ sth from sb** jdm etw wegnehmen; **to ~ sth from sth** *(MATH: subtract)* etw von etw abziehen; *(extract, quotation)* etw einer Sache *dat* entnehmen; **~ after** *vt fus* ähnlich sein +*dat*; **~ apart** *vt* auseinander nehmen; **~ away** *vt (remove)* wegnehmen; *(carry off)* wegbringen; **~ ˈ back** *vt (return)* zurückbringen; *(retract)* zurücknehmen; **~ down** *vt (pull down)* abreißen; *(write down)* aufschreiben; **~ in** *vt (deceive)* hereinlegen; *(understand)* begreifen; *(include)* einschließen; **~ off** *vi (plane)* starten ♦ *vt (remove)* wegnehmen; *(clothing)* ausziehen; *(imitate)* nachmachen; **~ on** *vt (undertake)* übernehmen; *(engage)* einstellen; *(opponent)* antreten gegen; **~ out** *vt (girl, dog)* ausführen; *(extract)* herausnehmen; *(insurance)* abschließen; *(licence)* sich *dat* geben lassen; *(book)* ausleihen; *(remove)* entfernen; **to ~ sth out of sth** *(drawer, packet etc)* etw aus etw herausnehmen; **~ over** *vt* übernehmen ♦ *vi:* **to ~ over from sb** jdn ablösen; **~ to** *vt fus (like)* mögen; *(adopt as practice)* sich *dat* angewöhnen; **~ up** *vt (raise)* aufnehmen; *(dress etc)* kürzer machen; *(occupy)* in Anspruch nehmen; *(engage in)* sich befassen mit; **~away** *adj* zum Mitnehmen; **~home pay** *n* Nettolohn *m*; **~n** *pp of* take; **~off** *n (AVIAT)* Start *m*; *(imitation)* Nachahmung *f*; **~out** *(US) adj* = takeaway; **~over** *n (COMM)* Übernahme *f*; **takings** |'teɪkɪŋz| *npl (COMM)* Einnahmen *pl*

talc |tælk| *n (also:* ~**um powder**) Talkumpuder *m*

tale |teɪl| *n* Geschichte *f*, Erzählung *f*; **to tell ~s** *(fig: lie)* Geschichten erfinden

talent |'tælnt| *n* Talent *nt*; **~ed** *adj* begabt

talk |tɔːk| *n (conversation)* Gespräch *nt*; *(rumour)* Gerede *nt*; *(speech)* Vortrag *m* ♦ *vi* sprechen, reden; **~s** *npl (POL etc)* Gespräche *pl*; **to ~ about** sprechen von +*dat or* über +*acc*; **to ~ sb into doing sth** jdn überreden, etw zu tun; **to ~ sb out of doing sth** jdm ausreden, etw zu tun; **to ~ shop** fachsimpeln; **~ over** *vt* besprechen; **~ative** *adj* gesprächig

tall |tɔːl| *adj* groß; *(building)* hoch; **to be 1 m 80 ~** 1,80 m groß sein; **~boy** *(BRIT) n* Kommode *f*; **~ story** *n* übertriebene Geschichte *f*

tally |'tælɪ| *n* Abrechnung *f* ♦ *vi* übereinstimmen

talon |'tælən| *n* Kralle *f*

tame |teɪm| *adj* zahm; *(fig)* fade

tamper |'tæmpəʳ| *vi:* **to ~ with** herumpfuschen an +*dat*

tampon |'tæmpɔn| *n* Tampon *m*

tan |tæn| *n (Sonnen)*bräune *f*; *(colour)* Gelbbraun *nt* ♦ *adj (colour)* (gelb)braun ♦ *vt* bräunen ♦ *vi* braun werden

tang |tæŋ| *n* Schärfe *f*

tangent |'tændʒənt| *n* Tangente *f*; **to go off at a ~** *(fig)* vom Thema abkommen

tangerine |tændʒə'riːn| *n* Mandarine *f*

tangible |'tændʒəbl| *adj* greifbar

tangle |'tæŋgl| *n* Durcheinander *nt*; *(trouble)* Schwierigkeiten *pl*; **to get in(to) a ~** sich verheddern

tank |tæŋk| *n (container)* Tank *m*, Behälter *m*; *(MIL)* Panzer *m*; **~er** |'tæŋkəʳ| *n (ship)* Tanker *m*; *(vehicle)* Tankwagen *m*

tanned |tænd| *adj* gebräunt

tantalizing |'tæntəlaɪzɪŋ| *adj* verlockend; *(annoying)* quälend

tantamount |'tæntəmaunt| *adj:* **~ to** gleichbedeutend mit

tantrum |'tæntrəm| *n* Wutanfall *m*

tap |tæp| *n* Hahn *m*; *(gentle blow)* Klopfen *nt* ♦ *vt (strike)* klopfen; *(supply)* anzapfen; *(telephone)* abhören; **on ~** *(fig: resources)* zur Hand; **~-dancing** *n* Steppen *nt*

tape |teɪp| *n* Band *nt*; *(magnetic)* (Ton)band *nt*; *(adhesive)* Klebstreifen *m* ♦ *vt (record)* aufnehmen; **~ deck** *n* Tapedeck *nt*; **~ measure** *n* Maßband *nt*

taper |'teɪpəʳ| *vi* spitz zulaufen

tape recorder *n* Tonbandgerät *nt*

tapestry |'tæpɪstrɪ| *n* Wandteppich *m*

tar |tɑːʳ| *n* Teer *m*

target |'tɑːgɪt| *n* Ziel *nt*; *(board)* Zielscheibe *f*

tariff |'tærɪf| *n (duty paid)* Zoll *m*; *(list)* Tarif *m*

tarmac |'tɑːmæk| *n (AVIAT)* Rollfeld *nt*

tarnish |'tɑːnɪʃ| *vt* matt machen; *(fig)* beflecken

tarpaulin |tɑːˈpɔːlɪn| *n* Plane *f*

tarragon |'tærəgən| *n* Estragon *m*

tart |tɑːt| *n* (Obst)torte *f*; *(inf)* Nutte *f* ♦ *adj* scharf; **~ up** *(inf) vt* aufmachen; *(person)* auftakeln

tartan |'tɑːtn| *n* Schottenkaro *nt* ♦ *adj* mit Schottenkaro

tartar |'tɑːtəʳ| *n* Zahnstein *m*

tartar(e) sauce |'tɑːtə-| *n* Remouladensoße *f*

task |tɑːsk| *n* Aufgabe *f*; **to take sb to ~** sich *dat* jdn vornehmen; **~ force** *n* Sondertrupp *m*

tassel |'tæsl| *n* Quaste *f*

taste |teɪst| *n* Geschmack *m*; *(sense)* Geschmackssinn *m*; *(small quantity)* Kostprobe *f*; *(liking)* Vorliebe *f* ♦ *vt* schmecken; *(try)* probieren ♦ *vi* schmecken; **can I have a ~ of this wine?** kann ich diesen Wein probieren?; **to have a ~ for sth** etw mögen; **in good/bad ~** geschmackvoll/geschmacklos; **you can ~ the garlic (in it)** man kann den Knoblauch herausschmecken; **to ~ of sth** nach einer Sache schmecken; **~ful** *adj* geschmackvoll; **~less** *adj (insipid)* fade; *(in bad ~)* geschmacklos; **tasty** |'teɪstɪ| *adj* schmackhaft

tattered |'tætəd| *adj* = in tatters

tatters ['tætəz] *npl:* **in ~** in Fetzen
tattoo [tə'tu:] *n* (MIL) Zapfenstreich *m*; (*on skin*) Tätowierung *f* ♦ *vt* tätowieren
tatty ['tætɪ] (BRIT: inf) *adj* schäbig
taught [tɔ:t] *pt, pp of* teach
taunt [tɔ:nt] *n* höhnische Bemerkung *f* ♦ *vt* verhöhnen
Taurus ['tɔ:rəs] *n* Stier *m*
taut [tɔ:t] *adj* straff
tawdry ['tɔ:drɪ] *adj* (bunt und) billig
tax [tæks] *n* Steuer *f* ♦ *vt* besteuern; (*strain*) strapazieren; (*strength*) angreifen; **~able** *adj* (*income*) steuerpflichtig; **~ation** [tæk'seɪʃən] *n* Besteuerung *f*; **~ avoidance** *n* Steuerumgehung *f*; **~ disc** (BRIT) *n* (AUT) Kraftfahrzeugsteuerplakette *f*; **~ evasion** *n* Steuerhinterziehung *f*; **~-free** *adj* steuerfrei
taxi ['tæksɪ] *n* Taxi *nt* ♦ *vi* (*plane*) rollen; **~ driver** *n* Taxifahrer *m*; **~ rank** (BRIT) *n* Taxistand *m*; **~ stand** *n* Taxistand *m*
tax: ~payer *n* Steuerzahler *m*; **~ relief** *n* Steuerermäßigung *f*; **~ return** *n* Steuererklärung *f*
TB *n abbr* (= tuberculosis) Tb *f*, Tbc *f*
tea [ti:] *n* Tee *m*; (*meal*) (frühes) Abendessen *nt*; **high ~** (BRIT) Abendessen *nt*; **~ bag** *n* Teebeutel *m*; **~ break** (BRIT) *n* Teepause *f*
teach [ti:tʃ] (*pt, pp* taught) *vt* lehren; (SCH) lehren, unterrichten; (*show*): **to ~ sb sth** jdm etw beibringen ♦ *vi* lehren, unterrichten; **~er** *n* Lehrer(in) *m(f)*; **~er's pet** *n* Lehrers Liebling *m*; **~ing** *n* (~er's work) Unterricht *m*; (*doctrine*) Lehre *f*
tea: ~ cloth *n* Geschirrtuch *nt*; **~ cosy** *n* Teewärmer *m*; **~cup** *n* Teetasse *f*; **~ leaves** *npl* Teeblätter *pl*
team [ti:m] *n* (*workers*) Team *nt*; (SPORT) Mannschaft *f*; (*animals*) Gespann *nt*; **~work** *n* Gemeinschaftsarbeit *f*, Teamarbeit *f*
teapot ['ti:pɔt] *n* Teekanne *f*
tear[1] [tɛə*] (*pt* tore, *pp* torn) *n* Riss *m* ♦ *vt* zerreißen; (*muscle*) zerren ♦ *vi* (zer)reißen; (*rush*) rasen; **~ along** *vi* (*rush*) entlangrasen; **~ up** *vt* (*sheet of paper etc*) zerreißen
tear[2] [tɪə*] *n* Träne *f*; **~ful** ['tɪəful] *adj* weinend; (*voice*) weinerlich; **~ gas** ['tɪəgæs] *n* Tränengas *nt*
tearoom ['ti:ru:m] *n* Teestube *f*
tease [ti:z] *n* Hänsler *m* ♦ *vt* necken
tea set *n* Teeservice *nt*
teaspoon ['ti:spu:n] *n* Teelöffel *m*
teat [ti:t] *n* Brustwarze *f*; (*of animal*) Zitze *f*; (*of bottle*) Sauger *m*
tea time *n* (*in the afternoon*) Teestunde *f*; (*mealtime*) Abendessen *nt*
tea towel *n* Geschirrtuch *nt*
technical ['teknɪkl] *adj* technisch; (*knowledge, terms*) Fach--; **~ity** [teknɪ'kælɪtɪ] *n* technische Einzelheit *f*; (JUR) Formsache *f*; **~ly** *adv* technisch; (*speak*) spezialisiert; (*fig*)

genau genommen
technician [tek'nɪʃən] *n* Techniker *m*
technique [tek'ni:k] *n* Technik *f*
techno ['teknəu] *n* Techno *m*
technological [teknə'lɔdʒɪkl] *adj* technologisch
technology [tek'nɔlədʒɪ] *n* Technologie *f*
teddy (bear) ['tedɪ-] *n* Teddybär *m*
tedious ['ti:dɪəs] *adj* langweilig, ermüdend
tee [ti:] *n* (GOLF: *object*) Tee *m*
teem [ti:m] *vi* (*swarm*): **to ~ (with)** wimmeln (von); **it is ~ing (with rain)** es gießt in Strömen
teenage ['ti:neɪdʒ] *adj* (*fashions etc*) Teenager-, jugendlich; **~r** *n* Teenager *m*, Jugendliche(r) *mf*
teens [ti:nz] *npl* Teenageralter *nt*
tee-shirt ['ti:fə:t] *n* T-Shirt *nt*
teeter ['ti:tə*] *vi* schwanken
teeth [ti:θ] *npl of* tooth
teethe [ti:ð] *vi* zahnen; **teething ring** *n* Beißring *m*; **teething troubles** *npl* (*fig*) Kinderkrankheiten *pl*
teetotal [ti:'təutl] *adj* abstinent
tele: ~communications *npl* Fernmeldewesen *nt*; **~conferencing** *n* Telefon- or Videokonferenz; **~gram** *n* Telegramm *nt*; **~graph** *n* Telegraf *m*; **~graph pole** *n* Telegrafenmast *m*
telephone ['telɪfəun] *n* Telefon *nt*, Fernsprecher *m* ♦ *vt* anrufen; (*message*) telefonisch mitteilen; **to be on the ~** (*talking*) telefonieren; (*possessing phone*) Telefon haben; **~ booth** *n* Telefonzelle *f*; **~ box** (BRIT) *n* Telefonzelle *f*; **~ call** *n* Telefongespräch *nt*, Anruf *m*; **~ directory** *n* Telefonbuch *nt*; **~ number** *n* Telefonnummer *f*; **telephonist** [tə'lefənɪst] (BRIT) *n* Telefonist(in) *m(f)*
telephoto lens ['telɪ'fəutəu-] *n* Teleobjektiv *nt*
telesales ['telɪseɪlz] *n* Telefonverkauf *m*
telescope ['telɪskəup] *n* Teleskop *nt*, Fernrohr *nt* ♦ *vt* ineinander schieben
televise ['telɪvaɪz] *vt* durch das Fernsehen übertragen
television ['telɪvɪʒən] *n* Fernsehen *nt*; **on ~** im Fernsehen; **~ (set)** *n* Fernsehapparat *m*, Fernseher *m*
teleworking ['telɪwə:kɪŋ] *n* Telearbeit *f*
telex ['teleks] *n* Telex *nt* ♦ *vt* per Telex schicken
tell [tel] (*pt, pp* told) *vt* (*story*) erzählen; (*secret*) ausplaudern; (*say, make known*) sagen; (*distinguish*) erkennen; (*be sure*) wissen ♦ *vi* (*talk*) sprechen; (*be sure*) wissen; (*divulge*) es verraten; (*have effect*) sich auswirken; **to ~ sb to do sth** jdm sagen, dass er etw tun soll; **to ~ sb sth** or **sth to sb** jdm etw sagen; **to ~ sb by sth** jdn an etw *dat* erkennen; **to ~ sth from** etw

unterscheiden von; **to ~ of sth** von etw sprechen; **~ off** vt: **to ~ sb off** jdn ausschimpfen

teller ['tɛləʳ] n Kassenbeamte(r) mf

telling ['tɛlɪŋ] adj verräterisch; (blow) hart

telltale ['tɛltɛl] adj verräterisch

telly ['tɛlɪ] (BRIT: inf) n abbr (= television) TV nt

temp [tɛmp] n abbr (= temporary) Aushilfskraft f ♦ vi als Aushilfskraft arbeiten

temper ['tɛmpəʳ] n (disposition) Temperament nt; (anger) Zorn m ♦ vt (tone down) mildern; (metal) härten; **to be in a (bad) ~** wütend sein; **to lose one's ~** die Beherrschung verlieren

temperament ['tɛmprəmənt] n Temperament nt; **~al** [tɛmprə'mɛntl] adj (moody) launisch

temperate ['tɛmprət] adj gemäßigt

temperature ['tɛmprətʃəʳ] n Temperatur f; (MED: high ~) Fieber nt; **to have** or **run a ~** Fieber haben

template ['tɛmplɪt] n Schablone f

temple ['tɛmpl] n Tempel m; (ANAT) Schläfe f

temporal ['tɛmpərl] adj (of time) zeitlich; (worldly) irdisch, weltlich

temporarily ['tɛmpərərɪlɪ] adv zeitweilig, vorübergehend

temporary ['tɛmpərərɪ] adj vorläufig; (road, building) provisorisch

tempt [tɛmpt] vt (persuade) verleiten; (attract) reizen, (ver)locken; **to ~ sb into doing sth** jdn dazu verleiten, etw zu tun; **~ation** [tɛmp'tɛɪʃən] n Versuchung f; **~ing** adj (person) verführerisch; (object, situation) verlockend

ten [tɛn] num zehn

tenable ['tɛnəbl] adj haltbar

tenacious [tə'nɛɪʃəs] adj zäh, hartnäckig

tenacity [tə'næsɪtɪ] n Zähigkeit f, Hartnäckigkeit f

tenancy ['tɛnənsɪ] n Mietverhältnis nt

tenant ['tɛnənt] n Mieter m; (of larger property) Pächter m

tend [tɛnd] vt (look after) sich kümmern um ♦ vi: **to ~ to do sth** etw gewöhnlich tun

tendency ['tɛndənsɪ] n Tendenz f; (of person) Tendenz f, Neigung f

tender ['tɛndəʳ] adj zart; (loving) zärtlich ♦ n (COMM: offer) Kostenanschlag m ♦ vt (an)bieten; (resignation) einreichen; **~ness** n Zartheit f; (being loving) Zärtlichkeit f

tendon ['tɛndən] n Sehne f

tenement ['tɛnəmənt] n Mietshaus nt

tennis ['tɛnɪs] n Tennis nt; **~ ball** n Tennisball m; **~ court** n Tennisplatz m; **~ player** n Tennisspieler(in) m(f); **~ racket** n Tennisschläger m; **~ shoes** npl Tennisschuhe pl

tenor ['tɛnəʳ] n Tenor m

tenpin bowling ['tɛnpɪn-] n Bowling nt

tense [tɛns] adj angespannt ♦ n Zeitform f

tension ['tɛnʃən] n Spannung f

tent [tɛnt] n Zelt nt

tentacle ['tɛntəkl] n Fühler m; (of sea animals) Fangarm m

tentative ['tɛntətɪv] adj (movement) unsicher; (offer) Probe-; (arrangement) vorläufig; (suggestion) unverbindlich; **~ly** adv versuchsweise; (try, move) vorsichtig

tenterhooks ['tɛntəhʊks] npl: **to be on ~** auf die Folter gespannt sein

tenth [tɛnθ] adj zehnte(r, s)

tent peg n Hering m

tent pole n Zeltstange f

tenuous ['tɛnjuəs] adj schwach

tenure ['tɛnjuəʳ] n (of land) Besitz m; (of office) Amtszeit f

tepid ['tɛpɪd] adj lauwarm

term [tə:m] n (period of time) Zeit(raum m) f; (limit) Frist f; (SCH) Quartal nt; (UNIV) Trimester nt; (expression) Ausdruck m ♦ vt (be)nennen; **~s** npl (conditions) Bedingungen pl; **in the short/long ~** auf kurze/lange Sicht; **to be on good ~s with sb** gut mit jdm auskommen; **to come to ~s with** (person) sich einigen mit; (problem) sich abfinden mit

terminal ['tə:mɪnl] n (BRIT: also: **coach ~**) Endstation f; (AVIAT) Terminal m; (COMPUT) Terminal nt or m ♦ adj Schluss-; (MED) unheilbar; **~ly** adj (MED): **~ly ill** unheilbar krank

terminate ['tə:mɪneɪt] vt beenden ♦ vi enden, aufhören

termini ['tə:mɪnaɪ] npl of **terminus**

terminus ['tə:mɪnəs] (pl **termini**) n Endstation f

terrace ['tɛrəs] n (BRIT: row of houses) Häuserreihe f; (in garden etc) Terrasse f; **the ~s** npl (BRIT: SPORT) die Ränge; **~d** adj (garden) terrassenförmig angelegt; (house) Reihen-

terrain [tɛ'reɪn] n Gelände nt

terrible ['tɛrɪbl] adj schrecklich, entsetzlich, fürchterlich; **terribly** adv fürchterlich

terrier ['tɛrɪəʳ] n Terrier m

terrific [tə'rɪfɪk] adj unwahrscheinlich; **~!** klasse!

terrified ['tɛrɪfaɪd] adj: **to be ~ of sth** vor etw schreckliche Angst haben

terrify ['tɛrɪfaɪ] vt erschrecken

territorial [tɛrɪ'tɔ:rɪəl] adj Gebiets-, territorial

territory ['tɛrɪtərɪ] n Gebiet nt

terror ['tɛrəʳ] n Schrecken m; **~ism** n Terrorismus m; **~ist** n Terrorist(in) m(f); **~ize** vt terrorisieren

terse [tə:s] adj knapp, kurz, bündig

test [tɛst] n Probe f; (examination) Prüfung f; (PSYCH, TECH) Test m ♦ vt prüfen; (PSYCH) testen

testicle ['tɛstɪkl] n (ANAT) Hoden m

testify ['tɛstɪfaɪ] vi aussagen; **to ~ to sth** etw

bezeugen

testimony |ˈtestɪmənɪ| n (JUR)
Zeugenaussage f; (fig) Zeugnis nt

test match n (SPORT) Länderkampf m

test tube n Reagenzglas nt

tetanus |ˈtetənəs| n Wundstarrkrampf m,
Tetanus m

tether |ˈteðəʳ| vt anbinden ♦ n: **at the end of
one's ~** völlig am Ende

text |tekst| n Text m; (of document) Wortlaut
m; **~book** n Lehrbuch nt

textiles |ˈtekstailz| npl Textilien pl

texture |ˈtekstʃəʳ| n Beschaffenheit f

Thai |taɪ| adj thailändisch ♦ n
Thailänder(in) m(f); **~land** n Thailand
nt

Thames |temz| n: **the ~** die Themse

than |ðæn, ðən| prep (in comparisons) als

thank |θæŋk| vt danken +dat; **you've him to
~ for your success** Sie haben Ihren Erfolg
ihm zu verdanken; **~ you (very much)**
danke (vielmals), danke schön; **~ful** adj
dankbar; **~less** adj undankbar; **~s** npl Dank
m ♦ excl danke!; **~s to** dank +gen;
T~sgiving (Day) (US) n Thanksgiving Day
m

that |ðæt, ðət| adj (demonstrative: pl those)
der/die/das; jene(r, s); **that one** das da
♦ pron **1** (demonstrative: pl those) das;
who's/what's that? wer ist da/was ist das?;
is that you? bist du das?; **that's what he
said** genau das hat er gesagt; **what
happened after that?** was passierte
danach?; **that is** das heißt

2 (relative: subj) der/die/das, die; (: direct
obj) den/die/das, die; (: indirect obj) dem/
der/dem, denen; **all (that) I have** alles, was
ich habe

3 (relative: of time): **the day (that)** an dem
Tag, als; **the winter (that) he came** in dem
Winter, in dem er kam
♦ conj dass; **he thought that I was ill** er
dachte, dass ich krank sei, er dachte, ich sei
krank
♦ adv (demonstrative) so; **I can't work that
much** ich kann nicht so viel arbeiten

thatched |θætʃt| adj strohgedeckt; (cottage)
mit Strohdach

thaw |θɔː| n Tauwetter nt ♦ vi tauen; (frozen
foods, fig: people) auftauen ♦ vt (auf)tauen
lassen

the |ðiː, ðə| def art **1** der/die/das; **to play the
piano/violin** Klavier/Geige spielen; **I'm
going to the butcher's/the cinema** ich
gehe zum Fleischer/ins Kino; **Elizabeth the
First** Elisabeth die Erste

2 (+adj to form noun) das, die; **the rich and
the poor** die Reichen und die Armen

3 (in comparisons): **the more he works the
more he earns** je mehr er arbeitet, desto
mehr verdient er

theatre |ˈθɪətəʳ| (US **theater**) n Theater nt;
(for lectures etc) Saal m; (MED)
Operationssaal m; **~goer** n
Theaterbesucher(in) m(f); **theatrical**
|θɪˈætrɪkl| adj Theater-; (career) Schauspieler;
(showy) theatralisch

theft |θeft| n Diebstahl m

their |ðeəʳ| adj ihr; see also **my**; **~s** pron
ihre(r, s); see also **mine²**

them |ðem, ðəm| pron (acc) sie; (dat) ihnen;
see also **me**

theme |θiːm| n Thema nt; (MUS) Motiv nt; **~
park** n (thematisch gestalteter) Freizeitpark
m; **~ song** n Titelmusik f

themselves |ðəmˈselvz| pl pron (reflexive)
sich (selbst); (emphatic) selbst; see also
oneself

then |ðen| adv (at that time) damals; (next)
dann ♦ conj also, folglich; (furthermore)
ferner ♦ adj damalig; **from ~ on** von da an;
by ~ bis dahin; **the ~ president** der
damalige Präsident

theology |θɪˈɒlədʒɪ| n Theologie f

theoretical |θɪəˈretɪkl| adj theoretisch; **~ly**
adv theoretisch

theory |ˈθɪərɪ| n Theorie f

therapist |ˈθerəpɪst| n Therapeut(in) m(f)

therapy |ˈθerəpɪ| n Therapie f

there |ðeəʳ| adv **1**: **there is, there are** es
or da ist/sind; (there exists/exist also) es gibt;
there are 3 of them (people, things) es gibt
3 davon; **there has been an accident** da
war ein Unfall

2 (place) da, dort; (direction) dahin, dorthin;
put it in/on there leg es dahinein/
dorthinauf

3: **there, there** (esp to child) na, na

there: **~abouts** |ˈðeərəˈbauts| adv (place)
dort in der Nähe, dort irgendwo; (amount):
20 or ~abouts ungefähr 20; **~after**
|ðeərˈɑːftəʳ| adv danach; **~by** |ˈðeəbaɪ| adv
dadurch, damit

therefore |ˈðeəfɔːʳ| adv deshalb, daher

there's |ˈðeəz| = **there is**; **there has**

thermometer |θəˈmɒmɪtəʳ| n Thermometer
nt

Thermos |ˈθɜːməs| ® n Thermosflasche f

thesaurus |θɪˈsɔːrəs| n Synonymwörterbuch nt

these |ðiːz| pron, adj (pl) diese

theses |ˈθiːsiːz| npl of **thesis**

thesis |ˈθiːsɪs| (pl **theses**) n (for discussion)
These f; (UNIV) Dissertation f, Doktorarbeit f

they |ðeɪ| *pl pron* sie; *(people in general)* man; **~ say that …** *(it is said that)* es wird gesagt, dass …; **~'d = they had; they would; ~'ll = they shall; they will; ~'re = they are; ~'ve = they have**

thick |θɪk| *adj* dick; *(forest)* dicht; *(liquid)* dickflüssig; *(slow, stupid)* dumm, schwer von Begriff ♦ *n*: **in the ~ of** mitten in +*dat*; **it's 20 cm ~** es ist 20 cm dick *or* stark; **~en** *vi* *(fog)* dichter werden ♦ *vt* *(sauce etc)* verdicken; **~ness** *n* Dicke *f*; Dichte *f*; Dickflüssigkeit *f*; **~set** *adj* untersetzt; **~-skinned** *adj* dickhäutig

thief |θiːf| *(pl* **thieves***) n* Dieb(in) *m(f)*

thieves |θiːvz| *npl of* **thief**

thieving |'θiːvɪŋ| *n* Stehlen *nt* ♦ *adj* diebisch

thigh |θaɪ| *n* Oberschenkel *m*

thimble |'θɪmbl| *n* Fingerhut *m*

thin |θɪn| *adj* dünn; *(person)* dünn, mager; *(excuse)* schwach ♦ *vt*: **to ~ (down)** *(sauce, paint)* verdünnen

thing |θɪŋ| *n* Ding *nt*; *(affair)* Sache *f*; **my ~s** meine Sachen *pl*; **the best ~ would be to …** das Beste wäre, …; **how are ~s?** wie gehts?

think |θɪŋk| *(pt, pp* **thought***) vt, vi* denken; **what did you ~ of them?** was halten Sie von ihnen?; **to ~ about sth/sb** nachdenken über etw/jdn; **I'll ~ about it** ich überlege es mir; **to ~ of doing sth** vorhaben *or* beabsichtigen, etw zu tun; **I ~ so/not** ich glaube (schon)/glaube nicht; **to ~ well of sb** viel von jdm halten; **~ over** *vt* überdenken; **~ up** *vt* sich *dat* ausdenken; **~ tank** *n* Expertengruppe *f*

thinly |'θɪnlɪ| *adv* dünn; *(disguised)* kaum

third |θəːd| *adj* dritte(r, s) ♦ *n* *(person)* Dritte(r) *mf*; *(part)* Drittel *nt*; **~ly** *adv* drittens; **~ party insurance** *(BRIT) n* Haftpflichtversicherung *f*; **~-rate** *adj* minderwertig; **T~ World** *n*: **the T~ World** die Dritte Welt *f*

thirst |θəːst| *n* *(also fig)* Durst *m*; **~y** *adj* *(person)* durstig; *(work)* durstig machend; **to be ~y** Durst haben

thirteen |θəː'tiːn| *num* dreizehn

thirty |'θəːtɪ| *num* dreißig

KEYWORD
---

this |ðɪs| *adj (demonstrative: pl* these*)* diese(r, s); **this evening** heute Abend; **this one** diese(r, s) (da)
♦ *pron (demonstrative: pl* these*)* dies, das; **who/what is this?** wer/was ist das?; **this is where I live** hier wohne ich; **this is what he said** das hat er gesagt; **this is Mr Brown** dies ist Mr Brown; *(on telephone)* hier ist Mr Brown
♦ *adv (demonstrative)*: **this high/long** *etc* so groß/lang *etc*

thistle |'θɪsl| *n* Distel *f*

thorn |θɔːn| *n* Dorn *m*; **~y** *adj* dornig; *(problem)* schwierig

thorough |'θʌrə| *adj* gründlich; **~bred** *n* Vollblut *nt* ♦ *adj* reinrassig, Vollblut-; **~fare** *n* Straße *f*; **"no ~fare"** „Durchfahrt verboten"; **~ly** *adv* gründlich; *(extremely)* äußerst

those |ðəʊz| *pl pron* die (da), jene ♦ *adj* die, jene

though |ðəʊ| *conj* obwohl ♦ *adv* trotzdem

thought |θɔːt| *pt, pp of* **think** ♦ *n* *(idea)* Gedanke *m*; *(thinking)* Denken *nt*, Denkvermögen *nt*; **~ful** *adj* *(thinking)* gedankenvoll, nachdenklich; *(kind)* rücksichtsvoll, aufmerksam; **~less** *adj* gedankenlos, unbesonnen; *(unkind)* rücksichtslos

thousand |'θaʊzənd| *num* tausend; **two ~** zweitausend; **~s of** tausende *or* Tausende (von); **~th** *adj* tausendste(r, s)

thrash |θræʃ| *vt* verdreschen; *(fig)* (vernichtend) schlagen; **~ about** *vi* um sich schlagen; **~ out** *vt* ausdiskutieren

thread |θrɛd| *n* Faden *m*, Garn *nt*; *(TECH)* Gewinde *nt*; *(in story)* Faden *m* ♦ *vt* *(needle)* einfädeln; **~bare** *adj* fadenscheinig

threat |θrɛt| *n* Drohung *f*; *(danger)* Gefahr *f*; **~en** *vt* bedrohen ♦ *vi* drohen; **to ~en sb with sth** jdm etw androhen

three |θriː| *num* drei; **~-dimensional** *adj* dreidimensional; **~-piece suite** *n* dreiteilige Polstergarnitur *f*; **~-wheeler** *n* Dreiradwagen *m*

thresh |θrɛʃ| *vt, vi* dreschen

threshold |'θrɛʃhəʊld| *n* Schwelle *f*

threw |θruː| *pt of* **throw**

thrift |θrɪft| *n* Sparsamkeit *f*; **~y** *adj* sparsam

thrill |θrɪl| *n* Reiz *m*, Erregung *f* ♦ *vt* begeistern, packen; **to be ~ed with** *(gift etc)* sich unheimlich freuen über +*acc*; **~er** *n* Krimi *m*; **~ing** *adj* spannend; *(news)* aufregend

thrive |θraɪv| *(pt, pp* **thrived***) vi*: **to ~ (on)** gedeihen (bei); **thriving** |'θraɪvɪŋ| *adj* blühend

throat |θrəʊt| *n* Hals *m*, Kehle *f*; **to have a sore ~** Halsschmerzen haben

throb |θrɒb| *vi* klopfen, pochen

throes |θrəʊz| *npl*: **in the ~ of** mitten in +*dat*

throne |θrəʊn| *n* Thron *m*; **on the ~** auf dem Thron

throng |'θrɒŋ| *n* (Menschen)schar *f* ♦ *vt* sich drängen in +*dat*

throttle |'θrɒtl| *n* Gashebel *m* ♦ *vt* erdrosseln

through |θruː| *prep* durch; *(time)* während +*gen*; *(because of)* aus, durch ♦ *adv* durch ♦ *adj* *(ticket, train)* durchgehend; *(finished)* fertig; **to put sb ~ (to)** jdn verbinden (mit); **to be ~** *(TEL)* eine Verbindung haben; *(have finished)* fertig sein; **no ~ way** *(BRIT)* Sackgasse *f*; **~out** |θruː'aʊt| *prep (place)* überall in +dat; (time) während +gen ♦ adv überall; die ganze Zeit

throw |θrəu| (pt threw, pp thrown) n Wurf m ♦ vt werfen; **to ~ a party** eine Party geben; **~ away** vt wegwerfen; (waste) verschenken; (money) verschwenden; **~ off** vt abwerfen; (pursuer) abschütteln; **~ out** vt hinauswerfen; (rubbish) wegwerfen; (plan) verwerfen; **~ up** vt, vi (vomit) speien; **~away** adj Wegwerf-; **~-in** n Einwurf m; **~n** pp of **throw**

thru |θru:| (US) = **through**

thrush |θrʌʃ| n Drossel f

thrust |θrʌst| (pt, pp thrust) vt, vi (push) stoßen

thud |θʌd| n dumpfe(r) (Auf)schlag m

thug |θʌg| n Schlägertyp m

thumb |θʌm| n Daumen m ♦ vt (book) durchblättern; **to ~ a lift** per Anhalter fahren (wollen); **~tack** (US) n Reißzwecke f

thump |θʌmp| n (blow) Schlag m; (noise) Bums m ♦ vi hämmern, pochen ♦ vt schlagen auf +acc

thunder |ˈθʌndəʳ| n Donner m ♦ vi donnern; (train etc): **to ~ past** vorbeidonnern ♦ vt brüllen; **~bolt** n Blitz nt; **~clap** n Donnerschlag m; **~storm** n Gewitter nt, Unwetter nt; **~y** adj gewitterschwül

Thursday |ˈθɜːzdɪ| n Donnerstag m

thus |ðʌs| adv (in this way) so; (therefore) somit, also, folglich

thwart |θwɔːt| vt vereiteln, durchkreuzen; (person) hindern

thyme |taɪm| n Thymian m

thyroid |ˈθaɪrɔɪd| n Schilddrüse f

tiara |tɪˈɑːrə| n Diadem nt

tic |tɪk| n Tick m

tick |tɪk| n (sound) Ticken nt; (mark) Häkchen nt ♦ vi ticken ♦ vt abhaken; **in a ~** (BRIT: inf) sofort; **~ off** vt abhaken; (person) ausschimpfen; **~ over** vi (engine) im Leerlauf laufen; (fig) auf Sparflamme laufen

ticket |ˈtɪkɪt| n (for travel) Fahrkarte f; (for entrance) (Eintritts)karte f; (price ~) Preisschild nt; (luggage ~) (Gepäck)schein m; (raffle ~) Los nt; (parking ~) Strafzettel m; (in car park) Parkschein m; **~ collector** n Fahrkartenkontrolleur m; **~ inspector** n Fahrkartenkontrolleur m n (THEAT etc) Kasse f; (RAIL etc) Fahrkartenschalter m

tickle |ˈtɪkl| n Kitzeln nt ♦ vt kitzeln; (amuse) amüsieren; **ticklish** |ˈtɪklɪʃ| adj (also fig) kitzlig

tidal |ˈtaɪdl| adj Flut-, Tide-; **~ wave** n Flutwelle f

tidbit |ˈtɪdbɪt| (US) n Leckerbissen m

tiddlywinks |ˈtɪdlɪwɪŋks| n Floh(hüpf)spiel nt

tide |taɪd| n Gezeiten pl; **high/low ~** Flut f/ Ebbe f

tidy |ˈtaɪdɪ| adj ordentlich ♦ vt aufräumen, in Ordnung bringen

tie |taɪ| n (BRIT: neck) Krawatte f, Schlips m; (sth connecting) Band nt; (SPORT) Unentschieden nt ♦ vt (fasten, restrict) binden ♦ vi (SPORT) unentschieden spielen; (in competition) punktgleich sein; **to ~ in a bow** zur Schleife binden; **to ~ a knot in sth** einen Knoten in etw acc machen; **~ down** vt festbinden; **to ~ sb down to** jdn binden an +acc; **~ up** vt (dog) anbinden; (parcel) verschnüren; (boat) festmachen; (restrictions) fesseln; **to be ~d up** (busy) beschäftigt sein

tier |tɪəʳ| n Rang m; (of cake) Etage f

tiff |tɪf| n Krach m

tiger |ˈtaɪgəʳ| n Tiger m

tight |taɪt| adj (close) eng, knapp; (schedule) gedrängt; (firm) fest; (control) streng; (stretched) stramm ♦ an)gespannt; (inf: drunk) blau, stramm ♦ adv (squeeze) fest; **~en** vt anziehen, anspannen; (restrictions) verschärfen ♦ vi sich spannen; **~-fisted** adj knauserig; **~ly** adv eng; fest; (stretched) straff; **~rope** n Seil nt; **~s** npl (esp BRIT) Strumpfhose f

tile |taɪl| n (on roof) Dachziegel m; (on wall or floor) Fliese f; **~d** adj (roof) gedeckt, Ziegel-; (floor, wall) mit Fliesen belegt

till |tɪl| n Kasse f ♦ vt bestellen ♦ prep, conj = **until**

tiller |ˈtɪləʳ| n Ruderpinne f

tilt |tɪlt| vt kippen, neigen ♦ vi sich neigen

timber |ˈtɪmbəʳ| n (wood) Holz nt

time |taɪm| n Zeit f; (occasion) Mal nt; (rhythm) Takt m ♦ vt zur rechten Zeit tun, zeitlich einrichten; (SPORT) stoppen; **in 2 weeks' ~** in 2 Wochen; **a long ~** lange; **for the ~ being** vorläufig; **4 at a ~** zu jeweils 4; **from ~ to ~** gelegentlich; **to have a good ~** sich amüsieren; **in ~** (soon enough) rechtzeitig; (after some ~) mit der Zeit; (MUS) im Takt; **in no ~** im Handumdrehen; **any ~** jederzeit; **on ~** pünktlich, rechtzeitig; **five ~s 5** fünfmal 5; **what ~ is it?** wie viel Uhr ist es?, wie spät ist es?; **at ~s** manchmal; **~ bomb** n Zeitbombe f; **~less** adj (beauty) zeitlos; **~ limit** n Frist f; **~ly** adj rechtzeitig; günstig; **~ off** n freie Zeit f; **~r** n (~r switch: in kitchen) Schaltuhr f; **~ scale** n Zeitspanne f; **~-share** adj Timesharing-; **~ switch** (BRIT) n Zeitschalter m; **~table** n Fahrplan m; (SCH) Stundenplan m; **~ zone** n Zeitzone f

timid |ˈtɪmɪd| adj ängstlich, schüchtern

timing |ˈtaɪmɪŋ| n Wahl f des richtigen Zeitpunkts, Timing nt

timpani |ˈtɪmpənɪ| npl Kesselpauken pl

tin |tɪn| n (metal) Blech nt; (BRIT: can) Büchse f, Dose f; **~foil** n Stanniolpapier nt

tinge |tɪndʒ| n (colour) Färbung f; (fig) Anflug m ♦ vt färben; **~d** with mit einer Spur von

tingle |ˈtɪŋgl| n Prickeln nt ♦ vi prickeln

tinker |ˈtɪŋkəʳ| n Kesselflicker m; **~ with** vt

fus herumfuschen an +*dat*
tinkle ['tɪŋkl] *vi* klingeln
tinned [tɪnd] (*BRIT*) *adj* (*food*) Dosen-,
Büchsen-
tin opener [-ˌəupnəˡ] (*BRIT*) *n* Dosen- or
Büchsenöffner *m*
tinsel ['tɪnsl] *n* Rauschgold *nt*
tint [tɪnt] *n* Farbton *m*; (*slight colour*) Anflug
m; (*hair*) Tönung *f*; **~ed** *adj* getönt
tiny ['taɪnɪ] *adj* winzig
tip [tɪp] *n* (*pointed end*) Spitze *f*; (*money*)
Trinkgeld *nt*; (*hint*) Wink *m*, Tipp *m* ♦ *vt*
(*slant*) kippen; (*hat*) antippen; (~ *over*)
umkippen; (*waiter*) ein Trinkgeld geben
+*dat*; **~-off** *n* Hinweis *m*, Tipp *m*; **~ped**
(*BRIT*) *adj* (*cigarette*) Filter-
tipsy ['tɪpsɪ] *adj* beschwipst
tiptoe ['tɪptəu] *n*: **on ~** auf Zehenspitzen
tiptop ['tɪp'tɔp] *adj*: **in ~ condition** tipptopp,
erstklassig
tire [taɪəˡ] *n* (*US*) = **tyre** ♦ *vt*, *vi* ermüden,
müde machen/werden; **~d** *adj* müde; **to be
~d of sth** etw satt haben; **~less** *adj*
unermüdlich; **~some** *adj* lästig
tiring ['taɪərɪŋ] *adj* ermüdend
tissue ['tɪʃuː] *n* Gewebe *nt*; (*paper
handkerchief*) Papiertaschentuch *nt*; **~
paper** *n* Seidenpapier *nt*
tit [tɪt] *n* (*bird*) Meise *f*; **~ for tat** wie du mir,
so ich dir
titbit ['tɪtbɪt] (*US* **tidbit**) *n* Leckerbissen *m*
titillate ['tɪtɪleɪt] *vt* kitzeln
title ['taɪtl] *n* Titel *m*; **~ deed** *n*
Eigentumsurkunde *f*; **~ role** *n* Hauptrolle
f
titter ['tɪtəˡ] *vi* kichern
titular ['tɪtjulaˡ] *adj* (*in name only*) nominell
TM *abbr* (= *trademark*) Wz

KEYWORD

to [tuː, tə] *prep* **1** (*direction*) zu, nach; **I go to
France/school** ich gehe nach Frankreich/
zur Schule; **to the left** nach links
2 (*as far as*) bis
3 (*with expressions of time*) vor; **a quarter
to 5** Viertel vor 5
4 (*for, of*) für; **secretary to the director**
Sekretärin des Direktors
5 (*expressing indirect object*): **to give sth to
sb** jdm etw geben; **to talk to sb** mit jdm
sprechen; **I sold it to a friend** ich habe es
einem Freund verkauft
6 (*in relation to*) zu; **30 miles to the gallon**
30 Meilen pro Gallone
7 (*purpose, result*) zu; **to my surprise** zu
meiner Überraschung
♦ *with vb* **1** (*infin*): **to go/eat** gehen/essen; **to
want to do sth** etw tun wollen; **to try/start
to do sth** versuchen/anfangen, etw zu tun;
he has a lot to lose er hat viel zu verlieren
2 (*with vb omitted*): **I don't want to** ich will

(es) nicht
3 (*purpose, result*) um; **I did it to help you**
ich tat es, um dir zu helfen
4 (*after adj etc*): **ready to use**
gebrauchsfertig; **too old/young to ... zu**
alt/jung, um ... zu ...
♦ *adv*: **push/pull the door to** die Tür
zuschieben/zuziehen

---

toad [təud] *n* Kröte *f*; **~stool** *n* Giftpilz *m*
toast [təust] *n* (*bread*) Toast *m*; (*drinking*)
Trinkspruch *m* ♦ *vt* trinken auf +*acc*; (*bread*)
toasten; (*warm*) wärmen; **~er** *n* Toaster *m*
tobacco [təˈbækəu] *n* Tabak *m*; **~nist**
[təˈbækənɪst] *n* Tabakhändler *m*; **~nist's
(shop)** *n* Tabakladen *m*
toboggan [təˈbɔgən] *n* (*Rodel*)schlitten *m*;
~ing *n* Rodeln *nt*
today [təˈdeɪ] *adv* heute; (*at the present time*)
heutzutage
toddler ['tɔdləˡ] *n* Kleinkind *nt*
toddy ['tɔdɪ] *n* (*Whisky*)grog *m*
to-do [təˈduː] *n* Theater *nt*
toe [təu] *n* Zehe *f*; (*of sock, shoe*) Spitze *f* ♦ *vt*:
to ~ the line (*fig*) sich einfügen; **~nail** *n*
Zehennagel *m*
toffee ['tɔfɪ] *n* Sahnebonbon *nt*; **~ apple**
(*BRIT*) *n* kandierte(r) Apfel *m*
together [təˈgeðəˡ] *adv* zusammen; (*at the
same time*) gleichzeitig; **~ with** zusammen
mit; gleichzeitig mit
toil [tɔɪl] *n* harte Arbeit *f*, Plackerei *f* ♦ *vi* sich
abmühen, sich plagen
toilet ['tɔɪlət] *n* Toilette *f* ♦ *cpd* Toiletten-; **~
bag** *n* Waschbeutel *m*; **~ paper** *n*
Toilettenpapier *nt*; **~ries** ['tɔɪlətrɪz] *npl*
Toilettenartikel *pl*; **~ roll** *n* Rolle *f*
Toilettenpapier; **~ water** *n* Toilettenwasser
nt
token ['təukən] *n* Zeichen *nt*; (*gift* ~)
Gutschein *m*; **book/record ~** (*BRIT*) Bücher-/
Plattengutschein *m*
Tokyo ['təukjəu] *n* Tokio *nt*
told [təuld] *pt*, *pp of* **tell**
tolerable ['tɔlərəbl] *adj* (*bearable*) erträglich;
(*fairly good*) leidlich
tolerant ['tɔlərnt] *adj*: **be ~ (of)** vertragen
+*acc*
tolerate ['tɔləreɪt] *vt* dulden; (*noise*) ertragen
toll [təul] *n* Gebühr *f* ♦ *vi* (*bell*) läuten
tomato [təˈmɑːtəu] (*pl* **~es**) *n* Tomate *f*
tomb [tuːm] *n* Grab(mal) *nt*
tomboy ['tɔmbɔɪ] *n* Wildfang *m*
tombstone ['tuːmstəun] *n* Grabstein *m*
tomcat ['tɔmkæt] *n* Kater *m*
tomorrow [təˈmɔrəu] *n* Morgen *m* ♦ *adv*
morgen; **the day after ~** übermorgen; **~
morning** morgen früh; **a week ~** morgen in
einer Woche
ton [tʌn] *n* Tonne *f* (*BRIT* = 1016 kg; *US* =
907 kg); **~s of** (*inf*) eine Unmenge von

tone |təun| n Ton m; **~ down** vt (criticism, demands) mäßigen; (colours) abtonen; **~ up** vt in Form bringen; **~-deaf** adj ohne musikalisches Gehör

tongs |tɔŋz| npl Zange f; (curling ~) Lockenstab m

tongue |tʌŋ| n Zunge f; (language) Sprache f; **with ~ in cheek** scherzhaft; **~-tied** adj stumm, sprachlos; **~ twister** n Zungenbrecher m

tonic |'tɔnɪk| n (drink) Tonic nt; (MED) Stärkungsmittel nt

tonight |tə'naɪt| adv heute Abend

tonsil |'tɔnsl| n Mandel f; **~litis** |tɔnsɪ'laɪtɪs| n Mandelentzündung f

too |tu:| adv zu; (also) auch; **~ bad!** Pech!; **~ many** zu viele

took |tuk| pt of **take**

tool |tu:l| n (also fig) Werkzeug nt; **~box** n Werkzeugkasten m

toot |tu:t| n Hupen nt ♦ vi tuten; (AUT) hupen

tooth |tu:θ| (pl **teeth**) n Zahn m; **~ache** n Zahnschmerzen pl, Zahnweh nt; **~brush** n Zahnbürste f; **~paste** n Zahnpasta f; **~pick** n Zahnstocher m

top |tɔp| n Spitze f; (of mountain) Gipfel m; (of tree) Wipfel m; (toy) Kreisel m; (~ gear) vierte(r)/fünfte(r) Gang m ♦ adj oberste(r, s) ♦ vt (list) an erster Stelle stehen auf +dat; **on ~ of** oben auf +dat; **from ~ to bottom** von oben bis unten; **~ off** (US) vt auffüllen; **~ up** vt auffüllen; **~ floor** n oberste(s) Stockwerk nt; **~ hat** n Zylinder m; **~-heavy** adj kopflastig

topic |'tɔpɪk| n Thema nt, Gesprächsgegenstand m; **~al** adj aktuell

top: **~less** |'tɔplɪs| adj (bather etc) oben ohne; **~-level** |'tɔplevl| adj auf höchster Ebene; **~most** |'tɔpməust| adj oberste(r, s)

topple |'tɔpl| vt, vi stürzen, kippen

top-secret |'tɔp'si:krɪt| adj streng geheim

topsy-turvy |'tɔpsɪ'tə:vɪ| adv durcheinander ♦ adj auf den Kopf gestellt

torch |tɔ:tʃ| n (BRIT: ELEC) Taschenlampe f; (with flame) Fackel f

tore |tɔ:r| pt of **tear**[1]

torment |n 'tɔ:ment, vb tɔ:'ment| n Qual f ♦ vt (distress) quälen

torn |tɔ:n| pp of **tear**[1] ♦ adj hin- und hergerissen

torrent |'tɔrnt| n Sturzbach m; **~ial** |tɔ'renʃl| adj wolkenbruchartig

torrid |'tɔrɪd| adj heiß

tortoise |'tɔ:təs| n Schildkröte f; **~shell** |'tɔ:təʃel| n Schildpatt m

torture |'tɔ:tʃər| n Folter f ♦ vt foltern

Tory |'tɔ:rɪ| (BRIT) n (POL) Tory m ♦ adj Tory-, konservativ

toss |tɔs| vt schleudern; **to ~ a coin** or **to ~ up for sth** etw mit einer Münze entscheiden; **to ~ and turn** (in bed) sich hin

und her werfen

tot |tɔt| n (small quantity) bisschen nt; (small child) Knirps m

total |'təutl| n Gesamtheit f; (money) Endsumme f ♦ adj Gesamt-, total ♦ vt (add up) zusammenzählen; (amount to) sich belaufen auf

totalitarian |təutælɪ'tɛərɪən| adj totalitär

totally |'təutəlɪ| adv total

totter |'tɔtər| vi wanken, schwanken

touch |tʌtʃ| n Berührung f; (sense of feeling) Tastsinn m ♦ vt (feel) berühren; (come against) leicht anstoßen; (emotionally) rühren; **a ~ of** (fig) eine Spur von; **to get in ~ with sb** sich mit jdm in Verbindung setzen; **to lose ~** (friends) Kontakt verlieren; **~ on** vt fus (topic) berühren, erwähnen; **~ up** vt (paint) auffrischen; **~-and-go** adj riskant, knapp; **~down** n Landen nt, Niedergehen nt; **~ed** adj (moved) gerührt; **~ing** adj rührend; **~line** n Seitenlinie f; **~-sensitive screen** n (COMPUT) berührungsempfindlicher Bildschirm m; **~y** adj empfindlich, reizbar

tough |tʌf| adj zäh; (difficult) schwierig ♦ n Schläger(typ) m; **~en** vt zäh machen; (make strong) abhärten

toupee |'tu:peɪ| n Toupet nt

tour |'tuər| n Tour f ♦ vi umherreisen; (THEAT) auf Tour sein; auf Tour gehen; **~ guide** n Reiseleiter(in) m(f)

tourism |'tuərɪzm| n Fremdenverkehr m, Tourismus m

tourist |'tuərɪst| n Tourist(in) m(f) ♦ cpd (class) Touristen-; **~ office** n Verkehrsamt nt

tournament |'tuənəmənt| n Turnier nt

tousled |'tauzld| adj zerzaust

tout |taut| vi: **to ~ for** auf Kundenfang gehen für ♦ n: **ticket ~** Kundenschlepper(in) m(f)

tow |təu| vt (ab)schleppen; **on** (BRIT) or **in** (US) **~** (AUT) im Schlepp

toward(s) |tə'wɔ:d(z)| prep (with time) gegen; (in direction of) nach

towel |'tauəl| n Handtuch nt; **~ling** n (fabric) Frottee nt or m; **~ rack** (US) n Handtuchstange f; **~ rail** n Handtuchstange f

tower |'tauər| n Turm m; **~ block** (BRIT) n Hochhaus nt; **~ing** adj hochragend

town |taun| n Stadt f; **to go to ~** (fig) sich ins Zeug legen; **~ centre** n Stadtzentrum nt; **~ clerk** n Stadtdirektor m; **~ council** n Stadtrat m; **~ hall** n Rathaus nt; **~ plan** n Stadtplan m; **~ planning** n Stadtplanung f

towrope |'təurəup| n Abschlepptau nt

tow truck (US) n Abschleppwagen m

toxic |'tɔksɪk| adj giftig, Gift-

toy |tɔɪ| n Spielzeug nt; **~ with** vt fus spielen mit; **~shop** n Spielwarengeschäft nt

trace |treɪs| n Spur f ♦ vt (follow a course)

nachspüren +dat; (find out) aufspüren; (copy) durchpausen; **tracing paper** n Pauspapier nt

track |træk| n (mark) Spur f; (path) Weg m; (racetrack) Rennbahn f; (RAIL) Gleis nt ♦ vt verfolgen; **to keep ~ of sb** jdn im Auge behalten; **~ down** vt aufspüren; **~suit** n Trainingsanzug m

tract |trækt| n (of land) Gebiet nt

traction |'trækʃən| n (power) Zugkraft f; (AUT: grip) Bodenhaftung f; (MED): **in ~** im Streckverband

tractor |'træktər| n Traktor m

trade |treɪd| n (commerce) Handel m; (business) Geschäft nt, Gewerbe nt; (people) Geschäftsleute pl; (skilled manual work) Handwerk nt ♦ vi: **to ~ (in)** handeln (mit) ♦ vt tauschen; **~ in** vt in Zahlung geben; **~ fair** n Messe nt; **~-in price** n Preis, zu dem etw in Zahlung genommen wird; **~mark** n Warenzeichen nt; **~ name** n Handelsbezeichnung f; **~r** n Händler m; **~sman** (irreg) n (shopkeeper) Geschäftsmann m; (workman) Handwerker m; (delivery man) Lieferant m; **~ union** n Gewerkschaft f; **~ unionist** n Gewerkschaftler(in) m(f)

trading |'treɪdɪŋ| n Handel m; **~ estate** (BRIT) n Industriegelände nt

tradition |trə'dɪʃən| n Tradition f; **~al** adj traditionell, herkömmlich

traffic |'træfɪk| n Verkehr m; (esp in drugs): **~ (in)** Handel m (mit) ♦ vi: **to ~ in** (esp drugs) handeln mit; **~ calming** n Verkehrsberuhigung f; **~ circle** (US) n Kreisverkehr m; **~ jam** n Verkehrsstauung f; **~ lights** npl Verkehrsampel f; **~ warden** n ≈ Verkehrspolizist m (ohne amtliche Befugnisse), Politesse f (ohne amtliche Befugnisse)

tragedy |'trædʒədɪ| n Tragödie f

tragic |'trædʒɪk| adj tragisch

trail |treɪl| n (track) Spur f; (of smoke) Rauchfahne f; (of dust) Staubwolke f; (road) Pfad m, Weg m ♦ vt (animal) verfolgen; (person) folgen +dat; (drag) schleppen ♦ vi (hang loosely) schleifen; (plants) sich ranken; (be behind) hinterherhinken; (SPORT) weit zurückliegen; (walk) zuckeln; **~ behind** vi zurückbleiben; **~er** n Anhänger m; (US: caravan) Wohnwagen m; (for film) Vorschau f; **~er truck** (US) n Sattelschlepper m

train |treɪn| n Zug m; (of dress) Schleppe f; (series) Folge f ♦ vt (teach: person) ausbilden; (: animal) abrichten; (: mind) schulen; (SPORT) trainieren; (aim) richten ♦ vi (exercise) trainieren; (study) ausgebildet werden; **~ of thought** Gedankengang m; **to ~ sth on** (aim) etw richten auf +acc; **~ed** adj (eye) geschult; (person, voice) ausgebildet; **~ee** n Lehrling m;

Praktikant(in) m(f); **~er** n Ausbilder m; (SPORT) Trainer m; **~ers** npl Turnschuhe pl; **~ing** n (for occupation) Ausbildung f; (SPORT) Training nt; **in ~ing** im Training; **~ing college** n pädagogische Hochschule f, Lehrerseminar nt; **~ing shoes** npl Turnschuhe pl

traipse |treɪps| vi latschen

trait |treɪt| n Zug m, Merkmal nt

traitor |'treɪtər| n Verräter m

trajectory |trə'dʒektərɪ| n Flugbahn f

tram |træm| (BRIT) n (also: **~car**) Straßenbahn f

tramp |træmp| n Landstreicher m ♦ vi (trudge) stampfen, stapfen

trample |'træmpl| vt (nieder)trampeln ♦ vi (herum)trampeln; **to ~ (underfoot)** herumtrampeln auf +dat

trampoline |'træmpəliːn| n Trampolin n

tranquil |'træŋkwɪl| adj ruhig, friedlich; **~lity** |træŋ'kwɪlɪtɪ| (US **~ity**) n Ruhe f; **~lizer** (US **~izer**) n Beruhigungsmittel nt

transact |træn'zækt| vt abwickeln; **~ion** |træn'zækʃən| n Abwicklung f; (piece of business) Geschäft nt, Transaktion f

transcend |træn'send| vt übersteigen

transcription |træn'skrɪpʃən| n Transkription f; (product) Abschrift f

transfer [n 'trænsfəː, vb træns'fəːr] n (transferring) Übertragung f; (of business) Umzug m; (being ~red) Versetzung f; (design) Abziehbild nt; (SPORT) Transfer m ♦ vt (business) verlegen; (person) versetzen; (prisoner) überführen; (drawing) übertragen; (money) überweisen; **to ~ the charges** (BRIT: TEL) ein R-Gespräch führen; **~ desk** n (AVIAT) Transitschalter m

transform |træns'fɔːm| vt umwandeln; **~ation** |trænsfə'meɪʃən| n Umwandlung f, Verwandlung f

transfusion |træns'fjuːʒən| n Blutübertragung f, Transfusion f

transient |'trænzɪənt| adj kurz(lebig)

transistor |træn'zɪstər| n (ELEC) Transistor m; (RAD) Transistorradio nt

transit |'trænzɪt| n: **in ~** unterwegs

transition |træn'zɪʃən| n Übergang m; **~al** adj Übergangs-

transit lounge n Warteraum m

translate |trænz'leɪt| vt, vi übersetzen; **translation** |trænz'leɪʃən| n Übersetzung f; **translator** |trænz'leɪtər| n Übersetzer(in) m(f)

transmission |trænz'mɪʃən| n (of information) Übermittlung f; (ELEC, MED, TV) Übertragung f; (AUT) Getriebe nt

transmit |trænz'mɪt| vt (message) übermitteln; (ELEC, MED, TV) übertragen; **~ter** n Sender m

transparency |træns'pɛərnsɪ| n Durchsichtigkeit f; (BRIT: PHOT) Dia(positiv) nt

transparent [træns'pærnt] adj durchsichtig; (fig) offenkundig

transpire [træns'paɪəʳ] vi (turn out) sich herausstellen; (happen) passieren

transplant [vb træns'plɑːnt, n 'trænsplɑːnt] vt umpflanzen; (MED, also fig: person) verpflanzen ♦ n (MED) Transplantation f; (organ) Transplantat nt

transport [n 'trænspɔːt, vb træns'pɔːt] n Transport m, Beförderung f ♦ vt befördern; transportieren; **means of ~** Transportmittel nt; **~ation** ['trænspɔː'teɪʃən] n Transport m, Beförderung f; (means) Beförderungsmittel nt; (cost) Transportkosten pl; **~ café** (BRIT) n Fernfahrerlokal nt

trap [træp] n Falle f; (carriage) zweirädrige(r) Einspänner m; (inf: mouth) Klappe f ♦ vt fangen; (person) in eine Falle locken; **~door** n Falltür f

trappings ['træpɪŋz] npl Aufmachung f

trash [træʃ] n (rubbish) Plunder m; (nonsense) Mist m; **~ can** (US) n Mülleimer m; **~y** (inf) adj minderwertig, wertlos; (novel) Schund-

traumatic [trɔː'mætɪk] adj traumatisch

travel ['trævl] n Reisen nt ♦ vi reisen ♦ vt (distance) zurücklegen; (country) bereisen; **~s** npl (journeys) Reisen pl; **~ agency** n Reisebüro nt; **~ agent** n Reisebürokaufmann(-frau) m(f); **~ler** (US **~er**) n Reisende(r) mf; (salesman) Handlungsreisende(r) m; **~ler's cheque** (US **~er's check**) n Reisescheck m; **~ling** (US **~ing**) n Reisen nt; **~sick** adj reisekrank; **~ sickness** n Reisekrankheit f

trawler ['trɔːləʳ] n (NAUT, FISHING) Fischdampfer m, Trawler m

tray [treɪ] n (tea ~) Tablett nt; (for mail) Ablage f

treacherous ['tretʃərəs] adj verräterisch; (road) tückisch

treachery ['tretʃərɪ] n Verrat m

treacle ['triːkl] n Sirup m, Melasse f

tread [tred] (pt trod, pp trodden) n Schritt m, Tritt m; (of stair) Stufe f; (on tyre) Profil nt ♦ vi treten; **~ on** vt fus treten auf +acc

treason ['triːzn] n Verrat m

treasure ['treʒəʳ] n Schatz m ♦ vt schätzen

treasurer ['treʒərəʳ] n Kassenverwalter m, Schatzmeister m

treasury ['treʒərɪ] n (POL) Finanzministerium nt

treat [triːt] n besondere Freude f ♦ vt (deal with) behandeln; **to ~ sb to sth** jdm etw spendieren

treatise ['triːtɪz] n Abhandlung f

treatment ['triːtmənt] n Behandlung f

treaty ['triːtɪ] n Vertrag m

treble ['trebl] adj dreifach ♦ vt verdreifachen; **~ clef** n Violinschlüssel m

tree [triː] n Baum m; **~ trunk** n Baumstamm m

trek [trek] n Treck m, Zug m; (inf) anstrengende(r) Weg m ♦ vi trecken

trellis ['trelɪs] n Gitter nt; (for gardening) Spalier nt

tremble ['trembl] vi zittern; (ground) beben

tremendous [trɪ'mendəs] adj gewaltig, kolossal; (inf: good) prima

tremor ['treməʳ] n Zittern nt; (of earth) Beben nt

trench [trentʃ] n Graben m; (MIL) Schützengraben m

trend [trend] n Tendenz f; **~y** (inf) adj modisch

trepidation [trepɪ'deɪʃən] n Beklommenheit f

trespass ['trespəs] vi: **to ~ on** widerrechtlich betreten; "**no ~ing**" „Betreten verboten"

trestle ['tresl] n Bock m; **~ table** n Klapptisch m

trial ['traɪəl] n (JUR) Prozess m; (test) Versuch m, Probe f; (hardship) Prüfung f; **by ~ and error** durch Ausprobieren; **~ period** n Probezeit f

triangle ['traɪæŋgl] n Dreieck nt; (MUS) Triangel f; **triangular** [traɪ'æŋgjuləʳ] adj dreieckig

tribal ['traɪbl] adj Stammes-

tribe [traɪb] n Stamm m; **~sman** (irreg) n Stammesangehörige(r) m

tribulation [trɪbju'leɪʃən] n Not f, Mühsal f

tribunal [traɪ'bjuːnl] n Gericht nt; (inquiry) Untersuchungsausschuss m

tributary ['trɪbjutərɪ] n Nebenfluss m

tribute ['trɪbjuːt] n (admiration) Zeichen nt der Hochachtung; **to pay ~ to sb/sth** jdm/ einer Sache Tribut zollen

trick [trɪk] n Trick m; (CARDS) Stich m ♦ vt überlisten, beschwindeln; **to play a ~ on sb** jdm einen Streich spielen; **that should do the ~** das müsste eigentlich klappen; **~ery** n Tricks pl

trickle ['trɪkl] n Tröpfeln nt; (small river) Rinnsal nt ♦ vi tröpfeln; (seep) sickern

tricky ['trɪkɪ] adj (problem) schwierig; (situation) kitzlig

tricycle ['traɪsɪkl] n Dreirad nt

trifle ['traɪfl] n Kleinigkeit f; (COOK) Trifle m ♦ adv: **a ~ ...** ein bisschen ...; **trifling** adj geringfügig

trigger ['trɪgəʳ] n Drücker m; **~ off** vt auslösen

trim [trɪm] adj gepflegt; (figure) schlank ♦ n (gute) Verfassung f; (embellishment, on car) Verzierung f ♦ vt (clip) schneiden; (trees) stutzen; (decorate) besetzen; (sails) trimmen; **~mings** npl (decorations) Verzierung f, Verzierungen pl; (extras) Zubehör nt

Trinity ['trɪnɪtɪ] n: **the ~** die Dreieinigkeit f

trinket ['trɪŋkɪt] n kleine(s) Schmuckstück nt

trip [trɪp] n (kurze) Reise f; (outing) Ausflug m; (stumble) Stolpern nt ♦ vi (stumble) stolpern; **on a ~** auf Reisen; **~ up** vi stolpern;

(fig) stolpern, einen Fehler machen ♦ *vt* zu
Fall bringen; *(fig)* hereinlegen
tripe |traip| *n (food)* Kutteln *pl*; *(rubbish)* Mist *m*
triple |'trɪpl| *adj* dreifach
triplets |'trɪplɪts| *npl* Drillinge *pl*
triplicate |'trɪplɪkət| *n*: **in ~** in dreifacher
Ausfertigung
tripod |'traɪpɔd| *n (PHOT)* Stativ *nt*
trite |traɪt| *adj* banal
triumph |'traɪʌmf| *n* Triumph *m* ♦ *vi*: **to ~
(over)** triumphieren (über +*acc*); **~ant**
|traɪ'ʌmfənt| *adj* triumphierend
trivia |'trɪvɪə| *npl* Trivialitäten *pl*
trivial |'trɪvɪəl| *adj* gering(fügig), trivial
trod |trɔd| *pt of* tread; **~den** *pp of* tread
trolley |'trɔlɪ| *n* Handwagen *m*; *(in shop)*
Einkaufswagen *m*; *(for luggage)* Kofferkuli *m*;
(table) Teewagen *m*; **~ bus** *n*
Oberleitungsbus *m*, Obus *m*
trombone |trɔm'bəun| *n* Posaune *f*
troop |tru:p| *n* Schar *f*; *(MIL)* Trupp *m*; **~s** *npl*
(MIL) Truppen *pl*; **~ in/out** *vi* hinein-/
hinausströmen; **~ing the colour** *n*
(ceremony) Fahnenparade *f*
trophy |'trəufɪ| *n* Trophäe *f*
tropic |'trɔpɪk| *n* Wendekreis *m*; **~al** *adj*
tropisch
trot |trɔt| *n* Trott *m* ♦ *vi* trotten; **on the ~**
(BRIT: fig: inf) in einer Tour
trouble |'trʌbl| *n (problems)* Ärger *m*; *(worry)*
Sorge *f*; *(in country, industry)* Unruhen *pl*;
(effort) Mühe *f*; *(MED)*: **stomach ~**
Magenbeschwerden *pl* ♦ *vt (disturb)* stören;
~s *npl (POL etc)* Unruhen *pl*; **to ~ to do sth**
sich bemühen, etw zu tun; **to be in ~**
Probleme *or* Ärger haben; **to go to the ~ of
doing sth** sich die Mühe machen, etw zu
tun; **what's the ~?** was ist los?; *(to sick
person)* wo fehlts?; **~d** *adj (person)*
beunruhigt; *(country)* geplagt; **~-free** *adj*
sorglos; **~maker** *n* Unruhestifter *m*;
~shooter *n* Vermittler *m*; **~some** *adj* lästig,
unangenehm; *(child)* schwierig
trough |trɔf| *n* Trog *m*; *(channel)* Rinne *f*,
Kanal *m*; *(MET)* Tief *nt*
trousers |'trauzəz| *npl* Hose *f*
trout |traut| *n* Forelle *f*
trowel |'trauəl| *n* Kelle *f*
truant |'truənt| *n*: **to play ~** *(BRIT)* (die
Schule) schwänzen
truce |tru:s| *n* Waffenstillstand *m*
truck |trʌk| *n* Lastwagen *m*; *(RAIL)* offene(r)
Güterwagen *m*; **~ driver** *n* Lastwagenfahrer
m; **~ farm** *(US)* *n* Gemüsegärtnerei *f*
trudge |trʌdʒ| *vi* sich (mühselig)
dahinschleppen
true |tru:| *adj (exact)* wahr; *(genuine)* echt;
(friend) treu
truffle |'trʌfl| *n* Trüffel *f or m*
truly |'tru:lɪ| *adv* wirklich; **yours ~** Ihr sehr
ergebener

trump |trʌmp| *n (CARDS)* Trumpf *m*
trumpet |'trʌmpɪt| *n* Trompete *f*
truncheon |'trʌntʃən| *n* Gummiknüppel *m*
trundle |'trʌndl| *vt* schieben ♦ *vi*: **to ~ along**
entlangrollen
trunk |trʌŋk| *n (of tree)* (Baum)stamm *m*;
(ANAT) Rumpf *m*; *(box)* Truhe *f*,
Überseekoffer *m*; *(of elephant)* Rüssel *m*; *(US:
AUT)* Kofferraum *m*; **~s** *npl (also:* **swimming
~s)** Badehose *f*
truss |trʌs| *vt (also: ~ up)* fesseln
trust |trʌst| *n (confidence)* Vertrauen *nt*; *(for
land etc)* Treuhandvermögen *nt* ♦ *vt (rely on)*
vertrauen +*dat*, sich verlassen auf +*acc*;
(hope) hoffen; *(entrust)*: **to ~ sth to sb** jdm
etw anvertrauen; **~ed** *adj* treu; **~ee** |trʌs'ti:|
n Vermögensverwalter *m*; **~ful** *adj*
vertrauensvoll; **~ing** *adj* vertrauensvoll;
~worthy *adj* vertrauenswürdig; *(account)*
glaubwürdig
truth |tru:θ| *n* Wahrheit *f*; **~ful** *adj* ehrlich
try |traɪ| *n* Versuch *m* ♦ *vt (attempt)*
versuchen; *(test)* (aus)probieren; *(JUR:
person)* unter Anklage stellen; *(: case)*
verhandeln; *(courage, patience)* auf die Probe
stellen ♦ *vi (make effort)* versuchen, sich
bemühen; **to have a ~** es versuchen; **to ~ to
do sth** versuchen, etw zu tun; **~ on** *vt
(dress)* anprobieren; *(hat)* aufprobieren; **~
out** *vt* ausprobieren; **~ing** *adj* schwierig
T-shirt |'ti:ʃə:t| *n* T-Shirt *nt*
T-square |'ti:skwɛəʳ| *n* Reißschiene *f*
tub |tʌb| *n* Wanne *f*, Kübel *m*; *(for margarine
etc)* Becher *m*
tubby |'tʌbɪ| *adj* rundlich
tube |tju:b| *n* Röhre *f*, Rohr *nt*; *(for toothpaste
etc)* Tube *f*; *(underground)* U-Bahn *f*; *(AUT)*
Schlauch *m*
tuberculosis |tjubə:kju'ləusɪs| *n* Tuberkulose
f
tube: **~ station** *n (in London)* U-Bahnstation
f; **tubing** *n* Schlauch *m*; **tubular** *adj*
röhrenförmig
TUC *(BRIT)* *n abbr* = **Trades Union Congress**
tuck |tʌk| *n (fold)* Falte *f*, Einschlag *m* ♦ *vt
(put)* stecken; *(gather)* fälteln, einschlagen;
~ away *vt* wegstecken; **~ in** *vt*
hineinstecken; *(blanket etc)* feststecken;
(person) zudecken ♦ *vi (eat)* hineinhauen,
zulangen; **~ up** *vt (child)* warm zudecken; **~
shop** *n* Süßwarenladen *m*
Tuesday |'tju:zdɪ| *n* Dienstag *m*
tuft |tʌft| *n* Büschel *m*
tug |tʌg| *n (jerk)* Zerren *nt*, Ruck *m*; *(NAUT)*
Schleppdampfer *m* ♦ *vt, vi* zerren, ziehen;
(boat) schleppen; **~ of war** *n* Tauziehen *nt*
tuition |tju:'ɪʃən| *n (BRIT)* Unterricht *m*;
(: private) Privatunterricht *m*; *(US: school
fees)* Schulgeld *nt*
tulip |'tju:lɪp| *n* Tulpe *f*
tumble |'tʌmbl| *n (fall)* Sturz *m* ♦ *vi* fallen,

stürzen; **~ to** vt fus kapieren; **~down** adj
baufällig; **~ dryer** (BRIT) n Trockner m; **~r**
['tʌmbləʳ] n (glass) Trinkglas nt
tummy ['tʌmɪ] (inf) n Bauch m; **~ upset** n
Magenverstimmung f
tumour ['tjuːməʳ] (US **tumor**) n Geschwulst
f, Tumor m
tumultuous |tjuːˈmʌltjuəs| adj (welcome,
applause etc) stürmisch
tuna ['tjuːnə] n T(h)unfisch m
tune [tjuːn] n Melodie f ♦ vt (MUS) stimmen;
(AUT) richtig einstellen; **to sing in ~/out of
~** richtig/falsch singen; **to be out of ~ with**
nicht harmonieren mit; **~ in** vi einschalten;
~ up vi (MUS) stimmen; **~ful** adj melodisch;
~r n (RAD) Tuner m; (person)
(Instrumenten)stimmer m; **piano ~r**
Klavierstimmer(in) m(f)
tunic ['tjuːnɪk] n Waffenrock m; (loose
garment) lange Bluse f
tuning ['tjuːnɪŋ] n (RAD, AUT) Einstellen nt;
(MUS) Stimmen nt; **~ fork** n Stimmgabel f
Tunisia |tjuːˈnɪzɪə] n Tunesien nt
tunnel ['tʌnl] n Tunnel m, Unterführung f ♦ vi
einen Tunnel anlegen
turbulent ['təːbjulənt] adj stürmisch
tureen |təˈriːn] n Terrine f
turf [təːf] n Rasen m; (piece) Sode f ♦ vt mit
Grassoden belegen; **~ out** (inf) vt
rauswerfen
turgid ['təːdʒɪd] adj geschwollen
Turk [təːk] n Türke m, Türkin f
Turkey ['təːkɪ] n Türkei f
turkey ['təːkɪ] n Puter m, Truthahn m
Turkish ['təːkɪʃ] adj türkisch ♦ n (LING)
Türkisch nt
turmoil ['təːmɔɪl] n Aufruhr m, Tumult m
turn [təːn] n (rotation) (Um)drehung f;
(performance) (Programm)nummer f; (MED)
Schock m ♦ vt (rotate) drehen; (change
position of) umdrehen, wenden; (page)
umblättern; (transform): **to ~ sth into sth**
etw in etw acc verwandeln; (direct)
zuwenden ♦ vi (rotate) sich drehen; (change
direction: in car) abbiegen; (: wind) drehen;
(~ round) umdrehen, wenden; (become)
werden; (leaves) sich verfärben; (milk) sauer
werden; (weather) umschlagen; **to do sb a
good ~** jdm etwas Gutes tun; **it's your ~** du
bist dran or an der Reihe; **in ~, by ~s**
abwechselnd; **to take ~s** sich abwechseln;
it gave me quite a ~ das hat mich
schön erschreckt; **"no left ~"** (AUT)
„Linksabbiegen verboten"; **~ away** vi sich
abwenden; **~ back** vt umdrehen; (person)
zurückschicken; (clock) zurückstellen ♦ vi
umkehren; **~ down** vt (refuse) ablehnen;
(fold down) umschlagen; **~ in** vi (go to bed)
ins Bett gehen ♦ vt (fold inwards) einwärts
biegen; **~ off** vi abbiegen ♦ vt ausschalten;
(tap) zudrehen; (machine, electricity)

abstellen; **~ on** vt (light) anschalten,
einschalten; (tap) aufdrehen; (machine)
anstellen; **~ out** vt (prove to be) sich
erweisen; (people) sich entwickeln ♦ vt (light)
ausschalten; (gas) abstellen; (produce)
produzieren; **how did the cake ~ out?** wie
ist der Kuchen geworden?; **~ over** vi
(person) sich umdrehen ♦ vt (object)
umdrehen, wenden; (page) umblättern; **~
round** vi (person, vehicle) sich herumdrehen;
(rotate) sich drehen; **~ up** vi auftauchen ♦ vt
(collar) hochklappen, hochstellen; (nose)
rümpfen; (increase: radio) lauter stellen;
(: heat) höher drehen; **~ing** n (in road)
Abzweigung f; **~ing point** n Wendepunkt
m
turnip ['təːnɪp] n Steckrübe f
turnout ['təːnaut] n (Besucher)zahl f
turnover ['təːnəuvəʳ] n Umsatz m; (of staff)
Wechsel m
turnpike ['təːnpaɪk] (US) n gebühren-
pflichtige Straße f
turn: ~stile ['təːnstaɪl] n Drehkreuz nt;
~table ['təːnteɪbl] n (of record player)
Plattenteller m; (RAIL) Drehscheibe f;
~-up [təːnʌp] (BRIT) n (on trousers)
Aufschlag m
turpentine ['təːpəntaɪn] n Terpentin nt
turquoise ['təːkwɔɪz] n (gem) Türkis m;
(colour) Türkis nt ♦ adj türkisfarben
turret ['tʌrɪt] n Turm m
turtle ['təːtl] n Schildkröte f; **~ neck
(sweater)** n Pullover m mit
Schildkrötkragen
tusk [tʌsk] n Stoßzahn m
tussle ['tʌsl] n Balgerei f
tutor ['tjuːtəʳ] n (teacher) Privatlehrer m;
(college instructor) Tutor m; **~ial** [tjuːˈtɔːrɪəl]
n (UNIV) Kolloquium nt, Seminarübung f
tuxedo [tʌkˈsiːdəu] (US) n Smoking m
TV [tiːˈviː] n abbr (= television) TV nt
twang [twæŋ] n scharfe(r) Ton m; (of voice)
Näseln nt
tweezers ['twiːzəz] npl Pinzette f
twelfth [twelfθ] adj zwölfte(r, s)
twelve [twelv] num zwölf; **at ~ o'clock**
(midday) um 12 Uhr; (midnight) um null Uhr
twentieth ['twentɪɪθ] adj zwanzigste(r, s)
twenty ['twentɪ] num zwanzig
twice [twaɪs] adv zweimal; **~ as much**
doppelt so viel
twiddle ['twɪdl] vt, vi: **to ~ (with) sth** an
etw dat herumdrehen; **to ~ one's thumbs**
(fig) Däumchen drehen
twig [twɪg] n dünne(r) Zweig m ♦ vt (inf)
kapieren, merken
twilight ['twaɪlaɪt] n Zwielicht nt
twin [twɪn] n Zwilling m ♦ adj Zwillings-;
(very similar) Doppel- ♦ vt (towns) zu
Partnerstädten machen; **~-bedded room** n
Zimmer nt mit zwei Einzelbetten; **~ beds**

npl zwei (gleiche) Einzelbetten *pl*

twine |twaɪn| *n* Bindfaden *m* ♦ *vi* (*plants*) sich ranken

twinge |twɪndʒ| *n* stechende(r) Schmerz *m*, Stechen *nt*

twinkle |'twɪŋkl| *n* Funkeln *nt*, Blitzen *nt* ♦ *vi* funkeln

twinned *adj*: **to be ~ with** die Partnerstadt von ... sein

twirl |twɔːl| *n* Wirbel *m* ♦ *vt, vi* (herum)wirbeln

twist |twɪst| *n* (*~ing*) Drehung *f*; (*bend*) Kurve *f* ♦ *vt* (*turn*) drehen; (*make crooked*) verbiegen; (*distort*) verdrehen ♦ *vi* (*wind*) sich drehen; (*curve*) sich winden

twit |twɪt| (*inf*) *n* Idiot *m*

twitch |twɪtʃ| *n* Zucken *nt* ♦ *vi* zucken

two |tuː| *num* zwei; **to put ~ and ~ together** seine Schlüsse ziehen; **~-door** *adj* zweitürig; **~-faced** *adj* falsch; **~fold** *adj, adv* zweifach, doppelt; **to increase ~fold** verdoppeln; **~-piece** *adj* zweiteilig; **~-piece (suit)** *n* Zweiteiler *m*; **~-piece (swimsuit)** *n* zweiteilige(r) Badeanzug *m*; **~-seater** *n* (*plane, car*) Zweisitzer *m*; **~some** *n* Paar *nt*; **~-way** *adj* (*traffic*) Gegen-

tycoon |taɪ'kuːn| *n*: **(business) ~** (Industrie)magnat *m*

type |taɪp| *n* Typ *m*, Art *f*; (*PRINT*) Type *f* ♦ *vt, vi* Maschine schreiben, tippen; **~-cast** *adj* (*THEAT, TV*) auf eine Rolle festgelegt; **~face** *n* Schrift *f*; **~script** *n* maschinegeschriebene(r) Text *m*; **~writer** *n* Schreibmaschine *f*; **~written** *adj* maschinegeschrieben

typhoid |'taɪfɔɪd| *n* Typhus *m*

typical |'tɪpɪkl| *adj*: **~ (of)** typisch (für)

typify |'tɪpɪfaɪ| *vt* typisch sein für

typing |'taɪpɪŋ| *n* Maschineschreiben *nt*

typist |'taɪpɪst| *n* Maschinenschreiber(in) *m(f)*, Tippse *f* (*inf*)

tyrant |'taɪərnt| *n* Tyrann *m*

tyre |'taɪər| (*US* **tire**) *n* Reifen *m*; **~ pressure** *n* Reifendruck *m*

U, u

U-bend |'juːbɛnd| *n* (*in pipe*) U-Bogen *m*

udder |'ʌdər| *n* Euter *nt*

UFO |'juːfəʊ| *n abbr* (= *unidentified flying object*) UFO *nt*

ugh |əːh| *excl* hu

ugliness |'ʌglɪnɪs| *n* Hässlichkeit *f*

ugly |'ʌglɪ| *adj* hässlich; (*bad*) böse, schlimm

UHT *abbr* (= *ultra heat treated*): **~ milk** H-Milch *f*

UK *n abbr* = **United Kingdom**

ulcer |'ʌlsər| *n* Geschwür *nt*

Ulster |'ʌlstər| *n* Ulster *m*

ulterior |ʌl'tɪərɪər| *adj*: **~ motive** Hintergedanke *m*

ultimate |'ʌltɪmət| *adj* äußerste(r, s), allerletzte(r, s); **~ly** *adv* schließlich, letzten Endes

ultrasound |'ʌltrəsaʊnd| *n* (*MED*) Ultraschall *m*

umbilical cord |ʌm'bɪlɪkl-| *n* Nabelschnur *f*

umbrella |ʌm'brɛlə| *n* Schirm *m*

umpire |'ʌmpaɪər| *n* Schiedsrichter *m* ♦ *vt, vi* schiedsrichtern

umpteenth |ʌmp'tiːnθ| (*inf*) *adj* zig; **for the ~ time** zum x-ten Mal

UN *n abbr* = **United Nations**

unable |ʌn'eɪbl| *adj*: **to be ~ to do sth** etw nicht tun können

unacceptable |ʌnək'sɛptəbl| *adj* unannehmbar, nicht akzeptabel

unaccompanied |ʌnə'kʌmpənɪd| *adj* ohne Begleitung

unaccountably |ʌnə'kaʊntəblɪ| *adv* unerklärlich

unaccustomed |ʌnə'kʌstəmd| *adj* nicht gewöhnt; (*unusual*) ungewohnt; **~ to** nicht gewöhnt an *+acc*

unanimous |juː'nænɪməs| *adj* einmütig; (*vote*) einstimmig; **~ly** *adv* einmütig; einstimmig

unarmed |ʌn'ɑːmd| *adj* unbewaffnet

unashamed |ʌnə'ʃeɪmd| *adj* schamlos

unassuming |ʌnə'sjuːmɪŋ| *adj* bescheiden

unattached |ʌnə'tætʃt| *adj* ungebunden

unattended |ʌnə'tɛndɪd| *adj* (*person*) unbeaufsichtigt; (*thing*) unbewacht

unauthorized |ʌn'ɔːθəraɪzd| *adj* unbefugt

unavoidable |ʌnə'vɔɪdəbl| *adj* unvermeidlich

unaware |ʌnə'wɛər| *adj*: **to be ~ of sth** sich *dat* einer Sache *gen* nicht bewusst sein; **~s** *adv* unversehens

unbalanced |ʌn'bælənst| *adj* unausgeglichen; (*mentally*) gestört

unbearable |ʌn'bɛərəbl| *adj* unerträglich

unbeatable |ʌn'biːtəbl| *adj* unschlagbar

unbeknown(st) |ʌnbɪ'nəʊn(st)| *adv*: **~ to me** ohne mein Wissen

unbelievable |ʌnbɪ'liːvəbl| *adj* unglaublich

unbend |ʌn'bɛnd| (*irreg: like* **bend**) *vt* gerade biegen ♦ *vi* aus sich herausgehen

unbias(s)ed |ʌn'baɪəst| *adj* unparteiisch

unborn |ʌn'bɔːn| *adj* ungeboren

unbreakable |ʌn'breɪkəbl| *adj* unzerbrechlich

unbridled |ʌn'braɪdld| *adj* ungezügelt

unbroken |ʌn'brəʊkən| *adj* (*period*) ununterbrochen; (*spirit*) ungebrochen; (*record*) unübertroffen

unburden |ʌn'bɔːdn| *vt*: **to ~ o.s.** (jdm) sein Herz ausschütten

unbutton |ʌn'bʌtn| *vt* aufknöpfen

uncalled-for |ʌn'kɔːldfɔːr| *adj* unnötig

uncanny |ʌn'kænɪ| *adj* unheimlich

unceasing |ʌn'siːsɪŋ| *adj* unaufhörlich

unceremonious |ʌnsɛrɪˈməʊnɪəs| adj
(abrupt, rude) brüsk; (exit, departure)
überstürzt

uncertain |ʌnˈsəːtn| adj unsicher; (doubtful)
ungewiss; (unreliable) unbeständig; (vague)
undeutlich, vag(e); ~**ty** n Ungewissheit f

unchanged |ʌnˈtʃeɪndʒd| adj unverändert

unchecked |ʌnˈtʃɛkt| adj ungeprüft; (not
stopped: advance) ungehindert

uncivilized |ʌnˈsɪvɪlaɪzd| adj unzivilisiert

uncle |ˈʌŋkl| n Onkel m

uncomfortable |ʌnˈkʌmfətəbl| adj
unbequem, ungemütlich

uncommon |ʌnˈkɔmən| adj ungewöhnlich;
(outstanding) außergewöhnlich

uncompromising |ʌnˈkɔmprəmaɪzɪŋ| adj
kompromisslos, unnachgiebig

unconcerned |ʌnkənˈsəːnd| adj
unbekümmert; (indifferent) gleichgültig

unconditional |ʌnkənˈdɪʃənl| adj
bedingungslos

unconscious |ʌnˈkɔnʃəs| adj (MED)
bewusstlos; (not meant) unbeabsichtigt ♦ n:
the ~ das Unbewusste; ~**ly** adv unbewusst

uncontrollable |ʌnkənˈtrəʊləbl| adj
unkontrollierbar, unbändig

unconventional |ʌnkənˈvɛnʃənl| adj
unkonventionell

uncouth |ʌnˈkuːθ| adj grob

uncover |ʌnˈkʌvəʳ| vt aufdecken

undecided |ʌndɪˈsaɪdɪd| adj unschlüssig

undeniable |ʌndɪˈnaɪəbl| adj unleugbar

under |ˈʌndəʳ| prep unter ♦ adv darunter; ~
there da drunter; ~ **repair** in Reparatur

underage |ʌndərˈeɪdʒ| adj minderjährig

undercarriage |ˈʌndəkærɪdʒ| (BRIT) n (AVIAT)
Fahrgestell nt

undercharge |ʌndəˈtʃɑːdʒ| vt: **to** ~ **sb** jdm
zu wenig berechnen

undercoat |ˈʌndəkəʊt| n (paint)
Grundierung f

undercover |ʌndəˈkʌvəʳ| adj Geheim-

undercurrent |ˈʌndəkʌrnt| n Unter-
strömung f

undercut |ʌndəˈkʌt| (irreg: like cut) vt
unterbieten

underdeveloped |ˈʌndədɪˈvɛləpt| adj
Entwicklungs-, unterentwickelt

underdog |ˈʌndədɔg| n Unterlegene(r) mf

underdone |ʌndəˈdʌn| adj (COOK) nicht gar,
nicht durchgebraten

underestimate |ˈʌndərˈɛstɪmeɪt| vt
unterschätzen

underexposed |ˈʌndərɪksˈpəʊzd| adj
unterbelichtet

underfoot |ʌndəˈfʊt| adv am Boden

undergo |ʌndəˈgəʊ| (irreg: like go) vt
(experience) durchmachen; (test, operation)
sich unterziehen +dat

undergraduate |ʌndəˈgrædjuɪt| n
Student(in) m(f)

underground |ˈʌndəgraʊnd| n U-Bahn f
♦ adj Untergrund-

undergrowth |ˈʌndəgrəʊθ| n Gestrüpp nt,
Unterholz nt

underhand(ed) |ʌndəˈhænd(ɪd)| adj
hinterhältig

underlie |ʌndəˈlaɪ| (irreg: like lie) vt zugrunde
or zu Grunde liegen +dat

underline |ʌndəˈlaɪn| vt unterstreichen;
(emphasize) betonen

underling |ˈʌndəlɪŋ| n Handlanger m

undermine |ʌndəˈmaɪn| vt untergraben

underneath |ʌndəˈniːθ| adv darunter ♦ prep
unter

underpaid |ʌndəˈpeɪd| adj unterbezahlt

underpants |ˈʌndəpænts| npl Unterhose f

underpass |ˈʌndəpɑːs| (BRIT) n
Unterführung f

underprivileged |ʌndəˈprɪvɪlɪdʒd| adj
benachteiligt, unterprivilegiert

underrate |ʌndəˈreɪt| vt unterschätzen

undershirt |ˈʌndəʃəːt| (US) n Unterhemd nt

undershorts |ˈʌndəʃɔːts| (US) npl Unterhose
f

underside |ˈʌndəsaɪd| n Unterseite f

underskirt |ˈʌndəskəːt| (BRIT) n Unterrock m

understand |ʌndəˈstænd| (irreg: like stand)
vt, vi verstehen; **I** ~ **that ...** ich habe gehört,
dass ...; **am I to** ~ **that ...?** soll das (etwa)
heißen, dass ...?; **what do you** ~ **by that?**
was verstehen Sie darunter?; **it is**
understood that ... es wurde vereinbart,
dass ...; **to make o.s. understood** sich
verständlich machen; **is that understood?**
ist das klar?; ~**able** adj verständlich; ~**ing** n
Verständnis nt ♦ adj verständnisvoll

understatement |ˈʌndəsteɪtmənt| n
(quality) Untertreibung f; **that's an** ~! das
ist untertrieben!

understood |ʌndəˈstʊd| pt, pp of
understand ♦ adj klar; (implied)
angenommen

understudy |ˈʌndəstʌdɪ| n
Ersatz(schau)spieler(in) m(f)

undertake |ʌndəˈteɪk| (irreg: like take) vt
unternehmen ♦ vi: **to** ~ **to do sth** sich
verpflichten, etw zu tun

undertaker |ˈʌndəteɪkəʳ| n Leichenbestatter
m

undertaking |ˈʌndəteɪkɪŋ| n (enterprise)
Unternehmen nt; (promise) Verpflichtung f

undertone |ˈʌndətəʊn| n: **in an** ~ mit
gedämpfter Stimme

underwater |ʌndəˈwɔːtəʳ| adv unter Wasser
♦ adj Unterwasser-

underwear |ˈʌndəwɛəʳ| n Unterwäsche f

underworld |ˈʌndəwəːld| n (of crime)
Unterwelt f

underwriter |ˈʌndəraɪtəʳ| n Assekurant m

undesirable |ʌndɪˈzaɪərəbl| adj unerwünscht

undies |ˈʌndɪz| (inf) npl (Damen)unterwäsche f

undisputed [ˈʌndɪsˈpjuːtɪd] adj unbestritten

undo [ʌnˈduː] (irreg: like **do**) vt (unfasten)
öffnen, aufmachen; (work) zunichte machen;
~ing n Verderben nt

undoubted [ʌnˈdautɪd] adj unbezweifelt;
~ly adv zweifellos, ohne Zweifel

undress [ʌnˈdrɛs] vt ausziehen ♦ vi sich
ausziehen

undue [ʌnˈdjuː] adj übermäßig

undulating [ˈʌndjuleɪtɪŋ] adj wellenförmig;
(country) wellig

unduly [ʌnˈdjuːlɪ] adv übermäßig

unearth [ʌnˈɜːθ] vt (dig up) ausgraben;
(discover) ans Licht bringen

unearthly [ʌnˈɜːθlɪ] adj (hour) nachtschlafen

uneasy [ʌnˈiːzɪ] adj (worried) unruhig;
(feeling) ungut

uneconomic(al) [ˈʌniːkəˈnɒmɪk(l)] adj
unwirtschaftlich

uneducated [ʌnˈedjukeɪtɪd] adj ungebildet

unemployed [ʌnɪmˈplɔɪd] adj arbeitslos
♦ npl: **the ~** die Arbeitslosen pl

unemployment [ʌnɪmˈplɔɪmənt] n
Arbeitslosigkeit f

unending [ʌnˈɛndɪŋ] adj endlos

unerring [ʌnˈɜːrɪŋ] adj unfehlbar

uneven [ʌnˈiːvn] adj (surface) uneben;
(quality) ungleichmäßig

unexpected [ʌnɪksˈpɛktɪd] adj unerwartet;
~ly adv unerwartet

unfailing [ʌnˈfeɪlɪŋ] adj nie versagend

unfair [ʌnˈfɛəˈ] adj ungerecht, unfair

unfaithful [ʌnˈfeɪθful] adj untreu

unfamiliar [ʌnfəˈmɪlɪəˈ] adj ungewohnt;
(person, subject) unbekannt; **to be ~ with**
nicht kennen +acc, nicht vertraut sein mit

unfashionable [ʌnˈfæʃnəbl] adj unmodern;
(area etc) nicht in Mode

unfasten [ʌnˈfɑːsn] vt öffnen, aufmachen

unfavourable [ʌnˈfeɪvrəbl] (US **unfavor-
able**) adj ungünstig

unfeeling [ʌnˈfiːlɪŋ] adj gefühllos, kalt

unfinished [ʌnˈfɪnɪʃt] adj unvollendet

unfit [ʌnˈfɪt] adj ungeeignet; (in bad health)
nicht fit; **~ for sth** zu or für etw ungeeignet

unfold [ʌnˈfəuld] vt entfalten; (paper)
auseinander falten ♦ vi (develop) sich
entfalten

unforeseen [ˈʌnfɔːˈsiːn] adj unvorher-
gesehen

unforgettable [ʌnfəˈgɛtəbl] adj unver-
gesslich

unforgivable [ʌnfəˈgɪvəbl] adj unverzeihlich

unfortunate [ʌnˈfɔːtʃənət] adj unglücklich,
bedauerlich; **~ly** adv leider

unfounded [ʌnˈfaundɪd] adj unbegründet

unfriendly [ʌnˈfrɛndlɪ] adj unfreundlich

ungainly [ʌnˈgeɪnlɪ] adj linkisch

ungodly [ʌnˈgɒdlɪ] adj (hour) nacht-
schlafend; (row) heillos

ungrateful [ʌnˈgreɪtful] adj undankbar

unhappiness [ʌnˈhæpɪnɪs] n Unglück nt,
Unglückseligkeit f

unhappy [ʌnˈhæpɪ] adj unglücklich; **~ with**
(arrangements etc) unzufrieden mit

unharmed [ʌnˈhɑːmd] adj wohlbehalten,
unversehrt

UNHCR n abbr (= United Nations High
Commission for Refugees) Flüchtlings-
hochkommissariat nt der Vereinten Nationen

unhealthy [ʌnˈhɛlθɪ] adj ungesund

unheard-of [ʌnˈhɜːdɒv] adj unerhört

unhurt [ʌnˈhɜːt] adj unverletzt

unidentified [ʌnaɪˈdɛntɪfaɪd] adj unbekannt,
nicht identifiziert

uniform [ˈjuːnɪfɔːm] n Uniform f ♦ adj
einheitlich; **~ity** [juːnɪˈfɔːmɪtɪ] n
Einheitlichkeit f

unify [ˈjuːnɪfaɪ] vt vereinigen

unilateral [juːnɪˈlætərəl] adj einseitig

uninhabited [ʌnɪnˈhæbɪtɪd] adj unbewohnt

unintentional [ʌnɪnˈtɛnʃənəl] adj
unabsichtlich

union [ˈjuːnjən] n (uniting) Vereinigung f;
(alliance) Bund m, Union f; (trade ~)
Gewerkschaft f; **U~ Jack** n Union Jack m

unique [juːˈniːk] adj einzig(artig)

UNISON [ˈjuːnɪsn] n Gewerkschaft der
Angestellten im öffentlichen Dienst

unison [ˈjuːnɪsn] n Einstimmigkeit f; **in ~**
einstimmig

unit [ˈjuːnɪt] n Einheit f; **kitchen ~**
Küchenelement nt

unite [juːˈnaɪt] vt vereinigen ♦ vi sich
vereinigen; **~d** adj vereinigt; (together)
vereint; **U~d Kingdom** n Vereinigte(s)
Königreich nt; **U~d Nations
(Organization)** n Vereinte Nationen pl;
U~d States (of America) n Vereinigte
Staaten pl (von Amerika)

unit trust (BRIT) n Treuhandgesellschaft
f

unity [ˈjuːnɪtɪ] n Einheit f; (agreement)
Einigkeit f

universal [juːnɪˈvɜːsl] adj allgemein

universe [ˈjuːnɪvɜːs] n (Welt)all nt

university [juːnɪˈvɜːsɪtɪ] n Universität f

unjust [ʌnˈdʒʌst] adj ungerecht

unkempt [ʌnˈkɛmpt] adj ungepflegt

unkind [ʌnˈkaɪnd] adj unfreundlich

unknown [ʌnˈnəun] adj: **~ (to sb)** (jdm)
unbekannt

unlawful [ʌnˈlɔːful] adj illegal

unleaded [ˈʌnˈlɛdɪd] adj bleifrei, unverbleit; **I
use ~** ich fahre bleifrei

unleash [ʌnˈliːʃ] vt entfesseln

unless [ʌnˈlɛs] conj wenn nicht, es sei denn;
~ he comes es sei denn, er kommt; **~
otherwise stated** sofern nicht anders
angegeben

unlike [ʌnˈlaɪk] adj unähnlich ♦ prep im

Gegensatz zu

unlikely [ʌn'laɪklɪ] *adj (not likely)*
unwahrscheinlich; *(unexpected: combination etc)* merkwürdig

unlimited [ʌn'lɪmɪtɪd] *adj* unbegrenzt

unlisted ['ʌn'lɪstɪd] *(US) adj* nicht im Telefonbuch stehend

unload [ʌn'ləʊd] *vt* entladen

unlock [ʌn'lɒk] *vt* aufschließen

unlucky [ʌn'lʌkɪ] *adj* unglücklich; *(person)* unglückselig; **to be ~** Pech haben

unmarried [ʌn'mærɪd] *adj* unverheiratet, ledig

unmask [ʌn'mɑːsk] *vt* entlarven

unmistakable [ʌnmɪs'teɪkəbl] *adj* unverkennbar

unmitigated [ʌn'mɪtɪgeɪtɪd] *adj* ungemildert, ganz

unnatural [ʌn'nætʃrəl] *adj* unnatürlich

unnecessary [ʌn'nesəsərɪ] *adj* unnötig

unnoticed [ʌn'nəʊtɪst] *adj*: **to go ~** unbemerkt bleiben

UNO ['juːnəʊ] *n abbr* = **United Nations Organization**

unobtainable [ʌnəb'teɪnəbl] *adj*: **this number is ~** kein Anschluss unter dieser Nummer

unobtrusive [ʌnəb'truːsɪv] *adj* unauffällig

unofficial [ʌnə'fɪʃl] *adj* inoffiziell

unpack [ʌn'pæk] *vt*, *vi* auspacken

unparalleled [ʌn'pærəleld] *adj* beispiellos

unpleasant [ʌn'plɛznt] *adj* unangenehm

unplug [ʌn'plʌg] *vt* den Stecker herausziehen von

unpopular [ʌn'pɒpjʊləʳ] *adj (person)* unbeliebt; *(decision etc)* unpopulär

unprecedented [ʌn'presɪdentɪd] *adj* beispiellos

unpredictable [ʌnprɪ'dɪktəbl] *adj* unvorhersehbar; *(weather, person)* unberechenbar

unprofessional [ʌnprə'feʃənl] *adj* unprofessionell

UNPROFOR *n abbr* (= *United Nations Protection Force*) UNPROFOR f

unqualified [ʌn'kwɒlɪfaɪd] *adj (success)* uneingeschränkt, voll; *(person)* unqualifiziert

unquestionably [ʌn'kwestʃənəblɪ] *adv* fraglos

unravel [ʌn'rævl] *vt (disentangle)* ausfasern, entwirren; *(solve)* lösen

unreal [ʌn'rɪəl] *adj* unwirklich

unrealistic ['ʌnrɪə'lɪstɪk] *adj* unrealistisch

unreasonable [ʌn'riːznəbl] *adj* unvernünftig; *(demand)* übertrieben

unrelated [ʌnrɪ'leɪtɪd] *adj* ohne Beziehung; *(family)* nicht verwandt

unrelenting [ʌnrɪ'lentɪŋ] *adj* unerbittlich

unreliable [ʌnrɪ'laɪəbl] *adj* unzuverlässig

unremitting [ʌnrɪ'mɪtɪŋ] *adj (efforts, attempts)* unermüdlich

unreservedly [ʌnrɪ'zɜːvɪdlɪ] *adv* offen; *(believe, trust)* uneingeschränkt; *(cry)* rückhaltlos

unrest [ʌn'rest] *n (discontent)* Unruhe f; *(fighting)* Unruhen pl

unroll [ʌn'rəʊl] *vt* aufrollen

unruly [ʌn'ruːlɪ] *adj (child)* undiszipliniert; schwer lenkbar

unsafe [ʌn'seɪf] *adj* nicht sicher

unsaid [ʌn'sed] *adj*: **to leave sth ~** etw ungesagt lassen

unsatisfactory ['ʌnsætɪs'fæktərɪ] *adj* unbefriedigend; unzulänglich

unsavoury [ʌn'seɪvərɪ] *(US* **unsavory**) *adj (fig)* widerwärtig

unscathed [ʌn'skeɪðd] *adj* unversehrt

unscrew [ʌn'skruː] *vt* aufschrauben

unscrupulous [ʌn'skruːpjʊləs] *adj* skrupellos

unsettled [ʌn'setld] *adj (person)* rastlos; *(weather)* wechselhaft

unshaven [ʌn'ʃeɪvn] *adj* unrasiert

unsightly [ʌn'saɪtlɪ] *adj* unansehnlich

unskilled [ʌn'skɪld] *adj* ungelernt

unspeakable [ʌn'spiːkəbl] *adj (joy)* unsagbar; *(crime)* scheußlich

unstable [ʌn'steɪbl] *adj* instabil; *(mentally)* labil

unsteady [ʌn'stedɪ] *adj* unsicher

unstuck [ʌn'stʌk] *adj*: **to come ~** sich lösen; *(fig)* ins Wasser fallen

unsuccessful [ʌnsək'sesful] *adj* erfolglos

unsuitable [ʌn'suːtəbl] *adj* unpassend

unsure [ʌn'ʃʊəʳ] *adj* unsicher; **to be ~ of o.s.** unsicher sein

unsuspecting [ʌnsəs'pektɪŋ] *adj* nicht ahnend

unsympathetic ['ʌnsɪmpə'θetɪk] *adj* gefühllos; *(response)* abweisend; *(unlikeable)* unsympathisch

untapped [ʌn'tæpt] *adj (resources)* ungenützt

unthinkable [ʌn'θɪŋkəbl] *adj* unvorstellbar

untidy [ʌn'taɪdɪ] *adj* unordentlich

untie [ʌn'taɪ] *vt* aufschnüren

until [ən'tɪl] *prep, conj* bis; **~ he comes** bis er kommt; **~ then** bis dann; **~ now** bis jetzt

untimely [ʌn'taɪmlɪ] *adj (death)* vorzeitig

untold [ʌn'təʊld] *adj* unermesslich

untoward [ʌntə'wɔːd] *adj* widrig

untranslatable [ʌntrænz'leɪtəbl] *adj* unübersetzbar

unused [ʌn'juːzd] *adj* unbenutzt

unusual [ʌn'juːʒʊəl] *adj* ungewöhnlich

unveil [ʌn'veɪl] *vt* enthüllen

unwanted [ʌn'wɒntɪd] *adj* unerwünscht

unwavering [ʌn'weɪvərɪŋ] *adj* standhaft, unerschütterlich

unwelcome [ʌn'welkəm] *adj (at a bad time)* unwillkommen; *(unpleasant)* unerfreulich

unwell [ʌn'wel] *adj*: **to feel** *or* **be ~** sich nicht wohl fühlen

unwieldy [ʌnˈwiːldɪ] *adj* sperrig
unwilling [ʌnˈwɪlɪŋ] *adj*: **to be ~ to do sth** nicht bereit sein, etw zu tun; **~ly** *adv* widerwillig
unwind [ʌnˈwaɪnd] (*irreg: like* wind²) *vt* abwickeln ♦ *vi* (*relax*) sich entspannen
unwise [ʌnˈwaɪz] *adj* unklug
unwitting [ʌnˈwɪtɪŋ] *adj* unwissentlich
unworkable [ʌnˈwəːkəbl] *adj* (*plan*) undurchführbar
unworthy [ʌnˈwəːðɪ] *adj* (*person*): **~ (of sth)** (einer Sache *gen*) nicht wert
unwrap [ʌnˈræp] *vt* auspacken
unwritten [ʌnˈrɪtn] *adj* ungeschrieben

KEYWORD
---

up [ʌp] *prep*: **to be up sth** oben auf etw *dat* sein; **to go up sth** (auf) etw *acc* hinaufgehen; **go up that road** gehen Sie die Straße hinauf
♦ *adv* **1** (*upwards, higher*) oben; **put it up a bit higher** stell es etwas weiter nach oben; **up there** da oben, dort oben; **up above** hoch oben
2: **to be up** (*out of bed*) auf sein; (*prices, level*) gestiegen sein; (*building, tent*) stehen
3: **up to** (*as far as*) bis; **up to now** bis jetzt
4: **to be up to** (*depending on*): **it's up to you** das hängt von dir ab; (*equal to*): **he's not up to it** (*job, task etc*) er ist dem nicht gewachsen; (*inf: be doing: showing disapproval, suspicion*): **what is he up to?** was führt er im Schilde?; **it's not up to me to decide** die Entscheidung liegt nicht bei mir; **his work is not up to the required standard** seine Arbeit entspricht nicht dem geforderten Niveau
♦ *n*: **ups and downs** (*in life, career*) Höhen und Tiefen *pl*

up-and-coming [ʌpəndˈkʌmɪŋ] *adj.* aufstrebend
upbringing [ˈʌpbrɪŋɪŋ] *n* Erziehung *f*
update [ʌpˈdeɪt] *vt* auf den neuesten Stand bringen
upgrade [ʌpˈgreɪd] *vt* höher einstufen
upheaval [ʌpˈhiːvl] *n* Umbruch *m*
uphill [ˈʌpˈhɪl] *adj* ansteigend; (*fig*) mühsam ♦ *adv*: **to go ~** bergauf gehen/fahren
uphold [ʌpˈhəuld] (*irreg: like* hold) *vt* unterstützen
upholstery [ʌpˈhəulstərɪ] *n* Polster *nt*; Polsterung *f*
upkeep [ˈʌpkiːp] *n* Instandhaltung *f*
upon [əˈpɔn] *prep* auf
upper [ˈʌpəʳ] *n* (*on shoe*) Oberleder *nt* ♦ *adj* obere(r, s), höhere(r, s); **to have the ~ hand** die Oberhand haben; **~-class** *adj* vornehm; **~most** *adj* oberste(r, s), höchste(r, s); **what was ~most in my mind** was mich in erster Linie beschäftigte; **~**

sixth (*BRIT: SCH*) *n* Abschlussklasse *f*
upright [ˈʌpraɪt] *adj* aufrecht
uprising [ˈʌpraɪzɪŋ] *n* Aufstand *m*
uproar [ˈʌprɔːʳ] *n* Aufruhr *m*
uproot [ʌpˈruːt] *vt* ausreißen
upset [*n* ˈʌpset, *vb, adj* ʌpˈset] (*irreg: like* set) *n* Aufregung *f* ♦ *vt* (*overturn*) umwerfen; (*disturb*) aufregen, bestürzen; (*plans*) durcheinander bringen ♦ *adj* (*person*) aufgeregt; (*stomach*) verdorben
upshot [ˈʌpʃɔt] *n* (End)ergebnis *nt*
upside-down [ˈʌpsaɪd-] *adv* verkehrt herum
upstairs [ʌpˈsteəz] *adv* oben; (*go*) nach oben ♦ *adj* (*room*) obere(r, s), Ober- ♦ *n* obere(s) Stockwerk *nt*
upstart [ˈʌpstɑːt] *n* Emporkömmling *m*
upstream [ʌpˈstriːm] *adv* stromaufwärts
uptake [ˈʌpteɪk] *n*: **to be quick on the ~** schnell begreifen; **to be slow on the ~** schwer von Begriff sein
uptight [ʌpˈtaɪt] (*inf*) *adj* (*nervous*) nervös; (*inhibited*) verklemmt
up-to-date [ˈʌptəˈdeɪt] *adj* (*clothes*) modisch, modern; (*information*) neueste(r, s)
upturn [ˈʌptəːn] *n* Aufschwung *m*
upward [ˈʌpwəd] *adj* nach oben gerichtet; **~(s)** *adv* aufwärts
uranium [juəˈreɪnɪəm] *n* Uran *nt*
urban [ˈəːbən] *adj* städtisch, Stadt-; **~ clearway** *n* Stadtautobahn *f*
urchin [ˈəːtʃɪn] *n* (*boy*) Schlingel *m*; (*sea ~*) Seeigel *m*
urge [əːdʒ] *n* Drang *m* ♦ *vt*: **to ~ sb to do sth** (*dazu*) drängen, etw zu tun
urgency [ˈəːdʒənsɪ] *n* Dringlichkeit *f*
urgent [ˈəːdʒənt] *adj* dringend
urinal [ˈjuərɪnl] *n* (*public*) Pissoir *nt*
urinate [ˈjuərɪneɪt] *vi* urinieren
urine [ˈjuərɪn] *n* Urin *m*, Harn *m*
urn [əːn] *n* Urne *f*; (*tea ~*) Teemaschine *f*
US *n abbr* = **United States**
us [ʌs] *pron* uns; *see also* **me**
USA *n abbr* = **United States of America**
usage [ˈjuːzɪdʒ] *n* Gebrauch *m*; (*esp LING*) Sprachgebrauch *m*
use [*n* juːs, *vb* juːz] *n* (*employment*) Gebrauch *m*; (*point*) Zweck *m* ♦ *vt* gebrauchen; **in ~** in Gebrauch; **out of ~** außer Gebrauch; **to be of ~** nützlich sein; **it's no ~** es hat keinen Zweck; **what's the ~?** was solls?; **~d to** (*accustomed to*) gewöhnt an +*acc*; **she ~d to live here** (*formerly*) sie hat früher mal hier gewohnt; **~ up** *vt* aufbrauchen, verbrauchen; **~d** *adj* (*car*) Gebraucht-; **~ful** *adj* nützlich; **~fulness** *n* Nützlichkeit *f*; **~less** *adj* nutzlos, unnütz; **~r** *n* Benutzer *m*; **~r-friendly** *adj* (*computer*) benutzerfreundlich
usher [ˈʌʃəʳ] *n* Platzanweiser *m*; **~ette** [ʌʃəˈret] *n* Platzanweiserin *f*
usual [ˈjuːʒuəl] *adj* gewöhnlich, üblich; **as ~**

wie üblich; **~ly** adv gewöhnlich
usurp [ju:'zə:p] vt an sich reißen
utensil [ju:'tensl] n Gerät nt; **kitchen ~s** Küchengeräte pl
uterus ['ju:tərəs] n Gebärmutter f
utilitarian [ju:tılı'teərıən] adj Nützlichkeits-
utility [ju:'tılıtı] n (usefulness) Nützlichkeit f; (also: **public ~**) öffentliche(r) Versorgungsbetrieb m; **~ room** n Hauswirtschaftsraum m
utilize ['ju:tılaız] vt benützen
utmost ['ʌtməust] adj äußerste(r, s) ♦ n: **to do one's ~** sein Möglichstes tun
utter ['ʌtə'] adj äußerste(r, s), höchste(r, s), völlig ♦ vt äußern, aussprechen; **~ance** n Äußerung f; **~ly** adv äußerst, absolut, völlig
U-turn ['ju:'tə:n] n (AUT) Kehrtwendung f

V, v

v. abbr = **verse; versus; volt;** (= vide) siehe
vacancy ['veıkənsı] n (BRIT: job) offene Stelle f; (room) freie(s) Zimmer nt; **"no vacancies"** „belegt"
vacant ['veıkənt] adj leer; (unoccupied) frei; (house) leer stehend, unbewohnt; (stupid) (gedanken)leer; **~ lot** (US) n unbebaute(s) Grundstück nt
vacate [və'keıt] vt (seat) frei machen; (room) räumen
vacation [və'keıʃən] n Ferien pl, Urlaub m; **~ist** (US) n Ferienreisende(r) f(m)
vaccinate ['væksıneıt] vt impfen
vaccine ['væksi:n] n Impfstoff m
vacuum ['vækjum] n Vakuum nt; **~ bottle** (US) n Thermosflasche f; **~ cleaner** n Staubsauger m; **~ flask** (BRIT) n Thermosflasche f; **~-packed** adj vakuumversiegelt
vagina [və'dʒaınə] n Scheide f
vague [veıg] adj vag(e); (absent-minded) geistesabwesend; **~ly** adv unbestimmt, vag(e)
vain [veın] adj eitel; (attempt) vergeblich; **in ~** vergebens, umsonst
valentine ['væləntaın] n (also: **~ card**) Valentinsgruß m; **V~'s Day** n Valentinstag m
valet ['vælıt] n Kammerdiener m
valiant ['væliənt] adj tapfer
valid ['vælıd] adj gültig; (argument) stichhaltig; (objection) berechtigt; **~ity** [və'lıdıtı] n Gültigkeit f
valley ['vælı] n Tal nt
valour ['vælə'] (US **valor**) n Tapferkeit f
valuable ['væljuəbl] adj wertvoll; (time) kostbar; **~s** npl Wertsachen pl
valuation [vælju'eıʃən] n (FIN) Schätzung f; Beurteilung f
value ['vælju:] n Wert m; (usefulness) Nutzen m ♦ vt (prize) (hoch) schätzen, werthalten;

(estimate) schätzen; **~ added tax** (BRIT) n Mehrwertsteuer f; **~d** adj (hoch) geschätzt
valve [vælv] n Ventil nt; (BIOL) Klappe f; (RAD) Röhre f
van [væn] n Lieferwagen m; (BRIT: RAIL) Waggon m
vandal ['vændl] n Rowdy m; **~ism** ['vændəlızəm] n mutwillige Beschädigung f; **~ize** ['vændəlaız] vt mutwillig beschädigen
vanguard ['vænga:d] n (fig) Spitze f
vanilla [və'nılə] n Vanille f; **~ ice cream** n Vanilleeis nt
vanish ['vænıʃ] vi verschwinden
vanity ['vænıtı] n Eitelkeit f; **~ case** n Schminkkoffer m
vantage ['va:ntıdʒ] n: **~ point** gute(r) Aussichtspunkt m
vapour ['veıpə'] (US **vapor**) n (mist) Dunst m; (gas) Dampf m
variable ['veərıəbl] adj wechselhaft, veränderlich; (speed, height) regulierbar
variance ['veərıəns] n: **to be at ~ (with)** nicht übereinstimmen (mit)
variation [veərı'eıʃən] n Variation f; (in prices etc) Schwankung f
varicose ['værıkəus] adj: **~ veins** Krampfadern pl
varied ['veərıd] adj unterschiedlich; (life) abwechslungsreich
variety [və'raıətı] n (difference) Abwechslung f; (varied collection) Vielfalt f; (COMM) Auswahl f; (sort) Sorte f, Art f; **~ show** n Varietee nt, Varieté f
various ['veərıəs] adj verschieden; (several) mehrere
varnish ['va:nıʃ] n Lack m; (on pottery) Glasur f ♦ vt lackieren
vary ['veərı] vt (alter) verändern; (give variety to) abwechslungsreicher gestalten ♦ vi sich (ver)ändern; (prices) schwanken; (weather) unterschiedlich sein
vase [va:z] n Vase f
Vaseline ['væsıli:n] ® n Vaseline f
vast [va:st] adj weit, groß, riesig
VAT [væt] n abbr (= value added tax) MwSt f
vat [væt] n große(s) Fass nt
vault [vɔ:lt] n (of roof) Gewölbe nt; (tomb) Gruft f; (in bank) Tresorraum m; (leap) Sprung m ♦ vt (also: **~ over**) überspringen
vaunted ['vɔ:ntıd] adj: **much-~** viel gerühmt
VCR n abbr = **video cassette recorder**
VD n abbr = **venereal disease**
VDU n abbr = **visual display unit**
veal [vi:l] n Kalbfleisch nt
veer [vıə'] vi sich drehen; (of car) ausscheren
vegan ['vi:gən] n Vegan m, radikale(in) Vegetarier(in) m(f)
vegeburger ['vedʒıbə:gə'] n vegetarische Frikadelle f
vegetable ['vedʒtəbl] n Gemüse nt ♦ adj

Gemüse-; **~s** npl (CULIN) Gemüse nt

vegetarian [vedʒɪ'teərɪən] n Vegetarier(in) f(f) ♦ adj vegetarisch

vegetate ['vedʒteɪt] vi (dahin)vegetieren

veggieburger ['vedʒɪbɜːɡəʳ] n = **vegeburger**

vehement ['viːɪmənt] adj heftig

vehicle ['viːɪkl] n Fahrzeug nt; (fig) Mittel nt

veil [veɪl] n (also fig) Schleier m ♦ vt verschleiern

vein [veɪn] n Ader f; (mood) Stimmung f

velocity [vɪ'lɒsɪtɪ] n Geschwindigkeit f

velvet ['velvɪt] n Samt m ♦ adj Samt-

vendetta [ven'detə] n Fehde f; (in family) Blutrache f

vending machine ['vendɪŋ-] n Automat m

vendor ['vendəʳ] n Verkäufer m

veneer [və'nɪəʳ] n Furnier(holz) nt; (fig) äußere(r) Anstrich m

venereal disease [vɪ'nɪərɪəl-] n Geschlechtskrankheit f

Venetian blind [vɪ'niːʃən-] n Jalousie f

vengeance ['vendʒəns] n Rache f; **with a ~** gewaltig

venison ['venɪsn] n Reh(fleisch) nt

venom ['venəm] n Gift nt

vent [vent] n Öffnung f; (in coat) Schlitz m; (fig) Ventil nt ♦ vt (emotion) abreagieren

ventilate ['ventɪleɪt] vt belüften; **ventilator** ['ventɪleɪtəʳ] n Ventilator m

ventriloquist [ven'trɪləkwɪst] n Bauchredner m

venture ['ventʃəʳ] n Unternehmung f, Projekt nt ♦ vt wagen; (life) aufs Spiel setzen ♦ vi sich wagen

venue ['venjuː] n Schauplatz m

verb [vɜːb] n Zeitwort nt, Verb nt; **~al** adj (spoken) mündlich; (translation) wörtlich; **~ally** adv mündlich

verbatim [vɜː'beɪtɪm] adv Wort für Wort ♦ adj wortwörtlich

verbose [vɜː'bəus] adj wortreich

verdict ['vɜːdɪkt] n Urteil nt

verge [vɜːdʒ] n (BRIT) Rand m ♦ vi: **to ~ on** grenzen an +acc; **"soft ~s"** (BRIT: AUT) „Seitenstreifen nicht befahrbar"; **on the ~ of doing sth** im Begriff, etw zu tun

verify ['verɪfaɪ] vt (über)prüfen; (confirm) bestätigen; (theory) beweisen

veritable ['verɪtəbl] adj wirklich, echt

vermin ['vɜːmɪn] npl Ungeziefer nt

vermouth ['vɜːməθ] n Wermut m

versatile ['vɜːsətaɪl] adj vielseitig

verse [vɜːs] n (poetry) Poesie f; (stanza) Strophe f; (of Bible) Vers m; **in ~** in Versform

version ['vɜːʃən] n Version f; (of car) Modell nt

versus ['vɜːsəs] prep gegen

vertebrate ['vɜːtɪbrɪt] adj Wirbel-

vertical ['vɜːtɪkl] adj senkrecht

vertigo ['vɜːtɪgəu] n Schwindel m

very ['verɪ] adv sehr ♦ adj (extreme) äußerste(r,

s); **the ~ book which** genau das Buch, welches; **the ~ last ...** der/die/das allerletzte ...; **at the ~ least** allerwenigstens; **~ much** sehr

vessel ['vesl] n (ship) Schiff nt; (container) Gefäß nt

vest [vest] n (BRIT) Unterhemd nt; (US: waistcoat) Weste f

vested interests ['vestɪd-] npl finanzielle Beteiligung f; (people) finanziell Beteiligte pl; (fig) persönliche(s) Interesse nt

vestige ['vestɪdʒ] n Spur f

vestry ['vestrɪ] n Sakristei f

vet [vet] n abbr (= veterinary surgeon) Tierarzt(-ärztin) m(f) ♦ vt genau prüfen

veteran ['vetərn] n Veteran(in) m(f)

veterinarian [vetrɪ'neərɪən] (US) n Tierarzt m/-ärztin f

veterinary ['vetrɪnərɪ] adj Veterinär-; **~ surgeon** (BRIT) n Tierarzt m/-ärztin f

veto ['viːtəu] (pl **~es**) n Veto nt ♦ vt sein Veto einlegen gegen

vex [veks] vt ärgern; **~ed** adj verärgert; **~ed question** umstrittene Frage f

VHF abbr (= very high frequency) UKW f

via ['vaɪə] prep über +acc

viable ['vaɪəbl] adj (plan) durchführbar; (company) rentabel

vibrant ['vaɪbrnt] adj (lively) lebhaft; (bright) leuchtend; (full of emotion: voice) bebend

vibrate [vaɪ'breɪt] vi zittern, beben; (machine, string) vibrieren; **vibration** [vaɪ'breɪʃən] n Schwingung f; (of machine) Vibrieren nt

vicar ['vɪkəʳ] n Pfarrer m; **~age** n Pfarrhaus nt

vice [vaɪs] n (evil) Laster nt; (TECH) Schraubstock m

vice-chairman [vaɪs'tʃeəmən] n stellvertretende(r) Vorsitzende(r) m

vice-president [vaɪs'prezɪdənt] n Vizepräsident m

vice squad [vaɪs-] n ≈ Sittenpolizei f

vice versa ['vaɪsɪ'vɜːsə] adv umgekehrt

vicinity [vɪ'sɪnɪtɪ] n Umgebung f; (closeness) Nähe f

vicious ['vɪʃəs] adj gemein, böse; **~ circle** n Teufelskreis m

victim ['vɪktɪm] n Opfer nt

victor ['vɪktəʳ] n Sieger m

Victorian [vɪk'tɔːrɪən] adj viktorianisch; (fig) (sitten)streng

victorious [vɪk'tɔːrɪəs] adj siegreich

victory ['vɪktərɪ] n Sieg m

video ['vɪdɪəu] adj Fernseh-, Bild- ♦ n (~ film) Video nt; (also: ~ **cassette**) Videokassette f; (also: ~ **cassette recorder**) Videorekorder m; ~ **tape** n Videoband nt; ~ **wall** n Videowand m

vie [vaɪ] vi wetteifern

Vienna [vɪ'enə] n Wien nt

Vietnam ['vjet'næm] n Vietnam nt; **~ese** [vjetnə'miːz] adj vietnamisch ♦ n inv (person)

Vietnamese *m*, Vietnamesin *f*

view |vju:| *n* (*sight*) Sicht *f*, Blick *m*; (*scene*) Aussicht *f*; (*opinion*) Ansicht *f*; (*intention*) Absicht *f* ♦ *vt* (*situation*) betrachten; (*house*) besichtigen; **to have sth in ~** etw beabsichtigen; **on ~** ausgestellt; **in ~ of** wegen +*gen*, angesichts +*gen*; **~er** *n* (*PHOT: small projector*) Gucki *m*; (*TV*) Fernsehzuschauer(in) *m(f)*; **~finder** *n* Sucher *m*; **~point** *n* Standpunkt *m*

vigil |'vidʒil| *n* (Nacht)wache *f*; **~ant** *adj* wachsam

vigorous |'vigərəs| *adj* kräftig; (*protest*) energisch, heftig

vile |vail| *adj* (*mean*) gemein; (*foul*) abscheulich

villa |'vilə| *n* Villa *f*

village |'vilidʒ| *n* Dorf *nt*; **~r** *n* Dorfbewohner(in) *m(f)*

villain |'vilən| *n* Schurke *m*

vindicate |'vindikeit| *vt* rechtfertigen

vindictive |vin'diktiv| *adj* nachtragend, rachsüchtig

vine |vain| *n* Rebstock *m*, Rebe *f*

vinegar |'vinigər| *n* Essig *m*

vineyard |'vinja:d| *n* Weinberg *m*

vintage |'vintidʒ| *n* (*of wine*) Jahrgang *m*; **~ car** *n* Oldtimer *m* (*zwischen 1919 und 1930 gebaut*); **~ wine** *n* edle(r) Wein *m*

viola |vi'əulə| *n* Bratsche *f*

violate |'vaiəleit| *vt* (*law*) übertreten; (*rights, rule, neutrality*) verletzen; (*sanctity, woman*) schänden; **violation** |vaiə'leiʃən| *n* Übertretung *f*; Verletzung *f*

violence |'vaiələns| *n* (*force*) Heftigkeit *f*; (*brutality*) Gewalttätigkeit *f*

violent |'vaiələnt| *adj* (*strong*) heftig; (*brutal*) gewalttätig, brutal; (*contrast*) krass; (*death*) gewaltsam

violet |'vaiələt| *n* Veilchen *nt* ♦ *adj* veilchenblau, violett

violin |vaiə'lin| *n* Geige *f*, Violine *f*; **~ist** *n* Geiger(in) *m(f)*

VIP *n abbr* (= *very important person*) VIP *m*

virgin |'və:dʒin| *n* Jungfrau *f* ♦ *adj* jungfräulich, unberührt; **~ity** |və:'dʒiniti| *n* Unschuld *f*

Virgo |'və:gəu| *n* Jungfrau *f*

virile |'virail| *adj* männlich; **virility** |vi'riliti| *n* Männlichkeit *f*

virtually |'və:tjuəli| *adv* praktisch, fast

virtual reality |'və:tjuəl-| *n* (*COMPUT*) virtuelle Realität *f*

virtue |'və:tju:| *n* (*moral goodness*) Tugend *f*; (*good quality*) Vorteil *m*, Vorzug *m*; **by ~ of** aufgrund or auf Grund +*gen*

virtuous |'və:tjuəs| *adj* tugendhaft

virulent |'virulənt| *adj* (*poisonous*) bösartig; (*bitter*) scharf, geharnischt

virus |'vaiərəs| *n* (*also COMPUT*) Virus *m*

visa |'vi:zə| *n* Visum *nt*

vis-à-vis |vi:zə'vi:| *prep* gegenüber

viscous |'viskəs| *adj* zähflüssig

visibility |vizi'biliti| *n* (*MET*) Sicht(weite) *f*

visible |'vizəbl| *adj* sichtbar; **visibly** *adv* sichtlich

vision |'viʒən| *n* (*ability*) Sehvermögen *nt*; (*foresight*) Weitblick *m*; (*in dream, image*) Vision *f*

visit |'vizit| *n* Besuch *m* ♦ *vt* besuchen; (*town, country*) fahren nach; **~ing hours** *npl* (*in hospital etc*) Besuchszeiten *pl*; **~or** *n* (*in house*) Besucher(in) *m(f)*; (*in hotel*) Gast *m*; **~or centre** *n* Touristeninformation *f*

visor |'vaizər| *n* Visier *nt*; (*on cap*) Schirm *m*; (*AUT*) Blende *f*

vista |'vistə| *n* Aussicht *f*

visual |'vizjuəl| *adj* Seh-, visuell; **~ aid** *n* Anschauungsmaterial *nt*; **~ display unit** *n* Bildschirm(gerät *nt*) *m*; **~ize** *vt* sich +*dat* vorstellen; **~ly-impaired** *adj* sehbehindert

vital |'vaitl| *adj* (*important*) unerlässlich; (*necessary for life*) Lebens-, lebenswichtig; (*lively*) vital; **~ity** |vai'tæliti| *n* Vitalität *f*; **~ly** *adv*: **~ly important** äußerst wichtig; **~ statistics** *npl* (*fig*) Maße *pl*

vitamin |'vitəmin| *n* Vitamin *nt*

vivacious |vi'veiʃəs| *adj* lebhaft

vivid |'vivid| *adj* (*graphic*) lebendig; (*memory*) lebhaft; (*bright*) leuchtend; **~ly** *adv* lebendig; lebhaft; leuchtend

V-neck |'vi:nek| *n* V-Ausschnitt *m*

vocabulary |vəu'kæbjuləri| *n* Wortschatz *m*, Vokabular *nt*

vocal |'vəukl| *adj* Vokal-, Gesang-; (*fig*) lautstark; **~ cords** *npl* Stimmbänder *pl*

vocation |vəu'keiʃən| *n* (*calling*) Berufung *f*; **~al** *adj* Berufs-

vociferous |və'sifərəs| *adj* lautstark

vodka |'vɔdkə| *n* Wodka *m*

vogue |vəug| *n* Mode *f*

voice |vɔis| *n* Stimme *f*; (*fig*) Mitspracherecht *nt* ♦ *vt* äußern; **~ mail** *n* (*COMPUT*) Voice-Mail *f*

void |vɔid| *n* Leere *f* ♦ *adj* (*invalid*) nichtig, ungültig; (*empty*): **~ of** ohne, bar +*gen*; *see* **null**

volatile |'vɔlətail| *adj* (*gas*) flüchtig; (*person*) impulsiv; (*situation*) brisant

volcano |vɔl'keinəu| *n* Vulkan *m*

volition |və'liʃən| *n* Wille *m*; **of one's own ~** aus freiem Willen

volley |'vɔli| *n* (*of guns*) Salve *f*; (*of stones*) Hagel *m*; (*tennis*) Flugball *m*; **~ball** *n* Volleyball *m*

volt |vəult| *n* Volt *nt*; **~age** *n* (Volt)spannung *f*

volume |'vɔlju:m| *n* (*book*) Band *m*; (*size*) Umfang *m*; (*space*) Rauminhalt *m*; (*of sound*) Lautstärke *f*

voluntarily |'vɔləntrili| *adv* freiwillig

voluntary ['vɔləntərɪ] *adj* freiwillig

volunteer [vɔlən'tɪə'] *n* Freiwillige(r) *mf* ♦ *vi* sich freiwillig melden; **to ~ to do sth** sich anbieten, etw zu tun

vomit ['vɔmɪt] *n* Erbrochene(s) *nt* ♦ *vt* spucken ♦ *vi* sich übergeben

vote [vəʊt] *n* Stimme *f*; *(ballot)* Abstimmung *f*; *(result)* Abstimmungsergebnis *nt*; *(franchise)* Wahlrecht *nt* ♦ *vt, vi* wählen; **~ of thanks** *n* Dankesworte *pl*; **~r** *n* Wähler(in) *m(f)*; **voting** ['vəʊtɪŋ] *n* Wahl *f*

voucher ['vaʊtʃə'] *n* Gutschein *m*

vouch for [vaʊtʃ-] *vt* bürgen für

vow [vaʊ] *n* Versprechen *nt*; *(REL)* Gelübde *nt* ♦ *vt* geloben

vowel ['vaʊəl] *n* Vokal *m*

voyage ['vɔɪɪdʒ] *n* Reise *f*

vulgar ['vʌlgə'] *adj (rude)* vulgär; **~ity** [vʌl'gærɪtɪ] *n* Vulgarität *f*

vulnerable ['vʌlnərəbl] *adj (easily injured)* verwundbar; *(sensitive)* verletzlich

vulture ['vʌltʃə'] *n* Geier *m*

W, w

wad [wɔd] *n (bundle)* Bündel *nt*; *(of paper)* Stoß *m*; *(of money)* Packen *m*

waddle ['wɔdl] *vi* watscheln

wade [weɪd] *vi*: **to ~ through** waten durch

wafer ['weɪfə'] *n* Waffel *f*; *(REL)* Hostie *f*; *(COMPUT)* Wafer *f*

waffle ['wɔfl] *n* Waffel *f*; *(inf: empty talk)* Geschwafel *nt* ♦ *vi* schwafeln

waft [wɔft] *vt, vi* wehen

wag [wæg] *vt (tail)* wedeln mit ♦ *vi* wedeln

wage [weɪdʒ] *n (also: ~s)* (Arbeits)lohn *m* ♦ *vt*: **to ~ war** Krieg führen; **~ earner** *n* Lohnempfänger(in) *m(f)*; **~ packet** *n* Lohntüte *f*

wager ['weɪdʒə'] *n* Wette *f* ♦ *vt, vi* wetten

waggle ['wægl] *vi* wackeln

wag(g)on ['wægən] *n (horse-drawn)* Fuhrwerk *nt*; *(US: AUT)* Wagen *m*; *(BRIT: RAIL)* Wag(g)on *m*

wail [weɪl] *n* Wehgeschrei *nt* ♦ *vi* wehklagen, jammern

waist [weɪst] *n* Taille *f*; **~coat** *(BRIT)* *n* Weste *f*; **~line** *n* Taille *f*

wait [weɪt] *n* Wartezeit *f* ♦ *vi* warten; **to lie in ~ for sb** jdm auflauern; **I can't ~ to see him** ich kanns kaum erwarten ihn zu sehen; **"no ~ing"** *(BRIT: AUT)* "Halteverbot"; **~ behind** *vi* zurückbleiben; **~ for** *vt fus* warten auf *+acc*; **~ on** *vt fus* bedienen; **~er** *n* Kellner *m*; **~ing list** *n* Warteliste *f*; **~ing room** *n* *(MED)* Wartezimmer *nt*; *(RAIL)* Wartesaal *m*; **~ress** *n* Kellnerin *f*

waive [weɪv] *vt* verzichten auf *+acc*

wake [weɪk] *(pt* **woke, waked,** *pp* **woken)** *vt* wecken ♦ *vi (also: ~ up)* aufwachen ♦ *n* *(NAUT)* Kielwasser *nt*; *(for dead)* Totenwache *f*; **to ~ up to** *(fig)* sich bewusst werden *+gen*

waken ['weɪkn] *vt* aufwecken

Wales [weɪlz] *n* Wales *nt*

walk [wɔːk] *n* Spaziergang *m*; *(gait)* Gang *m*; *(route)* Weg *m* ♦ *vi* gehen; *(stroll)* spazieren gehen; *(longer)* wandern; **~s of life** Sphären *pl*; **a 10-minute ~** 10 Minuten zu Fuß; **to ~ out on sb** *(inf)* jdn sitzen lassen; **~er** *n* Spaziergänger *m*; *(hiker)* Wanderer *m*; **~ie-talkie** ['wɔːkɪ'tɔːkɪ] *n* tragbare(s) Sprechfunkgerät *nt*; **~ing** *n* Gehen *nt*; *(hiking)* Wandern *nt* ♦ *adj* Wander-; **~ing shoes** *npl* Wanderschuhe *pl*; **~ing stick** *n* Spazierstock *m*; **W~man** ['wɔːkmən] ® *n* Walkman *m* ®; **~out** *n* Streik *m*; **~over** *(inf)* *n* leichte(r) Sieg *m*; **~way** *n* Fußweg *m*

wall [wɔːl] *n (inside)* Wand *f*; *(outside)* Mauer *f*; **~ed** *adj* von Mauern umgeben

wallet ['wɔlɪt] *n* Brieftasche *f*

wallflower ['wɔːlflaʊə'] *n* Goldlack *m*; **to be a ~** *(fig)* ein Mauerblümchen sein

wallop ['wɔləp] *(inf)* *vt* schlagen, verprügeln

wallow ['wɔləʊ] *vi* sich wälzen

wallpaper ['wɔːlpeɪpə'] *n* Tapete *f*

walnut ['wɔːlnʌt] *n* Walnuss *f*

walrus ['wɔːlrəs] *n* Walross *nt*

waltz [wɔːlts] *n* Walzer *m* ♦ *vi* Walzer tanzen

wan [wɔn] *adj* bleich

wand [wɔnd] *n (also: magic ~)* Zauberstab *m*

wander ['wɔndə'] *vi (roam)* (herum)wandern; *(fig)* abschweifen

wane [weɪn] *vi* abnehmen; *(fig)* schwinden

wangle ['wæŋgl] *(BRIT: inf)* *vt*: **to ~ sth** etw richtig hindrehen

want [wɔnt] *n (lack)* Mangel *m* ♦ *vt (need)* brauchen; *(desire)* wollen; *(lack)* nicht haben; **~s** *npl (needs)* Bedürfnisse *pl*; **for ~ of** aus Mangel an *+dat*; mangels *+gen*; **to ~ to do sth** etw tun wollen; **to ~ sb to do sth** wollen, dass jd etw tut; **~ed** *adj (criminal etc)* gesucht; **"cook ~ed"** *(in adverts)* „Koch/Köchin gesucht"; **~ing** *adj*: **to be found ~ing** sich als unzulänglich erweisen

wanton ['wɔntn] *adj* mutwillig, zügellos

war [wɔː'] *n* Krieg *m*; **to make ~** Krieg führen

ward [wɔːd] *n (in hospital)* Station *f*; *(of city)* Bezirk *m*; *(child)* Mündel *nt*; **~ off** *vt* abwenden, abwehren

warden ['wɔːdn] *n (guard)* Wächter *m*, Aufseher *m*; *(BRIT: in youth hostel)* Herbergsvater *m*; *(UNIV)* Heimleiter *m*; *(BRIT: also: traffic ~)* ≈ Verkehrspolizist *m*, Politesse *f*

warder ['wɔːdə'] *(BRIT)* *n* Gefängniswärte *m*

wardrobe ['wɔːdrəʊb] *n* Kleiderschrank *m*; *(clothes)* Garderobe *f*

warehouse ['wɛəhaʊs] *n* Lagerhaus *nt*

wares [wɛəz] *npl* Ware *f*

warfare ['wɔːfɛə'] *n* Krieg *m*; Kriegsführung *f*

warhead ['wɔːhed] *n* Sprengkopf *m*

warily |'wεərɪlɪ| adv vorsichtig

warlike |'wɔːlaɪk| adj kriegerisch

warm |wɔːm| adj warm; (welcome) herzlich
♦ vt, vi wärmen; **I'm ~** mir ist warm; **it's ~** es
ist warm; **~ up** vi aufwärmen ♦ vi warm
werden; **~-hearted** adj warmherzig; **~ly** adv
warm; herzlich; **~th** n Wärme f; Herzlichkeit
f

warn |wɔːn| vt: **to ~** (of or against) warnen
(vor +dat); **~ing** n Warnung f; **without**
~ing unerwartet; **~ing light** n Warnlicht nt;
~ing triangle n (AUT) Warndreieck nt

warp |wɔːp| vt verziehen; **~ed** adj wellig;
(fig) pervers

warrant |'wɔrnt| n (for arrest) Haftbefehl m

warranty |'wɔrntɪ| n Garantie f

warren |'wɔrən| n Labyrinth nt

Warsaw |'wɔːsɔː| n Warschau f

warship |'wɔːʃɪp| n Kriegsschiff nt

wart |wɔːt| n Warze f

wartime |'wɔːtaɪm| n Krieg m

wary |'wεərɪ| adj misstrauisch

was |wɔz| pt of **be**

wash |wɔʃ| n Wäsche f ♦ vt waschen; (dishes)
abwaschen ♦ vi sich waschen; (do ~ing)
waschen; **to have a ~** sich waschen; **~**
away vt abwaschen, wegspülen; **~ off** vt
abwaschen; **~ up** vi (BRIT) spülen; (US) sich
waschen; **~able** adj waschbar; **~basin** n
Waschbecken nt; **~ bowl** (US) n
Waschbecken nt; **~ cloth** (US) n (face cloth)
Waschlappen m; **~er** n (TECH) Dichtungsring
m; (machine) Waschmaschine f; **~ing** n
Wäsche f; **~ing machine** n Waschmaschine
f; **~ing powder** (BRIT) n Waschpulver nt;
~ing-up n Abwasch m; **~ing-up liquid** n
Spülmittel nt; **~-out** (inf) n (event) Reinfall
m; (person) Niete f; **~room** n Waschraum m

wasn't |'wɔznt| = **was not**

wasp |wɔsp| n Wespe f

wastage |'weɪstɪdʒ| n Verlust m; **natural ~**
Verschleiß m

waste |weɪst| n (wasting) Verschwendung f;
(what is wasted) Abfall m ♦ adj (useless)
überschüssig, Abfall- ♦ vt (object)
verschwenden; (time, life) vergeuden ♦ vi: **to**
~ away verfallen, verkümmern; **~s** npl (land)
Einöde f; **~ disposal unit** (BRIT) n
Müllschlucker m; **~ful** adj verschwenderisch;
(process) aufwändig, aufwendig; **~ ground**
(BRIT) n unbebaute(s) Grundstück nt; **~land**
n Ödland nt; **~paper basket** n Papierkorb
m; **~ pipe** n Abflussrohr nt

watch |wɔtʃ| n Wache f; (for time) Uhr f ♦ vt
ansehen; (observe) beobachten; (be careful
of) aufpassen auf +acc; (guard) bewachen
♦ vi zusehen; **to be on the ~** (for sth) (auf
etw acc) aufpassen; **to ~ TV** fernsehen; **to ~**
sb doing sth jdm bei etw zuschauen; **~ out**
vi Ausschau halten; (be careful) aufpassen; **~**
out! pass auf!; **~dog** n Wachhund m; (fig)

Wächter m; **~ful** adj wachsam; **~maker** n
Uhrmacher m; **~man** (irreg) n (also: **night**
~man) (Nacht)wächter m; **~ strap** n
Uhrarmband nt

water |'wɔːtəᵊ| n Wasser f ♦ vt (be)gießen;
(river) bewässern; (horses) tränken ♦ vi (eye)
tränen; **~s** npl (of sea, river etc) Gewässer nt;
~ down vt verwässern; **~closet** (BRIT) n
(Wasser)klosett nt; **~colour** (US **~color**) n
(painting) Aquarell nt; (paint) Wasserfarbe f;
~cress n (Brunnen)kresse f; **~fall** n
Wasserfall m; **~ heater** n Heißwassergerät
nt; **~ing can** n Gießkanne f; **~ level** n
Wasserstand m; **~lily** n Seerose f; **~line** n
Wasserlinie f; **~logged** adj (ground) voll
Wasser; **~ main** n Haupt(wasser)leitung f;
~mark n Wasserzeichen nt; (on wall)
Wasserstandsmarke f; **~melon** n
Wassermelone f; **~ polo** n Wasserball(spiel)
nt; **~proof** adj wasserdicht; **~shed** n
Wasserscheide f; **~-skiing** n Wasserskilaufen
nt; **~ tank** n Wassertank m; **~tight** adj
wasserdicht; **~way** n Wasserweg m;
~works npl Wasserwerk nt; **~y** adj
wäss(e)rig

watt |wɔt| n Watt nt

wave |weɪv| n Welle f; (with hand) Winken nt
♦ vt (move to and fro) schwenken; (hand,
flag) winken mit ♦ vi (person) winken; (flag)
wehen; **~length** n (also fig) Wellenlänge f

waver |'weɪvəᵊ| vi schwanken

wavy |'weɪvɪ| adj wellig

wax |wæks| n Wachs nt; (sealing ~) Siegellack
m; (in ear) Ohrenschmalz nt ♦ vt (floor)
(ein)wachsen ♦ vi (moon) zunehmen;
~works npl Wachsfigurenkabinett nt

way |weɪ| n Weg m; (method) Art und Weise
f; (direction) Richtung f; (habit) Gewohnheit
f; (distance) Entfernung f; (condition)
Zustand m; **which ~? - this ~** welche
Richtung? - hier entlang; **on the ~** (en route)
unterwegs; **to be in the ~** im Weg sein; **to**
go out of one's ~ to do sth sich besonders
anstrengen, um etw zu tun; **to lose one's ~**
sich verirren; **"give ~"** (BRIT: AUT) „Vorfahrt
gewähren!"; **in a ~** in gewisser Weise; **by**
the ~ übrigens; **in some ~s** in gewisser
Hinsicht; **"~ in"** (BRIT) „Eingang"; **"~ out"**
(BRIT) „Ausgang"

waylay |weɪ'leɪ| (irreg: like **lay**) vt auflauern
+dat

wayward |'weɪwəd| adj eigensinnig

W.C. (BRIT) n WC nt

we |wiː| pl pron wir

weak |wiːk| adj schwach; **~en** vt schwächen
♦ vi schwächer werden; **~ling** n Schwächling
m; **~ness** n Schwäche f

wealth |welθ| n Reichtum m; (abundance)
Fülle f; **~y** adj reich

wean |wiːn| vt entwöhnen

weapon |'wεpən| n Waffe f

wear |wɛəʳ| (pt **wore**, pp **worn**) n (clothing): **sports/baby ~** Sport-/Babykleidung f; (use) Verschleiß m ♦ vt (have on) tragen; (smile etc) haben; (use) abnutzen ♦ vi (last) halten; (become old) (sich) verschleißen; **evening ~** Abendkleidung f; **~ and tear** Verschleiß m; **~ away** vt verbrauchen ♦ vi schwinden; **~ down** vt (people) zermürben; **~ off** vi sich verlieren; **~ out** vt verschleißen; (person) erschöpfen

weary |'wɪərɪ| adj müde ♦ vt ermüden ♦ vi überdrüssig werden

weasel |'wi:zl| n Wiesel nt

weather |'wɛðəʳ| n Wetter nt ♦ vt verwittern lassen; (resist) überstehen; **under the ~** (fig: ill) angeschlagen (inf); **~-beaten** adj verwittert; **~-cock** n Wetterhahn m; **~ forecast** Wettervorhersage f; **~ vane** n Wetterfahne f

weave |wi:v| (pt **wove**, pp **woven**) vt weben; **~r** n Weber(in) m(f); **weaving** n (craft) Webkunst f

web |wɛb| n Netz nt; (membrane) Schwimmhaut f; **the (World-Wide) W~** das Web

website |wɛbsaɪt| n (COMPUT) Website f, Webseite f

wed |wɛd| (pt, pp **wedded**) vt heiraten ♦ n: **the newly~s** npl die Frischvermählten pl

we'd |wi:d| = we had; we would

wedding |'wɛdɪŋ| n Hochzeit f; **silver/ golden ~ anniversary** Silberhochzeit f/ goldene Hochzeit f; **~ day** n Hochzeitstag m; **~ dress** n Hochzeitskleid nt; **~ present** n Hochzeitsgeschenk nt; **~ ring** n Trauring m, Ehering m

wedge |wɛdʒ| n Keil m; (of cheese etc) Stück nt ♦ vt (fasten) festklemmen; (pack tightly) einkeilen

Wednesday |'wɛdnzdɪ| n Mittwoch m

wee |wi:| (SCOTTISH) adj klein, winzig

weed |wi:d| n Unkraut nt ♦ vt jäten; **~-killer** n Unkrautvertilgungsmittel nt

weedy |'wi:dɪ| adj (person) schmächtig

week |wi:k| n Woche f; **a ~ today/on Friday** heute/Freitag in einer Woche; **~day** n Wochentag m; **~end** n Wochenende nt; **~ly** adj wöchentlich; (wages, magazine) Wochen- ♦ adv wöchentlich

weep |wi:p| (pt, pp **wept**) vi weinen; **~ing willow** n Trauerweide f

weigh |weɪ| vt, vi wiegen; **to ~ anchor** den Anker lichten; **~ down** vt niederdrücken; **~ up** vt abschätzen

weight |weɪt| n Gewicht nt; **to lose/put on ~** abnehmen/zunehmen; **~ing** n (allowance) Zulage f; **~lifter** n Gewichtheber m; **~lifting** n Gewichtheben nt; **~y** adj (heavy) gewichtig; (important) schwerwiegend, schwer wiegend

weir |wɪəʳ| n (Stau)wehr nt

weird |wɪəd| adj seltsam

welcome |'wɛlkəm| n Willkommen nt, Empfang m ♦ vt begrüßen; **thank you – you're ~!** danke – nichts zu danken

welder |'wɛldəʳ| n (person) Schweißer(in) m(f)

welding |'wɛldɪŋ| n Schweißen nt

welfare |'wɛlfɛəʳ| n Wohl nt; (social) Fürsorge f; **~ state** n Wohlfahrtsstaat m; **~ work** n Fürsorge f

well |wɛl| n Brunnen m; (oil ~) Quelle f ♦ adj (in good health) gesund ♦ adv gut ♦ excl nun!, na schön!; **I'm ~** es geht mir gut; **get ~ soon!** gute Besserung!; **as ~** auch; **as ~ as** sowohl als auch; **~ done!** gut gemacht!; **to do ~** (person) gut zurechtkommen; (business) gut gehen; **~ up** vi emporsteigen; (fig) aufsteigen

we'll |wi:l| = we will; we shall

well: ~-behaved |'wɛlbɪ'heɪvd| adj wohlerzogen; **~-being** |'wɛl'bi:ɪŋ| n Wohl nt; **~-built** |'wɛl'bɪlt| adj kräftig gebaut; **~-deserved** |'wɛldɪ'zə:vd| adj wohlverdient; **~-dressed** |'wɛl'drɛst| adj gut gekleidet; **~-heeled** |'wɛl'hi:ld| (inf) adj (wealthy) gut gepolstert

wellingtons |'wɛlɪŋtənz| npl (also: **wellington boots**) Gummistiefel pl

well: ~-known |'wɛl'nəun| adj bekannt; **~-mannered** |'wɛl'mænəd| adj wohlerzogen; **~-meaning** |'wɛl'mi:nɪŋ| adj (person) wohlmeinend; (action) gut gemeint; **~-off** |'wɛl'ɔf| adj gut situiert; **~-read** |'wɛl'rɛd| adj (sehr) belesen; **~-to-do** |'wɛltə'du:| adj wohlhabend; **~-wisher** |'wɛlwɪʃəʳ| n Gönner m

Welsh |wɛlʃ| adj walisisch ♦ n (LING) Walisisch nt; **the ~** npl (people) die Waliser pl; **~ Assembly** n walisische Versammlung f; **~man, ~woman** (irreg) n Waliser(in) m(f)

went |wɛnt| pt of go

wept |wɛpt| pt, pp of weep

were |wə:ʳ| pt pl of be

we're |wɪəʳ| = we are

weren't |wə:nt| = were not

west |wɛst| n Westen m ♦ adj West-, westlich ♦ adv westwärts, nach Westen; **the W~** der Westen; **W~ Country** (BRIT) n: **the W~ Country** der Südwesten Englands; **~erly** adj westlich; **~ern** adj westlich, West- ♦ n (CINE) Western m; **W~ Indian** adj westindisch ♦ n Westindier(in) m(f); **W~ Indies** npl Westindische Inseln pl; **~ward(s)** adv westwärts

wet |wɛt| adj nass; **to get ~** nass werden; **"~ paint"** „frisch gestrichen"; **~ blanket** n (fig) Triefel m; **~ suit** n Taucheranzug m

we've |wi:v| = we have

whack |wæk| n Schlag m ♦ vt schlagen

whale |weɪl| n Wal m

wharf |wɔ:f| n Kai m

wharves |wɔːvz| npl of **wharf**

what |wɒt| adj **1** (in questions) welche(r, s), was für ein(e); **what size is it?** welche Größe ist das?

2 (in exclamations) was für ein(e); **what a mess!** was für ein Durcheinander!

♦ pron (interrogative/relative) was; **what are you doing?** was machst du gerade?; **what are you talking about?** wovon reden Sie?; **what is it called?** wie heißt das?; **what about …?** wie wärs mit …?; **I saw what you did** ich habe gesehen, was du gemacht hast

♦ excl (disbelieving) wie, was; **what, no coffee!** wie, kein Kaffee?; **I've crashed the car – what!** ich hatte einen Autounfall – was!

whatever |wɒtˈevəʳ| adj: **~ book** welches Buch auch immer ♦ pron: **do ~ is necessary** tu, was (immer auch) nötig ist; **~ happens** egal, was passiert; **nothing ~** überhaupt or absolut gar nichts; **do ~ you want** tu, was (immer) du (auch) möchtest; **no reason ~** or **whatsoever** überhaupt or absolut kein Grund

whatsoever |wɒtsəuˈevəʳ| adj see **whatever**

wheat |wiːt| n Weizen m

wheedle |ˈwiːdl| vt: **to ~ sb into doing sth** jdn dazu überreden, etw zu tun; **to ~ sth out of sb** jdm etw abluchsen

wheel |wiːl| n Rad nt; (steering ~) Lenkrad nt; (disc) Scheibe f ♦ vt schieben; **~barrow** n Schubkarren m; **~chair** n Rollstuhl m; **~clamp** n (AUT) Parkkralle f

wheeze |wiːz| vi keuchen

when |wɛn| adv wann
♦ conj **1** (at, during, after the time that) wenn; (in past) als; **she was reading when I came in** sie las, als ich hereinkam; **be careful when you cross the road** seien Sie vorsichtig, wenn Sie über die Straße gehen **2** (on, at which) als; **on the day when I met him** an dem Tag, an dem ich ihn traf **3** (whereas) wo … doch

whenever |wɛnˈevəʳ| adv wann (auch) immer; (every time that) jedes Mal wenn ♦ conj (any time) wann

where |wɛəʳ| adv (place) wo; (direction) wohin; **~ from** woher; **this is ~ …** hier …; **~abouts** |ˈwɛərəbauts| adv wo ♦ n Aufenthaltsort m; **nobody knows his ~abouts** niemand weiß, wo er ist; **~as** |wɛərˈæz| conj während, wo … doch; **~by** pron woran, wodurch, womit, wovon; **~upon** conj worauf, wonach; (at beginning of sentence) daraufhin; **~ver** |wɛərˈevəʳ| adv wo (immer)

wherewithal |ˈwɛəwɪðɔːl| n nötige (Geld)mittel pl

whet |wɛt| vt (appetite) anregen

whether |ˈwɛðəʳ| conj ob; **I don't know ~ to accept or not** ich weiß nicht, ob ich es annehmen soll oder nicht; **~ you go or not** ob du gehst oder nicht; **it's doubtful/unclear ~ …** es ist zweifelhaft/nicht klar, ob …

which |wɪtʃ| adj **1** (interrogative: direct, indirect) welche(r, s); **which one?** welche(r, s)?

2: in which case in diesem Fall; **by which time** zu dieser Zeit

♦ pron **1** (interrogative) welche(r, s); (of people also) wer

2 (relative) der/die/das; (referring to people) was; **the apple which you ate/which is on the table** der Apfel, den du gegessen hast/der auf dem Tisch liegt; **he said he saw her, which is true** er sagte, er habe sie gesehen, was auch stimmt

whichever |wɪtʃˈevəʳ| adj welche(r, s) auch immer; (no matter which) ganz gleich welche(r, s); **~ book you take** welches Buch du auch nimmst; **~ car you prefer** egal welches Auto du vorziehst

whiff |wɪf| n Hauch m

while |waɪl| n Weile f ♦ conj während; **for a ~** eine Zeit lang; **~ away** vt (time) sich dat vertreiben

whim |wɪm| n Laune f

whimper |ˈwɪmpəʳ| n Wimmern nt ♦ vi wimmern

whimsical |ˈwɪmzɪkəl| adj launisch

whine |waɪn| n Gewinsel nt, Gejammer nt ♦ vi heulen, winseln

whip |wɪp| n Peitsche f; (POL) Fraktionsführer m ♦ vt (beat) peitschen; (snatch) reißen; **~ped cream** n Schlagsahne f

whip-round |ˈwɪpraund| (BRIT: inf) n Geldsammlung f

whirl |wɜːl| n Wirbel m ♦ vt, vi (herum)wirbeln; **~pool** n Wirbel m; **~wind** n Wirbelwind m

whirr |wɜːʳ| vi schwirren, surren

whisk |wɪsk| n Schneebesen m ♦ vt (cream etc) schlagen; **to ~ sb away** or **off** mit jdm davon sausen

whisker |ˈwɪskəʳ| n: **~s** (of animal) Barthaare pl; (of man) Backenbart m

whisky |ˈwɪskɪ| (US, IRISH **whiskey**) n Whisky m

whisper |ˈwɪspəʳ| n Flüstern nt ♦ vt, vi flüstern

whistle |ˈwɪsl| n Pfiff m; (instrument) Pfeife f

♦ vt, vi pfeifen

white |waɪt| n Weiß nt; (of egg) Eiweiß nt
♦ adj weiß; **~ coffee** (BRIT) n Kaffee m mit
Milch; **~-collar worker** n Angestellte(r) m;
~ elephant n (fig) Fehlinvestition f; **~ lie** n
Notlüge f; **~ paper** n (POL) Weißbuch nt;
~wash n (paint) Tünche f; (fig)
Ehrenrettung f ♦ vt weißen, tünchen; (fig)
rein waschen

whiting |'waɪtɪŋ| n Weißfisch m

Whitsun |'wɪtsn| n Pfingsten nt

whittle |'wɪtl| vt: **to ~ away** or **down**
stutzen, verringern

whizz |wɪz| vi: **to ~ past** or **by** vorbeizischen,
vorbeischwirren; **~ kid** (inf) n Senkrecht-
starter(in) m(f)

who |huː| pron **1** (interrogative) wer; (acc)
wen; (dat) wem; **who is it?, who's there?**
wer ist da?
2 (relative) der/die/das; **the woman/man
who spoke to me** die Frau/der Mann, die/
der mit mir sprach

whodu(n)nit |huː'dʌnɪt| (inf) n Krimi m

whoever |huː'ɛvəʳ| pron wer/wen/wem auch
immer; (no matter who) ganz gleich wer/
wen/wem

whole |həʊl| adj ganz ♦ n Ganze(s) nt; **the ~
of the town** die ganze Stadt; **on the ~** im
Großen und Ganzen; **as a ~** im Großen und
Ganzen; **~food(s)** f 'həʊlfuːd(z)| n(pl)
Vollwertkost f; **~hearted** |həʊl'hɑːtɪd| adj
(agreement etc) rückhaltlos; **~heartedly** adv
von ganzem Herzen; **~meal** adj (bread,
flour) Vollkorn-; **~sale** n Großhandel m ♦ adj
(trade) Großhandels-; (destruction) Massen-;
~saler n Großhändler m; **~some** adj
bekömmlich, gesund; **~wheat** adj =
wholemeal

wholly |'həʊlɪ| adv ganz, völlig

whom |huːm| pron **1** (interrogative: acc)
wen; (: dat) wem; **whom did you see?**
wen haben Sie gesehen?; **to whom did
you give it?** wem haben Sie es gegeben?
2 (relative: acc) den/die/das; (: dat) dem/
der/dem; **the man whom I saw/to whom
I spoke** der Mann, den ich sah/mit dem ich
sprach

whooping cough |'huːpɪŋ-| n Keuchhusten
m

whore |hɔːʳ| n Hure f

whose |huːz| adj (possessive: interrogative)
wessen; (: relative) dessen; (after f and pl)
deren ♦ pron wessen; **~ book is this?, ~ is
this book?** wessen Buch ist dies?; **~ is this?**
wem gehört das?

why |waɪ| adv warum, weshalb
♦ conj warum, weshalb; **that's not why
I'm here** ich bin nicht deswegen hier;
that's the reason why deshalb
♦ excl (expressing surprise, shock) na so was;
(explaining) also dann; **why, it's you!** na so
was, du bist es!

wick |wɪk| n Docht m

wicked |'wɪkɪd| adj böse

wicker |'wɪkəʳ| n (also: **~work**) Korbgeflecht
nt

wicket |'wɪkɪt| n Tor nt, Dreistab m

wide |waɪd| adj breit; (plain) weit; (in firing)
daneben ♦ adv: **to open ~** weit öffnen; **to
shoot ~** danebenschießen; **~-angle lens** n
Weitwinkelobjektiv nt; **~-awake** adj
hellwach; **~ly** adv weit; (known) allgemein;
~n vt erweitern; **~ open** adj weit geöffnet;
~spread adj weitverbreitet, weit verbreitet

widow |'wɪdəʊ| n Witwe f; **~ed** adj
verwitwet; **~er** n Witwer m

width |wɪdθ| n Breite f, Weite f

wield |wiːld| vt schwingen, handhaben

wife |waɪf| (pl **wives**) n (Ehe)frau f, Gattin f

wig |wɪg| n Perücke f

wiggle |'wɪgl| n Wackeln nt ♦ vt wackeln mit
♦ vi wackeln

wild |waɪld| adj wild; (violent) heftig; (plan,
idea) verrückt; **~erness** |'wɪldənɪs| n Wildnis
f, Wüste f; **~-goose chase** n (fig) frucht-
lose(s) Unternehmen nt; **~life** n Tierwelt f;
~ly adv wild, ungestüm; (exaggerated)
irrsinnig; **~s** npl: **the ~s** die Wildnis f

wilful |'wɪlful| (US **willful**) adj (intended)
vorsätzlich; (obstinate) eigensinnig

will |wɪl| aux vb **1** (forms future tense)
werden; **I will finish it tomorrow** ich
mache es morgens zu Ende
2 (in predictions): **he will** or **he'll be there
by now** er dürfte jetzt da sein; **that will be
the postman** das wird der Postbote sein
3 (in commands, requests, offers): **will you
be quiet!** sei endlich still!; **will you help
me?** hilfst du mir?; **will you have a cup of
tea?** trinken Sie eine Tasse Tee?; **I won't put
up with it!** das lasse ich mir nicht gefallen!
♦ vt wollen
♦ n Wille m; (JUR) Testament nt

willing |'wɪlɪŋ| adj gewillt, bereit; **~ly** adv
bereitwillig, gern; **~ness** n (Bereit)willigkeit f

willow |'wɪləʊ| n Weide f

willpower |'wɪlpaʊəʳ| n Willenskraft f

willy-nilly |'wɪlɪ'nɪlɪ| adv einfach so

wilt |wɪlt| vi (ver)welken

wily |'waɪlɪ| adj gerissen

win |wɪn| (*pt*, *pp* **won**) *n* Sieg *m* ♦ *vt*, *vi* gewinnen; **to ~ sb over** *or* **round** jdn gewinnen; jdn dazu bringen

wince |wɪns| *vi* zusammenzucken

winch |wɪntʃ| *n* Winde *f*

wind[1] |wɪnd| *n* Wind *m*; (*MED*) Blähungen *pl*

wind[2] |waɪnd| (*pt*, *pp* **wound**) *vt* (*rope*) winden; (*bandage*) wickeln ♦ *vi* (*turn*) sich winden; **~ up** *vt* (*clock*) aufziehen; (*debate*) (ab)schließen

windfall |ˈwɪndfɔːl| *n* unverhoffte(r) Glücksfall *m*

winding |ˈwaɪndɪŋ| *adj* (*road*) gewunden

wind instrument |ˈwɪnd-| *n* Blasinstrument *nt*

windmill |ˈwɪndmɪl| *n* Windmühle *f*

window |ˈwɪndəʊ| *n* Fenster *nt*; **~ box** *n* Blumenkasten *m*; **~ cleaner** *n* Fensterputzer *m*; **~ envelope** *n* Fensterbriefumschlag *m*; **~ ledge** *n* Fenstersims *m*; **~ pane** *n* Fensterscheibe *f*; **~-shopping** *n* Schaufensterbummel *m*; **to go ~-shopping** einen Schaufensterbummel machen; **~sill** *n* Fensterbank *f*

wind: **~pipe** *n* Luftröhre *f*; **~ power** *n* Windenergie *f*; **~screen** (*BRIT*) *n* Windschutzscheibe *f*; **~screen washer** *n* Scheibenwaschanlage *f*; **~screen wiper** *n* Scheibenwischer *m*; **~shield** (*US*) *n* = **windscreen**; **~swept** *adj* vom Wind gepeitscht; (*person*) zerzaust; **~y** *adj* windig

wine |waɪn| *n* Wein *m*; **~ bar** *n* Weinlokal *nt*; **~ cellar** *n* Weinkeller *m*; **~glass** *n* Weinglas *nt*; **~ list** *n* Weinkarte *f*; **~ merchant** *n* Weinhändler *m*; **~ tasting** *n* Weinprobe *f*; **~ waiter** *n* Weinkellner *m*

wing |wɪŋ| *n* Flügel *m*; (*MIL*) Gruppe *f*; **~s** *npl* (*THEAT*) Seitenkulisse *f*; **~er** *n* (*SPORT*) Flügelstürmer *m*

wink |wɪŋk| *n* Zwinkern *nt* ♦ *vi* zwinkern, blinzeln

winner |ˈwɪnəʳ| *n* Gewinner *m*; (*SPORT*) Sieger *m*

winning |ˈwɪnɪŋ| *adj* (*team*) siegreich, Sieger-; (*goal*) entscheidend; **~ post** *n* Ziel *nt*; **~s** *npl* Gewinn *m*

winter |ˈwɪntəʳ| *n* Winter *m* ♦ *adj* (*clothes*) Winter- ♦ *vi* überwintern; **~ sports** *npl* Wintersport *m*; **wintry** |ˈwɪntrɪ| *adj* Winter-, winterlich

wipe |waɪp| *n*: **to give sth a ~** etw (ab)wischen ♦ *vt* wischen; **~ off** *vt* abwischen; **~ out** *vt* (*debt*) löschen; (*destroy*) auslöschen; **~ up** *vt* aufwischen

wire |ˈwaɪəʳ| *n* Draht *m*; (*telegram*) Telegramm *nt* ♦ *vt* telegrafieren; **to ~ sb** jdm telegrafieren; **~less** (*BRIT*) *n* Radio(apparat *m*) *nt*

wiring |ˈwaɪərɪŋ| *n* elektrische Leitungen *pl*

wiry |ˈwaɪərɪ| *adj* drahtig

wisdom |ˈwɪzdəm| *n* Weisheit *f*; (*of decision*) Klugheit *f*; **~ tooth** *n* Weisheitszahn *m*

wise |waɪz| *adj* klug, weise ♦ *suffix*: **time~** zeitlich gesehen

wisecrack |ˈwaɪzkræk| *n* Witzelei *f*

wish |wɪʃ| *n* Wunsch *m* ♦ *vt* wünschen; **best ~es** (*on birthday etc*) alles Gute; **with best ~es** herzliche Grüße; **to ~ sb goodbye** jdn verabschieden; **he ~ed me well** er wünschte mir Glück; **to ~ to do sth** etw tun wollen; **~ for** *vt fus* sich *dat* wünschen; **~ful thinking** *n* Wunschdenken *nt*

wishy-washy |ˈwɪʃɪˌwɒʃɪ| (*inf*) *adj* (*ideas*, *argument*) verschwommen

wisp |wɪsp| *n* (*Haar*)strähne *f*; (*of smoke*) Wölkchen *nt*

wistful |ˈwɪstful| *adj* sehnsüchtig

wit |wɪt| *n* (*also*: **~s**) Verstand *m no pl*; (*amusing ideas*) Witz *m*; (*person*) Witzbold *m*

witch |wɪtʃ| *n* Hexe *f*; **~craft** *n* Hexerei *f*

KEYWORD

with |wɪð, wɪθ| *prep* **1** (*accompanying, in the company of*) mit; **we stayed with friends** wir übernachteten bei Freunden; **I'll be with you in a minute** einen Augenblick bitte, ich bin sofort da; **I'm not with you** (*I don't understand*) das verstehe ich nicht; **to be with it** (*inf*: *up-to-date*) auf dem Laufenden sein; (: *alert*) (voll) da sein (*inf*) **2** (*descriptive, indicating manner etc*) mit; **the man with the grey hat** der Mann mit dem grauen Hut; **red with anger** rot vor Wut

withdraw |wɪðˈdrɔː| (*irreg*: *like* **draw**) *vt* zurückziehen; (*money*) abheben; (*remark*) zurücknehmen ♦ *vi* sich zurückziehen; **~al** *n* Zurückziehung *f*; Abheben *nt*; Zurücknahme *f*; **~n** *adj* (*person*) verschlossen

wither |ˈwɪðəʳ| *vi* (ver)welken

withhold |wɪðˈhəʊld| (*irreg*: *like* **hold**) *vt*: **to ~ sth (from sb)** (jdm) etw vorenthalten

within |wɪðˈɪn| *prep* innerhalb +*gen* ♦ *adv* innen; **~ sight of** in Sichtweite von; **~ the week** innerhalb einer Woche; **~ a mile of** weniger als eine Meile von

without |wɪðˈaʊt| *prep* ohne; **~ speaking/ sleeping** *etc* ohne zu sprechen/schlafen *etc*

withstand |wɪðˈstænd| (*irreg*: *like* **stand**) *vt* widerstehen +*dat*

witness |ˈwɪtnɪs| *n* Zeuge *m*, Zeugin *f* ♦ *vt* (*see*) sehen, miterleben; (*document*) beglaubigen; **~ box** *n* Zeugenstand *m*; **~ stand** (*US*) *n* Zeugenstand *m*

witticism |ˈwɪtɪsɪzəm| *n* witzige Bemerkung *f*

witty |ˈwɪtɪ| *adj* witzig, geistreich

wives |waɪvz| *pl of* **wife**

wk *abbr* = **week**

wobble |ˈwɒbl| *vi* wackeln

woe |wəʊ| *n* Kummer *m*

woke |wəʊk| *pt of* **wake**

woken |ˈwəʊkn| *pp of* **wake**

wolf [wulf] (*pl* **wolves**) *n* Wolf *m*
woman ['wumən] (*pl* **women**) *n* Frau *f*; ~
doctor *n* Ärztin *f*; **~ly** *adj* weiblich
womb [wu:m] *n* Gebärmutter *f*
women ['wimin] *npl of* **woman**; **~'s lib** (*inf*)
n Frauenbewegung *f*
won [wʌn] *pt, pp of* **win**
wonder ['wʌndəʳ] *n* (*marvel*) Wunder *nt*;
(*surprise*) Staunen *nt*, Verwunderung *f* ♦ *vi*
sich wundern ♦ *vt*: **I ~ whether** ... ich frage
mich, ob ...; **it's no ~ that** es ist kein
Wunder, dass; **to ~ at** sich wundern über
+*acc*; **to ~ about** sich Gedanken machen
über +*acc*; **~ful** *adj* wunderbar, herrlich
won't [wəunt] = **will not**
woo [wu:] *vt* (*audience etc*) umwerben
wood [wud] *n* Holz *nt*; (*forest*) Wald *m*; ~
carving *n* Holzschnitzerei *f*; **~ed** *adj*
bewaldet; **~en** *adj* (*also fig*) hölzern;
~pecker *n* Specht *m*; **~wind** *n*
Blasinstrumente *pl*; **~work** *n* Holzwerk *nt*;
(*craft*) Holzarbeiten *pl*; **~worm** *n* Holzwurm
m
wool [wul] *n* Wolle *f*; **to pull the ~ over sb's
eyes** (*fig*) jdm Sand in die Augen streuen;
~len (*US* **~en**) *adj* Woll-; **~lens** *npl*
Wollsachen *pl*; **~ly** (*US* **~y**) *adj* wollig; (*fig*)
schwammig
word [wə:d] *n* Wort *nt*; (*news*) Bescheid *m*
♦ *vt* formulieren; **in other ~s** anders gesagt;
to break/keep one's ~ sein Wort brechen/
halten; **~ing** *n* Wortlaut *m*; **~ processing** *n*
Textverarbeitung *f*; **~ processor** *n*
Textverarbeitung *f*
wore [wɔ:ʳ] *pt of* **wear**
work [wə:k] *n* Arbeit *f*; (*ART, LITER*) Werk *nt*
♦ *vi* arbeiten; (*machine*) funktionieren;
(*medicine*) wirken; (*succeed*) klappen; **~s** *n sg*
(*BRIT: factory*) Fabrik *f*, Werk *nt* ♦ *npl* (*of
watch*) Werk *nt*; **to be out of ~** arbeitslos
sein; **in ~ing order** in betriebsfähigem
Zustand; **~ loose** *vi* sich lockern; **~ on** *vi*
weiterarbeiten ♦ *vt fus* arbeiten an +*dat*;
(*influence*) bearbeiten; **~ out** *vi* (*sum*)
aufgehen; (*plan*) klappen ♦ *vt* (*problem*)
lösen; (*plan*) ausarbeiten; **it ~s out at £100**
das gibt or macht £100; **~ up** *vt*: **to get
~ed up** sich aufregen; **~able** *adj* (*soil*)
bearbeitbar; (*plan*) ausführbar; **~aholic**
[wə:kə'hɔlik] *n* Arbeitssüchtige(r) *f(m)*; **~er**
n Arbeiter(in) *m(f)*; **~ experience** *n*
Praktikum *nt*; **~force** *n* Arbeiterschaft *f*;
~ing class *n* Arbeiterklasse *f*; **~ing-class**
adj Arbeiter-; **~man** (*irreg*) *n* Arbeiter *m*;
~manship *n* Arbeit *f*, Ausführung *f*; **~sheet**
n Arbeitsblatt *nt*; **~shop** *n* Werkstatt *f*; ~
station *n* Arbeitsplatz *m*; **~-to-rule** (*BRIT*) *n*
Dienst *m* nach Vorschrift
world [wə:ld] *n* Welt *f*; **to think the ~ of sb**
große Stücke auf jdn halten; **~ly** *adj*
weltlich, irdisch; **~-wide** *adj* weltweit; **W~-**

Wide Web *n* World Wide Web *nt*
worm [wə:m] *n* Wurm *m*
worn [wɔ:n] *pp of* **wear** ♦ *adj* (*clothes*)
abgetragen; **~-out** *adj* (*object*) abgenutzt;
(*person*) völlig erschöpft
worried ['wʌrid] *adj* besorgt, beunruhigt
worry ['wʌri] *n* Sorge *f* ♦ *vt* beunruhigen ♦ *vi*
(*feel uneasy*) sich sorgen, sich *dat* Gedanken
machen; **~ing** *adj* beunruhigend
worse [wə:s] *adj* schlechter, schlimmer ♦ *adv*
schlimmer, ärger ♦ *n* Schlimmere(s) *nt*,
Schlechtere(s) *nt*; **a change for the ~** eine
Verschlechterung; **~n** *vt* verschlimmern ♦ *vi*
sich verschlechtern; **~ off** *adj* (*fig*) schlechter
dran
worship ['wə:ʃip] *n* Verehrung *f* ♦ *vt* anbeten;
Your W~ (*BRIT: to mayor*) Herr/Frau
Bürgermeister; (: *to judge*) Euer Ehren
worst [wə:st] *adj* schlimmste(r, s),
schlechteste(r, s) ♦ *adv* am schlimmsten, am
ärgsten ♦ *n* Schlimmste(s) *nt*, Ärgste(s) *nt*;
at ~ schlimmstenfalls
worth [wə:θ] *n* Wert *m* ♦ *adj* wert; **it's ~ it** es
lohnt sich; **to be ~ one's while (to do sth)**
die Mühe wert sein(, etw zu tun); **~less** *adj*
wertlos; (*person*) nichtsnutzig; **~while** *adj*
lohnend, (der Mühe wert); **~y** *adj* wert,
würdig

KEYWORD

would [wud] *aux vb* **1** (*conditional tense*): **if
you asked him he would do it** wenn du
ihn fragtest, würde er es tun; **if you had
asked him he would have done it** wenn
du ihn gefragt hättest, hätte er es getan
2 (*in offers, invitations, requests*): **would you
like a biscuit?** möchten Sie ein Plätzchen?;
would you ask him to come in? würden
Sie ihn bitte hineinbitten?
3 (*in indirect speech*): **I said I would do it**
ich sagte, ich würde es tun
4 (*emphatic*): **it WOULD have to snow
today!** es musste ja ausgerechnet heute
schneien!
5 (*insistence*): **she wouldn't behave** sie
wollte sich partout nicht anständig
benehmen
6 (*conjecture*): **it would have been
midnight** es mag ungefähr Mitternacht
gewesen sein; **it would seem so** es sieht
wohl so aus
7 (*indicating habit*): **he would go there on
Mondays** er ging jeden Montag dorthin

---

would-be ['wudbi:] (*pej*) *adj* Möchtegern-
wouldn't ['wudnt] = **would not**
wound¹ [wu:nd] *n* (*also fig*) Wunde *f* ♦ *vt*
verwunden, verletzen (*also fig*)
wound² [waund] *pt, pp of* **wind²**
wove [wəuv] *pt of* **weave**; **~n** *pp of* **weave**
wrangle ['ræŋgl] *n* Streit *m* ♦ *vi* sich zanken

wrap |ræp| vt einwickeln; **~ up** vt einwickeln; (deal) abschließen; **~per** n Umschlag m, Schutzhülle f; **~ping paper** n Einwickelpapier nt

wrath |rɔθ| n Zorn m

wreak |riːk| vt (havoc) anrichten; (vengeance) üben

wreath |riːθ| n Kranz m

wreck |rɛk| n (ship) Wrack nt; (sth ruined) Ruine f ♦ vt zerstören; **~age** n Trümmer pl

wren |rɛn| n Zaunkönig m

wrench |rɛntʃ| n (spanner) Schraubenschlüssel m; (twist) Ruck m ♦ vt reißen, zerren; **to ~ sth from sb** jdm etw entreißen or entwinden

wrestle |'rɛsl| vi: **to ~ (with sb)** (mit jdm) ringen; **~r** n Ringer(in) m(f); **wrestling** n Ringen nt

wretched |'rɛtʃɪd| adj (inf) verflixt

wriggle |'rɪgl| n Schlängeln nt ♦ vi sich winden

wring |rɪŋ| (pt, pp wrung) vt wringen

wrinkle |'rɪŋkl| n Falte f, Runzel f ♦ vt runzeln ♦ vi sich runzeln; (material) knittern; **~d** adj faltig, schrumpelig

wrist |rɪst| n Handgelenk nt; **~watch** n Armbanduhr f

writ |rɪt| n gerichtliche(r) Befehl m

write |raɪt| (pt wrote, pp written) vt, vi schreiben; **~ down** vt aufschreiben; **~ off** vt (dismiss) abschreiben; **~ out** vt (essay) abschreiben; (cheque) ausstellen; **~ up** vt schreiben; **~-off** n: **it is a ~-off** das kann man abschreiben; **~r** n Schriftsteller m

writhe |raɪð| vi sich winden

writing |'raɪtɪŋ| n (act) Schreiben nt; (handwriting) (Hand)schrift f; **in ~** schriftlich; **~ paper** n Schreibpapier nt

written |'rɪtn| pp of **write**

wrong |rɔŋ| adj (incorrect) falsch; (morally) unrecht ♦ n Unrecht nt ♦ vt Unrecht tun +dat; **he was ~ in doing that** es war nicht recht von ihm, das zu tun; **you are ~ about that, you've got it ~** da hast du Unrecht; **to be in the ~** im Unrecht sein; **what's ~ with your leg?** was ist mit deinem Bein los?; **to go ~** (plan) schief gehen; (person) einen Fehler machen; **~ful** adj unrechtmäßig; **~ly** adv falsch; (accuse) zu Unrecht

wrong number n (TEL): **you've got the ~** Sie sind falsch verbunden

wrote |rəut| pt of **write**

wrought |rɔːt| adj: **~ iron** Schmiedeeisen nt

wrung |rʌŋ| pt, pp of **wring**

wry |raɪ| adj ironisch

wt. abbr = **weight**

WWW n abbr (= World Wide Web): **the ~** das WWW

X, x

Xmas |'ɛksməs| n abbr = **Christmas**

X-ray |'ɛksreɪ| n Röntgenaufnahme f ♦ vt röntgen; **~s** npl Röntgenstrahlen pl

xylophone |'zaɪləfəun| n Xylofon nt, Xylophon nt

Y, y

yacht |jɔt| n Jacht f; **~ing** n (Sport)segeln nt; **~sman** (irreg) n Sportsegler m

Yank |jæŋk| (inf) n Ami m

yap |jæp| vi (dog) kläffen

yard |jaːd| n Hof m; (measure) (englische) Elle f, Yard nt (0,91 m); **~stick** n (fig) Maßstab m

yarn |jaːn| n (thread) Garn nt; (story) (Seemanns)garn nt

yawn |jɔːn| n Gähnen nt ♦ vi gähnen; **~ing** adj (gap) gähnend

yd. abbr = **yard(s)**

yeah |jɛə| (inf) adv ja

year |jɪər| n Jahr nt; **to be 8 ~s old** acht Jahre alt sein; **an eight-~-old child** ein achtjähriges Kind; **~ly** adj, adv jährlich

yearn |jɔːn| vi: **to ~ (for)** sich sehnen (nach); **~ing** n Verlangen nt, Sehnsucht f

yeast |jiːst| n Hefe f

yell |jɛl| n gellende(r) Schrei m ♦ vi laut schreien

yellow |'jɛləu| adj gelb ♦ n Gelb nt

yelp |jɛlp| n Gekläff nt ♦ vi kläffen

yes |jɛs| adv ja ♦ n Ja nt, Jawort nt; **to say ~** Ja or ja sagen; **to answer ~** mit Ja antworten

yesterday |'jɛstədɪ| adv gestern ♦ n Gestern nt; **~ morning/evening** gestern Morgen/ Abend; **all day ~** gestern den ganzen Tag; **the day before ~** vorgestern

yet |jɛt| adv noch; (in question) schon; (up to now) bis jetzt ♦ conj doch, dennoch; **it is not finished ~** es ist noch nicht fertig; **the best ~** das bisher Beste; **as ~** bis jetzt; (in past) bis dahin

yew |juː| n Eibe f

yield |jiːld| n Ertrag m ♦ vt (result, crop) hervorbringen; (interest, profit) abwerfen; (concede) abtreten ♦ vi nachgeben; (MIL) sich ergeben; **"~"** (US: AUT) „Vorfahrt gewähren"

YMCA n abbr (= Young Men's Christian Association) CVJM m

yob |jɔb| (BRIT: inf) n Halbstarke(r) f(m), Rowdy m

yoga |'jəugə| n Joga m

yoghourt |'jəugət| n Jog(h)urt m

yog(h)urt |'jəugət| n = **yoghourt**

yoke |jəuk| n (also fig) Joch nt

yolk |jəuk| n Eidotter m, Eigelb nt

you [ju:] pron **1** (subj, in comparisons: familiar form: sg) du; (: pl) ihr; (in letters also) du, ihr; (: polite form) Sie; **you Germans** ihr Deutschen; **she's younger than you** sie ist jünger als du/Sie
2 (direct object, after prep +acc: familiar form: sg) dich; (: pl) euch; (in letters also) dich, euch; (: polite form) Sie; **I know you** ich kenne dich/euch/Sie
3 (indirect object, after prep +dat: familiar form: sg) dir; (: pl) euch; (in letters also) dir, euch; (: polite form) Ihnen; **I gave it to you** ich gab es dir/euch/Ihnen
4 (impers: one: subj) man; (: direct object) einen; (: indirect object) einem; **fresh air does you good** frische Luft tut gut

you'd [ju:d] = **you had; you would**
you'll [ju:l] = **you will; you shall**
young [jʌŋ] adj jung ♦ npl: **the ~** die Jungen pl; **~ster** n Junge m, junge(r) Bursche m, junge(s) Mädchen nt
your [jɔ:ʳ] adj (familiar: sg) dein; (: pl) euer, eure pl; (polite) Ihr; see also **my**
you're [juəʳ] = **you are**
yours [jɔ:z] pron (familiar: sg) deine(r, s); (: pl) eure(r, s); (polite) Ihre(r, s); see also **mine²**
yourself [jɔ:ˈsɛlf] pron (emphatic) selbst; (familiar: sg: acc) dich (selbst); (: dat) dir (selbst); (: pl) euch (selbst); (polite) sich (selbst); see also **oneself; yourselves** pl pron (reflexive: familiar) euch; (: polite) sich; (emphatic) selbst; see also **oneself**
youth [ju:θ] n Jugend f; (young man) junge(r) Mann m; **~s** npl (young people) Jugendliche pl; **~ club** n Jugendzentrum nt; **~ful** adj jugendlich; **~ hostel** n Jugendherberge f

you've [ju:v] = **you have**
YTS (BRIT) n abbr (= Youth Training Scheme) staatliches Förderprogramm für arbeitslose Jugendliche
Yugoslav [ˈjuːgəʊslɑːv] adj jugoslawisch ♦ n Jugoslawe m, Jugoslawin f; **~ia** [ˈjuːgəʊˈslɑːvɪə] n Jugoslawien nt
yuppie [ˈjʌpɪ] (inf) n Yuppie m ♦ adj yuppiehaft, Yuppie-
YWCA n abbr (= Young Women's Christian Association) CVJF m

Z, z

zany [ˈzeɪnɪ] adj (ideas, sense of humour) verrückt
zap [zæp] vt (COMPUT) löschen
zeal [zi:l] n Eifer m; **~ous** [ˈzɛləs] adj eifrig
zebra [ˈziːbrə] n Zebra nt; **~ crossing** (BRIT) n Zebrastreifen m
zero [ˈzɪərəʊ] n Null f; (on scale) Nullpunkt m
zest [zɛst] n Begeisterung f
zigzag [ˈzɪgzæg] n Zickzack m
Zimbabwe [zɪmˈbɑːbwɪ] n Zimbabwe nt
Zimmer frame [ˈzɪmə-] n Laufgestell nt
zip [zɪp] n Reißverschluss m ♦ vt (also: ~ up) den Reißverschluss zumachen +gen
zip code (US) n Postleitzahl f
zipper [ˈzɪpəʳ] (US) n Reißverschluss m
zit [zɪt] (inf) n Pickel m
zodiac [ˈzəʊdɪæk] n Tierkreis m
zombie [ˈzɔmbɪ] n: **like a ~** (fig) wie im Tran
zone [zəʊn] n (also MIL) Zone f, Gebiet nt; (in town) Bezirk m
zoo [zu:] n Zoo m
zoology [zuːˈɔlədʒɪ] n Zoologie f
zoom [zu:m] vi: **to ~ past** vorbeisausen; **~ lens** n Zoomobjektiv nt
zucchini [zuːˈkiːnɪ] (US) npl Zucchini pl

GERMAN IRREGULAR VERBS
*with 'sein'

infinitive	present indicative (2nd, 3rd sg.)	imperfect	past participle
aufschrecken*	schrickst auf, schrickt auf	schrak *or* schreckte auf	aufgeschreckt
ausbedingen	bedingst aus, bedingt aus	bedang *or* bedingte aus	ausbedungen
backen	bäckst, bäckt	backte *or* buk	gebacken
befehlen	befiehlst, befiehlt	befahl	befohlen
beginnen	beginnst, beginnt	begann	begonnen
beißen	beißt , beißt	biss	gebissen
bergen	birgst, birgt	barg	geborgen
bersten*	birst, birst	barst	geborsten
bescheißen*	bescheißt, bescheißt	beschiss	beschissen
bewegen	bewegst, bewegt	bewog	bewogen
biegen	biegst, biegt	bog	gebogen
bieten	bietest, bietet	bot	geboten
binden	bindest, bindet	band	gebunden
bitten	bittest, bittet	bat	gebeten
blasen	bläst, bläst	blies	geblasen
bleiben*	bleibst, bleibt	blieb	geblieben
braten	brätst, brät	briet	gebraten
brechen*	brichst, bricht	brach	gebrochen
brennen	brennst, brennt	brannte	gebrannt
bringen	bringst, bringt	brachte	gebracht
denken	denkst, denkt	dachte	gedacht
dreschen	drisch(e)st, drischt	drasch	gedroschen
dringen*	dringst, dringt	drang	gedrungen
dürfen	darfst, darf	durfte	gedurft
empfehlen	empfiehlst, empfiehlt	empfahl	empfohlen
erbleichen*	erbleichst, erbleicht	erbleichte	erblichen
erlöschen*	erlischt, erlischt	erlosch	erloschen
erschrecken*	erschrickst, erschrickt	erschrak	erschrocken
essen	isst, isst	aß	gegessen

infinitive	present indicative (2nd, 3rd sg.)	imperfect	past participle
fahren*	fährst, fährt	fuhr	gefahren
fallen*	fällst, fällt	fiel	gefallen
fangen	fängst, fängt	fing	gefangen
fechten	fichtst, ficht	focht	gefochten
finden	findest, findet	fand	gefunden
flechten	flichtst, flicht	flocht	geflochten
fliegen*	fliegst, fliegt	flog	geflogen
fliehen	fliehst, flieht	floh	geflohen
fließen*	fließt, fließt	floss	geflossen
fressen	frisst, frisst	fraß	gefressen
frieren	frierst, friert	fror	gefroren
gären*	gärst, gärt	gor	gegoren
gebären	gebierst, gebiert	gebar	geboren
geben	gibst, gibt	gab	gegeben
gedeihen*	gedeihst, gedeiht	gedieh	gediehen
gehen*	gehst, geht	ging	gegangen
gelingen*	– –, gelingt	gelang	gelungen
gelten	giltst, gilt	galt	gegolten
genesen*	gene(se)st, genest	genas	genesen
genießen	genießt, genießt	genoss	genossen
geraten*	gerätst, gerät	geriet	geraten
geschehen*	– –, geschieht	geschah	geschehen
gewinnen	gewinnst, gewinnt	gewann	gewonnen
gießen	gießt, gießt	goss	gegossen
gleichen	gleichst, gleicht	glich	geglichen
gleiten*	gleitest, gleitet	glitt	geglitten
glimmen	glimmst, glimmt	glomm	geglommen
graben	gräbst, gräbt	grub	gegraben
greifen	greifst, greift	griff	gegriffen
haben	hast, hat	hatte	gehabt
halten	hältst, hält	hielt	gehalten
hängen	hängst, hängt	hing	gehangen
hauen	haust, haut	haute	gehauen
heben	hebst, hebt	hob	gehoben
heißen	heißt, heißt	hieß	geheißen
helfen	hilfst, hilft	half	geholfen
kennen	kennst, kennt	kannte	gekannt
klimmen*	klimmst, klimmt	klomm	geklommen
klingen	klingst, klingt	klang	geklungen

infinitive	present indicative (2nd, 3rd sg.)	imperfect	past participle
kneifen	kneifst, kneift	kniff	gekniffen
kommen*	kommst, kommt	kam	gekommen
können	kannst, kann	konnte	gekonnt
kriechen*	kriechst, kriecht	kroch	gekrochen
laden	lädst, lädt	lud	geladen
lassen	lässt, lässt	ließ	gelassen
laufen*	läufst, läuft	lief	gelaufen
leiden	leidest, leidet	litt	gelitten
leihen	leihst, leiht	lieh	geliehen
lesen	liest, liest	las	gelesen
liegen*	liegst, liegt	lag	gelegen
lügen	lügst, lügt	log	gelogen
mahlen	mahlst, mahlt	mahlte	gemahlen
meiden	meidest, meidet	mied	gemieden
melken	melkst, melkt	melkte	gemolken
messen	misst, misst	maß	gemessen
misslingen*	– –, misslingt	misslang	misslungen
mögen	magst, mag	mochte	gemocht
müssen	musst, muss	musste	gemusst
nehmen	nimmst, nimmt	nahm	genommen
nennen	nennst, nennt	nannte	genannt
pfeifen	pfeifst, pfeift	pfiff	gepfiffen
preisen	preist, preist	pries	gepriesen
quellen*	quillst, quillt	quoll	gequollen
raten	rätst, rät	riet	geraten
reiben	reibst, reibt	rieb	gerieben
reißen*	reißt, reißt	riss	gerissen
reiten*	reitest, reitet	ritt	geritten
rennen*	rennst, rennt	rannte	gerannt
riechen	riechst, riecht	roch	gerochen
ringen	ringst, ringt	rang	gerungen
rinnen*	rinnst, rinnt	rann	geronnen
rufen	rufst, ruft	rief	gerufen
salzen	salzt, salzt	salzte	gesalzen
saufen	säufst, säuft	soff	gesoffen
saugen	saugst, saugt	sog	gesogen
schaffen	schaffst, schafft	schuf	geschaffen
scheiden	scheidest, scheidet	schied	geschieden
scheinen	scheinst, scheint	schien	geschienen
schelten	schiltst, schilt	schalt	gescholten

infinitive	present indicative (2nd, 3rd sg.)	imperfect	past participle
scheren	scherst, schert	schor	geschoren
schieben	schiebst, schiebt	schob	geschoben
schießen	schießt, schießt	schoss	geschossen
schinden	schindest, schindet	schindete	geschunden
schlafen	schläfst, schläft	schlief	geschlafen
schlagen	schlägst, schlägt	schlug	geschlagen
schleichen*	schleichst, schleicht	schlich	geschlichen
schleifen	schleifst, schleift	schliff	geschliffen
schließen	schließt, schließt	schloss	geschlossen
schlingen	schlingst, schlingt	schlang	geschlungen
schmeißen	schmeißt, schmeißt	schmiss	geschmissen
schmelzen*	schmilzt, schmilzt	schmolz	geschmolzen
schneiden	schneidest, schneidet	schnitt	geschnitten
schreiben	schreibst, schreibt	schrieb	geschrieben
schreien	schreist, schreit	schrie	geschrie(e)n
schreiten	schreitest, schreitet	schritt	geschritten
schweigen	schweigst, schweigt	schwieg	geschwiegen
schwellen*	schwillst, schwillt	schwoll	geschwollen
schwimmen*	schwimmst, schwimmt	schwamm	geschwommen
schwinden*	schwindest, schwindet	schwand	geschwunden
schwingen	schwingst, schwingt	schwang	geschwungen
schwören	schwörst, schwört	schwor	geschworen
sehen	siehst, sieht	sah	gesehen
sein*	bist, ist	war	gewesen
senden	sendest, sendet	sandte	gesandt
singen	singst, singt	sang	gesungen
sinken*	sinkst, sinkt	sank	gesunken

infinitive	present indicative (2nd, 3rd sg.)	imperfect	past participle
sinnen	sinnst, sinnt	sann	gesonnen
sitzen*	sitzt, sitzt	saß	gesessen
sollen	sollst, soll	sollte	gesollt
speien	speist, speit	spie	gespie(e)n
spinnen	spinnst, spinnt	spann	gesponnen
sprechen	sprichst, spricht	sprach	gesprochen
sprießen*	sprießt, sprießt	spross	gesprossen
springen*	springst, springt	sprang	gesprungen
stechen	stichst, sticht	stach	gestochen
stecken	steckst, steckt	steckte *or* stak	gesteckt
stehen	stehst, steht	stand	gestanden
sitehlen	stiehlst, stiehlt	stahl	gestohlen
steigen.	steigst, steigt	stieg	gestiegen
sterben*	stirbst, stirbt	starb	gestorben
stinken	stinkst, stinkt	stank	gestunken
stoßen	stößt, stößt	stieß	gestoßen
streichen	streichst, streicht	strich	gestrichen
streiten*	streitest, streitet	stritt	gestritten
tragen	trägst, trägt	trug	getragen
treffen	triffst, trifft	traf	getroffen
treiben*	treibst, treibt	trieb	getrieben
treten*	trittst, tritt	trat	getreten
trinken*	trinkst, trinkt	trank	getrunken
trügen	trügst, trügt	trog	getrogen
tun	tust, tut	tat	getan
verderben	verdirbst, verdirbt	verdarb	verdorben
verdrießen	verdrießt, verdrießt	verdross	verdrossen
vergessen	vergisst, vergisst	vergaß	vergessen
verlieren	verlierst, verliert	velor	verloren
verschleißen	verschleißt, verschleißt	verschliss	verschlissen
wachsen*	wächst, wächst	wuchs	gewachsen
wägen	wägst, wägt	wog	gewogen
waschen	wäschst, wäscht	wusch	gewaschen
weben	webst, webt	webte *or* wob	gewoben
weichen*	weichst, weicht	wich	gewichen
weisen	weist, weist	wies	gewiesen
wenden	wendest, wendet	wandte	gewandt
werben	wirbst, wirbt	warb	geworben

infinitive	present indicative (2nd, 3rd sg.)	imperfect	past participle
werden*	wirst, wird	wurde	geworden
werfen	wirfst, wirft	warf	geworfen
wiegen	wiegst, wiegt	wog	gewogen
winden	windest, windet	wand	gewunden
wissen	weißt, weiß	wusste	gewusst
wollen	willst, will	wollte	gewollt
wringen	wringst, wringt	wrang	gewrungen
zeihen	zeihst, zeiht	zieh	geziehen
ziehen*	ziehst, zieht	zog	gezogen
zwingen	zwingst, zwingt	zwang	gezwungen

UNREGELMÄSSIGE ENGLISCHE VERBEN

present	pt	pp	present	pt	pp
arise	arose	arisen	do (3rd	did	done
awake	awoke	awoken	person;		
be (am, is,	was,	been	he/she/it/		
are;	were		does)		
being)			draw	drew	drawn
bear	bore	born(e)	dream	dreamed,	dreamed,
beat	beat	beaten		dreamt	dreamt
become	became	become	drink	drank	drunk
begin	began	begun	drive	drove	driven
behold	beheld	beheld	dwell	dwelt	dwelt
bend	bent	bent	eat	ate	eaten
beset	beset	beset	fall	fell	fallen
bet	bet,	bet,	feed	fed	fed
	betted	betted	feel	felt	felt
bid	bid,	bid,	fight	fought	fought
	bade	bidden	find	found	found
bind	bound	bound	flee	fled	fled
bite	bit	bitten	fling	flung	flung
bleed	bled	bled	fly (flies)	flew	flown
blow	blew	blown	forbid	forbade	forbidden
break	broke	broken	forecast	forecast	forecast
breed	bred	bred	forget	forgot	forgotten
bring	brought	brought	forgive	forgave	forgiven
build	built	built	forsake	forsook	forsaken
burn	burnt,	burnt,	freeze	froze	frozen
	burned	burned	get	got	got, (US)
burst	burst	burst			gotten
buy	bought	bought	give	gave	given
can	could	(been	go (goes)	went	gone
		able)	grind	ground	ground
cast	cast	cast	grow	grew	grown
catch	caught	caught	hang	hung,	hung,
choose	chose	chosen		hanged	hanged
cling	clung	clung	have (has;	had	had
come	came	come	having)		
cost	cost	cost	hear	heard	heard
creep	crept	crept	hide	hid	hidden
cut	cut	cut	hit	hit	hit
deal	dealt	dealt	hold	held	held
dig	dug	dug	hurt	hurt	hurt

present	pt	pp	present	pt	pp
keep	kept	kept	set	set	set
kneel	knelt, kneeled	knelt, kneeled	shake	shook	shaken
			shall	should	—
know	knew	known	shear	sheared	shorn, sheared
lay	laid	laid			
lead	led	led	shed	shed	shed
lean	leant, leaned	leant, leaned	shine	shone	shone
			shoot	shot	shot
leap	leapt, leaped	leapt, leaped	show	showed	shown
			shrink	shrank	shrunk
learn	learnt, learned	learnt, learned	shut	shut	shut
			sing	sang	sung
leave	left	left	sink	sank	sunk
lend	lent	lent	sit	sat	sat
let	let	let	slay	slew	slain
lie (lying)	lay	lain	sleep	slept	slept
light	lit, lighted	lit, lighted	slide	slid	slid
			sling	slung	slung
lose	lost	lost	slit	slit	slit
make	made	made	smell	smelt, smelled	smelt, smelled
may	might	—			
mean	meant	meant	sow	sowed	sown, sowed
meet	met	met			
mistake	mistook	mistaken	speak	spoke	spoken
mow	mowed	mown, mowed	speed	sped, speeded	sped, speeded
must	(had to)	(had to)	spell	spelt, spelled	spelt, spelled
pay	paid	paid			
put	put	put	spend	spent	spent
quit	quit, quitted	quit, quitted	spill	spilt, spilled	spilt, spilled
read	read	read	spin	spun	spun
rid	rid	rid	spit	spat	spat
ride	rode	ridden	split	split	split
ring	rang	rung	spoil	spoiled, spoilt	spoiled, spoilt
rise	rose	risen			
run	ran	run	spread	spread	spread
saw	sawed	sawn	spring	sprang	sprung
say	said	said	stand	stood	stood
see	saw	seen	steal	stole	stolen
seek	sought	sought	stick	stuck	stuck
sell	sold	sold	sting	stung	stung
send	sent	sent	stink	stank	stunk

430

present	pt	pp	present	pt	pp
stride	strode	stridden	**think**	thought	thought
strike	struck	struck, stricken	**throw**	threw	thrown
			thrust	thrust	thrust
tread	trod	trodden	**wake**	woke, waked	woken, waked
strive	strove	striven			
swear	swore	sworn	**wear**	wore	worn
sweep	swept	swept	**weave**	wove, weaved	woven, weaved
swell	swelled	swollen, swelled	**wed**	wedded, wed	wedded, wed
swim	swam	swum			
swing	swung	swung	**weep**	wept	wept
take	took	taken	**win**	won	won
teach	taught	taught	**wind**	wound	wound
tear	tore	torn	**wring**	wrung	wrung
tell	told	told	**write**	wrote	written